PSYCHOLOGY
An Introduction

PSYCHOLOGY
An Introduction

Josh R. Gerow
Indiana University—Purdue University at Fort Wayne

Scott, Foresman and Company
Glenview, Illinois
London, England

Dedicated to Nancy, Howard, and J. R.

Credit lines for photos, illustrations, and other copy-
righted materials appearing in this book are in the
Acknowledgments section beginning on page 690.
This section is to be considered an extension of the
copyright page.

Library of Congress Cataloging-in-Publication Data

Gerow, Joshua R.
  Psychology: an introduction.

  Bibliography: p. 678
  Includes index.
  1. Psychology. I. Title.
BF121.G44   1986   150   85-18945
ISBN 0-673-18097-2

123456789—RRW—91908988878685

PREFACE

A NOTE TO THE STUDENT

Welcome to psychology. Your instructor and I believe that psychology is an exciting, useful, and important science. This term we are going to do our best to share with you some of our enthusiasm for and understanding of the science that studies behavior and mental processes. Psychology is a broad field that covers many different topics, as a quick survey of the table of contents will show you. Indeed, at the moment, the prospect of covering all—or most—of the material in this text in one term may seem rather overwhelming. There *is* a good deal of information contained in this course, and to help you learn and remember the material that is presented in this book, turn to the section of this Preface called "How to Get the Most from This Text."

A NOTE TO THE INSTRUCTOR

Many months ago, I spent two days discussing with editors at Scott, Foresman and Company my vision for an introductory psychology text. Everyone listened carefully and seemed to know much more about psychology and psychology textbooks than I thought editors were supposed to know. At the conclusion of our conversations and meetings, Jim Levy, General Manager of the College Division, said casually, "Okay, let's do it. We'll give you whatever help you'll need." They did. And this text reflects precisely what I had in mind at the time of those initial meetings—and more.

What I wanted to write was an introductory-level textbook that spoke directly to students. My image throughout was that I was talking to a student in my office about psychology, and trying to do two things: make the basic subject matter of psychology as clear as possible and convince the student why she or he should care about it. Just because you and I may appreciate the relevance or application of some aspect of psychology, we should not always assume that the relevance or application is equally obvious to our beginning students. I thought that a conversational tone—without being "cute" or talking down to the reader—would be particularly appropriate for the beginning psychology student. I could see no reason why psychology texts had to be dry and encyclopedic in style.

I wanted the text to be a manageable one for both the instructor and the student. I wanted to provide the instructor with as much flexibility as possible. And although the text had to be reasonably brief, it also had to be reasonably comprehensive. That is, if concepts, or theories, or research studies were to be introduced, they needed to be explained in enough detail to make them understandable. It makes more sense, I argued, to explain a few things well than to try to explain many things poorly. I wanted the text to be up-to-date and to reflect current thinking in psychology, but it also had to acknowledge our history, not leaving the unfair and untrue impression that everything of worth in psychology has happened within the last decade. Surely, I wanted the text to be accurate and an honest reflection of psychology in the mid-1980s. That would mean making certain that students realized that in many areas "all the data are not in yet," that there remain many intriguing and important questions in psychology to which we do not have adequate answers. This, it seems to me, is one of the most exciting aspects of psychology.

Finally, I wanted to use effective pedagogy in such a way that it would not be objectionably intrusive. I wanted to do everything that could be done to help the student-reader appreciate general psychology without interfering with the flow of the text.

With the help of many dedicated colleagues in psychology and a group of exceptionally talented people at Scott, Foresman, this text does exactly what I wanted it to do. In the next section, I'll briefly point out some of the specific features of this text that help it meet my original vision.

Features of the Text

A glance at the table of contents will reveal that *Psychology: An Introduction* has been organized in a standard 15-chapter format suitable for a one-semester course. We begin with a definition of psychology and its methods, discuss physiological bases of behavior, move to basic psychological processes, consider the development, motivation, and personality of the individual, introduce the notion of psychopathology and therapy, examine the individual in a social context, and finally address specific areas of application of psychology. Within each chapter, there are two or three related, but focused, topics. The idea behind this organization is to foster flexibility and to keep individual units at a reasonable length. I suspect that few instructors will choose to assign all the topics of every chapter. Leaving out a topic or two here or there should not present any problems.

Within every topic, a number of components can be found. To begin with, there is a topic outline, which provides, at a glance, the basic structure within the topic. Brief topic openers follow. These opening pieces vary: some engage the student in a brief exercise, some present material of historical interest, some summarize relevant research, and others are clearly autobiographical. All are intended to informally introduce the student to the content of the topic, and they are referred to again throughout the body of the text.

The first formal section of each topic is appropriately called *Why We Care.* There are two goals for this short section: to answer the question of why *we* care about this topic as psychologists and why *students* should care about the material, and to present a more formal introduction to each topic, specifically detailing the issues to be discussed. In this latter sense, the *Why We Care* sections serve as topic previews.

Throughout each topic, we have inserted a number of short questions, labeled *Before You Go On.* The intent here should be obvious. For many years now, psychologists have documented the advantages of distributed practice. Learning accomplished in relatively short doses, with rest intervals interspersed, is more efficient and effective learning than that attempted in large chunks. Designing each chapter to include shorter topics and each topic to include *Before You Go On* questions helps reinforce study through distributed practice. We also recognize that there is a considerable difference between ''reading a book'' and ''studying a book.'' Study is an active process involving the elaborative rehearsal of presented information. *Before You Go On* questions prompt students to pause and consider what they have just read, to summarize and consolidate before they go on with their reading. The questions are designed to be brief and simple enough to be unobtrusive. In every case, the answers to *Before You Go On* questions are readily available in the previous few paragraphs. Each *Before You Go On* question is repeated and answered in the *Topic Summary* at the end of each topic.

To a large degree, introductory psychology is a matter of vocabulary development. To aid in this process, all *key terms* appear in **boldface** print in the text where they are defined. Definitions are provided in the text margins for ready reference and are also compiled in a complete page-referenced *Glossary* at the end of the text.

Each topic also includes a *Topic Expansion* designed to do just what its name suggests—to expand on some aspect of the material presented within the topic. In some cases, additional details are provided for issues addressed within the topic; in others, new material is introduced. *Topic Expansion* sections are free-standing, and they can be used as optional assignments.

Psychology: An Introduction includes a complete package of ancillary materials. The *Instructor's Manual* is available in a convenient, adaptable, three-ring binder format. It has profited from the contributions of a number of skilled and experienced teachers of psychology. It has been structured into two major sections, one offering suggestions for organizing and teaching the introductory psychology course in general, and the other for teaching with this text. The latter includes for each topic an expanded outline and summary, the author's comments, lecture expansion ideas, classroom demonstrations and exercises, and suggested film resources. As they are developed, supplements to the *Instructor's Manual* will be furnished to users of the text.

The *Study Guide* is an unusually effective supplement for introductory students. It provides an overview of each topic, specific learning objectives, and a series of objective sample test items (and answers) for each topic. A computerized version of the *Study Guide, STUDYWARE,* is also available. The field-tested *Ory Testing System* provides 100 multiple-choice test questions per chapter and 50 questions on the Statistical Appendix. Items in the *Testing System* have been carefully screened by William Dwyer of Memphis State University and John Ory of the University of Illinois for quality and accuracy and are classified as covering definitions, factual content, or applications of concepts. The *Testing System* is available in perforated-page format or on *EXAM,* Scott, Foresman's flexible test generator. It is compatible with either IBM or Apple microcomputers.

In addition, sets of 60 four-color *Transparencies* or *35 mm. slides* that illustrate major concepts in the text are available, as is *SIMLAB,* a collection of seven computer-simulated laboratories, each containing three experiments or tests that students can work through at IBM or Apple II microcomputer terminals.

A softbound copy of *How to Succeed in College* is included with each student's copy of *Psychology: An Introduction.* This class-tested book, written by your text author and R. Douglas Lyng, an associate professor of biological sciences, offers students a number of practical suggestions on how to handle college-level work in any discipline.

ACKNOWLEDGING THOSE WHO HELPED

In my initial conversations with Scott, Foresman and Company, there was one point that I made repeatedly and forcefully: I could not do the type of job I wanted to do without considerable help from others. I needed the help of colleagues in psychology who were familiar with and active in the discipline and were at the same time committed to the teaching of psychology. I needed the help of an experienced publisher to turn the ideas of psychologists into a sensible text that reflected our vision. I also needed the help of friends and colleagues in my own department to allow me the time and flexibility of scheduling required to make this project a top priority. I have been impressed and gratified by the extent and quality of the assistance that I have been offered from all quarters.

I have always been suspicious of authors who credit their spouses for being so understanding and helpful during the writing of their books. To all such authors I now apologize. I know of what you speak. Nancy has not only put up with my preoccupations (awakening at 3:00 in the morning to note a different way to handle the discussion of negative reinforcers, for example), but has proven to be my best reviewer and critic. She has read this text completely in all of its many versions. Her knowledgeable attention to details and to style has been of great help.

If it were not for the cooperation of my colleagues at Indiana University—Purdue University at Fort Wayne, this text would still be "in progress." Dr. Joanne Lantz, my chair, has allowed me a choice of teaching schedules to accommodate my writing schedule. I have constantly shared ideas and asked for input from my fellow department members. Their suggestions have been useful and are appreciated.

I had no idea just how helpful a publisher could be in turning a plan and prospectus for a text into an actual book. When I began this project, I had little idea of what textbook editors did. They make books happen. *Psychology: An Introduction* has been largely the responsibility (in every sense of the word) of Scott Hardy. It reflects the careful attention of Trig Thoreson (in the early going) and Joanne Tinsley, who served as developmental editors. That this text has the form and style that it does reflects the input of Joanne Tinsley, who has contributed substantially to this project. Barbara Schneider should be credited with the attractive and functional design of the book, and Sandy Schneider with the excellent pictures throughout. Two others from Scott Foresman deserve special mention: Marisa L. L'Heureux, who copy-edited the entire manuscript in a most vigilant and professional manner, and Iris Ganz, who managed to keep thousands of pages of manuscript organized and directed to the right people at the right time.

Most gratifying to me was the assistance I received from fellow psychologists who became involved in this project. I am impressed with the number of teachers of psychology who provided encouragement when it was warranted and criticism when it was deserved. Reviewers were willing to provide suggestions and guidance all along the way. I trust that they will find their good work reflected in these pages. Some commented on a chapter or two. Some provided reactions to the entire text. I thank them all and simply list here their names and affiliations:

Kenneth Bordens
Indiana University—Purdue University at Fort Wayne

Lynn Brokaw
Portland Community College

Gary P. Brown
Kellogg Community College

William O. Dwyer
Memphis State University

Barbara Engler
Union County College

Cynthia Ford
Jackson State University

Leon Keys
Ferris State College

Errol M. Magidson
Kennedy-King College

Terry Maul
San Bernardino Valley College

Rick McNeese
Sam Houston State University

Steve A. Nida
Franklin University

Faye Tyler M. Norton
Charlottesville, VA

Daniel W. Richards III
Houston Community College

Joan Rosen
Miami-Dade Community College, South

Connie Sanders
University of Tennessee

Freddie Shannon
Wayne County Community College

Raymond Shrader
University of Tennessee

Thomas Tighe
Maraine Valley Community College

Wayne Von Bargen
Psychological Service Associates—Fort Wayne, IN

Phyllis Walrad
Macomb Community College

Linda L. Wickstra
St. Louis Community College

Paul Wilson
Park Center—Fort Wayne, IN

Every student has his or her own favorite way of studying a textbook, and I won't suggest that you change "your way." But in this section I'd like to offer some advice on how you can best take advantage of the features we have built into this textbook in order to make your learning as easy as possible. Based on sound psychological research, the two major goals we had in mind were to keep units relatively brief (which is why we divided chapters into topics) and to help make the material meaningful (which is why we inserted many examples and *Before You Go On* questions throughout each topic). Here are the steps that will help you learn as you study this text:

1. Begin by surveying the *outline* for the assigned topic. This will give you a general sense of what the topic will be covering.

2. Read the topic opener. These have been designed to "set the stage" and get you involved with some of the relevant issues in the topic.

3. Read the *Why We Care* section. These brief sections attempt to tell you why psychologists care about the content of the topic, and, more importantly perhaps, why *you* should care. The *Why We Care* section also serves as a topic preview, letting you know in some detail precisely what will be covered.

4. Read the topic. This includes not only the prose, but also all the figures, graphs, and illustrations. After each major section, you will encounter a *Before You Go On* question. These are simple questions that can be easily answered if you have understood what you have just read. They serve to provide a quick a review of what you have been studying. If you cannot answer a *Before You Go On* question, reread the previous section. (There's little point in going on with your reading if you don't fully understand what you've just read.) Each *Before You Go On* question is answered in the *Topic Summary,* but try to avoid referring to the *Summary* during your first reading of the topic.

5. Note key words and concepts. These are printed in the text in **boldface** type. Each key word is defined in the text and also in the margin for ready reference. To a large degree, learning about psychology is learning to use the proper vocabulary. Having important words in the margin should help you develop that vocabulary.

6. Throughout your reading, try to relate the material you are studying to what you already know. Studying is a more active process than simple reading. The more meaningful you can make the material, by relating it to your own experiences, the easier it will be to remember.

7. After you have read the topic, read the *Topic Summary.* As I said, these repeat each of the *Before You Go On* questions and provide a short answer for each.

8. To review for an examination, it should not be necessary to have to reread all of the assigned material. To review for an exam and remind yourself of the issues covered in a topic, reexamine the topic outline, reread the *Topic Summary* (and see if you can now answer each question without reference to the text), and make sure that you know the definitions for all the key words and concepts.

9. Finally, there is a *Study Guide* to accompany *Psychology: An Introduction* (code number 18216-9). It comes in workbook and disc formats. If you want a copy of the workbook and it is not available in your bookstore, contact either your professor or the publisher (Marketing Support Services, College Division / Scott, Foresman and Company / 1900 East Lake Avenue / Glenview, IL 60025) for information on how to order a copy. To obtain a copy of *STUDYWARE,* the disc format study guide, see the order form on the following page.

Your instructor will have additional advice for you on how to get the most out of your introductory psychology class. I hope and trust that you will find the experience pleasurable as well as informative. I wish you the very best and would like to hear from you to know how you liked this book and how we might make it a better one.

Josh R. Gerow

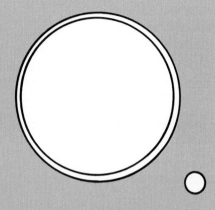

Dan Murphy
to accompany

_____

PSYCHOLOGY: An Introduction
_____

Josh Gerow

STUDY-WARE WORKS

The Study-Ware software is a computerized learning guide designed to check and test whether you've retained the material presented in PSYCHOLOGY: AN INTRODUCTION as well as whether you have understood its relevance. Study-Ware will reinforce your conceptual understanding of psychology and also improve your test-taking skills. Study-Ware will help you now and make your study of psychology much more enjoyable.

STUDY-WARE ORDER CARD

(Clip along dotted line and mail card below)

- -

NAME _____ SCHOOL _____

ADDRESS _____

CITY _____ STATE _____ ZIP _____

Please send me Study-Ware
for **PSYCHOLOGY: AN INTRODUCTION**
by **Josh Gerow**

_____Apple $14.95   _____IBM $14.95

Please send me **AMAZE**

_____Apple $12.95   _____IBM $12.95

_____Studyware +   _____Studyware +
Amaze $19.95   Amaze $19.95

Year in College   SR   JR   SO   FR
                              (circle one)

My Major_____

Other courses I'd like to have Study-Ware for_____

Please indicate method of payment
_____Personal Check _____VISA _____MasterCard

Accnt. #_____

Expiration Date_____

Signature_____
                    (required on all charges)

Make checks payable to Soft Productions, Inc.
Indiana residents add sales tax.

STUDY-WARE

School is tough enough. Get an edge on studying this semester with Study-Ware.

Study-Ware is an electronic learning system that not only evaluates your knowledge of text content but also helps diagnose your specific learning skills. Designed for the Apple 11+, 11e, and 11c, Macintosh, and the IBM PC computers, Study-Ware is keyed directly to PSYCHOLOGY: AN INTRODUCTION for easy reference and learning.

After reading each chapter in the text, Study-Ware allows you to check how much you have learned with fill-in-the-blank, multiple-choice, and matching review exercises and self-tests, and short essay questions.

Automatic scoring allows you to check yourself as you learn.

And Study-Ware is easy to use. Three simple keystrokes are all you need to get started.

The system was designed for use on your own computer or any computer available to you on campus.

To order, complete and mail the card below. Be sure to indicate the type of computer disk you want and your method of payment.

A-MAZE!

A computerized psychology adventure, A-MAZE asks students to wander the corridors of a psychology maze in search of doorways. Upon finding a door and opening it, students try to answer three types of questions covering the broad topics in introductory psychology. They are awarded or docked pellets accorded to each question type. Students can exit A-MAZE by acquiring 250 pellets—or lose by starving!

A-MAZE has three goals. The first is to help the student acquire an historical overview of important names, places, and events in psychology. The second is to help review some of the basic facts surrounding these people and events. The third is the game element that allows challenging competitions among students. For Apple and IBM Systems.

Mail to:

Soft Productions, Inc.
P. O. Box 1003
Notre Dame, Indiana 46556

CONTENTS

PSYCHOLOGY
An Introduction

CHAPTER ONE

THE NATURE OF PSYCHOLOGY

Topic 1   Defining Psychology

Topic 2   The Methods of Psychology

TOPIC

How would you feel about starting off with a test? This is a short, true-false test about psychology. It has two possible advantages over tests that you may take later this term: (1) You can score it yourself—answers can be found at the end of this topic, and (2) it will give you some idea of the issues and questions we will be covering in the rest of this book.

T F 1. Most psychologists engage in research and are employed by colleges and universities.

T F 2. If two events are correlated, we know that one is the cause of the other.

T F 3. If a person's right side is paralyzed due to a stroke, it is the right side of the person's brain that is damaged.

T F 4. Everybody dreams, usually several times a night.

T F 5. The average adult human can adequately attend to about 15–20 things at one time.

T F 6. In daylight, red is the easiest color to see.

T F 7. People can be forced to do things under the influence of hypnosis that they would not do otherwise.

T F 8. LSD and cocaine are physically addictive drugs.

T F 9. Most elderly people can remember the remote past better than they can remember recent events.

T F 10. Paying attention to the inappropriate behaviors of children usually acts to punish and eliminate those behaviors.

T F 11. Principles of learning that are derived from research with rats and dogs can seldom be applied to human learning.

T F 12. The fear of snakes, bees, rats, and/or the dark is instinctive, or unlearned.

T F 13. Childhood development passes through five distinct stages.

T F 14. People who take a long time to learn something generally remember what they have learned better than those who learn quickly.

T F 15. The amount of water (or liquid) that we drink throughout the day is determined by the dryness of our mouth and throat.

T F 16. Alcoholism runs in families.

T F 17. Sigmund Freud based his theories of personality on a series of experiments he performed in Vienna early in the twentieth century.

T F 18. Stress is a fact of life.

T F 19. Threatening suicide is a sure sign that the person will *not* actually commit suicide.

T F 20. Most people in psychiatric (or "mental") institutions are there because they are a danger to others.

T F 21. Schizophrenics have "split personalities."

T F 22. If neurotics "get worse," they become psychotic.

T F 23. If you are in danger or in trouble, you are more likely to get help if there are many people around instead of just a few.

T F 24. Extreme attitudes are easier to change than moderate attitudes.

T F 25. Humans are the least social of all the mammals.

Why We Care

We will be spending the next few hundred pages together reviewing some of the basic topics of general psychology. In this text we'll summarize some of the theories and data of psychology. We'll discuss some of the questions that psychologists have raised and look at how they have attempted to answer them. We will always be looking for ways in which the study of psychology can be applied to our everyday life experiences. Hopefully, this introduction will stimulate you to look beyond this text and this course for more information about psychology.

It seems reasonable to begin our discussion by trying to develop a sense of just what psychology *is*. This is the major goal of this first topic. To more fully appreciate what psychology is today, we will take a brief look at where psychology has been. Psychology as we know it today has had a brief history— it's just over 100 years old—but that history has deep roots in both philosophy and science.

A glance at our table of contents indicates that psychology covers a wide range of different topics. Before we review in Topic 2 *how* psychologists go about their work, we'll examine *where* psychologists work and, in general, *what* they do.

DEFINING PSYCHOLOGY

psychology
the scientific study of behavior and mental processes

Psychology is the scientific study of behavior and mental processes. Most psychologists would agree that this definition summarizes the essential character of psychology. It may leave something to be desired in terms of telling us precisely what it is that psychologists do. And it isn't as specific in terms of subject matter as we might like it to be. As a working definition, however, it does make a couple of very important points about psychology: (1) It is a science, and (2) it studies behavior and mental processes. Before we see if we can generate a more specific, or alternative, definition, let's see what these two points mean.

Psychology Is a Science

science
an organized body of knowledge gained through application of scientific methods

If psychology claims scientific status for itself, we should ask what it means to be a science. A **science** is an organized body of knowledge gained through application of scientific methods. If we accept this general definition for science, does psychology qualify? To do so requires two things: (1) an organized body of knowledge and (2) scientific methodology.

1. An Organized Body of Knowledge   Psychologists have accumulated a great deal of information over the years. We are coming to appreciate how thoughts and behaviors affect our nervous systems, and vice versa. We are beginning to discover how we find out about the world in which we live. We can specify some of the major determinants of personal growth and development. We know how many of the processes of learning and memory work. We have isolated many of the variables that influence the adjustments that people make to their environments and to each other. Throughout this book we will be looking at some of what psychologists have learned.

To be sure, we can still ask many interesting (and important) questions for which we have no good answers as yet. Not having all the answers can be frustrating at times, but it is also part of the excitement of psychology; there are still so many important issues to be resolved, so many questions to be answered. The truth is, nonetheless, that psychologists *have* learned a great deal about their subject matter. What we know is well organized and systematic. You have in your hands one version of the systematic, organized collection of knowledge that is psychology. In terms of point 1, psychology does qualify as a science.

2. Gained Through Scientific Methods

What we have learned in psychology we have learned through the application of **scientific methods**, which are a set of systematic procedures involving observation, description, control, and replication used to gain knowledge. The specific techniques or procedures that a psychologist may use to study some aspect of behavior or mental processes vary widely. We'll review some of psychology's more commonly used methods in Topic 2. The one thing that all of our methods have in common is that they are scientific.

Scientific methods do not rely solely on common sense. They do not even rely solely on logic. They rely on careful observation, description, control, and replication. To explain something scientifically is to rule out alternative explanations.

The way psychologists use scientific methods goes something like this: The scientist (psychologist) makes observations about his or her subject matter (behavior and/or mental processes). On the basis of these observations, a **hypothesis** is developed. A hypothesis is a tentative explanation that can be tested, confirmed, or rejected. In a sense, it is an educated guess about one's subject matter. Now, new observations and descriptions of events relevant to the hypothesis are made. These are then analyzed to see if the hypothesis was well founded. Alternative hypotheses are tested. If alternative hypotheses can be eliminated, and if the observations continue to support the scientist's hypothesis, a tentative conclusion is reached. This conclusion is communicated to others who may similarly test it to see if it can be confirmed.

Hypotheses become conclusions only if alternative explanations cannot be used to explain the same events. Observations, descriptions, and measurements must consistently reflect the same conclusion before they are accepted as part of the knowledge base of a science. Thus, through its use of scientific methods, psychology fulfills the second requirement for qualifying as a science.

scientific methods
systematic procedures involving observation, description, control, and replication used to gain knowledge

hypothesis
a tentative proposition, or explanation, that can be tested, confirmed, or rejected

Before you go on

What two points do we have to demonstrate in order to claim that psychology is a science?

The Subject Matter of Psychology

Simply skimming through the chapters of this book should convince you that trying to list everything that psychologists study would be pointless. The list would be much too long to be useful. However, it would be fair to suggest as a broad statement that psychology studies the behavior and mental processes of organisms.

Psychologists Study Behavior

By **behavior** we mean what organisms *do*: how they act and react and how they respond. The behaviors that we study must be observable; they should be measurable. If I am concerned with whether or not a rat presses a lever, I can directly observe the rat's behavior. If I wonder if Susie can draw a circle, I can ask her to do so and observe her efforts. Such behaviors have an advantage as the subject matter

behavior
any action or reaction of an organism that can be observed and measured

Psychologists study behavior in a number of ways. For example, because they cannot observe stress directly, psychologists often monitor how people react to stressful situations. In this way, they can provide an operational definition of stress.

public verifiability
the agreement (verifiability) of observers (public) that an event did or did not take place

operational definition
a definition given in terms of the operations used to measure or create the concept being defined

of a science because they are **publicly verifiable.** That is, we can demonstrate that a number of observers (public) can agree on (verify) the behavior of the organism being studied. We can all agree that the rat did or did not press the lever, or that Susie drew a circle, not a triangle. Events and behaviors that cannot be publicly verified lose status or credibility in science.

Remember we said psychologists study what organisms do, but some of the reactions that organisms have are not so easily observed. Reactions can, however, be measured in such a way as to make them verifiable. For example, I may not be able to tell by looking at you whether or not you are anxious at this moment. I could, however, monitor your blood pressure, rate of breathing, sweat gland activity, and a host of other internal physiological events. By observing the gauges, meters, and dials of my instruments, I can observe subtle changes that would not otherwise be obvious to me, or to you either for that matter. I would not be observing anxiety directly. But I might be willing to propose that the reactions I am observing are consistent with those we associate with anxiety.

In taking this approach, we say that we are providing an **operational definition** of anxiety. We are defining anxiety in terms of the "operations" that we use to measure or produce it. We might have chosen to operationally define anxiety in terms of responses that you might have to an anxiety test or questionnaire. Similarly, we might wonder how our rat's lever pressing would be affected if it were hungry. How do we know when a rat is hungry? Simple: We operationally define a hungry rat as one that has been deprived of food for 24 hours. That is, we can define hunger in terms of the procedures or operations used to produce it. We may also want to operationally define a lever press (i.e., how far down the rat will have to press the lever to qualify as a full lever press).

There are some limitations with operational definitions, but they do allow us to specify the exact nature of the behavior we are studying, and they allow us to communicate accurately with others. These are both critical aspects of science. Operational definitions can also be used to avoid lengthy philosophical discussions. Rather than agonizing over the true nature of intelligence, we may choose to operationally define intelligence as "that which an IQ test measures."

Psychologists Study Mental Processes   When it first began, psychology was defined as the science of **mental processes.** Yet for nearly 50 years in this century, mental activities were virtually ignored by most psychologists. Instead, psychologists focused almost exclusively on observable behavior. No one proposed that mental processes were unimportant. However, it was felt that such activities should not be included in the science of psychology. The argument was that mental processes were too personal and lacked public verifiability.

The study of mental processes is returning to the mainstream of psychology. We now believe that we *can* use scientific methodology to study **cognitions**—the sensing, perceiving, knowing, judging, and problem-solving skills involved in the processing of information about the world in which we live—and **affect**—the feelings associated with emotional responses.

Cognitions and affect are clearly mental events. They are our thoughts, ideas, beliefs, likes, dislikes, and feelings. Because such mental processes are not directly observable, they are difficult to study scientifically. But, people do think and reason, make judgments, form images, dream, and experience a wide range of feelings. These are the stuff of mental life. By carefully defining terms and drawing inferences from measurable behaviors, mental processes *can* be studied scientifically, even if indirectly. Modern psychology now appears to be secure enough with its own position to once again seriously pursue the study of such processes.

mental processes
those activities of consciousness not normally observable by others, including cognitions and affect

cognitions
the mental process of "knowing," of thinking, attending, perceiving, remembering, and the like

affect
the feelings or mood that accompany emotional reactions

The Variability of Psychology's Subject Matter   It is generally recognized that, as a science, psychology often lacks the accuracy and precision that we would like. The "facts" of psychology occasionally seem less certain than do the "facts" of other sciences, such as chemistry, physics, or biology. There are two reasons why this is so. One is that psychology is still a young science. As we shall soon see, the roots of psychology are ancient, but as a science, psychology emerged just over a century ago. In many ways, 100 years is a long time, but compared to other sciences, we are youngsters.

The second reason for the uncertainty in psychology has to do with its subject matter. The subject matter is complex and complicated, but so is the subject matter of other sciences. A major problem that we have in the science of psychology that is not shared by most other sciences is that our subject matter is variable. The behaviors and mental processes of our subjects change all the time.

In one sense, this is the familiar snowflake argument: "No two snowflakes are exactly alike." Indeed, no two organisms are exactly alike either. We are each different. In fact, when we contemplate the number of ways in which people can be (and often are) different from one another, it is sometimes a wonder that we can get along with each other at all. Many of the ways in

Psychologists must remember that their subject matter is variable. Not only do individuals differ one from another, but each individual changes from moment to moment. What you are feeling now may be completely different from what you will feel 5 minutes from now.

which persons differ may not be relevant for the particular behavior or mental process we are studying at the moment, but some may be.

Not only is each organism unique and different from all others, but it is also true that no one organism is exactly the same from one moment to the next. You are not the same person today that you were yesterday. You have changed, depending on your experiences, behaviors, and mental processes over the past 24 hours. Most likely, you have not changed in any noticeably significant way, but you have changed. You will not be exactly the same person tomorrow as you are right now. Simply by living, you will be changed.

Now imagine that a psychologist wants to study you and your behavior and mental activity and draw some conclusions that she can apply to people in general. Do you see a problem she is going to have? You are not exactly like everyone else; you are not even exactly the same after her study as you were before it began. This variability can cause problems. As it happens, science has devised techniques for dealing with such variability, but so long as such variability exists in psychology's subject matter, our understanding will lack the complete precision and accuracy we might desire.

You may have noticed that nowhere in our discussion have we specifically limited psychology to the study of *people*. To be sure, most psychologists are interested in people more than in rats, or monkeys, or other organisms. However, many psychologists have found that nonhuman organisms are more appropriate to study than are people. Many of the so-called "lower" species are studied by psychologists whose main concern is with humans. Other psychologists study rats or chimpanzees simply because they are interested in these animals and their behaviors. Psychology is not necessarily a science of humans only.

Before you go on
In what way does the variability of its subject matter affect the science of psychology?

THE HISTORY OF PSYCHOLOGY

In order to better appreciate the nature of psychology today, let's take a brief look at psychology's past. Our hope is that an examination of where we've been will help us understand where we are now and where we may be going.

Many of the basic concerns of psychology in the 1980s have been with us for a very long time. Certainly the early Greek philosophers wrote at length about issues that are essentially psychological in nature. The physicians, biologists, and physiologists of the eighteenth and nineteenth centuries were also interested in many psychological processes, but from their own, unique perspective. Still, it is not inaccurate to say that psychology as we know it today is a twentieth-century science. Where did psychology come from and with what issues did the early psychologists concern themselves?

Psychology's Roots in Philosophy and Science

Philosophy   Although we might go further back in time, there is good reason to begin with the French philosopher René Descartes (1596–1650). Descartes was interested in how the human body functions. He envisioned elaborate and mechanical schemes for its operation. Indeed, he thought of the human body as a complicated piece of machinery. He believed that the body functions according to rules, or laws, and that these laws are knowable.

Significantly, Descartes believed that humans possess more than just a body—that they have souls or minds. He suggested that the human mind also operates according to laws that are knowable, but which are different from those that affect the body. Descartes proposed that these two entities, mind and body, interact. It is through this interaction that we can come to know about the mind. Mind and body are different (dualism), but they interact with each other, a notion we call **interactive dualism.** For the first time, with the writings of Descartes, we have a clear focus on the possibility of understanding the mind, how it works, and how it interacts with the body.

Somewhat later, across the English Channel, a school of thought that we now identify as British Empiricism brought philosophy to the threshold of psychology. First with John Locke (1632–1704), and later with George Berkeley (1685–1753), David Hume (1711–1776), and David Hartley (1705–1757), attention was focused on how we represent the external world in the internal world of the mind.

René Descartes   John Locke

Descartes had raised this very question, and he had proposed a partial answer: Much of the content of our mind is innate. That is, Descartes claimed that we are born with certain basic notions about the world and about God. The empiricists thought otherwise. **British Empiricism** focused on the source of mental processes, claiming that they are learned through experience. The empiricists believed that we are each born into this world with our minds as blank slates. (The mind as a blank slate, or *tabula rasa,* was not new with Locke; the term had been introduced by Aristotle.) The question then became: "How does the mind come to be filled with all its ideas, and memories, and abilities?" To this question Locke answered, "In one word, from *experience.*"

With Locke and those who followed in his intellectual footsteps, at least a segment of philosophy turned its attention to the contents and nature of the mind. Mental life results from experience, from our perceptions of and interactions with the environment, the empiricists argued. Berkeley, in fact, equated knowledge with perception. What is, is what we perceive—knowing is perceiving.

Our perceptions, then, become real, at least in our minds. The contents of our minds can be manipulated. Ideas can be associated, one with another, to form new and different ideas. The empiricists wondered about *how* ideas become associated, and suggested a number of "laws of association." Although they never put their theories and ideas to experimental or scientific tests, their philosophy was becoming remarkably psychological in its concerns and questions. All it lacked was the appropriate methodology to become "scientific" and a separate discipline.

Science   During the nineteenth century, natural science was making tremendous progress on virtually every frontier. In 1860, a German physicist, Gustav Fechner (1801–1887), published a volume that was unique as a physics text. Fechner chose to apply his training in the methods of physics to an issue that involved the basic psychological process of sensation. What, Fechner wondered, was the relationship between the physical characteristics of a stimulus and the psychological experience of that stimulus? If the intensity of a light source is doubled, will an observer now experience that light as being twice as bright as it was before? Fechner was able to apply precise scientific techniques and measurements to a fundamentally psychological question about experience. We'll discuss Fechner's studies in more depth in Topic 5.

Also in the mid-1800s, the science of physiology was reaching a much fuller understanding of how the human body functions. It was clear by then

interactive dualism
Descartes's notion that a separate body and mind interact and influence each other

British Empiricism
the school of thought (associated with John Locke among others) that focused on the source of mental processes, claiming them to be learned through experience.

Hermann
von Helmholtz

Wilhelm Wundt

that nerves carry electrical messages to and from different parts of the body, and that the nerves that serve vision are different from those that serve hearing and the other senses. Hermann von Helmholtz (1821–1894) was a pioneer in areas of physiology that have direct impact on psychology. Although a physician/surgeon by trade, von Helmholtz's true love was pure science, the laboratory, and research. Here, from a point of view quite different from philosophy, grew an interest in matters clearly psychological. But remember, in the mid-1800s there was no psychology. Von Helmholtz's interests and experiments in sensation, perception, and the operation of the nervous system were getting very close, however.

By the late nineteenth century, psychology's time had come. From one direction philosophy had become intrigued with mental processes, the nature of ideas, and the perception of reality. From another, physiology and physics had begun to focus on the operation of sensory and perceptual systems and were using a scientific, laboratory methodology. All that was needed was someone to unite these two areas of interest and method and establish a separate discipline. Such a person was Wilhelm Wundt.

Before you go on

In what way did the philosophy of Descartes and Locke prepare the way for psychology?

In what way did Fechner and von Helmholtz influence the emergence of psychology?

Experimental Psychology Begins: Structuralism and Functionalism

Simply for the convenience of having a date to refer to, we generally say that psychology "began" in 1879 when Wilhelm Wundt (1832–1920) founded his laboratory at the University of Leipzig. Wundt was trained to enter medicine as a profession, and he studied physiology. In fact, at Heidelberg University he served as a laboratory assistant to von Helmholtz. He also held an academic position in philosophy. Wundt was a scientist/philosopher with an interest in such psychological processes as sensation, perception, attention, word associations, and feelings.

For Wundt, psychology was the study of the mind, of consciousness. The study was to be scientific. He was a strict scientist who left nothing to chance; all of his ideas were to be tested and then retested in the laboratory under carefully controlled conditions.

In keeping with the science of its day, Wundt's laboratory was seriously concerned with structure. Physics was searching for the elemental units of nature. Chemistry was studying the structure of chemical compounds and elements. Biology was engrossed in studying and classifying the structure of living things. How sensible it was then for Wundt to want to study the structure of consciousness, the structure of the mind. What, wondered Wundt, were the elements, or atoms, of the mind? Of what basic units are thoughts constructed? Can ideas be broken down into elements? What are the essential structures of our emotions? Although he did not use the term, it seems reasonable now to refer to the type of psychology engaged in by Wundt and his students—that is, the study of the structure of the human mind or consciousness—as **structuralism.**

structuralism
the school of psychology (associated with Wundt) interested in the structure or elements of the human mind or consciousness

At about the same time that Wundt's laboratory was flourishing in Germany, an American philosopher at Harvard University, William James (1842–1910), was taking issue with the formidable structuralists. James taught a course called "Psychology" and opened a laboratory to be used in the class for demonstrations—4 years before the founding of Wundt's lab. James wrote a classic psychology textbook in 1890 *(Principles of Psychology)*. But, James never did any experiments of his own and never really founded a formal school of psychology to oppose structuralism.

James agreed that psychology should rightfully study the mind and consciousness. He defined psychology as the "science of mental life." However, James argued that consciousness should not and could not be broken down into elements or particles or structures. James believed that consciousness is dynamic, a stream of events, personal, changing, continuous, active, and not a static structure that can withstand analysis into parts and subparts. Psychology should be concerned not with the structure of the mind, but with its function. That is, to what practical use can the mind and mental life be put?

William James

James' practical approach to psychology found favor in this country, and a new brand of psychology did emerge, largely at the University of Chicago. Under the guidance of James Angell and John Dewey, this new school of psychology was called **functionalism,** which focused on how the mind and consciousness help an organism adapt to its environment. By the 1920s, it was a well-established school of thought.

functionalism
the school of psychology that studied the function of the mind and consciousness in helping the organism to adapt to its environment

Functionalism concerned itself with consciousness, with mental life, as James had suggested. Functionalists were also influenced by the theories of Charles Darwin (1809–1882). Evolutionary theory drew the Chicago psychologists to wonder about the adaptive, utilitarian *functions* of the mind. What was thinking *for?* How can the mind adapt and change? How can the mind help the organism adapt, change, and survive? How is mental life affected by the environment, and how might it act to operate on its environment?

Focusing on the functions of mental life, and imbued with a spirit of useful application, the functionalists branched rapidly into child psychology, educational psychology, the study of learning and memory, and applications of psychological principles to business and industry.

As more and more bright young scientists were drawn to the study of psychology, academic departments and laboratories began to prosper. Now into the twentieth century, experimental psychology was well under way. Whether from a structuralist or functionalist perspective, psychology was the scientific study of the mind, its structure and/or its function.

Before you go on
Briefly compare and contrast structuralism and functionalism.

Gestalt Psychology

In the first quarter of this century, functionalism was well established in the United States and structuralism was holding its own in Germany. At the same time, a new group of German psychologists was taking a different approach to psychology. Under the leadership of Max Wertheimer (1880–1943), this school of thought became known as Gestalt psychology.

Gestalt is one of those words that is very difficult to translate literally into English. It basically means "whole," or "configuration," or "totality." In general terms, if you can "see the big picture," you may be said to have developed a gestalt. It was the "big picture" that intrigued the Gestalt psychologists.

gestalt
whole, totality, configuration, or pattern; the whole (gestalt) being perceived as more than the sum of its parts

Gestalt psychologists argued against trying to analyze perception, or awareness, or consciousness as if each is a discrete, separate entity. "The whole is *more* than the sum of its parts," they argued. When we look at a

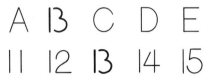

drawing of a cube, we do not see individual lines or surfaces. We combine these elements to form a whole, a gestalt, which we call a cube. When we listen to someone speak, we do not hear individual speech sounds; rather, we form gestalts—words, phrases, sentences, ideas—and we attend to these larger units.

Focusing largely on perception, Gestalt psychologists also argued that all perceptions, and thus all knowledge, cannot be considered in isolation. Everything occurs in a context or frame of reference. It is often the context in which something occurs that gives it its meaning (see Figure 1.1).

Unlike the functionalists who subscribed to Locke's view that experience provides the contents of the mind, Gestalt psychologists believed (as did Descartes) that some basic, set ways of perceiving the world were innate and unlearned. We see the world in three dimensions; we attend to contrasts between adjacent stimuli; stimuli in motion tend to grab our attention. Why? Gestalt psychologists would be willing to say "because"—because that's the way we were born to see, and learning has little or nothing to do with it.

Gestalt psychology, as a formal approach, lost momentum in the 1930s as Nazism gained power in Germany, and the leaders of Gestalt psychology emigrated to the United States. The influence of this school, however, is still very much with us. In Topic 12, we'll be reviewing some of the data and conclusions of Gestalt psychology as they relate to the selection and organization of our perceptions.

Before you go on

What does "gestalt" mean?

What do Gestalt psychologists study?

Behaviorism

John B. Watson (1878–1958) was born on a farm in South Carolina in 1878. After the death of his mother he no longer felt compelled to enter the ministry, as she had wished. Instead, he enrolled as a graduate student in psychology at the University of Chicago. There he had little choice but to study the functional psychology of the resident experts. He apparently had little flair for or sympathy with the study of mental activity, but he remained a psychology major, studying the behavior of animals, white rats in particular.

With his PhD in hand, at the age of 29, Watson moved to Johns Hopkins University where he had a spectacular, if brief, academic career. (After becoming involved in a scandal, he was fired in 1920 and left psychology to begin a successful career in advertising.) In fact, few individuals have had as much influence on American psychology as did John Watson.

Watson argued that if psychology were to become a mature, productive, scientific enterprise, it had to give up its preoccupation with the mind and mental activity. Psychology should concentrate on that which is observable and measurable, such as *behavior*: hence the name of a new school of psychology—**behaviorism.**

behaviorism
the school of psychology, associated with Watson and Skinner, that focuses on the observable, measurable behavior of organisms

Watson never claimed that people do not think, have ideas, or form mental images. He did argue that such things are not the proper subjects of scientific investigation. Science should focus on those events that observers can measure and agree upon, and behaviors fit the bill. No one else, after all, can exactly share your thoughts, ideas, and images. We have no way of seeing what you see in your mind's eye. So let us leave all these private, internal events to philosophy or religion, and make psychology as rigorously scientific as possible. Psychology should concentrate on the effects that overt, measurable stimuli (S) have on overt, measurable responses (R). Given this emphasis, behaviorism is often referred to as "S-R psychology."

John B. Watson   *B. F. Skinner*   *Carl Rogers*   *Abraham Maslow*

No one has characterized the behavioristic, S-R approach to psychology more than B. F. Skinner (b. 1904). Skinner took Watson at his word and has spent his long and productive professional career in psychology attempting to demonstrate that we can predict the behavior of organisms by observing the lawful relationship between the effect of stimuli on organisms and the responses of the organisms.

Skinner has avoided any reference to the internal states of his subjects, be they rats, pigeons, or people. What matters for Skinner is how organisms modify their behaviors through their interactions with their environments. Our behaviors are modified by learning. As we come to recognize the consequences of our behaviors, we change our behaviors accordingly. The behaviorists would not have us ask why a rat turns left in a maze by wondering what the rat wanted or what it was thinking about as it turned. Rather, they would have us see if we can specify the environmental conditions (stimuli) under which a rat is likely to make left turns (response). They would suggest that we focus on stimuli and responses and leave the internal affairs of the organism out of our explanations.

Humanism and Cognitive Psychology

The S-R behaviorism of Watson and Skinner has remained very popular, at least in American psychology. Its popularity is based largely on the fact that in many ways the approach is a logical one, and it works. The behavioristic approach has not gone unchallenged, however. We'll mention just two reactions that we can find clearly reflected in psychology today.

A type of psychology we call **humanism** is in many respects a reaction against behaviorism. Its leaders are Carl Rogers (b. 1902) and Abraham Maslow (1908–1970). Humanist psychologists believe that the individual or the self should be a central concern of psychology. It is their argument that we need to get the "person" back into psychology. A disregard for the organism that does the responding to stimuli is dehumanizing. Humanists feel we need to put the person, the self back into the S-R equation. Humanists argue that we need an O (for organism) between the S and the R; an S-O-R approach, if you will. Such matters as intention, will, caring, concern, love, and hate are real phenomena and worthy of scientific investigation. Any attempt to understand people without considering such processes will be doomed. Taking this approach led Maslow to develop a theory of human motivation (see Topic 20) and led Rogers to develop a system of psychotherapy (see Topic 30).

humanism
a point of view associated with Maslow and Rogers that focuses on the person or self as a central matter of concern

Another shift away from behaviorism that has occurred in recent years is the emergence, in fact reemergence, of **cognitive psychology**. Cognitive psychology deals with a myriad of topics: attention, perception, memory, consciousness, concept formation, language, problem solving, and thinking in general. Now you may recognize these as many of the same topics that entertained experimental psychologists back at the turn of the century, and you're right. "Mental" issues are coming back into vogue, but very carefully, very scientifically, trying to avoid the fuzzy, nonscientific problems that Watson pointed out so clearly.

A number of reasons have been offered to explain why cognitive, or mental, issues are returning to psychology. Two important considerations are (1) the inherent interest in such topics, long ignored by behaviorists, and (2) our increased understanding of internal processes that comes from our appreciation of computer science and the study of memory. The attempt to build machines that can think has forced us to look more closely at what thinking *is*.

Before you go on

What is the major position of behaviorism?

Which two psychologists do we associate with behaviorism?

Identify two approaches to psychology that take issue with behaviorism.

A Focus on Application: Mental Measurement and Psychoanalysis

So far, our review of history has focused on academic approaches to behavior and mental processes. Paralleling these developments, others were taking a more pragmatic, or applied, approach to psychology. These pioneers in psychology directed their attention to individual differences and mental disorders.

Mental Measurement   Sir Francis Galton (1822–1911) was a first cousin of Charles Darwin and was very influenced by him. Galton was in no literal sense a psychologist, but he was a very busy scientist. He was intrigued by the theory of evolution and the possibilities for improving the human race. Galton reasoned that before one could improve the human condition, one first needed to measure and catalog the range of human abilities and aptitudes as they exist at the moment. He set about devising countless ingenious tests and measurements of individual differences. Most of Galton's work was done in the late nineteenth century. From his efforts comes the tradition in psychology of recognizing individual differences and attempting to measure them accurately and reliably. In many ways it is quite fair to consider Galton the founder of psychological testing. Galton also devised many statistical procedures to help him deal with the vast amount of data (numbers) that his mental tests generated.

At the turn of the century, Alfred Binet (1857–1911) advanced Galton's work on testing. Binet was given a real, practical problem by the French Ministry of Education: Could he devise an instrument to assess the educational potential of young schoolchildren? Could intelligence be measured? Binet thought that it could, and by 1900 he had devised a number of tests to do just that. Aided by Théophile Simon, Binet published an individually-

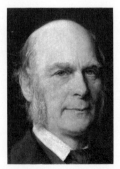

Sir Francis Galton

administered intelligence test in 1905. The original Binet-Simon test has undergone a number of major revisions. One of the most notable revisions was published in 1916 by Lewis Terman at Stanford University. Naming the new test after his university, the now Americanized test became known as the Stanford-Binet Intelligence Scale. (We'll discuss this classic test in some detail in Topic 27.)

Psychoanalysis   We will have ample opportunity to discuss many of the specific ideas and theories of Sigmund Freud (1856–1939) in later chapters. We will find ourselves referring to Freud in topics on child psychology, memory, consciousness, personality theory, and therapy. Few individuals in history have had as great an impact on the way we think about ourselves as this Viennese physician/psychiatrist.

Freud was in no way a laboratory scientist. He was a practitioner. Although his methods were largely unscientific, and some of his conclusions have turned out to be in error, his insights into the workings of the human mind are profound and influential. Through careful study of his patients, self-examination, beautifully written volumes of text, a unique force of will, and charisma, Sigmund Freud began and sustained psychiatry through its early years. From Freud, his students, his intellectual followers, and his opponents has come the clinical tradition in psychology—the concern with the diagnosis and treatment of behavior disorders.

Before you go on
In what ways did Sir Francis Galton, Alfred Binet, and Sigmund Freud shape psychology in its early history?

MAJOR AREAS OF MODERN PSYCHOLOGY

So far in this topic we have defined psychology as the scientific study of behavior and mental processes, and we have taken a brief look at psychology's past. In this last section, let's follow some of our own advice. We suggested that when psychologists are faced with a difficult concept to define, they often rely on operational definitions. Might we not offer the following as a sort of operational definition of psychology? "Psychology is that which persons who call themselves psychologists do." You probably recognize this definition as being somewhat tongue-in-cheek, but there is something to be said for it. In a sense, this whole book provides a definition of psychology. If you were to ask me what psychology really is, I might answer, "Everything in this text—and more."

For now, let's examine a listing of some of the major areas of concern that make up psychology today. The professional organization of psychology, the American Psychological Association, lists forty divisions to which its members may belong, and many belong to more than one (see Figure 1.2). One danger inherent in lists like the one here is that someone may infer that it provides a ranking in some order of importance. Be assured, none is intended.

Physiological/biological psychology is a growing and exciting area of psychology that concerns itself with the functions of the nervous system and its effect on behavior and mental processes. How does the brain influence what we do, how we feel, and how we think? What effects do drugs have on behavior? How are physiological and biological activity reflected in psycho-

Figure 1.2

The Divisions of the American Psychological Association

APA division number	APA division name
1	Division of General Psychology
2	Division on the Teaching of Psychology
3	Division of Experimental Psychology
5	Division of Evaluation and Measurement
6	Division of Physiological and Comparative Psychology
7	Division on Developmental Psychology
8	The Society of Personality and Social Psychology—A Division of the APA
9	The Society for the Psychological Study of Social Issues—A Division of the APA
10	Division of Psychology and the Arts
12	Division of Clinical Psychology
13	Division of Consulting Psychology
14	The Society for Industrial and Organizational Psychology, Inc—A Division of the APA
15	Division of Educational Psychology
16	Division of School Psychology
17	Division of Counseling Psychology
18	Division of Psychologists in Public Service
19	Division of Military Psychology
20	Division of Adult Development and Aging
21	Division of Applied Experimental and Engineering Psychologists
22	Division of Rehabilitation Psychology
23	Division of Consumer Psychology
24	Division of Theoretical and Philosophical Psychology
25	Division for the Experimental Analysis of Behavior
26	Division of the History of Psychology
27	Division of Community Psychology
28	Division of Psychopharmacology
29	Division of Psychotherapy
30	Division of Psychological Hypnosis
31	Division of State Psychological Association Affairs
32	Division of Humanistic Psychology
33	Division of Mental Retardation
34	Division of Population and Environmental Psychology
35	Division of Psychology of Women
36	Psychologists Interested in Religious Issues (PIRI)—A Division of the APA
37	Division of Child, Youth, and Family Services
38	Division of Health Psychology
39	Division of Psychoanalysis
40	Division of Clinical Neuropsychology
41	Division of Psychology and Law
42	Division of Psychologists in Independent Practice
43	Division of Family Psychology
44	The Society for the Psychological Study of Lesbian and Gay Issues—A Division of the APA

(There are no divisions 4 or 11)

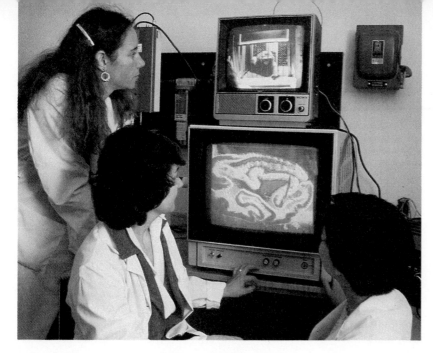

Psychologists often use neurobiology to study the effects of brain activity on behavior. Here, psychologists are studying the metabolic activity of a monkey's brain.

logical processes such as experience, dreaming, and memory? To what extent can behavior disorders be caused by (or treated with) physiological changes? These are just a few of the questions that physiological psychologists are asking.

Developmental psychology is concerned with the physical and psychological development of the individual. Often thought of only in terms of child psychology, some developmental psychologists focus on adolescence, some on adulthood, some on old age, and some prefer to take a broad life span approach. A developmental psychologist searches for biological and environmental influences on patterns of growth and development. In many ways, developmental psychology cuts across many other subfields in psychology because it deals with many basic psychological functions: intellectual and cognitive development, emotional and motivational development, social and moral development, and sensory and perceptual development, to name just a few.

Educational/instructional psychology is largely devoted to the study of the processes of learning and memory and the application of what we know about these processes to real-life situations. In both academic and business settings, educational psychologists often serve as consultants to improve training and education programs.

Clinical psychology includes those psychologists whose concern is with the psychological well-being of the individual. The training and experience of clinicians provide them the means to diagnose and treat individuals with behavior disorders. Clinicians have PhDs in clinical psychology, which distinguishes them from psychiatrists, who have earned a medical degree (MD) and may dispense drugs and use other forms of medical treatment. There are many subfields within clinical psychology, defined largely in terms of the type of therapy or the type of patient or client the psychologist deals with.

Counseling psychology is very much like clinical psychology, and most of the training is the same for both types of psychologists. Counseling psychologists, however, tend to serve those persons with less severe and less chronic (long-lasting) disorders.

Cognitive psychology is the field for psychologists who investigate the basic processes of the mind: perception, learning, memory, and thinking. Here, too, there are specialties. Psycholinguists, for example, are interested in language: how it is acquired, how it is produced, and how it is perceived and interpreted. Some cognitive psychologists are interested in artificial intelligence and how computers may be used to increase our understanding of the human mind.

Psychometrics is that field of psychology involved in psychological testing and measurement and the statistical interpretation of data. Psychological testing is a big business in our society. The construction of good, reliable, valid testing instruments is not easy. These psychologists give us the means to evaluate new tests as they are developed.

Social psychology responds to the observation that many organisms do not and cannot live without the company of others. How the behaviors of an individual affect others, and vice versa, is the general concern of social psychology. Predictably, this too is a field with many subfields, with interests in sex roles, attitudes, prejudice, intergroup conflict, conformity. interpersonal attraction, aggression, and the like.

Industrial/organizational psychology is defined mostly by where the psychologist tends to work. What he or she may do there covers a wide range of possibilities. Some industrial/organizational psychologists are concerned with marketing and advertising; some are concerned with group productivity; some are concerned with the design of equipment so that it can be used easily and safely; others are concerned with personnel decisions of hiring and firing; still others may help those suffering from the stress of the workplace.

Of course, this list is incomplete and provides only an overview. As of January of 1982, there were 51,341 U.S.-resident members of the American Psychological Association (Stapp & Fulcher, 1983) and many psychologists have chosen not to join this association or reside in other countries and have their own associations. No doubt, many psychologists would claim they do not fit any of the categories we have listed above. Others would claim that they fit two or more. This diversity and richness help make psychology such an exciting field to study.

Before you go on
Name nine areas of psychology and identify the sort of activity we might expect of a psychologist working in each area.

As we have seen, psychology is the scientific study of behavior and mental activity. It has had an exciting history with roots in philosophy and physiology. Psychology can be defined by its methods and its goals; that is, it can be defined by what psychologists do. It is to these issues that we now turn.

Answers to opening T-F test: Items 4, 16, and 18 are true; all the others are false.

Since 1976, the American Psychological Association (APA) has conducted a large-scale survey of its membership on a regular basis. The main purpose of the survey is to determine the type and setting of employment and the kind of activities in which APA members are engaged. The most recent Human Resources Survey, which was conducted in 1982, sought responses from 10,108 members of the APA who live in the United States. Just over 65 percent of those surveyed returned completed questionnaires. The results of this 1982 survey are reported in detail in the December 1983 issue of the *American Psychologist* (Nelson & Stapp; Stapp & Fulcher; Vandenbos & Stapp). Here we'll summarize some of the most relevant findings of this survey.

The APA's survey included both doctoral level and master's level members. One thing the survey tells us is that psychologists enjoy rather full employment—only 0.6 percent of the doctoral level respondents and 1.3 percent of the master's level respondents are unemployed and actively seeking employment. The survey revealed that psychologists work in a wide variety of settings, as reported in Figure 1.3. Most psychologists work in university and college settings (38.1 percent), while the second most common place to find psychologists is in hospitals, clinics, or counseling centers (25.0 percent). Since the 1976 survey, there has been a slight drop in the number of psychologists with doctoral degrees employed in university psychology departments. At the same time, the number of psychologists involved in private practice has increased from 12.2 percent in 1976 to 15.8 percent in the 1982 survey.

What do psychologists claim as their area of expertise or their specialty area? The answer to this question is provided in Figure 1.4. In this figure we have included specialty areas for both doctoral and master's level psychologists.

Figure 1.3

Employment settings for APA members with full-time positions (Based on Stapp & Fulcher, 1983.)

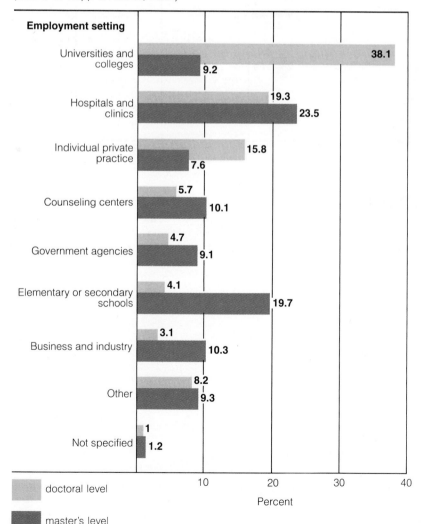

Here we can clearly see that most APA-member psychologists specialize in clinical and counseling psychology (59.8 percent for doctoral level psychologists and 53.0 percent for master's level psychologists). We have to remember that these labels only represent categories. Even though they may agree to the same category label, there is diversity within each category. As is the case for everyone, no two psychologists are exactly alike.

Figure 1.4
Specialty areas of APA members
(Based on Stapp & Fulcher, 1983.)

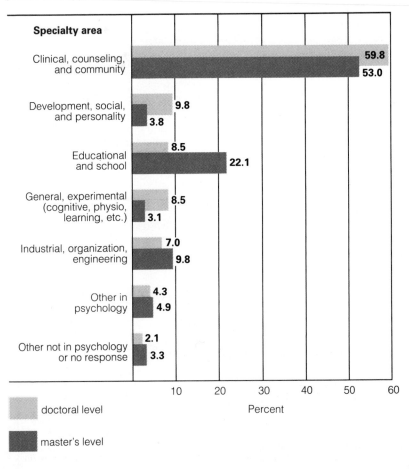

What two points do we have to demonstrate in order to claim that psychology is a science?

To prove that a discipline qualifies as a science requires demonstrating (1) that it has an organized body of knowledge and (2) that it uses scientific methods. / 5

What is the subject matter of psychology?

What are operational definitions?

Why do we use them?

Psychology is the scientific study of behavior and mental processes. Operational definitions define concepts in terms of the operations used to create or measure them. We use them to increase specificity and communicability and to minimize philosophical discussions about definitions. / 7

Compare and contrast the mental processes of cognition and affect.

Cognitions are intellectual mental processes, such as perceiving, remembering, and problem solving, while affect deals with the feelings of emotional responses. / 7

In what way does the variability of its subject matter affect the science of psychology?

The variability of behavior and mental processes reduces the accuracy and precision of the understanding of our subject matter. / 8

In what way did the philosophy of Descartes and Locke prepare the way for psychology?

In what way did Fechner and von Helmholtz influence the emergence of psychology?

Both René Descartes (with interactive dualism) and John Locke (with empiricism) directed the attention of philosophers to the mind—how it interacts with the body and how it comes to be filled with information.

Both Gustav Fechner (from physics) and Hermann von Helmholtz (from physiology) used scientific, experimental methods to ask basically psychological questions. / 10

Briefly compare and contrast structuralism and functionalism.

Both structuralism (Wundt) and functionalism (James, Angell, and Dewey) defined psychology in terms of mental activity, but the former looked for the structure or elemental particles of the mind, while the latter focused on the utilitarian usefulness or function of the mind or consciousness. / 11

What does "gestalt" mean?

What do Gestalt psychologists study?

"Gestalt" means whole or configuration. Gestalt psychologists study many things, focusing on factors that affect the selection and organization of perceptions. / 12

What is the major position of behaviorism?

Which two psychologists do we associate with behaviorism?

Identify two approaches to psychology that take issue with behaviorism.

Behaviorism (associated with John B. Watson and B. F. Skinner) holds that the true subject matter of the science of psychology should be measurable and observable—thus, behavior. Both humanistic psychology (Maslow and Rogers), which focuses on the self or person, and cognitive psychology, which focuses on mental processes, have taken issue with the behaviorists. / 14

In what ways did Sir Francis Galton, Alfred Binet, and Sigmund Freud shape psychology in its early history?

Galton may be called the founder of psychological testing, having devised many measures of behavior and mental processes. Binet authored the first truly successful intelligence test. Freud provided a foundation for psychologists who later devised theories of personality and engaged in the practice of trying to aid people with mental disorders. / 15

Name nine areas of psychology and identify the sort of activity we might expect of a psychologist working in each area.

Physiological psychologists study the nervous system and how it affects behavior and mental processes. *Developmental* psychologists study the life span growth and development of the individual. *Educational* psychologists study and try to improve the processes of learning and memory. *Clinical* psychologists have many sub-specialties, but are generally involved in the diagnosis and treatment of behavior disorders, not unlike *counseling* psychologists who tend to focus on less severe problems. *Cognitive* psychologists study mental processes such as memory and thinking. *Psychometric* psychologists are involved in the construction and assessment of psychological tests. *Social* psychologists study how the behavior of an individual influences and is influenced by others. *Industrial* psychologists work in business and industry in attempts to help solve the many problems that arise there. / 18

TOPIC

Let's suppose that you had a big biology mid-term exam this morning. You have been worried about this exam. For a number of reasons, you haven't been able to keep up with your studying as well as you would have liked. This mid-term will account for one third of your final grade. Late in the afternoon you stop by the biology department offices to see if grades have been posted. There they are. You quickly scan the list of identification numbers and locate your score: an A! Your score of 94 was the second highest in the class!

Once you recover from your initial excitement over having done so well, you stop to wonder why. Although you hadn't prepared as much as you could have, you recognize that you *did* put in a very good session of study and review last night. Everything seemed to come together and make sense. Why was last night's studying so much more effective than usual? Was there anything about your studying last night that was out of the ordinary? As you reflect on your efforts of the previous night, only one thing seems to have been different. It doesn't seem very significant at first, but last night you studied with classical music playing in the background. Everything else was basically the same as always. But usually you try to study in the quietest place you can find. Sometimes you have to study in noisy, crowded places; sometimes you go to the library. You've never studied with classical music playing before— you don't even like classical music. Can classical background music improve the effectiveness of studying? This strikes you as a reasonable (and potentially important) psychological question. How might you go about answering it?

You immediately recognize that your experience might simply reflect a unique coincidence. You realize that you cannot draw any general conclusions based on just one isolated incident. You need to find additional support for what has now become a hypothesis: Classical music is an aid to study. As is usually the case with such psychological questions, you will find that there are many ways you could go about confirming or rejecting your hypothesis. You might ask other students about the conditions under which they study. You might examine the study habits of good students and poor students. You might observe students studying and note background conditions. You might keep careful, complete records of your own studying experiences. You will have to generate some operational definitions for the relevant aspects of your basic question. That is, how will you define "effective or ineffective studying"? What sorts of background conditions will you investigate?

Even if you were to discover that students who earn high grades *do* tend to listen to classical music more frequently than do those who earn low grades, will you be able to conclude that it was the music that *caused* the higher grades? If you *can* generalize your experience to others, you may have discovered that there is a relationship between effective study and classical music, but you won't be able to conclude that classical music causes better studying. To be able to draw that kind of conclusion, you'll need to do an experiment.

As a science, psychology uses a number of different techniques for answering questions about behavior and mental processes. We'll use this question of the impact of classical music on the effectiveness of studying as an example throughout this topic.

What effect does listening to music have on studying? Studies have found that listening to music while studying can interfere with learning.

Why We Care

In Topic 1, we defined psychology as the *science* of behavior and mental processes. We also said that one of the main criteria for a science was the use of scientific methods. In this topic, we'll examine some of the scientific methods psychologists use. Throughout this text we'll review a number of specific applications of these methods to specific questions about behavior and mental processes. For now, we just want to present an overview of how these methods may be used within the context of psychology.

The goals of psychology are very much like those of any science. We want to be able to understand and explain our subject matter: behavior and mental processes and the relationships between them. We would like to be able to use what we know to make predictions. On the basis of our understanding, can we make any predictions, general or specific, about what an organism may do, think, or feel in the future? When appropriate, we would also like to be able to exercise some control over our subject matter. On the basis of our understanding of behavior and mental processes can we effect change? Can we improve an organism's quality of life? Can we help make the world a better place in which to live?

These are difficult and far-reaching goals: understanding, prediction, and control. As we mentioned in Topic 1, these are goals that we haven't always been able to attain. Our hope of reaching these goals hinges on our ability to use the methods of science as they can be applied to behavior and mental processes.

THE RELATIONSHIPS THAT PSYCHOLOGISTS STUDY

Psychologists seek to understand and explain the relationships that exist between behaviors and mental processes. How they go about doing that is the major subject of this topic. However, before we start examining methods, we should take a moment to look at the general nature of those relationships that psychologists study. In the most general sense, we can argue that there are two relationships: R-R and S-R relationships (in which the Rs stand for *response* and the S stands for *stimulus*), but we will soon recognize that these are oversimplifications.

R-R Relationships

R-R relationships
Statements of correlation that are used to tell us about the strength and nature of relationships between responses

response
any observable or measurable reaction of an organism

Statements of **R-R relationships** tell us how one set of **responses** is related to another set of responses. A response is any observable or measurable reaction of an organism. When we examine R-R relationships, what we find often goes something like this: "Whenever we have *those* responses, we also tend to find *these* responses," or, "These two responses go together."

For example, it is generally held that there is an R-R relationship between scores on a college entrance exam (one set of responses) and college grade point averages (another set of responses). Students who do well on entrance exams tend to do well in college. Students who do poorly on entrance exams tend to do poorly in college. Thus, we can state an R-R relationship here: These two responses are related to each other or are co-related. People who are good at diving (R) also tend to be good at gymnastics (R). You may discover that students who earn high grades (R) generally do listen to classical music (R).

R-R relationships are very useful in psychology. They can be used to help us make predictions. If the relationships we just listed are, in fact, true, I could better predict your grade point average if I knew your entrance exam score. In the same way, I could predict your diving ability if I knew how good a gymnast you are.

Before we go on, we need to make two important points about R-R relationships. First, as helpful as they may be in predicting behavior, they are seldom true every single time for every single individual. That is, there are usually exceptions. Some students who perform poorly on entrance exams have been known to graduate with honors, and some who do well on entrance exams end up flunking out of college. All our relationship suggests is that "in general," "by and large," "more often than not," the two responses we have measured are associated with each other. (Perhaps you recognize this as another way of saying that relationships in psychology often lack the precision and accuracy we would like them to have.)

The second important point about R-R relationships is that we cannot interpret them in terms of cause and effect. Just because two responses are related to each other does not mean that one *causes* the other. Good scores on entrance exams do not *cause* high grades in college courses. They just happen to occur together. Perhaps both are caused by some other factors, such as intelligence and motivation. All we can say about the responses of an R-R relationship is that they are related or associated.

Before you go on

What do R-R relationships tell us?

How can they be used?

Give one example of an R-R relationship.

S-R Relationships

S-R relationships tell us what is likely to happen in response to a **stimulus.** (A stimulus is any condition or event that produces a reaction or response.) Because they tell us about cause and effect, S-R relationships are often thought of as more important than R-R relationships. They work something like this: "When this stimulus (S) is presented, this response (R) will tend to occur."

S-R relationships
cause and effect statements relating stimuli to the responses they produce

stimulus
any event or energy that produces a reaction or response in an organism

If I blow in your eye (S), you will blink (R). When someone strikes your knee correctly (S), your leg will jerk (R). These are very simple S-R relationships, but they should give you the basic idea. If you were to discover that classical background music (S) does produce more effective learning (R), you would have demonstrated a useful cause-and-effect S-R relationship.

Complications with Stimulus-Response Relationships

There are two complications with S-R relationships. First, single stimuli seldom produce single responses. Most behaviors (beyond simple reflexes like eye blinks and knee jerks) have multiple causes. Stimuli seldom cause one and only one response. Second, stimuli act on organisms that produce responses. Stimuli and responses do not occur in a vacuum. Let's look at these two complications in more detail.

Multiple Causes (S) and Multiple Effects (R) First, let's look at what appears to be a simple S-R relationship, but is, in fact, quite complex. In a typical classroom setting, an instructor asks her students to listen to a word she is going to say. The students are then to say, out loud, the first word that they think of in response to her stimulus word. The instructor says "hot" and virtually every student in the class responds in unison, "cold." It looks like we have a simple S-R relationship here—the stimulus word "hot" results in the response word "cold." This relationship is depicted in Figure 2.1(A).

Now consider the stimulus more carefully. To be sure, the most important stimulus in this demonstration is the word "hot." Many other stimuli were relevant, however, in producing the response of "cold." The instructions the instructor used were a very important part of the overall stimulus situation. She simply asked for the first word the students thought of. She could have asked for a response word that means the same thing as her word or a word that rhymes with her word. It's hard to imagine what her students might have said in these situations, but it is unlikely that they would have said "cold." The fact that the demonstration took place in a classroom may have been critical. Would any of the students have said "cold" if they were on the beach, or out shopping, or standing on a street corner? There may have been other stimuli present in the situation that helped bring about the response "cold" from the students. The real stimulus in this demonstration, then, is really a collection of many stimuli. Instead of a simple S-R relationship, what we have is a sort of multiple S-R relationship.

We also have to consider the responses the subjects are likely to have to this collection of stimuli. It is true that for our example almost all of the students would respond by saying "cold." But there is certainly no guarantee that *every* student would. Someone might blurt out "fire," or "fudge," or "dog," or any number of perfectly reasonable things. For that matter, any one subject, even in the same stimulus situation, may not always have precisely the same response. As was the case for R-R relationships, the best we can do is to make probability statements: "Subjects will *probably* or *usually* say 'cold,' but they may make other (less probable) responses." So now we have multiple Ss resulting in multiple Rs. This may be more complicated, but it is also more realistic. This more realistic depiction is presented in Figure 2.1(B).

Figure 2.1
A simple S-R relationship and its more complex forms

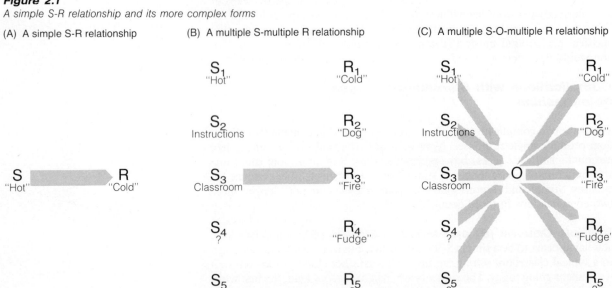

(A) A simple S-R relationship

(B) A multiple S-multiple R relationship

(C) A multiple S-O-multiple R relationship

Getting the Organism Involved   Finally, we have to acknowledge that S-R (and R-R) relationships require that we specify some characteristics of the organisms for which the relationships are true. Again, stimuli and responses do not operate in a vacuum.

Let's go back to our classroom example. We might now predict that in response to the stimulus word "hot," subjects will probably say "cold." In order to draw this conclusion, or make this prediction, we have to assume some things about the subjects, or organisms, involved in our demonstration. We'll assume that they are college students who are familiar with the English language and the common association between hot and cold. If none of the subjects in our demonstration speak English, they might not say anything at all. (They won't even understand our instructions!) What if the subjects were all 6-month-old infants? Or even rats?

The point is that we have to specify the nature of the organism (O) for which our S-R relationship holds. We may not need to know *everything* about our subjects. In this example, the sex or income of the subjects does not matter—"cold" will still be the most probable response. For different stimulus words in a similar demonstration, the sex and income of the subjects might be critical. S-R relationships that are true for rats may or may not be true for humans, and vice versa. Even the simplest of S-R relationships generally take the form of multiple S-O-multiple R (see Figure 2.1(C)).

Before you go on

What is the nature of S-R relationships?

Why should we think of them as multiple S-O-multiple R relationships?

METHODS: CORRELATIONAL STUDIES

Assessing **correlation** is a way to discover R-R relationships. Correlational studies tell us how and to what extent two sets of responses are related to each other, or are co-related (correlated). In order to study correlations, psychologists must come up with good, consistent ways of measuring the responses in which they are interested. This is no small task. It may involve generating operational definitions of the responses of interest. If no measuring device is readily available, one may need to be devised. Psychological tests (see Topic 24) are often developed for just this purpose.

correlation
a largely statistical method used to discover R-R relationships

As an example, let's say that we're interested in whether or not there is a correlation between reading ability and performance in introductory psychology. We first need to decide how we will measure, or operationally define, the two responses in which we are interested. We then measure the responses using the same set of subjects for both measurements. We now have two sets of measurements, or numbers, that we can study to determine if there is, indeed, a correlation between reading ability and performance in introductory psychology. Let's look at this study step by step.

First, we need to come up with some operational definitions for the measurements we want to take. "Performance in introductory psychology" isn't difficult to deal with. We'll take that to mean the total number of points earned by a student on classroom exams over the course of the semester. "Reading ability" is a little more difficult. We could design our own test to measure what we mean by reading ability, but instead we'll use a test published by someone else—the Nelson Denny Reading Test (Brown, 1973). After we have determined our operational definitions, we will give a large group of students our reading test. The results will give us one set of numbers. At the end of the semester, we'll add up all exam points for the same group of students and have a second set of numbers. So, for each student in our study we have a pair of numbers, one indicating reading ability and one indicating performance in the introductory psychology course. We want to know if these responses are correlated. From here on, our method is more statistical than psychological.

We enter our pairs of numbers into a calculator (or a computer if we have a very large set of numbers). A series of arithmetic procedures is applied. (Computer people call this massaging the data.) Then, out comes a single number, called the **correlation coefficient**, which tells us about the strength and nature of the relationship between the measured responses. This number is symbolized "r" and ranges in value from −1.00 to +1.00. What does this number r mean? It takes some experience to be truly comfortable with this statistic, but we can make some general observations.

First, let's deal with the *sign* of the correlation coefficient, whether it is positive (+), or negative (−), or zero. A positive correlation would tell us that our two responses *are* related to each other and that high scores on one response are associated with high scores on the other. It would also tell us that low scores on one measure are associated with low scores on the other. Because our two responses are positively correlated, we can make predictions of one response if we know the other. If a student does well on the reading test, we can predict that she or he will probably do well in introductory psychology. If someone does poorly on the reading test, we can expect that student to have a hard time in the class. We can make these predictions only if the two responses are correlated, only if we have an R-R relationship. For the record, for our example experiment, there is ample evidence that the correlation would be positive (Gerow & Murphy, 1980).

What if our calculations tell us that r is a negative (−) number? Here, too, we would have a useful R-R relationship. We could use scores on one response to predict scores on the other. The only difference is that the relationship is, in a way, upside down. Here, *high* scores on one response are associated with *low* scores on the other measured response. If we measured body size to see if it were related to gymnastic ability, we would find a negative correlation: Large body size is associated with poor gymnastic ability, and small body size is associated with good gymnastic ability. We can still use body size to predict gymnastic ability, but now high scores on one measure are related to low scores on the other, and vice versa. There is also a negative relationship between the weight of clothing you are likely to be wearing and the outside temperature. As temperatures go down, weight of clothing tends to go up, and we can use one measure to predict the other.

What happens if our correlation coefficient turns out to be zero, or nearly so? A zero correlation coefficient indicates the absence of an R-R relationship. If r equals zero, the two responses we have measured are not related in any useful way. Let's say I worked from the faulty logic that intelligence is a function of brain size and that head size tells us how big a person's brain is. On this basis, I suggest that we can measure intelligence by measuring head size. No doubt if I were to measure the head size of a large number of students and also measure, say, grade point average for the same students, I would find a correlation coefficient very close to zero. As correlations approach zero, predictability decreases.

So much for the sign of the correlation coefficient. Now what about its actual numerical value? More details are available in the Statistical Appendix, but for now we can suggest that the closer we get to the extremes of +1.00 or −1.00, the better or stronger the relationship between the two responses that we have measured. The closer our coefficient, r, gets to zero, the weaker the relationship, and the less useful it is for making predictions.

correlation coefficient
a statistic (a number, r) that indicates the nature (positive or negative) and strength of the relationship between measured responses

As we go through this text, we will encounter a number of studies that use correlational methods. Most of them involve the use of psychological tests to predict other behaviors. If we want to know if a new college aptitude test can be used to predict college grades, we will have to administer the test to a large number of entering freshmen, compute their grade point averages later on, and see if the test and grade point averages are correlated.

Before we examine other methods, remember the two important points we made about R-R relationships earlier. Even if two responses are correlated, we cannot use correlation to support the claim that one *causes* the other—they are simply related. Even if two responses are correlated, we cannot make precise predictions for all individual cases. Reading ability and introductory psychology grades are correlated. We can use reading tests to predict grades, but we have to allow for exceptions; some poor readers do well and some good readers do poorly in the course. Our correlation only holds in general.

Before you go on

What is the purpose of correlational methods?

What is the difference between positive (+) and negative (-) correlations?

What does a correlation coefficient of zero mean?

METHODS: EXPERIMENTS

It is safe to say that most of what we know in psychology today we have learned through doing **experiments**. Experiments are operations in which the scientific method is used to establish the relationship between manipulated events and measured events while other events are controlled. Experiments are designed to uncover S-R, or cause and effect, relationships. After we define a few terms we'll look at a couple of examples.

In order to see if a cause-and-effect relationship exists between two variables, an experimenter will manipulate one and look for measurable changes in the other. (Variables are simply things that can vary—measurable events that can take on different values.)

The conditions the experimenter manipulates are called **independent variables**. What the experimenter measures are **dependent variables**. The hope is that manipulations of some independent variable will produce consistent, predictable changes in the dependent variable. Or, put another way, what one manipulates (S) will cause changes in what one measures (R).

If there *are* systematic changes in what is measured, the experimenter would like to claim that these changes are due solely to the influence of the manipulated independent variable. In order to make such a claim, it must be demonstrated that all other variables that might have affected what is being measured have been controlled or eliminated. Because these other variables are not a part of the S-R relationship being studied, but may have an effect on it, they are called **extraneous variables**. So, to do an experiment, one manipulates independent variables, measures dependent variables, and controls extraneous variables. That may sound a little confusing in the abstract. Let's look at an example.

Does classical music playing in the background serve to improve learning? This is an ultimately experimental question. We want to know if music (S) causes a change in behavior (R). So, we manipulate background music, our independent variable—the variable that we believe will have an effect on behavior. One way to do this would be to have a number of subjects study

experiment
the scientific method used to establish the relationship between manipulated events (independent variables) and measured events (dependent variables) while other events (extraneous variables) are controlled

independent variables
those events in an experiment, manipulated by the experimenter, that are expected to have an effect on behavior

dependent variables
those responses or behaviors that are measured in an experiment and are expected to "depend" on manipulations of the independent variables

extraneous variables
those variables in an experiment that need to be controlled or eliminated so as not to affect the dependent variable

some material under different conditions. One group studies in a quiet room, a second group studies with rock music in the background, and a third group listens to classical music as they study.

Now that we have manipulated one variable, we need to measure another to see if our manipulations have any effect. We might ask all of our subjects to memorize a list of 20 words. All subjects will get 10 minutes to study the list. Then we will take away the list and see how many words the subjects have learned by asking them to write the words on a sheet of paper. Our hypothesis is that what we are measuring (number of words learned) will depend on what we have manipulated (background music).

Let's suppose that when we are done we find that those who studied their word list in the quiet setting did the best on the learning task, and that the other two groups did equally well, but much worse than the subjects who studied in the quiet room. It seems as if our experiment has suggested a possible S-R relationship: Quiet conditions (S) yield Increased learning (R). Or, we might say that background music interferes with learning, and it matters little whether that music is classical or rock. A manipulated independent variable has produced a change in a measured dependent variable.

Before we get too carried away, we had better consider the possible extraneous variables that might have been operating in our experiment. These, remember, are those factors that might have had an impact on what we are measuring (learning words) over and above what we have manipulated (background music). Obviously, we would want to consider these factors and control for them before we actually do our experiment. What extraneous variables would we have to consider in this experiment?

Our basic concern in this experiment is that the three groups we are using are treated as equally as possible in all aspects except for the background music they hear while studying a word list. A few questions come to mind. Did each of the groups get the same list of words to memorize? (Some word lists might be easier to learn than others.) Is there any evidence that the three groups are in any way equal in their ability to learn? (Maybe the one group did so well not because of the quiet background, but because they were better at learning in the first place.) Were all three groups tested at about the same time of day? (It's harder to learn words late in the afternoon than it is in mid-morning.) Were the physical conditions of the studying and testing rooms the same for all three groups? (Additional background noises may interfere with studying.) Did the subjects in the experiment have any preferences for types of music before the experiment began? (Some students may have preferred classical music to rock music, or vice versa.) Under what conditions do the subjects usually study? (With or without music? Of what kind?) As you can imagine, such lists of extraneous variables can be very long indeed. It is the extent to which these variables have been adequately controlled that most directly determines the quality of an experiment. (See Figure 2.2.)

Let's take a quick look at another potentially experimental question. Suppose you believe that a stimulating environment during early childhood improves intellectual functioning at adolescence. You propose to do an experiment to find evidence to support your belief. You have two groups of newborn children, say 20 in each group. One group will be reared for 3 years in a very stimulating environment filled with toys and games, bright wallpaper and pictures in the nursery, and many adults around every day. The other group of children will be reared in isolation, in quiet, empty rooms, with only their basic biological needs attended to. Wait a minute! This sort of experimental manipulation is unethical and would be out of the question (see topic expansion). You wouldn't isolate and deprive some children—particularly if your own hypothesis is that doing so will have negative consequences.

This problem provides a good example of an experiment that you might want to do with rats. Rats could be raised in cages that provide differing amounts of environmental stimulation. When the rats approach maturity, you could test their ability to negotiate mazes and/or learn a variety of responses. Early exposure to stimulation would be your independent variable, and your tests of learning ability would be your dependent variables.

One nice thing about using rats for your experiment is that extraneous variables are generally easy to control. You don't have to worry about previous experience, inherited differences, parental influence, and the like (all of your rats have a known genetic history and have been reared in very similar environments). You can exercise rather complete control over the rats you'll use in your experiment. The problem with using rats is obvious. Even if you demonstrate your point with rats, you will then have to argue that the data you have collected for rats is, in some direct way, applicable to humans. As we shall see, in many cases that argument is not too difficult to make. The advantage of being able to easily control extraneous variables makes the use of nonhuman subjects commonplace in psychology.

Rats are often used for experiments because the experimental variables are easy to control and the genetic history of rats is known. Sometimes data based on the behavior of rats can be applied to human behavior as well.

Figure 2.2

The stages of our example experiment illustrate the different types of variables.

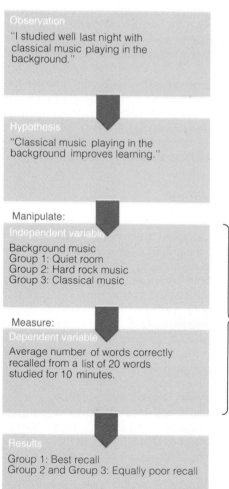

Observation

"I studied well last night with classical music playing in the background."

Hypothesis

"Classical music playing in the background improves learning."

Manipulate:

Independent variable

Background music
Group 1: Quiet room
Group 2: Hard rock music
Group 3: Classical music

Measure:

Dependent variable

Average number of words correctly recalled from a list of 20 words studied for 10 minutes.

Control:

Extraneous variables

Subject differences:
  learning ability
  music preferences } Random assignment to groups
  study habits
Same word list for all groups
Similar rooms for study and recall
Same instructions
Same time of day
Etc.

Results

Group 1: Best recall
Group 2 and Group 3: Equally poor recall

We don't have to spend a lot of time dealing with the details of experimental design here. Though it is important to remember that experiments are the most commonly used method for testing hypotheses in psychology, there are a few other ideas you should think about, too.

Generalizing Results

No one does an experiment simply because of an interest in the subjects who happen to be involved. We always want to be able to generalize whatever we find for our experimental subjects to a larger population of subjects. You would not be interested in the effects of background music on only the 60 subjects who happened to be in your experiment. You would want to discover an S-R relationship that you could generalize to virtually all college students.

Our ability to generalize our experimental findings beyond the subjects in our experiment depends on a number of factors. The most important is the extent to which our subjects provide an adequate **sample** of the population in which we are ultimately interested. That is, to what extent do the subjects we have chosen for our experiment adequately represent the larger group from which they were chosen? Our experimental results should be based on reasonably large numbers of observations.

The subjects about whom these observations are made should be demonstrably representative of the population to which we want to generalize our findings. It often seems that experimental psychology is becoming the psychology of college sophomores because college students so frequently serve as subjects in experiments. So, one of the questions we should ask about experimental results is: "Did the experiment adequately sample the population of subjects to which the results are being applied?"

Experimental and Control Groups

The most difficult extraneous variables to control are often those that involve the past experience of the subjects. In a typical experiment, the independent variable is manipulated by presenting one group of subjects with some treatment (such as background music) and withholding that treatment from another group of subjects. Subjects in both groups are measured to see if the treatment produced any measurable differences in the chosen independent variable. By definition, those subjects who receive some treatment, or manipulation, are said to be *experimental group* subjects. Any experiment may have a number of experimental groups. Our example on background music used two: one group heard classical music, the other heard rock music. Subjects who do not receive the experimental treatment are said to be in the *control group*. Each experiment should have one control group of subjects; in our example, these were the students who learned with no music.

To make sure that your experimental and control groups of subjects begin the experiment on an equal footing, you could do one of two things. You could try to match your subjects on your characteristic of interest. That is, if you were going to measure learning ability as a function of background music, you could give all your subjects a test of their learning ability and then systematically place subjects into groups so that all groups were of equal ability.

sample
a chosen portion of the population of interest

A more common technique would be to assign subjects to groups through **random assignment,** in which each subject has an equal chance of being assigned to any one of the groups you are using in your experiment. If assignment is truly random, then those subjects who learn well are just as likely to be in one group as another, and those subjects who learn with difficulty are equally likely to be in any one of your three groups—classical, rock, or no background music.

Overcoming Bias

Human subjects in psychology experiments are usually very helpful and well motivated to do whatever is asked of them. In their efforts to please, they may very well act in the experimental situation in ways they would never act otherwise. In other words, subjects sometimes do what they think the experimenter wants them to do. If subjects are reacting to their perception of the experimenter's wishes, they are not responding to the independent variables of the experiment. In order to overcome this difficulty, subjects are generally not told just what it is that the experimenter wants or expects the subjects to do. The subjects are kept in the dark concerning the purpose or goals of the experiment. This is called a **single-blind technique;** that is, only the subject is not informed about the hypothesis of the experiment.

For similar reasons, it is often helpful for the experimenter measuring the dependent variable to be kept in the dark concerning the goals or hypotheses of the experiment. It is very easy to misread a clock, or misperceive a turn in a maze, or misinterpret a subject's response. As we will see in Topic 11, we often tend to perceive what we want to perceive or what we expect to perceive whether it's really there or not. Notice that we're not talking about downright dishonesty here; we're talking about the honest errors that can be made in analyzing data when one has a stake in the outcome of the analysis. To offset this possible source of bias, we can use a **double-blind technique** in which neither the subject nor the experimenter analyzing the data knows what the hypothesis of the experiment is. (Obviously *somebody* has to know what the hypothesis is, but that somebody does not record or analyze the data.)

For example, in our study of the effect of background music on learning, we might make sure that the people scoring the lists of recalled words do not know which of the three groups of subjects produced the lists they are scoring. In our example of raising rats under different levels of stimulation, we would see to it that the experimenters rating the learning ability (dependent variable) of the rats did not know (were blind to) the conditions under which the rats were raised (independent variable).

Before you go on

What is meant by random assignment?

How does a double-blind procedure protect against subject and experimenter bias?

METHODS: NATURALISTIC OBSERVATION

One of the problems with experiments, even good ones, is that they are often artificial. By definition, when you do an experiment you have to manipulate and control certain variables. The more variables you have to control, the less like real life the situation may become.

Let's review a classic experimental technique for studying conformity behavior (Asch, 1952). A group of subjects is asked to make judgments about the length of lines (see Figure 2.3). They are to say which of three lines is the same length as a standard line. Because there are not many judgments to make, and only seven subjects in the group, they are asked to call out their answers one at a time.

In fact, the first six of the seven "subjects" in the group are the experimenter's assistants. From time to time they purposely give incorrect answers. The real subject here is the last person in the group, who may either go along with the group's obviously wrong answers (and thus conform), or be tough and call out the right answer (and be independent).

In many cases, subjects will indeed conform—they will yield to the pressure of the group and give an obviously wrong answer. This sort of experimental design is very useful. We can find out a number of things about conformity with this procedure. How much yielding to group pressure will we find? What sorts of people tend to conform the most? What sorts of manipulations (independent variables) can be used to increase or decrease the amount of conformity (dependent variable) we observe? (See Topic 32 for more on conformity.)

A problem with this sort of conformity experiment is that it is not very much like real life. After all, when was the last time you were with a group of strangers when someone came up and asked you to judge the length of lines? That sort of thing just doesn't come up very often. One alternative to conducting experiments is to study behavior as it occurs naturally—in the real world. This methodological approach is called **naturalistic observation**. As its name implies, this procedure involves carefully watching behaviors as they occur naturally. The observer makes careful notes, perhaps using a prepared record form or rating scale.

There is a strong logical appeal to the naturalistic method. If you are trying to understand what organisms do in real life, watch them while they are doing it. Indeed, it is the careful observations of everyday behaviors that usually give us ideas of what to do experiments on in the first place.

As sensible and appealing as naturalistic observation may sound, there are a few potential problems with it that we need to acknowledge. First, if we truly do want to observe people the way they naturally act, we must make sure that they do not know we are watching them. As you know from your own experience, people may act differently when they think they're being watched. You may do all sorts of things in the privacy of your own home that you would never do if you thought someone was watching you.

naturalistic observation
the psychological method in which behavior is observed as it occurs naturally

Naturalistic observation involves studying behaviors as they occur naturally. Here, a psychologist takes notes while watching a child at play.

Second, we must be wary of observer bias. The people doing the observing may let their own motivation and expectations interfere with the objectivity of their observations. This is the same basic problem that we may have with experiments. It again may be helpful to have observers noting behaviors without full knowledge of what it is they are looking for—a sort of double-blind technique. As a protection against observer bias, we may want to check the reliability (or dependability) of observations by using a number of observers and only relying on those observations that can be verified by a number of observers.

A third potential problem with naturalistic observation is even more difficult to deal with. The behaviors that you want to observe may not always be there when you are. If, for example, you are interested in conformity behaviors and want to observe them as they occur naturally, just where do you go to watch conformity happen? To use naturalistic observation, you may have to be clever, or lucky, and you will almost certainly have to be very patient.

Although it has its problems, there are occasions when naturalistic observation is about the only option we have. Studying chimpanzees in zoos and laboratories will not tell us everything about how they behave naturally in the wild. Many psychologists have been frustrated trying to do experiments on language acquisition with very young children. By the time they are 3 years old, children demonstrate all sorts of interesting language behaviors. However, they may be too young to understand and properly follow the sorts of instructions that many experiments would require. Perhaps all we can do is carefully observe and listen to young children using language and try to determine what they are doing by watching them in their natural environments.

Before you go on
What are some of the advantages and disadvantages of using naturalistic observation in psychology?

OTHER METHODS: SURVEYS, CASE HISTORIES, AND CROSS-CULTURAL STUDIES

From time to time the data that psychologists might want to use are not to be found by applying the standard methods we have reviewed thus far. In this last section, we'll summarize three additional techniques that psychologists have found useful.

Surveys

When we want to make relatively simple observations about large numbers of subjects, we may use a **survey** method. Doing a survey involves asking the same question or questions of large samples of respondents. The questions may be asked in a personal or telephone interview, or they may be asked in the form of a written questionnaire. Such studies yield data that would be very difficult to gather otherwise.

survey
a means of collecting data from large numbers of subjects, either by interview or questionnaire

Surveys provide us with information that we can use as a general data base. As we saw in Topic 1, the American Psychological Association regularly surveys its members to discover where they are employed and the area of psychology in which they are specializing. To find out whether or not your fellow students tend to study with music playing in the background, you might design a survey to ask them.

The critical aspect of survey data is the size and representativeness of the sample that is surveyed. As is the case for all research in psychology, we would like to be able to generalize our findings beyond those who participate in the survey. The American Psychological Association does not question all of its members; rather, it samples those who are typical of the entire membership. If we want to draw conclusions about the conditions under which college students *in general* do their studying, we need to adequately sample all sorts of college students from different types of institutions and from different parts of the country. Simply asking a few of your friends how they study would obviously not suffice. The advantage of this method is that we can collect data from large numbers of people. The disadvantage is that the information we collect is seldom very detailed or in depth.

Case Histories

case history
an intensive, detailed study of certain aspects of one (or a few) individual(s)

The **case history** provides yet a different sort of information. In the case history method, one person, or a small sample of persons, is studied in depth over an extended period of time. The method involves an intense and complete examination of a wide range of variables. It is usually retrospective, meaning that we start with some given condition today and go back in time in order to determine some of the factors that may have contributed to this present condition. We may use interviews, psychological testing, and observation to collect our data.

As an example, let's say we are interested in determining factors that have led to Mr. X becoming a child abuser. Our suspicion is that Mr. X's own childhood experiences might provide us with some insight. We talk to Mr. X at length and we interview his family and friends—those people who knew him as a child—trying to form a (retrospective) picture of Mr. X's childhood. If we find some clues, we will then do the same with other known child abusers, looking to find commonalities in their experiences that might have led them to become child abusers.

As we shall see, Freud based most of his theories of personality on the case histories he derived from examination of his patients and himself. The advantage of the case history method is that it provides us with a wealth of information about individual cases. The disadvantage is that we may not be able to generalize our findings beyond the individuals we have studied.

Cross-cultural Studies

As we explore the potential R-R and S-R relationships of behavior and mental processes, it is often useful to look beyond the confines of just one culture. We are seeking to make general observations about our subject matter.

A very basic question that will come up over and over again in many different contexts throughout this book is the extent to which human behaviors are determined by innate, unlearned factors, or are learned and molded by experience. One way to find out is to look at the behaviors of people from different cultures whose learning experiences are markedly different. Knowing that Americans tend to smile when they are happy is one thing. If we were to discover that all people of all cultures make the same facial expression when they are happy, we would have extended an important observation. As we will see when we get to Topic 27, what we call abnormal, or disordered, behavior often varies considerably from culture to culture.

Before you go on
How can surveys, case histories, and cross-cultural studies be used to help us understand R-R and S-R relationships?

As we will see throughout the book, psychologists study the behavior and mental activity of organisms. They are interested in the relationships that exist between organisms, stimuli, and responses. Although the techniques that are used to study these relationships are many and varied, they are all scientific.

Ethical and moral concerns can be found in all the sciences. In most sciences, ethical issues usually center on the *application* of information. We know how to split an atom; should we build a bomb? We can manufacture effective insecticides; should we use them? We can devise means to render people infertile; should we? We can use machinery to keep a person alive indefinitely; should we? We can bury radioactive waste; should we?

Psychology has something of a unique problem in that ethical issues are often raised about the actual *collection* of information. After all, the objects of study in psychology are living organisms. Their physical and psychological welfare needs to be protected as we investigate their behaviors and mental processes. Psychologists have long been concerned with the ethical implications of their work. In 1973, and again in 1981, the American Psychological Association published strict guidelines for the ethical conduct of research with either animal or human subjects. Here we will examine some of the issues that these guidelines address.

As one plans his or her research, the degree to which subjects in the experiment will be put at risk should be assessed. What are the potential dangers, physical or psychological, that might result from participation in this experiment? Even if potential risks are deemed to be slight, they should be considered and balanced in the light of what potential good might come from the proposed experiment. Seldom will one psychologist have to make the ultimate decisions about risk and/or potential benefits of a research program. Advisory committees of researchers, familiar with the techniques and problems of the proposed research, will have to approve it before the project begins.

What are some other ethical issues related to research in psychology? (1) The subject's *confidentiality* must be guaranteed. Often, the subject's name is not even used, replaced instead with an identification number. (2) Participation in research should be *voluntary*. No one should be coerced into being a subject in a psychology experiment. Volunteers should be allowed the option to drop out of any research project, even after it has begun. Colleges cannot offer extra credit to experimental subjects unless all students are given an opportunity to participate and unless nonexperiment options are also available for earning the same extra credit. (3) Subjects should participate in experiments only after they have given their *advised consent.* Within reason, subjects must know what is going to be expected of them when they participate in an experiment. They should be told the potential dangers, if any, why the project is being done, and what they will be expected to do. Obviously, it is sometimes necessary to withhold some information to get satisfactory results. If Asch told his subjects that all the other "subjects" were just friends of his and in on the experiment, he would not have found out much about conformity. Even so, the desire for results should be balanced with concern for the well-being of the subjects. (4) Particularly if subjects have been kept in the dark about the nature of the experiment, and even if they haven't, all subjects should be *debriefed* after the research has been completed. That means that, if nothing else, the true nature of the project, and its basic intent, should be explained to those who participated in it. Because they have something of a stake in it, subjects should be provided a copy of the results of the research when they become available.

Published ethical guidelines for the use of animals in research are also quite stringent. Only those who are trained and experienced in animal housing and care can be deemed responsible for laboratory animals. Those experts, in turn, must train all others working with the animals in the proper humane treatment of the animals under their care. Every effort must be taken to minimize the discomfort, illness, and pain of animals. Subjecting animals to stress, or pain is acceptable *only* if no other procedure is available, and the goal is justified by its prospective scientific, educational, or applied value. As with human subjects, there are usually review committees that must approve the design of any research using nonhuman animals in research because of concern for the ethical protection of the subjects.

TOPIC SUMMARY

What do R-R relationships tell us?

How can this information be used?

Give one example of an R-R relationship.

R-R relationships are statements of correlation that can be used to predict one response on the basis of knowing the other. For example, knowing college entrance exam scores are correlated with grade point averages, the latter may be predicted from the former. They do not imply cause and effect. / 25

What is the nature of S-R relationships?

Why should we think of them as multiple S-O-multiple R relationships?

S-R relationships are meant to be cause and effect statements: "This stimulus 'causes' this response." All responses are "caused" by more than one single stimulus (S), operating on an organism (O), to provide a variety of possible responses (R). / 27

What is the purpose of correlational methods?

What is the difference between positive (+) and negative (−) correlations?

What does a correlation coefficient of zero mean?

Correlational methods tell us about the strength and nature of R-R relationships. Positive correlations indicate that high scores on one response are associated with high scores on another response and that low scores on one response are associated with low scores on another. Negative correlations tell us that high scores on one response are associated with low scores on the other, and vice versa. Zero correlations tell us that the responses are not related. / 29

What is the essence of doing an experiment?

Define independent, dependent, and extraneous variables in the context of an experiment.

An experiment involves manipulating independent variables to see if they bring about hypothesized changes in some measured dependent variable while all other extraneous variables are controlled or eliminated. / 32

What is meant by random assignment?

How does a double-blind procedure protect against subject and experimenter bias?

A random sample is one in which all members of the population have an equal chance of inclusion. In an experiment, subjects should be randomly (by chance alone) assigned to receive the treatment (independent variable) or not. Single- and double-blind techniques protect against bias by keeping the subject (single-blind) or the experimenter *and* the subject (double-blind) uninformed of the hypothesis of the investigation. / 33

What are some of the advantages and disadvantages of using naturalistic observation in psychology?

Naturalistic observation overcomes the artificiality of experiments by observing behavior as it occurs naturally, but it may require good fortune, patience, and creativity so that those being observed do not know they are being watched. Some behaviors occur infrequently and are difficult to observe. / 35

How can surveys, case histories, and cross-cultural studies be used to help us understand R-R and S-R relationships?

Surveys provide large samples of data from many respondents, whereas case histories provide considerable depth and detailed information from just a few subjects. Cross-cultural studies help us make observations and draw conclusions that we can generalize to people in any culture. / 36

CHAPTER TWO

THE BIOLOGICAL BASES OF BEHAVIOR

Topic 3   Basic Structures and Functions

Topic 4   The Brain

TOPIC

Imagine the following scenario. You are wandering down the hall late at night in your bare feet. Suddenly, "Ouch!" You've stepped on a tack. You are now hopping around on one foot while you try to grab the other foot.

We will leave you there for now and ask simply, "What happens next?" What happens next goes something like this (with some questions interspersed that you probably wouldn't ask yourself at the time but which are an integral part of the experience you are having).

Your injured foot jerks up off the floor, and your arms flail out so you can maintain your balance. *(What stimulated the muscles of my leg to pull up my foot? How do my arms know what to do to keep me in balance?)* You realize that your foot hurts. *(Where does realization happen? In my brain?)* Perhaps we'd better be more specific. The point of the tack enters the sole of your foot and stimulates a nerve cell. *(How are nerve cells usually stimulated? What kind of nerve cell responds to tacks? For that matter, what's a nerve cell?)*

The cell that is stimulated by the tack sends a message to other nerve cells. *(Wait a minute! What do you mean by "message"? How do messages get from one cell to another?)* This message now races up your leg to the base of the spinal cord. *(How fast? What does the spinal cord look like? What does it do?)* From the spinal cord, messages go off in two directions: up toward the brain and back down to the muscles in the leg. *(How do messages get to my brain? And how do they get back down to my leg?)* Messages from the spinal cord to the leg stimulate muscles to quickly lift the leg off the floor. At the same time, messages to your brain are being interpreted. *(Do you mean to say that my leg lifts up off the floor without my even thinking about it? Doesn't my brain have to control the movement?)* Your brain will direct your eyes to focus on your foot. You'll identify the source of pain as a tack. Still hopping on one foot, you'll wonder who left a tack on the kitchen floor, and you may even get angry thinking about it. *(What part of the brain directs the movement of my eyes? To recognize the tack implies that I'm using memory. How are memories stored in the brain, and where? Are there separate parts of the brain that are involved in emotional responses like anger?)*

Even in a stimulus-response chain of events as simple as that involved in stepping on a tack, a remarkable series of biological, physiological, and biochemical reactions takes place. Ultimately, all of our behaviors and mental processes—from the simple blink of an eye to profound and abstract thought—are no more (and no less) than the integrated reactions of our nervous systems.

Why We Care

We have defined psychology as the science of behavior and mental processes. From its earliest days, psychology has been concerned with how the mind and body interact. To even begin to understand how and why organisms behave, think, and feel as they do, we must understand at least the fundamentals of the biology and physiology of the organism. Our aim is not to become amateur biologists or physiologists. We needn't become experts in all areas of human anatomy. We need have little concern for bones, blood, or muscle tissues, or how the lungs pass oxygen into the bloodstream, or how digestion works. We are primarily interested in the operation of the nervous system, and most of our attention will be focused on the brain. We choose to direct our attention there because we believe that it is the brain and the nerve cells leading to it and away from it that are most intimately involved in behavior and mental processes.

How our nervous systems work is an exciting area of study in modern psychology. New discoveries and new theories are rushing at us at a mind-boggling (or brain-boggling) pace. In this topic, we'll review some of what we know about the nervous system below the brain, saving the brain itself for our next topic. We'll take a building block approach, first describing the single, individual nerve cell, then seeing how these cells communicate, or interact, with others. We'll discuss the billions of nerve cells that work together in the major nervous systems of the human body, and we'll also consider another biological system (the endocrine system) that influences our behaviors and mental processes.

THE NEURON

neuron
a nerve cell that is the basic building block of the nervous system; transmits neural impulses

Our exploration of the nervous system begins at the level of the single cell. Individual nerve cells are called **neurons.** They are almost unimaginably small—microscopically small. It is appropriate to think of neurons as the basic building blocks of the nervous system. They exist throughout our nervous system by the billions. Neurons are so tiny and complex that estimating their number is clearly very difficult. For example, three recent sources give the number of neurons contained in the brain alone as "about 12 billion" (Bennett, 1982, p. 26), "50 billion or so" (Bloom et al., 1985, p. 33), and "on the order of 10^{11} (a hundred billion)" (Hubel, 1979, p. 45). The largest estimate is probably the most accurate.

Neural Structure

Nerve cells are like people (and snowflakes) in that no two are exactly alike. Though there is no such thing as a typical neuron most *do* have many structures in common. Figure 3.1 illustrates these common structures, while Figure 3.2 shows what neurons really look like.

cell body
the largest mass of a nerve cell. The cell body contains the cell's nucleus and "receives" neural impulses

dendrite
a branchlike extension of the neuron's cell body. Dendrites receive neural impulses

axon
the long taillike extension of a neuron that carries an impulse away from the cell body toward the synapse

One structure that all neurons have is a **cell body.** The cell body is the largest concentration of mass of the cell. It contains the nucleus of the cell, which, in turn, contains the genetic information that keeps the cell functioning and "doing its thing."

Extending away from the cell body are a number of tentaclelike structures, called **dendrites** and **axons.** As you can see, our drawing is very much simplified, showing only a few dendrites and but one axon. The dendrite extensions reach out to receive messages (called neural impulses) from other nearby neurons and send them toward the cell body. From there, impulses travel down the axon toward other neurons or to muscle fibers. Some axons

Figure 3.1

A schematic drawing of a typical neuron showing its major structures.

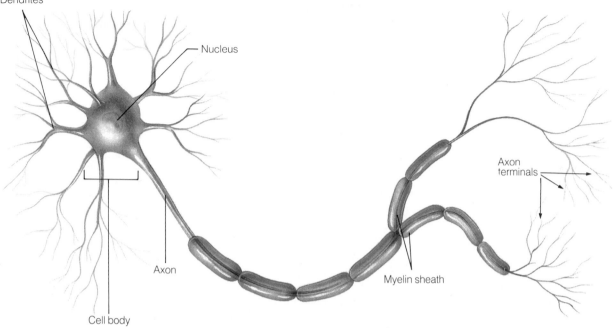

Dendrites

Nucleus

Axon
terminals

Axon

Myelin sheath

Cell body

can be quite long—as long as 2 or 3 feet in the spinal cord. It is generally true, then, that *within the neuron* impulses travel from dendrite to cell body to axon.

The neuron we have pictured in Figure 3.1 has a feature not found on all neurons. Here you can see that the axon is surrounded by a covering or sheath of **myelin.** Myelin is a white, fatty, lumpy substance that is found on about half the neurons in an adult's nervous system. It is the presence or absence of myelin that allows us to tell the difference between the gray matter (unmyelinated neurons) and the white matter (myelinated neurons) that is obvious on the visual inspection of the nervous system.

Myelin is a feature of neurons that is not fully developed at birth—it develops as the nervous system matures. Myelin serves to protect the long, delicate axon and helps speed neural impulses along their way. The differences in the rate of impulse transmission within a neuron are quite striking. Small, unmyelinated axons may transmit impulses at about 0.5 meters per second, while large, myelinated axons may speed impulses along at a rate of 120 meters per second. Thus, we tend to find myelin sheaths on those neurons that have to transmit messages relatively long distances throughout the body.

Axons end in a branching series of end points called **axon terminals.** It is at the axon terminals that each neuron connects with the dendrites and cell bodies of neighboring neurons to transmit impulses along to other neurons. The spreading axon terminals and the large number of dendrite extensions make it possible for one tiny neuron to interact with hundreds, even thousands, of other neurons.

One far-reaching observation about neurons is that we are born with about as many neurons as we will ever have. As we grow and develop, our neurons may become larger, grow new dendrites and axon terminals, form new connections with other neurons, and develop myelin sheaths, but they do not increase in number. A related observation is that if our neurons die

Figure 3.2

A photograph of neurons taken through a powerful microscope.

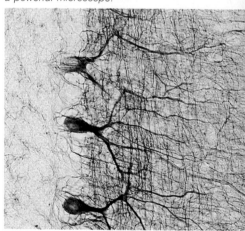

myelin
a white, fatty covering found on some axons that serves to protect the axon and increase the speed of neural impulses

axon terminals
a series of branching extensions at the end of an axon that form synapses with other neurons

(or are killed by injury or drug use) new ones are *not* generated to take their place. This feature makes neurons unique. We are constantly producing new blood cells to replace lost ones. If we didn't, we could never donate a pint of blood. Skin cells are constantly being replaced by new ones. You rinse away skin cells by the hundreds each time you wash your hands. But neurons are different; once they are gone, they are gone forever. Because remaining neurons can develop new dendrites and axon terminals, the function performed by dead neurons can often be taken over by surviving neurons, particularly if only a few are lost at any one time.

One way in which we can sensibly classify neurons is in terms of how and where they fit into general nervous system activity. Many neural impulses begin at our sense receptors (our eyes, ears, skin, etc.). There, receptor cells pick up energy from the world around us and change it into the energy of the nervous system. We'll discuss how receptor cells function in Chapter 4. Once receptor cells receive energy from the environment, impulses are relayed by **sensory neurons** *toward the brain or spinal cord.* The neurons that carry impulses *away from the brain or spinal cord* toward our muscles and glands are called **motor neurons.** Those nerve cells that transmit impulses from one part of the brain or spinal cord to another (i.e., *within* the brain or spinal cord) are called **interneurons.** So, it's a matter of *toward* the brain or spinal cord on sensory neurons, *within* on interneurons, and *away* on motor neurons. Remember that a neuron is a single cell. Neurons do tend to work together, organized in nerves or nerve fibers, which contain many individual nerve cells and axons.

sensory neurons
neurons carrying impulses from receptor cells toward the brain or spinal cord

motor neurons
neurons that carry impulses away from the brain or spinal cord toward the muscles and/or glands

interneurons
neurons within the brain or spinal cord

Before you go on
Describe the main structural features of a neuron, and classify neurons into three types.

Neural Function: The Impulse

Neurons transmit **neural impulses** from one place in the nervous system to another. The actual detailed story of how these impulses are generated and transmitted is a very complex one having to do with electrical and chemical changes that are extremely delicate and subtle. That the process is as well understood as it is is a wonder in itself. Here we'll describe it in very general terms.

Neurons do not exist in a vacuum. As living cells they are filled with and surrounded by fluids. Only a thin membrane (something like the skin) of a neuron separates the fluid inside the cell from the fluid outside the cell. These fluids contain dissolved chemical particles called **ions.** Chemical ions carry a very small, but measurable, electric charge, either positive (+) or negative (−). These ions float around in all the fluids of the body, but are heavily concentrated around the cells of the nervous system.

Neurons just "lying about," not doing anything are said to be at rest. "At rest" hardly seems an appropriate term for this situation—there seems to be little restful about it. A tension develops between the electric charge of ions *inside* the neuron and the electric charge of ions *outside* the neuron. Ideally, positive and negative electrical charges would be balanced on both sides of the neuron's membrane, but such is not the case. The neuron's membrane, when it is at rest, forces the inside to be too negative (that is, too many negative ions are trapped inside the cell) while the outside is too positive (too many positive ions are trapped outside the cell). Hence, the tension. The positive and negative ions, like poles of a magnet, are drawn toward each other, but cannot become balanced because of the neural membrane that separates them. (See Figure 3.3.)

neural impulse
the discharge of electrically charged chemical ions through the neural membrane that travels down a neuron when it is active or fires

ion
an electrically charged (either + or −) chemical particle

Figure 3.3

The transmission of a neural impulse in a section of an axon.

(A) The axon at rest, with negative ions (−) on the inside and positive ions (+) on the outside of the axon.

(B) The impulse: here the membrane reverses itself and negative ions race outside the neuron while positive ions race inside. The axon returns to a state of rest (A). In this illustration, the impulse is traveling from left to right.

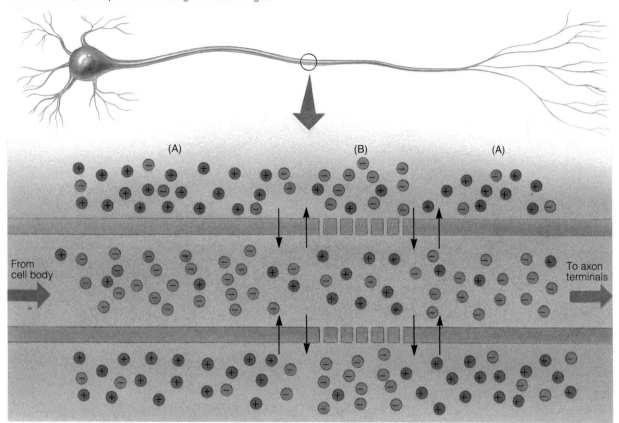

When a neural impulse reaches a given neuron and stimulates it to fire, or to produce an impulse of its own, what happens is something like this. At the region on the neuron where it is stimulated, the membrane no longer separates the charged chemical ions. Positive ions from the outside rush in as negatively charged ions race out through the membrane. For an instant, the electric charges are balanced, then they are imbalanced in the *opposite* direction (now, too many positive ions inside and too many negative ions outside). At almost the same time, the membrane changes back again to its original state, forcing the positive ions out again and drawing the negative ions back inside, and tension begins to develop again as the neuron returns to its resting state. It's all rather dramatic and exceedingly quick. The entire process usually takes about 1/10 of a second!

When a neuron fires, when an impulse "travels down a neuron," nothing physically moves from one end of the neuron to the other. The rush of ions is in and out through the neural membrane. What moves down the neuron is *where* the release of tension through the neural membrane occurs. Isn't it remarkable to think that everything we do ultimately comes down to small bits of electrically-charged chemical particles racing in and out of tiny neurons?

One aspect of neural activity is of particular interest to us because it relates directly to a psychological question. The question deals with how the nervous system reacts to differences in stimulus intensity. How do we react to the difference between a bright light and a dim one, a soft sound and a loud one, a tap on the shoulder and a slap on the back? It would be simple to imagine that for low intensity stimuli, neurons fire weakly, with only a few ions crossing the neural membrane and that for high intensity stimuli, neurons fire more forcefully or vigorously. This would be simple, but it is not true.

A neuron either fires or it doesn't. Chemical ions either penetrate the neural membrane full force, or they don't penetrate it at all. There is no in between, no degree of firing. This observation is referred to as the **all-or-none principle.**

It is also true that neurons do not necessarily fire every time they are stimulated. Each neuron has a level of stimulation that must be reached to get it to transmit an impulse. The minimum level of stimulation required to get a neuron to fire is called the **neural threshold.** These two notions, that of threshold and the all-or-none principle, give us some insight as to how the nervous system processes differences in stimulus intensity. High intensity stimuli (bright lights, loud sounds, etc.) don't get neurons to fire more vigorously, but they may stimulate *more* neurons to fire and may get them to fire more *frequently*. High intensity stimuli would be above the necessary threshold for firing for a greater number of neurons than low intensity stimuli. So, the difference in your experience of a flashbulb going off in front of your face and a candle viewed at a distance is largely a difference in the *number* of neurons involved and the *rate* at which they fire, not the *way* in which those neurons are responding.

all-or-none principle
the notion that a neuron will either fire, and generate a full impulse, or will not fire at all

neural threshold
the minimum amount of stimulation required to produce an impulse within a neuron

Before you go on
What is the basic process involved when a neuron fires?

What does the ''all-or-none principle'' state?

FROM ONE CELL TO ANOTHER: THE SYNAPSE

We have seen that neurons are very active cells that transmit electrochemical impulses (involving electrically-charged chemical particles) from dendrite to axon. Individual neurons, however, do not get much done by themselves. Neural impulses must be transmitted from neuron to neuron. This transmission takes place in the space between neurons, which is called the **synapse.** The essential structures of a synapse are shown in Figure 3.4.

At the very end of each axon are a number of axon terminals. These terminals contain small packets of chemical molecules. These packets are called **vesicles.** When a neural impulse reaches the axon terminal, some of these vesicles release the chemical they are holding. These chemicals, called **neurotransmitters,** released from their vesicles, flood out into the space between the axon of one neuron and the dendrite (or cell body) of the next neuron. Notice that the two neurons involved do not touch; they are separated by a very small space called the **synaptic cleft.**

At the synapse, then, neurotransmitters pass through the membrane of the axon *(presynaptic membrane)*, cross the synaptic cleft, and slip into spaces in the membrane of the next neuron *(postsynaptic membrane)*. Usually, this action stimulates the next neuron in the sequence to fire and thus begin the exchange of positive and negative ions. A new impulse then races

synapse
the junction of two neurons where an impulse is relayed from the axon of one to the dendrite (or cell body) of another through the release of a neurotransmitter

vesicles
the small containers, or packets, of neurotransmitter substance found in axon terminals

neurotransmitters
chemical molecules released at the synapse that either excite a subsequent neuron or inhibit impulse transmission

synaptic cleft
the space between the presynaptic membrane of one neuron and the postsynaptic membrane of the next neuron

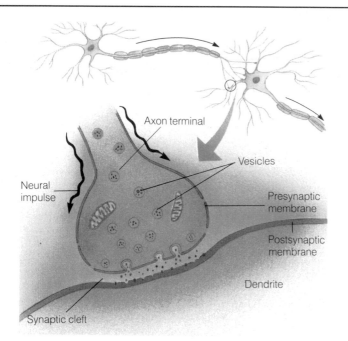

Figure 3.4
A synapse, in which transmission is from upper left to lower right. As an impulse enters the axon terminal, vesicles release neurotransmitter chemicals through the presynaptic membrane into the synaptic cleft. The neurotransmitter then stimulates the postsynaptic membrane of the next dendrite.

down the second neuron, new vesicles are opened, new transmitter substances are released, and the next neuron is stimulated to fire. It is indeed a remarkable chain of events. Now that we've covered the basics, let's add a few complications.

Recall that in our last section we suggested that each neuron has a threshold of stimulation required to get it to fire and generate a new impulse. Now, perhaps, we can get a better picture of what that means. It may mean that the second neuron in our illustration has a threshold so high that if neurotransmitters from only one presynaptic axon terminal were to stimulate it, nothing would happen. More chemical may be needed to get it to fire than that one axon terminal can provide. It may not fire until a number of axon terminals secrete large amounts of chemical into the synaptic cleft. Or the same axon may have to deliver its chemical a number of times in rapid succession to produce enough stimulation to be above threshold and to produce a new impulse.

We must also point out that some neurons hold an altogether different sort of chemical in their vesicles. These neurons do not stimulate new impulses at the synapse; they do just the opposite. Their neurotransmitters cross the synaptic cleft and inhibit, or decrease, the likelihood of an impulse moving from one neuron to the next, usually by blocking the neurotransmitter receptor sites on the postsynaptic membrane.

Not long ago it was believed that neurons contained one of just two types of neurotransmitters. Some were excitatory and stimulated new impulses, and others were inhibitory and stopped impulse transmission. We now recognize that such a view is too simplistic. There are now dozens of known neurotransmitters, and there is a good chance that there are more that are not known. Each may have its own unique influence on what happens at the synapse, although we continue to group them together as being basically excitatory or inhibitory. (See our Topic Expansion for more about neurotransmitters.)

Finally, so that our simplified drawing and description do not leave a false impression, let's make one point clear: Neural impulse transmission is not a matter of one neuron simply stimulating one other neuron that in turn stimulates but one more. Remember that any one neuron may have hundreds or thousands of axon terminals and synapses. Any one neuron, then, has the potential for exciting (or inhibiting) many others.

As we study behavior and mental processes in future topics, we should always try to keep in mind the incredibly fragile workings of neurons and synapses. Without these, nothing would follow. What changes might take place at the level of the neuron and synapse as we learn and remember? How is psychological growth and development influenced by neural growth and development, and vice versa? How is consciousness to be understood in terms of neural functioning? What effects do drugs have on the chemical activity of the synapse? These are but a few of the questions to which we shall be returning.

Before you go on
Summarize neural impulse transmission at the synapse.

NERVOUS SYSTEMS: THE BIG PICTURE

Now that we have a sense of how neurons work, individually and in pairs, let's step back for a moment to consider the broader context in which they actually operate. We've already made the point that very little gets accomplished through the action of just a few individual neurons. Behavior and experience require large numbers of neurons working together in complex, organized systems. Figure 3.5 diagrams the overall organization of the nervous systems.

Figure 3.5
The organization of the human nervous systems

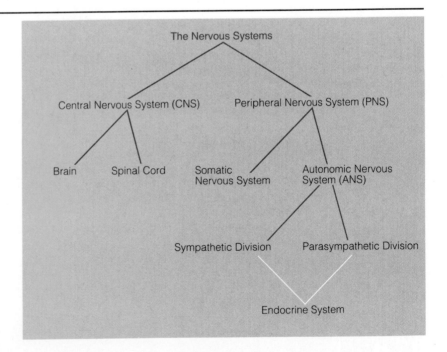

The first major division of the nervous system is determined largely on the basis of anatomy. The **central nervous system (CNS)** includes all the neurons and nerve fibers found in the spinal cord and the brain (see Topic 4). In many ways, this system of nerves is the most complex and the most intimately involved in the control of our behaviors and mental processes.

The **peripheral nervous system (PNS)** is quite simply composed of all the other nerve fibers in our body—those in our arms, legs, face, fingers, intestines, and so forth. In general, neurons in the PNS carry impulses either *from* the CNS to muscles and glands (with motor neurons, remember) or *to* the CNS (with sensory neurons) from receptor cells.

The peripheral nervous system is divided into two parts, based largely on the part of the body being served. The **somatic nervous system** includes those neurons outside the CNS that serve the skeletal muscles and that pick up impulses from the major receptors—the eyes, ears, and so forth. It is your somatic nervous system that will relay the impulses from your foot to your spinal cord and back to your leg when you step on a tack.

The other major division of the PNS is the **autonomic nervous system (ANS),** where "autonomic" means essentially the same thing as "automatic." The implication is that the activity of the ANS is in large measure (but not totally) independent of CNS control. The fibers of the ANS are involved in activating smooth muscles (like those of the stomach and intestines) and glands. The ANS also provides feedback to the CNS about the activity of these internal processes.

Because the autonomic nervous system is so involved in emotional responding, we'll return to it again in that context in Topic 21. For now we only note that the ANS is itself made up of two parts, the **sympathetic division** and the **parasympathetic division.** These two divisions of the ANS commonly work in opposition to each other, the former becoming active when we are in states of emotional excitement, the latter becoming active when we are relaxed and quiet. An overview of the structures affected by the ANS and its two divisions is presented in Figure 3.6.

As you can see, there is one other system reflected in our Figure 3.5—the **endocrine system.** Although the endocrine system is affected by the central nervous system, and can, in turn, affect nervous system activity, it is not itself a system of nerves. It is an interconnected network of glands that affect behavior through the secretion of **hormones** into the bloodstream. The endocrine system's glands and hormones operate on many of the same structures as does the autonomic nervous system, which is why we have pictured it as we have in Figure 3.5.

There is good reason to separate out all of these different organizations of neurons, fibers, and glands. It helps make a very complex system easier to deal with. But, we have to keep in mind that the outline of Figure 3.5 is arbitrary and somewhat artificial. All of the nerve fibers in each of these differently labeled systems have profound influences on each other. They are not as independent as our diagram might imply.

For example, let's go back once again to your stepping on a tack. Receptor cells respond to the tack and send impulses up your leg (somatic division of the PNS) to your spinal cord (CNS). There, some impulses are sent back down to your leg (PNS again) to get it to jerk up off the floor. Other impulses are sent to your brain (CNS) where you "know" what has happened. At about the same time, you become angry that someone would have left a tack on the floor. Hence, your autonomic nervous system becomes active, particularly the sympathetic division. It may also be the case that in your excitement of hopping about the kitchen, your endocrine system will be stimulated to provide extra doses of hormones. As you settle back down, the parasympa-

central nervous system (CNS)
those neurons in the brain and the spinal cord

peripheral nervous system (PNS)
those neurons throughout the body that are not in the brain or spinal cord; that is, those located in the periphery

somatic nervous system
sensory and motor neurons outside the CNS that serve the sense receptors and skeletal muscles

autonomic nervous system (ANS)
those neurons that activate smooth muscles and glands

sympathetic division
(of ANS) neurons that activate those organs involved in states of emotionality

parasympathetic division
(of ANS) neurons that activate those organs involved in maintenance of states of relaxation

endocrine system
a network of glands that secrete hormones directly into the bloodstream

hormones
chemical compounds, secreted by endocrine glands, carried through the bloodstream in order to have their effect on behavior

Figure 3.6

The division of the autonomic nervous system. The parasympathetic division becomes active when we are relaxed and quiet, while the sympathetic division is active when we are aroused or excited.
(Adapted from Gardner, 1963.)

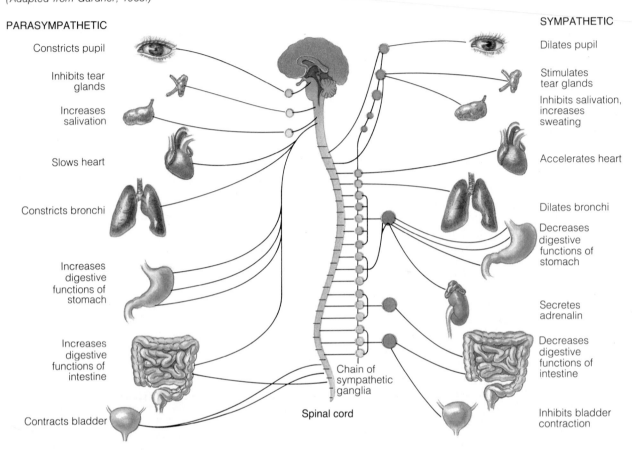

PARASYMPATHETIC

Constricts pupil

Inhibits tear glands

Increases salivation

Slows heart

Constricts bronchi

Increases digestive functions of stomach

Increases digestive functions of intestine

Contracts bladder

SYMPATHETIC

Dilates pupil

Stimulates tear glands

Inhibits salivation, increases sweating

Accelerates heart

Dilates bronchi

Decreases digestive functions of stomach

Secretes adrenalin

Decreases digestive functions of intestine

Inhibits bladder contraction

Chain of sympathetic ganglia

Spinal cord

thetic division of your ANS takes over again. So even though we may classify a certain behavior as being largely determined by some part of the human nervous system, we need to recognize that no division of the nervous system operates without the others.

Before you go on
Reproduce the outline of the nervous system without looking at it.

THE SPINAL CORD

As we have seen, the central nervous system consists of the brain and the spinal cord. In this section, we'll describe the structure and function of the spinal cord, reserving our next topic for the brain alone. As we examine the spinal cord, we can see for the first time the nervous system's involvement in the behavior of organisms.

Structure

The **spinal cord** is a massive collection of neurons that extends from the base of the brain nearly to the tail bone. It is surrounded and protected by the hard bone and cartilage of the vertebrae. It is sometimes difficult to remember that the spinal cord itself is a ropelike structure made up of soft, delicate nerve fibers living inside our "backbone."

A cross-section view of the spinal cord is illustrated in Figure 3.7. There are a couple of structural details that should be pointed out. They will become relevant very shortly when we talk about the function of the spinal cord. First, note the orientation of the section of spinal cord we are viewing in this diagram. *Dorsal* means toward the back; *ventral* means toward the front. We can see, then, that nerve fibers *enter* the spinal cord from the side, but toward the back (dorsal root), and *leave* toward the front (ventral root).

Second, notice that the center area of the spinal cord is made up of a dark gray matter—rather in the shape of a butterfly—while the outside area is a light white matter. Remember that this means that the center portion is filled with cell bodies and unmyelinated axons, while the outer portion contains myelinated axons. Both of these observations about the structure of the spinal cord provide keys to understanding its function.

Function

One of the two major functions of the spinal cord is to rapidly transmit neural impulses to and from the brain. Whenever sensory messages originate below the neck and go to the brain, they do so through the spinal cord. Whenever the brain transmits impulses to parts of the body below the neck, those impulses travel first down the spinal cord.

If you glance back at Figure 3.7, you can get an idea of just how important this function is. As this figure suggests, impulses to and from different parts of our body leave and enter the spinal cord at different levels (impulses to and from the legs, for example, enter and leave at the base of the spinal cord). If the spinal cord, or the fibers leading in and out of it, is damaged or destroyed, the consequences can be disastrous, resulting in a loss of sensation or feeling from the part of the body served and in a loss of voluntary

spinal cord
a collection of neurons within the spine that conveys impulses to and from the brain and is involved in some reflex behaviors

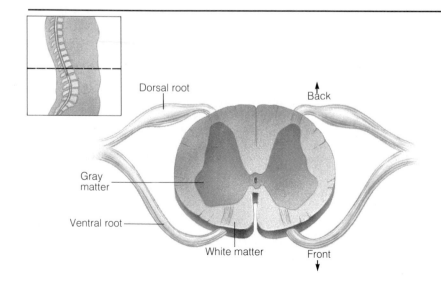

Figure 3.7
A cross-section view of the spinal cord showing dorsal and ventral roots and gray matter and white matter.

Dorsal root

Back

Gray matter

Ventral root

White matter

Front

Figure 3.8

A spinal reflex. Stimulation of the
receptor in turn stimulates sensory
neurons, interneurons, and motor
neurons. Impulses also ascend to the
brain through tracts in the white matter.

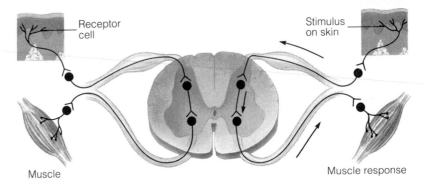

Receptor cell

Stimulus on skin

Muscle

Muscle response

movement (paralysis) of the muscles in the region. Quite clearly, the higher
in the spinal cord that such damage takes place, the greater will be the resulting losses.

Once inside the spinal cord, impulses race up and down the ascending and
descending pathways found in the white matter areas of the spinal cord.
Remember that this area appears white because of the myelin covering the
axons found there. Remember, also, that one of the functions of myelin is to
help speed impulses along their way—in this case up and down the spinal
cord.

The second major function of the spinal cord is its involvement in **spinal
reflexes.** These are very simple automatic behaviors that occur without the
conscious, voluntary action of the brain. To understand how these reflexes
work look at Figure 3.8. Here we have another drawing of a section of the
spinal cord, but we have added receptor cells, sensory neurons, interneurons,
and motor neurons.

For one last time, let's trace the reaction to your stepping on a tack. The
receptor cells initiate neural impulses and transmit them to sensory neurons
that enter through the dorsal root into the spinal cord. Now two things happen at almost the same time. Impulses race up the ascending tracts (pathways) of the spinal cord's white matter to your brain. Impulses also synapse
through interneurons and go right back out again through the ventral root on
motor neurons back down to your leg where muscles are stimulated to contract, and your foot stays suspended in midair.

Here, then, we have a simple reflex. Impulses travel *in* on sensory neurons, *within* on interneurons, and *out* on motor neurons. This is like our
basic S-O-R model in Topic 2 isn't it? *Stimulus* (S, sensory neurons)-*Organism* (O, the spinal cord)-*Response* (R, motor neurons). We are now clearly
involved with behavior.

There are two oversimplifications in Figure 3.8 that need to be mentioned
before we go on. First, the fact that impulses do synapse and go up the spinal
cord to the brain is not indicated, and second, the figure gives the impression, if you didn't know better, that reflex behaviors can be produced with
just three or four neurons. Such behaviors will, in fact, involve the stimulation of thousands of neurons along the way. We are really dealing here with
sensory and motor nerve fibers (bundles of neurons and axons), not just
single neurons.

spinal reflex

an automatic, involuntary response to a
stimulus that involves sensory neurons,
interneurons in the spinal cord, and
motor neurons

Before you go on

Why does spinal cord injury sometimes cause paralysis?

What are the major features of a spinal reflex?

THE ENDOCRINE SYSTEM

Most of our behaviors are influenced by neural activity in a rather immediate and direct fashion. Neural impulses race from the peripheral nervous system into the central nervous system and quickly back out again to the muscles that produce some behavioral reaction. In some cases, the chain of neural events involved seems instantaneous (remember, neural impulses can travel as fast as 120 meters per second).

Some of our behavioral reactions are much slower. They are produced by glands that secrete complex chemicals called hormones into our bloodstream. The hormones then stimulate other organs to respond in turn. The interconnected network of glands in our body is called the endocrine system. It is comprised of a number of different glands, as pictured in Figure 3.9. We'll cover just three of these glands to try to give you the general idea of how this system operates: the pituitary gland, the thyroid gland, and the adrenal glands. (There are some glands in our bodies that are not part of this endocrine system because their secretions do not enter the bloodstream—tear glands and sweat glands are two examples.)

The most important of our endocrine glands is the **pituitary gland.** It is often referred to as the master gland, reflecting the fact that it directly controls the activity of many other glands in the system. The pituitary is located deep in the middle of the brain. (Though it may be a master gland, it doesn't operate on its own: Its output is greatly influenced by brain activity.) One reason why the pituitary is such an important gland is that it secretes so many different hormones. Hormones, which are secreted by all the endocrine glands, travel through the bloodstream and have their effect on specific sites or on specific organs at some distance from where they were produced. The hormones from the pituitary have a wide range of effects on a large assortment of different locations.

One hormone released by the pituitary is called the growth hormone. It regulates the overall growth of the body during development. Extremes of overproduction or underproduction cause the development of giants or dwarfs. The so-called growth spurt associated with early adolescence is indirectly due to the activity of the pituitary gland.

It is the pituitary gland that stimulates the release of a hormone (that is actually produced elsewhere) that acts on the kidneys to regulate the amount of water held in the body. It is the pituitary that directs the mammary glands in the breasts to release milk after childbirth. In its role as master over other glands, the pituitary regulates the output of the thyroid gland and the adrenal glands, as well as the sex glands.

The **thyroid** is an endocrine gland located in the neck. It produces a hormone called thyroxin. Thyroxin regulates the *pace* of the body's functioning—the rate at which oxygen is used and the rate of body function and growth. When people are excitable, edgy, having trouble sleeping, and start to lose weight, they may have too much thyroxin in their system, a condition called hyperthyroidism. Too little thyroxin leads to complaints of fatigue, lack of energy, and a general inability to do much of anything (a condition called hypothyroidism).

The **adrenal glands**, located on the kidneys, secrete a variety of hormones into the bloodstream. The hormone adrenalin (more accurately referred to as *epinephrine*) is very useful in times of stress or threat. Its effects are felt throughout the body. Adrenalin quickens breathing, causes the heart to beat faster, directs the flow of blood away from the stomach and intestines and out toward the limbs, and increases perspiration. When our adrenal glands

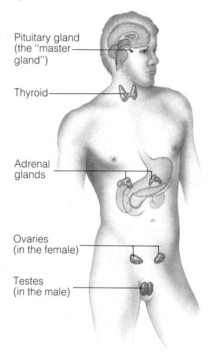

Figure 3.9
The locations of glands in the endocrine system

Pituitary gland (the "master gland")

Thyroid

Adrenal glands

Ovaries (in the female)

Testes (in the male)

pituitary gland
the master gland of the endocrine system that directly controls other glands and overall growth and development of the body

thyroid gland
an endocrine gland that regulates the rate, or pace, of the body's functioning

adrenal glands
endocrine glands that secrete a number of hormones, including those that mimic sympathetic nervous system activity

flood epinephrine into our system during a perceived emergency, we can usually feel the resulting reactions. But these reactions may be delayed.

For example, as you drive down a busy city street, a child suddenly darts out in front of you from behind a parked car and races to the other side of the street. Your defensive reaction is immediate as you slam on the brake and twist the steering wheel, swerving to avoid hitting the youngster. As the child scampers away, oblivious to the danger just past, you proceed down the street. Then, about half a block later, your hormone-induced reaction strikes. You feel your heart rate increase, feel a lump in your throat, and sense your mouth going dry as your palms turn sweaty. Why *now*? The incident is past. The child is safely across the street. You are in no danger, so why the reaction now? Because that reaction is largely hormonal, involving the adrenal glands, and it takes that long for the epinephrine produced by those glands to get through the bloodstream to have their various effects.

Before you go on
What is the endocrine system, and how does it operate?

The workings of the human nervous systems are marvelous and complex. That something as tiny as neurons can provide the impulses for all our actions is mind-boggling. What happens to neural impulses once they reach the brain is another fascinating process, as we will see in our next topic.

Neural impulses pass from neuron to neuron because of chemical reactions that take place at the synapse. Some chemical reactions are excitatory and stimulate a new impulse to begin at the postsynaptic membrane. Some chemical reactions inhibit the neural impulse at the postsynaptic membrane. This much we have already covered. Now we'll examine this process in a little more detail.

As an impulse enters an axon terminal, vesicles filled with a neurotransmitter (chemical molecules) adhere to the presynaptic membrane, break open, and allow the transmitter substance to flood out into the synaptic cleft. On the other side of the cleft, the postsynaptic membrane awaits the molecules of neurotransmitter substance. These molecules "fit" into specific "slots" in the postsynaptic membrane. Each slot will accept only one specified neurotransmitter—a lock and key analogy is often used. Just any molecule floating around in the synaptic cleft cannot fit into the postsynaptic membrane (see Figure 3.10).

As we have said, when some transmitters fit into their slots, an impulse is generated. Other transmitter substances inhibit impulses. What then happens to these neurotransmitters? Apparently, one of two things: Either they decompose and get washed away as waste, or they are taken back up into the axon terminal from which they came to be used again (a process called "reuptake"). Now that we have a general idea of the process, let's look at the specific actions that some chemicals (or drugs) have on synaptic activity.

One of the most common neurotransmitters in the nervous system is *acetylcholine (ACh)*. Acetylcholine is an excitatory substance of the sort that does not re-enter the axon from which it came. Levels of acetylcholine in the brain are low when we are asleep or under anesthetic, but are high when we are very active and aroused. The deadly poison curare paralyzes its victims by filling the "slots," or receptor sites, in the postsynaptic membrane of neurons that are usually reserved for acetylcholine. Botulism, an occasionally deadly form of food poisoning, is caused by a different poison, or toxin, that actually prevents the acetylcholine from being released through the presynaptic membrane.

Figure 3.10

A lock and key view of a neural impulse. The slots in the postsynaptic membrane will accept only the neurotransmitter that "fits."

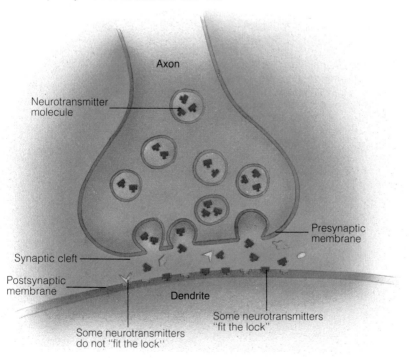

Axon

Neurotransmitter molecule

Presynaptic membrane

Synaptic cleft

Postsynaptic membrane

Dendrite

Some neurotransmitters "fit the lock"

Some neurotransmitters do not "fit the lock"

As we shall see, acetylcholine may be intimately involved in learning and memory (Drachman, 1977). Symptoms of senility—and of Alzheimer's disease—may be a behavioral consequence of decreases in levels of acetylcholine (Gibson, Peterson, & Jenden, 1981).

Norepinephrine (NE) is secreted by the adrenal gland, enters the bloodstream, and activates structures in the sympathetic nervous system. It is also a neurotransmitter that is found in the brain and spinal cord, where its effects are largely inhibitory. Norepinephrine is often taken back up into the presynaptic axon. A number of drugs, including cocaine, block this reuptake process. As a result, the norepinephrine stays at the synapse, continuing to excite the next neuron. Amphetamines act by mimicking the action of norepinephrine and stimulating its production and secretion into the synaptic cleft.

Serotonin is a neurotransmitter that is quite localized in a lower region of the brain associated with sleeping, dreaming, arousal, hunger, thirst, and sexual activity. It seems that the hallucinatory drug LSD inhibits the activity of serotonin in the brain, the most reasonable assumption being that molecules of LSD take up those receptor sites on the postsynaptic membrane usually reserved for serotonin. *GABA* (for gamma-aminobutyric acid) is the most common inhibitory neurotransmitter in the central nervous system. The effects of GABA end with reuptake. The relaxing, or tranquilizing, effects of some drugs, most notably Valium, are thought to be due to a facilitation of GABA activity, which is to say, an inhibition of neural impulse transmission.

As we mentioned earlier, the list of known and suspected neurotransmitters and drugs that affect neurotransmitter processes is now a long one and getting longer. Some have most intriguing capabilities. *Substance P,* for example, seems to be a neurotransmitter, found mostly in the spinal cord, that is thought to have an excitatory role in the transmission of pain (Snyder, 1980). Fortunately, its effects seem to be blocked by the action of GABA. *Dopamine* is an inhibitory substance in the brain that acts very much like norepinephrine and may be implicated in certain behavior disorders, such as schizophrenia.

In 1973, within weeks of each other, three separate laboratories published evidence of "slots," or "locks," or receptor sites, for opiate drugs like morphine (Levinthal, 1983, p. 152). It was then reasoned that these receptor sites would not be there just for opiate drugs unless the brain were capable of producing its own opiatelike drug. There are now known to be several neurotransmitters, collectively called *endorphins,* that act as the brain's own opiates, or painkillers. Whenever a painful stimulus occurs somewhere in our bodies, we seem to produce excess amounts of endorphins to combat the pain (Snyder, 1977). We'll return to many of these neurotransmitters, and their actions, throughout this book as we study the effects of drugs on consciousness, learning and memory, and causes and treatment of behavior disorders.

TOPIC SUMMARY

Describe the main features of a neuron, and classify neurons into three types.

Neurons are microscopically tiny living cells that are made up of a cell body, which contains the cell's nucleus, a number of dendrites, and an axon that extends from the cell body. Sensory neurons carry impulses *to* the central nervous system; motor neurons carry impulses *away* from the CNS; and interneurons are those found *within* the CNS. / 44

What is the basic process involved when a neuron fires?

What does the "all-or-none principle" state?

A neural impulse is essentially the movement of electrically-charged chemical ions in and out through the neuron's membrane. The neuron depolarizes by allowing negative ions to escape to the outside while positive ions are allowed, simultaneously, inside the neuron, after which a return to the resting state quickly occurs. The all-or-none principle suggests that the firing process either takes place or it doesn't; that is, there is no such thing as a partial firing of a neuron. / 46

Summarize neural impulse transmission at the synapse.

At the synapse, an impulse triggers the release of a neurotransmitter from the vesicles found in the axon terminal. These chemicals flood into the synaptic cleft, adhere to the postsynaptic membrane and either stimulate a new impulse or inhibit impulse transmission. / 48

Reproduce the outline of the nervous system without looking at it.

See Figure 3.5. / 50

Why does spinal cord injury sometimes cause paralysis?

What are the major features of a spinal reflex?

If the spinal cord is damaged, impulses originating in the brain to voluntarily move parts of the body cannot get out to activate the appropriate muscles, resulting in paralysis. In a spinal reflex, impulses enter the spinal cord on sensory neurons, synapse with interneurons, and exit the spinal cord on motor fibers to activate a muscle response. At the same time, impulses are sent to the brain on ascending tracts in the white matter. / 52

What is the endocrine system, and how does it operate?

The endocrine system is a network of glands that secrete chemical substances called hormones into the bloodstream. These hormones then regulate or stimulate behavioral reactions in some organ located at a distance from where the hormones are produced. The action of the endocrine system is most noticeable in states of emotionality. / 54

TOPIC

In the mid-1800s very little was known about the specific functions of different parts of the human brain. Indeed, one of the most heated debates among scientists of this era was whether or not specific behaviors or functions *could be* localized in specific areas of the brain.

Very early in the nineteenth century, Franz Joseph Gall (1758–1828) and one of his students, Johann Spurzheim (1776–1832), proposed that a long list of abilities (a sense of time, language, verbal memory, etc.) and personality characteristics (hate, love, destructiveness, benevolence, etc.) each had their own special location on the surface of the brain. Moreover, they argued that strengths and weaknesses in these faculties could be determined by the external examination of the skull (see Figure 4.1). For example, they argued that people with large ridges at the level of the eyebrows had good verbal memories because that's where such memories are processed in the brain. Gall and Spurzheim's theories never found favor in the scientific community, but became quite popular outside of science—and they did stimulate further research.

Marie-Jean Pierre Flourens (1794–1867) was a skilled surgeon who chose to use experimental techniques to study the localization of function in the brain. Using animals (mostly pigeons) he carefully removed small portions of brain tissue and noted the effects of his surgery on the behavior of his subjects. His experiments convinced him, and he in turn convinced others, that the brain operates in very general ways. Yes, some gross functions might be localized (coordinated movement, thought and intellectual functions in general, for example). But, for Flourens, the grand principle of the brain was its unity, the integration of its specific

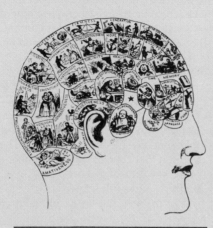

Figure 4.1
A phrenology map illustrating the brain sites where specific abilities and characteristics were thought to be located.

functions, and the observation that all its parts worked together. Searches for specific locations associated with specific functions were bound to fail. Scientists were generally pleased to find experimental evidence with which to refute Gall and Spurzheim.

Jean Baptiste Bouillaud (1796–1881) had once studied under Gall and was not ready to give up the notion of localization of function so easily. He felt that he had evidence that language abilities were located in the frontal part of the human brain. Bouillaud and his son-in-law, Ernest Auberton (1825–1893), collected data on a number of cases of individuals who had suffered damage in the front part of their brain and had great difficulty with or a complete loss of speech, a condition known as *aphasia*. Convinced that he was right about having localized a language center in the brain, Bouillaud offered a reward of 500 francs to anyone who could find brain damage in that center that was not accompanied by a loss of speech.

In early April of 1851, a patient was transferred to the care of the eminent neurologist and surgeon Pierre-Paul Broca (1824–1880). This patient had been hospitalized for 32 years! When he was admitted, at the age of 21, he was aphasic; he could not speak, except to occasionally utter the sound "tan" and had, as a result, become known as Tan. Except for his inability to speak, Tan appeared to be of normal intelligence. Broca's examination of Tan revealed no obvious reason why he could not speak. On April 17, 1851, Tan died, and Broca immediately performed an autopsy. There, in the left frontal portion of Tan's brain, Broca found a cavity the size of an egg, filled with fluid. This extreme damage in this specific region was the only damage to be found. Auberton and Bouillaud had been right. After similar evidence was found in eight more patients, Broca was willing to conclude that he had found the region of the brain responsible for the production of speech. This section of the brain is now called *Broca's area*. With Broca's discovery, the search was on again to find correlations between areas of the brain and the functions they perform.

Describing the structures and functions of the human brain presents authors with a very unique problem. We have run out of adjectives to describe this major structure of the central nervous system. How does one characterize a living structure so marvelously complex, so capable, so subtle, so dynamic? Is the brain a vast computer, a great woven knot of nerve tissue, the seat of understanding, a warehouse of memories and past experiences, a reservoir of emotion, the source of motivation? Yes, it is all these, and more.

Because of its very complexity, we will devote this entire topic to the study of the major structures and functions of the brain. If we are to have any hope of appreciating the intricacies of this organ, we have to break down our discussion to focus on small areas of the brain one at a time. We'll begin by looking at how the brain is studied. Then we'll discuss those "lower" areas of the brain that control very basic functions. Finally, we will study the cerebral cortex, the area of the brain most fully developed in humans. When we dissect the brain in this way (if only for the purpose of discussion), we often lose sight of the fact that it is a unified organ in which all the various parts work together. In many ways, both Bouillaud and Flourens were correct in their analyses of the brain. Some of its functions can be identified as occurring in different areas or locations of the brain, but the adaptability of the brain and the integration of those individual functions force us to consider it as a whole, as more than simply the sum of its various parts.

Discussions of brain structures and functions often tend to sound rather impersonal, as if we were talking about some strange mass of tissue in a glass jar. You'll need to constantly remind yourself that in this topic we're talking about *your* brain, and mine too. As you read these words, it is *your* brain that directs your eyes to move across the page, *your* brain that is seeking understanding, and *your* brain that keeps your heart pumping and keeps you breathing as you read.

HOW TO STUDY THE BRAIN

Before we start looking at different brain structures and what they do, we need to pause and discuss how we find out about such things. Because it is so complex, finding out how the brain works has not been an easy task. Our level of understanding has continued to increase as technology has provided us with new and more exact ways of studying the brain. In this section, we'll review five major techniques that have helped us to learn about the brain.

Accident and Injury

One way to figure out how parts of the brain operate is to work backward. What happens to someone's behavior or mental processes if a portion of his or her brain is damaged or destroyed by injury or disease? If, for example, a person is found to be blind after suffering a wound to the back of the head, we might hypothesize that vision is normally coded there, in the back of the brain. This was precisely the methodology used by Broca to discover that speech production is processed in a small area toward the front, and usually on the left side, of the brain. Broca's conclusions were based on the observation of human brains during autopsies. People with similar speech disorders commonly had damage in the same area of the brain. Logic leads to the suspicion that normal speech functions are controlled by structures at the left front of the brain.

One of the strangest cases of brain injury that helped our understanding of brain function is found in the story of Phineas Gage. In 1848, Gage, a 25-year-old railroad construction foreman, had the misfortune of being too close to an explosion. The explosion, which he accidentally caused himself, drove an iron bar into his head through his left jaw and out through the top of his skull (Figure 4.2). Much to everyone's surprise, Gage survived this massive injury to his brain. He was declared recovered in just a few weeks. Although he survived until 1861, his behavior—in fact his whole personality—changed completely. He became loud, profane, and irresponsible, and he seemed unable to plan and think ahead—an almost total reversal from the Phineas Gage his friends had known before the accident. The change in his behavior was directly related to the damage to Gage's brain. Important pathways in the front, upper part of his brain (the frontal lobes), which would normally exert voluntary control over the emotional behaviors originating in his lower brain centers, had been severed. After the accident, his emotions were expressed directly, without the supervision of the higher, frontal lobes.

Cutting and Removing

By definition, we cannot control the location or the extent of brain damage that occurs by accident or disease. What we may do is destroy or remove some particular part of the brain to see what effect may result. This is the procedure that Flourens used in his studies of the brain. Quite obviously we don't go around cutting into human brains motivated solely by curiosity, just to see what might happen. This procedure is used sparingly and almost always with nonhuman subjects.

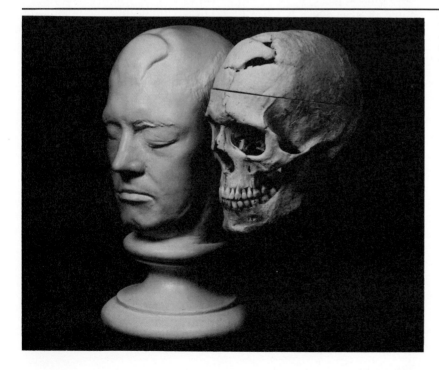

Figure 4.2
A cast of the head and the actual skull of Phineas Gage. Note the places in the skull pierced by the iron rod.

lesion
a cut or wound made on neural tissue to study the impact of the destruction of specific brain areas

lobotomy
a psychosurgical procedure in which the connections of the frontal lobes are severed from the rest of the brain

electrode
a fine wire used to either stimulate or record the electric activity of neural tissue

The logic of this method is the same as for naturally occurring brain damage. A **lesion**, or cut, is made in a particular place in, say, a rat's brain. That rat then refuses to eat, even if food is readily available. We may then assume, or hypothesize, that the lesioned part of the brain plays some role in feeding behavior.

Not long ago in our history (roughly 1930–60), the lesioning of parts of the human brain was an accepted treatment for some types of extreme mental disorder. The most commonly used procedure, called a **lobotomy**, severed the connections of rather large portions of the front part of the brain (the frontal lobes again, the same area destroyed in Phineas Gage's accident). There was enough evidence that the procedure worked (reduced the severity of some symptoms) that it was used with regularity—estimates are that over 50,000 lobotomies were performed in this country alone between 1936 and 1950 (Levinthal, 1983, p. 358).

There are many drawbacks to lobotomies, not the least of which is that it is an irreversible procedure. There were often unfortunate side effects of the procedure, including inappropriate emotional responding and impairment of intellectual functioning. In addition, lobotomies didn't always produce the desired results. Lobotomies are no longer being performed as a treatment of behavior disorders. We now have alternative treatment plans that are just as, or more, effective. Some varieties of psychosurgery (brain surgery used to alleviate psychological disturbances or to improve psychological functioning) are still being used, but only as a treatment of last resort and always with the patient's informed consent (Valenstein, 1973, 1980).

Electrical Stimulation

One of the most significant advances in technology that has aided our study of the brain was the development of the **electrode**. An electrode is a very fine wire (often made of platinum) that can be eased into a specific area of the brain. Once in position, the electrode can be used to deliver a mild electric current (a small shock if you will), artificially stimulating the brain to respond. This technique was first used successfully back in the early 1870s by Gustav Fritsch and Eduard Hitzig (Sheer, 1961). In many cases, stimulating the brain in this manner has no discernible effects at all. Sometimes, however, the results are quite dramatic. Let's look at an example of how this procedure may be used to increase our understanding of the brain.

When electric stimulation is used on humans, it is in conjunction with some other procedure that requires gaining access to the brain. Brain tissue itself contains virtually no receptor cells that cause a feeling of pain when they are stimulated, so brain surgery can be, and often is, done under local anesthetic. Thus, a patient may be tranquilized, but is otherwise fully conscious and aware of her or his surroundings. The patient's scalp is anesthetized, skin is folded back, a portion of the skull is removed, some tissue is pulled out of the way, and finally the brain itself is exposed. Again, this isn't done just to go poking around in the brain. The assumption is that you are there to remove scar tissue left from a stroke, or to remove a small tumor, or for some other good reason.

By using an electrode probe, you can map out many functions of different parts of the brain. (A pioneer in this effort was Wilder Penfield. See, for example, Penfield, 1975, or Penfield & Rasmussen, 1950.) A mild stimulus current is presented to the outer layer of the back of the brain. A subject reports a visual experience, perhaps a flash of lights, not unlike fireworks— thus reinforcing your hypothesis that vision is coded in the back of the brain. A stimulus to the left side of the brain produces a twitching movement in the right arm, even though your patient claims not to have moved on purpose. Perhaps *this* area of the brain controls the muscles in the right arm. We'll take a closer look at this sort of finding later in this topic when we discuss the activity of the cerebral cortex.

When we use nonhuman subjects, we can permanently implant electrodes in different parts of the brain. Although the procedure may sound (and look) gruesome, it is a painless one that appears to have no negative effects on the animals at all. What happens when an implanted electrode is turned on and delivers a stimulus to the brain depends, of course, on where it is implanted.

In a very dramatic exhibition of the power of electric stimulation of the brain, José Delgado entered a bull ring armed only with a cape and a small radio transmitter. A raging, charging bull then entered the ring. Attached to the bull's horns was a radio receiver that was, in turn, attached to an electrode implanted deep within the bull's brain. The bull charged Delgado who pushed a button on his transmitter that delivered a pulse to the bull's brain. The bull stopped his charge toward the unprotected Delgado and meekly turned aside (Figure 4.3).

This demonstration, as impressive as it was, has often been overinterpreted. At first it was thought that Delgado had found an antiaggression center in the brain. (What a boon to law enforcement *that* would be!) In fact, it is more likely that he stimulated a portion of the brain that simply caused the bull to pull away involuntarily. An excellent review of brain control through surgery and stimulation is provided by Valenstein (1973) who discusses Delgado's charging bull in some detail.

Recording Electrical Activity

Not only can electrodes be used to stimulate brain tissue, they can also be used to measure or record the electrical activity of the nervous system. Remember that nerve impulses are largely changes in electric charges that

Figure 4.3
Jose Delgado is a pioneer in the brain implantation of radio-activated electrodes. Here, even after the bull has started to charge, Delgado can stop it by a radio message to electrodes planted in the brain. After repeated experiences such as this, the animal becomes permanently less aggressive.

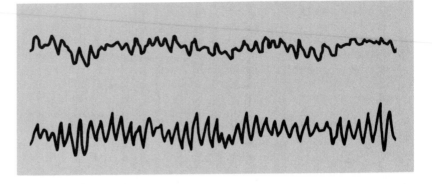

sweep down nerve fibers. In 1929 it was reported (by a German psychiatrist, Hans Berger, who had been using the technique for nearly 20 years) that electrodes attached to the scalp of an individual could pick up and record the electrical activity of the brain. Recordings of such brain activity are called **electroencephalograms,** or **EEGs** for short. Electroencephalograms do not provide very much in the way of detailed information about the specific activity of small areas of the brain, but they do provide a wealth of information about overall brain activity (Figure 4.4). Electroencephalograms can be used to tell us about a person's level of arousal, or what stage of sleep they are in (see Topic 9). The technique is sensitive enough to reinforce impressions we may have gotten from other sources. For example, when looking at a colorful, detailed picture, EEG activity at the back of the brain increases, suggesting once again that vision is in some way located at the back of the brain.

Recording electrodes are now available that are so small and so sensitive that they can be used to detect electrical changes in individual neurons! Most recordings of nerve cell activity are made using nonhuman subjects, particularly those animals that have large neurons, such as the squid. It is largely through the use of these tiny recording electrodes that we have learned about the true nature of the neural impulse and impulse transmission. Single-cell recordings also allowed David Hubel and T. N. Wiesel (1979) to discover individual cells in the brains of cats and monkeys (and by implication in humans) that respond only to very specific types of visual stimulation, and to propose that the entire visual field (what we see) is completely represented in the brain, although in quite a distorted form.

Observing the Brain Directly and Indirectly

Certainly one way to study the brain is simply to look at it. The development of the microscope helped a great deal in this regard, making small anatomical details of structure visible. The more powerful electron microscope allows us to look even closer and to take the sort of photographs we use in Topic 4. But normal microscopic examination restricts us to looking at dead tissue—cells removed from their usual surroundings. What a great advantage there would be in having a detailed look at the brain of a living, behaving organism. To a degree, X-ray technology allows us to do just that. Particularly when dyes or radioactive substances are injected into the brain, we can get a fairly good view of what is going on there, but the picture is not a clear one. Important structures, like tumors, may be hidden behind less important ones.

electroencephalogram (EEG)
direct measures of the electrical activity of the brain made through electrodes attached to the scalp

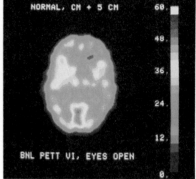

This is a PET scan taken of a subject with eyes open. Note the activity (the red areas) in the occipital area of the brain.

Recently, computer technology has joined with X-ray technology to do what is called a **CAT scan** of the brain. The "CAT" is an abbreviation for "computerized axial tomography." In essence, this device (see Figure 4.5) takes a series of X-ray pictures of the brain from many different angles. The pictures are fed into a computer that enhances their quality and focuses on any specified area of the brain. Now what one can get is a view of just a thin slice of living brain, showing the details of the structures found there. Of course, it still takes an expert to interpret what a CAT scan picture is showing, but the job is much easier and more reliable than with the simple X ray.

Since the CAT scan became generally available in the early 1980s, two newer methods of imaging the human brain have been developed. One, the **PET scan** (for "positron-emission tomography"), involves injecting very small doses of radioactive substance into the brain. Detectors then record the location of these radioactive substances in the brain. The usefulness of this PET scan procedure hinges on the fact that the radioactive substance being measured tends to be greatest in those areas of the brain that are most active. PET scans of subjects who are looking at a complex visual stimulus show increased activity in the back regions of the brain. When the same subject is listening to a Sherlock Holmes story, for example, the PET scan shows increased activity toward the sides of the brain, near the temples.

Even more recent is the technique of seeing the living brain through nuclear magnetic resonance techniques, or **NMR.** This technique allows for very precise and detailed high-resolution pictures of brain structures. Not only are the pictures very clear, but there is no need to inject the brain with any substance and there is no danger of overexposure to radiation with NMR use. The problem is that the technology involved is very new and terribly expensive.

CAT scan
(computerized axial tomography) a method of imaging brain structure through the computer enhancement of X-ray pictures

PET scan
(positron-emission tomography) a method of imaging the brain, and its activity, through the injection of radioactive substances into the brain

NMR
(nuclear magnetic resonance) a recently developed, high resolution method of imaging brain structures

Before you go on
Briefly summarize five major techniques used to study the brain.

"LOWER" BRAIN CENTERS

We've already indicated in this topic that there are many different ways in which we could organize our discussion of the brain. Let's choose a very simple one and divide the brain into two parts: the cerebral cortex and everything else. In a sense that hardly seems fair, but for the human brain, where the cerebral cortex plays so many important roles, this division is a reasonable one.

What we are here calling "lower" brain centers are lower in two ways. First, they are physically located below, or underneath, the cerebral cortex, and second, they are the brain structures first to develop, both in an evolutionary sense and within the developing human brain. They are the brain structures we most clearly share with other animals. In no way should you think of "lower" centers as being less important. As you will soon see, our very survival depends on them. You can use Figure 4.6 as a guide to locate the different structures as we discuss them.

The Brain Stem

As you look up the spinal cord toward the brain, you really can't tell where the spinal cord ends and the brain begins. There is no abrupt line separating these two components of the central nervous system. At its very base, there are two important brain structures that look as much like a widening of the spinal cord as anything else. Together they form the **brain stem.**

The very lowest structure is the **medulla** (or more formally, the medulla oblongata). In a real sense, the medulla acts as if it were an extension of the spinal cord because its major functions involve involuntary reflexes. There are all sorts of important little structures—called nuclei—within the medulla. They control such functions as reflexive eye movements and tongue movements; you don't, for example, have to think about blinking your eye as something rushes toward it; your medulla will control that blink reflexively. Other centers control sensory and motor fibers to and from the head and face.

brain stem
the portion of the brain just above the spinal cord, comprised of the medulla and the pons

medulla
the lowest structure of the brain that controls reflex functions such as respiration and heartbeat and where many nerve fibers cross from the left side of the brain to the right side of body, and vice versa

Figure 4.6
The major structures of the human brain. Note the orientation of the "lower" brain centers—the medulla, pons, cerebellum, and reticular activating system.

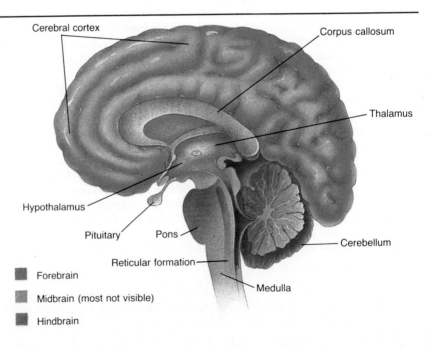

Cerebral cortex

Corpus callosum

Thalamus

Hypothalamus

Pituitary

Pons

Reticular formation

Cerebellum

Medulla

■ Forebrain

■ Midbrain (most not visible)

■ Hindbrain

Most important, perhaps, are those centers that control breathing reflexes and that stimulate the muscles of the heart to keep it beating rhythmically. We *can* exercise higher level control over the centers of the medulla, but only within limits. The medulla controls our level of respiration (breathing), but clearly we can override the medulla and hold our breath. We cannot, however, hold our breath until we die (as some children occasionally threaten). We can hold our breath until we lose consciousness, which is to say, until we lose higher level control, and then the medulla picks up where it left off, and we continue breathing.

It is at the level of the medulla that many nerve fibers to and from the brain (about 80 percent of them) cross over from left to right and vice versa. By and large, centers in the left side of the brain receive impulses from and send impulses to the right side of the body. Similarly, the left side of the body sends impulses to and receives messages from the right side of the brain. (Which explains why stimulating the correct portion of the *left* side of the brain may produce a movement in the *right* arm.) This crossing over from one side to another takes place here, in the brain stem.

Just above the medulla is another area of widening, a structure called the **pons**. (The pons is one structure—there is no such thing as a "pon.") Primarily, the pons serves as a relay station, or bridge (which is what "pons" means), sorting out and relaying sensory messages from the spinal cord and the face up to higher brain centers and reversing the relay for motor impulses coming down from higher centers. Damage that severs the pons, then, would effectively cut off the brain from the rest of the body.

pons
part of the brain stem forming a bridge, or relay station, between the brain and spinal cord

Before you go on
Name the two brain stem structures, and describe where they are and what they do.

The Cerebellum

Your **cerebellum** is about the size of your closed fist. It is more or less spherical in shape and sits right behind your pons, tucked up under the base of your skull. The cerebellum itself looks like a small brain. Its outer region is very convoluted, meaning that the tissue there is folded in upon itself, creating many deep crevices, lumps, and valleys.

cerebellum
spherical structure at lower rear of brain that is involved in the coordination and smoothing of muscular activity

The major role of the cerebellum is in smoothing and coordinating body movements. Most intentional, voluntary movements originate in higher brain centers and are only coordinated in the cerebellum, but some movements may actually originate there. Because body movement is so closely tied to vision, many eye movements seem to originate here. Remember the episode of stepping on a tack that we used in the last topic? As you step on the tack and lift your foot, your arms may flail out to the side to maintain balance—a movement probably originated and coordinated at the cerebellum.

Our ability to casually stoop, pick up a dime from the floor, and slip it into our pocket involves a series of movements made smooth and casual by our cerebellum. When athletes train a movement, like a golf swing or a gymnastic routine, we sometimes say that they are trying to get "into a groove" so that the trained movement can be made simply and smoothly. In a real sense, such athletes are training their cerebellum.

Few of our behaviors are as rapid or as well coordinated as the movements required to make speech sounds. Next time you're talking to someone, pause to consider just how quickly and effortlessly your lips, mouth, and tongue are moving (thanks to your cerebellum) to form the sounds of your speech. Cerebellum damage disrupts fine coordinated movements. Speech becomes slurred; one staggers when walking; smoothly touching the end of the nose is difficult to do with closed eyes. In fact, a person with cerebellum damage may appear quite drunk. (On what region of the brain do you suppose that alcohol has a direct influence? The cerebellum, of course!)

Damage to the cerebellum may disrupt motor activity in other ways. If the outer regions of the cerebellum are damaged, patients suffer jerky **tremors** (involuntary trembling movements) when they try to move (called intention tremors). Damage to inner, or deeper, areas of the cerebellum lead to tremors at rest, where the limbs and/or head may shake or twitch even when the patient tries to remain still.

tremors
involuntary, trembling, jerky movements that are usually associated with damage in the cerebellum

Before you go on
Where is the cerebellum located, and what is its major function?

The Reticular Activating System

reticular activating system (RAS)
a network of nerve fibers extending from the brain stem to the cortex that is involved in the level of arousal or activation

The **reticular activating system,** or **RAS,** is a different sort of brain structure. In fact, it is hardly a brain structure at all. It is a complex network of nerve fibers that begins down in the brain stem and works its way up through and around other structures, all the way to the top portions of the brain (see Figure 4.6).

Just precisely what the reticular activating system does, and how it does it, remains something of a mystery. As its name implies, however, the RAS is very much involved in determining our level of activation or arousal. It no doubt influences whether we're awake and attentive or drowsy or asleep, or at some level in between. Electrical stimulation of the RAS can produce EEG patterns of brain activity associated with being awake and alert. Lesions of the RAS cause a condition of constant sleep in laboratory animals (Lindsley et al., 1949; Moruzzi and Magoun, 1949). In a way, then, the RAS acts like a valve that either allows sensory messages to pass from lower centers up to higher centers of the brain, or shuts them off, partially or totally. The mystery is how the RAS does its thing, and what prompts it to do what it does.

The Limbic System

limbic system
a collection of small structures, including the amygdala, septal area, and hippocampus, involved in emotional and motivational responding and in the transfer of memories to long-term storage

The **limbic system** is a collection of small structures rather than a single, unified one. It is of the utmost importance in controlling the behavior of nonhuman mammals, which do not have as large or well-developed a cerebral cortex as humans do. The limbic system controls the complex behavior patterns we usually think of as instinctive (Figure 4.7).

Even within the human brain, parts of the limbic system are intimately involved in the display of emotional reactions. One center, the amygdala, produces reactions of rage and aggression when stimulated, while another area, the septum, seems to have the opposite effect, suppressing emotional responses when it is stimulated. The influence of the amygdala and the septum on emotional responding is rather direct in nonhumans. In humans it is more subtle, being influenced by other brain centers as well.

Another part of the limbic system, called the hippocampus, seems to be less involved with emotion and more involved with the processing of memories. People with a damaged hippocampus are often unable to move experiences into permanent memory storage. They may remember events for short periods of time. They may also be able to remember events from the distant past, but only if those events happened before their hippocampus was damaged.

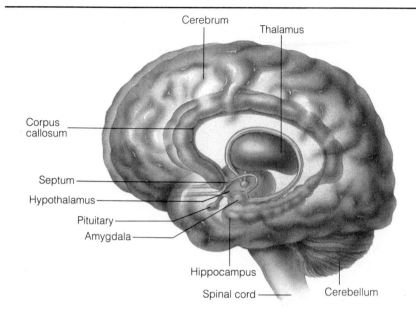

Figure 4.7

A number of small structures make up the limbic system, including the amygdala, septum, hypothalamus, thalamus, and hippocampus.

Labels on figure: Cerebrum, Thalamus, Corpus callosum, Septum, Hypothalamus, Pituitary, Amygdala, Hippocampus, Spinal cord, Cerebellum

The Hypothalamus

The first thing to say about the **hypothalamus** is that it is often considered to be part of the limbic system. It is located near it, and it is also very much involved in our motivational and emotional behaviors. Among other things, it influences (usually through the pituitary gland) many functions of the endocrine system, which, as we have seen, is involved in emotional responding (see Topic 3).

The major responsibility of the hypothalamus seems to be to monitor critical internal bodily functions. It has centers (nuclei again) that control feeding behavior. It is sensitive to the amount of fluid in our body and indirectly gives rise to the feeling of being thirsty. The hypothalamus acts something like a thermostat, making physiological adjustments should we become too hot or too cold. This small structure is also very much involved in aggressive and sexual responding. It acts as a regulator of many hormones. To be sure, we'll discuss the hypothalamus again in more detail when we study motives, needs, and emotions in later topics.

hypothalamus
a small structure near the center of the brain involved in feeding, drinking, aggression, and sexual behaviors; also involved in stimulation of the endocrine system

The Thalamus

The last structure to discuss as a lower brain center is the **thalamus**. It sits right below the covering of the cerebral cortex and is very involved with its functioning. It is a busy place. Like the pons, it acts as a relay station for impulses to and from the cerebral cortex.

Many impulses from the cerebral cortex to lower brain structures, the spinal cord, and eventually out to the peripheral nervous system first pass through the thalamus. Overcoming the normal function of the medulla (voluntarily holding our breath, for example) involves messages passing through the thalamus.

The thalamus also collects and spreads incoming sensory messages to the appropriate area of the cerebral cortex. Sensory messages from our lower

thalamus
the final sensory relay station, just below the cerebral cortex that projects sensory fibers to the proper cortical location

body, our eyes, ears, and all senses (except for taste and smell) pass through the thalamus. (Taste and smell have their own special, direct routes.) At the thalamus, a nerve fiber, say from an eye, is unwound, spread out, and projected onto the back of the cerebral cortex.

Before you go on
Where are the following structures and what do they do: the RAS,
the limbic system, the hypothalamus, and the thalamus?

THE CEREBRAL CORTEX

cerebral cortex
(cerebrum) the large, convoluted outer covering of the brain that is most fully developed in humans and is the seat of intellectual functions

The human brain is a homely organ. There's just nothing very pretty about it. When we look at a human brain, the first thing we are likely to notice is the large, lumpy, creviced outer covering of the **cerebral cortex** (in fact, "cortex" means outer bark or covering). It is this part of the brain that is the last to develop. The cerebral cortex (or cerebrum) of the human brain is much larger than any other brain structure. Indeed, it is the relative size and intricate development of our cerebrum that makes us uniquely human. It is our center for the processing of information about the world in which we live.

Lobes and Localization

Figure 4.8 presents two views of the human brain, one a view of the top of the brain, the other a side view. You can see from these illustrations that the deep folds of tissue of the human cerebral cortex provide us with a system for dividing the cerebrum into major areas. The most noticeable division of the cortex can be seen in the top view. Here, we can clearly see the very deep fold or crevice that runs down the middle of the cerebrum from front to back, dividing it into the left and right cerebral **hemispheres.**

hemispheres
the two halves of the cerebral cortex, separated by a large, deep fissure running from front to back

frontal lobe
the largest of the four lobes of the cerebrum; in front of the central fissure and above the lateral fissure

occipital lobe
the lobe of the cerebrum at the back and lower back of the brain

parietal lobe
the lobe of the cerebrum behind the frontal lobe, in front of the occipital lobe, and above the lateral fissure

temporal lobe
the lobe of the cerebrum located at the temples

A side view of one hemisphere allows us to see the four major divisions of the cerebrum that are found in each hemisphere. These divisions are referred to as *lobes* of the brain. The **frontal lobe** is the largest and is defined by two large crevices, called the central fissure and the lateral fissure. The **occipital lobe** is defined somewhat more arbitrarily; it is the area at the back and lower back of the brain. The **parietal lobe** is wedged behind the frontal lobe, in front of the occipital lobe, and above the lateral fissure. Finally, the **temporal lobe** is located roughly at the temples, below the lateral fissure, and in front of the occipital lobe. Remember that the brain is divided into two symmetrical hemispheres, giving us what amounts to a left and right frontal lobe, a left and right parietal lobe, and so on.

Using the methods we discussed at the beginning of this topic, we have come to learn a lot about what happens in different areas of the cerebral cortex. Primarily using stimulating electrodes, scientists have mapped out what normally goes on in the cerebrum. There are three major areas that have been mapped: (1) *sensory areas* where data from our sense receptors are sent, (2) *motor areas* where voluntary movements originate, and (3) *association areas* where sensory and motor functions are integrated and where higher mental processes are thought to occur.

Sensory Areas   Let's review for just a minute. Receptor cells in our senses respond to stimulus energy from the environment. These cells then pass neural impulses along sensory nerve fibers to the brain. Impulses from senses in our head usually pass through the pons in the brain stem, then up through the thalamus. Senses in our body below our neck first send impulses

Figure 4.8

The human cerebrum is divided into the left and right hemispheres, which in turn are divided into four lobes that house various functional areas.

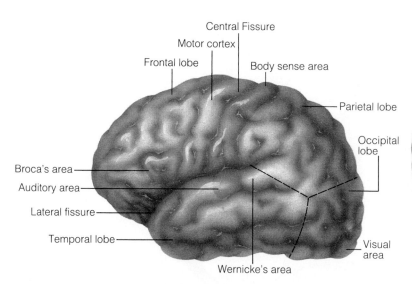

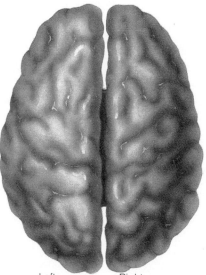

to the spinal cord. Then, it's up the spinal cord, through the brain stem and thalamus and beyond. Where do the impulses from our senses go after they leave the thalamus? It depends upon the sense.

Reflecting their relative importance to us, two large areas of the cortex are involved with vision and hearing. Virtually the entire occipital lobe handles visual information, labeled "visual area" in Figure 4.8. We have been suggesting that vision is processed back there since early in this topic. Auditory (hearing) impulses end up in large centers in the temporal lobes.

Our body senses (touch, pressure, pain, etc., from different parts of our body) send impulses to a strip at the front of the parietal lobe, labeled "body sense area" in Figure 4.8. Within this area of the parietal lobe, we can map out specific regions of the body. When we do so, we find that some parts of the body—the face, lips, fingers, and so forth—reflecting their sensitivity, are overrepresented in the body sense area of the cerebrum. See Figure 4.9 for a drawing of how the body senses are represented in the cerebral cortex.

It is at this point that we need to consider the notion of **cross-laterality.** This is the term that describes the fact that sensory information from the left side of our body (usually) ends up in the right hemisphere of our cerebral cortex. Likewise, sensory impulses from the right side of our body end up in the left parietal lobe. Remember, also, that most of the crossing over of sensory fibers takes place well below the cerebrum in the brain stem. The fact that someone touches your right hand is registered in the left parietal lobe of your cerebrum. We'll soon see how this observation can help us to understand the different functions of the two cerebral hemispheres.

Motor Areas We have already seen that some of our behaviors—at least very simple and reflexive ones—originate in our central nervous system below the cerebral cortex. Conscious, voluntary cerebral control of muscle activity begins in a strip at the back of our frontal lobes. This **motor area** of the cerebrum is directly across the central fissure from the body sense area in the parietal lobe (see Figure 4.8).

cross-laterality
the principle that, in general, sensory and motor impulses to and from the brain cross from the left side of the body to the right side of the brain, and vice versa

motor area
that portion of the parietal lobe directly behind the central fissure in which are found the centers that control the voluntary movement of muscles

Figure 4.9

The primary motor and somatosensory areas of the cortex can be mapped out to indicate the specific regions responsible for controlling the various parts of the body.

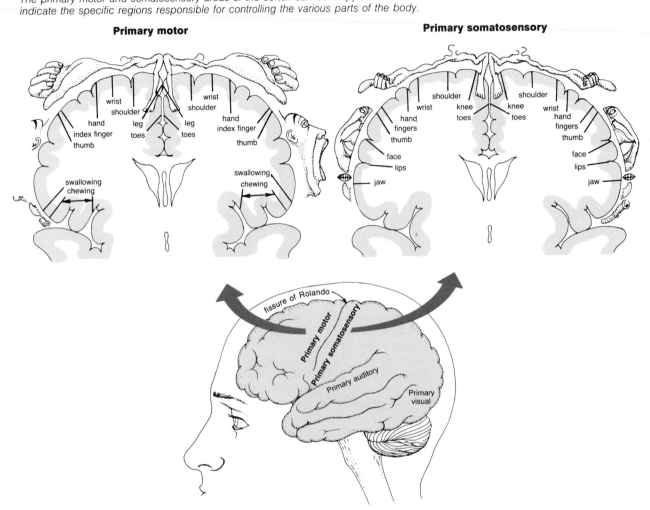

Once again, electric stimulation techniques have allowed us to map out locations in the motor area that control specific muscles or muscle groups. This mapping is shown in Figure 4.9. As with the body sense mapping, note that different parts of the body, and the muscles serving them, are disproportionally represented in the cerebral cortex's motor area.

We also find cross-laterality with the motor area. It is your left hemisphere's motor area that controls the movements of the right side of your body, and vice versa. As you raise your right arm, impulses instigating that behavior are coming from your left cerebral cortex—your left motor area.

Association Areas   Once we have located areas of the cerebral cortex that process sensory information and originate motor responses, we find that we've still got a lot of brain left over. The remaining areas of the cerebrum are called **association areas.** As you can see from Figure 4.8, there are three of them: frontal, parietal, and temporal. The occipital lobe is so "filled" with vision, there is no room left over for an occipital association area.

Exactly what happens in our association areas is not well understood. We assume that it is here that incoming sensory information is associated with

association areas
those areas in the frontal, parietal, and temporal lobes that are neither sensory nor motor in function where cognitive functioning is assumed to take place

outgoing motor responses—hence, association area. There is general support for the idea that it is in our association areas that so-called "higher" mental activities are processed.

As Broca discovered more than a century ago, some language and speech behaviors are located in the frontal association area (others are located in the temporal association area—see Topic Expansion). Frontal association areas (remember there are two of them, left and right) seem to be involved in a number of mental processes. Damage to the frontal lobes (as in a frontal lobotomy) seems to interrupt or destroy the ability to plan ahead, to think quickly, or to think things through.

In this context, we ought to remind ourselves of a point we made earlier. We should not get too carried away with cerebral localization of function. Let's not fall into the trap of coming to believe that separate little parts of the cortex operate independently. This is a point Flourens made more than 100 years ago, and that Marcel Kinsbourne has made more recently: "There are no discontinuities in the brain. No independent channels traverse it, nor is its territory divisible into areas that house autonomous processors" (1982, p. 412). This will be particularly important to remember as we now look at the division of the cerebral cortex into the right and left hemispheres.

Before you go on

Given a side view of the brain, can you locate the four lobes of the cerebral cortex?

Can you locate the primary sensory, motor, and association areas of the cerebrum?

The Two Cerebral Hemispheres

Even the ancient Greeks appreciated that the cerebral cortex was divided into two major sections or hemispheres. That there should be a division of the cerebrum into two halves seems quite natural, and not at all surprising. After all, we have two arms, legs, lungs, kidneys, and so forth. Why not two major divisions of the brain? Within the last 20 years, interest in the division of the cerebral cortex has heightened as we have accumulated more information that suggests that each half of the human cerebrum has primary responsibility for different functions.

The left hemisphere is usually the larger of the two halves, usually contains a higher proportion of gray matter, and is thought to be the dominant hemisphere. We have already noted that language behaviors are usually processed in the left cerebral hemisphere. At least this is true for virtually all right-handed people. For some—but not all—left-handers, language may "live" in a dominant right hemisphere. Because humans are so language oriented, not much attention was given to the lowly right hemisphere. Then, a remarkable surgical procedure, first performed regularly in the 1960s, provided us with new insights about the two cerebral hemispheres (Sperry, 1968; Springer & Deutsch, 1981).

Splitting the Brain   Normally, the two sides of the cerebral cortex are interconnected by a series of fibers called the **corpus callosum** (shown in Figure 4.6). Through the corpus callosum, one side of our cerebrum remains in constant contact with the other. Separating the functions of the two hemispheres is possible through a **split brain procedure** that is neither as complicated nor as dangerous as it might sound. The procedure amounts to destroying the corpus callosum connection between the two hemispheres. The

corpus callosum
the network of nerve fibers that normally transmit impulses between the two hemispheres of the cerebral cortex

split brain procedure
the surgical procedure of separating the functioning of the two cerebral hemispheres by destroying the corpus callosum

procedure was first tried on humans in 1961 by Joseph Bogen in an attempt to lessen the severity of the symptoms of epilepsy. As a treatment of last resort, it was found to be very successful.

Most of what we know about the activities of the cerebral hemispheres we have learned from split brain subjects—both human and animal. One thing that makes this procedure remarkable is that under normal circumstances split brain patients appear to behave normally. Only in the laboratory can we clearly see the results of having made the hemispheres of the cerebrum function independently (for example, Gazzaniga and LeDoux, 1978). To be sure, all the answers aren't in, but we can draw some tentative conclusions.

Experiments with split brain patients confirm very clearly that speech is a left cerebral hemisphere function. Suppose you have your hands behind your back. If I place a house key in your left hand and ask you to tell me what it is, your left hand will feel the key. Impulses will travel up your arm and cross over to your *right* cerebral hemisphere—remember cross-laterality. You can readily tell me that the object in your hand is a key because your brain is intact. Your right hemisphere tells your left hemisphere about the key, and your left hemisphere directs you to say "key." If your corpus callosum were cut, if you were a split brain patient, you couldn't answer my question. Your right brain would know that the object in your left hand is a key, but it would have no way of communicating its knowledge to the speech centers in your left brain. You would be able to pick out the key from among other objects; you just wouldn't be able to tell me about it.

So, a major activity of the left brain is the use of speech and language. Simple tasks of calculation are also left hemisphere functions. In addition, there is evidence that the left hemisphere is analytical, formalized, and almost rigid in the way it operates. The left hemisphere seems to process information sequentially, handling one thing at a time.

On the other hand, our right hemisphere seems better able to grasp the big picture, to see the overall view of an issue, and to be more creative. It is thought to be more visually and spatially oriented than the left hemisphere. Our right hemisphere is useful in solving spatial relations tasks such as jigsaw puzzles. Its activity involves more visual imagery than does the left hemisphere, and it is believed to be more musical, at least for nonmusicians. Some recent research also suggests that our right cerebral cortex is more involved than our left in our expression and interpretation of emotions.

To gain a better idea of where these tentative conclusions come from, let's examine a typical split brain experiment in some detail.

A Split Brain Experiment Roger Sperry is credited with bringing split brain subjects into the psychology laboratory. His efforts were rewarded with a Nobel Prize in 1981. Sperry and his students, most notably Michael Gazzaniga, have performed many ingenious experiments to determine the different roles of the right and left cerebral hemispheres. One such experiment was reported in the journal *Brain,* in 1972, by Levy, Trevarthan, and Sperry. In many ways it is typical of research in this area. The following discussion is based on the results of this experiment.

Let's first review some of the relevant ideas we have already covered regarding brain function. Even a split brain patient, with cerebral hemispheres divided, receives much the same sensory information in *both* hemispheres. Each eye, for example, provides information to both the left and right hemispheres of the occipital lobes. So, to study each hemisphere independently requires that sensory input be delivered to just one side of the brain or the other. We can do this without additional surgery because of the way the visual system works. Following our general principle of cross-laterality, everything in our left visual field (i.e., everything we see that

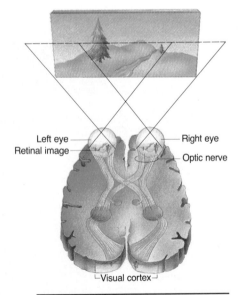

Figure 4.10
According to the principle of cross-laterality, stimuli entering our left visual field are sent to the right occipital lobe for processing, while stimuli in the right visual field are sent to the left occipital lobe. Though the lens of the eye turns the images upside-down, we do not perceive the images that way.

Left eye
Retinal image
Right eye
Optic nerve
Visual cortex

is located off to our left) gets sent to our right occipital lobe. Similarly, everything off to our right ultimately ends up in the occipital region of our left hemisphere. (Figure 4.10 diagrams this rather strange-sounding arrangement.)

If a split brain patient is asked to stare at a spot on a screen, everything projected to the right of that spot will go to the left hemisphere and everything to the left of the spot will go to the right hemisphere. What the split brain subject is shown is a strange picture. At least it looks strange to us. It is made up of two halves of photographs of different people (see Figure 4.11). If this combined picture is flashed before subjects staring at the middle of the picture, what will the split brain subject report seeing? It depends upon which side of the brain we ask.

If we ask the subject to *tell us* about the picture that flashed before her, she will use her language-governed left brain. She will tell us what the left hemisphere saw. She will describe the characteristics of the person on the *right side* of the combined photo. And, she will describe the picture as being a complete, normal, full-face photograph.

If we show the subject a series of portraits of people, including the two who made up the combined stimulus photo, she will, when asked to do so, *point* to the picture of the person on the left. This pointing behavior is controlled by the right side of the brain that only "saw" the left side of the stimulus picture.

Before you go on
Briefly summarize the different functions of the left and right cerebral hemispheres of the human brain.

How is a split brain procedure done?

Though we have learned a great deal about the human brain, there are still many mysteries to be solved. The methods we have for studying the brain and its activities are becoming more refined and exact as medical technology improves. As our understanding of the brain increases, so will our knowledge of the psychological working of the human mind.

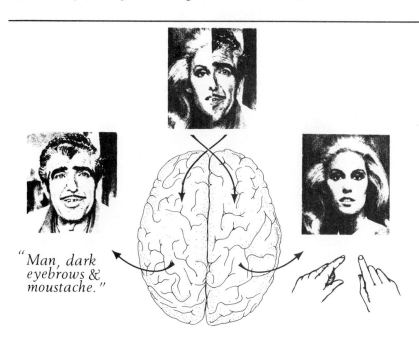

"Man, dark eyebrows & moustache."

Figure 4.11
When split-brain subjects are asked to verbally describe the photo with two different faces, they describe the man because the verbal left hemisphere, which received the images from the right eye, is being called into action. When the subjects are asked to point to the photo that matches the original, they choose the woman—a response controlled by the visual right hemisphere.

TOPIC

aphasia

a disorder or loss of speech caused by damage to some portion of the brain

Aphasia is a general term used to describe a loss of language function resulting from brain damage. As you'll recall, it was a case of aphasia that prompted Pierre-Paul Broca to perform an autopsy in 1851 that led to the discovery of a speech center in the left frontal lobe. Broca's area, as it is now called, is only one of the areas of the brain directly involved in language processing. In this Topic Expansion, we'll examine some of the other brain regions that are involved and describe what they do. As was the case for Broca, almost all we know about normal brain functioning with regard to language we have learned through the examination of cases of language disorder.

There's no doubt that Broca's area is intimately involved in language behavior, but only in one particular way. Broca's area (see Figure 4.12) controls the actual pro-

duction of speech sounds when we talk. Damage to this area results in a condition known as Broca's aphasia, or expressive aphasia, indicating that the major problem is one of speaking. Language comprehension is intact; reading and writing are unimpaired. The person knows what to say and wants to say it, but is unable to speak. (That Broca's area, with its main function of motor control of speech, lies so close to the major motor area of the frontal lobe is not surprising, is it?)

A few years after Broca's area was established as a speech center, Carl Wernicke (in 1874) discovered another language center in the brain, now called Wernicke's area. This brain region, which is located in the left temporal lobe, is normally involved in the comprehension of speech. Located near the primary auditory center of the cerebrum, Wernicke's area produces a different sort of language disorder when

---

Figure 4.12

The primary language areas of the brain: Broca's area, Wernicke's area, the angular gyrus, and the arcuate fasciculus.

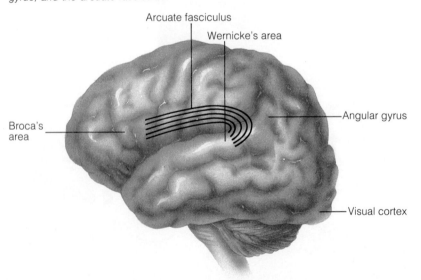

it is damaged. In Wernicke's, or receptive, aphasia, patients do not understand what is said to them, nor are they able to read. Patients with Wernicke's aphasia produce a strange sort of language behavior—very fluent, very rapid, but essentially devoid of meaning. Such a patient may say something like, "I don't know what to do after they fell through the other side, but didn't tell me if I could or not." Such utterances are made with conviction, with proper intonation and stress—they just don't make sense.

There's more to normal language production and reception than just these two areas, Broca's and Wernicke's (Geschwind, 1979). For example, there is a bundle of fibers that richly interconnect Wernicke's area and Broca's area (called the arcuate fasciculus). If these fibers are damaged, we find a different sort of language disorder called conduction aphasia. In this case, a person hears a phrase that is relayed to Wernicke's area and is understood. The person then wants to simply repeat the same phrase, but is unable to because it cannot be relayed to Broca's area for production if the arcuate fasciculus is damaged. (Self-generated speech is less impaired, although not quite normal.)

Wernicke's area processes speech *sounds* from the primary auditory area of the temporal lobe. Is there a language center that processes written language signals that go to the occipital lobe? Yes, there is. It's called the angular gyrus and is located right behind Wernicke's area (see Figure 4.12 again). The major symptom of a person with damage in this area is an inability to name objects (called anomic aphasia). It is sometimes the case that a person's brain damage is so severe or widespread that a number, or all, of these language centers are damaged. In such cases, language impairment will also be general, a condition called global aphasia.

Consider this chain of events: A written word is flashed on a screen. You are simply to say the word out loud. The first cerebral processing of the message takes place in the occipital lobes (reception). From there the message travels to the angular gyrus (written forms matched to auditory sounds) and from there to Wernicke's area (comprehension of form and meaning) and on to the arcuate fasciculus (passage to Broca's area). The message travels from here to Broca's area (speech is composed) and finally on to the motor area of the frontal lobe (to actually move the muscles as directed by Broca's area). The process is indeed a marvelously complex one, and surely you recognize that this skeletal description of the chain of events does little more than to raise even more interesting questions.

TOPIC SUMMARY

Briefly summarize five major techniques used to study the brain.

We can study the brain by (1) observing the effects of brain injury on behavior, (2) lesioning parts of the brain to see the resulting effects, (3) electrically stimulating parts of the brain, (4) recording the electrical activity of nerve cells and larger areas of the brain, and (5) looking at the brain with X rays, CAT scans, PET scans, or NMR imaging procedures. / 65

Name the two brain stem structures, and describe where they are and what they do.

The brain stem is made up of the *medulla,* which controls certain important reflexes such as breathing and heart rate and is where cross-laterality largely occurs, and the *pons,* which acts like a bridge, passing impulses between the spinal cord and the brain. / 67

Where is the cerebellum located, and what is its major function?

The cerebellum is located at the base of the brain and is most involved in the smooth coordination of muscular responses. / 68

Where are the following structures and what do they do: the RAS, the limbic system, the hypothalamus, and the thalamus?

The RAS (reticular activating system) reaches from the brain stem to the cerebral cortex and is involved in maintaining one's level of arousal. The limbic system, just above the brain stem, is involved in emotional responses (the amygdala and septum in particular) and the transfer of information to long-term memory storage (the hippocampus). The hypothalamus, near the limbic system, is a small structure very much involved in motivated behaviors such as feeding, drinking, sex, aggression, and temperature regula-

tion. The thalamus is a final relay station for sensory messages that get projected to the cerebral cortex. Motor impulses from the cerebrum also pass through the thalamus. / 70

Given a side view of the brain, can you locate the four lobes of the cerebral cortex?

Can you locate the primary sensory, motor, and association areas of the cerebrum?

See Figures 4.8 and 4.9 to review the locations of the four lobes of the cerebral cortex and the primary sensory, motor, and association areas. / 73

Briefly summarize the different functions of the left and right cerebral hemispheres of the human brain.

How is a split brain procedure done?

In a split brain procedure, the two hemispheres of the cerebrum are separated by lesioning or removing the corpus callosum. This procedure reinforces the notion that the left hemisphere is primarily concerned with language, sequential thinking, and analytic thinking. The right hemisphere seems to be more creative, more global in its approach to thinking, and more involved in tasks requiring spatial relations abilities. The right hemisphere may also be more involved than the left in emotional responding. / 75

CHAPTER THREE

SENSORY PROCESSES

You want to paint just one wall of your kitchen because it has faded over the years. You still have some of the original paint left, but it appears much darker than what is now on the walls. How much white paint will you have to add to your original paint to make it match what is on the walls now?

An instructor claims to have heard you whisper to your friend sitting next to you in a large classroom. Is it possible that he heard you, or is he just guessing?

You want to design a remote control device for a television set so that each click of the volume control raises the volume enough to make a noticeable difference. How would you proceed?

I apply a slight pressure to your forearm. Now I apply exactly twice as much pressure. Does my touch feel exactly twice as hard?

If you can clearly see a night-light when it is dark in the room, why can't you see the same light in the daylight?

How much salt do you have to add to your soup so that it is neither too bland nor too salty?

Can advertisers insert commercial messages into movies or videotapes that flash on the screen so quickly that they can influence our behavior even though we don't "know" they're there?

Each of these apparently unrelated questions deals with the relationship between events in our environment and our experience with them. In this topic, we'll examine some of the psychology that can help us answer questions like these.

The study of sensation begins our discussion of how we come to find out about the world, make judgments about it, learn from it, and remember what we have learned. In this topic, we'll begin that study by considering the limits of sensory systems.

It is an old truism that things are not always as they appear. For example, without additional information, you cannot really tell if Figure 5.1 is the picture of a real car, the picture of a model of a car, or the picture of a very good painting of a car. The best that our senses can do is to *represent* the physical world in psychological terms. The study of the relationship between stimuli in the physical world and our psychological representation of them is called **psychophysics.**

This topic is about psychophysics and is divided into three major sections. The first section puts sensation in a broader context of psychological processes. The second deals with the sensitivity of our senses and their ability to detect the presence of stimuli. The third section also deals with sensitivity, but as an ability to detect the differences between stimuli. We'll also consider how we might construct measurement scales for sensory psychological experiences.

psychophysics
the study of the relationship between the physical attributes of stimuli and the psychological experience that they produce

perception
the complex internal process of selecting, identifying, organizing, and interpreting stimuli

sensation
the process of receiving stimulus input from the environment and changing that input into nervous system activity

DEFINING SOME BASIC TERMS

In a direct way, this topic on sensory processes begins our discussion of memory (which we will cover formally in Chapter 6). This observation is based on a series of assumptions that we make about how the mind—or the brain, if you prefer—comes to process information.

Let's work this series of assumptions through—backward. If you can remember something, you are demonstrating that you have that information stored away someplace and that somehow you are able to retrieve it. The remembered information must be inside you (no doubt in your brain, but we'll get to that later).

In order to remember something, the argument goes on, you must have perceived it in the first place. You selected that information from your environment, identified it, organized it in some meaningful way, and interpreted it. Selection, identification, organization, and interpretation are rather complex skills. Collectively they are referred to as **perception.**

Perception, like memory, is an internal process. Somehow, the bits and pieces of information that make up your perceptions and become your memories have to get from the outside world to the inner environment of your nervous system. That is where **sensation** comes in. Our sensory processes receive stimulation from the world around us and change that stimulation into the activity of our nervous systems. Indeed, what our senses do, each in its own way, is pick up and respond to energy from our environment, changing it into the energy of our nervous systems. Sensation is a *psychological* process—it requires *stimuli*, an *organism* to do the sensing, and a *response.* In brief: Sensation picks up energy, perception selects and organizes it, and memory forms a record of it.

Although it may be convenient for us to separate sensation and perception in this way, we need to keep in mind that the distinction is somewhat arbitrary. In real life we are often hard-pressed to specify exactly where one process leaves off and the other begins. In fact, there are some psychologists (Dember & Warm, 1979, for example) who argue that we should not even try to separate these two functions.

Figure 5.1
Is this a picture of an actual car, a picture of a model of a car, or a picture of a painting of a car? Our senses provide us with pictures of the physical world.

A **stimulus** is what our senses respond to. It is the energy (or, as we shall see, the change in energy) we can detect that is given off by objects or events in our environments. Our senses, then, are receptors of energy from the environment. Their major functions are to *detect* environmental energy and to *change* that energy into nervous system energy.

stimulus
physical energy in the environment to which organisms can respond or that can be detected by a receptor

All this probably sounds much too complex and technical, but it will pay off to be somewhat particular here at the start. Let's look at a couple of examples. The light energy in the room at the moment bounces off your left hand and is reflected into your eyes. If there is enough light present, it stimulates receptor cells in your eyes. This means that sensation has taken place; light energy from the environment has been changed—by the receptor cells in your eyes—into the energy of the nervous system. The receptor cells of your eyes send neural impulses to your brain (eventually to your occipital lobe, you may recall). When your brain analyzes the information it has just received from your visual receptors, it perceives that you're looking at your own hand, an event that will probably not be given a special place in your memory.

As you sit there contemplating the nature of stimuli and the relationship between sensation and perception, someone slams a nearby door. The sound waves from the door travel through the air and stimulate the receptors in your ears. Deep in your ears, this physical energy of pulsating air pressure is transformed into neural impulses that race toward your brain (this time to the vicinity of your temporal lobe). A stimulus has been detected by a receptor, and energy has been transformed: A sensation has occurred.

Virtually all we know, all our memories, at some time entered our internal environment through our senses. Once again, the chain of logic: Without sensation there is no perception and without perception there is no memory. Even though these processes are very much intertwined, and even though there may be some exceptions to this chain of events, we'll use it as a guide and will explore each phase separately. In this topic, our main concern is with the very first step: relating the physical stimuli of the environment to psychological processing—the basic thrust of psychophysics.

Before you go on
Although they are clearly related, how might we differentiate between sensation and perception?

ABSOLUTE THRESHOLDS: THE SENSITIVITY OF OUR SENSES

Imagine the following simple experiment. You are seated in a dimly lighted room, staring at a small box. The side of the box facing you is covered by a sheet of cloudy plastic. Behind the plastic sheet is a light bulb. I can decrease the physical intensity of the light bulb to the point where you cannot see it at all. I can also increase the light's intensity to the point where you can see it very clearly. I also have many intensity settings available between these extremes. My basic question is: At what point of physical intensity will the light first become visible to you?

In theory, there should be some intensity below which you cannot see the light and above which you can. That point, for you, would be your absolute threshold. The term threshold here means the same thing that it means in other contexts—a point of crossing over. (You cross the threshold of a door as you move from outside to inside, or vice versa.) The notion of threshold is very much related to the notion of *sensitivity*, but in a backward sort of way.

That is, as threshold levels decrease, we say that sensitivity increases. The lower the threshold of a sense receptor, the more sensitive it is.

Now let's return to our imaginary experiment in which I am trying to determine your absolute threshold for sensing the light in the box. I systematically vary the light's intensity. I ask you to respond "Yes, I see the light," or "No, I don't see the light," depending on your experience. (In this experiment I'll not allow you the luxury of saying that you don't know or aren't sure.)

When this experiment is actually done, we find something that at first seems strange. Surely we can reduce the intensity of the light so low that you never report seeing it. And we can present intensities so high that you always say you see it. However, there are many intensities in between where your responses are inconsistent over many presentations of the same light intensity. That is, there are intensities of light to which you sometimes respond "yes" and sometimes respond "no"—even though the intensity of the light is unchanged!

In reality, there just isn't very much absolute about our absolute thresholds at all. They keep changing from moment to moment, reflecting small, subtle changes in the sensitivity of our senses from moment to moment. (They also reflect momentary shifts in our ability to pay attention to the task at hand.) Figure 5.2 shows (A) what we might like to happen in an experiment like the one we've just described, and (B) what does happen in such an experiment.

This sort of result occurs for all our senses, not just for vision. I would have the same general result if I tested your ability to detect intensities of sound, smell, touch, or taste. Because there are no literally absolute measures of our senses' sensitivity, we must resort to the following operational definition of **absolute threshold:** "the physical intensity of a stimulus that a subject reports detecting 50 percent of the time." Thus, intensities below threshold are detected fewer than 50 percent of the time, and intensities above threshold are detected more than 50 percent of the time.

So what good is the notion of an absolute threshold and why should we care? Determining absolute thresholds is not just a purely academic exercise. For one thing, as a measure of sensitivity, absolute threshold levels can be used to discover if one's senses are operating properly and are detecting low intensity levels of stimulation. Engineers who design sound systems need to

absolute threshold
the intensity of a stimulus that one can detect 50 percent of the time

---

Figure 5.2
Determining absolute threshold values.
(A) The idealized case, in which there is a point before which the stimulus is never detected and after which it is always detected, and (B) the realistic case, where absolute threshold is the intensity of stimulation that is detected 50 percent of the time.

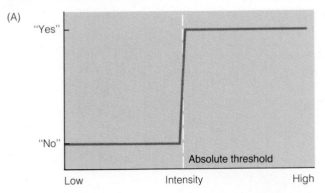

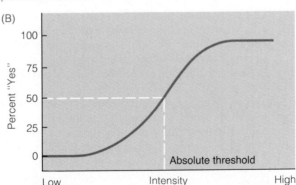

Figure 5.3

Examples of absolute threshold values for five senses
(i.e., these stimuli would be noticed at least 50 percent of the time)
(From Galanter, 1962.)

Vision	a candle flame seen from a distance of 30 miles on a clear, dark night
Hearing	the ticking of a watch under quiet conditions from a distance of 20 feet
Taste	1 teaspoon of sugar dissolved in 2 gallons of water
Smell	one drop of perfume in a three-room apartment
Touch	the wing of a bee dropped on your cheek from a height of one centimeter

know about absolute thresholds—speakers that do not reproduce sounds above threshold levels aren't of much use. Warning lights must be designed to be well above absolute threshold if they are to be of any use to us. How much perfume is required for it to be noticed? How low must you whisper so as not to be overheard in a classroom? Can one basil leaf in the tomato sauce be detected or will two be required? These are psychophysical questions about absolute thresholds.

Remember, psychophysics is the study of the relationship between physical stimuli and our psychological representation of them. Of major concern, then, will be the sensitivity of sensory mechanisms. Unless physical stimuli exceed absolute threshold levels, they may not be represented at all. As it happens, our sense receptors are remarkably sensitive, as the oft-quoted examples in Figure 5.3 attest.

Before you go on

What is meant by absolute threshold?

How does it relate to sensitivity, and how might it be measured?

DIFFERENCE THRESHOLDS: SENSITIVITY FROM A DIFFERENT PERSPECTIVE

In our everyday experiences, we seldom encounter situations that test our abilities to detect the presence of low-intensity stimuli. It is more common that we are called upon to detect differences between or among stimuli that are above the level of our absolute thresholds. Detecting such differences involves the concept of *difference threshold.*

The Basic Concept of Difference Threshold

Difference thresholds deal with stimuli that are clearly above our absolute threshold. The issue is not whether the stimuli can be detected, but whether or not we can detect a *difference* between stimulus attributes. Hence, a difference threshold is defined as the minimal difference that can be detected between stimulus attributes.

Let's deal with a stimulus attribute other than intensity for a moment and return to a question like the one we asked at the beginning of this topic. Here are two cans of paint of two shades of red, let's say. They are clearly different colors, one being much more toward pink than the other. As we slowly add white paint to the darker red, it more and more closely resembles our other pinkish-red paint. At what point can you no longer tell the two paints apart?

difference threshold
the minimal difference in some stimulus attribute, such as intensity, that one can detect 50 percent of the time

The point at which a difference between the paints is first detectable would be your difference threshold—for colors of paint, anyway.

Now let's return to intensity measures, but with sound for a change. I present you with two tones. You claim to be able to hear them both (they're above your absolute threshold), and as best you can tell, they are equally loud. If I gradually increase (or decrease) the intensity of one of the tones, I will eventually reach a point where you can just notice a difference between the loudness of the two tones. As it happens, **just noticeable difference,** or **j.n.d.,** is a technical term in psychology that can be defined as the amount of change in a stimulus attribute (such as intensity) that makes it just noticeably different from what it was.

As you might have anticipated, we do have the same complication here that we have when we actually try to measure absolute thresholds. That is, to very slight degrees, the actual value of a j.n.d., or difference threshold, tends to vary from moment to moment. As before, we simply operationalize our definition and say that to be above one's difference threshold, differences between stimuli need to be detected more than 50 percent of the time.

just noticeable difference (j.n.d.)
the minimum amount of change in a stimulus required for detection

Before you go on
What is a j.n.d., or difference threshold, and how might it be determined?

Weber's Law

Another complication with difference thresholds is not so easily dismissed. This is the idea that the amount of change in a stimulus necessary to produce a j.n.d. depends a great deal on the value of the stimulus with which you start.

You may be just barely able to detect the difference between a 40 pound weight and a 41 pound weight—a j.n.d. of 1 pound. But isn't it unlikely that you could tell the difference between a 100 pound weight and a 101 pound weight? Starting with 100 pounds, we might have to add 4 pounds before the weight felt noticeably heavier. So what *is* the j.n.d. for lifting weights: 1 pound, or 4 pounds? It depends. It depends on the weight you start with or use as a standard for comparison. Formalizing this idea leads us to two of the true pioneers of early psychology, Ernst Weber and Gustav Fechner.

Nearly 150 years ago (1843), Ernst Weber formulated a law that described the relationship between changes in physical intensity and changes in sensory experience. It was Weber's belief that the change in stimulus intensity (symbolized ΔI) needed to produce a j.n.d. change in experience was a constant fraction when divided by the original stimulus intensity. That is, the ratio of j.n.d. to standard is always a constant. In algebraic terms, **Weber's law** states:

$$\Delta I/I = C, \text{ where: } \Delta I = \text{change in intensity, or j.n.d.}$$
$$I = \text{standard, original intensity}$$
$$C = \text{a constant value (a fraction)}$$

Don't let this little equation confuse you. The basic idea is a simple one, and quite clever. Perhaps an example would help. Imagine that you are blindfolded, sitting at the middle of the 50-yard line in a large football stadium. On my command, 10 people up in the stands let out a yell. An eleventh person joins the group. Eleven people now yell, and you say that the yelling sounds louder than it did before. So, when I start with 10 people, just one additional person is above your difference threshold.

Weber's law
the statement that the size of a j.n.d. divided by standard intensity is a constant ratio ($\Delta I/I = C$)

Now I ask 100 people to yell. When I add just one person to *this* group of 100, you cannot tell the difference. Even two, or three, or six more people do not make a difference. When 10 more are added to the 100, however, you report that the yell you hear is louder. So, when I = 100, the j.n.d. = 10. Starting with 1,000 people, you would hardly notice the addition of one or even 10 more yellers. I would have to add 100; or, if I = 1,000, then the j.n.d. = 100. In each case—at least for people yelling in a football stadium—we find that $\Delta I/I$ is a constant, in this case 1/10. If I had 3,000 people yelling in that stadium, how many more would I have to add to make the cheering seem louder? Of course, 1/10 of 3,000, or 300 more.

Notice that Weber's fraction (1/10 for our imaginary example) is an indirect measure of a person's sensitivity. The smaller the fraction, the more sensitive the subject. That is, with 100 people yelling, 10 had to be added before you could tell the difference. Someone with more sensitive hearing might have been able to detect a difference with the addition of only 5 yellers (a Weber fraction of 5/100, or 1/20). Someone with poor hearing may have required 20 additional yellers before a j.n.d. in yelling could be detected (a Weber fraction of 1/5). Our example is fictitious. Weber fractions for some more common stimulus intensities are listed as follows (Schiffman, 1976):

Ernst Weber

Vision (brightness of white light)	1/60
Kinesthesis (lifted weights)	1/50
Pain (by heat on skin)	1/30
Hearing (loudness; midpitch)	1/10
Cutaneous (pressure on skin)	1/7
Smell (raw rubber)	1/4
Taste (salt solution)	1/3

I trust that you can find many examples of the relevance of difference thresholds and just noticeable differences in your everyday experiences. You probably would not notice the loss of one light bulb at a night baseball game, but you would immediately recognize that you had a problem if one of the three 100-watt bulbs in the kitchen light fixture burned out. The difference between a large and extra large milk shake had better be above your difference threshold or you'll never spend the additional money for an extra large one again. Isn't an hour's overtime more noticeable when you're only working 20 hours per week rather than 40 hours per week? For most students, there is more than a j.n.d. between a grade of A and a grade of B on an exam.

Scales of Sensation: Fechner and Stevens

Weber's law holds true for a wide range of stimulus values and for all of our senses. The problem is that is lacks precision for very high and very low stimulus intensities. At the extremes of intensity, $\Delta I/I$ no longer remains a constant fraction. Weber's basic idea was a good one, but it was an idea that he never fully put to the test himself. That job was taken on by Gustav Fechner.

Picking up on Weber's insight, Fechner realized that one's *sensation* of physical intensity cannot be *directly* related to measurements of physical intensity. A light that is physically twice as intense as another does not necessarily *appear* to be twice as bright. A different sort of technique was needed to construct a scale for measuring sensations, which are, after all, psychological processes. Yes, there is a relationship between physical intensity and psychological sensation, but the two are not the same.

Gustav Fechner

Fechner's law
the statement that the magnitude of psychological sensation is a logarithmic function of physical magnitude (S = C logI)

magnitude estimation
Stevens's method of psychophysical scaling in which subjects assign numbers directly to their psychological experience of the intensity of stimuli

Stevens's law
the statement that the magnitude of a psychological sensation is an exponential function of physical magnitude ($S = CI^h$)

Fechner's law (1860) states that one's sensation (S) is equal to a constant (C) multiplied by the logarithm of stimulus intensity (I). In equation form, that looks like:

$$S = C \times \log I.$$

Once again, don't get lost in the arithmetic of logarithms. The idea is a simple one. Noticeable differences between stimuli of low intensity (I) require little change in intensity to be sensed (S). Differences between stimuli of high intensity (I) require very large changes before they are noticed, or sensed (S). With his law, Fechner did two things: He converted Weber's fraction into a general statement about the relationship between psychological sensation and physical intensity, and he allowed for huge ranges of stimulus intensity by making the scale logarithmic.

Nearly 100 years after Fechner published his law, the psychologist S. S. Stevens (1961) proposed a different technique for establishing the relationship between physical attributes and psychological experiences. It was Stevens's belief that subjects could estimate the magnitude of sensations directly and assign them numbers. Stevens's method is called **magnitude estimation**, and it's really quite simple.

Subjects are presented with a series of stimuli and are asked to assign them numbers representing the value of some sensory attribute, such as brightness. If one light appears twice as bright as another, its numerical value should be twice as large. If you were to give one light a numerical value of 12, the number you would assign to a light that appears twice as bright would be 24, half as bright would be 6, three times as bright would be 36, and so on. Notice that in Stevens's method, determining difference thresholds, or j.n.d.s, is irrelevant. We don't ask about the differences between two dim lights and two bright ones—we simply ask for direct numerical estimates of the magnitude of the brightness of the lights.

When Stevens asked a number of subjects to make direct estimations of sensory magnitude, he discovered two things: (1) Once the basic rules were understood, subjects had very little difficulty doing what was asked of them. They could, in fact, directly and reliably rate their sensory experience on a numerical scale. (2) There is (as Fechner had proposed) a relationship between subjects' subjective estimations of sensory magnitude (S, again) and the physical intensity of the stimulus (I, again). However, Stevens found that the nature of the relationship is better expressed by an exponential (or power) function than by a logarithmic one. So what we have is **Stevens's law,** which says that (psychological) sensation equals a constant multiplied by (physical) intensity raised to a fixed power (or exponent), or:

$$S = C \times I^n, \text{ where: } S = \text{sensation (psychological)}$$
$$C = \text{a constant}$$
$$I = \text{physical intensity}$$
$$n = \text{a constant exponent}$$

In addition to modifying the basic arithmetic of Fechner's formulation, Stevens's law also argues (1970) that the relationship between sensation and stimulus can be different for different sensory dimensions. The relationship between actual physical intensity and brightness, for example, may take one form (have one value of n), while the relationship between the intensity of an electric shock and our subjective experience of that shock may be altogether different and have a different exponent. What this means is that high intensity lights may need to have their intensities increased considerably before they are judged as being brighter, while high intensity shocks may require only small increases before subjects recognize that they are stronger.

Let me caution you once again not to get lost in the mathematics of Weber, Fechner, and Stevens. The precise formulation of their laws is less important than the insight that they share. This insight is that with psychophysical methods we can do something that early philosophers thought impossible: We can measure or assign numbers to (or scale) subjective, psychological, sensory experiences. It is probably true that Stevens's formulation of how to go about doing so is more accurate than Fechner's, but Stevens would be the first to credit Fechner (and Weber) for demonstrating that it could be done.

Before you go on

What were Weber, Fechner, and Stevens trying to do with their laws?

What essential characteristic is common to all three characterizations?

SIGNAL DETECTION THEORY

We have already made the point that thresholds (both absolute and difference) are not stable, fixed values. They vary from moment to moment and have to be operationally defined in terms of probability—as a 50 percent point above which stimuli (or differences) can be detected.

In other words, the sensitivity of our senses is not constant. It changes. It changes because of momentary shifts in our attention and because of the random activity of the nerve cells in our sensory systems. Sometimes nerve cells may fire without any direct stimulation from the external environment. This random firing of nerve cells creates a sort of background noise that varies from moment to moment. (Even if you were standing in a deep cave, where there was no light, with your eyes closed, you would still have something of a visual experience—you would sense small flashes of light, your background visual noise.)

When we are asked to judge whether or not a stimulus has been presented, we have to make a judgment in the context of a shifting background of noise created by other stimuli in our environment and by our own nervous system activity. Basically what we have to do is determine whether or not we can *detect* a *signal* against a background of noise. Putting the issue this way, we can consider what is called **signal detection theory,** which is the theory that stimulus detection involves a decision-making process of separating a signal from background noise (Green & Swets, 1966).

Signal detection theory addresses two issues that earlier psychophysical theories tended to ignore: (1) the varying degrees of background noise in our sensory systems, and (2) the subject's attention, expectations, and biases. The first point is clear, but what do we mean by the second? In a basic detection threshold experiment in which we are trying to determine sensory thresholds, we ask subjects to report whether or not they detect a stimulus (or a difference between two obvious stimuli). Why should we believe that the subject—even a well-motivated subject—is telling us the truth? It is at least imaginable that some subjects will frequently say yes even when the stimulus is not detected (there is evidence (Block, 1965) that, when in doubt, subjects are more likely to say yes than no, a phenomenon known as acquiescence). Other subjects may be overly cautious, wanting to be sure before they respond yes. And, of course, some subjects simply don't pay much attention to what they are doing during the course of the experiment and say yes or no virtually at random.

signal detection theory
the view that stimulus detection is a matter of decision-making, of separating signal from noise

Figure 5.4

The possible outcomes of a signal detection experiment.

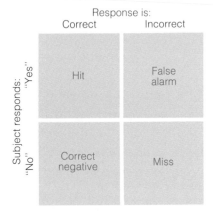

In a signal detection procedure, a number of "blank" trials, in which the stimulus to be detected is in fact *not presented,* are included in a series of many standard detection trials. Subjects are still to respond "yes (I detect the stimulus)" or "no (I do not detect the stimulus)." On some trials, the stimulus will be there as a signal, but on blank trials, the subjects are presented only with noise.

Notice that with this procedure there are four possible outcomes. A subject may say yes and be right or wrong, and a subject may say no and be right or wrong. In signal detection terminology, saying yes correctly is called a hit. Saying no correctly is called a correct negative. Saying yes incorrectly is called a false alarm, and saying no incorrectly is called a miss. These terms are summarized in Figure 5.4.

Now the experimenter can manipulate a number of things. She can vary the probability that the signal *will* actually be presented. She can vary the physical intensity of the stimulus. *And,* she can manipulate the bias, or the motivation, of the subject by manipulating payoffs and penalties for correct and incorrect responses.

For example, a subject may be offered a dollar for every correct detection of a signal. If there is no penalty for false alarms, the subject may very well say yes on every trial, not wanting to miss out on an opportunity to collect a dollar. If rewards are given for correct negatives, and if there are penalties for false alarms, the subject may become exceedingly conservative in responding.

In a typical signal detection experiment, a number of these variables are manipulated over a series of many trials. For our purposes, let us just say that using the logic of the theory, experimenters can precisely calculate the subject's sensitivity to the stimulus being used by mathematically eliminating the effects of response bias and background noise. Thus, signal detection theory views the limits of sensation not so much as a matter of threshold, but as a decision-making process. Taking a number of factors into account (the strength of the signal, the level of noise, the payoffs involved), the subject is asked—as we are often asked in everyday experience—to *decide* whether or not something really happened.

Before you go on

Briefly summarize the basic ideas of signal detection theory.

In this topic, we have addressed some technical but very basic psychological issues. All that we have come to know about this world in which we live entered our minds through our senses. In order to stimulate our senses, stimuli need to be of sufficient intensity; that is, they need to be above our absolute thresholds. In order for us to be able to detect differences among stimuli, those differences need to be above the level of our difference thresholds. By investigating sensory thresholds, the psychophysicist has shown us the lawful relationships that exist between physical stimuli and our subjective psychological experiences of them.

Stimuli that are below threshold levels of intensity cannot be detected; that is what makes them below threshold. The German word for threshold (often used in psychophysics) is *limen*. Stimuli below threshold may thus be referred to as subliminal. If stimuli are subliminal, by definition they cannot be perceived. Yet one of the more controversial debates in psychology today revolves around the reality of subliminal perception. On the face of it, the term is a contradiction. It implies that stimuli beyond (or below) a subject's awareness can be used to influence that subject's behavior. Research investigating this possibility dates to the mid-1800s (Murch, 1973).

The classic experiment, the one that captured the imagination of many people outside of psychology, was reported in 1951 by Lazarus and McCleary. In brief, the experimenters visually presented subjects with a list of 10 syllables, one at a time. Half the syllables were paired with a rather unpleasant electric shock. When the 10 syllables were shown again, subjects predictably responded to the 5 syllables that had previously been paired with the shock. The response that was measured was the GSR, or galvanic skin response, commonly taken as a physiological indication of emotionality. That there should be an emotional reaction (a GSR) to these 5 syllables was not surprising. Then the 10 syllables were presented again, in random order, *at below threshold levels*. Still, even though subjects could not recognize or identify the syllables, a marked GSR was noted in reaction to the syllables previously paired with the shock.

The results were clear, at least to Lazarus and McCleary. An awareness of the stimuli had taken place at some level below consciousness— a subliminal perception. It did not take long for others to point out some serious flaws in Lazarus and McCleary's procedures and in their interpretations. We needn't go through these arguments here (see Erikson, 1956, for a thorough analysis). Suffice it to say that the issue was far from settled. Many experiments tried to replicate what Lazarus and McCleary had reported. Some showed modest successes— most failed.

What certainly did not fail was the ability of the basic idea of subliminal perception to catch the fancy of the American public. Rumors of mind control and subliminal advertising techniques were everywhere in the mid-1950s. This idea of the subliminal control of people's minds and behaviors is still very much with us 30 years later despite the lack of evidence that it works.

Here's the way it's *supposed* to work. You go to a theater to watch a movie. At random intervals throughout the movie, short messages are flashed on the screen— "visit our snack bar," "buy popcorn," "have a cola." These messages are too brief and/or too faint to be clearly and consciously seen (detected). But, they subliminally enter your subconscious, control your behavior, and have you standing at the snack bar ordering popcorn and cola.

Whether the messages are placed in movies to tempt you to buy something, or implanted in videotapes to encourage you to stop smoking, or slipped into background music to dissuade you from shoplifting the basic idea is the same, and *it doesn't work*.

We really need not be concerned about the legal and ethical issues of subliminal advertising because there is virtually no evidence that it works (George & Jennings, 1975; Goldiamond, 1966; Murch, 1973). The basic problem is one of the difference between detection and identification (Dember, 1960). It's one thing to be able to detect (i.e., sense) that something has been flashed on a screen. It's quite another matter to be able to identify or recognize (perceive) what that something was and to respond to it an *any* level of consciousness.

In fairness, we must say that although the line of research that followed Lazarus and McCleary in the realm of application and advertising has not fared well, there is increasing evidence of *some* sort of subliminal perception (Dixon, 1971; Nisbett & Wilson, 1977; Shevrin & Dickman, 1980). Today, many researchers are convinced that stimuli presented at below threshold levels can and do have some effect on us—even though it may be a short-term effect. Wild claims of mass hypnosis and mind control through subliminal perception are just that, however—wild claims, unsubstantiated by scientific evidence.

TOPIC SUMMARY

Although they are clearly related, how might we differentiate between sensation and perception?

Although they both may be viewed as being different stages of the same process, sensation involves responding to environmental stimuli and changing energy from the environment into the energy of the nervous system, whereas perception acts on stimuli once they have been sensed, selecting, identifying, organizing, and interpreting them. / 83

What is meant by absolute threshold?

How does it relate to sensitivity, and how might it be measured?

An absolute threshold is the intensity of a stimulus that can be detected 50 percent of the time. It is measured by varying the intensity of a stimulus and asking subjects if they can detect its presence. The lower one's threshold for any sense, the more sensitive that sense is; that is, sensitivity and threshold are inversely related. / 85

What is a j.n.d., or difference threshold, and how might it be determined?

A j.n.d. is a just noticeable difference. That is, it is a difference between stimuli that can be detected 50 percent of the time. It is determined by asking subjects to detect differences between stimuli on some attribute where values on that attribute are systematically changed. / 86

What were Weber, Fechner, and Stevens trying to do with their laws?

What essential characteristic is common to all three characterizations?

Weber, Fechner, and Stevens all recognized that the value of a j.n.d. is a function of the value of a standard stimulus. That is, they all recognized that psychological experience (sensation) cannot be measured using physical scales. Whereas Fechner believed the relationship between psychological experience and physical intensity to be logarithmic, Stevens believed the relationship to be exponential. / 89

Briefly summarize the basic ideas of signal detection theory.

Signal detection theory assesses the value of thresholds in terms of detecting a signal against a background of noise, where motivational and attentional factors of the subject may also have an effect. / 90

TOPIC

What you see when you see a red barn is light—the light reflected from the barn—not the barn itself. Remember: The stimulus for vision—for seeing—is *light*. Now if the farmer who owns the barn paints it red, the light that bounces off it and is reflected into your eyes will be a red light. The barn now reflects red light (and absorbs and diffuses all other colors of light) because the farmer coated it with a chemical that has the ability to reflect red light. There are other chemicals that have the property of reflecting yellow light or blue light. If the farmer had covered his barn with such chemicals, the barn would appear yellow or blue, but only because it was reflecting those lights into your eyes.

In fact, paint (or crayons, or watercolors, or dyes, or any pigments for that matter) is itself without color. Color is a property of light and light is the stimulus for vision. Paint is a chemical that has the property of being able to absorb some colors of light while reflecting others. In this sense, paint has no color. If you doubt the truth of this, go to the hardware store and buy a small can of the chemical labeled red paint. Now take it into the closet, close the door, turn off the light in the closet, and open the can. What color do you see? Right, you obviously don't see any color. Color "belongs" to light, not to paint.

Remember this: The stimulus for vision is light. Now that you've stored that tidbit away, let me ask you a question. "What color is a barn that has been painted red?"

Even if you figure that there's a catch to this question someplace, you must have a strong desire to answer that the color of a barn that has been painted red is red. And if this weren't a psychology textbook, you'd know that you were right. But if I wanted to be particular, and as accurate as possible, I could argue that the red barn is really not red at all. It isn't green or any other color either. A barn that has been painted red is black if it is any color at all. *Black!* Where did I get that foolish idea? Well, I'm being very picky.

Why We Care

There are some people who would argue about which of our senses is the most important. Such arguments, or discussions, are generally pointless. Each of our senses is very important to us; each provides us with a wealth of information. There is no doubt, however, that vision is a major sense. A great deal of information about our environments comes to us through our eyes. The entire occipital lobe of the cerebral cortex is devoted to the processing of visual information.

Vision is also the sensory modality about which we know the most. We will devote this entire topic to vision, combining all the other senses in a briefer discussion in the next topic. In this topic, we have three main tasks: (1) to appreciate the nature of light, (2) to examine how different physical characteristics of light are correlated with psychological experiences, and (3) to understand how the eye works as the receptor organ for vision. Along the way, we'll encounter some intriguing minor issues, such as how our vision changes as the level of illumination changes and why tennis balls and golf balls are now often painted a gaudy yellow-green.

THE STIMULUS FOR VISION: LIGHT

We don't have to become physicists to understand how vision works, but it will be helpful to have some appreciation of the physical characteristics of light, which is, you'll recall, the stimulus for vision. For one thing, **light** can be thought of as a *wave form of radiant energy.* Quite simply that means that light radiates from its source in the form of waves (light waves). Light waves have a number of physical characteristics that we can use to describe them. From a psychological perspective, we need to concern ourselves with only three: wave amplitude, wavelength, and wave purity. Each of these physical characteristics produces its own psychological experience, which we'll discuss on the following pages.

light
a radiant energy that can be represented as a wave form with wavelengths between 380 and 760 nanometers

Wave Amplitude (Intensity)

One of the ways in which light energy may vary is in its intensity. If we think about light as traveling in the form of waves of energy, we can represent differences in intensity as differences in the **wave amplitude** of light. The amplitude of a wave is represented by its height. Refer to Figure 6.1 and assume that the two waves in the drawing represent two different light waves. One of the differences between light (A) and light (B) is in the height of the waves, or wave amplitude.

wave amplitude
a characteristic of wave forms (height of the wave) that indicates intensity

The amplitude of a light wave is the representation of a light's *physical intensity.* Our *psychological experience* of intensity is what we call **brightness.** The difference between a dim light and a bright light is due to the difference in wave amplitude. Of the two lights in Figure 6.1, light (A) has the higher amplitude and thus would be seen as the brighter light. So when I increase the amplitude of a light wave, I experience that as an increase in *brightness.* For example, dimmer switches that control the brightness of some light fixtures are in essence controlling the amplitude of light waves.

brightness
the psychological experience associated with a light's intensity or wave amplitude

Wavelength

A second physical characteristic of waves (such as light waves) is **wavelength,** which is the distance between any point in a wave and the corresponding point on the next cycle—the distance from peak to peak, for exam-

wavelength
a characteristic of wave forms that indicates the distance between any point on a wave and the corresponding point on the next cycle of the wave

nanometer
the unit of measurement for the wavelength of light that is equal to one millionth of a millimeter

hue
the psychological experience associated with a light's wavelength

ple. In Figure 6.1, one difference between waves (A) and (B) is their wavelength, where (A) has the longer wavelength. Although it is difficult to imagine distances so tiny, we *can* measure the length of a light wave. Our unit of measurement here is the **nanometer,** which is equal to one billionth of a meter or one millionth of a millimeter!

As it happens, there are many types of radiant energy that can be thought of as traveling in waves. However, the human eye can only respond to radiant energy in wave form that has a wavelength between (roughly) 380 and 760 nanometers (nm). This is the range of light waves that makes up what we call the visible spectrum. Wave forms of energy with wavelengths shorter than 380nm (such as X-rays and ultraviolet rays) are so short that they pass right through our eyes unnoticed. Wave forms of energy with wavelengths in excess of 760nm also pass through our eyes without stimulating the receptor cells (microwaves and radar are two examples).

Wave amplitude determines our experience of brightness, and wavelength determines our experience of **hue.** Hue is the attribute of light that determines the color we perceive. As light waves increase in length from the short 380nm wavelengths to the long 760nm lengths, our perception/experience of them changes—from violet to blue to green to yellow-green to yellow to orange to red along the color spectrum (see Figure 6.2).

Just so that we have a few examples to work with, let's agree that a 440nm wavelength of light is one that we'll call blue, 550nm is yellow-green, and 700nm is red. Indeed, an energy source that radiates energy with a 700 nanometer wavelength *is* a red light. (A bright red light has a high amplitude, and a dim red light has a low amplitude, but both have 700nm wavelengths.) If a light generated waves 550nm long, it would be a yellow-green light, and so on. (Notice that yellow-green is a single hue produced by a given wavelength of light. It is *not* some sort of combination of yellow and green. We simply have no one name for this hue, so we call it yellow-green.) That red barn we talked about earlier, then, must be one that reflects light waves that are approximately 700nm in length.

Given what we have so far, let me present an apparently simple problem: "I have two lights, one yellow-green (550nm) and the other red (700nm). I have adjusted the *amplitudes* of these two light sources so that they are exactly *equal.* They are of different hues because their wavelengths are different. What about their brightness? With both amplitudes equal, will the lights appear equally bright?"

As a matter of fact, they won't. The yellow-green light will appear much brighter than the red light. We seem to have a problem here with apparent brightness. We say that wavelength and wave amplitude interact to produce apparent brightness. Wavelengths of light in the middle of the range of visible spectrum (such as yellow-green) appear brighter than do wavelengths of light from the extremes—**if** amplitudes are equal.

I *can* get a red light to appear as bright as a yellow-green one, of course, but to do so I'll have to increase its amplitude (or physical intensity, if you prefer). Put another way, what all this means is that, *everything else being equal,* lights of different wavelengths do not appear equally bright, even if their amplitudes are the same. The relationship between wavelength and apparent brightness is shown in Figure 6.3.

If red wavelengths are comparatively more difficult to see than yellow-green wavelengths, why do we paint emergency vehicles like firetrucks and ambulances red? As a matter of fact, as you may have noticed, we don't anymore. More and more emergency vehicles are being painted a gaudy yel-

Figure 6.1
Representations of light waves differing in wavelength and wave amplitude. See text for explanation of how these physical characteristics are related to our psychological experience of light.

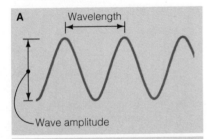

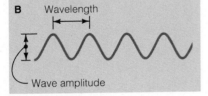

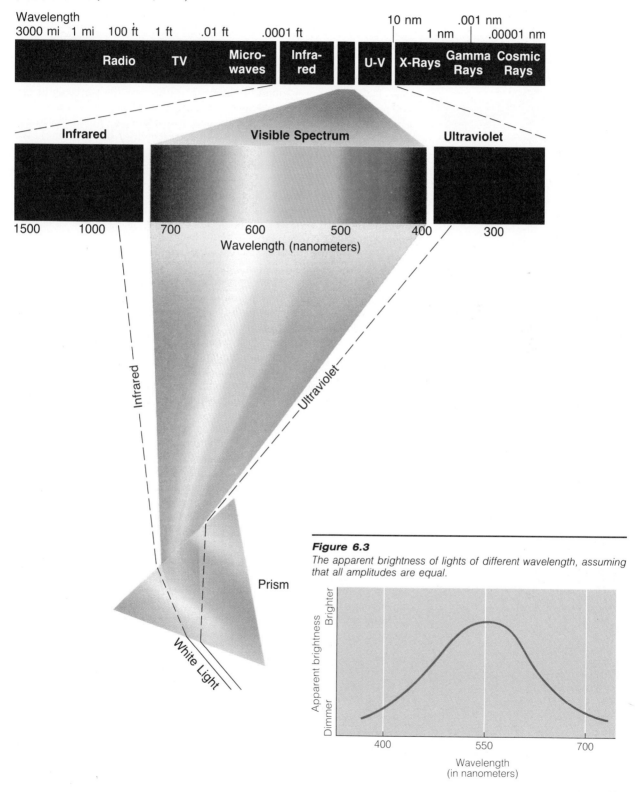

Figure 6.2

The visible spectrum, in which wavelengths of approximately 400–700 nanometers are visible to the human eye and are perceived as various hues.
(Based on Lindsay & Norman, 1977.)

Wavelength

| 3000 mi | 1 mi | 100 ft | 1 ft | .01 ft | .0001 ft | | 10 nm | .001 nm | | .00001 nm |

| | | | | | | | | 1 nm | | |

| Radio | TV | Micro-waves | Infra-red | | U-V | X-Rays | Gamma Rays | Cosmic Rays |

Infrared

Visible Spectrum

Ultraviolet

1500 1000 700 600 500 400 300

Wavelength (nanometers)

Infrared

Ultraviolet

Prism

White Light

Figure 6.3

The apparent brightness of lights of different wavelength, assuming that all amplitudes are equal.

Apparent brightness Brighter Dimmer

400 550 700

Wavelength
(in nanometers)

Figure 6.4

The physical characteristics of light waves influence our psychological experience of light.

Physical characteristic	Psychological experience
Wave amplitude (intensity)	Brightness
	These two interact
Wave length	Hue
Wave purity	Saturation

monochromatic
a pure light made up of light waves that all have the same wavelength

saturation
the psychological experience associated with the purity of a light wave; monochromatic lights are as highly saturated as possible

white light
a light of lowest possible saturation, containing a mixture of all visible wavelengths

low-green. The fact that red is harder to see than yellow-green is not a new discovery. So why did we ever paint firetrucks red? The answer is probably learning and experience: We have generations of people who have simply learned to associate red with danger. What we need to do now is train new generations to associate yellow-green with danger.

Wave Purity

Imagine a light of medium amplitude with all its wavelengths exactly 700nm long. It would be of medium brightness. And because the wavelengths are 700 nanometers long it would appear red. More than that, it would appear as a pure, rich red. Such a light would be **monochromatic,** or "pure," because it is made up of light waves all of one (mono) length or hue (chroma). We would seldom see such a light outside the laboratory because producing such a pure light is an expensive thing to do. ("Laser" beams are monochromatic lights.)

Even the reddest of red lights that you and I see in our everyday environments have other wavelengths of light mixed in along with the predominant 700nm red. Even the red light on top of a police car has some violet and green and yellow wavelengths of light in it.

The purity (or the opposite, mixture) of a light determines the color characteristic that we call **saturation.** Pure, monochromatic lights are highly saturated. They are highly saturated, or filled with themselves, leaving no room for mixing in anything else. As more and more different wavelengths get mixed into a light, it becomes lower and lower in saturation—in a sense it starts to look pale and washed out.

Here is a good question: "Of what hue is a light that is of the lowest possible saturation; a light that contains a random mixture of *all* possible wavelengths of light?" That is, by definition, what **white light** is. It is something of a curiosity that white light is in fact as *impure* a light as possible. A pure light has but one wavelength; a white light contains all the wavelengths.

True white light is as difficult (and as expensive) to produce as is a pure monochromatic light. Fluorescent light bulbs are reasonable approximations, but they still contain too many wavelengths from the short (or blue-violet) end of the spectrum. Regular incandescent light bulbs contain too many light waves from the orange and red end of the spectrum. A prism can take a beam of white light—sunlight is a reasonable approximation—and break it down into its various parts, giving us the experience of a rainbow of hues. Where did all those hues come from? They were there all along—mixed together to form the white light.

We have seen that three of the major characteristics of light influence the quality of our experience of light. Wave amplitude is the primary determinant of brightness, wavelength determines hue, and wave purity determines saturation. These various relationships are summarized in Figure 6.4, and all three dimensions are represented in the color solid presented in Figure 6.5.

Before you go on

In what ways do the major physical characteristics of light waves of energy (amplitude, length, and purity) affect our psychological experience of light?

Figure 6.5

The color tree illustrates the psychological experiences of light: the circumference of the tree illustrates the experience of hue, the radius illustrates saturation, and the arrangement of "leaves" from top to bottom illustrates brightness.

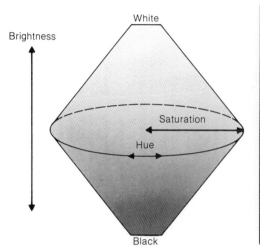

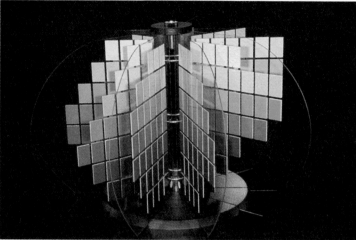

THE RECEPTOR FOR VISION: THE EYE

Vision involves changing light wave energy into the neural energy of the nervous system. This transformation of energy obviously takes place in the eye. Yet most of the structures of the eye have very little to do with the actual process of vision. Instead, they are there to ensure that the light waves that enter the eye are well focused by the time they get back to the layer of tissue that directly responds to light waves—where light waves are changed into neural impulses.

Structures That Focus Visual Images

Using Figure 6.6 as a guide, let's trace the path of light as it enters the eye from the environment and produces a visual experience. Light first enters the eye through the **cornea.** The cornea is the hard, round, virtually transparent outer shell of the eye. If you were to stick your finger in your eye, it would strike your cornea. The cornea has two major functions. One is to serve as a protector of the delicate structures behind it. The other is to start the process of bending the entering light waves to focus an image on the back surface of the eye.

Having passed through the cornea, light then travels through the **pupil,** which is an opening in the **iris.** The iris is that part of your eye that is pigmented, or colored. When we say that someone has blue, brown, or green eyes, we are really referring to the color of the iris. The iris contracts or widens, changing the size of the pupil. This is largely a reflexive reaction—it's not something you can control by conscious effort. Iris contractions that change pupil size are most commonly made in response to the level of light present—opening the pupil wide when small amounts of light are present

cornea
the outermost structure of the eye that protects the eye and helps focus light waves

pupil
the opening in the iris that changes size in relation to the level of light available

iris
the structure of the eye that reflexively opens or contracts the pupil

Figure 6.6

The major structures of the human eye.

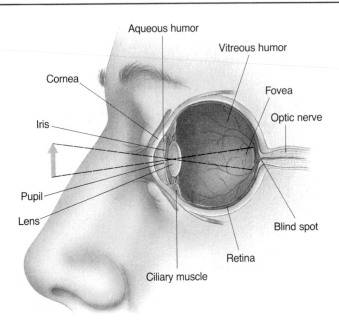

and reducing its size (protectively) in response to high intensity lights. Increasing pupil size is also one of the automatic responses that is produced with heightened levels of emotionality.

After the pupil, the next structure light encounters is the **lens.** As in a camera, the main function of the lens of the eye is to *focus* a visual image. The lens changes shape to bring an image into focus—becoming flatter when we try to focus on an object at a distance and becoming fatter, or rounder, when we try to view something up close. This too is largely a reflexive reaction. It is obvious that our lenses are not normally glass hard or they wouldn't be able to change shape. (Sometimes, with age, our lenses tend to harden, making it difficult to focus and requiring that we use glasses to help out.)

Some very powerful little muscles control the shape of our lens. They are called **ciliary muscles,** and they push and pull the lens to change its shape. The process in which the ciliary muscles change the shape of the lens is called **accommodation.** It is often the case that an image does not focus as it should either because of the general shape of the lens or through a failure of accommodation. The result is nearsightedness or farsightedness. Figure 6.7 shows examples of what happens in these cases.

There is a space between the cornea and the lens that is filled with a clear watery fluid called **aqueous humor.** This humor (which means "fluid") provides nourishment to the cornea and the other structures at the front of the eye. It would hardly make sense to have the cornea and lens surrounded by blood vessels and capillaries—light would not be able to pass through. This aqueous humor is constantly being produced and supplied to this space behind the cornea, filtering out blood to keep the fluid clear. If the fluid cannot easily pass back out of this space, pressure builds within the eye causing visual distortions, or, in extreme cases, blindness. This disorder is known as **glaucoma.**

lens
the structure of the eye behind the iris that changes shape to focus visual images

ciliary muscles
small muscles that control the shape (focusing capability) of the lens

accommodation
the process in which the shape of the lens is changed (by the ciliary muscles) in order to focus an image on the retina

aqueous humor
watery fluid found between the cornea and lens that nourishes the structures at the front of the eye

glaucoma
a vision disorder caused by an increase in pressure of aqueous humor on the lens and cornea

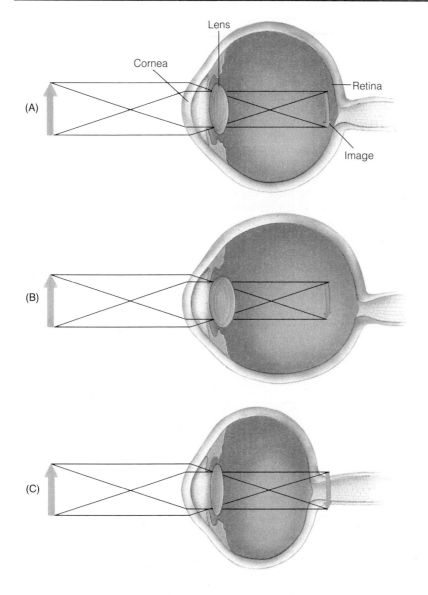

Figure 6.7
Sightedness:

(A) Normal vision, where the inverted image is focused by the cornea and lens on the retina.

(B) Nearsightedness, where the focused image falls short of the retina because the eyeball is too rounded.

(C) Farsightedness, where the focused image falls beyond the retina because the eyeball is too short or the lens too flattened.

There is another, larger space *behind* the lens that is also filled with a fluid or humor. This fluid is called **vitreous humor.** It is not nearly as watery as aqueous humor. It is thick and filled with tiny structures that give it substance. Its major function is to keep the eyeball rounded.

vitreous humor
the thick fluid behind the lens of the eye that functions to keep the eyeball spherical

The Retina

retina
layers of cells at the back of the eye that contain the photosensitive rods and cones

So far we have listed a number of structures, each important in its own way, but none of them doing much more than passing light waves back through the eye to other structures, perhaps in more focused form. It is at the next structure of the eye that vision takes place. Light energy is changed into neural energy at the **retina.**

The retina is really a series of layers of very specialized cells located at the back of the eye. These cells are nerve cells and in a true sense can be thought

photoreceptors
light-sensitive cells (rods and cones) of the retina

rods
the photoreceptor cells of the retina that are thought to be most active at low levels of illumination and to be essentially color-blind

cones
the photoreceptor cells of the retina that are thought to operate best in bright light and to be responsible for perceiving colors

optic nerve
the layer of nerve cells that transmits neural impulses from the eye to the occipital lobe of the brain

of as part of the brain. The location of the retina and its major landmarks are shown in Figure 6.6, while Figure 6.8 shows the retina in more detail.

To describe the retina, let's move in the opposite direction—from back to front. The layer of cells at the very back of the retina are the light-sensitive cells, or **photoreceptors,** of the eye. It is here that light energy is transformed into neural energy.

There are two types of photoreceptor cells: **rods** and **cones.** They are very aptly named, because that's just what they look like: small rods and cones. Their ends or tips respond to light wave energy and begin a neural impulse. These impulses travel down the rods and cones and pass on to (technically, *synapse with* is more correct) a number of other cells, also arranged in layers.

At these layers of nerve cells there is considerable combination and integration of neural impulses. Each rod and each cone does not have a single direct pathway to the brain. Impulses from many rods and cones are combined right in the eye (by horizontal cells, bipolar cells, amacrine cells, and ganglion cells, in order). Fibers from ganglion cells gather together to form the **optic nerve,** which leaves the eye and starts back toward the brain.

Notice again the arrow in Figure 6.8 that indicates the direction of the light entering the retina. It is correctly drawn. Yes, light waves first pass through all those layers of cells, past all those nerve cells, to reach the tips of the rods and cones where they are transformed into neural impulses. The layering of structures in the retina does seem to be somewhat inside-out. It would seem to make more sense to point the light-sensitive tips of the rods and cones out toward the incoming light, yet virtually all mammalian retinas are constructed in the manner shown in Figure 6.8.

Figure 6.8
The major features of the human retina.

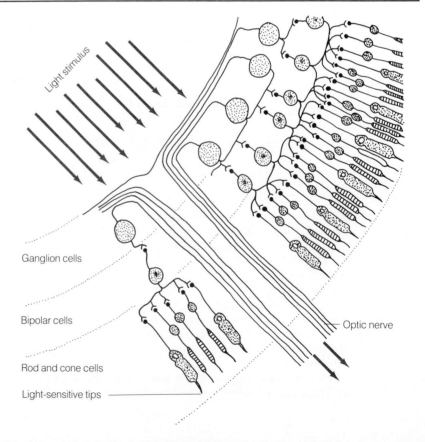

Figure 6.9

Finding your blindspot.

(1) Close your right eye and stare at the cross. Hold the page about a foot from your eye. Move the page until the star falls on your blindspot and disappears.

(2) Close your right eye and stare at the cross. Hold the page about a foot from your left eye and move the page until the break in the line falls on your blindspot. The line will look unbroken.

The two main structures of the retina that are depicted in Figure 6.6 are the **fovea** and the **blindspot.** The fovea is a small area of the retina where there are very few layers of cells between the light and the cone cells that fill the area. There are virtually no rods in the fovea, only cones. And the cones of the fovea are unusually tightly packed together. It is here at the fovea that our vision is best, that our acuity, or ability to discern detail, is best—at least in daylight or at reasonably high levels of illumination. If you were to try to thread a needle, you would want to focus the image of the needle and thread directly on the fovea.

The blindspot of the retina is where the nerve impulses from the rods and cones, having passed through all those other layers of cells, exit the eye. At the blindspot there are no rods and cones—there's nothing here but optic nerve on its way back to the brain. Because there are no rods or cones, there is no vision here—hence, blindspot. Every eye has to have a blindspot. There has to be a place where impulses from the retina can pass back to the brain. An eye without a blindspot is totally blind. Figure 6.9 provides you with a way to locate your own blindspot.

The eye is a marvelous organ. Most of its structures function to focus an image on the photosensitive rods and cones of the retinal layer at the back of the eye. If you think about all that light has to go through to get to the photosensitive rods and cones, you have to wonder how it is that we can see *anything* clearly. The corneas of our eyes are seldom perfectly rounded, and they are often less than totally clear, occasionally scratched or covered with dust and dirt. Aqueous humors are also filled with small particles of impurities. Light has to pass through a lens that is seldom perfectly shaped (most have flat spots and lumps that distort images). Then light has to go through a large volume of vitreous humor that contains all sorts of small structures and particles that can interfere with it. And finally, the light must pass through layer after layer of nerve cells (and the blood vessels that serve them) before reaching its destination at the rods and cones.

fovea
the region of the retina of greatest acuity due to a high concentration of cones

blindspot
the region of the retina, containing no photoreceptors, where the optic nerve leaves the eye

Before you go on

List the major structures of the eye and describe the function of each.

RODS AND CONES: A DUPLICITY THEORY OF VISION

It may have already struck you as odd that there are *two* separate photosensitive receptor cells in the retina of the eye: rods *and* cones. They are clearly different in their structure, as we have noted. Not only are there two different kinds of cells in our retinas, but they are not there in equal number. There are approximately 120 million rods and only 6 million cones, which means that rods outnumber cones in the human eye at a ratio of about 20 to 1.

Not only are rods and cones found in unequal number, but they are not evenly distributed throughout the retina. As we have already indicated, cones tend to be concentrated in the center of the retina, at the fovea. Rods also have an area of concentration in a band surrounding the fovea, out toward the periphery of the retina. I call this area the "ring around the fovea."

What the Theory Claims

These observations have led psychologists to wonder if the rods and cones of our eyes have different functions. They don't look alike. They're not found in equal numbers. They're not evenly distributed throughout the retina. Maybe they operate differently. The theory that our rods and cones have different (duplicitous) functions is called the **duplicity theory of vision.**

duplicity theory of vision
the theory that the rods are twilight receptors and color-blind, whereas the cones are daylight receptors and responsible for color vision

The evidence seems to support the belief that our cones are our daylight receptors. They function best under conditions of high illumination (as in daylight) and are responsible for our experience of color. On the other hand, our rods are essentially color-blind and operate best under conditions of low or reduced illumination. They are often referred to as our twilight receptors.

Evidence to Support the Duplicity Theory

Some of the evidence supporting this point of view can be verified by our own experiences. Isn't it difficult to distinguish among different colors at night or in the dark? The next time you are at the movies eating some candy the pieces of which are of different colors, see if you can tell them apart without holding them up to the light of the projector. You probably won't be able to tell a green piece from a red one—something of a problem if you happen to have a favorite flavor. You can't discriminate colors well in a dark movie theater because you are seeing primarily with your rods, which are very good at seeing in the reduced light of the theater but which don't respond differentially to different wavelengths of light.

If you are looking for something outside at night, you will probably not see it if you look directly at it. Say you're changing a tire along the road at night. You're replacing the wheel and can't find one of the lug nuts that you know is there someplace amidst the gravel. If you were to look directly at it, the image of the nut would fall on your fovea. Your fovea is made up almost entirely of cones. Cones do not operate well in relative darkness, and you'll not see the nut. To have the best chance of finding it, you have to get the image of the nut to fall out toward the periphery of your eye where your rods are concentrated (in the "ring around the fovea").

One of the reasons why nocturnal animals (such as many varieties of owls) get along so well at night is that they can see well in the dark. They see well because their eyes are filled with rods. Such animals necessarily have fewer cones and are demonstrably color-blind. (How you might test the color vision of an owl is discussed in Topic 11.) Let's now review two types of experimental evidence that support the view that our rods and cones have different functions.

Dark Adaptation   Additional evidence in support of the duplicity theory comes from the way that our eyes adapt to the dark. The phenomenon is a familiar one. You walk into a movie theater for a matinee on a sunny afternoon and at first cannot see much of anything. In a few minutes you can make out some rough forms, and you may not trample anyone on the way to your seat. After about 20 or 30 minutes you find that you are seeing rather well—about as well as you are going to in the darkened environment. The longer we stay in the dark, the more sensitive our eyes become to what light *is* available. (If the environment were entirely dark, with no light available, you would not see anything, no matter how long you waited. The stimulus for vision is light, remember.)

Figure 6.10 is a graphic representation of the dark adaptation process. With time spent in the dark our sensitivity increases, or our threshold decreases. (Threshold here means the least amount of light that we can see.) At first, we can only see very bright lights, the dimmer and dimmer ones are detected as our threshold drops. As Figure 6.10 indicates, the whole process takes about 20 to 30 minutes.

But there is something strange going on. The dark adaptation curve is not a smooth, regular one. At about the 7-minute mark there is a change in the shape of the curve. The break in the smoothness of the curve is called the rod-cone break. At first, and for 6 or 7 minutes, both rods *and* cones increase their sensitivity (represented by the first part of the curve). But our cones are basically daylight receptors, remember. They're just not cut out for seeing in the dark, and after that first few minutes they have become as sensitive as they are going to get. The rods, on the other hand, keep right on lowering their threshold, becoming more and more sensitive (represented by the second part of the curve).

The Purkinje Shift   Further evidence for the duplicity theory of vision comes from a phenomenon called the **Purkinje shift**. The Purkinje shift explains the change in the perceived brightness of lights as a function of overall light levels. That is, lights may change their apparent brightness as daylight changes to twilight. Let's explore this in a little more detail.

Because we know exactly where the rods and cones of the human eye are located, we can stimulate each kind of receptor cell independently. We can test the sensitivity of rods and cones to different intensity levels of light and to lights of different wavelength. When this is done, it turns out that our rods, not surprisingly, are much more sensitive to low intensity lights than are our cones, regardless of the hue (wavelength) of the light. What is curious is that the wavelength of light used to test sensitivity *does* make a difference, depending upon which type of receptor cell we are testing. Cones reach their maximum sensitivity when they are stimulated by wavelengths of light from the long end of the spectrum—toward the yellows and oranges. Rods, on the other hand, are most sensitive to wavelengths more toward the middle of the spectrum—toward the greens and blue-green.

Suppose that I have an apparatus (I call it a rainbow generator) that produces all the wavelengths of light of the visible spectrum, from 380 to 760 nanometers. I can adjust all of the wavelengths of light so that their intensity levels (amplitudes) are exactly equal. You are sitting in a brightly lighted room, looking at my device. What will you see when I turn on the device? You'll see a rainbow of light from violet on the left to red on the right. And because all of the wave amplitudes are equal, they will not appear equally bright (remember that wave amplitude and length interact to produce the impression of brightness). Now I dim the lights in the room and the

Figure 6.10
The dark adaptation curve.

(A) At first, both rods and cones lower thresholds, or increase sensitivity.

(B) In 6–8 minutes, the cones have become as sensitive as possible, adaptation then is due to the rods alone.

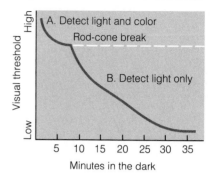

Purkinje shift
the phenomenon of perceived levels of brightness changing as a function of overall illumination levels

Figure 6.11

Perceived relative brightness is a function of wavelength for both daylight (cone) vision and twilight (rod) vision, illustrating the Purkinje shift.

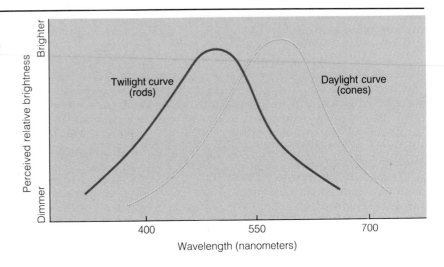

relative brightness of the lights in the rainbow shift toward the left, toward the blue end of the spectrum (see Figure 6.11). This is the Purkinje shift.

To demonstrate the Purkinje shift, we need not be so fancy. You can see it for yourself without a rainbow generator. You only need to look closely at a red flower and its green leaves sometime during a bright, sunny day, noting the relative brightness of the red and the green. Return to the same flower shortly after sunset and note the change in the relative brightness of the blossom and the leaves. Although the green leaves (to which the rods are sensitive) are still relatively bright, the red flower (to which the cones are sensitive) now appears quite dark, almost black.

In a literal sense then, we might claim that there are two different sorts of seeing—daylight, color vision that is accomplished mostly by our cones, and a color-blind, twilight vision that is accomplished mostly by our rods.

Before you go on

What is the duplicity theory of vision, and what evidence can you cite to support it?

In this topic, we have discussed the physical characteristics of light and how they affect our psychological perceptions of light. Remember, the stimulus for vision is light. The minute and complex structures of our eyes receive the stimuli from our senses and transform them into visual representations of the world we live in. As we will see in the next topic, our senses of hearing, smell, touch, and taste are equally complex and wonderful in their functions.

Explaining how the eye codes (or responds to) different intensities of light is not too difficult. Coding is largely determined by the frequency of the firing of the receptor cells in the retina. High intensity lights cause more rapid firings of neural impulses than do low intensity lights. How the eye codes different *wavelengths* of light to produce different experiences of color, however, is another story. Here things are not simple at all. To be honest about it, we should say that we really don't know exactly how the process occurs, but we do have two theories of color vision that have received research support. As is often the case with competing theories that try to explain the same phenomenon, both theories are probably partially correct.

The older of the two theories of color vision is called the *trichromatic theory*. It was first proposed by Thomas Young very early in the nineteenth century and then revised by Hermann von Helmholtz, a noted physiologist, about 50 years later. As its name suggests, the *trichromatic theory* proposes that the eye contains *three* separate and distinct receptors for color.

Although there is considerable overlap, each type of receptor responds best to one of three primary colors of light: red, green, and blue. These colors are primary because by the careful combination of these three wavelengths of light, all other colors can be produced. Your color television screen works according to this principle. The picture on your TV screen is made up of a pattern of very small dots, each one being either red, green, or blue, of a given intensity. From these three wavelengths all other colors are constructed, or integrated.

Because the sensitivity of the three types of receptors in our eyes overlaps, when our eyes are stimulated by a nonprimary color, such

as orange, the orange-hued light will stimulate each receptor to varying degrees in such a way as to produce the sensation of orange. What gives this theory credibility is that there really *are* such receptor cells in the human retina. Obviously they are cones (which are responsible for color vision). The relative sensitivity of these three cone systems is shown in Figure 6.12.

Ewald Hering thought that the Young-Helmholtz theory left a good bit to be desired, and in 1870 he proposed a theory of his own. This theory has come to be called the *opponent-process theory*. Hering's theory suggests that there are three *pairs* of visual mechanisms that respond to different light wave characteristics. One mechanism is a blue-yellow processor, one a red-green processor, and the third processes black-white differences.

Each mechanism is capable of responding to *either* of the two characteristics that give it its name, but not both. That is, the blue-yel-

low processor can respond to blue *or* to yellow, but can't handle both at the same time. The second mechanism responds to red *or* green, but not both, and the third processor codes brightness. Thus, the members of each pair work to oppose each other, giving the theory its name. If blue is excited, then yellow is inhibited. If red is excited, then green is inhibited. A light may appear to be a mixture of red and yellow perhaps, but cannot be seen as a mixture of blue *and* yellow because both blue and yellow cannot be excited at the same time. (It is rather difficult to imagine what a reddish-green would look like, isn't it? Can you picture a light that is bright and dim at the same time?)

Although the opponent-process theory may at first appear overly complicated, there are some strong signs that Hering was on the right track. In the first place, excitatory-inhibitory mechanisms such as he proposed for red-green, blue-yellow, and black-white have been found.

Figure 6.12

The relative sensitivities of three different kinds of cones to light of different wavelengths. Note that although there is considerable overlap, each cell is maximally sensitive to different wavelengths (or colors).

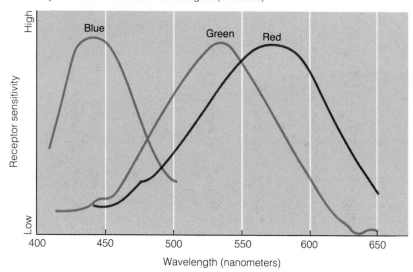

As it happens, they are not at the level of rods and cones in the retina (as Hering had thought), but at the layer of the ganglion cells (see Figure 6.8) and also in a small portion of the thalamus called the lateral geniculate body.

Hering's theory also makes some observations about color-blindness sensible. Although some people are totally color-blind, much more commonly, people are blind only to certain wavelengths of light. Blindness to colors usually occurs in pairs: Some people are red-green color-blind and some (fewer) are yellow-blue color-blind, suggesting a problem with one of the opponent-process mechanisms. Two sample tests for color-blindness are presented in Figure 6.13.)

Yet another piece of support comes from our experiences with *negative afterimages*. If you stare at a bright green figure for a few minutes and then shift your gaze to a white surface, you will notice an image of a red figure. The explanation for the appearance of this image is as follows: While you were staring at the green figure, the green component of the red-green process became fatigued because of all the stimulation it was getting. When you stared at the white surface, both the red and green components of the process were equally stimulated, but because the green component was fatigued, the red predominated, producing the experience of seeing a red figure. (Figure 6.14 provides an example for you to try.)

Because cone cell systems that respond differentially to red, blue, and green light have been found in the retina, we cannot dismiss the trichromatic theory. Because there are cells that operate the way the opponent-process theory predicts, we cannot dismiss this theory either. Well, which one is right? Probably they both are. Our experience of color probably depends upon the interaction of different cone cells *and* different ganglion cells in our retinas—a marvelous system indeed.

Figure 6.13

An illustration of the effect of red-green color-blindness. People with normal vision will be able to distinguish the images from the backgrounds, while people who are red-green color-blind will not.

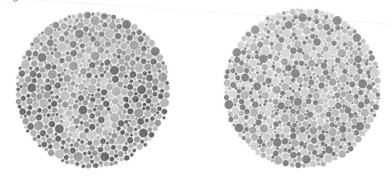

Figure 6.14

To illustrate the experience of color fatigue, stare at the green figure for 30 seconds, and then shift your gaze to a completely white surface. You should see the same figure, but it will appear red because the green receptors are fatigued. Now try the same experiment with the blue figure. What color do you see when you shift your gaze?

TOPIC SUMMARY

In what ways do the major physical characteristics of light waves of energy (amplitude, length, and purity) affect our psychological experiences of light?

We can think of light as a wave form of radiant energy having three major physical characteristics: wave amplitude, wavelength, and wave purity (or its opposite, mixture), which determine the brightness, hue, and saturation of the light as we perceive it. / 98

List the major structures of the eye and describe the function of each.

Before light reaches the retina, it passes through a number of structures, the major function of which is to focus an image. In order, light passes through the cornea, the pupil (or opening in the iris), aqueous humor, lens, and vitreous humor. Then, at the retina, light is changed into neural energy by the photosensitive rods and cones that pass neural impulses through a series of nerve cells to the optic nerve that carries the impulses to the occipital lobe. / 103

What is the duplicity theory of vision, and what evidence can you cite to support it?

The duplicity theory asserts that rods and cones function differently: the cones responding to high levels of illumination and color while the rods do not discriminate colors and respond to low levels of light. Evidence for this theory comes from common experience, the examination of the visual system of nocturnal animals, and data on dark adaptation and the Purkinje shift. / 106

TOPIC

Have you ever wished for a little peace and quiet? I mean *real* peace and quiet, where you could be free from virtually all outside stimulation: no bright lights, no screeching traffic noise, no kids racing around, no TV, no changes in temperature, no strong odors or tastes, no *anything*, just perfect peace and quiet? Sounds rather pleasant doesn't it—to be cut off from the intrusions of external sensory stimulation?

In fact, a number of psychologists over the years have constructed artificial environments that have been as free from such stimulation as possible. The results of their research have been rather surprising. In the mid-1950s, Heron and his associates (1956) asked volunteer college students to spend as long as they wanted in a sound-proof chamber. They stretched out on a soft bed with their eyes covered with goggles that let in only small amounts of diffuse light. They had their arms and hands cushioned in large cardboard tubes so they could feel nothing. During their stay in this sensory deprivation chamber, subjects were given short breaks for meals and to go to an adjacent bathroom. Otherwise, they were instructed to lie perfectly still and relax. At first, most of the volunteers thought that being paid $20 for the opportunity to experience such peace and quiet seemed almost like stealing.

But after just 2 or 3 days, subjects absolutely refused to reenter the deprivation chamber—even for rather hefty financial rewards. The experience was too intolerably negative. Subjects lost all track of time. Many experienced visual hallucinations—they thought they saw things that were not there to be seen. When subjects were tested after leaving the deprivation chamber, learning and problem-solving skills showed marked impairment. Many subjects became disoriented, confused, and emotionally upset—some displaying very atypical emotional outbursts.

It may very well be the case that we are too often *over*stimulated by the events of the world around us. A brief retreat from hectic overstimulation wouldn't hurt anyone. But it is also true that too *little* sensory stimulation has negative side effects as well. Our brain seems to need the stimulation it gets from our various senses.

Why We Care

We mentioned in the last topic that vision is a very important sense and that we happen to know more about it than we do the other senses. But consider for a moment the quality information that we *do* receive from our other, "lesser" senses. Try a little experiment on your own. Bypass your heavy reliance on vision by trying to spend the better part of a day doing without it. Blindfold yourself and try to go about your normal everyday activities.

One thing you will realize almost immediately is just how heavily you do rely on vision. You may also come to a new appreciation of your other senses as they inform you of the wonder of your environment: the aroma and taste of well-prepared barbecue, the sounds of birds and music, the touch and feel of textures and surfaces, the sense of where your body is and what it's doing, the feedback from your muscles as you move—all these and more, all through our "lesser" senses.

In this topic, we'll briefly review a number of senses, noting the relevant stimulus for each and indicating how each sense receptor works. We'll start with hearing and then move to the chemical senses of taste and smell. Then we'll consider the skin senses of touch, pressure, and temperature. Finally, we'll cover those senses that tell us where our body is in relation to gravity and how different parts of our body are positioned.

Figure 7.1

Sound waves are produced as air pressure is spread by the tine of a tuning fork vibrating to the right (a) and left (b). The point of highest pressure is the high point of the wave; lowest pressure is indicated by the low point of the wave

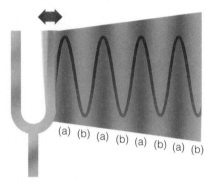

(a) (b) (a) (b) (a) (b) (a) (b)

HEARING

Hearing is a major sense. Hearing provides us with nearly as much information about our environment as does vision. One of its main roles is its involvement in our development of language and speech. Without hearing, these uniquely human skills are difficult to acquire.

The Stimulus for Hearing: Sound

The stimulus for vision is light; for hearing (or, more formally, *audition*), the stimulus is sound. Sound does not really travel in waves. Sound is, in fact, made up of a series of pressures of air (or some other medium, like water) against our ear, which we can represent as a wave. As a source of sound vibrates, it pushes waves of air against our ears. Figure 7.1 shows how sound may be depicted as a wave form of energy.

As was the case for light waves, there are three major physical characteristics of sound waves—amplitude, frequency (or length), and purity—and each of them is responsible for a different psychological experience. Let's briefly consider each in turn.

loudness

the psychological experience correlated with the intensity, or amplitude, of a sound wave

decibel

the unit of measurement for loudness in which 0 represents the absolute threshold and 140 is sensed as pain

Wave Amplitude (Intensity)   The amplitude of a sound wave depicts its intensity—the force with which the air beats against our ear. The physical characteristic of intensity determines the psychological experience we call **loudness**. That is, the higher its amplitude, the louder we perceive the sound to be. Soft, quiet sounds have low amplitudes (see Figure 7.2).

Measurements of the physical *intensity* of sound—the amplitude of sound waves—are given in units of force (or pressure) per unit area. The scale that is most commonly used is the **decibel** scale. (The construction of the decibel scale followed directly from Fechner's work on psychophysical scaling.)

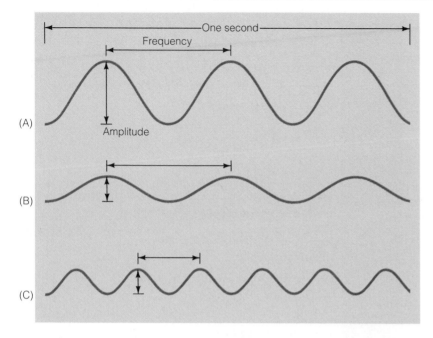

Figure 7.2

An illustration of how the physical characteristics of sound waves influence our psychological experiences of sound.

(1) Though waves (A) and (B) have the same frequency, wave (A) has a higher amplitude and would be experienced as a louder sound.

(2) Though waves (B) and (C) have the same amplitude, wave (C) would be experienced as having a higher pitch because of its greater frequency.

Loudness is a psychological characteristic. It is measured by people, not by instruments. The decibel scale of sound intensity has been contructed so that it reflects perceived loudness. Its zero point is the very lowest intensity of sound that can be detected, or the absolute threshold. Our ears are very sensitive receptors and respond to very low levels of sound intensity. (In fact, if our ears were much more sensitive we would hear molecules of air bouncing off our eardrums.) We can also respond to extremely intense, high amplitude sounds such as those produced by jet aircraft engines, large machines in factories, and rock concerts. Figure 7.3 lists decibel levels for some of the sounds we might find in our environment.

Wave Frequency   When we discussed light, we talked about the length of light waves and saw that wavelength was responsible for our perception of hue. With sound, we translate wavelength into *wave frequency*. Wave frequency is a measure of the number of times a wave repeats itself within a given period of time, usually one second. For sound, frequency is measured in terms of how many waves of pressure are exerted every second. The unit of sound frequency is the **Hertz**, abbreviated **Hz**, or wave cycles per second. If a sound wave repeats itself 50 times in one second, it is a 50Hz sound; 500 repetitions is a 500Hz sound, and so on.

If you keep in mind where sounds come from, it is clear that a 50Hz sound, for example, is being produced by something that is vibrating back and forth, creating pressures of air at the rate of 50 vibrations per second. Waves of different frequency are shown in Figure 7.2, where you should be able to see the relationship between wavelength and frequency.

The psychological experience that is produced by sound wave frequencies is **pitch**. When we differentiate between high sounds and low sounds, we are doing so on the basis of pitch. The musical scale represents differences in pitch.

Just as the human eye cannot respond to all possible wavelengths of radiant energy, so the human ear cannot respond to all possible sound wave

hertz (Hz)
the standard measure of sound wave frequency that is the number of wave cycles per second

pitch
the psychological experience that corresponds to sound wave frequency and influences our perception of tones as being high or low

Figure 7.3

Loudness values in decibel units for various sounds.

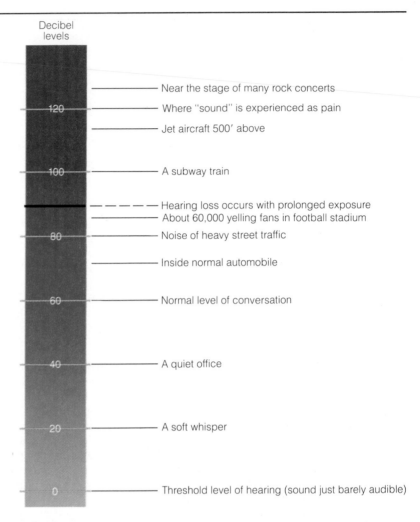

Decibel levels

— Near the stage of many rock concerts

120 — Where "sound" is experienced as pain

— Jet aircraft 500' above

100 — A subway train

– – – Hearing loss occurs with prolonged exposure
— About 60,000 yelling fans in football stadium

80 — Noise of heavy street traffic

— Inside normal automobile

60 — Normal level of conversation

40 — A quiet office

20 — A soft whisper

0 — Threshold level of hearing (sound just barely audible)

frequencies. The good, undamaged human ear can hear sound wave frequencies between 20 and 20,000Hz. If air pounds against our ears at a rate less than 20 times per second, we'll not hear it. Sound vibrations faster than 20,000 cycles per second cannot be heard either—at least by the human ear. Many animals, including dogs, *can* hear sounds with frequencies above 20,000Hz, such as those produced by dog whistles.

As sound wave frequencies increase from low frequencies (down at the 20Hz range) to high frequencies (up at the 20,000Hz end of the audible spectrum), our experience of pitch changes. Low frequencies produce low, bass sounds, such as those produced by foghorns or tubas. High frequency vibrations give rise to the experience of high-pitched sounds, such as the musical tones produced by flutes or the squeals of smoke detectors.

You will recall that for light, wave amplitude and wavelength interact so that lights of different wavelengths do not appear to be equally bright, even if all their intensities are adjusted to be equal. We have the same sort of interaction when we deal with sound and sound waves. Sound wave intensities and frequencies interact.

What this means is that all wave frequencies of sound do not *sound equally loud* (a psychological experience) even if all their *intensities are equal* (a physical reality). That is, sounds of high and low frequency do not appear as loud as sounds of midrange frequency, everything else being equal. Put another way, to have a high frequency sound appear as loud as a medium frequency sound, we would have to raise the amplitude of the high frequency sound. Fortunately, most of the sounds that are most relevant to us everyday—speech sounds, for example—are generally of mid range frequency, and thus are easily heard. This relationship between sound wave frequency and amplitude is depicted in Figure 7.4.

Wave Purity   A third characteristic of sound waves that we need to consider is wave purity or complexity. You'll recall that we seldom experience pure, monochromatic lights because they are difficult to produce. A pure sound is also uncommon in our normal experience. A pure sound would be one in which *all* of the waves from the sound source were vibrating at exactly the same frequency. Such sounds can be produced electronically, and tuning forks produce reasonable approximations, but most of the sounds we hear every day are complex sounds, composed of many sound wave frequencies.

A tone of middle C on the piano is a tone of approximately 256Hz. (Again, this means that the source of the sound, here a piano string, is vibrating 256 times per second.) A *pure* 256Hz tone is composed of sound waves of only that frequency. As it happens, even the middle C of the piano has many other wave frequencies mixed in with the predominant 256Hz wave frequency. (If the 256Hz wave did not predominate, the tone wouldn't sound like middle C!) For musical instruments, most of the other sound waves that are mixed in are some multiple of the basic frequency being produced. That means that the other wave frequencies in a tone of middle C tend to be 512Hz (256×2), or 768Hz (256×3), or 1024Hz (256×4), and so on. These added tones are called overtones, or harmonics.

The psychological quality of a sound that reflects its level of purity is called **timbre.** For example, each musical instrument produces a unique variety or mix of overtones, so each type of musical instrument tends to sound a little different from all others. If a trumpet, a violin, and a piano were each to play the same note (say that middle C of 256Hz), we could still tell the instruments apart because of our experience of timbre. (In fact, any one instrument may display different timbres, depending on how it is played.)

With light, we found that the opposite of a pure light was a white light, made up of all the wavelengths of the visible spectrum. Again, the parallel between vision and hearing holds. Suppose that I have a sound source that can produce all of the possible sound wave frequencies. I produce a random mixture of these frequencies from 20Hz to 20,000Hz. What would that sound like? Actually it would sound rather like a buzzing noise. The best example would be the sound that one hears when a radio (as it happens, FM is better than AM) is tuned *in between* stations. The soft whispering, buzzing sound, which contains many audible frequencies of sounds, is useful in masking or covering other unwanted sounds. We call a random mixture of wavelengths of light *white light,* and we call a random mixture of sound frequencies **white noise.**

The analogy between light and sound, between vision and hearing, is striking. Both types of stimulus energy can be represented as waves. In both cases, each of the *physical* characteristics of the waves (amplitude, length or frequency, and purity or mixture) is correlated with a *psychological* experience. These relationships are summarized in Figure 7.5.

Before you go on

What are the three major physical characteristics of sound, and which psychological experiences do they produce?

Figure 7.4
An illustration of the relationship between loudness (threshold) and pitch (wave frequency). With amplitude equal, sounds in the midrange of pitch (1,000-1,200Hz) have the lowest threshold. (Notice the frequency scale is logarithmic.)

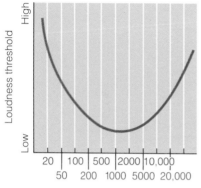

Sound wave frequency (pitch)

timbre
the psychological experience relating to sound wave purity by which we perceive the sharpness, clearness, or quality of a tone

white noise
a sound composed of a random assortment of wave frequencies from the audible spectrum

Figure 7.5
The physical characteristics of light and sound waves affect our psychological experiences of vision and hearing as illustrated in the table.

Physical characteristic	Psychological experience for vision	Psychological experience for hearing
Wave amplitude	Brightness	Loudness
Wavelength or frequency	Hue	Pitch
Wave purity or mixture	Saturation	Timbre

The Receptor for Hearing: The Ear

It is deep inside the ear that sound wave pressures are changed into neural impulses. As with the eye, most of the identifiable structures of the ear simply transfer energy from without to within. Figure 7.6 is a drawing of the major structures of the human ear, and we'll use it to follow the path of sound waves from the environment to the receptor cells for sound.

The outer ear is called the **pinna.** Its main function is to collect the sound waves from the air around it and funnel them to the **eardrum.** (Notice that when we are trying to hear soft sounds we sometimes try to help by cupping our hand around our pinna to gather in as much sound as we can.) Collected by the pinna, air waves push against the membrane of the eardrum, setting it in motion, vibrating it at the same rate as the sound source. Now the eardrum is vibrating back and forth, and the sound moves deeper inside the ear.

As you can see in Figure 7.6, there are three very small bones (collectively called *ossicles*) that make up the middle ear. Resting against the eardrum, the bones are, in order, the **malleus,** the **incus,** and the **stapes** (pronounced stape-ese). Because of their unique shapes, these bones are sometimes referred to as the *hammer, anvil,* and *stirrup.* These bones pass the vibrations of the eardrum along to the *oval window,* another membrane like the eardrum, only smaller. As the ossicles pass the sound wave vibrations along to the oval window, they concentrate them, increasing their force.

When sound is transmitted beyond the oval window, the vibrations are said to be in the inner ear. The inner ear is largely composed of the **cochlea,** a snaillike structure that contains the actual receptor cells for hearing. As the stapes vibrates against the oval window, it sets a fluid inside the cochlea in motion at the same rate.

There is yet another membrane in the ear, called the **basilar membrane,** that runs just about the full length of the cochlea, nearly in its center. As the fluid within the cochlea starts to move, the basilar membrane is bent up and down. Hearing takes place when very tiny **hair cells** (that's their name) are stimulated by the vibrations of the basilar membrane. Through a process not yet fully understood, the mechanical pressure of the basilar membrane on the hair cells starts a neural impulse that leaves the ear at the auditory nerve and travels toward the brain, to the temporal lobe.

The ear is the receptor for hearing. It translates physical energy into the psychological experience of sound. Most of the structures of the ear are responsible for focusing and directing waves of pressure to the hair cells where the neural impulse begins.

pinna
the outer ear which collects and funnels sound waves

eardrum
the outermost membrane of the ear which is set in motion by the vibrations of a sound and passes those vibrations to the ossicles

malleus, incus, and stapes
(collectively ossicles) Three small bones that transmit sound wave vibrations from the eardrum to the oval window

cochlea
the inner ear where sound waves become neural impulses

basilar membrane
a structure within the cochlea that vibrates and stimulates the hair cells of the inner ear

hair cells
the receptor cells for hearing, located in the cochlea, that are stimulated by the vibrating basilar membrane and transmit neural impulses to the brain

Before you go on
Summarize how sound wave pressures are transmitted through the different structures of the ear.

Figure 7.6

The major structures of the human ear.

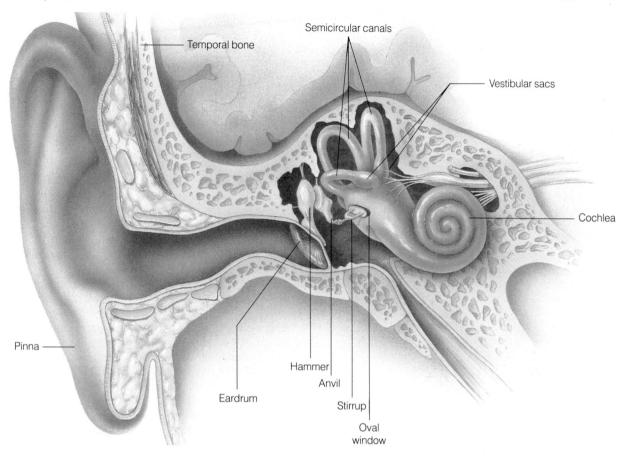

THE CHEMICAL SENSES

Taste and smell are referred to as chemical senses because the stimuli for both are molecules of chemical compounds. For taste, the chemical molecules are dissolved in liquid (usually the saliva in our mouths). For smell, the chemicals are dissolved in the air that reaches the smell receptors high inside our noses. The technical term for taste is *gustation;* for smell, it is *olfaction.*

If you have ever eaten while suffering from a severe head cold that has blocked your nasal passages, you appreciate the extent to which our experience of taste and smell are interrelated. Most foods seem to lose their taste when we cannot smell them—which is why we should differentiate between the *flavor* of foods (which includes such qualities as odor and texture) and the *taste* of foods. A simple test demonstrates this point very nicely. While blindfolded, eat a small piece of peeled apple and a small piece of peeled potato, and see if you can tell the difference between the two. You shouldn't have any trouble making this discrimination. Now hold your nose very tightly and try again. Without your sense of smell to help you, such discrimination— on the basis of taste alone—is very difficult. This demonstration will work with almost any two foods that have approximately the same texture. It's easy to discriminate between apples and bananas without taste or smell on the basis of texture alone.

Figure 7.7

This enlarged view of a taste bud shows how the sensation of taste travels from the gustatory receptor cells to the brain via the neurons.

Enlarged view of taste bud

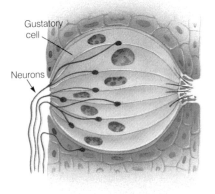

Gustatory cell

Neurons

Figure 7.8

The four primary qualities of taste are experienced in specific areas of the tongue, as illustrated below.

Top view of tongue

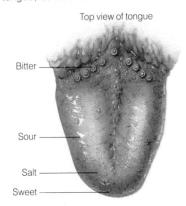

Bitter

Sour

Salt

Sweet

Taste (Gustation)

Our experience of the flavors of foods depends so heavily on our sense of smell and our sense of texture and temperature that we sometimes have to wonder if there is any sense of taste alone. Well, there is. Taste seems to have four basic psychological qualities—and many combinations of these four. The four primary qualities of taste are *sweet, salty, sour,* and *bitter.* You should be able to generate a list of foods that produce each of these basic sensations.

Some foods derive their special taste from their own unique combination of the four basic taste sensations. Have you noticed that it is more difficult to think of examples of sour and bitter tasting foods than it is to think of sweet and salty ones? This reflects the fact that we usually don't like bitter and sour tastes and have learned to avoid them.

The receptors for taste are located on (*in* might be more precise) the tongue, of course. The receptors for taste are called **taste buds.** We all have about 10,000 taste buds, and each one is made up of a number of separate parts. Fortunately, when parts of taste buds die (or are killed by foods that are too hot, for example), new segments are regenerated. We are always growing fresh new taste receptor cells. A schematic diagram of a taste bud is shown in Figure 7.7.

Different taste buds respond primarily to chemicals that represent or produce the four basic taste qualities. That is, some receptor cells respond mostly to salts, while others respond primarily to sweet-producing chemicals, like sugars. As it happens, these specialized cells are not evenly distributed on the surface of the tongue. Receptors for sweet are at the very tip of the tongue; receptors for salty tastes are at the front; sour receptors are on the sides; and bitter receptors are at the back of the tongue. A sour vinegar solution dropped right at the tip of the tongue might very well go unnoticed until some of it gets over to the side of the tongue. To best savor a lollipop, children learned ages ago to lick it with the tip of the tongue. The locations of the receptors for the primary tastes are illustrated in Figure 7.8.

Smell (Olfaction)

Smell is the sense we understand the least. It is a sense that often gives us great pleasure—think of the aroma of bacon frying over a wood fire or of freshly picked flowers. It also produces considerable displeasure—consider the smell of old garbage or the sulfur dioxide odor of rotten eggs.

We do know that the sense of smell originates in cells located high in the nasal cavity, very close to the brain itself. We also know that the pathway from these receptors to the brain is the most direct and shortest of all the senses. (See Figure 7.9.) What we don't understand well is how molecules suspended in air (or some other gas) stimulate the small hair cells of the olfactory receptor to begin to fire neural impulses.

We know that the sense of smell is one of the most important senses for nonhumans. The dog's sense of smell is legendary. Many organisms emit chemicals, called **pheromones,** that produce an odor that attracts members of the opposite sex. Japanese beetles are a common pest, particularly for people who grow roses. They are very difficult to kill (safely) with standard poisons. Japanese beetle traps are now available which contain a small amount of pheromone attractive to Japanese beetles. The beetles smell the odor the trap gives off, come rushing over to investigate, and slide off a slippery plastic platform to their doom in a disposable bag. It *is* rather gruesome, but it does attract many beetles. It may be that pheromones are stimulated by sex hormones. And it may be that humans emit similar pheromones, perhaps to attract members of the opposite sex (Wallace, 1977). If we do, the real effect is no doubt very small, although perfume and cologne salespeople would love to have us think otherwise.

For many years, psychologists have been trying to determine if there are primary odors. We have seen that there is reason to talk about primary colors and even primary tastes. What about primary odors? There have been a number of schemes proposed, and each seemed reasonable in its day. One scheme suggests that there are four basic odors from which all others may be constructed: *fragrant, acid, burnt,* and, of all things, *goaty.* Another scheme cites six primary odors. Yet another plan (Amoore, 1970) names seven primary qualities of smell and further suggests that each primary quality is stimulated by a unique type or shape of chemical molecule. For the moment, however, we can't be any more definite. There seems to be evidence both for and against Amoore's theory.

Before you go on

Discuss the chemical senses of taste and smell, noting the stimulus and receptor for each.

Do taste and smell each have primary qualities?

THE SKIN SENSES

Most of us take our skin for granted—at least we seldom sit around thinking about it very much. We often abuse our skin by overexposing it to the sun's rays in summer and to excess cold in winter. We scratch it, cut it, scrape it, and wash away millions of its cells every time we shower or bathe.

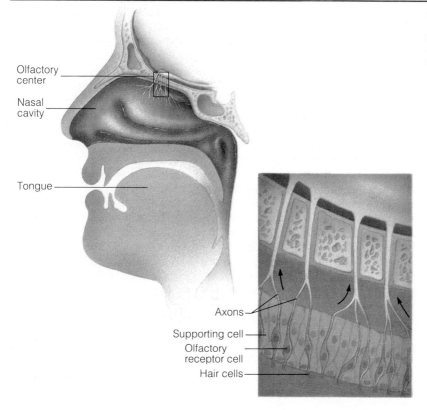

Figure 7.9
This illustration of the olfactory system shows its proximity to the brain and the relationship between the sensations of taste and smell.

Olfactory center

Nasal cavity

Tongue

Axons

Supporting cell

Olfactory receptor cell

Hair cells

Figure 7.10

This illustration of a patch of hairy skin shows the different layers of the skin and the various nerves.

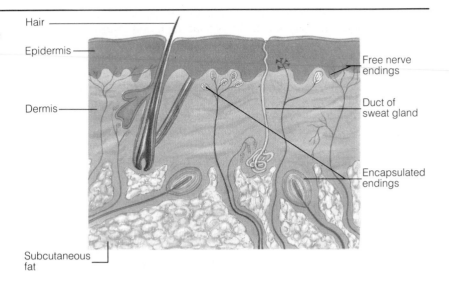

Hair

Epidermis

Dermis

Free nerve endings

Duct of sweat gland

Encapsulated endings

Subcutaneous fat

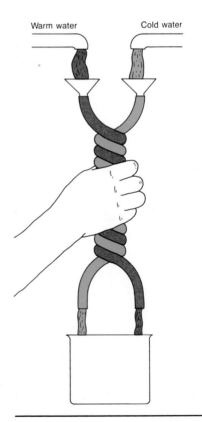

Warm water

Cold water

Figure 7.11

A demonstration that our sensation of hot may be constructed from the sensations of warm and cold. Even if you know the coiled tubes contain only warm and cold water, if you grasp the tubes you will experience the sensation of heat.

Figure 7.10 is a diagram of some of the major features of an area of skin from a hairy part of the human body. Each square inch of the layers of our skin contains nearly 20 million cells, including a large number of special sense receptors. Some of the skin receptor cells have *free nerve endings,* while most have some sort of small covering over their ends. We call these latter ones *encapsulated nerve endings,* and there are many different types. It is our skin that somehow gives rise to our psychological experience of touch or pressure, of pain (see Topic Expansion), and of warmth and cold. It would be convenient if each of the different types of receptor cells within the layers of our skin independently gave rise to a different type of psychological sensation, but such is not the case.

Indeed, one of the problems in studying the skin senses (or the *cutaneous* senses) is trying to determine just which cells in the skin give rise to the different sensations of touch and temperature. We can discriminate clearly between a light touch and a strong jab in the arm and between vibrations, tickles, and itches. A simple proposal would be that there are different receptors in the skin that are responsible for each of these different sensations. Unfortunately, this proposal is, in fact, not supported by the facts. Although *some* types of receptor cells *are* more sensitive to *some* types of stimulation, the best guess at the moment is that our ability to discriminate among different types of cutaneous sensation is due to the unique combination of responses that the many receptor cells have to different types of stimulation.

By carefully stimulating small areas of the skin with stimuli of different temperatures, we can locate areas that are particularly sensitive to temperature. We are convinced that warm and cold temperatures each stimulate different locations on the skin. Even so, there is no consistent pattern of receptor cells found at these locations, or temperature spots, as they are called. That is, we have not yet located specific receptor cells for cold or hot. As a matter of fact, our experience of hot seems to come from the simultaneous stimulation of both warm and cold spots. A rather ingenious demonstration shows how this works. Cold water is run through one metal tube and warm water is run through another tube. The two tubes are coiled together (see Figure 7.11). If you were to grasp the coiled tubes, your experience would be one of heat—the tubes would feel hot even if you knew that they weren't.

Perhaps no single sense better illustrates the phenomenon of **sensory adaptation** than does our skin sense of temperature. Sensory adaptation is the name we give to the observation that there is a reduction in the level of sensation as a function of exposure to a constant stimulus. Adaptation underscores the idea that our senses respond best to *changes* in levels of stimulation rather than constant, stable levels. Once your hand is in hot water for a few minutes, the temperature of the water no longer feels hot, even if we maintain the high temperature of the water. The water does not get cooler in any physical way, it just seems to. We say that your sense of temperature has adapted. To make the water seem warm again, we would have to increase its actual physical temperature to a level higher than what it was when you first put your hand in it.

One of the oldest demonstrations of sensory adaptation (attributed to John Locke in the seventeenth century) is quite easy for you to do at home. You will need three large containers: one filled with very hot water, one filled with very cold water, and the third filled with lukewarm water. Place your left hand in the hot water and your right hand in the cold water. After a few minutes of adaptation, place both hands in the lukewarm water. The experience ought to be immediate and very noticeable—the same lukewarm water now seems very cool to your left hand and very warm to your right.

sensory adaptation
a condition in which there is a reduction in the level of sensation as a function of exposure to a constant stimulus

Before you go on

What are the cutaneous senses?

How can sensory adaptation be demonstrated with the sense of temperature?

THE POSITION SENSES

Another sensory capacity we often take for granted is our ability to know how our bodies are positioned in space. Although we seldom worry about it, we are always aware of how our bodies are positioned in regard to the pull of gravity. We also get sensory information about where different parts of our body are in relation to each other. We can tell if we are moving or standing still. And unless we are on a roller coaster, or racing across a field, we usually adapt to these sensory messages and pay them little attention.

Most of the information about where we are in space normally comes to us through our sense of vision. If we ever want to know just where we are, all we have to do is look around. But notice that we can make such a determination even with our eyes closed. We have two specific systems of the position sense over and above what vision can provide. One, the **vestibular** sense, tells us about balance, where we are in relation to gravity, and movement or acceleration. The other, the **kinesthetic** sense, tells us about the movement of our muscles and joints.

The receptors for the vestibular sense are located on either side of the head, near the inner ears. Five chambers are located there: three semicircular canals and two vestibular sacs. Their orientation is shown in Figure 7.6. Each of these chambers is filled with fluid. When our head moves in any direction, the fluid in the semicircular canals moves (drawn by gravity or the force of our head accelerating in space). The movement of the fluid stimulates small hair cells inside the canals, producing neural impulses. The vestibular sacs contain very small solid particles that float around in the fluid within the sacs. When these particles are forced against one side of the sacs, as happens when we move, they stimulate different hair cells that start neural impulses.

vestibular sense
the position sense that tells us about balance, where we are in relation to gravity, and movement or acceleration

kinesthetic sense
the position sense that tells us where the different parts of our bodies are and what our muscles and joints are doing

Overstimulation of the receptor cells in the vestibular sacs or semicircular canals can lead to feelings of dizziness or nausea, reasonably enough called motion sickness.

Receptors for our kinesthetic sense are located in our joints, muscles, and tendons. These receptors sense the position and movements of parts of the body—again, information to which we seldom attend. Impulses from these receptors get to our brain through pathways in our spinal cord. They provide excellent examples of reflex actions. As muscles in the front of your upper arm (your biceps) contract, the corresponding muscles in the back of your arm (triceps) must relax if you are to successfully bend your arm at the elbow. How fortunate it is that our kinesthetic receptors, operating reflexively through the spinal cord, take care of these details without our having to consciously manipulate all the appropriate muscular activity. In fact, about the only time we even realize that our kinesthetic system is functioning is when it *stops* working well, such as when our leg "falls asleep" and we stumble up (or down) stairs.

Before you go on
What are our position senses, and how do they operate?

In this topic, we have reviewed the structures and functions of a number of human senses. We have seen that hearing, like vision, is stimulated by waves, and that the physical characteristics of those waves give rise to our psychological experiences of sound. We have seen how marvelously interrelated taste and smell are, and we have discussed the many skin senses we experience. It is clear that at any one time, our brains are receiving a remarkable amount of information from all of our sensory receptors.

Our sense of pain is a very curious and troublesome one for psychologists who are interested in sensory processes. Pain, or the fear of it, can be a very strong motivator; we'll do all sorts of things to avoid it. We view our feelings of pain as being particularly private sensations—the sorts of psychological experiences that are difficult to communicate and share with others (Verillo, 1975).

But just what *is* pain? What causes the sensation of pain? What are its sensory receptors? At present, we really don't know, but we do appreciate that the very complexity of pain makes it a special sense.

Many stimuli can cause pain. Very intense stimulation of virtually any sense receptor can produce pain. Too much light, very strong pressures on the skin, extreme temperatures, and very loud sounds can all result in our experiencing pain. But the stimulus for pain need not be intense. Even a light pin prick can be very painful if it's in the right place.

Our skin seems to have many receptors for pain, but pain receptors must also be deep inside our bodies—consider stomachaches, lower back pain, and headaches. About the only common thread in pain is discomfort and unpleasantness. On that point we are all agreed.

At one time it was believed that there was one particular type of receptor (probably some form of free nerve ending) that responded uniquely to pain-producing stimuli. We now know that that theory is too simple. Free nerve endings in the skin often *do* respond whenever we sense pain, but there's got to be more to it. A theory that is still getting much attention (some of it supportive, some not) is that of Ronald Melzack and P. D. Wall (1965; Melzack, 1973). Their theory is called the *gate-control theory*. It suggests that our experience of pain is something that happens not so much at the level of the receptor (say, in the skin), but within the central nervous system. The theory proposes that pain centers in the brain are responsive to stimulation from a particular type of nerve fiber—one that "opens the gate" and allows for the sensation of pain. Further, the theory also proposes that there are other nerve fibers that can offset the activity of the pain-carrying fibers and effectively "close the gate."

There are a number of situations in which this notion of an opening and closing gate to pain seems reasonable. We know that there are many reports of people who, under certain circumstances, feel no pain, even when they should. The classic story of a football player who plays the entire second half of a game with a broken bone in his ankle comes to mind. We know that emotional excitement and the focusing of attention on other matters can alleviate the feelings of pain. If this does happen (as a number of natural childbirth methods propose), it is more likely that changes to reduce the sensation of pain have taken place within the brain rather than at the site of the receptors. Perhaps our football player, focusing his attention on the game and filled with excitement, was able to close the pain gate in his brain. Neural impulses from the damaged tissue in his ankle no doubt raced up his leg and spinal cord to his brain, but his brain did not notice them—at least during the game (Sternbach, 1978).

Also in support of the idea that pain is sensed more in the brain than at the site of some specialized receptor cell is the discovery, in the mid-1970s, of *endorphins* (Hughes et al., 1975). Endorphins are complex chemicals actually created by brain activity. They are a type of neurotransmitter (see Topic 4) that affect the passage of neural impulses from one neural cell to another. Endorphins have the ability to act as natural painkillers, or analgesics. Unlike most manufactured analgesics (such as aspirin, morphine, or codeine), natural endorphins are nonaddictive, and they are very powerful. Attempts to reproduce endorphins artificially have so far met with little success.

TOPIC SUMMARY

What are the three major physical characteristics of sound, and which psychological experiences do they produce?

Like light, sound may be thought of as a wave form of energy with three major physical characteristics: amplitude, frequency, and purity. These in turn produce the psychological experiences of loudness, pitch, and timbre. / 115

Summarize how sound wave pressures are transmitted through the different structures of the ear.

Most of the structures of the ear (the pinna, eardrum, malleus, incus, stapes, oval window, and cochlea) act to pass sound wave pressures to the fluid in the cochlea, which vibrates the basilar membrane, which in turn stimulates tiny hair cells to transmit neural impulses along the auditory nerve toward the brain. / 116

Discuss the chemical senses of taste and smell, noting the stimulus and receptor for each.

Do taste and smell each have primary qualities?

The senses of taste and smell are highly interrelated. Together they are referred to as the chemical senses because each responds to chemical molecules in solution or suspension. The receptors for smell are hair cells that line the upper regions of the nasal cavity; for taste, the receptors are cells in the taste buds located in the tongue. Taste appears to have four primary qualities (sweet, sour, bitter, and salt), but for smell, the issue of primary qualities is in doubt. / 119

What are the cutaneous senses?

How can sensory adaptation be demonstrated with the sense of temperature?

The cutaneous senses are our skin senses: touch, pressure, pain, warmth, and cold. Specific receptor cells for each identifiable skin sense have not been localized. The temperature sense readily demonstrates sensory adaptation: A hand that has been immersed in hot water, when reimmersed in lukewarm water, will sense it as cold. / 121

What are our position senses, and how do they operate?

One of our position senses is the vestibular sense, which, by responding to the movement of small particles suspended in solution within our vestibular sacs and semicircular canals, can inform us about our orientation with regard to gravity or accelerated motion. Our other position sense is kinesthesis, which, through receptors in our muscles and joints, informs us about the orientation of different parts of our body. / 122

CHAPTER FOUR

PERCEPTION AND CONSCIOUSNESS

TOPIC

8 Perception

I have never had the nerve to try this classroom demonstration—I've always thought it a little too dangerous. When I was a graduate student, however, I had the opportunity to observe it. The demonstration is something of a classic now, and it has been replicated in many forms.

I was able to find a seat in the back of the large introductory psychology class, unnoticed by the more than 600 students who had filed into the lecture hall. The instructor entered the room from a side door at the front and began his lecture on the basic principles of perception. After a few minutes, the class settled down to taking notes and listening to the professor lecture about the importance of attention in perception. The room was very quiet.

Suddenly, a screaming student burst through the large double doors at the rear of the lecture hall. I recognized this student as the professor's graduate student assistant, but no one else in the class knew who he was or what he was doing. I felt that he overacted a bit as he stomped down the center aisle of the lecture hall, yelling the foulest of obscenities at the professor, "Dr. XXXX, you failed me for the last time you *&*&@% so-and-so! You're going to pay for this you &*&#@%!" Needless to say, the class was stunned. Everyone gasped as the crazed student raced down the aisle and leaped over the lectern to grab the professor.

The student and the professor struggled briefly, and suddenly—in clear view of everyone—there was a bright silver, chrome-plated revolver! Down behind the lectern they fell. BANG!—the sound of a loud, sharp gunshot filled the room. No one moved; the students were frozen in their seats. The graduate student raced out the same side door through which the professor had entered a few minutes earlier. (Here is one dangerous part of this demonstration—ensuring the safe escape of the "assailant.") As the graduate student raced from the room, the professor lay sprawled on the floor, moaning loudly. (It was now *his* turn for some overacting.)

Still no one moved. Six hundred students sat stunned in their seats. At just the right dramatic moment, the professor slowly drew himself back up to the lectern, and in a quiet, soft voice said, "Now I want everyone to take out a pencil and some paper and write down exactly what you saw." (Here, I suspect, is the second dangerous part of the demonstration: Many of the students were quite upset and didn't appreciate having been put through such a trauma just for the sake of a classroom demonstration.)

I'm sure that I need not describe all of the results of this demonstration for you; you can guess what happened. I never did read all 600 descriptions of the events that had just taken place, but I did help summarize many of the responses. It was quite impressive. The graduate student was described as being from 5'4" to 6'3" tall and weighing between 155 and 235 pounds. Although there was some agreement, one would have a hard time coming up with a single physical description of the "suspect" in this "shooting."

The most remarkable misperception that took place had to do with the gun. As I watched the professor take his place at the front of the class before he began to lecture, I was sure that he had blown the entire demonstration. I clearly saw him remove the pistol from his suitcoat pocket and place it on top of his lecture notes. When the "crazed student" crashed into the classroom, the professor reached down, grabbed the gun and pointed it at the student as he came charging down the center aisle. In fact, the student *never* had the gun in his hand. The professor had it all along. The first move the student made was to grab the wrist of the professor to point the gun toward the floor. The professor fired the shot that startled us all. Fewer than 20 students reported seeing these events the way they actually occurred! Virtually everyone placed the gun in the hand of the crazed student. The perceptions of the students that morning in their psychology class were influenced by a number of factors over and above what actually happened. As we shall note repeatedly in this topic, seeing and believing are often two separate cognitive processes.

Perception is a complex, active, and often creative process. Perception acts on stimulation received by the senses; it involves the selection, organization, and interpretation of stimuli. Thus, perception may be thought of as a more cognitive and central process than sensation.

In this topic, we'll focus on two of the major issues involved in the psychology of perception: (1) *Selection.* We cannot process fully all the stimuli that are capable of producing a response at our receptors. Somehow we must select some stimuli while ignoring others. What determines which stimuli we pay attention to? (2) *Organization.* How do the bits and pieces of information relayed from our sense organs become organized and interpreted as meaningful events? We don't really "see" the dots of light and dark and color that our eyes respond to; we "see" horses and people and cars and *things.* We group and organize some stimulus events as belonging with others. What guides this process?

Although a number of issues of perceptual development will be covered in Chapter 8, Developmental Psychology, here we'll examine some of the evidence dealing with the extent to which perceptual processes are learned or inherited. That is, how much of our perceptual selectivity and/or organization is natural and inborn and how much is due to learning and experience?

As we go through this topic, it should become clear to you that perception, as a psychological process, is very much related to two other processes: sensation and memory. Perception is a process that makes some sense of the multitude of various stimuli that bombards us every moment of every day. By giving sensory information some meaning, perception is a process that readies information for storage in memory. In fact, perception may be thought of as bridging the gap between what our senses respond to and what we can later remember.

PERCEPTUAL SELECTIVITY: PAYING ATTENTION

Imagine that you are at a party, engaged in a dreadfully boring conversation with someone you've just met. From time to time it occurs to you that wearing your new shoes was not a good idea—your feet hurt. You're munching on an assortment of appetizers that the hosts have provided. Music is blaring from a stereo system at the other end of the room. Aromas of foods, smoke, and perfumes fill the air. There must be at least 50 people at this party, and you don't know any of them. Your senses are being bombarded by all sorts of information: sights, sounds, tastes, smells, and pains. All of your senses are being stimulated simultaneously. Suddenly, you think you hear someone nearby mention your name. You redirect your attention, now totally disregarding the person talking right in front of you. What factors determine which of many competing stimuli attract and hold our attention? In fact, there are many factors. In this section, we'll discuss some of the more important ones.

Gestalt Psychology and Figure-ground

The study of factors that affect the selection of perceptions is not a new one in psychology. This issue was one of the major concerns of a group of psychologists we now refer to as Gestalt psychologists. Originally all Germans, the founders of Gestalt psychology included Max Wertheimer (1880–1967), Kurt Koffka (1886–1941), and Wolfgang Kohler (1887–1967).

As you will recall from Topic 1, **gestalt** is a German word that is difficult to translate directly into English. It means something like "whole" or "configuration" or "totality." One forms a gestalt when one sees the overall scheme of things or can "see the forest for the trees." If you have a general idea of how something works or can appreciate the overall view of something without overattending to details, it can be said that you have formed a gestalt of the situation.

One of the basic principles of Gestalt psychology is that of the **figure-ground relationship.** Of all the stimuli in your environment at any one time, those you attend to are *figures,* the rest become the *ground.* As you focus your attention on the words on this page, they form *figures* against the *ground* (or background, if you prefer) of the rest of the page. When you hear your instructor's voice during a lecture, it is a *figure* against the *ground* of all the other sounds in the room that are entering your ear at the same time.

It was the Gestalt psychologists' belief that we can only attend to one figure at a time in any one sense or sense modality. That is, we can only hear one thing, or see one thing, or taste one thing clearly at a time. Furthermore, there are many examples of visual figure-ground patterns in which the figure and the ground can easily be reversed (usually called reversible figures). A classic example of this is presented in Figure 8.1.

In Gestalt psychology terms, the issue of perceptual selectivity is one of determining which stimuli become figures and which remain part of the ground. As we said, there are many factors that influence this selection process, and they all usually operate at once. These many factors can be divided into two general types: (1) stimulus factors and (2) personal factors. By stimulus factors we mean those *characteristics of stimuli* that make some stimuli more compelling (or attention-grabbing) than others, no matter who the perceiver is. By personal factors we mean those *characteristics of the perceiver* that influence which stimuli become figures.

Stimulus Factors

Some stimuli are more compelling than others; they are more likely to get our attention and more likely to be selected as figures for further processing and interpretation. There are some factors that determine attention regardless of *whom* the perceiver is. Because individual differences seem to matter little here, we'll call these *stimulus factors* in determining attention. Contrast and repetition are the two main stimulus factors we'll discuss here.

Contrast The most striking and overwhelming stimulus factor in perceptual selectivity is **contrast,** or the extent to which a given stimulus is in some (physical) way different from the other stimuli around it. One stimulus can contrast with other stimuli in many different ways. For example, we are more likely to attend to a stimulus if its *intensity* is different from the intensities of other stimuli. Generally speaking, the more intense a stimulus, the more likely we are to select it for further processing. Simply put, a shout is more compelling than a whisper; a bright light is more attention-grabbing than a dim one; an extreme temperature is more likely to be noticed than a moderate one.

But notice that intensity is a comparative matter. A shout may be more compelling than a whisper—*unless* everyone is shouting; then it may very well be the soft, quiet, reasoned tone that gets our attention. If we are faced with a barrage of bright lights, a dim one may, *by contrast,* be the one we process more fully.

gestalt
whole, totality, configuration, or pattern; the whole (gestalt) being perceived as more than the sum of its parts

figure-ground relationship
the Gestalt psychology principle that stimuli are selected and perceived as figures against a ground or background

Figure 8.1
A classic reversible figure-ground pattern. What do you see here? A white vase or a birdbath? Or do you see two black profiles facing each other? Can you clearly see both figures at the same time?

contrast
the extent to which a stimulus is in some physical way different from other surrounding stimuli

Contrast is an important factor in perceptual selectivity. For example, the intensity and motion of lightning stand out in vivid contrast to the usually dark, cloudy surroundings.

The same argument also holds for the stimulus dimension of physical *size*. By and large, the bigger the stimulus, the more likely we are to attend to it. There is little point in building a small billboard to advertise your motel or restaurant. You'll want to construct the biggest billboard you can afford in hopes of attracting attention to it.

But again, when we are faced with many large stimuli, one that is smaller may be the one we attend to. If you have ever seen a professional football game in person, you may have experienced this very phenomenon. When the players first take the field, all dressed in similar uniforms and in full pads, they look huge (and most of them are). Almost immediately your eyes fixate on one player who seems to stand out from the rest: the placekicker. The placekicker is generally much smaller than his teammates and seldom wears much protective padding. By *contrast,* his size makes him the object of our attention.

Another physical dimension that determines perceptual selectivity, and for which contrast is relevant, is *motion*. Motion is a powerful factor in determining visual attention. A bird in flight is much clearer to see (forms a much clearer figure) than a bird sitting in a bush. In the fall, walking through the woods, you may come close to stepping on a chipmunk before you notice it, so long as it stays still—an adaptive response of camouflage that chipmunks know well. But if that chipmunk makes a dash to escape, it becomes easily noticed scurrying across the leaves. Once again, *contrast* is important. As you enter a nightclub, your attention is immediately drawn to the dance floor by the bright lights and the moving throng dancing to the loud music. How easy it is to spot the one person, right in the middle of the dance floor, who, for whatever reason, is motionless, frozen against the ground of moving bodies, contrasting as an easily noticed figure.

Although intensity, size, and motion are three physical characteristics of stimuli that readily come to mind, there are many others. Indeed, any dimension in which two stimuli may be different (contrast) may be a dimension that determines which stimulus we attend to.

The importance of stimulus characteristics in determining attention has been nicely demonstrated in a number of experiments on selective listening tasks (Broadbent, 1958; Cherry, 1953). In these experiments, subjects wear stereo earphones that play a different message to each ear. Sometimes, subjects are required simply to follow the flow of a message in one ear while disregarding the other. In some experiments, the subjects are asked to shadow, or immediately repeat, one of the messages that is being played into one of their ears. When both messages are produced by speakers whose voice qualities are very similar, the job is a difficult one. If one speaker is female, with a high-pitched voice, and the other speaker male, with a low-pitched tone, the task of attending separately to either of the two messages is much easier. Here we have experimental verification of an everyday observation: Stimuli that are physically different (contrast) are easier to separate than are stimuli with similar physical characteristics.

Repetition   Another stimulus characteristic that often determines attention, and for which contrast is really not relevant, is repetition. The more often a stimulus is presented, the more likely it is that it will be attended to (everything else being equal, of course).

Instructors who want to get across an important point will seldom mention it just once, but rather will repeat it over and over. (Clever students recognize that there is a high correlation between the importance of a piece of information and the number of times it is mentioned in class.) Think again of your billboard. No matter how large or bright it is, and even if you have managed to build motion into it, you would be well advised to construct as

Teachers who want to get an important point across repeat it often. The more often a stimulus is presented, the more likely it is that it will be attended to and remembered.

many billboards as your budget will allow if you want to get the attention of as many people as possible. The people who write and schedule television commercials want you to attend to their messages, and repetition is obviously one of their main techniques.

To summarize, there are many ways in which stimuli may differ—brightness, size, motion, color, pitch, and loudness, for example. The greater the contrast between any one stimulus and the others around it, the greater the likelihood that that stimulus will capture or draw our attention. And, everything else being equal, the more often a stimulus is presented, the greater the likelihood that it will be perceived and that it will be selected for further consideration and processing.

Before you go on
What stimulus factors determine the selection of perceptions?

Personal Factors

Sometimes what we pay attention to is determined not so much by the physical characteristics of the stimuli present but by personal characteristics of the perceiver. For example, assume that we have two students watching a basketball game on television. Both are being presented with identical stimulation from the TV screen. One says, "Wow, did you see that rebound?" The other viewer responds, "No, I was watching the cheerleaders." The difference in perception here is hardly attributable to the nature of the stimuli since both students were watching the same TV. The difference is due to characteristics of the perceivers, which we'll call *personal factors*. Although there may be many personal factors that determine the selection of perceptions, we can categorize most of them as being a function of *motivation, expectation,* and *past experience.*

Motivation   Imagine that our two students watching the basketball game on television are supporters of different teams. One is an avid fan of Team A; the other is a staunch backer of Team B. Our TV viewers may have a small wager on the outcome of this important game. We'll say that Team A wins the hard-fought contest with a last second shot at the buzzer. Both students watched exactly the same game on TV, but which of the two is likely to have perceived the officiating of the game as honest, fair, and above reproach? Which student is likely to have seen the game as "one of the poorest refereed games ever"? The perception of the quality of the officiating may depend on who won and on the motivation of the perceiver. In large measure, the viewers saw what they *wanted* to see.

One thing that most people are interested in is themselves, whether they like to admit it or not. Hence, when we are at a party, perhaps bored with the conversations going on around us, we are often drawn to a nearby discussion if we hear our own name. Similarly, many instructors have learned the old lesson that to capture the drifting attention of a class, he or she need only say, "Now about your next exam . . . ," or, "With regard to sex . . . ." It's rather impressive to see so many heads turn at the slightest mention of these key, motivating terms.

Expectation   If it is true that we often perceive what we want to perceive, it is equally true that we often perceive what we *expect* to perceive, whether it's really there or not. When we are psychologically prepared, or set, to perceive something, when we have developed an expectation, we say that we have formed a **mental set.**

mental set
a predisposed (set) way to perceive something; an expectation

Figure 8.2

Our mental set affects our perception. How many "the"s did you see when you first glanced at this simple figure? Why?

Take just a second to quickly view the message embedded in Figure 8.2. What did the message say? (If you've seen this demonstration before, you'll have to try it with someone who hasn't.) Many people will claim that the message was "Paris in the Spring." In fact, there are two "the"s in the little message—"Paris in the the Spring." Most people familiar with the English language and with this particular phrase do not expect there to be *two* "the"s right next to each other. Following their mental set, they report seeing only one. Other people may develop a different mental set or expectation. Their line of reasoning goes something like this: "This is a psychology text so there's probably a trick here someplace, and I'm going to find it." In this particular instance, such skeptics get reinforced. There *is* a trick, and if their mental set (or expectation) was to find one, they did so.

Past Experience   Just as contrast may be said to be the most important of the stimulus factors that determine attention, so is past experience the most important of the personal factors in perceptual selectivity. One reason why past experience may be listed as the most important is that, in many ways, it includes both motivation and mental set. Much of our motivation comes from our past experience. For example, why did those two viewers of the basketball game root for Team A or for Team B in the first place? Their allegiance was certainly not inborn, but was rather a reflection of their past experience. Similarly, our expectations develop largely from past experiences. We are likely to expect to perceive, or be set to perceive, what we have perceived in the past in similar circumstances.

But past experience means more than the development of motivation and expectation. Perhaps two personal examples will make clear what I mean here.

I once took a course in comparative psychology that examined the behaviors of a number of nonhuman organisms. One of the coteachers of the course was an ornithologist (a scientist who studies birds). Part of the course requirement involved participating in two early morning outings to go bird-watching. The memory is very vivid to this day: Cold, tired, clutching my thermos of warm coffee, I slopped through the marshland looking for birds as the sun was just rising. After only 20 minutes of this unpleasantness, our instructor had identified 10 or 11 different birds. I wasn't quite certain, but I thought I had spied one duck. I wasn't at all sure just what sort of duck it was, but I did think that I had seen a duck. Now the differences in perception between my instructor and I that cold, wet morning could be explained in terms of motivation (he *did* care much more than I), but mostly, I suspect, his ability to spot birds so quickly and surely reflected his past experience at the task—he knew where to look and what to look for.

One other experience having to do with the selection of perceptions impressed me greatly. I had the opportunity to ride along with a city police officer during a normal working day. Many aspects of the experience impressed me, not the least of which was the extent to which that officer was seeing a totally different city from the one I was seeing. Because of his experience (and his motivation and mental set), he was able to select and respond to stimulus cues that I didn't even notice. For example, he spotted a car that was parked in an alley. I didn't even notice a car there, but he saw it immediately and recognized it as one that had been reported as stolen.

Our selection of stimuli from our environment is influenced by a number of factors. Some stimuli are compelling for all of us because they contrast with others or because they are frequently repeated. It is also the case that the determination of which stimuli become figures and which remain ground is made by the perceiver, whose motivation, mental set, and past experience may influence perceptual selectivity. Figure 8.3 summarizes the factors we have discussed.

Figure 8.3

Factors that can affect perceptual selectivity.

Stimulus Factors	Personal Factors
Contrast	Past experience
intensity	Expectation
size	Motivation
motion	
Repetition	

PERCEPTUAL ORGANIZATION: WHAT GOES WITH WHAT

One of the first things we do in response to our environments is to *select* certain stimuli from among all those that strike our receptors for further processing. Another perceptual process involves organizing the bits and pieces of sensory experience into useful, meaningful, integrated, organized wholes, or gestalts. Somehow we are able to organize the individual sounds of speech into words and phrases and sentences. Our visual experience is not one of tiny bits of color and light and dark, but of identifiable objects and events. We don't perceive a warm pat on the back as responses from thousands of individual receptors in our skin. As was the case for selection, there are many factors that influence how we organize and interpret our perceptual worlds, and again there is logic in considering stimulus and personal factors separately.

Stimulus Factors

By stimulus factors, we are referring to characteristics of stimuli that promote our perception of them as being organized together in one figure or gestalt. Not surprisingly, it was the Gestalt psychologists who first investigated this issue and who first listed such factors. We'll consider four of the most influential: proximity, similarity, continuity, and closure.

Proximity Glance quickly at Figure 8.4(A). Without giving it much thought, what did you see there? A bunch of Xs yes, but more than that, there were two separately identifiable groups of Xs, weren't there? The group of eight Xs on the left seems somehow separate from the group on the right. This illustration demonstrates what the Gestalt psychologists called **proximity,** or *contiguity.* What this means is that events that occur close together in space, or in time, are generally perceived as belonging together as part of the same figure or gestalt. In Figure 8.4(A) it's rather difficult to see the Xs as falling into four rows or four columns. They just belong together as two groups of eight Xs each.

   Proximity operates on more than just visual stimuli. For example, sounds that are bunched together (are *contiguous,* to use the technical term) in speech are perceived as going together to form words or phrases. Thunder and lightning are contiguous because they occur together in time. If two events consistently occur together, one always *following* the other, we often come to perceive contiguity as causality. What this means is that if B consistently follows right after A, we may come to perceive A as the cause of B. Many people believe that lightning causes thunder because it is always perceived just before the (slower moving) sound of the thunder. In fact, the two occur together, neither causing the other.

Similarity Now glance at Figure 8.4(B) and describe what you see there. We have a collection of Xs and Os that are clearly organized in a pattern. The usual way to organize these stimuli is to see them as two separate columns of Xs and two of Os. Seeing rows of alternating Xs and Os is very difficult. This figure demonstrates the Gestalt principle of **similarity.** Stimulus events that have properties in common, or are in some way alike, are grouped together in our perception—a "birds of a feather are perceived together" sort of thing. Perceived similarity and grouping is often the easy basis for the formation of

Figure 8.4(A)
These Xs are organized as two groups, not four rows or columns, because of proximity.

Figure 8.4(B)
Here we see two columns of Os and two of Xs because of similarity.

XOXO
XOXO
XOXO
XOXO

proximity
a Gestalt principle of organization in which stimuli are perceived as belonging together if they occur close together in space or time

similarity
in Gestalt psychology, the principle that stimuli are perceived together if they share common characteristic(s)

stereotypes: "Oh, he's one of *those*." Here the principle works in reverse. If someone is perceived as being a member of a given group, it is assumed (often incorrectly) that he or she will have characteristics in common with (similar to) others in the group.

Continuity   The Gestalt principle of **continuity,** or *good continuation* (so as not to confuse it with contiguity), suggests that we tend to see things as ending up the way they started off. Figure 8.4(C) illustrates this point with a simple line drawing. The clearest way to organize this drawing is as two separate but intersecting lines: one straight, the other curved. It's hard to imagine seeing this figure any other way. Very often our perceptions are guided by a logic that says, "Lines (for example) that start out straight, should continue as straight."

The related concept of *common fate* deals with stimuli in motion. When stimulus objects are viewed as moving in the same direction at the same speed, they are seen as belonging together. Remember that chipmunk sitting motionless on the leaves in the woods? So long as both the chipmunk and the leaves stay still, the chipmunk won't be noticed. Its coloration fits in and is organized with the ground. But when it moves, the moving parts of the chipmunk are organized together and we can see it scurrying away.

Closure   One commonly applied Gestalt principle of organization is **closure.** This is our tendency to fill in gaps in our perceptual world. This concept is illustrated by Figure 8.4(D). At a glance, anyone would tell you that this figure is the letter R, but of course it is not. That's not the way you make an R. However, it may be the way we *see* an R due to closure.

Closure occurs commonly during our everyday conversations. Just for fun some day, tape record a casual conversation with a friend. Then write down *exactly what was said* during the conversation. A true and faithful transcription will reveal that many words and sounds were left out. Even though they were not actually there as stimuli, they were not missed by the listener because he or she filled in the gaps (closure) and understood what was being said.

Personal Factors

We can cover the personal factors determining perceptual organization rather quickly because they are the same as those that affect selection: motivation, expectation, and past experience. We perceive things as belonging together because we want to, because we expect to, and/or because we have perceived them together in the past.

Think back to our opening description of the classroom demonstration with the "crazed student," the professor, and the gun. Virtually no one in that class organized the relevant stimuli in that situation the way they actually occurred. Most people thought the student, not the professor, had the pistol. No one was *mentally set* for or expected the professor to have a gun in class. Certainly no one *wanted* to see their professor with a gun. And, hopefully, no one had ever *experienced* a professor bringing a gun to class. (Seeing crazed students with guns is not a common experience either, but with television and movies, it's certainly a more probable one.) Notice that stimulus *selection* was not the problem here. Everyone saw the gun. Students' reports of their perceptions differed from reality in terms of how they *organized* the gun in the classroom scene.

Recognizing that expectations develop largely through past experience, we find that one very important factor in how we organize our perceptions of

continuity
the Gestalt principle that a line or movement is perceived as continuing in the same smooth direction as first established

closure
a Gestalt principle of organization concerning the tendency to perceive incomplete figures as whole and complete

Figure 8.4(C)
We tend to see this figure as two intersecting lines, one straight, one curved, because of continuity.

Figure 8.4(D)
This figure is perceived as the letter R—which it is not— because of closure.

stimuli is the *context* in which we perceive them. We are seldom asked to make perceptual judgments in a vacuum. Figures are usually presented in a given ground, or context. Context often affects what we expect to perceive or think we have perceived. We might be startled when we turn on our car radio and hear what sounds like a loud, piercing scream. In a moment—given a context—we realize that we have just tuned in to a fine arts station and have heard two notes from a soprano's rendition of an operatic aria, not a scream after all.

Figure 8.5 provides two examples of the affect of context on visual perception. In Figure 8.5(A), is the highlighted stimulus the letter H or the letter A? In fact, by itself, it doesn't seem to be a very good example of either! But in the proper context—and given our past experience with the English language—that same stimulus may appear to be an A *or* an H.

Figure 8.5(B) presents Boring's (1930) classic *ambiguous figure*. After you study this drawing for a while you may be able to see why it is called ambiguous. Looked at one way, it depicts a demure young lady, dressed in Victorian era clothing, a large feather in her hat, looking away from the viewer. Looked at another way, the same picture shows an old woman, chin tucked down into her collar, hair down to her eyes, with a rather large mole on her nose. If I had shown you a series of pictures of young men and women dressed in Victorian costume, as if they were at a grand ball, and *then* presented Figure 8.5(B), you almost certainly would have seen the young lady. In the context of a series of pictures of old, poorly dressed men and women, you might have organized the very same line drawing to depict the old woman.

How we organize the world we perceive depends on a number of factors. How we perceive the stimuli of our environments is influenced by the proximity and similarity of the stimulus events, our interpretations of closure and continuity, and our personal motivations, expectations, and past experiences.

Figure 8.5(A)

Is the highlighted letter an A or an H? In fact, it is neither and can be interpreted as one or the other only on the basis of context and our past experience with the English language.

THE CAT SAT
BY THE DOOR.

Figure 8.5(B)

This perceptually ambiguous drawing can be interpreted in different ways depending on the context in which it is viewed. Do you see a young, Victorian woman or an old woman.
(After Boring, 1930.)

Before you go on

List stimulus and personal factors that determine how we organize stimuli in perception.

THREE PERCEPTUAL PROCESSES

We have noted that perception is a more complex, cognitive process than the simple reception of information that we call sensation. Perception requires that we select and organize stimulus information. Perception also involves identification, recognition, and the assignment of meaning to stimulus events. In this last section, we'll examine three separate perceptual processes that we often come to take for granted: the perception of depth and distance, the perception of motion (both real and apparent), and perceptual constancies (perceptual givens that help us make sense of the world around us).

The Perception of Distance and Depth

One of the ways in which we organize visual stimuli is to interpret not only *what* it is that we are seeing, but *where* it happens to be. We perceive the world in which we live for what it is—three-dimensional. So long as we are paying attention (a required perceptual process), we don't run into buildings or fall off cliffs. We know (with considerable accuracy) just how far we are from objects in our environment. What is remarkable (and strange) about

Figure 8.6

When looking at one object, the right eye sees a different image than the left eye due to retinal disparity. This disparity gives us a cue that the object we are viewing is three-dimensional.

What the right eye sees   What the left eye sees

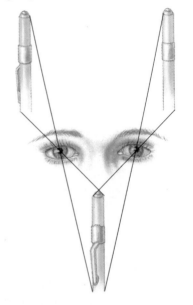

retinal disparity
the phenomenon in which each retina receives a different (disparate) view of the same three-dimensional object

convergence
the tendency of the eyes to move toward each other as we focus on objects up close

this ability is that the light reflected from objects and events in our environment falls on *two*-dimensional retinas. That there is depth and distance in our world is not something we *sense*; it is something we *perceive*.

The ability to accurately judge depth and distance is an adaptive skill that plays an important role in determining many of our actions. Our ability to make such judgments reflects the fact that we are simultaneously responding to a large number of clues or cues to depth and distance. Some of these cues are built into our visual systems and are referred to as *ocular cues*, while others are *physical cues* we receive from the environment itself. Let's examine both.

Ocular Cues   Some of the cues we get about depth and distance reflect the way our eyes work. Cues that involve both eyes are called binocular cues (*bi* means two); those cues that only require one eye are called monocular cues (*mono* means one).

One binocular cue for three-dimensionality comes from the fact that our eyes are separated. When we look at a nearby three-dimensional object, each eye gets a somewhat different view of it. Hold a pen with a clip on it a few feet in front of your eyes. Rotate the pen until the clip can be viewed by the right eye, but not the left. (You check that out by closing first one eye then the other as you rotate the pen.) Now each eye (retina) is getting a different (disparate) view of the same object. This phenomenon is called **retinal disparity.** It is a powerful cue that what we are looking at must be solid or three-dimensional. Otherwise, each eye would see the same identical image, not two disparate ones. See Figure 8.6.

Another binocular cue to depth and distance is called **convergence.** Convergence is the name we give to the action of our eyes turning inward, toward each other when we view something up close. Convergence also reflects the fact that we "know" how our eyes are aligned in our heads, even if we seldom pay it much attention. As we gaze off into the distance, our two eyes aim out in almost parallel fashion. As we focus our view on objects that are close to us, the two eyes come together, or converge. As our eyes move in toward each other, we interpret that convergence as indicating that what we are looking at is close to us. See Figure 8.7.

Figure 8.7

Our eyes turn inward (converge) when we look at things up close. Convergence helps us interpret our distance from the object we are viewing.

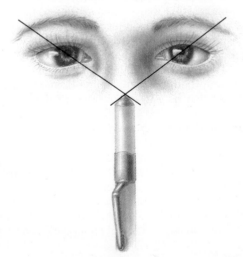

The rest of the cues we'll consider are monocular cues. Even the physical cues listed below are monocular because they can be appreciated by persons who can see with but one eye. A unique monocular cue to distance—at least short distances—is **accommodation.** This process, you'll remember, is the changing of the shape of the lens, by the ciliary muscles, to focus images on the retina of the eye. When we focus on distant objects, accommodation flattens our lens, and when we focus on nearby objects, our lens gets rounder or fatter, thanks to the action of the ciliary muscles. Although this process is reflexive and occurs automatically, our brain can and does react to the activity of our ciliary muscles in terms of the distance of an object from our eyes. That is, our brain "knows" what our ciliary muscles are doing to focus an image and interprets these actions in terms of distance. Accommodation probably does not function as an effective cue for distances beyond arm's length because the changes in the activity of the ciliary muscles in such cases are too slight to be noticed. But it is within arm's length that accurate decisions about distance are most critical.

accommodation
the process in which the shape of the lens is changed to focus an image on the retina

Physical Cues   The physical cues to distance and depth are those we get from the structure of our environment. These cues are sometimes called *pictorial cues* because they are the ones used by artists to create the impression of three-dimensionality on a two-dimensional canvas or paper. There are many pictorial cues. We'll list just six of the most important.

1. *Linear perspective* (See Figure 8.8.) As you stand on a railroad track, looking off into the distance, the rails—which you know are parallel—seem to come together in the distance. Using this pictorial cue in drawing obviously takes some time and experience to develop. Have you ever seen a child's drawing of his or her house that looked something like Figure 8.9? There are the roof, the chimney (always with smoke, of course), the windows, the front door, and the front sidewalk. Because the child *knows* that the sidewalk is as wide at the street as it is by the door, it is drawn as two parallel lines. The result looks like a house on a stick. Later the child will come to appreciate the usefulness of linear perspective and will make the sidewalk appear wider in the foreground at the street.

Figure 8.8
Though we know these railroad tracks run parallel, they appear to converge because of linear perspective, another clue to distance.

Figure 8.9
A house on a stick: the failure of linear perspective in a child's drawing.

Figure 8.10
Interposition of objects gives us information about the relative distance of various objects. Objects closer to us will cover or partially block more distant objects.

Figure 8.11
With no other cues, it is difficult to tell which object is closer. We interpret relative size to tell us that the larger object is closer to us.

2. *Interposition.* (See Figure 8.10.) This cue to distance reflects our appreciation that objects in the foreground tend to cover, or partially hide from view, objects in the background, and not vice versa. It seems like a silly thing to contemplate, but one of the reasons that I know that people sitting in the back of a classroom are farther away from me than people sitting in the front row is the information that I get from interposition. People in the front partially cover up people sitting behind them.

3. *Relative size.* (See Figure 8.11.) This is a commonly used clue to distance. As it happens, very few objects or events in this world change their size with any regularity. Lots of things get nearer or farther away from us. So, everything else being equal, we tend to judge the object that produces the larger retinal image as being closer to us. Bend down behind a friend's car. Open one eye and all you can see is license plate. Your entire visual field is filled with license plate. Slowly your friend drives away. In a second you can see the car's bumper, then the trunk, then the entire back of the car. As the car continues to drive away from you, the image it casts on your retina gets smaller and smaller and eventually disappears. Now you know that cars do not shrink or disappear, and you interpret the reduction in retinal size as a cue to distance—as retinal size gets smaller, the object is moving away.

4. *Texture gradient.* (See Figure 8.12.) Stand on a gravel road. As you look down at your feet you can clearly make out the details of the texture of the roadway. You can see individual pieces of gravel. But as you look down the gravel road, the texture gradually changes, details giving way to the smooth blending of the details into a textureless surface. We interpret this gradual change (which is what *gradient* means) in texture as indicating a gradual change in distance.

5. *Patterns of shading.* (See Figure 8.13.) Drawings that do not use patterns of shading and light appear flat and two-dimensional. Children eventually learn that if they want their pictures to look lifelike, they must shade in tree trunks and apples and show trees and houses as casting shadows. Two-dimensional objects do not cast shadows, and how objects create patterns of light and shade can tell us a great deal about their shape and solidity.

6. *Motion parallax.* (See Figure 8.14.) This rather technical sounding label names something with which we are all familiar. The clearest example may occur when we are a passenger in a car, looking out a side window. Even if the car is going at a modest rate of speed, the nearby utility poles and fence posts seem to race by. Objects slightly farther away from the car seem to be moving more slowly, and mountains or trees way off in the distance seem not to be moving at all. This apparent difference is known as motion parallax.

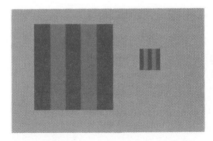

Figure 8.12
Changes in texture gradient are clues to distance. Objects or surfaces close to us will have a more detailed texture than those farther away.

Figure 8.13
Shading indicates to us that the objects we are looking at are three-dimensional. Patterns of light and shade give us information about the size, shape, and solidity of objects.

Thus, there are many cues that let us know how near or far we are from objects in our environment and that many objects in that environment are solid and three-dimensional. Some of these cues depend on the workings of our visual system while others depend on our appreciation of cues from the physical layout of objects in the world around us. Because we constantly get information from all of these factors at the same time, our judgments of distance and depth tend to be very accurate.

Before you go on

Name nine cues that provide us with information about depth and/or distance.

The Perception of Motion

How do we perceive motion? As an object moves across our field of view, say from right to left, how do we *know* that the object is moving? At first you may feel like ignoring what appears to be such a simple question. If you think about it for a while, however, you'll come to realize that our perception of motion is a complex process of perceptual organization. So long as our heads, our bodies, and our eyes are still, the answer to our question *is* fairly simple. Light reflected from the moving object produces an image on the retina that successively stimulates adjoining rods and cones and produces the perception of motion.

In reality, our heads and bodies are seldom perfectly still. For example, as our eyes scan a room, images of the objects in the room stimulate successive rods and cones on the retina. But we don't see everything in the room as moving. Somehow our brain compensates for eye and head and body movements. In fact, if we focus our attention on a flying moth (as an example), keeping its image at about the same place on our retina as it darts and dashes about the room, everything else in the room stimulates a series of different retinal areas. But because we *know* that we are moving our head and our eyes to focus on the moth, we perceive the moth as moving and the room as stationary. Of course it is also true that if we keep our head relatively still, and move our eyes to focus on that moth, we know that our eyes are moving to do so.

Our judgments of motion are influenced by details we seldom think about. Everything else being equal, we will tend to see small objects as moving faster than larger ones even if their actual speeds are the same. Objects that are seen moving against a plain, empty background are seen as moving more slowly than when they move against a patterned, complex background (Gregory, 1977). We have already discussed how factors such as motivation and past experience affect the organization of our perceptions. They may also affect our perception of motion. First we see a sleek sports car, driven by a teenager, traveling down the street. It is followed soon after by an old "clunker," driven by a "little old lady." Even though both cars are, in fact, traveling at the same rate of speed, we're more likely to perceive the first car as going faster.

Psychologically more interesting than our perception of real motion is our perception of motion when in fact there isn't any. When our (psychological) perceptions are at odds with (physical) reality, we say that we are experiencing an illusion. There are two main types of illusion of motion: the phi phenomenon and the autokinetic effect.

The **phi phenomenon** can be illustrated with just two lights. If two equally bright lights of the same color flash on and off alternately, it is very easy to

Figure 8.14
Motion parallax explains why objects close to us appear to pass more quickly than distant objects.

phi phenomenon
the visual illusion that explains the apparent motion of stationary lights flashing on and off in sequence

see them as one light moving back and forth. Look at Figure 8.15(A). Imagine that each small circle represents a stationary light bulb. One at a time, each light flashes on for a fraction of a second. The lights come on in order—Light 1, then 2, then 3, and so on. It is almost certain that an observer will see here a single light traveling in a circular path. This phi phenomenon illusion explains our perception of the movement of lights in theater marquees or in large signs (see Figure 8.15(B)). The arrow looks like it is moving through space, even though we know that it is securely fastened to the wall.

Our second illusion of motion is a very powerful one. The **autokinetic effect** is the apparent movement of a pinpoint source of light in an otherwise darkened environment. You might want to construct the apparatus for demonstrating this illusion yourself. To do so, you will first need to locate a rather large room that you can get completely dark. Now get a good flashlight and cover the lens with black paper or cloth so that no light escapes. Poke a very small hole in the paper or cloth covering so that only a small pinpoint of light can be seen. Secure the flashlight at one end of the room, with the hole pointed out toward the center of the room. Turn off all the lights except for your flashlight. Within seconds a strange thing happens: The stationary point of light starts to move and float around. Even though you know very well that the light is stationary, it will appear to move.

As it happens, we don't yet have a complete explanation for this phenomenon. The most commonly accepted view (for example, Pola & Matin, 1977) is that the apparent movement is produced by small head and body movements. As you try to focus on the light, your eyes, your head, and even your body move, causing the pinpoint of light to cast an image that moves across your retina. Because the image moves across your retina, your brain "sees" the light as moving. Even the slightest background light in the room destroys the illusion.

Figure 8.15(A)
The rapid consecutive flashing of these stationary lights will appear to be a single light traveling in a circle due to the phi phenomenon.

Figure 8.15(B)
Though these lights are stationary, the rapid consecutive lighting of them creates an illusion of motion.

The autokinetic illusion can sometimes be a problem for pilots or ships' captains who must navigate at night with only a single distance beacon or light source as a guide. With no other frame of reference but that one light source, the light will appear to move, making it difficult to determine exactly where it is. For the same reason, military pilots sometimes have difficulty maintaining flight formations at night if the only way they can tell where they are in the formation is to make judgments based on small lights on the wingtips of adjacent aircraft.

Before you go on

What are two illusions of motion?

How are they produced?

The Constancy of Perceptions

Another perceptual process that we usually take for granted is called *constancy*. Perceptual constancies help us organize and interpret the stimulus input we get from our senses. It is because of constancy that we can recognize a familiar object as being the same regardless of how far away it is, the angle from which we view it, or the color or intensity of the light that is reflected from it. You can recognize your textbook whether you view it from a distance or close up, straight on or from an angle, in a dimly or brightly lighted room, or whether the light in the room is blue, or red, or white—it will still be your textbook, and you will perceive it as such regardless of how your senses detect it. If it weren't for perceptual constancies, each individual sensation would be viewed as a new experience and little would appear familiar.

Size Constancy   We have already mentioned the role of **size constancy** in helping us determine how far away we are from an object. A friend standing close to us may fill our visual field. At a distance, the image of the same person may take up only a fraction of our visual field. We know very well, however, that our friend hasn't shrunk but has simply moved farther away.

Our tendency to view objects as remaining the same size depends on a number of factors, including the quality of the depth perception cues that are available and our familiarity with the stimulus object. To demonstrate the importance of depth cues, we can construct an environment in which they are virtually absent. Such an environment is created in a **ganzfeld**. Although there are many versions of ganzfelds, one of the most striking is a large, smooth, hollow sphere that is lighted indirectly. When you look inside the sphere there are no visual cues to tell you about up and down or front and back (see Figure 8.16). In this context, a balloon may be inflated in full view of a subject who will claim, because of size constancy, that she or he is watching a colored circle move closer and closer. As the air is released from the balloon, the subject will report that the circle is moving farther away. Once the stimulus is recognized as a balloon (a stimulus that *does* change its size), size constancy no longer dominates, and the subject's report of what is happening becomes accurate. In a ganzfeld, then, we are forced to perceive directly what our senses detect, without the added cues from the environment (or *surround*) that we usually use to interpret the world around us.

Shape Constancy   **Shape constancy** refers to our perception of objects as maintaining their shape even though the retinal image they cast may change. Shape constancy may be simply demonstrated with any familiar object, say the nearest door in your field of view. As you look at that door from

size constancy
the tendency to see objects as being of constant size regardless of the size of the retinal image

ganzfeld
an artificial environment in which physical cues to depth and distance have been removed

shape constancy
the tendency to see objects as being of constant shape regardless of the shape of the retinal image

Figure 8.16
Viewing a partially inflated balloon inside a ganzfeld.

different angles, the shape of the image of the door on your retina changes radically. Straight on it appears to be a rectangle; partially open, the image is that of a trapezoid; from the edge, fully open, the retinal image is of a straight line. But, regardless of the retinal image, because of shape constancy, you still see that object as a door. See Figure 8.17.

Brightness and Color Constancy   Our perception of brightness depends on the intensity of the light waves that reflect from objects in our environment. Due to **brightness constancy,** however, the relative brightness of familiar objects is perceived as the same regardless of the actual amount of light in which it is viewed. The white shirt that you put on this morning may be *sensed* as gray when you pass through a shadow, or as black when night falls, but it is still *perceived* as a white shirt—as bright as it was this morning.

brightness constancy
the tendency to see objects as being of the same brightness regardless of the intensity of light reflected from them

The same is true for color perception. If you know that you put on a white shirt this morning, you will still perceive it as white even if I illuminate it with a red light. Now most of the light waves reflected by the shirt into your eyes may be associated with the experience of red (about 700nm, remember), but you will still know the shirt is white. Someone else (who doesn't know any better) may perceive the shirt as red, but you'll perceive it as white because of color constancy.

Before you go on
Name and give an example of four types of perceptual constancy.

Perception is a complex cognitive process that involves the selection and organization of stimuli received by our senses. Many factors help determine which of the stimuli we sense become figures, or are attended to. Some factors involve characteristics of the stimuli themselves; others involve characteristics of the perceiver. The organization of the bits and pieces of sensory experience into meaningful integrated gestalts is also influenced by stimulus and personal factors. Perception is a psychological process we often take for granted, but without it there would be no way we could interpret or give meaning to the world around us.

Figure 8.17
Though we see four different images, we know we are looking at a door because of shape constancy.

One of the central questions of psychology deals with the extent to which human abilities and capacities are innate and due to one's *nature,* or learned and thus due to one's *nurture.* In this topic, we have reviewed a number of perceptual processes that seem quite basic and very important—selecting figures from grounds, organizing stimuli into coherent gestalts, perceiving the world as three-dimensional, perceiving motion, both real and apparent, and so on. Throughout the history of psychology, researchers have wondered where these perceptual skills come from. Indeed, debates over the role of experience versus inheritance in such matters predates scientific psychology by hundreds of years. Is perception an inherited ability or an acquired skill?

The Gestalt psychologists, who pioneered much of the experimental work on perception, were largely "nativists" in their approach to perception. That is, they believed that many of our most basic perceptual skills are inherited. In answer to questions like, "Why do we see the world in three dimensions?" or "Why do we tend to perceive unified figures against a diffuse background?" the Gestalt psychologist would answer, "Because you were born that way." The processes of selection, organization, and distance and motion perception were seen as innate predispositions that simply come with being human. Learning and/or experience were not viewed as necessary.

Opposed to the nativists are the "empiricists," who argue that one's learning and experience with one's environment dictate the manner in which perceptual abilities develop. Let's review two types of research investigations that bear directly on the question of nature versus nurture for perceptual processes.

What if we could find someone who was born blind and as an adult had his or her sight restored? We could then find out immediately what he or she could and could not perceive. What he or she could see, and how he or she saw it, would have to reflect innate abilities, because having been blind, there would have been no visual experience from which to learn. When the philosopher John Locke raised this possibility in the late seventeenth century, it was as a hypothetical case. Now, of course, we know that sight can be and has been restored to many individuals who had been blind since birth—most commonly through the removal of cataracts. A number of such patients have been studied in great detail (Gregory, 1977; Senden, 1960).

Unfortunately, the results of these studies are inconclusive at best. Virtually all subjects were able to make simple judgments about figure-ground relationships; that is, they could detect objects or drawings as figures against backgrounds. In some cases, the figures—even simple ones like triangles—could not be correctly identified through vision alone. In other cases, visual perception appeared to be very much intact and only slightly limited. Some patients had great difficulty adjusting to the new capacity to see and never fully recovered from the surgery that restored their sight (Gregory, 1977). Others reacted very positively.

The basic problem in this sort of research has to do with the extent of the experience adults have had compensating with other, nonvisual senses. The inabilities of some persons with newly restored sight may have more to do with their recovery from the operation itself than with the lack of any innate capacity.

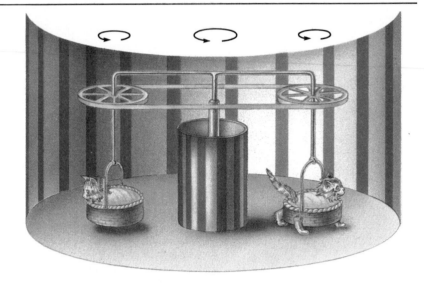

Another way of attacking the nature-nurture issue with regard to perception is to raise animals in environments where visual experience is severely limited or controlled. In one such study (Riesen, 1965), kittens were raised from birth wearing translucent goggles that let in some light but blurred all visual details. When the goggles were removed (at age three months), the kittens seemed able to make some simple visual discriminations, but were unable to detect distance, couldn't discriminate on the basis of stimulus shapes or sizes, and couldn't follow (or *track*) a moving object.

Held and Hein (1963) raised kittens in total darkness until they were a few months old. They were then allowed a few hours a day in a visual environment filled with vertical lines (see Figure 8.18). One kitten could walk around in the environment while a second one got a free ride in a small basket device. Still, both kittens experienced the same type of visual stimulation. When their visual capacities were tested, the kitten that had passively ridden around in the environment showed many deficits of vision. Most notably, it lacked normal depth perception, being unable to detect differences between near and far. The kitten that had walked around had virtually normal visual abilities. This research suggests that even though there may be some innate predispositions to view the world in certain ways, an *active* interaction with the environment is necessary for these abilities to develop.

It seems then that in the case of perception, our question of nature versus nurture remains without a definitive answer. It seems most reasonable to propose that, as is so often the case, both sides of the issue have some credibility. There may be some innate, inherited predispositions to organize the perceptual world, at very least into figures and ground. How and when perceptual *capacities* become perceptual *abilities* may depend on the extent and nature of early perceptual experience.

TOPIC SUMMARY

What stimulus factors determine the selection of perceptions?

From all of the information that stimulates our receptors, some is selected for further processing, or paid attention to. One of the factors that affects attention is the characteristics of the available stimuli. We are more likely to attend to a stimulus if it *contrasts* with others around it (contrast may be in terms of intensity, size, motion, or other physical characteristics). *Repetition* of a stimulus also increases the likelihood that we will attend to it. / 131

What personal factors are involved in perceptual selectivity?

The selection of stimuli is partly based on characteristics of the perceiver, such as motivation, expectation (or mental set), and past experience. / 133

List stimulus and personal factors that determine how we organize stimuli in perception.

The perceptual organization of stimuli depends on stimulus characteristics such as proximity, similarity, continuity, and closure. The personal factors that affect perceptual organization include motivation, expectation, and past experience. / 135

Name nine cues that provide us with information about depth and/or distance.

We are able to perceive three-dimensionality and distance because of the many cues with which we are provided. Some have to do with the visual system itself, such as retinal disparity, convergence, and accommodation. Other cues come from the environment, including the physical cues of linear perspective, interposition, relative size, texture gradient, patterns of light and shade, and motion parallax. / 139

What are two illusions of motion? How are they produced?

The perception of motion when there is none provides an example of an illusion. The phi phenomenon is demonstrated by lights flashing on and off in sequence giving the appearance of one light in motion. The autokinetic effect occurs when a stationary point of light is perceived as moving in an otherwise darkened environment. / 141

Name and give an example of four types of perceptual constancy.

Perceptual constancies bring stability to our perceptual world. With size constancy we perceive objects as remaining the same size even when the size of their retinal images changes. Similarly, shape constancy is the stability of our perception of an object's shape regardless of the shape of its retinal image. With brightness and color constancy, we are able to perceive an object's true color or brightness regardless of the intensity or wavelength of light that is reflected from it. / 142

At the 1980 annual meeting of the American Psychological Association, Professor Wilse B. Webb addressed a group of psychology teachers on the subject of consciousness. As a researcher in the field of sleep and dreaming, and with his interest in the history of psychology, Webb was an obvious choice to make such a presentation. When faced with having to define "consciousness," Webb said that the "expert on the matter is William James," and recommended "a reading of him" (Webb, 1981, p. 134). Let's follow Webb's advice.

In 1892, James had this to say about the reality of consciousness:

The first and foremost concrete fact which everyone will affirm—is the fact that consciousness of some sort goes on. "States of mind" succeed each other. If we could say in English "it thinks" as we say "it rains" or "it blows" we would be stating the fact most simply and with the minimum of assumptions. As we cannot, we must simply say that thought goes on (James, 1892, p. 152).

So, for James, consciousness is an obvious process—the process that involves thought and thinking. According to James (1890, 1904), there are four basic "realities" concerning consciousness. We are well advised to keep these following four notions in mind (in our own consciousness) as we read through this topic.

1. Consciousness is always *changing*. "No state once gone can recur and be identical with what was before," James wrote (1892, p. 152). It is from William James that we get the expression "stream of consciousness."

Consciousness, then, does not appear to itself chopped up in bits. Such words as "chain" or "train" do not describe it fitly as it presents itself in the first instance. It is nothing jointed; it flows. A "river" or "stream" is the metaphor by which it is most naturally described. In talking of it hereafter, let us call it the stream of thought, of consciousness . . . (James, 1890, p. 243).

2. Consciousness is a *personal* experience. Every thought is "owned" by some individual. Consciousness does not exist without a conscious individual. My consciousness and yours are different and separate.

3. Consciousness is *continuous*. Again, the stream metaphor works nicely. Thought goes on; it cannot be broken down into segments. There are no gaps in consciousness. There are differences in the flow of the stream of consciousness perhaps, but no real breaks. After gaps of sleep, we pick up and move on as if nothing truly affected the continuous flow of our mind's activity.

Like a bird's life, it [consciousness] seems to be made of an alteration of flights and perchings. The rhythm of language expresses this, where every thought is expressed in a sentence, and every sentence closed by a period (James, 1890, p. 158).

4. Consciousness is *selective*. Awareness is often a matter of making choices, of selectively *attending* to or focusing on some aspects of consciousness while ignoring others. In a way, then, consciousness and perception are related; we cannot perceive or be conscious of everything around us at any one time.

Now the study of the phenomena of consciousness . . . will show us that consciousness is at all times primarily a selecting agency. Whether we take it in the lowest sphere of sense, or in the highest of intellection, we find it always doing one thing, choosing one out of several of the materials so presented to its notice, emphasizing and accentuating that and suppressing as far as possible all the rest. The item emphasized is always in close connection with some interest felt by consciousness to be paramount at the time (James, 1890, p. 139).

Consciousness is such an integral part of our lives that we might argue that to be alive is to be conscious. As helpful as Webb's recommendation "to refer to the charm and wit of the master, William James" (1981, p. 142) may be, we will want to try to get a more complete sense of what psychologists mean by "consciousness."

As James first told us 100 years ago, consciousness is personal, always changing, continuous, and selective. It may also be true that our best chance of understanding consciousness will come from an examination of those situations in which the normal stream of consciousness is altered.

We will find two things helpful. First, let us consider some matters of definition. Is consciousness one unified process, or may we view consciousness as a process that occurs at different levels or to different degrees? Second, understanding "normal" consciousness may be easier if we look at "altered" states of consciousness. Hence, we'll examine four states in which our consciousness or awareness is altered: sleep, hypnosis, meditation, and under the influence of drugs.

Before you go on

According to William James, what are the four basic characteristics of consciousness?

LEVELS OF CONSCIOUSNESS

consciousness
our awareness, or perception, of the environment and of our own mental processes

Let us define **consciousness** as our awareness, or perception, of the environment and of our own mental processes. Consciousness then is a state of mind; it is a state of paying attention, a state of awareness, and a state of perception.

It is often helpful to think about consciousness as occurring at different levels. The differences here are not so much in *kind* as in *degree*. That is, the level, or extent, of our consciousness may vary widely throughout the course of a normal day (Hilgard, 1977).

Normal, waking, or immediate consciousness is the awareness of those thoughts, ideas, feelings, and perceptions that are active in our mind at any one time. As James said, and as we pointed out in the previous topic, there are limits on the *amount* of information we can attend to at this level of consciousness. You cannot be reading this text, reflecting on last night's dinner, wondering about this evening's television programs, listening to the president's speech on the radio, and realizing that you're hungry all at the same time. This level of consciousness is selective.

preconscious
that level of consciousness in which elements of memory and environment can quickly and easily be brought into awareness

Your **preconscious** level of awareness includes the ideas and feelings stored in your memory and the many stimuli in your environment to which you are not paying attention at the moment. The memories and stimuli are there, you are simply not conscious of them. However, they are readily accessible and you can *become conscious* of them quite easily.

With very little hesitation you *could* remember the details of last night's dinner. You could tell me (if you ever knew) what is on TV tonight. You could direct your attention to the radio, and you might (now that I've brought it up) realize that you *are* hungry and go off searching for food. These tidbits of information are not at the center stage of your awareness until you make them so, until you move them from the level of preconscious to conscious.

The notion of an **unconscious** level of mental activity is one we associate with Sigmund Freud. The unconscious is said to house all sorts of things—memories, thoughts, desires, feelings, etc. Thoughts are said to be in our unconscious if we cannot gain ready access to them. Memories, for example, may be stored at an unconscious level. These memories are thought to be in our mind and to be ultimately, or theoretically, *knowable,* but they cannot be dredged up easily.

To complete our outline, we need to acknowledge another possibility. There are some events or stimuli that stand no chance of ever getting into our normal, waking level of consciousness; they are beyond our consciousness. There are two commonly cited types of information that fit this category.

One type are those activities of our bodies of which we are not aware in any sense. We do not notice (are not conscious of) the vibrations of our eardrums or the digestive activities of our stomachs. We are not aware of the electrical activities of our own brains. Such processes are beyond awareness or consciousness. They enter our consciousness only when they are disrupted or heightened to extremes.

The other sort of information that is beyond consciousness are those events in our external environment that never stimulate our sense receptors. As you sit reading this topic, a group of engineers may be having a meeting at a nearby Holiday Inn. Because you are not there, and knew nothing about the meeting, you are unaware of its occurrence. It is beyond your consciousness.

To summarize, one approach to consciousness defines it as a state of awareness of our own mental activity and of the environment around us. This awareness can be thought of as occurring at a number of different levels, from normal waking consciousness, to preconscious, to unconscious. In each case, the issue is the extent to which information is available to awareness and centered in our attention. We must also acknowledge that some information is generally beyond any level of consciousness.

Before you go on
What is consciousness, and in what way may we speak of levels of consciousness?

SLEEPING AND DREAMING

In many ways, sleep is a scary state. We are not aware or conscious of our own sleeping. It is seemingly a temporary (one hopes) "loss of consciousness." We can know that we have been asleep and we can be certain that we will sleep again. But we can't be conscious of our sleep while we're sleeping!

The study of sleeping and dreaming as variants of consciousness has intrigued psychologists for many years. Webb (1981) reports that the number of sleep-related articles now exceeds 1500 per year. In this section, we'll examine some of what we know about this state of consciousness we call sleep.

Stages of Sleep

How do we know when someone is asleep? Self-reports of sleeping are notoriously unreliable. A person who claims that he or she "didn't sleep a wink last night" may have slept soundly for many hours. Our best, most reliable indicators of sleep are physiological measurements, usually of brain activity. The **electroencephalogram (EEG)** is an instrument that measures and records (on an electroencephalo*graph*) the electrical activity of the brain. It

Figure 9.1

The EEG records of sleeping subjects illustrate the brain wave activity associated with the different stages of sleep.

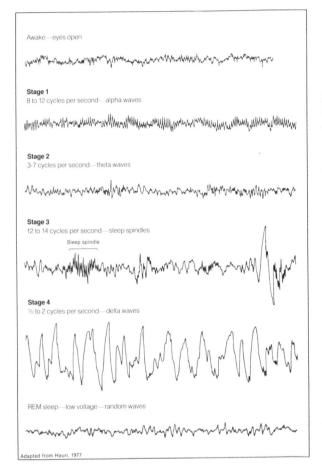

Awake—eyes open

Stage 1
8 to 12 cycles per second—alpha waves

Stage 2
3-7 cycles per second—theta waves

Stage 3
12 to 14 cycles per second—sleep spindles

Sleep spindle

Stage 4
½ to 2 cycles per second—delta waves

REM sleep—low voltage—random waves

Adapted from Hauri, 1977

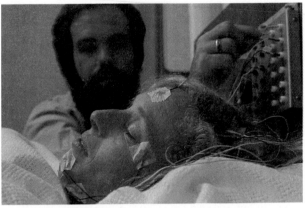

Subjects in sleep labs provide scientists with information about humans during sleep. By hooking the subjects to EEGs, scientists can study the activity of the brain during sleep.

does so through small electrodes that are pasted onto the scalp. The process may be slightly messy, but it is in no way painful.

The EEG tracings of sleeping subjects reveal that the process can be divided into four different stages. Figure 9.1 shows the electroencephalographs of a subject in each of these four stages.

When we are in a calm, relaxed state of wakefulness, with our eyes closed, but *not yet asleep,* our EEG pattern shows a rhythmic cycle of brain wave activity called **alpha activity.** Here, there are slow, relatively smooth waves of electrical reaction, with the waves cycling 8 to 12 times every second. If, as you sit or lie there, you start worrying about an event of the day, the smooth alpha waves become disrupted and are replaced by a random pattern of heightened electrical activity.

As you drift from rest and relaxation into sleep, your brain wave patterns change and you will normally progress through the following stages of sleep.

Stage 1. This is a very light stage of sleep from which an individual can be easily aroused. The smooth, cyclical alpha pattern disappears. The amplitude (or magnitude) of the electrical activity lessens considerably. At the same time, your breathing is becoming more regular, and your heart rate is decreasing. This stage doesn't last very long—generally less than 10 minutes. Then, you slide into stage 2 sleep.

Stage 2. The basic EEG pattern is the same in this stage as in stage 1—low amplitude and hardly any noticeable wavelike pattern. The difference is that we now see what are called **sleep spindles** in the EEG record. These are brief, high amplitude bursts of electrical activity that occur with regularity (about every 15 seconds or so). You're falling into a deeper sleep now, but still can be easily awakened.

Stage 3. Now you're getting into deep sleep. There is a reduction in the brain's electrical activity and we can clearly make out **delta wave** activity in your EEG. Delta waves are high, slow waves (from .5 to 3 cycles every second). In stage 3 sleep, delta waves constitute between 20 and 50 percent of your EEG pattern. Your internal functions (temperature, heart rate, breathing) are lowering and slowing. It's going to be hard to wake you now.

Stage 4. Now you're in deep sleep. Your EEG record is filled with slow delta waves, recurring over and over again. Delta waves now take up more than 50 percent of your brain wave pattern. At this point, even your muscles have become totally relaxed. It is difficult to rouse someone from this stage of sleep. About 15 percent of your night's sleep will be spent in stage 4 sleep.

It usually takes about an hour to go from stage 1 to stage 4. How long it actually takes will, of course, depend somewhat on how tired you are and the physical conditions surrounding the sleeper. We'll assume a nice, quiet, dark room and a comfortable and familiar bed. After an hour's passage through these four stages, the sequence reverses itself. The sleeper goes back through stage 3 to stage 2, but before he or she goes through the cycle again, something truly remarkable happens: The sleeper's eyes start to move rapidly under closed eyelids.

sleep spindles
very brief, high amplitude peaks in EEG pattern, found in stages 2 and 3 of sleep

delta wave
an EEG wave pattern (.5 to 3 cycles per second) indicative of deepening levels of sleep

Before you go on
What is the EEG?

What are the four stages of sleep?

REM and NREM Sleep

In the early 1950s, Nathaniel Kleitman and Eugene Aserinsky made quite a discovery. They noticed that as sleeping subjects began their second cycle into deeper levels of sleep, their eyes moved (Kleitman, 1963). This period of *rapid eye movement* sleep is called **REM sleep.** The most noteworthy aspect of this discovery is that when sleeping subjects are awakened during REM sleep, they report that they are dreaming. When awakened during sleep periods without rapid eye movements (NREM sleep), reports of dreams are significantly fewer in number and much more fragmented (Aserinsky & Kleitman, 1953). REM sleep appears to be an entryway to dreams.

REM sleep patterns occur throughout the night, normally lasting from a few minutes to half an hour. About 90 to 120 minutes each night is spent "REMing." During these REM periods, we are probably dreaming. Dream time seems very well correlated with real time. That is, if subjects are awakened after 5 minutes of REM sleep, they report that they had been dreaming for about 5 minutes. If they are left to REM for 20 minutes, they report that they have had a longer dream (Dement & Kleitman, 1957). So much for the notion that all our dreaming is jammed into the last few seconds before we wake! The normal pattern of REM occurrences is provided in Figure 9.2 from research by William Dement (1974). Notice in this figure that during the course of a night's sleep, one does not necessarily have to progress through all of the stages of sleep in an orderly fashion. That is, in some cycles, stage 2 may be passed over completely; in another cycle, stage 3 may be absent; in some cases, sleep returns to stage 4 between REM cycles, in some cases it doesn't.

REM sleep
rapid eye movement sleep during which dreaming occurs; also called paradoxical sleep because of high levels of physiological activity

Figure 9.2
This illustration shows the typical
sequence of sleep stages during a
typical night of a young adult. Notice the
recurring REM sleep throughout the
night.

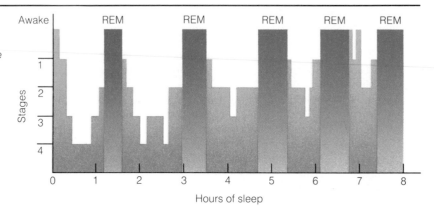

Dreaming isn't the only thing that happens during REM sleep. From the outside, a sleeper in REM sleep appears quiet and calm—except for those barely noticeable eye movements. On the inside, however, there is quite a different story. In many ways the REM sleeper is very active, although oblivious to most external stimulation. One noticeable change is a type of muscular immobility—not because muscles become tensed, but because they become so totally relaxed. This relaxation is occasionally interrupted by slight muscle twitches (which you may have observed if you've watched a sleeping dog that appears to be chasing some imaginary rabbit in its dreams). There is usually an excitement of the sex organs, males having a penile erection, females having a discharge of vaginal fluids. Breathing usually becomes shallow and rapid. Blood pressure levels may skyrocket, and heart rates increase, all while the subject lies "peacefully" asleep. Because all this physiological activity is going on, REM sleep is sometimes referred to as *paradoxical sleep*. There doesn't appear to be very much quiet and peaceful about it at all. These changes take place regardless of *what* the subject is dreaming about. It matters little whether one is dreaming about lying on the beach getting a tan or about hand-to-hand combat in World War II; physiologically, the reactions are the same.

Before you go on

What is REM sleep?

What occurs during REM sleep?

Why Do We Sleep?

We know a lot about sleep. We can trace sleep through its various stages and cycles and note when dreams are likely to occur. We know that everyone sleeps, although for varying lengths of time depending on one's age (see Figure 9.3). We know that everyone dreams, although many people cannot remember many of their dreams. What we don't know yet is *why* we sleep. "Perhaps sleep does not have a function. Perhaps, as some of my own students have argued with me, we should accept our failure to isolate a specific function of sleep as evidence for nonexistence of such a function" (Rechtschaffen, 1971, p. 87). We may not know why we sleep, but we have some hypotheses on the subject.

Deprivation Studies In 1960, William Dement reported the results of a sleep deprivation experiment he had performed. His report had quite an impact. Dement systematically deprived college student volunteers of the

Figure 9.3

This graph shows changes throughout the life cycle in amounts of sleep. Notice the decline in the amount of REM sleep.
(Adapted from Roffwarg et al., 1966.)

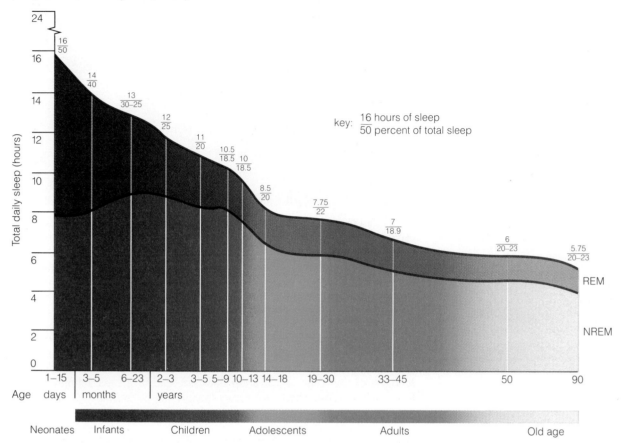

opportunity to engage in REM sleep. Whenever EEG records indicated that his subjects were falling into REM patterns of sleep, they were awakened. The number of REM deprivations increased as dawn approached; the experimenter had to awaken his subjects more and more frequently. After five nights of interrupted REM sleep, Dement's subjects showed a wide variety of strange behavioral reactions. They were irritable, grouchy, somewhat paranoid, noticeably anxious, and lacked the ability to concentrate once awake for the day. Subjects who were awakened just as frequently, but during NREM sleep, showed no such behavioral deterioration. Here seemed to be a major breakthrough! We sleep because we need to REM; we need to dream.

The catch is that even Dement was unable to replicate these findings in later studies (see, for example, Dement, 1974). In fact, most sleep deprivation studies (on animals as well as humans) show remarkably *few adverse side effects of deprivation* of any kind of sleep. Even with lengthy deprivation there are very few changes in the subjects' physiological reactions. If the task at hand is interesting enough, there is little impairment of intellectual functioning after prolonged sleep deprivation (Dement, 1974; Webb, 1975). Apparently, we can adapt to deprivation, perhaps by taking little cat naps while we're awake. Very short episodes of sleep (called *microsleeps*) can be found in the EEG records of waking subjects, both animal and human. Microsleeps increase in number when normal sleep is disrupted.

People who are deprived of sleep for any length of time will often become irritable, anxious, paranoid, and unable to concentrate. The effects of sleep deprivation are obvious in these subjects who were deprived of sleep for 72 hours.

That's not to say that there aren't *any* effects that result from being deprived of sleep. Subjects deprived of REM sleep for a few nights and then left alone will spend unusually long periods REMing, as if to catch up on lost REMs. But this rebound effect is generally only found for the first night after deprivation, and then patterns return to normal. There is similar evidence (although there is less of it) that NREM sleep also rebounds. This is particularly true when stage 4 deep sleep is disrupted (Agnew, Webb, & Williams, 1964).

The fact that deprivation does cause an increase in future sleeping suggests some sort of *need* to sleep—to REM for active sleep, to NREM for quiet sleep. At best, however, these needs are weak. Deprivation leads to rebounding, but *more* deprivation does not lead to greater rebounding effects. In this sense, then, sleep does not act like a "normal" physiological need.

An Evolutionary Perspective Sleeping does not seem to be a learned response. It just happens. That it happens is rooted in our biology. That it happens as it does is also rooted in our evolutionary history, according to Webb (1975). In this view, we sleep to conserve energy, if not actually restore it.

Sleeping is simply a part of being alive—a characteristic we share with many organisms. Some animals, given the way that they have evolved, sleep for only a few minutes or hours each day. Examples include those animals whose only defense against predators is to be vigilant and quick to run away, such as rabbits, sheep, and antelope. Other animals (lions and tigers, for example) sleep even more than humans because they are unthreatened by their environment and easily able to find food and shelter. Humans are diurnal (daytime) animals and are guided largely by their visual sense, which works best during daylight hours. At night we are free to rest and relax, preparing ourselves to face the new day in the morning. In this context, asking "Why do we sleep?" makes no more sense than asking "Why do we walk upright?"

Before you go on

What are the effects of depriving someone of sleep?

Is there any evidence that there is a need to sleep?

Dreaming

The discovery of the REM stage of sleep has given us a convenient and reliable indicator of dreaming. We dream five or six times during every night of every week of every year—that's a lot of dreams! Dreaming is simply a part of sleep. We may remember very few of our dreams, true, but that doesn't mean we haven't had them.

Those dreams that we do remember tend to be wild and bizarre dreams, often frightening, disjointed, and very vivid in some of their details. However, when we wake people during REM sleep and ask them to tell us about the content of their dreams, we discover that the great majority of them are about very commonplace, very usual, downright boring things (Hall, 1966; Webb, 1979). Still, we find dreams intriguing and have long sought to understand their nature.

Freud's View   Sigmund Freud considered dreams to be very significant events (1900). Analyzing and interpreting dreams was a major part of his technique of therapy. He saw dreams as a pathway (a *royal road* he called it) to the unconscious mind. Asleep, without the constant vigilance of awareness and attention, the mind is free to entertain itself with varieties of content that might be kept (or repressed) from conscious awareness. Freud told his patients to remember their dreams so they could be examined for clues and insights into the patient's present difficulties.

Freud was interested in the content of dreams at two levels. The first of these is the actual subject matter of the dream as it is recalled. This is called the **manifest content.** Ideas, thoughts, wishes, or desires might show up in dreams where they would not be expressed otherwise. More controversial is the Freudian notion of the **latent content** of dreams (many psychologists doubt that dreams *have* latent content). The latent content is the "true" meaning and significance of the dream for the dreamer. Understanding latent content often relies on interpreting the *symbolism* of dream content. That is,

manifest content
the literal content of a dream as it is recalled by the dreamer
latent content
the underlying meaning of a dream, thought to be symbolically representative

Dreams can sometimes be bizarre and frightening. It was once thought that nightmares were the work of demons who were visiting sleepers who had sinned. "Nightmare," by Fuseli, shows a demon sitting on a woman who is having a nightmare.

everything in a dream may not be as it appears: It may act as a symbol for something else.

Freud's theory of personality (see Topic 23) relies heavily on the role of sexual and aggressive motives. Hence, most Freudian symbolism in dream content revolves around these themes. Dreaming about almost any long, pointed object (e.g., pencils, telephone poles, rocket ships, rifles) is seen as symbolizing the male sex organs. Similarly, dreaming about caves, jars, closets, even coffee mugs, can be taken as symbolizing female sex organs. Entering a tunnel, driving a sports car (particularly at high speeds), and riding a horse symbolize sexual intercourse. Some psychoanalysts find this sort of symbolic interpretation useful in helping them understand some clients or patients. As a scientific theory of dreaming, however, a number of weaknesses arise, not the least of which is how to test the theory. Among other things, as we have already noted, very few dreams (of subjects awakened in the laboratory during REM sleep) tend to be sexual at all, either in actual, manifest content or in symbolic, latent content.

Other Views   Other psychologists have been less inclined to think of dreams as mechanisms for wish fulfillment of the unconscious. There are few elaborate theories yet—we just have bits and pieces of possibilities.

For example, some researchers believe that dreaming is an exercise in memory and problem solving. There are many reports of people who have "seen" the answer to a problem in a dream. In fact, if you are faced with a problem (either intellectual or psychological), there is a reasonably good chance that you will dream about that problem. You might then find, in your dreams, some possible solutions to test later.

The morning after a night of interrupted REM sleep, subjects are less able to remember stories they read before going to bed than they would be otherwise (Tilley & Empson, 1978). The notion that dreaming helps to form and save memories may account for the fact that we dream so much more when we are young than we do later in life (see again, Figure 9.3).

Another view of dreaming is that during REM sleep, different parts of the brain are stimulated and become active. Somehow the brain tries to make sense of all this activity and makes up a story to explain its own activity. The resulting story is what we remember dreaming (McCarley & Hoffman, 1981). In fact, dreams *are* sensitive to stimulation we receive when we are asleep. If we were to drip water on your foot, for example, you might dream of walking in the rain or swimming in an attempt to make sense of this stimulation (Kalat, 1984, p. 223).

Before you go on
Define manifest and latent dream content.

What is the function of dreams?

HYPNOSIS

hypnosis
an induced altered state of consciousness characterized by an increase in suggestibility, attention, and imagination

Hypnosis is an induced altered state of consciousness characterized by the following psychological traits: (1) a marked increase in suggestibility, (2) a focusing of attention, (3) an exaggerated use of imagination, (4) an inability/unwillingness to act on one's own, and (5) an unquestioning acceptance of distortions of reality (Hilgard & Hilgard, 1975). There is little truth, then, in the belief that being hypnotized is like "going to sleep." In fact, few of the characteristics of sleep are found in the hypnotized subject. EEG patterns, for example, are significantly different.

Hypnosis has been used, with varying degrees of success, for a number of different purposes. As you know, it has been used as entertainment, as a show business routine in which members of an audience are hypnotized to do usually silly things in public. It has long been viewed as a method for studying consciousness, particularly for gaining access to those levels of consciousness not in immediate awareness. Hypnosis has also been touted as a process of treatment for a wide range of psychological and physical disorders. In this section, we'll provide answers, as best we can, for some common questions about hypnosis.

1. Can everyone be hypnotized? No. The susceptibility to hypnosis varies rather widely from person to person. Some people resist and cannot be hypnotized. Contrary to popular belief, you cannot be hypnotized against your will. Other individuals are excellent subjects for hypnosis, can readily be put into deep hypnotic states, and may even be able to hypnotize themselves (Hilgard, 1975; 1978). What seems to matter most is a willingness to cooperate with the hypnotist.

2. Can I be made to do things under the influence of hypnosis that I would be embarrassed to do otherwise? Next to being unknowingly hypnotized, this seems to be the greatest fear associated with hypnosis. Again, the answer is generally no. Under the influence of a skilled hypnotist, you may very well do some pretty silly things, and do them publicly. But, under the right circumstances, you might do those very same things without being hypnotized. It is unlikely that you would do anything under hypnosis that you would not do otherwise.

3. Are hypnotized subjects simply more open to the suggestions of the hypnotist, or is their consciousness really changed? This question does not get a yes or no answer. The issue is in dispute. Some believe that hypnosis is no more than a heightened level of suggestibility (if not gullibility) (Barber, 1972; Spanos & Barber, 1974). Others believe it to be a special state, separate from the compliance of a willing subject. When hypnotized subjects are left alone, they maintain the condition induced by their hypnosis. Subjects not hypnotized, but complying as best they can with an experimenter, revert quickly to normal behavior when left alone (Hilgard, 1975; Orne, 1969).

4. Can hypnosis be used to alleviate pain—real, physical pain? Yes. It won't (can't) cure the cause of the pain, but it can be used to control the feeling of pain. Hypnosis can be used to create **hallucinations** in the hypnotized subject. Hallucinations are perceptual experiences that occur without sensory input—that is, false experiences. Some hallucinations are termed "positive" because the subject is led to perceive something that is not there. Pain reduction can be accomplished through the use of *negative* hallucinations: that is, the failure to perceive something (pain) that *is* there. **If** a subject is a good candidate for hypnosis in the first place, there is a good chance that at least a portion of perceived pain can be blocked from conscious awareness (Hilgard & Hilgard, 1975).

5. Is a hypnotized person in any sense aware of what she or he is doing? Yes, but in a very strange way. It seems that within the hypnotized subject is a "hidden observer" who may be quite aware of what is going on. In one study (Hilgard & Hilgard, 1975), a subject was hypnotized and told that he would feel no pain as his hand was immersed in a container of ice water (which is usually very painful indeed). When asked, the subject reported feeling very little pain, just as expected. The hypnotic suggestion was working. The Hilgards then asked the subject if "some part of him" was feeling any pain and to indicate the presence of such pain by using his free hand to press a lever (or even to write out a description of what he was feeling). Even though the subject continued to *verbally report* no pain sensations, the free hand (on the behalf of the "hidden observer") indicated that it "knew" there was considerable pain in the immersed hand.

Because hypnotized subjects are more open to suggestion, hypnotism is sometimes used to help change habits and reduce anxiety, but there are limits to what hypnosis can do.

hallucinations
perceptual experiences occurring without the benefit of sensory input; perceiving that which is not there to be perceived

6. Can I remember things under hypnosis that I couldn't remember otherwise? Probably not, although there is no more hotly contested issue with regard to hypnosis than this. In the everyday sense of, "Can you hypnotize me to remember my psychology material better for the test next Friday?" the answer is "Almost certainly not." I might be able to convince you under hypnosis that you should remember your psychology and lead you to *want* to remember your psychology, but there is no evidence that hypnotic suggestion can *directly* improve your ability to learn and remember new material.

In the more restrictive sense of, "I don't remember all the details of the accident and the trauma that followed. Can hypnosis help me remember those events more clearly?" the answer is less definite. When we get to our discussion of memory (Chapter 6), we'll see that distortions of memory in recollection can occur in normal states. In hypnotic states, the subject is suggestible and susceptible to distortions in recall furnished by the hypnotist (even assuming that the hypnotist has no reason to cause distortions). To the extent that hypnosis can reduce feelings of anxiety and tension, it may help in the recollection of anxiety-producing memories (Freud's repression notion again). The evidence is neither clear nor convincing on this issue in either direction.

Hypnosis does alter one's consciousness, does open one to suggestions of the hypnotist, can be used to treat symptoms (if not their underlying causes), and can distort one's view of reality. However, we are learning that it is neither mystical nor magical; there are limits to what hypnosis can do.

Before you go on

What changes in consciousness are associated with hypnosis?

MEDITATION

meditation
the focusing of awareness in order to arrive at an altered state of consciousness and relaxation

Meditation is a self-induced state of altered consciousness characterized by an extreme focusing of attention. Meditation is usually associated with ancient or Eastern cultures and has been practiced for many centuries. It did not become popular in this country until the 1960s. It was then that psychologists began to study meditation seriously. In this section we'll first review the process of meditation, and then we'll look at the claims that have been made about its potential benefits.

Though there are several different kinds of meditation, we'll concentrate on one of the most popular forms: *transcendental meditation,* or TM. To begin meditating, the meditator should be calm, relaxed, and comfortably positioned. He or she then directs attention toward one particular stimulus. This could be some simple bodily function, such as one's own breathing. Attention could be focused on some softly spoken or chanted word, or phrase, or **mantrum.** Mantra (the plural of mantrum) are to be easy, soft words or sounds, such as "ummm," or "one," or "calm."

mantrum
a soft word or sound chanted repeatedly to aid the meditation process

As attention becomes focused, all other stimuli are blocked from conscious consideration. The meditator ignores stimuli from the environment, either external or internal (like thoughts or feelings or bodily processes). Throughout, the attempt is to relax, to remain calm and peaceful. By definition, a state of meditation cannot be forced; it just happens, and its practitioners claim that to reach an altered state of awareness through meditation is not difficult (Benson, 1975).

Once in a meditative state, there *are* some measurable changes that take place that are neither quite like sleep nor quite like hypnosis. The most noticeable change is a predominance of alpha waves in the EEG record (re-

Practitioners of meditation claim it can be used to promote relaxation and to reduce stress and anxiety. Scientific studies, however, have found that the same relaxed state can be achieved merely by resting. There is also no evidence to show that meditators are better able to cope with stress.

member, such waves characterize a relaxed state just *before* one falls asleep). Breathing usually slows and becomes deeper. Oxygen intake is reduced, and heart rate may decrease (Wallace & Benson, 1972).

There is no doubt that many people can enter meditative states of consciousness. The doubts that have arisen about meditation center on the claims for the psychological experiences and benefits that can be derived from meditating.

One of the major claims for meditation is that it is a reasonably simple and very effective way to enter a state of relaxation. Indeed, the reduction of arousal is taken to be the main advantage of meditation. The claim is that by meditating, one can slow bodily processes and enter a state of physical as well as psychological calm.

Recently, David Holmes (1984) reviewed the experimental evidence for somatic (bodily) relaxation through meditation. On a number of different measures of arousal/relaxation, including heart rate, respiration rate, muscle tension, and oxygen consumption, Holmes found *no differences* between meditating subjects and subjects who were simply resting or relaxing. After reviewing the data of dozens of experiments, Holmes concluded, " . . . there is not a measure of arousal on which the meditating subjects were consistently found to have reliably lower arousal than resting subjects. Indeed, the most consistent finding was that there were not reliable differences between meditating and resting subjects. Furthermore, there appear to be about as many instances in which the meditating subjects showed reliably higher arousal as there are instances in which they showed reliably lower arousal than their resting counterparts" (1984, p. 5).

Another claim that is often made about meditation is that people who practice meditation are better able to cope with stress, or pressure, or threatening situations than are people who do not practice meditation. Once again, Holmes (1984) reports that he could find *no* evidence to support this claim. In fact, in four of the studies he reviewed, Holmes found that under mild threat, meditating subjects showed *greater* arousal than did nonmeditating subjects.

Some of the claims made for meditation techniques go beyond simple relaxation and arousal reduction. Those claims that meditation can raise one to transcendental heights of new awareness, and thus make you a better person, are viewed with even more skepticism. Some meditators claim that they have an enormous "openness" to ideas and feelings, that they have hallucinatory experiences, and that they can divorce themselves from their bodies and minds. Such experiences might, in some instances, be true. The idea that a meditator can exist apart from present experience and view life "as if from without" is not too far removed from Hilgard's notion of a "hidden observer" in hypnosis. Nonetheless, the majority of psychologists who have investigated meditation continue to question claims for a state of well-being that is achieved through such little effort and that relies more on testimonials of personal experience than on hard scientific evidence (Webb, 1981).

Before you go on

What is meditation?

Is meditation an effective means of relaxation and arousal reduction?

ALTERING CONSCIOUSNESS WITH DRUGS

In this section we will discuss some of those chemicals that alter our psychological processes of mood, perception, or behavior. Because of their effect on such processes, these chemicals are referred to collectively as **psychoactive** drugs.

psychoactive drug
a natural or synthetic chemical that has an effect on psychological processes and consciousness

There are many psychoactive drugs. We'll focus on four different types: stimulants, depressants, hallucinogens, and marijuana. The use of drugs as therapeutic agents in the treatment of psychological and behavioral disorders will be covered later (see Chapter 13, Topic 29).

(I will try to avoid any noticeable preaching in this section. I will point out, however, that the use (or misuse) of drugs that alter consciousness may have a number of negative outcomes.)

There are a few terms that will be relevant throughout our discussion, and we ought to agree on how we will be using them. For our purposes, we'll adopt the following definitions. *Tolerance*: in which the use of a drug leads to the condition where, physically, more and more of it is needed to reach a desired state. That is, as tolerance develops, usage must increase to achieve the same results. ("I used to get high with just one; now I need three.") *Dependence*: in which the user comes psychologically to need the use of a chemical to reach and maintain normal psychological states. ("I've just got to have my morning coffee before I can face the day.") *Addiction*: in which a tolerance to the chemical has probably developed, making withdrawal painful and difficult. ("There's no way I'll give it up; the pain is just too great without it.") The major difference between dependence and addiction is the extent and severity of withdrawal symptoms.

Stimulants

stimulants
those drugs (such as caffeine, cocaine, and amphetamines) that increase nervous system activity

Chemical **stimulants** do just that—they chemically stimulate, or activate, the nervous system. If nothing else, they produce a heightened sense of arousal. In general, they create not only an increase in activity, but also an elevation of mood.

The effect of stimulants on the nervous system seems to be twofold. On the one hand, they lower the threshold level of neurons so that they may be more easily activated or fired. On the other hand, they act as neurotransmitters (see Chapter 2) directly stimulating activity at the level of the neural synapse.

Caffeine is one of the most widely used of all stimulants. It is found in a variety of foods and drinks as well as in many varieties of over-the-counter and prescription painkillers. In moderate amounts it seems to have no dangerous or life-threatening effects on the user. At some point, a mild dependence of at least a psychological nature may develop, as in, "I just can't get going in the morning without two or three cups of coffee."

After excessive use, giving up sources of caffeine may result in the pain of withdrawal. There is usually a rebound sort of effect when caffeine intake is stopped. That is, you may drink many cups of coffee or tea to help stay awake and aroused enough to withstand an all-night study session. Within a few hours after you stop drinking the caffeine, you will rebound and experience a streak of real mental and physical fatigue—perhaps right at exam time!

Nicotine is another very popular stimulant drug. Its usual method of use is through smoking, and it is absorbed by the lungs. Nicotine is carried from the lungs to the brain in a matter of seconds. There is no doubt that nicotine is a stimulant of central nervous system activity, which makes it rather strange that people will claim that they need to relax by having a cigarette. Although nicotine is a nervous system stimulant, it does seem to relax muscle tone (Bennett, 1982).

Many individuals develop a tolerance to nicotine, requiring more and more of it to reach the desired state of stimulation. The drug often leads to dependency and, in many cases, addiction. Withdrawal can be accompanied by a wide range of unpleasant symptoms. How ultimately addictive nicotine (or perhaps any other drug) becomes may depend primarily on the rapidity with which it enters the brain. Thus, people who take many quick, deep puffs when smoking may become addicted more easily to nicotine than will people who take slow, shallow puffs (Bennett, 1980).

Cocaine is a naturally occurring stimulant derived from leaves of the coca shrub (native to the Andes mountains in South America). Some time periods seem to have drugs of their own (alcohol in the 1920s; marijuana in the 1960s). Cocaine appears to be *the* drug of the 1980s.

The main stimulant reaction of cocaine is produced by one of two physiological reactions, perhaps by both together. (1) Cocaine acts as if it were a natural neurotransmitter. It mimics the action of norepinephrine, an excitatory neurotransmitter manufactured in the human body. (2) Cocaine manages to keep normal amounts of norepinephrine from breaking down and being eliminated as waste. The result is an overall increase in the level of norepinephrine and the activity that it produces.

The allure of cocaine is the rush of pleasure—almost euphoria—that it produces when it first enters the bloodstream (through the mucus membranes when inhaled through the nose ("snorting"), or directly through injection). Some of the allure of the drug may be the fact that it is illegal and that many famous people have reportedly used it, but that's another story.

It's hard to see what's wrong, much less illegal, about a "natural" substance that creates a feeling of euphoria and good will. There's a lot of pain and misery in this world, what's wrong with something that introduces some pleasure? What's wrong is that continued use of the drug leads to an increasing tolerance for it. To reach the same level of pleasure, the user needs to keep increasing the dosage of the cocaine. As tolerances build, the likelihood of addiction to the chemical becomes greater (particularly if the drug is injected so that it gets to the brain quickly). Another problem is that while small amounts may simply lead to a mild sense of "high," larger dosages lead to levels of intoxication that are dangerous, not only to the user, but to others who happen to be around: Judgment, perception, problem-solving skills, and the like are sometimes seriously impaired with cocaine intoxication.

Cocaine is a stimulant that occurs naturally in the leaves of the coca shrub. The drug is usually "snorted," producing an artificial "high." Cocaine possession and use is illegal in the United States and repeated usage can lead to addiction and death.

Amphetamines are synthetically manufactured chemical stimulants that usually come in the form of capsules or pills under many brand names (and street names, such as bennies, uppers, wake-ups, cartwheels, dexies, or jellie babies). Amphetamines actually cause the release of the body's own store of norepinephrine. As a result, users feel alert, awake, aroused, filled with energy, and ready to go. Unfortunately, the results are short-lived and illusory. The drug does not create alertness so much as it masks fatigue, which will ultimately overcome the user when the drug wears off. Once again, tolerance and dependency build rather quickly, and withdrawing from the use of amphetamines can be a long and painful process.

Before you go on
What are stimulants, and what are their effects?

Depressants

depressants
those drugs (such as alcohol, opiates, sedatives, and heroin) that slow or reduce nervous system activity

In terms of their effects on consciousness, **depressants** are the opposite of the stimulants. They reduce one's awareness of external stimuli, slow normal bodily functioning, and decrease levels of overt behavior. Predictably, the reaction one has to depressants depends largely on how much is taken. In small doses, they can produce relaxation, freedom from anxiety, and a loss of stifling inhibitions. In greater amounts, they can produce sedation, sleep, coma, and even death.

Alcohol is doubtless the most commonly used depressant. It has been in use for thousands of years. In many ways, alcohol is the most dangerous of all drugs, largely because of its popularity and widespread use. It is certainly the most deadly of drugs. Alcohol-related traffic fatalities alone are enough to qualify alcohol for this distinction.

Perhaps the first thing to remember about alcohol is that it *is* a depressant. Some individuals may feel that they are stimulating when they drink alcohol, but their nervous system activity is actually being depressed.

The specific effects of alcohol on the drinker are a reflection of a number of factors. Primary among them (again) is *amount*. What matters most is the amount of alcohol that gets into the person's bloodstream, usually through the stomach. The amount of alcohol in one's bloodstream at any one time is affected by how much one drinks and by how fast the alcohol can get into the bloodstream, which in turn is affected by what else happens to be in the stomach at the time. Indeed, drinking on an empty stomach may be more dangerous than drinking while or after eating because the alcohol will be absorbed more quickly. In most states, 1/10 of 1 percent alcohol in the bloodstream is considered legally drunk. At this level, brain activity is so affected that decision making becomes distorted and motor coordination is impaired (both are the sorts of skills usually required to drive safely).

The effect that alcohol has on a person may also be a function of the person's frame of mind. Sometimes a few drinks seem to produce little effect on a person. Sometimes a couple of beers can have that same person dancing around the room, lampshade on head, acting in a generally foolish way. At other times, the same two cans of beer may turn the same person into a crying, "sad drunk." Reactions often reflect such cognitive variables as one's frame of mind and one's perception of what is going on in the environment at the time.

Opiates, such as morphine and codeine, are naturally occurring depressants that are artificially refined for human use as analgesics (they can reduce or eliminate sensations of pain). It was for this purpose that they were first

Alcohol is the most commonly used of all drugs. Because drinking is socially acceptable, overuse is not seen as a serious problem. Alcohol is, however, a drug that can lead to addiction, serious health problems, and even death.

commonly used. In small doses, they create feelings of well-being, ease, relaxation, and a trancelike state. Unlike alcohol, they seem to have little effect on motor behavior. The catch, again, is that they produce very strong dependence and addiction. Their removal results in extreme pain and depression.

Heroin is an opiate, originally (in the 1890s) derived from morphine, but thought not to be as addictive. That thought was soon proven wrong. Strong dependency and addiction grow rapidly as increased tolerance for the drug builds, leading to more and more chemical being required to produce the same effects that were once gained with small amounts. Once again we find that the addictive nature of heroin may be related to its rapid entry into the brain. (Methadone is a drug with many of the chemical properties of heroin, and one that has many of the same psychological effects. A major difference is that methadone is very slow to reach the brain and is essentially nonaddictive.)

The effects of heroin (above whatever painkilling use it might have) seem to be most related to one's emotional state and mood. Unlike alcohol, or the opiates like morphine, there are seldom hallucinations or thought disturbances associated with heroin use. But, as increased amounts of heroin are needed to produce the desired emotional states of pleasant euphoria, tolerance builds, and increased dosages of heroin can cause breathing to stop, often for periods long enough to result in death.

Sedatives, unlike opiates, are synthetically produced. Like opiates, there are many types and varieties. All types slow nervous system activity, producing a sense of relaxed tranquility in small amounts and producing sleep or coma in larger doses. Some sedatives are addictive (barbiturates, for example) and the user suffers strong withdrawal symptoms when their use is discontinued. All produce dependency if used with any regularity. As is generally the case, once addiction develops, getting off these drugs is very hard to do.

Before you go on
Identify four depressants, and summarize their effects.

Hallucinogens

Those chemicals we call **hallucinogens** have the most unpredictable effects on consciousness. One of the main reactions to these drugs is the formation of hallucinations, usually visual. That is, users often report having visual experiences even though there is nothing there to see, or they tend to see things in ways that others do not. Hallucinations of hearing, smell, touch, and taste are possible, but much less common.

LSD, or lysergic acid diethylamide, remains a popular hallucinogen. Chemically, it acts as if it were a neurotransmitter. Psychologically, it raises levels of emotionality and produces vivid visual hallucinations. The changes in mood that take place may simply be extreme exaggerations of one's present mood. From the start, this has been viewed as one of the dangers of LSD. Many individuals are drawn to drugs like LSD because things are not going well for them, and they are in a bad mood. They hope that LSD will help cheer them up. In fact, it will probably just make their moods worse, resulting in a "bad trip," by exaggerating the feelings they have when they take the drug.

The hallucinations that occur under the influence of LSD usually involve an exaggeration of some actual perception. That is, colors become much more vivid, stationary objects appear to move, dimly lit stimuli take on a glow, and otherwise unnoticed details become very apparent. Occasionally, LSD gives rise to an experience of **synesthesia.** In this condition, stimulus energy of one modality is perceived in a different modality—a crossing-over of sensory processing. For example, the individual may "hear" colored lights, "see" sounds, "feel" odors, and so forth. Whether people really experience synesthesia is hard to tell for sure. What matters is that the subjects themselves believe they experience synesthesia.

PCP (technically phencyclidine, commonly angel dust) is a relatively new hallucinogen, first available in 1959 and declared illegal just eight years later. Like LSD, it produces alterations in states of perception and hallucinations. Even more troublesome is that PCP causes distortions in judgment and decision-making. High doses seem to consistently produce aggressive and often violent behaviors. For example, some individuals on PCP have committed violent assaults on others. The drug does not seem to be addictive, but a strong dependency develops quickly.

Before you go on
What characterizes those drugs that are classified as hallucinogens?

Marijuana: A Special Case

Marijuana is a consciousness-altering drug that must be considered a special case because it doesn't fit neatly into any of the three categories we've used above. In many ways, marijuana acts as a depressant. In small dosages, its effects are very similar to those of alcohol: decreased nervous system activity and depression of thought and action. In higher doses, however, marijuana acts very much as if it were a hallucinogen, producing hallucinations and alterations in mood.

Marijuana is produced from the cannabis plant, which often grows wild as a weed. The active ingredient in marijuana is the chemical compound THC (tetrahydrocannabinol). THC is also the active ingredient in *hashish* (a similar, but more potent drug also made from the cannabis plant).

Though there is little evidence that smoking marijuana is addictive, it is harmful to the lungs and can cause impaired judgment, slower reflexes, and poor coordination. When smoked by pregnant women, marijuana also seems to result in smaller babies and more miscarriages.

Marijuana is a difficult drug for society to deal with. It is currently illegal to sell, possess, or use the drug. Yet, in many ways, the drug seems no worse than alcohol, which is legal. There is little evidence that marijuana tolerance develops and scant evidence that it is addictive. Is it dangerous? Certainly, if for no other reason than it is usually smoked, and smoking is clearly a danger to one's health. It is also dangerous in the sense that alcohol is dangerous. Excessive use leads to impaired judgment, impaired reflexes, unrealistic moods, and poor physical coordination (Bennett, 1982; Weil et al., 1968). Most of us would rather not have *that* sort of driver out on the same roads we're using.

The most debatable aspect of marijuana use is the implications of moderate to heavy long-term use. People are tired of hearing this response (users in particular), but the evidence just isn't in yet. The data are more suggestive than definitive. Marijuana use seems to cause bronchitis and other lung ailments (usually associated with smoking, but with marijuana, even more so). It may have genetic implications (it seems to in nonhumans at least). It may adversely affect the body's immune system and white blood cells. It seems to have predictably negative effects when taken during pregnancy, resulting in smaller babies and increased numbers of miscarriages, among other things (Grinspoon, 1977; Julien, 1978).

Before you go on

What is the active ingredient in marijuana, and what effects does it have on behavior, both in the short and long term?

To be conscious is to be aware of one's self and one's environment. Our consciousness is forever changing, personal, continuous, and selective. In this topic, we have reviewed different levels and states of consciousness as modified or altered by sleep, hypnosis, meditation, and drugs.

A good night's sleep is a wonderful and apparently necessary thing. Some people have no difficulty sleeping and seem able to sleep through anything. Others experience problems, either in getting to sleep in the first place or during sleep itself. Perhaps as many as 10 million Americans "suffer from sleep disorders that persist, and disrupt their lives, for months and years" (Mitler et al., 1975). As is the case for so many psychological processes, we generally take sleep for granted until we experience some abnormality of sleep. Here, we'll review three types of sleep disorder.

Insomnia. At some time or another, each of us has suffered from a bout of **insomnia**—an inability to fall asleep and/or stay asleep when one wants to. When we experience insomnia, we usually know why. We may be excited or worried about something that is going to happen the next day. We may have overstimulated our autonomic nervous system with drugs, such as the caffeine in coffee or tea. Many people who chronically (regularly) suffer from insomnia haven't the slightest idea why they are unable to get a good night's sleep.

An interesting finding from the sleep laboratory is that many individuals who *believe* that they are not getting any sleep are, in fact, sleeping much more than they think (Dement, 1974). Dement and his colleagues have called this phenomenon *pseudoinsomnia*. It is Dement's impression that such people spend a number of dream episodes dreaming that they are awake and trying to get to sleep! Pseudoinsomnia can usually be cured by simply demonstrating to patients that they are in fact getting a good night's sleep, as indicated by their EEG records.

Prescribing sleeping pills, or using over-the-counter medications to cure real insomnia may cause more problems than it solves. The pills (sedatives or depressants) may have a positive effect for a while, but eventually, dosages have to be increased as tolerance builds. When the drugs are discontinued, a rebound effect makes it even more difficult to get to sleep than it was before. Generally, insomnia is not considered to be a disease in any sense, but rather a symptom, probably of depression or anxiety.

Narcolepsy. **Narcolepsy** involves going to sleep, even during the day, without the intention of doing so. Sleep occurs in "sleep attacks," lasting from 5 to 30 minutes. The strangest thing about these sleep attacks is that they tend to be attacks of active REM sleep. The person quickly falls asleep and is immediately in REM sleep, dreaming. Narcoleptics generally skip over the initial, gradual staging of the sleep cycle, even at night when they sleep on purpose. They go very quickly to REMing. The biggest problem with narcolepsy (in addition to the embarrassment it sometimes causes) is that narcoleptic sleep attacks are sometimes accompanied by the total relaxation of muscle tone that is also associated with REM sleep (Dement, 1974; Lucas et al., 1979). The danger involved in suddenly going to sleep and losing muscle control during one's daily activity is obvious. Imagine such an attack occurring while a person is swimming, or driving a car, or crossing the street, for example.

Sleep apnea. "Apnea" means a sudden stop in breathing. If we stop breathing when we are awake and conscious, we can do something about it. We can exercise conscious, voluntary control over our breathing. We cannot do so, however, when we are asleep. **Sleep apnea** involves patterns of sleep during which breathing stops entirely. Usually, episodes are short and long-term dangers are few.

insomnia
the chronic inability to get an adequate amount of sleep

narcolepsy
a disorder characterized by brief, uncontrollable sleep attacks and an immediate descent into REM sleep

sleep apnea
patterns of sleep during which breathing stops momentarily

When apnea episodes are longer, a minute or two, carbon dioxide builds to such a level that the sleeper is awakened, draws a few gasps of air, and returns to sleep, perhaps oblivious to what just happened.

For reasons not clearly understood, sleep apnea appears most commonly in obese, middle-aged males. Sleep apnea is also a prime suspect in the search for the cause of Sudden Infant Death Syndrome, or SIDS for short. In this syndrome, young infants, apparently without any major illness, but sometimes with a slight cold or infection, suddenly die in their sleep. Such sudden death occurs in about two infants per thousand. As stated by Mary Ellen Avery and Ivan Frantz in a recent review of the literature on SIDS and apnea, "The relation of apneic spell, so commonly seen in premature infants, and sudden infant death remains speculative. The reasons for sudden death may be multiple, and our inability to determine a cause means only that we are asking the wrong questions or using the wrong investigative approaches. The final common event in sudden infant death is the quiet cessation of breathing during sleep. Further study of the factors that regulate sleep is surely warranted" (1983, pp. 107–108).

TOPIC SUMMARY

According to William James, what are the four basic characteristics of consciousness?

According to William James, consciousness can be characterized as (1) changing, (2) personal, (3) continuous, and (4) selective. / 148

What is consciousness, and in what way may we speak of levels of consciousness?

Consciousness can be defined as the perception or awareness of our environment and of our own mental processes. As such, consciousness may be thought of as a process that occurs at different levels: immediate, normal consciousness, preconscious, and unconscious. It is also true that some information is beyond our consciousness. / 149

What is the EEG?

What are the four stages of sleep?

The EEG is an instrument that measures the general pattern of the electrical activity of the brain, the most common indicator of sleep stages. In addition to a stage of relaxed wakefulness, characterized by EEG alpha waves, there seem to be four stages, or levels, of sleep: (1) light sleep characterized by low amplitude EEG waves; (2) low amplitude EEG waves with sleep spindles present; (3) delta waves enter the EEG pattern; and (4) deep sleep, with more than 50 percent delta wave activity. / 151

What is REM sleep?

What occurs during REM sleep?

REM sleep is rapid eye movement sleep, which occurs 4–7 times per night. A number of events occur during REM sleep, most notably dreaming. The physiological activities include loss of muscle tone, excitement of sexual organs, shallow, rapid breathing, and increased heart rate and blood pressure. / 152

What are the effects of depriving someone of sleep?

Is there any evidence that there is a need to sleep?

People who have been deprived of sleep show a rebound effect by making up for lost sleep at the earliest possible time. This is true for REM sleep more than for NREM sleep. In this sense, sleep acts like a biological need. However, more deprivation does *not* lead to more rebounding (after a point), which is not the way a biological need would act. Some suggest that the need to sleep is a need only in the evolutionary sense—it is simply a part of being alive, something we do from time to time. / 154

Define manifest and latent dream content.

What is the function of dreams?

Freud believed that dreams are the exercise of the unconscious mind and that interpreting dreams is a way to understand the unconscious. Both manifest content (the actual or reported content) and latent content (the symbolic, "true" content) of dreams mattered to Freud. Others have viewed dreaming as an opportunity for memory consolidation, or as the brain's way of "explaining" its activity during sleep. We do not know just why we dream, much less why we dream what we do. / 156

What changes in consciousness are associated with hypnosis?

There are clearly a number of changes in consciousness that occur during hypnosis, including an increase in suggestibility, a strict focusing of attention, an exaggeration of imagination, a reduction of spontaneous activity, and an unquestioning acceptance of distortions in reality. / 158

What is meditation?

Is meditation an effective means of relaxation and arousal reduction?

Meditation is an altered state of consciousness characterized by an extreme focusing of attention and an alteration of perceptions. It is usually self-induced. There are many claims for the benefits of meditation, including its effectiveness as a relaxation technique, but very few of these claims are supported by experimental evidence. / 160

What are stimulants, and what are their effects?

Stimulants include such drugs as caffeine, nicotine, cocaine, and amphetamines. Their basic effect is to increase the level of nervous system activity, almost always by affecting the activity of the neural synapse. With heavy use, tolerance may develop, as may dependence and addiction. / 162

Identify four depressants, and summarize their effects.

The depressants include such drugs as alcohol, the opiates (e.g., morphine, codeine), heroin, and a variety of synthetic sedatives. All slow nervous system activity, and, in small doses can alleviate feelings of nervousness and anxiety. In large doses, however, tolerance, dependency, and addiction can result. / 163

What characterizes those drugs that are classified as hallucinogens?

Hallucinogens are drugs that alter mood and perceptions. They get their name from their ability to induce hallucinations in which a user may have an experience that is not related to what is going on in the user's environment. / 164

What is the active ingredient in marijuana, and what effects does it have on behavior, both in the short and long term?

The active ingredient in marijuana is THC, or tetrahydrocannabinol. Listing its short- and long-term effects is difficult because of contradictory evidence. However, it does seem that in small doses there is nothing particularly dangerous about the drug, at least in terms of tolerance, dependence, or addiction. It is at least as dangerous as cigarette smoking, and it is illegal. Of more concern is long-term, heavy use. Here, many of the negative side effects that we associate with long-term alcohol use and smoking can occur. / 165

CHAPTER FIVE

LEARNING

TOPIC

It was the spring semester of Jerry's senior year in high school. Basketball season was over, and spring vacation was only a couple of weeks away. Jerry finally agreed that it was time to do something about his nose. Jerry had always been a clumsy youngster and more accident-prone than most. He had played basketball for the past four years and had broken his nose so many times that he had lost count. Now he suffered from chronic nosebleeds. If he sneezed, his nose might bleed for hours. Yes, the time had come to have surgery.

During the surgery, Jerry was under a local anesthetic and was quite aware of what was happening to him. He could smell the odors of the operating room. He recognized that the blood he saw was his own. He didn't feel pain perhaps, but he certainly felt discomfort. He could clearly hear the surgeon snipping off small pieces of bone and cartilage. It was a most unpleasant experience. Later that day, back in his room, discomfort changed to pain—real, numbing pain. He was in the hospital, face black-and-blue, for five days.

That was almost 25 years ago. Jerry is now a psychologist. He is 43 years old. To this day, whenever he goes to a hospital, his nose hurts! He need not be a patient. Even if he is just visiting a friend, after 10 or 15 minutes, his nose starts to ache. He's a psychologist, remember. He knows better. He knows that the pain is just in his head. But that doesn't make the pain seem any less real.

This true story makes two points. First, it demonstrates the lasting power of even simple types of learning. As we shall see, Jerry's experience is a good example of classical conditioning. The sights and sounds of the hospital, once paired with a traumatic experience and pain, can elicit at least some of that response later—even much later. Second, Jerry's aching nose is evidence of a point that we'll make concerning psychotherapy. Insight in itself is not necessarily therapeutic. Simply knowing what causes a problem may not be enough to make that problem go away.

Why We Care

Who we are as individuals, as people in this world, is ultimately a reflection of the unique combination of our inherited characteristics (our *nature*) and our experiences with our environment (our *nurture*). Our nature is largely established at the moment of conception. There isn't much we can do about the genes we have inherited from our parents. At least there is some hope that we *can* influence who we are—what we know, what we feel, what we do—by attending to how we learn, how we change our behaviors as a function of our experience.

How we change and learn and adapt to our environment is clearly a major issue in psychology. In this topic, we'll begin by defining learning. Then we'll concentrate on a deceptively simple form of learning: classical conditioning. Whether they realize it or not, most people are familiar with the basic work of Ivan Pavlov on classical conditioning, and for the sake of simplicity, most of our descriptions of classical conditioning will be based on Pavlov's work with salivating dogs. Once we have the basic procedures in hand, we'll consider why classical conditioning is so important to all of us and how the procedures of classical conditioning are found regularly in our daily lives.

A DEFINITION OF LEARNING

learning
demonstrated by a relatively permanent change in behavior that occurs as the result of practice or experience

Let's begin by defining learning. We shall say that **learning** is demonstrated by any relatively permanent change in behavior that occurs as the result of practice or experience. This definition is a rather standard one, and there are some key points about it that we should explore for a moment.

For one thing, learning involves *changes*. We say that these changes are demonstrated by changes in behavior. The issue here is that learning is a process that cannot be observed directly; it must be inferred from one's performance, from one's behavior. In a literal sense, there is no way that anyone can directly measure what you have learned. We have to ask you to perform and then make judgments about your learning on the basis of your performance. And sometimes we may be wrong.

For example, you may learn everything there is to know about the psychology of learning for your next exam. Just before your exam, someone you care about becomes seriously ill. As a result, you may not get much sleep, and then you develop a sinus headache and catch the flu. When you come in to take your exam, you feel miserable, and you fail the exam, answering only 15 percent of the questions correctly. Your instructor may infer (incorrectly in this case) that you haven't learned very much psychology. On the other hand, there may be someone else in class who has not studied at all and has actually learned very little. But her exam is of the multiple-choice type, and she guesses correctly the answer to 95 percent of the questions. Here your instructor might assume (incorrectly again) that this student has learned a great deal. One way that some psychologists deal with this complication is to say that what is learned is some behavior *potential*, or predisposition. Because what is learned is simply potential, we will not recognize that learning has taken place until the potential is realized in behavior; all we can measure is behavior, or performance, not potential.

We also say that the changes that take place in learning must be *relatively permanent*, or enduring, changes. They are not fleeting or cyclical changes such as those due to fatigue or temporary shifts in motivation. Imagine, for example, that you want to study the behavior of a skilled typist. Typing 60 to 65 words per minute is usually considered to be a good rate. You are going to

Many factors can infuence how well you do on an exam, including how much you study, your health and state of mind, and the type of exam. Because of the influence of such factors, written exams are only measurements of performance rather than potential.

observe Sharon, a secretary who reportedly types 85 words per minute without error.

Early Monday morning you go watch Sharon type. You find her typing only 54 words per minute and making an error every other line. Disappointed, you seek out another typist, but are told that there is none better than Sharon. Two hours later, you return to Sharon's desk and find her typing away at 91 words per minute without error. You wouldn't want to claim that between 8:15 and 10:15 on that Monday morning Sharon "learned" how to type. There's a better explanation for the change in behavior that you have observed. It's called warm-up. Sharon will probably go through this cyclical change in her behavior every Monday morning and to a lesser degree on every other morning of the week. And fatigue, not forgetting, would account for her decreased typing skills if you were to watch her again at the end of the day. These are important changes in behavior, but they are not due to learning. Remember, learned changes are relatively permanent.

We also say, by definition, that learned changes in behavior result from *practice* or *experience.* For one thing, such changes are not due to maturation (i.e., heredity). That we walk when we are about 1 year old probably has more to do with our genes and physical development than with our experience. Similarly, learned changes are not due to automatic physiological reactions, such as sensory adaptation. When we enter a darkened theater, we don't really "learn" to see in the dark. Our vision improves and our behaviors change as our eyes adapt to the lower level of light in the theater. Consider your own behavior when you sit in a tub of hot water. Your behavior changes as you settle down and relax as you adapt to the hot water—more of a physiological change than a learned one.

One final point about the nature of learning is worth mentioning. As students and parents and teachers, we often fall into the habit of thinking that learning is necessarily a good thing. Clearly, it isn't always so. We can learn bad or ineffective habits as readily as we learn good adaptive ones. No one I know ever honestly claimed to enjoy the first cigarette that he or she ever smoked. Yet many people have learned the habit, which is hardly a very adaptive one.

If we put these ideas together, we come up with our definition of learning: Learning is demonstrated by (or inferred from) a relatively permanent change in behavior that occurs as the result of practice or experience. In this topic and the next one, we will focus on two forms or varieties of learning called **conditioning.** Don't be misled into thinking that "conditioning" means something more than "learning." Conditioning and learning are synonymous terms; they have the same definition. We simply agree to call the basic, fundamental types of learning "conditioning."

conditioning
demonstrated by a relatively permanent change in behavior that occurs as the result of practice or experience

Before you go on

How do we define learning?

How do we define conditioning?

PAVLOV AND A CLASSIC DEMONSTRATION

When we think about learning, we generally think about such activities as memorizing the Bill of Rights, or studying for an exam, or learning to *do* something like ice skate. But, in fact, our examination of the psychology of learning begins in the laboratory of a Russian physiologist who taught dogs to salivate in response to tones. How salivating dogs could possibly be relevant to college students is difficult to imagine at first, but please be patient; the relevance will become apparent soon.

Psychology was just beginning to emerge as a separate discipline late in the nineteenth century. At this time, Ivan Pavlov was using his skills as a physiologist to try to understand the basic processes of digestion—work for which he was awarded the Nobel Prize in 1904. His experimental subjects were dogs. Focusing on the salivation reflex, Pavlov knew that he could produce salivation in his subjects by blowing food powder into their mouths. It was simple: Every time he presented the food powder, the dogs began to salivate.

Pavlov's fame in psychology stems from the fact that he noticed and pursued something not so simple. Occasionally, his dogs would salivate *before* the food was put in their mouths. They would salivate at the very sight of the food or at the sight of the laboratory assistant who delivered the food. With this observation, Pavlov was off on a tangent that he pursued for the rest of his life. We now call the procedure he studied **classical conditioning**—a type of learning in which an originally neutral stimulus comes to evoke a new response after having been paired with a stimulus that reflexively evokes that same response. In his honor, we sometimes refer to this type of learning as Pavlovian conditioning. Some psychologists use the term "respondent conditioning," indicating that the response that is learned is directly under the control of (or predicted by) a particular stimulus. We'll stick with the term "classical conditioning" as we examine what is involved in this learning process.

Classical conditioning is a simple procedure that is difficult to describe in words. To keep matters as straightforward as we can, we'll describe classical conditioning as Pavlov demonstrated it (Pavlov, 1927; 1928).

To demonstrate classical conditioning, we first need a stimulus that reliably (consistently) produces a predictable response. The relationship between this stimulus and the response it evokes is usually a natural, unlearned, reflexive one. Given this stimulus, the same response always follows. Here is where Pavlov's food powder comes in. If we present the stimulus food powder, the salivation response reliably follows. There is no learning in this reflexive S-R association, so we call the stimulus an **unconditioned stimulus (UCS)** and the response an **unconditioned response (UCR)**. So now we have the UCS (food powder) producing the UCR (salivation).

To get classical conditioning under way, we need a second, neutral stimulus that, when presented, produces a minimal response or a response of no

classical conditioning
learning in which an originally neutral stimulus comes to evoke a new response after having been paired with a stimulus that reflexively evokes that same response

unconditioned stimulus (UCS)
in classical conditioning, a stimulus (e.g., food powder) that reflexively and reliably evokes a response (the UCR)

unconditioned response (UCR)
in classical conditioning, a response (e.g., salivation) reliably and reflexively evoked by a stimulus (the UCS)

Pavlov and his staff studying the effect of classical conditioning on his famous dog.

Figure 10.1

Pavlovian classical conditioning. See text for explanation.

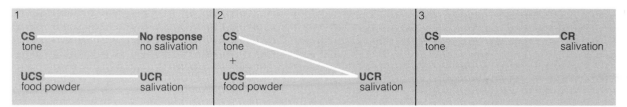

particular interest. For this stimulus, called the **conditioned stimulus (CS)**, Pavlov chose a tone. At first, when a tone is sounded a dog *will* respond. It will, among other things, perk up its ears and try to "orient" toward the source of the sound. After awhile, however, the dog will get used to the tone ("habituate" we say) and will essentially ignore it.

Now we are ready to go. We have two stimuli, a tone (CS) that produces a minimal response of no particular interest and food powder (UCS) that reliably produces salivation (UCR).

Once we get our stimuli and responses straight, the rest is easy. The two stimuli are paired. That is, they are presented at about the same time—first, the tone, then the food powder, CS then UCS. The salivation response occurs automatically in response to the food powder. So we have CS then UCS, followed by UCR, or tone-food-salivation. Each pairing of the CS and the UCS may be considered a conditioning *trial*. If we repeat this procedure a number of times—have a number of trials–conditioning (learning) takes place. We produce a relatively permanent change in behavior as a result of experience. Now when we present the tone by itself, the dog salivates, something it did not do before. Now the dog salivates not just in response to the food powder, but also in response to the tone, or the CS. To keep *this* salivation separate from salivation in response to the food powder, we call it a **conditioned response (CR),** indicating that it has been learned or conditioned.

Let's review this one more time, referring to Figure 10.1 which presents the procedure in a schematic diagram. (1) We start with two stimuli—the CS, which evokes no response, and the UCS, which evokes the UCR. (2) We repeatedly present the two stimuli together. (3) We find that when we present the CS alone it now produces a CR.

Before we examine some of the phenomena associated with classical conditioning, there are two technical points to make. First, the CR never quite reaches the strength of the UCR no matter how many times the CS and the UCS are paired. In Pavlov's demonstration, for example, the CR salivation is the same *type* of response as the UCR, but we never get as much salivation in response to the tone as we originally got in response to the food powder. Second, *how* the CS and the UCS are paired does matter. If you think about it, you'll realize that there are many ways in which two stimuli can be presented at about the same time. One method works best: The CS comes first, followed by the UCS about 0.5 seconds later, or tone-food-salivation again. (For an apparent exception to this rule of thumb, see the Topic Expansion.)

conditioned stimulus (CS)
in classical conditioning, an originally neutral stimulus (e.g., a tone) that, when paired with a UCS, comes to evoke a new response

conditioned response (CR)
in classical conditioning, the learned response (e.g., salivation) evoked by the CS after conditioning

Before you go on

Summarize the essential procedures of Pavlovian classical conditioning.

CLASSICAL CONDITIONING PHENOMENA

Now that we have the basics of Pavlovian conditioning in mind, we can consider some of the details that go along with it—some of the insights developed in Pavlov's laboratory. We'll first see how a classical conditioning experiment actually proceeds. Then we'll see what happens if we continue to present the CS without pairing it with the UCS. Finally, we'll consider what happens when new stimuli, similar to the CS, are presented to a classically conditioned organism. Just to keep our terminology firmly in mind, we'll continue to refer to the original Pavlovian example of salivating dogs.

Acquisition

acquisition
the process in classical conditioning in which the strength of the CR increases with repeated pairings of the CS and UCS

The stage of conditioning during which the strength of the CR is increased—where a dog acquires the new response of salivating to a tone—is called **acquisition.** When classical conditioning begins, the conditioned stimulus does not produce a conditioned response. After a few pairings of the CS and UCS together (conditioning trials), we can demonstrate the presence of a CR. There will be some saliva produced in response to the tone presented alone. The more trials, or presentations of the CS and UCS together, the more the dog will salivate in response to the tone when it is presented alone. Over repeated trials, the increase in CR strength (here, the amount of saliva in response to the tone) is rather rapid at first, but soon starts to slow and eventually levels off. Figure 10.2 illustrates this acquisition phase of a classical conditioning demonstration.

Extinction and Spontaneous Recovery

Assume that we now have a dog that salivates at the sound of a tone. Acquisition is complete. Now suppose that we go through a series of trials during which the CS (the tone) is presented, but is *not* paired with the UCS (no more food powder). The result of this procedure is that the CR will weaken. The dog will eventually stop salivating to the tone. This process is called **extinction,** and we say that the CR has extinguished.

extinction
the process in classical conditioning in which the strength of the CR decreases with repeated presentations of the CS alone

It would appear that we're right back where we started. Because the CR has extinguished, when we present the tone, our dog does nothing—at least it no longer salivates. Let's give our dog a rest and return it to the kennel. When the dog is returned to the laboratory later and the tone is sounded, the dog salivates again! Not a lot, perhaps, but the CR salivation does return, or

---

Figure 10.2

The stages of conditioning.

(1) Acquisition is produced by repeated pairings of the CS and the UCS. The strength of the CR increased, rapidly at first, then more slowly.

(2) Extinction is produced by presenting the CS without the UCS. The strength of the CR decreases.

(3) After a rest interval, spontaneous recovery produces a partial return of the CR.

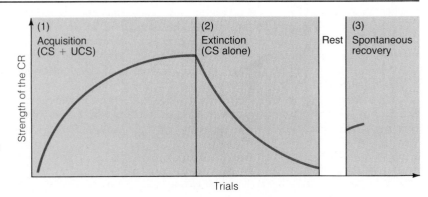

recover. It recovers automatically, or spontaneously. We call this phenomenon **spontaneous recovery.** Both extinction and spontaneous recovery are illustrated in Figure 10.2.

That spontaneous recovery typically takes place after extinction, and following a rest interval, indicates two things. First, one series of extinction trials may not be sufficient to eliminate a conditioned response. To get our dog to *stop* salivating altogether, we may have to run a series of extinction trials, many of which may be followed by a small spurt of spontaneous recovery. Second, what is happening during extinction is not literally "forgetting"— at least not in the usual sense. It seems that the response is not forgotten so much as it is *suppressed.* That is, the salivation response is still there, but it is not showing up in performance during extinction; it returns later, in spontaneous recovery.

spontaneous recovery
the phenomenon in classical conditioning in which a previously extinguished CR returns after a rest interval

generalization
the phenomenon in classical conditioning in which a CR is evoked by stimuli different from, but similar to, the CS

discrimination
the phenomenon in classical conditioning in which an organism learns to make a CR in response to only one CS, but not to other stimuli

Before you go on

In classical conditioning, what are acquisition, extinction, and spontaneous recovery?

Generalization and Discrimination

Before we consider the application of classical conditioning to human behaviors, we should introduce two important concepts that were identified and studied in Pavlov's laboratory.

During the usual course of conditioning, a tone of a given pitch is consistently used as the conditioned stimulus. After repeated pairings of this tone with food powder, a dog comes to salivate when the tone is presented alone.

What will happen if we present a different tone, one that the dog has not heard before? Typically, the dog will salivate in response to it also. This response may not be as strong as the original CR. How strong it is, or how much saliva is produced, depends primarily on how similar the new tone is to the original CS. The closer it is to the original, the more saliva it will generate. This process is called **generalization,** and we say that the conditioned response will generalize to other new, yet similar stimuli.

This is a powerful phenomenon. It means that an unconditioned stimulus need not be paired with all possible conditioned stimuli. If you choose an average, or midrange conditioned stimulus, the conditioned response will automatically generalize to many other similar stimuli. Conditioning trials do not have to be applied over and over again for separate stimuli. A graph of the generalization process is presented in Figure 10.3.

So if a dog is conditioned to salivate to a middle-pitch tone, it will also salivate to higher and lower tones through generalization. What if we do not want it to? What if we want our dog to salivate to the CS alone and not to other tones? We would use **discrimination** training. Discrimination is, in a sense, the opposite of generalization. In discrimination training, we would present the dog with many tones, but would pair the UCS food powder with only one of them, the chosen CS. We might, for example, pair the food powder with a tone of middle C. A lower tone, say A, would also be presented to the dog, but would not be followed by food powder. At first, there would be some saliva produced in response to the A tone (through generalization). Eventually, however, our subject would learn to discriminate and would no longer respond by salivating to the A tone.

Some discriminations may be too difficult to make. One of Pavlov's students conditioned a dog to salivate to a stimulus circle. The circle was paired with food powder, and after awhile the dog learned to salivate when the CS

Figure 10.3
Generalization. Presenting stimuli other than the CS may produce a CR. How much CR is produced depends on the similarity between the new stimulus and the original CS.

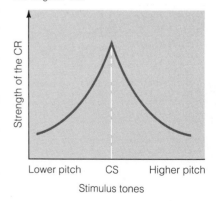

circle was presented. When the dog was presented with a stimulus in the shape of an ellipse, salivation followed—generalization again. The circle and the ellipse were then presented many times. Now the circle was always followed by food powder; the ellipse never was. Eventually, the dog learned to discriminate, salivating only to the circle and never to the ellipse. This procedure was repeated, gradually changing the shape of the oval to make it rounder and more similar to the conditioned stimulus circle. The circle was always followed by food powder; the ellipses were not.

At one point, the dog could no longer discriminate between the two stimuli. The oval now looked too much like the circle. Because it was unable to discriminate between the two stimuli, we might predict that the dog would simply salivate to both of them. However, the behavior of the animal in this situation changed markedly. It stopped salivating altogether. It began to bark and whimper and tried to escape.

To Pavlov, the dog appeared to be nervous and anxious. The dog was being asked to make a discrimination that it could not make. It was in conflict. Pavlov referred to the dog's reactions as **experimental neurosis.** In describing the dog's behavior, Pavlov wrote, " . . . in short, it presented all the symptoms of acute neurosis" (Pavlov, 1927, p. 291). Now whether or not the reaction of this laboratory animal provides us with insight about neuroses in humans is open to debate. Do anxiety and nervousness originate simply from an inability to make proper discriminations among stimuli? Probably not, but as Barry Schwartz (1984, p. 128) says, it is tempting to think of neurosis in such terms, and, if nothing else, "What Pavlov's demonstration showed is that a very specific, isolated conditioning experience can transform the general behavior of an animal. It is not implausible that some human neuroses might stem from particular conditioning experiences of this sort."

experimental neurosis
a condition of anxiety and agitation evidenced by subjects that are asked to make too fine a discrimination in a classical conditioning task

Before you go on

In classical conditioning, what are generalization and discrimination?

THE SIGNIFICANCE OF CLASSICAL CONDITIONING: WHAT ABOUT PEOPLE?

It is time to leave our discussion of dogs and salivation and Pavlov's laboratory. There is, of course, some practical application to all of this. Applications of classical conditioning are all around us. In this section, we'll review three areas in which Pavlovian conditioning can influence human behavior: in the laboratory, in the acquisition of emotional responses, and in the development of the connotative meanings of words.

In the Laboratory

Of one thing we can be sure: We can bring the Pavlovian procedure directly into the human learning laboratory. Here is a laboratory demonstration that you can do with a friend. Have your subject seated at a desk, relaxed and staring straight ahead. Position a drinking straw just off to the side of your subject's face so that it cannot be seen.

Your UCS (unconditioned stimulus) will be a strong puff of air through the straw into your subject's eye. The obvious UCR (unconditioned response) will be an involuntary, sudden blink of the eye. For a CS (conditioned stimulus), just tap on the desk. After a brief habituation period, your subject will not respond to your tap, and you'll be ready to go. Remember the best sequence: CS-UCS-UCR, or tap-puff-blink. Repeat this procedure a dozen times or so and then present the CS alone. Tap on the desk and your subject will (should) respond with the CR (conditioned response) by blinking to the tap on the desk.

This does qualify as conditioning. There is a relatively permanent change in your subject's behavior as a result of the experience of pairing a tap and a puff of air together. As it happens, it is not a terribly useful or significant sort of learning—the response here is rather trivial—but it is learning.

Conditioned Emotional Responses

One of the most significant aspects of classical conditioning is its role in affecting our emotional responses to stimuli in our environment. There are very few stimuli that naturally, or instinctively, produce a specific emotional response. Yet think of all those things that *do* directly influence how we feel.

For example, very young children seldom seem afraid of spiders, airplane rides, or snakes. (Some children actually seem to enjoy each of these.) Now consider how many people *are* afraid of these things. There are many stimuli in our environments that cause us to be afraid. Many of our fears are quite rational and realistic. When we claim that many emotional responses are learned through classical conditioning, we are not just referring to intense, irrational, phobic fears.

Childhood experiences often influence our adult likes, dislikes, and fears. A pleasant, nonfearful experience with swimming early in life will usually lead to healthy attitudes toward swimming and water later in life.

What scares you? What makes you feel at ease, pleasant, comfortable? Why? Might you not feel particularly upset or distressed in a certain store because you once had an unpleasant experience there? Might you fondly anticipate a vacation at the beach because of a very enjoyable vacation you had there as a child? Do you shudder at the sight of a police car? Do you smile at the thought of a payroll envelope? Does walking into the classroom on the day of an exam cause you some anxiety? In each of these cases, are we not talking about classical conditioning? (To be fair, we must say that not all of our learned emotional reactions are acquired through classical conditioning alone. As we shall see in our next two topics, there are other possibilities.)

Think back to Jerry and his experience with hospitals. For Jerry, the CS of hospital sights and sounds was paired with the UCS of an operative procedure that caused a UCR of pain. After just one experience, the pairing led to a CR of discomfort associated with the CS of the hospital. Notice, too, that Jerry's conditioned response generalized to many other hospitals, not just the one in which his surgery was performed. And the conditioned response has obviously lasted a long time.

Let's take a detailed look at one example of the conditioning of an emotional response. In 1920, John B. Watson and Rosalie Raynor published a summary article on a series of experiments they performed with Little Albert. Little Albert's experiences have become quite famous, although even Watson and Raynor's summary of their own work tended to oversimplify matters somewhat (Samuelson, 1980).

At least on the surface, the Little Albert experiments provide a good model for the classical conditioning of emotional responses. Eleven-month-old Albert was given many toys to play with. Among other things, he was allowed to play with a live white rat. Albert seemed to enjoy the rat—he certainly showed no signs of fearing it. Then conditioning began. As Albert reached for the rat, one of the experimenters made a loud sudden noise by banging on a metal bar with a hammer. The loud noise was frightening—that much Watson and Raynor had established two months earlier when they first

Rosalie Raynor and John B. Watson with Little Albert. Albert's conditioned fear of a white rat generalized to other similar stimuli, including a mask with a beard and mustache.

observed Albert in the hospital laboratory. At least Albert made responses that Watson and Raynor felt indicated fear.

After repeated pairings of the noise and the rat, Albert's reaction to the rat underwent a relatively permanent change. Now when presented with the rat, Albert would at first start to reach out toward the rat, then he would recoil and cry, often trying to bury his head in his blanket. He was clearly making emotional responses to a stimulus that did not evoke those responses before it was paired with loud sudden noises. This sounds like classical conditioning: The rat serves as the CS and the loud sudden noise as the UCS that evokes the UCR of an emotional fear response. After repeated pairings of the rat and the noise (the CS and UCS), the rat evoked the same sort of fear response (or CR).

Watson and Raynor claimed that Albert's fear of the white rat *generalized* to all sorts of other stimuli, a dog, a ball of cotton, and even a mask with a beard and mustache. Albert's emotional reaction probably did generalize to other similar stimuli, but in a number of instances, Watson and Raynor did not test for generalization in a straightforward way. They occasionally paired the loud noise (UCS) with new stimuli (S) before testing to see what reaction they might produce (Harris, 1979).

As it happens, there are a number of problems with the Watson and Raynor demonstration of learned fear—not the least of which is the unethical treatment administered to poor Albert. Watson had previously argued (1919) that emotional experiences of early childhood could affect an individual for a lifetime, yet here he was purposely frightening a young child (without the advised consent of his mother). In fact, Albert's mother removed him from the hospital and Watson and Raynor's experiment before they had a chance to undo what they had done. They were convinced that they could uncondition Little Albert, but as fate would have it, they never got the chance. It should also be mentioned that a number of researchers tried to replicate Watson and Raynor's experiment (despite ethical considerations), but they were generally not successful (Harris, 1979).

Even with all these technical disclaimers, it is not difficult to see how the Little Albert demonstration can be used as a model for describing how fear and other emotional responses can develop. When they began their project, Albert didn't respond fearfully to the rat, or to the cotton, or to the mask.

After a few trials of pairing a neutral stimulus (the rat) with an emotion-producing stimulus (the loud noise), Albert appeared afraid of a number of white, furry, fuzzy objects.

Before you go on
Briefly summarize the Little Albert experimental demonstration.

The Meaning of Words

Consider the meaning of words. The meaning of a word is more than just its definition. *Mother* may be defined as a "child-bearing member of the species." That may be how *mother* is *defined*, but that is not what mother *means. Mother* means all sorts of things—apple pie, comfort, love, warmth, acceptance, etc. Indeed, part of what *mother* means involves how you *feel* about mother. This aspect of the meaning of a word is called its *connotative meaning.*

How you feel about *mother* is largely a reflection of classical conditioning—the pairing of feelings in the presence of your mother and hearing the word *mother*. Words that are paired with pleasant situations tend to take on pleasant connotations, such as *money, love, baby*. Words that are heard in unpleasant contexts tend to become unpleasant words, for example, *war, death, final exam.*

As a last example, assume that I have before me two small boys, each 3 years old. I ask them to say quickly, out loud, everything they think of when I say a word. I say "dog." Boy 1 responds, "oh, doggie; my doggie; Spot; my friend; good dog; go fetch; friend; my dog; Spot." Boy 2 responds, "Oooo dog; bite; teeth; blood; bad dog; hurts me; bad dog." Now both of these boys know what a dog *is*. How they feel about dogs is another matter and is quite obviously a function of their experience with dogs—a classically conditioned reaction.

Before you go on
What is connotative meaning, and what does it have to do with classical conditioning?

Words mean different things to different people. For example, young children who have pleasant experiences with dogs will probably have pleasant thoughts and feelings about dogs as they grow older.

"How to study" books often recommend that students find one special place to study. In this way, being in that place is associated with studying due to classical conditioning.

APPLYING CLASSICAL CONDITIONING TO YOUR STUDY OF PSYCHOLOGY

Every so often, it is a good idea to pause and reflect on the psychology you have been reading to see if you can find a practical application for what you have been learning. As we come to the end of this topic, now might be just such a time. We have spent a lot of time talking about Pavlov and salivating dogs. You should be convinced that classical conditioning can be applied to human behaviors. Is there any example you can think of where classical conditioning could be relevant for studying psychology?

One thing "how to study" books often recommend is that students find one special place to do most of their studying. This place may be at home or somewhere on campus, but the suggestion is usually given that this place be reserved *only* for studying. What is behind this recommendation is the logic of classical conditioning. We shouldn't recommend that someone study in bed. Being in bed has been associated with anything but studying—being sick perhaps, or just sleeping. Studying at the kitchen or dining room table is seldom a good idea either for the same sort of reason: Those places have been conditioned to a different set of responses (eating) that are not compatible with effective studying.

You should condition yourself to always study in the same place, or, at most, two or three places. Do nothing there but study. For this purpose, college libraries serve very well. It even makes sense to slip into an unused classroom during the day to study. There is an advantage to studying and learning in the same physical environment in which you will be tested later.

Learning is a process that cannot be observed directly. It is inferred from our observation of relatively permanent changes in behavior (or performance) that occur as the result of practice or experience. In this topic, we have reviewed the procedures of classical, or Pavlovian, conditioning. One of the major applications of Pavlovian conditioning is its role in emotional behavior. Many of the stimuli to which we respond emotionally do not evoke that response naturally or reflexively; rather, they do so through classical conditioning. In other words, many of the stimuli in our environments that give rise to pleasant and unpleasant feelings do so because they have been previously paired with more inherently pleasant or unpleasant experiences or situations. In the next topic, we will discuss another type of learning—operant conditioning.

Two conclusions about classical conditioning that were formulated in Pavlov's laboratory persisted unchallenged for nearly 40 years. One conclusion was that the best way to quickly establish a strong conditioned response (CR) is to present the unconditioned stimulus (UCS) shortly after the conditioned stimulus (CS). Years of research suggested that an interval of approximately 0.5 seconds between the CS and the UCS works best. The second assumption that was commonly made about classical conditioning was that virtually any neutral conditioned stimulus could be paired with an unconditioned stimulus to produce effective classical conditioning. That is, if we found a reliable UCS-UCR, any CS paired with the UCS could be used to develop a CS-CR.

It now appears that there is at least one excellent example of classical conditioning in which the CS-UCS interval may be much longer than 0.5 seconds—even hours long. This same example also suggests that some stimuli make more effective conditioned stimuli than others. The example is found in the research on the formation of aversions (very strong dislikes) to certain tastes.

First let's explore the time interval issue. Many studies have confirmed that rats, and probably people, can be classically conditioned to avoid particular foods (Garcia, Ervin, & Koelling, 1966; Revulsky & Garcia, 1970). In the rat experiments, subjects eat (or drink) a food that has been given a distinctive taste. The rats are also poisoned, or treated with X rays, so they will develop nausea. The feelings of nausea do not occur until *hours after the food has been eaten.* (In a few days, the rats are perfectly normal and healthy again.)

Even though there has been a delay between the flavored food (CS) and the feelings of nausea (UCS), in just one trial the rats learn to avoid the food. Similarly, children undergoing treatment for cancer typically experience nausea as an unpleasant side effect of chemotherapy. Such children often show a strong taste aversion for whatever they ate hours before their treatment—even if the food was ice cream (Bernstein, 1978).

The time delay between the CS and UCS here is obviously at odds with the standard belief that, to be effective, CS and UCS need to be paired together in time. Another difficulty centers on why the *taste* of previously eaten food should serve as the CS for nausea that occurs hours later. That is, why is the nausea associated with the taste of food instead of some other stimulus event that could be paired with the nausea? Think of this experience happening to you. You go to a restaurant and order a piece of pumpkin pie and a cup of coffee. Hours later, you suffer severe stomach cramps and nausea. Why should you associate these with the pie and/or coffee and not the type of chair you sat on, or the color of car you drove to the restaurant, or who you happened to eat with? As it happens, we may have a predisposition, or bias, toward associating some things with others. Consider the following experiment.

Rats are allowed to lick at a tube that delivers a strongly flavored solution to their cage. Each time they lick at the tube, they experience the taste of the solution, a clicking sound is produced, and a light flashes. So the rats are presented with three stimuli simultaneously: taste, click, and light. Then some of the rats have their feet shocked (painfully) every time they lick the tube of solution. Other rats are given a drug that makes them very sick.

Then all the rats are given a choice of the type of solution they can drink. They can drink a strongly flavored solution that is quiet and dark (not accompanied by a click or a light). Or, they can drink a tasteless solution from a tube that presents a click and a light at each lick (a bright, noisy solution). The results of such a procedure are very clear-cut: (1) Rats that are poisoned now avoid the solution with the distinctive taste and drink the bright, noisy solution. (2) Rats who had been shocked now avoid the solution with the click and light and choose to drink the tasty solution (Garcia & Koelling, 1966). The point is that associating nausea and sickness with taste is much more natural than associating them with noises and lights. Noises and lights, on the other hand, show an *associative bias* (Schwartz, 1984) to shock rather than to nausea.

What these studies on taste aversion tell us, then, is that CS-UCS intervals may, in some cases, be considerably longer than the nominal 0.5 seconds, and that organisms may be more prepared (or biased toward) forming some associations than others through classical conditioning.

TOPIC SUMMARY

How do we define learning?

How do we define conditioning?

Learning and conditioning have the same definition. Both are demonstrated by a relatively permanent change in behavior that occurs as a result of practice or experience. / 173

Summarize the essential procedures of Pavlovian classical conditioning.

In classical, or Pavlovian, conditioning, a stimulus that originally evokes a response of no particular interest (a conditioned stimulus) is paired with a stimulus (an unconditioned stimulus) that reliably produces a response (an unconditioned response). As a result of this pairing, the CS comes to evoke a response (a conditioned response) that is the same as the original UCR. / 175

In classical conditioning, what are acquisition, extinction, and spontaneous recovery?

In classical conditioning, acquisition is an increase in the strength of the CR after it is repeatedly paired with the CS and the UCS. Extinction is a noticeable decrease in the strength of the CR that occurs when the CS is repeatedly presented without the UCS. Spontaneous recovery is the return of the strength of the CR after extinction, following a rest interval. / 177

In classical conditioning, what are generalization and discrimination?

In generalization, we find that a response (CR) conditioned to a specific stimulus (CS) will also be evoked by other, similar stimuli. The more similar the new stimuli are to the original CS, the greater the CR. In many ways, discrimination is the opposite of generalization. It is a matter of learning to make a CR in response to a specific CS and learning not to make a CR in response to other stimuli. / 178

Briefly summarize the Little Albert experimental demonstration.

The Watson and Raynor Little Albert demonstration involved pairing a loud sudden noise (the UCS) with the neutral stimulus of a white rat (the CS). As a result of presenting these two stimuli together, Albert came to display a learned fear response (a CR) to the originally neutral rat. It was claimed that the conditioned fear generalized to other similar stimuli. This model has been used to explain learned emotional reactions to events in our environments. / 181

What is connotative meaning, and what does it have to do with classical conditioning?

The connotative meaning of a word is the emotional response or feeling that the word evokes. It is thought that how we feel about words is largely classically conditioned. / 181

TOPIC

There were approximately 25 students enrolled in the Psychology of Learning class that met every Monday, Wednesday, and Friday morning from 9:00 to 9:50. The instructor was a dynamic lecturer. The topic for the week was operant conditioning. After describing the procedures of operant conditioning and stressing its importance in everyday life, the instructor suggested that the class try to use operant conditioning principles to change the behaviors of one of its professors.

The idea seemed like a good one, and the choice was easy to make. Following the learning class, most of the students moved across the hall for a class in child psychology. It was a larger class, with as many as 75-80 students in attendance on a good day. The professor in the child psychology class had a very boring lecture style: He simply read his notes to the class. Every day he would go through the same ritual. He would find his place in his notes, check the time on his pocket watch, and then read to the class for 50 minutes. He wasn't a poor reader, and what he was reading was no doubt quality psychology. But his classroom style, the students thought, left much to be desired. They decided to condition his behavior.

The class decided to reward the professor for doing what they wanted him to do by smiling, looking attentive, and appearing to take many notes. When he did what the students did not want him to do, they would look away, appear bored, and stop taking notes.

The project began on a Wednesday. When the students assembled after class that day, they realized that they weren't very well organized. They hadn't specifically defined exactly *what* it was they wanted to reward. They only thought that they wanted their professor to stop reading to them. The students thought that after that first day the professor *was* looking up from his notes a bit more than usual, but because they did not have a good baseline for comparison, they weren't even sure of that.

After their first "failure" on Wednesday, the students did get some results on Friday. By the end of class, the professor was looking up from his notes more than usual and he was moving around in his chair. Monday's class brought a major breakthrough: The professor rose from the chair! From time to time he would sit down again (only to be ignored), and he would not give up physical contact with his notes. He was still reading, but occasionally he would stand to do so.

On the first Wednesday: nothing. The following Friday: some movement. The next Monday: standing. By the following Friday, about halfway through the class period, the professor was standing in the corner; notes still on his desk, he was talking to the class about child psychology. Think about that. In just five days these students lifted their professor from his chair and placed him in the corner! The students had no doubt that within 10 minutes they could have moved their professor from one corner to another. All this was done simply by rewarding some behaviors with attention and ignoring others—and in fewer than five classes. The class was impressed.

This is a true story. I was one of those 25 students, and I was very impressed indeed. The sight of our instructor leaning back in the corner of our classroom is still a vivid memory. The end of this story is not a happy one. As you might imagine, when our instructor got to the corner, we could no longer control ourselves. We started laughing, and our instructor demanded to know what was going on. When he was told, he did not take kindly to having been the subject in our little experiment and went back to reading his notes to us. If you try this exercise, choose the subject of your experiment and the behaviors you want to condition with care.

Why We Care

In our last topic, we examined the basic procedures and phenomena associated with classical conditioning. In this topic, we turn our attention to operant conditioning. Remember our definition of conditioning in general: Conditioning is demonstrated by a relatively permanent change in behavior that occurs as a result of practice or experience. In classical conditioning, relatively permanent changes in behavior arise through the experience of pairing two stimuli, a CS and a UCS. As a result of this pairing, the CS comes to evoke a response that it did not evoke before, called a CR. We saw that one of the major applications of classical conditioning was in establishing emotional reactions to originally neutral stimuli.

In operant conditioning, what matters most are the consequences of an organism's behavior. The basic premise is that our behaviors are controlled by the consequences they produce. Learning is a matter of increasing the rate of those responses that produce positive consequences and decreasing the rate of responses that produce negative consequences. We shall see in this topic that a great deal of human behavior can be explained in terms of operant conditioning.

First, we'll define some of the terminology of operant conditioning. What is operant conditioning, and how might it be demonstrated? As we did with classical conditioning, we'll then look at a laboratory demonstration of operant conditioning. Because the concept of reinforcement is so important in operant conditioning, we'll spend a good deal of time examining some of the principles of reinforcement—and punishment.

THE BASICS OF OPERANT CONDITIONING

Most of the early work on operant conditioning was done by B. F. Skinner and is sometimes called "Skinnerian conditioning" for that reason. Skinner did not "discover" operant conditioning, however. The techniques of operant conditioning had been applied for hundreds of years before Skinner was born. Skinner brought that earlier work, most of it casual, some of it scientific, into the psychology laboratory. There he investigated the procedures of operant conditioning with a unique vigor and helped the rest of us realize the significance of the process.

Toward a Definition

You'll recall that describing classical conditioning in words alone was difficult, so we relied on a diagram of the procedure to help us understand it. For operant conditioning, we have the opposite problem. Diagrams are difficult, the words are easy. **Operant conditioning** is changing the probability or rate of a response on the basis of the consequences that result from that response. Responses followed by reinforcement tend to increase in rate; those not followed by reinforcement tend to decrease in rate.

operant conditioning
changing the rate of a response on the basis of the consequences that result from that response

As it happens, the words that describe the essential nature of operant conditioning are not Skinner's, but those of E. L. Thorndike (1911). It was Thorndike's observation (his "law of effect") that responses are learned when they are followed by a "satisfying state of affairs" (p. 245). If an organism makes a response and then experiences a satisfying state of affairs (is reinforced), the organism will tend to make that response again. On the

E. L. Thorndike

other hand, if a response is *not* followed by a satisfying state of affairs (is not reinforced), then the organism will tend *not* to make that response again. Thorndike seemed to be saying something like, "We tend to do, and continue to do, whatever makes us feel good." This simple and seemingly trivial observation is in fact a profound one—profound because it is true. Our behaviors *are* shaped by their consequences.

Examples of operant conditioning are all around us. One hardly needs special apparatus or a laboratory to observe the principle at work. Imagine a mother rushing through the supermarket with her toddler seated in the shopping cart. The youngster is screaming at the top of his lungs for a candy bar. Over and over, echoing throughout the store, "I wanna candy bar! I wanna candy bar!" Mother is doing a good (and appropriate) job of ignoring this monstrous behavior until she spies a neighbor coming down the next aisle. The neighbor has her three children with her, and all three are acting like perfect, quiet angels. What's a mother to do? She races by the checkout lanes, grabs a chocolate bar, and gives it to her child. Does one have to be an expert in child psychology (or operant conditioning) to predict what will happen on the next visit to the store? Reinforced behaviors tend to recur. Screaming "worked" this time so it will be tried again.

As we did with classical conditioning, we'll use examples from the laboratory to summarize the basic procedures and phenomena of operant conditioning. Once again, see if you can find examples from your own personal experience that make the same points.

Before you go on
What is the essence of operant conditioning?

The Procedures of Operant Conditioning

To demonstrate operant conditioning in the controlled environment of the laboratory, Skinner built a special piece of apparatus. He called it an operant chamber. Although Skinner never uses the term and says he doesn't like it (Skinner, 1984), we now often call this device a Skinner box. There's not much to it. Figure 11.1 shows a standard Skinner box. The chamber pictured here is designed for rats. The box is empty except for a small bar or lever that protrudes from one wall and a small cup to hold a piece of rat food. Pellets of food are automatically dispensed from a pellet holder through a tube into the food cup. Pellets are released one at a time when a switch is closed, and depressing the bar or lever all the way down is one way to close the switch and release a pellet.

Now that we have our chamber, we need a subject. If we place a hungry rat (operationally defined as one deprived of food for a certain period of time) into the chamber *and do nothing else,* the rat will occasionally press the bar. There is very little else for it to do in there. The rat is freely emitting a response that its environment allows. (Such responses are called "operants," indicating that they are freely emitted and not under the direct control of some stimulus.) The rate at which the rat emits such a response is called its *base rate* (or baseline rate) of responding. Over the course of an hour, our rat may press the lever 8 to 10 times.

After a reasonable period of observation, we activate the food dispenser so that a pellet of food is delivered every time the bar is pressed. In accord with Thorndike's law of effect, the rate of the bar pressing response increases. The rat may reach the point of pressing the bar not 8-10 times per hour, but at a rate of as many as 500-600 times per hour. Learning has taken place. There has been a "relatively permanent change in behavior as a result of experience."

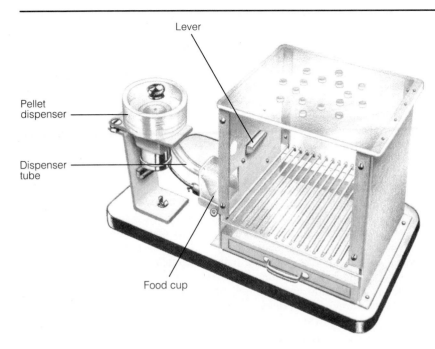

Lever

Pellet
dispenser

Dispenser
tube

Food cup

Figure 11.1
A drawing of an operant chamber, or Skinner box.

Here is a little subtlety: Has the rat learned to press the bar? In any sense can we say that we have taught the rat a bar-pressing response? No. The rat knew how to press the bar, and did so, long before we introduced the food pellets as a reward for its behavior. What it did learn—the change in behavior that took place—was a change in the *rate* of response, not in response per se.

The Stages of Operant Conditioning

Now that we have the basic idea of operant conditioning in mind, let's explore just how one goes about using the procedure. A couple of related questions need to be addressed: How do you get your organism to make the response you want it to in the first place? What happens if you stop reinforcing a respone?

Shaping. One of the problems with operant conditioning is that before you can reinforce a response, you have to get that response to occur in the first place. If your rat never pressed the bar, it would never get a pellet. What if you place your rat in an operant chamber and discover that after grooming itself and wandering about, it stops, stares off into space, and settles down, facing away from the lever and the food cup. Your apparatus is prepared to deliver a food pellet as soon as your rat presses the bar, but it appears that you may have a long wait. You want to get going now.

In such a circumstance, you could use the procedure called **shaping**. Shaping involves reinforcing *successive approximations* of the response that you ultimately want to condition. We say that you can "shape the bar-pressing response."

You have a button that delivers a pellet to the food cup even though the bar is not pressed. When your rat turns to face the lever you deliver a pellet, reinforcing that behavior. It's not exactly the response you want, but at least the rat is now facing in the right direction. You don't give your rat another pellet until it moves toward the bar. It gets another pellet for moving even closer to the bar. The next pellet doesn't come until the rat touches the bar.

shaping
a procedure of reinforcing successive approximations of a desired response until the actual desired response is made

Each reinforcement, then, is delivered as your rat successively approximates the bar-press response you are looking for. Eventually the rat will press the bar far enough to close the switch and deliver a pellet. Shaping is over, and the rat is on its own.

In practice this procedure is not as easy as it may sound. You have to be quick with your button, and you must make sure that each reinforced response is really closer to the one you ultimately want. Remember that your rat will continue to do whatever it was doing just before it got reinforced. If you're not careful, your rat may be reinforced for running to the lever alone, or bobbing its head up and down, or turning circles, instead of pressing the lever. This point is an important one: To be effective at increasing the rate of a response, reinforcers need to be delivered immediately after the desired response takes place. The greater the delay of reinforcement, the less effective the conditioning.

Our opening story described what was basically a shaping procedure. We did not start off by reinforcing our instructor for standing in the corner. If we had waited for that behavior to occur, we would have had nothing to reinforce ("corner-standing" behavior had a base rate of nearly zero). We started reinforcing him just for looking up from his notes. Then we reinforced movements in his chair and standing. Eventually we came to reinforce movements toward the corner. Then, once our professor got to the corner, we lost control of our experiment.

Before you go on

Why do we need shaping, and how does it work?

Acquisition, Extinction, and Spontaneous Recovery Once an organism begins to freely emit the responses you wish to reinforce, the procedure of operant conditioning is simple. Immediately following a desired response, a reinforcer is provided to the organism. As responses produce reinforcement, they become more and more likely to occur. The increase in response rate that we find following reinforcement will generally be slow at first, then become more rapid, and eventually will level off. We call this phase or stage of operant conditioning "acquisition." Figure 11.2 is a curve depicting the stages of operant conditioning, including acquisition. It is very important to note that the Y-axis in this curve is a measure of *rate* of response, not response strength. That is, what increases in acquisition for operant conditioning is the rate of a response.

Once an organism is responding at a high rate of response, what happens if reinforcement is withheld? Let's say that because we have reinforced its bar pressing, a rat is pressing a bar at a rate of 550 presses per hour. From now on, however, it will receive no more pellets of food for its efforts—no more reinforcement. What happens is predictable: The rat's rate of bar-pressing response decreases gradually until it returns to the low baseline rate at which the experiment began. That is, eventually the conditioned response (bar pressing) will extinguish. (This is the same term we used in classical conditioning.)

After extinction has occurred, we remove the rat from the operant chamber and return it to its cage for a few days. When we again deprive it of food and return it to the chamber, what will it do? It will go right over to the bar and begin to press it again. Even though it has gone through extinction training, and even though the last time we saw this rat in the operant chamber it was not pressing the bar, it will again press the bar after a rest interval. Remember, this return of an extinguished response following a rest interval is called spontaneous recovery. As was the case in classical conditioning, the

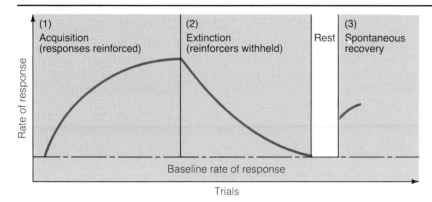

Figure 11.2

The stages of operant conditioning.

(1) During acquisition, response rates increase when responses are reinforced.

(2) In extinction, reinforcers are withheld and the response rate returns to operant rate.

(3) During spontaneous recovery, an increase in response rate is noted following a rest interval after extinction.

The stages here are the same as those found in classical conditioning.

significance of spontaneous recovery is that once acquired, a conditioned response can seldom be eliminated in just one series of extinction trials. Figure 11.2 also shows extinction and spontaneous recovery for operant conditioning.

> **Before you go on**
>
> **Describe acquisition, extinction, and spontaneous recovery as they occur in operant conditioning.**

REINFORCEMENT

From what we have said so far, it is obvious that reinforcement is an important concept in operant conditioning. Reinforcement is a process—the process of administering, or delivering, a reinforcer. In this section, we'll examine different types of reinforcers: positive reinforcers, negative reinforcers, primary reinforcers, and secondary reinforcers. We'll also see that we can schedule the administration of reinforcers in a variety of ways.

A Definition of Reinforcer

What qualifies as a good reinforcer? What creates the satisfying state of affairs that Thorndike suggests is necessary to increase response rate? For hungry rats in operant chambers, the answer seems to be deceptively simple. Here we can ensure that a rat is hungry, and we can confidently predict that the delivery of food will be reinforcing. For people, or for rats who are no longer hungry, the answer may not be so obvious.

Skinner's Operational Approach   Skinner and his students argue that we should define reinforcers operationally. That is, we should define reinforcers in terms of their effect on behavior. We need to remember that reinforcers are stimuli. Stimuli that increase the rate or the probability of the responses they follow are **reinforcers**.

At first reading, that logic may appear somewhat backward. A reinforcer is something that increases the rate of those responses it follows. This line of reasoning suggests that nothing is *necessarily* going to be a reinforcer. Reinforcers are defined only after we have noted their effect on behavior. Thus, we never know ahead of time what will or will not produce an increased rate of response—or a satisfying state of affairs, if you prefer. We may have some strong suspicions, based on what has worked in the past, but we will not know for sure until we try.

reinforcer
a stimulus that increases the rate or probability of the response that it follows

For example, for many people money is a powerful reinforcer. Your instructor might decide to offer you $10 for every test item you answer correctly this term. Such a reinforcement scheme might drastically increase the rate of students' studying behavior. But (as hard as this may be to believe) some students might not be interested in such financial reinforcement. For them, the monetary reward would not be at all reinforcing. It would not lead to an increase in their studying. Farfetched, perhaps, but the point is that we cannot always tell whether or not a given stimulus will be reinforcing until we try it. It is reinforcing *only* if it increases the rate or the likelihood of the response that it follows (Kimble, 1981).

Premack's Preference Approach   People often seem to prefer doing some things rather than others. Even rats show marked preferences. Rats, for example, prefer dark places to brightly lighted ones. At least they appear to. Given a choice, they spend more time where it is dark than where it is light. Some people prefer rhubarb pie to pumpkin pie. Some people don't like rhubarb pie at all. The point is that we can often establish an ordered list (a hierarchy) of preferences for any learner. Some behaviors are more preferred than others, and favored behaviors go to the top of the list while less favored go to the bottom of the hierarchy.

It is David Premack's position (called the **Premack Principle**) that organisms will do something low on their list of preferred activities just for the opportunity to do something that they would prefer to do more (Premack, 1965). This view defines reinforcers in terms of preferences, and vice versa. For example, some children may be reinforced for working on math problems by being given an opportunity to play video games for 15 minutes. Other children, perhaps with many video games at home, might find playing the games of no interest whatever. They *prefer* to work on math problems. As a result, they will play video games only if reinforced by being given the opportunity to do math problems for 15 minutes.

Premack Principle
the theory that more preferred activities can be used as reinforcers for less preferred activities

Before you go on
Provide an operational definition of reinforcer.

What is the Premack Principle?

Positive Reinforcers

Now that we know what a reinforcer is, we need to distinguish between positive and negative reinforcers. A **positive reinforcer** is a stimulus presented to an organism that increases (or maintains above baseline) the rate of a response that precedes it. The term does appear to be somewhat redundant: If something is positive, it certainly ought to be reinforcing. Positive reinforcers are sometimes like rewards. Examples include such stimuli as food for hungry organisms, water for thirsty ones, high letter grades for well-motivated students, and money, praise, and attention for most of us.

We need to be a little careful when we attemp to equate positive reinforcers with rewards, however. We usually think of rewards as being pleasant, but positive reinforcers do not always appear to be pleasant. For instance: A mother fusses at her daughter for not cleaning her room. She soon discovers that, "the more I yell and scream at her, *the worse she gets!*" If, indeed, her daughter's messiness gets worse, it is because the messy behavior is being

positive reinforcer
a stimulus that increases the rate of a response when that stimulus is presented to an organism after the response is made

strengthened. The yelling and screaming are acting as positive reinforcers, increasing the rate of a behavior. Now yelling and screaming do not appear to be very pleasant, yet here they are, acting as reinforcers.

Before you go on
What is a positive reinforcer?

Negative Reinforcers

A Definition   A **negative reinforcer** is a stimulus that increases the rate of a response that precedes *its removal.* Now that's going to require some explanation. Negative reinforcer is a strange term. There is something contradictory about the very sound of it. If something is negative, how can it be a reinforcer? The secret is to remember that the key word here is *reinforcer* and that reinforcers increase the rate of responses. Thus, negative reinforcement must produce some sort of satisfying state of affairs. That it does. The reinforcement comes not from the delivery or presentation of negative reinforcers, but with their removal. (Another secret is to remember that reinforc*ement* is a process. It is something that happens in response to stimuli called reinforc*ers.*)

So, negative reinforcers are stimuli that, when removed or withheld, increase the probability of a response. They may include such stimuli as shocks, enforced isolation, and threats of low letter grades. They are exactly the sorts of things that an organism would work (respond) to avoid or escape. A child who cleans her room to get her mother to *stop* nagging is responding to a negative reinforcer.

negative reinforcer
a stimulus that increases the rate of a response when that stimulus is removed after the response has been made

Examples in Escape and Avoidance Conditioning   One clear demonstration of negative reinforcement can be found in a type of operant conditioning called **escape conditioning.** In this procedure, an organism learns to escape from a painful, noxious, or aversive situation. If an appropriate response is made and the escape is successful, the organism is reinforced and will tend to make the same response again in the future. Notice that the reinforcement comes not from giving the organism a positive reinforcer, but from its escaping a negative reinforcer.

Do people ever respond to escape conditioning? All the time. For example, bully Ken has little Wayne's arm twisted up behind his back, demanding that Wayne say "uncle." The longer Wayne resists, the harder Ken twists. Finally, Wayne reluctantly mutters "uncle," and Ken releases his grasp. Wayne has probably learned how to escape from Ken's bullying in one trial: submit to his demands. The next time Ken grabs Wayne's arm, Wayne is likely to say or do whatever Ken asks. (Note that if all Ken wanted was for Wayne to say "uncle," he could have used positive reinforcement, offering Wayne a quarter for saying "uncle." The behavioral result would have been the same. But Ken has probably chosen *this* approach because he has been reinforced for doing so in the past; that is, he has found that being a bully works.)

escape conditioning
a form of operant conditioning in which an organism learns to escape from a negative reinforcer

Another example of negative reinforcement in action is **avoidance conditioning.** In avoidance conditioning, an organism learns to *avoid* an unpleasant, painful, aversive situation *before* it occurs. The major difference between avoidance conditioning and escape conditioning is the addition of a cue or signal for the presentation of the negative reinforcer.

avoidance conditioning
a form of operant conditioning in which an organism learns to respond to a signal or cue in order to avoid a negative reinforcer

Figure 11.3

A shuttle box apparatus of the sort used to demonstrate avoidance conditioning.

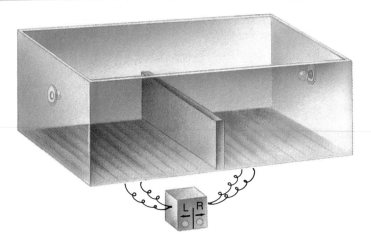

Let's look at a laboratory example of avoidance conditioning that uses a *shuttle box apparatus*—a long, narrow empty box, separated into two compartments by a divider, or hurdle (see Figure 11.3). The divider is high enough to present some obstacle yet low enough so that it can be jumped over with some effort. There is a signal light in each compartment of the box. In addition, the metal flooring of each side of the shuttle box is wired to a device that can deliver a painful shock to the feet of an animal in the box.

A dog is placed in the left compartment of a shuttle box. A light (signal) comes on. Five seconds later, a strong, painful shock is delivered to the floor of the left compartment. The dog hops around, squeals, barks, and eventually jumps the hurdle into the right compartment where there is no shock. Thus, the dog is negatively reinforced for jumping. A light comes on in the right compartment, followed five seconds later by a shock to the floor. Rather quickly now the dog jumps back to the left. One more trial: light, five second delay, shock, jump. Now the dog is once again in the right compartment of the box. The next time the signal light comes on the dog jumps into the left side of the box within five seconds, thus *avoiding* the shock. On each subsequent trial, the dog jumps the hurdle when the light comes on. It has learned to avoid the shock.

This example is impressive in a number of ways. Here, a painful, aversive stimulus (a shock) is used to bring about a relatively permanent change in behavior. In just three trials, after only three shocks, we have trained a dog to hop from one side of a box to the other when a light is turned on. One of the most noteworthy aspects of avoidance conditioning is that responses acquired in this way are highly resistant to extinction. After all, once the jump is made in response to the signal light, the shock is no longer required. Our dog will continue to jump from side to side for a long time.

We have to remember, of course, that in this demonstration, we are using the shock as a negative reinforcer, not as a punisher. The first thing we should realize is that we are not shocking the dog for doing something that it has already learned how to do. We are not punishing any particular response. Indeed, when the appropriate response is made, the shock is avoided.

Notice that in both escape and avoidance conditioning, we make no special effort to introduce any motivational state into this procedure other than the escape or avoidance of the shock. These are not hungry or thirsty dogs, for example. The dog is motivated solely to escape or avoid the shock, the negative reinforcer.

It is also important to note that a response for avoiding the shock is readily available to the subject. There is something the dog *can* do to avoid getting shocked. All it has to do is jump to the other side of the box. When dogs, for example, are shocked at random intervals in a situation in which there is no way to escape or avoid the shock, an unusual thing happens. The dogs eventually reach a state where they appear to give up. They just lie down and passively take administered shock. This pattern of behavior is called **learned helplessness**. One curiosity of this research is that once a learned helplessness response is acquired, it is difficult to overcome. That is, if dogs are then placed in a situation in which escape from shock is possible, it is very difficult for them to learn to escape, and some dogs never learn it at all (Maier & Seligman, 1976; Seligman, 1975).

learned helplessness
a condition in which a subject does not attempt to escape from a painful or noxious situation after learning in a previous, similar situation that no escape was possible

Before you go on

What is a negative reinforcer?

How are negative reinforcers used in escape and avoidance conditioning?

Punishment

While we're at it, let's consider punishment. **Punishment** occurs when a stimulus delivered to an organism *decreases* the rate or the probability of occurrence of the response that preceded it. In common usage, punishment may be painful—either physically (a spanking) or psychologically (ridicule). Determining ahead of time what stimulus will be punishing is often as hard to do as determining ahead of time what will serve as a reinforcer. We only know for sure that something is a punisher in terms of its effect on behavior.

For example, we may *think* that we are punishing Richard by sending him to his room because he has begun to throw a temper tantrum. It may be that "in his room" is exactly where Richard would like to be. We may have reinforced his behavior rather than punished it. Once again, the only way to know for certain is to note the effect on behavior. If stimuli decrease the rate

punishment
the administration of a punisher, which is a stimulus that decreases the rate or probability of a response that precedes it

In punishment, a stimulus is used to decrease the rate of the behavior that precedes it. In this manner, undesirable behaviors will occur less frequently.

of the behaviors they follow, those stimuli may be called punishers. So if Richard's tantrum-throwing behaviors become less frequent as a consequence of our actions, sending him to his room may indeed be a punishing thing to do.

Before you go on

What is a punisher?

Primary and Secondary Reinforcers

Reinforcers are defined in terms of their effects on behavior. Positive and negative reinforcers increase response rate; punishers decrease response rate. Now we need to make a distinction between primary and secondary reinforcers.

A Definition   The distinction between primary and secondary reinforcers is more one of degree than of either/or. What is at issue here is the extent to which reinforcers are natural and unlearned, or learned through experience. **Primary reinforcers** are those that do not require any previous experience to be effective. They are, at least in some way, related to the organism's survival. They are usually biological or physiological in nature. Food for a hungry organism, or water for a thirsty one, are common examples. Some believe that attention, at least for children, may qualify as an unlearned, primary reinforcer.

Suggesting the underlying principle involved, **secondary reinforcers** are often referred to as learned or conditioned reinforcers. There is nothing about them that suggests that they are inherently reinforcing or satisfying in any biological sense, yet they operate to strengthen preceding responses.

Most of the reinforcers that you and I work for are of this sort. Money, praise, letter grades, and promotions are good examples. Money, in and of itself, is not worth much. But our previous learning experiences have convinced most of us of the reinforcing nature of money, and it can serve to increase the rate of a wide variety of responses.

Examples from Behavior Modification   Operant conditioning procedures have been used as a technique of therapy to modify maladaptive or deviant behaviors. The systematic application of conditioning principles in situations that are essentially designed as therapy is called **behavior modification.** In many cases, it can be an extremely effective way of increasing the incidence of appropriate behaviors and minimizing inappropriate behaviors.

The success of behavior modification often hinges on the therapist's ability to use secondary rather than primary reinforcers. For example, directing the attention of a severely retarded child to some task may at first be accomplished by seeing to it that the child is somewhat hungry and providing a small piece of chocolate or a raisin whenever the child makes the desired response. At best, the process is tedious, and even children soon tire of raisins and chocolate pieces.

How much more convenient to be able to switch to secondary reinforcement. During initial trials, every time a food reward is presented, the therapist declares, "Good girl, Sarah, good girl," and pats Sarah on the shoulder. Over and over again—response, then raisin, accompanied by "Good girl, Sarah." Obviously, the hope is that Sarah will reach a point where the "Good girl, Sarah" becomes reinforcing because of its association with the

primary reinforcers
stimuli (usually biologically or physiologically based) that increase the rate of a response with no previous experience required

secondary reinforcers
stimuli that increase the rate of a response because of their being associated with other (primary) reinforcers; also called conditioned *or* learned *reinforcers*

behavior modification
a therapeutic technique of modifying behavior by reinforcing appropriate behaviors and extinguishing inappropriate behaviors

primary reinforcer—the praise will become a secondary reinforcer through classical conditioning. Then Sarah will modify her behavior for the praise alone.

A slightly more sophisticated approach is to use what is called a "token economy" system of secondary reinforcement. Such a system might work as follows. Mickie's parents have been having trouble getting babysitters for Mickie, who is a real terror of considerable reputation in the neighborhood. Mom and Dad make a deal, a signed contract with Mickie. Every time they go out and a babysitter is required, Mickie can earn five marbles. If he is very good for the sitter, he gets five marbles; if he is bad, he gets none. When Mickie has earned 25 marbles (or stamps, or poker chips, or marks on a record sheet), he can cash them in for a toy of his choice. If Mickie's behavior with babysitters improves (and it should), then the marbles are acting as reinforcers, but no doubt only because Mickie has learned the economy for which the marbles are tokens.

Such schemes are often remarkably effective. Perhaps because of their effectiveness, some students find these techniques offensive. "You're only bribing the child to behave," they claim. In a sense, they may be right, but the procedure does work. And our hope is, as Skinner has pointed out repeatedly, that sooner or later Mickie will come to appreciate the consequences of his appropriate behaviors with babysitters. That is, he will come to learn that behaving himself with babysitters leads to other rewards, such as praise, being allowed to stay up a little later than usual, and so on. In time, appropriate behaviors in the presence of babysitters should become self-sustaining, and the marbles (or tokens) will no longer be necessary.

Before you go on

What is the difference between primary and secondary reinforcers?

How might the latter be used in behavior modification?

Schedules of Reinforcement

In all of our discussions and examples so far we have implied that operant conditioning requires that we provide a reinforcer after every desired response. In fact, at the start, it *is* best to reinforce each response as it occurs, but once the response rate begins to increase, there may be good reason for doing otherwise—for reinforcing responses intermittently.

The procedure of reinforcing each and every response after it occurs is called a **continuous reinforcement (CRF) schedule**. One minor problem with CRF schedules is that one may quickly run out of reinforcers. Giving a rat a pellet of food each time it presses a bar may soon deplete pellet supplies. More importantly, earning and eating all those pellets soon reduces the reinforcing nature of the pellets. Once the rat has eaten its fill (is satiated), it will have to be removed from the operant chamber until it becomes hungry again (Skinner, 1956).

In general, alternatives to reinforcing every response are called **partial** (or intermittent) **reinforcement schedules.** One advantage they provide is that they conserve reinforcers. The most significant advantage of partial schedules of reinforcement becomes apparent when we consider the *extinction* of well-conditioned responses. A continuous schedule of reinforcement may soon lead to a high rate of some desired response, but when reinforcers are withheld (extinction begun), the rate of response will drop rather quickly.

continuous reinforcement (CRF)
a reinforcement schedule in which each and every response is followed by a reinforcer

partial reinforcement schedules
systems by which responses are not reinforced every time they occur

Figure 11.4

The effects of a schedule of reinforcement on extinction are illustrated below. Three hypothetical extinction curves following operant conditioning under (1) continuous reinforcement (CRF), (2) a fixed schedule, and (3) a variable schedule of reinforcement.

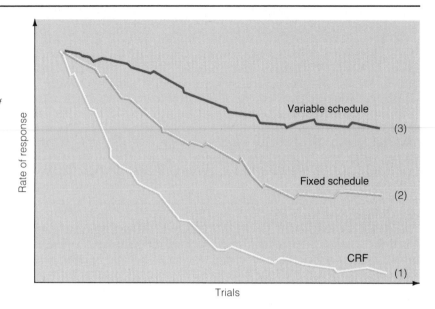

fixed ratio (FR) schedule
a system in which one reinforcer is administered only after a fixed number of responses

fixed interval (FI) schedule
a system in which the first response that occurs after a fixed time interval is reinforced

variable ratio (VR) schedule
a system in which a reinforcer is administered only after a randomly varied number of responses has occurred

variable interval (VI) schedule
a system in which a reinforcer is administered after the first response made following the end of a varying time interval

Up to now, the learner has not experienced making a response that is not followed by a reinforcer. When reinforcers are withheld, responses soon return to their base rate (see Figure 11.4).

There are many ways in which one can reinforce less than every desired response. We'll review four such procedures: fixed ratio, fixed interval, variable ratio, and variable interval schedules.

With a **fixed ratio (FR) schedule,** one establishes (fixes) a ratio of reinforcers to responses. In a 1:5 FR schedule, for example, one reinforcer would be delivered after every five responses. A 1:10 fixed ratio schedule for a rat in a Skinner box means that the rat would earn a pellet only after it had pressed the bar 10 times. Piecework is an example of a fixed ratio schedule: "I'll pay you a dollar for every six pints of strawberries you pick," or "You'll get 50¢ for every 12 widgets you assemble," or "You'll earn one point of extra credit for every three book reports you hand in."

With a **fixed interval (FI) schedule,** *time* is broken down into established (fixed) intervals. After each fixed time interval a reinforcer is delivered when the next response occurs. A 30-second FI schedule, for example, would call for the delivery of a food pellet for the first bar-press a rat makes after each 30-second interval passes. With such a schedule, you know from the start that you won't be dispensing more than two pellets every minute. Those of us who are salaried employees generally work on a fixed interval schedule, getting paid after a given interval of time (a week, two weeks, a month, etc.), and only if we show up for work at the end of each interval. Both the FR and the FI schedules of reinforcement can be used to establish responses that are much more resistant to extinction than those learned on a CRF schedule (see again, Figure 11.4).

There are two variable schedules of reinforcement, the **variable ratio (VR) schedule** and the **variable interval (VI) schedule.** From the learner's point of view, these schedules are very much alike. They are mostly different from the perspective of the teacher, or the dispenser of reinforcers. For the VR schedule, one chooses a ratio of reinforcers to responses. Then the ratio is changed, and changed again; it is variable. For a VR 1:5 schedule, for example, the experimenter will administer one reinforcement for every five responses *on the average,* but always in a different ratio. That is, the first reinforcer may come after five responses, the next after two, the next after eight, the next after just one, and so on. On the average, the ratio of reinforcers to responses is 1:5, but the pattern of actual ratios is variable. From the learner's point of view, this is essentially a random schedule of reinforcement. Only the experimenter/teacher knows when the next reinforcer is scheduled.

The most commonly cited example of a variable ratio reinforcement schedule is gambling devices, such as slot machines. They are usually programmed to pay off (reinforce) on a variable ratio schedule where the ratios are usually quite small. Gambling devices serve well to stress again an important benefit of partial schedules—their resistance to extinction (see Figure 11.4).

Variable interval schedules follow the same logic as do variable ratio schedules. Here, time intervals are established in a random fashion. For a rat in an operant chamber, the first food pellet may come following the first response after a 30-second interval; the next following the first response after a 90-second interval; then after a 10-second interval, and so on. A VI 30-second schedule would be one in which the varied time intervals *average* 30 seconds in length. An instructor who wants to keep a class on its toes and studying regularly may schedule short pop quizzes on a variable interval schedule. The students may learn that quizzes are coming, but never know when.

The terminology we have used here is standard, but somewhat technical. The main point to remember is that operant conditioning does not require that each and every response be reinforced. There are advantages to partial reinforcement schedules, one of the most important being their resistance to extinction.

Slot machines use variable ratio reinforcement schedules. They are programmed to pay off at variable intervals.

Before you go on

Define FR, FI, VR, and VI schedules of reinforcement.

GENERALIZATION AND DISCRIMINATION

In classical conditioning, we saw that a response conditioned to one particular stimulus could be evoked by other, similar stimuli. We have the same phenomenon occurring in operant conditioning, and again we call it **generalization**—reinforced responses that have been conditioned to a specific stimulus may appear in response to other, similar stimuli.

For example, Priscilla may be reinforced for saying "doggie" as a neighbor's poodle wanders across the front yard. "Oh yes, Priscilla, good girl. That's a doggie." Having learned that calling the neighbor's poodle a "doggie" earns parental approval, the response is tried again, this time with a German shepherd from down the street. That is, Priscilla's operantly conditioned response of "doggie" in the presence of a poodle generalizes to the German shepherd. When it does, it will no doubt also be reinforced. The problem is, of course, that Priscilla may overgeneralize to virtually all furry four-legged animals and start calling cats and cows "doggie" also. When a child turns to a total stranger and utters "dada," generalization can (usually) be blamed for the embarrassing mislabeling.

The process of generalization can be countered with the reverse process of **discrimination** conditioning. Discrimination learning is basically a matter of differential reinforcement. What that means is that responses made to appropriate stimuli will be reinforced, while (differential) responses made to inappropriate stimuli will be ignored or extinguished (not punished, please note).

generalization
the process by which a response that was reinforced in the presence of one stimulus appears in response to other, similar stimuli

discrimination
the process of differential reinforcement wherein one (positive) stimulus is reinforced while another (negative) stimulus is not

Figure 11.5

Discrimination training. Response rates
of a pigeon pecking at a green disk and
a red disk presented together. Pecks at
the green disk are reinforced; those to
the red disk are not.

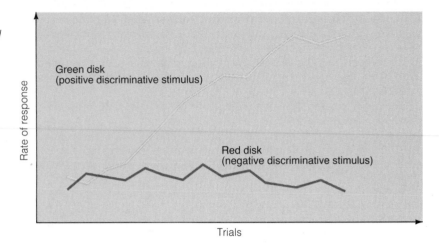

To demonstrate how discrimination training works, let's consider a strange question: Are pigeons color-blind? Disregarding for the moment why anyone would care, how might you go about testing the color vision of a pigeon? The standard tests we use for people certainly wouldn't work. What we do is take advantage of something pigeons can do.

Pigeons *can* be trained to press levers in operant chambers, but they are better at pecking at things, so we usually use a pecking response when we demonstrate operant conditioning with pigeons. A pigeon can be readily trained to peck at a single lighted disk in order to earn a food reward. A pigeon in an operant chamber pecks at a lighted disk, and a grain of food is delivered. Soon the pigeon pecks the disk at a high rate.

Now let's present the pigeon with *two* lighted disks. One disk is red and one is green. Otherwise, they are identical: the same shape, size, brightness, etc. Our basic question is whether or not the pigeon can tell the difference between red and green. So we decide that we'll make the green disk the positive discriminative stimulus. The red disk, then, will be the negative discriminative stimulus. This means that every peck at the green disk will be followed by a piece of grain, and that pecks at the red disk will not be reinforced.

The results of this sort of manipulation are depicted in Figure 11.5. At first, the red and green lighted disks are responded to at an approximately equal rate. But in short order the pigeon is ignoring the red disk and pecking only at the green one, for which it receives its reinforcer.

In order to maintain such behavior, the pigeon must be able to discriminate between the two colored disks. We still do not know what green and red look like to a pigeon, but we may conclude that pigeons can tell the difference between the two. This is sensible and predictable because in many ways the eyes of pigeons are like those of humans. They contain many cones in their retinas, and as you'll recall, cones are the receptors for color vision. Some varieties of owls are virtually without cone receptor cells in their retinas and are color-blind. They cannot make the discrimination between red and green, for example, and appear very frustrated in a discrimination learning task based on color.

Before you go on

In the context of operant conditioning, what are generalization and discrimination?

CAN ANY RESPONSE BE OPERANTLY CONDITIONED?

Rats can be operantly conditioned to press lighted disks on the side of an operant chamber. Pigeons can be trained to press bars or levers in a Skinner box. Yet, typically, we demonstrate operant conditioning with these organisms by having rats increase lever-pressing rates and pigeons increase disk-pecking rates. Somehow these responses seem more natural for the animals we're using. Even so, it was commonly believed for a long time that if we could find the right reinforcer, we could train almost any animal to do almost any thing.

Keller and Marion Breland, psychologists who had worked with B. F. Skinner, were convinced of the power of reinforcement and operant conditioning as a means of modifying the behavior of organisms. They chose to apply their expertise in psychology to the practical matter of animal training, and many of their trained animals became quite popular and famous. Along with their many successes at training animals to do a number of very involved things, the Brelands experienced failures. Some of their animals seemed totally contrary and unable to learn apparently simple routines. They described their frustrations in a 1961 article titled "The Misbehavior of Organisms," a take-off on the title of Skinner's classic book *The Behavior of Organisms* (1938).

As an example of the sort of difficulty the Brelands encountered, consider their efforts to teach a raccoon and a pig to deposit large coins in a bank. Both the raccoon and the pig had previously demonstrated that they were capable of responding to operant conditioning. They were not in any way unintelligent animals. But the raccoon never quite learned to drop his coins into the bank. He would grab the coins, rub them together, begin to enter them into the bank's slot, and then withdraw them at the last moment, rubbing them together again. The pig never got that close. The pig would drop the coins from its mouth and then push them around the floor with its nose. When the coins were put back into the pig's mouth, they were promptly dropped again and pushed around the ground.

What was happening here, the Brelands concluded, was that their animals were simply acting naturally. They were acting toward the coins the way they would naturally, or instinctively, act toward food—the raccoon manipulating the coin (food) with its hands, the pig rooting it around the ground. No training or reinforcement was sufficient to overcome this instinctive predisposition for long. Yes, reinforcement could get an animal to perform some task, but eventually it would drift back to more typical, natural, or instinctive patterns of behavior. The Brelands labeled this phenomenon **instinctive drift**. It suggests that there *are* indeed limits on what an organism can learn, and many of these limits are established by the organism's genetic history.

Keller and Marion Breland studied the effect of reinforcement and operant conditioning on animals. They found that it is difficult to permanently overcome an animal's natural or instinctive behaviors. Here, a rabbit demonstrates a natural food-getting behavior—scratching for food. Only in this case, the rabbit is scratching at a piano keyboard.

instinctive drift
the tendency of behaviors that have been conditioned to eventually revert to more instinctive behaviors

Before you go on
What is instinctive drift, and what does it tell us about the limits of conditioning?

APPLYING OPERANT CONDITIONING TO YOUR STUDY OF PSYCHOLOGY

In educational settings, we tend to think of teachers and professors as being the sole dispensers of reinforcers and punishers. Now it is true that your instructor will ultimately dispense letter grades (secondary reinforcers) based on the behavior of you and your classmates this term. Effective studying and learning will (should) be reinforced, and ineffective studying and learning will (should) not be reinforced.

It is clear, too, that as students you need not wait for your instructor to dispense reinforcers. You can do that yourself. You can reinforce yourself. In terms of study, plan to work very hard for, say, one hour. *If* at the end of that hour you feel that you have indeed studied very hard and learned some things, go ahead and reinforce your effort. How can you do that? Well, that's up to you. You know best what might work as a reinforcer for you—extra TV time, a candy bar, something to drink, etc.—something that will create for you a satisfying state of affairs. Now we all hope that you will find effective studying inherently reinforcing, and that you will feel reinforced simply for having done a good job, but it won't hurt to provide yourself some extra bonus for a job well done.

For this to work, you have to be very honest with yourself. Good work gets reinforced, poor work does not. You have to be willing to withhold reinforcers when the quality of study is not up to standard. After a few weeks, you should be able to tell if your reinforcement plan is working: Has your rate of effective study increased? If it has, you have chosen an appropriate reinforcer.

In this topic, we have found that operant conditioning is a procedure in which the rate of one's response is changed by the systematic manipulation of the consequences of that response. As with classical conditioning, we have seen that a variety of factors affect the outcome of operant conditioning trials. The more we study the acquisition of knowledge in humans and animals, the more we can hope to improve learning ability. Many psychologists study learning, and it is to some of their theories and studies that we turn in the next topic.

Until the 1960s, it was commonly held that operant conditioning was effective only for those responses that were under a subject's voluntary control. Attention was focused on overt responses such as bar-pressing, disk-pecking, studying, and tantrum-throwing behaviors. Involuntary reactions such as blood pressure level, pulse rate, or muscle tension due to stress were thought to be beyond the control of reinforcers and operant conditioning. These internal, visceral, physiological responses were thought to be best suited for classical conditioning.

Research by Neal Miller (1969) and many others (see Kimmel, 1967 and Yates, 1980, for reviews), indicates that one *can* learn to exercise control over internal, supposedly involuntary responses. The procedure for doing so is called **biofeedback.** Biofeedback is "the process of providing information to an individual about his [or her] bodily processes in some form which he

[or she] might be able to use to modify those processes" (Hill, 1985, p. 201). The basic insight that initiated experimentation in biofeedback was that we are seldom aware of the subtle changes that take place within the normal activity of our bodies. What is needed is a system for letting the subject/learner know when his or her blood pressure, for example, is rising, steady, or falling.

The technology for providing us with the instrumentation to "feed back" to an individual the state of his or her internal physiological conditions is readily available (although occasionally quite expensive). How does biofeedback work? One's heart rate, let's say, is constantly monitored, and the rate is fed back to the subject, perhaps in the form of an audible tone. As heart rate increases, the pitch of the tone becomes higher. With a lowering heart rate, the pitch becomes lower and lower. Once the learner knows (through the feedback) what the heart rate (or blood pressure, or

biofeedback
the operant conditioning procedure of providing information to an individual about internal bodily processes so that those processes can be modified

Biofeedback helped this woman raise her blood pressure to the point where she could sit up after having been flat on her back for 5 years. Though still paralyzed, being able to sit up has enabled her to lead a more normal life.

muscle tension, etc.) is doing, a certain degree of control can be gained over the responses. The reinforcement involved here is usually just the newly gained information that a desired change in response is being made. That is, the lower tone indicating a decrease in heart rate is the reinforcer in our example. As a result of being reinforced, these responses increase in their rate or frequency (Kimmel, 1974; Miller, 1978).

When the reports of early successes became widely known, claims for the wonders of biofeedback were often wildly exaggerated, and biofeedback as a treatment technique was generally oversold (Simkins, 1982). Following the initial exaggeration, skepticism followed. According to Miller (1985, p. 58), the field "then settled down and we began to make steady progress."

There remains a number of problems with biofeedback techniques as a means of treating a wide range of disorders. For example, it still remains much easier to use biofeedback techniques to train an individual to raise blood pressure levels than it is to train people to lower their blood pressure levels. It is nonetheless true that biofeedback procedures hold great promise for the treatment of a number of disorders. A pamphlet from the National Institute of Mental Health (1983), for example, claims that biofeedback training is currently widely used to treat "migraine headaches, tension headaches, . . . disorders of the digestive system, high blood pressure and its opposite, low blood pressure, cardiac arrhythmias, . . . Raynaud's disease (a circulatory disorder that causes uncomfortably cold hands), epilepsy, paralysis and other movement disorders," and a number of other ailments.

TOPIC SUMMARY

What is the essence of operant conditioning?

Operant conditioning is that type of learning in which the probability or rate of a response is changed as a result of its consequences. That is, reinforced responses increase in rate while non-reinforced responses decrease in rate. / 188

Why do we need shaping, and how does it work?

Shaping is a procedure used in operant conditioning to establish a response that can then be reinforced. We shape a desired response by reinforcing successive approximations to that response. / 190

Describe acquisition, extinction, and spontaneous recovery as they occur in operant conditioning.

In operant conditioning, acquisition is produced by reinforcing a desired response so that its rate will increase. Extinction is the phenomenon of decreasing the rate of a response (return to baseline) by withholding reinforcement. A previously extinguished response will return to a rate above baseline after a rest interval; that is, in the same situation it will spontaneously recover. / 191

Provide an operational definition of reinforcer.

What is the Premack Principle?

A reinforcer is a stimulus that increases the rate or probability of a response that precedes its administration. The Premack Principle suggests that those behaviors that are more preferred can serve as reinforcers for behaviors that are less preferred. / 192

What is a positive reinforcer?

A positive reinforcer is a stimulus that increases the rate of a response when it is presented following that response. / 193

What is a negative reinforcer?

How are negative reinforcers used in escape and avoidance conditioning?

A negative reinforcer is a stimulus that increases the rate of a response that precedes its removal. In escape conditioning, an organism is reinforced by escaping from a negative reinforcer, while in avoidance conditioning, an organism is reinforced for avoiding a negative reinforcer before it occurs by reacting to a cue or signal. / 195

What is a punisher?

A punisher is a stimulus that decreases the rate or probability of a response that precedes it. / 196

What is the difference between primary and secondary reinforcers?

How might the latter be used in behavior modification?

Primary reinforcers are stimuli (reinforcers) that are in some way biologically important or related to an organism's survival, whereas secondary reinforcers act to increase the rate of a response because of the organism's previous learning or conditioning experience. That is, secondary reinforcers are learned reinforcers. They are very useful in behavior modification programs (token economies, in particular) where an individual can be conditioned to modify his or her behavior for secondary reinforcers such as praise, or approval, or tokens, rather than primary reinforcers such as food and drink. / 197

Define FR, FI, VR, and VI schedules of reinforcement.

Partial schedules of reinforcement call for the delivery of a reinforcer for something less than every desired response. For example, the FR (fixed ratio) schedule calls for a reinforcer after a set number of responses (for example, one reinforcer after every five responses). A VR (variable ratio) schedule randomly changes the ratio of reinforcers to responses, but maintains some given ratio as an average. An FI (fixed interval) schedule calls for the administration of a reinforcer for the first response after a specified time interval. A VI (variable interval) schedule calls for a reinforcer for the first response at the end of a time interval, where the length of the time interval is randomly varied. / 199

In the context of operant conditioning, what are generalization and discrimination?

In operant conditioning, generalization occurs when a response reinforced in the presence of one stimulus is also made in the presence of other, similar stimuli. Discrimination, on the other hand, is a matter of differential reinforcement: reinforcing responses to appropriate stimuli and extinguishing responses to inappropriate stimuli. / 200

What is instinctive drift, and what does it tell us about the limits of conditioning?

Instinctive drift is the term used by the Brelands to note that some behaviors are more difficult to condition than others, and that over time, an organism is going to "drift" toward doing what comes naturally, or instinctively, no matter how much we may condition to the contrary. / 201

TOPIC

The year is 1949. You are a psychologist with the Yerkes Laboratory of Primate Biology in Orange Park, Florida. You happen to be near Madison, Wisconsin, and decide to visit the laboratory of Harry Harlow, a University of Wisconsin psychologist who is working on discrimination learning problems with rhesus monkeys.

You have done some of this sort of work yourself. You know that if you present a monkey with two small, inverted cups, each with a different design on it, the monkey will eventually learn to overturn the cup that always hides a small piece of food. Sooner·or later your monkey will learn to ignore one cup and always grab for the one that hides the food. You also know from your experience that it takes monkeys quite a few trials, or presentations of the two cups, before they catch on and learn this type of visual discrimination.

When you get to his lab, Professor Harlow tells you that he has a particularly smart monkey he wants to show you. This monkey is so smart that it can learn to make a visual discrimination in just one trial! If it makes the correct response on the first trial, it won't make any errors at all. This you have to see, and Harlow sets up a demonstration for you.

Harlow's monkey is presented simultaneously with two cups. One is marked with a division sign ($\div$) and the other with a series of dots (:::). A raisin is placed under the "$\div$" cup; nothing is placed under the ":::" cup. On the first presentation of the stimulus cups, the monkey makes the wrong choice, overturning the cup with the dots on it. You smile at the monkey's error, but Harlow doesn't look the least bit worried. Then, for 20 straight trials, the monkey makes no more mistakes! You are impressed. No matter where it is positioned, the monkey grabs for the cup that hides the raisin, overturns it, and enjoys his reward. The monkey seems to have learned this discrimination in just one trial. Yes, you're convinced, and you're impressed, but you also suspect that there is more going on here than meets the eye. You're right, there is, and we'll find out what in this topic.

There is no doubt that classical and operant conditioning can and do account for many of our learning experiences. Each of these procedures is, in its own way, a matter of forming associations. We associate pleasant or unpleasant feelings with certain situations. We associate some responses with reinforcers and others with punishers. In either case, we make relatively permanent changes in our behaviors on the basis of our experiences. Both classical and operant conditioning are behavioristic in their orientation. They focus on observable events (stimuli) in the environment and on observable behaviors (responses) of the learner. That these two procedures have been the focus of our attention in the psychology of learning for so long is an indication of the influence of behaviorism on American psychology.

But now it is time to look beyond conditioning. The data from a number of experiments, and from our own experiences, suggest that there is more to learning than just the simple formation of associations between stimuli and between stimuli and responses. There seem to be a number of situations in which an organism's behaviors are changed that stretch the credibility of explanations given only in terms of observable stimuli and responses.

In a broad sense, it is time for us to consider the "O," or organism, in our S-O-R formulation (see Topic 1, p. 13). That is, to understand some types of learning, we may have to consider the nature of the learner (organism) in addition to considering the nature of stimuli and responses. Such approaches go by a number of different labels, but we may refer to them all as being basically **cognitive**. That is, these approaches emphasize the mental processes or mental activity (cognitions) of the organism involved in the learning task. They argue that learning often involves the acquisition of information and knowledge.

cognitive
having to do with cognitions—mental representations of information and knowledge

In this topic, we'll examine a sample of the views of psychologists who have argued that we should consider more than a simple conditioning approach to learning. We'll begin with Edward Tolman and his notion that we (and rats) learn without even trying. Then we'll move to Wolfgang Köhler and his view that even chimps can learn through insight. We'll also return to Harlow and see why his monkey seemed so smart, and we'll review Albert Bandura's evidence that learning can result from the simple observation of others. Finally, we'll introduce Konrad Lorenz's concept of a biologically-based sort of acquisition called imprinting.

Before you go on

In general, what characterizes a cognitive approach to learning?

TOLMAN: LATENT LEARNING AND COGNITIVE MAPS

Do rats have brains? Of course they do. They aren't very large brains, and the cerebral cortex of a rat's brain is small indeed. A more intriguing question about rats is whether or not they have minds. Can they figure things out? Can they understand? Can they manipulate cognitions? Surely they can form simple associations. They can learn to associate a light with a shock. They can associate a bar-press response with a reinforcer. And they can modify their behaviors on the basis of these associations. Can they do more?

Consider a now-classic experiment performed more than 50 years ago by Tolman and Honzik (1930). Even at that time it was well established that a rat could learn to run through a complicated maze of alleyways and dead ends to get to a goal box where it would receive a food reward. Tolman and Honzik wanted to understand just *what* the rats were learning when they learned to negotiate such a maze. They used three different groups of rats with the same maze.

One group of hungry rats was given a series of exposures to the maze (trials). Each time they ran from the starting point to the goal box they were given a food reward for their efforts. Over the course of 16 days, the rats in this group showed a steady and predictable improvement in their maze-running behavior. Their rate of errors, for example, dropped from approximately nine per trial to just two. They had learned their way around the maze. Getting quickly and errorlessly from the start box to the goal box was what they were reinforced for doing.

A second group of rats was also given an opportunity to explore the same maze for 16 days of test trials. They were never given a food reward for making it to the end of the maze. When they got to the goal box they were removed from the maze. Curiously enough, the average number of errors made by the rats in this group also dropped over the course of the experiment (from about nine errors per trial down to about six). That the rats in this group *did* improve their maze-running skills suggested to the researchers that simply being removed from the maze provided some measure of reinforcement. Even so, after 16 days of experience, this group was having much more difficulty in their maze running than was the group being given a food reinforcer.

Now for the critical group of rats. A third group of rats was allowed to explore the maze on their own for 10 days. They were *not* given a food reward upon reaching the goal box. Beginning with day 11, a food reward was introduced when they reached the end of the maze. The food was provided as a reinforcer on days 11 through 16. The introduction of the food reward had a very significant effect on the rats' behaviors. Over the course of the first 10 days in the maze (without the food), their maze running showed only a slight improvement. Soon after the food was introduced, their performance improved markedly. In fact, on days 13 through 16, they made even fewer errors than did the rats reinforced with food all along. A graph showing the relative performance of these three groups of rats is shown in Figure 12.1.

What do you make of this experiment? Why did that third group of rats perform so much better after the food reward was introduced? Might they have learned something about the pattern of that maze *before* they were explicitly reinforced for getting to the goal box? Might they have figured out the maze early on, but failed to rush to the goal box until there was some good reason to do so?

Tolman thought that the rats had, indeed, figured out the maze. Tolman argued that the food only rewarded a change in the rats' performance, and that the actual learning had taken place earlier. This sort of learning is called **latent learning** because it is, in a sense, hidden and not shown in behavior at the time it occurs.

During those first 10 days in the maze, the rats developed what Tolman called a **cognitive map** of the maze; that is, they formed a mental picture, or representation, of what the maze was like. The rats "knew" about the maze, but until food was provided at the goal box, there was no reason, or purpose, for getting there in any big hurry. This sort of logic leads us to refer to Tolman's approach to learning as "purposive behaviorism" (Tolman, 1932). By introducing the notion of purpose and drawing a distinction between performance and what was actually learned, Tolman forced attention on the O in S-R, stimulus-response psychology to make it an S-O-R psychology.

Edward Tolman

latent learning
hidden learning that is not reflected in performance until performance is reinforced

cognitive map
a mental representation of the learning situation or physical environment

Figure 12.1

The performance of rats in a maze that (1) were never rewarded, (2) were rewarded on every trial, or (3) were rewarded only on trials 11–16. (After Tolman & Honzik, 1930.)

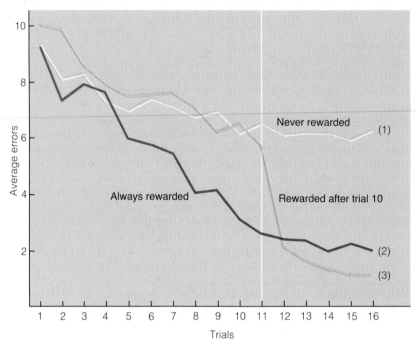

Here then was Tolman arguing that even rats form a mental representation, or cognitive map, of their environment at the very time that behaviorism was dominating American psychology. Interest in cognitive maps died out for awhile, but has recently been making a comeback, thanks to a series of well controlled experiments by David Olton (1976, 1978, 1979). Let's briefly review just one.

The maze pictured in Figure 12.2 is an unusual one. It is certainly more complex than the usual T-shaped mazes often used in animal learning experiments. In one of Olton's experiments, a piece of food is placed at the end of each of the eight arms, or runways, that extend from the center of the maze. In order to solve this maze, a rat placed at the center has to learn to run to the end of each arm, eat the food there, and move on to other runways where food could still be found. Going back to a runway arm already visited constitutes an error—there is no food there.

As it happens, rats perform beautifully in this maze. Within 20 trials, they race from arm to arm without ever retracing their path down an "old" runway. What's more, on each trial the rats run around the maze in a different pattern. Their behavior does not seem rigidly compulsive. They don't simply start with one arm and then move around the maze in one direction. Their pattern of visits seems almost random. But, remember, they don't go down the same arm twice on any one trip around the maze!

The rats' performance is not disrupted even if odor cues are removed by splashing a strong-smelling after-shave lotion on the maze. (That is, the rats cannot smell—or see, for that matter—where the food is and isn't. And they cannot tell by smell where they have and have not been before. The lotion masks all these odors.) On the other hand, if the maze is rotated after a trial has begun, the rats *do* make errors and go down runways they have traveled before, even though food is not present there. They may be "old" runways, but after the maze is rotated, they are in new positions. What Olton and his colleagues argue they have demonstrated is that their rats have learned a mental representation of the maze (a cognitive map) and have learned where they have and have not been to get food.

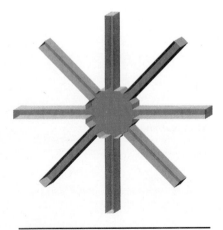

Figure 12.2

An eight-arm maze of the sort used by Olton to demonstrate the formation of cognitive maps in rats. (After Olton, 1976.)

There is a very important point that we need to make before we leave Tolman, Olton, latent learning, and cognitive maps. So far we have only talked about rats. What about people? For one thing, there is a compelling argument that suggests that if we can demonstrate that a cognitive restructuring takes place when *rats* learn, it seems rather clear that such processes will also occur with humans.

You should be able to find examples from your own experiences that very closely approximate the latent learning and cognitive maps of Tolman. You may take the same route between home and campus every day. If an accident blocked your path one day, wouldn't you be able to use your knowledge of other routes (a cognitive map) to get where you are going?

Although cognitive map may at first sound like a strange term, upon reflection, there are a number of occasions where the concept is useful. On one of my first trips to the offices of Scott, Foresman and Company in Glenview, Illinois, I parked my rented car in a huge parking lot reserved for employees. (Not having yet formed a proper cognitive map, I did not know where "Visitor Parking" was.) As I left my car and headed to the building, it occurred to me that I probably would forget where I had parked. So I took a few minutes to develop a mental image, a cognitive representation of the parking lot and some of its major features. Once I appreciated the general shape of the parking lot, its relation to the building, and where my car was in it, the rest was relatively easy.

Another setting in which we may find an application of Tolman's purposive behaviorism is in athletics. Before the "big game," the coaching staff may devise a perfect game plan—basically a set of cognitions dealing with what the team should do. The team members may learn the appropriate defensive strategy and may understand a number of offensive formations and plays. In theory, they know what they are supposed to do if they want to win. But what will ultimately decide the contest is not their understanding, but their performance. In sports, this is usually called execution. *Knowing what to do* and *doing it* are often two different things.

Coaches often devise a cognitive plan (a game plan) of perfect strategies that will lead to victory. Though the players may learn these strategies, it is their performance that will ultimately decide the outcome of the game.

Before you go on

What is learned when one forms a cognitive map?

What is latent learning?

KÖHLER: LEARNING THROUGH INSIGHT

Another form of learning that does not seem to fit neatly into the mold of classical or operant conditioning takes us back to some research that predates Tolman's. It comes from the work of Wolfgang Köhler, a German psychologist of the Gestalt tradition. As a Gestalt psychologist, Köhler's interests were focused on cognitive issues, although he did not use the term "cognitive" in quite the same way that we use it today. Köhler's psychology dealt with attention, perception, and problem solving.

Köhler came to the United States as a visiting professor in 1925. He left Germany permanently when Hitler came to power; he then taught, retired, and died here (in 1967). Even though he spent much of his professional life in the United States, he was little influenced by American behaviorism. Thorndike's law of effect and the notion that organisms learn by being rewarded for trial and error responses did not fit well with Köhler's view of learning.

From 1913 to 1920, Köhler was in charge of a large primate research station on Tenerife, one of the Canary Islands. His observations at Tenerife led him to believe that learning could be explained in terms of restructuring cognitions. He suggested that much learning results from **insight**—a (usually) sudden reorganization of perceptions and cognitions that leads to problem solution.

To test his hypothesis about learning, Köhler presented his chimpanzees with a series of problems to solve. Typically, the problem involved getting to some fruit or food that was clearly in view, but well out of reach. For example, food might be placed outside a chimp's compound, beyond arm's reach, or suspended by a rope well above the chimp's grasp. For a time, the chimps would engage in fruitless trial and error behaviors, but soon they seemed to realize that they could not reach the food by ordinary means.

Suddenly, in what has been called an "aha experience," the chimps would seem to "see" the solution to their problem. They would quickly drag a box or crate under a suspended banana, scurry up the box, and retrieve the fruit. If one crate would not do, two or three would be piled in a stack. Some chimps saw (in*sight*) a different way to the food: They would grab a long stick or pole and swat at the food above their heads to knock it to the ground.

One particularly bright chimp, upon discovering that one stick was not long enough to reach a banana outside his cage, suddenly grabbed a second stick, jammed it into the end of the first, and made a two-piece pole long enough to retrieve the banana. Occasionally a chimp would combine two problem solutions, dragging a box under a suspended piece of fruit, then swatting at the prize with a stick while balanced on the box (Köhler, 1925). See Figure 12.3.

So chimpanzees are clever. Any of us who have watched monkeys at the zoo know that they are clever. What relation does all this have to learning? The main point is that Köhler's observations and demonstrations provided a serious challenge for S-R association approaches to learning that fail to take into account the cognitions of the learner. Even though there were attempts at trial and error responding, Köhler's chimps usually responded quickly and without error once they had developed their insight. And once learned, their solutions generalized. Once a chimp understood the value of a stick as a tool for retrieving food, it would use a stick for that purpose in a variety of set-

Figure 12.3
Köhler's chimps solving problems.

tings. Once learned, the chimps' responses to a problem were performed without effort or confusion, as if the chimps *knew* exactly what they were doing.

You and I have certainly had similar experiences. Once we "see" the solution to a difficult or tricky problem, we usually do not forget it. Often, once we have insight—once we see the solution—we just know that our solution will work, even before we try it. In Topic 16 we'll consider a number of problem-solving tasks for which Köhler's notion of insight will prove to be a very useful explanatory concept.

Before you go on
What is insight?

In what way is insight a cognitive process?

HARLOW: LEARNING SETS

Now is a good time to return to our opening story of Harry Harlow and his smart monkey. You'll recall that Harlow was able to impress you (at least in our story) by showing you a monkey that could make a correct visual discrimination in just one trial. Your experience told you that monkeys generally require many trials before they catch on, or develop insight, about such a discrimination task. You suspected that Harlow was not telling you the whole story.

In truth, Harlow's monkey had not seen either of these two stimuli before (the "÷" or the ":::"). They were brand new stimuli for this rhesus monkey. *But,* this monkey *had* already solved 311 two-choice visual discrimination problems just like this one—only the designs were changed. During those previous 311 problems, Harlow's monkey did indeed learn something over and above "÷ gets me raisin, ::: does not."

In Harlow's terms, his monkey had developed a **learning set,** a prepared, expected way to go about solving such problems. We say that it had gone through a process of "learning to learn." Even though it had never seen the "÷" and the ":::" stimuli before, the monkey had seen many pairs of stimuli in a similar discrimination task. It learned that one of them would be associated with a food reward and one would not (Harlow, 1949).

learning set
an acquired, expected way to go about learning or problem solving; learning to learn

Harlow's is an important demonstration. It shows that previous learning experiences can affect present ones, in this case making them easier. Much of your learning in school has been of this sort. We often claim that education (as opposed to training) is a matter of establishing the proper learning sets. We cannot teach anyone *all* the answers to all of the questions and problems that she or he may face in a lifetime. Our best hope is that we can teach people how to learn to solve their own problems and answer their own questions.

For example, college seniors generally earn higher grades than do college freshmen. There are many reasons for this. Poor students may flunk out early and never make it to their senior year. Seniors usually take fewer required courses and take more meaningful courses in their major area of study. And, importantly, by the time they get to be seniors, most students have learned how to learn. They have acquired the learning sets that help them study more efficiently and take exams more effectively.

Before you go on
How might we demonstrate the formation of a learning set?

BANDURA: SOCIAL LEARNING AND MODELING

So far we have reviewed three approaches to learning that stress the importance of cognitive activity: Tolman's latent learning, Köhler's insight learning, and Harlow's learning sets. In this section, we'll examine a fourth approach that is also cognitive in nature, but that adds a decidedly social flavor to the process: the **social learning theory** of Albert Bandura (1977). The central idea of Bandura's theory is that learning often takes place through observation and the imitation of models. Indeed, what makes social learning theory *social* is the notion that we often learn from others. What makes it *cognitive* is that what is learned through observation usually involves changes in cognitions—cognitions that may never be expressed as behavior nor be reinforced.

The classic demonstration of observational learning was reported in 1963 by Bandura, Ross, and Ross. Let's take a look at this famous experiment.

For this demonstration, 96 preschool children were randomly assigned to one of four experimental conditions or treatments:

> (1) Children in this condition observed an adult model act aggressively toward an inflated plastic "Bobo" doll toy. The adult model attacked the doll repeatedly in the same unusual way.

> (2) Children in this condition watched the same aggressive behaviors directed toward the "Bobo" doll, but the episode was on film, not "live and in person."

> (3) Children in this condition watched a cartoon version of the same behaviors, this time performed by a cartoon cat.

> (4) Children in this condition comprised the control group and did not watch anyone (or anything) interact with "Bobo" dolls, either live or on film.

Then the test began. Each child (tested individually) was given a variety of new and interesting toys to play with, but only for a brief time. The child was then led to another room that contained fewer, older, and less interesting toys, including a small version of the inflated "Bobo" doll. Each child was left alone in the room while experimenters watched the child's behavior. The children did not know they were being observed.

There was no doubt that the children who had seen the aggressive behaviors of the model—whether live, on film, or in cartoon form—were themselves more aggressive in their play than were the children who did not have the observational experience. Children who were in the first three experimental conditions attacked the "Bobo" doll. What's more, they attacked it in the same stereotyped sort of way that the model they had viewed had!

You'll have to admit that explaining the behavior of these young children in terms of trial and error, or classical or operant conditioning, is difficult to do. According to social learning theory, they learned simply by observing. Once again, as we saw with latent learning, the learning was separated from performance. The children had no opportunity to imitate (to perform) what they had learned until they had a "Bobo" doll of their own. The learning that took place during observation was symbolic, or cognitive. As Bandura put it, "Observational learning is primarily concerned with processes whereby observers organize response elements into new patterns of behavior at a symbolic level on the basis of information conveyed by modeling stimuli" (Bandura, 1976, p. 395).

Later studies on observational learning have shown that reinforcement and punishment do play a role. For example, a new twist was added to an

social learning theory
the theory that learning takes place through the observation and imitation of models

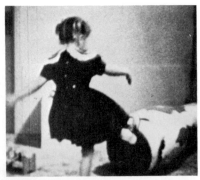

In Albert Bandura's classic study, children who watched adults behave aggressively toward the "Bobo" doll displayed the same sort of behavior themselves. The children learned aggressive behavior through observation.

experiment that basically replicated the one just described. The difference was that after attacking the "Bobo" doll, the adult models were either rewarded or punished for their behavior by another adult. As you might guess, children who saw the model punished for attacking the doll engaged in very little aggressive behavior toward their own "Bobo" dolls. Those who saw the model reinforced for attacking the doll acted very aggressively, again imitating the model's behaviors in considerable detail (Bandura, 1965).

The application of this sort of data is very straightforward. For example, most of Bandura's research suggests that children can and do learn all sorts of potential behaviors by watching TV. The only real concern, however, should be for those occasions where behaviors deemed inappropriate are left unpunished. So long as children are exposed to the consequences of inappropriate behaviors, they will be less likely to imitate them. This logic suggests that what would be most unfortunate would be for one of a child's TV heroes to "get away with murder," or even be reinforced for doing so. Reinforced behaviors of valued models are more likely to be imitated than punished behaviors of less valued models (for example, Bandura, 1965).

Learning about the consequences of one's behaviors by observing the consequences of someone else's behavior is called **vicarious reinforcement** or **vicarious punishment.** Our own experiences speak to the usefulness of these concepts. You are much more likely to imitate (as best you can) the behaviors of a person who is rewarded for his or her efforts than you are to imitate the behaviors of someone who gets punished. A child, for example, does not *have to* burn her fingers in a fire to learn to avoid the fireplace. Just watching someone else getting burned (or pretending to get burned) will usually suffice.

In fact, learning through observation and the imitation of models (modeling) is a common form of human learning. Your television on any Saturday will provide many examples, particularly if you choose to watch a PBS station. All day long there are people (models) trying to teach us how to paint landscapes, build solar energy devices, do aerobic exercises, remodel a base-

vicarious reinforcement (or) punishment
the strengthening (reinforcement) or weakening (punishment) of responses due to observing the consequences of someone else's behaviors

Children learn through observation and modeling. They often imitate the behavior of their parents and, thus, learn through doing.

ment, improve our golf games, replace a carburetor, or prepare a low-calorie meal. The basic message is one of, "Here, you watch me, see how I do it, then try it yourself." Simply watching children trying to imitate the behaviors of mommy and daddy should convince you of the reality of social learning.

Before you go on
Summarize the basic concepts of social learning and modeling.

APPLYING COGNITIVE THEORIES OF LEARNING TO YOUR STUDY OF PSYCHOLOGY

We have seen that many of the principles of classical and operant conditioning can be applied to your study of psychology. It should also be clear that you can apply many of the ideas we have introduced in this topic to your studying. After all, most of what you will be asked to learn this term is conceptual, or cognitive, in nature. Do you *understand* what is meant by vicarious reinforcement? Do you *know* what a cognitive map is? Much of your learning may be latent: You may never be asked about some of what you learn.

Here are two practical applications. (1) Choose an appropriate model to imitate. Is there someone in your class who is doing very well, perhaps better than you are? What is she or he doing that you are not? Ask them. How are they studying and preparing for exams? By imitating an appropriate model, you may develop some of the same effective behaviors.

(2) Treat your class as an opportunity for you to develop an appropriate learning set. See if you can profit in some general way from past successes or failures. What study strategies have paid off in the past? Which have not worked so well? Be ready to learn how to learn, and adapt your behaviors so that your performance will improve in the future. Such insights should generalize to be helpful in other classes as well.

In many cases, learning is directly reflected in observable behaviors. It is often the case, however, that what is learned—the relatively permanent change that takes place—is *not* reflected in behavior, at least not at the time of learning. What is learned in such circumstances are new cognitions, ideas, or mental representations. Cognitive psychologists argue that learning involves the acquisition (or restructuring) of knowledge, comprehension, and understanding. Evidence for such learning can be found in the cognitive maps and latent learning demonstrations we associate with Tolman, the formation of insights as in Köhler's demonstrations, Harlow's demonstration of the formation of learning sets, and the social learning and imitation studies of Bandura.

imprinting
the simple acquisition of a response (e.g., following) based on exposure to the proper stimulus during a critical period

critical period
the time interval during which an imprinted response is most easily and effortlessly acquired

We noted earlier that an organism's biology places some constraints on what can and cannot be learned through conditioning. That is, some responses are more naturally associated with some stimuli in classical conditioning than with others (aversion and tastes, for example). Some responses seem particularly resistant to changes through reinforcement (instinctive drift).

Imprinting is the name we give to an unusual process: the acquisition of a response (usually a following or attachment response) early in life that occurs during a critical period and with very little effort. The process of imprinting as a special form of learning was introduced to psychology by ethologists (scientists who study the behaviors of animals in their natural habitats), most notably Konrad Lorenz (1981) and Ekhard Hess (1959, 1972).

Ethologists noted that very young ducklings and goslings in the wild typically follow their mothers. You've seen pictures of this response, if not the response itself—a single-file row of little ducks waddling after mother duck down to the pond for a morning swim. The question was *why* the baby ducklings did so. Was the response learned or conditioned in some way, or was it a natural, instinctive reaction without any need for practice and experience? The answer to this question turns out to be "yes"; that is, both factors are involved. This following response, which we say is imprinted, does require experience, but it also requires a built-in, inherited predisposition.

Here's how we can demonstrate imprinting in the laboratory. A duckling is hatched and raised in isolation for the first week or so of its life. At this point, the duckling will not follow anything, not even its mother. So the following response is not automatic. It is not instinctive in

the sense that it will occur no matter what. Some experience is necessary.

There is for ducklings a **critical period** during which the following response will be acquired very rapidly and very easily. This period is usually within the first two days after hatching, with the most sensitive time occurring about 15 hours after hatching. If a larger, moving object is present during this critical period, imprinting will occur—the duckling will "attach" and follow that object regardless of what it is.

In fact, if *you* were wandering around some newly hatched ducklings, and if their mother was kept away from their view, you'd have taken on quite a responsibility. These ducklings would thereafter ignore their mother and follow you. If mother duck walked away in one direction, honking loudly, and you took off in the opposite direction, the ducklings would be close behind you (see Figure 12.4).

So, following its mother is *not* something that a duckling does automatically or instinctively. The following response—a relatively permanent change in behavior—requires experience. But the required experience is very minimal, the effort small, and the reinforcement difficult to see. Now if a baby duckling fails to imprint and follow its mother, it *can* be taught to do so. However, if the critical period has passed, the process is a long and difficult one, usually involving shaping and reinforcement of the sort we find in operant conditioning. By contrast, the formation of attachment and a following response is very simple and rapid during a duckling's normal development.

One might ask if there are any human behaviors that result from imprinting. At the moment there is no sure answer to this question. There is some evidence that a sort

Figure 12.4
Ethologist Konrad Lorenz followed by some ducklings that imprinted on him.

of bonding or attachment does occur early and easily between infants and mothers (or primary caregivers) (Ainsworth, 1979). And there are some psychologists (for example, Lenneberg, 1967; McNeill, 1970) who argue that at least some aspects of human language acquisition follow the patterns of imprinting. Consider how easy it is to acquire one's language during the critical period of ages one to four. Consider how effortlessly children around the world acquire a language (or two or three languages) usually by the time they are 4 years old. Yet, if we wait too long, acquiring a language is very difficult, as any of us who have suffered with French or Spanish in high school or college will attest. Imprinting appears to be a real process in the lives of a number of nonhuman organisms. It may also provide a convenient model for explaining the acquisition of some complex human behaviors.

TOPIC SUMMARY

In general, what characterizes a cognitive approach to learning?

Cognitive approaches to learning emphasize changes that occur within an organism's system of cognitions—its mental representations of itself and its world. Cognitive learning involves the acquisition of knowledge, information, and understanding. Such learning need not be directly reflected in behavior. / 208

What is learned when one forms a cognitive map?

What is latent learning?

According to Tolman, when one acquires a cognitive map, one develops a mental representation (or picture) of one's surroundings—an appreciation of general location and where objects are located. Tolman also argues that much of our learning is latent. That is, learning is the acquisition of information that may not be put into performance until some time later, if at all. / 211

What is insight?

In what way is insight a cognitive process?

Insight involves the sudden reorganization of perceptions and cognitions that leads to the solution of a problem. As a result of insight, learning takes place, and the relatively permanent change that occurs is clearly cognitive, involving perceptions and understanding. / 213

How might we demonstrate the formation of a learning set?

Learning sets are acquired expectations of how to go about learning effectively. It is a matter of learning to learn. Through repeated experience with a particular type of learning task, one develops an effective strategy for similar tasks that are encountered in the future. / 213

Summarize the basic concepts of social learning and modeling.

Bandura's social learning theory emphasizes the role of observation and imitation in the acquisition of cognitions and behaviors. We often learn by imitating successful models through vicarious reinforcement. / 216

CHAPTER SIX

MEMORY

TOPIC

Having studied psychology for 3 hours, you decide to reinforce yourself and order a pizza. You decide to splurge and have your pizza delivered. (You heard this afternoon that Pizza City now delivers free of charge.) Never having called Pizza City before, you have to turn to the yellow pages to find the number: 555-5897. You repeat it to yourself as you think about your choice of pizza toppings—555-5897. Confident that you know the number, you close the phone book and return it to the desk drawer. You dial the number without error—555-5897. Buzzz-buzzz-buzzz-buzzz. Darn, the number's busy! Well, you'll call back in a minute.

Just as you hang up the phone, the door bell rings. "Now who can that be?" you wonder. It's the paper boy. You owe him $11.60 for the past 2 weeks' deliveries. Discovering that you don't have enough cash on hand to pay for the newspaper *and* a pizza, you write a personal check. "Let's see, today's date? What *is* today's date? Oh yes, 10-15-86. How much did you say I owed you? Oh yes, $11.60, plus a dollar tip, comes to $12.60. This is check number 1079; I better write that down. Number 1079. There you go; thanks a lot."

The paperboy leaves. You return to your studying and suddenly remember that you were going to order a pizza. Only 5 or 6 minutes have passed since you last got a busy signal from Pizza City. As you go to dial the phone, however, you cannot for the life of you remember their phone number. Back to the yellow pages.

This experience demonstrates the operation of a rather peculiar type of memory. Pizza City's phone number was clearly in your memory; you remembered it long enough to dial it. But, unable to rehearse the number (and not thinking to write it down), when you needed it again just a few minutes later, it was lost. By the way, without looking, what is the telephone number of Pizza City?

For a long time in psychology, the study of memory was quite simple and straightforward. Memory was viewed as a static, passive storehouse of information. Things somehow got stored away in memory and there they stayed until we wanted to get them out. Psychology textbooks often pictured memory as a large file cabinet, crammed with papers and folders, or as bookshelves in a crowded library. There was thought to be just one type of memory and one kind of storage that either worked when we wanted it to or failed.

Remembering was viewed as being almost automatic. Psychology followed the tradition of the philosopher Plato, who saw memory as being like a block of wax. According to Plato, experiences made impressions, or imprints, in the wax. Sometimes the wax would be soft and malleable, and the impression would be a good, clear one. Sometimes the wax would be hard, and our memories would be only faint, imperfect impressions of our experiences. Plato also recognized individual differences in memory abilities and argued that some people were born with larger and softer "blocks of wax" than others (Adams, 1980).

Of the many changes that have taken place in psychology over the past 30 years, few have been as striking as the changes in the way we view memory. Two of these changes form the focus of this topic and the next one. The first of these changes involves the belief that memory may not be one, unified structure or process; rather, there may be a number of types or levels of memory. This view suggests that all the information stored in memory does not necessarily get stored in the same way or in the same place. There may very well be two (or three, or even more) memory storehouses or processes. The idea that there may be different types of memory or levels of processing information provides the centerpiece for our discussion in this topic. First, we'll formulate a general definition of memory. Then we will explore this notion of there being different kinds of memory and review some of the data that supports this way of looking at memory.

The second change in our way of thinking reflects the idea that memory is not simply a passive receptacle of information. We now view memory as an *active,* creative process, whereby information is actively encoded into memory, stored there, and then actively retrieved. This topic will focus on getting information into memory and storing it there. Our next topic will deal with the practical matter of retrieval, or getting that information out of our memory when we want it.

Before you go on

Over the past 30 years, there have been two major changes in the way we think about memory. What are they?

INTRODUCTION: WHAT IS MEMORY?

Remembering is a mental process that involves the recall or recognition of past experiences. We may say that we demonstrate a **memory** when we can respond to a stimulus in its absence. This is a rather unusual way to think about memory. What does it mean?

Responding to a stimulus that is right in front of you may very well *involve* your memory. But responding to a stimulus that is no longer physically present, no longer available to any of your senses, indicates that you are certainly using memory.

memory
the ability to encode, store, and retrieve information no longer physically present

If I draw a triangle on the blackboard and ask you to identify it, you are using your memory to name the figure, but the task is basically one of perception: Do you perceive the triangle? Then I erase the figure and ask you to tell me what *was* on the blackboard. To do so, you must demonstrate a memory of the stimulus because the stimulus itself is no longer there; you are responding to a stimulus in its absence and are demonstrating a memory.

We can think about memory as being the final step in a series of psychological activities that deal with information processing. We come into this world knowing very little about it. By the time we are adults, we know an incredible number of things about ourselves and the world in which we live. Much of that information may be trivial and irrelevant, but much of it is essential for survival.

How do our minds come to be filled with so much information? As we pointed out in Chapter 3, the processing of information begins with sensation, as our sensory receptors are stimulated to respond. Then, through the process we labeled perception, sensory information is selected and organized. Through learning, some experiences bring about relatively permanent changes in our behaviors. With memory, we have the formation of a record of our information processing.

Following the information processing approach to memory, we see that remembering something involves three separate processes. First, we speak of putting information *into* memory. This process we call **encoding**. Once information is in memory, we must keep it there. This process we call **storage**. And, of course, to use the stored information, we need to be able to get it out again. This process we call **retrieval**. We will have occasion throughout this topic and the next to refer to these three aspects of memory.

As we have said, modern views of memory see it as being more than one, simple, unified process. That is, not all of the information that gets stored in memory necessarily gets stored in the same way or in the same place. Some psychologists (for example, Atkinson & Shiffrin, 1968; Tulving, 1985) argue that there are a number of different types of memory that have different characteristics and different mechanisms for processing information. These psychologists talk about separate, distinct memories, or memory stores. Others (for example, Cermak & Craik, 1979) argue that there is one memory, but within that memory, there are different levels of processing of information. Their argument is that some information simply gets more or less processing than other information.

In this topic, we will examine the basic idea of, and supporting research evidence for, three types or levels of memory: a sensory memory, a short-term memory, and a long-term memory. Sometimes we will refer to sensory, short-term, and long-term stores as if they were *places* or *structures* (or something you put memories in). Sometimes we'll refer to *processing* information at different levels, as if the stores referred to activities, not places (something you do with information to remember it). This mixing of viewpoints is intentional, because at the moment we cannot declare with any certainty which way of viewing memory is "the right one." In either case, we will have a number of questions to ask about each memory structure or level. For example, what is its capacity? That is, how much information can it deal with? What is its duration, or how long will information be held there? How do we know this sort of memory exists? Is there any practical relevance for this memory?

encoding
the active process of putting information into memory

storage
the process of holding encoded information until the time of retrieval

retrieval
the process of locating, removing, and using information that is stored in memory

Before you go on
How do we define memory?

What are three stages of processing information in memory?

SENSORY MEMORY

Sensory memory involves the storage of large amounts of sensory information for very short periods of time (less than 1 second). This notion of a very brief, sensory memory is a strange, difficult, and controversial concept in cognitive psychology.

A sensory memory does fit the overall picture of information processing. All of the information that gets stored in our memories must enter through our senses. To be able to remember what a lecturer says, you must first hear the lecture. To remember a drawing from this book, the image of the drawing must enter your visual system. You couldn't remember the aroma of fried onions if you'd never smelled them in the first place.

The basic idea of sensory memory is that information does not pass directly through our sensory systems; instead, it is held at *sensory registers* for a brief period of time. Even after a stimulus has left our environment and is no longer physically present, it leaves its imprint on our sensory registers, forming a sensory memory.

The *capacity* of sensory memory seems, at least in theory, to be very large indeed. Apparently, we are able to keep as much in our sensory memories as our sense receptors can respond to at any one time. Everything above our sensory thresholds—everything to which our senses can react—gets stored in our sensory memories.

The problem with sensory memory lies in its *duration*. We may easily be able to get vast amounts of information into our sensory memories (encoding), but we aren't able to keep it there (storage) very long. What *is* the duration of sensory memory? It's difficult to say exactly, but memories last in sensory memory less than 1 second—about 0.5 seconds. It certainly won't be of much help for your next psychology exam if you can process information to this store or level and no further.

Sensory memory is viewed as being a rather physical or mechanical type of storage. The information stored there cannot be acted upon. You can't *do* anything with it, manipulate it, or reorganize it. You simply have to take the information in your sensory registers the way your receptors deliver it to you. It is as if stimuli from the environment become burned into our sensory systems and then rapidly fade or are replaced by new stimuli.

For example, did you ever play with a flashlight in the dark when you were a child? Remember how you could see the light of the bulb and a tail of light that followed along behind as someone moved the flashlight about? With a little practice, perhaps you could spell out words in the dark by quickly moving your flashlight. This was possible because your sensory memory made brief memories of the light's locations as it moved through space. In a fraction of a second, your memory of the light's path was gone, but it had been there for a moment. In such a situation, you were seeing not only what *was happening*, but you were also aware of what *had just happened*. You could see the light *and* remember where it had been.

Before you go on

What is sensory memory?

What is its capacity and duration?

Where did this notion of a split-second sensory memory come from? The classic research on sensory memory is that of George Sperling (1960, 1963). Sperling's experiments dealt with visual sensory memory. Let's examine his research in some detail.

Sperling wanted to determine the capacity of sensory memory. He already knew that if a visual display is flashed very briefly (50 milliseconds, or 1/20 of a second) to subjects instructed to remember what they are shown, recall is not very good. That is, presented with a display of letters and digits like the one in Figure 13.1, subjects correctly recalled three or four items. Obviously then, the 1/20 of a second display was long enough for subjects to recognize what they were being shown, but even with the strong possibility of guessing, they could remember only a few specific items. We have claimed that sensory memory has a very large capacity, but three or four letters and digits hardly seems like much of a load.

Sperling's investigation of sensory memory involved a modification of standard recall procedures. Asking subjects to recall *all* the material they have been shown, or as many items as they can recall, is called the **whole report method.** Subjects are asked to *report* the *whole* of what they have been shown.

Having demonstrated that subjects can correctly recall three or four items from a display like the one in Figure 13.1 using the whole report method, Sperling then used a **partial report method**. That is, he didn't ask subjects to recall all of the letters and digits in the display, just those in the first row, or second column, or third row, and so on. With this procedure, subjects performed much better, recalling almost all of the items in one row or column, compared to only one-third or one-fourth of the items in the whole display.

Then Sperling added a new twist. He presented a display of digits and numbers for 1/20 of a second, and then played a tone as soon as the display left the subjects' view. Subjects were told that the tone should act as a cue for recall. If a high-pitched tone was heard, items from the top row were to be recalled. A tone of medium pitch indicated that the letters and/or numbers from the middle row should be recalled, and a low-pitched tone signaled recall from the bottom row.

With this *modified partial report* method, subjects did an impressive job of recalling the required stimulus material. If they were shown a 9-item display, they seldom made an error in recalling the items from any signaled row. They correctly recalled (on the average) 3 of the 4 items from a signaled row when they were shown a 12-item display. Before we go any farther, it's time for a "so what?"

Data from the whole report method seems to indicate that only 3 or 4 letters or digits from a group of 9 or 12 are available in subjects' memories after a brief exposure. Only 25 to 33 percent of the items (3 of 12, 3 of 9) are stored. In many ways, this is not new. Psychologists have long known that we really can't pay attention to more than a few things in a short period of time.

Now think about what the modified partial report method data suggest. It is Sperling's interpretation that in order to do well in recalling items from any line in the display, *the entire matrix must be available* in some form of memory when the tone sounds. Remember that subjects didn't know what they were supposed to recall until they heard the signal tone, which was sounded *after* the display of stimuli was no longer present. If subjects can respond so well at the cue of the tone after stimuli have left the screen, it must be that the entire display is somehow in the memory and available for the required recall.

Sperling's data suggest that approximately nine digits or letters are well within the capacity of some sort of memory, but only if that memory is tapped very quickly. In his research from the early 1960s, Sperling also examined the duration of this special type of memory. If the signal tone in the modified partial report method was played immediately after the stimulus

Figure 13.1
A matrix of letters and digits of the sort that Sperling (1960) used to demonstrate sensory memory.

G	6	N	3
4	8	B	T
A	X	5	7

whole report method
a recall procedure in which a subject is asked to recall all of the material presented earlier

partial report method
a recall procedure in which a subject is asked to recall only a specified portion of the material presented earlier

Figure 13.2

The number of letters available in sensory memory as a function of time or delay. Note that almost 10 letters (of 12) are available immediately, but that with a 1 second delay, fewer than five are available, which matches performance under the whole report conditions. (After Sperling, 1960.)

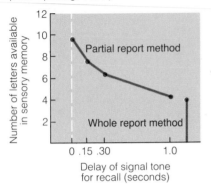

display left the screen, subjects' recall indicated that about nine letters or digits were available. What if there was a delay between when the display left the subjects' view and when the tone was sounded? The answer to this question is depicted in Figure 13.2.

As the interval between the display and the recall cue (the tone) increased, the quality of recall decreased rapidly. In fact, if only 1 second passed between the presentation of the stimulus materials and the signal tone, subjects' recall of items from the signaled row dropped to about the same rate as they demonstrated for the whole report method. In other words, to tap this memory and make use of whatever is stored there, one needs to use it quickly.

We may tentatively draw two conclusions from Sperling's work: (1) There is a register (sensory memory) that holds a good deal of visual information, and (2) that information is available if we get to it very quickly, because most of it is lost within 1 second.

Extending Sperling's partial report method directly to senses other than vision has not been easy to do. There is considerably more evidence for a visual sensory memory than for any other sense. However, a good deal of research has been done involving the sense of hearing, and there is evidence for a similar sort of memory register in audition as in vision (for example, Darwin et al., 1972; Massaro, 1975).

Before you go on

What evidence can you cite that supports the basic idea of a sensory memory?

SHORT-TERM MEMORY (STM)

When they are learning math, children often count on their fingers. As they become more familiar with math fundamentals, their short-term memories can help them solve simple problems in their heads.

At this point in our discussion we have seen that a good deal of information can be stored in our sensory registers. We've also seen that it doesn't take much effort on our part to get information into our sensory memories. But that information stays there for only a fraction of a second, which, on the one hand, is too bad since some of that information might be useful if we could hold on to it longer. On the other hand, it might be just as well that our memories don't get overloaded with masses of useless and irrelevant information.

Once information gets to sensory memory, where does it go next? As we have noted, most of it rapidly fades or is quickly replaced with new stimuli. With a little effort, however, we can process material in our sensory memories more fully by moving it on to our short-term memory.

I am willing to assume that you can multiply 789 by 546 and come up with the right answer. I'll only make this assumption if I further assume that you'll have as long as you'd like to work on the problem, and that you'll be allowed to use paper and pencil. (The use of a calculator in this instance shall constitute cheating.)

Now, can you solve this simple multiplication problem in your head, without the benefit of paper and pencil? Probably not; few of us can. Why not? We obviously know how to multiply two, 3-digit numbers. Why can't we do so without paper and pencil? At least part of the answer is that to do so puts too great a strain on our memories. As we move along into the problem, there are just too many numbers to keep track of, to keep alive in memory.

By the time we get around to multiplying 789 by 5, we've forgotten the result of multiplying it by 6.

The type of memory that fails us as we try to work on such multiplication problems is called **short-term memory (STM)**. Short-term memory has a limited capacity and, without rehearsal, a brief duration. To encode information into STM requires that we attend to the information. Short-term memory is frequently referred to as working memory. It is viewed as something like a workbench or desk top where we can use and manipulate the information we pay attention to from our sensory memories. Because of its limited duration and capacity, STM acts like a bottleneck in the processing of information from our senses into long-term storage. Let's see just how limited our short-term memories are.

The Duration of STM

Interest in short-term memory processing can be traced to two similar experiments reported independently in the late 1950s (Brown, 1958; Peterson & Peterson, 1959). The experimental procedure for demonstrating STM is not unlike our example of trying to remember the telephone number of Pizza City after first getting a busy signal. Let's review the Petersons' experiment.

On a typical trial, a subject is shown three consonants, such as KRW, for 3 seconds. Presenting the letters for 3 seconds assures that they are attended to and, hence, encoded into STM. The subject is then asked to recall the three letters after retention intervals ranging from 0 to 18 seconds. This doesn't sound like a very difficult task, and it isn't. Almost anyone can remember three letters for as long as 18 seconds. However, in this experiment, subjects are prohibited from rehearsing the three letters during the retention interval. They are given another task to perform right after they see the letters. They are asked to count backward, by threes, from a three-digit number supplied by the experimenter.

For example, if you were a subject, you would be shown a letter sequence, say KRW, and then you would have to count backward from, say, 397, by threes, or 397, 394, 391, 388, and so forth. You'd be pressed to do your counting out loud and as rapidly as possible. The idea is that the counting task interferes with your rehearsal of the three letters you were just shown.

Under these conditions, your ability to recall the letters correctly *depends on the length of the retention interval.* If you are asked to recall the letters after just a few seconds of counting, you won't do too badly. If you have to count for as long as 15 to 20 seconds, your ability to recall the letters drops to almost zero (see Figure 13.3). Unable to rehearse them and distracted by the counting task, the letters are soon unavailable to you.

One way to increase or stretch the duration of short-term memory is to rehearse the information stored there. The type of rehearsal that we use simply to keep material active in our short-term, working memory is called **maintenance rehearsal,** or rote rehearsal, which amounts to little more than simple repetition of the information already in our STM. Remember, to get information into STM (encoding), we merely have to attend to it. By repeating the information over and over (as we might if we wanted to remember a telephone number until we could dial it), we are essentially reattending to it with each repetition.

So one reason why STM is a bottleneck in our processing of information is that it does not store information for very long. By attending to information, however, we keep it available in memory well beyond the limits of sensory memory. As a rule of thumb, we can say that, if left unrehearsed, material

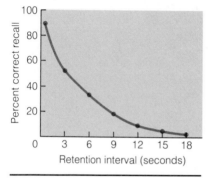

Figure 13.3
Recall of letters as a function of retention interval where maintenance rehearsal is minimized.
(Adapted from Peterson & Peterson, 1959.)

will stay in STM for about 15 to 20 seconds. That's better than sensory memory, but it still won't help much when it comes to taking an exam next week.

At least the duration of STM is long enough to allow us to use it occasionally in everyday activities. Again, our telephone number example is relevant. Usually all we want to do with a telephone number is remember it long enough to dial it. It's not often that we feel the need to make a permanent record of a telephone number. Using STM in mathematical computations is another good example, although multiplying 789 by 546 may exceed STM capabilities. And, as you read one of my longer sentences, it is useful to have a short-term storage place to keep the beginning of the sentence that you are reading in mind until you finally get to the end of the sentence, so that you can figure out the basic idea of the sentence. Now let's deal with the capacity of STM. Just how much information can we hold in STM for that 15 to 20 seconds?

Before you go on

How long is information stored in STM?

How do we know?

What is required to get material into STM in the first place?

The Capacity of STM

In 1956, George Miller wrote a charming paper on "the magical number seven, plus or minus two." In it, he argued convincingly that the capacity of our working memories is very small—limited to just 5 to 9 (7 ± 2) bits, or chunks, of information.

As we all know, we can readily store a telephone number in our short-term memories. Adding an area code makes the task somewhat harder because the 10 digits now come fairly close to the upper limit of our capacity. Notice, though, how we tend to cluster, or chunk, the digits of a phone number into a pattern. The digit series 2194935661 is more difficult to deal with as a simple string than when it is seen as a telephone number: (219) 493-5661 (Bower & Springston, 1970).

By chunking bits and pieces of information together, we can add meaningfulness to what we are attending to and storing in our memories. Can you hold this number in your STM: 49162536496481? The 14 digits here are beyond the capacity of most people's STM. *But,* if you recognize these as a series of numbers, each being the *square* of the digits 2 through 9 (4/9/16/25/36/49/64/81), the task is an easy one because you have chunked the material in a meaningful way. Using a similar system of chunking digits into meaningful clusters, one student demonstrated an ability to recall more than 80 randomly presented digits (Ericsson & Chase, 1982).

Let's try one more. Try to remember these letters: EVOLNILRIGDNAYOBA. Now *that* will strain your STM capacity. But how simple it is to remember this string if it is seen as being organized or chunked as a simple phrase in reverse: A BOY AND GIRL IN LOVE. The six *words* are well within your STM capacity, and, using memory as an active process, the letters are now easily remembered.

Thus, STM is a bottleneck, working something like a leaky bucket. From the vast storehouse of information available in sensory memory, STM scoops up some (and not much at that) and holds it for a while until we either use it, maintain it, move it on to long-term storage, or lose it.

How Information Is Encoded in STM

The material or information that is stored in our sensory memories is encoded there in virtually the same form in which it was presented. Visual stimuli form visual memories or impressions, auditory stimuli form auditory memories, and so on. It is for this reason that some psychologists prefer to talk about separate memory registers, one for each sense modality.

We recognize that getting information into STM is not necessarily an automatic process. We have to first attend to the material to encode, or process, it into short-term memory. How, then, is information stored in STM?

Conrad was one of the first to argue that information is stored in STM with an acoustic code (1963, 1964). What this means is that material tends to be processed in terms of what it *sounds* like. Conrad's conclusion was based on his interpretation of the errors that subjects make in short-term memory tasks.

For example, he would present subjects with a series of letters to remember. The letters were presented *visually*, one at a time, and then subjects were asked to recall the letters they had just seen. It was not surprising that many errors were made over the course of the experiment. It *was* surprising that when subjects responded with an incorrect letter, it was very frequently with a letter that *sounded* like the correct one. For example, if subjects were supposed to recall the letter E and failed to do so, they would commonly recall in error V, G, or T, or a letter that sounded like the E they were supposed to recall. They rarely responded F, which certainly looks more like the E they had seen than does V, G, or T.

Experiments by Baddeley (1966) made the same point, but with a different technique. In these experiments, subjects were asked to recall short lists of common words. Some lists were made up of words that all sounded alike (e.g., man, ban, fan, can). Other lists contained words that had similar meanings; that is, they were semantically alike (e.g., large, huge, giant, big). A third type of list contained a random assortment of words. Lists were only five words long, and, hence, were well within the capacity of short-term memory. The lists that were hardest to recall were those that contained acoustically similar items (i.e., the "man, ban, fan" list). Baddeley's argument is that the acoustic similarity caused confusion within STM, whereas semantic similarity did not.

It seems then that using short-term memory is a matter of talking to ourselves. We tend to code and process information, no matter how it is presented, acoustically, the way it sounds. At least that's what most of the early evidence seemed to suggest. Subsequent research has not changed the view that acoustic coding is the most important method of coding for STM, but it has presented the possibility that some material may be encoded in STM in other ways—such as being represented visually or semantically (Cooper & Shepard, 1973; Martindale, 1981; Wickens, 1973). Presently, perhaps the most we can say is that there appears to be a tendency to rely heavily on the acoustic coding of information in short-term memory, but other codes (visual or semantic, in particular) may be used.

LONG-TERM MEMORY (LTM)

Long-term memory (LTM) is memory as we usually think of it—memory for large amounts of information over long periods of time. As we did for sensory memory and short-term memory, we'll begin by considering two basic issues: capacity and duration.

Our own experiences tell us that the capacity of our long-term memories is huge, virtually limitless. At times we even impress ourselves with the amount of material we have stashed away in LTM (for example, when we play games such as Trivial Pursuit). Just how much can be stored in human memory may never be measured, but we can rest assured that there is no way we will ever learn so much that there won't be room for more.

For an example of memory's huge capacity, consider an experiment by Standing, Conezio, and Haber (1970). Over the course of 5 days, they presented subjects with 2500 different pictures and asked them to try to remember them all. Even a day or so later, subjects correctly identified, in a new collection of pictures, 90 percent of the ones they had seen before. Standing (1973) then increased the number of pictures that subjects viewed to 10,000. It took quite awhile simply to view 10,000 pictures! Again, subjects later correctly recognized more than 90 percent of them.

There seems to be no practical limit to the amount of information we can process (or encode) into this long-term store of memory. (Getting information out again when we want it is another matter. We'll get to that issue in our next topic.) How long will information stay in LTM once it is there? Assuming that you remain free from disease or pathology, you are likely never to forget your own name, or your parents' names, or the words to "Twinkle, Twinkle Little Star."

At the moment, it is impossible to even imagine an experiment that could tell us with any certainty how long our memories remain stored in LTM. One thing we know for a fact is that we often cannot remember things we know we once knew. We do tend to forget things. The issue is *why*. Do we forget because the information is no longer *available* to us in our long-term memories, simply not there any more? Or do we forget because we are unable to get the information out of LTM, implying that the information is still available, but somehow not *accessible?*

Our long-term memories can store vast amounts of information—both important and trivial. A wide variety of life situations, even game playing, call on our ability to retrieve information from our long-term memories.

For a very long time in psychology we believed that once information was processed into LTM, it stayed there until we died. Forgetting was viewed as a failure of *retrieval* of retained information. George Mandler (1967), among others, made this case very forcefully, proposing that memories were always retained and available, though not necessarily accessible. He used an analogy of a house on an island in the middle of a large lake. From the edge of the lake, ". . . one can see the house, which is certainly available, but in the absence of rowboats, helicopters, or bridges, the house is not accessible" (p. 25). And so it is with many memories: They are there, but not accessible. There is a good deal of comfort to be derived from this view. How pleasant it is to think that everything we ever knew, everything that ever happened to us, is still there someplace, ultimately retrievable if we only knew how to get it out.

As comforting as this view may be, there is reason to believe that it is not totally accurate. A review article by Loftus and Loftus (1980) has raised again the issue of the relative permanence of long-term memories. Suggesting that long-term memories are not necessarily permanent involved a two-pronged attack. First the Loftuses reviewed the data supporting the argument for permanence and found that "the evidence in no way confirms the view that all memories are permanent and thus potentially recoverable" (p.

409). They claim that the bulk of such evidence is anecdotal and should be interpreted as suggesting that people who remember once-forgotten information are merely reconstructing a reasonable facsimile of the original information from bits and pieces of their past experiences. That is, when we remember something that happened to us a long time ago, we don't recall the events *as they happened* (as if our memories work like video recorders). Rather, we remember a specific detail or two and actively reconstruct what amounts to new memories.

Let's examine one study (Loftus et al., 1978) that raises serious doubts about the permanence of long-term memories. Subjects are shown a series of slides that show a red Datsun approach an intersection, turn right, and knock down a pedestrian who is crossing at the crosswalk. Some subjects see a yield sign at the intersection, while others are shown a stop sign at the intersection. In all other respects, the slides are identical. After viewing the slides, subjects are asked a series of questions about what they have just seen. Some are asked, "Did another car pass the red Datsun while it was stopped at the *stop sign?*" Others are asked the same question, with *"yield sign"* used in place of *"stop sign."*

Then all the subjects are shown a series of pairs of slides and are asked to identify the one slide in each pair that was in the series they had seen earlier. As you can guess, the critical slide pair for these subjects is the pair showing the red Datsun at a stop sign and at a yield sign. By now you might also guess the result. Eighty percent of the subjects choose the slide that contained the sign consistent with the question they had been asked, but not consistent with the sign they had actually seen. That is, if you were a subject who had seen the Datsun at a *stop sign* and were then asked about the car being passed by another while at a *yield sign,* chances are that you would remember the sign as a yield sign, not a stop sign. The later question would replace the previous information in your LTM.

There are a number of implications of this line of research that have practical importance. One of the most obvious applications is in the area of eyewitness testimony. If it is in fact true that long-term memories are not permanent and can be distorted or replaced by later information, we may be forced to reconsider the weight that is given to eyewitness testimony in courts of law (Buckhout, 1975; Loftus, 1984).

Inaccurate eyewitness testimony indicates that our long-term memories are not perfect and are subject to distortion. On the basis of eyewitness testimony, the man on the top was imprisoned for 5 years for a crime committed by the man on the bottom.

Before you go on
Are long-term memories necessarily permanent?

Encoding in LTM: A Matter of Repetition and Rehearsal

We have already seen how simple, rote repetition (called maintenance rehearsal) can be used to keep material active in short-term memory. There is reason to believe that this simple sort of rehearsal is also one way to move information from STM to LTM. The basic idea is that the more one repeats a bit of information, the more likely it will be remembered—even beyond the limits of short-term memory.

One experimental demonstration of this rather common-sense notion is that of Rundus (1971). Rundus presented subjects with a list of words to memorize. The words were presented one at a time and recall was requested well beyond the limits usually associated with STM. When asked to learn a list of words under conditions like these, most subjects repeat some of the words (rehearse them) silently, talking to themselves. Rundus asked his subjects to do this rehearsing out loud. He recorded their rehearsal and looked at

Figure 13.4

*Recalling and recognizing stimulus
words as a function of rehearsal.
(Data from Rundus, 1971.)*

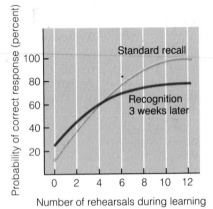

the relationship between the probability that a word would be recalled and the number of times it was repeated during the presentation of the list. The correlation was almost perfect: The more frequently a word was repeated, the more likely it was to be recalled. (And the more likely it was to be recognized even 3 *weeks later.*) So it seems that the simple repetition of information (at least for words and letters) will move it along to LTM. (See Figure 13.4.)

However, the simple repetition of material may not be sufficient to process it into LTM. We have just seen that it can be helpful, but getting some material into long-term memory may require more. Some of the most damaging evidence against the argument that repetition alone is all that is needed to encode information into LTM is provided by Craik and Watkins (1973). They presented subjects with a rather long list of apparently random words. Subjects were told to listen carefully to the entire list. They were also instructed to try to recall the *last word that began with a certain letter,* say D. So when the first word beginning with a D appeared on the list, subjects started to rehearse and repeat it, thinking that they would have to recall it. But as soon as the next D-word appeared, subjects would begin repeating *it* to themselves since they were only responsible for remembering the *last* word beginning with a D, not all of them. The lists presented to the subjects had a number of different D-words on them. Some D-words were rehearsed only once (before being replaced by another), while some were rehearsed as many as 12 times.

After the list was presented, subjects responded with the last D-word they had heard and seldom had much trouble doing so. Then, after a couple of minutes of polite conversation, the experimenters surprised the subjects by asking them to recall the entire list of stimulus words! What Craik and Watkins were interested in was the probability of correctly recalling a word that had been repeated a number of times during the list's presentation—in our case, D-words. Craik and Watkins found that it didn't much matter how many times a word is repeated or rehearsed with simple maintenance rehearsal. All the words were recalled with approximately the same (low) probability.

It does seem that to get information into LTM, we need to rehearse it. But it also seems clear that if we want to ensure that material is well processed into LTM, we need to do more than simply repeat it over and over. We need to think about it, reorganize it perhaps, form images of it, try to make it meaningful, or relate it to something already in our long-term memories. In other words, to get information into LTM we need to "elaborate" on it, to use the term proposed by Craik and Tulving (1975). We need to process it more fully, using what is called **elaborative rehearsal**.

elaborative rehearsal

a mechanism for processing information into LTM that involves the meaningful manipulation of the information to be remembered

Do you see how the distinction between maintenance and elaborative rehearsal fits a model of memory that deals with levels of processing? For sensory memory, we need do very little to process information; stimuli are stored automatically at this level. To get to the next level requires deeper processing; attention and acoustic coding are required for STM. LTM, then, represents the deepest level of processing. Items must be elaborated, expanded, and made meaningful to reach this level. Simple acoustic talking to ourselves is no longer sufficient.

Before you go on

Can repetition alone process information from STM to LTM?

What kind of rehearsal works best for LTM encoding?

What Is Stored in LTM and How Is It Stored There?

Our own experiences tell us that the information we have stored away in LTM can be retrieved in many different forms. We can remember the definitions of words. We can picture or visualize people and events from the past. We can remember the melodies of songs and can recall the feel of a fastball slamming into our baseball gloves. We can recall how our bodies moved when we first tried to ski or roller skate.

Episodic and Semantic Memories Endel Tulving (1972) has suggested that the information we have stored in LTM is of two different types. Although the two may interact with each other, he sees them as being basically different. One type of memory is called **semantic memory**. In it we have stored all our vocabulary, simple concepts, and rules (including the rules that govern our use of language). In a way, our semantic memories are crammed with facts (both important and trivial), such as:

> **semantic memory**
> *in LTM, where vocabulary, facts, simple concepts, and rules are stored*

Who opened the first psychology laboratory in Leipzig in 1879?

How many stripes are there on the American flag?

How is an omelet made?

If we can recall the answers to these questions, we have found them in our long-term semantic memories.

The other type of memory proposed by Tulving is called **episodic memory**. It is here that we store our life events and experiences. It is a time-related memory, and, in a sense, it is very autobiographical. For example:

> **episodic memory**
> *in LTM, where life events and experiences are stored*
>
> *episode—events*

What were you doing the day John Lennon was killed?

When and where did you first learn how to ride a bike?

What did you have for lunch yesterday?

The answers to these sorts of questions are stored in our episodic memories.

Our semantic memories store vocabulary, simple concepts, and rules, including the rules of spelling.

Our episodic memories store our life events and experiences. Being in a fire is an experience few of us would ever forget.

The Organization of Semantic Memory

The facts in our semantic long-term memories are clearly stored in an organized fashion. On this point we are agreed. What is much less certain is *how* the information in our semantic memories is organized. Although we cannot review all the possibilities here, we'll take a look at some of the data and hypotheses that have emerged concerning how we store words in our long-term memories.

A classic experiment on the organization of memory is that of Bousfield (1953), who demonstrated the phenomenon of **category clustering.** Bousfield showed that in recall we tend to group words together in conceptual categories, even if they were presented in a random order. For example, subjects are presented with a list of words to learn: *Howard, spinach, zebra, plumber, Bernard, dentist, carrot, weasel,* etc. There are 60 words on the list. After listening to the list, subjects are asked to write down, in any order, as many of the words from the list as they can recall. Subjects are told nothing about the nature of the list of words, but it is in fact made up of 15 words from each of four different conceptual categories: animals, men's names, professions, and vegetables (which you may have noticed as you read the sample list above).

When subjects recall such a list, they almost always do a rather strange thing. They do not write down their recall in a random order, or in the order in which the words were presented, but group them together into categories. For example, they might write down a number of men's names, then six or seven animals, then a string of professions, followed by a few vegetables. Then, at the end of their recall, they may just add a random word or two from any category. So one organizational scheme for long-term memory takes advantage of our knowledge of categories. Particularly for nouns, when we can sort and store information in clusters or categories, we do so.

What about words that do not fit so neatly into categories? How might they be organized? Research by Endel Tulving (1962) shows just how powerful our tendency to organize verbal material is. Tulving presented subjects with a list of 16 random and apparently unrelated words to be learned and later recalled. He presented the same list to subjects over and over, each time in a different order until the list was learned. Because there was no organization in the list itself, any consistency at recall must reflect an organization imposed by the subject recalling the list.

Tulving found a strong tendency for subjects to recall words together, in the same sequence, on successive recall trials. Each subject tended to organize his or her own recall in his or her own way, consistently grouping together clusters of two or three words in the same order on different recall attempts, even though the items were always presented in a different order. Tulving referred to this type of clustering as **subjective organization.**

Collins and Quillian (1969) have suggested that our semantic memories are organized in hierarchies of information. To see what that means, refer to Figure 13.5, which presents a very small segment of a possible hierarchy for a few of the words that you and I have in our semantic memories. At the top of this flow chart of semantic organization is the term *animal.* Associated with it are some of its defining characteristics, "has skin," "can breathe," "moves around." Below *animal* are found (among others) two concepts: *bird* and *fish,* each with their defining characteristics. Below this level we find even more specific examples, including *canary, robin, shark,* and *salmon,* each with its defining characteristics. It is possible, of course, to go even farther. That is, if you once had a canary named Pete, your semantic memory might include a level below *canary,* separating Pete and his (or her) characteristics from all other canaries. Or, you might have a level above *animal* called *living things.*

category clustering
the tendency of subjects during recall to group words together into categories even if they are presented in random order

subjective organization
the tendency for subjects to impose some subjective, personal order on their recall of random events or items

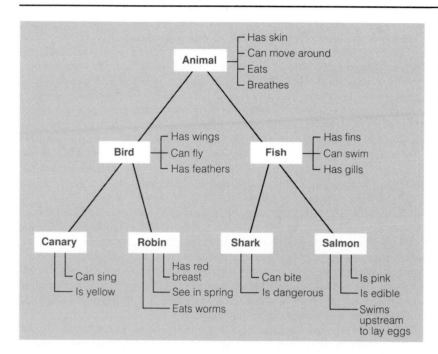

Figure 13.5

An illustration of how information is organized in semantic memory. Members of a category are organized in a hierarchy. The information to be retrieved must be located within the hierarchy to be recalled.
(Adapted from Collins & Quillian, 1969.)

This system appears quite complicated as presented in Figure 13.5, and we have to remember that in this figure we've left out many of the things that we know about animals, fish, birds, and canaries just to make it reasonably simple. Is there any evidence that memories are stored in this fashion? Yes, there is. Suppose I ask you the following three questions about canaries and ask that you respond "yes" or "no."

1. Can canaries sing?
2. Do canaries have feathers?
3. Do canaries have skin?

I suspect that none of these questions gave you a hard time. But if we were to have measured how long it took you to answer these three questions, we might have found what Collins and Quillian found. The first was answered most quickly, the second took longer, and the third, longer yet. Each question required that you search a higher and higher level of memory to find the answer (singing is associated directly with canaries, feathers with birds in general, and skin with animals in general). There is an assumption in this model that concepts can be clearly and neatly defined and organized. Such is not always the case, as we shall see in Topic 15. The exercise we just went through for *canary* might yield different results if our example hadn't been such an obvious example of a bird (Rosche, 1973). How might you answer the same three questions if they dealt with an ostrich or a penguin?

It would be altogether improper to leave the impression that we know how words, concepts, and facts are organized in our semantic memories. We are quite sure that there is organization, but we have conflicting data on what that organization is. It may be categorical, it may be hierarchical, it may be in some combination, or it may be in some totally unknown way.

Before you go on

Compare and contrast semantic and episodic memories.

serial position effect
the observation that items from the middle of a list are more difficult to recall than are items from either the beginning or end of a list

The **serial position effect** conforms to our own experience: When we are asked to remember a list of items, it is much easier to recall items from the beginning and end of the list than it is to recall items from the middle of the list. In other words, the *position* of items in a *series* affects our ability to recall them. Figure 13.6 shows typical serial position effect curves.

One doesn't need lists of words to demonstrate the serial position effect. Almost any task that requires that we memorize material in order will do. For example, have you ever listened carefully to young children learning to sing "The Star Spangled Banner"? They start off like gangbusters, "Oh, say can you see . . . ." Then they mutter and mumble their way through the middle of the song, all mysteriously ending up in unison, and with great confidence, ". . . and the home of the brave."

Being able to recall items from the beginning of a list is called the *primacy effect*. We call the spurt of improved recall for items at the end of a list the *recency effect*. I hope that you recognize that labeling these phenomena *explains* nothing. Explaining the serial position effect by saying that it is due to primacy and recency effects simply *names* what's happening. It doesn't explain it. The most generally (though not universally) accepted explanation of the serial position effect hinges on our understanding of STM and LTM and of maintenance and elaborative rehearsal.

The gist of the argument is this: Items from the beginning of the list are easy to recall because there has been ample time to rehearse and elaborate these items into long-term memory from which they are retrieved (primacy effect). Because recall is asked for immediately after the list's presentation, items from the end of the list are easy to recall because they are still active and available in short-term memory (recency effect). Items from the middle of the list are difficult to recall because they have not yet been elaborated into LTM, and they have slipped beyond the limits of STM retention. Assuming that all this sounds reasonable, let's review some data from Glanzer and Cunitz (1966) that supports it.

Figure 13.6
Serial position curves for lists of 20 and 40 words, presented at a rate of 1 second per item.
(Adapted from Murdock, 1962.)

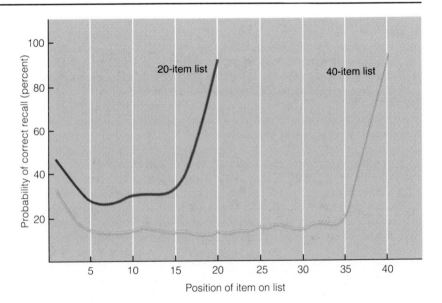

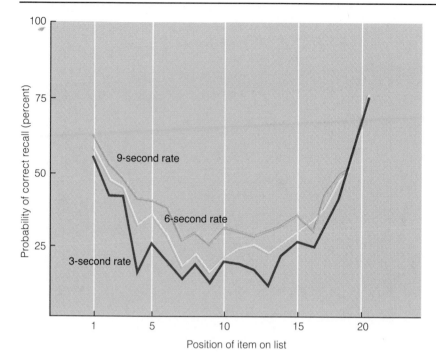

Figure 13.7

Data from Glanzer and Cunitz (1966) illustrating that slower presentation rates allow more time for elaboration, enhancing primacy effects, but not affecting recency effects.

If the primacy effect depends on our elaborating items into LTM, then the more time we have to do so, the better. In one of Glanzer and Cunitz's experiments, subjects were asked to recall a list of 20 words. The list was presented at rates of 3, 6, or 9 seconds per item. The slower presentation rates should allow more time for subjects to elaboratively rehearse items from the beginning of the list, and, thus, should show a stronger, steeper, primacy effect. Rate of presentation should have little effect on maintenance rehearsal for items at the end of the list. The data presented in Figure 13.7 show that this is exactly what happened.

If the recency effect depends on our retrieval of items from STM, then tasks that interfere with immediate recall should disrupt the recency effect. To see if this is the case, subjects were presented with 15-word lists (all at the same rate of presentation). Recall was requested either immediately following the presentation of the list (0 delay), after a 10-second distraction of a counting task, or after a 30-second delay and distraction. By the time subjects finish with a 30-second counting task that interferes with maintenance rehearsal, items in STM should be lost and the recency effect should disappear. It did. See Figure 13.8.

This experiment shows us two things. On the one hand, it helps us understand an observation about recall that has been recognized for a long time: the serial position effect. In so doing, it also gives strength to the argument that short-term and long-term memories are different mechanisms that operate under different principles. This dual-memory viewpoint is not universally held in psychology, but data such as these help reinforce the distinction.

Before you go on

What is the serial position effect, and how can STM and LTM processes be used to explain it?

Figure 13.8

The effects of a distracting task (of 0, 10, or 30 seconds) between the presentation of the list and the request for recall. The major effect is on STM-related recency effect.
(After Glanzer & Cunitz, 1966.)

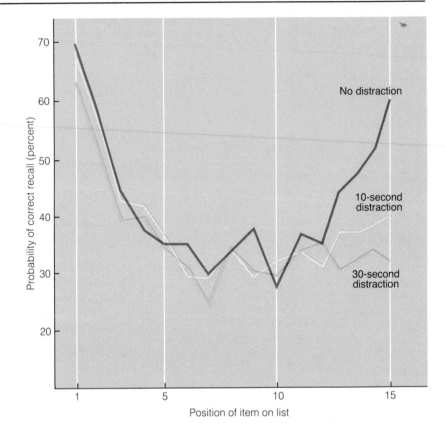

We have covered a lot of ground in this topic, much of it very technical. We have tried to show that memory is not a simple receptacle for information that passively enters our bodies and gets dumped someplace where we can get it out whenever we wish. To encode and store information in our memory requires a series of processes to move it from sensory registers to short-term storage and from short-term to long-term storage. What ultimately matters for most of us, day in and day out, is whether or not we can get material out of our memory system when we want to. We'll consider this process of retrieval in our next topic.

We may all safely assume that memories are stored in our brains. Precisely where and how they are stored in our brains is something we simply do not know. The search for physiological and biochemical foundations for memory has been a very active, exciting, and controversial one. In few areas of science can we find so much conflicting evidence and theory. One of the major problems facing researchers in this area is that memories seem to form so quickly and last for such a long time. Finding biochemical processes that can reflect such rapid modification on the one hand, and then maintain such a long-term stability on the other, is not going to be easy. Just to provide an idea of what this sort of research is like, let's consider two different views of how memories may be represented in the brain.

One area of research that seemed very promising when it first began centered its attention on the RNA molecule. RNA (ribonucleic acid) is a complex chemical molecule, found in the nucleus of all cells, that is involved in the transmission of inherited characteristics. Part of the logic behind pursuing the RNA molecule was that it obviously could store large amounts of genetic information, so perhaps it could also serve as a storage mechanism for information gained through experience. The theory was that a particular experience would modify the complex structure of the RNA molecule and that the newly restructured molecule could serve as the storage mechanism for that experience.

What made all of this complex chemistry seem feasible was a series of remarkable experimental demonstrations by James McConnell and his associates (McConnell, 1962; McConnell et al., 1959; Thompson & McConnell, 1955). These experiments seemed to demonstrate that RNA extracted from a small flatworm (planaria) that had learned a response (coiling in response to a light) could transfer that response to naive flatworms.

Planaria learned to coil their bodies in response to a light. Classical conditioning was used: The light was paired with a shock that naturally produced the coiling response. The conditioned planaria were then ground up and fed to planaria who had not learned this response to light. Upon eating the conditioned planaria, the naive planaria also tended to coil in response to a light. It was as if the memory of the conditioning experience had been transferred from one organism to another.

You might imagine the excitement that followed reports of this research. Wild claims were found in the press as people wondered about transferring RNA from intelligent individuals to individuals of lesser intelligence. Some replications were reported. For example, rats were trained in a variety of tasks, and, after their death, RNA was extracted from their brains and injected into untrained rats. When these naive rats were tested, they either showed the responses learned by the RNA donors or took many fewer trials to learn the same responses (Babich et al., 1965).

The problem that soon developed was the lack of a consistent ability to replicate these experiments. Sometimes they worked and sometimes they didn't, and there was no obvious reason why. As Kalat (1984) put it, reviewing a number of these early studies, "Science cannot make use of an experiment whose results are not replicable. Within a few years, research interest began to fade rapidly. By the end of the 1970s, most biological psychologists had come to regard the whole line of research as a blind alley" (p. 342).

As interest in RNA molecules faded, other biochemical mechanisms took over center stage. One biochemical process that is currently attracting much attention is the transmission of neural impulses at the synaptic level in the brain. The synapses in the brain that are most suspect are those which are activated by the neurotransmitter acetylcholine (ACh). A number of lines of evidence point to acetylcholine's role in memory. For one thing, we recognize that memory failure is, to some degree, normally associated with old age. It is also true that ACh levels decrease with age. ACh has also been strongly implicated in the extreme memory loss of Alzheimer's disease (see Topic 28) (Bartus et al., 1982). Experimental tests on young adult subjects show that an artificially lowered ACh level inhibits ability on memory tasks, and that low doses of drugs that temporarily increase ACh levels tend to improve memory abilities (Kalat, 1984).

Unfortunately, there is as yet no good, or safe, way to consistently raise acetylcholine levels in the brain (in hopes of thereby improving memory skills). At best, positive effects are short-lived, and, at worst, the side effects may be quite harmful (Bartus, 1982). And it is still the case that we really don't know precisely what effect acetylcholine has on memory, whether it is specific or general in its action (Levinthal, 1983).

As we've suggested, there are other avenues of research being actively pursued; some involve how small bits of protein are synthesized within nerve cells, while others involve physical changes at the synapse and an alteration of neurotransmitter receptor sites. The research is tedious, but obviously very important. Imagine how much more likely it would be that we could improve our memories if we better understood the basic biochemical processes involved in the encoding, storage, and retrieval of memories.

TOPIC SUMMARY

Over the past 30 years, there have been two major changes in the way we think about memory. What are they?

As opposed to 30 years ago, psychologists now view memory as an active process, not a passive receptacle of information. Also, memory is no longer viewed as being a single, unified structure. Rather, it is seen as being composed of different levels of processing, or stores of information. / 224

How do we define memory?

What are three stages of processing information in memory?

One can be said to demonstrate a memory if one can respond to a stimulus in its absence. Memory involves the encoding, storage, and retrieval of information. It is a mental process that involves the recall or recognition of past experiences. / 225

What is sensory memory?

What is its capacity and duration?

Sensory memory involves the very brief (less than 1 second) storage of large amounts of information in sensory registers. We cannot manipulate information in these registers; thus, the information is assumed to be stored exactly as it is received by our sense receptors. / 226

What evidence can you cite that supports the basic idea of a sensory memory?

George Sperling's use of the partial report method demonstrated that if we can access the sensory registers quickly enough (within 1 second), recall reflects the storage of large amounts of material presented visually for just a fraction of a second. That is, when cued to recall visually presented material within 0.5 seconds after the material was no longer in the subject's environment, a subject could demonstrate that large amounts of information were available for recall. / 228

How long is information stored in STM?

How do we know?

What is required to get material into STM in the first place?

When we pay attention to information in our sensory memories, we move it on to our short-term memories. Although we cannot hold much information there, it will stay in STM for approximately 15–20 seconds before fading or being replaced by new information. Material that has been attended to cannot be recalled after about 20 seconds if maintenance rehearsal is prohibited. / 230

How much information can be held in STM?

How can chunking affect the capacity of STM?

It is reasonable to say that the capacity of STM is limited to approximately five to nine bits of information. This assumes the information to be unrelated and meaningless. By chunking bits and pieces of information together into meaningful clusters, more of it can be processed at the level of STM. / 231

What evidence do we have that information tends to be encoded acoustically in STM?

Information in STM may be processed there in any number of forms, but acoustic coding seems most likely. When errors in short-term memory are made, those items recalled in error are most likely to *sound* like the items that were to be recalled. Words that sound alike are more likely to cause STM confusion than are words that mean the same thing. / 231

Are long-term memories necessarily permanent?

Although LTM may hold information for a very long time, it should not necessarily be thought of as being a literally permanent memory. Information in LTM seems to be subject to distortion, replacement, and reconstruction. / 233

Can repetition alone process information from STM to LTM?

What kind of rehearsal works best for LTM encoding?

Although the simple repetition of information may sometimes be sufficient to encode material from STM to LTM, there seems little doubt that the best mechanism for placing information into LTM is elaborative rehearsal; that is, to think about the material, forming associations or images of the material and relating it to something already stored in LTM. / 234

Compare and contrast semantic and episodic memories.

Within LTM, episodic memories are those that store our life experiences and events. They are somewhat autobiographical and time-ordered. On the other hand, our semantic memories are those that store our facts, knowledge, and vocabularies. Although it seems reasonable to assume that episodic memories store information sequentially, semantic memories seem to operate with a number of possible organizational schemes. / 237

What is the serial position effect, and how can STM and LTM processes be used to explain it?

The serial position effect is the name we give to the observation that it is harder to remember items from the middle of a list than it is to remember items from either the beginning or the end of the list. Items at the beginning of the list are thought to be easier to recall because they had ample time to be elaborated into LTM, while items at the end of the list are still being maintained in STM. Items in the middle of the list are no longer in STM, but have not yet been elaborated into LTM, and, hence, are more difficult to recall. / 239

TOPIC

I'd like you to take a short vocabulary test. This test is a little different from most because I'll provide you with the definitions, and I want you to come up with the word described by my definition. These are not easy words, but perhaps you have heard them before. Before you go looking down the page for the answers to these three questions, look for them carefully in your long-term memory. See if you can notice what you are doing as you search for answers.

What words fit the following definitions:

— "A small flat-bottomed boat or skiff used along rivers and coastal regions of China and Japan."

— "A navigational instrument used in measuring angular distances, especially the altitude of the sun, moon and stars."

— "Favoritism, especially in governmental patronage, based on family relationships rather than merit."

Did you get any of those? Were you able to find in your memory the words for which these definitions are appropriate? These words, and others, were used in a 1966 experiment by Roger Brown and David McNeill to demonstrate what they labeled a "tip-of-the-tongue" phenomenon, or TOT. This same sort of procedure was used to create a condition we're all familiar with: the sense of *knowing* that you know something, being unable to fully recall it when it is wanted, but feeling that it is right at the tip of your tongue. What Brown and McNeill discovered was that many of their college student subjects didn't have the faintest idea what one calls a

"small flat-bottomed boat or skiff used along rivers and coastal regions of China and Japan." A number of their subjects did know immediately what the correct response was. But many subjects experienced a TOT—a condition that these researchers likened to "mild torment, something like the brink of a sneeze," (p.326) as they fought to pull the word out of their long-term memories.

When asked about the word for which they were searching, Brown and McNeill's subjects could often correctly report the letter with which the word began, the number of syllables it contained, and which syllable is stressed when the word is pronounced. For example, in response to the first question, subjects often responded with words that sounded like the correct response—for example, "Saipan," "Siam," "Cheyenne," "sarong," "sanching," and "sympoon." Subjects recognized that these weren't correct responses, but felt that they were close. Other subjects responded with words that were semantically similar, but also recognized that the words were incorrect—for example, "barge," "houseboat," and "junk." When the correct response was provided (in this case, "sampan"), the reaction was common: "Oh yes! That's right!" Correct words were easily recognized by subjects who had experienced a TOT. Did you have a TOT for any of the three words for which you were searching? By the way, the other two words that are defined as indicated above are "sextant" and "nepotism." Did either of these provide a tip-of-the-tongue experience for you?

Obviously, TOT states can be found in many retrieval tasks, not just those requiring a search for words. A friend of mine has an audio tape of theme songs from television shows past and present. None of the themes include words, only the melody is provided. More than half of the themes provide me with a TOT experience as I struggle to remember the name of the show that goes with a given theme song. I can often categorize the show as "action-adventure," or a "sitcom," or a "detective-type" show. And I may even be able to remember who starred in the program, but I cannot recall its name. Tip-of-the-tongue phenomena provide evidence, both in the laboratory and real life, that we often have information stored in our memories that we cannot get out when we want to; there are some things we simply cannot seem to remember.

Why We Care

In this topic, we will address an issue of practical importance to all of us: What factors affect our ability to remember? In our last topic we saw that material can be encoded and stored in a number of different stores or levels of memory. In this topic, the focus of our attention is on long-term memory (LTM). Our concern will be with a question of practical significance. Why is it that we can remember some things (even when we may not want to) and cannot remember others?

We'll organize this topic into four major sections, each dealing with memory retrieval. The first thing we will discover is that how we ask for retrieval influences the amount of information retrieved. We'll also explore how the *quantity* of one's learning has an effect on retrieval. Then we'll shift our attention to the *quality* of learning and look at some ways to improve the coding of information into LTM that may help us retrieve that information later. Finally, we'll see that there are some processes that tend to inhibit the retrieval process. As we have done before, we'll review some data on each of these issues and try to point out how you can apply what we know about memory retrieval in your everyday life.

MEASURING RETRIEVAL: RECALL AND RECOGNITION

One of the factors that affects our ability to retrieve information from our long-term memories is how we are asked to go about retrieval. This is a factor over which you and I seldom have much control. For instance, unless you have a very democratic instructor, you will not be allowed to decide what kind of exams will be given. You will generally be asked to retrieve information in one of a number of standard exam formats chosen by your instructor.

Let's design a laboratory example to work with for a while. Imagine that we have subjects come to the laboratory on a given Tuesday to learn a list of 15 randomly chosen words. Some subjects take longer than others, but eventually all come to demonstrate that they have learned the list. All subjects report back to the laboratory 2 weeks later when our basic question is: "How many of the words you learned last week do you still remember?"

One thing we might do is ask for simple **recall** of the list of words. To do so, we need only provide the subjects with a blank sheet of paper and ask them to write down, in any order, as many of the words from the previously learned list as they can remember. This is a very difficult type of retrieval task. For recall, we provide the fewest possible cues to aid their retrieval. We merely specify the information we want and essentially say, "There, now go into your long-term memories, find that information, get it out, and write it down." Let's assume that one subject correctly recalls six words. So, for our working example, we have a subject who can remember six words.

What if we furnished our subject with a list of 50 words, including those on the previously learned list? Now our instructions are to "circle the words on this list that you *recognize* from the list you learned 2 weeks ago." In this case, we would not be asking for recall, but for **recognition**, a retrieval task requiring a subject to simply identify material previously learned as being familiar. Isn't it likely that our subject will do better on this task? If she recalled 6 words of the original 15, she might now recognize as many as 11. Now, in a way, we are in a slight dilemma: Should we say that our subject remembered 6 words or 11 words? The answer is, "Both or either." Whether our subject remembered 6 words or 11 words depends on how we asked her to go about remembering.

recall
a method of retrieval in which the individual is provided with the fewest possible cues to aid retrieval

recognition
a method of retrieval in which the individual is asked to identify previously learned material as being familiar

Figure 14.1

Two curves demonstrating retention for nonsense syllables over a 2-day period. In one case, retention is measured with a test for recognition, while the other tests for recall.
(From Luh, 1922.)

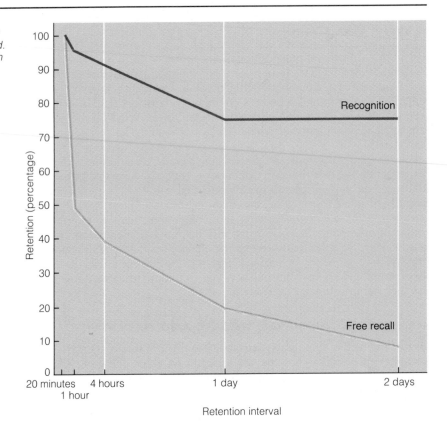

In virtually all cases, retrieval by recognition will be superior to retrieval by recall. Figure 14.1 provides some clear-cut data to support what we have been saying. Over a 2-day period, tests of retrieval by recognition are superior to tests of retrieval by recall. (Noting the source of these data—Luh, 1922—should also show you that this is not a new discovery.) With recall, we provide minimal retrieval cues; with recognition, we provide maximum cues and ask the subject to recognize a stimulus as being one that she or he has seen before (Mandler, 1980). Most students I know would much rather take a multiple-choice exam, in which they only have to recognize the correct response from a small number of alternatives, than a fill-in-the-blank test that requires recall.

In fact, it is reasonable to propose that the greater the number of retrieval cues provided, the better retrieval will be. Even within the basic format of a recall task, compare these two questions: (1) Which psychologist is associated with early experiments on conditioning? (2) Which Nobel Prize-winning Russian physiologist, who studied the salivation reflex of dogs at the turn of the century, is associated with early experiments on classical conditioning? The added cues provided in the second question should lead to higher recall scores. Now we need to consider some of the factors affecting retrieval over which we can usually exercise more control.

Before you go on

How do retrieval cues of the sort provided in recall and recognition tasks affect retrieval?

RETRIEVAL AND THE QUANTITY OF LEARNING

Here's a statement with which I suspect you will agree: "Our ability to retrieve information from our memories is a function of how well it was learned in the first place." Now I'm not going to dispute the reasonableness of this statement, but I am going to suggest that it really doesn't tell us much. As true as it may be, we need to be more specific about what we mean when we say "how well it was learned." One approach we can take is to say that the ability to remember material depends on both the *quantity* and the *quality* of our practice or experience with that material. In this section, we'll deal with the first of these two factors.

We have already noted that there is a relationship between the number of times stimulus material is presented and a subject's ability to retrieve that material from memory. One of the reasons why some students do not do as well on classroom exams as they would like is that they simply do not have (or make) enough time to study or practice the material covered on the exams.

Overlearning

What you and I often do once we decide to learn something that we want to remember is read, practice, and study the material until we know it. We practice until we are satisfied that we have stored the required information in our memories, and then we quit. Another way of expressing this is to say that we often fail to engage in **overlearning**, which is the process of practicing or rehearsing material over and above what is needed to just barely learn it. Consider another fictitious laboratory example, and see if you can't extend this logic to study habits.

overlearning
the practice or rehearsal of material over and above what is needed to just barely learn it

A subject comes to the laboratory to learn a list of nonsense syllables, verbal items such as *dax, wuj, lep, pib, zuw,* etc. There are 15 items on the list, and the material has to be presented repeatedly before our subject can recall all of the items correctly. Having correctly recalled the items once, our subject is dismissed with instructions to return to the laboratory two weeks later for a test of his recall of the nonsense syllables. Not surprisingly, our subject doesn't fare too well on the retrieval task.

What would have happened to that subject's recall if we had continued to present him with the list of syllables over and over at the time of learning, well beyond the point where he first learned them? Say the list was learned in 12 trials. We have the subject practice the list for six more presentations (50 percent overlearning, or practice 50 percent over and above that required for learning). Or let's require an additional 12 trials of practice (100 percent overlearning). What if we required an *additional 48 trials* of practice (400 percent overlearning)?

The effects of such overlearning practice are well documented and predictable. The recall data for this imaginary experiment might look like the data presented in Figure 14.2. Notice three things about these data: (1) If we measure retrieval at different times after learning, forgetting is rather impressive and quite sudden. Most of what is going to be forgotten will be forgotten soon after learning takes place. (This observation dates way back to Ebbinghaus (1885) and the first book on memory in psychology.) (2) Overlearning improves retrieval, having its greatest effects with longer retention intervals. (3) Sooner or later there is a "diminishing returns" phenomenon. That is, 50 percent overlearning is much more useful than no overlearning, 100 percent overlearning is better than 50 percent, and 400 percent is better than 100 percent, but not by very much. For any task or individual, there is probably a realistic optimum amount of overlearning.

Figure 14.2

Idealized data showing the effect of overlearning on retrieval. Note the "diminishing returns" with additional overlearning.
(Based on Krueger, 1929.)

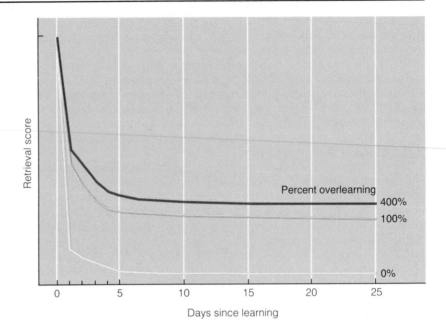

Obviously, the more we practice what we are learning, the easier it will be to retrieve it. Unfortunately, this statement is overly simplistic because it doesn't say anything about the *nature* or the quality of the practice. How one *schedules* one's practice or learning time is an important factor in determining the likelihood of retrieval, and it is to this issue that we turn next.

Before you go on

What is meant by overlearning, and how does it affect retrieval?

Scheduling Practice

Some of the oldest data in psychology supports the notion that the quality of learning is improved if it is spread out over time with rest intervals spaced in between. The data presented in Figure 14.3 is fairly standard. In fact, this 1946 experiment provides such reliable results that it is commonly used in psychology laboratory classes. The task is to write the alphabet, but upside-down and from right to left. If you think that sounds easy, you should give it a try.

Subjects are given the opportunity to practice this task under four different conditions. The **massed practice** group works on the task without a break between trials. The three **distributed practice** groups receive the same amount of actual practice, but get rest intervals interspersed between each 1-minute practice trial. One group gets a 3- to 5-second break between trials, a second group receives a 30-second rest, and a third group gets a 45-second break between practice trials.

As we can see in Figure 14.3, subjects in all four groups begin at about the same (poor) level of performance. After 20 minutes of practice, the performance of all the groups shows improvement. By far, however, the massed practice (no rest) group did the poorest, and the 45-second rest group did the best.

massed practice
rehearsal in which there is no break in one's practice

distributed practice
rehearsal in which practice is done in segments with rest intervals interspersed

The conclusion to be drawn from years of research like this is that, almost without exception, distributed practice is superior to massed practice. There are exceptions, however. There are some tasks that suffer from having rest intervals interspersed between practice trials. In general, whenever you must keep track of many things at the same time, you should mass your practice until you have finished whatever it is you are working on. If, for example, you are working on a complex math problem, you should work through the problem to a solution, whether it's time for a rest break or not.

Quite clearly what we are talking about here is scheduling of study time. Discussions of study schedules make up the major part of any how-to-study book. The message is always the same: Many short study periods with rest periods interspersed are more efficient than a few study periods massed together.

Imagine, for example, that I have two students in my introductory psychology class who are equally able, equally well motivated, and facing an exam in 10 days. One student will study for 5 *hours* this weekend: 1 hour on Saturday and 4 hours on Sunday. The second student will study for only *4 hours*. She will spend 30 minutes a day for 8 days preparing for the exam. Everything else being equal, there is no doubt that the second student will learn more psychology than the first and will be able to retrieve more of what she learned on the exam than the first student, even though she studied for 1 hour less. I have seen this demonstrated again and again, yet some students refuse to believe it.

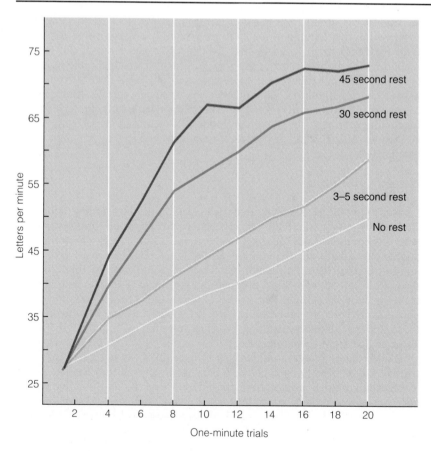

Figure 14.3
Improvement in performance as a function of distribution of practice time. The task was the printing of inverted capital letters, with twenty 1-minute trials separated by rest intervals of varying lengths.
(After Kientzle, 1946.)

Now let us assume that you are going to follow this advice and use a 45-minute break between classes to study. Unless you are an outstanding student, it is unlikely that you can usefully study an entire chapter of any college-level textbook in that time frame. There is simply too much material within a chapter to deal with. So, distribute your practice. Break it down into little chunks. Study one section at a time. (To help you do just that with this text is one of the reasons we included the "Before You Go On" questions and divided lengthy chapters into shorter topics to help you distribute your practice.)

Before you go on
Compare and contrast massed and distributed practice, noting their effects on retrieval.

RETRIEVAL AND THE QUALITY OF LEARNING

Retrieval can be improved by increasing the quantity of original learning and properly scheduling one's practice time. As we know from personal experience, time spent learning, no matter how it is distributed, is only part of the story. We now need to consider the *quality of the time spent in learning*. Passively sitting in a comfortable chair, turning the pages of a textbook, is not very effective, high quality practice. There is more to studying a text than reading it.

To once again use the term of Craik and Tulving (1975), to practice material in such a way as to maximize the chances of being able to retrieve it when we want it, we need to use *elaborative rehearsal*. We need to do something with the information (elaborate it) to meaningfully process it into our long-term memories in such a way that we can easily get it out again. In this section, we'll examine some of the ways in which we can elaborate information to improve our chances of retrieval. Specifically, we'll deal with what we mean by "meaningfulness," and then we'll review some specific strategies we can use to improve memory retrieval. These strategies are often referred to as **mnemonic devices** (after the Greek goddess of memory, Mnemosyne). They all involve using existing memories in a way to make new information more meaningful.

mnemonic devices
strategies for improving retrieval that take advantage of existing memories in order to make new material more meaningful

Meaningfulness

I have a hypothesis. I believe that I can determine the learning ability of students by noting where they sit in a classroom. The good, bright students tend to choose seats on the side of the room farthest from the door. The poor, dull students sit by the door, primarily interested in easily getting in and out of the room. (Although there may be some truth to this, I'm not serious.) To prove my point, I propose an experiment. Students seated away from the door are asked to learn a list of words that I read aloud only once. Because they have already heard my first list, I need a second list of words for those students seated by the door. Students seated in the middle of the room are excluded from the experiment.

The list that my smart students hear is made up of words such as *cat, dog, mother, father, black, white,* and so forth. As I predicted, they have no problem recalling this list after just one presentation. The students huddled by the door get my second list: *insidious, tachistoscope, sophistry, flotsam, episcotister,* and so forth. Needless to say, my hypothesis will be confirmed.

This is obviously not a very fair experiment. The students sitting by the door will yell foul. My second list of words is clearly more difficult to learn and recall than the first. The words on the first list are shorter, more familiar, and easier to pronounce. However, the major difference between these two lists is in the **meaningfulness** of the items—the extent to which they evoke existing associations in one's memory. The *cat, dog* list is easy to learn and remember because each word in it is meaningful. Each word makes us think of many other things, or produces many associations. Words like *tachistoscope* are more difficult because they evoke few, if any, associations.

meaningfulness
the extent to which information to be retrieved evokes existing associations in one's memory

An important point to keep in mind is that meaningfulness is not a characteristic built into materials to be learned. Meaningfulness resides in the memory of the learner. *Tachistoscope* may be a meaningless collection of letters for many people, but for others it may be a word rich in associations. What is meaningful and what is not is a function of our individual experiences.

It then follows that one of your tasks as a learner is to do whatever you can to make the material you are learning meaningful. You need to seek out and establish associations between what you are learning and what you already know. You need to be prepared to ask yourself a series of questions about what you are studying. What does this mean? What does it make me think of? Does this remind me of something I already know? Can I make this more meaningful? If you cannot, there is little point in going on to more confusing material. Perhaps you now recognize another reason for our including "Before You Go On" questions within each topic.

Before you go on

What is meaningfulness?

How does meaningfulness relate to retrieval?

Mnemonic Devices: Making Material Meaningful

Retrieval is enhanced if we can actively elaborate the material we are learning, if we can make it meaningful and organize it in some meaningful way. Often this is simply a matter of reflecting on what we are learning and actively forming associations with previously stored memories. Now let's examine some specific encoding techniques we can use that will aid our retrieval later.

Figure 14.4

Percent correct recall for words from 12 lists learned under two conditions. In the narrative condition, subjects made up short stories to aid recall, while in the control condition, rote memorization—no mnemonic device—was used.
(After Bower & Clar, 1969.)

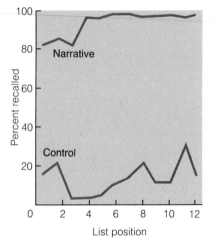

PATO — POT — DUCK

Figure 14.5

An illustration of how the key word method can help foreign vocabulary retention.
(After Atkinson, 1975.)

The Use of Narrative Chaining An experiment by Bower and Clark (1969) indicates that we may improve our retrieval of otherwise unorganized materials if we can weave that material into a meaningful story. One group of college students was asked to learn a list of 10 simple nouns in order. It's not a difficult task, and subjects had little trouble with it. Then they were given another list of 10 nouns to learn, and then another—12 lists in all. These subjects were given no instructions other than to remember each list of words in order.

A second group of subjects was given the same 12 lists of 10 nouns each to learn. It was suggested to them that they make up little stories that used each of the words on the list in turn. Many of the stories were rather silly, such as: "One night at *dinner,* I had the *nerve* to bring my *teacher.* There had been a *flood* that day and the rain *barrel* was sure to *rattle.* There was, however, a *vessel* in the *harbor* carrying this *artist* to my *castle.*"

Right after each list was presented, both groups were asked to recall the list of words they had just heard. There was virtually no difference in the recall scores for the two groups.

Then came a surprise. After all 12 lists had been presented and recalled, subjects were told that they were going to be tested again on their recall for each list. The experimenters provided 1 word from 1 of the 12 lists, and the subjects were to recall the other 9 words from that list. The difference in recall between the two groups of subjects in this instance was striking (see Figure 14.4). Those who used a narrative chaining technique (made up stories) recalled 93 percent of the words (on the average), whereas those who did not so organize the random words recalled only 13 percent of them.

The message seems clear and consistent with what we have said so far. A technique that adds organization and meaningfulness to otherwise meaningless material is a means of elaborative rehearsal that will improve retrieval.

The Use of Visual Imagery Organizing disconnected words into meaningful stories helps us remember them. Forming visual images or pictures in our minds can also be very helpful. Assume, for example, that you have to memorize a large number of Spanish words and what they mean. The basic task is one of forming an association between the Spanish words and their English equivalents. You could use simple rote memorization, but it is tedious at best and not very efficient.

Atkinson (1975) suggests that to help your memory of foreign language vocabulary, it is useful to imagine some connection tying the two words together. (He calls this the *key word* method of study.)

For example, the Spanish word for "horse" is "caballo," which is pronounced "cab-eye-yo." To help remember this association you might choose "eye" as the key word and picture a horse actually kicking someone in the eye. Or, if you're not prepared to be that gruesome, you might imagine a horse with a very large eye. The Spanish word for "duck" is "pato." Here your key word might be "pot," and you could picture a duck wearing a pot on its head (see Figure 14.5) or sitting in a large pot on the stove. I realize that this sounds strange, but research data suggests that it works (Pressley, Leniv, & Delaney, 1982).

The same basic technique works whenever you need to remember any paired sort of information. It needn't be restricted to foreign language vocabulary building. Gordon Bower (1972), for example, asked students to learn lists of pairs of English words. Some subjects were instructed to form a mental image that showed some interaction between the two words. One pair, for instance, was *piano-cigar.* There are many ways to form an image of a piano and a cigar: The cigar could be balanced on the edge of the piano, for one. Recall for word pairs was much better for those subjects who formed mental images than it was for those who did not. In fact, recall was best when bizarre or unusual images were created—a "picture" of a piano actually smoking a cigar, for example (see Figure 14.6). If you wanted to remember that it was Bower and Clark who did the experiment on narrative chaining, you might try to picture two *story-tellers, chained* together, each holding a *Clark Bar* in their hands as they take a *bow* on a theater stage. It sounds silly, but it works.

One of the better-known mnemonic devices that involves imagery is called the *peg word* method by its originators Miller, Galanter, and Pribram (1960). This strategy is most useful when we have to remember a series of items *in order*. Using this device is a two-step process.

The first step is to associate common nouns (peg words) that rhyme with the numbers from 1 to 10 (and beyond 10 if you're up to it). Figure 14.7 is the scheme of associations that Miller and his colleagues suggested. Now if you have a list of words to memorize, the second step is to form an interactive image of the word you're memorizing and the appropriate peg word; again, the more bizarre the image, the better.

To see how this might work, suppose that you have to remember the following words in order: *textbook, glass, ring, nose.* Having already memorized your peg word scheme, you make an image association between each word on the list and its peg word, perhaps: (1) a *textbook* in the middle of a hamburger *bun,* (2) a *shoe* in a *glass,* (3) a wedding *ring* around the trunk of a *tree,* (4) someone's *nose* stuck in a *door,* and so on. At retrieval, you first recall the peg words in order (*bun, shoe, tree,* and *door*), and then recall the word from the list that you've associated with each peg word. This may sound like a lot of extra work to go through, but once you've mastered your peg word scheme, the rest is remarkably easy.

The last imagery-related mnemonic device we'll mention may be the oldest in recorded history. It is attributed to the Greek poet Simonides and is called the *method of loci* (Yates, 1966). The idea here is to get in mind a well-known location (hence *loci*), say the floor plan of your house or apartment. Visually place the material you are trying to remember in different locations throughout your house in some sensible order. Then, when the time

Figure 14.6
The key word method can also be used to help remember pairs of English words. A bizarre image showing the interaction of the two words proves to be quite memorable.
(After Wollen, Weber, & Lowry, 1972.)

Piano   Cigar

Figure 14.7
The peg-word mnemonic scheme proposed by Miller, Galanter, and Pribam (1960).

One is a Bun

Two is a Shoe

Three is a Tree

Four is a Door

Five is a Hive

Six are Sticks

Seven is Heaven

Eight is a Gate

Nine is a Line

Ten is a Hen

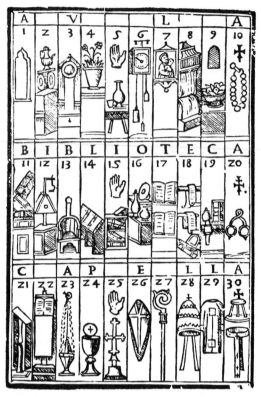

The method of loci is an ancient mnemonic device. This illustration was done by a Dominican monk in the sixteenth century. On the left are the abbey and the surrounding buildings through which the speaker will mentally walk, picking up the ideas (illustrated on the right) that he or she needs to recall.

comes for you to retrieve the material, visually walk through your chosen location, recalling (or retrieving) the information you have stored at different places.

Not long ago I was asked to present a short talk at a high school. There were a number of points I wanted to make in my speech, and as an experienced lecturer, I didn't want to use written notes to aid my recall. I also didn't want to appear as nervous as I knew I was going to be, so I decided to try the method of loci. I divided my talk into five or six major ideas, imagined my house, and walked through it in my mind. I stored my introduction at the front door, point 1 got me to the living room, point 2 to the dining room, and so on through the house until I got to my conclusion at the back door. Even though I had been telling others about the method of loci for many years, this was the first time I had actually used it, and I was very impressed with how easy it was to remember my little speech.

In this section, we've reviewed a number of specific techniques that we can use to improve retrieval of information from memory. In each case, the basic idea is to organize otherwise unrelated information in a meaningful way, whenever possible taking advantage of (bizarre) mental images of what we are trying to remember.

Before you go on

Describe the processes involved in the key word method, the peg word method, and the method of loci.

FACTORS THAT INHIBIT RETRIEVAL

Think back to when you were 5 years old. Can you remember all the gifts you got for your birthday that year? Can you remember *any* of them? I know I can't. Given the reconstructive nature of memory (see Topic Expansion), I suspect that I can guess what I might have gotten for birthday presents that year and generate a fairly reasonable list. But there is no way that I can directly retrieve that information from my long-term memory with any certainty. Now one possibility is that that information is no longer there. It may in some literal sense be lost forever. Another possibility is that that information is in fact available in memory, but inaccessible at the moment because I have had so many birthdays since my fifth one, and so much has happened and entered my memory since then, that the material I am looking for is covered up and being *interfered with* by information that entered later.

How about your last birthday? Can you recall the gifts you received for your last birthday? That's a little easier, but remembering with confidence is still not that easy. Here again, our basic retrieval problem may be one of interference. Assuming that what we are searching for is still there (and that *is* an assumption), we may not be able to retrieve it because so many *previous* experiences (presents received earlier) are getting in the way, interfering with retrieval.

In addition to interference, the process of repression can also be seen as one that actively inhibits the retrieval of information from memory. We'll review both of these processes in this section. Neither interference nor repression can always be avoided. Neither is easily overcome, but any steps we can take to do so may prove to be worthwhile.

Interference—Retroactive and Proactive

The basic idea that activity that follows the learning of material can interfere with the retrieval of that material, is an old one in psychology. Some of the early experiments, for example, demonstrated that subjects who were active for a period after learning remembered what they had learned less well than subjects who used the intervening period for sleeping. The graphs in Figure 14.8 show apparently comparable data from two experiments—one with college students who had learned nonsense syllables, the other with cockroaches that had learned to avoid an area of their cage. In either case, subjects who engaged in normal waking activity did worse on tests of retrieval over different retention intervals.

When interfering activities come *after* the learning of material to be remembered, we are dealing with **retroactive interference.** Let's first go to the laboratory. We will need two groups of subjects randomly assigned to either the experimental group or the control group. The subjects in both groups are asked to learn something (almost anything will do; we'll assume a list of nonsense syllables). Having learned their lists, the groups are then treated differently. Experimental group subjects are now asked to learn something else, perhaps another list of nonsense syllables. At the same time, the control group subjects are asked to do nothing, which is impossible, of course, in a literal sense. Control group subjects might be asked to rest quietly or engage in some simple game.

Now for the test. Both groups of subjects are asked to retrieve the material presented in the *first* learning task. In almost every conceivable instance, the control group subjects will show a higher retrieval score than the experimental group subjects. For the latter group, the second set of learned material is

retroactive interference
the inhibition of retrieval of previously learned material caused by material learned later

Figure 14.8

These graphs illustrate how activity following learning can interfere with the retrieval of the learned material. In both cases, normal waking activity caused more interference with retrieval than did forced inactivity (for cockroaches) or sleeping (for students).
(Based on Minami & Dallenbach, 1946.)

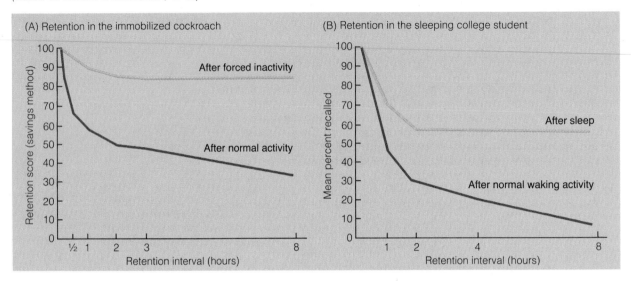

interfering with the retrieval of the material learned first. Figure 14.9(A) presents this experimental design in more simple terms.

Most of us are familiar with examples of retroactive interference from our own educational experiences. A student who studied French in high school takes a few courses in Spanish at college and now can't remember much French at all. The Spanish keeps getting in the way. I have two students who are to take a psychology exam tomorrow morning at 9:00. Both are equally able and equally well motivated. One is taking only one class—mine. She studies her psychology for 2 hours, watches TV for 2 hours, and goes to bed. She comes in the next morning to take the exam. The other student also studies her psychology for 2 hours, but then must read a chapter and a half from her sociology text, just in case she is called on in class. After reading sociology, she goes to bed, comes to class, and takes the exam. Everything else being equal, this second student will be at a disadvantage. The sociology that she has studied will retroactively interfere with her retrieval of the psychology she has learned. What is this student to do? She *has* to study her psychology, and she *knows* she had better read her sociology. If the psychology exam is an important one to her, I might suggest that she set herself up for proactive interference, rather than retroactive interference. She should read her sociology assignment and then study for her psychology exam. Even then she'll be at a disadvantage, but generally, the effects of proactive interference are not as powerful as those of retroactive interference.

proactive interference
the inhibition of retrieval of recently learned material caused by material learned earlier

Proactive interference occurs when previously learned material interferes with the retrieval of material learned later. Follow along in Figure 14.9(B). Again we have two groups of subjects, experimental and control. The experimental group again starts off by learning something, that same list of syllables perhaps. Now the control group subjects begin by doing nothing, by resting quietly while the experimental group goes through the learning task. Both groups then learn some new material, say a second list of syllables. We now test for retrieval, but this time we test for the retrieval of the more recently learned material. Once again, the control group subjects will be at an advantage. They have none of that first list in their memories to interfere with the retrieval task. But the advantage is not as great as it was in the case of retroactive interference. As we said, proactive interference is generally not as detrimental as retroactive interference.

One simple way to demonstrate proactive interference is to ask subjects to learn a series of word lists. As subjects go through learning and trying to remember more and more lists, their recall tends to get worse. As subjects try to recall the items from list 5, for example, the words from lists 1 through 4 interfere with retrieval. By the time subjects are trying to recall words from list 10, they have nine other lists causing interference (Underwood, 1957).

Although both retroactive and proactive interference effects are well documented, there are many factors that influence the *extent* of such interference. For example, it seems that meaningful, well-organized material is less susceptible to interference than is less meaningful material, such as nonsense syllables. It should also strike you as reasonable that *the nature of the interfering task* matters a great deal. As a general rule of thumb, the more similar the interfering material is to the material being retrieved, the greater will be the interference. Think back to my student who had to study for her psychology exam *and* read a sociology assignment. She will experience more interference (retro- *or* pro-) than will a student who has to study for the psychology exam and work on calculus problems. In this context, I might be so bold as to suggest that working on calculus is rather like doing nothing in that there is little about the calculus that is going to get in the way, or interfere, with the psychology lesson. Hence the advice that suggests that if you're going to take more than one course at a time, the courses should be as different from each other as possible to minimize possible interference effects.

Before you go on

What is the difference between retroactive interference and proactive interference?

Which of these two generally has the greater impact on retrieval?

Repression

It was the view of Sigmund Freud that the contents of our minds (including our memories) are not always available to us. Some thoughts, ideas, desires, motives, *and memories* are pushed out of our conscious awareness into our unconscious minds. This is particularly true for those memories (or thoughts, or desires, etc.) that cause us to feel anxiety, dread, or discomfort when we think about them.

Figure 14.9
Designs of experiments to demonstrate retroactive and proactive interference

(A) Retroactive interference

Group	Learn	Learn	Test
Experimental	Task A	Task B	Retrieval of task A
Control	Task A	Nothing	Retrieval of task A

(B) Proactive interference

Group	Learn	Learn	Test
Experimental	Task A	Task B	Retrieval of task B
Control	Nothing	Task B	Retrieval of task B

Note: If interference is operating, the control group will demonstrate better retrieval than will the experimental group.

The process of forcing anxiety-producing events into our unconscious is called **repression**. Repression is an automatic process; it happens without our awareness. We cannot purposely repress something. When we do it, we don't know we're doing it.

The basic notion, then, is that we (conveniently) forget some things because retrieving them would be unpleasant. For this reason, repression is commonly called *motivated forgetting*. Coming up with hard experimental evidence on *how* (and if) repression occurs is clearly difficult to do. That such a process *does* occur is generally well accepted, however.

Perhaps your doctor or dentist charges a fee for patients who miss scheduled appointments. Many do so because missing appointments is quite common, and repression may explain why, at least in some instances. Let's say that you *really* don't like going to the dentist; you shudder at the very thought of it. But today you can readily recall that you have a dentist's appointment scheduled for next Friday. As Friday approaches, and your anxiety builds (the theory goes), you become more and more likely to repress your appointment. On the preceding Thursday, a friend asks you to join him on a shopping trip the next day. "Let's see, Friday afternoon. No, I'm not doing anything tomorrow afternoon. I'll meet you at one o'clock." Friday night at dinner your memory of your appointment returns to you in a flash, "Oh no! I had a dental appointment this afternoon. I forgot!" How easy it is to recall the appointment that evening, secure in the knowledge that you won't even be able to call and reschedule the appointment until Monday morning. The pressure is off, and there's no longer any reason to repress the dreaded event.

Now it is very unlikely that you'll be able to convince your instructor that you forgot the difference between retroactive and proactive interference because you repressed it. To the extent that repression works at all, it operates on material that is emotionally laden and anxiety producing.

Before you go on
What is repression?

A Footnote: The Practice of Retrieval

In this topic, we have reviewed quite a bit of data and have summarized a number of laboratory experiments dealing with factors that affect our ability to retrieve information from our memories.

We need to add one final point to our discussion. We have seen that the quantity and quality of one's learning have a definite influence on memory. We do need to spend time with the material we are learning. We need to try to make that material meaningful and well organized. We need to try to avoid interference effects, and so on. Something else that we can do to improve our ability to retrieve information from memory is to *practice retrieval* itself.

Perhaps you'll recall from our discussion about learning that we cannot assess or measure learning directly. We can only measure performance and, on that basis, make inferences about what someone may have learned. Classroom exams, for example, are designed to measure what you have learned in a given course. But they do so indirectly by measuring what you can remember or retrieve at the time of the test. Why don't we spend more time, then, practicing what is really going to matter—getting learned material *out of* our memories? In short: Retrieval is a skill that can be practiced. The more you practice it, the better you will be at it. Try to anticipate test questions and work example problems at the end of textbook chapters or in accompanying study guides, if they are available. Ask yourself questions about the material you are studying. The time spent doing so will pay off.

One of the most influential studies of memory retrieval was reported by Sir Frederic Bartlett in his book *Remembering, A study in experimental and social psychology* (1932). Bartlett's experiments were important because they clearly indicated that retrieval is often an active reconstruction of stored memories, not just a simple recitation of past experiences. Bartlett was not much interested in how people remember unrelated words or nonsense syllables. He was more intrigued with how we remember life events and stories.

Among other projects, Bartlett asked subjects (often friends of his) to read a short story twice. He then asked them to reproduce the story 15 minutes later. He kept in touch with many of his subjects and asked them to reproduce the same story after a few days, weeks, months, and even years later. Bartlett's analysis focused on the distortions in the story that occurred after different retention intervals. One of his stories he called "The War of the Ghosts." It is presented in its original form in Figure 14.10(A). Figures 14.10(B) and (C) are reproductions made by one subject after a 15-minute retention interval and a 4-month retention interval. In many ways they are typical.

Bartlett found that stories tended to be shorter in recall. Many of the details of the original (particularly names and places) were quickly lost. It is not too surprising that some aspects of the original were forgotten. What was forgotten *first* tended to be those details that were most foreign to the experience of the subjects.

Notice from the examples in Figure 14.10 the tendency to make the remembered details consistent with good story-telling. Most significantly, subjects often *added* details to the story to make it more sensible. (Bartlett called these additions *ra-*

tionalizations.) It is as if subjects were unable or unwilling to recall any part of the story without making some attempt to fit it in (organize it) to their new rendition.

Bartlett's studies tell us much about how memory works and how it doesn't. Virtually no one remembered his stories verbatim or appeared to even try to. People tend not to *recall* stories so much as *reconstruct* them, to use Bartlett's term. Story reconstruction reflects both information contained in the original material and information that subjects have gathered from other experiences. And, as Bransford points out, ". . . reconstructive memory is especially important because people can think they are remembering accurately and yet be failing to do so" (1979, p. 162).

Figure 14.10

(A) *The Original Story*

One night two young men from Egulac went down to the river to hunt seals, and while they were there it became foggy and calm. Then they heard war-cries, and they thought: "Maybe this is a war-party." They escaped to the shore, and hid behind a log. Now canoes came up, and they heard the noise of paddles, and saw one canoe coming up to them. There were five men in the canoe, and they said:

"What do you think? We wish to take you along. We are going up the river to make war on the people."

One of the young men said: "I have no arrows."

"Arrows are in the canoe," they said.

"I will not go along. I might be killed. My relatives do not know where I have gone. But you," he said turning to the other, "may go with them."

So one of the young men went, but the other returned home.

And the warriors went on up the

river to a town on the other side of Kalama. The people came down to the water, and they began to fight, and many were killed. But presently the young man heard one of the warriors say: "Quick, let us go home: that Indian has been hit." Now he thought: "Oh, they are ghosts." He did not feel sick, but they said he had been shot.

So the canoes went back to Egulac, and the young man went ashore to his house, and made a fire. And he told everybody and said: "Behold I accompanied the ghosts, and we went to fight. Many of our fellows were killed, and many of those who attacked us were killed. They said I was hit, and I did not feel sick."

He told it all, and then be became quiet. When the sun rose he fell down. Something black came out of his mouth. His face became contorted. The people jumped up and cried.

He was dead.

(B) *First attempt at recall about 15 minutes after reading the story.*

Two young men from Egulac went out to hunt seals. They thought they heard war-cries, and a little later they heard the noise of the paddling of canoes. One of these canoes, in which there were five natives, came forward towards them. One of the natives shouted out: "Come with us: we are going to make war on some natives up the river." The two young men answered: "We have no arrows." "There are arrows in our canoes," came the reply. One of the young men then said: "My folk will not know where I have gone"; but, turning to the other, he said: "But you could go." So the one returned whilst the other joined the natives.

The party went up the river as far as a town opposite Kalama, where they got on land. The natives of that part came down to the river to meet them. There was some severe fighting, and many on both sides were slain. Then one of the natives that had made the expedition up the river shouted: "Let us return: the Indian has fallen." Then they endeavored to persuade the young man to return, telling him that he was sick, but he did not feel as if he were. Then he thought he saw ghosts all round him.

When they returned, the young man told all his friends of what had happened. He described how many had been slain on both sides.

It was nearly dawn when the young man became very ill; and at sunrise a black substance rushed out of his mouth, and the natives said one to another: "He is dead."

(C) *Second recall attempt about 4 months later.*

There were two men in a boat, sailing towards an island. When they approached the island, some natives came running towards them, and informed them that there was fighting going on on the island, and invited them to join. One said to the other: "You had better go. I cannot very well, because I have relatives expecting me, and they will not know what has become of me. But you have no one to expect you." So one accompanied the natives, but the other returned.

Here there is a part I can't remember. What I don't know is how the man got to the fight. However,

anyhow the man was in the midst of the fighting, and was wounded. The natives endeavored to persuade the man to return, but he assured them that he had not been wounded.

I have an idea that his fighting won the admiration of the natives.

The wounded man ultimately fell unconscious. He was taken from the fighting by the natives.

Then, I think it is, the natives described what happened, and they seem to have imagined seeing a ghost coming out of his mouth. Really it was a kind of materialisation of his breath. I know this phrase was not in the story, but that is the idea I have. Ultimately the man died at dawn the next day." (From Bartlett, 1932.)

TOPIC SUMMARY

How do retrieval cues of the sort provided in recall and recognition tasks affect retrieval?

When we ask for retrieval by recall, we provide an individual with the fewest possible retrieval cues. With recognition, we provide the information to be retrieved and ask that it be identified as being familiar. Retrieval by recognition is always more effective than retrieval by recall. / 246

What is meant by overlearning, and how does it affect retrieval?

Overlearning involves the rehearsal of information (learning) above and beyond that needed for immediate recall. Within limits, the more one overlearns, the greater the likelihood of accurate retrieval. / 248

Compare and contrast massed and distributed practice, noting their effects on retrieval.

In massed practice, study or rehearsal is massed together without intervening rest intervals. In distributed practice, rehearsal is done in shorter segments interspersed with rest intervals. In almost all cases,

distributed practice leads to better recall than massed practice. / 250

What is meaningfulness?

How does meaningfulness relate to retrieval?

Meaningfulness is the extent to which material to be retrieved can be related to or associated with information already stored in memory. In general, meaningful material (or material that can be made meaningful) is easier to retrieve than meaningless material. / 251

Describe the processes involved in the key word method, the peg word method, and the method of loci.

In general, mnemonic devices are strategies used to increase the meaningful organization of material to be retrieved from memory, thus making retrieval easier. The key word method involves forming an interactive visual image that depicts how two items can be associated. The peg word method requires first learning a word associated with the numbers 1–10 (if there are 10 items to be learned), and then forming an

interactive image of these words and items that need to be recalled in order. The method of loci involves mentally placing terms to be retrieved in a sequence of familiar locations. / 254

What is the difference between retroactive interference and proactive interference?

Which of these two generally has the greater impact on retrieval?

Retroactive interference occurs when previously learned material cannot be retrieved because it is inhibited or blocked by material learned *later*. Proactive interference occurs when information cannot be retrieved because it is inhibited by material learned *previously*. Retroactive interference is generally more detrimental to retrieval than the proactive interference. / 257

What is repression?

Repression, often called motivated forgetting, occurs when anxiety-producing or traumatic events are forced into the unconscious level of the mind. Repression interferes with retrieval. / 258

CHAPTER SEVEN

HIGHER COGNITIVE PROCESSES

TOPIC

— *Rogaritz* is usually white.

— *Rogaritz* is hard and dry.

— *Rogaritzen* (the plural of *rogaritz*) can be of any color.

— *Rogaritzen* can be used to write on a blackboard.

— A piece of *rogaritz* will fit comfortably in one hand.

— You shouldn't put *rogaritz* in your mouth.

— Using *rogaritzen* usually creates messy dust.

Have you figured out what *rogaritz* is? Would you recognize one if you saw it? Have you ever used *rogaritzen*? How many uses for *rogaritzen* can you think of? If you can answer these questions—if you know now what *rogaritz* is—you have acquired a new concept: the concept of *rogaritz*. You recognize it as being basically the same thing we call *chalk*. Because we already have a perfectly good word to label this concept, I suppose there's no compelling reason to try to remember the new concept label *rogaritz*.

Did you attend to what you were doing when you tried to identify the nature of *rogaritz*? Some of the descriptive information was very useful; for example, it was helpful to know that *rogaritz* is usually white and used to write on blackboards. Some information didn't help much, such as the clue that *rogaritzen* can be of any color and shouldn't be put in your mouth. These latter two statements are true concerning *rogaritzen*, but not central to it.

They could apply to many other concepts. Notice also that to form the concept of *rogaritz*, you needed to already know about other concepts, such as *white, blackboard, dust,* and *plural*.

A mere seven statements provided you with more than enough information to develop the concept of *rogaritz*. Can you list seven comparable statements to reflect the essence of concepts like *truth, God, consciousness,* or *entity*? Clearly, some concepts are more difficult to define, or are more abstract than others. *Abstraction* is itself a very abstract concept.

Why We Care

cognitions
ideas, beliefs, thoughts, images, concepts, memories, and the like

cognitive processes
the mental activities that involve forming and using cognitions

Broadly speaking, a **cognition** can be thought of as an idea, belief, thought, or image. When we know or understand something, we use cognitions to do so. **Cognitive processes** are mental activities that involve forming, using, and manipulating cognitions. Cognitive processes are many and varied. They include a number of processes we have already discussed, such as perception, learning, and memory.

In this chapter, we'll consider three complex cognitive tasks: concept formation, language, and problem solving. Topic 15 deals with concepts and how they are formed, and how they are used to communicate using language. In Topic 16, we'll discuss how we use concepts to solve problems. Because these cognitive tasks rely heavily on our perceptual, learning, and memory experiences, we can refer to them as "higher" cognitive processes.

In this topic, we will generate a working definition of what a concept *is*. As Howard Pollio expressed it, "Right at the beginning it is important to emphasize how difficult a concept is the concept of concept" (1974, p. 98). We'll discover that there are a number of types of concepts: some commonly found in psychology laboratories, others found in nature and our everyday life experiences.

Having defined concepts, we will turn our attention to how they are acquired or learned. Most psychologists agree that concepts *are* learned. *How* they are learned is the debatable issue.

The second higher cognitive process we will examine in this topic is language. Our use of language is a remarkable mental process. Again, our first step will be to define what language is. Then we'll review some research and theory that deal with our ability to rapidly and effortlessly produce and comprehend language. Finally, we'll review the question of whether or not non-human organisms can be said to use language.

Before you go on
What is meant by cognition, and what are cognitive processes?

DEFINING THE CONCEPT OF CONCEPT

Think about chairs. Really. Take a minute or two and just think about chairs. As you do this, try to notice what is happening.

Images come to mind. You can "see" a large variety of chairs in different contexts. You may have thought about armchairs, dining-room chairs, rocking chairs, high chairs, chairs in a classroom, easy chairs, chairs with smooth leather seats, overstuffed chairs upholstered with flowery fabric, broken chairs, kitchen chairs, and so on. We all know what a chair is. We have all formed a category or concept that we've agreed to label chair.

As you thought about chairs, did any one particular chair—a standard, definitional chair—come to mind? As you contemplated chairs, were there any features or attributes that all (or most) had in common? Are there defining characteristics of chairs? Most have four legs, although bean-bag chairs have no legs at all. Most chairs are used primarily for sitting, although we often stand on a chair to reach high places. Many are used in association with tables and some with desks. Most chairs have a back. However, if the back gets too low, you have a stool, not a chair. Each chair has a limited width: they can usually accommodate only one person. If they are wider, they become love seats or sofas. Chairs are usually seen as pieces of furniture. Can you describe chair in the same way we described *rogaritz* earlier?

I've asked you to go through these mental gymnastics so that you can appreciate our definition of concept. A **concept** is a *mental* event used to represent a category or class of events or objects. Note that concepts represent categories, classes, or groups of things, not just single individual cases.

A world without concepts would be unimaginable. If we had no way to organize or classify our experiences, our impressions of our environments (and of ourselves) would be chaotic. Because we have a *concept* of chair, for example, we do not have to treat each and every encounter with a chair as a new experience. We do not have to make up a new and different label or word for every single chair we see. We only have to recognize an object as having the characteristics appropriate for this category and refer to it as a chair. This is one of the most important reasons why concepts are so valuable to us.

We can define a concept, then, in terms of a set of attributes or features that are related according to some rule or rules. This *attribute-rule* approach works fairly well for a concept like chair. We've listed above some of the *attributes* associated with the category of events called chair. Perhaps you've thought of others. The *rule* that relates these features states that chairs share many (if not all) of these attributes at the same time. According to this view of concepts, learning a concept is a matter of learning the attributes that characterize it and the rule that relates those attributes (Bourne et al., 1979).

concept
a mental event used to represent a category or class of events or objects

Formal Concepts

Defining concepts in the psychology laboratory is fairly easy. We can take the attribute-rule approach to concepts and apply it quite literally and formally. First we decide which attributes we'd like to deal with—perhaps color, shape, and size. Then we provide a limited number of values for each of our attributes. *Color:* Our possible values of this attribute may be red, green, or blue. *Shape:* The possible values may be round, square, or triangular. *Size:* The values may be small, medium, or large. So, we have chosen three attributes, each of which may have one of three values. All we need to do is decide what rules we'll use to relate these values to form concepts.

Let's say that we want to define a new concept: the concept of *wug.* To do so, we need a rule that tells us the relationships among the values of our attributes. Let's say a *wug* is square, blue, and small. We have thus assigned *wug* a value on each of the three attributes. Moreoever, we have specified that to qualify as a *wug,* an event must have all three values. More simply put, *wugs* are small blue squares. We might use these same attributes to define *luks* as large red triangles, and so on. Look at Figure 15.1. Given these items, can you find the *wugs* and the *luks?* Doing so demonstrates that you've learned a couple of new (formal) concepts.

There are a number of ways in which the values of attributes can be combined by rules to define formal concepts. Let's briefly mention just four attribute-rule combinations.

First, rules specifying that concepts must have each one of a number of values define **conjunctive concepts.** In that case, *wug* is a conjunctive concept because *wugs* must be small *and* blue *and* square. Blueness, or squareness, or smallness alone do not define a *wug.* Each value of our three attributes must be present for us to have a *wug.* Another example might be the concept of short-term memory that we discussed in our last chapter. The defining characteristic of this memory is that it has a limited capacity *and* a limited duration.

In the second combination, membership in a concept is defined by an "either/or" rule regarding attributes. Such concepts are called **disjunctive concepts.** For example, a *dax* is defined as being *either* red *or* large. Can you find a *dax* in Figure 15.1? There are many more *daxs* than *wugs*—18 in all. In baseball, the concept of a strike provides us with a reasonable example of

conjunctive concepts
concepts that are defined by "and" rules; that is, having all attributes of the concept

disjunctive concepts
concepts defined by "either/or" rules; that is, either having some attributes or others

Figure 15.1
Stimuli of the sort used in studies of formal concepts.

a disjunctive concept. One may define a strike as being either a "pitch that crosses home plate within a prescribed area," *or* "a ball batted into foul territory," *or* "a pitch swung at and missed."

Affirmation rules represent a third attribute-rule combination. They simply specify membership in a concept by stating or affirming just one attribute value. They define **affirmative concepts;** for instance, *all green objects.* In this case, size and shape do not matter at all. An item is a member of an affirmative concepts category if it has the affirmed value of one given attribute.

A fourth attribute-rule combination involves a formal concept with which you are familiar—the **relational concept.** These concepts are defined in terms of comparisons of values on some dimension or attribute. The concepts of *larger than,* or *nearer than,* or *smarter than* are relational concepts. When we identify a concept as being bigger than a bread basket or faster than a speeding bullet, we are using a relational rule (bigg*er,* fast*er*) to tell us about attributes (size and speed) that are important for that concept.

affirmative concepts
concepts defined by the presence of one particular attribute

relational concepts
concepts defined in terms of their comparative relation to other concepts

Before you go on
How can we use attributes and rules to define concepts?

Natural Concepts

Talking about attributes with values and the rules that combine them may be reasonable for the sorts of concepts we study in psychology laboratories. But what about concepts as they occur in real life? Is it always possible to define concepts in terms of attributes and rules? Remember the problems we had when we tried this with *chair?* Real or natural concepts are often not easily defined and may be referred to as "fuzzy" concepts (Labov, 1973; Zadeh, 1965).

How would you characterize the difference between a river and a stream? Somehow we know what a river is, and we know what a stream is, but because *each* is a fuzzy concept, there is no clear distinction between the two. This is precisely why we often find ourselves saying things like, "Technically speaking, a tomato is a fruit, not a vegetable." Or, "In a way, a bat is rather like a bird." Or, "Actually, a spider isn't really an insect." We didn't have this problem with *wugs* and *daxs,* but we encounter it regularly when we use natural concepts.

One way to deal with this complication is to follow the lead of Eleanor Rosch (1973, 1975, 1978). She has proposed that we think about naturally occurring concepts or categories in terms of **prototypes.** A prototype is a member of a category that best typifies or represents the category to which it belongs.

prototype
the member of a concept or category that best typifies or represents that concept or category

What Rosch is suggesting is that within our concept of chair, there are some instances that are more typical and better examples—more "chair-ish" than others. A robin may be a prototypic bird. Crows are less prototypic. Vultures are even less typical, and the fact that a penguin even *is* a bird is occasionally hard to remember because a penguin is so nonprototypic. Figure 15.2 lists the elements in Rosch's furniture category. You can see which are the *best* examples of the concept of furniture. Within this category, *lamp* turns out to be a poor example, and of the 60 items rated, *ashtray, fan,* and *telephone* ranked at the bottom of the list, just barely qualifying as furniture at all. Automobile manufacturers recently created something of a concept-definition problem when they introduced a new vehicle generally called a mini-van. Mini-vans are not real vans, but they aren't cars either, nor are they station wagons. Hence, a new label for a new concept was devised: mini-van.

Figure 15.2
Goodness of example rankings for the furniture category. (From Rosch, 1975.)

Member	Goodness of example rank	Member	Goodness of example rank	Member	Goodness of example rank
chair	1.5	vanity	21	mirror	41
sofa	1.5	bookcase	22	television	42
couch	3.5	lounge	23	bar	43
table	3.5	chaise lounge	24	shelf	44
easy chair	5	ottoman	25	rug	45
dresser	6.5	footstool	26	pillow	46
rocking chair	6.5	cabinet	27	wastebasket	47
coffee table	8	china closet	28	radio	48
rocker	9	bench	29	sewing machine	49
love seat	10	buffet	30	stove	50
chest of drawers	11	lamp	31	counter	51
desk	12	stool	32	clock	52
bed	13	hassock	33	drapes	53
bureau	14	drawers	34	refrigerator	54
davenport	15.5	piano	35	picture	55
end table	15.5	cushion	36	closet	56
divan	17	magazine rack	37	vase	57
night table	18	hi-fi	38	ashtray	58
chest	19	cupboard	39	fan	59
cedar chest	20	stereo	40	telephone	60

In Rosch's view, then, some categories are rather poorly delineated and may very well spill over into others. This view argues that there is structure *within* concepts—some instances providing good examples, others providing poorer examples. Excellent examples (prototypes) share the largest number of attributes common to members of the category *and* have few attributes that cause them to be confused with others.

Before you go on
How does the concept of prototype help our understanding of what a concept is?

FORMING CONCEPTS

By the time we get to be college students, our minds are crammed with a huge variety of formal and natural concepts. How were those concepts acquired? Where did they come from? As the philosopher John Locke asked, "How comes it [the mind] to be furnished?" To his own question, Locke had a ready answer, ". . . I answer in one word, from experience." Few psychologists today would argue with Locke's conclusion that concepts are learned. Concepts develop through experience. Psychologists have found that the basic process of concept formation can be studied in the laboratory, and that people develop predictable strategies for acquiring concepts.

A Classic Experimental Demonstration

Figure 15.3 shows some of the stimulus materials that Edna Heidbreder used in her 1946 study of concept formation. Each item in a set was presented to a subject *one at a time.* (As you can see, there are five sets.) As each picture was presented, Heidbreder would name it, using the nonsense label that is

Though we usually associate the concept of body building with males, a growing number of females are also involved in the sport.

Figure 15.3

The sets of images Heidbreder used in her experiments on concept formation. As each image was presented, it was given a nonsense label (which labels are shown in the first three sets). The subjects were presented with the images and the nonsense labels until they could supply the label themselves. Thus, they came to label drawings of trees as "mul"—a new concept had been formed.

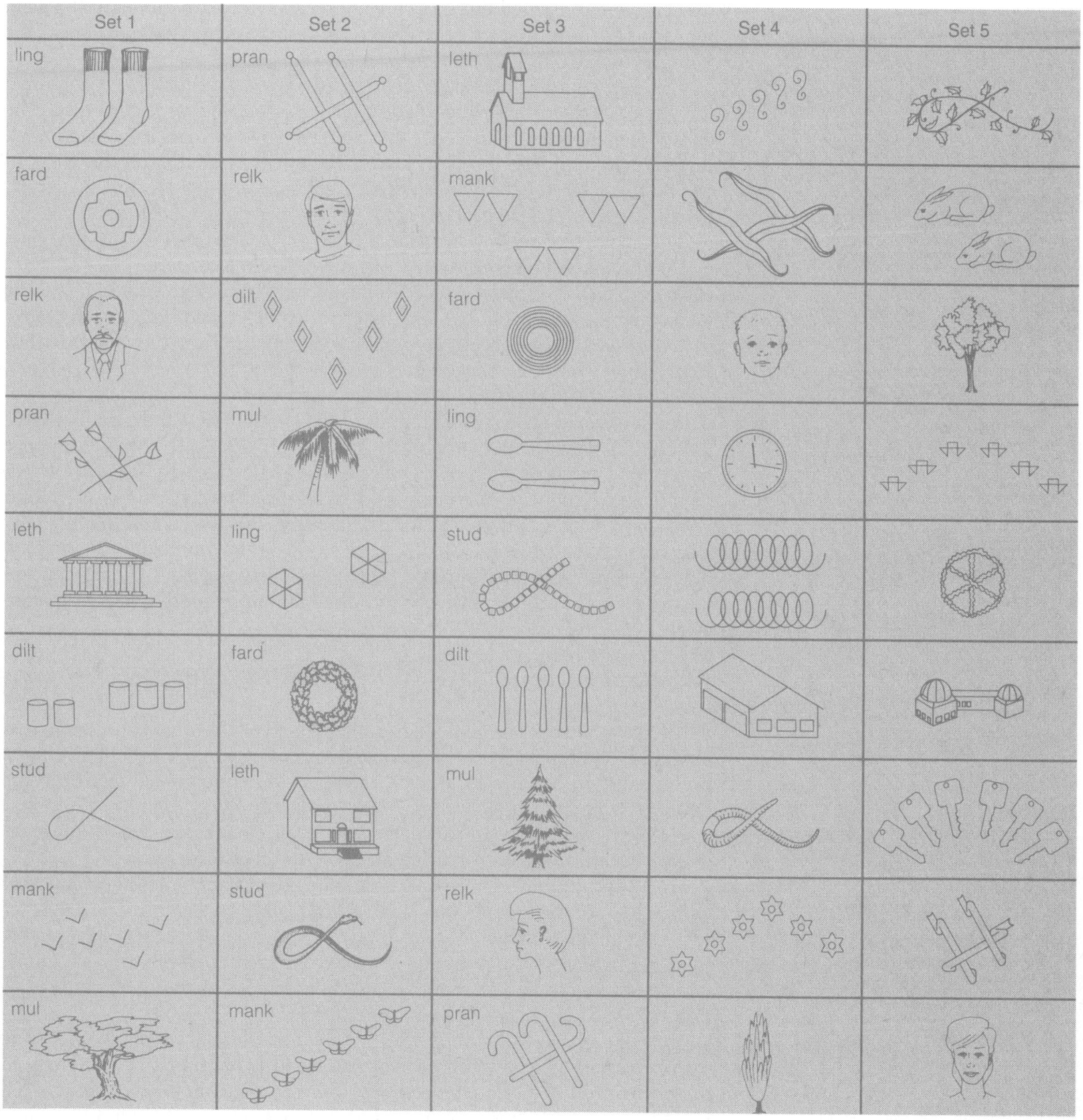

included in the figure for the first three sets. The subjects in the experiment did not see these names.

Subjects were told to learn simply the name associated with each picture. A set of pictures was presented over and over until the subject could supply the correct name associated with each picture. This wasn't too hard to do, and soon subjects could provide a label for each item in set 1. Then the items in set 2 were presented one at a time. Subjects were asked to learn the label for each of *these* little pictures. As you can see, the names for the items of set 2 are *the same as those used for set 1.*

This procedure was repeated for 16 different sets of pictures. Each time, the subject had to learn the label or name associated with a picture. The pattern behind what Heidbreder was doing is obvious to us as we look at all the pictures and their labels in Figure 15.3. It is clear that all drawings of people are labeled *relk.* Collections of six small things are named *mank.* Circular items are *fards,* and so on. *Ling* thus becomes a label for a concept; roughly, things appearing in pairs.

Heidbreder's subjects eventually formed the same concepts that you and I can see so clearly in Figure 15.3. Remember though, they were seeing these items one at a time, couldn't see the provided label, and didn't even realize that they were in a concept formation experiment. They thought that they were simply learning verbal labels for little pictures.

As subjects progressed through the sets of picture-label pairs, they required fewer and fewer presentations of the stimuli to form the picture-label association. Toward the end, some subjects provided the correct response name for a pictured item even before Heidbreder had a chance to say it. Significantly, subjects often could not state exactly what rule *or* attributes were underlying a particular concept, like *ling,* but they could identify new members of the category. Heidbreder's study not only added to the data on how we form concepts, but also convinced psychologists that the concept formation task could be brought into the laboratory and studied systematically.

Developing Strategies and Testing Hypotheses

Subjects in concept learning studies often go about forming concepts in systematic ways. To be sure, some people just guess at random whether or not a presented item belongs in a given category. Most, however, develop some **strategy** to guide their responding (Bruner, Goodnow, & Austin, 1956; Johnson, 1978). In this context, strategy means a systematic plan or procedure for identifying members of a particular category or concept.

Acquiring formal concepts—those with identifiable attributes and specific rules—often follows one of two strategies: conservative focusing or focus gambling (Bruner et al., 1956). Let's look at both. **Conservative focusing** involves examining, or focusing, on each attribute, one at a time, and attempting to find the appropriate value for that attribute before considering the next. Let's consider this strategy.

Imagine an array of stimuli like those we considered in Figure 15.1. The experimenter has in mind a concept, let's call it *yuf* this time. *Yufs* are all members of the same category: simply *blue objects.* You realize that this is a category for which there is only one relevant attribute (color) and for which the formal rule is one of affirmation. If an object of any shape or size is blue, it is a *yuf.*

A subject has to find all the *yufs* in Figure 15.1. A first choice might be a small red circle. "No, that's not a *yuf,*" you say. The subject then chooses a

strategy
a plan or procedure for identifying members of a particular category or concept

conservative focusing
a concept formation strategy of choosing one attribute at a time to see if it forms part of a given concept

large blue square. "Yes, that's a *yuf*." Now the strategy comes into play. A subject using the conservative focusing strategy would pick (focus on) the large blue square and try to see which other items might be included in the same category. On successive attempts, just one attribute at a time is changed. A next choice, for example, might be a large blue circle. When the subject discovers that this too is a *yuf*, he or she has learned that shape is irrelevant—*yufs* can be square or circular. The next test might be for size. "How about a small blue square?" "Yes, that is also a *yuf*." "Aha! Size doesn't seem to matter." Now, the subject, still focusing on the large blue square known to be correct, changes color. "Is a large green square a *yuf*?" "No, it isn't." Now the subject knows that color is a relevant attribute, and apparently the *only* relevant attribute, in defining a *yuf*.

When we are faced with a very large number of stimuli that vary on a large number of attributes, and when concept rules are more complicated than the simple affirmation rule, conservative focusing may not be a very economical strategy. In such cases, subjects often use the strategy of **focus gambling.** In this strategy, once a positive instance of a category is identified, the subject makes virtually random choices, looking for other items that share at least some of the attributes of the known category member. They gamble and take chances. Occasionally they get lucky and guess correctly. Many subjects employed this strategy, at least for a while, in the concept identification experiment used by Bruner et al. The strategy seemed reasonable to subjects because the task involved many more attributes and values than we used in our example. Sometimes, hopping around from item to item (gambling) is more time-consuming and wasteful than a systematic examination of one attribute at a time.

focus gambling
A concept formation strategy of finding a positive instance of a concept and then guessing that other events that share some of the same attributes are also members of the concept

A third way to think about concept formation is to say that subjects go through a process of *hypothesis testing.* That is, they develop a hypothesis, or guess, about what is going on, and then they test that hypothesis when presented with new stimuli. Saying to yourself, "I think that all members of this concept are green," is a hypothesis. You test it by finding another green stimulus and seeing if it fits within the category also.

Notice that this approach to concept formation works whether we think of concepts in terms of attributes and rules or in terms of prototypes. In the former case, hypotheses about specific attributes and rules are formed and tested. In the latter case, new stimuli are tested or judged in terms of their similarity to a prototype. For example, "I think that a spider looks a lot like my notion of an insect. I don't know how else to categorize it, so I'm going to call it an insect. It may not be the best example of an insect, but it sure looks like one to me." When you test that hypothesis (at least in a biology class), you discover that you're wrong, because as much as a spider may appear similar to your prototypic insect, it belongs in a different category (*arachnid*).

What many experiments since Heidbreder's in 1946 have demonstrated is that subjects form concepts in a very systematic way, developing strategies and testing hypotheses. In discussing this cognitive process, Howard says, ". . . this tendency to formulate and test hypotheses is a salient feature of human performance, reflecting our inherent propensities to organize and impose regularity upon experience. In fact, people engage in such hypothesis testing even in tasks in which the stimuli are not rule-governed at all" (1983, p. 497).

Before you go on
In the context of concept formation, what is a strategy?

LANGUAGE

When we use our language, we are engaging in a marvelously complex cognitive activity. As the philosopher Suzanne Langer put it, "Language is, without a doubt, the most momentous and at the same time the most mysterious product of the human mind. Between the clearest animal call of love or warning or anger, and a man's least, trivial *word,* there lies a whole day of Creation—or in modern phrase, a whole chapter of evolution" (1951, p. 94).

In this section, we'll briefly review some of the concerns of those scientists interested in **psycholinguistics.** Psycholinguistics is a hybrid, interdisciplinary pursuit. Psycholinguists "are interested in the underlying knowledge and abilities which people must have in order to use language and to learn language in childhood" (Slobin, 1979, p. 2). First, let's formally define language.

psycholinguistics
the science that studies the cognitive processes involved in the acquisition and use of language

A Definition of Language

How shall we characterize this "momentous and mysterious product of the human mind" called language? The following definition is somewhat complex, but it makes a number of psychologically important points about language. It is a paraphrase of a definition offered by Charles Morris (1946). **Language** is a large collection of arbitrary symbols that have significance for a language-using community and that follow certain combinatorial rules. Now let's pull this definition apart and examine some of the points that it raises.

language
A collection of arbitrary symbols that have significance for a language-using community and that follow certain rules of combination

First, language is made up of a large number of *symbols.* The symbols that make up language are commonly referred to as words. In many cases, words are labels that we assign to concepts. We've just talked about concepts and how they are defined and formed. The symbols of language represent something else. When we use the word chair as a symbol, we don't use it to label one specific instance of a chair. We use the word as a symbol to represent our concept, our mental idea, of chair. Words stand for our cognitions and concepts; and we have a great number of words. They allow us to communicate about what we know. Hence, language involves a large collection of symbols.

It is important that we define the symbols of language as being *arbitrary.* By that we mean simply that there is no *necessary* reason why we have to represent anything with the particular symbol we do. You call what you are reading a book (or a textbook, to use a more specific symbol for a more specific concept). We have all agreed (in English) that *book* is the appropriate symbol for what you are reading. But we don't *have to.* We could all agree to call it a *fard,* if we'd like. Or a *relm.* The symbols of a language are arbitrary. They can be whatever we like.

To be part of a language, however, our symbols need to *have significance for members of a language-using community.* That is, a number of people need to agree on the symbols that are used in a language and need to agree on what those symbols mean. For example, there is a language-using community for which the utterance, "Kedinin üstünde halt var" makes sense or has significance. I'm not part of that community, but many people are. To them, the statement reads roughly, "The cat is on the mat" (from Slobin, 1979, p. 4).

The final part of our definition *(that follow certain combinatorial rules)* is a critical one. What this means, of course, is that language is made up of much more than just a large collection of arbitrary symbols or words. Language is rule-governed. That is, there are rules about how we can and cannot string symbols together in a language. These rules are reflected in a lan-

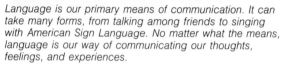

Language is our primary means of communication. It can take many forms, from talking among friends to singing with American Sign Language. No matter what the means, language is our way of communicating our thoughts, feelings, and experiences.

guage's grammar or syntax. In English, we can say "The small boy slept late." We cannot say "Slept boy late small the." Well, we can say it, but no one will know what we mean by it and everyone will recognize the utterance as not belonging in the English language.

Even with this lengthy definition of language, there are a few important points we've left out. For one, using language is a remarkably creative, generative process. What that means is that very few of the utterances we make are utterances we've ever made before or even encountered before. It's unlikely, for example, that you have ever before encountered a sentence just like this one. I know for a fact that I never wrote one like it before. Virtually every time we use our language, we use it in a new and creative way.

Another important observation about language reflects its use as a means of communication (at least within that language-using community we mentioned above). We use our language to share our private thoughts and feelings with others. What humans seem able to do with their language that no other organism can (see Topic Expansion) is to communicate about the *not here and the not now.* The linguist Hockett (1960) calls this feature of language *displacement.* It allows me to tell you about last night's dinner and to ask you to tell me about your plans for dinner tomorrow night. It also allows us to communicate about the *never was and never will be.* We can talk about all sorts of things, like owls and pussycats in teacups, and four-dimensional, time-warped hyperspace, and a beagle that flies his doghouse into battle against the Red Baron.

One final point: Language and speech are not synonymous terms. Speech is simply one common form (using the vocal-auditory channel) in which language is expressed as behavior. There are others, including writing, reading, coding (as in Morse code), or signing (as in American Sign Language).

Before you go on
What are some of the defining characteristics of language?

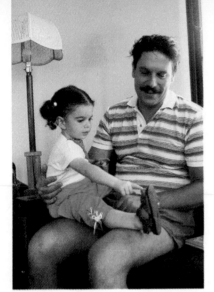

Learning a language involves learning the rules that govern the language. From the time a child begins to talk, she or he learns to combine the phonemes of her or his language into words, such as toe in this case.

phonemes
the smallest unit of sound in the spoken form of a language

morpheme
the smallest unit of meaning in a language

The Rules of Language

One way that we can characterize language is to say that language behavior is rule-governed. Those of us who know a language also know the rules of that language.

When we study language, we usually do so at three levels. At all three levels, we can see rules at work. The first level involves the system of sounds that are used to produce the language as speech. The individual sounds of a language are called **phonemes**. There are approximately 45 different individual speech sounds, or phonemes, in English. How they are combined to produce words and phrases is very lawful, or, as we have said, rule-governed (Reynolds & Flagg, 1983).

The difference between the utterances "time," "clime," "rhyme," and "grime," is in the initial phoneme of each word. We recognize each of these as being acceptable words in English. We also recognize that "blime" and "frime" are not English words, although they *could be*. The "bl" and "fr" sound combinations of "blime" and "frime" are acceptable in English: They follow the rules. Even if you could manage to pronounce them, you'd recognize that utterances such as "hklime" or "gzlime" or "wbime" are clearly not words and never can be. They violate the rules for combining sounds into words in English. They are not lawful phoneme combinations.

Having analyzed a language's phonemes, noting which sounds are relevant for that language and which combinations are possible, the next level of analysis involves *meaning*. A **morpheme** is the smallest unit of meaning in a language. In most cases, psychologists are willing to take "morpheme" and "word" as synonymous terms, although there are more morphemes in any language than there are words. For one thing, morphemes include all of the prefixes and suffixes of a language. For example, the utterance "write" is a morpheme and a word; it has meaning and it's not possible to subdivide it into smaller, meaningful units. The utterance "rewrite" is also a word and has meaning, but it is composed of *two* morphemes, *write* and *re,* which in this context does have meaning—roughly, "write it again." When we change a noun from singular to plural, boy to boys, or ox to oxen, for example, we are adding a morpheme to the noun—a morpheme that indicates plurality.

Notice that how we generate morphemes is also rule-governed. For example, we cannot go around making nouns plural any old way. The plural of ox is oxen, not oxes. The plural of mouse is mice, not mouses, or mousen, or meese. If I want you to write something over again, I have to ask you to *rewrite* it, not *write-re* it.

© 1985 United Feature Syndicate, Inc.

The most obvious aspect of our language that involves the use of rules, is reflected in our ability to generate sentences—to string words (or morphemes) together in order to create meaningful utterances. The rules that govern the way sentences are formed in a language are referred to as the **syntax** of a language. Let's now examine what we know when we know the syntax of our language.

Before you go on
Define phoneme, morpheme, and syntax.

Syntactic Competence   To know the syntax, or syntactic rules, of one's language involves a peculiar sort of knowledge or cognitive ability. We all know what the rules are in the sense that we can and do use them, but few of us know what the rules are in the sense that we can tell anyone else what they are. What psycholinguists say is that we have developed a *competence*— a cognitive ability that governs our use of language behavior or performance. Our competence with the syntactic rules of English can be demonstrated with a few examples of what we call *linguistic intuitions* (Howard, 1983; Slobin, 1979).

For example, we know that "The small boy slept late" fits the rules of English, and that "Slept boy late small the" does not. We recognize that the utterance, "Colorless green ideas sleep furiously" fits the rules of English, even though it doesn't make any sense (Chomsky, 1957). It may be a silly thing to say, but we realize intuitively that it is a legal thing to say.

We are also able to recognize that these two utterances are communicating the same message, even though they look quite different:

"The student read the textbook."
"The textbook was read by the student."

Not only do we recognize that these are acceptable sentences in English, we recognize that they reflect the same basic idea. In either case, we know who is doing what.

Another way in which we demonstrate our cognitive competence with the rules of our language is in our ability to detect ambiguity. Consider, for example, these two sentences:

"They are cooking apples."
"They are cooking apples."

Now there's no doubt that they appear identical, but we can also see that they may be communicating very different (ambiguous) ideas. In one case, we may be talking about what some people are doing (cooking apples as opposed to spaghetti). In the other, we may be identifying a variety of apple (cooking apples as opposed to eating apples.)

Somehow we need to devise a set of rules that can be used to explain these intuitive cognitive abilities that we all have. When we acquire the rules of our language, just what do we learn? We will consider two theories of syntactic rules (such theories are called *grammars*). One is called a *phrase-structure grammar,* and the other is called *transformational grammar.* These theories have found favor in psychology because they help us understand the cognitive skills of language users. Let's now review briefly the basic idea behind each of these grammars.

Phrase-structure and Transformational Grammars   One approach to syntactic rules (e.g., Clark & Clark, 1977) suggests that we analyze sentences into phrases. That is, when we produce a sentence, we combine words into phrases and phrases into sentences. And when we comprehend a sentence, we break it down into phrases and analyze phrases into words. Let's look at an example of how this might work. Let's take the simple sentence:

The young man killed the fat rat.

Rather than treating this sentence as a sequence of one word following another, we can organize the sentence into phrases. In this case, there are two major phrases: a noun phrase "The young man" and a verb phrase "killed the fat rat." The noun phrase is made up of three words: an article (The), an adjective (young), and a noun (man). The verb phrase is made up of a verb (killed) and another noun phrase (the fat rat). If we were to draw a diagram reflecting the structure of this sentence, it would look like the diagram in Figure 15.4.

This diagram does two things. It gives us a sense of which words go together in this particular sentence (the rat is fat, while the man is young and killed the rat, not the other way around.) This basic diagram can also be used to describe a very large (potentially infinite) number of acceptable sentences. The same diagram can be used for the sentence "The old woman crushed the tin can," or "The fat rat killed the young man," or even "The colorless idea loved the maroon psychologist." That is, if we know the appropriate phrase structure of an acceptable sentence in English, all we have to do is fill in the blanks with the right sort of word, and we're bound to produce an acceptable sentence, whether it makes any sense or not.

Let's go back now to our ambiguous "cooking apples" sentence. Figure 15.5 provides the phrase-structure diagram for both versions of this sentence. Now we can see clearly that in sentence (A) "cooking" is a verb and is something that "they" are doing. In sentence (B), "cooking" is an adjective and describes a variety of apple.

There are a few problems with this phrase-structure approach to grammar, however. To know all of the possible grammatically correct utterances in English would require knowing a huge number of possible phrase-structure diagrams. Given the capacity of our long-term memory, this may be

Figure 15.4
A diagram illustrating how a phrase-structure analysis can be used to reflect the structure, or rules, of a simple sentence.

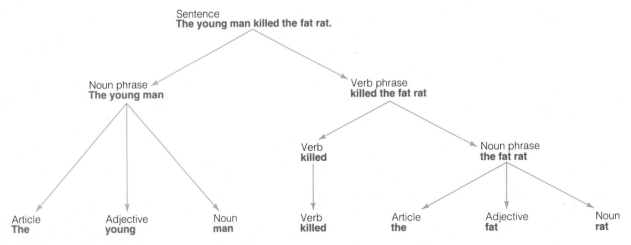

possible, but it's not very economical. Another problem is that there are many ambiguous sentences for which a phrase-structure analysis doesn't tell us anything about the intention of the speaker. All that phrase-structure diagrams do is analyze sentences that have already been produced; they don't tell us anything about what the producer of the sentence had in mind when the sentence was generated. Another problem is that phrase-structure grammars don't tell us anything about the obvious relationship between sentences like, "The student read the textbook" and "The textbook was read by the student." The phrase-structure analysis of these two sentences is quite different, even though they are both communicating the same basic idea.

The approach of Noam Chomsky (1957, 1965), called *transformational grammar,* does help in these situations. The theory of transformational grammar is quite complex and we can hardly do it justice here. But we can suggest that one of the major ideas of the theory is the distinction between **surface structure** and **deep structure.** The surface structure of a sentence is the syntactical structure of the sentence as it is produced. This structure can be adequately analyzed with phrase-structure diagrams. The deep structure of an utterance is, in a sense, the intention or idea behind the sentence as it is produced. Thus, "The student read the textbook" and "The textbook was read by the student" both have the same basic deep structure. They are both communicating the same basic idea or cognition. They are different only in their surface structure—in how that idea is expressed. According to Chomsky, then, what we learn when we learn the rules of syntax is how to take simple, basic ideas and *transform* them into a number of different forms, such as the passive form (The textbook was read by the student.), question form (Did the student read the textbook?), or negative form (The student didn't read the textbook.), or even passive questions (Was the textbook read by the student?).

Clearly some of the transformational rules that we know, that change simple sentences into more complex ones, are themselves quite complex. But with the knowledge and the competence of only a few dozen such rules, we can generate virtually every grammatically acceptable sentence possible in our language.

surface structure
in transformational grammar, the structure of an utterance as it is produced

deep structure
in transformational grammar, the basic idea, cognition, or message that is to be communicated with language

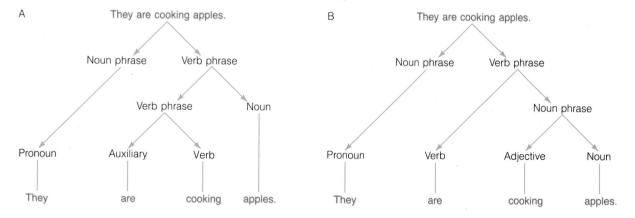

Figure 15.5
An illustration of how a phrase-structure analysis can remove ambiguity from a sentence. In (A), we see that what they are cooking are apples. In (B), we see that the apples are cooking apples, as opposed to some other sort of apples.

The study of language that is psycholinguistics has set for itself some very high goals. To understand the underlying knowledge and abilities which people must have in order to use language requires understanding how we use the sounds (phonemes) of spoken language, how we assign meaning to sounds (morphemes), and how we combine morphemes to form syntactically acceptable utterances. Our study of language involves us with the most complex of cognitive tasks. We have only begun to realize what some of the relevant questions are. Some of the issues of language *development* are presented in Topic 18 of our next chapter.

Before you go on

What are the essential characteristics of phrase-structure and transformational grammars?

Cognition is the mental process through which we come to know about ourselves and the world in which we live. Cognitive processes involve perception, learning, and memory. Concepts are our mental representations of our experiences. Concepts represent classes, or categories, of objects and events, and in so doing, help us to bring order and meaningfulness to our observations. Most of our concepts are symbolized words, the meaningful and arbitrary units of our languages. Language use provides an excellent example of rule-governed behavior. All language users demonstrate a knowledge—a competence—of the rules of their language, whether or not they can explicitly state the nature of those rules. In this topic, we have reviewed the complex cognitive processes of concept acquisition and the use of concepts to communicate with language.

None of us doubt that animals can and do communicate. They communicate with each other on a regular basis, and, for that matter, can communicate with humans if need be. If you have a dog or a cat, you surely know when it is hungry or needs to go outside. Your dog or cat can even communicate to you how it feels at the moment: happy, sad, angry, and so on. Of much greater interest to cognitive psychologists is the question of whether or not nonhuman animals are capable of using *language* as a means of communication. We recognize the use of language as being an incredibly complex cognitive ability. It is an ability readily apparent among humans and difficult to find among nonhumans. Can nonhumans be taught to use language as a means of communication?

Early attempts to teach language to chimpanzees did not fare well (Hayes, 1952; Kellogg, 1968). These efforts failed largely because the researchers tried to teach their chimps to *speak* language. The chimp raised by the Kelloggs (named Gua) never learned to say even one word; and Vickie (raised by the Hayeses) managed only three words (mamma, papa, and cup), and she learned these only with great difficulty.

One breakthrough in the study of chimpanzees' use of language came with the research of Beatrice and Roger Gardner (1969, 1975), who taught a male chimp named Washoe to communicate with American Sign Language (ASL) rather than speech. Progress was slow at first, but Washoe's vocabulary eventually grew to include more than 150 signs (Fleming, 1974). More than that, Washoe would string signs together to make short sentences, such as, "Gimme water" or "Washoe sorry." Sometimes Washoe produced three-sign strings, such as "Roger tickle me."

Other researchers have devised different means of demonstrating languagelike communication with chimpanzees. The Premacks (1972) taught Sarah to use small plastic shapes as symbols. Sarah has demonstrated the ability to order these plastic shapes to form reasonable approximations of sentences, such as "Mary give Sarah banana." Duane Rumbaugh and his associates (1977) taught another chimpanzee, Lana, to communicate with the aid of a computer that has a large keyboard composed of visual signs. Lana learned to use the computer-generated signs to communicate a range of ideas and demands, often stringing together a number of signs into sentences.

Washoe learning the American Sign Language word for brush.

Lana and the computer with which she communicates. The keyboard is composed of visual signs that Lana strings together to form sentences.

Patterson (Patterson & Linden, 1981) has had great success teaching ASL signs to a gorilla (Koko) that has acquired more than 800 signs.

What have we learned from these studies of chimpanzees and apes? We have learned that chimpanzees are capable of more complex cognitive activities than we previously realized. But, have we demonstrated that chimps can learn language? Here the answer is not at all clear.

One of the most severe critics of chimp language studies is Herbert Terrace, who himself tried to teach sign language to a chimp. (He named his pupil Nim Chimpsky.) It is Terrace's view (1979) that although chimps and apes can learn a number of clever response patterns, they haven't yet demonstrated a true use of language.

Even with reasonably generous criteria for defining a language, Terrace argues that the data do not support the conclusion that chimps can use language. For one thing, he says, there is no evidence of an appreciation of syntax or grammar. Washoe would combine signs, but would often combine them in different ways to communicate the same thing. There was no apparent difference in Washoe's mind between "Gimme water" and "Water gimme," for instance. There is also no evidence yet of a chimp's ability to deal with the sort of abstractions that human language allows. That is, chimpanzee "language" is very concrete, very here-and-now oriented. And, significantly, chimps have yet to show any evidence of using their "language" to talk about language—something we have been doing for the past several pages. It is also true that the ability to communicate with signs and symbols of the sort used so far is an ability that develops very slowly and with great difficulty, as opposed to the rapid, virtually effortless way in which humans acquire their native language.

The issue of chimpanzee language is far from settled, and it is far from trivial. Some people believe that the question of whether or not animals other than humans can use language is related to claims of human superiority. Such is not the issue at all. As we continue to explore the use of cognitive and language skills in the controlled environments of chimpanzees and gorillas, we can, perhaps, learn more about the essential features of languages and how languages are acquired by humans.

TOPIC SUMMARY

What is meant by cognition, and what are cognitive processes?

Cognitions are what we use to understand ourselves and the world in which we live. Generally speaking, they are ideas, beliefs, thoughts, and images. They are mental representations. Cognitive processes are the mental activities involved in knowing and understanding, including perception, learning, memory, concept formation, problem solving, and the use of language. / 264

How can we use attributes and rules to define concepts?

Concepts are mental representations of categories or classes of objects and events. They are often defined in terms of attributes of objects or events that are associated by rules. Formal concepts may be defined by conjunctive rules, disjunctive rules, affirmation rules, or relational rules. / 267

How does the concept of prototype help our understanding of what a concept is?

A prototype is the best example or most typical member of a category or concept. It is the member of a concept class that has the most of the attributes that define that concept and few attributes that cause it to be confused with other concepts. / 268

In the context of concept formation, what is a strategy?

Concepts are usually learned by developing a plan or strategy for most conveniently discovering the essential attributes of a concept and the rule that unites those attributes. In large measure, concept formation is a matter of generating and testing hypotheses about potential class or concept membership. / 271

What are some of the defining characteristics of language?

Language is a complex and creative cognitive skill used for communication. A language is made up of a large number of arbitrary symbols (words that stand for our conceptualization of events) that have meaning for users of that language and are combined in accordance with certain rules. Language allows us to communicate about the not here and the not now. / 273

Define phoneme, morpheme, and syntax.

A phoneme is the smallest unit of sound in the spoken form of a language. A morpheme is the smallest unit of meaning in a language. The syntax of a language is the set of rules that dictate how the morphemes of a language can be combined to form acceptable utterances. / 275

What are the essential characteristics of phrase-structure and transformational grammars?

Grammars are theories of language syntax. The phrase-structure grammar proposes analyzing sentences in terms of the phrases that make them up and further analyzing phrases into individual words or morphemes. A transformational grammar suggests that each sentence as it is produced, or as it forms a surface structure, is a transformed version of the language user's intention, or deep structure. / 278

TOPIC

Here are some problems for you to solve. We'll return to each of these problems within this topic and provide answers. For now, see how well you can do.

1. (From Posner, 1973) "Two train stations are fifty miles apart. At 2:00 P.M. one Saturday afternoon two trains start toward each other, one from each station. Just as the trains pull out of the stations, a bird springs into the air in front of the first train and flies ahead to the front of the second train. When the bird reaches the second train it turns back and flies toward the first train. The bird continues to do this until the trains meet.

"If both trains travel at the rate of twenty-five miles per hour and the bird flies at one hundred miles per hour, how many miles will the bird have flown before the two trains meet?"

2. (From Reynolds and Flagg, 1983) "What English word has been scrambled to make *teralbay*?"

3. (From Duncker, 1945) "One morning, exactly at sunrise, a Buddhist monk began to climb a tall mountain. A narrow path, no more than a foot or two wide, spiraled around the mountain to a glittering temple at the summit. The monk ascended at varying rates of speed, stopping many times along the way to rest and eat dried fruit that he carried with him. He reached the temple shortly before sunset. After several days of fasting and meditation, he began his journey back along the same path, starting at sunrise again walking at variable speeds with many pauses along the way. His average speed descending was, of course, greater than his average climbing speed. Show that there is a spot along the path that the monk will occupy on both trips at precisely the same time of day."

4. (From Köhler, 1969) "The diameter of this circle is exactly 10 inches long. What is the length of line 'L'?"

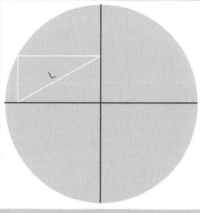

5. (From Greeno, 1974) "Hobbits" and "orcs" are characters from Tolkien's classic *Lord of the Rings*. Orcs are monsters. Hobbits are very small humanlike dwarfs, usually eaten by orcs. "Three hobbits and three orcs stand on one side of a river. On their side of the river is a boat that will hold a maximum of two creatures. All six creatures need to get to the other side of the river, using just the one boat. However, if at any time orcs outnumber hobbits (on either side of the river), the orcs will eat the hobbits. How can all the creatures make it across the river without any hobbits being eaten by the hungry orcs?"

6. (From Scheerer, 1963) "Connect the nine dots below with four straight lines, drawn in such a way that your pen or pencil never leaves the page."

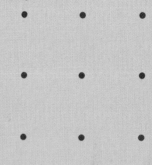

In their 1954 text, *Experimental Psychology,* Woodworth and Schlosberg began their chapter on problem solving with this observation, "If the experimentalist could show us how to think clearly, and how to solve our problems successfully and expeditiously, his social contribution would be very great" (p. 814). The study of problem-solving behaviors is a classic one in psychology. You will notice that many of the references that we will cite in this topic are quite old, reflecting this long-standing interest. We have learned a lot about problem-solving behaviors since Woodworth and Schlosberg published their textbook, but the hope implied in their introductory statement is still largely unfulfilled.

Our daily lives are filled with problems of various sorts. Some of them are simple and trivial; others are very important to us. In this topic, we'll focus our attention on cognitive, or intellectual, problems: those that require the manipulation of cognitions for their solution. The first thing we'll do is define the nature of problems, and then we'll consider how we can go about solving them.

Solving problems requires a number of interrelated processes. We must first recognize that a problem exists. Then we must decide how we will represent the problem in such a way as to maximize our chances of solving it. Then we devise some strategy to help us reach the goal of solving the problem. Finally, we must assess whether or not our proposed solution actually does solve the problem at hand.

That problem solving is a "higher" cognitive process is intuitively obvious. It requires that we *perceive* the nature of the problem and *learn* the most efficient path toward a solution, using our *memories* as we go along.

WHAT IS A PROBLEM?

Sometimes our goals are obvious, our present position is obvious, and the path between where we are and where we want to go is obvious. In such cases, we really don't have a problem. Say you want to have a nice breakfast. You have eggs, bacon, and bread available. You also have the implements needed to prepare these foods, and you know how to use them. You know that a nice breakfast would be two eggs over-easy, three strips of fried bacon, and a piece of buttered toast. With little hesitation, you can engage in the appropriate behaviors and reach your goal.

problem
a situation in which there is a discrepancy between one's situation at the moment and one's desired situation with no clear way of getting from one to the other

A **problem** exists when there is a discrepancy between your present state and your perceived goal state and no readily apparent way to get from one to the other. In situations where the path to goal attainment is not clear or obvious, a problem exists, and you will have to engage in problem-solving behaviors.

A problem-solving situation can thus be thought of as having three major components: (1) an *initial state,* which is the situation as it exists at the moment, or the cognitions of the individual faced with the problem; (2) a *goal state,* which is the situation as the problem solver would like it to be, or the end product; and (3) possible routes or strategies for getting from the initial state to the goal state.

Psychologists make the distinction between well-defined and ill-defined problems. Well-defined problems are those in which the initial state and the goal state are clearly delineated. We know what is available, know what the goal is, and may even know some of the possible ways to go about getting from one to the other. "What English word can be made from the letters

Problems come in a variety of forms, from solving architectural dilemmas to piecing together a map of the United States. The nature of the problem often determines the method used to solve it.

teralbay?'' We recognize this question as presenting a problem. We understand what the question is asking, have some ideas about how we might go about answering it, and we'll know when we have succeeded. "How do you get home from campus if you discover that your car, which is in the campus parking lot, won't start?" Again, we know where we are (on campus), we'll know when we have reached our goal (at home), but we have to discover a new or different way to get there.

Many of the problems that you and I face every day tend to be of the ill-defined variety. In such cases, we *do not* have a clear idea of what we are starting with, and we may not be able to identify any one ideal or correct solution. "What should my college major be?" Many high-school seniors (and some college seniors) do not even know what their options are. They have few ideas about how to find out about possible college majors. And, once they have selected a major, they are not sure that their choice was the best one. (Which perhaps explains why so many college students change their majors so often.)

"Write the script for a movie that will be a smashing success." The screenwriter certainly knows what a script is and probably knows what the producers mean by "smashing success." Beyond that, however, this problem is certainly ill-defined. This is the same sort of ill-defined problem you may face when assigned a term paper. All you may know is that the paper must be on some topic in psychology, at least 15 pages long, and well-written and original!

Because ill-defined problems usually involve many variables that are difficult to define, much less control, psychologists tend to study problems that are at least reasonably well-defined. In the setting of the psychology laboratory, we at least try to present subjects with a complete description of the initial state of the problem and specify what a solution or goal state would be. Each of the six problems with which we started this topic is a well-defined problem. You should be able to understand what each question is asking. You'll know when you have solved the problem. The issue is: "How will you progress from the presented initial state to the desired goal state?

Before you go on

What are the three components of a problem?

Contrast well-defined and ill-defined problems.

PROBLEM REPRESENTATION

The first thing we have to do when we set out to solve a problem is to put it in some form that allows us to think about it in familiar terms. We need to come up with some way to *represent* it in our own minds, interpreting the problem so that the initial state and the goal state are clear to us. In short, we need to understand the nature of the problem. Is the problem a mathematical one? Can it be represented visually? Can the information with which I am provided be translated into terms with which I am more familiar, without significantly changing the problem itself?

By examining a few of the problems with which we began this topic, we can see that the choice of how to represent a problem is critical. For example, consider our problem 4. At first inspection, you might decide that this problem is too difficult to even attempt, perhaps requiring an in-depth knowledge of trigonometry or geometry. But if you work with the representation of the problem for a moment, you may recognize that if you know the diameter of the circle is 10 inches, then any radius of the circle must be 5 inches long. That in itself doesn't help much until you also see that line L is a diagonal of the rectangle in the drawing, and that the other diagonal happens to be a radius of the circle. It then becomes obvious that line L must also be 5 inches long (see Figure 16.1). If the problem's initial state is not restated, or represented, in *this* way, the problem is very difficult to solve.

Now refer to the problem concerning the mountain-climbing monk (problem 3). Thinking about this problem as it is presented can be maddening. You may picture yourself walking up and down a mountain on two different days, mentally visualizing a narrow path, trying to locate a point on the path where you might be at precisely the same time on two different days.

As is often the case with real-life problems, this statement of the problem contains a good deal of irrelevant information. *Problem representation* often involves sorting out what matters and what doesn't. Certainly the fact that we're dealing with a monk is not relevant and neither are the temple, the dried fruit, the fact that the path is narrow or spirals, *or* that the trip was made on different days.

You might think about (represent) this problem in terms of one climber making the trip in one day. Or, better still, imagine that there are two monks involved: one starting from the top of the mountain, the other from the bottom. Surely they will meet somewhere on that mountain trail sometime during the day (see Figure 16.2). When you represent the problem in this way, the solution becomes readily apparent.

So, it might help to represent this mountain-climbing problem visually, actually drawing out the ascending and descending pathways on a sheet of paper. Choosing to visually represent problem 1 in this way would not be helpful. It's easy to imagine a subject working on this problem by drawing little train stations and the trains moving toward each other, and tracing the path of the bird racing back and forth between the trains. If you tried this, you discovered that it didn't help very much.

Instead of visualizing this problem, think about the logic and the arithmetic involved. The stations are 50 miles apart. The trains each travel at 25

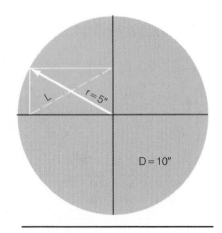

Figure 16.1
A way to represent problem 4 in order to make its solution more obvious.

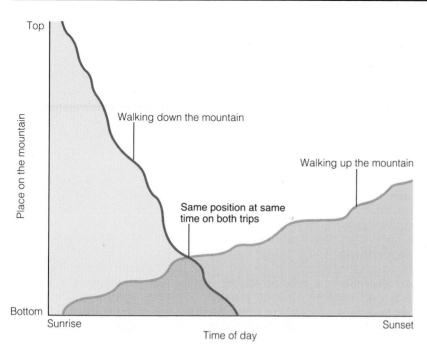

Top

Place on the mountain

Walking down the mountain

Walking up the mountain

Same position at same
time on both trips

Bottom

Sunrise

Sunset

Time of day

Figure 16.2
*A graphic representation of problem 3
that makes the solution easier to see.*

miles per hour. At that rate, how long will it take the trains to meet? Exactly
1 hour. You also know that the bird flies at a rate of 100 miles per hour. If
it has to fly (back and forth or anyplace else) for just 1 hour, how far will it
have flown? Right! Exactly 100 miles. As in the previous example, the solution becomes obvious as soon as the problem is stripped to its essentials and
is mentally represented in such a way that a solution is possible.

Here's one final example of the importance of problem representation
(from Adams, 1974). "Imagine that you have a very large sheet of paper,
1/100 of an inch thick. Imagine folding it over onto itself so that you now
have two layers of paper. Fold it again so that there are four layers. It is
impossible to actually fold one sheet of paper 50 times, but imagine that you
could. About how thick would the paper be if it were folded 50 times?"
Trying to picture just what a piece of paper folded 50 times would look like is
very difficult. Some subjects guess a few inches, while some imagine that the
folded paper would be several feet thick. Actually, 50 folds would increase
the paper's thickness by a factor of 2^{50}! That comes out to nearly
1,100,000,000,000,000 inches, and the resulting paper would be so high as
to nearly reach from the earth to the sun!

I would not suggest that choosing the best way to represent a problem is
a simple task. Very often problem representation provides *the* stumbling
block to problem solution (Bourne et al., 1983). Once you realize that you
are faced with a problem, your first step in solving it should be to represent it
in a variety of ways. Eliminate unessential information. Relate the problem to
other problems of a similar type that you have solved before. Having done so,
if the solution is still not obvious, you may have to develop some strategy to
move from your representation of the problem to the goal of its solution. We
now turn to how one might go about generating possible problem solutions.

Before you go on

*In the context of problem solving, what is meant by problem
representation?*

PROBLEM-SOLVING STRATEGIES

Once you have represented the initial state of a problem and have a clear notion of what an acceptable goal state might be, you still have to figure out how to get to your goal. Even after you have adequately represented a problem, how to go about solving it may not be readily apparent. You might spend a few minutes guessing wildly at a solution, but soon you have to settle on some strategy. In this context, strategy means a systematic plan for generating possible solutions that can be tested to see if they are correct. The main advantage of cognitive strategies appears to be that they permit the learner or problem solver to "exercise some degree of control over the task at hand. They allow learners to choose the skills and knowledge that they will bring to bear on any particular problem at any time" (Gagné, 1984, p. 381). There are a number of possible strategies that you might choose to try. In this section, we'll consider two different types of strategies—algorithms and heuristics—each appropriate for different tasks.

Algorithms

algorithm
a problem-solving strategy in which all possible solutions are generated and tested and an acceptable solution is guaranteed

An **algorithm** is a problem-solving strategy that *guarantees* that you will eventually arrive at a correct solution. It involves systematically exploring and evaluating *all* possible solutions until the correct one is found. It is sometimes referred to as a *generate-test* sort of strategy where one generates hypotheses about potential solutions and then tests each one in turn. Perhaps you recognize the concept formation strategy of conservative focusing that we discussed in our last topic as a type of algorithmic strategy. In that case, each attribute of a concept is examined and tested, one at a time, to determine if that attribute is part of the concept's definition.

Simple anagram problems (letters of a word presented in a scrambled fashion) can be solved using an algorithm. "What English word has been scrambled to make *ttse*?" With sufficient patience, you can systematically rearrange these four letters until you hit on a correct solution: *ttse, ttes, tste, tset, tets, test*! There it is—*test*. With only four letters to deal with, finding a solution generally doesn't take very long.

On the other hand, consider problem 2 where we have an anagram composed of eight letters: *teralbay*. As it happens, there are 40,320 possible combinations of these eight letters (Reynolds and Flagg, 1983, p. 243). Unless your system for moving letters around just happens to start in a good place, you could spend a lot of time trying to come up with a combination that produces an English word.

Heuristics

heuristic
a problem-solving strategy in which hypotheses about problem solutions are generated and tested in a time-saving and systematic way, but that does not guarantee an acceptable solution

A **heuristic** strategy is a more economical technique for generating possible solutions to a problem. Such a strategy acts like a rule of thumb and guides the systematic generation and testing of problem solutions. But it does not guarantee success. With a heuristic strategy, there *is* a possibility of failure. However, heuristic strategies are usually much less time-consuming than algorithm strategies and do lead searches for paths toward goals in a logical, sensible way. We'll review two heuristic strategies: *means-ends analysis* and *working backward*.

If you tried problem 2 (the *teralbay* anagram problem), it is likely that you employed a heuristic strategy. To do so, you would rely on your experience with the English language (remember that cognitive processes such as the use of memory are relevant for problem solving). You would then seriously consider only those letter combinations that you know occur frequently. You would probably generate and test the most common combinations first. You wouldn't worry too much about the possibility that the solution contained a combination like *brty.* Nor would you search for a word with an *aae* string in it. You might explore words that end in *able,* because you know these to be fairly common. But that wouldn't work. How about *br* words? No, that doesn't work either. How about words with the combination *tray* in them? *Traybeal?* No. *Baletray?* No. "Oh! Now I see it: *betrayal.*"

This type of heuristic strategy is called a *means-ends analysis* (Newell & Simon, 1972). In this strategy, one always keeps the final goal in mind, but first works toward the establishment of subgoals. In the *teralbay* example, subgoals might be defined in terms of letter combinations that make sense or are commonly found. Once the subgoals are reached, they are manipulated in an attempt to reach the final goal.

The means-ends heuristic strategy might also prove helpful in solving the Hobbits and Orcs problem. In this problem, the goal state is well-defined: get all the creatures to the other side of the river. The means to reach that end is also specified. The problem here is that there is no way to reach the goal in just one step or procedure. You may find it useful to think in terms of getting just one Hobbit or Orc across the river at a time. A serious constraint is put on this particular problem because Orcs can never outnumber Hobbits—a sort of subgoal routine in itself.

Figure 16.3 shows a solution to this problem. In words, the first few steps go like this: Let's get an Orc across the river. (1) I'll send two Orcs over, leave one, and have the other return (2). Now Hobbits outnumber Orcs, but that's okay. That worked well, let's get a second Orc across the river the same way. Two Orcs cross the river (3); one stays, the other returns (4). So far so good. Now I've got to start moving Hobbits. If I send two Hobbits across the river (5) they'll be even on the other side, but if one Hobbit returns then there will be two Orcs and only one Hobbit on the other side of the river, and I'll have a problem. Hmm. I know, I'll have one of each, one Hobbit and one Orc, return (6). That will keep everything equal. From this subgoal on, the solution is relatively easy.

This sort of heuristic strategy is not as far-fetched as it may appear in these examples. If John has decided that it is his goal to be a family-practice physician, he cannot simply rent an office and begin to practice medicine. To get to that ultimate goal of being a physician (or almost anything else) will involve establishing a series of subgoals and procedures for reaching those subgoals before moving on to others. The final goal state may always be in John's mind, but right now he has to get a good grade in introductory psychology (one subgoal along the way) or he's going to have difficulty even getting into medical school.

Another type of heuristic strategy that you have probably used involves the procedure of *working backward.* In this strategy, the goal state of a problem may be better defined than either the initial state *or* the means to get to the goal. Sometimes it is easier to trace a path from the goal of a maze to its starting point than it is to trace the same path in the other direction.

Suppose that you know what you want to have for supper tonight: a Chinese dinner of eggrolls, shrimp in lobster sauce, and fried rice. There's your goal state, now how do you get there? "What would I have to do to get that dinner on my table tonight? I'd have to fry rice. In order to fry rice, I'll need something to fry it in. No problem; I'll use my new wok. But I need the rice to fry. How *do* you fry rice, anyway?" When you check your Chinese cookbook, you discover that to fry rice you need to first cook the rice, then let it cool, or chill it, before frying. "I haven't got the time to buy rice, then

Figure 16.3

A visual representation of the Hobbits and Orcs problem. See text for an explanation and constraints on the problem.

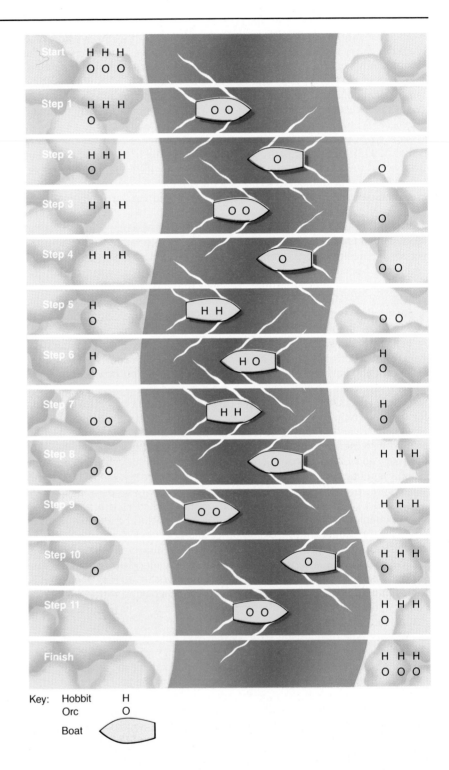

Key: Hobbit   H
       Orc   O

       Boat

boil it, then cool it, then fry it. How else could I get fried rice to the table?" It may be at this point that you decide that your problem has no reasonable solution, and you may decide to stop at your neighborhood Chinese restaurant on the way home and buy your supper.

If you have the problem of wanting to get an A on your next psychology exam, wouldn't you try to solve that problem by working backward? "What would it take for me to get an A?" As is so often the case with such real-life, ill-defined problems, there are many different ways that one could go about answering such a question. I'll leave those possibilities to you.

Before you go on
Compare and contrast algorithmic and heuristic strategies in problem solving.

BARRIERS TO EFFECTIVE PROBLEM SOLVING

By and large, it is difficult to solve problems without relying heavily on one's memory. If you failed to remember that a circle's radius is equal to one half its diameter, you couldn't solve problem 4. If you kept forgetting that Orcs eat Hobbits, you couldn't solve problem 5. If you couldn't remember what you wanted to have for supper, you would have a hard time trying to figure out what to buy when you went to the grocery store. Regardless of the type of problem or the type of strategy employed to solve it, solving problems requires that we use our memories.

There are times, however, when our memories may create difficulties in problem solving. We'll look at two such cases in this section.

Mental Set

In Chapter 4, Topic 8, we suggested that our perceptions are often influenced by our expectations. We said that we often perceive what we are set to perceive. This notion of **mental set** is also relevant in problem solving. A mental set is defined as a tendency to perceive or respond to something in a given (set) way. We often form set tendencies or expectations when we go about problem solving, and these often interfere with what we're doing.

mental set
a tendency to perceive or respond to something in a predetermined, set way

One clever (though somewhat unpleasant) demonstration of mental set involves giving a class a lengthy surprise test, perhaps 50 true-false items. The instructions at the top of the first page state clearly: "Place all of your answers on the attached answer sheet. Do not write on this exam. *Read all of the items on this test before making any marks on the answer sheet.*" Having taken so many true-false tests before, many students do not even read the instructions. They just start into the test, working away. Some students read the instructions and choose to ignore the warning about reading all of the items first. Only those students who do so get to read item 50 before they begin to answer the questions. Item 50 reads, "This is not really a test. I just wanted to see if you would follow directions. Just sit quietly until I collect the papers."

Probably *the* classic example of mental set in problem solving is provided by Luchins (1942). His "water jar" problem is presented in Figure 16.4. This won't work very well with you because you are no longer a naïve subject. You might want to try it on a friend.

The job here is to take the provided jars, each with a specified capacity, and using only the provided jars, get a prescribed amount of water into a large empty basin. Your subjects should be asked to express their answers

Figure 16.4

Luchin's water jar problem (1942) as an example of how mental set can affect problem solving. The simple equation B − A − 2C can be used to come up with the required amount of water in all items except item 9 (the solution for which is discussed in the text).
(From Luchin, 1942.)

Item	Size of jars (in ounces)			Water required
	A	B	C	
1	29	3	0	20
2	21	127	3	100
3	14	163	25	99
4	18	43	10	5
5	9	42	6	21
6	20	59	4	31
7	23	49	3	20
8	15	39	3	18
9	28	76	3	25

algebraically. For example, in the first problem they are given only two jars: a 29-ounce jar and a 3-ounce jar. They are to get 20 ounces into the basin. You can help them out with this first one, which isn't very hard. Your subject will soon see that pouring in 29 ounces of water, and then removing 3 ounces, three times, will result in the required 20 ounces in the basin.

The second problem is only slightly more difficult. Eventually, your subject will find the solution: Fill jar B (127 ounces) and empty it into the basin. Use jar A to remove 21 ounces, leaving 106 ounces in the basin. Use jar C to remove 3 ounces twice. The result will be 100 ounces in the basin. In symbolic terms, that would be B − A − C − C, or B − A − 2C, or 127 − 21 − 6 = 100. Off your subject goes, merrily solving the problems, and soon discovering that B − A − 2C will work in every case. Look at item 7. Yes, B − A − 2C will work to get 20 ounces in the basin (49 − 23 = 26 and 26 − 3 − 3 = 20). But there's a much simpler solution: A − C, or 23 ounces minus 3 ounces equals 20 ounces. Because B − A − 2C has worked so well in the past, many subjects adopt it as their *set* way to go about solving the problems. It will also work for item 8, even though an easier solution is available there.

The real test comes with item 9. I have had subjects swear that this item cannot be solved. "Look," they say, "B − A − 2C, or 76 minus 28 is 48, and 48 minus 3 is 45, and 45 minus 3 is 42, not 25!" When I tell them that problem 9 can be solved, they get anxious, upset, and even occasionally aggressive. When they just can't take it any longer, I point out the solution to them: "Why not just take A (28 ounces) and subtract C (3 ounces)? That'll give you the 25 ounces you need." Their response is often, "Well! You didn't tell me I could do it *that way!*" Indeed. No one told them they had to do it *any* way. But their B − A − 2C scheme worked so well for so long that they developed a mental set that this was the only way to solve the problem.

Our problem 6 was included to provide an example of how an inappropriate mental set can interfere with problem solving. Most subjects when first presented with this problem make an assumption (form a mental set). They assume that the nine dots form a square, and that their lines somehow must stay within that square. Only when this mental set is "broken" can the problem be solved (see Figure 16.5).

You should be able to find examples from your own experience in which you have developed mental sets that interfered with efficient problem-solving strategies. For example, have you ever had a car with some chronic problem, perhaps a poor carburetor? Every time the car wouldn't run properly, the problem was with the carburetor. Then, even when a much less serious problem arose (let's say that you simply ran out of gas), the first thing you did was raise the hood and start tinkering with the carburetor. Have you ever found your frequently used route to a goal blocked? Let's say that every time

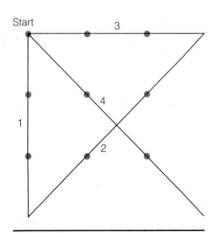

Figure 16.5

A solution to the "nine dot" problem.

you drive home from campus you take the same route because you believe that that route best solves your problem of how to get home from campus. What will you do if road construction blocks your route? Some people have such a mentally set way of getting from one place to another that they are at a great loss if that way no longer works.

Before you go on

What is a mental set, and how might a mental set affect problem solving?

Functional Fixedness

The phenomenon of **functional fixedness** is rather like that of mental set. The process is defined by Duncker (1945) as the inability to discover an appropriate new use for an object because of experience using the object in some other function. That is, the problem solver may fail to see the solution to a problem because he or she has "fixed" some "function" to an object that would be useful in solving the problem if it were used in a new and different way.

A standard example is that of Maier (1931). Two strings are dangling from the ceiling. They are so far apart that a subject cannot reach both at the same time. The subject's problem is to do just that: hold both strings at once. If there were nothing else in the room, this problem might never get solved. However, there are other objects in the room, including a pair of pliers (see Figure 16.6). A common solution to this problem is to tie the pliers to one string and swing the pliers and string like a pendulum. As the subject holds the other string, the string with the pliers attached can be grasped as it swings over to the subject. Because many subjects fail to see the pliers as useful (functioning) for anything but grabbing onto things, they fail to see the pliers as a potential pendulum weight, and thus may fail to solve the problem. They have "fixed" the "function" of the pliers in their mind.

Another famous experiment that demonstrates functional fixedness is reported by Duncker (1945). Here, subjects are provided with a box of tacks, a candle, and some matches. The task is to use these materials to mount the candle on the wall and light it. Obviously, one cannot just tack a candle to the wall. The solution to this problem requires breaking the functional fixed-

functional fixedness
the phenomenon in which one is unable to see a new use or function for an object because of experience using the object in some other function

Figure 16.6
Maier's two-string problem. The subject is to manage to get both strings in his grasp. They are separated so that when holding one string, the other cannot be reached. See text for an explanation of the solution.
(Adapted from Maier, 1931.)

Figure 16.7
*The materials provided in the candle
problem, and how the problem can be
solved.*
(After Duncker, 1945.)

ness set of the box in which the tacks are presented, seeing it as a potential candleholder, tacking *it* to the wall, and mounting the candle on the box (see Figure 16.7).

There have been a number of experiments (for example Glucksberg and Danks, 1968) that have shown that some subtle changes in the way in which the materials are presented have an effect on solving this problem. For example, when the box of tacks is labeled *tacks,* the problem is much harder to solve than when the tacks and the box are labeled separately. For that matter, just using an empty box and a scattered assortment of tacks increases the likelihood that subjects will overcome the functional fixedness of seeing the box as something that holds things.

Solving a problem often requires that we break out of the restraints that mental set and functional fixedness put on how we represent the problem, how we define a problem solution, and how we view the path between initial and goal states. In large measure, being able to overcome these barriers is to be able to solve problems creatively, and it is to this subject that we turn next.

Before you go on
What is functional fixedness, and how might it affect problem solving?

Overcoming Barriers with Creative Problem Solving

Creative solutions to problems are new, innovative, and useful. It is important to note that in the context of problem solving, creative means more than unusual, rare, or different. Someone may generate a very original plan to solve a given problem, but unless that plan *works,* we shouldn't view it as creative (Newell, Shaw, & Simon, 1962; Vinacke, 1974). Creative solutions should be put to the same test as more ordinary solutions: Do they solve the problem at hand?

Creative solutions generally involve a new and different organization of the elements of the problem. As we mentioned earlier, it is at the stage of problem representation that creativity may be most noticeable. Seeing a problem in a new light, or combining elements of a problem in a new and different way, may lead to creative solutions.

We say that creative problem solving often involves **divergent thinking;** that is, starting with one idea and generating from it a large number of alternative possibilities and new ideas, the more the better (Dirkes, 1978). When we engage in **convergent thinking,** we take many different ideas and try to focus and reduce them to just one possible solution. Obviously, convergent thinking has its place in problem solving. But for creative problem solving, divergent thinking is generally more useful because many new and different

divergent thinking
the creation of many ideas or potential problem solutions from one idea
convergent thinking
the reduction or focusing of many different ideas into one possible problem solution

possibilities are explored. We need to remember, however, that all these new and different possibilities for a problem's solution need to be judged ultimately in terms of whether or not they really solve the problem.

For example, if you let your mental activity take you off into divergent thinking about the problem of keeping warm on a cold winter's night, you might come up with the idea of popping bushels of warm popcorn. The popped corn would keep everyone warm. Now there's little doubt that such a solution at least borders on the unique, unusual, and creative, but it certainly doesn't seem very workable, no matter how divergent it may be.

Creative problem solving may be analyzed into four interrelated stages. This view of the problem-solving process is another old one in psychology, but it has held up rather nicely over the years (Wallas, 1926).

(1) *Preparation:* This is not unlike our problem representation. The basic elements of the problem are considered. Past experience becomes relevant, but should not become restrictive. It is at this stage of problem solving that it is most important to overcome the negative effects of mental set and functional fixedness. Different ways of expressing the problem are considered, but a solution is not found.

(2) *Incubation:* In this stage, the problem is put away for a while and not thought about. Perhaps fatigue can then dissipate. Perhaps inappropriate strategies can be forgotten. Perhaps unconscious processes can be brought to bear on the problem. Why setting aside a problem may lead to its creative solution we cannot say. We do know, however, that it is often very useful.

(3) *Illumination:* This is the most mysterious stage of the problem-solving process. Not unlike insight, a potential solution to a problem seems to materialize as if from nowhere. Some critical analogy becomes apparent, as does a new path to the problem's solution (Glass, Holyoak, & Santa, 1979).

(4) *Verification:* Now the proposed solution must be tested (or verified) to see if it does in fact provide an answer to the question posed by the problem.

You have probably noted that there is really nothing that extraordinary about Wallas's description of the creative problem-solving process. It sounds very much like the sort of thing that anyone should do when faced with a problem to solve. The truth is, however, that we often fail to go through these stages in any systematic fashion. To do so consciously is often a help to problem solving. It has long been recognized that good problem solvers show more conscious awareness of what they are doing during the course of problem solving than do poor problem solvers (Glaser, 1984).

Before you go on

What is the difference between divergent and convergent thinking?

What are the four stages of creative problem solving, according to Wallas?

Problem solving is certainly a higher cognitive process. It involves our perceptions, our learning experiences, and our memories. To solve a problem requires that we understand the situation as it exists, understand the situation as we would like it to be, and discover some way to reach our desired goal state. To do so effectively and efficiently often requires that we represent the problem appropriately, generate the proper problem-solving strategy, and overcome the inhibiting influence of past experience as reflected in mental set and functional fixedness.

It is not uncommon to hear parents say something like, "We do not want our schools to teach our children just the facts, but to teach them to think, as well." Many psychologists believe that thinking and problem-solving skills are somehow "teachable," and that these are cognitive abilities that *ought* to be taught. In the 1930s and 1940s, education often tended to focus on drill, repetition, and rote practice, with little regard for higher cognitive functions. In the 1950s and 1960s, Skinner's behaviorism and reinforcement theory spilled (or flooded) into the classroom with programmed instruction and teaching machines. Within the past 25 years, there has been a rebirth of interest in cognitive processes in psychology and an increased call for educators to be sensitive to such cognitive abilities as concept formation and problem solving (Glaser, 1984).

As it happens, an increased interest in teaching cognitive skills has not been reflected in the performance of school children. A major study of the impact of education in this country provided evidence that basic fundamental skills are improving and that higher cognitive skills are declining. For example, in mathematics, "there appears to be an increase in the performance associated with basic skill and computation, but little improvement and even a reported decline in mathematical understanding and problem solving" (cited in Glaser, 1984, p. 94).

What can be done to improve the problem-solving skills of students? This very question is one of the most actively researched questions in cognitive psychology today. It has a number of tentative answers. For one thing, it *is* helpful for students to simply know about the basic nature of problem solving.

Teaching students about problem representation, algorithms, heuristics, mental sets, and functional fixedness is in itself a helpful thing to do (for example, Adams, 1974; Greeno, 1978; Hayes, 1981; Newell & Simon, 1972). Most programs of this sort are "knowledge-free" in the sense that they do not require any particular expertise on the part of the student. ". . . In large part, abstract tasks, puzzle-like problems, and informal life situations are used as content" (Glaser, 1984, p. 96). In other words, most of the material used to teach students about problem solving has been the sort of material we have used in this topic: puzzles and informal life situations.

It is the position of cognitive psychologist Robert Glaser (1984) that instruction in problem-solving strategies and techniques needs to rely on a knowledge base. Ability to solve problems is, in this position, a reflection of an interaction between general cognitive abilities to manipulate information (higher cognitive processes) *and* a base level of adequate information to manipulate (knowledge). The essence of this argument is: If you don't *know* much about the particular elements of a given problem, you are going to have difficulty solving it, regardless of how much you know about heuristics, strategies, and problem solving in general.

Consider an experiment by Chi (1978). When their memory was tested with a standard test of memory for digits, 10-year-old children predictably performed significantly less well than adults. The children in Chi's experiment were expert chess players, however, and the adults were not. When children and adults were tested on their memory of chess pieces arranged on a chessboard, the children's memories were far superior to those of the adults. The adults probably had better, more efficient strategies for performing the task at hand, but the children simply had more knowledge about chess, and that gave them the advantage.

One of Glaser's arguments, then, is that problem-solving skills can be taught, but need to be taught in the context of a specific domain of knowledge and understanding. On the one hand, it makes little sense to try to teach students the higher cognitive skills of concept formation and problem solving if they do not have an adequate base of knowledge or information with which to work. On the other hand, it makes little sense to do no more than drill students over and over again on basic facts without exploring theories, concepts, relationships, and how such facts can be used to solve problems. Or, as Glaser puts it, "As individuals acquire knowledge, they also should be empowered to think and reason" (1984, p. 103).

TOPIC SUMMARY

What are the three components of a problem?

Contrast well-defined and ill-defined problems.

We can say that a problem has three components: (1) an initial state—the situation as it exists at the moment, (2) a goal state—the situation as the problem solver would like it to be, and (3) routes or strategies for getting from the initial state to the goal state. Whether or not a problem is well-defined or ill-defined is a matter of the extent to which the elements of the initial state and goal state are well delineated and clearly understood by the problem solver. / 286

In the context of problem solving, what is meant by problem representation?

In the context of problem solving, problem representation involves the mental activity of representing the problem in our minds in a fashion in which we can deal with the problem (mathematically, visually, etc.). In essence, it involves putting the problem into familiar terms. / 287

Compare and contrast algorithmic and heuristic strategies in problem solving.

Algorithms and heuristics are strategies we can use to solve problems. Algorithms involve a systematic search of all possible solutions until the goal is reached; with algorithms, a solution is guaranteed. A heuristic strategy involves generating and testing hypotheses that *may* lead to a problem solution in a sensible, organized way. / 291

What is a mental set, and how might a mental set affect problem solving?

A mental set is a tendency or predisposition to perceive or respond in a particular way. Mental sets generally develop from past experience and involve the continued use of strategies that have been successful in the past even though they may no longer be appropriate for the problem at hand. Mental sets often interfere with effective problem solving by blocking from our consideration either new and different ways to represent the problem or new and different strategies for problem solution. / 293

What is functional fixedness, and how might it affect problem solving?

Functional fixedness is a type of mental set in which an object is seen as serving a few fixed functions. Because we may not see a familiar object as being able to serve different functions, fixedness often interferes with effective problem solving. / 294

What is the difference between divergent and convergent thinking?

What are the four stages of creative problem solving, according to Wallas?

Divergent thinking is seen as a useful technique in problem solving in which a large number of alternative possibilities of problem solution are generated to be tested later for usefulness. Convergent thinking involves taking a large number of ideas or possibilities for problem solution and reducing them to one or a few. Problem solving in general, and creative problem solving in particular, is said to have four interrelated stages: preparation (in which the problem is represented mentally), incubation (in which the problem is put aside for a while), illumination (in which a potential solution becomes known), and verification (in which the potential solution is tested to see if it does indeed solve the problem at hand). / 295

CHAPTER EIGHT

DEVELOPMENTAL PSYCHOLOGY

TOPIC

Let's consider Emily for a moment. Emily is 10 years old and a third-grade student in public school. She is a slightly above-average student, reporting that spelling and recess are her two favorite subjects in school. In most regards, she seems to be a normal 10 year old but Emily *is* different. It is apparent to everyone who knows her that Emily is a very talented young girl.

Emily is very musical. She can play the piano exceptionally well, even without sheet music to guide her. She has given a number of recitals and has recently been invited to be a guest artist with the local symphony orchestra for next year's concert season. Emily has always enjoyed listening to music. When she was only 3 years old, she entertained her relatives by singing along with the radio or television. It was when she was 3 that she began taking piano lessons. Our question is: Why is Emily such an unusual 10 year old? Many 10-year-old girls (and boys) take lessons and play the piano, but why is Emily so much better than most? This sort of question has been at the core of a controversy in psychology that continues unresolved even today—a controversy over the relative importance or impact of one's inheritance (one's nature) and one's experiences and interactions with the environment (one's nurture).

Emily's father never showed much talent for music. He never learned to play an instrument. He can barely carry a tune when he tries to sing, which, mercifully, isn't very often. Emily's mother, on the other hand, is an accomplished musician. When she was a teenager, she earned money by playing the piano in a band. She studied music in college. It seems clear to everyone that Emily inherited her musical abilities from her mother's side of the family. Even her maternal grandmother was known to be quite a musician.

It is very easy, and convenient, in situations such as these to talk about inheriting musical talent, or aggressiveness, or intelligence, or artistic ability, or a host of other traits and characteristics. But we'd better be careful. Just what does it mean to say that Emily inherited her musical ability from her mother? If Emily had a sister, would *she* necessarily be as talented as Emily? Might Emily have turned out to be so musically inclined if she had been reared by foster parents who had neither the interest nor the ability of her biological parents? In such cases, we have to answer, "maybe, maybe not." The issue here is not a simple one. But it is an issue that permeates all of psychology and is of special interest in this topic and this chapter: What are the roles of nature and nurture in development?

From conception through death, all of us as human beings share certain developmental experiences that unite us as one species. As we have already mentioned a number of times, it is also true that each of us is unique and, in our own way, different from everyone else. Developmental psychologists are interested in those experiences that we all have in common and in the ways that we differ as we grow and develop from conception through death.

Our normal sequence of development usually appears to be continuous, slow, and gradual. You probably don't believe that you are much different today than you were yesterday. You probably won't feel significantly changed by tomorrow or the next day either. Though development may appear very slow and gradual to us now, it is not necessarily so throughout our life span. Young children often seem to grow and change on a day-to-day basis. Physically and psychologically, we experience spurts of growth, periods of leveling off, and times of decline. Rates of development change throughout the life's cycle—sometimes fast, sometimes slow. What we will be searching for in this chapter is orderliness, for the patterns and sequences of development common to us all.

We tend to think of a person's development as beginning at birth. In fact, one's patterns and sequences of development begin much earlier—at **conception** and with the first division of one cell into two. This topic focuses on those factors that help mold the human organism before it is born. We'll begin by reviewing the mechanics of heredity. Although we'll make the point that we do not directly inherit behaviors, thoughts, or feelings, it is quite clear that what we do, what we think, and what we feel are influenced by our genetic constitution. We need to appreciate what our genetic constitution *is,* where it comes from, and what it can and cannot do.

conception
the uniting of a father's sperm cell and a mother's ovum

We'll also examine the course of development from conception to birth— the *prenatal period* of development. We'll first summarize the normal sequence of growth and development, and then consider some of the environmental influences that may have an impact on that growth and development. Throughout this topic, and especially in the Topic Expansion, the interaction alluded to in our description of Emily—the interaction between the forces of nature and nurture—will be apparent.

THE MECHANICS OF HEREDITY

Here I sit, all 6′4″ of me. More than 200 pounds of billions upon billions of individual living cells: skin cells, blood cells, nerve cells, bone cells, hair cells, and more. It is very difficult for me to imagine that this mass of interconnected cells that is me was ever just one single cell. But I was. And so were you.

Much of who we are was determined before we were born, when we were each but one cell. That I am a male was determined then. That I am 6′4″ tall and not 4′6″ tall may have been influenced by the fact that I have been well fed and cared for, but it also reflects the fact that my parents and grandparents happened to have been taller than average. Many of the characteristics that affect how we feel, what we think, and how we behave were determined, at least in part, long before we were born. They are the results of the mechanics of heredity.

Chromosomes, Genes, and DNA

Each of the billions of living cells in our bodies has a job to do. It may be to produce long strands of hair (hair cells). It may be to transmit neural impulses (nerve cells). It may be to transport oxygen from the lungs and waste matter to the lungs (blood cells). It may be to form rigid structures that support our weight (bone cells). This list could clearly be a long one. The structure and function of each individual cell in our bodies are under the control of the nucleus of each cell. A cell's **nucleus** is a dense region near its center which is the *master control* for cellular activities (Bennett, 1982). The precise nature of the structure and function of each cell is what is transmitted through heredity from one generation to another. It is within the nucleus of a cell that we find the building blocks of hereditary transmission: the chromosomes, genes, and DNA molecules.

DNA (deoxyribonucleic acid) is a complex protein molecule, the structure of which was first described in 1953 by James D. Watson and Francis Crick. This long chemical molecule is able to unwind, separate, and duplicate itself as two new molecules, thus restructuring the genetic "blueprint," or plan, for each cell's structure and function.

These complex DNA molecules (and parts of DNA molecules) make up **genes.** We think of genes as the basic structures of heredity. It is the genes that carry the genetic code laid down in the DNA molecules. Individual genes are located on very tiny strips of protein called **chromosomes.** Chromosomes (literally meaning *colored bodies*) are carriers of genes. We don't know exactly, but the standard estimate is that each chromosome carries, or holds, more than 1,000 different genes. Each cell of the human body contains, in its nucleus, 23 pairs of chromosomes. (Different kinds of organisms have different numbers of chromosomes; chickens, for example, have 39 pairs of chromosomes in the nucleus of each cell in their bodies.) Figure 17.1 is a picture of what human chromosome pairs look like.

We must keep in mind that genetic information—coded in DNA molecules that make up genes that are arranged on chromosomes—can be found in every single cell of the body. Even a hair cell has the genetic information stored within its nucleus that can be used to create blood cells or nerve cells. Every bit of genetic information received from one's parents is duplicated in

nucleus
the dense area of a cell (near its center) that contains genetic material and acts as master control for the cell's structure and function

DNA (deoxyribonucleic acid)
complex protein molecules that make up genes and that contain the blueprint for genetic transmission

genes
the basic structure of heredity; found on chromosomes

chromosomes
tiny threads of protein, found in pairs in the nucleus of a cell, that carry genes

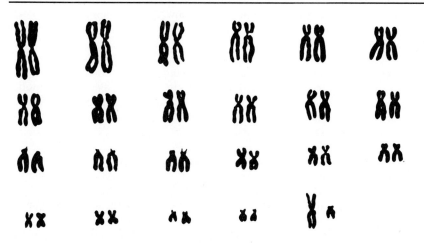

Figure 17.1
Illustrations of human chromosomes arranged in pairs.

the genes found in each and every cell. Now let's summarize how this information gets passed from parents to child.

Before you go on

Define DNA, gene, and chromosome, and indicate the relationship among these three terms.

Genetic Transmission

As we have said, each cell in the human body contains 46 chromosomes arranged in 23 pairs. It is the genetic code found in the genes on these chromosomes, working together in pairs, that determines the structure and function of each cell. As it happens, there is an important exception to this observation. There are cells that contain 23 single chromosomes, not 23 pairs. These are the sex cells: the **ovum** in females and the **sperm** in males.

In their last stage of development, sex cells divide in such a way as to create two new cells, each with half the usual number of chromosomes. The genes found on the 23 chromosomes in the sperm or ovum are an essentially random collection of the genes available.

At the moment of conception, a sperm cell from the father penetrates the membrane of the ovum from the mother, and a new cell is formed, called the **zygote.** The zygote will now have a complete set of 23 pairs of chromosomes and a full complement of genes. Half of the zygote's genes and chromosomes will have come from the mother's ovum and half from the father's sperm. So from each parent, we get a random assortment of half the genes available, and these are then combined at random into 23 new pairs of chromosomes and genes. Within hours, the newly formed zygote divides into two new cells. Each of these two cells contains in its nucleus a complete and accurate copy of each of the genes contributed by each parent to the zygote. Now let's examine some of the implications of this genetic transmission.

Female or Male, XX or XY?   Of our 23 pairs of chromosomes, one pair, usually counted as the 23rd pair, determines our sex. This, too, is a characteristic established at conception. It is basically a simple matter, although complications do arise occasionally.

The chromosomes that determine a person's sex are called the **X and Y chromosomes.** As is usually the case, neither can do much by itself; they have their effect by working in pairs. Being female results from receiving an X chromosome from each parent, forming an XX pair. Being male is determined by having one X chromosome and one Y chromosome, or an XY pair. (See Figure 17.1.)

Females have XX sex chromosome pairs, so each ovum contains one X chromosome. Males have XY sex chromosome pairs, so that half the sperm have an X chromosome and half have a Y chromosome. Because the mother always contributes an X chromosome, and because fathers contribute either an X or a Y, we can say that the sex of a child is determined by the father—or at least by the father's chromosomes.

Dominant and Recessive Genes   To repeat, any inherited characteristic reflects the interaction of at least one pair of genes—one inherited from mother, the other from father.

Now let's consider an example: eye color. Let's agree for the moment to forget all those people we know who have green eyes or gray eyes and pretend that there are only two possibilities: being blue-eyed or brown-eyed.

ovum
the sex cell of the mother that contains 23 single chromosomes

sperm
the sex cell of the father that contains 23 single chromosomes

zygote
the single cell that results from conception; contains 23 chromosomes from the father's sperm and 23 chromosomes from the mother's ovum

X and Y chromosomes
the chromosomes that determine an individual's sex; paired as XX for females and XY for males

Let's further assume that there is but one separate gene for each possibility—one directs the iris of the eye to appear blue, the other directs the iris to appear brown. Whether or not a child ends up with brown eyes or blue eyes will be determined by the genes that she or he gets from her or his parents.

Eye color follows a pattern commonly found with inherited characteristics: the gene determining eye color is a **dominant** gene, and the other is **recessive.** In order to be expressed, the code in recessive genes has to occur in *both* the appropriate genes in a pair. The code in a dominant gene may be expressed if it is paired with a similarly dominant gene *or* with a recessive gene.

Let's see how that works with blue and brown eyes. In this case, genes that produce brown eyes are dominant—we'll call them *B genes.* Genes that produce blue eyes are recessive—we'll call them *b genes.* The child in our example will get one eye-color gene from each parent when the father's sperm cell unites with the mother's ovum at conception. At that moment, eye color is determined.

Now, we need to make one more assumption to go through our example. Let's assume that both mother and father have brown eyes. But, each has brown eyes only because each carries one *B* gene and one *b* gene. Even though each has (or is a carrier of) a blue-eye gene (*b*), each will have brown eyes because brown is the dominant gene and the recessive blue-eye gene does not get expressed. What will be the eye color of a child born to these parents? The answer is that the child's eye color will quite literally be a matter of chance.

Step by step, it works like this. (You may want to follow along in Figure 17.2, which depicts these possibilities schematically.) The child may get one *b* (blue-eye) gene from each parent, and if she has two blue-eye genes working together as a pair, she'll certainly have blue eyes. What if she receives a brown-eye *(B)* gene from *either* parent? Then, it doesn't matter what gene she gets from the other, she'll have brown eyes. If she gets a brown-eye gene from both parents, she'll have brown eyes. If she gets a blue-eye gene from only one parent, she'll still have brown eyes, because the brown-eye gene is dominant and will be expressed over the recessive blue-eye gene. If you work through this example as depicted in Figure 17.2, you'll see that it's not as complicated as it may appear on first reading.

dominant gene
a gene whose characteristics will be expressed regardless of the gene with which it is paired

recessive gene
a gene whose characteristics will be expressed only if it is paired with a similar recessive gene

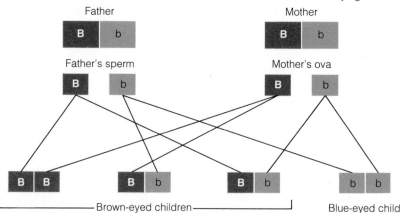

Each parent has brown eyes, but each also carries a recessive blue-eye gene.

Brown-eyed children — **Blue-eyed child**

Figure 17.2
Genetic transmission of dominant/recessive traits. Here, two brown-eyed (B) parents each carry a recessive blue-eye gene (b). Only a child who receives the recessive gene (b) from both parents will, in fact, have blue eyes.

genotype
an individual's characteristics as determined by his or her genes

phenotype
an individual's characteristics as actually expressed

There is an important distinction we need to make here with regard to inherited characteristics. Those traits or characteristics that we inherit from our parents are said to comprise our **genotype.** With eye color, for example, we only know one's genotype for sure if that person has blue eyes. In order to have blue eyes, the person must have two blue-eye genes. The inherited characteristic *as it is expressed,* or as it shows itself, is one's **phenotype.** We may easily determine that someone has brown eyes, and that's their phenotype. But knowing that, we really don't know their genotype for eye color. That brown-eyed person *may* have two brown-eye genes *or* may have one blue-eye gene that is dominated by a paired brown-eye gene. That is, the genotype for a brown-eyed person may be *BB* or *Bb.*

You probably realize that genetic transmission of characteristics is seldom this straightforward. Most physical characteristics are determined by the combined activity of many genes, not just a pairing of two individual genes. Even eye color is seldom a matter of one *B* gene versus one *b* gene fighting for expression in the phenotype. There are a number of genes involved in determining the color of one's eyes. The various combinations of dominant and recessive possibilities give rise to many different shades of blue, brown, green, and gray eyes. More complicated characteristics, such as height and skeletal bone structure, may involve hundreds of genes working together. Remember, there are nearly 1,000 genes on each chromosome—approximately 50,000 genes in each cell. Thus, the number of possible combinations is huge.

Before you go on

What determines the sex of a child?

What are genotype and phenotype, and how are they related to dominant and recessive characteristics?

An Abnormality of Chromosomes: Down's Syndrome

Down's syndrome
a disorder leading to mental retardation that is caused by having three chromosomes, instead of the normal pair, in position 21

Occasionally, the normal transmission of genetic characteristics does not go well. Such is the case in the chromosomal abnormality called **Down's syndrome.** In 1866, Langdon Down first described the collection of symptoms that now carries his name. Down's syndrome individuals can have a number of symptoms, including a slanted fold of skin over their eyes, a small head, a flat nose, a protruding tongue, and almost certainly some degree of mental retardation. Most persons with Down's syndrome have IQs in the 30 to 50 range, where 100 is average, and 70 usually defines mental retardation (MacMillan, 1982).

In the late 1950s, it was discovered that the cause of Down's syndrome—long suspected to be genetic—was a chromosome abnormality. Whereas most people have 46 chromosomes arranged in 23 pairs, individuals with Down's syndrome have 47 chromosomes. Chromosome pair number 21 has three chromosomes, rather than the normal two.

In many cases, Down's syndrome seems to be associated with some subtle change in the chromosomes in the ovum before conception occurs. Apparently, as the age of the mother increases, the ovum deteriorates slightly, and an extra chromosome remains in position 21. Support for this line of reasoning comes from the observation that Down's syndrome seems to be related to the mother's age at conception. There is an increasing probability of Down's syndrome with the increasing age of the mother (Apgar & Beck, 1974; Smith & Berg, 1976).

The deterioration of the ovum may be due to factors other than simply age alone. The ovum is influenced by many environmental factors, such as X-rays

Infant-stim programs train parents to provide extra stimulation—visual, auditory, and physical—for their Down's syndrome child. This extra stimulation often leads to higher IQ scores in Down's children.

and viral infections that may cause the chromosome abnormality that results in Down's syndrome (Clarke-Stewart et al., 1985, p. 60). Furthermore, some malformation or malfunction of the father's sperm cell has been implicated in about one fourth of Down's syndrome cases (Abroms & Bennett, 1981; Magenis et al., 1977; Stene et al., 1981). As with the mother, the age of the father is a significant predictor of Down's syndrome probabilities.

Fifty years ago it was thought that the symptoms of Down's syndrome were irreversible and that little could be done to improve the quality of life of people with the disorder. We have since learned that not all intellectual abilities are necessarily affected by Down's syndrome. What are most affected are language and verbal skills, but other intellectual abilities may be nurtured by a helpful, stimulating environment. Indeed, an intensive program of infant stimulation, called *infant-stim,* has been shown to produce significant improvements in overall IQ scores (Pines, 1982). Infant-stim programs require a lot of effort, usually by parents and usually at home. Parents are trained in methods of providing extra experiences of stimulation—visual, auditory, and physical—to their Down's syndrome child. Training is often provided by instructors at local associations for retarded citizens. This intense stimulation reportedly raises IQs an average of 15 points.

Infant-stim programs are not without their critics. The programs are time consuming and expensive, and positive results are not always found. But at least there is the hope that increasing environmental stimulation early in infancy can help offset the severity of the intellectual deficit caused by the chromosomal abnormality we call Down's syndrome.

Before you go on

What is Down's syndrome, and what causes it?

PRENATAL DEVELOPMENT: INFLUENCES BEFORE BIRTH

Human development begins at conception, when the father's sperm cell unites with the mother's ovum. At that time, the 23 chromosomes from each parent pair off within a single cell, the zygote. Within the next 30 hours or so, that one cell will divide and become two. In 3 days, there will be approximately 10–15 cells; after 5 days, there will be slightly more than 100 (Moore, 1982; Torrey & Feduccia, 1979). No one knows how many cells the average human organism has at birth, and few are willing to even hazard a guess; to say "more than a trillion" cells is probably a conservative estimate (Moore, 1982).

The period from conception to birth is called the **prenatal period** of development. Until recently, this period of human development received only minor attention from psychologists. We now recognize that many of the factors that may determine life-long patterns of development have their effect during this very sensitive period. In this section, we'll review briefly the physical development of the organism during the prenatal period, and we'll look at some of the environmental, or external, factors that might have an impact on that development.

Physical Aspects of Prenatal Development

Prenatal development is usually divided into three different stages: the stage of the zygote, the stage of the embryo, and the stage of the fetus. These stages are not all of the same length, and each is characterized by its own landmarks of development.

The **stage of the zygote** is by far the shortest of the three prenatal stages of development, lasting from conception to a time approximately 2 weeks later when the zygote becomes implanted in the wall of the uterus. The female's ovum is generally fertilized as it moves along the fallopian tubes from the ovaries where ova (the plural of ovum) are stored and released, one at a time, at approximately 28-day intervals. It typically takes the zygote about 7 days to travel down the fallopian tube to the uterus and another 7 days to become firmly attached there (see Figure 17.3). At this point, the zygote has grown to include hundreds of cells, and, for the first time, it is clear that all the cells are not exact replicas of each other. That is, there is now clearly some differentiation among the cells in the zygote. Some of the cells, for example, de-

prenatal period
the period of development from conception to birth

stage of the zygote
in prenatal development, the period from conception through the first 2 weeks

Figure 17.3
A diagram of the female reproductive organs, indicating where fertilization and implantation take place.

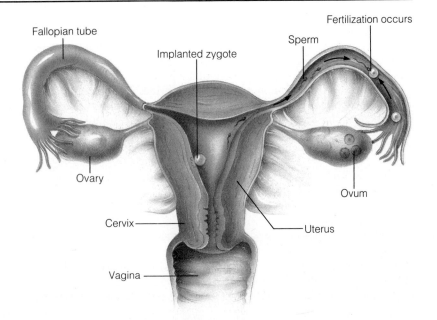

Fallopian tube
Fertilization occurs
Sperm
Implanted zygote
Ovary
Ovum
Cervix
Uterus
Vagina

Figure 17.4

A representation of prenatal development, indicating the most critical periods in which defects are likely to occur, and which aspect of the developing organism is likely to be affected.
(After Moore, 1982.)

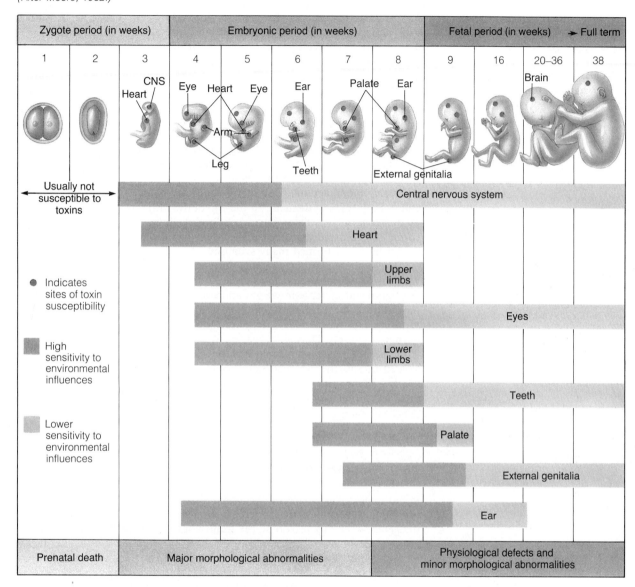

velop to form the protective placenta, while others form the umbilical cord that will ultimately supply nourishment to the developing organism.

Once implantation is complete, we say that the stage of the zygote is over, and we have entered the **stage of the embryo.** The embryonic stage lasts about 6 weeks, from week 2 to week 8. During this period, the embryo, as it is now called, develops at a tremendous rate. At the beginning of this stage, we can differentiate three types of cells: those that will become the nervous system, sense organs, and skin; those that will form the internal organs; and those that will become the muscles, skeleton, and blood vessels. By the end of this stage, we can clearly identify the face area, eyes, ears, fingers, and toes. That is, not only does the number of cells increase, but the types of cells present also increase.

stage of the embryo
in prenatal development, the period from 2 weeks to 8 weeks following conception

In many ways, this is the most critical stage of prenatal development. It is during this stage—or more conservatively, within the first 3 months—that the unborn organism is most sensitive to external or environmental influences. It seems that if there are going to be any problems, any birth defects, for example, they are most likely to develop during this stage. If heart, hands, eyes, and ears do not become differentiated and develop during this period, there is no way to compensate later (see Figure 17.4).

Two months after conception, the stage of the embryo draws to a close. The 1-inch-long embryo now has enough of a primitive nervous system to respond to a light touch with a simple reflex movement.

stage of the fetus
in prenatal development, the period from 2 months after conception until birth

The final stage of prenatal development is also the longest, the **stage of the fetus.** (See Figure 17.5.) This period includes months 3 through 9. Not only do the organs of the body continue to grow in size and complexity, but they begin to function. The arms and legs move spontaneously by the end of the third month. In two more months, these movements will be substantial enough for the mother to feel them.

During months 4 and 5, so many significant changes take place it's difficult to keep track of them all. At the end of the fifth month, the fetus is a full 10 inches long. Internal organs have developed, but not to the point of sustaining life outside the uterus. The brain has developed, but the neurons within have not formed many synapses.

Development continues rapidly during the last few months of pregnancy. The most noticeable change—certainly most noticeable to the mother—is the significant increase in weight and overall movement of the fetus. Sometime during the seventh month, most fetuses have reached the point of **viability.** This means that if they were forced to do so, they could survive if born prematurely. During its last few weeks in the uterus, the growth of the fetus slows. Its movements may be more powerful, but overall activity is also slowed due to the cramped quarters in which the fetus finds itself. After nearly 270 days, the fetus is ready to enter the world as a newborn. Development from that point on we leave to the next two topics.

viability
the point at which a fetus can survive outside the uterus, usually in the seventh month

Before you go on
Briefly summarize the three stages of prenatal development.

Environmental Influences on Prenatal Development

In most cases, the progressive growth and development of the human organism from zygote to embryo to fetus occurs strictly according to the plans of the genes—heredity providing the framework for prenatal development. As prenatal development takes place, the human organism is not immune to environmental influences, however. This is a reasonably new conclusion. "Until the early 1940s, it was generally accepted that human embryos were protected from environmental agents by their fetal membranes and their mother's abdominal walls and uterus" (Moore, 1982, p. 140). It was then discovered that birth defects often resulted when a pregnant woman contracted rubella (or German measles). Twenty years later, it became well established that many drugs taken by a pregnant woman ultimately had an effect on the development of the embryo and fetus. It has by now become common knowledge that during the very rapid period of prenatal development, even small environmental disturbances may have serious and lasting consequences. The prenatal human does not live in a vacuum after all, but in a uterine environment, tied through its umbilical cord to its mother. Most of the environmental influences on prenatal development that we know about are those that tend to be negative. Let's review a few.

Figure 17.5

A representation of the growth and development of the human fetus during the fetal stage. The illustrations here are about one half the actual size.
(After Moore, 1982.)

The Fetal Period

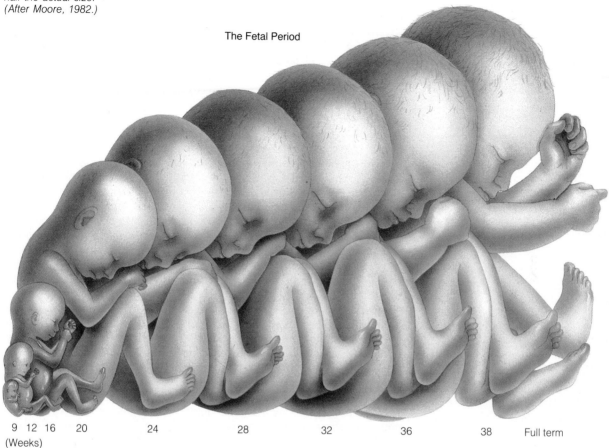

9 12 16   20   24   28   32   36   38   Full term
(Weeks)

Nourishment   Never meant to be taken literally, the old expression "You are what you eat" does have some truth to it. Before we are born, we are what our mothers eat. When pregnant women eat poorly, their unborn children may share in the consequences. Extreme cases of maternal malnutrition lead to increases in miscarriage, stillbirth, and premature births. At best, the newborn child of a malnourished mother can be expected to be similarly malnourished.

It is also the case that deficiencies in specific vitamins and minerals may also affect the prenatal organism. For example, calcium deficiencies affect the development of bones and teeth in the fetus. But, as is the case for many nutrients, it may very well be the mother who suffers most. That is, if there are inadequate supplies of calcium in the mother's system, "the fetal need for calcium will be met at the expense of the mother" (Hughes & Noppe, 1985, p. 140). So it may be the mother who suffers from a calcium deficiency more directly than her unborn fetus.

We shouldn't overinterpret the data here. Although the correlation between the diet of the mother and the health of her unborn child is well established, severe complications tend to develop only in extreme cases of malnourishment. It is advisable, however, to attend very carefully to what one eats during pregnancy, and to maintain a well-balanced, nutritious diet.

Drugs and Chemicals As evidence accumulates that smoking has adverse effects on the smoker, so is evidence accumulating that smoking by pregnant women has adverse effects on their unborn children. Exactly *how* smoking affects the fetus is not known for certain. It may simply be a matter of reducing the oxygen supply being passed on to the fetus. It may be that the tar and nicotine of the smoke act directly as poisons, or toxins. What we do know is that cigarette smoking is well-established as a cause for retarded prenatal growth (Globus, 1980); mothers who smoke a pack a day or more double the chances of having a low-weight baby. Furthermore, smoking mothers have many more miscarriages, stillbirths, and babies who die soon after birth than do mothers who do not smoke (Frazier et al., 1961).

As we indicated earlier, alcohol is perhaps the most commonly abused of all drugs. It is a drug that is certainly injurious to unborn children. Alcohol is quickly and directly passed through the umbilical cord from the drinking mother to the fetus. The effects are often stunning. In one study, women in their 37th to 39th weeks of pregnancy were given a drink of vodka. Within 3 to 30 minutes after the alcohol was ingested, the fetus stopped breathing, many for more than half an hour. Breathing began again only as the alcohol level in the mother's bloodstream began to drop (Fox et al., 1978, cited in Clarke-Stewart et al., 1985).

Heavy drinking (3 ounces or more per day) significantly increases the probability of having smaller babies and babies with retarded physical growth, intellectual retardation, and a host of other problems, collectively referred to as **fetal alcohol syndrome** (Jones et al., 1973). In the mid-1970s, it was believed that an occasional social drink or two had no particular effect on prenatal development. Now, the best advice seems to be total abstinence (Abel, 1981).

Some drugs taken by a mother during her pregnancy seem to have no noticeable effect on the developing child—penicillin, for example (Golbus, 1980). Others may have predictable effects—the antibiotic tetracycline, for example, passes through to the developing fetus and is deposited in the teeth and bones, coloring them yellow. Other drugs may have devastating effects. One of the best examples is the drug thalidomide, routinely prescribed in Europe in the early 1960s as a mild tranquilizer and treatment for morning sickness nausea. Thalidomide children, as they are called, developed shortened, malformed limbs, or no limbs at all, and very often were mentally retarded.

Also in the 1950s and 1960s, many women who had problems during earlier pregnancies were given DES (diethylstilbestrol) to reduce the likelihood of miscarriage. This synthetic hormone is now believed to be related to the development of cervical cancer in the *daughters* of women who took the drug years earlier. The bottom-line advice again seems quite clear: Pregnant women should use drugs of any sort only with great care and only after consultation with their physicians.

Maternal Stress There is a certain logic (and many old wives' tales) that suggests that a mother's emotional health will affect her unborn baby. There is even some logic to the physiology of the argument. As we will see, emotionality is accompanied by hormonal changes, and these hormonal changes may have some influence on the development of the embryo or fetus. It is also the case that when a pregnant mother is under stress, the blood flow in her body is, for a short while at least, diverted from the uterus to other

fetal alcohol syndrome
a collection of symptoms reflecting retardation of intellectual and physical development caused by a mother's ingestion of alcohol during pregnancy

organs in the body, reducing the amount of oxygen available to the prenatal organism (Stechler & Halton, 1982).

We have to remember, too, that stress during pregnancy is a two-way street. Being pregnant in and of itself is often quite stressful. That is, we may tentatively conclude that there is some support for the notion that stress leads to prenatal complications, but we should also follow the advice of Hughes and Noppe: "However, remember that a relationship between maternal stress and birth complications, infant irritability, and so forth does not demonstrate that stress actually causes pregnancy problems. In fact, stress may be the result rather than the cause of such difficulties. Perhaps a woman is more likely to be stressed if she is carrying a very active fetus or if she is experiencing a particularly difficult pregnancy. In any case, there is no link at all between minor everyday stress and the condition of the fetus" (1985, p. 141).

Before you go on

Briefly review the impact of diet, drugs, and stress on prenatal development.

Inherited characteristics are coded in the DNA molecules that make up the genes that are carried on chromosomes. Every cell of the human body contains, in its nucleus, 23 pairs of such chromosomes that provide the blueprint for growth and development. This genetic blueprint is provided at conception as the father's sperm unites with the mother's ovum to form a zygote. For the next 9 months (approximately 270 days), the human organism grows and develops in its mother's uterus. This period of development is called the prenatal period and has three stages: zygote, embryo, and fetus. During the prenatal period, the organism is subject to a number of environmental influences that may markedly affect the developmental process.

Long before scientists understood the intricacies of DNA molecules, psychologists had been debating the importance of heredity (nature) versus environment (nurture). In fact, the debate had begun long before psychology became established as an independent science.

Are we a direct reflection of our genes, our biology, unfolding according to the plans coded in DNA? Or, are we molded and shaped by our experiences and our interactions with our environments? How much of what we are as human beings is determined by heredity, and how much by environment? Are we the product of our natures or our nurtures?

These are very complex questions, and we cannot settle the matter here once and for all. But we can raise some issues for you to think about, particularly as we deal with developmental psychology. These issues have come up before, in perception and learning, and will come up again when we discuss intelligence, personality, and some social behaviors.

One point needs to be made clear: We do not inherit behaviors. We do not inherit skills, talents, or aptitudes—at least not in any literal sense. What we inherit are chromosomes, genes, and complex chemical molecules. Inherited packages of genetic information may guide and direct the physical development of our bodies, and may do so in very complex ways, but we do not inherit behaviors directly.

Remember Emily from our opening story? She was described as a talented 10-year-old musician who had inherited her musical talent from her mother. In what sense might this be true? What Emily may have inherited were genes that directed the development of her hearing in such a way that she can readily distinguish differences in pitch and tone. She may have inherited genes that ultimately led to the development of a skeletal and muscular system that allow for the rapid, fluid movement of her fingers on the piano keyboard. She may have inherited the genes that directed her brain to develop fully and richly in those areas that are involved in the making of music. Given those genes, what was then required was an environment to put those physical characteristics to good use. Without training, practice, encouragement, examples to imitate, and opportunities to perform, Emily's inherited characteristics might never have been realized.

Currently, most psychologists emphasize the *interaction* of inherited predispositions (possibilities for development) with environmental influences in development. The issue is no longer thought of as a matter of nature *versus* nurture. It no longer seems useful to ask *which* determines a given behavior.

How much of what we are is determined by heredity and how much by our environments? Though we may inherit a tendency to be artistic, this tendency must be nurtured for us to develop artistic talent.

The basic predisposition for intelligence may be inborn, but our childhood environments greatly influence how quickly and easily we learn many basic skills, such as reading.

It doesn't even make much sense to ask about relative influence, as in "Which is more important?" or "What percentage of a given ability is inherited, and what percentage is learned?" They are both important. What matters is how they interact.

Some psychologists suggest that inheritance places certain limits on development. They argue that what we inherit are predispositions to develop in certain ways. For example, a child may inherit the genes that predispose her or him to be quite tall. If that child is not fed properly or develops some serious illness, she or he may never grow to the height that her or his genes allowed. The child may still be taller than average, but not as tall as possible, if the environment does not sustain the potential.

This same argument can be made for more complex psychological processes, such as intelligence. We are not born with our memories filled with information and problem-solving skills. We do not automati-cally become smart just because our parents are. But some children may inherit the capacity, or predisposition, to learn and develop those traits that we associate with intelligence.

There is no denying that many complex psychological functions have a genetic basis. Many traits do run in families. Many of the similarities between identical twins, who have the same collection of genes, are much greater than can be attributed to their similar environments alone. IQ scores of adopted children are better correlated with the IQs of their biological parents than with the IQs of their adoptive parents. Children of schizophrenic parents are more likely to become schizophrenic than are children of nonschizophrenic parents. Levels of emotionality appear to have a genetic basis, too. There are many such examples, and we shall encounter this issue periodically throughout the rest of this book.

TOPIC SUMMARY

Define DNA, gene, and chromosome, and indicate the relationship among these three terms.

DNA (deoxyribonucleic acid) is a complex protein molecule that contains the genetic code of one's heredity. Such molecules make up genes, the basic units of heredity, that are found on tiny ribbons of protein called chromosomes. Chromosomes, and the genes they carry, are found in 23 pairs in the nucleus of each cell of the human body. / 304

What determines the sex of a child?

What are genotype and phenotype, and how are they related to dominant and recessive characteristics?

One's sex is determined at conception by the 23rd pair of chromosomes. Females carry XX pairs, while males carry XY pairs. Hence, a child receives an X chromosome from its mother and either an X or a Y chromosome from its father. One's genotype is one's genetic make-up; here, we may find recessive genes not expressed in an observable trait or characteristic. One's phenotype is one's inherited characteristic as expressed. That is, a person may have a genotype that includes a dominant and a recessive gene (for eye color, for example). The phenotype, however, will only show the coloration that is dominant. / 306

What is Down's syndrome, and what causes it?

Down's syndrome is the name given to a collection of symptoms associated with a chromosomal abnormality. Down's syndrome individuals generally have a small head, flat nose, and almost certainly some degree of intellectual retardation. The syndrome is caused when chromosome pair number 21 contains three chromosomes instead of the normal two. Why this should happen is as yet unknown for sure, but there is a correlation between the likelihood of having a Down's syndrome child and the age of the parents at conception. / 307

Briefly summarize the three stages of prenatal development.

Prenatal development begins at conception and ends at birth. This period is generally divided into three stages: the stage of the zygote (conception to 2 weeks), at which time the zygote becomes implanted in the uterus; the stage of the embryo (week 2 to week 8), during which there is rapid growth and differentiation of developing cells; and the stage of the fetus (month 3 until birth), during which the organs begin to function. / 310

Briefly review the impact of diet, drugs, and stress on prenatal development.

There is little doubt any longer that a mother's diet and the use of drugs have potentially profound effects on prenatal development. A mother's generalized malnutrition, or deficiencies of specific vitamins and minerals, is usually shared by the embryo or fetus. Smoking and alcohol use during pregnancy have well-documented negative effects. The rule of thumb is typically to avoid drugs of any sort unless prescribed by a physician. Research on the effects of maternal stress on prenatal development has not produced clear-cut results. Severe, chronic stress may (at least indirectly) have negative consequences. We need to remember that stress during pregnancy may very well be caused by the pregnancy itself. / 313

TOPIC

In 1966, Doris Entwistle of Johns Hopkins University published a major study entitled *Word Associations of Young Children*. In her book, Entwistle claimed that very young children produce word association responses of a different sort than do older children or adults. Intrigued by her findings, I decided to do an experiment of my own that involved measuring how long it took children of different ages to produce word associations. The procedure was a simple one: Present a stimulus word, have the child respond with the first thing that comes to mind, and time how long it takes for him or her to respond.

Having secured the cooperation of a number of nursery schools in the area, two undergraduate research assistants went off to collect data. I couldn't go with them on the first day because I had a class to teach. When I met the assistants upon their return, they were frustrated and upset, and one was on the verge of tears. When I asked how everything had gone, she responded, "It was awful! The darn kids wouldn't do it! It was just a mess." I became very paternalistic and reassured the assistants, "Now, now, don't worry. Dr. Gerow will go with you tomorrow and everything will be all right." It wasn't. My assistants were right. To a large degree, the darned kids wouldn't do it.

I approached a 4-year-old with a proposition: "Hi. How are you? Let's play a game, okay? Let's play a game with words. Do you want to play a game with words?" My first result was that 8 percent of the children simply didn't want to play. They just walked away and went back to their sandbox or some other activity. When children did agree to play, they did some most peculiar things. I'd give my simple instructions: "I'm going to say a word, and then you tell me the first word that my word makes you think of. Okay? My first word is *black*." After a moment's pause, my first subject responded, "My Mommy has a black dress and she wears it to church sometimes."

"Okay, that's fine," I'd say, "but next time only tell me *one word*. Don't tell me a story. For example, you could just say 'dress' if that's what *black* makes you think of. Okay?" I gave the next word on the list. "My next word is *happy*." "Dress," the child quickly responded. "No, no, you have to tell me what *happy* makes you think of." "Oh, I'm happy when we have ice cream for dessert."

Some children demonstrated that they were learning how to spell. "What's the first thing you think of when I say *black*?" The response: "bee." To "man," the response was "em," and so on. Some children responded with sounds I didn't even know how to record: In response to "black," one child responded "b-b-b-b." To "happy," the response was "hap-hap-hap."

I eventually included more than 300 children in this research, just to see how children *would* respond to my little "word game." In fact, most of the responses produced by the children were nonword responses. With the word association procedure, we have one of the easiest, most straightforward techniques in all of psychology. But "playing the game" is a task that some children may do with their own set of rules, and others may simply not be ready to play such a game. The point of all this is that doing even simple experiments with young children is often not as simple as it may sound. If children do not understand the instructions of the experimenters, or if they bring their own sets of beliefs to the task, the results may be misleading at best. To scientifically study the behaviors of young children often requires that we be particularly clever or very patient. Experiments may not work, and other research methods, such as naturalistic observation, may be all we can use.

Why We Care

To their parents, children are a source of great joy and considerable aggravation. Quiet, peaceful angels one minute, noisy screamers demanding attention the next. Children are a source of joy and aggravation to psychologists as well. They are living laboratories, changing from week to week and even from day to day. Sometimes children seem to change by the hour.

The psychology of child development is particularly important when we realize how many traits, ideas, attitudes, and habits are formed in this period that remain with us well into adulthood.

In this topic, we'll consider some of the major landmarks in the development of children. We'll summarize physical-motor, sensory-perceptual, and cognitive-social development. In each case, we'll focus attention first on the capabilities of the newborn child before tracing further development through childhood. Even though we will be looking at these three areas of development separately, it is important to remember that the divisions are really very artificial—each area of development is continually interacting with and influencing the others.

PHYSICAL AND MOTOR DEVELOPMENT

Before we address the psychological development of children, let's briefly review patterns of their physical and motor development. In this section, we'll focus on the physical growth of the child and note the orderly sequence of the development of their motor responses—their abilities to do things with their bodies. We'll begin by considering some of the abilities of the newborn infant, or the neonate.

The Neonate

As recently as 20 years ago, textbooks on child psychology seldom devoted more than a few paragraphs to the behaviors of the **neonate**—the newborn through the first 2 weeks of life. It seemed as if the neonate did not do much worth writing about. Today, most child psychology texts devote substantially more space to discussing the abilities of newborns. It is unlikely that over the past 20 years neonates have gotten smarter or more able. Rather, psychologists have. They have devised new and clever ways of measuring the abilities and capacities of neonates.

When a baby is first born, it appears that it just can't do a thing. Oh, it can cry, and it can dirty a diaper, but it seems that mostly it just sleeps. In fact, most newborns *do* sleep a lot, about 15–17 hours each day. As parents are quick to discover, that sleep tends to occur in a series of short naps, seldom lasting more than a few hours at a time.

A careful examination of babies, however, reveals that they are capable of a wide range of behaviors. Almost all of these behaviors are reflexive—simple, unlearned, involuntary reactions to specific stimuli. Many of the neonate's reflexive responses serve a useful purpose; they help to respond to a basic need. Some do not seem to have any particular survival value, but even these are very important to know about because they can be used as a measure of the adequacy of the neonate's development.

Blinking is a reflex present at birth. Suddenly closing both eyes at the presentation of a bright light serves to protect the delicate light-sensitive cells in the retinas. The blinking reflex is one that remains with us for the rest of

neonate
the newborn child, from birth through the first 2 weeks

The rooting reflex helps newborns locate sources of nourishment, whether at their mothers' breasts or from bottles.

our lives. Most other reflexes that we can observe in newborn babies eventually disappear, to be replaced later with more voluntary reactions. Let's discuss a few.

The **rooting reflex** causes the baby to turn toward a light touch on its cheek. The neonate's mouth opens and attempts at sucking motions are made (sucking responses are also reflexive in newborns). For a hungry newborn, this rooting reflex is very handy because it helps him or her find mother's breast or a bottle. In about 3 or 4 months, a light touch on the cheek no longer produces the rooting reflex, but by then it is no longer needed; the infant will have learned how to locate the source of its nourishment.

The grasping reflex is another reflexive behavior that disappears after 3 or 4 months, to return yet another month later as a voluntary behavior. If you press your index finger against a neonate's palm, the baby will quickly grasp it. The grasp of a newborn is quite impressive in its strength. You can usually lift a newborn with your fingers if it has grasped them tightly. If this reflex is not present within a few days after birth, we may suspect some developmental delay or difficulty.

Another reflex that is quite noticeable during the first 2 weeks of life is the walking/stepping reflex. It is produced by holding a baby above a flat surface so that its feet just touch. The baby raises its legs and feet alternately, as if he or she were walking without going anyplace. This stepping reflex also disappears after 3 or 4 months, to be replaced later (at about 1 year) with voluntary walking movements. (There is some evidence that if this reflex is exercised early, the practice may have small, but lasting effects in that voluntary walking responses may be made sooner than otherwise expected (Bower, 1976).)

The **Moro reflex** is produced by a sudden noise or a sudden loss of support. The neonate's fingers separate and the arms are thrust out to the sides and then quickly brought back to the chest, now with fists clenched. Whereas the usefulness of a rooting or sucking reflex or even a grasping reflex seems quite clear, other reflexes do not appear to be so useful. What is the purpose of the Moro reflex? We simply do not know, although we may speculate that it is in some way related to a clinging response commonly found among nonhuman primates. This reflex also disappears after 4 or 5 months. Although it may have no known purpose, the Moro reflex is one of the most diagnostically significant of the neonate's reflexes. Failure to exhibit a strong Moro reflex is often (but not always) associated with some central nervous system disturbance.

In all, there are more than a dozen reflexes that can be observed and measured (for strength and duration, for example) in the newborn child. Although only some of them serve the purpose of meeting the newborn's needs at the time, all can be used as diagnostic indicators of the quality of the neonate's development.

rooting reflex
the neonatal reflex in which a child turns toward a light touch on its cheek and then makes sucking motions

moro reflex
the neonatal reflex, which is caused by a sudden noise or loss of support, in which a child thrusts its arms out to the sides with fingers open, only to quickly return the arms to the chest with fists clenched

Before you go on

What are some of the reflexes that can be observed in neonates?

Why do we care about neonatal reflexes?

The Motor Development of Children

Parents trying to keep their young children in properly fitting clothes know very well how quickly children can grow. In their first 3 years, children will increase in height and weight at a rate never again equaled. Although their changes in size and motor skills are rapid, such changes tend to be orderly and well sequenced, following a prescribed pattern. It is with that pattern that we are concerned here.

As we have said repeatedly, one of psychology's most reliable observations is that individuals differ. No two children are alike. No two children can be expected to grow at exactly the same rate or to develop control over their bodies at the same time. Joanne may walk unaided at the age of 10 months. Bill may not venture forth on his own until he's 13 months old. Differences between children are often as great as their similarities. And those children who happen to develop more slowly might benefit from having their parents appreciate the notion of individual differences in developmental rates.

Regardless of the *rate* of one's motor development, there are regularities in the *sequence* of one's development. No matter when Joanne does walk, she will first sit, then crawl. It's an old adage, and it's true: We have to stand before we walk and walk before we run.

A summary of the development of common motor skills is presented in Figure 18.1. There are two important things for you to notice about this Figure: (1) The sequence of events is very regular, and (2) *when* each stage develops includes a wide range of ages that should be considered normal. It is also true that the sequence and timing of the events listed in this Figure hold equally for males and females. That is, in these basic motor skills, there are no significant sex differences. Figure 18.2 reflects some of the motor skills that can be found among school-aged children and notes sex differences when they are present.

No two children grow and develop at the same rate. This 8 month old is learning to walk, but other babies might not develop this motor skill until 14 or 15 months.

Before you go on

Briefly summarize some of the landmarks of early motor development.

Figure 18.1

The increasing mobility of a child is illustrated in this time-sequence chart. As the child increases in age, so does he or she increase in strength and mobility. Though merely able to hold its head up at 2 months, the child can usually walk by 12 months.

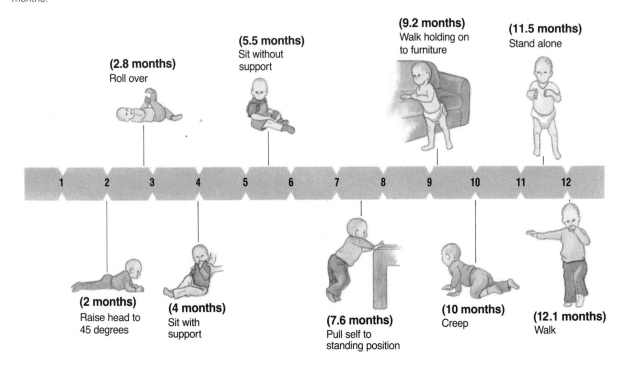

Figure 18.2

Typical behaviors found in school children. Note the orderly progression, but now some gender differences are apparent. (Based on Cratty, 1970.)

Age	Selected behaviors
6 years	Girls superior in movement accuracy; boys superior in forceful, less complex acts. Skipping acquired. Throwing with proper weight shift and step.
7 years	One-footed balancing without vision becomes possible. Can walk 2 in. balance beams. Can hop and jump accurately into small squares. Can execute accurate jumping-jack exercise.
8 years	12 lb. pressure on grip strength by both sexes. The number of games participated in by both sexes is greatest at this age. Can engage in alternate rhythmical hopping in 2–2, 2–3, 3–3 pattern.
9 years	Girls can throw a small ball 40 ft. Girls can vertical jump 8-1/2 in. and boys 10 in. over their standing height-plus-reach. Boys can run 16½ ft. per second.
10 years	Boys can throw a small ball 70 ft. Can judge and intercept pathways of small balls thrown from a distance. Girls can run 17 ft. per second.
11 years	Standing broad jump of 5 ft. possible for boys. 6 in. less for girls.
12 years	Standing high jump of 3 ft. possible.

SENSORY AND PERCEPTUAL DEVELOPMENT

One of the reasons psychologists used to think that newborn children couldn't do much was that it was commonly believed that newborns could not sense or perceive much. We now understand that neonates can and do respond to a wide range of stimuli in their environments.

Their ability to detect even small subtle changes in the world around them is quite remarkable. However, there *are* limitations. The ability of the eyes to focus on an object, for example, does not develop fully until the child is about 4 months old. Neonates can focus well on objects held at about their arms' length, but everything nearer or farther appears blurred or out of focus.

For their first few weeks, babies have difficulty coordinating the movements of their eyes, although within hours after birth they can follow (track) a stimulus object that is swung slowly back and forth in front of them. Newborns can detect differences in brightness, and soon develop the ability to detect edges or borders and to differentiate among colors (Cohen, DeLoache, & Strauss, 1978).

An issue that has been of considerable interest to psychologists is just when the perception of depth and distance develops. Apparently, even newborns have some simple reflexive reactions to depth. They will close their eyes and squirm away if you rush some object, such as your hand, toward their face. Like so many other reflexes, however, this one too seems to disappear in a few months.

In the late 1950s, two Cornell University psychologists, Eleanor Gibson and Richard Walk (1960) constructed an apparatus to test the depth perception of very young children. The *visual cliff,* as it is called, is a deep box, covered by a sheet of thick, clear plexiglass. It is divided into two sides, one shallow, one deep. The deep and shallow sides are separated by a center board (see Figure 18.3).

Gibson and Walk discovered that 6-month-old children would not leave the center board to venture out over the deep side of the box, even to get to their mothers. By crawling age, then, the child seems able to perceive depth *and* judge it to be dangerous.

But, neonates obviously cannot crawl. When they are placed on the plexiglass over the deep side of the visual cliff, their heart rate decreases, indicating that at least they notice the change in visual stimulation (Campos, Langer, & Krowitz, 1970). When 9-month-old infants are placed over the deep side of the visual cliff, their heart rates *increase*. This increase in heart rate is believed to indicate fear, a response that develops after the ability to discriminate depth (Campos, 1976). So it seems that in some rudimentary form even a neonate may sense depth, but knowing how to react appropriately to depth may require experience and learning that come later.

What about the other senses: hearing, smell, taste, and so on? Newborn infants can hear very well. They can certainly direct their attention to the source of a sound—even a faint sound. Sounds probably don't *mean* much to neonates, but they can respond differently to sounds of different pitch and loudness. Even 3-day-old newborns are able to discriminate the sound of their mother's voice from other sounds (DeCasper & Fifer, 1980).

Newborns can also respond to differences in taste and smell. They clearly discriminate among the four basic taste qualities of salt, sweet, bitter, and sour. They even display a distinct preference for sweet-tasting liquids. Although they are unable to use the ability then, the sense of smell seems to be established before birth. Right after birth neonates respond predictably—drawing away and wrinkling their noses—to a variety of strong odors.

In summary, a wide range of sensory and perceptual capabilities appears to be available to the newborn child. The neonate may require some time to

Figure 18.3
The visual cliff was designed to determine if depth perception is innate or learned. By the time they can move about, most infants will avoid the "deep" side of the apparatus. There does seem to be an innate ability to sense depth, but the ability to react to it apparently needs to be learned.

learn what to do with sensory information that it acquires from its environment, but many of its senses are operational. The newborn can see, hear, smell, and taste, and has developed a sense of touch. What the newborn makes of the sensations it receives will depend upon the development of its mental or cognitive abilities, and it is to this subject that we now turn.

Before you go on
Summarize the basic sensory capacities of the neonate.

COGNITIVE AND SOCIAL DEVELOPMENT

In preceding topics, we have had occasion to refer to cognitive skills and abilities many times. Cognitive skills are those that enable us to know and understand ourselves and the world around us. In this section, we'll summarize how these skills develop throughout childhood; we'll begin with a summary of the cognitive capacities of the newborn infant. We'll focus on the theory of Jean Piaget. We'll also consider the theory of Erik Erikson, whose approach to development is as much social as it is cognitive.

The Cognitive Abilities of the Neonate

As we have seen, reflex reactions can help neonates survive. For long-term survival, however, neonates must learn to adapt to their environments, and profit from experience. Neonates will have to begin forming memories of their experiences and learn to make discriminations among the many stimuli with which they are presented. Are any of these cognitive processes possible in a baby just a couple of weeks old? In a number of specific ways, the answer seems to be yes.

Friedman (1972) reported a demonstration of what we might call memory in neonates only 1 to 4 *days* old. Babies were shown a picture of a simple figure, say a checkerboard pattern, for 60 seconds. Experimenters recorded how long the baby looked at the stimulus pattern. After the same pattern was shown over and over, the baby appeared to be bored with it, and gave the pattern less of its attention. When a different stimulus pattern was introduced, the baby stared at it for almost the full 60 seconds of its exposure.

So what does this have to do with memory? The argument is that for the young neonate to stare at the new stimulus, it must have formed some memory of the old one. Otherwise, how would it recognize the new pattern as being new or different? In fact, if the new stimulus pattern was very similar to the old one, the baby would not give it as much attention as it would if it were totally different. It is as if a judgment were being made about the distinctiveness of the new stimulus and the old (remembered) ones.

In talking about recognizing visual patterns, we should mention the research of Robert Fantz (1961, 1963). Fantz presented newborn children with pairs of visual stimuli. In most pairs, one stimulus was more complex than the other. As the babies lay on their backs, looking up at the stimuli, the experimenters could note which one of the two stimuli received the most attention from the child. In almost every case, a preference was shown for the more complex stimulus pattern.

This in itself is interesting—and not easy to explain. The major finding of these studies is that the babies could at least discriminate between the two stimuli. That attention equals preference is more of an assumption than a research finding. Fantz also discovered something curious when he found that even newborn infants showed a distinct preference for (chose to attend

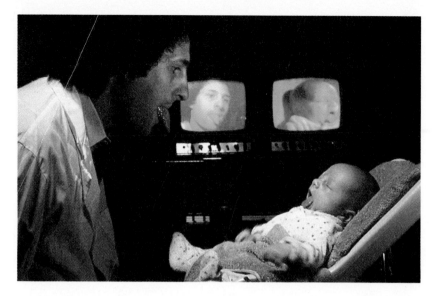

Babies often imitate facial expressions they see, as this 23-day-old newborn is doing.

to) drawings of a human face. They chose the face pattern as the focus of their attention no matter what it was paired with.

One more step takes us to the research of Meltzoff and Moore (1977) who discovered something in the controlled setting of a laboratory that many parents have discovered by accident. Not only do newborns look at a human face, but they often try to imitate facial expressions. When experimenters stuck out their tongues at babies, the babies stuck out their tongues. Infants opened their mouths to imitate the same facial expression of the experimenter. These attempts at imitation—a cognitive skill indicating an appreciation of the environment—were clearly present by the age of 2 weeks, and were often found in neonates only 1 hour old!

Before you go on

Cite an example that demonstrates more than a simple reflexive reaction by a neonate to environmental stimuli.

Piaget's Theory of Cognitive Development

The physical growth and development of a child is quite remarkable. Even more impressive are the increases in cognitive and intellectual abilities that occur during childhood. By the time the human organism reaches adolescence, it has acquired an enormous stockpile of information. More than just learning facts, the child comes to appreciate how to learn. Strategies for survival and/or success have begun to develop (Siegler, 1983).

Accounting for how children's intellectual capacities and abilities change is a difficult business. The theory that has attracted the most attention in this regard is that of the Swiss psychologist Jean Piaget (1896–1980). Though there *are* others, Piaget's theory of cognitive development (Piaget, 1948, 1954, 1967) has been so influential that it will be the focus of our discussion.

In Piaget's scheme, children progress through four stages of development. Determining *precisely* when each stage begins or ends is not always possible. It is also assumed that two adjacent stages may overlap and blend for a while. Even so, each stage is characterized by its own cognitive methods, insights, and abilities. The four stages are summarized in Figure 18.4, and are described more fully in the following sections.

Jean Piaget

Figure 18.4

A summary of Piaget's stages of cognitive development

1. **Sensorimotor stage** (birth to age 2 years)
"knows" through active interaction with environment
becomes aware of cause-effect relationships
learns that objects exist even when not in view
imitates crudely the actions of others
2. **Preoperational stage** (ages 2 to 6 years)
begins by being very egocentric
language and mental representations develop
objects are classified on just one characteristic at a time
3. **Concrete operations stage** (ages 7 to 12 years)
develops conservation of volume, length, mass, etc.
organizes objects into ordered categories
understands relational terms (e.g., bigger than, above)
begins using simple logic
4. **Formal operations stage** (ages over 12)
thinking becomes abstract and symbolic
reasoning skills develop
a sense of hypothetical concepts develops

Sensorimotor Stage (Ages 0 to 24 months) For children under age 2, language isn't terribly relevant. Such very young children are unable to discover much about their world by asking questions about it or by trying to understand long-winded explanations. Trying to explain to a 10-month-old baby *why* it shouldn't chew on an electrical extension cord is likely to be an unrewarding piece of parental behavior. In this sensorimotor stage, children discover by sensing (sensori-) and by doing (motor) and by attending to the relationships that may exist between the two processes. The child may come to appreciate, for example, that a yank on the dog's tail (a motor activity) reliably produces a loud yelp (a sensory experience), perhaps followed in turn by parental attention.

One of the most useful concepts to develop in the sensorimotor stage is that of *causality*. Infants gradually come to the realization that events sometimes have knowable causes, and that some behaviors cause predictable reactions. Pushing a bowl of oatmeal off the high chair causes a mess and gets Mommy's attention: If A then B—a very practical insight.

Another important discovery that occurs during this stage of development is that objects may exist even when they are not immediately in view. Early in

Figure 18.5

The older infant (bottom) has developed the concept of object permanence. The infant sees the toy and even when it is blocked from view, he realizes it is still there and crawls under the blanket to get it.

this stage, an object that is out of sight is more than out of mind. The object ceases to exist for the child. Games of peek-a-boo are a real thrill to the child as you disappear below the side of the crib only to magically reappear from time to time. By the end of the sensorimotor period, children have learned that objects can exist even if they are not physically present, and children can anticipate their reappearance. This awareness is called **object permanence** (see Figure 18.5).

object permanence
the realization that objects that are not physically present are not gone forever and may still reappear

One of the skills that best characterizes the sensorimotor period of development is that of imitation. As we have seen, the ability to imitate some facial expressions may be present at a very early age. By the end of this period, however, imitation skills are well developed. So long as it is within the baby's range of abilities, the baby will imitate almost any behavior that it sees. A cognitive strategy has developed, one that will be used for a lifetime: trying to imitate the behaviors of a model.

Before you go on

Briefly summarize some of the cognitive skills that develop during the sensorimotor stage.

Preoperational Stage (Ages 2 to 6 years) By the end of the sensorimotor stage, a child has recognized that he or she is a separate, independent person in the world. Throughout most of the preoperational stage, a child's thinking is self-centered, or **egocentric.** According to Piaget, the child has difficulty understanding much of anything from someone else's perspective. In this stage, the world is very much *me* and *mine* and *I* oriented.

egocentric
seeing everything from one's own point of view, unable to appreciate someone else's perspective

Perhaps you have seen two preschool children at play. They are right next to each other, one playing with a truck, the other coloring in a coloring book. They are jabbering at each other, taking turns, but obviously quite oblivious to what the other is saying:

"This sure is a neat truck!"

"I think I'll paint the sky a kinda purple."

"I'm gonna be a truck driver some day."

"But if I make the sky a kinda purple, what'll I make the trees?"

"Maybe I'll drive a milk truck. Broooom!"

"I know, blue."

Such exchanges, often called *collective monologues,* demonstrate the egocentrism of children's thinking in this stage.

One of the major cognitive achievements that occurs during this period is the child's use of symbols, or mental representations, for things in the real world. This is most clearly evidenced with the rapid development of language. The problem for children in this preoperational stage is that although they form and use symbols, they haven't yet learned how to use symbolic rules. They don't know how to operate on, or with, these symbols (hence, *pre*operational). Perhaps this is part of the problem I had with the experiment that I described at the beginning of this topic. Perhaps this also explains children making strange sounding statements, such as "I goed to the store."

One of the most actively researched of Piaget's concepts is that of **conservation.** In general, the principle explains that changing the form of something does not necessarily change what it really is. Many experiments convinced Piaget that conservation is not present at the beginning of the preoperational stage, but clearly marks its end.

conservation
the understanding that changing something's form does not change its essential character

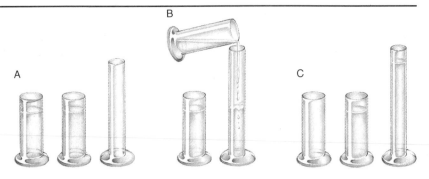

Figure 18.6

A test of conservation of volume. In (A), the child acknowledges that there is an equal amount of liquid in both beakers. In (B), the child watches the liquid being poured from one short beaker into a taller one. In (C), the child in the preoperational stage will report that there is more liquid in the taller beaker.

To demonstrate the conservation of volume, for example, exactly the same amount of colored water is placed in two tall, slender beakers. Water is then poured from one of them into a wide, shorter beaker. The preoperational child will claim that there is less water in the short beaker (see Figure 18.6). Two equal-sized balls of clay are given to a 4 year old. One is then rolled into a long cigar-shape, and the child will assert that it has more clay in it than the ball does. Have you ever found it surprisingly easy to swap your (larger) nickel for a preschooler's dime?

Before you go on

In Piaget's theory, what is meant by egocentrism and conservation?

Concrete Operations Stage   (Ages 7 to 12 years) As we have implied, one of the major landmarks of development from the preoperational to the concrete operations stage is the acquisition of the principle of conservation. But the ability to conserve volume, length, or weight is not the only sign of a more mature level of cognitive abilities.

As they enter the concrete operations stage, children begin to develop a number of concepts and can manipulate some of these concepts. They can organize objects into classes or categories of things. That is to say, they can classify things: balls over here, blocks over there, plastic soldiers in a pile by the door, and so on. Each of these is recognized as a toy, ultimately to be put away in the toy box and not to be stored in the closet, where clothes are supposed to go. Thus, it is in this period that we may say that rule-governed behavior begins. The concrete, observable, perceivable objects and events of the world can be classified, ranked, ordered, or separated into more than one category.

During the concrete operations stage, children enjoy simple games. They can follow simple rules and can move pieces around a board specified numbers of spaces.

During this stage, the youngster enjoys simple games, if the rules are easy. Moving pieces around a board to squares that match the color indicated by a spinner is easy; so is moving pieces along a board the same number of spaces as indicated on a pair of dice. Problems arise when choices need to be made that force decisions beyond the here and now: "Should I buy this piece of property now or build a house on Boardwalk?" "Should I save 7s or go for a run of clubs?" "If I move my piece there, I'll get jumped, but then I can jump two of his pieces."

As its name suggests, in the stage of concrete operations, children begin to operate on (use and manipulate) concepts and ideas. However, their manipulations are still very concrete, very much tied to real objects in the here and now. For example, an 8 year old can easily be expected to find her way to and from school, even if she throws in a side trip or two along the way. What she will have a hard time doing is telling you with any precision just how she gets from one place to another. Drawing a sensible map is very difficult for her. If she actually stands right on the corner of Maple Street and Oak Avenue, she knows where to go next to get home. Dealing with such knowledge later, in abstract terms, is what is difficult.

Before you go on

What cognitive skills might we expect from a child in the concrete operations stage of development?

Formal Operations Stage   (Ages over 12 years) The logical manipulation of abstract, symbolic concepts does not appear to develop until the last of Piaget's stages—formal operations. The key to this stage, usually begun at adolescence, is abstract, symbolic reasoning. By the age of 12, most children have developed the ability to develop and mentally test hypotheses—to work through problems in their minds. Many of the problem-solving strategies that we discussed in Topic 16 develop at this stage.

It is only at the stage of formal operations that youngsters are able to reason through hypothetical problems: "What if you were the only person in the world who liked rock music?" "If nobody had to go to school, what would happen then?" Similarly, children are now able to deal with questions that are literally contrary to fact: "What if Walter Mondale had been elected president in 1984 instead of Ronald Reagan?" Piaget (1967) has suggested that the ability to reason and think abstractly may occasionally overwhelm an adolescent. Instead of focusing on the realities of the moment, many teenagers prefer to engage in the abstract consideration of possibilities in a best of all possible worlds. As a result, "we often see the adolescent as an idealist; as a nonconformist; as a daydreamer; and, in the minds of some people, as a troublemaker" (Hughes & Noppe, 1985, p. 230).

Before you go on

What cognitive ability characterizes the stage of formal operations?

Reactions to Piaget—and Beyond

There can be no doubt of Piaget's influence on the study of the cognitive abilities of children. His observations, insights, and theorizing about intellectual development spanned decades. However, there has been a sizable quantity of research that has brought into question some of Piaget's basic ideas. The two major criticisms of Piaget's theory are that the border lines between his proposed stages are much less clear-cut than the theory allows, and that Piaget significantly underestimated the cognitive talents of preschool children (Flavell, 1982; Gelman, 1978). Let's examine just a few examples of these criticisms.

The egocentrism said to characterize the preoperational preschool child may not be as flagrant as Piaget would have us believe. For instance, in one study (Lempers, Flavell, & Flavell, 1977), children were shown a picture that was pasted inside a box. They were asked to show the picture to someone else. Not only did they do so, but in showing the picture, they turned it so that it would be right-side up to the viewer. In fact, every child over 2 years of age in the study indicated such an appreciation of someone else's point of view. Similarly, there is now ample evidence that object permanence may be neither universal nor consistently found in any one child—it depends on how you test for it (Harris, 1983).

Even Piaget's well-researched notion of conservation may not be such an obvious indicator of cognitive development as was once thought. When experimenters pour liquid from a short beaker into a tall one, a 5 year old will probably say that the taller beaker now holds more liquid—evidence of a failure to conserve in the preoperational stage. However, if the *child* actually does the pouring from one beaker to the other, as opposed to just watching, even 5 year olds show definite signs of conservation and recognize that the amount of liquid is the same in both containers (Rose & Blank, 1974).

A further criticism is that Piaget's theory, focusing from the start on a stage approach, gives little attention to the impact of language development on cognitive development in general. Piaget had little to say about the smooth and gradual increase in the capacity of a child's memory. Indeed, some children may appear to fail at a task designed to measure a cognitive skill simply because they lack the words to describe what they know, or because the task puts too great a strain on their abilities to remember (Pines, 1983). We must also keep in mind that just because a child—of whatever age—*can* demonstrate some cognitive skill is no guarantee that the child normally *does* use that skill in her or his daily activities.

Before you go on
Cite two criticisms of Piaget's theory of cognitive development.

Erikson's Theory of Psychosocial Development

Erik Erikson

Erik Erikson (b. 1902) is a psychologist who, like Piaget, proposed a stage theory of human development. Unlike Piaget, his theory focuses on much more than cognitive and intellectual development, although these aspects are clearly included. What matters most for Erikson is how an individual grows and develops in a social environment. Erikson's theory is based on his observations of a wide range of different sorts of people of different ages. Many of his observations were made in the context of therapy or analysis, not the research laboratory. He did not just concentrate on children. His theory extends, as we shall see, through adolescence into adulthood. Many of his observations had more of a cross-cultural basis than did Piaget's. Erikson was born in Germany, studied with Freud in Vienna, and came to the United States to do research on a wide variety of subjects, including college students, American Indians, and soldiers in World War II.

Erikson's theory lists eight stages of development through which an individual passes. These stages are quite different from the developmental periods of Piaget's theory. They are not so much periods of time as they are a series of conflicts, or—as Erikson calls them—*crises* that need to be resolved. Each of the eight stages is named by a pair of terms that indicates the nature of the conflict that needs to be resolved at this point in development.

As a stage theory, Erikson's implies that we naturally go through the resolution of each conflict or crisis in order, and that facing any one type of crisis usually occurs at about the same age for all of us. Figure 18.7 provides a summary of each of the eight stages of development, or psychosocial crises, according to Erikson. Also included are very brief descriptions of how each crisis might be resolved.

As you can see, only the first four stages or crises are thought to be relevant for children. One of the major strengths of Erikson's view of development is that it encompasses the entire life span. While Piaget (and, as we shall see, Freud, p. 422) focused only on the stages of development of children, Erikson extended his views to late adulthood. For now, we'll leave Erikson's theory as summarized in Figure 18.7, but we will return to his theory in our next topic.

Before you go on
What are the four crisis stages of development in childhood according to Erikson?

Figure 18.7

Erikson's eight stages of development
(Based on Erikson, 1963.)

Approximate age	Crisis	Adequate resolution	Inadequate resolution
0–1½	Trust vs. mistrust	Basic sense of safety	Insecurity, anxiety
1½–3	Autonomy vs. self-doubt	Perception of self as agent capable of controlling own body and making things happen	Feelings of inadequacy to control events
3–6	Initiative vs. guilt	Confidence in oneself as initiator, creator	Feelings of lack of self-worth
6–puberty	Competence vs. inferiority	Adequacy in basic social and intellectual skills	Lack of self-confidence, feelings of failure
Adolescent	Identity vs. role confusion	Comfortable sense of self as a person	Sense of self as fragmented; shifting, unclear sense of self
Early adult	Intimacy vs. isolation	Capacity for closeness and commitment to another	Feeling of aloneness, separation; denial of need for closeness
Middle adult	Generativity vs. stagnation	Focus of concern beyond oneself to family, society, future generations	Self-indulgent concerns; lack of future orientation
Later adult	Ego-integrity vs. despair	Sense of wholeness, basic satisfaction with life	Feelings of futility, disappointment

Language Development

One of the most significant cognitive developments of children is the free and skilled use of language. Few cognitive skills can compare to language in complexity and usefulness. As we saw in Topic 15, where we discussed the basic nature of language, to know how to use language requires that children acquire competence at three levels. They must know the *sounds* that allow for the expression of language in speech. They must know the *words,* or meaningful units, of their language. And they must know the *rules* that allow words to be combined in sequences that produce well-formed sentences. How the sounds and words of one's language are acquired is thought to be comparatively easy to deal with. The difficulties in accounting for language acquisition become most obvious when we consider the acquisition of language rules; but let's review each aspect of language one at a time.

Language Sounds   The basic units of speech sounds in a language are called **phonemes.** They are the consonant and vowel sounds of a spoken language. There are approximately 45 such phonemes in standard English. That there are many more sounds in our language than we have letters in our alphabet with which to express them is one of the reasons why learning to read and spell is often so difficult. How much easier it would be if each sound in English were represented by just one letter; for example, does one represent a /k/ sound with a k as in key, or a c as in car?

Learning speech sounds does not start from scratch. Infants freely produce a wide variety of sounds as they coo and babble. Indeed, children seem to gain some pleasure in producing such vocalizations. They spontaneously produce a very wide range of sounds, including many of the phonemes of their language and of other languages, too. Children who will grow up speaking English often babble with the guttural sounds of German, the trilled sounds of French, and even the clicks and clacks of Swahili.

phoneme
the smallest unit of sound in the spoken form of a language

So acquiring the phonemes of one's language seems to be a relatively straightforward process. The child learns, through imitation and reinforcement, which of the sounds it produces need to be "saved." Those that are not appropriate for the child's language are simply not used and disappear from the child's repertoire (deVilliers and deVilliers, 1978).

Word Meanings   The acquisition of meaningful units of a language is more difficult. Linguists refer to meaningful speech sounds as **morphemes.** In most cases, morphemes are the same as words. *Table* is a word and a morpheme—it cannot be broken down into smaller meaningful units. The word *tablecloth,* however, is made up of *two* morphemes: *table* and *cloth.*

Psychologists agree that children learn the particular words (or morphemes) of their language. Again, they learn through imitation and reinforcement at first (see Chapter 5). A child's first words are usually nouns. More than that, the first words of a child are usually nouns that stand for concrete objects in the child's immediate experience: mommy, da-da, doggie, and the like.

Even very early in language development (around 1 year of age), we often notice one of the important characteristics of language: it is generative, or creative. Children often create or generate utterances they could not possibly have heard before. For reasons I'm sure I'll never understand, my first-born insisted on referring to his pacifier as his *abu* (or *aboo?*). Once everyone else learned what it was that he was talking about, *abu* became a meaningful word—in this case, one generated by the child.

Rules of Combination   An important observation about language is that it is *rule-governed* behavior. There are rules in every language that prescribe how words can be combined to form phrases and sentences. We just can't string words together in any old order. The rules of English may be different from those of German or Spanish or Russian, but all languages have such rules, which combine to form the **syntax** of the language. The utterance "Colorless green ideas sleep furiously," may strike you as a silly sort of thing to say, but somehow or another, you recognize that at least the words are put together in the right order—following the syntactic rules of English.

How do young children acquire the knowledge of the rules of their language? This is a controversial question in developmental psychology that does not yet have a satisfactory answer, but we can look at some of the issues involved. By the time children start elementary school, they give evidence of understanding and producing sentences in such a way as to demonstrate knowing virtually all of the rules of language. That is, children normally know their language by the time they are 4 years old.

It seems clear that the rules of English, for example, are not taught and/or learned in any direct way. Most of us don't even understand the rules of English well enough to specify what they *are.* Surely we can *use* them, but we'd have a hard time trying to *state* them, much less teach them directly to a child. In fact, when parents correct their child's speech, they more often correct on the basis of *what* is said, rather than on the basis of *how* it is said (Brown, Cazden, & Bellugi, 1969). For example, if a child says, "Me no like oatmeal," a parent is likely to respond with a statement such as, "Sure you do. You eat it all the time." Even explanations in terms of learning through imitation are strained by the observation that children seldom mimic or even *try* to mimic what adults say, but continuously create and generate completely *new* utterances.

An intriguing point of view that psychologists have been grappling with for some time is that many aspects of language, including a search for rules

morpheme
the smallest unit of meaning in a language

syntax
the rules that govern how the morphemes of a language may be combined

and syntax, are based on innate, unlearned predispositions (Ainsfeld, 1984; Chomsky, 1967). Support for this view of language acquisition stems from the observation that children go through what appears to be a definite sequence of development of their language. Moreover, this sequence of development appears relatively unaffected by differences in environment and seems to be about the same regardless of which language the child is acquiring (Slobin, 1979).

Limited by vocabulary and memory capacity, children first produce language utterances that are only one word long. **Holophrastic speech,** as it is called, uses but one word—in a variety of contexts and accompanied by gestures and changes in pitch—to communicate a wide range of things. Words are no longer simple labels for objects, as they were when they were first learned. The vocal utterance "milk" can now be used to communicate such things as, "I want more milk," "Oh-oh, I spilled my milk," or "Yuck, not milk again!"

At about the age of 2 years, the child begins producing utterances that are two words long. When analyzed carefully, these two-word utterances are very regular—as if they were put together according to some rather strict rules. Given an understanding of the words "BIG" and "LITTLE," and many nouns, one child was heard to say "big ball," "big plane," "big stick," "little stick," "little ball," and so on, but he never reversed the order. He would *not* say "plane big," or "ball little" (Braine, 1976). It was as if, even with just two words to work with, the child appreciated that order matters, that one way to combine them was okay and the other was not.

Overregularization is a phenomenon that convinces some of us that children acquiring their language are strongly inclined to search for rules. Here we find children saying strange things, particularly when forming the plural of nouns or the past tense of verbs. They will say "two foots," or "four mans," or "he goed," even *after* they have previously used the words "feet," "men," and "went." Obviously, the argument is that the child is so predisposed to find and use rules that she or he will do so with great consistency, even when the rule is wrong. In fact, "two foots" is much more reasonable than "two feet," even though "two foots" is not likely to have been heard in adult speech (Anisfeld, 1984).

Before you go on

What are phonemes, morphemes, and syntax, and how might each develop in or be acquired by young children?

As we have seen, the neonatal period is one of great growth and development. Motor, perceptual, cognitive, and social skills are being developed and strengthened. While Piaget's theory of child development outlined four stages through which children pass, Erikson expanded the developmental stages to eight that encompassed the entire life span. We have also seen that the complex process of language development is most difficult in relation to the acquisition of the rules that govern language usage. For all types of development, we have seen that there are wide ranges of ages for attainment of various skills, and though these ranges can be useful in watching for signs of development in children, they should not be thought of as being exact. Every child develops according to his or her own developmental schedule, and variation from the "norm" is usually no cause for alarm.

Human beings are social animals. To a large degree, we adapt and thrive in this world to the extent that we can profit from our interpersonal relationships. The roots of our social development can be found in early infancy—in the formation of **attachment**. Attachment is defined as a strong, two-way emotional bond, usually referring to the bond or relationship between a child and its mother, or primary caregiver.

The place to begin our discussion on attachment is with Harry Harlow and his experiences raising rhesus monkeys (Harlow, 1959; Harlow, Harlow, & Suomi, 1971). Harlow and his colleagues raised some baby monkeys with their biological mothers, and others in cages that

attachment
a strong, two-way emotional/social relationship, usually between a child and its mother or primary caregiver

Figure 18.8
One of Harlow's monkeys and its artificial terry cloth mother. Harlow found that the contact comfort mothers provide is essential for normal social development.

contained "artificial mothers." These "mothers" were models made of a harsh wire mesh and fitted with wooden heads (see Figure 18.8). Small doll-sized baby bottles positioned within the models provided nourishment to the baby monkeys. One style of artificial mother was covered with a soft, terry cloth wrap, while the other was left as bare wire.

There was no doubt which model the young monkeys preferred. Whether it provided food or not, the baby monkeys clung tightly to the soft terry cloth model. It seemed clear to Harlow that mother rhesus monkeys provide more to their young than just food. The opportunity to cling to something soft and cuddly (Harlow called it *contact comfort*) is equally important.

What were the long-term implications of raising baby rhesus monkeys under these different conditions? Monkeys raised in isolation, or with bare wire model mothers, or, to a lesser degree, even with the cloth-model mothers, all showed definite signs of abnormal development. As adults they tended to show inappropriate social behaviors, either withdrawing or acting aggressively violent. Normal sexual behavior patterns were disrupted— many never successfully mated. When mating was possible, females turned out to be very poor mothers. For rhesus monkeys, then, forming an early attachment bond is apparently an important step in social development.

As is usually the case, we need to exercise caution when translating data from the animal laboratory to humans. It does seem that a strong attachment bond is often (though not always) formed between a human child and its primary caregiver(s).

Forming an attachment between infant and mother (as an example) involves a constant interaction and an active give-and-take between the two. Strong attachments are most likely to be formed (we say the two become *securely attached*) if the mother is sensitive to the needs of the child, picking up the baby when he or she cries, changing the diaper as soon as it is soiled, feeding on a regular schedule, and so on. Attachment is also prompted by spontaneous hugging, eye contact, smiling, and vocalizing. But remember that forming an attachment is a two-way street. The bond will be most secure when baby reciprocates, by smiling, cooing, and clinging to mother when attended to (Ainsworth, 1979).

It may be tentatively concluded that forming secure attachments is important for the later development of the human infant, just as contact comfort is important for the later development of the rhesus monkey. Because we have not been able to do the sort of controlled experiment with human infants that Harlow did with monkeys, the data are not as impressive. However, they do suggest that there are long-term benefits (from improved emotional stability to improved problem-solving skills) to be derived from strong attachments formed early in childhood (Bowlby, 1969; Etaugh, 1980; Schwartz, 1983).

Before we leave this section, we need to mention that infants can and do form attachments with people other than their mothers. Although it is true that, *in general,* fathers spend less time with very young children than do mothers (father's time increases as children get older), father-child attachments are quite common and very helpful for the long-term development of the child (Lamb, 1979; Lynn, 1974). There is no evidence that fathers are any less sensitive to the needs of their children than are mothers. There is evidence, however, that fathers' play with their children is usually more boisterous and vigorous than mothers'.

What are some of the reflexes that can be observed in neonates? Why do we care about neonatal reflexes?

Some reflexes have obvious survival value for the neonate; for example, the rooting reflex in which the newborn turns toward a slight pressure on its cheek, or the sucking reflex, or even the grasping reflex. Other reflexes, such as the Moro reflex (thrusting arms to the sides and then quickly bringing them back to the chest in reaction to a sudden noise or loss of support), or the walking reflex, seem to serve no particular function for the neonate but may be used to diagnose developmental delays or confirm normal physical development. / 320

Briefly summarize some of the landmarks of early motor development.

Although the particular age at which motor abilities develop does show considerable variability from child to child, the sequence is usually quite regular and predictable. In order, and with approximate ages, a child can hold his or her chin up at 1 month; reach for an object at 3 months; sit with support at 4 months; sit alone at 7 months; stand with help at 8 months; crawl at 10 months; walk if led at 11 months; pull up at 12 months; walk alone at 13 months. / 321

Summarize the basic sensory capacities of the neonate.

The neonate's senses function quite well right from birth. The eyes can focus well at arm's length, although they will require a few months to focus over a range of object distances. Rudimentary depth perception seems to be present even in the neonate. Hearing and auditory discrimination are quite good, as are the senses of taste, smell, and touch. / 324

Cite an example that demonstrates more than a simple reflexive reaction by a neonate to environmental stimuli.

We have recently come to appreciate that neonates can demonstrate memory. They will attend to a new and different visual pattern after coming to ignore a familiar one, showing an appreciation of the difference between familiar and new. They show definite preferences for complex visual patterns over simple ones and seem most to prefer (attend to) visual representations of the human face. Even babies only 1 hour old make attempts to imitate the facial expressions of someone in their field of view. / 325

Briefly summarize some of the cognitive skills that develop during the sensorimotor stage.

During Piaget's sensorimotor stage of cognitive development, the child learns through an active interaction with the environment, by sensing and doing. The baby appreciates some cause and effect relationships, imitates the actions of others, and, by the end of the period, develops a sense of object permanence. / 327

In Piaget's theory, what is meant by egocentrism and conservation?

Egocentrism is one of the most notable cognitive reactions during the preoperational stage of cognitive development. The child becomes very *me* and *I* oriented, unable to appreciate the world from anyone else's perspective or point of view. The cognitive skills of conservation are not acquired until the end of the preoperational stage and mark the beginning of the concrete operations stage. Conservation involves understanding that changing something's form (rolling out a ball of clay, pouring liquid from one size container into another) does not change its essential nature. / 328

What cognitive skills might we expect from a child in the concrete operations stage of development?

In the concrete operations stage of cognitive development, the child develops conservation, organizes concepts into categories or classes, begins to use simple logic, and comes to understand relational terms. / 329

What cognitive ability characterizes the stage of formal operations?

The essential nature of the formal operations stage of cognitive development is the display of the ability to think, reason, and solve problems symbolically, or in abstract rather than concrete, tangible form. / 329

Cite two criticisms of Piaget's theory of cognitive development.

As influential as Piaget's theory of cognitive development has been, it has not escaped criticism. Two of the major criticisms of the theory are that (1) there is little actual evidence that cognitive abilities develop in a series of well-defined, sequential stages (i.e., the borders between stages are very poorly defined), and (2) preschool children, in particular, seem to have more cognitive strengths and abilities than Piaget's theories credit them with. / 330

What are the four crisis stages of development in childhood according to Erikson?

Of Erikson's eight stages, or crises, of development, four occur during childhood: (1) trust versus mistrust, which deals with whether the child develops a sense of security or anxiety; (2) autonomy versus shame and doubt, which deals with whether the child will develop a sense of self and competence or shame and guilt; (3) initiative versus guilt, which deals with whether the child will gain confidence in his or her own ability or develop a sense of guilt and inadequacy; and (4) industry versus inferiority, which deals with whether the child develops a sense of confidence in intellectual and social skills or develops a sense of failure and lack of confidence. / 330

What are phonemes, morphemes, and syntax, and how might each develop in or be acquired by young children?

Phonemes are the basic sounds of language; morphemes are the smallest meaningful units of sound in one's language. It seems quite reasonable to propose that these aspects of language are learned through the processes of imitation and reinforcement. Syntax is the set of rules that govern how the phonemes and morphemes of one's language can be combined to form acceptable phrases and sentences. Although all language users know how to use such rules, few can actually state them, which is but one of the reasons why some psychologists believe that simple learning cannot be used to account for the acquisition of syntax. They propose instead that there is some innate mechanism, the nature of which is as yet unknown, that assists in the acquisition of language at an early age. / 333

TOPIC

Ageism is the name given to a prejudice against anyone because of her or his age. When a teenager is told that she can't get a job simply because she is too young, even though she is clearly able, she may be the victim of ageism. However, prejudice and negative stereotypes relating to age are usually reserved for the elderly. As we shall see, there are many ways of defining "old age." Let's use a definition in terms of chronological age (time from birth), and define old age as being over 65. Before we get to our discussion of adulthood and old age in this topic, try the following true-false questions concerning the elderly, just to see if there is any ageism in your attitude toward people over 65 years of age.

T F 1. Those over 65 constitute a minority of the population in the United States, numbering fewer than 5 million, or 2½% of the population.

T F 2. The number of people in this country who are over the age of 65 is decreasing.

T F 3. Most elderly people live alone and will probably die alone.

T F 4. Most elderly people do little more than sit around watching TV or just sleeping.

T F 5. The use of mental health services is higher among the elderly than for any other age group.

T F 6. When elderly people do have jobs, they tend to show low productivity and high absenteeism.

T F 7. Nearly one third of those over 65 live in nursing homes.

T F 8. A large majority of people over the age of 65 wish that they had never retired and are generally dissatisfied with the quality of their lives.

T F 9. Most elderly people have a physical disease or disorder that limits their freedom.

T F 10. Old people tend to be quite lonely and depressed.

You have probably recognized that each of these true-false statements is false. Not only is each false, but in a number of cases, as we shall see, the truth of the matter is almost the exact opposite of the statement as it appears above.

In this topic, we acknowledge that one's growth and development do not come to a halt when one is no longer a child. We continue to develop, in fact, through adolescence, into adulthood, and in most cases, until the day we die. Many of the changes that reflect our development as adults and adolescents are more gradual and subtle than those that occur in childhood. They are more difficult to observe, but they are no less significant.

After first defining adolescence, we'll review the physical changes that usually occur during this developmental period, and then we'll focus on two of the major issues in the lives of adolescents: sexuality and identity.

The psychology of adulthood as an area within developmental psychology is a recent one. As more and more Americans enter the age group we classify as *elderly*, interest in this segment of our population has increased. We'll arbitrarily divide adulthood into three segments and examine some of the psychologically important milestones of each.

ADOLESCENCE

adolescence
the developmental period between childhood and adulthood, often begun at puberty, which ends when full physical growth is achieved

The period of development that we call **adolescence** is an exciting one. It is a period filled with discovery, turmoil, growth toward independence, and the beginning of lifelong commitments. It is very difficult to specify exactly when one's adolescence begins, or when it ends.

We may choose to view adolescence in biological terms. In that case, adolescence begins with the onset of puberty (sexual maturity; a readiness to reproduce), and ends with the end of physical growth. An individual's developing sexuality and physical growth certainly have psychological implications and need to be addressed, but there are other ways of defining adolescence.

A more psychological perspective to this period emphasizes the development of the cognitions, feelings, and behaviors that characterize adolescence. This approach views adolescence "as a psychological process occurring within the individual" (Forisha-Kovach, 1983, p. 8).

It is also possible to think about adolescence from a social perspective, examining the role of adolescents in society. Such views generally define adolescence in terms of being in between, not yet an adult, but no longer a child. In this context, the period usually lasts from the early teen years through one's highest level of education, when the individual is thought to enter the adult world. Actually, whether we accept a biological, social, or psychological approach to defining adolescence, we usually are talking about people between the ages of approximately 12 and 20.

This period has long been viewed as an important one for physical, social, and cognitive growth, but different psychologists have tended to approach adolescence from different theoretical perspectives. Freud, for example, saw adolescence as a natural stage in sexual development, referring to it as a *genital stage*, characterized by increasingly mature sexual relationships. For Erikson, the main task of adolescence is to establish one's sense of identity as a unique person and to minimize identity confusion. Piaget chose to address the cognitive developments of the period—his formal operations stage— where abstract reasoning and an appreciation of alternative hypotheses first appear. Whereas some psychologists consider the period in terms of growth and positive change, others have viewed adolescence as a period of great turmoil, stress, rebellion, and negativism (Conger & Peterson, 1984).

Before you go on
How might adolescence be defined from a physical, social, and psychological point of view?

Physical Changes of Adolescence

The onset of adolescence is generally marked by two biological or physical changes. For one, there is a marked increase in height and weight, known as a *growth spurt,* and for the other, there is sexual maturation.

The growth spurt of early adolescence usually occurs in girls at an earlier age than it does in boys. Girls begin their growth spurt as early as 9 or 10 years of age, and then slow down at about age 15. Boys generally show their increased rate of growth between the ages of 12 and 17 years. Indeed, males usually don't reach their adult height until their early 20s, whereas girls generally attain their maximum height by their late teens (Roche & Davila, 1972). Figure 19.1 presents one way to represent the adolescent growth spurt in graphic form.

At least some of the potential psychological turmoil of early adolescence may be a direct result of the growth spurt. It is not uncommon to find increases in weight and height occurring so rapidly that they are accompanied by real, physical growing pains, particularly in the arms and legs. Unfortu-

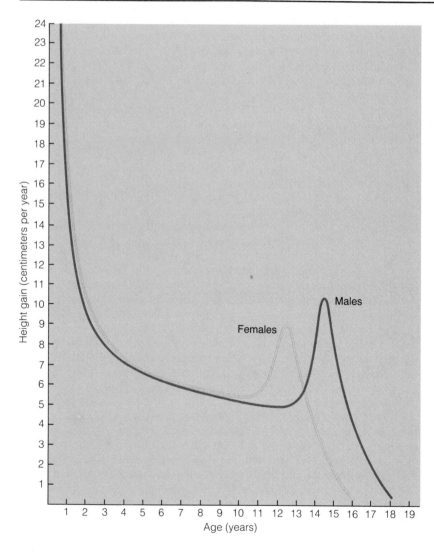

Figure 19.1

Females begin their main growth spurt at around age 10, while the growth spurt in males does not begin until about age 12. In general, males will grow faster and for a longer period of time than females.

(After Tanner, Whitehouse, & Takaishi, 1966.)

Adolescent boys often seem gangly, awkward, and clumsy as different parts of their bodies grow at different rates and at different times.

nately, the spurt of adolescent growth seldom affects all parts of the body uniformly—especially in boys. Thirteen- and 14-year-old boys often appear incredibly clumsy and awkward as they try to coordinate their large hands and feet with the rest of their body. One of the most noticeable areas of growth in boys is that of the larynx and vocal cords. As the vocal cords grow and lengthen, the pitch of the voice is lowered. Much to the embarrassment of many a teenaged boy, this transition is seldom a smooth one, and he may suffer through weeks or months of a squeaking, crackling change of pitch right in the middle of a serious conversation.

Remember that the data presented in Figure 19.1 for the growth spurt represent averages. There are large variations from individual to individual. The possible advantages or disadvantages of being an "early bloomer" or a "late bloomer" compared with age mates is the subject of our Topic Expansion. For now, we can say with reasonable confidence that whatever the advantages or disadvantages of being an early or late maturing adolescent may be, they are not lasting.

It is with **puberty** that there is a noticeable increase in the production of the sex hormones; primarily the androgens in males and the estrogens in females. In fact, all of us have both androgens *and* estrogens in our bodies. Males simply have more androgens, and females have more estrogens.

Boys seldom know when puberty begins for them. For some time they have been experiencing penile erections and nocturnal emissions of seminal fluid. Biologically, we identify puberty in males with the appearance of live sperm in the testes and ejaculate of males, and most males have no idea when that happens—such determinations require a laboratory test.

With females, puberty is quite noticeable. It is indicated by the first menstrual period, which is called **menarche.** With puberty, both boys and girls are ready, in a biological sense, to reproduce. However, coming to deal with that readiness and making the adjustments that we associate with psychological maturity do not come automatically with sexual maturity.

In addition to simply growing larger at a rapid pace and becoming sexually able to reproduce, the physical changes we call the *secondary sex characteristics* are also of concern to the teenager. These changes are also under the control of the sex hormones that become active in puberty and they are taken as indirect evidence of sexual maturity. In males, the neck and shoulders expand, hips narrow, and facial and body hair begin to develop. In females, the hips become broader and rounder, the shoulders narrow, and breasts develop.

puberty
the stage of physical development at which one becomes capable of sexual reproduction

menarche
a female's first menstrual period; often taken as a sign of the beginning of adolescence

Let's mention just one other physical change here that is often of supreme importance to the adolescent: acne. The occurrence of acne appears to be a normal consequence of physical development and the enlargement of the pores of the skin. Stimulated by androgens, it is more common in boys than girls, and it affects as many as 85 percent of all adolescents to some degree. Although American youngsters spend untold millions of dollars for prescription and over-the-counter treatments for acne, there is little evidence that *any* treatment really helps (Katchadourian, 1977).

With all of the physical and physiological changes that occur in early adolescence, it is easy to see why G. Stanley Hall, in the first textbook written about adolescence, was moved to describe the period as one of "second birth" (Hall, 1905).

Before you go on
Briefly describe the physical changes that accompany the beginnings of adolescence.

Adolescent Sexuality

Sexual behaviors are rooted in physiology. True sexual behaviors require the physiological basis that develops at puberty. For rats and most species of "lower" animals, about the only requirement for skilled sexual behaviors is the presence of an adequate supply of sex hormones (and opportunity, of course). With sufficient sex hormones available, the sexual behaviors of a naive, virgin rat are not much different from those of an experienced rat. Normally, the whole cycle appears very straightforward: Maturity brings hormones, hormones give rise to a sex drive, and the drive results in appropriate sexual behavior—hormones, drive, and behavior. This straightforward relationship between hormones and behavior may be true for rats. It is certainly not that simple for humans.

A certain level of sex hormones may be necessary for sexual behavior in humans, but hormones alone are not sufficient. Skilled sexual behaviors in humans require learning, experience, and, if you will, practice. It is during adolescence that practice takes place and that attitudes and values concerning sexual behaviors develop. Although the physiological ability to reproduce is present in most humans soon after puberty, expressing that ability in appropriate behavior often requires accommodating to social pressures, cognitive developments, and religious and moral values. In this section, we'll review some of the data concerning adolescent sexual behaviors, focusing on masturbation and heterosexual intercourse. In the next section, we'll consider identity formation and how our sexuality influences our views of who we are.

Masturbation   A common outlet of adolescent sexuality is **masturbation**—the self-stimulation of the genitals to levels of sexual arousal, often to orgasm. Although masturbation may begin, in an exploratory sort of way, in childhood, it is most common in adolescence and continues throughout adulthood. Masturbation is often the source of great stress and feelings of guilt among teenagers. Yet from Kinsey's first major study in 1948 to more recent surveys (for example, Haas, 1979), it seems that masturbation among adolescent males is virtually universal, with almost 90 percent of those questioned responding that they masturbate at least occasionally. Teenage females appear to masturbate less frequently (about half as often as males), although with females the numbers are increasing.

masturbation
self-stimulation of the genitals to the point of arousal, often to orgasm

It is during adolescence that sexual attitudes and values develop. Though they are physiologically able to reproduce, adolescents often find that they are not emotionally ready for sexual activity because of social and religious values.

Bizarre horror stories concerning the ill effects of masturbation can still be heard, but the truth is that "there is no evidence that masturbation is a harmful activity" (Lerner and Hultsch, 1983, p. 380). Indeed the only harmful side effects of masturbation are the guilt and shame that the individual may feel about his or her behavior. In this regard, I have always appreciated the humorous wisdom of Ginott (1969, p. 170) who quotes the line, "What's wrong with masturbation is that one does not meet interesting people that way."

Intercourse and Pregnancy As you might imagine, collecting quality data on the sexual behaviors of adolescents is not easily done. Many surveys are biased because sample size is small or is not representative of the general population of adolescents. Truthfulness is always a potential problem with survey data, even if anonymity is assured. This is particularly true when we are asking questions about as sensitive an issue as sexual behaviors. Some respondents may tend to stretch reality with tales of numerous sexual exploits, while others, perhaps more anxious or guilt-ridden, tend to minimize reports of their sexual activities.

One of the first large-scale national studies of teenage sexual practices was that of Sorenson (1973) who found that by age 19, more than half the females (57%) and almost three quarters of the males (72%) reported having had sexual intercourse. These figures are consistent with similar data collected from females only for the year 1971 (Zelnik & Kantner, 1980). This survey indicated that 46.4 percent of never-married females aged 19 had had sexual intercourse.

With some minor changes in methodology, Zelnik and Kantner replicated their 1971 survey twice—once in 1976 and again in 1979. Their samples of subjects were drawn from large metropolitan areas. The 1971 and 1976 surveys included responses from females only. Males were added to the 1979 survey.

Figure 19.2 summarizes some of the findings from these three investigations. The data are subdivided each year by race. Take a few minutes to identify some of the major trends. Note that for the combined sample, the percentage of women reporting intercourse rose from about 30 percent in 1971 to 43 percent in 1976 to nearly 50 percent in 1979. Also, note that the increase between 1976 and 1979 is totally attributable to increases in activity among white females. The average age of first intercourse has remained quite stable over the years, but is almost 1 full year younger for black teenage females (15½) than for whites (16½). Comparable data for males are also in Figure 19.2. They are higher than for females, but race differences are much smaller.

With all this sexual activity among adolescents, it is not surprising that teenage pregnancy in this country is a major problem. In 1980, there were 562,330 babies born to adolescent mothers, and about half of these teenage mothers were unmarried at the time. Nearly 10,000 babies were born to mothers age 14 or younger. It is difficult to assess the number of abortions or miscarriages that occurred, but estimating teenage pregnancies at approximately 1,110,000 in 1980 alone is probably not far off (Auletta, 1984). The data of Zelnik and Kantner (1980) reflect a _doubling_ of teenage pregnancies between 1971 and 1979.

The large number of teenage pregnancies reflects two realities: (1) there is a high, and increasing, rate of sexual activity among adolescents, and (2) effective means of contraception are not being used by teenage couples engaged in such activity. Only 34 percent of the respondents in Zelnik and Kantner's 1979 study reported that they always used *some* form of contra-

Increased sexuality has led to growing numbers of teen pregnancies. Few adolescents are emotionally, physically, and financially able to support and care for a baby.

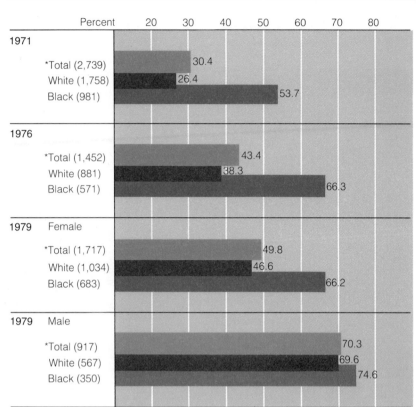

Figure 19.2
Percent of females aged 15–19 (1971, 1976, 1979) and males ages 17–21 (1979) who had premarital intercourse; by race.

*The total is an average that represents the combination of white and black respondents.

ception. Thirty-six percent said that they never did. And some of the more commonly used methods of contraception (e.g., withdrawal) are demonstrably unreliable at best.

Once pregnant, fewer teenagers now consider marriage an acceptable alternative, while more and more are turning to abortions. The increase in abortions, however, has clearly not kept pace with the number of premarital pregnancies. Conger (1975) is willing to call teenage pregnancy an epidemic, reporting that more than 25 percent are terminated by induced abortions, 10 percent result in marital births that were conceived premaritally, and over 20 percent result in out-of-wedlock births. Further, 14 percent end in miscarriages, and the rest are born to teenagers who have remained single.

Before you go on

Cite some of the data that suggests that adolescents are sexually active, and may be more so than in the past.

Identity Formation in Adolescence

Adolescents give the impression of being great experimenters. They experiment with hair styles, music, religions, drugs, sexual outlets, fad diets, part-time jobs, part-time interpersonal relationships, and part-time philosophies

Adolescence is a time of identity crisis, a time of questioning, as teens struggle to define who and what they are and what they believe and feel.

Adolescence is a time of identity formation. Adolescents often achieve their identities and develop a sense of self, goals, and direction, including vocational goals and direction. For instance, the desire to be a musician may lead adolescents to join various musical groups.

identity crisis
the struggle to define and integrate one's sense of self, and to decide what one's attitudes, beliefs, and values should be

of life. In fact, it often seems that teenagers' commitments are made on a part-time basis. They are busily trying things out, doing things their way, playing around, off on a grand search for Truth.

This view of adolescents as experimenters is not without foundation. It is consistent with the view that one of the major tasks of adolescence is the resolution of an **identity crisis**—the struggle to define and integrate the sense of who one is, what one is to do in life, and what one's attitudes, beliefs, and values should be. During adolescence, the individual comes to grips with many questions: "Who am I?" "What am I going to do with my life?" "What is the point of it all?" Needless to say, these are not trivial questions. One's search for his or her identity may lead to a number of conflicts. Some conflicts may be resolved very easily, some may continue into adulthood.

As we saw in our last topic, the concept of identity formation is associated with the personality theorist Erik Erikson (1963). For Erikson, the search for identity is the fifth of eight stages of psychosocial development (see Figure 18.7). It is the stage that occurs during the adolescent years. For many youngsters, adolescence brings very little confusion or conflict at all in terms of attitudes, beliefs, or values. Many teenagers are quite able and willing to accept without question the values and sense of self that they began to develop in childhood.

For many teenagers, however, the conflict of identity is quite real. They have a sense of giving up the values of parents and teachers in favor of new ones—their own. Physical and physiological changes, an increased sexuality, and perceived societal pressures to decide what they want to be when they "grow up" may lead to what Erikson calls *role confusion*. Wanting to be independent, to be one's own self, often does not fit in with the values of the past, of childhood. Hence, the teenager tries to experiment with different possibilities, trying to see what works out best, occasionally to the dissatisfaction of bewildered parents.

James Marcia (1980) has expanded upon Erikson's basic ideas of identity formation. It is Marcia's view that identify formation takes place in four stages. Each stage defines a different **identity status**—different levels of commitment in the search for the sense of one's self. These statuses include: (1) Identity diffusion, which is characterized by a lack of commitment, but at the same time no real conflict because the individual has yet to question her or his identity. (2) Foreclosure, in which there are no real problems or conflicts either because the individual simply accepts, without question, the attitudes, goals, and values prescribed by family or society. (3) Moratorium, which is the stage of real conflict and crisis. The search is on, and goals and values are being carefully examined. No commitment has yet been made. (4) Identity achieved, in which the struggle is over, the conflict resolved, and a satisfying integration of alternatives has been accepted. The individual has a good sense of self, goals, and direction. Notice that this highest level or stage of identity achieved requires a probing, questioning attitude on the part of the adolescent. It is as if true identity formation results only from a struggle—at least according to Erikson and Marcia.

There is value in Marcia's approach to teenage identity formation. But matters may be more complicated than he suggests. It may be that different sorts of identity crises are resolved sooner than others. For example, in a study of junior and senior high school students, Archer (1982) found that many students had reached the higher stages of moratorium and identity achieved in terms of their vocational goals. That is, in terms of their vocation, or future employment, many subjects had a good sense of what they wanted to be when they grew up. There was some evidence that the students had begun to question their religious beliefs. In terms of sex-role preferences, 132 of the 160 subjects were found to be still at the foreclosure level of development. And of the total sample, 157 had yet to begin struggling with their political philosophies, with 142 never having considered the question (identity diffusion), and 15 simply accepting parental values (foreclosure).

So it seems that when we ask about a teenager's developing identity, we need to specify the domain or area in which we are interested. It all doesn't just come together at once.

identity status
a level of commitment in the development of identity or a sense of self

Before you go on
Summarize the adolescent's search of identity as described by Erikson and Marcia.

Sex-role Identity It is during adolescence that girls and boys become women and men—at least in the physical sense. It is also during adolescence that individuals come to more fully appreciate the expectations that others have of them *because* they are female or male.

Expectations that other people form about us on the basis of our positions in society are called **social roles.** People form many attitudes and expectations about our behaviors (how we *should* act) on the basis of our sex alone. These are called **sex (or gender) roles.** We begin to appreciate what is expected of us as very young children. For instance, children's choices of toys, playmates, or clothing are often made on the basis of their understanding of what is "acceptable" for them as boys or girls (Schau et al., 1980).

Indeed the argument is commonly made that the differentiation of sex-appropriate behaviors begins in the delivery room with the exclamation, "It's a boy!" or "It's a girl!" It is still a very common practice to surround infant girls in pink and boys in blue. From day one, we are led to believe that there

social roles
expectations that others form about us on the basis of our positions in society
sex (or gender) roles
social roles based on one's sex, or gender

From the day we are born, we are taught that certain behaviors are appropriate and some are not, solely on the basis of gender. Children's choices of toys are often made on the basis of their understanding of what is acceptable for them as girls and boys; thus, little girls play with dolls and little boys play with trucks. An increasing number of parents are raising their children without these traditional sex roles as the concept of androgyny gains wider acceptance.

androgyny
a social role that includes both feminine and masculine traits, attitudes, beliefs, values, and so on

are, and ought to be, significant psychological and behavioral differences based on sex. From such beginnings, many false beliefs develop.

The psychological reality of perceived sex differences in behavior has been a very active field of study over the past 20 years. One of the most influential investigations of sex differences (Maccoby & Jacklin, 1974) concluded that most of our common beliefs ought to be classified as myths because they have no evidence to support them.

To claim that there are no differences between boys and girls, or between men and women, is naive and obviously untrue. However, the major issue is the extent to which observed differences are real and *necessarily* a product of being male or female. That from adolescence on males perform better than females on tasks requiring mathematical reasoning, or that school-age girls tend to earn higher grades than boys, are two conclusions that are supported by data and research. But are these differences due to biologically based differences between males and females? Probably not. They more likely reflect differences in attitudes and beliefs about how boys and girls *should* perform on these tasks. In fact, one major conclusion of sex-difference research is often overlooked. This is the finding that in most cases where some difference between the sexes *is* found, there is more variability *within* either sex than there is *between* the two (Maccoby & Jacklin, 1974; 1980).

Androgyny Fortunately, sharp distinctions between male-appropriate and female-appropriate behaviors are softening. An increasing number of parents are not so quick to claim that "big boys don't cry." Girls are not so automatically pushed away from toy cars and trucks toward dolls and frilly things. Boys playing with dolls are becoming a more common sight.

To be sure, movement away from a sharp distinction between sex-role behaviors is slow and far from universal. However, there does seem to be an increasing appreciation in today's society of a concept that psychologists call **androgyny**—the notion that masculinity and femininity are not opposites of the same dimension, but characteristics that can be evidenced in either males or females to greater or lesser degrees. Although she did not coin the term, androgyny is commonly associated with Sandra Bem (1974) who developed a very convenient test (the Bem Sex Role Inventory, or BSRI) to measure it.

The basic idea of androgyny is that people need not be *either* masculine *or* feminine. It is possible to rank high on masculine traits or characteristics *and* high on traits or characteristics traditionally associated with being feminine. That is, one need not be strong and assertive in interpersonal relationships ("masculine" traits) at the expense of being sensitive and sympathetic to the feelings of others ("feminine" traits). It is Bem's argument that characteristics called "masculine" or "feminine" are appropriate for certain situations and are equally appropriate for both males and females (Bem. 1975). Indeed, becoming androgynous to some degree is rather like indicating that one doesn't hold to sex-role distinctions, and that a certain way of behaving is neither right nor wrong simply because one is a female or a male.

Before you go on
What is meant by sex-role identification, and how is the concept of androgyny relevant?

ADULTHOOD

Growth and development are life-long processes. The changes that occur during our adult years may not appear as striking or dramatic as those that typify our childhood and adolescence, but they are no less real. Many of the adjustments that we make as adults may go unnoticed by others as we accommodate to physical changes that force our bodies to slow and lose strength. As adults, the status of one's health may become a real concern for the first time. Psychological and social adjustments need to be made to marriage, parenthood, job and career, the death of friends and family, retirement, and, ultimately, one's own death.

Our adult lives end with our deaths. Just when adulthood begins is difficult to say. In a legal sense, adult status is granted by governments—at age 18 for some activities, or at age 21 for others. Psychologically speaking, adulthood is marked by two possibilities that at first seem almost contradictory: (1) *independence,* in the sense of taking on responsibility for one's actions and no longer being tied to parents, and (2) *interdependence,* in the sense of commitment and intimacy in interpersonal relationships.

Following the lead of Erikson (1968) and Daniel Levinson (1974), we can consider adulthood as being comprised of three overlapping periods: young adulthood (roughly ages 18 to 40), the middle years (roughly 40 to 65), and old age (over 65).

Young Adulthood

If anything marks the transition from adolescence to adulthood it is choice and commitments independently made. The sense of identity fashioned during adolescence now needs to be put into action. There are choices to be made. They tend not to be simple. Advice may be sought from elders, parents, teachers, or friends, but as an adult, the individual makes his or her own choices. Should I get married? Should I remain single? Perhaps I should live with someone. Should I get a job? Which one? To what sort of work shall I devote my life? Is more schooling or education required? What sort of schooling? Where? How? Should we have children? How many? When? Now while we're young, or should we wait until we're more experienced and have our careers established? Many of these issues are first addressed in adolescence, in Erikson's stage of identity formation. But now these questions are no longer abstract. They are often very real questions that demand some sort of response.

One of the major issues of young adulthood revolves around the issue of intimacy versus isolation. During this stage, people consider whether to marry or stay single. This is a time when we need to develop close, loving, intimate relationships to avoid loneliness.

It is Erikson's claim (1963) that early adulthood revolves around the basic choice of *intimacy versus isolation.* A failure to establish close, loving, or intimate relationships may result in loneliness and long periods of social isolation. Marriage is certainly not the only source of interpersonal intimacy, but it is still the first choice for most Americans. More young adults than ever before are postponing marriage plans, but fully 95 percent of us do marry (at least once). In fact, we are more likely to claim that happiness in life depends more on a successful marriage than any other contributor, including friendship, community activities, or hobbies (Glenn and Weaver, 1981).

Individuals reach the point of being ready to marry at different ages. Some may decide to marry simply because they perceive that it is the thing to do. Others choose marriage as an expression of an intimacy that has already developed. In addition to the choices of *when* (and *how*) to marry, of no small consequence is the choice of *who* to marry. If we have learned nothing else about the choice of marriage partners over the last 30 years, it is that mate selection is a complex process.

There are at least three factors that influence the choice of a marriage partner (Newman & Newman, 1984). The first factor deals with availability. Before we can develop an intimate relationship with someone, there needs to be the opportunity to develop the relationship in the first place. Availability is one thing, eligibility may be another. Here, matters of age, religion, politics, and background come into play. Available and eligible, yes; now how

Figure 19.3

Characteristics sought in mates
(From Buss, 1985.)

Rank (most important)	Male choices	Female choices
1	kindness and understanding	kindness and understanding
2	intelligence	intelligence
3	physical attractiveness	exciting personality
4	exciting personality	good health
5	good health	adaptability
6	adaptability	physical attractiveness
7	creativity	creativity
8	desire for children	good earning capacity
9	college graduate	college graduate
10	good heredity	desire for children
11	good earning capacity	good heredity
12	good housekeeper	good housekeeper
13	religious orientation	religious orientation

about attractive? To a degree, attractiveness here means physical attractiveness, but as we all know, judgments of physical beauty often depend on who's doing the judging. Attractiveness also involves judgments about psychological characteristics such as understanding, emotional supportiveness, similarity in values and goals, and so on.

Psychologist David Buss recently reviewed the available evidence on mate selection, with a particular focus on the question of whether or not opposites attract (Buss, 1985). He concluded that, at least in marriage, they do not. He found that "we are likely to marry someone who is similar to us in almost every variable" he examined (p. 47). Most important are the variables of age, education, race, religion, and ethnic background (in order), followed by attitudes and opinions, mental abilities, socioeconomic status, height, weight, and even eye color. More than that, he found that men and women are in nearly complete agreement on those characteristics they commonly seek in a mate. Figure 19.3 presents 13 such characteristics, ranked by men and women. There is a significant difference in ranking for only two: physical attractiveness and good earning capacity.

You should not conclude from this discussion that choosing a marriage partner is always a matter of making a sound, rational decision. Clearly it isn't. The truth is that many factors, including romantic love, affect such decisions. That approximately 40 percent of all first marriages end in divorce is an unsettling reminder that the choices people make are not always the best.

Beyond establishing an intimate relationship, becoming a parent is generally taken as a sure sign of adulthood. For many young couples, parenthood has become more a matter of choice than ever before because of more available means of contraception and new treatments for infertility. Having one's own family helps foster the process of *generativity* that Erikson associates with middle adulthood. This process reflects a growing concern for family and for one's impact on future generations. Although such concerns may not become central until one is over 40, parenthood usually begins much sooner.

There is no doubt that having a baby around the house significantly changes established routines. The freedom for spontaneous trips, intimate outings, and privacy is in large measure given up in trade for the joys of parenthood. As parents, men and women take on the responsibilities of new social roles—that of father and mother. These new roles of adulthood add to the already established roles of being a male or a female, a son or a daughter, a husband or a wife, and so on.

Though parenthood entails a great loss of freedom and spontaneity, most people feel that the joys of sharing and togetherness compensate for these losses.

The Middle Years

As the middle years of adulthood approach, life often starts to settle down. By the time most people reach the age of 40, their place in the framework of society is fairly well established. They have settled down to have a family (or have decided not to). They have established what is to be their major life work or career. If anything, the movement to middle age involves a transition filled with reexamination (Levinson et al., 1974).

During the middle years, one is forced to contemplate one's own mortality. The so-called middle-age spread and loss of muscle tone, accompanied by facial wrinkles, and graying hair or signs of impending baldness, are evident each day in the mirror. You now tend to notice obituaries in the newspaper where more and more people of your age (or younger) are listed every day.

For some people, this realization that time is running out produces something of a crisis, even approaching panic. For most, however, middle age is a time of great satisfaction and opportunity (Rossi, 1980). In most cases, children are grown, some are off having families of their own. Careers are in full bloom. Time is available as never before for leisure and commitment to community, perhaps in the form of volunteer work.

It is during these years that the individual faces what Erikson calls the crisis of *generativity vs. stagnation.* The individual often shifts from thinking about all that they have done with their life to considering what they will do with what time is left for them and how they can leave a mark on future generations (Erikson, 1963; Harris, 1983). Careers and jobs begin to draw to a close and retirement nears. Preparations begin to get the most out of old age.

The middle years of adulthood are ones of settling down and reflecting. During this period, children are often grown and gone, careers are well-established, and there is more time for leisure and commitment to community.

Old Age

Now we can return to some of the questions we raised at the very beginning of this topic, where we introduced the concept of ageism and attitudes about the elderly, here taken to be those over 65 years of age.

The first thing we need to realize is that persons over the age of 65 comprise a sizable proportion of the population in the United States. More than 25.5 million Americans are in this age bracket, and the numbers are increasing by an average of 1,400 per day (Kermis, 1984; Storandt, 1983). Given the fact that people are living longer, coupled with the declining birth rates in this country, it is no surprise that the U.S. population now includes more people over the age of 65 than ever before. And the trend should continue for some time. By the year 2020, Americans over 65 will comprise nearly 20 percent of the population (Eisdorfer, 1983).

One misconception about the aged is that they live in misery. Yes, there are often some miseries that have to be attended to. Sensory capacities are not what they used to be. But, as Skinner (1983) suggests, "If you cannot read, listen to book recordings. If you do not hear well, turn up the volume of your phonograph (and wear headphones to protect your neighbors)." Yes, death becomes a reality. As many as 50 percent of the women in this country over 65 are widows. But many elderly people (3,000 in 1978) choose this time of their lives to marry for the *first time* (Kalish, 1982).

Yes, children have long since "left the nest," but they are still in touch, and now there are grandchildren with whom to interact. Moreover, the children of the elderly have themselves now reached adulthood and are more able and likely to provide support for aging parents. In fact, only about 5 percent of elderly Americans live in nursing homes, and fewer than 20 percent are unable to get around, to come and go as they please (Harris, 1975, 1983). Yes, many individuals dread retirement, but most welcome it as an opportunity to do those things they have planned on for years (Haynes *et al.,* 1978). Many people over 65 become *more* physically active after retiring from a job where they were tied to a desk all day long.

Although we often assume that old age necessarily brings with it the curse of poor health, a 1981 Harris survey tells us that only 21 percent of the respondents over age 65 claimed poor health to be a serious problem. That compares to 8 percent in the 18 to 54 age range, and 18 percent in the 55 to 65 age range. So although health problems are more common, they are not nearly as widespread or devastating as we might think. (It should also be noted that poor health among the elderly is very much related to income and educational levels. For example, 31 percent of those with incomes below $5,000 reported serious health problems.)

In the introduction to a series of articles on aging published in the American Psychological Association's journal in 1983, James Birren made this summary statement, "Generally, the quality of life for most older adults is far from bad" (p. 298). One of the findings of the 1975 Harris poll dispelled another myth of ageism: that old people are lonely. Eight percent claimed that they had no close person to talk to, but 5 percent of those surveyed who were younger than 65 agreed to the same statement. In short, old age is not as bad as we sometimes let ourselves believe; that is, it is not necessarily so.

To return one last time to Erikson, we find that his final stage of psychosocial development is reserved for this period beyond the age of 65. According to Erikson, it is at this stage that it is common for individuals to pause and reflect on their lives, what they have accomplished, the mark they have left, and what they might do with the time remaining. If all goes well with this self-examination, the individual develops a sense of *ego identity*—a sense of wholeness, an acceptance that all is well and can only get better. If self-examination results in regret, if life seems unfulfilled, with choices badly made, then one may face despair and turn only to death.

Of the two sure things in life, death and taxes, the former is the surer. There are no loopholes. Dealing with the reality of our own deaths is the last major conflict or crisis that we face in life. As it happens, many people never have to deal with their own death in psychological terms. These are the people who die young, or suddenly, either from natural or accidental causes. But many individuals have the time to contemplate their own dying, and this usually takes place in old age.

Much attention was focused on the confrontation with death in the popular book *On Death and Dying* by Elisabeth Kübler-Ross (1969). Her description of the stages that one goes through when facing death was based upon hundreds of interviews with terminally ill patients who were aware that they were dying. Kübler-Ross suggests that the process takes place in five stages: (1) *Denial*—a firm, simple avoidance of the evidence; a sort of, "No, this can't be happening to me" reaction. (2) *Anger*—often accompanied by resentment and envy of others, along with a realization of what is truly happening; a sort of "Why me? Why not someone else" reaction. (3) *Bargaining*—a matter of dealing, of barter, usually with God; a search for more time; a sort of "If you'll just grant me a few more weeks, or months, I'll go to church every week; no, every day" reaction. (4) *Depression*—a sense of hopelessness; that bargaining won't work, that a great loss is imminent; a period of grief and sorrow both over past mistakes and what will be missed in the future. (5) *Acceptance*—a rather quiet facing of the reality of death, with no great joy or sadness; a realization that the time has come.

It turns out that the Kübler-Ross description is an idealized one—perhaps too much so. Many dying patients do not seem to fit this pattern at all. Some may show behaviors consistent with one or two of the stages, but seldom all five. There is also a concern that this pattern of approaching death may be viewed as the "best" or the "right" way to go about it. Fears are that caretakers may try to force dying people into and through these stages, instead of letting each face the inevitability of death in his or her own way (Kalish, 1976).

Although elderly people may be more preoccupied with dying and death than are younger people, they are no more morbid about it. In one study (Kalish and Reynolds, 1976), adults over 60 did more frequently think about and talk about death than did the younger adults surveyed. However, of all the adults in the study, the oldest group expressed the least fear of death, some even admitting they were eager for it.

Old age is a time for reflecting on one's life and achievements. If an individual has a sense of wholeness and acceptance, he or she can face the rest of life and death calmly and gladly.

Before you go on

Summarize some of what we know about the elderly in this country.

If you have read all three topics in this chapter, you might now be quite impressed with how orderly and lawful human development can be. Chromosomes line up to form zygotes. Zygotes become embryos, fetuses, and, through birth, neonates. Neonates are born with a range of adaptive reflexes and sensory capabilities. Motor development progresses through identifiable stages. Cognitive development progresses through five stages, and psychosocial development passes through eight stages. Many of the conflicts of adolescence are predictable. Adulthood moves from choice to commitment to preparation for death.

As easy as it is to be impressed with the lawful orderliness of human development, we must always remember not to take all of this too literally. Orderly sequences of development emerge from examining averages and progressions *in general.* Developmental trends and stages are like so many other things: If one looks hard enough, they can be found. But, the individual differences that we see around us constantly remind us that for any *one individual,* child, adolescent, or adult, many of our observations may not hold true. It is important to keep in mind that the picture we have drawn in this chapter is one of general conclusions to which there will always be exceptions.

By now you are aware that the ages that we indicate for major developmental landmarks are not to be taken as being applicable to every individual. Some people go through developmental stages at different ages. Such is the case for puberty—the biological indicator of adolescence, marked by a growth spurt and the capability for sexual reproduction. Many boys and girls reach this level before or after most of their peers, or age-mates. They are commonly referred to as early and late bloomers. The consequences of attaining puberty significantly sooner or later than average are often quite important at the time, although we should mention right at the start that few of these consequences are long-lasting, particularly for girls.

Let's first get an idea of what early and late maturation means. Figure 19.4 depicts, for males and females, the age ranges during which the major developments associated with puberty may be expected. Notice that for boys, the spurt in height may *begin* as early as 10½ and may not end for some until 17½. Pubic hair may start to grow at age 11, or not until age 14. Some 13-year-old boys may look very childlike, short and immature in appearance, while others the very same age may have already taken on the appearance of young men. Similarly for girls, note that enlargement of the breasts may begin for some as early as age 8, or as late as age 13. As we have already indicated, the first menstrual period (menarche) may be experienced at about age 10, or not until age 15. Early maturing girls at age 13 may look like young women while late bloomers still appear very "girlish" and childlike.

What are the advantages and disadvantages of early maturation? A girl who is an early bloomer is not only taller than other girls her age, but often towers over the *boys* her own age. She may be more athletic, stronger, and faster than the boys in her class. Given her appearance, she is more likely to be approached for dates, although she may not date more often. She may have more early sexual encounters and may marry at a younger age than her age-mates, particularly those who are late bloomers (Hughes & Noppe, 1985). The early maturing girl often has problems with her self-image, particularly if she puts on extra weight and shows marked breast development.

Because of the premium put on physical activity in boys, the early maturing boy is at a greater advantage than is the early maturing girl. Because of his appearance, the early blooming boy will have more dating and sexual experiences than the average boy. And whereas early dating and sexual experiences may have negative consequences for females (they may be viewed as being "loose" or immoral), they often raise the status of young boys, particularly among their peers.

For young teenagers, being a late bloomer is more negative in its impact than being an early bloomer. A late-maturing girl will have difficulty establishing relationships with boys and will show less interest in them than average (Hughes & Noppe, 1985). The late maturing boy finds himself in an equally unpleasant position. Not only will his athletic abilities tend to be below average, but he will not generally find success with members of the opposite sex, which won't help to enhance his self-esteem any. There is some evidence (Jones, 1957) that late-maturing boys carry a sense of

Figure 19.4

These graphs illustrate the ages at which certain physical changes occur in the average male and female during puberty.
(After Tanner, 1973.)

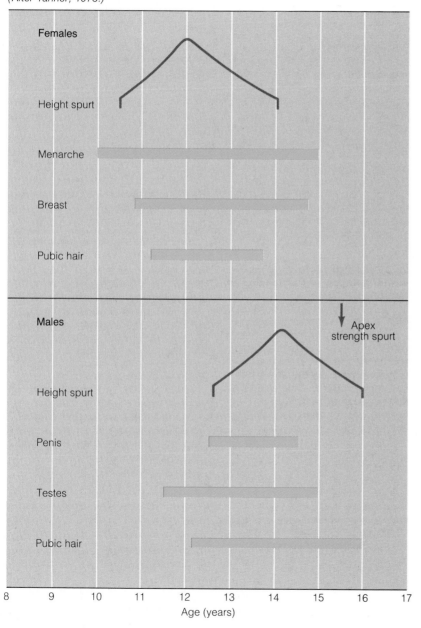

inadequacy and poor self-esteem into adulthood. Late maturity for girls seems to have very little long-term negative consequences. Some feel—in retrospect—that being a late bloomer was turned to an advantage because it afforded them an opportunity to develop other, broadening interests, rather than becoming "boy crazy" like so many of their peers in early adolescence (Tobin-Richards et al., 1984).

How any one child/adolescent responds to her or his physical maturity at puberty will be ultimately affected by many variables: peer-group reaction, parental and family support, cognitive and social skills that develop at the same time, and so on. Summary generalizations are tentative, but we may suggest that (1) early maturity is more advantageous than late maturity, at least at the time of one's adolescence, (2) boys profit from early maturity more than do girls, but may also suffer more from late maturity, and (3) it is difficult if not impossible to attribute any individual differences that appear after adolescence to one's age at puberty.

TOPIC SUMMARY

How might adolescence be defined from a physical, social, and psychological point of view?

Adolescence may be defined in a number of ways. Physically, it is said to begin with puberty and last until the end of one's physical growth. Psychologically, it is defined in terms of the cognitions and feelings that characterize the period, searching for identity and awareness of one's sexuality. Socially, it is a marginal period, coming between childhood and adulthood, and is defined in terms of how the adolescent is viewed by others. / 340

Briefly describe the physical changes that accompany the beginnings of adolescence.

Two significant physical developments mark adolescence: a spurt of growth (seen at an earlier age in girls than in boys) and the beginnings of sexual maturity. That is, as adolescents, individuals are for the first time physically prepared for sexual reproduction. / 343

Cite some of the data that suggests that adolescents are sexually active, and may be more so than in the past.

By 1980, surveys of adolescents indicated that, as a group, teenagers were engaging in sexual intercourse at rates higher than those found in earlier, similar surveys. Whereas a 1971 survey suggested that about 30 percent of female respondents had had sexual intercourse, 43 percent reported having had intercourse in a 1976 sample, and nearly 50 percent of a 1979 sample reported having had sexual intercourse. Slightly more than 70 percent of male respondents in the 1979 survey reported that they had had intercourse. In 1980, more than half a million births in the United States were to adolescent mothers, nearly 10,000 to mothers 14 or younger. / 345

Summarize the adolescent's search of identity as described by Erikson and Marcia.

The search for one's identity—a sense of who one is and what one is to do with one's life—is, for Erikson, the major conflict of adolescence. Most teenagers develop such a sense of identity, while some enter adulthood in a state of role confusion. Garcia has proposed that searching for one's identity is a process that itself goes through stages, from a lack of commitment, to acceptance of attitudes, goals, and values of others, to a challenge and examination of one's own goals, values, and attitudes, to finally resolving the conflict and fixing one's identity. All aspects of self-awareness and identity may not be resolved or fixed at the same time. / 347

What is meant by sex-role identification, and how is the concept of androgyny relevant?

Sex-role identification deals with the appreciation, begun in childhood and central to adolescence, and learning of the accepted attitudes and expectations that others have of how one *should* act and what one *should* think or feel as a function of being either female or male. The concept of androgyny implies that any individual need not be masculine *or* feminine, but may encompass the values, attitudes, and behaviors traditionally associated with either sex to different degrees. / 348

What developments may be said to characterize young adulthood?

Young adulthood encompasses roughly those years between the ages of 18 and 40. In this period, one assumes responsibilities, becomes independent (at least from parental control), and is faced with decisions concerning career, marriage, and family. For Erikson, the period is marked by the conflict between intimacy and social relationships on the one hand and social isolation on the other. / 351

What issues are faced during the middle years of adulthood?

In many ways, the middle years of adulthood (roughly ages 40 to 65) define a period of settling down and reexamination of one's life goals. The individual comes to accept his or her own mortality in a number of ways. This is the period, according to Erikson, of generativity—a sense of leaving one's mark and making a contribution for future generations, or a sense of stagnation. / 351

Summarize some of what we know about the elderly in this country.

There are now more than 25 million Americans over the age of 65, and the number of elderly is growing daily. Although there are often sensory and physical limits placed by old age, only 21 percent of elderly people rate health problems as a major concern (and one's economic status is a major predictor of problems in this area). Although some elderly persons are isolated and lonely, fewer than 5 percent live in nursing homes and only 8 percent consider themselves lonely. And although older people are more concerned about death than are younger people, they are neither consumed nor morbid about it. / 353

CHAPTER NINE

MOTIVATION, EMOTION, AND STRESS

TOPIC 20 Motivation

See if you can remember what it was like to start grade school. Can you remember the excitement, the anticipation, the scary feeling of leaving home to go to school? It's unlikely that you had any specific educational or career goals in mind as you began your school years. After a few years in grade school, however, a definite goal begins to take shape for many youngsters: to get out of grade school and go to junior high.

"In junior high, they have different teachers and change classes and have athletics instead of recess and everything." Upon entering junior high school, you probably felt quite pleased with yourself; you had reached your goal. But soon, a new goal became clear in your mind: You wanted "to get out of junior high school and go to senior high school, with all the big kids."

As your final spring term approached in high school, you may have suffered from a common ailment: "senioritis." More than anything else, you wanted high school to be over with. You were motivated to finish to get out. What mattered then was a new goal: to go to college.

Well, here you are. You're in college. You're taking an introductory psychology course and have probably just recently begun your college career. If you're like many other students, a new goal may have entered your life: You want to get on with it; you want to get out of college so you can get a job. The goals have changed, yet remained very much the same: You want to finish the job at hand so that a new one can be attempted.

There are three points that can be made about this scenario, and they will be relevant throughout this topic. (1) The description of the chain of events we've described here certainly does not apply to everyone. It may not apply to you. There are any number of people who never had much desire to get out of junior high school and go to high school. Many more have no desire or motivation to go to college. Getting out of high school, one way or another, was good enough for them; going to college was unthinkable. And not all college students enter college and immediately start dreaming about graduation—although that goal is clear in the minds of some. The point is that different people, even in the same situation, are often motivated by different needs and goals.

(2) A second point that this example makes about motivation is that it draws our attention to the *cyclical nature* of motivation. In a way, to be a motivated organism is to be in a cycle. Soon after one goal is reached (getting out of grade school, for instance), another often comes to take its place (getting out of junior high), and then another and another. Think of this motivational cycle in terms of something very basic, such as hunger and eating. If you are hungry, you are motivated to eat; getting something to eat is your goal. No matter how much you eat, however, you will not eat so much that you won't be hungry again. Soon the need for food and the goal of eating will reappear.

(3) A third point about this discussion is that motivational cycles imply no value judgment, no right or wrong, good or bad. Some students see the cyclical nature of motivation as downright depressing. "What's the point," they argue, "if everytime I finally reach a goal, there's just going to be another one there to take its place; I'll never be happy."

Such arguments miss an important point. In order for new goals to become established, old ones often need to be satisfied first. It may be true that many of us do not spend enough time reflecting on past goals achieved. Instead of focusing on how long it's going to take to graduate from college, reflect on the fact that you *have* graduated from high school. It is a good idea to remember how badly you wanted to do that and get into college.

Why We Care

motivation
those forces that arouse and direct behavior in order to satisfy needs or reach goals

In this topic, we will address some important practical issues. We are going to deal with questions concerning the *why* of behavior. In many ways, these are the most difficult types of questions in psychology. These are questions dealing with **motivation,** the process that arouses and directs behavior in order to satisfy needs or reach goals.

You don't need a psychologist to convince you that motivation is an important concept in your daily life. We have already seen that motivation affects virtually everything we do. Motivation influences our ability to learn, affects our memory, and even has an impact on so basic a process as perception.

We'll get our discussion underway by considering some different ways in which psychologists have approached the study of motivation, and we'll define some basic terms. The theoretical approaches presented here are not necessarily mutually exclusive. They have much in common, and we will be able to find a number of useful ideas within each approach.

The remainder of the topic will be spent reviewing what we know about two different sorts of motives: (1) those that are very basic, related to our survival, and rooted in our biology or physiology, (we'll call these physiologically-based drives), and (2) those motives that are not rooted in biology, but are more clearly learned and/or social in nature (we'll call these psychologically-based motives).

THEORETICAL APPROACHES TO MOTIVATION

arousal
one's level of activation or excitement; indicative of a motivational state

An assumption that we make about motivation is that it involves two subprocesses. First, we see motivation as providing the **arousal,** or activation, of behavior. Here we are using the term motivation in the sense of a force that gets behaviors going, gets an organism to do something. The second process of motivation is that of providing *direction* or focus to our behaviors. Here we are using the term motivation in the sense of answering the question, "Why did he or she do *that*?" In this sense, a motivated organism's behavior is viewed as being goal-directed and in some way purposeful. There are obviously many reasons why people do what they do. We are subject to the influences of a great number of individual motives that activate and direct our behaviors.

From its earliest days, psychology has attempted to find some systematic approach, or theory, that could summarize and organize what different motives or motivational states have in common. In this section, we'll review some of these approaches in a somewhat chronological order.

Instinct

instinct
an unlearned, complex pattern of behavior that occurs in the presence of particular stimuli

In the early days of psychology, explaining a person's behavior was a rather simple matter. Behaviors could be explained in terms of innate **instincts.** Instincts are complex patterns of behavior that occur in the presence of certain stimuli. These complex behavior patterns are unlearned. They are inherited, or innate. Why do birds build nests? A nest-building instinct. Why do salmon swim upstream to mate? Instinct, of course.

That may explain some of the behavior of birds and salmon, but what about people? Do people have instincts, too? William James (1890) thought

Many complex behaviors can be explained in terms of innate instincts. For example, spiders build webs and bees pollinate flowers because of instinct.

that they do. In fact, James reasoned that humans, as more complex beings, no doubt had many more instincts than did "lower" animals.

No one expressed the instinctual explanation of human behaviors more forcefully than William McDougall (1908). He suggested that human behaviors were motivated by 11 basic instincts (repulsion, curiosity, flight, parental, reproductive, gregarious, acquisitive, constructive, pugnacity, self-abasement, and self-assertion). Soon he extended his list to include 18 instincts. As new and different behaviors required explanation, new and different instincts were devised to explain them. What began as a serious and sensible scientific enterprise soon became rather pointless, as lists of human instincts became longer and longer.

A man who often got into brawls at the local tavern was said to be motivated by an aggressiveness-pugnacity instinct. A woman who frequently attended meetings and quilting bees was responding to her gregariousness instinct. Some people were thought to have cleanliness instincts, while others could be said to have sloppiness instincts.

As lists of human instincts got longer and longer, the basic problem with this approach became obvious. Particularly for humans, explaining behavior patterns by alluding to instinct simply renamed or relabeled them and didn't explain anything at all. But, lest we simply dispense with this approach totally, the psychologists who argued for instincts did introduce and draw attention to an idea that is still very much with us today—that we may engage in some behaviors for reasons that are basically physiological and more inherited than learned.

Needs and Drives

An approach that provided an alternative to explaining behavior in terms of instincts was one that attempted to explain the "whys" of behavior in terms of needs and drives. This approach, dominant in the 1940s and 1950s, is best associated with Clark Hull (1943).

A **need** is a lack or shortage of some biological essential required for survival. Needs arise from deprivation. When an organism is kept from food, it develops a need for food. If deprived of water, a need develops. A need

need
lack or shortage of some biological essential that is required by an organism for survival

drive
the arousing and directing experience of a state of need, thus motivating behavior

then gives rise to a drive. A **drive** is a state of tension, arousal, or activation. When an organism is in a *drive state,* it is motivated. It is aroused and directed to do something to satisfy the drive by reducing or eliminating the underlying need.

This approach is much less circular than an appeal to instincts. A need gives rise to a drive. For example, having gone without food for some time, a need develops. The need for food may give rise to a hunger drive. Then what? Here is where learning, experience, and reinforcement can come into play. Whereas instincts are directly tied to a specific pattern of behavior, needs and drives are not. They are concepts that can be used to explain why we do what we do, while still allowing for the influence of experience and the environment.

There are some complications that arise with a need-drive theory of motivation. One complication concerns the relationship between the strength of a need and the strength of the drive that results from it. As needs increase in strength, so do drives. But if needs become *too* great, drives often start to weaken. For example, we may become *so* deprived of water (i.e., have such a strong need) that we become weak and disoriented. In such a condition, our behavior may become *less* aroused or directed toward finding and consuming water (i.e., the drive becomes weaker). Here, increasing the need too much causes a decrease in the drive.

A second complication of a need-drive approach centers on the biological nature of needs. To claim that needs arise only from biological deprivations seems unduly restrictive.

Why did you have breakfast this morning? Because you were hungry. You experienced a hunger drive based on your physiological need for food. That seems reasonable enough. Unfortunately, however, such explanations often seem less helpful when we try to account for many human behaviors. It seems that not all of the drives that activate a person's behavior are based on biological needs. Humans often engage in behaviors to satisfy *learned* needs. Drives based on learned needs are called *secondary,* as opposed to *primary drives* that are based on unlearned, physiological needs. In fact, *most* of the needs that you and I work so hard to reduce have little to do with our physiology at all.

You may feel that you need a new car this year. I may convince myself that I need a new set of golf clubs, and we'll both work very hard to save the money to buy what we need. It is difficult to imagine how your car or my golf clubs could be satisfying a biological need.

It does seem that people often behave in such a way as to reduce drives and thus satisfy needs. Sometimes, drives are produced by biological, tissue needs, and we can speak of primary drives. At other times, our needs are learned or acquired and give rise to secondary drives. The ultimate goal of drives in most cases is the fulfillment of the needs that produced them, whether those needs are learned or unlearned. How that goal is reached will reflect the learning history of the organism.

Incentives

incentive
a goal that an organism may be motivated to approach or avoid

An alternative to a drive-reduction approach to motivation focuses not on what *starts* the behavior, but on the *end state,* or goal, of behavior. According to this approach, external stimuli serve as motivating agents, goals, or **incentives** for our behavior. Incentives act to *pull* our behavior, as opposed to drives, which *push* our behavior. Incentive theory frees us from relying on biological or physiological concepts to explain the "whys" of one's behaviors.

When a mountain climber says that he or she climbs a mountain "because it is there," the climber is indicating a type of motivation through incentive. You may not read this topic because you need to, but because reading it will help you reach your goal of a good grade on the next exam. After a very large meal, we may order a piece of cherry cheesecake, not because we need it in any physiological sense, but because it's there on the dessert cart and looks so good.

Some parents want to know how to motivate their child to clean up his or her room. A teacher wants to know how to motivate a student to earn high grades. A supervisor want to know how to motivate employees to work harder. Each of these cases may be interpreted in terms of establishing incentives.

What those parents *really* want to know is how they can get their child to value, work for, and be reinforced by a clean room. The teacher wants to know how to get a student to view learning and high grades as incentives worth working for. Similarly, the supervisor is looking for some technique to convince employees that hard work is a worthwhile thing to do. None of these people have problems that are easily solved, but it would help if they understood the nature of their own questions.

Let's take the parents as an example. First, let's recognize that they don't necessarily want to motivate anyone. What they want is a clean room, and they'd like to have the child clean it. If they do want the child to be motivated to clean his or her room, he or she needs to learn the value or incentive of having a clean room. You can imagine the child's response: "Why should I?" "Because I told you to," becomes the almost reflexive response. Now, *how* to teach a child that a clean room is a thing to be valued is, in fact, another story, probably involving other incentives that the child does value. We reviewed these issues back in Topic 11. For now, let's simply acknowledge that establishing a clean room as a valued goal is the major task at hand. Having a clean room is obviously not an innate, inborn need. The parents have learned to value clean rooms, and there is hope that their child can also learn to be similarly motivated.

People often do things because they are motivated by some incentive. People climb mountains because they are motivated to conquer the mountain—that is their incentive; that is what drives them.

Before you go on

How have the concepts of instinct, drive, and incentive been used to explain motivated behaviors?

PHYSIOLOGICALLY-BASED DRIVES

The motives that activate and direct our behaviors can be classified or organized in a number of different ways. We'll use a very simple system that suggests that there are just two major types of motivators: those that have a biological basis, which we will call *physiological-based drives,* and those that are more clearly learned or social in nature, which we'll call *psychologically-based motives.*

There are a few important points that you'll need to keep in mind about this classification scheme. For one thing, note that we will use the term *drive* for those activators of behavior that have a biological or physiological basis and the term *motive* for those that do not. In all other ways, drive and motive may be thought of as synonymous terms. Second, you should note that even drives that are rooted in an organism's physiology may be affected by psychological processes. Hunger, for example, is clearly a physiologically-based drive, but what we eat, when we eat, and how much we eat are often influenced by psychological and social factors.

Homeostasis

A concept of central importance in our consideration of physiologically-based drives is **homeostasis.** This term means *equal state,* and it is usually used to refer to the optimum balance of internal physiological processes. In a way, the need to maintain homeostasis is the most general of all physiological needs. It is our need to find and maintain a state of equilibrium, or balance, among internal conditions.

The concept was first introduced to the mainstream of psychology by Walter Cannon in 1932. The idea is that each of our physiological processes has a normal, balanced, "set point" of operation. Whenever anything happens to disrupt this balance, we become motivated. We are driven to do whatever we can to return to our homeostatic level. If we drift only slightly from our balance point, our own physiological mechanisms may act to return us to homeostasis without our intention or awareness. If these automatic processes are unsuccessful, we may then act, motivated by the basic need to maintain homeostasis. Just how homeostasis can be used to explain behavior may be more clear after we look at a few examples.

Temperature Regulation

Most of us seldom give our own body temperature much thought. We all have a fuzzy notion that 98.6 °F is our normal, homeostatic body temperature. That body temperature has anything to do with motivation becomes sensible in the context of homeostasis. Whenever anything happens to elevate or depress our body temperature above or below its homeostatic level, we become motivated. We become motivated to return our body temperature to its normal, balanced 98.6°.

Let's say you are outside on a very cold day, and you are improperly dressed for the low temperature and high wind. Soon your body temperature

When our body temperature is above or below its normal level, we are motivated to return the temperature to its normal 98.6°. Feeling cold may motivate you to put on more clothes before the big snowball fight. Feeling hot may motivate you to douse yourself with water after running a long race.

Figure 20.1
A number of small structures make up the limbic system, including the amygdala,
septum hypothalamus, thalamus, and hippocampus.

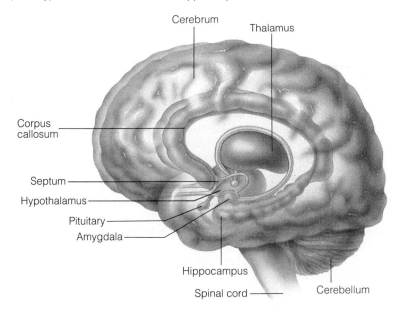

Cerebrum

Thalamus

Corpus
callosum

Septum

Hypothalamus

Pituitary

Amygdala

Hippocampus

Spinal cord

Cerebellum

starts to drop. Automatically, your body starts to respond to do what it can to
elevate your temperature back to its normal level: blood vessels in the hands
and feet constrict, forcing blood back to the center of the body to conserve
heat (as a result, your lips turn blue); you start to shiver, and the involuntary
movements of your muscles create small amounts of heat energy.

Or, imagine that you are walking across a desert, fully dressed, at noon on
a day in August. Your body temperature begins to rise. Automatically, blood
is forced to the body's surface where it can deflect heat. You begin to per-
spire, and the moisture on the surface of the skin evaporates, cooling the
skin—all in an attempt to return your body's temperature to its homeostatic
level.

There are two centers in your brain that act as a thermostat and instigate
these attempts at temperature regulation. Both are located in the
hypothalamus deep inside the brain (see Figure 20.1). One center is particularly sensitive to elevated body temperatures, the other to lowered temperatures. Together they act to mobilize the internal environment when normal
balance is upset.

Note that if these reactions are not successful, you may be motivated to
take some voluntary action on your own. You may have to get inside, out of
the cold or heat. You may need to put on or take off some clothes. You may
need to turn on the furnace or the air conditioner. Over and above what your
body can do automatically, you may have to engage in (learned) voluntary
behaviors to maintain homeostasis.

hypothalamus
*a small structure at the base of the brain
involved in many drives, including thirst,
hunger, sex, and temperature regulation*

Before you go on
**Given the concept of homeostasis, how might temperature
regulation be thought of as a physiologically-based drive?**

We drink because we need to, because we are driven by thirst to satisfy our needs for liquids.

Thirst and Drinking Behavior

Surely we need water for survival. If we don't drink, we die. As the need for water increases, it gives rise to a thirst drive. The intriguing issue is not so much that we need to drink, but how we *know* that we're thirsty. What actually causes us to seek liquid and drink it?

Internal, Physiological Cues For a very long time, we thought that we knew the simple answer: We drink to relieve the discomfort caused by the dryness of our mouths and throats. No doubt, the unpleasantness of a dry mouth and throat *does* cause us to drink. But there must be more to drinking behavior than this.

Animals with no salivary glands, whose mouths and throats are constantly dry, drink no more than normal animals (more frequently, yes, but no more in terms of quantity). Normal bodily processes (urination, perspiration, exhaling, etc.) cause us to lose about 2½ liters of water a day (Levinthal, 1983). That water needs to be replaced, but how do we know when to do so?

About two thirds of the fluid in our bodies is contained *within* our body's cells (intracellular), and about one third is held in the spaces *between* cells (extracellular). There appear to be two separate mechanisms sensitive to losses of fluid from each of these areas. Intercellular loss of fluid is monitored by regions of the hypothalamus. One small center seems to "turn on" the thirst drive when fluid levels are low, and another center "turns off" thirst when fluid levels are adequate. Thirst that stems from extracellular fluid loss is monitored (in a complex chain of events) by the kidneys, which stimulate the production of a hormone that leads to a thirst drive.

External, Psychological Cues Often our drinking is motivated by a physiological drive that arises from our physiological need for water. Sometimes, however, our drinking behavior may be influenced by external factors, or incentives. The implication here, as we have mentioned earlier, is that we may become motivated to drink, not in response to internal needs, but in response to external stimulation. For example, the aroma of freshly brewed coffee may stimulate us to order a second (unneeded) cup. A frosty glass of iced tea may look too good to refuse. We may drink a cold beer or soda simply because it tastes so good, whether we *need* the fluid they contain or not.

Notice also that once motivated, *what* we drink may be strongly influenced by our previous learning experiences. Some people prefer Coke; some prefer Pepsi. Others would choose a different brand. Some people do not like cola drinks at all. Choices and preferences for what we drink are shaped by availability (people from New England seldom drink coconut milk) and past experience.

Before you go on

List some of the factors that may influence drinking behavior.

Hunger and Eating Behavior

Our need for food is as obvious as our need for water. If we don't eat, we die. Again, the interesting question involves what it is that gives rise to the hunger drive? The answer to this question is very complex indeed. There are many factors that motivate a person to eat. Some of them are physiological in nature. Some are more psychological, reflecting learning experiences. Some involve social pressures. Let's briefly summarize some of the evidence.

Internal, Physiological Cues   We are often driven to eat by the discomforting feelings associated with having an empty stomach. As the walls of our stomach begin to rub against each other, making disturbing sounds, we interpret these signs as indicating a need for food.

Once again, however, eating is also motivated in other ways. People and animals with no stomachs still feel hungry periodically and eat amounts of food not unlike those eaten by people with stomachs intact. Beyond the stomach itself, the two structures that now seem most involved in the hunger drive are the hypothalamus and the liver.

Theories of hunger that focus on the role of the hypothalamus are referred to as *dual-center theories.* This label is used because such views suggest that there are *two* regions in the hypothalamus that regulate food intake. One is an "eat" center that gives rise to feelings of hunger, while the other is a "no eat" center that let's us know when we've had enough.

There are two centers (called *nuclei*) in the hypothalamus that have predictable effects on eating behavior when they are either electrically stimulated or destroyed by surgical lesion. Removing, or lesioning, the "eat center," for example, leads to starvation; while lesioning the "no eat center" leads to extreme overeating (Friedman & Stricker, 1976; Keesey & Powley, 1975).

Although the hypothalamus may be involved in eating behaviors, normal eating patterns are not under the influence of artificial electrical stimulation and lesioning procedures. What activates the brain's food-regulating centers in a normal organism? Here, we are still very much at the level of hypothesis, not fact.

A long-accepted view was that the body responds to levels of blood sugar, or glucose, in our blood. When glucose levels are low—which they are when we haven't eaten for awhile—we are stimulated to eat. When blood sugar levels are adequate, we are stimulated to stop eating. And, it may be that our *liver* is the organ that most closely monitors such blood chemistry for us.

Another view holds that we respond (through a complex chain of events) to levels of fat stored in our bodies. When fat stores are adequately filled, we feel no hunger. When fat supplies are depleted, a hunger drive arises.

We probably receive a number of internal cues that simultaneously inform us of our physiological need for food. Many of the cues may be subtle and effective in the long term (such as a sensitivity to stored fat levels), others may be more immediate and attention-grabbing (such as "hunger pangs" from an empty stomach). Eating behaviors, however, may also be influenced by factors over and above those from our physiology.

External, Psychological Cues   We often respond to external cues that stimulate us to engage in eating behavior. Here we'll list a few of the nonphysiological influences that may motivate us to eat.

Sometimes, just the *stimulus properties* of foods—their aroma, taste, or appearance—may be enough to get us to eat. You may not want any dessert after a large meal until the waitress shows you a piece of creamy cheesecake with cherry topping. Ordering and eating that cheesecake has nothing to do with your internal physiological conditions.

Sometimes people eat more from *habit* than from need. "It's twelve o'clock. It's lunch time; so let's eat." We may fall into habits of eating at certain times, tied more to the clock than to internal cues from our bodies. Some people are virtually unable to watch television without poking salty foods in their mouths—a behavioral pattern motivated more by learning than by physiology.

Occasionally, we find that we eat simply because others around us are eating. Such *socially facilitated* eating has been noted in a number of species

Though we need to eat to survive, there are people who consume more calories than they burn off and become obese. Bad eating habits and lack of exercise are often contributing factors in cases of obesity.

(for example, Harlow, 1932; Tolman, 1969). A caged chicken, for example, is allowed to eat its fill of grain, and eventually it stops eating. When other hungry chickens are placed in the cage and begin to eat, the "full" chicken starts right in eating again, its behaviors not noticeably different from those just added to the cage.

Obesity—An Example There is no doubt that ours is a weight-conscious society. The odds are good that you are on some weight-reduction program or at least know someone who is. People try to lose weight for cosmetic reasons (to look better) or for health reasons (being obese can cause health problems), or both. The basic reason for obesity is that a person is consuming more calories than he or she is burning off with mental or physical activity. Other than that, about all we know about obesity is that it is a complex condition, with many interacting causes.

There *are* biological differences between obese people and those of normal body weight. One notable biological difference is that obese individuals have a greater *number* of fat cells (and larger fat cells) than normal-weight individuals (Nisbett, 1972). Evidence seems to suggest that this higher number of cells is largely due to genetic influences (overweight parents tend to have overweight children). It may also be the case that the number of fat cells in a person's body may be influenced by feeding patterns established in infancy. Beyond childhood, the number of fat cells in the body remains quite stable, although they may change in size (Knittle, 1975).

Some (though probably few) obese individuals have some sort of hypothalamic problem that stimulates a higher than normal desire for food (Nisbett, 1972). It is Nisbett's view that some people have an established homeostatic level (in this context called a *set point*) with regard to food that is simply higher than average. As a result, when such people diet and lose weight, they may be upsetting a homeostatic balance, which for them requires that they weigh more than others of the same age and height.

Most cases of obesity probably involve more than just internal, physiological causes. They may also reflect learning histories and responsiveness to external cues (Rodin, 1981).

Stanley Schachter (1971) is the psychologist most closely associated with the view that argues that overweight people tend to be less sensitive to internal hunger cues from their bodies and more sensitive to external eating cues from the environment.

In one demonstration, Schachter provided normal-weight and overweight subjects with a bowl of almonds to eat while they filled out a questionnaire. In one condition, the almonds were shelled and ready to eat. In the other experimental condition, the almonds were in the shell and effort was required to eat them. Normal-weight subjects ate the same amount of nuts in either case, relying, Schachter claimed, on internal hunger mechanisms: If they felt hungry, they would eat the almonds, whether they needed to be shelled or not. The overweight subjects ate many more nuts when they could be consumed without effort, hardly touching them if they had to be shelled first. They weren't hungry enough to bother shelling the nuts, but if they were there ready to eat, the nuts were eaten in large quantities.

For those people who are overweight, it would be nice to know that there is some simple, foolproof way to lose weight. Given that there are so many factors that influence eating, such a hope seems unlikely to be fulfilled in the near future. It seems that no one physiological mechanism has the sole control of our hunger drive. And it seems that no one personality trait leads to obesity (Leon & Roth, 1977).

Before you go on
List those internal and external factors that influence our drives to eat.

Sex Drives and Sexual Behavior

As a physiologically-based drive, the sex drive is unique in a number of ways. First, the survival of the individual does not depend on its satisfaction. If we don't drink, we die; if we don't regulate our temperature, we die; if we don't eat, we die. If we don't have sex—well, we don't die. The survival of the *species* requires that an adequate number of its members respond successfully to a sex drive, but an individual member can get along without doing so.

Second, most physiologically-based drives, including hunger, thirst, and temperature regulation, provide a mechanism to replenish and maintain the body's energy. When satisfied, the sex drive depletes bodily energy. In fact, the sex drive motivates the organism to seek tension, as opposed to those drives that seek to reduce tension to return to homeostasis.

Third, to the extent that the sex drive is physiologically based, it is based in the activity of the autonomic nervous system and the hormones produced there. Although hormones may play a role in the other physiologically-based drives, their influence is thought to be minimal; in relation to sex drive, hormones are often of prime importance. The hypothalamus does play a role in the sex drive, but hormones are most immediately involved in activating sexual responsiveness.

Fourth, a related point about the sex drive that makes it different from the rest is that it is not present at birth, but requires a level of maturation (puberty) before it is apparent. The other drives are present, and even most critical, early in life.

A fifth unique quality of the sex drive is the extent to which internal and external influences have different degrees of impact depending on the species involved. The importance of internal, physiological states is much greater in "lower" species than it is in primates and humans. At the level of human responding, hormones may be necessary, but they are seldom sufficient for

The sex drive is a physiologically-based drive. It satisfies both physical and emotional needs. Unlike the eating, drinking, and temperature regulation drives, the sex drive is not present at birth, but requires a certain level of maturation.

the maintenance of sexual responding, and for an experienced human, may not even be necessary. We'll see this complication as we consider the internal and external cues for the sex drive.

Internal, Physiological Cues   With rats, the matter of sex is quite simple and straightforward. In the male rat, if adequate supplies of **testosterone** (the male sex hormone) are present, and if there is the opportunity, the rat will respond to the hormone-induced sex drive, and will engage in sexual behaviors. In the female rat, if adequate supplies of **estrogen** and **progesterone** (the female sex hormones) are present, and if the opportunity is available, the female rat will also engage in appropriate sexual behaviors. For rats, learning and experience seem to have little to do with sexual behaviors—they are tied closely to hormonal levels. It is very difficult to tell the difference between the mating behaviors of sexually experienced rats, virgin rats, or naive rats that have mated only once or twice.

If the sex hormones of a female rat are removed, there will be a complete and immediate loss of sexual receptivity. If these sex hormones are then replaced by injection, sexual behaviors return to normal (Davidson et al., 1968). Removing the sex hormone from male rats produces a slightly different story. Sexual behaviors diminish and may eventually disappear, but they take longer to do so. Again, injections of testosterone quickly return the male rat to normal sexual functioning.

Removal of the sex hormones from male dogs or cats ("higher" species than rats) also produces a reduction in sexual behaviors, but much more gradually than for rats. An experienced male primate ("higher" still) may persist in sexual behaviors for the rest of his life even after his sex hormones have been removed. (The same also seems true of human males, although the data here are sketchy.)

Even in primate females, removal of the sex hormones (by removing the ovaries) results in a rather sudden loss of sex drive and a cessation of sexual behaviors. In normal female primates (and in dogs, cats, and rats, etc.), sexual responsiveness is well predicted by the hormone-driven fertility cycle. The period during which ovulation (the release of the eggs or ova from the ovary) occurs is the time of greatest sexual drive and activity.

In the human female, we find a different situation. The human female's receptiveness to sexual activity appears to be in no way related to the fertility, or estrous, cycle (Bennett, 1982). And, menopause, the period after which the ovaries no longer produce ova and sex hormone is no longer produced, does *not* bring about an end in sexual interest or in sexual behavior for the human female.

So, what we find is that the sex drive in "lower" species is tied to its physiological, hormonal base. As the complexity of the organism increases, from rats, to dogs, to primates, to humans, the role of internal cues becomes less certain and less noticeable.

External, Psychological Cues   No one would get far arguing that sex is not an important human drive. However, it *is* easy to lose sight of the fact that it is basically a *biological* drive. Particularly in societies like ours, where so much learning (and unlearning: Satisfying the sex drive may involve unlearning many prohibitions acquired in childhood and adolescence) is involved, one could easily come to believe that sexual drives are learned through experience and practice alone. Hormones may provide humans with an arousing force to do something, but *what* to do and *how* to do it often seem to require training and practice.

testosterone
the male sex hormone, produced by the testes, important to the sex drive and the development of secondary sex characteristics

estrogen
a female sex hormone, produced by the ovaries, important in the sex drive and the development of secondary sex characteristics

progesterone
a female sex hormone, produced by the ovaries, important in the sex drive and in preparing the female for pregnancy

Sex manuals of a "how to" nature sell well, and sex therapy has become a standard practice for many clinical psychologists trying to help people cope with the pressures that external factors put on their "natural" sexual motivation.

In addition to the internal forces produced by the sex hormones, sex drives can be stimulated by a wide range of environmental stimuli. Some people engage in sexual behaviors simply to reproduce; others do so for the physical pleasure they experience; others because they feel it demonstrates a romantic "love" for another; yet others want to demonstrate their femininity or masculinity. In other words, sexual drives in humans are seldom satisfied with "just anybody." Many social and cognitive (external) constraints are often placed on the choice of a sexual partner. (For a brief discussion of the choice of a mate in marriage, see Topic 19, pp. 349–350.) What "turns someone on" sexually varies considerably from person to person. Virtually any of the senses—touch, smell (particularly important in lower mammals and primates), sight, and sound—can stimulate sexual arousal.

Homosexuality—An Example   The complexities of human sexual responsiveness are no more apparent than when we consider those persons who are **homosexual.** Homosexuality is not a new phenomenon by any means, but we are just now getting to the point of discussing it freely and openly. Homosexuals are those individuals who are sexually attracted to and aroused by members of their own sex, as opposed to heterosexuals who seek outlets for their sexual drives among members of the opposite sex. Most psychologists agree that homosexuality and heterosexuality are not mutually exclusive categories, but rather end points of sexual preference, and that many combinations are possible. It is likely that about 2 percent of American males and approximately 1 percent of American females can be classified as exclusively homosexual in their sexual preferences.

In most ways, there is very little difference between homosexuals and heterosexuals, including the pattern of their sexual responsiveness. Homosexual couples are often more at ease and comfortable with their sexual relationship than are most heterosexual couples (Masters & Johnson, 1979). Even now in the 1980s we have no generally accepted theory on the causes of homosexuality. (Some homosexuals may wonder if there is an acceptable theory to explain the causes of heterosexuality.)

As we have seen before, what we do know is that the matter is not a simple one. "Explaining" homosexuality will almost certainly involve internal, biological and external, psychological factors. We cannot state with certainty why some people become homosexual, that is true; but there are a few things we do know. In the first place, homosexuals are not simply lacking in proper hormone balance (although some small differences have been found occasionally, and sexual preferences among rats can be influenced by the manipulation of hormone levels).

In the second place, sexual preference cannot be attributed to some simple early childhood phenomenon. This was the commonly held view as recently as 15 years ago: The male homosexual was reared by a domineering, overly affectionate mother and a detached—often absent—father. Female homosexuals were reared by cold, aloof mothers and close—often abusive—fathers. Such "theories" never did have much experimental support (the subjects of early studies of homosexuality were almost always in therapy at the time; homosexuals not in therapy were not included in such early studies). Although psychologists are not about to abandon early childhood as a potential time period for the development of sexual preferences, we have

homosexual
an individual with sexual preference for and sexually aroused by members of his or her own sex

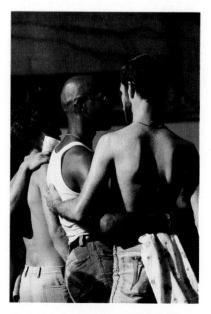

Though homosexuality is becoming more prevalent and homosexuals are able to be more open about their sexual preferences, homosexuality is still a controversial issue.

learned that we cannot attribute a "cause" of homosexuality to any particular parenting style. Indeed, most homosexuals themselves claim that their parents had little influence on their adult sexual preferences (Bell, Weinberg & Hammersmith, 1981).

Before you go on

In what ways is the sex drive a unique physiologically-based drive?

What is homosexuality, and what causes it?

PSYCHOLOGICALLY-BASED MOTIVES

From time to time you may be able to analyze your own behavior in terms of physiologically-based needs and drives. For example, you woke up this morning for reasons largely biological. The fact that you had breakfast might be explained in terms of a hunger drive. That you got dressed might have been your attempt to do what you could to control your body temperature. Control of body temperature might have influenced your choice of clothes. Perhaps some sexual motivation affected what you chose to wear today.

Many of our behaviors seem to be aroused and directed (i.e., motivated) by forces that are more subtle and less clearly biological in origin. Let's briefly review some of the motivators that psychologists have investigated that are more clearly learned and social in nature. Remember that we are going to refer to these psychologically-based drives as *motives*. Although there are potentially a large number of such motives, we'll review four that received considerable attention as mechanisms for "explaining" human behavior: achievement, power, affiliation, and competency motivation.

Achievement Motivation

need to achieve (nAch)
the (learned) need to meet or exceed some standard of excellence in performance

thematic apperception test (TAT)
a projective personality test requiring a subject to tell a series of short stories about a set of ambiguous pictures

The notion that some people are motivated by a **need to achieve**—referred to in brief as **nAch**—was introduced to the literature of psychology in 1938 by Henry Murray. Measuring nAch and determining its sources and its implications has been a major contribution of David McClelland and his associates (for example, McClelland et al., 1953; McClelland, 1975, 1985). Achievement motivation is defined by one's need to attempt and succeed at tasks in such a way as to meet or exceed some standard of success or excellence.

Although there are short, paper-and-pencil tests for the same purpose, achievement motivation is usually assessed by means of the **thematic apperception test,** or **TAT.** This test is a *projective test* (see Topic 24). Subjects are asked to tell short stories about a series of rather ambiguous pictures that depict people in various settings (see Figure 20.2). Subjects' stories are interpreted and scored according to a series of objective criteria that note references to trying difficult tasks, succeeding, being rewarded for one's efforts, setting short-term and long-term goals, and so on. Because there are no right or wrong responses to the pictures of the TAT, judgments can be made about the references to achievement that a subject "projects" into the picture and his or her story describing it.

One of the first things that McClelland and his coworkers found was that there *were* differences in measured levels of nAch among the male subjects they tested. One of the most consistent findings concerning people with high needs for achievement involves the nature of tasks they choose to attempt. When given a choice, they generally try to do things where success is not guaranteed (no challenge otherwise), but where there is a reasonable chance of success. Both young children (McClelland, 1958) and college students (Atkinson & Litwin, 1960) who were high in nAch were observed playing a ring-toss game, where the object was to score points by tossing a small ring over a peg from a distance. The farther from the peg one stood, the more points could be earned with success. High nAch subjects in both studies chose to stand at a moderate distance from the peg. They didn't stand so close as to guarantee success, but they didn't choose to stand so far away that they would almost certainly fail. Subjects with low nAch scores tended to go to either extreme—very close, earning few points for their successes, or so far away they hardly ever succeeded.

McClelland would argue that you are, in fact, reading this text at this moment because you are motivated by a need to achieve. You want to do well on your next exam. You want a good grade in this course, and you have decided that to do so, you need to study the assigned text material. Some students read text assignments not because they are motivated by a need to achieve, but because they are motivated by a *fear of failure* (Atkinson & Feather, 1966). In this case, the incentive that is relevant is a negative one (wanting to avoid an F), which is a different matter than working toward a positive incentive (wanting to earn an A). Individuals motivated by a fear of failure tend to take very few risks. They either choose to attempt tasks on which they are bound to do well, or to attempt tasks that are virtually impossible (if the task is impossible, they can't blame themselves for their failures).

In this regard, we should mention the concept of *fear of success.* This concept, introduced in 1969 by Horner, is said to account for the motivation of many women who are said to back off from competition for fear of succeeding and thereby losing popularity and femininity. It turns out that although there may be some merit in the notion of fear of success as an explanatory mechanism, it has not fared well under the experimental test (e.g., Jackaway & Teevan, 1976; Mednick, 1979).

There seems little doubt that the need to achieve is learned, usually in early childhood. Children who show high levels of achievement motivation are generally those who have been encouraged in a positive way to excel ("Billy, that grade of B is very good; do you think you could make an A next time?" as opposed to, "What! only a B!"). High nAch children are generally encouraged to work things out for themselves, independently, with parental support and encouragement ("Here, Billy, you see if you can do this" as opposed to, "Here, dummy, let me do it; you'll never get it right!"). McClelland is convinced that achievement motivation can be specifically taught and acquired by almost anyone, of any age, and he has developed training programs designed to increase achievement motivation levels (for example, McClelland & Winter, 1969).

Figure 20.2
In a thematic apperception test, subjects would view pictures like these and be asked to make up short stories about them. The stories are interpreted and scored, thus providing a measure of the subjects' needs to achieve.

Before you go on

What is achievement motivation, and how is it usually measured?

Power Motivation

Some people are motivated not only to excel, but also to be in control, to be in charge—of the situation and of others. In such cases, we may speak of a **need for power** (McClelland, 1982; Winter & Stewart, 1978). Power needs are generally measured in the same way as achievement needs, through the interpretations of stories generated with the thematic apperception test.

People with high power needs like to be admired. They prefer situations in which they can control the fate of others, usually by manipulating access to information. They present an attitude of, "If you want to get this job done, you'll have to come to me to find out how to do it." Individuals with low power needs tend to avoid situations in which others would have to depend upon them. They tend to be rather submissive in interpersonal relationships.

need for power
the need to be in control of events or persons, usually at another's expense

Many behaviors can be explained on the basis of a need for affiliation. We all feel the need to be with others, to work toward a common goal, and to form associations and partnerships.

Affiliation Motivation

A psychologically-based motivator that has been found to be very helpful in explaining the behaviors of some people is the **need for affiliation.** As its name suggests, this motive involves a felt need to be with others, to work together toward some end, and to form friendships and associations.

One interesting implication of having a high need for affiliation is that it is often at odds with a need for power. As you might imagine, if you are simultaneously motivated to be in control and to be with others (in a supportive way), conflicts may arise. Simply put, it is more difficult to exercise power over people whose friendship you value than it is to exercise power and control over people whose friendship is of little concern to you. It is also the case that affiliation and achievement motives are somewhat independent. Achievement and success can be earned either with others (high affiliation), or on one's own (low affiliation).

Although we might be quite confident that achievement and power motives are learned, we are less confident about the sources of affiliation motivation. There is a reasonable argument that to some degree, the need to affiliate and be with others is biologically based. We are to some degree social animals for whom complete social isolation is quite difficult (particularly when we are young). On the other hand, it seems clear that the extent to which we value affiliation relationships can be attributed to our learning experiences.

need for affiliation
the need to be with others and to form friendships and associations

need for competence
the need to meet the challenges (large and small) provided by one's environment

Competency Motivation

Robert White (1959, 1974) has proposed that all people are motivated by a **need for competence.** To be competent does not imply excellence, nor does it suggest success at the expense of others. It simply means managing to cope, on one's own, with the challenges of everyday living.

More general than either the needs for achievement, power, or affiliation, the need for competence can be used to account for a wide range of behaviors. Some people develop competence with musical instruments, others in their jobs, others at some hobby, still others in story-telling, or weight lifting,

Our behaviors are often motivated by a need for competence. We are all motivated to find something we can do well—perhaps some artistic or creative hobby that we can enjoy and master.

or break dancing. The point is that we are all motivated to find something we can do well—some way to demonstrate that we are effective in dealing with our environments.

When you try to help a child who is attempting to do something that you judge it cannot do, the child may respond, "I can do it myself!" The child is trying to maintain (or develop) a sense of competence, which you may have challenged simply by offering to help.

As with other types of human motivation, we can see individual differences in the degree of a need for competency. Some people are satisfied with being able to handle a small number of everyday tasks. Others seek to find new and different ways to express their competency or mastery over the environment (Harter, 1978).

The motivational concepts we have briefly introduced here might be useful in trying to understand why students decide to attend college. Although there may be many reasons, all operating at once, some people become college students because they want to achieve. Some see a college education as a means of gaining power. Some students see attending college as providing opportunities for meeting new people and establishing relationships. Others try college just because they want to see if they can do it—they appreciate the incentive value of a challenge.

Before you go on
Define the needs for power, affiliation, and competence.

In this topic, we have discussed a number of approaches to questions concerning *why* organisms behave as they do. We've also summarized some specific sources of human motivation. It would be helpful if we had some scheme we could use to provide an overall picture of how drives and motives are organized and how they interact. In this regard, one of the most commonly cited theories of motivation is that of Abraham Maslow (1943, 1970). Maslow has proposed that we think about drives and motives as being organized in a hierarchical fashion, with basic *survival needs* on the bottom of the hierarchy and more general *growth needs* at the top. Figure 20.3 summarizes Maslow's hierarchy of needs.

Maslow's theory is essentially a stage theory. It supposes that the very first things that motivate organisms are their *physiological needs*. These include basic needs that are related to our survival—for example,

hierarchy of needs
Maslow's theoretical arrangement, in which needs are satisfied in order, from physiological needs to self-actualization

our need for food, water, shelter, and so on. Until these needs are satisfied, there is little reason to suspect that an individual would be concerned with anything else. Once our physiological needs are under control, we are motivated by *safety needs*—the needs to feel secure and protected from dangers that might arise in the future. We are thus motivated to see to it that the cupboard has food for later, that we won't freeze this winter, and that there's enough money saved to protect against sudden calamity. Surely we're not going to worry much about what we'll eat tomorrow if there's not enough to eat today; but if today's needs are taken care of, we can then focus on the future.

Assuming that our present and future survival needs are satisfied, we move to the next level of the hierarchy—*love and belongingness needs*. At this level, our concerns are with acceptance by others; we have a need to belong in some

Figure 20.3
Maslow's hierarchy of needs.

way—to a group or to another individual. Our physical needs satisfied, we become motivated to find friendship, love, and acceptance. Once belongingness needs are met, our next concern is with *esteem*. Now we seek some confirmation of our worth as a person. We seek self-esteem and the esteem of others. Needs to achieve, or gain power, or feel competent are esteem-type needs. We develop esteem by convincing ourselves and others that we are capable of dealing with challenges of the environment.

The highest level of needs in Maslow's hierarchy are *self-actualization needs*. These are the most difficult to achieve, and often are the hardest to understand. We are self-actualized when we have become the best person that we can be, when we have taken the fullest advantage of our potential as human beings. We are self-actualizing when we strive to be as creative and/or productive as possible.

In many ways, Maslow's arrangement of needs in a hierarchical fashion seems to conform to common sense. We can hardly expect someone to be motivated to grow and achieve when they are concerned about survival on a day-to-day basis. And, when a person's needs for safety, belongingness, and esteem are met, they don't just stop behaving, unmotivated to do anything else. The concept of a drive to self-actualize and continue growing as a person is a convenient way to explain their behavior.

However, as a comprehensive theory of the motivation of the human organism, Maslow's hierarchy has some serious difficulties. Perhaps the biggest stumbling block is the idea that one can assign ranks to needs and put them in a neat order regardless of what that order might be. It is quite clear that many people are motivated in ways that violate the stage ap-

proach of Maslow's theory. Many individuals will, for example, freely give up satisfaction of basic survival needs for the sake of "higher" principles (as in hunger strikes). For the sake of love and belongingness, people may abandon their own needs for safety and security.

Another complication with this organizational scheme is that we have to remember that needs are often cyclical—as we pointed out in our topic opening. For example, you may have your physiological and safety needs under control at the moment and may be motivated largely by achievement and esteem needs. But soon you may face a situation in which the more basic biological needs return to attract your attention. Or more simply, once you have satisfied your physiological needs, they do not stay satisfied forever. Having just eaten, you will soon be hungry again. At any one time, any one individual is probably being motivated by a number of different *types* of needs, from different locations in the hierarchy.

The Army uses advertisements that encourage people to become self-actualized. The slogan "Be All You Can Be" urges people to be as productive as possible in order to reach their fullest potential.

TOPIC SUMMARY

How have the concepts of instinct, drive, and incentive been used to explain motivated behaviors?

In trying to explain why organisms do what they do, three concepts have proven useful. *Instincts* are complex patterns of behavior that occur in the presence of certain stimuli. Instinct approaches take the position that complex behavioral patterns are unlearned (innate). Although there may be an instinctive basis for some human behaviors, the concept has proven to be less than satisfactory. *Needs* are shortages of some biological necessity. Deprivation leads to a need, which leads to a drive, which arouses and directs the organism's behavior. The relationship between deprivation, need, drive, and behavior is often not very straightforward; and many needs are more learned than biologically based. Focusing on *incentives* explains behaviors more in terms of their goals and outcomes rather than their driving forces. We say that incentives "pull" behavior, whereas drives "push" behavior. In this sense, we are motivated to reach some desired end-state. These three approaches are not necessarily mutually exclusive, and each may be used to explain some types of motivated behavior. / 363

Given the concept of homeostasis, how might temperature regulation be thought of as a physiologically-based drive?

Homeostasis is a general need to maintain a state of balance, or equilibrium, among internal physiological conditions. In this sense, temperature regulation can be viewed as a physiological drive, because we clearly need to (and are driven to) keep our body temperatures within certain (homeostatic) limits. / 365

List some of the factors that may influence drinking behavior.

We are motivated to drink for a number of reasons: to relieve dryness in our mouths and throats and to maintain a homeostatic level of fluid within our bodies (as monitored by the hypothalamus). We also engage in drinking behavior in response to external cues (stimulus values), such as taste, aroma, or appearance. What we drink is often influenced by our learning experiences. / 366

List those internal and external factors that influence our drives to eat.

There are a number of factors that lead to eating behaviors, some internal, some external. Internal cues for eating include sensations arising from an empty stomach and cues mediated by the hypothalamus, which may be responding to fat store levels, blood sugar levels, or some other indicator that our normal homeostatic balance has been disrupted. The stimulus properties of foods may motivate eating, as may habit patterns and social pressures. / 367

In what ways is the sex drive a unique physiologically-based drive? What is homosexuality, and what causes it?

There are five ways in which the sex drive is an unusual physiological drive. (1) Individual survival does not depend on its satisfaction. (2) The drive involves seeking tension rather than seeking relief from tension. (3) It is hormonally based. (4) It is not present at birth, but matures later. (5) The extent to which it is influenced by learned or external influences varies from species to species. Homosexuality involves sexual attraction and arousal by members of one's own sex. Its specific causes are as yet un-

known. If there are hormonal differences between homosexuals and heterosexuals, the differences appear to be quite small. If there are early childhood learning experiences involved, we do not know with any certainty what they might be. / 372

What is achievement motivation, and how is it usually measured?

Achievement motivation (nAch) is defined as one's need to attempt and succeed at tasks in such a way as to meet or exceed some standard of excellence. Achievement motivation is usually assessed through the interpretation of short stories generated in response to the thematic apperception test, in which one looks for themes of striving and achievement. / 373

Define the needs for power, affiliation, and competence.

The need for power is defined as the need to be in charge, to be in control of a situation or of others, and usually at the expense of others. Affiliation needs involve being motivated to be with others, to form friendships and interpersonal relationships. A need for competence implies a need to demonstrate the ability to do something, to cope on one's own with the challenges of daily living. / 375

TOPIC

It has been a glorious day. You and some friends have spent the day backpacking in the mountains. The signs of Spring are everywhere to be found, and you enjoyed each minute spent searching for them. The day was so perfect that you decided to hike all the way around Lake Willoweemoc. That hike was tiring and getting back to camp for dinner was welcomed by all.

After a full day in the fresh mountain air, no one was terribly choosy about what to have for dinner. The volume of food seemed much more relevant than the quality or elegance. Large, heaping piles of beans and stew were consumed by all. Somehow you even managed to find room for dessert: a toasted marshmallow and a piece of chocolate bar squeezed between two graham crackers. As hungry as you had been, there is no doubt that you overdid it. As your friends settle around the campfire, darkness just beginning to overtake the campsite, you excuse yourself. You need to "walk off" some of that dinner and decide to stroll down a trail that leads away from the campsite.

As you stroll down the trail, you feel totally relaxed, at peace with the world. Your mind seems to be flowing along of its own will, reflecting briefly on the pleasantness of the day, noting the smell of wild flowers, wondering what tomorrow will bring. When you are about 200 yards from the campsite, you think you hear a strange sound in the woods. Looking back, you notice that you can barely see the campfire's glow through the trees, even though their leaves are not yet fully formed. Well, maybe you'd better not venture too much farther, perhaps just over that ridge. Suddenly, without warning, from behind a dense thicket, a large, growling, black bear appears. It takes one look at you, bares its teeth and roars. *What will you do now?*

Why We Care

_____ Humans seem to prefer to think of themselves as rational, reasonable, intellectual organisms. We like to talk about our cognitive skills and abilities—perceiving, learning, remembering, and problem solving. But the truth is, I suspect, that if we were totally honest with each other, we would admit that it is our *emotions* we think about most. We enjoy reflecting on our pleasant emotions and are concerned with finding ways to minimize our unpleasant emotions.

Some emotional reactions are quite unpleasant—fear, rage, jealousy, shame, and so on. Just the same, we would not want to give up our ability to experience emotions. To do so would be to surrender love, joy, pride, satisfaction, and ecstasy.

Psychology has been interested in emotional reactions since its very earliest days in the late 1800s. I have always found the psychology of emotions somewhat disappointing. My expectations—and those of many others—have always been too high, perhaps. We want psychology to tell us precisely what emotions are. We want to know where they come from. And we want to know what we can do to increase the "good" ones and eliminate the "bad" ones. It is in regard to our emotional reactions that we most want simple, easy, and direct answers. These are the very reactions about which we get emotional.

In the last 100 years, psychologists have learned a great deal about what emotions are and where they come from. There are good reasons, however, why psychology may not be able to provide direct and simple answers to all our questions about emotions.

In a way, our problems with the study of emotion involve limits on our methodology. In Chapter 1, we made the case that psychology's best method was the experimental method. We noted that most of what we know in psychology today we have learned through doing experiments. One of the problems we have when studying emotions is that we often find our best method difficult or impossible to use—at least with humans.

We might want to measure the physiological changes that occur in subjects who are very afraid, very angry, and very happy. We do have at our disposal many techniques for monitoring physiological changes. But ethical considerations (and common sense) prohibit us from wiring subjects to measuring devices and then scaring them out of their wits, making them very angry, and then making them very happy just because we want to observe physiological changes! Even if we were not concerned about ethics, how could we ever be sure that our subject's reactions of fear, anger, and joy were in any way equal in magnitude or strength? For that matter, how could we manipulate these emotional reactions in the laboratory in the first place?

Because of considerations like these (and others that you might imagine), experimental manipulations are usually performed on nonhuman subjects. We have often noted the difficulty of making inferences about human reactions from studies that use nonhuman subjects.

Doing experiments is not psychology's only method, however. Why not use naturalistic observation? Why not observe emotional behaviors as they occur naturally, outside the laboratory? The problem here, at least with adults, is that it is often very difficult to accurately assess someone's emotional state on the basis of observable behaviors and reactions.

Growing up, becoming a mature adult, often involves learning to control or hide one's true feelings and emotions. No matter how sad they may be, children may learn that "big boys don't cry." We learn that, in some circumstances at least, it is inappropriate to display our happiness outwardly in the presence of others. When we're angry, we are taught that we should "count to 10" and try to control our expressions of anger. As a result, it is often very difficult to make accurate observations about a person's emotional state by simple observation.

Even though two of our best and most reliable methods—experiments and naturalistic observation—have not always been of much use, we do know a number of things about emotions. We will review some of what we know in this topic. First we'll tackle the matter of definition. Then we'll see how emotions tend to be expressed in behavior. We'll examine the aspect of emotionality we probably know most about: the physiological reactions that accompany emotions. Finally, we'll review some of the theoretical approaches that try to tie it all together.

Before you go on

What are two reasons why the study of emotional responses in adult humans is so difficult?

DEFINING AND CLASSIFYING EMOTION

Let's go back to your chance encounter with a bear in the woods. The question was, "What will you do now?" Certainly, you would have an emotional reaction. Most of us would. This would hardly be the time for a prolonged, thoughtful exercise in problem solving. Your response would be one that would qualify as an emotion.

A careful analysis suggests that there are four components to your emotional reaction. First, you will experience a *feeling*—in this case, one that you might call fear (if not panic). You will have a *cognitive* reaction—you will "know" what has just happened to you. You will realize that you have just met a bear, and you would rather that you hadn't. You will have an internal, *physiological* reaction. This reaction will be largely visceral, involving your glands, hormones, and internal organs. And you will engage in an observable, *behavioral* reaction—most likely, you'll either freeze in your tracks, or you'll run back to your campsite just as fast as you can.

In this scenario, we can see four (interacting) dimensions of emotion: subjective feelings, cognitive interpretations, bodily or physiological reactions and overt expression or behavioral response. If this way of thinking about emotion seems "right" to you, you are not alone. If, by chance, you think that this is the *only* way to think about emotion, you may need to reconsider.

There is currently quite a debate going on over just what the components of emotion are, which might be the most important, and which "come first" in an emotional response. Two researchers in emotion, R.B. Zajonc of the University of Michigan and Richard S. Lazarus of the University of California at Berkeley, represent different views on these matters. They are exchanging views in the way that scientists do: in the journals and meetings of psychologists. The exchange is a heated one, even emotional at times.

At the heart of the controversy is the role of cognition in emotion. Zajonc and others have taken the position that cognition is not really necessary for our experience of emotion, although cognitive reactions often may follow along with feelings (Zajonc, 1980, 1984).

Lazarus is not convinced that feelings and thoughts can be separated and dismisses most of Zajonc's evidence to the contrary as irrelevant. For Lazarus and others there is little point in talking about feeling without thought (Lazarus, 1982). "Cognitive activity is a necessary precondition of emotion

Emotions have four components: subjective feelings, cognitive interpretations, bodily reactions, and behavioral response. What do you think this woman's emotions are as she opens presents on her birthday?

Figure 21.1
Plutchik's eight primary emotions and how they relate to adaptive behaviors

Emotion, or feeling	Common stimulus	Typical behavior
1. Anger	blocking of goal-directed behavior	destruction of obstacle
2. Fear	a threat or danger	protection
3. Sadness	loss of something valued	search for help and comfort
4. Disgust	something gruesome or loathsome	rejection; pushing away
5. Surprise	a sudden, novel stimulus	orientation; turning toward
6. Curiosity	a new place or environment	explore and search
7 Acceptance	a member of own group; something of value	sharing; taking in; incorporating
8. Joy	potential mate	reproduction; courting; mating

because to experience an emotion, people must comprehend . . . that their well-being is implicated in a transaction, for better or worse," he argues (Lazarus, 1984, p. 124). Can you *feel* afraid without *knowing* it? Lazarus would say no.

This central, definitional issue will not be resolved in the very near future. For now, we're going to have to settle on a working definition of **emotion** as a reaction that includes the subjective experience of a *feeling,* a *cognitive* interpretation, an internal *physiological* reaction, and some *behavioral* expression. That may seem a little too intellectual and devoid of emotion, but that's the best we can do. Although one's cognitions, physiology, and overt behavior are usually involved in an emotional reaction, there does seem to be little doubt that the most important aspect is the subjective feeling component. Perhaps it would help if we could devise a scheme or plan to describe and classify different, specific emotional reactions.

Our vocabularies are filled with words we use to describe different emotional states. Simple names for emotions can be found by the dozen. If we are to study emotional reactions scientifically, it would be most helpful if we could categorize or organize emotions in some systematic way.

In fact, there are a number of ways to classify emotional responses, and each has its own supporters. Wilhelm Wundt, back in that first psychology laboratory in Leipzig in the late 1800s, was very concerned with emotional reactions. He organized emotions along three intersecting dimensions: pleasantness/unpleasantness, relaxation/tension, and calm/excitement.

Carroll Izard has proposed a classification scheme that calls for nine primary emotions (Izard, 1972). From these nine, all others can be constructed. Izard's nine primary emotions are fear, anger, shame, contempt, disgust, distress, interest, surprise, and joy. These emotions are primary because they cannot be dissected into simpler, more basic emotions. Any other known emotion is thought to be a combination of any two or more of these nine.

Robert Plutchik (1980a), on the other hand, argues for eight basic emotions. What makes these primary is that each can be directly tied to some adaptive pattern of behavior; they are emotions that can be related to survival. Plutchik's eight primary emotions, and their adaptive significance, are listed in Figure 21.1.

Plutchik also believes that emotions in addition to these eight can be seen as variants or combinations of the primary emotions. While rage, for example, may be an extreme emotion, it is viewed as being essentially the same as anger. Anger in a yet weaker form becomes annoyance (Plutchik, 1980b). (See Figure 21.2.)

emotion
a reaction involving subjective feelings, physiological response, cognitive interpretation, and behavioral expression

Figure 21.2
Plutchik's emotion solid

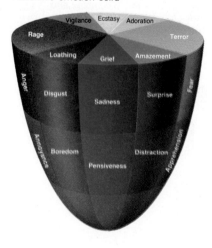

Whether there are eight or nine primary emotions (or fewer or more) and how they might be combined to form different emotions will depend on one's theoretical perspective. There isn't even complete agreement on how to distinguish between positive and negative emotions. Fear, for example, seems like a reasonable candidate for a list of negative emotions. Yet it is clear that fear can be useful and act in many ways to protect and guide one's behavior in adaptive ways. So, on what basis shall we make our judgments of positive and negative?

Now that we have in mind a general definition of emotion, we can turn to the *expression* of emotional states.

Before you go on

An emotional state can be said to involve which four possible reactions?

Can emotions be classified?

OUTWARD EXPRESSIONS OF EMOTION

It is very useful for one organism to be able to let another know how it is feeling. As one wild animal approaches a second, the second had better have a good idea about the emotional state of the first. "Is it angry?" "Does it come in peace?" "Is it just curious, or is it looking for dinner?" "Is it sad, looking for comfort, or is it sexually aroused, looking for a mating partner?" An inability to make such determinations—quickly—can be disastrous. Animals need to know the emotional state of other animals if they are to survive for long.

Charles Darwin (1872) was among the first to recognize the importance of the ability to display one's emotions accurately to others. Nonhuman animals have many ritualistic, complex, and instinctive patterns of behavior to communicate aggressiveness, interest in courtship, submission, and many other emotional states (see Figure 21.3).

Humans can also express their emotional state in a variety of ways, including verbal report. Surely, if I am happy, or sad, or angry, or jealous, I can try to *tell* you how I feel. The human ability to communicate with language often puts us at a great advantage.

Figure 21.3
Animals have many complex and instinctual patterns of behavior that communicate emotion. To display aggression and threat, mandrills bare their teeth and grimace, while Australian frilled lizards unfurl flaps of skin on their necks in order to appear larger than they really are.

Even without verbal language, there is a school of thought that suggests that the human animal, like the nonhuman, uses a *body language* to communicate its emotional condition (for example, Birdwhistell, 1952; Fast, 1970). Someone quietly sitting, slumped slightly forward with head down, may be viewed as feeling sad, even from a distance. We may similarly interpret postural cues and gestures as being associated with fear, happiness, anger, and so on. But, as we have already noted, such expressions are often the result of learning or may be modified by cultural influences.

Darwin recognized facial expression as a common cue to emotion in animals, especially mammals. Might facial expression provide a key to underlying emotions in humans, too? Might there be a set of facial expressions of emotional states that is universal among the human species, just as there appears to be among nonhumans? A growing body of evidence supports the idea that *facial* expressions of one's emotional state may be an innate response, only slightly sensitive to cultural influence (see Topic Expansion).

Paul Ekman has conducted a number of studies to see if there is a reliable relationship between emotional state and facial expression and if such relationships can be found in a number of different cultures. In one large cross-cultural study, Ekman and his associates (1973) showed college students six pictures of people's faces. In each picture, a different primary emotion was being displayed—happiness, disgust, surprise, sadness, anger, and fear. When students from the United States, Argentina, Japan, Brazil, and Chile were asked to identify the emotion experienced by the people in the photographs, their agreement was remarkable (see Figure 21.4).

A problem with this study is that all of the subjects did have many shared experiences, even though they were from basically different cultures. They were, after all, college students and had many experiences in common (seen

Figure 21.4

Photos with these types of facial expressions were shown to subjects from the United States, Brazil, Chile, Argentina, and Japan. The subjects were asked to identify the emotion being displayed. The percentage of subjects who identified the photographs with the emotions listed is indicated.

	Happiness	Disgust	Surprise	Sadness	Anger	Fear
United States (N = 99)	97%	92%	95%	84%	67%	85%
Brazil (N = 40)	95%	97%	87%	59%	90%	67%
Chile (N = 119)	95%	92%	93%	88%	94%	68%
Argentina (N = 168)	98%	92%	95%	78%	90%	54%
Japan (N = 29)	100%	90%	100%	62%	90%	66%

Figure 21.5

Paul Ekman went to New Guinea to study the relationship between facial expression and emotional state. The man at top left was told that he was happy because a friend was coming. The man at top right was told that his child had died. The man at bottom left was told he was angry and about to fight. And the man at bottom right was told he had just seen a dead pig that had been lying in one place for a long time. People from any culture would have no trouble identifying their facial expressions as indicating happiness, grief, anger, and disgust, respectively.

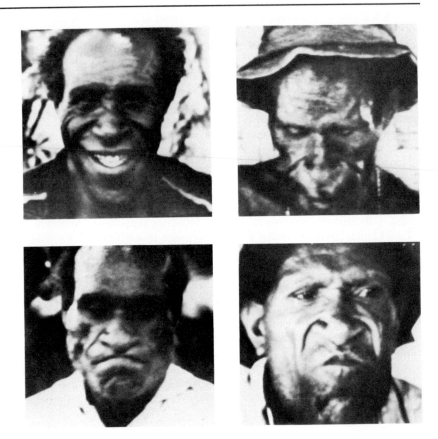

the same movies, watched the same TV shows, etc.). So, even though Ekman's subjects came from different countries, perhaps their agreement as raters could be explained in terms of the similarities of their experiences, rather than some innate tendency to express emotions through facial expression.

An argument against this line of reasoning may be found in another project by Ekman (1972). Here, natives of a remote New Guinea tribe were asked to make faces depicting different emotional reactions (e.g., "A friend has come and you are happy.") No one in our culture (or any other) would have much difficulty deciding what emotion the subjects (who were videotaped) were trying to display (see Figure 21.5).

In a more recent follow-up, Ekman, Levenson, and Friesen (1983) have shown that simply moving one's facial muscles into the positions that are associated with emotional expression can actually cause distinctive physiological changes associated with an emotional state. As bizarre as that sounds, the implication is that if you raise your eyebrows, open your eyes widely, and raise the corners of your mouth, you will produce an internal physiological change not unlike that which occurs when you are happy, and you will smile as a result! (This line of evidence is one that Zajonc uses to support his theory that emotion does not *require* a cognitive component.)

Before you go on

Is there any evidence that the facial expression of emotion may be innately determined?

PHYSIOLOGICAL ASPECTS OF EMOTION

Return once again to our imaginary encounter with the bear in the woods. You will probably agree that a significant part of your reaction in this situation (or one like it) would be internal, physiological, and "gut-level."

Responding to a bear is not something that most people would do in a cognitive, intellectual sort of way. When we are emotional, we respond with our insides; our visceral organs respond.

Our biological reaction to emotional situations takes place at a number of different levels. Of primary interest is the activity of our autonomic nervous system (ANS). We first mentioned the ANS in Topic 4. At that time, we said we would delay our discussion of details until now—in our topic on emotion. The brain has a role to play in emotion and so does the endocrine system, but first we'll consider the autonomic response.

The Role of the Autonomic Nervous System

The **autonomic nervous system, or ANS,** is made up of two parts, or *divisions,* that serve many of the same organs, but have quite the opposite effect on those organs. The **parasympathetic division** is actively involved in maintaining a relaxed, calm, and unemotional state. As you sat there at the campfire, the parasympathetic division of your ANS actively directed your digestive processes to do the best they could with all that stew and beans and dessert. Blood was diverted from the extremities to the stomach and intestines. Saliva flowed freely. Even in the twilight, as you relaxed, the pupils of your eyes contracted, conserving the retinas against excess light. Your stomach full, and blood diverted to it, you tended to feel somewhat sleepy as your brain began to respond to the lower levels of blood supply. Your breathing was slow, deep, and steady, as was your heart rate. All of these internal activities were under the control of the parasympathetic division of your autonomic nervous system.

Suddenly, there's that bear! The **sympathetic division** of your autonomic nervous system takes over. Automatically (which is essentially what *autonomic* means) all sorts of physiological changes take place. And these changes are usually quite adaptive.

A number of things happen under the direction of your sympathetic system. (1) The pupils of your eyes dilate, letting in as much of what light there is available so you can see clearly. (2) Your heart rate and blood pressure are elevated—you've got a bear here, and energy needs to be mobilized as fast as possible. (3) Blood is diverted away from the digestive tract toward the limbs and brain, and digestion stops; again, you've got a bear to deal with; dinner can wait until later. Let's get the blood supply out there to the arms and legs where it can do some good (with what is called the "fight or flight" response).

(4) Even without your doing so purposely, respiration increases, becoming deeper and more rapid—you'll need all the oxygen you can get. (5) Moisture is brought to the surface of the skin in the form of perspiration—as it evaporates, the body is cooled, conserving energy. (6) Blood sugar levels increase, making more energy readily available. (7) Blood will tend to clot more readily than usual—again for obvious but hopefully unnecessary reasons.

The sympathetic system makes some of these changes rather directly (stopping salivation and stimulating the cardiac muscle, for example). The rest are made indirectly through the secretion of hormones (mostly **epinephrine** and **norepinephrine** from the **adrenal glands** of the endocrine system.

autonomic nervous system (ANS)
the system of nerves that serves the smooth muscles, glands, and internal, visceral organs

parasympathetic division
division of the ANS that maintains a calm, relaxed state of the organism

sympathetic division
division of the ANS that becomes active during emotional states

epinephrine
(adrenalin) a hormone produced by the adrenal glands that is involved in emotional activity, mostly affecting heart activity

norepinephrine
a hormone secreted by the adrenal glands; involved in emotional arousal

adrenal glands
located on the kidneys, part of the ANS especially involved in emotional reactions

Because part of the physiological component of emotion *is* hormonal, under the control of the endocrine system, it *does* take a few seconds for the hormones to have their ultimate effect. As a result, we sometimes sense a delayed reaction of an emotional response. If you were, in fact, confronted by a bear in the woods, you probably would not have the presence of mind to notice, but the physiological reaction of sweaty palms, gasping breaths, and a "lump in your throat" take a few seconds to develop.

Is the autonomic and endocrine system reaction exactly the same for each and every emotion that we experience? *That* is a very difficult question. There is some evidence that there may be some differences. There appears to be a small difference in the hormones produced during rage and fear reactions. Consistent differences in physiological reactions for different emotional states are, at best, very small indeed. This issue has been very controversial in psychology for many years and is likely to remain so (Levinthal, 1983; Selye, 1976).

Before you go on
Summarize the activities of the sympathetic division of the autonomic nervous system during states of emotionality.

The Role of the Brain

When we become emotional, our sympathetic nervous system does not spring into action on its own. Autonomic nervous system activity is closely related to, and coordinated by, central nervous system activity.

There seems little doubt that the two brain structures most intimately involved in emotionality are the **limbic system,** deep in the brain, and the hypothalamus, that small structure at the base of the brain so involved with physiological needs and drives. The limbic system is a "lower" center in the brain made up of a number of small structures (of which the amygdala may be the most important center for emotionality). These centers are lower in the sense of being well below the cerebral cortex, and also in the sense of being present in the brains of "lower" animals, such as rats and cats.

The limbic system (see Figure 20.1) seems most involved in those emotional responses that call for defensive or attacking responses—those emotions stimulated by threat. Electrical stimulation and/or destruction through lesioning of portions of the limbic system reliably produce a variety of intense emotional reactions.

It is almost to be expected that the hypothalamus would have a role to play in emotionality. It is very involved in many motivational states. The observation that the hypothalamus is involved in emotion dates back to the 1920s and some of W. R. Hess's early work on electrical stimulation of brain mechanisms (Levinthal, 1983). Strong emotional reactions can be produced by hypothalamic stimulation—including reactions that lead to attacking and killing any nearby prey (Flynn et al, 1970).

Precisely how these lower brain centers of the limbic system and hypothalamus are involved in the normal experience and expression of emotion is not yet fully understood. However, there is little doubt that they are involved.

The role of the cerebral cortex in emotionality is also poorly understood. Its role seems to be largely inhibitory That is, the limbic system and hypothalamus appear to act as the sources for extreme and poorly directed emotional reactions. The cortex interprets impulses from these lower centers and other information available to it, and then modifies and directs the emotional reaction accordingly.

limbic system
a set of small structures located low in the brain; involved in motivational and emotional states

Perhaps the clearest involvement of the cerebral cortex in emotionality is in the *cognitive* aspect of an emotional response. It is clearly the cerebral cortex that is involved in the interpretation and memory of emotional events. When you get back to the campfire, having just been frightened by a black bear, you will use your cortex to tell all the emotional details of your story.

There is also some evidence that emotional reactions tend to be processed more in the right hemisphere of the human brain, and that the left hemisphere is usually rather unemotional (Tucker, 1981). The data are quite weak, however, and split-brain researcher Roger Sperry (1982) is cautious in drawing conclusions about which hemisphere of the brain is most involved in emotionality.

To review: The limbic system and hypothalamus, two lower brain structures, appear to be centers of emotional reaction. These centers are coordinated and controlled by higher centers in the cerebral cortex, which, among other things, provides the cognitive interpretation of emotional responses.

Before you go on
What brain centers are involved in emotionality?

THEORIES OF EMOTION

Psychologists have long sought a theoretical model of emotion. Theories of emotion are attempts to state, in a systematic way, just how we become emotional, and how the various components of an emotional state interact. In this section, we'll review some of the theories that have found favor in psychology.

James-Lange

In the late 1880s, William James in the United States and (somewhat later) Carl Lange in Denmark both arrived at essentially the same view of emotion, now called the *James-Lange theory.* Think back again to your meeting with a bear in the woods. A common sense argument might be that after you saw the bear, you raced back to the campfire because you were afraid. James and Lange would suggest a different chain of events.

According to their theory, you were afraid because you ran! You saw the bear, turned, and started to run—*then* you felt afraid because you noticed that you were running. If you had noticed that you were laughing and smiling, you would have interpreted your reaction as pleasant and might have felt joy or happiness.

The James-Lange theory claims that we experience an emotion as we do because of the physiological, bodily response we make to a stimulus situation. We are sad because we cry, afraid because we tremble, and happy because we smile. If nothing else, the James-Lange theory was the first to make a statement about the possible relationships among the components of an emotional reaction.

Cannon-Bard

One of the most severe critics of the James-Lange view was Walter Cannon, who objected to the theory on a number of grounds (1927). Of prime concern for Cannon was an assumption, made by both James and Lange, that people can differentiate among the physiological changes that accompany an emotional reaction and can thereby identify the emotion they are experiencing. We may be able to tell the difference between a physiological response of crying and one of trembling, but most physiological reactions in emotional situations are much more subtle. In fact, there is little evidence to support the idea that we can differentiate among these internal physiological changes very well at all.

It seemed to Cannon that the internal, visceral changes that we were supposed to be responding to when we identified our emotional state were very slow in coming. Often stimulated by hormonal changes, they would be too slow to give rise to identifiable emotional feelings quickly enough. There was also evidence that producing physiological changes like those that occur in emotion does not produce the true sensation of an emotional response (all sorts of aerobic exercise can produce physiological reactions very much like those we would experience if we were emotional). Cannon proposed a theory of his own, which was later expanded upon by Philip Bard (1934), and has come to be called the *Cannon-Bard theory.*

Cannon and Bard proposed that a lower brain center, the *thalamus,* receives emotion-producing stimulation and immediately sends messages to the cerebral cortex for interpretation *and* to yet lower brain centers to initiate a physiological response. (We now would feel more comfortable replacing the role of the thalamus with that of the limbic system, but the idea is the same in either case.)

So, for this theory, the perception of an emotion-producing stimulus goes first to a lower brain center, and then simultaneously to the cortex for interpretation and to the sympathetic division of the autonomic nervous system for expression. Although Cannon's focusing on the thalamus may have been misplaced, it did direct attention to lower centers, and it did suggest that higher brain centers also become involved early on in an emotional response.

Schachter-Singer

The model of emotion proposed by Stanley Schachter and Jerome Singer (1962) is much more cognitive in its orientation. It is the claim of the *Schachter-Singer theory* that how we "feel" at any one time is a result of a number of interacting factors. First, there is some stimulus from the environment. Then there is a sense of heightened physiological arousal. And there is the person's cognitive appraisal of the situation—the memory of similar situations from the past and an interpretation of what is going on in the environment. The critical thing is how the person uses his or her cognitive skills to interpret the situation at the moment. Without this cognitive appraisal, there would be too much ambiguity for us to know just how we feel.

In one classic test of this theory, subjects reported to the laboratory, thinking that they were to participate in an experiment on the effects of a vitamin injection. In fact, subjects received an injection of epinephrine, which, in many ways, mimics the activity of the sympathetic nervous system. Having received their injection, subjects were asked to wait in a room with another person who was actually part of the study.

Some of the subjects were told about the true nature of the injection and what possible side effects might be expected. Predictably, their behaviors were not influenced by the behavior of the person with whom they were waiting. They "knew" (had a cognition) that there would be some internal physiological reaction to the drug they had just received.

Other subjects were *not* told about the possible side effects. Their behavior was very much influenced by the behavior of the person with whom they were waiting. In one case, the other person in the room acted in a euphoric, silly way, laughing and dancing. The real subjects joined in, following the example of the other person. In another case, uninformed subjects were placed in the waiting room with a person who acted angry and hostile at having to fill out a "stupid questionnaire." Even though they were given the same drug as the subjects who joined in the silly behavior—and had the same physiological reactions—these subjects became angry and hostile.

When there was nothing specific to which they could attribute their physiological arousal (here, drug-induced), subjects responded in ways consistent with their cognitive appraisal of what was going on around them. Not only did the uninformed subjects respond differently in different contexts, but they also reported *feeling* different. Their labeling of their emotional state depended on cognitive factors.

Not everyone has been able to replicate the results of this experiment (for example, Marshall & Zimbardo, 1979; Maslach, 1979). In these attempts at replication, subjects were not as able to identify their emotional state through cognitive appraisal of what was happening around them. Schacter and Singer (1979) believe that they can account for some of the discrepancies. It may be, for example, that the dosage of epinephrine administered to produce the level of physiological arousal is critical. Schacter and Singer also acknowledge that if arousal is too high, and if the subject has no good idea why (hasn't been told what the drug will do), it is likely that the arousal will be interpreted as a negative emotion, which is certainly more adaptive; that is, when in doubt, assume there's a problem.

Fear and relief are two emotions that can be paired and explained by the opponent-process theory. For example, on their first jump, skydivers will often feel extreme fear while in flight, followed by a great sense of relief once they land safely. On subsequent jumps, neither the fear nor the relief will be felt as strongly.

Opponent-process Theory

A rather different sort of theoretical approach to emotion has been gaining attention lately. The *opponent-process theory* (Solomon & Corbit, 1974; Solomon, 1980) sees emotions as occurring in pairs that are essentially opposite in nature (fear and relief, pleasure and pain, depression and elation, for example.)

When one member of a pair is stimulated (fear at the sight of our bear again), the other is suppressed. If the stimulus that causes the first emotional reaction remains (neither you nor the bear run away), the level of the first reaction drops slightly as the second starts to take effect. (After a few minutes, there is some relief in knowing that the bear is not going to attack immediately.)

If the emotion-arousing stimulus is no longer present (let's say the bear runs away this time), the first emotional reaction (fear) drops to zero, and the opponent emotion (relief) becomes the experienced emotional reaction. That relief has been there for awhile, but because the bear was there also, the fear overrode it. Now, no bear = no fear = a sense of relief—the opponent process.

One good example of this procedure involves skydivers. On their first attempt (and on the way down), fear predominates, followed by a happy sense of relief only after being earthbound for some time. On subsequent jumps, because the initial fear is not as great when leaping from the plane, the sense of relief (or accomplishment, or utter joy) is not as great either (Epstein, 1967; Solomon & Corbit, 1974). The same sort of explanation has been used to explain drug use and dependence. After one's first initial "rush" or "high," there is usually an opponent reaction of crashing, of feeling down. The more experienced one becomes with drugs, the less the "high," but the less the subsequent "low" also.

Before you go on
Name four theories of emotion and briefly summarize each.

There seems little doubt that the expression of how we feel is influenced by our learning history. We have learned when it is inappropriate to behave emotionally (e.g., as a customer in a bank lobby) and when it is appropriate (e.g., as a contestant on a TV game show). We learn how to interpret and label our emotions when we acquire the words of our language. Although learning may mold and influence emotion development, is there any evidence—as Darwin believed—that certain basic emotions are innate, and that facial expressions provide a direct window to underlying emotional states? Studies of the emotional development of very young children are suggesting that the answer to both these questions is yes; certain emotions may be innate, and facial expression provides a reliable means of assessing those emotions.

There is clearly survival value in an infant's ability to communicate how he or she feels. A child less than 1 year old has few avenues through which to communicate. Communicating about feelings is of prime interest to both child and caregiver. Although there are useful signals of a vocal sort (screams and coos, for example), the best indicator of emotional state seems to be facial expression.

A psychologist who has been doing research on the facial expression of emotion in infants for many years is Carroll Izard (Izard, 1971; Izard et al., 1980; Izard, 1984; Trotter, 1983). Izard and his colleagues have devised a coding scheme to classify infants' facial expressions, a scoring system they call MAX (for Maximally Discriminative Facial Movement Coding System). MAX's coding system is based on the position of different facial features, such as the corners of the mouth, the position of the eyebrows, openness of the eyes, and so on. Although these facial features can vary and be combined in an infinite number of ways, Izard believes that they can be used to categorize expressions of 10 discrete emotions: distress, disgust, shame, fear, surprise, anger, interest, joy, guilt, and contempt. Figure 21.6 provides examples of some of the primary emotions as expressed in the faces of infants. (Perhaps you will recall that for adults, Izard has proposed nine primary emotions; guilt is the

Figure 21.6

Izard's studies of emotions in infants led him to devise the MAX system of coding, which interprets infants' emotions based on the position of different facial features. For example, the raised eyebrows, wide eyes, and open mouth of the baby on the left indicate surprise, according to the MAX system. The lowered brows and narrowed eyes of the baby on the right indicate anger.

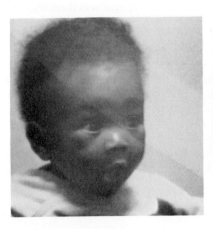 

one that seems not to have staying power.)

To demonstrate the ease with which infants' facial expressions can be coded, Izard asked untrained college undergraduates to watch videotapes of young children (between the ages of 1 and 9 months). The students' job was to classify the responses of the children they were watching. Mothers, experimenters, and others attempted to evoke different emotions. For example, one taped segment showed the faces of children receiving regularly scheduled inoculations.

Some subjects were asked to name the emotion being expressed by the baby on the videotape; others were asked to choose a label from a list of nine that best described the expression on the baby's face. Other subjects were asked to match the baby's facial expressions with those made by adults. Remember that all these untrained undergraduates had to go by was the facial expression of the infant. Subjects were agreed and accurate in their assessment to a remarkable degree. They correctly identified joy 81 percent of the time, sadness 72 percent of the time, and disgust 37 percent of the time (the poorest match, but still considerably more accurate than chance would predict). Raters trained in the MAX coding system reliably identified emotional expressions almost 90 percent of the time.

What does this sort of research tell us? For one thing, it suggests that a number of different types of emotion (not just an overall emotionality) may have a very strong genetic, inherited basis. Although learning may very well influence emotional expression, even in young children, the consistency of expression and classification over many many children from different backgrounds and experiences suggests, at least, an innate basis for emotion.

We also have here confirmation of the notion that facial expression is a useful indicator of inner states of emotion. With coding systems such as MAX at our disposal, we can now imagine experiments of a cross-cultural nature, or a developmental nature, and can at least think about using coded facial expression of emotion as a sign or symptom of developmental delay or retardation. The study of emotion in infants and adults has gained (or regained) a measure of respect in scientific circles, largely because of the development of the precise and reliable measuring devices that are now available to code and classify emotional reactions.

What are two reasons why the study of emotional responses in adult humans is so difficult?

It is difficult to study emotions in humans because (1) ethical considerations make it impossible to do many experiments, and (2) adults usually have learned to hide their emotions from public view, making the use of naturalistic observation questionable. / 382

An emotional state can be said to involve which four possible reactions?

Can emotions be classified?

There are four possible components of an emotional reaction: the experience of a subjective *feeling;* a *cognitive* appraisal or interpretation; an internal, visceral, *physiological* reaction; and an overt *behavioral* response. There have been a number of attempts to sort or categorize emotional reactions into primary and secondary types, dating back to Wundt in the late 1800s. Carroll Izard has one scheme that calls for nine primary emotions: fear, anger, shame, contempt, disgust, distress, interest, surprise, and joy. (Izard adds guilt when considering prime emotions of infants.) Robert Plutchik argues that there are eight basic emotions and many combinations and degrees of these eight. Thus, there appears to be some sense in attempting to classify basic emotions. / 384

Is there any evidence that the facial expression of emotion may be innately determined?

It is a common observation that facial expressions can indicate the internal, emotional state of an individual. What leads us to believe that facial expression of emotion is unlearned (and, hence, innate) is that there is such universal reliability in the interpretation of facial expressions, even across widely different cultures. / 386

Summarize the activities of the sympathetic division of the autonomic nervous system during states of emotionality.

Among the many changes that take place when we become emotional are those produced by the sympathetic division of the autonomic nervous system. Occurring to varying degrees and dependent upon the situation, these reactions include dilation of the pupils, increased heart rate and blood pressure, cessation of digestive processes, deeper and more rapid breathing, increased perspiration, and elevated blood sugar levels. / 388

What brain centers are involved in emotionality?

The cerebral cortex is involved in the cognitive interpretation of emotional events and also acts as an inhibitory mechanism, controlling and coordinating the activity of lower brain centers for emotionality (largely the limbic system and the hypothalamus). Basically, the brain coordinates the physiological aspect of emotionality. / 389

Name the four theories of emotion and briefly summarize each.

There have been a number of theories proposed over the years, trying to describe the relationships between the various components of emotional reactions. The *James-Lange* theory claims that we perceive an emotion-producing stimulus, which produces a bodily reaction. We then interpret our bodily reaction to identify our emotional state; that is, we are afraid because we tremble. The *Cannon-Bard* theory proposes that emotion-producing stimuli are processed by lower brain centers, which then send the messages simultaneously to the cortex for interpretation and to yet lower centers to produce physiological reactions. The *Schachter-Singer* model theorizes that one's interpretation of an emotional state involves the interpretation of diffuse physiological arousal in terms of the cognitive appraisal of the environment at the moment. The *opponent-process* theory suggests that any emotional reaction is soon accompanied by an opposite reaction, which persists after the emotion-producing stimulation is no longer present. / 391

TOPIC

**STRESS AS A RESPONSE:
THE GENERAL ADAPTATION SYNDROME**

STRESSORS: CAUSES OF STRESS
Frustration-induced Stress
Conflict-induced Stress
  Approach-approach Conflicts
  Avoidance-avoidance Conflicts
  Approach-avoidance Conflicts
  Multiple Approach-avoidance Conflicts
Life Change-induced Stress

REACTIONS TO STRESS
Reacting to Stress with Learning
Reacting to Stress with Aggression
Reacting to Stress with Defense Mechanisms
  Repression
  Denial
  Rationalization
  Compensation
  Fantasy
  Projection
  Regression
  Displacement
  *The Use and Misuse of Defense Mechanisms Against the
  Feelings of Stress*

TOPIC EXPANSION: COPING WITH EVERYDAY STRESS

— It's Friday afternoon. You have a chance to get away for the weekend with friends. Unfortunately, you have two big exams scheduled for Monday and need the weekend to study.

— I put 25¢ in the vending machine, expecting to get a cup of coffee. The paper cup comes down the chute upside-down, and my coffee runs down the drain.

— Cindy and Jerry have known each other since grade school. They dated throughout high school. Next week, family and friends will join in the celebration of their wedding.

— The Dean has to make a decision. If he chooses Plan A, the faculty may be outraged. If he opts for Plan B, the students may riot. If he does nothing, he may be fired.

— Ken wants to make the basketball team, but the coach informs him that in spite of his efforts, he's just too short.

— Joanne has enough change to buy one single-dip ice cream cone. When she walked into the store, she wanted a cherry-vanilla cone. Now that she sees that the flavor of the month is "Fresh Peach," she can't make up her mind.

— After 11 years on the road as a salesman, Mike is being promoted to sales manager—an office job with a substantial raise in pay.

— For the first time in his life, Jim is standing on the high diving board. He wants to dive (or jump) off to impress his friends, but now that he's up there, he realizes just how high that diving board really is. There's no way he'll climb back down the ladder.

— Three-year-old Mindy keeps asking her mother for a cookie. Mother steadfastly refuses because it's almost dinner time. Mindy returns to her room and promptly pulls an arm off her favorite doll.

— Christmas vacation is coming.

— It's raining.

Life is filled with stress, frustration, and conflict. This list provides only a very small sample of different types of stress, frustration, and conflict that we may encounter on a daily basis. In this topic, we'll discuss stress: where it comes from, and how it may be responded to.

Why We Care

Stress is a strange concept. It is a commonly used term that has become one of the "buzzwords" of the 1980s. One reason stress is a strange concept is that we all know what stress means, but we have a difficult time defining it precisely. Part of this problem reflects the fact that "stress" has become a general label; in fact, it has come to mean a number of different things.

Stress is a complex set of reactions made by an individual under pressure to adapt. It is a response made to a real or perceived threat to one's well-being that motivates further adjustment.

In this sense, stress is something that happens inside people. It is the way we respond to certain circumstances. In some ways, stress is like an emotion—there are definite physiological reactions and unpleasant feelings associated with stress. In some ways, stress is like a motivator: People under stress are motivated to do something to lessen the stress they experience. Thinking about stress as a response allows us to discuss the reactions that people have to stress, what people do when they feel stressed.

Thinking about stress as a response also allows us to consider the possible sources or stimuli that produce stress. Those events or stimuli that are real or perceived threats to well-being and produce stress are called **stressors**.

The structure of this topic will follow the logic of our definition. First, we'll expand on our definition of the stress response and consider the physiological nature of a stress reaction. Then we'll turn our attention to stressors. Although there are many potential stimuli for stress, we'll focus on frustration-induced stress, conflict-induced stress, and stress induced by life events. Finally, we will consider some of the more common ways people can and do react to stress when it occurs. We'll see that some reactions to stress are clearly more adaptive than others.

Before we get into the causes of and adjustments to stress, there are two important points that should be understood. One is that stress is not necessarily *bad*. We tend to think of stress as a reaction to disasters (large and small), which reaction in turn produces disastrous consequences. Reflection should convince us that a certain amount of stress is not only necessary, but sometimes even *good*. To be stressed is to be alive (Selye, 1974). Many of the events and activities in our lives that cause a stressful reaction are, in their own way, very positive and pleasant—promotions, weddings, births, or admission to college, for example. Even some of our worst experiences of great stress provide opportunities for learning, growth, and development.

A second point to keep in mind while reading this topic has to do with individual differences in responding *with* stress or *to* stress. What constitutes a stressor, and what an individual may do in response to stress, varies considerably from person to person. Some people fall apart at weddings; others don't find them stressful at all. For some people, even simple choices are difficult to make; for others, choices are not enough—they seek challenges. The variability in stress levels that we see among different people can usually be found within each individual at different times. You know this from your own experience. On one day, being caught in slow-moving traffic may drive you up the wall. In the very same situation a few days later, you may find that you couldn't care less. So, we need to remember that reactions *of* stress and adjustments *to* stress vary from time to time and from person to person.

stress
a complex pattern of reactions to real or perceived threats to one's sense of well-being that motivate adjustment

stressors
real or perceived threats to one's sense of well-being; sources of stress

Before you go on
Define stress and stressor.

STRESS AS A RESPONSE: THE GENERAL ADAPTATION SYNDROME

One approach to stress views it as a physiological reaction to stressors. Using this approach, stress can be seen as a type of emotional response with associated physiological changes. A demand is made on the physiological systems of the body, and the demand is interpreted as a challenge to the person's well-being.

The most complete description of this approach to stress is described in Hans Selye's **general adaptation syndrome,** or **GAS.** According to Selye (1956, 1974), one's pattern of reaction to stressors occurs in three stages: alarm, resistance, and exhaustion (see Figure 22.1).

The first response to the perception of stress is *alarm.* A perceived threat produces rapid and noticeable changes in the sympathetic division of the autonomic nervous system. Consistent with changes that accompany any emotional response, the sympathetic division directly, or indirectly, causes an increase in blood pressure and heart rate, pupilary dilation, a cessation of digestion, and a rerouting of blood supply to the extremities of the body. The adrenal glands secrete norepinephrine into the bloodstream and mobilize the body's resources, providing increased levels of blood sugar. All of these reactions are very much like those we experience in any extremely emotional situation.

This strong reaction is one that cannot last long. We cannot maintain high levels of sympathetic activity for more than a few minutes, a few hours at the most.

Let's illustrate this process with an example. We must remember that the severity of a stressor for one person may be quite different for someone else. With that in mind, imagine a student, Pam, in the midst of a very important semester. Pam is strongly motivated to do well this term in all of her courses. Just past mid-term, she gets word from home that her father has had a massive heart attack. She leaves school and rushes home to the hospital. Her father had never been seriously ill before; now he's in the coronary intensive care unit. The shock and disbelief are overwhelming. Pam doesn't know what to do.

In *resistance,* the second stage of the general adaptation syndrome, the stressor remains present. Pam's father begins to show some signs of recovery, but will be in intensive care for at least another week and will be hospitalized for a long time. There is a real risk of another heart attack. There's little that Pam can do to help her father, but she feels that she can't leave to go back to school; and every day that she stays home, she gets farther behind in her classes.

Pam's bodily resources were mobilized in the alarm stage of the GAS. Now she discovers that there is no escape from or means of removing the source of her stress. The drain on her body's resources continues, often with negative results. If other stressors appear, she will be less able to deal with them effectively. Pam will become vulnerable to physical illness and infection to a greater degree than she would be without the constant stress she is experiencing. Her internal, sympathetic response seems to return to normal levels of functioning (it can't stay at the high level of an alarm stage). As she continues to search for ways to reduce or eliminate the stress, Pam's physiological response continues to resist and mobilize: high blood pressure, ulcers, skin rashes, or respiratory difficulties may develop. Pam may appear to be in control, but the reality of her father's condition and the approach of final exams continue to eat away at her, intruding into her awareness from time to time.

general adaptation syndrome (GAS)
a pattern of physiological reactions to stressors including alarm, resistance, and exhaustion

Figure 22.1
When we are first exposed to stress, our bodily resources are mobilized in an alarm reaction, which raises our resistance above normal levels. Our resistance is maintained at this high level during the stage of resistance. If the stressor remains, resistance may eventually fall below normal levels, depicted here as the stage of exhaustion.
(From Selye, 1956.)

If Pam cannot discover some useful way to deal with her stress, her physiological reaction to the still-present stressor may produce a condition of *exhaustion.* In this stage, her bodily resources become nearly depleted. She is running out of energy and out of time. If effective means of coping with her father's condition and her college courses are not found, Pam may break down—psychologically and/or physically. Although the resistance stage may last several months, eventually one's bodily resources become expended. In extreme cases, the exhaustion stage of the general adaptation syndrome may result in death.

As we shall see, the extent of one's reaction to stressors depends on many factors. Selye's view of stress as a physiological response implies that there is some patterned reaction of alarm, resistance, and exhaustion that *is* stress. Stress is the mobilization of the body's resources to combat real or perceived threats to our well-being. We have limited supplies of such resources. Repeated stress reactions tend to have cumulative effects. Dire consequences can follow when a person is simultaneously or successively faced with a number of stressful situations.

Hans Selye

Before you go on

Name and describe the three stages of the general adaptation syndrome.

STRESSORS: THE CAUSES OF STRESS

We have defined stressors in general as events or stimuli that are real or perceived threats to one's sense of well-being. Many events or stimuli can qualify as stressors. In this section, we'll consider three classes of stressors: frustration, conflict, and life events. In each case, we'll provide examples. Some of our examples can be viewed as quite trivial—choosing a flavor of ice cream, for instance. This is done to remind us that stress is not necessarily a response to some overwhelming, catastrophic event, such as the death of a loved one.

Frustration-induced Stress

Let us begin with a premise. We can't prove this, but we can take it as a basic assumption: *All behavior is goal-directed.* In a way, this is saying that all behavior is motivated, or that an unmotivated organism is a dead organism. In all of our behavior, we are pushed or pulled toward positive goals and away from negative goals.

Notice that there are a couple of assumptions that we are *not* making here. We are not willing to assume, for example, that you can always tell what goals are directing your behavior. In a real sense, you may not know. I may ask you why you did something, "What was the goal behind that behavior?" Your honest answer may be, "I really don't know." But just because you may not be aware of or able to tell me about the goals that direct your behavior does not mean that our basic assumption is wrong.

Another reality about goals and behavior is that it is often difficult to directly infer one from the other. For example, many people engage in the same behaviors, but for a variety of different reasons—to reach different goals. Many students have registered for a course in introductory psychology this term. Why? In order to reach what goal? There are probably as many reasons as there are students in your class. It is also true that many people

Figure 22.2

A depiction of frustration. A person's
goal-directed behavior is being blocked
or thwarted.

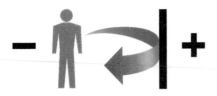

frustration

the blocking or thwarting of goal-
directed behavior

Frustration comes from the blocking of
goal-directed behavior. Being caught in
a traffic jam, unable to get where we
want to go, can cause great frustration.

share the same goal, but engage in a wide variety of different behaviors in
order to reach that goal. For example, a goal for many people is "acquiring
lots of money." To reach this end, some work very hard, some enroll in
college classes, some rob gas stations, some try to "marry money," and so on.

So one assumption that we can make about behavior is that it is goal-directed. Our second assumption is: *Organisms don't always reach all of their
goals.* Have you always gotten everything you've ever wanted? Have you
always been able to avoid unpleasantness, pain, or sorrow? Do you know
anyone who has?

Sometimes we are totally prohibited from ever reaching a certain goal. At
other times our progress toward a goal may be slower or more difficult than
we would like. In either case, we are being frustrated. **Frustration,** then, is
the blocking of goal-directed behavior (see Figure 22.2). The blocking may
be either total and permanent or partial and temporary.

Seen in this way, stress that results from frustration is a normal, commonplace reaction. It is, again, a fact of life. It does not imply weakness, or
pathology, or illness. What will ultimately matter is how individuals react to
the frustrations and stressors of their lives. Before we consider adjustments
to frustration, let's look at some of its major sources.

To someone who feels the stress that results from frustration, the source
of that frustration may be of little consequence. However, in order to respond adaptively to frustration-induced stress, it is helpful to be able to recognize the source of the blocking that is keeping us from our goals. There are
basically two types of frustration: environmental and personal.

Environmental frustration implies that the blocking or thwarting of goal-
directed behaviors is being done by something or someone in the environment. (We should talk about the *source* or *origin* of frustration, not *fault* or
blame, which are evaluative terms. All we are trying to do here is describe,
not evaluate.)

Our opening example of losing 25¢ in a coffee vending machine is a simple type of environmental frustration. I wanted a cup of coffee. Goal-directed
behavior led me to slip a quarter into the coin slot. Something in my environment—here a piece of faulty machinery—interfered with my goal-directed
behavior and kept me from reaching my goal. You may want to be outside
and find that it's raining. As a result, you may be under some stress because
your goal-directed behavior is being thwarted by your environment.

Three-year-old Mindy (from another opening example) is also being envir-
onmentally frustrated, but in a slightly different way. She wants a cookie and
her mother is blocking that motivated behavior. This type of environmental
frustration, in which the source of the blocking is another individual, is often
called *social frustration.*

Sometimes we are frustrated, not so much because someone or something
in our environment is blocking our progress toward our goals, but because of
some more internal or personal reason. Ken's failure to make the basketball
team was due mostly to the fact that he is too short. Someone wanting to be
a concert pianist may be frustrated in her attempt to do so because she
happens to have short, stubby fingers and can only reach half an octave on
the piano keyboard. She may learn to be a good pianist, but she probably
won't make it in the world of classical piano. Her frustration is not the fault
of people who write piano music or build piano keyboards. Her inability to
play some piano music is not her fault, but if she persists in this goal-directed
behavior, she will be frustrated, and the source of her frustration will be
more personal than environmental.

A high school student with a C- average may face frustration if he continues to hold out serious hope of being a nuclear physicist. The source of his

frustration can be said to be personal if he has neither the educational background nor the intellectual aptitude to major in physics and do well.

As adults, you and I seldom encounter stressful situations that result from personal frustration anymore. We have gained a useful sense of what we can and cannot do (occasionally through painful experience). We have changed some of the goals that we may have had as youngsters because we have recognized that there are some goals we cannot reach. (We do need to acknowledge that coming to grips with personal frustration is not always easy or successful. As we will see in Chapter 12, many people become alcoholics or drug abusers, develop psychological disorders, or attempt suicide when faced with personal (or environmental) frustrations that they cannot solve on their own.)

Before you go on

What is meant by frustration-induced stress?

Define environmental, social, and personal frustration.

Conflict-induced Stress

It is sometimes the case that we are unable to satisfy a particular drive or motive because it is in **conflict** with another drive or motive that is influencing us at the same time. Stress may then result, not from the frustration caused by the blocking of our goal-directed behaviors, but because our own motivational system is causing a conflict.

conflict
a source of stress in which some goals can be reached only at the expense of others

With conflict there is always the implication of a decision or a choice that has to be made. Sometimes the decision is relatively easy to make; sometimes it is very difficult. In discussing conflict, it is useful to talk about positive goals or incentives we wish to approach and negative goals or incentives we wish to avoid.

Approach-approach Conflicts Conflicts are unpleasant and stressful situations. In most cases, the type of conflict that produces the least amount of stress is the *approach-approach conflict* (see Figure 22.3). Here an organism is caught between two alternatives, and both of them are potentially reinforcing. If the subject chooses alternative A, he or she will reach a desirable goal. If alternative B is chosen, a different desirable goal will be attained. What makes this a conflict is that *both* alternatives are not simultaneously available. It has to be one or the other. A choice has to be made.

In a way, these can be thought of as simple conflicts, since the subject ends up with some desired goal no matter which alternative is chosen. Our opening example of Joanne in the ice cream store was an example of an approach-approach conflict situation. She could have one dip of ice cream, but she was torn between two flavors. Typical of conflict, we'd probably notice some vacillation in Joanne's behavior, some swaying back and forth between the two alternatives. But the conflict will eventually be resolved with a choice, and Joanne will at least walk out of the store with an ice cream cone of one flavor or the other. Her life might have been easier (less stressful) if the store provided just one flavor and she didn't have to make such choices, but she'll contemplate that possibility with an ice cream cone in hand.

Not all approach-approach conflicts are so trivial. For one thing, there is always the possibility that a person will be faced with many more than two positive alternatives from which to choose. In fact, if she had been paying attention, Joanne might have faced the fact that she really had as many as 31

Figure 22.3
A diagram of an approach-approach conflict. Here, the subject is faced with two (or more) positive, attractive goals and must choose from among them.

Figure 22.4

A diagram of an avoidance-avoidance
conflict. Here, the subject is faced with
two (or more) negative, unattractive
goals, and one must be chosen. This is
a no-win situation.

choices to make in that ice cream store. Even if there are many more than
two choices available, we still use the simple "approach-approach" label,
assuming, of course, that all the alternatives are reinforcing ones.

Sometimes the choices we are called upon to make are much more serious
than those involving ice cream flavors. What will be your college major? On
the one hand, you'd like to go to medical school and be a surgeon (that's a
positive goal, or incentive). On the other hand, you'd like to cultivate your
aptitude for music and study composition and conducting at a school of
music (also a clear positive incentive). At the moment, you cannot do both.
The courses you'd take as a pre-med student are quite different from those
you'd take if you were to follow music as a career path. Both avenues are
good, constructive, desirable alternatives. But now, at registration, you have
to make a choice—a choice that may have long-lasting repercussions.

Avoidance-avoidance Conflicts   There is little doubt that among
the most stressful and unpleasant conflicts are those characterized as *avoidance-avoidance conflicts* (see Figure 22.4). In this type of conflict, the subject is faced with a number of alternatives, and each of them is negative or
punishing. No matter which way he or she turns, he or she is going to "get
burned." Remember our example of the Dean who had to choose between
alternatives that upset the students or faculty, or lose his job? In many ways,
he was in a no win situation. No matter what he chooses, someone is going to
be unhappy—yet he has to choose. To be in an avoidance-avoidance conflict
is, in a way, to be boxed in, so that no matter what you do, the result will be
punishing.

We have a number of clichés in the English language that seem to be
describing such conflicts: "Caught between the devil and the deep blue sea,"
"Out of the frying pan, into the fire," "Stuck between a rock and a hard
place," are three that come to mind. In each case, we seem to be describing a
situation from which a pleasant reprieve seems unlikely.

Approach-avoidance Conflicts   It may be easier for us to generate
examples of either approach-approach or avoidance-avoidance conflicts than
it is to come up with good examples of simple *approach-avoidance conflicts*
(see Figure 22.5). The problem here is that our subject is considering only
one goal. What makes this situation a conflict is that the subject would very
much like to reach that goal, but, at the same time, would very much like not
to. It's a matter of "yes, I'd love to. Well, as a matter of fact, I'd rather not.
Well, maybe I would. No, I wouldn't . . . yes . . . no." Typical of conflicts in
general, what we see here is vacillation, a swinging back and forth—
motivated to approach and, at the same time, motivated to avoid.

It's easy to see how we might set up such a conflict situation for a rat.
Brown (1948) and Miller (1959) have demonstrated all of these conflicts
using rats rather than humans as subjects. We'd place a nice, attractive pile
of rat food at the end of a runway. We would also arrange to shock the
portion of the runway floor around the food. A hungry rat on that runway
would be in a true approach-avoidance conflict. It would want to get to the
end of the runway to get the food, but it would also want to avoid that same
end to avoid getting shocked.

You and I usually try not to get into simple approach-avoidance conflicts
in the first place. We generally try to arrange things so that we are not faced
with just one possibility. Our opening example of Jim on the high diving
board was meant as an example of this sort of conflict. Having gotten up

Figure 22.5

A diagram of a simple approach-
avoidance conflict. Here, the subject is
faced with but one goal. What puts the
subject in conflict is that the goal has
both positive and negative features.

there in the first place, Jim virtually removed any hope of gracefully retreating down the ladder. He had but one option. On the one hand, he badly wanted to jump; on the other, he realized he could get hurt. He was in an approach-avoidance conflict. And, predictably, he probably spent a good deal of time up there just jumping and bouncing around, trying to come to some resolution of his conflict.

Multiple Approach-avoidance Conflicts The type of motivational conflict most commonly found among adult humans is the *multiple approach-avoidance conflict* (see Figure 22.6). As its name implies, this type of conflict arises when an individual is faced with a number of alternatives, each one of which is in some way positive and in some way negative at the same time.

Perhaps you and some friends are out shopping on a Saturday morning. You suddenly discover that it's getting late and you're all hungry. Where will you go to lunch? You may have a multiple approach-avoidance conflict here. "We could go to Bob's Diner, where the food is cheap and the service is fast, but the food is terrible. Or we could go to Cafe Olé, where the food is better, but service is a little slower, and the food is more expensive. Or, we could go to The Grill, where the service is elegant and the food superb, but the price is very high." Granted this is not an earth-shaking dilemma, but in each case there is a plus and a minus to be considered in making the choice.

Our first opening example was of this sort of conflict. Should you get away for the weekend with friends or stay home and study? One alternative is to stay at home—you'll surely do well on the exam (+), but you'll miss out on the fun (−). The other alternative is to go away for the weekend (+), but you'll probably flunk the exam (−).

Life is filled with such conflicts, and some of them can be severe and stressful. They may very well encompass questions of the "what shall I do with the rest of my life?" sort. "Should I stay at home and raise the children (+ and −), or should I have a career (+ and −)?" "Should I get married or stay single, or is there another way (again, + and − in each case)?" "Should I work for Company A (+ and −), or should I work for Company B (+ and −)?" Quite clearly, lists like this could go on and on. You might want to reflect on the conflicts you have faced during the past few weeks. You should be able to categorize each of them into one of the four types we have listed here.

Before you go on
Name four types of motivational conflict, and provide an example of each.

Life Change-induced Stress

Stress demands that we make adjustments. Stress involves real and/or perceived threats to our sense of well-being. It is clear that frustration and conflict are potent sources of stress in our lives and are often unavoidable consequences of being a motivated organism. Within the last 20 years, psychologists have also attempted to deal with those sources of stress that do not fit neatly into our descriptions of either frustration or conflict. One useful approach has been to look at the changes that occur in one's life as potential sources of stress.

In 1967, Holmes and Rahe published their first version of the Social Readjustment Rating Scale, or SRRS (see also Holmes & Holmes, 1970). The

Figure 22.6
A diagram of a multiple approach-avoidance conflict. Here, the subject is faced with a number of alternative goals, each of which has positive and negative characteristics, and a choice must be made.

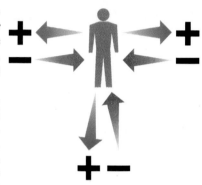

basic idea behind this scale is that stress naturally results whenever our life situation changes. These changes may be for the worse or for the better, but negative changes are more stressful (Sarason *et al.,* 1978). The scale's authors provided subjects with a list of life events that might be potentially stressful. The original list of such events was drawn from the reports of patients suffering from moderate to high levels of stress in their lives. Marriage was arbitrarily assigned a value of 50 stress points (technically called *life change units*). With marriage = 50 as their guide, subjects rated a number of other more-or-less typical life changes in terms of the amount of stress they might provide. Figure 22.7 is a version of the 1970 modification of the original scale.

In a rather direct way, the SRRS gives us a way to measure the stress in one's life. Psychologists have reported a positive correlation between scores on the SRRS and the incidence of physical illness and disease (Rahe & Arthur, 1978). People with SRRS scores between 200 and 299 have a 50-50 chance of developing noticeable symptoms of physical illness within the next 2 years. *Eighty* percent of those with scores above 300 may develop physical symptoms within the same time period. The logic is that stress causes illness, particularly cardiovascular disorders. But we must remember what we said back in our first chapter about correlations: They do not tell us about cause-and-effect. After all, some of the SRRS items themselves are related to physical illness or are in some way health related. It may not be much of a surprise, then, to find scores on this scale related to levels of physical illness.

Richard Lazarus (1981) argues that we ought to focus more of our attention on those causes of stress that are less dramatic than big life changes such as the death of a family member or marriage. What often matters most, at least in the short term, is life's little hassles—the traffic that goes too slowly, the toothpaste tube that splits, ants at a picnic, the cost of an ice cream cone (compared to what it was just a few years ago), and so on.

Part of Lazarus' argument is that big crises or major life change events are often too large to have an impact on us directly. What may cause us to feel stressed are the ways in which these big events produce little changes in our lives. For example, being in jail may mean that one can't watch a favorite TV program. Being retired may mean a lack of access to friendly conversation at coffee break time. A spouse who starts to work may make life a little more difficult; the other spouse may have to cook dinner for the first time. Thus, stress results not so much from the event itself, but from the little hassles it creates. Clearly we could go down the entire list of life events in Figure 22.7 and see that in each case, the event itself is often a collection of small, stress-inducing hassles.

Before you go on

What is the SRRS?

What is it meant to measure?

REACTIONS TO STRESS

So far we have defined stress and reviewed a number of potential stressors—frustration, conflict, and life events that involve making changes. Now we need to consider what someone might do when under stress. How might we respond when stressed; that is, what can be done about it? In this sense, we are now treating stress as a motivator, a reaction that in turn causes us to do something else.

Figure 22.7

The Social Readjustment Rating Scale
(From Holmes & Rahe, 1967.)

Life event	Mean value
1. Death of spouse	100
2. Divorce	73
3. Marital separation from mate	65
4. Detention in jail or other institution	63
5. Death of a close family member	63
6. Major personal injury or illness	53
7. Marriage	50
8. Being fired at work	47
9. Marital reconciliation with mate	45
10. Retirement from work	45
11. Major change in health or behavior of a family member	44
12. Pregnancy	40
13. Sexual difficulties	39
14. Gaining a new family member (e.g., through birth, adoption, oldster moving in, etc.)	39
15. Major business readjustment (e.g., merger, reorganization, bankruptcy, etc.)	39
16. Major change in financial state (e.g., a lot worse off or a lot better off than usual)	38
17. Death of a close friend	37
18. Changing to a different line of work	36
19. Major change in the number of arguments with spouse (e.g., either a lot more or a lot less than usual regarding child-rearing, personal habits, etc.)	35
20. Taking out a mortgage or loan for a major purchase (e.g., for a home, business, etc.)	31
21. Foreclosure on a mortgage or loan	30
22. Major change in responsibilities at work (e.g., promotion, demotion, lateral transfer)	29
23. Son or daughter leaving home (e.g., marriage, attending college, etc.)	29
24. Trouble with in-laws	29
25. Outstanding personal achievement	28
26. Wife beginning or ceasing work outside the home	26
27. Beginning or ceasing formal schooling	26
28. Major change in living conditions (e.g., building a new home, remodeling, deterioration of home or neighborhood)	25
29. Revision of personal habits (dress, manners, associations, etc.)	24
30. Trouble with the boss.	23
31. Major change in working hours or conditions	20
32. Change in residence	20
33. Changing to a new school	20
34. Major change in usual type and/or amount of recreation	19
35. Major change in church activities (e.g., a lot more or a lot less than usual)	19
36. Major change in social activities (e.g., clubs, dancing, movies, visiting, etc.)	18
37. Taking out a mortgage or loan for a lesser purchase (e.g., for a car, TV, freezer, etc.)	17
38. Major change in sleeping habits (a lot more or a lot less sleep, or change in part of day when asleep)	16
39. Major change in number of family get-togethers (e.g., a lot more or a lot less than usual)	15
40. Major change in eating habits (a lot more or a lot less food intake, or very different meal hours or surroundings)	15
41. Vacation	13
42. Christmas	12
43. Minor violations of the law (e.g., traffic tickets, jaywalking, disturbing the peace, etc.)	11

Figure 22.8

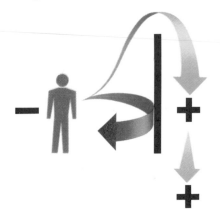

Some of the possible responses to stress—particularly repeated, severe stress—are clearly pathological. That is, they are maladaptive and inappropriate responses of the sort that we associate with mental illness or abnormal behavior. We'll discuss these reactions in Chapter 12. For now, we'll consider only those reactions that are "normal," and which are not considered to be a sign of illness or pathology.

The way we react to stress will, to some degree, depend upon the source of the stress in the first place. Did the stress come from frustration of goal-directed behaviors, or from conflict, or from a stress-producing life event?

Reacting to Stress with Learning

One of the most effective ways to deal with stress is to bring about relatively permanent changes in our behaviors as a result of the experience of stress. That is, to learn and adapt in such a way as to eliminate the source of the stress.

This response makes particularly good sense when we consider frustration-induced stress. Here, our path to a goal is being blocked or thwarted. An adaptive way to handle such stress is to find some new way to reach our goal or to learn to modify our goal (see Figure 22.8).

In fact, a great deal of our everyday learning is motivated by such frustration-induced stress. We have had to learn many new responses as a means of coping with stress. Let's look at a few imaginary examples. Having been frustrated once (or twice) by locking yourself out of your house or apartment, you have learned to hide a second set of keys somewhere you can easily find them. Having been denied promotion because you didn't have a college degree, you are learning about general psychology on the way toward earning such a degree. Having been caught at home in a blizzard with no cookies in the house, you learned to bake them yourself. Having discovered that you're too short to make the basketball team, you learned to play golf. You may have learned as a child to get what you wanted from your parents by smiling sweetly and asking politely. In each of these cases, what prompted the learning of new responses or the establishment of new goals was stress—stress resulting from frustration.

Learning through experience with stress may also have taught you the value of escape and avoidance (and the usefulness of negative reinforcers). You now know how to avoid getting into many motivational conflicts. You try to plan things so as to keep your options open to avoid getting into avoidance-avoidance conflicts. You may have learned that the only sensible thing to do once in such a conflict is to escape, or to make major changes in what is motivating you.

This is one way in which stress can be seen as a positive force in our lives. If we were never challenged, if we never set difficult goals, if we never faced stressful situations, we would miss out on many opportunities for growth and learning. The stress we experience might be quite unpleasant at the time, but it may produce positive consequences.

Before you go on
How can learning be seen as a reaction to stress?

Reacting to Stress with Aggression

frustration-aggression hypothesis
the point of view (now discredited) that all aggression stems from frustration

It is clear that there are many sources and causes of aggression and that one of those causes is frustration. At one time, it was proposed that frustration was *the* major cause of aggression, the so-called **frustration-aggression**

hypothesis (Dollard et al., 1939). This point of view claimed that frustration could produce a number of reactions, including aggression, but that aggression was always caused by frustration. Even though there *are* other sources of aggression (some view aggression as innate and instinctive, while others see it as a response learned through reinforcement or through modeling that need not be stimulated by frustration), stress and frustration remain prime candidates as the cause of a great deal of aggression. It doesn't do much good in the long run, but a flash of aggressive behavior often accompanies the stress of frustration (Berkowitz, 1982).

There you are in the parking lot, trying to get home from class, and your car won't start. Over and over you crank the ignition. Frustrated, you swing open your door, get out, kick the front left fender, throw up the hood, and glower at the engine. You're good and mad. Being angry and kicking at the car (or yelling at someone who offers to assist) won't help you solve your problem, but such anger and aggression are common reactions to frustration.

Before you go on
What is the frustration-aggression hypothesis?

Reacting to Stress with Defense Mechanisms

Stress may occasionally promote positive outcomes. Motivated to overcome stress and the situations that produce it, we may learn new and adaptive responses. It is also clear, however, that stress involves a very unpleasant emotional component. **Anxiety** is a general feeling of tension or apprehension that often accompanies a perceived threat to one's well-being. It is this unpleasant emotional component that often prompts us to learn new responses to rid ourselves of stress.

There are a number of techniques, essentially self-deceptive, that we may employ to keep from feeling the unpleasantness associated with stress. These techniques, or tricks we play on ourselves, are not adaptive in the sense of helping us to get rid of stress by getting rid of the source of stress. Rather, they are mechanisms that we can and do use to defend ourselves against the *feelings* of stress. They are called **defense mechanisms.** Freud believed defense mechanisms to be the work of the unconscious mind. He claimed that they are ploys that our unconscious mind uses to protect us (our *self* or *ego*) from stress. There are many psychologists who would take issue with Freud's interpretation of defense mechanisms. Psychologists now tend to think of defense mechanisms in more general terms than did Freud, but few will deny that defense mechanisms exist. It *is* true that they are generally ineffective if consciously employed. The list of defense mechanisms is a long one. Here, we'll review some of the more common defense mechanisms, providing an example of each, to give you an idea of how they might serve as a reaction to stress.

Repression The notion of **repression** came up in an earlier discussion of memory (pp. 257–258). In a way, it is the most basic of all the defense mechanisms. It is sometimes referred to as *motivated forgetting*, which gives us a good idea of what is involved.

Repression is a matter of conveniently forgetting about some stressful, anxiety-producing event, conflict, or frustration. Paul had a teacher in high school he did not get along with at all. After spending an entire semester trying his best to do whatever was asked, Paul failed the course. The following summer, while walking with his girlfriend, Paul encountered this teacher. When he tried to introduce his girlfriend, Paul could not remember his teach-

anxiety
a general feeling of tension or apprehension accompanied by a perceived threat to well-being

defense mechanisms
techniques, often beyond one's conscious control, employed to protect against the feelings of stress

repression
"motivated forgetting," in which stressful events are forced from awareness and cannot be remembered

er's name. He had repressed it. As a long-term reaction to stress, repressing the names of people we don't like or that we associate with unpleasant, stressful experiences is certainly not a very adaptive reaction. But at least it can protect us from dwelling on such unpleasantness.

denial
refusing to acknowledge the presence of stressors

Denial **Denial** is a very basic mechanism of defense against stress. In denial, a person simply refuses to acknowledge the realities of a stressful situation. When a physician first tells a patient that he or she has a terminal illness, a common reaction is denial; the patient refuses to believe that there is anything seriously wrong.

Other less stressful events than serious illness sometimes evoke denial. Many smokers are intelligent individuals who are well aware of the data and the statistics that can readily convince them they are slowly (or rapidly) killing themselves by continuing to smoke. But they deny the evidence. Somehow they are able to convince themselves that they aren't going to die from smoking; that's something that happens to other people. The same phenomenon is often found among drug addicts and alcoholics who deny their true condition, claiming they can stop whenever they wish, though reality seems to indicate otherwise.

rationalization
generating excuses to explain one's behaviors rather than dealing with the real reasons for one's behaviors

Rationalization **Rationalization** amounts to making excuses for our behaviors when facing the real reasons for our behaviors would be stressful. The reason Kevin failed his psychology midterm is that he didn't study for it and has missed a number of classes. Kevin hates to admit, even to himself, that he could have been so stupid as to flunk that exam because of his own actions. As a result, he rationalizes: "It wasn't really my fault. I had a lousy instructor. We used a rotten text. The tests were grossly unfair. I've been fighting the darn flu all semester. And Marjorie had that big party the night before the exam." Now Suzie, on the other hand, really did want to go to Marjorie's party, but she decided that she wouldn't go unless somebody asked her. As it happens, no one did. In short order, Suzie rationalized that she "didn't want to go to that dumb party anyway"; she needed to "stay home and study."

compensation
a mechanism through which extraordinary resources are invested in some trait or ability to offset deficits in other traits or abilities

Compensation We might best think of **compensation** in the context of personal frustration. This defense mechanism is a matter of overemphasizing some positive trait or ability to counterbalance a shortcoming in some other trait or ability. If some particular goal-directed behavior becomes blocked, a person may compensate by putting extra effort and attention into some other aspect of behavior. For example, Karen, a seventh grader, wants to be popular. She's a reasonably bright and pleasant teenager, but is—in the judgment of her classmates—very plain, if not downright homely. Karen *may* compensate for her lack of good looks by studying very hard to be a good student, or by memorizing jokes and funny stories, or by becoming a good musician. Compensation is not just an attempt to be a well-rounded individual. It is a matter of expending *extra* energy and resources in one direction to offset shortcomings in other directions.

fantasy
an escape from stress through imagination and daydreaming

Fantasy As a defense mechanism, **fantasy** and daydreaming are very much alike. Fantasy is one of the more common defense mechanisms among college students. It is a very pleasant mechanism. Particularly after a hard day when stress levels are high, isn't it pleasant to sit in a comfortable chair, kick off your shoes, lie back, close your eyes, and daydream, perhaps about graduation day, picturing yourself walking across the stage to pick up your diploma.

When things are not going well for us, we may retreat into a world of fantasy where everything always goes well. Remember that to engage from time to time in daydreaming is normal and an acceptable response to stress. You should not get worried if you daydream occasionally. On the other hand, you should realize that there are some potential dangers here. You need to be able to keep separate those activities that are real and those that occur in your fantasies. And you should realize that fantasy in itself will not solve whatever problem is causing you stress. Daydreaming about academic successes may help you feel better for awhile, but it is not likely to make you a better student.

Projection

Projection is a matter of seeing in others those very traits and motives that cause us stress when we see them in ourselves. Under pressure to do well on an exam, Mark may want to cheat, but his conscience won't let him. Because of projection, he may think he sees cheating going on all around him.

Projection is a mechanism that is often used in conjunction with hostility and aggression. When people begin to feel uncomfortable about their own levels of hostility, they often project their aggressiveness onto others, coming to believe that others are "out to do me harm," and "I'm only defending myself."

projection
seeing in others those very characteristics and motives that cause stress in one's self

Regression

To employ **regression** is to return to earlier, even childish, levels of behavior that were once productive or reinforced. Curiously enough, we often find regression in children. Imagine a 4-year-old who until very recently was an only child. Now Mommy has returned from the hospital with a new baby sister. The 4-year-old is no longer "the center of the universe," as his new little sister now gets parental attention. The 4-year-old reverts to earlier behaviors and starts wetting the bed, screaming for a bottle of his own, and crawling on all fours in an attempt to get attention. He is regressing.

Many defense mechanisms can be seen on the golf course, including regression. After Doug knocks three golf balls into the lake, he throws a temper tantrum, stamps his feet, and tosses his three-iron in the lake. His childish regressive behavior won't help his score, but it does act as a release from the tension of his stress at the moment.

regression
when under stress, a return to earlier, childish levels of previously productive behaviors

Displacement

The defense mechanism of **displacement** is usually discussed in the context of aggression. Your goal-directed behavior becomes blocked or thwarted. You are frustrated, under stress, and somewhat aggressive. You cannot vent your aggression directly at the source of the frustration, so you displace it to a safer outlet. Dorothy expects to get promoted at work, but someone else gets the new job she wanted. Her goal-directed behavior has been frustrated. She's upset and angry at her boss, but feels (perhaps correctly) that blowing her top at her boss will do more harm than good. She's still frustrated, so she displaces her hostility toward her husband, children, and/or the family cat.

Displacement doesn't have to involve hostility and aggression. A young couple discovers that having children is not going to be as easy as they thought. They want children badly, but there's an infertility problem that is causing considerable stress. Their motivation for love and sharing and caring may be displaced toward a pet, or nephews and nieces, or some neighborhood children—at least until their own goals can be realized with children of their own.

displacement
directing one's motives at some substitute person or object rather than expressing them directly

***The Use and Misuse of Defense Mechanisms Against
the Feelings of Stress***   The list of defense mechanisms provided
above is not an exhaustive one. These are among the most common, and this
list gives you an idea of what defense mechanisms are like. There are a couple
of important points about them that deserve special mention.

First, using defense mechanisms is a normal reaction to stress. You
shouldn't be alarmed if you find that many of the defense mechanisms listed
here sound like reactions you have used. In moderation, they help us to cope
with some of the stresses of life and the frustrations and conflicts that we
face from day to day because they reduce levels of felt anxiety. Second, although they are normal, defense mechanisms can be maladaptive. So long as
we can defend ourselves against the unpleasant feelings of stress, we will be
less motivated to take any direct action to ultimately get rid of that stress. We
will be less likely to try to solve those conflicts, remove those sources of
frustration, or adapt to those life changes that are causing the stress in the
first place. Finally, another possible danger in using defense mechanisms is
that the user will lose sight of what is real and what is defensive. Largely
because defense mechanisms are employed without our conscious awareness, it sometimes becomes difficult to separate rationalizations from reasons, fantasy from truth, repression from forgetfulness, displaced aggression
from real aggression, and so on.

Before you go on

*Define repression, denial, rationalization, compensation, fantasy,
projection, and regression.*
In what ways are these defense mechanisms?

In this topic, we have repeatedly made the observation that frustration, conflict, and life events make stress a natural and common fact of life. As unavoidable as stress may be, we need to develop effective ways of dealing with it. Are there any practical suggestions that we can make to help someone faced with stress? Listed below are some of the questions that you might contemplate when under stress.

(1) Is the threat to my well-being real or imagined? You'll recall that we defined stress as a real or *perceived* threat to an individual's sense of well-being. One of the first things you should do when you feel under stress is try to assess whether or not you really have a reason to feel so stressed. Are you really in a conflict? Are your motives truly being frustrated? Is this change in your life necessarily stressful? Or are you imagining more problems than actually exist? We may, for example, believe that someone is out to "do us in" and block our goal-directed behavior. We may imagine that a coworker is plotting against us so that we won't get the raise we feel we have earned. Before we do anything else, we should try to determine whether or not our perception is accurate. Is that coworker *really* trying to thwart your goal-directed behavior? You may discover that there is no justifiable reason to feel stress in the first place.

(2) What is the source of my stress? In addition to determining if your stress is real, you should do whatever you can to discover the exact origin of your felt stress. What is causing it? Are you in a motivational conflict? Of what sort? Are your goal-directed behaviors being frustrated? By whom? By what?

What is the nature of the life event that is causing you to feel stressed? The more specific you can be in locating the source of your stress, the more likely you will be to find ways of adjusting to it.

(3) Can the stressor be removed? There is no doubt that the most satisfying way to adapt to stress in the long run is to remove its source—if that's possible. Are you finding it difficult to reach a certain goal? Is there another way of reaching the same end? Can you modify your goal so that you stand a better chance of reaching it? Do you really want to make the track team as a runner, or do you just want to be part of the action? Maybe you could be a team manager. Would that be good enough?

Can you resolve the conflict that is causing your stress? Can you manage to go to the party and still find time to do the studying that needs to be done? If you have three exams scheduled for one day, can you have one of them postponed? Is there some way you can get the extra money to buy that second dip of ice cream rather than having to choose between two flavors? If your conflict cannot be resolved, can you escape from the situation altogether? If you can't decide between alternative A and alternative B, might you get by without choosing at all? If being promoted will carry more responsibility and stress than you'd like to deal with, can you refuse the promotion? Uppermost in your mind should be the notion that, when possible, dealing with stress by removing its source is the best reaction.

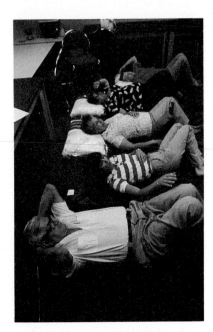

One of the best ways to avoid the ill effects of stress is to learn to cope with it. Stress management workshops teach people to manage stress and to react calmly to stressful situations. In this way, people can lessen the impact of stress on their lives.

(4) Can an incompatible response be acquired? Obviously, we can't always avoid stress by removing or escaping from its source. Some stress will simply be unavoidable. One way to cope with the feelings of stress and the physiological changes that underlie them is to develop patterns of response that are inconsistent with those associated with stress. What does *that* mean? To be stressed is to be emotional, riled up, with the sympathetic division of your autonomic nervous system churning away at your insides. Perhaps you can lessen these effects by developing different, opposite reactions. In the simplest sense, learn to relax. Relaxation training is not difficult to master, but you may require someone else to help you at first. You need to train yourself so that you can voluntarily, on command, get your parasympathetic division to overcome the sympathetic division. Meditation may help (see pp. 158–160). Biofeedback training may help you to relax (see pp. 203–204). Hypnosis may help (see pp. 156–158). Even vigorous physical exercise may help. The basic idea is that so long as you feel calm and relaxed, it will be impossible to feel stressed and emotionally upset at the same time—the two responses are incompatible.

Meichenbaum (1977) argues that we can learn to deal with stress by talking to ourselves, replacing negative statements (such as, "Oh am I in trouble now; I'm sure to be called on, and I'll embarrass myself in front of the class") with coping statements (such as "I know I'll do as well as I can, and in a little while this will all be over"). This cognitive approach of essentially talking one's self out of stress does take a good bit of practice, but it can be effective as a means of what Meichenbaum calls "stress innoculation." Of course, none of these techniques will truly rid you of stress. What they may do is help make the stress of your life more bearable.

(5) Can I find support when stressed? There is considerable evidence (Gottlieb, 1981; Janis, 1983, for example) that suggests that facing stress alone is more difficult than facing it with the social support of others. There *is* truth to the notion that "talking about it" does help. Support when you are under stress can be found in two general ways. The first place to look for social support is among friends and family—those who care about you and are willing to help you deal with whatever is causing your stress. Simply being with others, discovering that others have had the same sorts of stress in their lives, goes a long way toward helping someone adjust to stress. Another obvious place to look for support (although many people are less willing to look here) is from mental health professionals. It may be that just a few short sessions at a crisis intervention center, community mental health center, or private clinic will be enough to help you through whatever stressful situation you may be facing.

Define stress and stressor.

Stress is the term we use to label a complex set of reactions that are made in response to real or perceived threats to one's sense of well-being. Stress is very much like an emotional reaction that motivates the individual to do something to lessen stress levels. Stressors are the sources, or causes, of stress and include frustration, conflict, and life events. / 397

Name and describe the three stages of the general adaptation syndrome.

According to Hans Selye, a prolonged stress reaction progresses through three stages: the general adaptation syndrome. At first, there is the mobilization of the sympathetic division of the ANS in the *alarm* reaction as the body prepares to cope with stress. If the stressor is not removed, the body then goes through a stage of *resistance,* when resources continue to be mobilized, but when new stressors will be difficult to deal with, and physical illness becomes more likely. If the stressor remains, one may finally enter a stage of *exhaustion,* where the body's resources become depleted, adaptation breaks down, and death may result. / 399

What is meant by frustration-induced stress?

Define environmental, social, and personal frustration.

Frustration-induced stress is that stress caused by the blocking or thwarting of goal-directed behaviors. The specific type of frustration that leads to stress is named according to what is blocking the goal-directed behavior. If the source of the blocking is something in the environment, we call the frustration *environmental.* If the source of the frustration is a person in the environment, we call the frustration *social.* If the source of the frustration is from within, from the person herself or himself, we call it *personal.* / 401

Name four types of motivational conflict, and provide an example of each.

In an *approach-approach* motivational conflict, an organism is faced with two (or more) attractive goals and must choose among them. All are not available. Deciding what to order in a restaurant from among a number of alternatives on the menu would be an example. In an *avoidance-avoidance* conflict, a choice must be made among unpleasant, potentially punishing alternatives, as when a parent gives a child the choice of cleaning the garage or mowing the yard. In an *approach-avoidance* conflict, there is but one goal under consideration; in some ways, the goal is attractive, while in others, it is not. Someone nominated for a committee membership might be in an approach-avoidance conflict. He wants to serve and to help out, but really doesn't want to give up the time to do so. Perhaps the most common conflict is the *multiple approach-avoidance* conflict in which a person is faced with a number of alternatives and each has its own strengths and weaknesses, as in trying to decide on a college major or a career. / 403

What is the SRRS?

What is it meant to measure?

The SRRS (or Social Readjustment Rating Scale) acknowledges that some of the day-to-day events and changes that are a part of living often act as stressors. The SRRS is an attempt to measure the severity of stress in one's life by having the person indicate how many life change events have recently occurred. Some events are more stress-producing than others. High scores on the SRRS have been correlated with increased incidence of physical illness. / 404

How can learning be seen as a reaction to stress?

We have defined learning as a relatively permanent change in behavior that occurs as the result of practice or experience. In many cases, stress (and frustration in particular) provides experiences for learning. We often have to learn new responses to acquire our goals, and sometimes we must learn to modify our goals when attempts to reach old goals lead to stress. / 406

What is the frustration-aggression hypothesis?

The frustration-aggression hypothesis is the view, first proposed by Dollard, that the blocking or thwarting of goal-directed behaviors (i.e., frustration) is often (if not always) the cause of aggression. That is, frustration may produce a number of reactions, but aggression can always be traced to frustration. This view is now seen as an overly simplistic theory of aggression. / 407

Define repression, denial, rationalization, compensation, fantasy, projection, and regression.

In what ways are these defense mechanisms?

Defense mechanisms protect the individual from the felt emotional component of stress. They do not solve conflicts, nor do they resolve stress, but they make stress less unpleasant. There are many defense mechanisms including: (1) repression—unconsciously forgetting an anxiety-producing or stressful event or experience; (2) denial—a refusal to acknowledge the realities of a stressful situation; (3) rationalization—attempts to find reasonable excuses for one's behavior rather than facing the real reasons for one's behaviors; (4) compensation—overemphasizing some positive trait to make up for a lacking in some other trait; (5) fantasy—engaging in daydreaming or imaginary thoughts of successes and achievements; (6) projection—seeing in others those traits and motives that cause us stress when we see them in ourselves; (7) regression—retreating to earlier levels of behavior that were productive in the past; and (8) displacement—directing aggression at some safe outlet rather than the true source of frustration. / 410

CHAPTER TEN

PERSONALITY

TOPIC

THE PSYCHOANALYTIC APPROACH

Freud's Approach

Levels of Consciousness
Basic Instincts
The "Structure" of Personality
The Development of Personality

The Psychoanalytic Approach After Freud

Alfred Adler
Carl Jung
Karen Horney

Evaluating the Approach

THE BEHAVIORAL/LEARNING APPROACH

John B. Watson
John Dollard and Neal Miller
B. F. Skinner
Albert Bandura
Julian Rotter
Evaluating the Approach

THE HUMANISTIC/PHENOMENOLOGICAL APPROACH

Carl Rogers
Abraham Maslow
Evaluating the Approach

THE TRAIT APPROACH

Gordon Allport
Raymond B. Cattell
Hans Eysenck
Evaluating the Approach

TOPIC EXPANSION: IS THERE CONSISTENCY IN PERSONALITY?

Most of us like to think that we understand ourselves fairly well. We feel that we have a sense of who we are, how we tend to think and feel, and what we are likely to do in almost any situation. To a lesser degree, we also feel that we understand a few other people we know particularly well, such as very close friends and family members. What is more difficult is to understand the *personality* of those people we do not know well. Wouldn't it be convenient if there were some simple way to quickly make judgments about the characteristics of others, perhaps just by observing some noticeable physical characteristic? Such is the hope of approaches to personality called *constitutional theories*. The basic idea of these theories is that there is a correlation between one's physical appearance (one's constitution) and one's significant psychological characteristics (one's personality). A number of constitutional theories have been proposed, but none has gained as much attention as that of William H. Sheldon (1940, 1942, 1944, 1954).

Sheldon claimed that people could be classified in terms of their body type. He used a three part classification system. People who are soft, flabby, rounded, and unmuscled he called *endomorphs*. Those who are hard, tough, rectangular of build, and well-muscled are *mesomorphs*. Individuals who are extremely thin, fragile, and delicately boned are called *ectomorphs*. Although people can be found who characterize each of these types to an extreme, Sheldon allowed for degrees of each of these body types. That is, some people who are basically well-built and athletic in appearance may (with age perhaps) develop a softness of muscle tone or a pot belly. Hence, they are mesomorphs with a tendency toward endomorphy. Sheldon's scheme for classifying body

types yields a numerical score and is quite reliable; that is, there is usually a high level of agreement among raters on an individual's body-type score.

Sheldon further proposed that personality, or temperament, could also be measured using a three-dimensional rating scheme. His three dimensions of temperament included *viscerotonia* (including such things as love of physical comfort, love of eating, complacency, and evenness of emotional flow), *somatotonia* (including love of physical adventure, need and enjoyment of exercise, love of chance and risk, and competitive aggressiveness), and *cerebrotonia* (including overly fast reactions, love of privacy, mental overintensity, and poor sleep habits). In fact, each of these three temperament types was defined by 20 separate rating scales and yielded a numerical score. Now all that remained was for Sheldon to demonstrate a relationship between body type and temperament type. That he did, and with outstanding success.

Over a 5-year period, Sheldon interviewed, tested, and rated 200 men. He found extremely high correlations between body type and temperament. Endomorphs tended to be viscerotonic, mesomorphs were somatotonic, and ectomorphs were clearly cerebrotonic (see Figure 23.1). Sheldon's reported correlations were all around +0.80, a degree of correlation never found before in personality research—and never found again.

There were two major flaws with Sheldon's efforts. First, many of his temperament scales *insured* that there would be a correlation; it's hardly surprising that people who love to eat and love relaxation should turn out to be overweight and somewhat flabby, or that people who love exercise and physical adventure should turn out to be ath-

Figure 23.1
*Illustrations of Sheldon's body types and
the temperaments that correspond to
each type.*
(After Sheldon, 1942.)

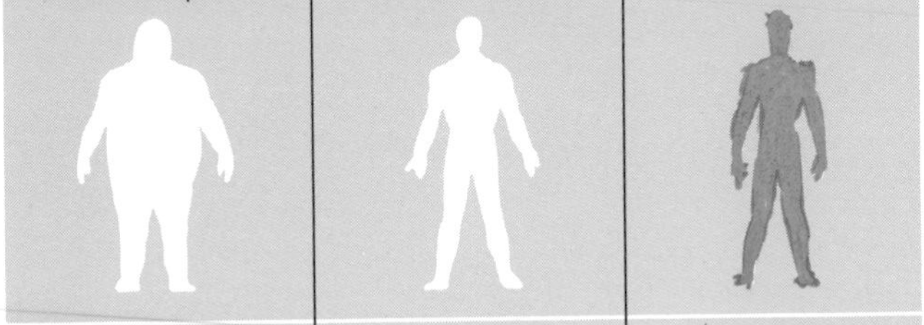

	Endomorphic	Mesomorphic	Ectomorphic
Body type	Soft and round	Muscular and strong	Thin and fragile
Temperament	Relaxed, sociable, and fond of eating	Energetic, courageous, and assertive	Brainy, artistic, and introverted

letic and well-muscled. Second, the measurements of body type and temperament type were both made by the same person—Sheldon. Sheldon thus placed himself in an excellent position to be accused of experimenter bias (see Topic 2). When judgments of constitution and personality are made by independent raters, correlations are still positive, but drop to less impressive levels (Stager & Burke, 1982).

We need not simply dismiss Sheldon's approach to personality. There *is* some truth to the notion of a relationship between physical characteristics and personality or temperament. It's just not as compelling as we might like it to be. Our physical stature may very well set limits on what we can and cannot do and may limit the range of our possible reactions. Our personalities may have direct effects on our physical appearances through overindulgence, vanity, or neglect. But as much as stereotypes still exist, fat people are not necessarily jolly, and people who have a "lean and hungry look" do not necessarily think too much, nor are they necessarily dangerous (Shakespeare, *Julius Caesar*; act I, scene II).

Why We Care

In this topic, we will be examining a number of theories about personality. We'll organize specific theories into four basic types, or approaches. Before we do so, we'll consider what we mean by *theory* and what we mean by *personality*.

A **theory** is a series of assumptions; in our particular case, these are assumptions about people and their personalities. The ideas or assumptions that comprise a theory are reasonably and logically related to each other. Further, the ideas of a theory can lead (through reason) to specific, testable hypotheses. In short, a theory is an organized collection of ultimately testable ideas used to explain a particular subject matter.

Once you recognize that we are devoting this topic to *theories* of personality, you may conclude that psychologists really don't know for sure what personality is, where it comes from, or how it works. Although we do have many generally accepted ideas about personality, your conclusion would be basically correct.

Now then, what is **personality**? Few terms have been as difficult to define as personality. In many ways, each of the approaches we will study in this topic generates its own definition of personality. What we are basically looking at are the *cognitions* (thoughts, beliefs, ideas, etc.), *affect* (feeling, mood, or emotion), and *behaviors* of people that we claim can characterize them in a number of situations over time and help them to adapt to their environments. Personality also includes those dimensions we can use to judge people to be different from one another. As psychologist David Buss put it recently, "The field of personality psychology is centrally concerned with the traits that characterize our species as well as the major ways in which individuals characteristically differ" (1984, p. 1143).

theory
a collection of related assumptions, used to explain some phenomenon, which lead through logical reasoning to testable hypotheses

personality
relatively enduring and unique traits (including cognitions, feelings, and behaviors) that can be used to characterize an individual in different situations

Before you go on
What is a theory of personality?

THE PSYCHOANALYTIC APPROACH

We will begin our study of personality theories by considering the **psychoanalytic** approach. This is the approach associated with Sigmund Freud and his students. We begin with Freud because he was the first to present a truly unified theory of personality.

Freud's theory of personality has been one of the most influential and, at the same time, most controversial in all of science. Although there are many facets to Freud's theory (and the theories of the neo-Freudians), two basic assumptions characterize the psychoanalytic approach: (1) a reliance on innate, inborn instincts as explanatory concepts for much of human behavior, and (2) an acceptance of the power and influence of unconscious forces to mold and shape our behavior.

psychoanalytic
the approach to personality associated with Freud and his followers that relies on instincts and the unconscious as explanatory concepts

neo-Freudians
those theorists of the psychoanalytic school who have taken issue with some parts of Freudian theory, including Adler, Jung, and Horney

Freud's Approach

Sigmund Freud was born in Moravia (now a part of Czechoslovakia) in 1856. After a brief stay in Leipzig, his family moved to Vienna when Freud was 4 years old. Freud remained a resident of Vienna until the Nazi invasion in 1938. He then moved to England and died in London on September 23, 1939.

Sigmund Freud

The son of a Jewish wool merchant, Freud graduated from the University of Vienna Medical School in 1881. He didn't want to enter the private practice of medicine, favoring instead scientific research and study. However, economics (and a growing family) forced him into practice at the General Hospital of Vienna, where he became interested in nervous disorders. He was struck with how little was known about the cause or treatment of such disorders, and he chose to specialize in psychiatry. His theories about the nature of personality arose largely from observations of his patients and intense self-examination. This context provided Freud with the experience he needed to propose a general theory of personality and to develop a technique of therapy called *psychoanalysis*. A discussion of psychoanalysis appears in Topic 30. For now, let's review some of Freud's basic ideas about the structure and dynamics of the human personality.

Levels of Consciousness   We have already discussed Freud's views on consciousness (Topic 9). As you may recall, it was Freud's view that only a small portion of mental life was readily available to a person's awareness at any one time. Ideas, memories, motives, and desires of which we are actively aware are said to be conscious.

Aspects of our mind that are not conscious at the moment, but can be easily brought to awareness for consideration, are stored or housed at a preconscious level. For example, right now you may not be thinking about what you had for dinner last night or what you might do for dinner tonight. But with very little effort, the matter of tonight's and last night's dinner can be brought into your conscious awareness.

Cognitions, feelings, and motives that are not available to the conscious mind are said to be at the unconscious level. At this level, we have stored a number of ideas, memories, and desires of which we are not and cannot easily become aware. This is a strange notion—that there are ideas, thoughts, and feelings stored away in our minds of which we are completely unaware. However, the contents of the unconscious mind do influence us. Unconscious content passing through the preconscious may show itself in slips of the tongue, humor, neurotic symptoms, and, of course, dreams. There was no doubt in Freud's mind that unconscious forces could be used to explain much of one's behavior that otherwise seemed irrational and beyond description.

As we shall see, a good deal of Freudian psychoanalysis as a psychotherapeutic technique is aimed at helping a patient get in touch with the contents of the unconscious level of the mind. A husband, for instance, who constantly forgets his wedding anniversary and occasionally cannot remember his wife's name when he tries to introduce her may be experiencing some unconscious conflict or doubts about being married in the first place. (There *are*, of course, other possibilities.)

Before you go on

What are the three levels of consciousness proposed by Freud?

life instincts (eros)
those inborn impulses proposed by Freud that compel one toward survival, including hunger, thirst, and sex

libido
the energy that activates the life (sexual) instincts (largely of the id)

Basic Instincts   According to Freudian theory, our behaviors are governed largely by the operation of a number of instincts. These are inborn impulses or drives, forces that rule our personalities. There may be many individual instincts, but they can be grouped into two categories.

On the one hand are **life instincts** (*eros*), which are impulses for survival, in particular those that motivate sex, hunger, and thirst. Each instinct has its own energy that compels us into action. Freud called the energy through which the sexual instincts operate **libido.** Opposed to the life instincts are **death instincts** (*thanatos*). These are impulses toward destruction. Directed inward, they give rise to feelings of depression or suicide; directed outward, they result in aggression toward other people or their property. In large measure, life (according to Freud) is an attempt to resolve conflicts between these two natural and diametrically opposed instincts.

The "Structure" of Personality Freud believed that the mind operates on one of three levels of awareness: unconscious, preconscious, and conscious. Freud also proposed that the human mind or personality is composed of three separate, though interacting, structures or subsystems: the id, ego, and superego. Each of these subsystems has its own job to do, its own principles to follow.

The **id** is the inborn or inherited portion of personality. The id resides in the unconscious level of the mind, and it is through and in the id that one's basic instincts develop. The driving force of the id is libido, or sexual energy, although it may be more fair to Freud to say "sensual" than "sexual."

The id constantly seeks satisfaction for instinctual impulses, regardless of the consequences. It operates on what Freud labelled the **pleasure principle,** indicating that the major function of the id is to find satisfaction of pleasurable impulses. Although two other divisions of personality develop later, our id remains with us always and constantly provides a major force in our lives.

The **ego** is that part of the personality that develops through our experience with reality. In many ways, it is our self, the rational, reasoning part of our personality. The ego operates on the **reality principle.** One of the ego's main jobs is to try to find satisfaction for the id, but in ways that are reasonable. The ego may have to delay gratification of some libidinal impulse, or may need to find an acceptable outlet for some desire. When the ego cannot find acceptable ways to satisfy the drives of the id, conflict and anxiety result. Then ways must be found to deal with the resulting anxiety. It was for this purpose that Freud suggested the notion of defense mechanisms.

The last of the three structures to develop is the **superego,** which we can liken to one's sense of morality, or conscience. It is said that the superego operates on an **idealistic principle.** One problem we have with our superegos is that they—like the id—have no contact with reality. Again, it falls to the ego to try to maintain a realistic balance between the conscience of the superego and the libido of the id.

Now this isn't as complicated as it may sound. Let's suppose a bank teller discovers an extra $20 in her cash drawer at the end of the day. She certainly could use an extra $20. "Go ahead. Nobody will miss it. The bank can afford a few dollars here and there," is the basic message from her id. "The odds are that you'll get caught if you take this money. You may get away with it, but if you *are* caught, you may lose your job, then you'll be in a sorry state," reasons her ego. "But you shouldn't even consider taking that money. Shame on you! It's not yours. It belongs to someone else and should be returned," the superego protests. Clearly, the interaction of the three components of one's personality is not this simple and straightforward, but perhaps this example illustrates the general idea.

death instincts (thanatos)
those inborn impulses proposed by Freud that compel one toward destruction, including aggression

id
that instinctive aspect of personality that seeks immediate gratification of impulses and operates on the pleasure principle

ego
that aspect of personality that encompasses the sense of self, in contact with the real world; operates on the reality principle

superego
that aspect of personality that refers to ethical or moral considerations and operates on the idealistic principle

pleasure principle
the impulse of the id to seek immediate gratification to reduce tensions

reality principle
the impulse that governs the ego, arbitrating between the demands of the id, the superego, and the real world

idealistic principle
the impulse that governs the superego, opposed to the id, seeking adherence to standards of ethics and morality

Before you go on
According to Freud, what are the three structures of personality, and by what principle does each operate?

During the oral stage, babies find pleasure and satisfaction in oral activities, such as feeding, sucking, and making noises.

During the phallic stage, children sometimes develop an Electra (for girls) or Oedipus (for boys) complex in which they form close, sexually based relationships with their opposite-sex parent and exhibit jealousy and/or fear of their same-sex parent.

The Development of Personality   Freud obviously put a lot of stock in the biological basis of personality, relying as he did on concepts like instinct. This same orientation flavored his view of how one's personality develops. According to Freud, the personality develops naturally, in a series of overlapping stages. The events that occur in early stages have the potential to profoundly influence later development.

One of Freud's most controversial assumptions was that even infants and young children are under the influence of sexual strivings of the id and its libidinal energy. The outlet for the sexual (again, *sensual* may be a better term) impulses of young children is not the reproductive sex act. But Freud claimed that much of the pleasure derived by children is often essentially sexual in nature, hence the reference to Freud's stages of development as *psychosexual*. Freud claimed that there are five such stages:

(1) Oral stage (birth to 1 year). Pleasure and satisfaction come from oral activities: feeding and sucking and making noises. The mouth continues to be a source of pleasure for many people long into adulthood, as demonstrated by overeating, fingernail biting, smoking, or talkativeness.

(2) Anal stage (ages 1 to 3 years). Sometime in their second year, children develop the ability to control their bowel and bladder habits. At this time, the anus becomes the focus of pleasure. Satisfaction is gained through bowel control. Aggressiveness (the id again) can be displayed (particularly against parents) by either having bowel movements at inappropriate times or by refusing "to go" when placed on the "potty chair." Here we can clearly see the thoughtful, reasoning ego emerging and exercising control. After all, the parents can't *make* their child do what they want it to. The child is in control, and that control leads to great satisfaction.

(3) Phallic stage (ages 3 to 5 years). Here there is an awareness of one's sexuality. The genitals replace the mouth and anus as the source of pleasure, and masturbation or fondling of the genitals may become a common practice. It is during this stage of development that children form close (sexually based) attachments to the parent of the opposite sex and feelings of jealousy and/or fear of the same-sex parent may arise. This pattern of reaction is called the *Oedipus complex* in boys and the *Electra complex* in girls. It is in the phallic stage that the superego begins to develop.

(4) Latency stage (ages 6 years until puberty). At this point in one's life, sexual development gets put on hold. Now the ego is developing very rapidly. There is much to be learned about the world and how it operates. Sexual development can wait. Sexuality becomes suppressed. Children essentially become asexual. Friends tend to be of the same sex. You have no doubt heard the protestations of a 9-year-old boy, "Oh yuck, kiss a girl! Never! Yuck!" And you counsel, "Just wait, soon girls won't seem so 'yucky.' "

(5) Genital stage (from puberty on). With puberty, there is a renewal of the sexual impulse, a reawakening of desire and an interest in matters sexual, sensual, and erotic.

Before you go on
Briefly review Freud's five psychosexual stages of development.

During the latency stage, sexuality is suppressed and children focus on same-sex friendships.

The Psychoanalytic Approach After Freud

Sigmund Freud was a persuasive communicator. In person, he was a powerful speaker. In his writings, he was without peer. His ideas were new and different, and they attracted many students. Freud founded a psychoanalytic society in Vienna. He had many friends and colleagues who shared his ideas and his theories, but some of his colleagues did not entirely agree with his theory. They were bothered by the focus on biological instincts and libido and the lack of concern for social influences. Some of these psychoanalysts left Freud and proposed theories of their own; they became known as *neo-Freudians*. Because they had their own ideas, they had to part from Freud; he apparently would not tolerate disagreement with the basic ideas of his theory. One had to accept all of psychoanalysis—including psychoanalysis as a treatment for mental disorders—or one rejected Freud and his theories.

Remembering that a theory is made up of a series of logically interrelated, testable assumptions, it is obvious that we cannot do justice to someone's theory of personality in a short paragraph or two. What we can do, perhaps, is sketch the basic idea behind the theories of a few selected neo-Freudians.

Alfred Adler (1870–1937)   At first, as the psychoanalytic movement was beginning to take shape, Adler was one of Freud's closest associates. However, Adler left Freud, and, in 1911, founded his own version of a psychoanalytic approach to personality. Two things seemed to most offend Adler: the negativity of Freud's views (the death instinct, for example) and the idea of sexual libido as a prime impulse in life.

Adler proposed that we are very much a product of the social influences on our personality. We are motivated not so much by causes, such as in-

Alfred Adler

Carl Jung   Karen Horney

stincts, but by goals and incentives (pulled rather than pushed, as we noted earlier). The future and what it holds for us is more important than our past. Our major goal is the achievement of success or superiority. This goal is fashioned in childhood when, because we are weak and vulnerable, we develop an **inferiority complex.** Yes, we may seem inferior as children, but with the help of social influences and our own creativity, we can overcome and succeed. Thus, Adler's view of people is much more upbeat and positive than Freud's.

inferiority complex
the Adlerian notion that, as children, we develop a sense of inferiority in dealing with our environment

Carl Jung (1875–1961)   Adler left Freud's inner circle of associates in 1911. Two years later, another student, Carl Jung, left also. Jung was more mystical in his approach to personality and (like Adler) was certainly more positive about one's ability to control one's own destiny. He believed that our major goal in life was to bring together in unity all of the aspects of our personality, conscious and unconscious, introverted (inwardly directed) and extroverted (outwardly directed).

Jung accepted the idea of an unconscious mind, but expanded it, claiming that there are *two* types of unconscious: the *personal unconscious,* which is very much like Freud's view of the unconscious, and the *collective unconscious,* which contains very basic ideas and notions that go beyond an individual's own personal experiences. These ideas and notions are common to all of humanity and are inherited from generations past.

Karen Horney (1885–1952)   Trained as a psychoanalyst in Germany, Horney came to the United States in 1934. She preserved some Freudian concepts, but changed most of them significantly. Horney believed that levels of consciousness make sense, as do anxiety and repression. But she theorized that the prime impulses that motivate behavior are not biological and inborn, or sexual and aggressive. A major concept for Horney was *basic anxiety,* which grows out of childhood when the child feels isolated and alone in a hostile environment. If proper parental nurturance is forthcoming, this basic anxiety can be overcome. If, however, parents are inconsistent, indifferent, or overly punishing, children may also develop *basic hostility* and may feel very hostile toward their parents. Little children, however, cannot express hostility toward their parents, so the hostility gets repressed (into the unconscious) and even more anxiety builds. So, like Freud, Horney placed great emphasis on childhood experiences, but from a perspective of social interaction and personal growth.

Horney also disagreed with Freud's position regarding the biological necessity of differences between men and women. Freud's theories have been taken to task a number of times for their male chauvinist bias (Fisher & Greenberg, 1977). Horney was one of the first to do so.

Before you go on
Briefly summarize the contributions of Adler, Jung, and Horney to the psychoanalytic approach to personality.

Evaluating the Approach

There is a common misconception that when Freud died, psychoanalytic theory died with him. Psychoanalytic theory is still alive and well. It has changed and evolved (some would say matured) over the years, but it is very much with us (Silverman, 1976). Current psychoanalytic theory tends to emphasize the role of the ego more than the role of the id and superego (Kohut, 1977; Rappaport, 1951).

Two major criticisms of Freudian psychoanalytic theory are that it is largely based on the observations of disordered patients and that many of its assumptions are untestable. Freud thought of himself as a scientist, but he tested none of his theories experimentally. Some of them seem to be beyond testing. What, after all, *is* libidinal energy? How can it be measured? How would we recognize it if we saw it? It does seem that the heavy reliance on instincts as explanatory concepts—especially instincts with sexual and aggressive overtones—goes beyond where many psychologists are willing to venture.

On the other hand, Freud must be credited (along with other psychoanalytically oriented theorists) for focusing our attention on the importance of the early childhood years and for suggesting that some (even biologically determined) impulses affect our behaviors even though they are beyond our awareness. And although Freud himself may have overstated the matter, drawing attention to the impact of sexuality and sexual impulses as influences on behavior and personality was a major contribution to psychology.

THE BEHAVIORAL/LEARNING APPROACH

Many American psychologists in the early twentieth century did not think much of the psychoanalytic approach, regardless of its form or who happened to propose it. From its very beginnings, American psychology was oriented towards the laboratory and theories of learning. Explaining personality in terms of learning and focusing on observable behaviors seemed the reasonable course of action. In this section, we'll briefly review some of the approaches to personality that are behavioral, that rely on learning theory to explain personality.

John B. Watson

John B. Watson and his followers in behaviorism argued that psychology should turn away from the study of the mind and consciousness because they are unverifiable and ultimately unscientific. Behaviorists argue that psychologists should study observable behavior. Yet psychoanalysis was arguing for *un*conscious and *pre*conscious forces as determiners of behavior. "Nonsense," the behaviorist would say. "We don't even know what we mean by consciousness, and you want to talk about levels of unconscious influence!"

Among other things, Watson and his followers believed in the importance of the environment in shaping one's responses. They could not accept the Freudian notion of inborn traits or impulses, whether called id or libido or anything else. What mattered was *learning*. A personality theory was not needed. A theory of learning would include all the details about the so-called personality that one would ever need to know.

The behaviorists believe that who we are is determined by our early learning experiences. For example, to be artistically talented as adults, we need to be nurtured as children.

Who we are is determined by our learning experiences, and early experiences do count heavily—on that one point Watson and Freud might have agreed. Even our fears are conditioned (remember Watson's Little Albert study). So convinced was Watson that instincts and innate impulses had little to do with the development of behavior that he had no qualms about writing, "Give me a dozen healthy infants, well-formed, and my own specified world to bring them up in and I'll guarantee to take any one at random and train him to become any type of specialist I might select—doctor, lawyer, artist, merchant, chief, and yes, even beggarman and thief, regardless of his talents, penchants, tendencies, abilities, vocations, and race of his ancestors (1925)."

John Dollard and Neal Miller

John Dollard (1900–1980) and Neal Miller (b. 1909), as behaviorists and learning theorists, tried to see if they could use the basic principles of learning theory to explain personality and how it developed. What matters for one's personality, Dollard and Miller argued, was the system of habits one developed in response to various cues in the environment. Behavior was motivated by primary drives, upon whose satisfaction survival depended, and learned drives, which developed through experience. Motivated by drives, those habits that get reinforced are those that tend to be repeated, and eventually become part of the stable collection of habits that make up one's personality. For example, repression into the unconscious is a matter of learned forgetfulness—forgetting about some anxiety-producing experience is reinforcing and, consequently, tends to be repeated. It was Miller (1944) who proposed that conflict is explainable in terms of tendencies (habits) to approach or to avoid goals and has little to do with the id, ego, and superego, or with unconscious impulses of any sort.

B.F. Skinner

In this context, we should again mention B. F. Skinner, although he claims to have proposed no particular theory of learning, much less of personality. In many ways, Skinner's is a radical behaviorism, because he consistently refuses to refer to any sort of internal or "organism" variables to explain behavior. Look only at observable stimuli, observable responses, and relationships among these; do not go meddling about in the mind of the organism, Skinnerians argue.

Behavior is shaped by its consequences. Some behaviors result in reinforcement and tend to be repeated. Some behaviors result in punishment and tend not to be repeated. The question is, how shall external conditions be manipulated to produce the consequences we want?

Think back to our opening discussion of Sheldon and body type. A young boy who happens to be muscular and strong finds that he can get his way by acting like a bully, aggressively imposing his will on others. His behaviors pay off with reinforcement, and, as a result, he works to maintain his physical power and strength (his mesomorphic body type). Another young boy, frail and sickly, finds that physical aggressiveness doesn't work for him. He finds other ways to gain reinforcement—through diligent study or by learning to tell jokes well, perhaps. The key here is not some *necessary* bond between body type and behavior, but learning history. Remember, behaviors that are reinforced tend to increase in rate.

Albert Bandura

Albert Bandura (b. 1925) is a learning theorist who is more than willing to consider the internal, cognitive processes of the learner. Many aspects of our behavior, of our personality, are learned, but they are learned through observation and social influence. For Bandura, learning involves more than simple connections between stimuli and responses; it involves a cognitive rearrangement and representation. In simpler terms, this approach argues that you may very well learn to behave honestly, for example, through the observation of others. If you view your parents as being honest and see them and others being reinforced for their honest behaviors (vicarious reinforcement), you may acquire similar responses.

Bandura's approach to learning has a decidedly social flavor. We learn by observing others. When we see others being reinforced, we experience some

Albert Bandura

vicarious reinforcement ourselves. The theory also suggests that we can influence our environments and the people in them just as our environments can influence us.

Julian Rotter

Like Bandura, Rotter (b. 1916) has proposed a learning theory of personality that is characterized as a social learning theory. It is more cognitive than the approaches of either Dollard and Miller or Skinner. Rotter claims that events themselves have much less of an effect on behavior than do a person's perceptions of those events. An important component of Rotter's views about personality is one's perception of **locus of control.**

Rotter believes that some people develop attitudes or expectancies that reinforcement is controlled either by internal or external forces (1982). This is mostly a matter of learning the extent to which one's behaviors, and the consequences of one's behaviors, are under one's own control (internal) or under the control of others and the environment (external). Someone with an *internal locus of control* would tend to blame themselves for failures and congratulate themselves for successes. If they fail at something, it is because of lack of hard work on their part, and steps are taken to do better. A person with an *external locus of control* would tend to see failure *and* success as a result of chance, or luck, or the intervention of others. If they fail at something, they do not view their failure as their fault, nor do they take much credit should they succeed. Rotter believes that neither extreme is better than the other, and that most of us would fall between the extreme externalizer and internalizer when we seek to find attribution for our successes and failures.

locus of control
a general belief that what happens is either under our control (internal locus) or a matter of chance and environmental factors (external locus)

Before you go on
Specify a contribution to the notion of personality contributed by Watson, Skinner, Dollard and Miller, Bandura, and Rotter.

Evaluating the Approach

In a number of ways, the major strengths of a behavioral/learning approach to personality also constitute its major weaknesses. It is somewhat simplistic. It tends to focus only on the observable and measurable. A number of psychologists argue that Dollard and Miller and Skinner totally dehumanize personality, and that even the social learning approaches of Bandura and Rotter tend to be too deterministic. That is, virtually everything a person may do, think, or feel is in some way directly determined by his or her environment through learning or conditioning.

Behavioral/learning approaches to personality are often not theories at all—at least not comprehensive theories. They tend to be very specific and focused (again, a mixed blessing). They tend to avoid any mention of biologically determined characteristics. To their credit, they demand that terms be carefully defined and that assumptions be experimentally verified.

THE HUMANISTIC/PHENOMENOLOGICAL APPROACH

The humanistic/phenomenological approach to personality contasts sharply with both the psychoanalytic and behavioral approaches. For one thing, it is not deterministic. It claims that people have an ability to shape their own destiny, to chart and follow their own course of action, and that biological, instinctive, or environmental influences can be minimized. What matters most is how people view themselves and others, how they think, and, more importantly, how they *feel,* which is essentially what **phenomenological** means.

In many ways, the humanistic view is more positive and optimistic than either the Freudian view (with its death instincts and negative impulses of aggression) or the learning view (with its emphasis on control exerted by forces of the environment). It also tends to focus much more on the here and now than on early childhood experiences as important molders of personality. This point of view tends to emphasize the wholeness or completeness of personality, rather than focusing on its structural parts.

Carl Rogers

Carl Rogers' (b. 1902) view of personality is often referred to as a person-centered or self theory. Like Freud, Rogers developed his views of human nature through the observation of his clients (a term Rogers prefers to "patients") in a clinical setting. Unlike Freud, Rogers finds very little negative about basic human drives. For Rogers, the most overwhelming of human drives is the drive to become *fully functioning.*

To be fully functioning implies that the person has become all that he or she can be. But it means more than that. When we are children, some of what we do brings reinforcement and reward, but some of what we do does not. How we are regarded by those we care about is *conditional* upon how we behave. We tend to receive only conditional positive regard. *If* we do what is expected or desired, *then* we get reinforced. As a result, we try to act in ways that bring positive rewards, in ways that satisfy others, rather than satisfy ourselves. Our feelings of self and self-worth are thus dependent on the actions of others who either reward us or don't reward us.

So long as we are reacting only to please others, we are not fully functioning. To be fully functioning involves an openness to one's self and one's own feelings and desires, an accurate awareness of one's inner self, and a positive *self-regard.* Helping children to become fully functioning requires that we offer them more of what Rogers calls unconditional positive regard, and that we separate the child's behaviors from the child's self. What that means is that we may punish a child for doing a bad thing, but never for being a bad child (e.g., "I love you very much, but what you have done is inappropriate and, therefore, will be punished"). Helping clients to achieve positive self-regard is one of the major goals of Rogers' form of psychotherapy.

Notice that what matters here is often not so much what *is,* but what is *felt* or *perceived.* One's true self (whatever that may be) is less important than one's *image* of one's self. How the world is experienced is what matters. You may, in fact, be an excellent piano player (better, perhaps, than 98.8 percent of all of us). But if you feel that you are a rotten piano player, that perception of self-regard is what most matters.

Abraham Maslow

Abraham Maslow's (1908–1970) basic criticism of the psychology he had studied was that it was altogether too pessimistic and negative. The individual was seen as being battered about by either a hostile environment or by depraved instincts, many of which propelled the person on a course of self-destruction.

There must be more to living than this, thought Maslow. Someone should attend to the positive side of human nature. Maslow felt that people's needs are not base or evil, but are positive or neutral (Maslow, 1954). Our major goal in life is to actualize (realize and put into practice) those positive needs, to *self-actualize.*

Let's look, Maslow argued, at the very best among us. Let us examine the characteristics of those who have realized their fullest positive potential and have become self-actualized (see Figure 23.2). In his search for such individuals, Maslow couldn't find many. Most were historical figures, such as Thomas Jefferson and Eleanor Roosevelt (and the scientific status of Maslow's search for self-actualizers has been questioned by many psychologists).

As we have seen (Topic 20), one of Maslow's major concerns was the hierarchical arrangements of motives that activate our behaviors. At lower levels, and to be satisfied first, were basic needs (he called them *deficiency needs*). Some deficiency needs are physiological (need for water, sleep, etc.), others are psychological (need for security, self-esteem, etc.). Once the lower needs have been tended to, one can turn to higher needs, called *metaneeds* or *growth needs*. These needs include some rather abstract ideas, such as the need for justice, order, truth, and beauty.

Maslow believed that we all have a need to grow, to become the best we can be. For example, this disabled backpacker has overcome his handicap to enjoy an active outdoor life.

Before you go on

Briefly summarize the humanistic/phenomenological approach to personality as epitomized by Rogers and Maslow.

Evaluating the Approach

The humanistic/phenomenological approach has a number of strengths. For one thing, it does remind us of the wholeness of personality and of the danger in analyzing something complex in artificial segments. That the approach is positive and upbeat in its flavor also serves as a useful reminder that at least such views are possible. And, as we shall see in our topic on psychotherapy, this humanistic approach has had a considerable impact on many therapists and counselors.

Figure 23.2
Some of the characteristics or attributes of self-actualizers
(Adapted from Maslow, 1954.)

---

1. They tend to be realistic in their orientation.
2. They accept themselves, others, and the world for what they are, not for what they should be.
3. They have a great deal of spontaneity.
4. They tend to be problem-centered rather than self-centered.
5. They have a need for privacy and a sense of detachment.
6. They are autonomous, independent, and self-sufficient.
7. Their appreciation of others (and of things of the world) is fresh, free, and not stereotyped.
8. Many have spiritual or mystical (although not necessarily religious) experiences.
9. They can identify with mankind as a whole and share a concern for humanity.
10. They have a number of interpersonal relationships, some of them very deep and profound.
11. They tend to have democratic views in the sense that all are created equal and should be treated equally.
12. They have a sense of humor that tends more to the philosophical than the hostile.
13. They tend to be creative in their approach.
14. They are hard working.
15. They resist pressures to conform to society.

The basic problem with the approach is not unlike the basic problem with Freudian theory. It may make sense, but how does one go about scientifically testing any of the basic assumptions of the approach? As with Freudian theory, many of the key terms are defined in very general, fuzzy ways. What really is self-image? How would we recognize a self-actualizer if we saw one? How can one test the effects of delivering unconditional positive regard? In many ways, what we have here is more philosophical theory than psychological theory.

THE TRAIT APPROACH

Trait theories of personality have a markedly different flavor from any of the theories we have looked at so far. Trait theories tend to be more concerned with the adequate *description* of personality than with the *explanation* of personality. The trait approach is in some ways not unlike Sheldon's attempt to describe temperament. Trait approaches, however, acknowledge that an individual's personality is too complex to be adequately characterized by only three descriptive dimensions. (And they make no attempt to correlate traits with body types.)

With this approach, the argument is that an individual's personality can be adequately described on the basis of a reasonable number of personality **traits.** We may define a trait as "any distinguishable, relatively enduring way in which one individual differs from others" (Guilford, 1959, p. 5).

traits
distinguishable, relatively enduring ways in which individuals may differ

Traits are considered to be dimensions. That is, any trait (such as friendliness) is not a simple either/or proposition. Friendliness falls along a continuum, ranging from extremely unfriendly to extremely friendly, with many possibilities in between. To be useful, traits need to be measurable, and our measurements should yield numerical scores so we can assess the extent to which two people may differ on those traits.

Over the years, the issue for psychologists who have taken this approach has been which traits are the important ones. Which traits can best characterize a person and how she or he is different from everyone else? Is there any way in which our personality traits can be organized? The different answers to these (and related) questions have given rise to a number of trait theories. Let's briefly look at three: Allport's, Cattell's, and Eysenck's.

Gordon Allport

Gordon Allport (1897–1967) and his colleagues systematically examined an unabridged dictionary looking for words that could be used to describe people (Allport & Odbert, 1936). They found nearly 18,000 terms! Allport's logic was that if he could describe any person in terms of all 18,000 of the words he had found, he would have a complete description of that person's personality—at least he would have as complete a description as his language would allow. The problem, of course, is that nobody wants to deal with thousands of descriptive terms. In some sensible, reasonable way, Allport's 18,000 words had to be reduced to a manageable number that would serve the same basic purpose of description. The result became Allport's notion of traits and a scheme by which to organize them.

For Allport, a personality trait was a real force that existed within an individual and could be used to explain the consistency in a person's behaviors. In many different situations, for example, a trait of friendliness might produce a range of different specific responses, but those responses would be, in their essence, very much alike.

Perhaps you will recall, from Topic 1, our claim that psychologists often try to discover S-R (stimulus-response) relationships, and that S-R relationships often require that we know something about the organism (O) that is responding to stimulation. What we then had was an S-O-R relationship. Allport claims that the stable pattern of O variables we need to know about are personality traits. In order to predict how someone would act (R) in response to discovering that his or her books had been stolen (S) requires that we know something about the person involved (O). What we need to know, Allport claims, are his or her personality traits.

Allport's theory proposes that personality traits are of two types: *common traits* and *personal traits* (or personal dispositions). By common traits, Allport means those traits or dimensions of personality that are shared by almost everyone (to greater or lesser degrees perhaps, but shared in common with everyone else). Aggressiveness is a good example of a common trait, and so is intelligence. These are traits that can be readily used to make comparisons between people. Personal dispositions, on the other hand, are those traits that are unique to just some persons. How one displays a sense of humor (sharp wit, cutting sarcasm, dirty jokes, philosophical puns, etc.) is usually thought of as being a unique disposition.

Personal dispositions or traits can be analyzed into one of three types. A *cardinal trait* is a single trait that is so powerful, so overwhelming that it influences virtually everything that the person does. Very few people's personalities are ruled by cardinal traits. Even Allport could only imagine a few examples (Don Quixote, the Marquis de Sade, and Don Juan among them). No, what predominates in influencing your behavior and mine are not likely to be cardinal traits, but *central traits* or dispositions. These traits can generally be described in just one word, and are the 5 to 10 traits that best characterize any person (e.g., honest, friendly, outgoing, fair, kind, etc.).

Finally, each of us is occasionally influenced by *secondary dispositions.* These are traits that seldom govern many of our reactions and may be applied only in specific circumstances. Someone, for example, may be very calm and easy-going, even when threatened (a collection of central traits). However, when threatened in their own home (by unwanted intruders, let's say), we find that they can be very aggressive and not calm at all.

Allport believed that personality traits were actual forces in a person that could be used to explain the consistency of a person's behavior. For example, because this young boy is sharing his candy with his friends, we can guess that he shares other things with other people.

Raymond B. Cattell

Cattell's (b. 1905) approach to personality is an empirical one, relying on the results of psychological tests, questionnaires, and surveys. Talking about personality traits without talking about how they are measured would make little sense to Cattell.

Using a statistical technique called *factor analysis,* Cattell has looked at measurements of personality traits that give basically redundant information. (If you know that someone is outgoing, you really don't need to test them to see if they are sociable or extroverted.)

Cattell argues that there are two types of personality traits. *Surface traits* are the clusters of behaviors that go together, like those that make up curiosity, or trustworthiness, or kindliness. These traits are easily observed and can be found in a number of different settings. More important than these traits that can be seen on the surface are the fewer number of traits from which surface traits develop. These are called *source traits*. It is one's pattern of underlying source traits that determines which surface traits will get expressed in behavior. Obviously, source traits are not as easily measured because they are not directly observable. Cattell's list of source traits is presented in Figure 23.3.

Figure 23.3

Sixteen source traits as identified by Cattell (remember that each trait is a dimension)
(From Cattell, 1973, 1979.)

Reserved ←——→ Outgoing
(detached, aloof) (participating)

Less intelligent ←——→ More intelligent
(dull) (bright)

Affected by feelings ←——→ Emotionally stable
(easily upset) (calm)

Submissive ←——→ Dominant
(obedient, easily led) (assertive)

Serious ←——→ Happy-go-lucky
(sober, taciturn) (enthusiastic)

Expedient ←——→ Conscientious
(disregards rules) (moralistic, staid)

Timid ←——→ Venturesome
(shy, restrained) (socially bold)

Tough-minded ←——→ Sensitive
(rejects illusions) (tender-minded)

Trusting ←——→ Suspicious
(accepting) (circumspect)

Practical ←——→ Imaginative
(down-to-earth) (absent-minded)

Forthright ←——→ Shrewd
(unpretentious) (astute, worldly)

Self-assured ←——→ Apprehensive
(secure, complacent) (insecure, troubled)

Conservative ←——→ Experimenting
(disinclined to change) (experimenting)

Group-dependent ←——→ Self-sufficient
(a joiner) (resourceful)

Uncontrolled ←——→ Controlled
(follows own urges) (shows will power)

Relaxed ←——→ Tense
(tranquil, composed) (frustrated, driven)

Hans Eysenck

The theory of Hans Eysenck (b. 1916) combines some of the features of a simple, Sheldonlike type theory with the more detailed analysis of a trait theory like Allport's and Cattell's. He claims that personality can be viewed as basically divisible into two main *types*. Each type is defined by a dimension. On the one hand, there is the *extroversion-introversion* dimension. People high on extroversion seek stimulation; they are active and sociable. Introverts are reserved, cautious, and withdrawn. (Few people are pure extroverts or introverts—most of us fall somewhere in between.)

Eysenck's other major dimension is one of *stability-instability* (often called neuroticism). People high on stability tend to be calm and easygoing, while people at the other extreme tend to be moody, anxious, and temperamental. The interaction of these two types (dimensions) gives rise to a number of different, specific traits (see Figure 23.4).

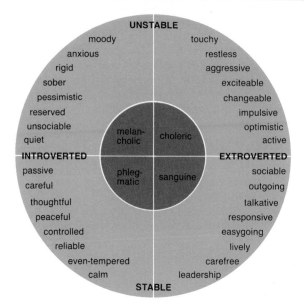

Figure 23.4
The interaction of Eysenck's extroversion-introversion and stability-instability dimensions and the traits they produce.
(From Eysenck, 1973.)

More recently (1976) Eysenck has proposed a third major type of personality, a *psychoticism* dimension that interacts with the first two. This dimension is essentially a measure of the degree to which a person takes a realistic view of life and of the world or is in some way out of touch with reality. Although the specific traits that develop through the interaction of these three personality types may be molded by learning and experience, Eysenck claims that one's position on his three main dimensions is largely inherited or instinctive.

Before you go on

What is a personality trait?

What are the major traits that influence personality, according to Allport, Cattell, and Eysenck?

Evaluating the Approach

Trait theories have some obvious advantages. They provide us not only with descriptive terms, but with the means of measuring or assessing those characteristics so that we can make comparisons among individuals. They suggest that we look at organism variables when we try to make predictions about behavior or mental processes.

On the other hand, as theories they offer little more than description. To say that someone acted in a certain way "because they are introverted" doesn't really *explain* their reaction, it just labels it. And, obviously, there is less than perfect agreement about which traits are the most important. How a person may be rated on any dimension may depend upon who does the rating and which types of measuring devices are used. And, as we will explore in our Topic Expansion, these theories suppose a consistency of reaction over time and in different situations that may be more fictional than real.

In this topic, we have briefly reviewed a number of different approaches to human personality and examined a sample of specific theories. Which of these various approaches or theories is the right one? Which is best? These are clearly unanswerable questions. Each approach is qualitatively different from the others, emphasizing different aspects of personality. The psychoanalytic approach emphasizes inborn impulses and the power of the unconscious. The behavioral learning approach emphasizes the influence of the environment, learning, and experience in molding the person. The humanistic/phenomenological approach emphasizes the power of the self, of conscious choices and personal growth. The trait approach emphasizes the measurement and organization of consistent patterns of behavior of individuals.

In their own separate ways, each approach has a contribution to make. In their own separate ways, each is "right" and the "best one." To be eclectic is to choose or select the best from all possible sources. That might be—for the time being—our wisest course of action: to pick and choose those aspects of each of these approaches that best serve whatever problem or aspect of human nature we may be dealing with at the moment.

Each of the approaches that we have reviewed in this topic brings its own unique flavor and point of view to the study of personality. There is one theme, however, that most have in common: They all address and focus on the *consistency* of personality. Someone with an overdeveloped superego should be consistently conscientious and feel guilty whenever established standards are not met. Someone who has learned, perhaps through modeling, to respond aggressively should be consistently aggressive in a range of settings. Someone attempting to grow personally and self-actualize should be consistently open to a wide variety of new ideas and opinions. Someone rated high on the trait of dominance should be consistently domineering, no matter who they are with.

Our personalities are not always consistent. Though we may have general personality characteristics, there will be times when our behaviors will deviate. For example, though we may generally be friendly and outgoing, there may be times when we prefer solitude.

A fundamental problem with this argument for the consistency of personality is that it may be wrong (Mischel, 1968 & 1979). It is logical and sensible, but in many cases it is not true. Think carefully about your own behavior and your own personality. Let's assume for the moment that you think of yourself as easygoing. Are you *always* easygoing, easy to get along with? Are there situations in which you would probably be easygoing, but yet other situations in which you might fight to have your way? Are there not some situations in which you tend to be social and outgoing, yet other, different situations in which your preference is to be alone and not mix in? Even if you are usually self-assured and confident, aren't there times when you feel (and act) unassured, timid, and apprehensive? Such is the thrust of Mischel's challenge: Personality characteristics only appear to be consistent when they are viewed in consistent (or similar) situations.

We may observe consistency in the personality of others for two reasons. (1) It is convenient. We like to think that we can quickly and accurately categorize people. We see someone do something dishonest—pick up change left as a tip for a waitress, perhaps—and find it convenient to label that person as being basically dishonest. We assume that the mean, aggressive football player will probably be mean and aggressive off the field. Such assumptions may not be true, but they make it easy to form judgments about others. (2) We probably see others only in a restricted range of situations, where their behaviors and attitudes may very well be consistent. The only real test would be to see those people in quite different situations on a number of occasions.

As you might suspect, Mischel's arguments challenging the very definition of personality have caused quite a stir. Over the past 15 years, there has been an exciting barrage of research and debate on this issue. Things may not be quite as unstable and situation-bound as Mischel first suggested. The issue is far from settled. One outcome of the rethinking about personality that theorists have been exploring lately is a point of view about personality and situational variables that has come to be known as *interactionism*. This approach is quite complex, reflecting the complexity of the issue, but we can summarize the basic idea (Bandura, 1978; Magnusson & Endler, 1977; Mischel, 1981).

As its name suggests, interactionism predicts that what a person will do, or how a person will react, is a function of the interaction of his or her stable personality characteristics *and* his or her perception of the situation. In a way, then, neither personality characteristics (inside the person) nor the situation (external environment) can be fully relied upon to explain an individual's reaction.

Let's say that Ken agrees to a friendly racquetball game, just for the exercise. At first, all goes well, and Ken, a superior player, really takes it easy on his opponent. After all, they're just playing for the exercise. During their second game, Ken's opponent makes a few good shots and actually moves ahead in the score. Ken notices that a small group of spectators is watching them play. Now Ken's perception of the situation starts to change. "This is no longer fun and games," he thinks to himself, as he starts smashing low line drives off the front wall of the racquetball court. Within just a few minutes, Ken's behaviors and reactions indicate a considerable change. The situation, at least in Ken's mind, has changed, and now his behavior is aggressive and forceful. As the situation changes, it brought about a change in Ken's personality (a perceived challenge to his ability brought out aggressive reactions). But Ken's personality also brought about a change in the situation (his very aggressiveness changed a friendly game into a competitive event). Thus, with interactionism we have an approach to explaining behavior that acknowledges the impact of the environment, but also allows for the influence of internal personality characteristics, as well.

TOPIC SUMMARY

What is a theory of personality?

A theory of personality is a series of related assumptions that, through logic and reason, lead to testable hypotheses that can be used to describe an individual and to differentiate an individual from others. / 419

What are the three levels of consciousness proposed by Freud?

Freud proposed that at any time we are only aware, or *conscious,* of a few things; some ideas or memories are accessible in our *preconscious,* while others may be accessed only with great difficulty—these are in our *unconscious* mind. / 420

According to Freud, what are the three structures of personality, and by what principle does each operate?

Three structures of personality according to Freud are the inborn, instinctive *id,* which operates on a *pleasure principle,* seeking immediate gratification, the *ego,* or sense of self, which operates on a *reality principle,* mediating needs in the context of the real world, and the *superego,* or sense of morality or conscience, which operates on an *idealistic principle.* / 421

Briefly review Freud's five psychosexual stages of development.

Freud believed that one's personality developed through five identifiable stages: the oral stage (birth to 1 year), the anal stage (ages 1–3), the phallic stage (ages 3–5), the latency stage (ages 6–puberty), and the genital stage (from puberty on). / 422

Briefly summarize the contributions of Adler, Jung, and Horney to the psychoanalytic approach to personality.

Adler, Jung, and Horney each parted with Freud on theoretical grounds, while remaining basically psychoanalytic in their approaches to personality. For Adler, social influences mattered much more than Freudian instincts. Jung was less biological, more positive, and expanded on Freud's view of the unconscious mind. Horney also rejected the notion of instinctual impulses and discussed instead the notion of basic anxiety and how one reacts to it as the molder of one's personality. / 424

Specify a contribution to the notion of personality contributed by Watson, Skinner, Dollard and Miller, Bandura, and Rotter.

A number of psychologists have argued that personality can be approached through an examination of learning principles and observable behavior. Watson first emphasized focusing on behavior and abandoning mental concepts. Dollard and Miller attempted to explain personality development in terms of learning theory and habits. Skinner emphasizes the notion of reinforcement and the consequences of one's behaviors. Bandura stresses the role of observation and social learning in the formation of personality. And Rotter believes that one's appraisal of control over behavior is an essential part of personality. / 427

Briefly summarize the humanistic/phenomenological approach to personality as epitomized by Rogers and Maslow.

The theories of Rogers and Maslow are alike in many ways, both emphasizing the integrity of the self and the positive power of personal growth and development, and both denying the negativity and biological basis of Freudian theory and the sterility of behaviorism. / 429

What is a personality trait?

What are the major traits that influence personality, according to Allport, Cattell, and Eysenck?

A personality trait is a characteristic and distinctive way in which one individual may differ from others. According to Allport, there are two kinds of traits: *common* and *personal,* the former found in virtually everyone, the latter unique just to some individuals. Cattell also feels that there are two kinds of traits: *surface traits,* which are readily observable, and *source traits,* from which surface traits evolve. Eysenck, on the other hand, believes that one's personality can be described somewhere among the intersections of three major dimensions: *extroversion-introversion,* *stability-instability,* and *psychoticism.* / 433

TOPIC

In Topic 1 you were asked to take a short true-false test about psychology. Here's another test for you to try. This one is in a multiple-choice format and ought to be easier. It's an adaptation of a personality test recently found in a national magazine. After you've taken the test, we'll let you know what it's about. In the meantime, try to guess what this test is supposed to be testing.

1. Suppose a shopping center was under construction in your neighborhood. Would you protest against it?
   (A) No.
   (B) Maybe. It would depend on which stores were in it.
   (C) Yes, I definitely would.

2. Do you feel that today's teenagers have looser morals than the teenagers of the 1960s?
   (A) Yes, definitely.
   (B) Some do and some don't.
   (C) No, I don't feel that things have changed that much.

3. How do you feel about modern art, compared to the art of the "great masters"?
   (A) I prefer it. It's fascinating.
   (B) It's ugly.
   (C) I don't like art of any sort.

4. Would you enjoy having your picture taken in the nude?
   (A) No, I would not under any circumstances.
   (B) Yes, I'd enjoy that.
   (C) Only if I were paid a lot of money.

5. When you visit a zoo, which animals do you most enjoy watching?
   (A) The monkeys. They're fun to watch.
   (B) The penguins.
   (C) The big cats—lions, tigers, and leopards.

6. How do you feel about young couples who choose to live together rather than marry?
   (A) It's a very good idea for most couples.
   (B) It's okay for a few, under certain circumstances.
   (C) It's wrong and a bad idea for any couple.

7. Should a person feel embarrassed or uncomfortable about getting their hair cut by a person of the opposite sex?
   (A) No, of course not. It's perfectly normal.
   (B) Yes, I think it would be embarrassing.
   (C) Maybe. It would depend on the people involved.

8. What do you think about women who never wear make-up?
   (A) It's their right, and it's perfectly okay with me.
   (B) They are crude and only trying to attract attention.
   (C) They are simply lazy.

9. Do you envy the good looks of television actors and actresses?
   (A) Yes, I wish I looked that good.
   (B) No, good looks are only skin deep.
   (C) Usually not, but there are definite exceptions.

10. Do you think a divorced father should be given custody of his children?
    (A) Yes, more often than not.
    (B) Occasionally.
    (C) No, never.

Now that you've taken this quiz, do you have any idea what it might be about? A test very much like this one was discovered in a magazine at the checkout stand of a supermarket. The test in the magazine claimed that it could indicate whether or not one was naturally sexy. According to the text that accompanies the quiz, being sexy is largely a state of mind, and "This test will help you find out just how much of this magical quality you are fortunate enough to possess." This "test" can serve as an example (and there are many such examples) throughout this topic. It *is* a psychological test. Whether or not it is a *good* psychological test remains to be seen. (If you're curious about how you scored, how "naturally sexy" you are, I suggest that you can score your responses on *this* quiz however you'd like. I suspect that your grading scheme would be as useful as mine.)

There is a certain logic to the claim that a science is only as good as its measurement. We tend to be impressed when physicists tell us precisely how much heat will be generated when a thermonuclear device is exploded. We tend to be unimpressed if the sun shines all day after a television weather forecaster tells us that there is a 40 percent chance of rain.

The ability to make accurate predictions often hinges on the ability to accurately *measure* or *assess* one's subject matter. Psychologists are interested in behavior and mental processes. Our ability to make sensible statements and predictions about our subject matter often depends on our ability to adequately measure those factors.

In a strict sense, **measurement** involves the assignment of numbers to some characteristic of interest according to rules or according to some agreed upon system. The rules for physical measurement are simple and well established. You are 5′10″ tall because from top to bottom your height equals 70 inches, where an inch is defined as a standard measure of length, and you have 70 of them. The rules for psychological measurement are seldom as clear-cut. Are you extroverted and outgoing, or are you shy and introverted? How extroverted are you? How do we know? What is the standard against which we can compare you and your behavior?

measurement
the assignment of numbers to some characteristic of interest according to rules or some agreed upon system

Much of the measuring that is done in psychology is done with psychological tests, and testing is one of the concerns of this topic. Here we will focus on tests designed to measure some aspect of personality, often referred to as **affective assessment** as opposed to **cognitive assessment,** which deals with the measurement of intelligence, aptitudes, and abilities. (The measurement of intelligence is covered in Topic 25.) Affective assessment is a measure of "typical behavior," while cognitive assessment attempts to measure "maximum performance" (Cronbach, 1984, p.26). With the former type of assessment, I want to know about how you *usually* perform, and with the latter, I want to know the *best* you can do.

affective assessment
the measurement of personality characteristics, one's typical behaviors

cognitive assessment
the measurement of intelligence, ability, or aptitude, one's best performance

If experience counts for anything, you are already something of an expert on psychological tests. At least you are an expert on *taking* tests. To have simply survived to this point in your education means that you have taken hundreds of tests—most of them of the cognitive sort.

As you know from your wealth of experience, there is a wide range of instruments that we can label as tests (including the exercise at the beginning of this topic). In this topic, we will do three things. We will (1) examine the nature and definition of psychological tests in general, (2) examine some of the criteria by which tests and other assessment techniques can be judged and compared, and (3) review and evaluate some of the more generally used instruments and procedures that are used in affective assessment.

Before you go on

Define measurement.

Compare and contrast affective and cognitive assessment.

THE NATURE OF PSYCHOLOGICAL TESTS

A Working Definition

psychological test
an objective, standardized measure of a sample of behavior

For quite some time now, a leading expert in this field (Anastasi, 1982) has defined a **psychological test** as "an objective, standardized measure of a sample of behavior." Let's take a close look at the terms within this definition.

A psychological test tells us about the extent or amount of some characteristic of interest. It yields a measure of something. At very least, we ought to be able to sort what we are measuring into categories. To be able to do so meaningfully is a type of measurement. For example, if we learn that some people are Republicans, some are Democrats, and some are Independents, while others aren't sure what they are, we have done a simple sort of measuring, because we have classified people according to some characteristic of interest (here, political affiliation). A psychological test can be used to indicate that some subjects are introverted, some are extroverted, and many are both. Even if we can do no more than that, we have measured a characteristic of interest.

A psychological test measures *behavior*. It measures behavior because that is all we can measure directly. We simply cannot measure those internalized concepts that we call feelings, or potential, or ability. All we can measure directly is overt, observable behavior. On the basis of our assessment of behaviors, we may be willing to make all sorts of inferences and assumptions about underlying, internal processes. But behavior is all we can measure directly. (We've encountered this situation before, most notably when we considered the difference between learning and performance.)

It should be clear that any one psychological test can measure only a *sample* of behavior. Let's say that I want to know about your tendency to be aggressive or the extent of your extroversion. I cannot very well ask you everything about you that relates to aggression or extroversion. ("List *all* of the situations in which you are likely to be aggressive or extroverted," for instance.) What we have to do instead is to sample (systematically draw a portion of) the behaviors in which we are truly interested. We then assume that responses to our sample of items can be used to predict responses to questions we have not asked.

Notice that psychological tests are twice removed from what we usually think we are doing when we test someone. For instance, let's say that I am interested in how you feel about psychology. Maybe I want to compare your feelings with those of someone who has never taken a psychology course. First, there is no way that I can get inside the two of you and view your feelings directly. I have to assume that your responses (behavior) to my test items accurately reflect your feelings (and that you're not just trying to be nice and make me feel good, for example). Second, because time prohibits me from asking everything that I might wish to ask, I have to assume that my questions and your answers provide an adequate sample of what I am interested in. So, instead of assessing your feelings directly, I end up making *inferences* based on a *sample* of behavior.

There are two other definitional points to consider. If a psychological test is to have any value, its administration must be *standardized* and its scoring should be *objective*. Here is where your experience as a test-taker may be relevant. Imagine taking a college placement test that will be used to determine which of a number of courses in English composition you will be required to take. You are given 45 minutes to answer 50 multiple-choice items *and* write a short essay on a prescribed topic. Later on you discover that many students were given the same examination, but with instructions to "take as long as you'd like to finish the test." You also discover that these students could write their essay on any one of three suggested topics. You would be justified in complaining that something is wrong with the testing system. What it lacks is standardization. As much as possible, everyone taking a test—any kind of test—should take it under the same standard conditions, follow the same instructions, have the same time limits, and so on.

A psychological test should be objective. In this context, objectivity refers to the evaluation of the responses that examinees make to test items—

scoring the test, in other words. Different examiners (at least those of the same level of expertise) should be expected to give the same interpretation and evaluation to a test answer or response. If the same responses to a psychological test lead one psychologist to declare a subject perfectly normal, a second psychologist to consider the subject a mass of inner conflict and over-ridden with anxiety, while a third wonders why this subject is not in a psychiatric institution, we have a problem. Assuming that the problem is with the test and not the three psychologists, the problem is one of objectivity. Although strict, literal objectivity is a goal seldom reached by psychological tests (particularly those designed for affective assessment), it is a worthy goal.

So it looks like all we need for a psychological test is a series of items or questions for subjects to respond to that are administered in a standard fashion and scored objectively. That doesn't sound very hard to do. It isn't. The world is full of tests that meet these minimal criteria (even our opening test on natural sexiness seems to do that). Weekly newspapers at supermarket checkout lanes, scores of magazines, newspapers, and even television programs regularly include psychological tests. As a consumer of such tests as well as a student of psychology, you should be able to assess the value or usefulness of measuring devices that we call psychological tests. It is to this matter that we turn next.

Before you go on
What is a psychological test?

Criteria for a Good Test

As easy as it may be to write a test, it is very difficult to construct a good one. To qualify as a good psychological test or assessment tool, a technique needs to have three characteristics: reliability, validity, and adequate norms. To demonstrate these characteristics takes time and effort (and money). It is for these reasons that many of the tests found in the popular press tend not to be good tests.

reliability
consistency or dependability

Reliability   In the context of psychological testing, **reliability** means the same thing that it means in other contexts: consistency or dependability. Someone gives you an objective, standardized measure of a sample of your behavior, and, on the basis of your responses, suggests that you have an IQ that is slightly below average—86, let's say. Two weeks later, you take the same test and are told that your IQ is now 127—nearly in the top 3 percent of the entire population! Something is terribly wrong. We have not yet discussed IQ, but surely we recognize that one's intelligence as indicated by an IQ score should not change by 40 points within 2 weeks.

A test is said to be reliable if it measures something (anything) consistently. Let's say that I have developed a short multiple-choice test that supposedly measures the extent of one's extroversion or introversion. I administer the test to a group of 200 college freshmen. If I administered the same test 1 month later to the same subjects, I would be surprised if everyone earned exactly the same score. I'll expect some random fluctuation in scores, but changes on the retest a month later should be small if I have a good, reliable instrument. If a test does not measure whatever it measures with some consistency, it will not be very useful. If a month ago your test scores indicated that you were a very extroverted person and today's test indicates tendencies toward introversion, which test administration am I to believe?

The type of reliability with which we are usually concerned is **test-retest reliability.** As its name suggests, test-retest reliability involves administering a test to the same group of subjects on two different occasions. Scores on the two administrations are then correlated with each other. Correlation will tell us directly if the test in question is reliable. If the correlation coefficient approaches zero, the test may be declared unreliable. Acceptable levels of reliability are indicated by correlation coefficients that approach +1.00.

The necessity for demonstrating test-retest reliability makes good sense when we are trying to measure consistent and stable characteristics like intelligence or extroversion. Test scores should be consistent because we assume that what we are measuring is itself reliable and consistent over time. What happens if the very characteristic we are trying to measure is known (or suspected) to change over time? Consider trying to develop a test for anxiety. If we realize nothing else about it, we recognize that how anxious we feel changes from week to week, from day to day, and even from hour to hour. That is, level of anxiety may not be a reliable characteristic.

So if I do write a test to measure anxiety, test-retest reliability will not be a sensible criterion to use in evaluating my test. A subject may get a very high score today, right before midterm exams, and a very low score just a few days later after having learned that she did well on all her exams. We do not abandon the notion of consistency and reliability altogether, however. There are two possible alternatives to test-retest reliability.

One thing I might do is make up two forms of my test. They will be very much alike in virtually every detail; they will ask the same sorts of questions about the same behaviors, but in slightly different ways. I will then ask that you take both forms of the test. Your score, or your reactions, should be very much the same on both forms if my test is reliable.

At the very least, we should expect a psychological test to demonstrate internal reliability. That is, we should require that the test be consistent from beginning to end. We might correlate the scores on items from the first half of the test with scores on the second half of the test. We might correlate scores on the odd-numbered items with scores on the even-numbered items. Such a measure would yield a **split-half reliability** score and would tell us if there is consistency *within* the test, even if consistency over time is irrelevant.

test-retest reliability
a check of consistency made by correlating the results of a test taken by the same subjects at two different times

split-half reliability
a check on the internal consistency of a test, which is found by correlating one part of a test with another part of the same test

Before you go on

What is reliability, and how do we measure the reliability of psychological tests?

Validity   When people worry about the usefulness of a test, they are usually concerned with its **validity.** Measures of validity tell us the extent to which a test actually measures what it says it's measuring. For example, the claim was made that the quiz at the beginning of this topic was a test of one's natural sexiness. For one thing, you should stop to wonder if there even *is* such a thing. Assuming that you think that there really is such a "magical quality" and state of mind, does this test actually measure the extent to which you are "naturally sexy?" If it does, it is valid. If it does not, it is not valid.

We determine a test's *reliability* by correlating the test with itself (at a later time with test-retest reliability, or at the same time with alternate forms or split-half reliability). We determine a test's *validity* by correlating test scores with some other, independent measure, or *criterion.* As it happens, there are a number of different types of validity that we might be concerned with.

validity
the extent to which a test measures what it claims to be measuring

predictive validity
the extent to which a test can be used to predict future behaviors

One of the most practical types of test validity is **predictive validity.** Here, a psychological test or assessment technique is used to predict some future behavior. The criterion is something that will or will not happen in the future. Does this test of extroversion predict which college students are most likely to join sororities or fraternities? Does this aptitude test predict who will do well in college and who will not? Does this typing test predict who will do well working with a word processor and who will not? Does this clinical assessment predict whether or not this subject, who has just attempted suicide, is likely to hurt himself or others in the future?

Establishing a test's predictive validity is a matter of correlation once again. The test in question is administered to a large group of subjects. All subjects are later measured on the independent criterion, and test scores are correlated with criterion scores. Now you find out if, in fact, those who earn high test scores, for example, also earn good grades in college courses. You now find out, for example, if those who get high scores on your extroversion test do, in fact, tend to join sororities and fraternities.

If a psychological test is well correlated with other established tests that purport to measure the same characteristic(s), then the test is said to have **concurrent validity.** If you generate a new test to measure test anxiety that is not at all correlated with any of the well-established tests already available that measure test anxiety, we may have to suggest that your test lacks concurrent validity.

concurrent validity
the extent to which a test is correlated with other tests claiming to measure the same characteristic

content validity
the extent to which a test provides an adequate and fair sample of the behaviors being measured

One additional form of validity ought to be mentioned here because it is very relevant for students taking classroom exams. It is **content validity,** which is the extent to which a test adequately samples the behaviors that it claims to be testing. For example, you may be told that you are to be given an exam covering all of learning and memory. The test is to be made up of 50 multiple-choice items. You might be more than a little upset if you were to find that 48 of the 50 items on the test dealt with Pavlovian classical conditioning. You would claim that the test was not fair. It would lack validity because it does not measure what it claims to measure. In this case, it would lack content validity because the content of the test does not cover a broad range of material on learning and memory.

Before you go on

What are predictive, concurrent, and content validity?

How is each of these measured?

Norms Let's say that you have just taken an objective, paper-and-pencil questionnaire, designed to measure the extent to which you tend to be extroverted or introverted. You know that the test is a reliable and valid instrument. You are told that you scored a 50 on the test. So what? What does a score of 50 mean? It doesn't necessarily mean that you answered 50 percent of the items correctly, because this is a test of typical performance and there are no right or wrong answers. Does a 50 mean that you are extroverted or introverted, or neither?

The point is that if you don't have a basis of comparison, any one test score by itself is meaningless. You need to compare your score of 50 with the scores of other people like yourself who have already taken the test. Results of a test taken by a large group of subjects whose scores can be used to make comparisons are called **norms.**

norms
results of a test taken by a large group of subjects whose scores can be used to make comparisons with or give meaning to new scores

You may discover, by checking with the norms, that a score of 50 is indeed quite average, and indicative of neither extreme extroversion nor extreme introversion. On the other hand, a 50 may be a very high score, indicating extroversion, or a very low score, indicating introversion. An aptitude test score of 134 sounds pretty good until you discover that the average score was 265, and that scores in the norms range from 115 to 360. If the norms tell you that the average score on this aptitude test was only 67, then your score of 134 would be a very good score indeed.

The usefulness of a test, then, often depends on the adequacy of the norms that are used to make comparisons or judgments about any one test score. If the extroversion-introversion test you took had been previously administered to only 40 or 50 high school students to compile its norms, it would hardly provide an adequate test of *your* extroversion or introversion. The scores that make up norms should be drawn from subjects similar to those who are going to be tested later—and the more the better.

So writing a good psychological test is not as easy as it may at first appear. Writing a series of questions and deciding on acceptable answers may be relatively simple, but the rest takes considerable time and effort. Let's now turn to a few of the techniques and tests that psychologists use to assess personality characteristics, always keeping in mind as students—and as consumers of psychological tests—the three major criteria for good tests: reliability, validity, and adequate norms.

Before you go on
In the context of psychological testing, what are norms, and for what purpose are they used?

PERSONALITY ASSESSMENT

In this section, we will summarize four ways to measure or assess an individual's personality: behavioral observations, interviews, paper-and-pencil tests, and projective techniques. Before we do so, we should review just what it is we are trying to assess, and why we generally want to make such assessments.

As we saw in our last topic, personality is a very difficult concept to define with precision. Common to many definitions, however, is the notion that there are characteristics of an individual that remain fairly consistent over time and over many (if not all) situations. Many of these characteristics can also be used to describe how one person is different from others. It is further reasoned that if we know which characteristics are typical of an individual, we can use that knowledge to make specific predictions about his or her behaviors or mental processes. The key, then, is to find those characteristics of a person that can be reliably and validly measured.

If we can find those characteristics, what then? Why do we bother? There are two major motives behind the measurement of personality. One is very practical, at least in a clinical sense. Regardless of the approach one takes, one of the first questions that a psychologist in a clinical setting may ask is "What is wrong with this person?" (Burisch, 1984). In fact, the basic question—one of diagnosis—may be, "*Is* there anything wrong with this person?" The issue is the extent to which the behaviors, feelings, or cognitions of an individual are abnormal, and, if so, in what way.

A second use for personality assessment is research, where there are two basic questions: (1) Which personality traits can be measured? How are different traits organized within the individual? Which traits are the most important or most fundamental for describing a person's personality? For personality trait theorists, this is obviously *the* purpose for constructing personality tests or measures. However, other theorists are also interested in this basic question. Psychologists of a psychoanalytic persuasion, for example, might like to develop reliable and valid measures of the influence of unconscious motives and impulses.

(2) Another research-oriented question that involves psychological tests goes a step farther. Here the question is whether a measured personality trait or characteristic can be used to predict some other, independent behavior. This concern has very practical implications. For example, if we know that Joe X is, in fact, dominant and extroverted, does that knowledge tell us anything about his leadership potential? Which measurable characteristics are best associated with success as a plant manager? What sorts of personality characteristics best describe a successful astronaut, or police officer, or secretary? If Susan hears voices telling her to do things and is uncontrollably anxious when left alone, what sort of treatment or therapy might best help her with her problems?

In brief, personality assessment has one of three major goals: clinical diagnosis, theory building, or behavioral prediction. There is no doubt that these three goals often interact. A clinical diagnosis is often made in the context of a particular theoretical approach and is often used to predict possible outcomes, such as which therapy technique may be most appropriate.

Before you go on
What are the basic goals of personality assessment?

Behavioral Observation

behavioral observation
the personality assessment technique in which one draws conclusions about an individual on the basis of observations of his or her behaviors

As you and I develop our own impressions of the personalities of our friends and acquaintances, we do so largely by relying on **behavioral observation.** As its name suggests, this approach involves drawing conclusions about an individual's personality on the basis of observations of his or her behaviors. We judge Dan as being bright because he was the only one who knew the answer to a question in class. We feel that Pam is submissive because she always seems to do whatever her husband demands.

Behavioral observation involves drawing conclusions about an individual's personality on the basis of his or her behaviors. Child psychologists will often observe and interact with children to determine the bases of their behaviors.

As helpful as our observations may be to us, there are real problems with such unstructured, uncontrolled observations. Because we have only observed a small range of behaviors in a small range of settings, we may be guilty of overgeneralizing when we assume that the same behaviors will show up in new, different situations. Dan may never again know the answer to a question in class. Pam may be giving in to her husband only because she knows that we are there. That is, the behaviors we happen to observe may not be typical at all.

Nonetheless, behavioral observation can be an excellent source of information. It is commonly a part of any clinical assessment. The clinical psychologist may note any number of behaviors of a client as being potentially significant—style of dress, manner of speaking, gestures, postures, and so on.

Let's consider an example. A small child is reportedly having trouble at school, behaving aggressively, starting fights, and being generally disruptive. One thing a psychologist may do is visit the school and observe the child's behaviors in the natural setting of the classroom. It may be that the child does behave aggressively and engage in fighting behavior, but only when provoked, or only when the teacher is in the room. Otherwise, the child is quite pleasant. It may be that the aggressive behavior of the child is simply a ploy to get the teacher's attention.

In an attempt to add some structure to her observations, a psychologist may use *role-playing* as a means to collect more information. Role-playing is a matter of acting out a given life situation. "Let's say that I'm a student, and that you're the teacher, and that it's recess time," the psychologist says to a child. "Let's pretend that somebody takes a toy away from me, and I hit him on the arm. What will you do?"

Some observational techniques are very structured. Instead of simply gathering general observations of behavior, some sort of *rating scale* is used (an example is provided in Figure 24.1). Rating scales provide a number of advantages over casual observation. For one thing, they focus the attention of the observer on a set of specified behaviors to be observed. Rating scales also yield a more objective measure of a sample of behavior. Using rating scales, one can arrange to have behaviors observed by a number of raters. If a number of raters are involved in the observation of the same behaviors (say, children at play in a nursery school), you can check on the reliability of the rater's observations. That is, if all five of your observers agree that Timothy engaged in "hitting behavior" on the average of five times per hour, the consistency (or reliability) of that assessment adds to its usefulness.

Aggressive behavior in a child is often an attempt to get attention. Once a psychologist has observed the behavior occurring naturally, he or she can often determine what causes the behavior and help the child learn to deal more effectively with his or her anger.

Before you go on

How is behavioral observation used to assess personality?

Interviews

We can find out some things about people by watching them. We can also gain insight about some aspects of their personality by simply asking them questions. In fact, the **interview** "remains the most important instrument of clinical assessment" (Korchin & Schuldberg, 1981). It is also "one of the oldest and most widely used, although not always the most accurate, of the methods of personality assessment" (Aiken, 1982, p. 296).

The basic data of the interview is what people say about themselves, rather than what they do. The interview is not, strictly speaking, a measure-

interview
the personality assessment technique involving a conversational interchange between an interviewer and a subject to gain information about the subject

Figure 24.1
A graphic rating scale such as this might be used by an employer in evaluating employees or potential employees. It could also be used by psychologists studying behavior.

Poor   Superior

Dependability				
Requires prodding and supervision	Needs occasional prodding	Steady, responsible worker	Needs little supervision; uses own judgment	Self-starter; needs no supervision
Personal relations				
Rude; causes trouble	Inconsiderate; unkind	Relations with others usually good	Helpful; kind; polite	Well liked; good social skills
Poise				
Nervous; ill at ease	Easily upset; tense	Average poise and self-assurance	Self-assured	Composed; handles crises well

ment technique, because the results of an interview are usually quite impressionistic and not easily quantifiable. It is more a technique of discovering generalities than specifics.

A major advantage of the interview is its flexibility. The interviewer may decide to drop a certain line of questioning if it seems to be producing no useful information and to pursue some other area of questioning. Unfortunately, there is scant evidence that unstructured interviews have much reliability validity. For example, in discussing interviews used to assess personality characteristics of job applicants, Tenopyr (1981) calls the history of validity for the interview "dismal." She says that the employment interview, "despite various innovations over the years, has never been consistently shown to improve selection" (p.1123).

As is the case for observational techniques, there is considerable variety in the degree to which interviews may be unstructured or structured. In the latter type of interview, there are a specific set of questions to be asked in a prescribed order. The structured interview, then, becomes more like a psychological test to the extent that it is objective, standardized, and asks about a particular sample of behavior.

Before you go on
Cite one advantage and one disadvantage of the interview as a technique of personality assessment.

Paper-and-Pencil Tests

Minnesota Multiphasic Personality Inventory (MMPI)
a paper-and-pencil inventory used to assess a number of personality dimensions

Observational and interview techniques barely qualify as psychological tests. They are neither as standardized nor as objective as we would like them to be. In this section, we'll focus on one of the best objective tests designed to assess personality: the **Minnesota Multiphasic Personality Inventory,** or the **MMPI** for short. The test is referred to as multiphasic because it measures a number of different personality dimensions all at once.

The MMPI was designed to help in the diagnosis of persons with mental disturbances and, hence, is not a personality test in the usual sense. The test was first made available just as World War II began and immediately became very popular. It is, no doubt, the most researched test in all of psychology, and remains one of the most commonly used (Lubin, Larsen, & Matarazzo, 1984). This is not to suggest that the MMPI is without its critics. Cronbach

(1984, p. 483) calls the test "long and inefficient," and claims that "A number of items are outdated, and the dimensions used in summarizing responses are—to put it mildly—relics of an antiquated psychiatry."

In many ways, the MMPI *looks* just like a number of other personality tests. It is composed of more than 550 statements to which a subject responds "true" or "false." The statements cover feelings, attitudes, physical symptoms, and past experiences. What makes the MMPI somewhat different is the method used to choose items to include in the inventory and the inclusion of validity scales.

In constructing the MMPI, the authors simply made up a large list of items to which a subject could respond "true" or "false." The authors began writing their test with no particular theory of personality in mind. They just made up items. The potential test items were then administered to subjects who had already been diagnosed as belonging to some psychiatric category: paranoid, schizophrenic, or depressed, for example. The items were also given to approximately 700 control group subjects who had no psychiatric diagnosis; they were taken to be normal. If any one item were answered by normals and subjects with psychiatric problems in the very same way, the item obviously did not discriminate normals from nonnormals, and was dropped as a potential item. Items were included only if they discriminated, or differentiated, among the different groups of subjects and patients responding to them.

Because of the way in which it was constructed, the MMPI is called a *criterion referenced* test. That means that each item on the test is referenced to one of the criterion groups—either normals or patients with a particular diagnosis. Some of the items appear quite sensible. "I feel like people are plotting against me," seems like the sort of item that paranoids would call "true," while normals would tend to respond "false." Many items, however, are not so obvious. "I like to visit zoos," is not an MMPI item, but it might be if subjects of one diagnostic group respond to the item differently from the way other subjects do. What the item looks like or what the item may actually mean is irrelevant. What matters, and the only thing that matters, is if subjects of different groups respond differently to the item. We should also add that no one will (or can) make a diagnosis of psychological disorder on the basis of a subject's response to just one item. What matters is one's *pattern* of responding to a large number of items. The different clinical scales for the MMPI are presented in Figure 24.2.

It is clear that the interpretation of one's responses to MMPI items is limited by the quality or validity of those responses. There are a number of factors that might interfere with validity here. Simple fatigue and lack of motivation to carefully respond to more than 500 items is one. Another is the possibility that a person will respond with what he or she believes to be good or socially acceptable answers rather than with responses that truly reflect the subject's personality. In order to monitor such possibilities, four validity scales were added to the standard clinical scales of the MMPI.

The *? scale* checks the number of items left unanswered. Skipping a few items is okay, but not responding to large numbers of items will invalidate the test. The *L-scale,* or lie scale, is made up of a number of items that are sensitive to a person's attempt to present themselves in an overly positive way. For example, responding "true" to "I always smile at everyone I meet," or "false" to "I sometimes get angry at others," would lead to an overly high score on this scale. In addition, there is a scale that indicates when a subject is trying to put himself or herself in an unfavorable light (agreeing with statements such as, "There is an international plot against me," for example). Finally, there is a validity scale that provides a correction factor to be used in the interpretation of the clinical scales when subjects are being slightly overcritical or overgenerous in evaluating themselves.

Figure 24.2
MMPI scales and descriptions.
(Based on Aiken, 1970.)

Validity scales

Cannot say scale (?)	Measures the total number of unanswered items.
Lie scale (L)	Measures the tendency to claim excessive virtue or to try to present an overall favorable image.
Infrequency scale (F)	Measures a tendency to falsely claim psychological problems.
Defensiveness scale (K)	Measures the tendency to see oneself in an unrealistically positive way.

Clinical scales

Scale 1	Hypochondriasis (Hs)	Measures excessive somatic concern and physical complaints.
Scale 2	Depression (D)	Measures symptomatic depression.
Scale 3	Hysteria (Hy)	Measures hysteroid personality features and the tendency to develop physical symptoms under stress
Scale 4	Psychopathic Deviate (Pd)	Measures antisocial tendencies.
Scale 5	Masculinity-Femininity (Mf)	Measures sex-role conflict.
Scale 6	Paranoia (Pa)	Measures suspicious, paranoid ideation.
Scale 7	Psychasthenia (Pt)	Measures anxiety and obsessive behavior.
Scale 8	Schizophrenia (Sc)	Measures bizarre thoughts and disordered affect accompanying schizophrenia.
Scale 9	Hypomania (Ma)	Measures behavior found in manic affective disorder.
Scale 0	Social Introversion (Si)	Measures social anxiety, withdrawal, and overcontrol.

Originally developed as an aid to diagnosis, the MMPI is still used largely for that same purpose. Making diagnoses directly from MMPI scores, however, is seldom done. The test is seen as an *aid* to diagnosis—a simple and straightforward way to collect a large amount of information. Years of research have indicated that a person's pattern of scores may be more significant than high or low scores on any one item or scale of the test. Because there are years of data to build upon, MMPI test results are often computer generated. An example of an MMPI profile and a (fictitious) MMPI computer-generated report are presented in Figure 24.3.

Although the MMPI is the most commonly used personality inventory, it is not the only acceptable paper-and-pencil personality test. There are dozens of such tests. The California Personality Inventory, or CPI, for example, was constructed following the same logic as was used for the MMPI. That is, potential test items were administered to subjects independently known to be different on some personality trait (on the basis of self-reports and the ratings of others who knew them well). If the test item discriminated between the two groups (if each group answered differently), it was included on the final scale. The major difference between the MMPI and the CPI is that the CPI was constructed using normal subjects, not people who were hospitalized for some psychological problem. The CPI assesses 18 "normal" personality traits, including self-acceptance, dominance, responsibility, and sociability. Because it is designed to measure a number of different traits, it can also be referred to as a multiphasic test.

Some multiphasic tests have been designed in conjunction with the development of a particular personality theory. Cattell's trait theory approach

Figure 24.3

A computerized printout from a Minnesota Multiphasic Personality Inventory profile. (From The Minnesota Report, 1984.)

PROFILE VALIDITY

This is a valid MMPI profile. The client was quite cooperative with the evaluation and appears to be willing to disclose personal information. There may be some tendency on the part of the client to be overly frank and to exaggerate her symptoms in an effort to obtain help. She may be open to the idea of psychological counseling if her clinical scale pattern reflects psychological symptoms in need of attention.

SYMPTOMATIC PATTERN

The client is exhibiting much somatic distress and may be experiencing a problem with her psychological adjustment. Her physical complaints are probably extreme, possibly reflecting a general lack of effectiveness in life. She is probably feeling quite tense and nervous, and may be feeling that she cannot get by without help for her physical problems. She is likely to be reporting a great deal of pain, and feels that others do not understand how sick she is feeling. She may be quite irritable and may become hostile if her symptoms are not given "proper" attention.

Many individuals with this profile have a history of psychophysiological disorders. They tend to overreact to minor problems with physical symptoms. Ulcers and gastrointestinal distress are common. The possibility of actual organic problems, therefore, should be carefully evaluated.

Her response content indicates that she is preoccupied with feeling guilty and unworthy, and feels that she deserves to be punished for wrongs she has committed. She feels regretful and unhappy about life, complains about having no zest for life, and seems plagued by anxiety and worry about the future. She has difficulty managing routine affairs, and the item content she endorsed suggests a poor memory, concentration problems, and an inability to make decisions. She appears to be immobilized and withdrawn and has no energy for life. According to her response content, there is a strong possibility that she has seriously contemplated suicide. A careful evaluation of this possibility is suggested. She views her physical health as failing and reports numerous somatic concerns. She feels that life is no longer worthwhile and that she is losing control of her thought processes.

INTERPERSONAL RELATIONS

She appears to be somewhat passive-dependent in relationships. She may manipulate others through her physical symptoms, and become hostile if sufficient attention is not paid to her complaints. Marital unhappiness is likely to be a factor in her present clinical picture. She is a rather

NOTE: This MMPI interpretation can serve as a useful source of hypotheses about clients. This report is based on objectively derived scale indexes and scale interpretations that have been developed in diverse groups of patients. The personality descriptions, inferences and recommendations contained herein need to be verified by other sources of clinical information since individual clients may not fully match the prototype. The information in this report should most appropriately be used by a trained, qualified test interpreter. The information contained in this report should be considered confidential.

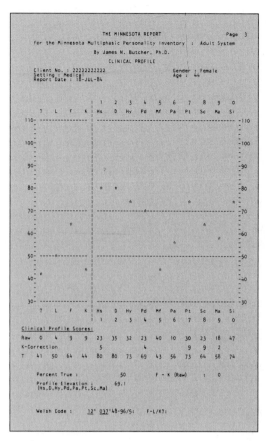

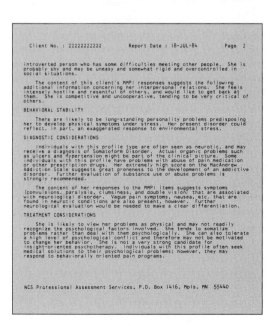

investigated a number of potential personality traits and settled on a few basic traits (see pp. 431–432). These traits are what are measured with Cattell's "16 PF" questionnaire (where PF stands for personality factors). Analyses of responses on this paper-and-pencil test (of more than 100 statements with which the subject responds "yes" or "no") results in a personality profile. That profile can then be compared with one gathered from a large norm group. Figure 24.4 shows the 16 personality factors test profile form.

Finally, we should mention that there are a number of personality questionnaires or inventories that are designed to measure just one trait and, thus, are not multiphasic. Probably the best example here is a commonly used test called the Taylor Manifest Anxiety Scale. Taylor used a different approach in constructing this test. She began with a very large pool of items—many of them from the MMPI—and asked psychologists to choose those items that they thought would measure anxiety. The 50 items most commonly chosen as indicators of anxiety make up this test, which has been widely used and is generally accepted as the best paper-and-pencil indicator of anxiety.

Figure 24.4
Cattell's 16 personality factor scales.

ipat

16 PF$_{T.M.}$ TEST PROFILE

Sten Score
FB ______
FG ______

FACTOR	Raw Score Form A/C/E	Raw Score Form B/D	Raw Score Total	Standard Score	MEANING OF SCORE ON LEFT	STANDARD TEN SCORE (STEN) 1 2 3 4 5 ←Average→ 6 7 8 9 10	MEANING OF SCORE ON RIGHT
A					**Cool,** Reserved, Impersonal, Detached, Formal, Aloof	A	**Warm,** Outgoing, Kindly, Easy-going, Participating, Likes People
B					**Concrete-thinking,** Less Intelligent	B	**Abstract-thinking,** More Intelligent, Bright
C					**Affected by Feelings,** Emotionally Less Stable, Easily Annoyed	C	**Emotionally Stable,** Mature, Faces Reality, Calm
E					**Submissive,** Humble, Mild, Easily Led, Accommodating	E	**Dominant,** Assertive, Aggressive, Stubborn, Competitive, Bossy
F					**Sober,** Restrained, Prudent, Taciturn, Serious	F	**Enthusiastic,** Impulsive, Heedless, Expressive, Cheerful
G					**Expedient,** Disregards Rules, Self-indulgent	G	**Conscientious,** Persistent, Moralistic, Staid, Rule-bound
H					**Shy,** Threat-sensitive, Timid, Hesitant, Intimidated	H	**Bold,** Venturesome, Uninhibited, Can Take Stress
I					**Tough-minded,** Self-reliant, No-nonsense, Rough, Realistic	I	**Tender-minded,** Sensitive, Over-protected, Intuitive, Refined
L					**Trusting,** Accepting Conditions, Easy to Get on with	L	**Suspicious,** Hard to Fool, Distrustful, Skeptical
M					**Practical,** Concerned with "Down to Earth" Issues, Steady	M	**Imaginative,** Absent-minded, Absorbed in Thought, Impractical
N					**Forthright,** Unpretentious, Open, Genuine, Artless	N	**Shrewd,** Polished, Socially Aware, Diplomatic, Calculating
O					**Self-assured,** Secure, Feels Free of Guilt, Untroubled, Self-satisfied	O	**Apprehensive,** Self-blaming, Guilt-prone, Insecure, Worrying
Q_1					**Conservative,** Respecting Traditional Ideas	Q_1	**Experimenting,** Liberal, Critical, Open to Change
Q_2					**Group-oriented,** A "Joiner" and Sound Follower, Listens to Others	Q_2	**Self-sufficient,** Resourceful, Prefers Own Decisions
Q_3					**Undisciplined Self-conflict,** Lax, Careless of Social Rules	Q_3	**Controlled,** Self-respecting, Socially Precise, Compulsive
Q_4					**Relaxed,** Tranquil, Composed, Has Low Drive, Unfrustrated	Q_4	**Tense,** Frustrated, Overwrought, Has High Drive

Name: ______
Second Orders: Extraversion ______ Anxiety ______ Tough Poise ______ Independence ______

A sten of	1	2	3	4	5	6	7	8	9	10	is obtained
by about	2.3%	4.4%	9.2%	15.0%	19.1%	19.1%	15.0%	9.2%	4.4%	2.3%	of adults

From 16 PF Test Profile by Raymond Cattell, Herbert Eber, Maurice Tatsuoka. Copyright © 1956, 1973, 1982 by the Institute for Personality and Ability Testing, Inc. Reproduced by permission.

Before you go on

Why was the MMPI constructed?

What does multiphasic mean?

How did the authors of the MMPI try to insure that the test would be valid?

Projective Techniques

A **projective technique** involves asking a subject to respond to an ambiguous stimulus. The stimulus involved can be any number of things, as we shall see, and there are clearly no right or wrong answers. The procedure is very unstructured and open-ended. In many ways, the projective technique is more of an aid to interviewing than it is a psychological test (Korchin & Schuldberg, 1981). The basic idea is that because there is, in fact, so little in the stimulus presented, the subject will project some of his or her own self into the response.

Some projective techniques are very simple and are given verbally. Indeed, the word association technique, first introduced by Galton in 1879 and used commonly in psychoanalysis, is a sort of projective technique. "I will say a word, and I want you to say the first thing that pops into your head. Do not think about your response; just say the first thing that comes to mind." There certainly are no right answers in this type of test, but there are lists of norms that indicate the associations most frequently given in response to some common stimulus words. The notion here is that the clinician can gain some insight, perhaps into the problems of a patient, by using this procedure.

Another similar technique is the *unfinished sentences* procedure. In this procedure, a sentence is begun, "My greatest fear _____," perhaps, and the subject is asked to complete the sentence. Although there are a number of published tests available, many clinicians prefer to make up their own forms. A commonly used instrument of this type is the Rotter Incomplete Sentences Blank, see Figure 24.5. Again, there are no right or wrong responses, and interpreting responses is rather subjective, but a skilled examiner-interviewer can use these procedures to gain new insights about a subject's personality.

projective technique
a personality assessment technique requiring subjects to respond to ambiguous stimuli, thus projecting some of their selves into their responses

---

Directions: Complete these sentences to show your real feelings.

1. I don't like_____.

2. My best friend_____.

3. I wish that_____.

4. I can't_____.

5. I want_____.

6. My parents_____.

7. I am very_____.

8. I need_____.

9. My school_____.

10. I feel_____.

Figure 24.5
Sentence completion exercise for young children.

Rorschach inkblot test
a projective technique in which the subject is asked to say what he or she sees in a series of inkblots

Of all the projective techniques, none is so famous as the **Rorschach inkblot test.** This technique was introduced in 1921 by Hermann Rorschach who believed that people with different sorts of personalities respond differently to inkblot patterns (see Figure 24.6). There are 10 stimulus cards in the test, 5 are black on white, 2 are red and gray, and 3 are multicolored. Subjects are asked to tell what they see in the cards, or what the inkblot represents.

Scoring of Rorschach responses has become quite controversial. Standard scoring procedures require attending to a number of different factors: what the subject says (or content), where the subject focuses attention (location), mention of detail versus global features, reacting to color or open spaces, and how many different responses there are per card. Many psychologists have questioned the efficiency of the Rorschach as a diagnostic instrument. Much of what it can tell an examiner may be gained directly. For example, Rorschach responses that include many references to death, dying, and sadness are probably indicative of a depressed subject. One has to wonder if inkblots are really needed to discover such depression. As a psychological test, the Rorschach inkblots seem neither reliable nor valid. Nonetheless, this test remains a very popular instrument. It is used primarily as an aid to general assessment and the development of subjective impressions.

thematic apperception test (TAT)
a projective technique in which the subject is asked to tell a story about an ambiguous picture

A projective device we discussed earlier (in the context of achievement motivation, Topic 20, p. 372), is the **thematic apperception test,** or **TAT.** You may recall that this test is made up of a series of ambiguous pictures about which a subject is asked to tell a story. The subject is asked to describe what is going on, what led up to this situation, and what the outcome is likely to be. The subject is asked to take about 5 minutes to tell his or her story.

The test is designed to provide a mechanism to discover the subject's hidden needs, desires, and emotions, which will be projected into their stories about the pictures. This test is called a *thematic test* because scoring depends largely on the interpretation of the themes of the stories that are told. Although some formal scoring schemes are available, scoring and inter-

Figure 24.6
A sample Rorschach inkblot. The subject is asked what the inkblot represents, or what he or she sees in the inkblot.

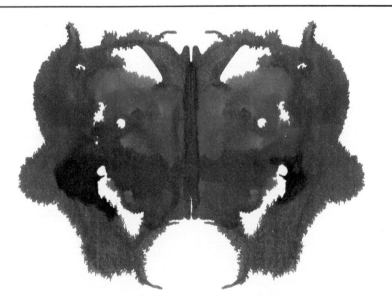

pretation are usually subjective and impressionistic. The examiner/scorer essentially develops hypotheses about the subject being tested on the basis of responses to one picture, and then tests these hypotheses on other stories. That is, one story may be filled with examples of aggression. Are there underlying needs for aggression here? Let's see if such aggressive themes also show up in other stories. It is likely that the TAT remains popular for the same reason as the Rorschach: Psychologists are used to it, comfortable with the data it provides, and willing to accept any source of additional information they can use to make a reasonable assessment or diagnosis.

Before you go on

What is the essence of a projective technique, the Rorschach and TAT in particular?

Measuring or assessing personality is a difficult business. We mentioned this at the start and need to reemphasize this point here at the end of this topic. Given the difficulty we have even defining personality, the fact that it is difficult to find reliable, valid, objective, and standardized ways of measuring it should not be surprising. If it is not apparent, we should mention in closing this topic that no psychologist will try to assess one's personality with just one of the tools or instruments we have described. In almost all cases, such assessments are made by pulling together data from interviews, observations, objective paper-and-pencil inventories, *and,* perhaps, some projective technique.

We opened this topic with a rather silly example of a personality test and claimed that writing such tests is easy. Problems arise in assessing whether or not such tests qualify as good tests; that is, whether or not they are reliable and valid instruments. Now let's review the two major techniques that have been used to construct personality inventories. We'll also review some evidence that suggests that these techniques may be more involved and difficult than is necessary.

Historically, there have been two major approaches to personality test construction: the empirical and the factor analytic. The empirical approach attempts to achieve validity through the way items are chosen for inclusion in the test. This is the method used to construct the MMPI and the CPI. Groups *known* to be different on some characteristic are given a large number of test items to which to respond. If both groups respond similarly to an item, it is eliminated from consideration. If an item is answered in one way by one group and in another way by the other group of subjects, it may be used in the final test because it discriminates between the two groups.

Notice that it does not matter at all what the item looks like. If a group of depressed subjects agrees with the statement "I like broccoli," while a group of nondepressed subjects disagrees with the statement, it may show up on the test as a "Depression Scale" item. These sorts of tests have a built-in validity (of a sort) because if items do not demonstrate differences between two groups of interest, those items never get in the test in the first place.

There are a couple of major problems with this approach. (1) One has to be certain that the groups used to test the items are

genuinely different. The validity of the test is limited by the validity of the diagnosis or classification made before items are even administered. (2) One has to generate a very large number of items—and some of them are strange looking items—in order to find enough items to discriminate between any two groups.

The factor analytic approach to personality test construction is the method associated with the trait theories of personality, such as Allport's, Eysenck's, and Cattell's. This approach was used to develop the Cattell Sixteen Personality Factor Inventory. Here, there are no assumptions made about the type of subjects being asked to respond to potential items. If anything, the subjects are taken to be a representative sample of a large population of subjects. The subjects respond to a large number of items generated by the test's author. Then a statistical manipulation called factor analysis is applied to the responses that subjects made to all the items.

This procedure is quite complex, but it is basically a correlational technique that seeks to find consistency among responses. What it amounts to is eliminating items that uncover the same, or redundant, information. That is, if everyone answered item 3 and item 48 in exactly the same way, we would be getting redundant information by using both items. What the test builder hopes to find is a small number of groups of items, each of which seems to be measuring the same general thing. These groups of items are called factors, and the psychologist can label them however she or he would like. When Cattell went through this process, he found 16 groups of items or factors (see Figure 24.4). The basic problem with this time-consuming approach is that the number of factors that emerge from one's analysis, and what those factors are, is in large measure determined by one's choice of original items and the characteristics of the groups of subjects who first respond to the items. It may be, for example, that if Cattell had administered his original items to a different group of subjects, his factor analysis might have resulted in 15 or 18 factors, rather than 16.

All of this seems like a lot of work just to measure a few personality traits. Matthias Burisch (1984) agrees that it is a lot of work and further argues that it is probably not necessary. Burisch argues that we need not be so clever or roundabout in our construction of personality scales. Let's use more common sense, he argues. Let's use our knowledge of psychology and personality and simply ask subjects about those aspects of their personality in which we may be interested. In this regard, Burisch quotes Allport (1941), "If we want to know how people feel, what they experience and what they remember, what their emotions and motives are like, and the reasons for acting as they do, why not ask them?" (p. 37).

Burisch reports data from 15 studies that have compared different techniques for constructing personality tests. In no case were the more difficult and more time-consuming types of tests found to be either more valid, more useful, or more economical (in either construction or administration). Arguing that we ought not abandon common sense in our attempts to develop reliable and valid personality inventories, Burisch offers the following example (1984, p. 218).

Consider the following three items:
I feel hungry nearly all the time.

I used to dream rather often.

I would rather live in a big city than in a quiet village.

Suppose a subject has said yes to all of them. Does any clear image of this person come to your mind? Yet the three items are all from the aggression scale of a much-used German inventory.

In contrast, consider the following three items:

Frankly, I start quarrels fairly often.

I frequently feel like attacking someone.

Sometimes I take pleasure in provoking others a little.

Someone who answers all these items positively admits to a tendency to spontaneous aggression, if only in verbal form, and thus communicates something about herself or himself.

TOPIC SUMMARY

Define measurement.

Compare and contrast affective and cognitive assessment.

Measurement involves assigning numbers to some characteristic of interest according to rules or some agreed upon system. Cognitive assessment involves attempts to measure intellectual abilities or aptitudes, where one tries to do one's best. Affective assessment, on the other hand, involves measuring typical behaviors—those associated with one's personality. / 440

What is a psychological test?

A psychological test is an *objective* (not open to multiple interpretation) *standardized* (administered and scored in the same way) *measure of a sample* (we cannot measure all behaviors) *of behavior* (because behavior is all we can measure). / 442

What is reliability, and how do we measure the reliability of psychological tests?

Reliability means consistency or dependability. With psychological tests, we measure reliability by administering the same test to the same people at different times (test-retest reliability) or we check the internal consistency of the test by comparing scores on some items with scores on other items (split-half reliability). / 443

What are predictive, concurrent, and content validity?

How is each of these measured?

Predictive validity tells us if a test predicts what it claims to predict. To measure it, test scores are correlated with some other, independent criterion measured after the test has been taken. Concurrent validity tells us if the test under consideration is at least correlated with other tests that claim to measure the same thing. Content validity is the extent

to which a test is composed of a fair and representative sample of the material or characteristic being tested. / 444

In the context of psychological testing, what are norms, and for what purpose are they used?

Test norms are scores on the test earned by a large number of subjects, similar to those for whom the test has been designed. It is against the standard of these scores that an individual's test score can be compared. / 445

What are the basic goals of personality assessment?

Personality assessment can be used for a number of reasons, including (1) making a clinical diagnosis about the presence and/or nature of a psychological disorder, (2) as a tool in building a theory of personality in order to see which traits are associated with others, and (3) for behavioral prediction in attempting to assess what someone might do in the future. / 446

How is behavioral observation used to assess personality?

One tries to draw conclusions about personality on the basis of the observations of behaviors. Behaviors should be observed in a variety of settings. Observations should be as objective as possible and may involve the use of behavioral rating scales to check reliability. / 447

Cite one advantage and one disadvantage of the interview as a technique of personality assessment.

The major advantage of the interview technique is its flexibility. The interviewer may pursue avenues of interest, while abandoning lines of questioning that are not fruitful. Unfortunately, there is very little data to support the notion that interviewing is a valid technique for most uses. / 448

Why was the MMPI constructed?

What does multiphasic mean?

How did the authors of the MMPI try to insure that the test would be valid?

The MMPI was originally designed (in 1941) as an aid to psychological diagnosis. As a multiphasic instrument, it measures a number of different personality traits at once. Validity of a sort was built into the test when the authors only used items that discriminated between subjects of different diagnostic categories. / 453

What is the essence of a projective technique, the Rorschach and TAT in particular?

With a projective technique, the assumption is that in responding to an ambiguous stimulus (inkblots with the Rorschach, pictures with the TAT), subjects will project some of their selves, perhaps even unconscious aspects of their selves, into their responses. / 455

CHAPTER ELEVEN

INTELLIGENCE

TOPIC 25

Allen spent most of his summer afternoons out in the backyard. Mostly, he just wandered around, staring at the railroad tracks that passed by the institution's property. As freight trains approached, Allen would hurry to the fence at the very end of the yard and watch intently as the trains rolled by. Some trains were 60 cars long. Everyone thought that Allen simply loved to watch trains—not unusual behavior for a young teenager, particularly one institutionalized as mentally retarded. It wasn't until Allen's fourth summer at the institution that it was discovered that he was doing more than just passively watching freight trains roll by. He was reading the serial numbers on the boxcars—many were 13 digits long—and was adding them together in his head! When his addition was checked, it was found that he added with great accuracy. (In fact, on the first test, the person operating the calculator made a mistake and computed the wrong sum, while Allen's total was correct.)

George was also institutionalized. His intellectual abilities were just too slight and few in number to allow him the full freedom of the community. George had an incredible ability, however. He maintained—in his head—a perpetual calendar. He could tell you the day of the week for any date you provided. "What day did July 20, 1940 fall on?" George would hesitate but a minute and reply, "Saturday." "There were four Sundays in July 1976. On what dates did they fall?" George answered, "July 4th, July 11th, July 18th, and July 25th." George could also tell you that in the year 2010, the Fourth of July would fall on a Tuesday.

Melissa had an IQ of 54, where 100 is average and an IQ of 69 or below defines mental retardation. As a 17 year old, Melissa knew about few of the things her peers, high school juniors, knew about. She did not know who was president of the United States. She was unsure about the colors of the American flag. She guessed that there were seven days in a week. She could read a few simple words, but could not write at all, and "Sesame Street" was her favorite television program. What Melissa *could* do was play the piano. With very few errors, she could reproduce on the piano almost any music she heard, from classical to jazz to popular. She could not read a note of music and could not explain her mysterious ability, but she *could* play the piano.

People like Allen, George and Melissa are few in number. There have been enough such cases now that we cannot deny the phenomenon: There are mentally retarded individuals, occasionally severely disabled, who possess some one single remarkable talent or ability, well beyond what we generally expect from people of normal intelligence. Such people have been given the rather unfortunate label of *idiot savants*. We do not know how to explain their abilities, but their very existence challenges our basic beliefs about the nature of intelligence and intelligence testing. It is as if all of one's intellectual aptitudes can become focused on one particular skill or in one particular area. It may very well be that the more well-rounded and generalized one's intellectual abilities, the less likely it is that that person will be outstanding in any one area (Restak, 1982).

Intelligence is a troublesome concept in psychology. We all know what we mean when we use the word, but we have a terrible time trying to define intelligence concisely. We wonder if Johnny's failure in school is due to his lack of intelligence or to some other factor, such as an emotional disorder. You may argue that locking my keys in my car was not a very intelligent thing to do. I may argue that anyone with any intelligence can see the difference between positive and negative reinforcement. We occasionally credit some people as being very intelligent in general, but suspect that they are unable to behave intelligently in specific circumstances, sometimes doing the dumbest things. As we saw with the idiot savants, sometimes intelligence is very narrow and focused.

In this topic, we'll review some of the views or models of intelligence that have found favor among psychologists. We'll then examine intelligence as it is measured by psychological tests. Intelligence tests are among the most commonly used of all psychological tests. We'll review the two major individual intelligence tests, the Stanford-Binet and the Wechsler tests, and then we'll look at a few of the more commonly used group tests of intelligence.

There are few concepts in all of psychology that are as controversial as intelligence. How it is to be measured and what social significance should be attached to different levels of intelligence are issues that have been debated since psychology's earliest days.

THE NATURE OF INTELLIGENCE

Problems of Definition

Intelligence has been variously defined as the sum total of everything that you know, or as the ability to learn and profit from experience, or as one's ability to solve problems and to cope with the environment. Of course, there is nothing wrong with any of these definitions or uses of the term intelligence. The problem is that none seem to say it all. We have gotten into the habit of using intelligence as such a general label for so many talents, abilities, and aptitudes that it virtually defies specific definition. (See Figure 25.1.)

Nonetheless, we should settle on some definition to guide our study through this chapter. I propose that we accept two definitions, one academic and theoretical, the other operational and practical. For a theoretical definition of **intelligence,** we can probably do no better than offer David Wechsler's: "the capacity of an individual to understand the world about him [or her] and his [or her] resourcefulness to cope with its challenges" (1975, p. 139).

This definition (and others like it) does present some problems. What does one mean by "capacity"? What is actually meant by "understand the world"? What if the world never really challenges one's "resourcefulness"? Will such people be less intelligent? Do you see the problem? What at first reading may seem like a very sensible and inclusive definition of intelligence may, upon reflection, pose even more definitional problems.

Perhaps we ought to follow our advice from Topic 1, where we suggested that defining concepts operationally often helped to overcome such difficulties. Let's continue to use the word intelligence as if we all know what it means. When pressed, we'll rely on an **operational definition:** Intelligence is that which intelligence tests measure. If we agree to use this definition, we

intelligence
the capacity to understand the world and the resourcefulness to cope with its challenges; that which an intelligence test measures

operational definition
a definition given in terms of the operations used to measure or to create the concept being defined

Figure 25.1

In a study on the characteristics of intelligent behavior, lay people and intelligence researchers emphasized different characteristics, as is evident on these lists. Though the elements on both lists are related, the emphases are clearly different. (From Sternberg, 1982.)

Lay people	Intelligence researchers
I. Practical problem-solving ability Reasons logically and well. Identifies connections among ideas. Sees all aspects of a problem. Keeps an open mind. Responds thoughtfully to others' ideas. Sizes up situations well. Gets to the heart of problems. Interprets information accurately. Makes good decisions. Goes to original sources for basic information. Poses problems in an optimal way. Is a good source of ideas. Perceives implied assumptions and conclusions. Listens to all sides of an argument. Deals with problems resourcefully.	**I. Verbal intelligence** Displays a good vocabulary. Reads with high comprehension. Displays curiosity. Is intellectually curious. Sees all aspects of a problem. Learns rapidly. Appreciates knowledge for its own sake. Is verbally fluent. Listens to all sides of an argument before deciding. Displays alertness. Thinks deeply. Shows creativity. Converses easily on a variety of subjects. Reads widely. Likes to read. Identifies connections among ideas.
II. Verbal ability Speaks clearly and articulately. Is verbally fluent. Converses well. Is knowledgeable about a particular field. Studies hard. Reads with high comprehension. Reads widely. Deals effectively with people. Writes without difficulty. Sets aside time for reading. Displays a good vocabulary. Accepts social norms. Tries new things.	**II. Problem-solving ability** Is able to apply knowledge to problems at hand. Makes good decisions. Poses problems in an optimal way. Displays common sense. Displays objectivity. Solves problems well. Plans ahead. Has good intuition. Gets to the heart of problems. Appreciates truth. Considers the result of actions. Approaches problems thoughtfully.
III. Social competence Accepts others for what they are. Admits mistakes. Displays interest in the world at large. Is on time for appointments. Has social conscience. Thinks before speaking and doing. Displays curiosity. Does not make snap judgments. Makes fair judgments. Assesses well the relevance of information to a problem at hand. Is sensitive to other people's needs and desires. Is frank and honest with self and others. Displays interest in the immediate environment.	**III. Practical intelligence** Sizes up situations well. Determines how to achieve goals. Displays awareness to world around him or her. Displays interest in the world at large.

need to see how intelligence tests work. But before we do, we should briefly consider some of the theoretical approaches to intelligence that psychologists have developed over the years.

Before you go on

Provide an operational definition of intelligence.

Can you offer a definition of intelligence that is not an operational definition?

Models of Intelligence

Models (or theories) of intelligence are attempts to categorize and organize different types of intellectual abilities into sensible groupings. In this section, we will look at a few of the models of intelligence that at some point in psychology's history have gained a reasonable measure of acceptance.

Spearman's "g" One of the first theories of intelligence was proposed by Charles Spearman (1863–1945). Spearman was one of the early pioneers in mental testing and invented a number of useful statistical procedures, including factor analysis.

Spearman's image of intelligence came from his inspection of the scores earned by a large number of subjects on a wide range of psychological tests that were all designed to assess cognitive, or intellectual, skills and abilities. His procedures were largely correlational. He looked at the extent to which abilities measured by these different instruments were related to each other.

What impressed Spearman was that no matter what a specific test was supposed to be measuring, some people always tended to do a little better than others, and some people always seemed to perform less well than most. Spearman (1904) concluded that intelligence is made up of two things: a general intelligence, called a **g-factor**, and a series of specific intellectual skills, called **s-factors.** As a result, Spearman's view of intelligence has come to be called a *two-factor theory* of intelligence.

g-factor
Spearman's name for general intelligence of the sort common to all intellectual tasks

s-factor
Spearman's term for the intellectual skills that are appropriate for specific tasks

Spearman believed that intelligence is made up of a general intelligence (g-factor) and a series of specific intellectual skills (s-factors). The ability to perform difficult tasks depends on these two factors. For example, being a chef requires a great deal of organization—a g-factor. Being a medical researcher, on the other hand, requires special learning skills in mathematics and the physical sciences—s-factors.

Figure 25.2

Thurstone's Seven Primary Mental Abilities
(After Thurstone, 1938.)

Verbal comprehension (V)	The ability to understand ideas, concepts, and words, as in a vocabulary test.
Number (N)	The ability to use numbers to solve problems quickly and accurately.
Spatial relations (S)	The ability to visualize and manipulate patterns and forms in space, as in the ability to recognize an object viewed from a different perspective.
Perceptual speed (P)	The ability to determine quickly and accurately whether or not two complex stimuli are identical or in some way different.
Word fluency (W)	The ability to use words quickly and fluently, as in the ability to solve anagrams and produce rhymes.
Memory (M)	The ability to remember lists of materials, such as digits, letters, or words presented previously.
Inductive reasoning (I)	The ability to discover a general rule from presented information, to discover relationships, as in, "what number comes next? 2, 4, 6, 8,—."

In other words, everyone has a certain level of general intelligence ("g"), which Spearman thought is probably inherited, *and* some specific skills that are useful in some tasks, but not in others. This point of view suggests that person A, with a high g-factor, will tend to do better than person B, with a low g-factor, on virtually all tests of intellectual functioning. However, it is quite possible that there is some specific skill (the ability to memorize strings of digits, perhaps) on which person B may perform at a *higher* level than person A because of a particular strength in his or her s-factor.

Looking at intelligence in terms of what a variety of different tests measure, and how such measures are related to each other, became a popular way to think about intelligence. Many psychologists followed Spearman's lead. They administered different kinds of tests to many different kinds of subjects. Then, using sophisticated statistical techniques (many of them devised by Spearman), they looked for areas of overlap and areas of independence.

Thurstone's Primary Mental Abilities   When L. L. Thurstone (1877–1955) examined the correlations among different types of ability tests, he found something different from what Spearman had noticed. Thurstone (1938) felt there was no evidence for a global, general intellectual ability, "g." He believed that intellectual abilities could be classified into seven different, separate factors or dimensions. These he called the seven **primary mental abilities** (see Figure 25.2). Each of the factors in this model is thought of as being independent and separately measurable. To know one's intelligence requires that you know how one fares on all seven of these factors.

primary mental abilities
according to Thurstone, the seven unique abilities that comprise intelligence

Guilford's Structure of Intellect   From Spearman's view that intelligence is made up of two factors, "g" and "s," we moved to Thurstone's theory that intelligence is made up of seven separate factors. Now things get more complicated. J. P. Guilford (1967) suggests that intelligence should be analyzed into three intersecting dimensions. Any intellectual task, Guilford claims, can be analyzed in terms of the mental *operations* that are used, the *content* or material upon which the operations are performed, and the *product* of applying a particular operation to a particular type of content. Each of these dimensions has a number of possible values. That is, there are five operations, four contents, and six products. These three dimensions and their values are depicted in Figure 25.3.

If you study Figure 25.3, you'll discover that there are 120 possible combinations of content, operation, and product in Guilford's scheme of intelligence. Remembering that Guilford's scheme is theoretical, we need to ask, "What does this mean in real life?"

Just to give you an idea of how this system works, let's choose one of the 120 possible "cells" or intersections of Figure 25.3—the one where *cognition, figural,* and *units* intersect. What would this intellectual skill be like? Guilford says it's a matter of recognizing (cognition) diagrams or pictures (figural) of simple, well-defined elements (units). To test this ability, one might be shown an incomplete drawing of a simple object and be asked to identify it as quickly as possible. The intersection of *cognition, semantic,* and *unit* values would be tested with a simple vocabulary test.

Figure 25.3

Guilford's model of intelligence. In this model, there are three major divisions (contents, products, and operations), each with its own subdivisions. Each subdivision may interact with all others, yielding 120 specific intellectual skills or abilities.
(After Guilford, 1967.)

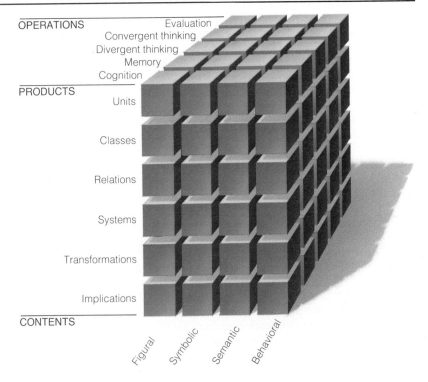

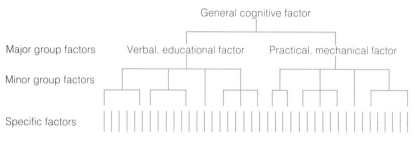

General cognitive factor

Major group factors — Verbal, educational factor — Practical, mechanical factor

Minor group factors

Specific factors

Figure 25.4
Intellectual abilities may be represented in a hierarchy from very general to very specific according to Philip Vernon. (After Vernon, 1963.)

Other Views   Philip Vernon (1960) has suggested that we should think of intelligence as a series of skills and abilities that are arranged in a hierarchy (see Figure 25.4). At the very top is a general cognitive or mental ability not unlike Spearman's "g." Under it are just two major factors: one is essentially a *verbal/academic* sort of intelligence, the other a *mechanical/practical* sort. These in turn can be thought of as being comprised of yet more specific factors. The verbal/academic, for example, is made up of *numerical* and *verbal* skills, among others. These skills, too, can be broken down still further (verbal skills include *vocabulary* and *word usage*); and further still (vocabulary may include *synonyms* and *antonyms*). Seeing cognitive skills as being arranged in a hierarchy is one way of combining the basic ideas of Spearman, Thurstone, and Guilford.

Raymond Cattell is a well-known personality theorist, associated with the trait theory approach to personality we discussed in Topic 23. Cattell saw from the start that in some way, one's intelligence is a major contributor to one's personality. Cattell's study of personality convinced him (1963) that general intelligence reflects two different kinds of cognitive skills—*fluid* and *crystallized* intelligence. These two types of intellectual ability are seen as being correlated, but different. Fluid intelligence is the more general of the two; it is, perhaps, innately determined and involves the ability to see relationships and solve problems in a wide variety of situations. It involves the ability to adapt to new and different situations. It may be that this is the sort of intellectual functioning that tends to decline in old age (Horn & Donaldson, 1976). Crystallized intelligence, on the other hand, is a function of one's experience, of the situations one has been in. It is a reflection of what has been learned—using one's fluid intelligence—and is thought of as being rather specific.

The theories of intelligence we've reviewed here are concerned mostly with the *structure* of intelligence. As is often the case with structural theories, each of these (and other similar ones) makes some valid points, but somehow fails overall to give us sufficient insight into how intelligence really works or where it comes from. Psychologists have certainly not stopped theorizing about intelligence, however. More recent approaches have tended to stress the cognitive *processes* involved in performing intellectual tasks (for example, Sternberg, 1979, 1981).

In large measure, our attitudes and feelings about intelligence have been molded by our experiences with tests designed to measure intelligence. Earlier, we suggested that we could define intelligence as "that which intelligence tests measure." Let's see how these tests do just that.

Fluid intelligence involves the ability to see relationships and solve problems—such as fixing a broken bike for a favorite friend.

Before you go on

Briefly summarize the basic idea behind three models or theories of intelligence.

MEASURING INTELLIGENCE: THE IQ TESTS

The Stanford-Binet Intelligence Scale

Alfred Binet

Historians of psychology would probably refer to the work of Alfred Binet (1857–1911) even if he hadn't written the first practical test of general intelligence. He was certainly the leading psychologist in France at the turn of the century. Although he had a law degree, he chose to pursue his interests in psychology. Binet was impressed with Jean Martin Charcot's work on hypnosis and studied with him in Paris. When psychology was first beginning to emerge as a science, Binet became associated with the psychology laboratory at the Sorbonne. He studied all sorts of things there: hypnosis, abnormal behaviors, optical illusions, and thinking processes. By far, however, his major interest was with individual differences. In particular, Binet was curious about how people differed in their abilities to solve problems.

It was not surprising then that Binet's expertise was sought on a wide range of educational issues. Of great concern in 1900 were those children in the Paris school system who seemed unable to profit from the educational experiences they were being given. What was the problem? Were they uninterested? Did they have some emotional sickness? Or were they simply intellectually unable to grasp and use the material they were being presented? With a number of collaborators, most notably Theodore Simon, Binet set out to construct an instrument to measure the intellectual abilities of children.

Binet's first test appeared in 1905, with a major revision in 1908 and a minor rewording of some items 3 years later. The test was an immediate success. It caught the attention of L. M. Terman at Stanford University, who translated it into English and supervised a revision of the test in 1916. (Terman's revision included changing some clearly French questions into items more suitable for American children.) Since 1916, the test has been referred to as the Stanford-Binet and has undergone a number of revisions. A 1937 edition provided two alternate forms of the test, labeled Form L and Form M (after Terman's initials). Revisions in 1960 and 1972 made few substantive changes, but did update some items and change the scoring scheme. So what is this test like?

The Structure of the Test   The Stanford-Binet is an individually-administered test made up of a series of subtests. The subtests are somewhat unusual in that they are not defined in terms of question type (the specific ability being tested), but in terms of *age level.* This division into age level subtests is based on Binet's observation that average children of different ages have different intellectual abilities and can do different things.

The Stanford-Binet provides subtests for age levels 2 through 4-1/2, at half-year intervals (i.e., 2, 2-1/2, 3, 3-1/2, 4, and 4-1/2). There is a subtest for each age level 5 through 14, and some subtests for average and superior adults. To qualify as an item for a given age-level subtest, an item must be one that most average children of that age (or older) can respond to correctly, while younger children cannot.

For example, an item at the 6-year-old level might ask a child to complete the sentence, "Feathers are soft; wood is _____." What makes this a 6-year-old level item is that average 6-year-olds (and 7- and 8-year-olds, to be sure) can usually answer it, while average 5-year-olds cannot. An average 3-year-old can make a bridge out of three wooden blocks, following a model, while average 2-year-olds cannot. Hence, "bridge-building with three blocks" becomes a 3-year level subtest item. Other typical Stanford-Binet items for different subtests are listed in Figure 25.5.

The *types* of questions that are asked and the sorts of skills that are tested tend to change from age level to age level, from subtest to subtest. That is, a 2-year-old may be asked to stack wooden blocks; 5-year-olds may have to follow a route through a simple maze; 7-year-olds may be asked to add some numbers; and 12-year-olds may be asked to define a few abstract words.

MA, CA, and IQ   Now that we have a sense of what the test is like, how is it used to determine intelligence? Assume that you are testing a 6-year-old child. Because she was born 6 years ago, we say that her **chronological age (CA)** is 6. What we want to know now is how her mental abilities compare to other children of her age. Physically, she is 6, but what is her **mental age**, or **MA**? By definition, if she can earn full credit for the 6-year-old items, but cannot pass the 7-year-old items, she is an average 6-year-old, and we say that her mental age is 6. If she goes beyond the 6-year level and correctly answers all the 7- and 8-year level items before failing at the 9-year level, she is acting (intellectually) like an average 8-year-old, and we can say that her MA is 8. If our examinee cannot pass the 6-year level, but can get full credit for the 5-year level, her MA would be 5.

We do not express scores earned on the Stanford-Binet directly with MA scores, but in terms of an **intelligence quotient**, or **IQ** score. IQ is simply defined as a quotient of MA divided by CA, multiplied by 100, or:

$$MA/CA \times 100 = IQ.$$

In our first example, our subject had a chronological age of 6, and her mental age was equal to 6, so her IQ would be exactly 100: $6/6 \times 100 = 100$. Notice that with this formula, anyone of average intelligence for his or her chronological age will *always* have an IQ of 100. For example, an average 12-year-old boy by definition has an MA of 12, and $12/12 \times 100 = 100$.

Let's work through another example. Imagine that you are asked to test an 8-year-old boy who has been having trouble in school. There is some concern that he might be slow or intellectually deficient. Having talked to the boy for

chronological age (CA)
a person's actual, biological age

mental age (MA)
on the Stanford-Binet test, the age level at which the subject is functioning intellectually

intelligence quotient (IQ)
the quotient of mental age divided by chronological age (MA/CA) multiplied by 100, taken to represent one's level of tested intelligence

Figure 25.5

Typical items from the Stanford-Binet intelligence scale; by age level (From Terman & Merrill, 1972.)

Two-year level	Asked to point out parts of the body on a large paper doll; asked to build a tower of four small blocks
Three-year level	Asked to copy a drawing of a circle; asked to repeat three digits in order.
Four-year level	Asked to fill in the blank: "In daytime it is light; at night it is _____;" asked to repond to: "Why do we have houses?"
Five-year level	Asked to fold a piece of paper into the form of a triangle; asked to define simple words, such as "hat."
Six-year level	Asked to tell the difference between "a slipper and a boot;" asked to hand the examiner nine small blocks.
Eight-year level	Asked to answer questions about a simple story; asked to tell the similarities and differences between "airplane and kite."
Ten-year level	Asked to define abstract words, such as "grief;" asked to repeat six digits from memory
Twelve-year level	Asked to say what is foolish about: "Bill's feet are so big that he has to put his pants on over his head;" asked to repeat five digits from memory in reverse order.

a few minutes, you have decided that you can skip over the 2- and 3-year level items and give him full credit for them. You start with the 4-year level items, and your subject does just fine. He also does well at the 5-year level. With some difficulty, he responds correctly to enough items to earn full credit at the 6-year level. He then fails to get credit for any 7-year level items, and you stop testing before he becomes too frustrated. Your subject has performed just as you would expect an average 6-year-old to perform. So his mental age is 6. But his chronological age is 8, leading you to the conclusion that his IQ is 75—6/8 x 100 = 75. Although not retarded (see our next topic), his IQ is, in fact, below average.

Indeed, whenever someone has a mental age that exceeds his or her chronological age, their IQ will be greater than 100. Whenever someone has the mental capacity (as measured by this test) of someone younger, her or his IQ will be below 100.

Evaluating the Instrument   The Stanford-Binet test has been used for a long time. There is much to be said for it. It is a well-recognized measure of those behaviors that we commonly label intelligent—at least in an educational or academic sense—and is, in that way at least, a valid instrument. It is also quite reliable, although we can expect a change in scores of as much as 10 points on repeated administrations (an IQ score of 100 ought to be thought of as representing a true IQ somewhere between 90 and 110).

The Stanford-Binet also has some drawbacks. It is an individual test (one subject and one examiner) and should be administered, scored, and interpreted only by well-trained professionals. The test takes as long as an hour to administer and, hence, is quite expensive.

The test is heavily weighted with verbal items—vocabulary, sentence interpretation, and the like. There are very few performance items, particularly at the older age levels. The test yields but one score—a general, overall IQ score—with no indication of any possible strengths or weaknesses in specific or particular intellectual tasks. The scoring of the test does not consider any of the factor-type theories or models of intelligence we discussed earlier. It is also true that the Stanford-Binet is best suited for young children, the group for which it was originally designed. Its value as a measure of intellectual ability for the normal college-aged population is questionable.

Before you go on

Briefly describe the Stanford-Binet intelligence scale.

What are MA and CA, and how are they used to calculate an IQ?

The Wechsler Tests of Intelligence

David Wechsler published his first general intelligence test in 1939. It was designed for use with adult populations; it was also designed to reduce the heavy reliance on verbal skills that Wechsler saw as one of the major shortcomings of the Stanford-Binet test. With a major revision in 1955, the test became known as the **Wechsler Adult Intelligence Scale (WAIS).** The latest revision (now called the WAIS-R) was published in 1981. The WAIS-R is appropriate for subjects between 16 and 74 years of age and is reported to be the most commonly used of all tests in clinical practice (Lubin et al., 1984).

A natural extension of the WAIS was the **Wechsler Intelligence Scale for Children (WISC),** which was originally published 11 years after the WAIS. After a major revision in 1974, it became known as the WISC-R. The WISC-R is appropriate for testing children between the ages of 6 and 17 (there is some overlap with the WAIS). A third test in the Wechsler series is designed for younger children between the ages of 4 and 6-1/2. It is called the **Wechsler Preschool and Primary Scale of Intelligence,** or **WPPSI.** It was first published in 1967.

Wechsler Adult Intelligence Scale-Revised (WAIS-R); Wechsler Intelligence Scale for Children-Revised (WISC-R); Wechsler Preschool and Primary Scale of Intelligence (WPPSI). David Wechsler's IQ tests, each for a different age range of subjects and all composed of both verbal and performance subtests

The Structure of the Test There are some subtle differences among the three Wechsler tests, but each is based on the same general logic. As such, we'll consider only one, the WAIS-R, in any detail.

The WAIS-R is made up of 11 subtests, or scales. Unlike the Stanford-Binet, the subtests of the WAIS-R are not arranged by age level, but by the *type* of information or skill being tested. The subtests are organized into two main categories. Six subtests define the *verbal scale,* and five subtests constitute a *performance scale.* Figure 25.6 lists the different subtests of the WAIS-R and describes some of the sorts of items found on each.

With the Wechsler scales, we have IQ tests that are quite different from the Stanford-Binet in both content and format. The most notable difference is the addition of performance items. With the Wechsler tests, we can now deal with three types of IQ—verbal IQ, performance IQ, and total IQ.

Determining IQs To administer the WAIS-R, you present each of the 11 subtests to your subject. The items within each subtest are arranged in order of difficulty. You start with relatively easy items—those you are confident that your examinee will respond to correctly—and then you progress to more difficult ones. You stop administering any one subtest when your subject fails a specified number of items in a row. You alternate between performance and verbal subtests. The whole process takes up to an hour and a half.

Each item on each subtest is scored. (Some of the performance items have strict time limits that affect scoring.) You now have 11 scores earned by your subject (called *raw scores*). Each subtest raw score is compared to the score provided with the test's norms appropriate for your subject's age. The WAIS-R was standardized on a large representative sample of nearly 2,000 adults in nine different age groups. How your subject's score compares to the score earned by subjects of the same age in the norm group determines your

The Wechsler Adult Intelligence Scale (WAIS-R) is a general intelligence test for subjects between 16 and 74. The WAIS-R tests a variety of different types of information and skills, such as the test of object assembly shown here.

Figure 25.6

The subtests of the Wechsler Adult Intelligence Scale-Revised (WAIS-R)

Verbal Scale

Information	(29 items) Questions designed to tap one's general knowledge about a variety of topics dealing with one's culture; e.g., "Who wrote *Huckleberry Finn*?" or "How many nickels in a quarter?"
Digit span	(7 series) Subject is read a series of 3 to 9 digits and is asked to repeat them; then a different series is to be repeated in reverse order.
Comprehension	(16 items) A test of judgment, common sense, and practical knowledge; e.g., "Why is it good to have prisons?"
Similarities	(14 pairs) Subject must indicate the way(s) in which two things are alike; e.g., "In what way are an apple and a potato alike?"
Vocabulary	(35 words) Subject must provide an acceptable definition for a series of words.
Arithmetic	(14 problems) Math problems must be solved without the use of paper and pencil; e.g., "How far will a bird travel in 90 minutes if it flies at the rate of 10 miles per hour?"

Performance scale

Picture completion	(20 pictures) Subject must identify or name the missing part or object in a drawing; e.g., a wagon with only three wheels.
Picture arrangement	(10 series) A series of cartoonlike pictures must be arranged in an order so that they tell a story.
Block design	(9 items) Using blocks whose sides are either all red, all white, or diagonally red and white, subject must copy a designed picture or pattern shown on a card.
Object assembly	(4 objects) Free-form jigsaw puzzles must be put together to form familiar objects.
Digit symbol	In a key, each of nine digits is paired with a simple symbol. Given a random series of digits, the subject must provide the paired symbol within a time limit.

subject's *standard score* for each of the Wechsler subtests. If your subject scores right at the average for his or her group, the resulting IQ will be 100. If his or her score is above that listed in the norms, the resulting IQ will be proportionately higher than 100. If your subject did not do as well as the subjects in the norm group, the resulting IQ will be below 100.

With the Wechsler tests, then, we do not compute IQ as a quotient (of MA over CA, or anything else). IQs are determined by comparing the score earned by a subject compared to scores earned by those subjects in the norm group and are called *deviation* IQs because they reflect the extent to which earned scores deviate from the norms. Scoring in this manner allows for sensible verbal IQ and performance IQ, as well as a full scale or total IQ.

The Wechsler scales provide a degree of insight that is not possible with the Stanford-Binet. By having separate subtest scores, we can look beyond the total IQ and see where that score comes from. Two subjects may each have an IQ of 115 as determined by the WAIS-R. An examination of their verbal and performance subtest scores may reveal that they earned that total score in quite different ways, however. One may have done very well on most of the performance subtests and only average on the verbal subtests, while the other subject may have shown the opposite pattern of scores. In fact, finding differences between verbal IQ and performance IQ levels is not at all uncommon. When these differences are large, we may have reason to suspect some sort of possible brain damage or psychopathology.

Before you go on
What are the major features of the Wechsler intelligence scales?

Group Tests of Intelligence

There are a number of advantages of individually administered tests, such as the Wechsler tests and the Stanford-Binet. Perhaps most important is that the examiner has the opportunity to meaningfully interact with the subject taking the test. The examiner can use the testing session to develop opinions about the examinee and can observe first-hand how the subject goes about responding to test items.

The major disadvantage of the individually administered tests is that they are time-consuming and expensive. There are, of course, alternative, group tests of intelligence available. Group IQ tests are generally paper-and-pencil tests that can be administered to many individuals at one time.

When World War I began, Binet's IQ test had already gained wide approval, and the notion of using psychological methods to measure abilities and aptitudes was generally accepted. There was good reason to know the intellectual capabilities of the thousands of recruits who were entering the armed services. All these men obviously could not be tested individually. A committee of psychologists was charged with the task of creating a group intelligence test. The result, published in 1917, was the Army Alpha test, a paper-and-pencil test that made rough discriminations among examinees on the basis of intelligence. We should note that in the same year, the same committee published the Army Beta test. The Beta was designed for illiterates who could not read the Army Alpha. It was largely a performance test, whose instructions were given orally, or were acted out to the examinees.

The military continues to be a major publisher and consumer of group intelligence tests. World War II provided the opportunity for a major revision of the Army Alpha and Beta. The revision was so total that a new test was born: the Army General Classification Test (AGCT). The AGCT was a paper-and-pencil test that was published in four alternate forms. Like the individual IQ tests, it was scored using standard scores, with average being equal to 100. It also allowed subscores for verbal ability, arithmetic compu-

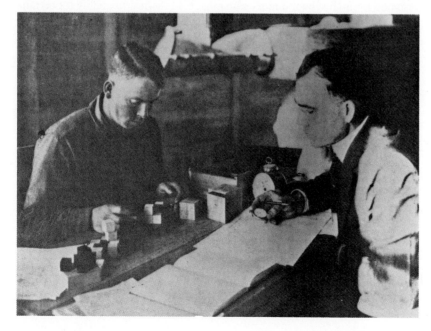

The first large-scale use of intelligence tests in America was during World War I when the Army tested potential recruits.

tation, arithmetic reasoning, and spatial relations. The AGCT has now been replaced by the Armed Forces Qualification Test (AFQT), and anyone who goes through the process of military induction will have first-hand experience with this group IQ test.

In addition to the military, the other large-scale consumer of group intelligence tests is the educational establishment. There are literally dozens of group-administered tests available that are designed to provide an assessment of overall intellectual ability. Let's name a few of the more commonly used tests.

There has been a long history of group IQ tests associated with Arthur Otis, one of Terman's students at Stanford. The one used most often was the Otis-Lennon Mental Ability Tests, designed for children from kindergarten through high school. It yields an IQ score. It has been replaced by the Otis-Lennon School Ability Test (OLSAT). This test is also appropriate for children throughout the school years and also yields IQ score approximations. Its main advantage is the huge sample of subjects who comprise the norm group.

The Cognitive Abilities Test, or CAT, is another group test that is popular in many school systems. It is really a series of tests, each appropriate for different age levels from kindergarten through grade 12. One advantage of the CAT is that it provides items and norms that allow for the calculation of verbal, quantitative, and nonverbal IQs, as well as an overall, general score.

When psychological tests are used to make predictions about future behaviors, we call them *aptitude tests*. However, the fact is that many of the aptitude tests used in the context of education are essentially tests of general intellectual ability. In their construction and administration, they are much like any general intelligence test. The difference is in the use to which the score is put: predicting future academic success. The two most commonly used college entrance tests are the SAT (Scholastic Aptitude Test), which yields verbal and mathematics subscores as well as an overall score, and the ACT (American College Testing Program). The College Entrance Examination Board, which publishes the SAT, also publishes the PSAT (Preliminary Scholastic Aptitude Test), which is becoming increasingly popular. It is designed for high school juniors who must take the test to qualify for certain scholarships; often it is taken as practice for the SAT.

As their college careers come to a close, students may once again face the task of taking a standardized aptitude test if they wish to go to graduate school or to a professional school. Each type of professional school—medical school, law school, and so on—has its own type of exam. The Graduate Record Exam (GRE) is more like an advanced form of the SAT. These tests, too, are essentially paper-and-pencil IQ tests, but are used for prediction purposes.

Before you go on
What are the advantages of group intelligence tests?

How are paper-and-pencil IQ tests and educational aptitude tests alike?

It may be acceptable to define intelligence as "that which an intelligence test measures." Such operational definitions do have a number of advantages. On the other hand, from time to time we need to remind ourselves that intelligence and IQ *are not* synonymous terms. Intelligence is a sort of personality trait. It is something that a person has. It is a system of complex cognitive skills and abilities. An IQ is simply a number. Yes, it is a number that we use to try to reflect the extent, or amount, of intelligence, but it is not intelligence itself.

Let's consider the tests we've reviewed in this topic in the light of the characteristics of good tests that we introduced in Topic 24. Are IQ tests reliable? That is, do they measure whatever they measure consistently? Yes, the individually-administered IQ tests are very reliable—among the most reliable psychological tests we have. The group intelligence tests are less consistent; scores on retesting with most of the group tests may vary considerably. For this reason, group-administered tests are usually recommended for rough screening purposes only. What all this means, of course, is that any one IQ score should not be taken too seriously. Even the best of tests is such that upon retesting, an IQ score may vary considerably. Max's parents know that an average IQ score is 100 and are very upset when Max brings home a test report from school indicating an IQ of 94. They know that's below average, and they begin to wonder if something is wrong with Max. Of course, if Max were to take the same test again, he might earn a score of 107, which, no doubt, would please his parents, but would also remind us that IQ tests are not perfectly reliable.

Are IQ tests valid? That is, do they really measure what they claim to measure? This is clearly a difficult question to answer directly. To assess a test's validity, one correlates test performance with performance on some other, independent criterion measure. What shall we take as the criterion measure for an intelligence test? What other, independent assessment of intelligence do we have when we can barely agree on a working definition of what intelligence *is*? Most intelligence tests have been validated against the criterion of success or failure within the educational system—how well one does in school. On this criterion, the most commonly used IQ tests are demonstrably quite valid. But is school and academic success a true independent assessment of intelligence? In fact, there has been a move lately to rename intelligence tests something like "general academic achievement tests," but such a well-intentioned idea is not likely to gain much general support.

The third criterion for a good test is that it has adequate norms, or standard scores, against which individual scores can be compared to give them meaning and significance. On this criterion, intelligence tests fare very well. All of the commonly used IQ tests—even of the group-administration type—have excellent norms. Given the popularity of these tests, new scores can constantly be added to available norms to keep them up to date.

When Terman and his associates at Stanford revised Binet's intelligence test, they did more than simply translate the test into English. They made a special effort to Americanize the test. They eliminated questions about French forms of government, for example, and included tasks and questions they felt were appropriate for average American children.

There is an appeal to the logic that a test ought to reflect the culture in which it is going to be used. This seems particularly true for tests designed to measure general intelligence. There is, however, a compelling alternative point of view. A test designed to reflect a given culture will almost surely reflect the mainstream values and experiences of that culture. By definition then, the test will be biased against anyone who has not had the opportunity to share in those mainstream cultural experiences.

Rural children may have no idea of what a subway is. Ghetto residents could hardly be expected to know that "bogey" means "one over par" on the golf course. Hispanics for whom English is a second language may have difficulty even understanding the examiner's questions. Do these examples reflect a lack of intelligence, or a lack of

Figure 25.7
Sample items from the Culture Fair Intelligence Test.
(From Cattell & Cattell, 1960.)

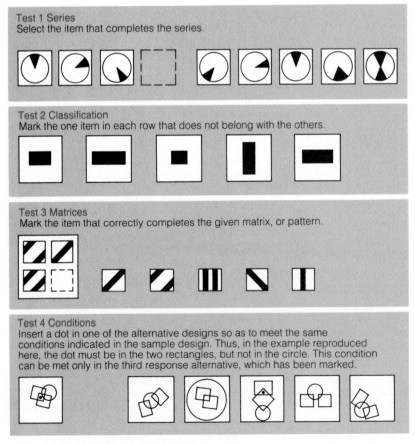

Test 1 Series
Select the item that completes the series.

Test 2 Classification
Mark the one item in each row that does not belong with the others.

Test 3 Matrices
Mark the item that correctly completes the given matrix, or pattern.

Test 4 Conditions
Insert a dot in one of the alternative designs so as to meet the same conditions indicated in the sample design. Thus, in the example reproduced here, the dot must be in the two rectangles, but not in the circle. This condition can be met only in the third response alternative, which has been marked.

From Culture Fair Intelligence Test *by R. B. Cattell and A. K. S. Cattell. Copyright © by the Institute for Personality and Ability Testing, Inc., 1949, 1960. Reproduced by permission.*

experience with standard, white, middle-class, well-educated, suburban society? After all, the people who write intelligence tests are seldom poor, uneducated, rural members of an ethnic minority.

Although this controversy is still very much with us, it is not a new one. It surfaced soon after intelligence tests first became popular. Psychologists then tried to write tests that were culture-free assessments of intellectual ability. Of necessity, they tended to be nonverbal, and often included items of the sort found on the performance scale of the Wechsler tests. Unfortunately, these tests did not meet with much success.

Early claims for culture-*free* tests soon softened. The intent of test writers became one of producing tests that were at least culture *fair* and that minimized the influence of any prevailing cultural experience. Although they are still used primarily for research purposes, some promising tests have emerged from this effort. We shall briefly consider two: the Culture Fair Intelligence Test and The Raven Progressive Matrices.

The Culture Fair Intelligence Test was first published in 1949. It was written by R. B. Cattell and K. S. Cattell and remains quite popular. It comes in three forms: for young children, for older children and adults, and for bright adults and college students. It is meant to be a test of reasoning ability rather than a test of what one has learned through experience with one's culture. Each scale is made up of four subtests, series, classifications, matrices, and conditions. Examples of items are shown in Figure 25.7.

The Raven Progressive Matrices test was published in its first edition in 1938 by L. S. Penrose and J. C. Raven. Since then, many different forms and versions have been published (Raven Court, & Raven, 1978). Like the Cattells' test, this one is also nonverbal and requires a sort of reasoning that should be free from cultural experience.

Do either of these tests do what their creators intended? Well, a little. Scores on both tests do correlate reasonably well with scores on the Stanford-Binet and the Wechsler—a degree of concurrent validity. Curiously, the Progressive Matrices test correlates as well with the verbal scale on the Wechsler as it does with the performance scale. As you may have guessed, scores on either of these tests are not particularly well correlated with academic performance (which designers of the test see as a plus—they measure something more basic than academic achievement perhaps). Even though designed to be as free from cultural bias as possible, it remains true that, in general, middle-class white subjects score higher on both these tests than do other ethnic or cultural groups.

Provide an operational definition of intelligence.

Can you offer a definition of intelligence that is not an operational definition?

Operationally defined, intelligence can be taken to be "that which an intelligence test measures." More generally, or theoretically, we may define intelligence as "the capacity of an individual to understand the world about him or her and his or her resourcefulness to cope with its challenges." / 464

Briefly summarize the basic idea behind three models or theories of intelligence.

Spearman viewed intelligence as being composed of one general factor (g) and a number of specific abilities (s). Thurstone argued that intelligence was a combination of seven primary and unique mental abilities. Guilford argues that there are as many as 120 different skills and abilities that constitute intelligence. Vernon suggests that intellectual skills and cognitive abilities can be arranged in a hierarchy, from very general on the top to very specific on the bottom. For Cattell, the major distinction with regard to intelligence is whether it is fluid, general, and basic, or crystallized, a reflection of what has been learned through experience in one's culture. Recently, psychologists like Sternberg have argued that intelligence should be thought of in terms of cognitive *processes*, not *structures*. / 467

Briefly describe the Stanford-Binet intelligence scale.

What are MA and CA, and how are they used to calculate an IQ?

The Stanford-Binet Scale is made up of a series of subtests. Each subtest is designed for a different age level and contains items that can be responded to correctly by children of that age. Many of the items are verbal in nature. The test is individually administered. It is used to assess a subject's mental age, or MA, which, when divided by the subject's chronological age, or CA, yields an intelligence quotient, or IQ. / 471

What are the major features of the Wechsler intelligence scales?

The Wechsler Scales are individually-administered tests of general intelligence. They are made up of a number of subtests of different content. The subtests are categorized as verbal or performance, and three IQ scores can be determined: verbal, performance, and full scale, or total, IQ. There are three Wechsler tests, each appropriate for different age groups, ranging from ages 4 to 74. / 472

What are the advantages of group intelligence tests?

How are paper-and-pencil IQ tests and educational aptitude tests alike?

Group intelligence tests, used largely in educational and the military, are far more economical than the individually-administered tests, even though they may not be as reliable. They can serve as screening devices. Many educational aptitude tests are essentially paper-and-pencil tests of general intellectual abilities that are used to make predictions about future academic performance. / 474

TOPIC

This topic is concerned with differences in intelligence, differences usually assessed through the use of intelligence tests. To get in the mood for our discussion, why not try the following, simple test of intellectual ability. Try to do your best. Answers are furnished below.

1. T-Bone Walker was famous for playing
   (a) trombone.
   (b) piano.
   (c) T-flute.
   (d) guitar.
   (e) hambone.

2. "Boogie Jugie" means the same as
   (a) tired.
   (b) worthless.
   (c) old.
   (d) well put together.

3. If you throw the dice and seven is showing on the top, what is facing down?
   (a) seven.
   (b) snake eyes.
   (c) boxcars.
   (d) little Joe.
   (e) eleven.

4. Black Draught is a
   (a) winter's cold wind.
   (b) laxative.
   (c) black soldier.
   (d) dark beer.

5. Hully Gully came from
   (a) East Oakland.
   (b) Fillmore.
   (c) Watts.
   (d) Harlem.
   (e) Motor City.

6. An alley apple is a
   (a) brick.
   (b) piece of fruit.
   (c) dog.
   (d) horse.

7. A gas head is a person who has a
   (a) fast-moving car.
   (b) stable of "lace."
   (c) process.
   (d) habit of stealing cars.
   (e) long jail record for arson.

8. A blood is
   (a) a vampire.
   (b) a dependent individual.
   (c) an injured person.
   (d) a brother of color.

9. A handkerchief head is
   (a) a cool cat.
   (b) a porter.
   (c) an Uncle Tom.
   (d) a hoddi.
   (e) a preacher.

10. "Boot" refers to
    (a) a cotton farmer.
    (b) a Black.
    (c) an Indian.
    (d) a Vietnamese citizen.

How do you suppose you did on this little test? The answers (honest) are as follows: 1–d; 2–b; 3–a; 4–b; 5–c; 6–a; 7–c; 8–d; 9–c; 10–b. As much as I might like to take credit for being creative enough to generate items like these, this quiz combines items from two well-known tests. The odd-numbered items are from the Counterbalance General Intelligence Test authored by Adrian Dove (1968), and the even-numbered items come from the BITCH test—that's the Black Intelligence Test of Cultural Homogeniety, by Robert Williams (1972).

Both of these tests make the basic point that when we consider any comparisons of individuals, or groups of individuals, in terms of their intelligence, we should seriously consider the fairness of the test used to assess that intelligence. Both Williams and Dove would argue that the above quiz is a reasonable test of intelligence for urban, ghetto blacks. Most white, middle-class, college students do not do very well on such tests.

Why We Care

Throughout this text we have repeatedly made the point that no two people are exactly alike, that everyone is different from everyone else. One of the most important ways in which people differ is in their intellectual abilities and capabilities. In this topic, we'll review some of the psychological literature on individual and group differences in intelligence.

There are many questions to ask. Who are smarter, men or women? Do people become less intelligent with old age? Are there truly any differences in intelligence between Blacks and whites? Answering these sorts of questions honestly, scientifically, and completely is not really possible at the present time. There are a number of reasons why we can't offer definitive answers to such questions. For one thing, as we saw in our last topic, there is less than perfect agreement on just what intelligence *is*. For another, there are serious questions about the precision, as well as the fairness, of even our best instruments for measuring intelligence.

So what we'll do in this topic is raise some interesting questions about differences in intelligence, provide the best quality answers we can at the moment, and continually caution against overinterpretation of incomplete data. We'll start with a general discussion of the roles of heredity and environment in determining intellectual functioning. We'll look at some data on differences in intelligence as a function of two different characteristics: sex and age. Finally, we'll consider the individual extremes of intelligence, the mentally gifted and the mentally retarded.

INTELLIGENCE: THE INFLUENCE OF HEREDITY AND ENVIRONMENT

Are the differences we observe in intelligence due to heredity or to environmental influences? This is one of the oldest and most enduring questions in all of psychology. As reasonable as the question may sound, it is one that does not have a certain answer. As we shall see, there is some evidence that intelligence tends to run in families and might be due in part to innate, inherited factors. There are also data (and common sense) that tell us that a person's environment can and does affect intellectual, cognitive functioning. After all these years of scientific investigation, why can't we provide an answer to this question?

Conceptual Problems with the Heredity vs. Environment Question

When we ask about the origin of intelligence, we have two large conceptual problems (and many smaller ones). One difficulty, which we discussed in Topic 25, is our inability to define intelligence to everyone's satisfaction. Unable to settle on just one definition, we usually end up relying on intelligence tests to provide operational measures of intelligence. But, as we have seen, there continues to be substantial disagreement about the quality and the fairness of our IQ tests.

Our second major problem has to do with the limitations of research design, specifically, the lack of adequate controls. Just how can we determine if *any* trait, such as intelligence, is genetic (inherited) or experiential (environmental) in origin? In theory, a couple of approaches come to mind. We could take individuals with exactly the same genetic constitution (such as identical twins) and rear them in different environments. Or, we could take people of clearly different genetic constitution and raise them in identical environments. Either sort of experimental manipulation might prove to be very helpful in separating the two major influences on intelligence.

It doesn't take very long to figure out why such manipulations are not possible—at least with human subjects. How could we ever guarantee that any two persons were raised in identical environments? How can we ever get more than two subjects at a time who have exactly the same genetic constitution? And even with pairs of subjects, who's to decide what kind of environments each would be assigned? No matter how important we feel our scientific question is, we cannot simply pluck children out of their homes and systematically assign them to different environmental conditions. We cannot raise children in cardboard boxes for a few years just to see what cognitive abilities might develop without the benefit of a stimulating environment. No, the ethical considerations are all too obvious.

Before you go on

What two major problems have inhibited our search for an answer to the heredity versus environment question with regard to intelligence?

A Tentative Answer

Before we examine any of the supporting evidence, we can offer a tentative answer to our opening question. Both one's heredity *and* the environment are critically important in determining one's intelligence. One's heredity may put limits on what environmental influences can accomplish. Without a nurturing, stimulating environment, even the best of inherited potential may be wasted.

Some people are born with the predisposition to become extremely intelligent. This inherited potential must be encouraged and nurtured in a stimulating environment to be fully realized.

Many programs are evolving that help children develop certain motor, intellectual, and social skills. Many feel that such early physical and intellectual stimulation helps children achieve their fullest potential.

A person does not inherit intelligence. A person inherits genes and chromosomes (see Topic 17). These physical entities may very well set limits for the potentials of our intellectual abilities. Some people may be born with the potential, or even the predisposition, to become very intelligent. If the environment does not encourage that predisposition, however, the potential will be wasted. Some individuals may be born with inherited predispositions that severely limit their intellectual growth. Even the best of stimulating environments may be insufficient to raise intellectual functioning above average levels. The point is that the two, environment and heredity, interact. Each may limit the other. Both are important.

What the Data Suggest: The Study of Twins

Maybe we can't all agree precisely on what intelligence is. But we *can* use IQ test scores as an approximation and as an operational definition. Perhaps we can't do the perfectly controlled heredity/environment experiment. But we *can* look at the relationships among the IQs of people with similar and different genetic histories who have been reared in similar and different environments. Such data may be flawed (Mackenzie, 1984), but perhaps they can give us some helpful leads.

As you might imagine, studies that examine the correlations of IQ test scores of persons with varying degrees of genetic similarity and those reared in similar and dissimilar environments have been done a number of times. The results of some of the better of these studies is summarized in Figure 26.1. These are oft-cited data, and we ought to be sure that we understand what they mean.

On the left side of the figure we have a listing of the types of subjects whose IQ scores have been correlated. As you can see, as we go down the list, the genetic similarity between the subjects increases, from unrelated individuals reared apart to identical twins reared together. The graph shows the average (in this case the median) correlation for each of the pairs of groups named under "Subjects." These correlations represent average values from many correlational studies. Quite clearly, such data, drawn from a number of studies conducted at different times, with different subjects, and with different intents, need to be interpreted with great caution. Even with the variability reflected in these data, however, a few general conclusions seem reasonable.

As genetic similarities between subjects increase, correlations also increase. Correlations between the IQ scores of individuals who are unrelated in any biological sense appear quite low. Remembering that fraternal twins are just brothers and sisters who happen to be born at about the same time, we find that IQs among family members in general are correlated somewhere near 0.50. When we examine the correlations of IQs of identical twins (whose genetic constitutions are the same, of course), we find very high correlations—as high as those usually reported as reliability coefficients for the IQ tests that were used. It seems quite obvious by inspection that genetic similarity and IQ scores are positively related.

You should also notice another apparent difference in the correlations presented in Figure 26.1. It seems that regardless of genetic similarity, correlations for subjects raised together are consistently higher than for subjects raised apart, in different environments. We do need to note that children raised apart need not necessarily be reared in significantly different environments, and being raised together does not guarantee that environments are identical. What these differences do suggest is that environmental influences may also affect IQ scores. As you can see, we are drawn to the conclusion we

The correlation of IQ scores of identical twins is very high (even when the twins are raised apart) due to identical genetic constitutions.

Figure 26.1

Correlations of IQ test scores as a function of genetic and environmental similarity. Vertical lines indicate average (median) correlations, and horizontal lines indicate the range of correlations from many different studies reviewed by Erlenmeyer-Kimling and Jarvik (1963).

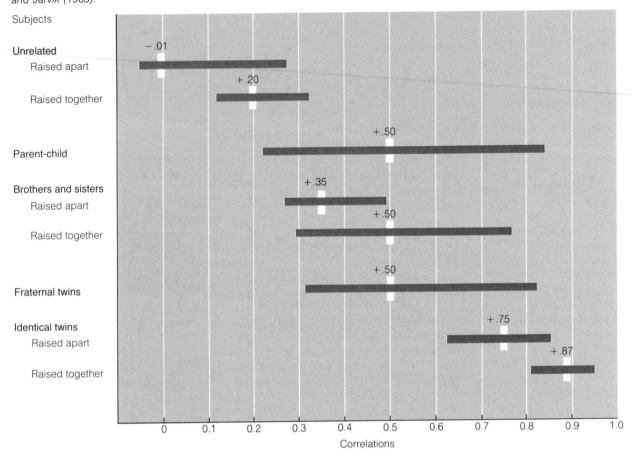

made earlier. Even though we are looking at grouped data, and even though many factors are left uncontrolled, inheritance clearly influences intelligence as measured by IQ test scores, but so does the environment.

A more recent survey of similar literature (Bouchard & McGue, 1981) draws the same general conclusion. After reviewing 111 studies, the authors concluded that genetic similarity is related to intercorrelations of IQ test scores. Identical twins produce correlations in IQ scores fully 20 points higher, on the average, than that found for fraternal twins. Again, however, we need to caution that identical twins are often treated in similar ways (dressed alike, for instance) more so than are fraternal twins.

Additional insight can be gained by examining the IQs of adopted children. This sort of research also focuses on correlational data. Are adopted children's IQs more strongly correlated with the IQs of their biological parents (genetic influence), or with the IQs of their foster or adoptive parents (environmental influence)? Once again, the data appear clear-cut, but their interpretation is not. With large groups of subjects, correlations between the IQs of children and their biological parents are significantly higher (around 0.48) than when correlations are computed between the IQs of children and their adoptive parents (around 0.20). This seems to imply that even changing environments cannot significantly lessen the relationship between the IQs of biological parents and their offspring. But we'd better not make any snap judgments.

Social agencies do not arrange adoption placements in order to satisfy psychologists' needs for adequate experimental control. What we don't know in most of these studies of adopted children is the degree to which the home environments of adoptive and biological parents are the same or different. One study (Scarr & Weinberg, 1976) reports very large increases in IQ scores for children from low socioeconomic background who were placed with families at a higher socioeconomic level. In this study, adoptive parents were of significantly higher educational level than were biological parents. Here, the environment appeared to have a major impact on IQ.

The same researchers, 2 years later (Scarr & Weinberg, 1978), reported another investigation in which socioeconomic status was controlled, at least to some degree. In this study, the researchers concerned themselves only with correlations between the IQs of children and their biological or adoptive parents if the socioeconomic level of both types of parent was approximately equal. The idea, of course, was to reduce environmental impacts that could be attributed to social class differences. In these conditions, there appears to be a much stronger relationship between a child's IQ and that of its biological parents than that of its adoptive parents. Support one more time for the role of inheritance.

To review, the perfect experiment, or correlational study, to determine the relative importance of heredity and the environment has not yet been done. In fact, there is an argument that suggests that it cannot be done. (There is also a compelling argument that there is no reason to even try such research if the only aim is to apportion the relative influence of heredity and environment. What is needed is a focus on the specific determinants of what we call intelligence (Mackenzie, 1984).) From the data that has been collected, there is evidence that can be used to justify almost any rationale: that one, or the other, or both are important. It does seem that, in general, IQ is strongly affected by heredity (at very least, by genetic predispositions). At the same time, it is true that IQ can be influenced or modified by the environment. The more extreme the environmental differences, the greater the predicted shifts in IQ.

Before you go on

In general, what has the study of twins and adopted children told us about the relative importance of heredity and the environment in determining intelligence as measured by IQ tests?

DIFFERENCES IN IQ AS A FUNCTION OF SEX AND AGE

Recognizing that there are individual differences in intelligence, can't we make any reasonable statements about differences in IQ in general? Here are those easy questions again. Who are smarter, women or men? Do we become less intelligent with old age? As you are probably coming to appreciate, straight answers are often misleading and, if interpreted incorrectly, can be dangerous.

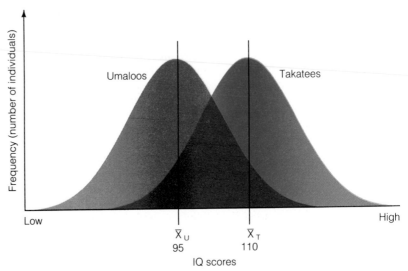

Figure 26.2

Hypothetical distributions of IQ scores for two imaginary groups (Umaloos and Takatees). The average IQ for Takatees ($\overline{X}_T$) is higher than that for Umaloos ($\overline{X}_U$), but there is considerable overlap in the two distributions. That is, some Umaloos have IQs that are higher than the average for Takatees (110) and some Takatees have IQs lower than the average for Umaloos (95).

One thing we have to ask ourselves is why we care. What motivates our interest in knowing about such group differences in IQ? Even the best scientific data can be put to questionable use. Unfortunately, issues of group differences are sometimes raised in order to justify what amounts to social or political ends. Some sexists (male and female), and some racists (black and white), and some ageists (young and old) like to point to any observed differences in IQ for groups of individuals to make claims of superiority or inferiority. It is in such cases that clear-cut straight answers can be dangerous.

More commonly, however, reported mean differences in intelligence test scores are simply misleading. Let's imagine for a moment that I have tested two large groups of people—1,000 Umaloos and 1,000 Takatees. On the average, the mean IQ score for Umaloos is found to be 95; for Takatees, it is 110. An appropriate statistical analysis tells me that this observed difference of 15 points is too large to have been expected by chance. Are Takatees smarter than Umaloos? Yes, *on the average* they are—that's what I just discovered.

Now look at Figure 26.2. Here we find two curves representing the distributions of IQ scores from my fictitious study. We can clearly see the difference in the averages of the two groups. However, there are some Takatees whose IQs are below the average IQ of Umaloos. And there are Umaloos whose IQs are above the average IQ of Takatees. We may be able to draw some conclusions about average IQ levels, but making statements about individual Takatees and Umaloos is difficult.

Perhaps the main reason we care about group differences in intelligence (over and above simple curiosity) is the hope that understanding such differences will help us to understand the true nature of intelligence and the factors that influence its development within individuals. Being able to demonstrate a significant difference between the average IQs of two groups of individuals in itself tells us nothing about why those differences exist. Are Takatees genetically superior to Umaloos? Maybe, maybe not. Have Umaloos had equal experiences with the sorts of things that IQ tests ask about? Maybe, maybe not. Are the tests themselves slanted to provide Takatees with an advantage? Maybe, maybe not. Discovering that two identifiable groups of individuals have different average IQ scores raises more questions than it answers.

Before you go on

If group A and group B have different IQ scores on the average, what may be true about two individuals, one from group A and the other from group B, with regard to intelligence?

Sex Differences and IQ

Now here's a question to which we almost have a definitive answer: Is there a sex difference in measured IQ? Answer: No. At least there are few studies that ever report any differences between men and women on any test of overall, general intelligence of the sort that is represented by an IQ score (Aiken, 1982). Of course, we have to keep in mind that there may be no measurable differences between the IQs of men and women because our IQ tests are constructed in such a way as to minimize or eliminate any such differences. Usually, if an item on an intelligence test clearly discriminates between women and men, it is dropped from consideration.

When we look beyond the global measure that IQ scores afford, there do seem to be some reliable indications of sex differences on specific intellectual skills (which balance each other out on general IQ tests). For example, it is generally the case that females score (on the average, remember) higher than males on tests of clerical speed and accuracy, verbal fluency, reading ability, and fine dexterity (the ability to manipulate small objects). Males, on the other hand, outscore females on tests of mathematical reasoning and spatial relations.

Because they have been encouraged to enroll in math and science classes, males generally outscore females on tests of math reasoning and spatial relations. The data may change in the future as females are encouraged to more fully develop this part of their education. Similarly, males are being encouraged to develop their reading and visual arts skills more.

Tests of spatial relations require the subject to visualize and mentally manipulate figures and forms. What is curious about this rather specialized ability is that males seem to perform better than females on such tasks from an early age, widening the gap through the school years, even though this particular ability seems to be only slightly related to any academic course-work (McGee, 1979). What this means is that sex differences here cannot be easily attributed to differences in educational opportunity.

On the other hand, educational experiences may have a great deal to do with observed differences in mathematical ability. Scores on tests of mathematics and arithmetic skills are very well correlated with the number and nature of math classes taken while a student is in high school (Welch, Anderson, & Harris, 1982). For many reasons, males tend to enroll in advanced math courses at a higher rate than females. It is not surprising, then, that by the time they leave high school, there are significant differences between men and women on tests of mathematical ability. Quoting from a recent article by Lyle Jones (1984) who has conducted many studies of racial differences in IQ, "At age 13, for neither blacks nor whites is there evidence for a mean [average] sex difference in mathematics achievement. . . . At age 17, for both blacks and whites, the mean for males is significantly higher than for females . . . . (p. 1210). This finding is consistent with reports from the College Entrance Examination Board (1982) reporting on sex differences in SAT math scores.

So it seems that any differences that can be found between males and females on intellectual tasks is reasonably small, quite specific, and probably due to environmental influences and schooling experiences—although on this last conclusion, all the data are not yet in.

Before you go on
Are there sex differences in IQ?

Age Differences and IQ

Throughout Chapter 8 (Topics 18 and 19 in particular), we discussed many of the cognitive changes that accompany one's life-long growth and development. Here we might review a few observations concerning the relationship between age and IQ.

You know a great deal more now than you did when you were 12 years old. You knew more when you were 12 than you did when you were 10. You learned a lot in fifth and sixth grade. In fact, when you were 12, you probably believed that you knew more than your parents did. Certainly, what we know generally increases with age. But what we know is not a direct measure of intelligence.

IQ scores are computed in such a way that they remain consistent with age. Remember, the IQ score of the average 12 year old is the same as the IQ of the average 30 year old and the average 60 year old—100. This is true if you use the MA/CA x 100 formula or standard score technique to compute IQs.

But what about the IQ of any one individual? If Kim's IQ is 112 at age 4, will it still be 112 at age 14, or 40, or 80? As it happens, the measured IQs of individuals much younger than 7 do not correlate very well with later IQ scores. We cannot put too much stock in IQs earned by 4 year olds as predictors of adult intellectual abilities. The data in Figure 26.3 are typical in this regard. They show the correlations between IQ scores earned at age 16 to 18 with IQ scores at some younger age. Notice that when previous testing was done before the age of 7 or 8 years, the correlations are quite low.

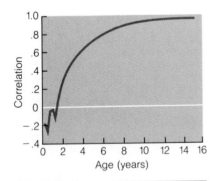

Figure 26.3
Correlations between IQ test scores earned by males between the ages of 16 and 18 with IQ test scores earned at a younger age by the same subjects. Note that there is no correlation (not even a negative one) between IQ at ages 16–18 and IQs determined at ages younger than 3 years. That is, infant and preschool IQ test scores are poor predictors of IQ at older ages. (From Bayley and Schaefer, 1964.)

This does not mean that the testing of young children is without purpose. Determining the intellectual abilities of young children is often very useful, particularly if there is some concern about retardation or developmental delay. The resulting scores may not predict adult intelligence well, but they do serve as a guide to assess the development of the child compared to other children. Even taken as a rough guide or indicator, knowing as early as possible that there may be some cognitive problem with a youngster is useful information.

What about intellectual changes throughout the life span? Does intelligence decrease with old age? You may have anticipated the answer: yes, no, and it depends. Much of the data we have on age differences in IQ scores have been gathered using a **cross-sectional method.** That is, IQ tests are given, at roughly the same time, to a large number of subjects of different ages. When this is done, the results seem to indicate that overall, global IQ peaks in the early 20s, stays rather stable for about 20 years, and then declines rather sharply (for example, Wechsler, 1958).

A different approach to the same question would be to test the same individuals repeatedly, over a long period of time. This is the **longitudinal method.** When this technique is used, things don't look so bad, usually showing IQ scores rising until the mid-50s and then very gradually declining (Schaie, 1974; Schaie & Strother, 1968).

So we have a qualified "yes" and qualified "no" as answers to our question about age and IQ so far. Probably the best answer is "it depends." Careful studies of cognitive abilities, some of which have combined the essential features of longitudinal and cross-sectional designs, demonstrate that we should ask about specific intellectual skills because they do not all decline at the same rate, and some do not decline at all. For example, tests of vocabulary often show no drop in scores with increasing age (Blum, Jarvik, & Clark, 1970), while tests of verbal fluency often show steep declines beginning at age 30 (Schaie & Strother, 1968).

Another "it depends" answer comes to the surface when we consider the distinction between fluid and crystallized intelligence (Horn & Cattell, 1966). It appears that fluid intelligence—abilities that relate to speed, adaptation, flexibility, and abstract reasoning—are the sorts of skills that show the greatest decline with age. On the other hand, it seems that crystallized intelligence—abilities that depend on acquired knowledge, accumulated experiences, and general information—are the sorts of skills that remain quite constant or even increase throughout one's lifetime (Horn, 1976; Vernon, 1979).

cross-sectional method
a research method in which a number of subjects of different ages are compared on some measure at the same time

longitudinal method
a research method in which measures are taken on the same subjects repeatedly over time

Before you go on
Does intelligence decline with age, increase with age, or stay the same?

THE EXTREMES OF INTELLIGENCE

When we look at the IQs earned by large, random samples of individuals, we find a predictable distribution of scores. The most common, or frequently occurring, score is the average IQ score, 100. Most of the other earned scores are relatively close to this average. In fact, virtually 95 percent of all IQ scores fall between 70 and 130. What we want to consider in this section of our topic are those individuals whose IQ scores place them in the extremes, in the "tails" of the IQ curve. First we'll look at the upper extreme, then the lower.

The Mentally Gifted

There are many ways in which a person can be gifted. A United States Office of Education report (1972) suggests that giftedness be defined as a demonstrated achievement or aptitude for excellence in any one of six areas:

(1) *Psychomotor ability.* This is one of the most overlooked areas in which some individuals can clearly excel. We are dealing here with people of outstanding abilities in skills requiring agility, strength, speed, quickness, coordination, and the like.

(2) *Visual and performing arts.* Some people, even as children, demonstrate an unusual talent for arts, music, drama, and writing.

(3) *Leadership ability.* Leadership skills are valued in most societies, and there seem to be individuals who are particularly gifted in this area. This is often true even with very young children. Youngsters with good leadership skills tend to be intellectually bright, but they are not necessarily the smartest of the group.

(4) *Creative or productive thinking.* This area of giftedness has received considerable attention over the past 25 years. Here we are talking about individuals who may be intellectually or academically above average, but, again, not necessarily so. Among other things, people with this type of giftedness are able to generate unique and different solutions to problems.

(5) *Specific academic aptitude.* In this case, we are talking about people who have a flair or special ability for a particular subject or two. Someone who is a real whiz in math, history, or laboratory science, without necessarily being outstanding in other academic areas, would fit this category. (A more common form of the idiot savant syndrome, perhaps.)

(6) *Intellectually gifted.* Inclusion in this group is based on scores earned on a general intelligence test, usually a Wechsler test or the Stanford-Binet Scale. It is most likely that when people use the term "mentally gifted," they are referring to individuals who would fit this category—people of exceptionally high IQ. (IQ scores of 130 or above usually qualify for inclusion in this category. Some prefer to reserve the label for those with IQs above 135. In either case, we are dealing with a very small portion of the population—fewer than 3 percent qualify.)

How can we describe intellectually gifted individuals? Most of what we know about the **mentally gifted** comes directly, or indirectly, from a classic study begun by L. M. Terman in the early 1920s. This is the same Terman who revised Binet's IQ test in 1916. With that test ready to go, Terman supervised the testing of more than a quarter of a million children throughout California. Terman's research group at Stanford University focused its attention on those children who earned the highest scores—about 1,500 in all, each with an IQ above 135.

Louis Terman died in 1956, but the study of those mentally gifted individuals—who were between the ages of 8 and 12 in 1922—still continues. Ever since their inclusion in the original study, and at regular intervals, they have been retested, surveyed, interviewed, and polled by psychologists still at Stanford (Goleman, 1980; Oden, 1968; Sears, 1977).

The Terman study has its drawbacks—choosing a very narrow definition of gifted in terms of IQ alone is an obvious one. Failing to control for factors such as socioeconomic level or parents' educational level is another. Nonetheless, the study is an impressive one—for having been continued for more than 60 years, if nothing else. What can this longitudinal analysis tell us about people with very high IQs?

Giftedness can be defined as a demonstrated achievement or aptitude for excellence in one of six areas, including the visual arts. Some people demonstrate great artistic ability, even as children.

mentally gifted
demonstrating outstanding ability or aptitude in a number of possible areas; usually general intelligence, where an IQ of 130 is a standard criterion

Most of Terman's results fly in the face of the common stereotype of the bright child as being skinny, anxious, clumsy, of poor health, and almost certainly wearing thick glasses (Sears, 1977). The data just do not support the stereotype. In fact, if there is any overall conclusion that might be drawn from the Terman-Stanford study, it is that, in general, the gifted children experienced advantages in virtually everything. They were taller, faster, better coordinated, had better eyesight, fewer emotional problems, and tended to stay married longer than average. All sorts of obvious things were also true of this sample of bright children, now oldsters. They received much more education, found better, higher-paying jobs, and had more intelligent children than did people of average intelligence. By now we certainly know better than to overgeneralize. Every one of Terman's children (sometimes referred to as "Termites") did not grow up to be rich and famous and live happily ever after. The truth is that many did, but not all.

Before you go on

List six ways in which individuals can be considered to be gifted.

Summarize the basic findings of the Terman-Stanford study of intellectually gifted youngsters.

The Mentally Retarded

Issues of Definition   Intelligence as measured by IQ tests is often used to confirm suspected cases of **mental retardation.** But, as is the case for the mentally gifted, there is more to retardation than IQ alone. The definition provided by the American Association on Mental Deficiency (AAMD) cites three factors to consider, "subaverage general intellectual functioning which originated during the developmental period and is associated with impairment in adaptive behavior" (Grossman, 1973). Let's look at each of these three points.

mental retardation
a condition, indicated by an IQ below 70, which begins during the developmental period and is associated with impairment in adaptive functioning

The IQ cutoff for mental retardation is usually taken to be 70. The AAMD further categorizes mental retardation as follows:

IQ 70–85—borderline or slow
IQ 50–69—mildly mentally retarded
IQ 35–49—moderately mentally retarded
IQ 20–34—severely mentally retarded
IQ less than 19—profoundly mentally retarded

As you review this list, you need to keep two things in mind. (1) These IQ test scores are suggested limits. Given what we know about IQ tests and their reliability, it is ridiculous to claim after one administration of a test that a person with an IQ of 69 is mentally retarded, while someone else with an IQ of 71 is not. (2) Diagnosis of mental retardation is not (should not be) made on the basis of IQ score alone.

To fit the definition of mental retardation given above, the cause or the symptoms of the below-average intellectual functioning must show up during the usual period of intellectual development (up to age 18). In many circles, the term "developmentally delayed" is coming to replace the narrower term "mentally retarded." Actual diagnosis may come only after the administration of an IQ test, but initial suspicions generally come from perceived delays in normal developmental or adjustive patterns of behavior.

By making "impairment in adaptive behavior" a part of their definition of mental retardation, the AAMD is acknowledging that there is more to getting along in this world than the intellectual and academic sorts of skills that IQ tests emphasize. Being mentally retarded does not necessarily mean being totally helpless, particularly for those who fall in the categories of more moderate levels of retardation. Of major consideration is (or ought to be) the individual's ability to adapt to his or her environment. In this regard, such skills as the ability to dress oneself, to follow directions, to make change, to find one's way home from a distance, and so on, become very relevant (Coulter & Morrow, 1978). As it happens, there are a number of psychological assessment devices that try to measure these very skills. Two of the more commonly used scales are the Vineland Social Maturity Scale (Doll, 1965), which yields a *social age* score, not unlike Binet's mental age score, and the AAMD's Adaptive Behavior Scale (1974).

Even without a simple, one-dimensional definition, it is clear that the population of retarded citizens is a large one. It is very difficult to obtain exact figures because many individuals who might fit the criteria and be classified as mildly retarded have never been diagnosed as such. Even so, standard estimates indicate that approximately 3 percent of the population at any one time falls within the IQ range for retardation. Let's now turn to a brief discussion of the causes, treatment, and prevention of mental retardation.

Before you go on

How might we best define mental retardation?

Causes, Treatment, and Prevention   We don't really know what causes *average* intelligence. We have little idea what causes someone to be mentally gifted. We can't begin to explain the causes of all mental retardation, but at least we have a number of good ideas. In fact, we suspect that there are hundreds of possible causes; at the moment, the list of known, or highly suspected, causes exceeds 100. The more we learn about the sources of mental retardation, the better able we will be to treat it or to prevent it altogether.

Approximately one quarter of all cases of mental retardation reflect some problem that developed before, during, or just after birth. Between 15 and 20 percent of those referred to as retarded were born prematurely, where prematurity is defined as being born at least 3 weeks before the due date *or* at a weight below 5 pounds, 8 ounces.

We are coming to appreciate more and more how the health of the mother during pregnancy can affect the health of her child. All sorts of prenatal conditions are thought to cause developmental delays, including hypertension, exposure to X-rays, lowered oxygen intake, rubella (German measles), maternal syphilis, and the mother's use of a wide range of drugs, from powerful narcotics to the frequent use of aspirin, from alcohol to nicotine. To greater and lesser degrees, all of these have been linked to mental retardation. In addition, of course, there are those cases that stem from difficulties or injuries during the birth process itself.

The extent to which normal levels of intelligence are inherited is open to debate. Some types of mental retardation, however, are clearly genetic in origin. One of the clearest examples of such a case is the intellectual retardation that accompanies Down's syndrome. We don't know why it happens, but occasionally a fetus develops with 47 chromosomes instead of the usual 46, or 23 pairs. (We do know that Down's syndrome becomes more likely as the age of the parents increases.) The clinical signs of Down's syndrome are well known: small round skull, flattened face, large tongue, short broad nose, broad hands, short stubby fingers, and so on (see Figure 26.4). During childhood, behavioral development is noticeably delayed. Down's syndrome children may fall into any of the levels of retardation listed above. Many are

Figure 26.4
Many Down's syndrome individuals are educable and can enjoy social interaction, though supervision is often required.

educable and lead lives of considerable independence, although it is generally true that even as adults, most will require supervision at least some of the time.

Most cases of mental retardation do not have such obvious causes. They are more subtle in their origin. They may by brought on by lack of decent nutrition in infancy (or prenatally). As we have already noted, anything approaching extremes of deprivation of any sort may lead to delays in intellectual functioning.

Quite clearly, our ability to treat and/or prevent mental retardation depends on our ability to specify its causes. More than that, however, history tells us that we will probably have better luck finding ways to prevent mental retardation than we will in finding ways to significantly change it. Special education programs have helped. Preparing teachers and mental health professionals to be sensitive to the wide range of behaviors and feelings that mentally retarded persons *are* capable of has helped. Impressive changes *can* be made in raising the IQs of some mildly retarded, and a few moderately retarded, children. For severely and profoundly retarded individuals, the outlook is not bright, at least not in terms of IQ points. (And we always need to remind ourselves that quality of life is not necessarily a function of IQ.) The emphasis in recent years has been to focus less on overall intellectual growth and more on those specific skills and abilities—social as well as intellectual— that *can* be improved.

There is greater hope in the area of prevention. As we come to appreciate the influences of the prenatal environment on the development of cognitive abilities, we can educate mothers (and fathers) about how their behaviors can affect their child even before it is born. Another excellent example of how mental retardation can be prevented concerns a disorder called **phenylketonuria,** or **PKU.** This disorder is genetic in origin, and 50 years ago it was discovered to be a cause of mental retardation. Soon thereafter, a simple test was developed that could detect the disorder in newborns (usually right in the delivery room). With detection, a simple prescribed diet can reduce or eliminate any of the retardation effects of the disorder.

phenylketonuria (PKU)
a genetically-caused disorder that produces mental retardation; it is now detectable and preventable

Before you go on
List some of the possible causes of mental retardation.

That there are significant differences between the IQ test scores of black and white Americans is not a new discovery. It was one of the first conclusions drawn from the testing program for Army recruits in World War I. Since then, many studies have reconfirmed the fact that whites score approximately 15 points higher on general IQ tests than blacks. Blacks even seem to earn lower scores than whites on performance tests and culture fair tests (Jensen, 1980). The nagging question, of course, is *why*.

The proposed answers have been very controversial and return us to three possibilities that we have touched on before in other contexts: (1) The *tests themselves* are slanted, biased, and unfair. Recalling the short quiz that opened this topic should remind you of the gist of this argument. (2) Black-white differences in IQ scores can be attributed to *environmental factors*. (3) There are *genetic factors* involved that place blacks at a disadvantage. Now, test bias may account for *some* of the observed differences between black and white IQ scores, but let's assume for the moment that our available intellectual assessment techniques are as valid as possible. What then?

In the 1950s and 1960s, psychologists were generally confident that the bulk of the difference between the IQ scores of whites and blacks could be explained in environmental terms. There weren't many quality studies available to support the position, but the logic was compelling and consistent with prevailing attitudes. Blacks were at a disadvantage on standard IQ tests, the argument went, because they were often denied access to enriching educational opportunities. Their overall lower socioeconomic status deprived them of many of the sorts of experiences that could affect IQ scores. Even the generally poorer health and nutrition of blacks was used to explain why their scores tended to be low.

In 1969, Arthur Jensen shocked the scientific community with a long, thoughtful article in the *Harvard Educational Review.* Quite simply, Jensen argued that there was insufficient evidence to warrant the conclusion that the environment could produce the large racial difference in IQ scores. The alternative was obvious to Jensen: The observed differences were attributable to genetic factors. Many readers took Jensen's claim to be that blacks are genetically inferior to whites. More recently, Jensen claims that his argument was meant as a reasonable hypothesis, intended to provoke scientific efforts to explore the possibility (Jensen, 1981). It should be kept in mind that Jensen never offered credible evidence to support a genetic-factors argument. Instead, he has accepted most of the data we have looked at concerning genetic factors and has largely attempted to discredit the adequacy of the environmental-factors argument.

Perhaps you can imagine the furor created by Jensen's 1969 article. Psychologists and sociologists took up the challenge and tried to find convincing evidence that the environment *is* the cause of lower black IQ scores. After reviewing the body of literature that has grown from these efforts, Brian Mackenzie (1984, p. 1217) is willing to assert that, "What is finally clear from such research, therefore, is that environmental factors have not been identified that are sufficient to account for all or even most of the 15-point mean difference in IQ between blacks and whites in the United States. Jensen's (1973) conclusion that half to two thirds of the gap remains unaccounted for by any proposed combination of environmental influences is still unrefuted."

Now what does *that* mean? Does that mean the racial differences in IQ *are* caused by genetic factors? *Are* blacks genetically inferior to whites? Of course not; at least there is not yet any evidence to support such a conclusion. To understand the reason requires that we understand two important points about this issue: (1) Just because there is ample evidence to strongly suggest that genetic factors affect differences in intelligence within races, that evidence cannot automatically (without more data) be used as evidence of genetic factors affecting differences in intelligence between races. (2) It is improper to assume that the failure to identify specific environmental causes of race differences in IQ is sufficient reason to drop the environmental-factors argument altogether. And just because we have not yet identified all of the environmental factors that can be said to cause racial differences in IQ does not mean that we must accept genetic explanations. To do so would be to accept what Mackenzie calls the "hereditarian fallacy."

So where do we stand on this issue? We stand in a position of considerable uncertainty. As we have seen, there is a body of research data that underscores the contribution of both genetic and environmental influences on what we call intelligence. Whether any of this data can be used to settle the issue of racial differences in IQ is debatable. In terms of accounting for racial differences in IQ scores, it seems at the moment as though there is little unambiguous data to support an environmentalist position, and virtually no unambiguous data to support a geneticist argument.

What two major problems have inhibited our search for an answer to the heredity versus environment question with regard to intelligence?

Two problems that have hindered our search for answers to the heredity vs. environment question have been (1) our failure to adequately define intelligence, and (2) the inability to exercise adequate experimental control over extraneous variables. / 482

In general, what has the study of twins and adopted children told us about the relative importance of heredity and the environment in determining intelligence as measured by IQ tests?

Although we cannot draw any definite conclusions, it seems reasonable to suggest that there are genetic factors that may place limits on one's intellectual potential, but the impact of the environment is needed to exercise such potential because both are ultimately important in determining intelligence as measured by IQ tests. / 485

If group A and group B have different IQ scores on the average, what may be true about two individuals, one from group A and the other from group B, with regard to intelligence?

Mean group differences tell us very little about individual differences. That is, two individuals may have the same IQ score or either may have a score higher than the other. / 487

Are there sex differences in IQ?

No and yes. There are no significant differences between men and women on virtually any test that yields a global, or general, IQ score. There are, however, some specific skills and abilities that demonstrate sex differences, although the assumption is that these differences are culturally determined. / 488

Does intelligence decline with age, increase with age, or stay the same?

The evidence suggests that overall intelligence tends to drop off slightly as one approaches the age of 50 or 60. There are, however, different skills and abilities that are differentially affected by age. Fluid intelligence, for example, may decline with age, while crystallized intelligence may remain constant or even increase slightly with age. / 489

List six ways in which individuals can be considered to be gifted.

Summarize the basic findings of the Terman-Stanford study of intellectually gifted youngsters.

Giftedness can mean a number of things in addition to (1) overall intellectual ability. Other abilities in which individuals may be gifted include: (2) visual and performing arts, (3) psychomotor, (4) leadership, (5) creative, and (6) specific academic areas. Individuals who are mentally gifted also experience a number of other physical, educational, social, and economic advantages. / 491

How might we best define mental retardation?

Mental retardation should be thought of as indicated by subaverage intellectual functioning (usually indicated by IQ scores below 70), originating during the developmental period (within 18 years), and associated with impairment in adaptive behavior (as well as academic behaviors). / 492

List some of the possible causes of mental retardation.

In addition to genetic causes, most of the known causes of mental retardation revolve around the health and care of the mother and fetus during pregnancy, where drugs, lack of oxygen, poor nutrition, and the like have been implicated in mental retardation. / 493

CHAPTER TWELVE

ABNORMAL PSYCHOLOGY

TOPIC

Iris *really* doesn't want to get out of bed this morning. She had another rough night—tossing and turning and getting very little sleep. She's been overly tired for weeks. Her main problem is that she feels nervous, anxious, and apprehensive, but doesn't know why. She's been yelling at the children and nagging her husband. Iris realizes that her outbursts have not been justified, but she can't seem to stop them. She has a whole day ahead of her. Nothing *has* to be done, but she just can't decide what to do. Should she go shopping? Play tennis? Clean the house? Sit by the pool? No, none of these options seem worth the effort. Once again, Iris doesn't want to do anything today. She's afraid she'll be too nervous.

Without warning, Mark's hands have become paralyzed. From the wrist down, there is a total loss of voluntary control and a total loss of feeling. Mark's tensely distorted hands can be held over a candle flame and he will not withdraw them, apparently feeling no pain. There seems to be no impairment at all in his forearms, upper arms, or shoulders. There is no known medical or physiological explanation for Mark's symptoms. What people who know Mark well find most difficult to understand is his apparent lack of concern about his new handicap. He attributes his paralysis and loss of feeling to "the will of God" and shows no visible anger, regret, or remorse.

David becomes absolutely petrified if he thinks he has to ride in an elevator. He has been known to walk dozens of flights of stairs to avoid taking an elevator. Recently, he was in a hotel that has glass-enclosed elevators that can be seen from the lobby. Even the sight of those moving elevators created a sense of panic in David. When others try to reassure David of the inherent safety of elevators, he becomes nervous and agitated.

Carol was found this morning wandering around in the central business district of a large northeastern city. She was ill-dressed for the cold winds and low temperatures. Her behavior seemed aimless, and she was stopped by a police officer who asked if he could be of assistance. It soon became apparent that Carol did not know where she was. The officer took her to a nearby hospital. It was discovered that she had no recollection of where she had been or what she had been doing for the past 5 weeks. She had no idea how she got to the city in which she was found (350 miles from where she lived). To Carol, the last 5 weeks seem never to have happened.

Iris, Mark, David, and Carol do have something in common: They each have a psychological or mental disorder. They are either suffering from distress (Iris and David) or from an impairment in functioning (Mark and Carol). Clearly, their symptoms are quite different. Indeed, each would be diagnosed and classified as having a different disorder. In this topic, we'll be reviewing these disorders and others like them.

In this topic, we begin a discussion of abnormal psychology—the study of psychological disorders of behavior and mental activity. Psychological or mental disorders are much more common than any of us would like to think. It is impossible to know with certainty exactly how many people are suffering from some form of psychological disorder, but we do have a general idea.

In late 1984, the National Institute of Mental Health (NIMH) began to release preliminary findings from the largest study yet attempted of the prevalence of mental problems. This ongoing study is massive in scope (about 17,000 community residents were interviewed in depth), and, in many respects, the results are astounding.

The NIMH study reported that approximately 43 million adult Americans were suffering from some sort of mental disorder when the survey was taken. That's about 19 percent of the adult population. These data become all the more impressive when we consider the very large number of people who were not included in the survey. The study dealt only with adults, leaving uncounted many children and adolescents who might qualify as mentally disordered. Thirteen percent of those originally selected to be in the NIMH sample refused to be interviewed. Individuals with psychosexual disorders were not included; homeless people were not included; individuals who were institutionalized were not included. Thus, it appears that as careful and concise as the NIMH study is, its estimate is no doubt very conservative.

Statistics such as these are impressive; they are also impersonal. It is difficult to conceptualize what it really means to say that 43 million people are suffering from a mental disorder. "While exactly how many people have mental or emotional problems is uncertain, the NIMH survey demonstrated that widespread, genuine distress does exist" (Albee, 1985). It seems unlikely that many of us will be exempt from intimate, personal contact with someone who has a psychological disorder; that is why we care.

In this topic, we'll begin our discussion as we often have, considering matters of definition. In no area of psychology are definitional issues as critical as they are in considering psychological disorders. Just what is *abnormal?* Related to defining abnormal in general is the issue of classifying and labeling various disorders, and we'll review the implications of classification systems before we turn our attention to specific disorders. Having tackled some large theoretical issues, we will then begin a brief description of some of the more common or typical psychological disorders. In this topic, we'll cover some of the anxiety disorders, somatoform disorders, dissociative disorders, personality disorders, and psychosexual disorders.

Before you go on

According to the National Institute of Mental Health, how prevalent are mental or psychological disorders in the U.S.?

PROBLEMS OF DEFINITION AND CLASSIFICATION

We all have a basic idea of what we mean by such terms as mental illness or psychological disorder. The more we think about abnormality and what it means, however, the harder it becomes to define. In this section, we'll do two things: (1) we'll consider some of the more common approaches to defining abnormal from a psychological perspective, and (2) we'll consider the implications of defining disorders in terms of specific symptoms by describing each disorder in detail and giving it a label.

Defining Abnormality

Defining what we mean by abnormal in psychology is not easily done. In order to be complete, our definitions often tend to get rather complicated. Here's the definition we'll use for the next two topics: In psychology, **abnormal** means statistically uncommon, maladaptive cognitions, affect, or behaviors that are at odds with social expectations and that result in distress and discomfort. This lengthy definition touches most of the bases that are usually considered relevant in defining abnormality. Let's now briefly review these points one at a time.

One way to think about abnormality is to take a *statistical* and *literal* approach. Literally, abnormal means "not of the norm or average." In this approach, any behaviors that are uncommon are then to be considered abnormal, and in a literal, statistical sense, of course, they are. The major flaw with this approach is that it would label the behaviors of Larry Bird, Itzak Perlman, Michael Jackson, and Barbara Walters as abnormal. In a statistical sense, they *are* abnormal; there are few others who act as these people do, yet none of these people is psychologically disordered. As it happens, most of the psychological disorders we'll consider are rare in a statistical sense, but rarity alone is not enough.

Perhaps more importantly, the reactions of people who are suffering from a mental disorder are not only statistically uncommon, but they are often *maladaptive.* Thoughts, feelings, and behaviors are such that these individuals cannot function as well as they could without the mental disorder. There is some degree of impairment here. That is, "behavior is abnormal if it is maladaptive; if it interferes with functioning and growth" (Coleman et al., 1984).

Another observation reflected in our definition is that abnormality may show itself at a number of different levels of functioning. That is, a person may engage in abnormal *behaviors,* have abnormal *cognitions* (thoughts, perceptions, and beliefs), experience abnormal *affect* (emotional reaction or feelings), or demonstrate any combination of these. Sometimes the most noticeable aspect of a disorder is behavioral (for example, Mark's paralyzed hands and his inability to use them). Sometimes the major psychological consideration is one of cognition, as was the case for Carol who found herself walking around in a strange city with no idea of where she'd been. Sometimes the major issue in abnormality is affective, such as Iris's inappropriate feelings of nervousness and anxiety that appeared for no apparent reason.

Any definition of abnormality should reflect social and/or cultural expectations. That is, deviance from the average, or the norm, needs to be assessed within some social context. What is clearly abnormal and disordered in one culture may be viewed as quite normal, if not commonplace, in another. In some cultures, crying and wailing at the funeral of a total stranger is considered to be strange or deviant; in others, it is common. In some cultures, to claim that you have been communicating directly with dead ancestors would be taken as a sign of severe disturbance; in others, it would be treated as a great gift.

Yet one other issue needs to be addressed when we consider a definition of psychological abnormality. This is to acknowledge that to a greater or lesser degree, psychological or mental disorders involve distress or discomfort. Typically, people who we consider to be abnormal are, in some way, suffering. They are experiencing emotional distress. But not all people with psychological disturbances feel the distress themselves. They might very well be quite happy in their own way. The likelihood is, however, that such individuals are the source of distress and discomfort to others around them,

abnormal
statistically uncommon, maladaptive cognitions, affect, and/or behaviors that are at odds with social expectations and that result in distress or discomfort

What is considered abnormal or deviant behavior in one society may be quite normal in another. Even the kinds of contests held vary from culture to culture, from a male beauty contest in the Bororo tribe of West Africa to a pie-eating contest in Massachusetts. Normal ideas of dress and adornment also vary, from the Asaro mudmen of New Guinea to the highly adorned women of Nigeria. What we consider normal may not be normal for everyone.

friends and family who care about them. Of the four people we mentioned at the beginning of the topic, Iris and David felt real distress and discomfort, but Mark and Carol did not. However, Mark and Carol's families have probably been worried about them for some time.

Now that we have a sense of what abnormal is, let's be sure that we understand a few things that it is *not*. (1) Abnormal and normal are not two separate and distinct categories. They may be thought of as endpoints on some dimension that we can use to describe people, but there is a considerable gray area between the two where distinctions get fuzzy indeed. (2) Abnormal does not mean dangerous. True, some people diagnosed as having a mental disorder *may* be dangerous, but most likely they are more dangerous to themselves than to others. And most people with psychological disorders are not dangerous at all. (3) Abnormal does not mean bad. People who suffer from psychological disorders are not necessarily bad people, or weak people, in any evaluative sense. They may do bad things, and bad things may have happened to them, but it is certainly not in psychology's tradition to make moral and ethical judgments about good and bad.

So where has this discussion led us? If nothing else, we can agree that psychological abnormality is not a simple, one-dimensional concept. It involves a number of different things: statistical rarity, behavioral, cognitive, and/or affective reactions that are maladaptive, the violation of social expectations, and feelings of distress or discomfort.

Before you go on
How do we define psychological abnormality?

The Classification of Abnormal Reactions

One way of dealing with a definition of psychological abnormality is to consider each individual psychological disorder separately. This approach involves describing the symptoms of specific disorders as completely as possible and then organizing or classifying disorders in some systematic way.

Systems of classification are quite common in science and are not at all new in psychology. In 1883, Emil Kraepelin published the first significant classification scheme for mental disturbances. It was based on the notion that each disorder has its own collection of symptoms (called a *syndrome*) and its own cause (at that time thought to be biological or organic). Some of Kraepelin's views have been found to be incorrect, but he clearly demonstrated the value of classifying psychological disorders in a systematic way.

The DSM Series In 1952, the American Psychiatric Association published a classification scheme for mental disorders. The book in which the scheme was presented was called the *Diagnostic and Statistical Manual of Mental Disorders.* In an ordered fashion, it listed the symptoms of 60 known disorders. Sixteen years later, a new version was published, referred to as the *DSM-II.* The *DSM-II* rearranged some classifications and expanded some categories and compressed others, but still listed 145 types and subtypes. The most recent version of the *Diagnostic and Statistical Manual,* the *DSM-III,* was written by a large committee of psychologists and psychiatrists and was published in 1980. The *DSM-III* has 230 separate entries that each constitute some form of psychological disorder.

Emil Kraepelin

Even before its publication, the *DSM-III* had attracted controversy. Classifying more than 200 behavioral patterns as disordered seemed to many to be going overboard. Some psychologists don't feel that conditions such as "Developmental Arithmetic Disorder" (characterized by arithmetic test scores that are below expected level, considering one's intellectual capabilities) or "Occupational Problem" (for example, job dissatisfaction and uncertainty about career choices) ought to be included in a classification scheme of psychological disorders.

Even though the *DSM-III* has its limitations, it is the system of classification most widely used in all mental health fields. We will follow the general outline of the *DSM-III* in these two topics on abnormal psychology. Figure 27.1 presents a partial listing of the disorders listed in the *DSM-III* and shows subtypes for each major category of disorder.

We should note that the *DSM-III* is more than just an organized listing of disorders in terms of their symptoms. The *DSM-III* recommends that diagnosis of a disorder be sensitive to (a) any physical illnesses or ailments that are present, (b) the amount of stress the individual has been under recently, and (c) the level of adaptive functioning that the individual has been able to manage over the past 3 years. The manual generally attempts to avoid any reference to the **etiology,** or causes, of disorders. It is meant to be as objective as possible, to describe as specifically and completely as possible, and to theorize as little as possible.

There are many advantages to having a single, if still imperfect, classification scheme for psychological disorders. The major advantage, of course, is communication. If I mean one thing when I use the term phobia and you mean something quite different, we can't hold a very reasonable conversation about your patient's phobia. If we both agreed on, say, the *DSM-III*'s definition, we would at least be using the term in the same way. A related advantage is that if we can develop a reliable (consistent) way of classifying disorders, we can begin thinking about how we might most effectively prescribe appropriate treatment or therapy. The logic is rather simple: If professionals can't even agree on what's wrong with people, how can they begin to know how to treat them? We can't leave the impression that there is only one prescribed treatment possible or most suitable for each of the diagnostic categories of the *DSM-III*. As we'll see in our chapter on treatment and therapy, that is far from the case. But it certainly makes sense that we must be able to classify disorders before we can treat them. However, classification can cause difficulties.

Problems with Classification and Labeling

As useful as it is to have a system for the classification of psychological disorders, we must also recognize that there are problems associated with any such scheme. First, applying labels to people may be convenient, but it is often dehumanizing. It is sometimes difficult to remember that Sally Jones is a complex and complicated human being with a range of feelings, thoughts, and behaviors, and not just a paranoid schizophrenic. In this regard, the *DSM-III* has an advantage over its predecessors. It refers to disordered behaviors and patterns of behaviors, not to disordered people. That is, it refers to paranoid reactions, and not to individuals who are paranoid.

A second problem inherent in classification and labeling is that it is so easy to fall into the habit of believing that labels *explain*. Clearly they don't. Being able to reliably and accurately diagnose and label a pattern of behaviors does not explain those behaviors. It does not tell us why such a pattern of behaviors developed, or what we can or should do about them now. Third, labels often create unfortunate and lasting stigmas of negative attitudes about people. Part of our definition of abnormal was the notion of statistical

etiology
the cause or predisposing factors of a disturbance or disorder

Jack Smith is a tragic example of the dangers of labeling. Smith was born in a mental hospital at which his parents were patients. He was assumed to be retarded and received no education until after age 12, despite having shown an interest in learning. His early childhood was spent in an orphanage, followed by 38 years in a mental hospital. In 1976, after extensive psychiatric evaluation, a judge declared that Smith was neither mentally ill nor dangerous. Unfortunately, by that time the 54-year-old Smith was considered too impaired to be released. He now lives in a nursing home.

disorder. Given the prevalence of mental disorders, however, it *is* possible, and you might want to explore finding professional help, but don't jump to conclusions without seeking professional diagnoses.

ANXIETY DISORDERS

As we mentioned in Topic 22, anxiety is a term that is difficult to define with precision. Everyone knows what anxiety is; everyone has experienced anxiety and recognizes it as unpleasant. We shall take **anxiety** to be a general feeling of apprehension or dread, accompanied by predictable physiological changes—increased muscle tension, shallow rapid breathing, a cessation of digestion, increased perspiration, and a drying of the mouth. Thus, anxiety involves two levels of reaction: subjective feelings (e.g., dread/fear) and physiological responses (e.g., sweaty palms). Anxiety is the definitional characteristic of the *anxiety disorders* (which used to be called *neuroses*).

anxiety
a general feeling of apprehension or dread, accompanied by predictable physiological changes

Anxiety disorders are among the most common of all the psychological disorders. The *DSM-III* (1980) estimates that 2 to 4 percent of the population experiences some form of anxiety disorder. The 1984 NIMH study reports much higher rates: from 7 to 15 percent with "one or more of the several anxiety diagnoses" (Freedman, 1984). In either case, percentages of this sort do not convey the enormity of the problem. Even if we take a rather conservative figure of 5 percent of the population, it's difficult to imagine that we are talking about more than 10,000,000 individuals at any one time. We'll consider three subtypes of anxiety disorder: phobic disorders, anxiety states, and obsessive-compulsive disorders.

Phobic Disorders

The essential feature of a **phobic disorder** (or phobia) is a persistent fear of some object, activity, or situation that leads a person to consistently avoid that object, activity, or situation. Implied in this definition is the notion that the fear is intense enough to be disruptive and/or debilitating. It is also implied that there is no real threat involved in the stimulus that gives rise to a phobic reaction; that is, the fear is unreasonable or inappropriate.

phobic disorder
an intense, irrational fear that leads a person to avoid the feared object, activity, or situation

Agoraphobia is a fear of open places. People with this phobic disorder often cannot leave their homes without experiencing extreme panic and anxiety. It sometimes reaches the point where they refuse to leave their homes at all.

Anxiety is a general feeling of apprehension or dread. Everyone experiences anxiety occasionally, and the DSM-III estimates that 2 to 4 percent of the population experiences some form of anxiety disorder.

Figure 27.2

A sample of phobic reactions

Phobia	Is a fear of
Acrophobia	High places
Agoraphobia	Open places
Algophobia	Pain
Astraphobia	Lightning and thunder
Autophobia	One's self
Claustrophobia	Small, closed places
Hematophobia	Blood
Monophobia	Being alone
Mysophobia	Dirt or contamination
Nyctophobia	The dark
Pathophobia	Illness or disease
Pyrophobia	Fire
Thanatophobia	Death and dying
Xenophobia	The unknown
Zoophobia	Animals

agoraphobia
a phobic fear of open places, of being alone, or of being in public places from which escape might be difficult

Let's look at that the other way around. There are a number of things in this world that are life threatening and downright frightening. If, for example, you are walking in the downtown center of a large city late at night and three huge thugs dragging bicycle chains and holding knives approach you, you are likely to feel an intense reaction of fear. Such a reaction is not phobic, because it is not irrational.

Similarly, there are few of us who truly enjoy the company of large numbers of bees. Just because we don't like bees and would rather they not be around does not qualify us as having a phobic reaction. What is missing here is *intensity* of response. People who have a phobic reaction to bees (mellissaphobia) will often refuse to leave the house in the summertime for fear of encountering a bee; they become genuinely upset and nervous at the buzzing sound of any insect, fearing it to be a bee, and may become uncomfortable simply reading a paragraph, such as this one, about bees.

There are many different types of phobic reaction. Most are named after the object or activity that is feared. Figure 27.2 lists some of the most common phobic reactions. It is probably the case that most phobias involve a fear of animals—although such phobias are not the type for which people most commonly seek treatment (Costello, 1982). In many such cases, the person with a phobic reaction may be successful in avoiding the feared animal and may never seek treatment. So long as David (from our opening descriptions) is able to avoid contact with elevators, and so long as he is able to walk many flights of stairs, his intense, irrational phobic fear may cause him little concern. Sometimes, however, avoiding the source of one's phobic reaction is virtually impossible.

One of the most commonly treated varieties of phobia is **agoraphobia,** which quite literally means "fear of open places." The fear here is not just reserved for those occasions in which one stands in the middle of a large open field, however. Most commonly, this diagnosis is used for people who have an exaggerated fear of being alone or of leaving their houses to venture forth into the world. Such people want to avoid crowds, streets, stores, and the like. They essentially establish for themselves a safe home base and may, in extreme cases, refuse to leave it altogether.

Before you go on

What are the essential characteristics of a phobic reaction?

Generalized Anxiety and Panic Disorders

generalized anxiety disorder
persistent, chronic, and distressingly high levels of unattributable anxiety

In phobic reactions we have a specific stimulus that brings about an intense fear response, and we have people who take steps to avoid the stimulus of their phobias. In *generalized anxiety disorder* and *panic disorder,* we have neither of these features. With **generalized anxiety disorders,** the anxiety is persistent (has lasted at least 1 month) and does not seem to be brought on by anything specific in the environment. The anxiety is diffuse and may come and go without reason or warning. People with this disorder are almost always in some state of uneasiness. If they are not experiencing a particularly high level of anxiety at the moment, they may be afraid that they soon will be. Iris's symptoms, which we described at the beginning of this topic, are illustrative of a person with this disorder. Although people with the disorder can function socially and occupationally (meaning with others and on the job), the symptoms may lead the individual to abuse alcohol, barbiturates, and antianxiety medications.

For the person suffering from **panic disorder,** there may be long periods of freedom from any real sense of anxiety. The major symptom of this form of anxiety disorder is the sudden, often unpredictable anxiety attack, or panic attack. These attacks may last for a few seconds or for hours, and involve "the sudden onset of intense apprehension, fear, or terror, often associated with feelings of impending doom" (*DSM-III,* 1980, p. 230). The subjective experience is similar to the fear of the phobic reaction, except that there is no apparent stimulus to bring it on. It just happens. And because it just happens, without warning, an obvious complication of this disorder is that the individual soon begins to fear the next attack and the loss of control that it will bring. Panic attacks are not that rare among people who are under stress. The likelihood is that you know from your own experience what such an attack feels like. To qualify as a psychological disorder in the *DSM-III,* such attacks must have occurred at a rate of at least three within a 3-week period, and they must be accompanied by a number of physiological symptoms (such as chest pain, hot and cold flashes, sweating, or trembling).

panic disorders
disorders in which anxiety attacks suddenly and unpredictably incapacitate; there may be periods free from anxiety

Before you go on

How are the two anxiety states of generalized anxiety disorder and panic disorder the same, and how are they different?

Obsessive-Compulsive Disorder

In a way, we really have three disorders here: an obsessive disorder, a compulsive disorder, and a combination—an obsessive-compulsive disorder. Obsessive disorders are characterized by recurrent **obsessions**—ideas or thoughts that involuntarily and constantly intrude into awareness. It is generally the case that obsessions are silly, pointless, or groundless thoughts (most commonly of violence, contamination, or doubt). As is the case with many psychological disorders, we have all experienced obsessive thoughts. Worrying throughout the first few days of a vacation if you remembered to turn off the stove would be an example. Or, have you ever awakened to a clock radio that was playing some particular song? As you take your morning shower, the lyrics keep coming to mind. As you get dressed, you hear yourself humming the same song. There you are, driving to work, still thinking about that same song. You have the feeling that "I can't get that song out of my head!" Imagine having a thought like that, constantly interrupting, constantly coming to mind whenever you weren't consciously focusing your attention on something else, day after day. As much as you try to ignore or fight off the thoughts, they keep popping into your awareness. Such thoughts would be anxiety-producing to say the least.

obsessions
ideas or thoughts that involuntarily and persistently intrude into awareness

Compulsions are constantly intruding acts or behaviors. They are repetitive. Again, from your own experience, have you ever found yourself walking along on a sidewalk, carefully avoiding the cracks in the pavement? To do so is a compulsive sort of response. It serves no real purpose in itself, and it provides no genuine satisfaction, although it is done very conscientiously. The most commonly reported compulsions involve handwashing and counting behaviors. The person recognizes that these behaviors serve no useful purpose, but cannot stop them. It is as if they engage in these pointless behaviors in order to prevent some other behavior from taking place.

compulsions
constantly intruding, stereotyped, and essentially involuntary acts or behaviors

Although you and I may experience similar sorts of reactions, the truly obsessive-compulsive reaction is often very debilitating and the source of great distress. In extreme cases, a particular obsession or compulsion may come to greatly influence a person's entire life.

Notice that we sometimes use "compulsive" in an inappropriate way, as when we refer to someone being a compulsive gambler, a compulsive eater, or a compulsive practical joker. What is inappropriate about the use of the term compulsive in such cases is that the individual may engage in habitual patterns of behavior, but usually gains pleasure from doing so. The compulsive gambler enjoys gambling; the compulsive eater loves to eat. Such people may not enjoy the ultimate consequences of their actions, but they feel little discomfort in the behaviors themselves. To qualify as a truly compulsive behavior requires that the behavior not be the source of pleasure and be recognized as senseless.

Before you go on

In the context of the obsessive-compulsive disorder, what is an obsession, and what is a compulsion?

SOMATOFORM DISORDERS

somatoform disorders
psychological disorders that reflect imagined physical or bodily symptoms or complaints

"Soma" is a word which translated from the Greek means "body." Hence, all of the **somatoform disorders,** in some way or another, have physical, bodily symptoms or complaints. What makes these *psychological* or *mental* disorders is that in each case, there is no known medical or biological cause for the symptoms. We should point out that *psychosomatic disorders* are *not* somatoform disorders. There is no actual physical damage or tissue involvement with the somatoform disorders; the symptoms are psychological. With the psychosomatic disorders, there *is* physical damage, as in skin rashes, respiratory ailments, or ulcers. What makes these disorders *psycho*somatic is that their basic cause is psychological (stress-related) in nature. Here we'll review three somatoform disorders: hypochondriasis, somatization disorder, and the rather dramatic conversion disorder.

Hypochondriasis

hypochondriasis
a mental disorder involving the fear of developing some serious disease or illness

Hypochondriasis is the appropriate diagnosis for someone who lives in extreme fear and dread of developing some serious disease. Such people are unusually aware of every ache and pain and tend to diagnose their own symptoms as being indicative of some terrible physical disorder. They tend to read popular magazines devoted to health issues, and they usually feel free to diagnose their own ailments. In fact, they have no medical disorder, illness, or disease, but they will not be persuaded by the best of medical opinion and reassurance.

A person with occasional chest pains diagnoses his own condition as cancer of the heart. When numerous physicians try to reassure him that his heart is perfectly fine, and that he has no signs of cancer, the patient's fears are not put to rest. "They're just trying to make me feel better by not telling me, because they know, as I do, that I have cancer of the heart and am going to die soon."

It's not too difficult to imagine why someone would develop the symptoms of hypochondriasis. If the individual truly comes to believe that he or she (and the disorder is found equally in men and women) is about to contract some serious disease, three possible problems might be solved: (1) The person now has a way to explain otherwise unexplainable anxiety. "Well, my goodness, if you had cancer of the heart, you'd be anxious too." (2) The illness may be used to excuse the person from those activities that he or she finds anxiety producing. "As sick as I am, you don't possibly expect me to go to work, do you?" (3) The illness or disease may be used as a way to gain

The vast array of over-the-counter medicines available testify to the preoccupation of many Americans with their health. Taken to extremes, this preoccupation with aches and pains can lead to hypochondriasis.

attention and/or sympathy. "Don't you feel sorry for me, knowing that I have such a terrible disease?"

Somatization Disorder

Somatization disorder is the rather fancy label given to a disorder that is in many ways very similar to hypochondriasis. The major difference is that with somatization disorder, there is a long history of complaint about some particular physical symptoms. Whereas the hypochondriac fears that he or she may have or get some disease or illness, the patient with somatization disorder has a long-standing list of actual physical complaints. As with hypochondriasis, there is no known physical cause, or etiology, for the complaints. These complaints typically begin before the age of 30. The debilitating nature of the disorder can be seen in the patient's altering of life-style to accommodate his or her symptoms. Unlike hypochondriasis, this diagnosis is much more commonly made for females than for males (*DSM-III*, 1980).

somatization disorder
a persistent distress over a chronic physical symptom for which there is no medical explanation

Conversion Disorder

Surely, **conversion disorder** is the most strange or bizarre of the somatoform disorders. Although it is rare, its symptoms are quite striking. Here we find an individual with a "loss or alteration in physical functioning suggesting a physical disorder, and it has been determined that the symptom is not under voluntary control" (*DSM-III*, 1980, p. 244). The loss in physical functioning is typically of great significance: paralysis, blindness, or deafness comprise classic examples. The symptoms are not imaginary; they are quite real in the sense that the person cannot see, hear, or feel. What makes the disorder psychological is that there is no known medical reason for the symptom.

conversion disorder
the display of a (severe) physical disorder for which there is no medical explanation; often accompanied by an apparent lack of concern on the part of the patient

Our opening description of Mark was meant as an example of this disorder. In Mark's case, his hands became paralyzed and lost all feeling. He developed a symptom known as *glove anesthesia.* Now, as it happens, it is physically impossible to have such paralysis and loss of feeling in the hands alone; normally there would also be some paralysis in the forearm, upper arm, and shoulder, as well.

One of the most remarkable secondary symptoms of this disorder (which occurs only in some patients) is known as *la belle indifference*—a seemingly inappropriate lack of concern over one's condition. Persons with this disorder seem to feel quite comfortable with and accepting of their infirmity. Here are people who are demonstrably blind or paralyzed who show very little concern over their condition.

This particular disorder holds an important position in psychology's history. This was the disorder that most intrigued Sigmund Freud in his clinical practice and ultimately led him to develop a new method of therapy, which we now call *psychoanalysis* (see Topic 30). This disorder was apparently known to the Greeks, who called it hysteria, a name which is still sometimes applied, as in hysterical blindness, for example. It was the Greek view that the disorder was only to be found in women and reflected a disorder of the uterus, or "hystera," hence the name hysteria. The notion was that the disordered uterus would float through the body and settle in the eyes, hands, ears, or whatever part of the body was affected. Of course, this notion is no longer thought to be valid, although the potential sexual basis for the disorder was one of the aspects that caught Freud's attention.

Before you go on
Describe the somatoform disorders hypochondriasis, somatization disorder, and conversion disorder.

DISSOCIATIVE DISORDERS

To dissociate means to become separate from or to escape. The underlying theme of disorders classified as **dissociative disorders** is that in some way a person dissociates or escapes from some aspect of life or personality that is seen as the source of stress and discomfort. These mental disorders are statistically quite rare, but they are quite dramatic and are often the subject of novels, movies, and television shows.

Psychogenic Amnesia and Fugue

Psychogenic means "psychological in origin." Thus, **psychogenic amnesia** is an inability to recall important personal information that is too extensive to be explained by ordinary forgetfulness. It is usually the case that what is forgotten is some traumatic incident and some or all of the experiences that led up to or followed the incident. As you might suspect, there is no identifiable, medical explanation for the loss of memory. As you might also suspect, there is a considerable range in the type and extent of the forgetting associated with psychogenic amnesia. In some cases, a person may lose entire days and weeks at a time; in others, only specific details cannot be recalled. Not surprisingly, cases of this disorder tend to be more common in wartime when traumatic experiences are more common.

Occasionally, forgetfulness is accompanied by a physical change of location. The person finds himself or herself in a strange and different place, with no reasonable explanation for how he or she got there. When this dimension is added, we have a disorder known as a **fugue state.** It is likely that this is the diagnosis that would apply to Carol in our opening descriptions.

These disorders are, in their own way, not unlike some of the somatoform disorders in that they involve an escape from stressful situations. In conversion disorders, for example, a person may escape from stress by taking on the symptoms of a major physical disorder. Here, escape is more literal. People escape by forgetting altogether, or they avoid conflict and stress by psychologically or physically "running away" (Coleman et al., 1984, p. 218).

dissociative disorders
disorders in which one separates or dissociates from aspects of one's personality

psychogenic amnesia
a psychologically caused inability to recall important personal information

fugue state
a condition of amnesia accompanied by unexplained travel or change of location

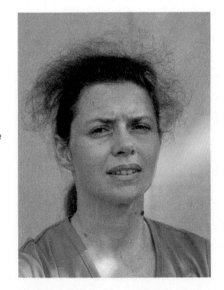

This woman, dubbed "Jane Doe," was found incoherent and near death in Florida in 1980. She was suffering from psychogenic amnesia and was unable to remember her name, her past, and how to read and write. After extensive publicity, a couple from Roselle, Illinois came forward and identified Jane Doe as their daughter who had moved to Florida and been missing since 1976. Despite the certainty of the couple, Jane Doe was never able to remember her past.

Multiple Personality

Perhaps the most important thing to recognize about the disorder called **multiple personality** is that it is listed here as a dissociative disorder, and *not* as "schizophrenia." The major symptom of multiple personality is "the existence within the individual of two or more distinct personalities, each of which is dominant at a particular time" (*DSM-III*, 1980, p. 257). A second thing to recognize is that the disorder is "extremely rare" (*DSM-III*, 1980, p. 258). Coleman (1984) claims that only slightly more than 100 cases have been reported in psychological and psychiatric records.

The very idea of split personality—of two or more personalities inhabiting the same person—is difficult for most of us to imagine. Perhaps it would help to contrast this disordered reaction with a pattern of behavior that is typical of all of us.

We all change our behaviors and, in some small way, our personalities every day, depending on the situations in which we find ourselves. We do not act (think or feel) exactly the same way at school as we do at work, or at a party, or at church. We change and modify our reactions to fit the circumstances. In a way, then, we are not exactly the same people at a party that we are at work. At a party, you may be a person who is carefree, uninhibited, happy, and filled with pleasant thoughts. At work, you may be a different person: reserved, quiet, serious, and concentrating on the task at hand. No, you and I do not have multiple personalities. What's the difference? There are three major differences

The main difference is one of degree. For a person with a multiple personality disorder, the change in personality is usually dramatic, complete, and extreme. We are not dealing with a person who slightly alters his or her behaviors; we are dealing with two distinct personalities. A second difference is that when you and I alter our behaviors or feelings or thinking, it is in response to the environment. That is, we change in reaction to the situations in which we find ourselves. Such is not the case for a person with this dissociative disorder—changes in personality usually take place without warning, often in response to stressors. The third major difference has to do with control. When we change our behaviors, we usually do so consciously and intentionally. Individuals with a multiple personality disorder can neither control nor predict which of their personalities will be dominant at any one time.

multiple personality
the existence within one individual of two or more distinct personalities, each of which is dominant at a particular time

Before you go on

What are the defining symptoms of the dissociative disorders?

PERSONALITY DISORDERS

All of the psychological disorders we have reviewed so far, and those we'll consider in our next topic, are disorders that seem to afflict people who previously were quite normal and undisturbed. In most cases, we can remember a time when the person did not show the symptoms of his or her disorder. That is much harder to do with the **personality disorders** because persons with these disorders have a long-standing history of symptoms. Personality disorders are found in those individuals whose "enduring patterns of perceiving, relating to, and thinking about the environment and one's self are inflexible and maladaptive," and cause either impaired functioning or distress (*DSM-III*, 1980). Significantly, these maladaptive and distressful per-

personality disorders
enduring patterns of perceiving, relating to, and thinking about the environment and one's self that are inflexible and maladaptive

Figure 27.3
The DSM-III clusters of personality disorders (1980).

CLUSTER 1   Disorders of odd or eccentric reactions

Paranoid personality disorder
an extreme sensitivity, suspiciousness, envy, and mistrust of others; the attitude of suspicion is not justified; shows a restricted range of emotional reactivity and avoidance of intimacy; rarely seeks help.

Schizoid personality disorder
an inability to form interpersonal relationships; little involvement in social affairs; tends to be a loner; appears cold and aloof; often involves excessive daydreaming.

Schizotypal personality disorder
experiences oddities or eccentricities in thought, perception, speech, or behavior of long-standing; tends to be very egocentric; although a basic contact with reality is maintained, there are occasional exceptions (e.g., strong belief in ESP, clairvoyance, or fantasy); extreme social isolation, a sense of being separated from one's own body, etc.

CLUSTER 2   Disorders of dramatic, emotional, or erratic reactions

Histrionic personality disorder
overly dramatic, reactive, and intensely expressed behavior; very lively, tending to draw attention to one's self; tends to overreact to matters of small consequence; seeking of excitement and avoiding of routine; a tendency for dependency on others with otherwise poor interpersonal relations.

Narcissistic personality disorder
a grandiose exaggeration of self-importance; displays a need for attention if not admiration; tendency to set unrealistic goals; maintains few lasting relationships with others; in many ways, a childish level of behavior.

Antisocial personality disorder
a history of continuous disregard for the rights and property of others; early signs include lying, truancy, stealing, fighting, and resisting authority; an inability to maintain a job is common; demonstrates poor parenting skills; a strong tendency toward impulsive behaviors with little regard for the consequences of that behavior.

Borderline personality disorder
(as its name suggests, there is no dominant pattern of deviance here) sometimes there is impulsivity; sometimes instability of mood; a pattern of extensive uncertainty about many important life issues; temper tantruming is not uncommon, and often appears unprovoked.

CLUSTER 3   Disorders involving anxiety and fearfulness

Avoidant personality disorder
oversensitive to the possibility of being rejected by others; an unwillingness to enter into relationships for fear of rejection; devastated by disapproval; there remains, however, a desire for social relations (i.e., does not enjoy being alone).

Dependent personality disorder
individual allows, and seeks, others to dominate and assume responsibility for actions; poor self-image and a lack of confidence; sees self as stupid and helpless, deferring to others.

Compulsive personality disorder
a restricted ability to show love, warmth, or tender emotions; an overconcern for rules and regulations and doing things in a prescribed way; becomes anxious about getting the job done, but not about being compulsive in doing so; rigid and stiff.

Passive-aggressive personality disorder
resistance to the demands of others is passive and indirect; tendency toward procrastination, dawdling, stubbornness, inefficiency, and forgetfulness; often tend to be whiners, moaners, and complainers.

---

sonality traits have existed for a considerable period of time. The problems are long-standing ones, usually identifiable in adolescence.

The *DSM-III* lists 11 different personality disorders, organized into three groups or clusters. Cluster 1 includes disorders in which the individual can be characterized as being odd or eccentric in some way. Cluster 2 includes disorders in which the individual appears overly dramatic, emotional, or erratic. Behaviors in this cluster seem quite impulsive. Cluster 3 adds the dimension of anxiety or fearfulness to the standard criteria for personality disorder. The **prognosis,** or prediction of the likely outcome of a disorder, is usually quite poor for personality disorders. These maladaptive patterns of behavior have often taken a lifetime to develop. Changing them is very difficult. Figure 27.3 provides a summary of the 11 types of personality disorders.

prognosis
the prediction of the likely outcome of a disorder

Before you go on
What are the defining characteristics of the personality disorders?

psychosexual disorders
impairment or discomfort associated with sexual activity that is not organic in origin

There are few psychological disturbances that are as capable of capturing the imagination of the general public as the **psychosexual disorders.** Societies usually have systems of expectations and rules for the conduct of sexual behaviors that are well known by all its members. Deviance from these expectations or rules, however, is only a part of the picture of the psychosexual disorders. Such disorders are usually accompanied by guilt, shame, or fear. Remember our discussion of "abnormal" at the beginning of this topic? Statistical infrequency alone is not enough to qualify a behavior as disordered. There must also be feelings of inappropriateness and/or distress. And there is usually at least the implication of a maladaptive pattern of responding. We *must* remember that these disorders of sexual functioning are *psychological* in their cause as well as their nature; that is, an inability to engage in sexual behavior as a result of spinal cord injury is not in itself to be considered a psychosexual disorder.

Psychosexual disorders are classified into three major categories and a fourth, catch-all sort of category. Rather than exploring all of the various types of psychosexual disorders in detail, a few have been summarized in Figure 27.4. Here we have listed the four major groups of disorder and have provided just an example or two from each group to give you an idea of what they are like.

It is important to note that there are two psychologically important terms that are *not* found in Figure 27.4: homosexuality and rape. As it happens, neither of these is listed in the *DSM-III* as a psychosexual disorder.

Homosexuality, the sexual preference for and activities directed toward a member of one's own sex, was dropped from the list of psychological disorders in 1973. Homosexuality is now seen as a disorder only for those individuals who would prefer to be heterosexual. Although homosexuality may be more common than most people believe it to be—one estimate suggests 1.4 million women and 2.6 million men in the United States are exclusively homosexual (Coleman et al., 1984, p. 480)—homosexuals do make up a definite minority of the population. There is much we don't know about homosexuality. We do not know why some persons develop homosexual patterns of behavior, nor are we sure why others develop heterosexual patterns. We might state a few things we have learned about homosexuality in terms of myths for which there is no credible evidence (taken from Bootzin & Acocella, 1984, pp. 324–325): (1) Many homosexuals develop mannerisms of the opposite sex, males being feminine; females very masculine. (2) There is a consistent pattern of personality traits among homosexuals and these are different from those found in heterosexuals. (3) Homosexuals experience a higher rate of psychological disorders than heterosexuals. (4) Homosexual behavior patterns are communicable to children who come into contact with homosexuals. (5) Homosexuals become either sexually active or passive in their sexual behaviors with other homosexuals. (6) Actual sexual practices of homosexuals are significantly different from those engaged in by heterosexuals. All six of these "known facts" are false.

As is the case for homosexuality, rape is not classified as a mental disorder in the *DSM-III*. Rape is clearly a sexual deviation. It is also a crime. Forceable rape involves the performance of a sexual activity with an unwilling partner. (Statutory rape involves sexual activities with a minor.) Coleman (1984, p. 474) cites FBI figures that indicate the rapid rate of increase in forceable rapes: from 55,000 reported cases in 1974 to 77,000 cases in 1982.

Figure 27.4
Varieties of psychosexual disorders

GENDER IDENTITY DISORDERS
involving confusion between one's sense of one's gender and one's actual, anatomical sex; a conflict between being male and feeling female or being female and feeling male.

Transsexualism
involves a persistent sense of discomfort and inappropriateness about one's anatomical sex; there is an equally persistent desire to be rid of one's genitals and to live as a member of the opposite sex; may engage in cross-dressing (dressing in clothes of the other sex); often the discomfort about one's sexual identity began in childhood.

PARAPHILIAS
involving unusual or bizarre fantasies or acts that are necessary for full sexual excitement; such acts are repetitive and involve either a nonhuman object for sexual arousal, or the use of real or imagined suffering or humiliation, or activity with nonconsenting partners. (nine are listed in the *DSM-III*)

Zoophilia
the act or fantasy of engaging in sexual activity with animals is a repeatedly preferred or exclusive method of achieving sexual excitement.

Exhibitionism
repetitive acts of exposing the genitals for the purpose of achieving sexual excitement; exposure is usually to total strangers; no further sexual activity is attempted; apparently occurs only in males; often reported to law enforcement agencies.

Sexual masochism
a condition in which sexual arousal is attained through being humiliated, bound, beaten, or otherwise made to suffer; voluntary and intentional participation in a harmful activity for the purpose of arousing sexual excitement.

PSYCHOSEXUAL DYSFUNCTIONS
involving impairment during some stage of the sexual response cycle; either an inability to complete the sex act, or an inability to derive pleasure from doing so; some disorders are clearly more associated with one sex than the other.

Inhibited sexual excitement
a recurrent and persistent inhibition of sexual excitement; in males, a partial or complete failure to maintain an erection, or similar failure to attain or maintain the lubrication-swelling response of sexual excitement in females; often referred to as impotence or frigidity.

Inhibited male orgasm
recurrent and persistent inability to ejaculate following an adequate phase of sexual excitement; not due to any organic factors, physical disorder, or medication.

Functional dyspareunia
intercourse (coitus) is associated with recurrent and persistent genital pain; in either male or female; not due to lack of lubrication or some organic disorder.

Functional vaginismus
a recurrent and persistent involuntary muscular contraction of vaginal muscles that interferes with coitus; again, not caused by organic disorder.

OTHER PSYCHOSEXUAL DISORDERS
Ego-dystonic homosexuality
a desire to acquire and/or increase heterosexual arousal so that heterosexual relationships can be initiated or maintained; category reserved for homosexuals for whom changing sexual orientation is a persistent concern; an unwanted state of homosexual orientation.

And these are just the *reported* cases. Actual numbers may be 5 to 10 times as large.

Many psychologists view rape, not as a crime of sex and passion, but as a crime of anger and violence. Rape often involves more than one offender. In most cases, rape is not a matter of a sudden loss of control. Most cases of rape are premeditated (Janda & Klenke-Hamel, 1980).

Many misconceptions about rape and rapists persist. Here are a few commonly held myths (taken from Coleman et al., 1980, 1984). (1) Women who are raped usually "ask for it," and have at least an unconscious desire to be raped. (2) Most persons who are accused of rape are convicted. (3) Rapists are oversexed and probably have a hormonal problem. (4) Most rapists are single men who hardly ever experience normal sexual relations with women. (5) Most rapes are stimulated by the viewing of pornography. (6) Rapists are usually repeat offenders, whose crimes tend to become more violent and frequent. (7) Most rapes occur at a considerable distance from the victim's home or place of work. (8) Achieving sexual satisfaction is the rapist's prime goal. Once again, each of these statements is demonstrably false.

There are, then, a number of reasons why neither homosexuality nor rape is listed as a category of mental disorder in the *DSM-III*. Homosexuality, in and of itself, meets few of the general definitions of abnormality that we have used throughout this topic. Rape, in and of itself, may be seen as a symptom of a disorder, perhaps, but as a behavior, it does not qualify as a mental disorder.

According to the National Institute of Mental Health, how prevalent are mental or psychological disorders in the U.S.?

Although it is obviously difficult to know the extent of mental disorders with any precision, a report of the National Institute of Mental Health released in the fall of 1984 claims that approximately 43 million noninstitutionalized, adult Americans (19 percent) were suffering from some sort of psychological disorder. / 500

How do we define psychological abnormality?

In the context of psychological disorders, we define abnormal to mean statistically uncommon maladaptive behaviors, cognitions, and/or affect, that are at odds with social expectations, and that result in distress and discomfort. It is recognized that all of the criteria listed in this definition need not necessarily be present simultaneously. / 502

What is the DSM-III?

What are some of its advantages and disadvantages?

The *DSM-III,* or the third edition of the *Diagnostic and Statistical Manual of Mental Disorders,* the "official" classification scheme for psychological disorders as decided by a large committee of psychologists and psychiatrists. The major advantage of this system is that it provides one standard label and cluster of symptoms for that label that all mental health practitioners can use; it is an aid in communication. It does have its limitations, however. It includes 230 separate entries, which some believe to be too many. On the other hand, there are deviations from social norms that are not included in the manual. Such schemes should not be used to confuse description with explanation; the *DSM-III* does the former, not the latter. / 506

What are the essential characteristics of a phobic reaction?

By definition, a phobic reaction is typified by an intense, persistent fear of some object, activity, or situation which is in no real sense a threat to the individual's well-being; an intense, irrational fear. / 508

How are the two anxiety states of generalized anxiety disorder and panic disorder the same, and how are they different?

Panic disorders and generalized anxiety disorders are alike in that their major defining characteristic is a high level of anxiety that cannot be attributed to any particular source. The major difference between the two is that for the generalized anxiety disorder, the felt anxiety is chronic, persistent, and diffuse. In the panic disorder, however, there may be periods during which the person is totally free from feelings of anxiety; the anxiety occurs in acute attacks. / 509

In the context of the obsessive-compulsive disorder, what is an obsession, and what is a compulsion?

An obsession is an idea or thought that constantly intrudes on one's awareness. A compulsion, on the other hand, is a repeated and stereotyped behavior or act that constantly intrudes on one's behavior. / 510

Describe the somatoform disorders hypochondriasis, somatization disorder, and conversion disorder.

By definition, each of the somatoform disorders reflect some physical or bodily symptom or complaint. In hypochondriasis, for example, a person lives in fear and dread of contracting some serious illness or disease, when there is no medical evidence that such fears are well founded. In the somatization disorder, the focus of attention is on some chronic, long-standing, anxiety-producing, physical symptom for which there is no medical explanation. And in conversion disorder, there is an actual loss or alteration in physical functioning—often dramatic, such as blindness or deafness—not under voluntary control, suggesting a physical disorder, but without medical basis. / 511

What are the defining symptoms of the dissociative disorders?

The defining characteristic of the dissociative disorders is a retreat or escape from (a dissociation with) some aspect of one's personality. It may be a matter of an inability to recall some life event (amnesia), sometimes accompanied by unexplained travel to a different location (fugue state). In some very rare cases, certain aspects of one's personality become so dissociated that we may say that the person suffers from multiple personality, where two or more personalities are found in the same individual. / 513

What are the defining characteristics of the personality disorders?

Personality disorders are enduring patterns of perceiving, relating to, and thinking about the environment and one's self that are inflexible and maladaptive. These are essentially life-long patterns of response, and may be classified as being odd, eccentric, dramatic, erratic, or fearful. / 514

TOPIC 28

Organic, Paranoid, Affective, and Schizophrenic Disorders

Before you sits George, a 26-year-old male Caucasian. His appearance is one of a person who has dressed hurriedly: hair disheveled, shirt partially buttoned. Throughout the interview George either looks down at the table or off into space, seemingly not focusing on anything.

Psychologist: Good morning, George. How do you feel today?

George: (with a sing-song tone) Better than yesterday; but not as good as tomorrow.

Psych: You think you'll feel better tomorrow?

G: Oh yeah. Gotta. Can't feel worse. Know what day this is?

Psych: No, what day is it?

G: My birthday. (In fact, it is not.) Gonna have a big party.

Psych: How old are you today?

G: 120

Psych: Really. You're 120 years old? That's really old.

G: Yes, but not many people know that (speaking now very rapidly and with no feeling or intonation in his voice). Last year I was 119 years old; now I'm 120. I was born in 1652 and know Christopher Columbus sailed the ocean blue. I told him to go even though he didn't want to. He didn't think it was safe, but I knew that it was safe and he wouldn't fall off. (long pause) You gonna be at my party?

Psych: Who's having this party for you, George?

G: My classmate students here at the college and some of the teachers, too. Those who know I'm not crazy. Those who know about the voices.

Psych: What voices?

G: (no response)

Psych: What voices are you talking about, George? What voices do they know about?

G: The voices that talk only to me. They tell me what to think when I can't figure it out.

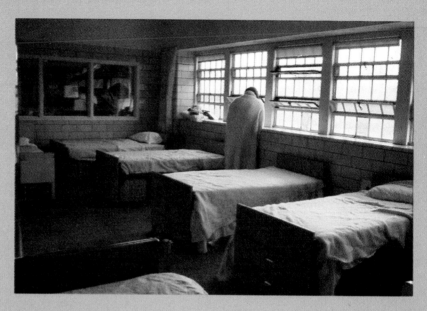

Psych: Can't figure what out?

G: Everything man. God, you're stupid. Are you one of the dumb teachers here? Sometimes I don't like this school. You're dumb, man.

Psych: I'd like to know more about these voices.

G: They're telling me not to talk to you anymore.

Psych: Are they telling you that right now?

G: I can't talk to you anymore. It would be a crime. And I'm not a bad person.

Psych: Of course you're not a bad person. I'd like to talk with you some more.

G: (For 20 minutes George says nothing and simply stares at the table. Occasionally he seems to chuckle softly to himself. He is then returned to his room.)

This is George's third day as an in-patient at a community mental health center. His parents brought him to the center when he unexpectedly returned from college, went into his room, and refused to come out because "voices" were telling him not to. He claimed that he came home because his "voices told him to." He had apparently neither bathed nor shaved for days. It took considerable coaxing to get him from his room. A check with college officials revealed that George had not attended classes for the past 3 weeks. George is obviously a severely disturbed young man. As we shall see, he is showing many of the symptoms of a devastating disorder that afflicts more than 2 million Americans: schizophrenia.

In this topic, we continue our discussion of mental or psychological disorders. It is probably inappropriate and in a sense unfair to classify some disorders as being more or less severe or debilitating than others. To the person who is experiencing the disorder, and to those who care about that person, *any* psychological disorder can seem severe and debilitating.

It is nonetheless the case that the disorders we'll introduce in this topic tend to be more disruptive and discomforting than those we reviewed in the last topic. Most forms of the disorders we'll cover in this topic are those that can be classified as **psychotic disorders.** That is usually taken to mean two things: a gross impairment in functioning (difficulty dealing with the demands of everyday life) and a gross impairment in reality testing (a loss of contact with the real world as the rest of us know it). As a result, persons with these disorders frequently require hospitalization.

The term *psychosis,* or psychotic disorder, is not a specific classification in the *Diagnostic and Statistical Manual of Mental Disorders (DSM-III)* of the American Psychiatric Association (1980). The term (rather like neurosis) has come to mean so many different things to different people that it has lost some of its usefulness. It is still quite clear, however, that at least some of the symptoms of the disorders we'll examine in this topic qualify as being psychotic—involving a loss of contact with reality and a gross impairment in functioning.

As was the case for the disorders we discussed in our last topic, we will again see that psychological disturbances often have an impact on each of three levels: behavioral, cognitive, and/or affective. In some cases, it is a disturbance in behavior that is most noteworthy—a person actually does strange and unusual things (in our opening example, George constantly stared at the table or gazed off into space throughout the entire interview, an inappropriate behavior). In some cases, the most noticeable symptoms are cognitive—a person has strange, unusual, and unreal thoughts or beliefs (this was George's major symptom during the interview, when he claimed to be hearing voices that controlled his thoughts). In some cases, the most obvious impairment is affective or emotional—a person may have flattened affect and show little or no emotional response, or may respond with inappropriate affect (George's chuckling to himself for no apparent reason, coupled with his lack of emotional tone when talking about his birthday would be an example).

We'll begin this topic by taking a brief look at two types of disorders that are often classified as psychotic: organic mental disorders and paranoid disorders. Then we'll discuss the two major psychotic disorders: the affective disorders and schizophrenic disorders.

psychotic disorders
psychological disorders that involve gross impairment in functioning and a loss of contact with reality

Before you go on
What criteria are used to classify a symptom or a disorder as psychotic?

ORGANIC MENTAL DISORDERS

A consideration of the label used to describe this collection of psychological disorders tells us what they have in common: a disordering of behavior or mental processes whose etiology (cause) involves some organic or brain function. As the *DSM-III* points out, it is assumed that in some way or another, brain function is involved in *all* mental disorders. Here, however, a specific brain function can be implicated as causing the psychological symptoms.

Our approach to organic mental disorders is a little different from the generally descriptive approach we have used so far. Any diagnosis, and resulting labeling, of organic mental disorders depends on two interacting factors: (1) an organic brain **syndrome,** which is a collection of psychological symptoms (and is simply descriptive), and (2) a statement of the known cause or etiology of the syndrome. That is, one group of symptoms may be associated with substance abuse or senility. In such instances, we would have two, separate disorders. Even though the symptoms are the same, they are caused by different factors. So that we can have the proper vocabulary available, some of the major organic brain syndromes are presented in Figure 28.1. With these in mind, we can review some of the typical organic mental disorders.

syndrome
a collection of symptoms used to describe a disorder

Degenerative Dementia

As the name **degenerative dementia** implies, the major syndrome of this disorder is dementia (see Figure 28.1). It is also degenerative, meaning that the symptoms tend to gradually worsen over time. It is a disorder of old age and is still often referred to as *senile psychosis*. It should be made clear, however, that this disorder is in no way a normal, natural, or necessary part of growing old, although cases in persons younger than 65 are relatively uncommon. The *DSM-III* states that "between 2 percent and 4 percent of the population over the age of 65 is estimated to have (this disorder), with the prevalence increasing with increasing age, particularly after 75" *(DSM-III,*

degenerative dementia
a marked loss of intellectual and cognitive abilities that worsens with age

---

Figure 28.1
Defining terms: The major organic brain syndromes and symptoms (Adapted from DSM-III, 1980.)

Delirium
a clouded state of consciousness; a lessening of one's awareness; difficulty in maintaining attention; accompanied by disturbances of thought; poor sleep habits; disorientation and confusion; episodes do not last long, a week or so at most; someone who is delirious cannot seem to relate what is happening now to what has happened in the past.

Dementia
a marked loss of intellectual abilities; attention is unaffected, but use of memory is poor and deteriorates; memory losses may be minor at first and progress to virtual total loss of memory; judgment and impulse control may also be adversely affected; person is not delirious.

Amnestic syndrome
impairment of memory occurring in normal state of consciousness; attention

and other intellectual skills and abilities remain intact.

Delusions
defined as a false personal belief; the belief is firmly held regardless of what others may say; there are many types, including delusions of being controlled, grandiose delusions, and delusions of persecution; basically coming to believe firmly in something that is clearly not true.

Hallucinations
defined as sensory perception without external stimulation of the relevant sensory organ; hallucinations may occur in any sense, but some are more associated with some causes than others, LSD and visual, alcohol and auditory, for example.

Affective syndrome
a disturbance in mood, either excited and manic or (more commonly)

depressed; delusions and hallucinations may occur.

Intoxication
major feature is the impairment of behavior and mental processes following the use of a drug; specific symptoms depend on the nature of the drug used; intoxication may involve any and all of the syndromes listed above; common changes involve disturbances in perception, attention, thinking, judgment, and emotional control.

Withdrawal
a set of symptoms that follow the reduction or cessation in intake of a drug previously used to reach a state of intoxication; particular symptoms depend on drug used; any of the above listed syndromes may be involved in withdrawal.

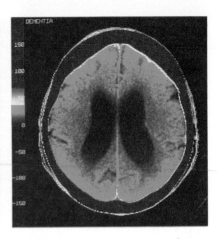

There are obvious differences in the CAT scans of a normal brain (left) and the brain of a person with degenerative dementia (right). The dark blue areas in the diseased brain indicate an enlargement of the ventricles (the large, hollow spaces in the brain) due to the degeneration of brain tissue.

1980, p. 125). One form of degenerative dementia that has recently attracted much attention is Alzheimer's disease, which is discussed in our Topic Expansion.

Substance-induced Organic Mental Disorders

In Chapter 4, Topic 9, we discussed some of the more common psychoactive drugs and noted their effects on consciousness. As we suggested, if these drugs or chemicals are used long enough, or in large enough doses or quantities, they may cause lasting damage to the central nervous system and produce a wide range of psychological reactions that we can classify as disordered. In this section, we'll take a brief look at some of the more commonly abused substances that produce organic mental disorders, and we'll indicate which of the syndromes listed in Figure 28.1 are most likely to be associated with such abuse.

Alcohol A psychoactive substance is one that has some effect on the user's psychological functioning. Alcohol is one of the most commonly used of such substances and certainly ranks as the most commonly abused. It is estimated that between 10 and 15 million Americans are alcohol abusers (Coleman, 1984; National Council on Alcoholism, 1979). The *DSM-III* lists six major ways in which alcohol use *may* lead to an organic mental disorder.

(1) Alcohol intoxication, which is indicated by maladaptive behavioral effects (such as fighting or impaired judgment), slurred speech, lack of coordination, mood change, irritability, impaired attention, and other signs; in a way, this is simply a matter of drinking too much.

(2) Alcohol withdrawal, which is indicated by tremors (involuntary shaking), nausea, vomiting, depressed mood, and other signs that occur after one has *stopped* drinking for a time.

(3) Alcohol withdrawal delirium, in which, in addition to the signs listed in (2) above, delirium also occurs, usually within 1 week after one stops drinking.

(4) Alcohol hallucinosis, the major sign of which is vivid hallucinations (usually auditory and unpleasant) that follow within 48 hours after drinking stops.

(5) Alcohol amnestic disorder, in which the major sign is the amnestic syndrome (Figure 28.1), brought on by prolonged, heavy use. Because this disorder can be anticipated for a person who is a long-term heavy drinker, it can be prevented with proper medication.

(6) Dementia is the major sign. To make sure these symptoms are not just those associated with intoxication, this diagnosis is not made until the person has been off alcohol for at least 3 weeks.

Virtually everyone over the age of 21 has had some experience with alcohol. The majority of the population has experienced at least one bout with alcohol intoxication. No other drug carries with it as much potential for the development of a long-term disorder than does alcohol. Its use and abuse are costly beyond measure. Dollar figures ($25 million lost each year attributable to alcohol use) become meaningless when compared to the personal and family losses that can be attributed to the mental disorders brought on by the abuse of alcohol.

Barbiturates   The abuse of barbiturates and other sedative drugs leads to three possible diagnosable mental disorders. One is a disorder of use: intoxication, which includes many of the same symptoms as alcohol intoxication—impaired judgment, interference with mental functioning, slurred speech, lack of bodily coordination, unstable mood, irritability, and the like. The other two disorders show up during withdrawal and include such symptoms as nausea, weakness, anxiety, depressed mood, tremors, and (within 1 week after one stops taking the drug) delirium and/or amnestic syndrome.

Opiates   The opiate drugs, or narcotics (including heroin), give rise to two possible mental disorders when abused, one from taking the drug, the other when drug use stops. Symptoms of opiate intoxication include constriction of the pupil of the eye, euphoria, apathy, drowsiness, and impairment of attention or memory. Withdrawal from heavy opiate use leads to a number of mental and physical symptoms, including dilation of the pupils, insomnia, weakness, diarrhea, hallucinations, or delusions.

Cocaine   Abuse of cocaine is different from abuse of many other drugs in that there is seldom any psychological disturbance associated with withdrawal. Psychotic symptoms are only associated with its use, hence the term cocaine intoxication. The symptoms here include an unfounded sense of well-being and confidence, with an apparent increase in sensitivity to sensations. Remember that cocaine is a stimulant and may lead to states of agitation, elevated blood pressure, and increased physical activity.

Amphetamines   Prolonged or excessive use of amphetamines (stimulants) may lead to a range of possible disorders, from intoxication (including agitation, elation, talkativeness, etc.) to delirium, to delusional disorders, to severe disorders associated with withdrawal (including disturbed sleep, fatigue, and increased dreaming). As we shall see, the wide range of symptoms induced by amphetamine use has provided scientists with an insight to one of the possible causes of a major psychotic disorder, schizophrenia.

Obviously, there are other substances that are psychoactive and can be abused, including PCP (or phencyclidine), which may cause delirium, the hallucinogens (such as LSD), which may cause hallucinations, delusions, and/or disorders of affect, and cannibis drugs (such as marijuana and hashish), which may cause intoxication disorders or delusions. The list of dis-

No other drug is as much abused as alcohol, but there is help available for alcoholics.

orders that are substance-induced is a long one, and the symptoms and syndromes associated with each can be very severe and debilitating. There is no way to avoid the obvious: Psychoactive drugs are dangerous.

Before you go on

What are some of the syndromes associated with organic mental disorders?

What gives rise to these syndromes?

PARANOIA

A 51-year-old single woman was brought to the hospital by her elderly parents—"My parents think I need to be here, but I'm not sick."
About a year before admission the patient had begun seeing her family physician for painful breasts, and was receiving male hormone injections. She began to believe that the doctor was maliciously trying to change her into a man, and wrote several letters to him complaining of this.

Shortly thereafter, she began to believe that her stepfather and certain government officials were involved in a plan to get her to give up a piece of land she owned in the country. She also accused her stepfather of telling various garages to perform improper repairs on her car and to overcharge her, as a means of harassment. She accused the neighbors of putting substances in her water that damaged the trees and grass. Drinking this water, she believed, caused her and her pets to have problems with receding gums. She wrote numerous letters to public officials complaining of these events, and sent soil and water samples to the agriculture department to be tested. Yet all the while she worked efficiently at her job examining real-estate tax forms.

She had no previous contact with mental health professionals. The mental status examination revealed no hallucinations, incoherence, or loosening of associations (Spitzer et al., 1981, pp. 67–68).

paranoid disorder
a rare psychotic mental disorder characterized by delusions of persecution, influence, grandeur, or jealousy

This case presents an excellent example of a **paranoid disorder,** the essential feature of which is a persistent delusion or set of delusions. One of the things that makes this case somewhat unusual is that it is so clear-cut and obviously a case of paranoia. In many cases, the delusions and symptoms are such that it is difficult to identify "pure" paranoia.

Paranoia is a disorder rarely encountered in clinical practice. On the one hand, the disorder may simply be rare. On the other hand, it may very well be that many individuals display the major symptom of paranoia—the false beliefs of a delusion—and go undiagnosed. In many cases, paranoia causes little or no impairment in intelligence and little or no difficulty on the job. Indeed, people with paranoid disorders tend to be of above average intelligence and hold good jobs of considerable responsibility. Impairment with this disorder is more typically found in social and marital relationships.

It should be remembered that the delusions that characterize the paranoid disorder tend to be delusions of persecution and/or jealousy. These delusions are seldom bizarre and outrageous. They are, in a way, well thought out, internally consistent, and, in a way, not unreasonable. Persons with this disorder can often convince others of the truthfulness of their delusions and will stick with the same delusions for a long period of time. The problem is, of course, that the delusions of a person with a paranoid disorder are, in fact, not true.

Before you go on

What is the defining characteristic of a paranoid disorder?

AFFECTIVE DISORDERS

As we already know, affect has to do with one's felt emotions, or mood. Hence, **affective disorders** clearly demonstrate some disturbance or disorder in mood or feeling. We have to be a little careful here. Almost all psychological disorders will have some impact on one's mood or affect. With affective disorders, however, the intensity and extremeness of mood are the primary characteristics.

affective disorders
disorders of mood or feeling; usually depression; less frequently mania and depression occurring in cycles

Another thing we must recognize is that we have all felt some degree of extreme mood. From time to time we have all felt depression, and at other times we have felt the elevated, heightened, euphoric mood of mania. These moods have not severely impaired our functioning for very long, however. And most importantly, when we are depressed or very happy we know why. We can attribute our depression or our mania to something that has happened to us—a close friend or relative has died, we have been denied admission to medical school, we have won a large prize, we fail to get an expected promotion, or have been chosen worker of the year.

Depression and Mania

Affective disorders are defined in terms of extremes of mood. There is no doubt that depression is the more common of the two extremes. Depression is usually found alone, whereas mania almost never is—it is associated with episodes of depression.

Seligman (1975) is credited as having first named depression "the common cold of mental illness." The *DSM-III* (1980) considers depression to be twice as likely in women than men (18–23 percent of females and 8–11 percent of males are likely to have at least one depressive episode). The 1984 study of the National Institute of Mental Health also recognizes depression as a prevalent disorder, suggesting that at any one time, approximately 1 person in 20 (of their sample) "had suffered a major depressive episode" (NIMH, 1984, p. 952). The symptoms of depression are summarized in Figure 28.2.

Mania is a condition of mood that cannot be maintained for long. It's altogether too tiring to stay extremely manic for an extended time. People are

Figure 28.2
Common symptoms of depression

1. Persistently unpleasant mood—feeling sad, blue, depressed, hopeless, low, down-in-the-dumps, irritable, and so on
2. Loss of pleasure or interest in all or almost all usual activities or pastimes
3. Poor appetite or weight loss (not due to dieting)
4. Insomnia
5. Agitation or slowing of motor behavior
6. Decrease in sexual activity and sexual drive
7. Loss of energy—fatigue
8. Feelings of worthlessness—self-reproach, inappropriate guilt feelings
9. Diminished ability to think—real or complained of, indecisiveness
10. Recurrent thoughts of death—ideas of suicide, wishes to be dead, actual suicide attempts

Figure 28.3
Common symptoms of mania

1. Elevated mood—feelings are expansive, euphoric, or irritable

2. Increase in activity—socially, at work, or sexually; physical restlessness; participation in multiple activities, all at the same time

3. More talkative than usual

4. Racing thoughts—ideas come quickly to mind

5. Decreased need for sleep

6. Distractibility—attention easily drawn to unimportant or irrelevant matters

7. Lack of appreciation of possible dangers of behaviors—shopping sprees, sexual indiscretions, foolish investments, reckless driving, and so on.
   (at least three of these should have occurred during a period of at least 3 weeks)

very rarely ever manic without showing interspersed periods of depression. Because such people swing back and forth between these two extremes of mood (with episodes of normal affect interspersed), they are said to have a *bipolar disorder*, commonly referred to as a manic-depressive disorder. Figure 28.3 lists some of the major defining characteristics of a manic reaction.

Unfortunately, the prognosis for either major depression or the manic-depressive disorder is not encouraging. Only about 40 percent can be said to be symptom-free for a period of 5 years (Coryell & Winokur, 1982), although we'll see that there are other disorders for which a 40 percent "cure rate" would be a marked improvement.

We've described the essential symptoms of affective disorders and have noted that depression is by far the more common of these disorders. Now let's ask why people become depressed. Where does depression come from?

Causes of Depression

The answers we find to the question "What causes depression?" depend in large measure on where and how we look for such answers. It seems most likely that depression is caused by a number of different, but potentially interrelated causes. Some of them are biological, others are more psychological. In this section, we'll briefly consider some of the factors that seem to influence the development of depression.

Biological Factors   Bipolar affective disorder is not very common in the general population. Anyone chosen at random would have less than a one half of 1 percent chance of developing the symptoms of the disorder. The chances of developing the symptoms rise to 15 percent if a brother, sister, or either parent ever had the disorder. This 15 percent figure seems to be true for fraternal twins, too. If, however, one member of a pair of identical twins has the disorder, the chances that the other twin will contract the disorder jump to more than 70 percent (Allen, 1976). What all this means, of course, is that there is excellent evidence that there is a genetic, or inherited, predisposition for the bipolar affective disorder. The data are not quite as impressive for the unipolar affective disorder (depression only), where the similar data for identical twins is 4 in 10, or 40 percent, compared to 11 percent for fraternal twins. We can suspect, however, that there is some sort of genetic basis to the disorder. Attempts to localize the specific genetic mechanism involved have, as yet, been inconclusive (Carson & Carson, 1983).

It is one thing to suspect a genetic basis for a disorder and yet another to specify the biological mechanism that produces its symptoms. Recently, attention has been focused on a number of neurotransmitters that seem to directly influence mood. Collectively they are referred to as *biogenic amines* and include such known transmitter substances as serotonin, dopamine, and norepinephrine. The major breakthrough in this research came when it was discovered that a drug (reserpine) used to treat high blood pressure also produced symptoms of depression. It was then discovered that reserpine depleted the brain's normal level of norepinephrine, and the search for neurotransmitter involvement in affective disorders was on (Bennett, 1982).

One current theory is that depression is caused by a reduction in the biogenic amines, and that mania is caused by an overabundance of these chemicals. It remains to be seen what produces these biochemical imbalances in some people and not others. Anisman and Zacharko (1982) have demonstrated that stress causes increased levels of these neurotransmitters in the brain. If these substances are overstimulated by prolonged stress, perhaps their supply becomes depleted in the long run, leading to symptoms of depression. The theory seems logical, but as yet there is insufficient evidence for us to draw any firm conclusions.

Learned and Cognitive Factors Learning theorists attribute depression to a number of learning phenomena, including most importantly, a lack of effectiveness of reinforcers. Given a history of having responses pass without reinforcement, an organism will tend to stop responding and will become withdrawn, quiet, passive, and, in many ways, depressed. Some people, lacking ability to gain (or earn) reinforcement, simply tend to respond less often to environmental cues. They enter into a long, generalized period of extinction, which ultimately leads to depression.

Other learning theory approaches to depression tend to be much more cognitive in their orientation. The best example of such an approach is that of Seligman (1975) and his concept of learned helplessness. The basic idea of learned helplessness is that an organism that was once faced with a number of unpleasant circumstances from which there is no escape, will soon come to give up trying to escape, even if escape is possible. A previous learning of the sort demonstrated by Seligman *might* account for the passivity and low level of responding of some depressed persons.

Other psychologists (most notably Beck, 1967, 1976) argue that although depression is shown as a disorder of affect, its causes are largely cognitive. Some people, the argument goes, tend to think of themselves in a poor light; they believe that they are, in many ways, ineffective people. They tend to blame themselves for a great many of their failures, whether deservedly so or not. Facing life with such a negative self-attitude tends to foster more failures and self-doubt, and such cycles inevitably lead to feelings of depression.

To be sure, there are other views about the causes of depression, including some psychoanalytic views that depression is a reflection of early childhood experiences that lead to inwardly directed anger. We do not yet understand all the possible causes of depression. Perhaps the only thing we can conclude with any certainty is that depression probably stems from a combination of genetic predispositions, biochemical influences, learning experiences, situational stress, and cognitive factors. Which of these is more, or most, important remains to be seen.

Before you go on
How are the affective disorders defined?

What do we know about their prevalence and their causes?

SCHIZOPHRENIA

schizophrenia
complex psychotic disorders characterized by impairment of cognitive functioning, delusions and hallucinations, social withdrawal, and inappropriate affect

We will now examine what many consider to be the ultimate psychological disorder: **schizophrenia.** In many ways, schizophrenia is "the most devastating, puzzling, and frustrating of all mental illnesses" (Bloom et al., 1985). Schizophrenia is the label given to a number of specific disorders, which have in common a retreat from reality and other people, accompanied by disturbances in perception, thinking, affect, and behavior.

One of the things that qualifies schizophrenia as the ultimate psychological disorder is that it seems to involve virtually every aspect of being. The possible range of symptoms is so great that it is nearly impossible to specify just which symptoms are basic or fundamental, and which are secondary.

Let's simply list some of the symptoms that are commonly associated with schizophrenia. There is usually a disturbance of thinking. As reflected in their delusions, schizophrenics come to believe strange and unusual things that are simply not true. The delusions of the schizophrenic tend to be bizarre, inconsistent, and clearly unsupportable. Perceptions are often distorted, most commonly with auditory hallucinations (hearing voices). Sometimes distortions of time are very compelling, in which a minute may seem to last for hours, or in which hours may race by in a matter of seconds. Schizophrenics may engage in a number of unusual behaviors, typically ritualized, stereotyped, and meaningless. One of the most obvious behavioral consequences of schizophrenia is found in language behavior. Some schizophrenics simply make up words *(neologisms)* as they talk. (I once had a schizophrenic tell me at great length and with great animation about a "rogaritz" and what that "rogaritz" was going to do with a tree once it caught it.) Others use English words, but mix them up and use them inappropriately (in "word salads").

It is also common to find affect involved in a schizophrenic disorder. Most commonly, we encounter flattened affect, meaning that a person shows no particular emotional response of any kind to external stimuli. Less commonly there is the inappropriate affect of the psychotic: giggling and laughing or crying and sobbing for no apparent reason. Our opening interview with George is typical of the sort of reactions one might expect from a person with a schizophrenic disorder.

We need to make two things clear. First, as unsettling as this list of symptoms may be, the average schizophrenic patient does not present the picture of the crazed, wild, lunatic that is often depicted in movies and on television. Day in and day out, the average schizophrenic patient is quite colorless, socially withdrawn, and of very little immediate danger to others. Although there are exceptions to this rule of thumb, it is particularly true when the schizophrenic patient is under treatment and/or under medication. Their "differentness" may be frightening, but schizophrenics are seldom dangerous people.

Second, when literally translated, schizophrenia means "split of the mind." This term was first used by a Swiss psychiatrist, Eugen Bleuler, in 1911. The split that Bleuler was addressing was a split of the mind of the schizophrenic from the real world and the social relationships that the rest of us enjoy. Never has the term been used to describe a multiple or split personality of the Dr. Jekyl and Mr. Hyde variety. Such disorders do occur, but they are rare, and we have already seen that they are classified as a variety of dissociative reaction.

Schizophrenia tends to occur around the world at approximately the same rate: 1 percent of the population at any one time. This figure has been stable for many years (Coleman et al., 1984). The 1984 NIMH survey revealed about 1 percent of their sample to be schizophrenic, with about half of these individuals actively in treatment for the disorder (NIMH, 1984). It is a common claim that schizophrenic patients fill more than half of the hospital beds in mental or psychiatric hospitals in this country (Bloom et al., 1985). Once again, however, the statistics are difficult to deal with on a personal level. We are certainly talking about very large numbers of persons, many of whom will be treated and will recover, while many others will spend the rest of their lives in and out of institutions, under rather constant care and supervision. Let's now consider some of the ways in which this collection of disorders can be classified.

Types and Varieties of Schizophrenia

Reactive and Process   Up to now, we have classified varieties of disorders in terms of specific, defining symptoms. With schizophrenia, there is at least one common distinction that is not made on the basis of the *nature* of symptoms, but on the basis of their onset. We use the term **process schizophrenia** to describe schizophrenic symptoms that have developed gradually, usually over a period of years. It is usually only in retrospect, after the diagnosis of schizophrenia has been made, that we realize that there has been a long history of symptoms that have gradually worsened to the point where intervention is required, treatment sought, and a diagnosis made.

process schizophrenia
schizophrenia in which the onset of the symptoms is comparatively slow and gradual

Reactive schizophrenia, on the other hand, is the term we use for the sudden onset of schizophrenic symptoms. Here we have a clinical picture of someone who was, by all accounts, quite normal and well adjusted, but who suddenly showed signs of having a psychotic break.

reactive schizophrenia
schizophrenia in which the onset of the symptoms is comparatively sudden

As we have found to be the case in other situations, we should not consider "reactive" and "process" as two separate and distinct varieties of schizophrenia. Rather, we should view them as poles, or extremes, of a dimension that can be used to describe the nature of the onset of schizophrenic symptoms.

The significance of this distinction is that there is reason to believe that the prognosis for schizophrenia can be, in large measure, based on the nature of its onset—the more toward the *process* variety, the worse the prognosis, and the more toward the *reactive* type of onset, the better the prognosis.

DSM-III Subtypes   The *Diagnostic and Statistical Manual of Mental Disorders* lists five types or categories of schizophrenic disorder. All of these varieties share many of the same symptoms of disorganized cognition, inappropriate affect, and strange behavior. But each has a particular symptom or cluster of symptoms that makes it different. The types of schizophrenia listed in the *DSM-III* are presented in Figure 28.4.

> **Before you go on**
>
> **What are the major symptoms of schizophrenia?**
>
> **How prevalent is the disorder?**
>
> **What characterizes the following varieties or types of schizophrenia: process versus reactive, paranoid, catatonic, and hebephrenic?**

Observations on the Causes of Schizophrenia

Schizophrenia is obviously a complex set of disorders. There is even some disagreement about how to define the disorder. (In one recent study, a sample of schizophrenics was reduced by more than half when the researchers

Undifferentiated type
a general classification; showing no particular symptom that qualifies as one of the other types, hence undifferentiated; shows hallucinations, delusions, incoherent speech, disorganized behaviors; in short, a little of everything and nothing in particular.

Paranoid type
major symptom is one of delusions (of persecution, grandeur, influence, or jealousy); often accompanied by hallucinations; delusions are usually auditory; delusions also tend to be absurd and illogical; may lead to anger and violence; behavior is not as disorganized, unless delusions are acted out.

Catatonic type
shows a tendency to remain motionless, impassive, not reacting to any environmental stimulation (catatonia); may assume and hold bizarre postures for long time periods; often displays extreme negativism; may, without warning, become very agitated and excitable and impulsive.

Disorganized (hebephrenic) type
a severe disturbance of entire personality; most noticeable is inappropriate affect; usually childish, silly, giggling; clear disturbances of language (neologisms and word salad, for example); extreme social withdrawal is common; absence of organized delusions.

Residual type
only following previous diagnosis of a specific schizophrenic disorder; a sort of general, but mild form of schizophrenic symptoms; no clearly psychotic symptoms, but with signs of inappropriate affect, withdrawal, illogical thinking, or eccentric behavior; reserved for persons recovering from the disorder of schizophrenia.

imposed the *DSM-III* criteria rather than the *DSM-II* criteria to define their subjects (Winters et al., 1981).) As you might suspect, our bottom-line conclusion on the cause of schizophrenia is going to be tentative and multidimensional. Although we don't know what causes the disorder, we do have a number of interesting ideas to consider.

Hereditary Factors   There is little doubt that schizophrenia tends to run in families (Kessler, 1980; Rosenthal, 1970). The data are not as striking as they are for the affective disorders, but it is clear that one is at a higher risk of being diagnosed as schizophrenic if there is a history of the disorder in one's family.

It is generally held that the risk of becoming schizophrenic is 4 to 5 times greater for an identical twin than it is for a fraternal twin if the other member of the twin pair has the disorder. Looked at another way, the odds of being diagnosed as schizophrenic are, in the general population, about 1 in 100. For those who are identical twins of schizophrenics, the odds jump to nearly 1 in 2 (Bloom et al., 1985). It is also true that when adopted children become schizophrenic, it is much more likely that schizophrenia will be found among members of that person's biological family than his or her adoptive family (Bootzin & Acocella, 1984). We need to remember, once again, that such data do not mean that schizophrenia is inherited. It is more correct to say that such data suggest that one may inherit a predisposition to become schizophrenic. This distinction may be somewhat subtle, but it is an important one, recalling our many earlier discussions about not drawing cause-and-effect conclusions from correlational data.

The genetic predisposition for schizophrenia is well illustrated by the Genain quadruplets, shown here celebrating their 51st birthday in 1981. All four women experienced a schizophrenic disorder of varying severity, duration, and outcome—facts that may suggest an environmental role in schizophrenia.

Biochemical Factors: The Dopamine Hypothesis   Dopamine is a neurotransmitter substance found in every human brain (see Topic 4). The implication of this particular neurotransmitter in schizophrenia has recently come to light from a couple of different lines of research.

For one thing, we know that the abuse of amphetamines often leads to the development of many schizophrenialike symptoms. We further observe that amphetamines are chemically similar to dopamine and may actually cause an increase in dopamine levels in the brain. Logic then leads us to the conclusion that perhaps schizophrenic symptoms are caused by excess amounts of dopamine.

Support for this view comes from examining the workings of various antipsychotic drugs that bring about a reduction in schizophrenic symptoms. Apparently, drugs that alleviate schizophrenic symptoms commonly block receptor sites for dopamine in the brain (Snyder, 1980). If reducing the effectiveness of dopamine by blocking its activity at the synapse can control schizophrenic symptoms, might we not assume that these symptoms are caused by dopamine in the first place?

The arguments for this hypothesis appear compelling, but they are far from certain. There are a number of problems that are difficult to deal with. For one thing, not all antipsychotic medication has its effect by blocking dopamine receptor sites. It is also troublesome that when drugs *are* effective, their effect generally takes a few weeks to show up. The effect of the drug is immediate—why isn't the effect on symptoms immediate also? We also have a "chicken-and-egg" problem with this hypothesis. Even if dopamine were shown to be related to schizophrenic symptoms, we would still have to ask if there is a direct causal relationship. That is, do increased levels of dopamine cause schizophrenic symptoms, or does the disorder of schizophrenia cause elevated dopamine levels? We do not as yet have good answers to these questions (Carson, 1983).

Psychological and Social Factors   It may be that genetic and/or biochemical factors predispose a person to develop the symptoms of schizophrenia. What sorts of events or situations tend to turn such predispositions into reality for the schizophrenic? To this question, our answers are very sketchy indeed. One of the standard views (Lidz, 1965, 1973) is that schizophrenia develops as a response to early experiences within the family unit.

The early family experiences of people who later develop schizophrenic symptoms seem qualitatively different from those who do not become schizophrenic. Contributing factors that have been isolated include such things as improper or inefficient means of communication within the family. That is, there seems to be an inability or unwillingness to share feelings and emotions, to talk openly about problems and conflicts. Early childhood experiences of schizophrenics seem filled with conflict, anxiety, doubt, and emotional tension. There also seems to be an unusually high incidence of double messages and double binds being presented to children who later tend to become schizophrenic. For example, a mother may tell her child that she becomes upset when everyone forgets about her birthday and then scold the child for spending lunch money to buy a birthday present. Parents who communicate something like, "We want you to be independent and show some responsibility, but so long as you live in this house, you'll do things the way we say, no questions asked," are certainly delivering a double message to their child.

A (female) psychiatrist coined the term "schizophrenogenic mother" to describe a pattern of mothering behaviors that are cold, aloof, and generally unaffectionate. Attributing such qualities to mothers alone, however, is not supported by the evidence. Fathers may show "schizophrenogenic" behaviors also. Hostile parent-child relationships that lack spontaneous displays of love, affection, and positive regard are commonly found for schizophrenics. But, once again, we should not overinterpret. Many people raised in such homes never develop any schizophrenic symptoms. And many schizophrenics were reared in normal homes with families who were loving and accepting. And it is certainly not uncommon to find one child from a family developing schizophrenia, while another reared in the same environment never develops any schizophrenic symptoms. There seems no doubt that one's family atmosphere and learning history *can* be a factor in schizophrenia. That such psychosocial factors might be the only factors involved seems very unlikely.

We will save our discussion of the treatment of schizophrenia until the next chapter. Quite obviously, however, one treatment method will involve the use of medication to lessen the symptoms of the disorder. Largely because of the introduction of antipsychotic medications, the outlook for patients with schizophrenia is not nearly as dismal as it was just 25 years ago. It seems reasonable to estimate now that nearly one third of all persons diagnosed as schizophrenic will recover (be symptom-free for at least 5 years). About one third will be at least partially recovered and may assume, at least to some degree, the normal responsibilities of adaptive living in society. It still remains, however, that nearly one third of all patients diagnosed as schizophrenic will never recover to the point where they will be freed from institutionalization or daily supervision (Bloom et al., 1985).

Before you go on
Describe three factors that have been implicated as possible
causes of schizophrenic symptoms.

Alzheimer's disease
a gradual, progressive loss of intellectual functioning (dementia) caused by abnormal changes in brain tissues

Alzheimer's disease is a gradual, progressive deterioration of intellectual functioning. It is an incurable disease caused by abnormal changes in the tissues of the brain (Aronson, 1982). Problems of recent memory are common in early stages. (For example, "Did I take my medicine this morning?" "Now that I'm here, why did I come to the hardware store?") Mild personality changes soon follow—less spontaneity, apathy, withdrawal (perhaps as attempts to hide one's symptoms from others). "As the disease progresses, problems in abstract thinking or in intellectual functioning take place. The individual may begin to have trouble with figures when working on bills, with understanding what is being read, or with organizing the day's work. Further disturbances in behavior, such as being

agitated, irritable, quarrelsome, and less neat in appearance, may also be seen at this point. Later in the course of the disease, the afflicted may become confused or disoriented about what month or year it is and be unable to describe accurately where they live or to name correctly a place being visited. Eventually they may wander, not engage in conversation, become inattentive and erratic in mood, uncooperative, incontinent with loss of bladder and bowel control, and in extreme cases, totally incapable of caring for themselves" (Cohen, 1980).

Alzheimer's is not new; it was first described in 1907 by Alois Alzheimer. The disease was thought to be an inevitable process of aging. It is not. Alzheimer's is a disease; it is not a natural, normal process. It is

Written reminders can help Alzheimer's victims lead a relatively normal life. In the early stages, they can remember how to do things once they are reminded to do them at all. Later on, they may lose the ability to do even simple tasks.

not the same as, nor is it caused by, hardening of the arteries, or arteriosclerosis.

Alzheimer's disease can be diagnosed with certainty only at autopsy, when microscopic analysis of brain tissue indicates the presence of the disease. So what we have are estimates, largely from psychological evaluations and secondary physical signs. These estimates suggest a widespread disorder. Alzheimer's disease afflicts between 1.5 and 2 million Americans, and at least 100,000 of these people die each year (Mace & Rabins, 1981; Wurtman, 1985). In terms of percentages, it is believed that 5 to 6 percent of persons over the age of 65 develop the disease. There are now nearly 28 million Americans in that age bracket, and, as we all know, that number is ever increasing.

At autopsy, there are four clear signs of Alzheimer's disease (Butler & Emr, 1982). One is a collection of tangles—a "spaghetti-like jumble of abnormal protein fibers" (Butler & Emr, 1982, p. 14). A second sign is the presence of "plaques"—basically waste material; degenerated nerve fibers surrounding a protein core. A third is the presence of a number of small cavities filled with fluid and debris. The fourth sign is an indication of atrophy, or shrunken structure. There are two problems we need to mention: (1) each of these signs can be found in a normal brain, particularly an older one (seldom more than one at a time, however), and (2) we don't know what causes these signs.

Richard Wurtman (1985), after reviewing the literature, suggests that there are a number of different models that are being used to explain Alzheimer's disease. Each is very complex, but we can at least list them: (1) The genetic model, which points to the fact that the disease runs in families. Although there *may* be a genetic basis, we don't know what it is or where to look for it. (2) The abnormal protein model. Because proteins are obviously involved in tangles and plaques, this model searches for these abnormal proteins and tries to determine where they come from. (3) The infectious-agent model, in which the search is to see if the abnormalities of brain structure might be caused by some (probably low-grade) infection. (4) The toxin model, which suggests that there is evidence that salts of the metal aluminum may act as a poison, or toxin, and thus bring on Alzheimer's disease. (5) The blood-flow model, which returns to the once popular idea that the symptoms of the disease are caused by a reduced blood flow and lack of oxygen to important areas of the brain. (6) The acetylcholine model, which is one of the most actively pursued, points to a decrease in activity in a brain enzyme that normally produces a very important neurotransmitter, acetylcholine. Acetylcholine levels are measurably low in Alzheimer's disease patients. (7) The elephant model, which combines the basic elements of all the others. Wurtman suggests this to be the most viable of the models. Indeed, there is good data to support all of the six approaches we've just listed, but none is *the* cause. The cause is quite possibly a combination of all six, or something yet to be discovered.

What criteria are used to classify a symptom or a disorder as psychotic?

To qualify as psychotic, a symptom or disorder should display a gross impairment of functioning and a loss of contact with reality. Impairment and loss of reality may be shown in thinking, affect, or behavior. / 520

What are some of the syndromes associated with organic mental disorders?

What gives rise to these symptoms?

The organic mental disorders may display any of a number of different syndromes, including: delirium, a clouded state of consciousness and lessening of awareness; dementia, a marked loss of intellectual abilities, including memory, judgment, and impulse control; amnestic syndrome, an impairment of memory with no other intellectual deficit; delusions, false personal beliefs; hallucinations, perceptions without sensory stimulation; and affective syndrome, a disturbance of mood, either manic or depressed. These syndromes arise through some form of brain dysfunction or damage, usually due to the aging process or the abuse of chemical substances such as alcohol, barbiturates, opiates, cocaine, amphetamines, or hallucinogenic drugs. / 524

What is the defining characteristic of a paranoid disorder?

Paranoia is a rare psychotic disturbance, the major symptom of which is a persistent delusion or set of delusions. The delusions tend to be quite systematic and consistent. They are, however, false beliefs. / 524

How are the affective disorders defined?

What do we know about their prevalence and their causes?

Disturbances of affect can be found in many psychological disorders. In the affective disorders, a disturbance in mood or feeling is the prime, and occasionally only, major symptom. Most commonly we find the disorder to be one of depression alone; less commonly we find mania and depression occurring in cycles. Depression is a common disorder, affecting as many as 20 percent of all women and 10 percent of all men at some time in their lives. The disorder seems to have a strong basis in heredity. Neurotransmitters (biogenic amines) such as serotonin and dopamine have been implicated in depression. Psychological explanations tend to focus on the learned ineffectiveness of reinforcers, cognitive factors, such as a poor self-image, and learned helplessness as models for explaining the causes of depression. / 527

What are the major symptoms of schizophrenia?

How prevalent is the disorder?

What characterizes the following varieties or types of schizophrenia: process versus reactive, paranoid, catatonic, and hebephrenic?

Schizophrenia is a label applied to a number of disorders that all seem to involve varying degrees of cognitive impairment (delusions, hallucinations, disturbances of thought, and the like), social isolation, and disturbances of affect and behavior. Process schizophrenia is the term used when symptoms tend to develop slowly and gradually, whereas we call those cases in which symptoms arise suddenly, reactive schizophrenia. The latter has a better prognosis than the former. Paranoid schizophrenia is characterized by delusions, usually absurd and illogical. Catatonic schizophrenia is characterized by catatonia (states of physical impassivity) and negativity. Hebephrenic schizophrenia is characterized by childish behaviors, inappropriate affect (giggling and laughing), and disordered language behaviors. / 529

Describe three factors that have been implicated as possible causes of schizophrenic symptoms.

Although we certainly do not know the causes of schizophrenia, three lines of investigation have produced hopeful leads. (1) there seems to be little doubt of at least a genetic predisposition for the disorder. Although schizophrenia is not inherited, it does tend to run in families. (2) Research on biochemical correlates of schizophrenia have localized the neurotransmitter dopamine as being involved in the production of schizophrenialike symptoms. (3) It also seems reasonable to hypothesize that early childhood experiences, particularly those involving parent-child interactions and communications, may predispose one toward schizophrenia. / 532

CHAPTER THIRTEEN

TREATMENT AND THERAPY

TOPIC

Philippe Pinel (1745–1826) was a French physician who, in the midst of the French Revolution (on April 25, 1793), was named Director of the Bicetre in Paris, a hospital-asylum for insane men. Two years later, he was also placed in charge of the Salpertiére, a similar institution for insane women.

We know of Pinel today largely because of an act of courage and compassion. On September 2, 1793, Pinel ordered the chains and shackles removed from about 50 of the inmates of his hospital. To do so required the permission of the French government, because the patients had been chained according to the law of the period. This humane gesture produced surprising effects: The condition of the patients, in many cases, improved markedly. This action of Pinel's "has become a symbol in men's minds of the humane and moral treatment of the insane" (Shipley, 1961, p. 311). Let us try to imagine the scene, as described in Pinel's own words.

On my entrance to the duties of that hospital, every thing presented to me the appearance of chaos and confusion. Some of my unfortunate patients laboured under the horrors of a most gloomy and desponding melancholy. Others were furious, and subject to the influence of a perpetual delirium. . . . Symptoms so different, and all comprehended under the general title of insanity, required, on my part, much study and discrimination; and to secure order in the establishment and success to the practice, I determined upon adopting such a variety of measures, both as to discipline and treatment, as my patients required, and my limited opportunity permitted.

* * *

I determined to turn my attention, almost exclusively, to the subject of moral treatment. The halls and the passages of the hospital were much confined, so arranged as to render

the cold of winter and the heat of summer equally intolerable and injurious. The chambers were exceedingly small and inconvenient. Baths we had none, though I made repeated applications for them; nor had we extensive liberties for walking, gardening or other exercises. So destitute of accommodations, we found it impossible to class our patients according to the varieties and degrees of their respective maladies.

* * *

A working man . . . was transferred to Bicetre. The idea of his death haunted him night and day, and he unceasingly repeated, that he was ready to submit to his impending fate. Constant employment at his trade, which was that of a tailor, appeared to me the most probable means of diverting the current of his morbid thoughts. I applied to the board for a small salary for him, in consideration of his repairing the clothes of the other patients in the asylum. This measure appeared to engage his interest to a very high degree. He undertook the employment with great eagerness, and worked without interruption for two months. A favourable change appeared to be taking place. He made no complaints nor any allusions to his supposed condemnation. He even spoke with the tenderest interest of a child of about six years of age, whom it seemed he had forgotten.

* * *

A young gentleman, twenty-two years of age, of a robust constitution was deprived of part of his property by the revolution. He gave way to melancholy, began to look forward to futurity with extreme despondency, and lost his sleep. He was, at length, seized by violent maniacal fury. . . . With his hands and feet tied he was suddenly immersed in the cold bath. Notwithstanding the violence with which he resisted this treatment, it was practiced upon him for some time. . . . Upon my first interview with him he appeared exceedingly enraged. . . . The bath was never mentioned to him. He was treated with mildness and put on a diluent regimen [bland diet], with the liberty of walking at all hours in a pleasant garden. The amusement which he derived from this liberty, exercise and familiar conversation, in which from time to time I would engage him, gradually induced a state of calmness, and toward the end of a month he was not remarkable either for haughtiness or diffidence. In about three months his delirium had completely left him. . . . Upon his departure he returned into the country, where, for the last two years, he has been occupied partly by literary pursuits, and partly by those of agriculture. No symptom of his delirium has since appeared.

In our last chapter, we reviewed a rather long list of mental or psychological disorders. We also noted that such disorders are, unfortunately, far from rare experiences. Tens of millions of Americans are afflicted with psychological disturbances, from mild disorders of stress and adjustment to devastating disorders of schizophrenia and other psychotic reactions. In this chapter, we turn our attention to what might be done to help people suffering from psychological disorders.

In many ways, we can claim that the humane treatment of persons with psychological problems is a twentieth-century phenomenon. As we have seen in our opening description of life in an asylum in the late 1700s, the basic notion that such persons should be treated humanely is less than 200 years old. Active intervention to improve the quality of life of people suffering from mental illness is much more recent than that. To begin this topic, we'll take a brief look at the history of treatment for psychological disorders.

The bulk of this topic will be devoted to those measures of treatment that generally fall outside the realm of psychology—medical or physical treatments. We'll examine psychosurgery and shock therapies, but will concentrate on the use of drugs and chemicals to control and treat the symptoms of mental illness. Psychological approaches—the psychotherapies—will be reserved for Topic 30.

AN HISTORICAL PERSPECTIVE

The history of the treatment of mental disorders is not a pleasant one. By today's standards, therapy—in the sense of doing something humane to improve the condition of a person in distress—does not even seem like an appropriate term to describe the way in which most disordered persons were treated in the past.

Mental illness is not a new phenomenon. Even the earliest of written records from the Babylonians, Egyptians, and ancient Hebrews clearly depict a variety of cases that we now recognize as describing psychologically disordered individuals (Murray, 1983). Many of the names, or labels, have changed, of course. By the seventeenth century, words such as melancholia (now depression), delirium, hallucination, delusion, and mania were well-established in medical terminology to describe the insane or demented. How individuals with such disorders were treated was consistent with the prevailing view of what caused the disorder.

The ancient Greeks and Romans believed that people who were depressed, irrational, manic, intellectually retarded, or experienced hallucinations and delusions had in some way offended the gods. In some cases, individuals were simply viewed as being out of favor with the gods, and it was believed that their condition might be improved through religious ritual and prayer. More severely disturbed patients were seen as being possessed of evil spirits. These were more difficult, often impossible, to cure. The aim of ancient therapists was to exorcize the evil spirits and demons that had inhabited the mind and soul of the mentally deranged. Treatment was seldom successful, and many unfortunates died as a result of their treatment or were killed outright when treatment failed. Treatment was left in the hands of priests who were, after all, thought to be skilled in the ways and means of spirits.

There were those in ancient times who had a more reasonable view (by today's standards) of psychological disorders. Among them was Hippocrates (460–377 B.C.) who believed that mental disorders had physical causes, not

Mental illness is not a new phenomenon. King Saul's mental problems were legendary. Here, the boy David is playing music to soothe the troubled Saul. The demon thought to be the cause of Saul's condition is above and behind his upraised arm.

spiritual ones. He identified epilepsy as being a disorder of the brain, for example. Some of his views were incorrect (that hysteria is a disorder of the uterus, for instance), but at least he attempted to demystify mental illness.

The impact of enlightened scientists, such as Hippocrates, was, in the long run, slight and short lived. The Middle Ages (1000 to 1500) was a period in history during which the oppression and persecution of the mentally ill was at its peak. During this period, there was a prevailing view that psychologically disordered people were bad people, sinners, under the spell of the devil and evil spirits. There was no hope for these people, except that they save their immortal souls and confess their evil ways and wickedness.

For hundreds of years, from the fourteenth century well into the eighteenth century, the attitude toward those who were mentally ill was that they were in league with the devil or that they were being punished for evil thoughts and deeds. They were seen as witches who could not be cured except through confession and denunciation of their evilness. When such confessions were not forthcoming, the prescribed treatment was torture. If torture failed to evoke a confession, death was the only recourse; often it was death by being burned at the stake.

A large volume, the *Malleus Maleficarum* (The Witches Hammer), was written by two priests, with the blessing of the pope, in 1478. It described in great detail the symptoms of witches, and how witches were to be interrogated so as to ensure a confession. The techniques described in *Malleus* comprise a listing of the most horrible of tortures. It has been estimated that between the early fourteenth and mid-seventeenth century, nearly 200,000 to 500,000 "witches" were put to their death (Ben-Yehuda, 1980). In 1652, Martin Luther described the mentally retarded as godless people, beyond salvation. "Furthermore, since the mentally disturbed did not behave like normal people, for centuries they were regarded as nonhuman and subject to the most barbaric abuses. Luther personally recommended that one retarded twelve-year-old boy be drowned" (Hothersall, 1984, pp. 197–198).

When the insane were not tortured or immediately put to death for their strange behaviors and thoughts, they were institutionalized in asylums. The first asylum was probably St. Mary of Bethlehem Hospital in London, given over to "fools" and "lunatics" in 1547. This place became known as Bedlam (apparently a cockney mispronunciation of Bethlehem). What a terrible place it was. Inmates were tortured, poorly fed, or starved to death. To remove the "bad blood" of their system (thought to be a cause of their melancholy or delirium), some were regularly led to bleeding chambers, where a small incision was made in a vein in the calf of their legs so that their blood would ooze into leather buckets. There was no professional staff at Bedlam. The keepers, as they were called, could make some extra money by putting their charges on view for the general public. Going down to see the lunatics of Bedlam became an established entertainment for the nobility. Those inmates who were able were sent into the streets to beg, wearing a sign that identified them as "fools of Bedlam."

It would be comforting to think that Bedlam was an exception, an abberration, but it was not. In the eighteenth and nineteenth centuries (and, in many places, well into the twentieth century), institutions not unlike Bedlam were commonplace. In our topic opening, we presented Philippe Pinel's impression of the asylum-hospital in Paris in 1793. He could have been describing Bedlam 250 years earlier.

Perhaps we should not be surprised that in some quarters yet today there are prejudices, negative attitudes, and fears of the mentally ill. Our history suggests that until very recently, the prevailing understanding of the psychologically disturbed was that they were bad people, possessed of demons and devils, unable to control their behaviors and thoughts, and unable to be

During the Middle Ages, the mentally ill were thought to be under the spell of unseen demons. This fifteenth-century painting, Mouth of Hell, *is an expression of the terrifying reality of these demons.*

As described in Malleus Maleficarum, one of the accepted punishments for alleged witchcraft was being burned alive, often after having been tortured into making a false confession.

This view of Bedlam is from Hogarth's Rake's Progress. In the eighteenth century, it was considered entertaining to visit Bedlam to view the lunatics, as the two ladies of fashion shown here are doing.

cured. The only recourse was to separate the mentally ill from everyone else. "Put them away." "They are evil." "They are not human."

As we have seen, the tide began to turn late in the 1700s. Pinel's unchaining of the insane and his belief in moral treatment for the mentally disturbed are generally viewed as the beginning of a very gradual enlightenment concerning mental illness. Unfortunately, we cannot report that Pinel's successes led to broad, sweeping reforms.

In the United States, three names stand out as pioneers of reform for the treatment of the mentally ill and retarded. The first is Benjamin Rush (1745–1813), who is considered to be the founder of American psychiatry, having published the first text on the subject of mental disorders in this country in 1812. Although many of the treatments recommended by Rush strike us as barbaric today (he was a believer in bleeding, for example), his general attitudes were comparatively humane. He essentially transported the moral consideration of the mentally ill to America. The second person we should mention is Dorothea Dix (1802–1887). Dix was a nurse and a person of poor health. In 1841, she took a position at a women's prison and was appalled at what she saw. Included among the prisoners, and treated no differently, were hundreds of persons who were clearly mentally retarded and/or mentally ill. Despite her slight stature and ill health, she entered upon a crusade of singular vigor. She went from state to state campaigning for reform in prisons and mental hospitals and asylums.

One of the ironic outcomes of Dix's crusade was that state governments agreed that the mentally ill should not be housed in prisons, and large state-run institutions and asylums were built. Although they began operation in the tradition of moral treatment, they often became no more humane or moral in their treatment than Bedlam had been.

In this brief historical sketch, one other name deserves mention: Clifford Beers. Beers was a graduate of Yale University who was institutionalized in a series of hospitals or asylums. It seems likely that he was suffering from what we now call an affective disorder. Probably in spite of his treatment, rather than because of it, Beers recovered and was released, in itself an unusual occurrence. He wrote a book about his experience, A Mind That Found Itself, in 1908. The book became a best seller and is often cited as providing the stimulus for a reform that we identify as the mental health movement.

Benjamin Rush   Dorothea Dix   Clifford Beers

Since the early 1900s, progress has been slow and unsteady. World War I and the Depression severely reduced monies available to support state institutions for mental patients. Within the past 50 years, conditions have improved immeasurably, but there is yet a long way to go. We are still fighting, even in the 1980s, the prejudice that persons suffering from psychological disorders are somehow weak or less than human.

Before you go on

List some of the ways in which persons with psychological disorders have been treated in the past.

BIOMEDICAL TREATMENT OF PSYCHOLOGICAL DISORDERS

As we have seen in our brief review of the history of the treatment of psychological disorders, biological and medical approaches can be traced to ancient times. By definition, treatments that are medical in nature are not those that psychologists use. To perform surgery, administer shock treatments, or prescribe medication requires a medical degree. Psychologists are often involved in biomedical approaches to treatment, however. Psychologists may recommend medical treatment and refer a client or patient to the care of a physician or psychiatrist (a person with a medical degree who specializes in mental disorders). The treatment alternatives that psychologists use, called psychotherapies, will be the subject of our next topic.

Here we'll review three types of biomedical treatment: psychosurgery, which was quite common just 50 years ago, but has been replaced by other methods; shock treatment, which is used less frequently now than it was 20 years ago, but is not uncommon; and chemotherapy, the use of psychoactive drugs, which is the newest and most promising development in the treatment of mental illness.

Psychosurgery

Psychosurgery is the name we give to surgical procedures (usually directed at the brain) designed to affect psychological or behavioral reactions. Although there are other psychosurgical procedures (to reduce chronic pain, for example), in many ways psychosurgery is synonymous with the procedure called a **prefrontal lobotomy,** or simply lobotomy. This surgery severs the major neural connections between the prefrontal lobes (the area at the very front of the cerebral cortex) and lower brain centers.

psychosurgery
a surgical procedure designed to affect psychological or behavioral reactions

prefrontal lobotomy
a psychosurgical technique in which the prefrontal lobes of the cerebral cortex are severed from lower brain centers

The technique was first "successfully" performed in 1935 by a Portuguese psychiatrist, Egas Moniz. For developing this procedure, Moniz was awarded the Nobel Prize in Medicine in 1949. The logic behind the procedure was that the frontal lobes of the cortex influence the more basic emotional centers of the brain (the thalamus and the hypothalamus). Severely psychotic patients were thought to have difficulty in coordinating these two parts of the brain. It was further reasoned that if they were separated surgically, the more depressed, agitated, or violent patients could be brought under control.

The operation often appeared to be successful. Used as a measure of last resort, stories of the remarkable changes it produced in chronic mental patients circulated widely. During the 1940s and 1950s, prefrontal lobotomies were performed with regularity. It's difficult to estimate precisely how many lobotomies were performed just within these two decades, but certainly they numbered in the tens of thousands.

Treating severely disturbed, depressed, and schizophrenic patients has always been difficult. And perhaps we shouldn't be surprised that a relatively simple surgical technique was accepted so widely and uncritically at first. The procedure was often done in the physician's office, under local anesthetic. An instrument that looks very much like an ice pick was inserted through the eye socket, on the nasal side, and was pushed up into the brain. A few simple movements of the instrument and the job was done—the lobes were severed. Within hours, the patient would be recovered from the procedure.

It was always appreciated that the procedure was an irreversible one. What took longer to realize was that it often carried with it terrible side effects. In fact, nearly one quarter of the patients receiving prefrontal lobotomies died (Coleman et al., 1984). Many of those who survived suffered seizures, memory loss, an inability to plan ahead, and a general listlessness and loss of affect. By the late 1950s, psychosurgery had virtually disappeared. Contrary to common belief, it is not an illegal procedure in this country, although the conditions under which it might even be considered are very restrictive. Psychosurgery is no longer practiced for the simple reason that it is no longer needed. There are other means—with fewer side effects—that can produce the same general results more reliably.

Before you go on

What is a prefrontal lobotomy?

Why was it ever used, and why is it not used today?

Electroconvulsive Therapy

electroconvulsive therapy (ECT)
a treatment (usually for the symptoms of severe depression) in which a high voltage current passed across a patient's head causes a seizure and loss of consciousness

As gruesome as are the procedures of psychosurgery, many people find the very notion of shock treatments, or **electroconvulsive therapy (ECT),** even more difficult to deal with. This technique, first introduced in 1938, involves passing an electric current (of between 70 and 150 volts) across a tranquilized patient's head for a fraction of a second. As a result, there is a physical seizure, followed by a loss of consciousness. True, it is not a pleasant procedure to watch. But one of the side effects of ECT is a memory loss for events just preceding the administration of the shock and for the shock itself.

At first, the treatment was devised to help schizophrenics, but it soon became clear that its most beneficial results were for those patients suffering from deep depression. For reasons that were not understood at the time, electroconvulsive shock therapy was often helpful. Why ECT produces the benefits that it does is not fully understood even today. That is, it alleviates the symptoms of depression and, in some cases, even has beneficial effects on

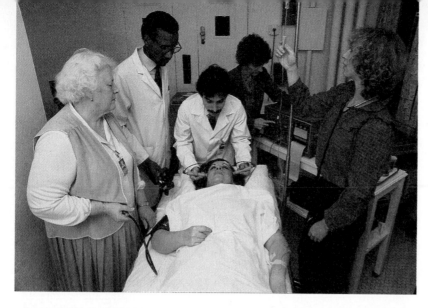

A patient is given electroconvulsive therapy (ECT).

other psychotic symptoms as well. The beneficial effects are reasonably long-lasting. Many patients remain symptom-free for months.

The poor reputation that ECT has among the general population did not develop without foundation. There are many horror stories of the negative side effects that can follow abuse of the procedure. Although it is now recommended that no more than a dozen treatments be given, and that these be administered over an extended period of time, such advice has not always been followed. There is little doubt that some patients in the past have received hundreds of ECT treatments. In such cases, there is often evidence of brain damage and permanent memory loss.

Even though we do not fully understand why ECT works, and even though it is a treatment that must be used with extreme care, ECT is still very much in practice today. With the introduction of psychoactive, antidepressant medications, there is less need to use ECT. ECT is now generally reserved for (1) patients for whom drug therapies seem ineffective, (2) patients with acute suicidal tendencies (because drugs often take weeks to have their full antidepressant effects), and (3) depressed patients who also suffer from delusions (Kalat, 1984). Recently, it has been noted that administering the shock to just one side of the brain (called a unilateral ECT) is a safer, yet equally effective procedure with fewer side effects (Squire & Slater, 1978).

Before you go on

What is ECT?

Why is it still being used?

Drug Therapy

As we stated in Topic 9 in our discussion of consciousness, chemicals that influence psychological functioning have been in use since the beginning of recorded history. Chemicals that have their effect on the cognitions, affect, or behavior of an individual are collectively referred to as psychoactive drugs. As we have seen, there are many of them, and most are used to artificially produce an altered state of consciousness or awareness. Effectively using drugs to improve the condition of the mentally disordered has been a much more recent development and one of the most significant scientific achievements of the last half of the twentieth century (Snyder, 1984). In this section, we'll examine the three main types of psychoactive drugs used as therapy: the antipsychotic, antidepressant, and antianxiety drugs.

Antipsychotic Drugs   The first **antipsychotic drug** used in this country was the compound *reserpine.* It is classified as an antipsychotic drug because it does just what its label suggests: It reduces the severity, and may even eliminate, psychotic symptoms. The introduction of the drug, in the early 1950s, was most welcomed. Unfortunately, reserpine has a number of side effects that made its use quite dangerous. True, it does have a demonstrably calming and settling effect on severely disturbed patients, but it also dangerously lowers blood pressure levels. Now, in small doses, reserpine (and variants of it) is used to treat chronic high blood pressure.

The real breakthrough in the use of antipsychotic medication came in the mid-1950s with the introduction of a class of drugs known as *phenothiazines,* the first of which was *chlorpromazine.* The major advantage of this drug is that it has all of the benefits of reserpine and none of its side effects.

The antipsychotic effects of chlorpromazine were discovered in France in the 1940s. A neurosurgeon, Henri Laborit, was searching for a drug that would calm his patients before surgery. Just before undergoing surgery, patients often feel nervous and anxious, and Laborit simply wanted to help them relax. A drug company supplied him with chlorpromazine. It worked even better than anyone had expected, and Laborit convinced some of his colleagues to try the drug on their patients, some of whom were suffering from psychological disorders. The experiments met with success, and by the late 1950s, the drug (with the trade name Thorazine) was widely used both in the United States and in Europe. The drug revolution had begun. With this success in hand, the search for other chemicals that could markedly improve the plight of the mentally ill began in earnest.

Needless to say, chlorpromazine is not the only antipsychotic drug that is currently being used with success. Most of the other commonly used antipsychotic medications are similar derivatives of the phenothiazines, however.

Although the effects of the antipsychotic drugs are remarkable and impressive, and although they have revolutionized the care of psychotic patients (see Topic Expansion), they should not be considered as an ultimate solution for disorders such as schizophrenia and the other psychoses. For one thing, there are some patients for whom the drugs either have no effect or have harmful effects. Although the most effective of the antipsychotic drugs clearly control symptoms, there is some question as to whether they are in any sense curing the disorder. Symptom-free patients, often released from institutional care to the outside world, soon stop using their medication, only to find that their psychotic symptoms return.

Before you go on

What are antipsychotic drugs, and what are their effects?

Antidepressant Drugs   **Antidepressant drugs** are those that elevate the mood of persons who are feeling depressed. The first effective antidepressant was *iproniazid,* originally used in the treatment of tuberculosis. One of the side effects of the drug was that it made tubercular patients feel cheerful and happy. When tested on depressed patients, it was found to have the same effect. Unfortunately, it was soon determined that iproniazid caused irreversible liver damage, and its use as an antidepressant was stopped.

The antidepressant medications that are used today are of two major types: *MAO inhibitors* (MAO, or monoamine oxidase, is a chemical found in the brain that reduces levels of two neurotransmitters; MAO inhibitors thus increase levels of these neurotransmitters), and *tricyclics* (which also affect the biochemistry of neurotransmitters, but in a different way).

These drugs would be of little use for you if, for example, you were depressed about doing badly on a history exam. They generally require weeks to have their maximum effect and need to be taken on a long-term basis to prevent a recurrence of the depression. And although they elevate the mood of many depressed individuals, they have virtually no effect at all on people who are not depressed. That is, they do not produce a euphoric high.

Of the two types of antidepressants, the tricyclic types (trade names Elavil or Tofranil, for example) are more commonly used. The tricyclics produce unfortunate side effects: intellectual confusion, increased perspiration, and weight gain. Some tricyclics have been implicated as a cause of heart disease. The MAO inhibitor drugs require adherence to a strict diet and carefully monitored dosages to have their best effect. They also produce more serious side effects. Unlike the antipsychotic drugs, however, there is evidence that when these drugs are effective, they may actually bring about long-term cures rather than symptom suppression. For those who do not respond to those medications presently available, many other varieties are being tested, and for such patients, electroconvulsive therapy may be indicated.

Before you go on
What are the two types of antidepressant drugs, and what do they do?

Antianxiety Drugs   **Antianxiety drugs** (or tranquilizers) help to reduce the felt aspect of anxiety. They are the most commonly prescribed of all drugs. One type of antianxiety drug, the *meprobamates* (trade names Miltown or Equanil, for example) are basically muscle relaxants. When muscular tension is reduced, the patient often reports feeling calm and at ease.

antianxiety drugs
chemicals, such as the meprobamates and benzodiazepines, that alleviate the symptoms of anxiety

The other major variety of antianxiety drug is the group of *benzodiazepines* (trade names Librium, Valium, and many others). These drugs act on the central nervous system. The impact of these drugs is significant. They help very anxious people feel better. At first, the only side effects appear to be a slight drowsiness, blurred vision, and a slight impairment of muscle coordination. Unfortunately, the tranquilizing effects of the drugs are not long lasting. Patients can easily fall into a pattern of relying on the drugs to alleviate even the slightest of fears and worries. Soon a dependency and addiction can develop, from which withdrawal can be painful. When too much antianxiety medication is taken (an overdose), death may result, and the fact that benzodiazepines and alcohol don't mix has been well documented. Valium plus alcohol can lead to death.

Before you go on
What are the common antianxiety drugs, and what are the dangers inherent in their use?

In summary, we can say that there is now great hope that biochemical techniques can be found to at least suppress, if not totally eliminate, many of the most severe symptoms associated with psychological disorders. At the moment, however, we should probably remain somewhat cautious. Remember that just 35 years ago it was widely believed that prefrontal lobotomies and other forms of psychosurgery would provide the ultimate long-term answer to the question of how to treat psychologically and emotionally disturbed patients. Drug therapy and psychosurgery cannot be equated in terms of the way in which they produce their effects, nor in their irreversibility. However, scientists are learning more about the chemistry of the nervous system and the delicate balance between brain and behavior. If we remain ever mindful of the harsh and inhumane treatment of the mentally ill that characterized our not-too-distant past, we can now, in the 1980s, be more cautiously optimistic than ever before.

As we noted above, the first institution expressly for the mentally ill was St. Mary of Bethlehem Hospital, so designated in 1547. Despite reform and well-intentioned efforts to promote mental health (rather than merely housing the disordered), by the middle of the twentieth century, large state-run or state-supported institutions were the commonplace residences of the chronically mentally ill and mentally retarded. Lack of public support, leading to a lack of appropriate funding for staff and facilities, led to what amounted to a national disgrace.

Mental institutions became unmanageably overcrowded. Individual therapy and/or personal care for patients was virtually unknown in such institutions. Privacy was unheard of, food inedible, and filth and squalor prevailed, not in all institutions, of course, but in most. Within the last 30 years, there has been a truly revolutionary shift. For a number of seemingly sound and sensible reasons, patients have been *deinstitutionalized*. They have been sent out from the large mental institutions to return to family and community. The drop in institutional patient population has been dramatic (see Figure 29.1). Compared to 1955, the number of patients in state and county mental hospitals has dropped by nearly 75 percent. What has brought about this great change, and has it been a change for the better?

There are a number of reasons we might list for the deinstitutionalization we have seen over the past 30 years. Some of them we have already alluded to. Let's list three.

Figure 29.1
The number of patients institutionalized in county and state mental hospitals. Also indicated is the approximate U.S. population. Remember that it was in the mid- and late-1950s that antipsychotic medications became widely used. (Adapted from NIMH, 1984.)

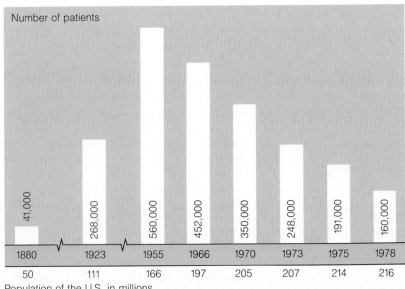

Number of patients

1880	1923	1955	1966	1970	1973	1975	1978
41,000	268,000	560,000	452,000	350,000	248,000	191,000	160,000
50	111	166	197	205	207	214	216

Population of the U.S. in millions

1. *A concern for the rights of the mental patient.* The overcrowded and virtually inhumane conditions that existed in many institutions simply became more than society was able to bear. The courts ordered that either the patients in mental institutions receive adequate and proper treatment or be released. The landmark decision of this sort was sent down in 1971 in the *Wyatt vs. Stickney* case in Alabama. Ricky Wyatt was a patient in a state hospital who felt that he (and his fellow patients who joined in his suit) was not being fairly or adequately treated. He filed suit against the Alabama Mental Health Commissioner, Stonewall Stickney. Not only did the judge in the case find in favor of Wyatt, he set down a list of conditions that state institutions must meet to ensure the adequate treatment of the people in their charge. He further specified that if significant changes were not made in a timely fashion, the patients were to be released.

2. *Symptom management through chemical means.* We have already touched on this matter. In the mid-1950s, the introduction of effective drugs that at least masked or suppressed psychotic symptoms made it more reasonable that patients no longer displaying bizarre or dangerous behaviors could be released from institutional care.

3. *The establishment of community mental health centers.* In 1963, Congress passed the Community Mental Health Centers Act. Among other things, the Act included a provision for the establishment of mental health centers in local communities. The plan was for there to be one easily accessible mental health center for every 50,000 people. These would be centers to ac-

commodate people on an out-patient basis and could particularly serve those recently discharged from large residential mental hospitals. (They were to provide many other services as well, including inpatient treatment, consultation and education, and prevention programs.)

Has the new system of deinstitutionalization worked? On this question, the house is divided. There are those who applaud the change (Braun et al., 1981), and argue that, within limits, "continued optimism about community care seems warranted" (Shadish, 1984, p. 725). Many, however, see deinstitutionalization as trading one problem for a host of others. Many of the patients released from mental institutions are, quite literally, "dumped" back into their home community. There, resources for their assistance are often few and limited. There is inadequate housing for those who have been released. Many become street people, particularly in large cities. Many require

the support of the welfare system. And no matter how capable a community mental health center may be (assuming there is one nearby), if patients do not seek its support, it will do them little good. And, as we have seen, most of the antipsychotic medication that deinstitutionalized patients require does not have lasting effects. As soon as such patients stop taking their medication, their symptoms return, and they will likely need to be institutionalized again. In fact, since deinstitutionalization has become a matter of policy, admissions have actually increased, although the average length of stay in institutions has decreased (Kiesler, 1982).

It appears that the trend to reduce the population of mental institutions is likely to continue. Effective community programs and resources are needed to assist those released from mental institutions, to ensure that their discharge is appropriate for them and for the community to which they return.

TOPIC SUMMARY

List some of the ways in which persons with psychological disorders have been treated in the past.

In ancient times, and through the Middle Ages, the prevailing view of the mentally ill was that they were possessed by evil spirits or the devil. As a result, treatment was often harsh, involving torture and placement in dungeonlike asylums for the insane, which, in many ways, were worse than prisons. It was not uncommon for the mentally ill, who were viewed as witches, to be put to death for their evil ways. Throughout history, there have been attempts by persons of compassion to treat the disordered humanely. It wasn't until the twentieth century that what we see now as a mental health movement began. This movement was started as a campaign to treat the mentally ill with an aim of curing them in the most humane way possible. / 543

What is a prefrontal lobotomy? Why was it ever used, and why is it not used today?

A prefrontal lobotomy is a psychosurgical technique that involves severing the connections between the front of the cerebral cortex and lower brain centers. It was first used in the mid-1930s and was a common treatment in the 1940s and 1950s. It was used as a treatment of last resort, because it was often successful in alleviating the worst of psychotic symptoms. Unfortunately, it also produced many mild to severe side effects, including death. Because of its inherent danger, and because safer, more reversible treatments (such as drug therapy) are available today, it is no longer used. / 544

What is ECT? Why is it still being used?

ECT stands for electroconvulsive therapy. In this treatment, a patient is rendered unconscious by passing a strong electric current across his or her head. Upon regaining consciousness, the patient's memory of the treatment is lost. Although there may be negative side effects, particularly with prolonged or repeated use, the technique is demonstrably useful (for most patients) as a means of reducing or even eliminating severe depression and some other psychotic symptoms. / 545

What are antipsychotic drugs, and what are their effects?

Most antipsychotic drugs are derivatives of the family of drugs called phenothiazines. The most common is chlorpromazine, produced in the 1940s and commonly in use by the mid-1950s to suppress the majority of symptoms associated with psychosis—hallucinations, delusions, disordered thought, inappropriate affect, and the like. Although these drugs definitely reduce the psychotic symptoms in many patients, it is not accurate to say that they cure the disorder, because symptoms often return when the drugs are discontinued. / 546

What are the two types of antidepressant drugs, and what do they do?

The two major types of antidepressant drugs are the MAO inhibitors and the tricyclics. Although their chemical composition is quite different, both seem to work in the same general sort of way by increasing the levels of two important neurotransmitters in the central nervous system. Unlike the antipsychotic drugs, these often have long-term beneficial effects, but they do take a couple of weeks to establish that effect, and they do not work for all patients. It is also true that long-term use of the drugs produces a number of potentially harmful or unpleasant side effects. / 547

What are the common antianxiety drugs, and what are the dangers inherent in their use?

The most common anxiety-alleviating drugs are the meprobamates and the benzodiazepines, including Valium and Librium, which are two of the most commonly prescribed of all drugs in the world. These drugs reduce felt levels of anxiety, generally without producing a total relaxation and loss of intellectual abilities. Unfortunately, there is evidence that persons who use them develop dependencies and addictions to them. And like many psychoactive drugs, even slight overdoses can lead to complications. Excessive overdoses (or use with alcohol) can lead to death. / 547

TOPIC

30 *The Psychotherapies*

Barbara is an 18-year-old freshman at City Community College. Still living at home with her parents and two younger brothers, she is having difficulty dealing with the demands on her time. She has a full-time job at a restaurant and is trying to manage four classes at college. The pressures of home, school, and work seem to be making Barbara uncharacteristically anxious and depressed. She is falling behind in her school work, performing poorly at her job, and is finding life at home almost unbearable. On the recommendation of her psychology instructor, Barbara has been seeing a counselor at the Student Services Center. She has had six visits there with a psychotherapist. Let's listen in on the first few minutes of their seventh session:

Psychotherapist: Good morning, Barbara; how do you feel today?

Barbara: [snapping back quickly] Good lord, can't you ever say anything but "how do you feel today?" I feel fine, just fine.

P: You sound angry.

B: [in a sarcastically mocking tone] "You sound angry today."

P: [silence]

B: Well I'm not angry, so there.

P: um. hmm.

B: Well, maybe a little angry.

P: So you feel "a little angry"?

B: Yeah, so I'm angry. Big deal. So what of it? Is there something wrong with being angry?

P: Of course not.

B: You'd be angry too.

P: Oh?

B: My old man threatened to kick me out of the house last night.

P: He threatened you?

B: He said that if I didn't get my act together and shape up, he'd send me packing. God knows where I'd go, but if he pulls that crap on me one more time, I'll show him. I will leave.

P: Would you like to leave?

B: Yes! No! No, I don't really want to. It's just that nobody cares about me around there. They don't know how hard it is trying to work and go to school and everything, ya' know?

P: [nods]

B: *They* never went to college. What do *they* know? They don't know what it's like.

P: You feel that your parents can't appreciate your problems?

B: Damn right! What do they know? They've never tried to work and go to college at the same time.

P: They just don't know what it's like.

B: Right. Of course it's not really their fault, I suppose. They've never been in this situation. I suppose I could try to explain it to them.

P: You mean that it might be helpful to share with them how you feel about this, that it's hard for you, and maybe they'll understand?

B: Yeah! That's a good idea! I'll do that. At least I'll try. I don't want to just whine and complain all the time, but maybe I can get them to understand what it's like. Boy, that would help—just to have somebody understand and maybe be on my side once in awhile instead of on my case all the time. That's a good idea. Thanks.

This dialogue is no doubt idealized, yet it reflects a number of principles of one approach to psychotherapy that we will examine later in this topic. We'll return to this interchange when we discuss client-centered therapies.

Attempts to treat mental disorders through psychological means are collectively referred to as **psychotherapy.** There are many different varieties of psychotherapy, which is why we have titled this topic "Psychotherap*ies.*" In this topic, we will examine some of the major forms of psychotherapy. Even when we recognize that a disorder may have a biological cause, or be (in part) genetically determined, that disorder will still involve the individual's cognitions, affects, and behaviors. The general goal of psychotherapy is to effect change in these psychological dimensions.

Different types of therapy often have different specific goals: some attempt to help the individual gain insight about the true nature of his or her disorder and its underlying cause or causes; some try to help the individual develop a stronger sense of self-identity and self esteem; yet others focus on bringing about lasting and measurable changes in overt behavior. Some varieties of psychotherapy are clearly better suited for some problems than they are for others.

We'll begin the topic by reviewing the different types of professionals who engage in psychotherapy. Then, we'll outline the major goals and methods of some of the more common types of psychotherapy. We'll divide this discussion into four main parts: psychoanalytic (or Freudian) techniques, humanistic techniques, behavioral techniques, and cognitive techniques. At the end of the topic, we'll provide some practical advice on choosing a psychotherapist.

psychotherapy
attempts to treat mental disorders through psychological means, effecting change in cognitions, affect, and/or behavior

WHO PROVIDES PSYCHOTHERAPY?

Psychotherapy is provided by a number of different types of professionals. Each has had a different educational background and may therefore have a different set of particular skills to bring to the therapeutic session. In this section, we'll list some of the most common types of mental health providers, as they are sometimes collectively referred to. Please remember that this is a list of generalities; our descriptions may not hold true for each person within a given category. Remember also that because of training or experience, some professionals develop specialties within their fields. That is, some therapists specialize in disorders of children and adolescents, others work with adults or families. Some therapists devote their efforts to alcohol and substance abuse problems, while others become involved in family and group therapies. And, finally, keep in mind that the nature of the therapy offered by the mental health professional is sometimes determined, at least in part, by the setting in which she or he chooses to work: the mental hospital, the community mental health clinic, private practice, schools, or industry, for example. The following may be considered psychotherapists:

1. *Clinical psychologist.* The clinical psychologist has usually earned a PhD degree in psychology that provides practical, applied experience, plus an emphasis on research. In addition to course work and supervised work in graduate school, the PhD clinician will spend a year on internship, usually at a mental health center or psychiatric hospital. The clinical psychologist usually has intensive training in psychological testing (in general, *psychodiagnostics).* Recently, some clinical psychologists have earned the terminal (highest) degree called a PsyD (a doctor of psychology rather than the more common doctor of philosophy). PsyD programs generally take as long to complete as PhD programs, but emphasize more practical, clinical work and less research.

Psychiatrists have an M.D. degree and usually spend a few years in residency at mental hospitals. They are allowed to use biomedical therapies to help their patients.

Counseling psychologists usually have a PhD in psychology and sometimes have an internship at some kind of counseling center.

Psychiatric social workers are usually involved in family and group therapy.

2. *Psychiatrist.* Psychiatry is a specialty in medicine. In addition to the course work required for an M.D. degree, the psychiatrist spends an internship (usually 1 year) and a residency (usually 3 years) in a mental hospital, specializing in the care of psychologically disturbed patients. The psychiatrist is the only kind of psychotherapist permitted to use the biomedical varieties of treatment we reviewed in our last topic.

3. *Counseling psychologist.* The counseling psychologist usually has a PhD in psychology. The focus of study (and the required 1-year internship), however, is generally on patients with less severe psychological problems. For instance, rather than spending one's internship in a psychiatric hospital, a counseling psychologist would more likely spend the time at a university counseling center.

4. *Psychoanalyst.* Psychoanalyst is a special label given to either a clinical psychologist at the PhD level or a psychiatrist who has also received intensive training in the particular methods of (Freudian) psychoanalysis.

5. *Psychiatric social workers.* The terminal degree for social workers is generally taken to be the Masters degree, although PhDs in social work are becoming more common. Social workers can and do engage in a variety of psychotherapies, but their traditional role has been involvement in family and group therapy.

6. *Others.* Psychotherapy may be offered by a number of other professionals and paraprofessionals. Some people practice therapy and counseling with a Masters degree in psychology (although because of licensing and certification laws in many states, they may not advertise themselves as psychologists). Occupational therapists usually have a bachelor's degree in occupational therapy, which includes many psychology courses, and internship training in aiding the psychologically and physically handicapped. Psychiatric nurses often work in mental hospitals and clinics. In addition to their R.N., psychiatric nurses have special training in the care of mentally ill patients. Pastoral counseling is a specialty of many individuals with ministerial de-

grees who have furthered their education with course work and experience in psychotherapy techniques. The mental health technician usually has an associate degree in mental health technology (MHT). Although MHT graduates are seldom allowed to provide unsupervised psychotherapy, they may be involved in the delivery of mental health services.

Although the psychoanalyst will be expected to provide a derivative of Freudian psychodynamic therapy, we can make no other general statement about the type of therapy that the above therapists may choose to use. It's worth pointing out that most psychotherapists are, in fact, somewhat eclectic in their approach to psychotherapy; that is, they will tend to use whatever aspect of a given variety of psychotherapy that seems best suited for their client or patient at the time. Now let's review those major types of psychotherapy.

Before you go on

Which professionals engage in psychotherapy, and what is their educational experience?

PSYCHOANALYTIC TECHNIQUES

We begin our review of the psychotherapies with **psychoanalysis**. Psychoanalysis began with the practice of Sigmund Freud toward the end of the nineteenth century. Psychoanalysis did not really evolve from Freudian personality theory (see Topic 23). If anything, the reverse is true. Freud was a therapist first, a personality theorist second. But his technique of therapy and theory of personality sprang forth from the same mind, and they are very much interrelated.

Psychoanalysis is based on a number of assumptions, most of them having to do with conflict and the nature of the unconscious. For Freud, one's life is often a struggle to resolve conflicts between naturally opposing forces: instincts for life and instincts for death. The biological, sexual, and aggressive strivings of the id are often in conflict with the superego, which is associated with guilt and overcautiousness. The rational, reality-based ego is to mediate between the id and the superego. Anxiety-producing conflicts that go unresolved are repressed; that is, they are forced out of awareness into the unconscious levels of the mind. Even conflicts and anxiety-producing traumas of childhood can be expected to produce symptoms of psychological disturbance.

According to Freud, the best way to truly rid one's self from anxiety is to enter the unconscious, identify the nature of the anxiety-producing conflict, and resolve it as best as possible. The first step is to gain insight into the nature of one's problems; only then can problem solving begin. This is the aim of Freudian psychoanalysis: insight and resolution of repressed conflict.

Sigmund Freud died in 1939, but his model for psychotherapy certainly did not die with him. It has been modified (as Freud himself modified it over the years), but it still remains true to the basic thrust of Freudian psychoanalysis. Before we consider how it has changed, let's examine Freudian psychoanalysis as he practiced it.

Freudian Psychoanalysis

Psychoanalysis with Sigmund Freud was probably going to be a long, often tedious process of self-examination and introspection. Aided by the careful interpretation of the analyst, and following rigorously the therapist's every suggestion, the patient was to search his or her unconscious mind for the sources of conflict and stress, which probably were established in childhood.

psychoanalysis
the form of psychotherapy, begun by Freud, aimed at helping the patient gain insight into unconscious conflicts

To help his patients relax, Freud had them lie on this couch while he sat out of view.

Once identified, the patient's conflicts could then be resolved. A number of procedures and processes were employed in this search for repressed conflicts. We'll list some of the primary ones.

Free Association   In 1881, Freud graduated from the University of Vienna Medical School (he had been a student there since 1873). From the start, he was interested in the treatment of what were then called nervous disorders. He went to France to study the technique of hypnosis, which many were claiming to be a worthwhile treatment for many mental disorders. Freud wasn't totally convinced, but when he returned to Vienna, he and a colleague, Josef Breurer, tried hypnosis as a means of treating neurotic disorders, conversion reaction hysteria in particular. They both became convinced that hypnosis itself was of little benefit in treating nervous disorders. What mattered, they believed, was to have the patient talk—talk about anything and everything. The therapist might occasionally try to guide the talking, but talking by itself seemed therapeutic.

Soon, the method of **free association** became the central procedure of psychoanalysis. Patients were told to say out loud whatever came into their minds. Sometimes the analyst would provide a stimulus word to get a chain of freely flowing associations going. To truly free associate the way Freud would have wanted you to is not an easy task. It often took many sessions for patients to learn the technique. Patients were not to edit their associations; they were to say *whatever* they thought of, and that is not always an easy thing to do. Here is where the "Freudian couch" came in. To help his patients relax, he would have them lie down, be comfortable, and avoid eye contact with the analyst. The job of the analyst through all this was to try to interpret the apparently free-flowing and random verbal responses, always looking for expressions of unconscious desires and conflicts.

Resistance   During the course of talking to a patient, and particularly during periods of free association, the psychoanalyst listens very carefully to what the patient is saying. The analyst also listens to what the patient is *not* saying. Freud believed that **resistance**—the inability or unwillingness to freely discuss some aspect of one's life—was a significant process in analysis. Resistance can show itself in many ways, from simply avoiding the mention of some topic, to joking about small matters as being inconsequential, to disrupting a session when a particular topic comes up for discussion, to missing appointments altogether. The logic here is fairly straightforward. If, for example, over the last 6 months you have talked freely about a wide variety of things, including your early childhood memories and all the members of your family except your older brother, we might suspect that there is some possible problem in your relationship with your older brother. For analysis to be successful, resistances need to be investigated and broken down.

Dream Interpretation   We examined Freudian dream analysis in Topic 9. That analyzing the nature of a patient's dreams is part of psychoanalysis is not at all surprising. Freud referred to dreams as the "Royal Road" to the unconscious mind. Freud would often have to train his patients to carefully recall and record their dreams. Then he would have them share the content of their dreams with him. Freud analyzed dreams at two levels: (1) manifest content—the dream as recalled and reported by the patient, and (2) latent content—the dream as a symbolic representation of the contents of the unconscious. The job for the analyst, Freud argued, was to interpret dreams in terms of what information and insights they could provide about the true nature of the patient's unconscious mind.

free association
the procedure in psychoanalysis in which the patient is to express whatever comes to mind without editing responses

resistance
in psychoanalysis, the inability or unwillingness to freely discuss some aspect of one's life

Transference   One of the most controversial aspects of Freudian psychoanalysis is his concept of **transference**. Transference occurs when the patient unconsciously comes to view and feel about the analyst in much the same way he or she feels about some other important person in his or her life, usually a parent. As therapy continues over a long period of time, the relationship between analyst and patient does become a complex and often emotional one. If feelings that were once directed toward someone else of significance are now directed toward the analyst, they are more accessible and observable and more readily interpreted and dealt with. Therapists have to guard against doing the same thing themselves—letting their own feelings and past experiences interfere with their neutral and objective interaction with their patients. Failing to do so is called *countertransference*.

transference
in psychoanalysis, the situation in which the patient comes to feel about the analyst in the same way he or she once felt about some other important person

Before you go on

Describe the essential nature of Freudian psychoanalysis, defining free association, resistance, dream interpretation, and transference.

Post-Freudian Psychoanalysis

Early in the twentieth century, Freudian psychoanalysis was the only form of psychotherapy. In the 1940s and 1950s, it was *the* psychotherapy of choice. "Psychoanalytic theory was the dominant force in psychiatry in the postwar period and was embraced by a large number of clinical psychologists. To a certain extent, and for all practical purposes, there was no rival orientation" (Garfield, 1981, p. 176). In the 1980s, psychoanalysis has become a much less common form of psychotherapy, and strict, Freudian-style psychoanalysis is getting very rare indeed. How has the Freudian notion of therapy been changed?

First, what hasn't changed? To still qualify as a psychoanalytic approach, one must hold that the basic aim of therapy is the uncovering of deep-seated, unconscious conflict, and that early childhood experiences can influence psychological adjustment in adolescence and adulthood. This general statement is about all that unites psychoanalytic approaches to therapy today.

Probably the most significant change since Freud's time is the concern for shortening the length of analysis. Today we talk about time-limited and short-form analysis, terms that Freud would not have approved of. Today's analyst will also take a more active, directive role than did Freud. The couch as a requirement is usually gone now; the comfort of the patient is what matters, and some patients feel more comfortable pacing or sitting than they do lying on a couch. Another major shift in emphasis is that modern psychoanalysts, although not insensitive to the effects of early childhood experiences, tend to spend more time exploring the present, the here and now.

Before you go on

How is psychoanalysis different today from when it was practiced by Freud?

Evaluating Psychoanalysis

Although we need to credit psychoanalysis for being the first, and lasting, psychotherapeutic technique, and although much of the procedure has an undeniable appeal, it is certainly fair to say that the critics have not been kind to psychoanalysis. Some of the arguments brought against analysis are more telling than others.

Even with the inherent difficulties of doing research on the outcomes of therapy, one might conclude that psychoanalysis has not fared well at all. One of the major blows to psychoanalysis came from Hans Eysenck in 1952, who, after reviewing much of the available research, claimed that there was no evidence that persons treated with psychoanalysis end up any better than persons not treated at all. Many psychoanalysts (and others) yelled foul at Eysenck's evaluation, but a more recent review by Erwin (1980) comes to the same conclusion. Further, in 1981, Joseph Wolpe made the following statements about psychoanalysis: "The clinical effectiveness of psychoanalytic therapy has never been established. . . . In actuality, not a single one of the theory's main propositions has ever been supported by scientifically acceptable evidence. . . . But this too is brushed aside. That this happens is a tribute to the expository brilliance with which Freud presented his theories. His writing weaves a magic web from which few can extricate themselves once enmeshed" (Wolpe, 1981, pp. 159–160). As we shall see, the picture is probably not all this bleak. Many well-controlled studies have demonstrated the effectiveness of psychoanalysis (Smith et al., 1980).

On a practical level, we may argue that even with today's briefer editions, psychoanalysis is a time-consuming and expensive process. When you reflect on what is required in analysis, it is also very obvious that it will be inappropriate for many. It won't be effective for severely disturbed, psychotic patients. It isn't likely to be effective for less intelligent and less insightful patients.

HUMANISTIC TECHNIQUES

There are many different brands of humanistic psychotherapy and its closely allied cousin, existential therapy. What these therapies have in common is a concern for self-examination and personal growth and development. The goal of these therapies is not to uncover deep-seated conflicts, but to foster psychological growth, to help one be the best that one can be. Based on the notion that we can all take charge of ourselves and our futures and grow and change, therapy is devised to assist that process.

Client-centered Therapy

client-centered therapy
the humanistic psychotherapy associated with Rogers, which is aimed at helping the client grow and change from within

Client-centered therapy is sometimes called Rogerian therapy after its founder, Carl Rogers. It is, perhaps, the therapy that best typifies the humanistic approach. As its name suggests, the client is the center of the client-therapist interaction (Rogers never uses the term patient and now prefers the term person-centered to client-centered). For Rogers, therapy is an opportunity to allow a person to engage in self-discovery.

What are the characteristics of client-centered therapy? Again, there are many variants, but the following generally characterize a client-centered approach. The focus is on the present, not the past or one's childhood. The focus is on feelings or affect, not beliefs or cognitions; that is, you are more likely to hear, "How do you feel about that?" not "What do you think about that?" The therapist will attempt to reflect or mirror—not interpret—how a client is feeling (using statements such as, "You seem angry about that." or "Does that make you feel sad?"). It should be pointed out that assessing the true nature of a client's feelings is not necessarily easy to do. To do so accurately requires that the therapist be an active listener and **empathic,** or able to understand and share the essence of another's feelings.

empathic
able to understand and share the essence of another's feelings; to view from another's perspective

558

Throughout each session, the therapist will express what is called *unconditional positive regard.* This is the expression of being accepting and noncritical. "I will not be critical." "If that is the way you feel, that is the way you feel." "Anything you say in here is okay." Our opening dialogue between Barbara and her therapist reflects a number of these principles.

A friend of mine, a Rogerian therapist, was once elated about how well a session with an undergraduate student had gone. When I asked him why he thought it had gone so well, he said that when the student entered his office and sat down, he asked her how she was feeling and what she'd like to talk about. She said that she didn't want to talk about anything. So my friend said, "Okay, if you don't want to talk, that's okay too. If you change your mind, I'm right here, and I'm willing to listen." For the next 50 minutes, the two of them sat there, neither doing or saying anything. At the end of their hour, the therapist said, "Well, our time's up. I'll see you next week." The student replied, "Right, see you then." It was my friend's point of view that the value of this (very quiet) session was that his client hopefully had learned something. She had learned that if she didn't want to talk about it, she didn't have to. That sort of acceptance (seldom found among family and friends) may then lead her to the realization that if she did want to talk about anything (no matter what), that would be okay too.

Evaluating Humanistic Therapies

Client-centered, nondirective approaches to therapy were at their peak of popularity in the 1960s. This was a period of individualization, of people "doing their own thing," and a technique that fostered positive regard and personal growth fit the times very well. As was the case with Freudian analysis, few psychotherapists presently practice a pure form of client-centered therapy. The client-person is still at the center of attention, but newer forms of humanistic therapy attempt to hasten the process by allowing the therapist to become more actively involved.

Also, like psychoanalysis, humanistic therapies, client-centered in particular, will not be effective for many individuals. The technique works best for mild adjustment problems (it will hardly be reasonable to try the technique with a psychotic patient) and for intelligent, sensitive, introspective people.

One problem of evaluating these therapies is that the criteria for success are particularly difficult to measure. How does one manage to get an adequate, reliable picture of someone else's personal growth or ego-strength enhancement? How do we know if therapy has helped someone to be the best they can be? We must usually take the client's word for the quality of changes that have taken place, and there are obvious problems with doing that (e.g., having invested considerable time and effort in "becoming," it might be difficult to admit that nothing much happened, even if that were the case).

Before you go on
What are the essential characteristics of client-centered therapy?

BEHAVIORAL TECHNIQUES

In a literal sense, there is no one **behavior therapy.** Behavior therapy is more a collection of many specific techniques. What unites these techniques is that they are "methods of psychotherapeutic change founded on principles of learning established in the psychological laboratory" (Wolpe, 1981, p. 159).

behavior therapy
techniques of psychotherapy founded on principles of learning established in the psychological laboratory

There are many different principles of learning, and there are many types of psychological disorder to which such methods and principles might be applied. In this section, we will list some of the more prominent applications that have become part of behavior therapy.

Systematic Desensitization

systematic desensitization
the application of classical conditioning procedures to alleviate extreme anxiety; anxiety-producing stimuli are presented while the subject is in a relaxed state

Systematic desensitization—the application of classical conditioning procedures to alleviate extreme feelings of anxiety—is one of the first applications of learning principles to meet with success and has experienced lasting acceptance. It was formally introduced by Joseph Wolpe in the late 1950s (Wolpe, 1958), although others had used similar procedures earlier. The procedure is designed to alleviate extreme anxieties, particularly those of the sort we find in phobic disorders.

In its standard form, there are three stages to systematic desensitization. The first thing the therapist does is instruct the subject to totally relax. There are many ways to go about such training. Some procedures use hypnosis, others biofeedback, but most simply have the subject relax a foot, then both feet, then one leg, then both legs, and so on, until the entire body is relaxed—a procedure called progressive relaxation. No matter which method is used, this phase generally doesn't take very long, an hour or two at the most.

The second step is to construct an anxiety hierarchy—a list of stimuli that gradually increase in their ability to evoke anxiety. The most feared, most anxiety-producing stimulus (the object of the phobia, for example) is placed at the top of the list. Each item that follows evokes less and less anxiety, until, at the bottom of the list, we find a stimulus that evokes no anxiety at all.

Joseph Wolpe is shown here conducting systematic desensitization therapy to reduce a client's anxiety. The client, in a relaxed state, is told to vividly imagine the weakest anxiety on her list. If she feels anxious, she is instructed to stop and relax again.

Now treatment is ready to begin. The subject is told to relax completely and think about the item lowest on the anxiety hierarchy. The subject is then told to think about the next highest stimulus, and the next, and so on, all the while remaining as relaxed as possible. As progress is made up the list, toward the most anxiety-producing stimulus at the top, the therapist constantly monitors the subject's tension/relaxation level. When anxiety seems to be overcoming relaxation, the subject is told to stop thinking about that item on the hierarchy and to think about an item lower on the list.

The logic here is obvious. A person cannot be relaxed and anxious at the same time—they are incompatible responses. Thus, if I pair a stimulus with relaxation, through classical conditioning it will come to produce a sense of calm, not the incompatible response of tension and anxiety. For most people, the technique works. It works best for those fears or anxieties that are specific, that are associated with easily identifiable, specific environmental stimuli, and works least well for a diffuse, generalized fear (for which hierarchies are difficult to generate).

Before you go on
Describe the three essential steps of systematic desensitization.

Flooding and Implosive Therapy

flooding
a technique of behavior therapy in which a subject is confronted with the object of his or her phobic fear, while accompanied by the therapist

Flooding is another procedure that is aimed at eliminating fears or anxieties based on specific stimuli. Bootzin and Acocella describe flooding as "a cold-turkey extinction therapy" (1984, p. 505). Flooding is referred to as an *in vivo* or in real life procedure. In this approach, the subject, accompanied by the therapist, is actually placed in his or her most fear-arousing situation. For example, someone afraid of heights would be taken to the top of a very tall building or to a very high bridge. Someone afraid of water would be taken out on a large lake or to a nearby swimming pool. There, with the therapist close at hand providing support and encouragement, the subject comes face to face with his or her most feared situation, survives (although the session may be terrifying for some), and comes to learn that the fear is irrational.

Implosive therapy is based on the very same premise, but involves the use of imagination rather than real life situations. In implosive therapy, you do not slowly work your way up or down any anxiety hierarchy. You are forced to come to imagine your worst fears, all at once, here and now. The therapist does not try to get the subject to relax, but rather to experience the full force of anxiety while in the ultimately safe surroundings of the therapist's office. Repeated trials of imagined fears and experienced anxiety paired with the safety and security of the office soon lead to the extinction of the maladaptive fear response.

Although these two techniques do sound somewhat bizarre, and they are definitely not for everyone (some therapists have difficulty dealing with such focused anxiety), they are demonstrably effective and usually require less time than does systematic desensitization.

implosive therapy
a behavior therapy in which one imagines one's worst fears, experiencing extreme anxiety in the safe surroundings of the therapist's office

aversion therapy
a technique of behavior therapy in which an aversive stimulus, such as a shock, is paired with an undesired behavior

Before you go on
In what ways are flooding and implosive therapy different from systematic desensitization?

Aversion Therapy

You should recognize **aversion therapy** as another form of classical conditioning applied to a psychological problem. In aversion therapy, a stimulus that produces a pleasant response is paired with an aversive, painful, unpleasant stimulus until the stimulus becomes unpleasant. For example, every time you put a cigarette in your mouth, I deliver a painful shock to your lip, or every time you take a drink of alcohol, you get violently sick to your stomach. Every time a child molester is shown a slide of a young child, he is shocked.

Now none of these techniques sounds like the sort of thing that anyone would agree to voluntarily. Many people do, however. They volunteer for such treatments for two reasons: (1) they are very effective at eliminating a specific behavior, and (2) they are seen as the lesser of two evils—the shocks and nausea-producing drugs are seen as being worse (by the subject or patient) than the behaviors they are designed to eliminate.

It is probably aversion therapy more than any other technique that has given behavior therapy a bad reputation among the general public, which often equates behavior therapy with cruel and unusual punishment and mind control. Assume that you, as prison warden, define as inappropriate the behavior of hanging one's arms over the bars of one's cell after the order for lights out. You see this behavior as inflammatory, ultimately dangerous, and a threat to your institution. To end it, you simply wire the bars of all the prison's cells to provide a strong shock when they are touched after the lights are turned off. Now, to justify your actions, you suggest that you were simply engaging in a form of behavior therapy, aversion therapy to be exact. Whether or not you have the right to instigate such a program is another

Aversion therapy is one method used to help alcoholics. Every time they take a drink, they receive a small shock. Through classical conditioning, the alcohol comes to be unpleasant and they will not want to drink anymore.

matter, but one thing seems certain: we should not refer to what you have done as aversion therapy. It's simply punishment. This example may seem a little exaggerated, but it does illustrate the important ethical issues involved in this kind of treatment.

Before you go on

What is aversion therapy?

Contingency Management and Contracting

As their names suggest, contingency management and contingency contracting borrow heavily from the learning principles of operant conditioning and are, in a sense, varieties of behavior modification (see Topic 11). The basic idea, of course, is to have the individual come to appreciate the consequences of his or her behaviors. Appropriate behaviors lead to rewards and opportunities to do valued things; inappropriate behaviors lead to aversive stimulation and fewer opportunities.

The basic procedures work very well. Their total effectiveness is, as operant conditioning would predict, a function of the extent to which the therapist has control over the situation. If the therapist can control rewards and punishments (contingency management), determining such matters as who gets dessert after dinner and who gets to watch television, he or she stands a good chance of modifying behaviors. As therapist, you modify behavior by managing the contingencies. *If* a patient (a severely disturbed, hospitalized schizophrenic, for example) engages in the appropriate response (leaving her room to go to dinner), *then* the patient will get something she really wants (an after-dinner cigarette).

Contingency contracting amounts to establishing a token economy of secondary reinforcers. What that means is that the patient is first taught that some token, which may be a checker, a poker chip, a bingo marker, or just a check mark on a pad, can be saved, and when enough tokens are accumulated, they can be cashed in for something of value to the patient. With contracting, the specific token, of specific value, for a specific behavior is spelled out ahead of time. Because control over the environment of the patient/learner is most complete in such circumstances, this technique is particularly effective in institutions and with young children.

Bandura uses modeling to help people overcome phobias. By watching other people handle snakes without fear, people can overcome their fears and handle the snakes themselves.

Modeling

Some learning cannot be explained in terms of classical or operant conditioning. It should be no surprise that behavior therapy, relying as it does on learning principles, uses learning principles beyond those of conditioning. **Modeling,** a term introduced by Albert Bandura (1977), involves the acquisition of a new, appropriate response through the imitation of a model. As we saw in Topic 12, modeling can be an effective means of learning.

modeling
the acquisition of a new appropriate response through the imitation of a model

In a therapeutic situation, modeling often amounts to having (or allowing) patients watch someone else perform a certain appropriate behavior, perhaps earning a reward for it (called vicarious reinforcement, you'll recall). Some phobias, particularly those in children, can often be overcome through modeling. A child who is afraid of dogs, for example, will profit from watching another child (more effective than an adult) playing with a dog. Some phobia treatments designed to alleviate phobic fears are of the "here, watch what I do and then you do it, too" sort. This works well with adults who are afraid of such objects as snakes.

Before you go on
Briefly summarize contingency management, contingency contracting, and modeling as means of psychotherapy.

Evaluating Behavior Therapy

The most commonly voiced criticism of behavior therapy is that it tends to focus only on the individual's maladaptive behavior and ignores inner matters such as early childhood experiences, subjective feelings, self-esteem, and personal growth. The behavior therapist claims that such criticisms are unfair on two grounds: (1) Behavior therapists *do* concern themselves with inner states of the individual. If there were not some inner distress, there would be little reason to engage in therapy of any kind. "It is the subjective problem, the complaint, that drives the neurotic patient to seek treatment, no matter of what kind" (Wolpe, 1981, p. 162). (2) Although such matters of deep-seated conflict resolution and personal growth and development are noble aims, there is no scientifically reasonable way to assess progress or achieve a cure using such concepts. The only reasonable alternative is to focus on behaviors and behavior change.

Although there are few quality research reports that behavior therapies are in any general way superior to other forms of psychotherapy, they are certainly every bit as effective in the short and long term. Thus, the advantage for the behavior therapies is that they tend to take much less time and, hence, are less expensive than many alternative treatment means.

COGNITIVE TECHNIQUES

Psychotherapists who use cognitive techniques do not deny the importance of a person's feelings or behavior (in fact, these therapies are often called *cognitive-behavioral).* Rather, they believe that what matters most in the therapeutic session is the subject's set of thoughts, perceptions, attitudes, and beliefs about himself or herself and the environment. To change how one feels and acts, therapy should first be directed at changing what one thinks. As we have seen with other approaches to psychotherapy, there is not just one type of cognitive-behavioral therapy; there are many. We'll examine two.

Rational-emotive Therapy

Rational-emotive therapy (RET) is associated with Albert Ellis (1970). Its basic premise is that psychological problems arise when a person tries to interpret (a cognitive activity) what happens in the world on the basis of irrational beliefs. Maladaptive behaviors stem from maladaptive cognitions, which in most cases are simply unrealistic beliefs about one's self and one's environment.

When compared to client-centered techniques, RET is quite directive. The therapist takes an active role in interpreting the reality or the irrationality of a client's system of beliefs and encourages active change. Therapists often act as role models and make homework assignments for clients that help them bring their expectations and perceptions in line with reality.

To give a very simplified example, think back to our opening dialogue with Barbara and her client-centered therapist. A cognitive therapist might see a number of irrational beliefs operating, including two that Ellis (1970) claims are very common ones: (1) a person should always be loved for everything they do, and (2) it is better to avoid problems than face them. These, claims Ellis, are exactly the sort of cognitions that many people hold and that create psychological difficulties (others are listed in Figure 30.1). Rather than waiting for self-discovery, which might never come, a cognitive therapist would point out to Barbara that the fact that her parents never went to college and don't understand what it is like to work and go to school at the same time is their problem, not hers. Rather than avoiding problems that arise from her parents' lack of appreciation, she needs to either set them straight or move out (there are a number of other possibilities, of course).

Cognitive Restructuring Therapy

Along the same lines as rational-emotive therapy is **cognitive restructuring therapy,** as proposed by Aaron Beck (1976). Although the basic idea is the same and the goals are similar, restructuring therapy is much less confrontational and direct than RET.

Beck's assumption is that psychological distress stems from a few simple, but misguided beliefs (cognitions, again). According to Beck, people with psychological disorders share certain characteristics. (1) They tend to have very negative self-images. They do not value themselves or what they do. (2)

Figure 30.1
Some of the major irrational beliefs that lead to maladjustment and disorder (From Ellis, 1970)

1. One should be loved by everyone for everything one does.
2. Certain acts are awful or wicked and people who perform them should be severely punished.
3. It is horrible when things are not the way we would like them to be.
4. Human misery is produced by external causes, or outside persons or events, rather than by the view that one takes of these conditions.
5. If something may be dangerous or fearsome, one should be terribly upset by it.
6. It is better to avoid life problems, if possible, than to face them.
7. One needs something stronger or more powerful than oneself to rely on.
8. One should be thoroughly competent, intelligent, and achieving in all respects.
9. Because something once affected one's life, it will indefinitely affect it.
10. One must have certain and perfect self-control.
11. Happiness can be achieved by inertia and inaction.
12. We have virtually no control over our emotions and cannot help having certain feelings.

They tend to take a very negative view of life experiences, and they over-generalize. For example, having failed one test, a person comes to believe that there is no way he can do college work and withdraws from school and looks for work, even though he believes there's little chance that anyone would offer a job to someone who is such a failure and a college drop-out. (3) They tend to seek out experiences that reinforce their negative expectations. The student in the above example may apply for a job as a law clerk or as a stockbroker. Lacking even minimal experience, he'll be offered neither job and, thus, will find confirmation of his own worthlessness. (4) They tend to hold a rather dismal outlook for the future. (5) They tend to avoid seeing the bright side of any experience.

In cognitive restructuring, a therapist offers the patient an opportunity to test or demonstrate her or his beliefs. The patient and therapist make up a list of hypotheses based on the patient's assumptions and beliefs and actually go out and test these hypotheses. Obviously, the therapist is going to exercise enough control over the situation so that most of the experiments will not confirm the patient's beliefs about himself or herself, but will lead instead to positive outcomes. This approach, of leading a person to the self-discovery that negative attitudes directed toward one's self are inappropriate, has proven very successful in the treatment of depression.

Before you go on
Briefly summarize the logic behind rational-emotive therapy and cognitive restructuring therapy.

GROUP APPROACHES

There are many other approaches to the treatment of mental disorders through psychological means. We have only listed here some of the more classic or more common. In this section, we'll identify a few additional types of psychotherapy.

Many patients profit from some variety of *group therapy*. Group therapy is a general label applied to a variety of situations in which a number of people are involved in a therapeutic setting at the same time. It is often the therapy of choice in family and marital counseling, where the very nature of the psychological problem is interpersonal and can best be solved by involving all parties to the problem. If a small child is having psychological problems, it may be appropriate to meet in therapy with the child alone, but it is almost certainly going to be necessary to also meet with the parent(s) to bring about lasting change in the child and his or her behavior.

In standard forms of group therapy, a number of patients are brought together at one time (under the guidance of a therapist) to share their feelings and experiences. There are a number of possible benefits from this procedure, including an awareness that "I'm not the only one with problems." The sense of support that one can get from someone else with psychological problems is occasionally even greater than that afforded by a therapist—a sort of "she really knows from her own experience the hell that I'm going through" logic. And there is truth in the basic idea that getting involved in helping someone else with a problem is, in itself, a therapeutic process.

Transactional analysis is a form of group therapy (usually for married couples or families) that was exceedingly popular in the 1970s. It was developed by Eric Berne (1964, 1969). The basic idea here is that everyone is governed by three aspects of personality: parent, which reflects the rules, regulations, and prohibitions of society; adult, which reflects the mature, reasonable, and rational; and child, which reflects spontaneous, unthinking,

Many distressed people profit from group therapy. Not only are they relieved to discover that other people have problems, too, but it is therapeutic for them to be able to help others.

Eric Berne

creative, and/or selfish aspects of personality. In Berne's mind, a healthy individual maintains a balanced state among these three components of personality. Interpersonal interactions are healthy and adaptive when they are carried out in such a way that all members of the interaction are operating on the same level. That is, husbands and wives normally communicate on an adult-adult level. If both engage in a child-child interaction ("I wanna get out of here and party!" "Great idea, let's do it!"), there won't be any problems. Problems develop when people consistently interact from different levels or aspects of personality. If a husband constantly and inappropriately communicates to his wife in the manner of parent, there will be conflict and problems (unless, of course, the wife constantly interacts as child). For Berne, therapy is a matter of educating people about the games they play with each other in their interpersonal relationships and trying to get communication to occur at appropriate levels.

Before you go on
What are the advantages of group therapy?

EVALUATING PSYCHOTHERAPY

Evaluating psychotherapy has proven to be a very difficult task. Is psychotherapy effective? Compared to what? Is any type of psychotherapy better than any other? The best we can do is offer very tentative answers. Yes, psychotherapy is effective. Compared to what? Compared to doing nothing. No, there is no evidence that, in general, any one type of therapy is significantly better than any other.

Let's mention just a few of the problems that are involved in doing quality research on the effectiveness of psychotherapy. First, we have little quality data on how people might respond without treatment. We do know that there is often a spontaneous remission of symptoms. That is, sometimes people get better without the formal intervention of a therapist. (To say that people get better on their own is not literally accurate. There are many factors that may improve one's mental health, even if one is not officially in therapy (Erwin, 1980).) What we don't know is how many people might recover from mental illness without psychotherapy—a baseline group against which we may compare recovery rates for different psychotherapies.

Second, we can't seem to agree on what we mean by recovery. For some, it is simply the absence of observable symptoms for a specified period of time. For others, however, the goal of therapy is something different—personal growth perhaps, or a restructuring of cognitions, or an insight into a deep-seated motivational conflict.

Finally, even when we can agree on criteria for a recovery, or cure, there is often great concern about how to measure or assess outcomes. It hardly seems scientific to ask therapists or their patients to report if therapy has been a helpful experience.

These are three of the most commonly cited general problems with designing research to evaluate the outcome of psychotherapy. Even so, a number of quality studies have been done. Most have focused on just one technique at a time (Erwin, 1980; Eysenck, 1952; Miller & Berman, 1983; Wolpe, 1981).

A recent evaluation study that shows very positive results for psychotherapy is that of Smith, Glass, and Miller (1980). Smith and her colleagues found that a variety of psychotherapeutic techniques (see Figure 30.2) produce results that are significantly better than what might be expected

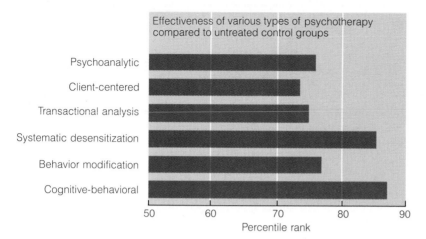

Effectiveness of various types of psychotherapy compared to untreated control groups

Psychoanalytic
Client-centered
Transactional analysis
Systematic desensitization
Behavior modification
Cognitive-behavioral

50   60   70   80   90
Percentile rank

Figure 30.2
A summary of the results of 475 studies that assessed the effectiveness of psychotherapy. These data reflect the percentage of clients treated with various forms of therapy who scored higher, or more favorably, on a number of outcome measures compared to similar clients who were not treated. That is, the average subject of behavior modification scored higher on outcome measures than did 75 percent of subjects not treated.

through spontaneous remission. According to Figure 30.2, an average patient in psychoanalysis scored more favorably on a number of outcome variables than did 75 percent of controls who received no treatment. Smith, Glass, and Miller did not go out and collect new data for their report. What they did was to carefully review 475 available studies on the effectiveness of psychotherapy. Clearly some of these studies were more flawed than others, but the overall conclusion of Smith and her colleagues is based on a large sample of data.

What about comparing psychotherapy methods? Here the answer is also quite clear: In general, there are no differences. No one type of therapy produced better results than any other. But remember that this conclusion is based on a broad generality. There is evidence that suggests that some types of therapy are better suited for some types of psychological problem than are other types of therapy. For example, systematic desensitization and other behavioral methods are demonstrably useful for phobic disorders, whereas cognitive therapies seem best suited to patients with depression.

Which particular therapy is best suited for which particular disorder is just one of the questions to which we do not have a definitive answer. In the 1970s and 1980s, the effectiveness, safety, and appropriateness of psychotherapy has become a question of public policy, debated on the floor of the United States Congress (DeLeon et al., 1983). The government, through Medicaid and Medicare, for example, invests millions of dollars each year in mental health and psychotherapy. Particularly in the context of spiraling health costs in general, it is not surprising that those who control the purse strings (including many insurance companies) are demanding accountability. The DeLeon article (1983) cited above has this title, "Psychotherapy—Is it safe, effective and appropriate?" As we have said, the answer seems to be "yes" to these three questions. But our "yes" is tentative and needs more data and more research before we can answer in the affirmative with confidence.

Before you go on

Is there any evidence that psychotherapy is effective?

Is any one type of psychotherapy better than the others?

Throughout the last two chapters we have repeatedly mentioned the reality that psychological disorders are very common. As you read these words, tens of millions of Americans are in need of, or could profit from, treatment for their psychological distress. What if *you* were such a person? What if you were to realize that you were showing the symptoms of a psychological disorder? Where would you turn? How would you begin?

The first thing you would need to do in this hypothetical situation is ask a lot of questions. Many people and agencies can serve as a good resource at this point. Do you have any family or friends who have been in therapy or counseling? What (or whom) do they recommend? If you get no useful information from friends or family, there are many other people you could ask (assuming that your symptoms are not acute and that time is not critical). You might check with your psychology instructor. He or she may not be a psychotherapist, but will probably be familiar with the mental health resources of the community. You might also see if your college or university maintains a clinic or counseling center service for students (if nothing else, this is often an inexpensive route to take). Check with your family physician. Among other things, a complete physical examination may turn up some leads about the nature of your problem. You might talk with your rabbi, priest, or minister. Clergypersons commonly deal with people in distress and, again, are usually familiar with community resources. If there is one in your community, call the local mental health center or mental health association. If all else fails, resort to the phone book; call and ask around. If you recognize that you have a problem, one that

you cannot deal with yourself, do not give up. Find help. And the sooner the better.

Now let's assume that a psychotherapist has been recommended to you. You have scheduled an appointment. How will you know if you have made a wise choice? To be sure, only you can be the judge of that. Two cautions are appropriate here: (1) Give the therapy and the therapist a chance. By now you recognize that psychological problems are seldom simply and easily solved. (In fact, a therapist who suggests that your problem can be simply and easily solved is probably a therapist of whom to be leery.) It may take three or four sessions before your therapist has learned (from you) what the exact and real nature of your problem is. Most psychological problems have developed over a long period of time. An hour or two per week for a week or two cannot be expected to automatically make everything right again, as if by magic. You can expect progress, and you might expect some sessions to be more helpful than others. To expect a miracle cure is unreasonable. (2) On the other hand, you may feel that you have given your therapy every opportunity to succeed. If you have been truly open and honest with your therapist and feel that you are in no way profiting from your sessions, say so. Express your displeasure and disappointment. After careful consideration, be prepared to change therapists. Starting over again with someone new may involve costs in time and effort, but occasionally it is the only reasonable option.

Now let's consider one more scenario. Imagine that you recognize some of the symptoms of mental illness in a close friend. You sense that this friend is under

stress, dealing with it poorly, and is showing inappropriate, maladaptive behaviors. In your judgment, your friend needs psychological help. What do you do now?

In many regards, this may be a more difficult situation than when you recognize a problem in yourself. You want to be helpful, but you also recognize that your friend needs professional help and that getting your friend to realize this may not be easy. The advice to you in such a situation is, in general, as follows. Be as honest with your friend as you can be. Indicate that you think that something is wrong. Listen carefully. Suggest that you would like to help. Don't try to bully or force the issue (unless you really believe that your friend could be dangerous). Listen. Be supportive. Make specific recommendations of specific actions that your friend might take. Listen patiently. Don't be judgmental. Volunteer to go with your friend to seek help or at least to make an initial contact. Don't try to be devious—setting up a surprise visit with a therapist, for instance. Listen closely to what your friend has to say and offer to help, but remember that, in the long run, only he or she can decide what to do.

Which professionals engage in psychotherapy, and what is their educational experience?

Many different kinds of mental health professionals can be referred to as psychotherapists. These include: clinical psychologists, PhDs or PsyDs in psychology with a 1-year internship; psychiatrists, M.D.s with an internship and residency in a mental hospital; counseling psychologists, PhDs in psychology specializing in less severe disorders and with an internship in a counseling setting; psychoanalysts, PhDs in psychology or psychiatrists who specialize in Freudian psychoanalysis; psychiatric social workers, usually with a Master's degree and tending to focus on family and group therapy techniques; and many others, including therapists with a Master's degree in psychology, pastoral counselors, and mental health technicians. / 555

Describe the essential nature of Freudian psychoanalysis, defining free association, resistance, dream interpretation, and transference.

Freudian psychoanalysis is a therapeutic technique aimed at uncovering repressed conflicts so they can be successfully resolved. Among other things, the process involves: (1) free association, in which the patient is encouraged to say anything and everything that comes to mind, without editing; (2) resistance, in which a patient seems unable or unwilling to discuss some aspect of their life; taken as a sign that the resisted experiences may be anxiety-producing; (3) dream interpretation, in which one analyzes both the manifest and latent content of dreams for insights into the nature of the patient's unconscious mind; and (4) transference, in which feelings that once were directed at some significant person in the patient's life become directed toward the analyst. / 557

How is psychoanalysis different today from when it was practiced by Freud?

Although the basis of psychoanalysis has remained unchanged since Freud's day, some changes have evolved. For example, there is now more effort to shorten the duration of analysis; there is less emphasis on childhood experiences and more concern with the here and now. Present-day analysis is also more directive than it was in Freud's day. / 557

What are the essential characteristics of client-centered therapy?

Client-centered therapy, which we associate with Carl Rogers, is based on the belief that people can control their own lives and, with help, solve their own problems if they can be helped to understand the true nature of their feelings and problems. It is a procedure of self-discovery and personal growth. The therapist reflects or mirrors the client's feelings, focuses on the here and now, and tries to be empathic, relating to the patient's feelings. Throughout therapy sessions, the therapist provides unconditional positive regard for the client. / 559

Describe the three essential steps of systematic desensitization.

Systematic desensitization is a behavior therapy technique particularly well suited for the treatment of phobic reactions. A subject is first taught to relax. Then an anxiety hierarchy is made, which lists stimuli in order of their capacity to evoke fear or anxiety. Desensitization is accomplished by gradually presenting more and more anxiety-producing stimuli from the hierarchy while the subject remains in a relaxed state, thus learning to be relaxed in the presence of stimuli that previously evoked anxiety. / 560

In what ways are flooding and implosive therapy different from systematic desensitization?

Flooding and implosive therapy are two rather dramatic forms of behavior therapy that are particularly useful in the treatment of phobias. In flooding, the subject is confronted with the object of her or his fear in person *(in vivo)*, accompanied by the therapist. Implosive therapy requires the subject to imagine his or her fears in the most vivid possible way in an effort to increase anxiety to very high levels in the safety and security of the therapist's office. Unlike systematic desensitization, neither procedure is gradual, and neither encourages the subject to remain relaxed; indeed, both require the subject to become anxious in order to face and deal with that anxiety. / 561

What is aversion therapy?

Aversion therapy is accomplished by pairing an unwanted behavior with a strongly negative stimulus, such as a shock or a nausea-producing drug. It is an effective means of reducing unwanted behaviors, but should only be thought of as therapy when subjects voluntarily agree to undergo the treatment after recognizing the long-term benefit of submitting to the aversive stimuli. / 562

Briefly summarize contingency management, contingency contracting, and modeling as means of psychotherapy.

Contingency management, contingency contracting, and modeling are three specific applications of accepted learning principles that are used as therapy to increase the likelihood of appropriate behaviors and/or decrease the likelihood of inappropriate behaviors. Contingency management amounts to exercising control over the pattern of rewards that a patient or subject may receive. Contracting usually involves secondary reinforcement and a token economy system in which a subject agrees (by contract) to engage in certain behaviors in order to earn specified rewards. Modeling comes from social learning theory and suggests that persons can acquire appropriate behaviors through the imitation of models, particularly when models are seen as reinforced for their behaviors. / 563

Briefly summarize the logic behind rational-emotive therapy and cognitive restructuring therapy.

Cognitive therapies are designed to alter the way a person perceives and thinks about himself or herself and the environment. Rational-emotive therapy (RET), for example, takes the premise that people with psychological problems are operating on a series of irrational assumptions about the world and themselves. RET is quite directive in its attempts to change people's cognitions. Cognitive restructuring therapy is somewhat less directive, but is based on the same sort of idea as RET. Here the underlying premise is that people with psychological disorders have developed negative self-images and negative views (cognitions) about the future. Here, the therapist provides opportunities for the patient to test those negative cognitions and discover that everything is not as bad as it may seem. / 565

What are the advantages of group therapy?

There are a number of advantages to group therapy. (1) The basic problem may be an interpersonal one and, thus, will be better understood and dealt with in an interpersonal situation. (2) There is value in realizing that one is not the only person in the world with a problem, and that there are others who may have even more difficult problems. (3) There is therapeutic value in providing support for someone else. (4) The dynamics of intragroup communication can be analyzed and changed in a group setting. / 566

Is there any evidence that psychotherapy is effective?

Is any one type of psychotherapy better than the others?

Scientifically evaluating the appropriateness and effectiveness of psychotherapy has proven to be very difficult to do. There are many conflicting research studies. It is safe to take as a tentative conclusion that, in general, psychotherapy is effective. It is significantly better than leaving disorders untreated. There are data that suggest that some therapies are better suited to some clients and to some disorders than they are to others. However, there is no evidence that, in general, any one type of therapy is any better than any other. / 567

CHAPTER FOURTEEN

SOCIAL PSYCHOLOGY

Written in collaboration with Steve A. Nida, Franklin University

TOPIC

In the late 1960s, a third-grade teacher in a small elementary school in Riceville, Iowa, wanted to provide her pupils with a first-hand experience of prejudice. Jane Elliott announced to her students that she had evidence that blue-eyed children were clearly superior to children with brown eyes. As a result, students with brown eyes were declared second class citizens. They were forced to sit at the back of the classroom. They had to stand at the end of the lunch line, allowing the blue-eyed children first choice; they were not allowed second helpings of food. They were not allowed to use the drinking fountain. The "superior" blue-eyed children were given special privileges, including extra recess time. To make them more visible, brown-eyed children were forced to wear paper collars that identified their lowly status from a distance.

It wasn't long before the children in Ms. Elliott's third-grade class became active participants in her experiment. The classroom performance of the brown-eyed children deteriorated; they performed below their usual levels on a number of academic tasks. The blue-eyed children performed better than usual. They voluntarily avoided contact with their "inferior" brown-eyed classmates. Fights and arguments broke out. The behavior of the blue-eyed students became aggressive, contemptuous, and occasionally vicious—and all in one day!

The next school day, Ms. Elliott informed the class that she had made a terrible mistake: she had gotten her evidence reversed. It was blue-eyed children who were inferior; the best people were those with brown eyes. With displays of great joy and enthusiasm, the brown-eyed children tore off their offensive collars and helped fit the blue-eyed pupils with paper collars

that identified *them* as inadequate and inferior. Even with their experience of the previous day, the behaviors of the children in the class were exactly the same, only the roles were reversed. Those who just the day before were the objects of prejudice now sat in the front of the class, performed well on classroom tests, rushed to be first in line at lunch time, and treated their blue-eyed classmates very badly.

On the third class day, Ms. Elliott shared her original intent with her pupils and told them that none of what she said the last two days was, in fact, true. The effects of this classroom demonstration were not long-lived. The children could, and did, soon return to their normal behaviors. The artificially-induced prejudice disappeared almost as fast as it had been created. But the experience was a meaningful one for those Iowa third-graders and a significant one for us, too. It tells us a great deal about the irrationality and fragility of a prejudice based on some physical characteristic (Elliott, 1977; Leonard, 1970; Peters, 1971). We will have occasion throughout this topic to return to Jane Elliott's classroom demonstration.

Why We Care

social psychology
the scientific study of how others influence the thoughts, feelings, and behaviors of the individual

The demonstration we have just described is filled with examples of social influence. **Social psychology** is the subfield of psychology that is concerned with how others influence the thoughts, feelings, and behaviors of the individual. Social psychologists focus on the *individual,* not the group (which is more likely to be the concern of sociologists).

There is no doubt that many areas of psychology are also interested in reactions that are essentially social in nature. Developmental psychologists, for example, are interested in how styles of cooperative and competitive play change and develop through the early years of life. Personality psychologists are interested in individual characteristics (traits) that affect interpersonal behavior, such as friendliness, aggression, and so on.

In this chapter, we will consider two major areas of interest in social psychology: (1) social thinking—the perception and evaluation of other people in social situations, and (2) social influence—how other people affect the psychological reactions of the individual.

This topic begins with a discussion of the perspective from which social psychologists study behavior and mental processes. We'll spend the bulk of this topic dealing with an important social-psychological phenomenon: attitudes. We'll see how psychologists define attitude, and we'll study how attitudes are formed and how they may be changed. We'll also review interpersonal (or social) attraction and consider some of the factors that determine how and why some people are attracted to or form positive attitudes about others.

THE SOCIAL-PSYCHOLOGICAL PERSPECTIVE

Since we are all social organisms, we are, each in our own way, amateur social psychologists. Getting along well with other people is considered to be an asset, and those of us who are able to do so easily may be good social psychologists in the sense that we are skilled in predicting the behaviors of others and understanding how others affect our own behaviors. All of us seem to put a great deal of effort into trying to understand social behavior.

To claim that we are all amateur social psychologists has both positive and negative implications. On the one hand, it means that social psychology tends to be perceived as interesting and relevant because it deals with familiar, everyday situations that affect us all. On the other hand, it also means that the average person is inclined to accept common sense, personal experience, and even folklore as the basis for making assumptions about social behavior. Although common sense often may be valid, it is not an acceptable basis for a scientific approach to social behavior. The social psychologist is distinguished, then, by a questioning perspective that relies on experimentation and other scientific research strategies as sources of knowledge about social behavior, even if the results of applying these strategies fly in the face of common sense. As we shall see in this chapter, some of the most influential discoveries in social psychology have been unexpected and counterintuitive.

During the last few years, social psychology has, like many other areas of psychology, taken on a clearly *cognitive* flavor. That is, social psychologists are attempting more and more to understand social behavior by examining the mental structures and processes that are reflected in such behavior.

To give you a feel for this approach, let's look again at the situation created in Ms. Elliott's third grade classroom. On the first day of that experi-

Stereotypes are generalized ideas about members of a group that do not allow for individual differences. Most often, stereotypes are negative views. And for almost every stereotype, there are people who support the opposite view.

ment, children with blue eyes developed (quickly) some rather unfavorable ideas about brown-eyed classmates. Pupils with brown eyes were thought of as inferior, lazy, and irresponsible. These cognitions developed without any real test. On the basis of very little actual evidence or data, blue-eyed children were willing to think of all brown-eyed children as inferior. They were willing to ignore their previous experiences and individual differences among their brown-eyed classmates. They mentally came to represent children with brown eyes as inferior. They formed a **stereotype**—a generalized mental representation of members of a group that is based on limited experience and that does not allow for individual differences.

Although this particular example of a stereotype has negative implications because it is based on erroneous information, stereotypes are not necessarily bad. When they are based on accurate information they are useful tools that help us simplify and deal more efficiently with a complex world. For instance, assume that your stereotype of law enforcement officers includes the cognition that they will arrest you for speeding. If you are out on the highway and see a law enforcement vehicle in your rearview mirror, you'll make sure that your speed is not exceeding the posted limit, regardless of whether you see that vehicle as belonging to a state trooper, a city police officer, or a county sheriff. You won't pause to wonder what that officer is doing out there on the highway until after you have checked your speed. Because you have formed a stereotype, your behavior has become predictable and virtually automatic.

Notice also that once the pupils in our opening story developed the idea of superiority and inferiority on the basis of eye color, their behaviors changed accordingly. The students had rather strong notions about how one deals with or reacts to classmates who are "inferior." They are to sit at the back of the class, they are to stand at the end of lunch lines, and they are not to be spoken to in a friendly manner, *because* they are inferior.

We all develop a complex set of rules or expectations about how to behave that guide and direct our social actions. These prescriptions or expectations are called social **norms.** Clearly, norms have a cognitive basis (a mental rep-

stereotype
a generalized mental (cognitive) representation of someone based on a small sample of experience

norms
rules or expectations that guide our behavior in certain social situations by prescribing how we ought to behave

resentation) if we are to use them consistently. Like stereotypes, they are cognitions that we may use to help simplify our social world. Because we have developed social norms, we know how we are to act in a wide variety of social situations.

Before you go on

What are stereotypes and norms, and in what way are they cognitive?

ATTITUDES

attitude
a general evaluative disposition directed toward some object, consisting of feelings, behaviors, and beliefs

Since the 1920s, a central concern in social psychology has been the nature of attitudes. An **attitude** is a general evaluative disposition directed toward some object; it consists of beliefs, feelings, and behaviors. One major dimension of an attitude, according to this traditional definition, is cognitive (beliefs); so in at least one respect, social psychology has nearly always been characterized by a cognitive orientation.

The concept of "evaluative" included in this definition refers to a dimension of attitudes that involves notions such as for or against, pro or con, and positive or negative. By "disposition" we mean a tendency or a preparedness to respond to the object of the attitude. Notice that by definition, attitudes have objects. We have attitudes *toward* or *about* something. We don't just have good attitudes or bad attitudes in general; we have attitudes about some attitudinal object.

Anything can be the object of an attitude, whether it is a person, a thing, or an idea. You may have attitudes about this course, the car you drive, your father, the President, or the fast-food restaurant where you occasionally eat lunch. Some of our attitudes are more important than others, of course, but the fact that we do have attitudes toward so many things is precisely the reason why the study of attitudes is so central in social psychology.

The Structure of Attitudes

Although many different definitions of attitude have been proposed over the years, most of them recognize that an attitude consists of three components. When we use the term *attitude* in everyday conversation, we most likely are referring to the *affective* component, which consists of our feeling or emotions about the attitudinal object. The *behavioral* component consists of our behavioral tendencies toward the object of our attitude. This component includes our actual behaviors and/or our intentions to act should the opportunity arise. The *cognitive* component includes our beliefs or thoughts about the attitudinal object. We sometimes refer to these three components as the ABCs of attitude (Myers, 1983), a memory device that you may find helpful (see Figure 31.1).

Notice that all three of these components are required to fit our definition. If you believe that brown-eyed children are lazy, you have a belief, not an attitude. If you hate brown-eyed children, you have an emotional reaction, not an attitude. If you make fun of brown-eyed children, you are engaging in behavior, but you do not necessarily have an attitude toward them. Strictly speaking, to say that you have an attitude toward brown-eyed children would require evidence of all three components.

In many cases, the cognitive, affective, and behavioral components of our attitudes are consistent. We think that classical music is relaxing and like to listen to it, so we buy classical music recordings. It is clearly the case, how-

Attitudes consist of beliefs, feelings, and behaviors. Thus, if we believe that nuclear power is dangerous and feel that it should be banned, we may choose to show our beliefs by demonstrating against nuclear power.

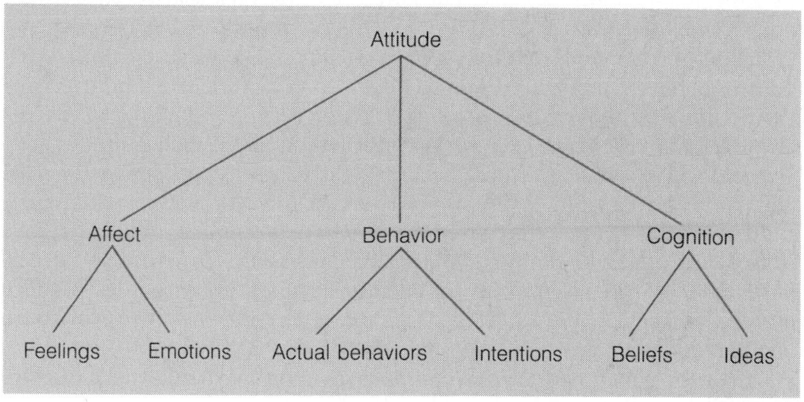

Figure 31.1
The ABCs of attitudes

ever, that there are a number of occasions when our behaviors are not consistent with our beliefs and our feelings. We may have unfavorable, stereotyped beliefs and negative feelings about someone, yet when we encounter that person at a social gathering, we smile, extend our hand, and say something pleasant.

Because our behavioral component often does not reflect our feelings or our beliefs, some social psychologists (e.g., Fishbein & Ajzen, 1975) prefer to exclude this component; they reserve the term *attitude* to refer only to the fundamental like or dislike for the attitudinal object, that is, the affective component.

Fishbein and Ajzen maintain that attitudes *may* lead to behavioral intentions which in turn *may* be correlated with actual behavior. Across a large sample of situations, there should, in fact, be consistency between one's attitude and *most* behaviors. But, predicting any single behavior on the basis of one's attitude is very difficult. The basic problem is that one's actual behaviors, particularly in social settings, are subject to many influences over and above one's underlying attitude.

Before you go on
What is an attitude and what are its three components?

The Usefulness of Attitudes

Attitudes are important for a variety of reasons that are readily apparent in everyday life. Have you ever noticed how quick people are to evaluate the unfamiliar? If a friend tells you that she just bought a new book, saw a new movie, or tried a new restaurant, one of the first things that you will probably want to know is if she liked it or not. Further questioning will most likely be required for you to go beyond a general evaluative comment (such as "I didn't like it") and explore the reasons behind the feeling. Such probing may reveal that your friend believes the book to be too difficult to understand, the movie to be too corny, or the service in the restaurant to be too slow. In short, we can see that our "attitudes serve as convenient summaries of our beliefs" (Petty & Cacioppo, 1981, p. 8).

Attitudes are also useful when they serve a **social identification function** (Greenwald, 1985). The attitudes of other people provide useful information about who they are, and, similarly, our attitudes tell others about us. Many

social identification function
the observation that attitudes communicate information useful in social evaluation

social evaluations are based on one's likes and dislikes (particularly if they are extreme).

Having information about someone's attitudes allows us to predict that person's behaviors more accurately than we could without such information. It is no accident that people in the process of getting to know one another devote a good bit of time exchanging information about their attitudes. You have probably experienced this social process yourself, perhaps when going on a date with someone for the first or second time. In this situation, don't you usually spend some time discussing the music you like, political preferences, what you enjoy doing in your spare time, and even where you like to go on dates? Such discussions about likes, dislikes, and attitudes produce information that people use to get to know each other, a process of social identification.

impression management function
the selective presentation or misrepresentation of one's attitudes in an attempt to present one's self in a particular way

Most people, of course, are aware that providing social information of this sort does influence what others may think of them. Consequently, people often tend to carefully select what information they choose to offer about their own attitudes. Sometimes they may choose to misrepresent their true attitudes completely. In such cases, we say that attitudes can serve an **impression management function** (Greenwald, 1985). Obviously, managing someone else's impression by providing misleading information about one's attitudes will only work for a limited amount of time.

Before you go on
What are some of the functions served by attitudes?

Attitude Formation

Given the usefulness of attitudes and the fact that we have attitudes toward so many things, we now need to consider where attitudes come from. Most experts agree that simple conditioning processes go a long way toward explaining the formation of attitudes. In other words, attitudes appear to be learned. Of interest is *how* they are learned, and there may be a number of viable answers to this question.

Classical Conditioning Some attitudes are no doubt acquired through the simple associative process of classical conditioning. As depicted in Figure 31.2, positive experiences (unconditioned stimuli) are paired with an attitudinal object (conditioned stimulus). As a result of this association, the attitudinal object comes to elicit the same good feeling (a positive evaluative response) that was originally produced by the unconditioned stimulus. The good feeling, originally an unconditioned response evoked by some positive experience, now becomes a conditioned response evoked by the attitudinal object. Of course, negative attitudes can be acquired in the same way.

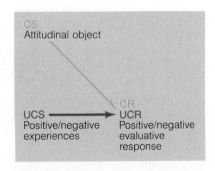

Figure 31.2
The classical conditioning of attitudes

Much advertising attempts to work in just such a way, by taking an originally neutral object (the product) and trying to create positive associations to it. Soft drink advertisements, for instance, frequently depict young, attractive people having a great deal of fun playing volleyball, dancing, or enjoying a concert while drinking some particular soft drink. The obvious intent is that you and I will associate the product with the good times. Advertising with sexual connotations (see Figure 31.3) operates along the same lines. As you realize, the positive experiences presented in the ads do not have to have any direct, logical relationship to the product. For example, those young people playing volleyball on the beach would probably be having a good time whether they were drinking one particular soft drink or not.

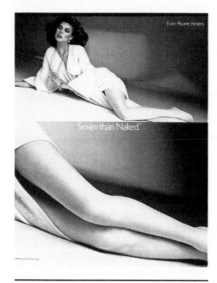

Figure 31.3

Figure 31.4

Operant Conditioning   Attitudes can also be formed as a result of the direct reinforcement of behaviors consistent with some attitudinal position. Several studies have shown that verbal reinforcement (saying "good," "fine," or "that's right") when someone claims agreement with attitudinal statements leads people to develop attitudes consistent with the position expressed in those statements (Insko, 1965). The blue-eyed children from our opening example no doubt received considerable reinforcement and social support from their peers for acting in negative and derogatory ways toward their "inferior" brown-eyed classmates. And it is no small matter that simply having others to view as inferior is in itself somewhat reinforcing. How much better one can feel about himself or herself if he or she comes to believe that others are somehow below them.

Observational Learning   As we discussed in Topic 12, people often tend to imitate behaviors that they have seen reinforced in others (called vicarious reinforcement). To the extent that we perceive that others are gaining reinforcers for having and expressing some attitude, we are likely to adopt that attitude ourselves.

Incidentally, advertising that relies on testimonials from satisfied customers is basically appealing to observational learning (see Figure 31.4). The potential consumer is shown that an actual consumer has used a certain product with success (i.e., has received reinforcement), and the advertiser hopes that this exposure will lead the potential buyer to develop a favorable evaluation of the product.

Before you go on

Briefly describe three ways in which attitudes might be acquired.

Attitude Change and Persuasion

Much of the social-psychological research on attitudes has been concerned with the very practical questions of when and how attitudes change. Some of this research has dealt with conscious, planned attempts to change some-

persuasion
the process of intentionally attempting to change an attitude

one's attitude(s), a process we call **persuasion.** In this section, we will examine some of the conditions that lead to attitude change, beginning with one of those unexpected and counterintuitive findings to which we referred earlier.

Cognitive Dissonance Theory Common sense would seem to suggest that the affective and cognitive components of an attitude will produce behaviors consistent with those feelings and beliefs. In other words, behavior should follow from attitudes, and attitude change should lead to behavior change. In 1957, Leon Festinger proposed a theory that suggested just the reverse: that attitudes follow from behavior. This theory has continued to stimulate research in social psychology for over 25 years now, and the bulk of the evidence has supported the notion that, at least in certain circumstances, behavior change *does* lead to attitude change.

Festinger and Carlsmith (1959) conducted a now classic experiment that illustrates this process. Let's review this study in some detail. Subjects reported for an experiment presumably dealing with human performance and eye-hand coordination. They were asked to perform an extremely boring task requiring them to rotate row after row of wooden knobs on a large board, first in one direction, and then back to their original position. After a lengthy knob-turning session, the experimenter explained that the research had to do with how expectations influence performance on such a task. The subject was told that the person sitting in a waiting area just outside the laboratory was to be the next subject in the experiment. This next subject was to be led to believe that the project was going to be fun, interesting, and educational. Explaining that his assistant, who was usually responsible for telling this "lie," was absent, the experimenter asked the subject to do this "selling job" for him and offered to pay for the subject's service. The subjects invariably agreed and actually worked very hard at trying to convince the next subject in the waiting room (who was actually a confederate working with the experimenter) that the experiment was in fact enjoyable and interesting. Having finished this task, all subjects were later asked to fill out a simple questionnaire that asked about their reactions to the knob-turning experiment itself.

The major experimental manipulation was a simple one: Some of the subjects were paid $20 for trying to convince the waiting subject that the clearly boring task was fun and interesting, while others were paid only $1. Now, finally, comes the counterintuitive part. Which subjects do you suppose expressed more positive attitudes about the experiment in which they had participated: those paid $20, or those paid $1? Although it does seem logical to expect that the larger reward ($20) would produce the more positive attitudes, Festinger and Carlsmith predicted just the opposite. They reasoned that subjects paid only $1 would feel that their behavior had not been sufficiently justified. They had told a lie and had been given only a trivial amount of money for doing so. Consequently, these subjects would experience a great deal of unpleasant tension or discomfort about this inconsistency, called **cognitive dissonance.** "I lied for a lousy dollar." One way to resolve their dissonance (which means inharmoniousness or incongruence) would be to modify their attitude toward the experiment so that it better fit their behavior (was now consonant). Essentially, these subjects would convince themselves that they hadn't lied at all; the experiment *had* been fun and interesting.

cognitive dissonance
the state of tension or discomfort that exists when we hold inconsistent cognitions

The subjects paid $20, on the other hand, would have plenty of justification for their action (in 1959, $20 was no small amount of extra cash). They had lied, too, but they had had a "good reason" to do so. These subjects would experience very little dissonance and should not be expected to change their attitude toward the boring experiment. "Yeah I lied, but I got paid 20 bucks." Figure 31.5 presents the results of this experiment in graphic form.

The results of this study (and numerous others) suggest that one good way to change peoples' attitudes may be to get them to change their behavior first. Not only that, but there is a clear advantage in offering as *little* incentive to bring about the change in behavior as possible. Simply buying someone off to change her or his behavior will not create the sort of cognitive dissonance required to bring about lasting attitude change.

To turn to advertising once again, is it not the case that some advertising appeals may be seen as an attempt to arouse cognitive dissonance? Consider, for instance, the magazine ads that request the reader to sponsor an underprivileged child in a foreign country. The reader sees a picture of the unfortunate child, reads about the extreme poverty, and, at the same time, recognizes how much better off he or she is than the child in the ad: cognitive dissonance. One way to reduce such dissonance is to convince one's self that he or she is really no better off than the child in the ad. The hope is, however, that the reader will choose to eliminate dissonance by mailing in a large contribution.

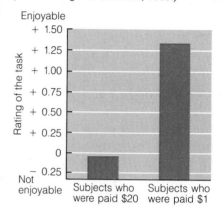

Figure 31.5
After being paid either $1 or $20 to "lie" about a boring task, subjects were later asked to rate the task in terms of enjoyment and interest. As can be seen in this figure, those paid $1 (with cognitive dissonance) gave the task much higher ratings.
(After Festinger & Carlsmith, 1959.)

Before you go on

What is cognitive dissonance, and how is it relevant to attitude change?

Cognitive Response Theory   A theory of attitude change that is more recent than Festinger's, but that is still cognitive in its orientation is one often called cognitive response theory (Petty, Ostrom & Brock, 1981). This theory proposes that the recipient of a persuasive communication (an attempt to change an attitude) is not at all passive. Rather, the person receiving a persuasive message is an active information processor who generates *cognitive responses* or thoughts about the message being received. These cognitive responses can be favorable, agreeing with and supportive of the message. Or they can be unfavorable, disagreeing and counterarguing with the message. This line of reasoning has led researchers to examine variables that may affect persuasion and the cognitive responses persuasive messages engender. Two interesting variables that have been under study are *message quality* and *distraction.* Let's see what is involved in this sort of research.

Imagine that you are headed for a career in medical research and that you believe very strongly that research with animals is well justified because of its ultimate benefits for humankind. You hear that an animal rights group is holding a rally on your campus and, mostly out of curiosity, you decide to attend to hear what they have to say about why animals should not be used in laboratory research. Cognitive response theory says that you are going to be generating counterarguments (disagreeing thoughts or cognitions) as you listen to the speeches at the rally.

Let's further assume that there is some very loud construction going on nearby. The noise generated by the construction may interfere with the production of your counterarguments, and you may not be as able to resist the persuasive speeches as you might be otherwise. On the other hand, a person who supports the animal rights group will generate cognitive responses that

Figure 31.6

An illustration of the amount of agreement with a persuasive message that contained strong or weak arguments and was heard under conditions of low or medium distraction. Distraction lowered agreement when strong arguments were used and raised agreement when weak arguments were used.
(After Petty, Wells, & Brock, 1976.)

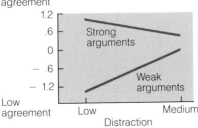

We are more likely to be persuaded by communicators we perceive as having expertise and trustworthiness.

agree with the speeches. For this person, the construction noise may cause the speech to be less influential than it would be without the distraction.

Distraction and message quality have been studied experimentally by Petty, Wells, and Brock (1976). In one experiment, message quality was either high or low; that is, the persuasive speech contained either strong or weak arguments about an attitudinal object. Subjects heard one of these two messages under conditions involving either low or moderate distraction. As Figure 31.6 shows, when the message consisted of strong arguments, agreement with the message was reduced when the level of distraction was increased. This occurred, presumably, because the distraction interfered with the production of cognitive responses that were in favor of the persuasive message. Increasing distraction had the opposite effect when weak arguments were presented, presumably because the distraction interfered with the listener's ability to generate counterarguments.

Research suggests that cognitive response theory may also be usefully applied to advertising. Advertisers frequently make strong claims about their products and do not want potential consumers in the audience to counterargue or even begin to question the validity of their claims. Since distractions can interfere with the production of these cognitive responses, distractions would leave the consumer more vulnerable to the persuasive message of the advertiser. Catchy (or loud) music, humor, and novelty are commonly used as ways of creating distraction and, thus, enhancing the effectiveness of the advertising.

The Source of Persuasive Communication   The effectiveness of a persuasive communication is almost always influenced by its source. In general, a highly credible (believable) source will induce more change than will a less credible source. Although there are probably several factors that make up what we call credibility, there are two that seem especially important: expertise and trustworthiness.

A number of studies (Aronson, Turner & Carlsmith, 1963; Hovland & Weiss, 1951, for example) have indicated that the greater the perceived expertise of the communicator, the greater the amount of persuasion that occurs. For example, I am much more likely to be influenced by Pete Rose (player/manager of the Cincinnati Reds baseball team) if he is trying to influence my attitudes toward baseball than I would be if he were trying to persuade me to buy a certain brand of toaster oven.

A second factor likely to enhance a communicator's credibility is a high degree of trustworthiness. Studies by Walster and Festinger (1962) demonstrated that more attitude change resulted when subjects overheard a persuasive communication than when they believed that the communication was directed at them. Trustworthiness and credibility were apparently enhanced by the perceived lack of intent to persuade ("Why should they lie; they don't even know we can hear them?").

Cognitive response theory also speaks to this issue of source credibility. Haas (1981) maintains that persuasive information will be examined in an attempt to assess its validity. People are simply less likely to question and counterargue information they get from a source they rate as credible; they expect it to be accurate.

Before you go on

Other than cognitive dissonance, what are some factors associated with persuasion?

ATTRIBUTION THEORY

Another facet of the cognitive orientation that we find in social psychology is the area of study known generally as **attribution theory.** Social psychologists working with this theory are interested in understanding the cognitive rules we use in trying to explain behavior, both our own and that of others. In other words, the fundamental question here is "To what causes do we attribute a particular behavior?" An attribution, then, is an explanation that we generate for some behavior.

Social psychologists have found it useful to distinguish between two basic types of attributions: internal and external. This distinction comes down to whether behavior is caused by the person or by the environment. **Internal attributions** explain the source of behavior in terms of some characteristic of the person, often a personality trait or disposition, and for this reason internal attributions are sometimes called *dispositional attributions.* **External attributions,** on the other hand, explain the cause of behavior in terms of something outside the individual; they are referred to as *situational attributions.*

The evidence does indicate that people tend to consistently rely on certain types of information when making judgments about the causes of behavior. Imagine, for example, that your best friend shows his temper only when he is with his girlfriend. That information is useful because of its *distinctiveness,* and it may very well signal a troubled relationship. As a different example, imagine that you have just received an A on a test in your history class. In this case, you could (and probably would) use information about how well everyone else did on the test before you decide about your own superiority; this kind of information is concerned with *consensus.* In fact, using information about a behavior's distinctiveness and consensus, along with information about its *consistency* over time, is the basis of one major theory about how we explain or attribute the causes of behavior (Kelley, 1973). Figure 31.7 illustrates how these types of information may lead to different types of attribution.

One currently active area of research deals with the errors we tend to make in our social thinking. One well-documented example of a cognitive bias involves an attributional process. It's something called the **fundamental attribution error** (Ross, 1977), and it has to do with the basic discrepancy between the way we tend to explain someone else's behavior and the way we explain our own.

It seems that people have a compelling need to organize and make sense out of the world in which they live. This observation applies both to our physical world and to our social world. The fundamental attribution error is, in a sense, an outgrowth of this need to perceive order and consistency in our social world. Because they summarize a lot of information, an awareness of personality characteristics serves as a handy tool for organizing information about people. That is to say, we tend to rely heavily on *internal attributions* in explaining other peoples' behavior. Since we are usually quite aware of the situation or environmental factors that are influencing our own behaviors, we use mostly *external attributions* to explain them. More simply: We believe that others do what they do because that's the way they are, and we believe that we do whatever we do under the influence of the environment (except when we are successful; then we may credit ourselves and not the environment). Most researchers believe that this bias, or error, in attribution is a direct result of selective attention in the two different circumstances. We just

attribution theory
a theory that tries to describe how we explain the causes of behavior

internal attribution
an explanation of behavior in terms of something within the person; a dispositional attribution

external attribution
an explanation of behavior in terms of something outside the person; a situational attribution

fundamental attribution error
the tendency to use internal attributions when explaining the behavior of other people

Figure 31.7
Attributing behavior: some important considerations and possible outcomes. (After Baron & Byrne, 1984.)

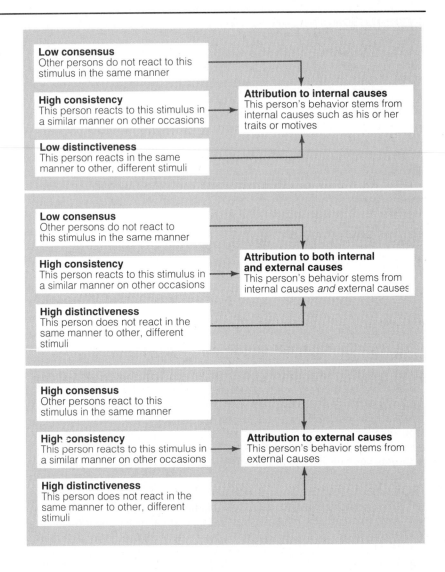

Low consensus
Other persons do not react to this stimulus in the same manner

High consistency
This person reacts to this stimulus in a similar manner on other occasions

Low distinctiveness
This person reacts in the same manner to other, different stimuli

Attribution to internal causes
This person's behavior stems from internal causes such as his or her traits or motives

Low consensus
Other persons do not react to this stimulus in the same manner

High consistency
This person reacts to this stimulus in a similar manner on other occasions

High distinctiveness
This person does not react in the same manner to other, different stimuli

Attribution to both internal and external causes
This person's behavior stems from internal causes *and* external causes

High consensus
Other persons react to this stimulus in the same manner

High consistency
This person reacts to this stimulus in a similar manner on other occasions

High distinctiveness
This person does not react in the same manner to other, different stimuli

Attribution to external causes
This person's behavior stems from external causes

don't notice (or attend to) those environmental influences that affect other's behaviors, but we notice (or attend to) such factors when they affect us.

Before you go on

What are the two basic types of attribution, and how does the fundamental attribution error affect social judgment?

INTERPERSONAL ATTRACTION

You may wonder why interpersonal attraction—a process that clearly involves overt behavior—is included here, in a topic on social thinking. In addition to behavior, attraction also involves feelings that one person has about another. But attraction also includes beliefs and ideas (cognitions) about some other person. Attraction then can be seen as an attitude—a favorable and powerful attitude at that.

A Simple Theory of Attraction

Several social psychologists (for example, Clore & Byrne, 1974; Lott & Lott, 1974; Myers, 1983) have suggested that a straightforward learning model can explain interpersonal attraction quite nicely. This model implies that we tend to like people we associate with rewards. This view claims that we learn to like people and become attracted to them through conditioning, by associating them with rewards or reinforcers that are present when they are. We are thus attracted to (have positive attitudes toward) those people we associate with rewarding experiences. Let's look at how this might work in more detail.

Factors Affecting Attraction

What determines who you will be attracted to? What factors tend to provide the rewards that serve as the basis of liking? Here we'll list four of the most common principles of interpersonal attraction.

Reciprocity Our first principle is perhaps the most obvious one. The simplest way to become associated with rewards is to provide them directly. Not surprisingly, we tend to value and like people who like us back. Remember that we've already noted, in our discussion of operant conditioning (Topic 11), that the attention of others is often a powerful reinforcer. This is particularly true if the attention is positive, supportive, and affectionate. And research indicates that the reward value of someone else caring for us is particularly powerful when that someone initially seemed to have neutral or even negative attitudes toward us. That is, we are most attracted to people who like us now, but who didn't originally (Aronson & Linder, 1965).

Proximity Our second principle suggests that physical closeness, or proximity, tends to produce liking. Sociologists, as well as your own personal experience, will tell you that people tend to establish friendships (and romances) with others with whom they have grown up, worked, or gone to school. Similarly, social psychological studies have consistently found that residents of apartments or dormitories tend to become friends with those other residents living closest to them (Festinger, Schachter, & Back, 1950). Being around others gives us the opportunity to discover just who can provide those interpersonal rewards we seek in friendship.

There is, nonetheless, another social-psychological phenomenon at work here, called the **mere exposure phenomenon.** A great deal of research, pioneered by Robert Zajonc (1968), has shown with a variety of novel social and nonsocial stimuli that liking tends to increase with repeated exposure to stimuli. Examples of this phenomenon are abundant in everyday life. Have you ever bought a record album that you have not heard previously, assuming that you will like it because you have liked all the other albums made by this performer? The first time you listen to your new album, however, your reaction may be lukewarm at best, and you may be disappointed in your purchase. Not wanting to feel that you've wasted your money, you play the album a few more times over the next several days. What often happens is that you soon realize that you like this album after all, even more than some of the old ones. The mere exposure effect has occurred, and this commonly happens in our formation of attitudes about other people as well.

For anyone thinking about putting this bit of information to practical use, there is a slight catch. That is, if you are interested in helping yourself strike up a new relationship with someone by increasing the number of "acciden-

Proximity leads to liking, which is why next-door neighbors are often good friends.

mere exposure phenomenon
the tendency to increase our liking of people and things the more we see of them

tal'' encounters you have with this person, you might want to be careful. The mere exposure phenomenon tends to occur only when the initial attitude is neutral or slightly favorable to start with. Repeated exposure to an unliked stimulus tends to decrease liking in the long run. Aside from this qualification, though, there is some truth to the adage that familiarity breeds liking, not contempt.

Physical Attractiveness   Our physical appearance is one personal characteristic that we cannot easily hide. It is always on display in social situations, and it communicates something about us. People are aware of the role of appearance in nonverbal, interpersonal communication and may spend many hours each week doing whatever can be done to improve the way they look.

The power of physical attractiveness in the context of dating has been demonstrated experimentally in a classic study directed by Elaine Hatfield Walster (Walster et al., 1966). Over 700 University of Minnesota freshmen completed a number of psychological tests as part of an orientation program. Couples of these freshmen were then randomly matched for dates to an orientation dance, during which they took a break and evaluated their assigned partners. This study was particularly significant because it allowed researchers the possibility of uncovering intricate, complex, and subtle facts about attraction, such as which personality traits might tend to mesh in such a way as to produce attraction. As it turned out, none of these complex factors, so carefully controlled for, was important. The effect of physical attractiveness was so powerful that it wiped out all other effects. For both men and women, the more physically attractive their date, the more they liked the person and the more they wanted to go out again with that individual.

Numerous studies of physical attractiveness followed this one. Some of these studies simply gave subjects a chance to pick a date from a group of several potential partners (usually using descriptions and pictures). Not surprisingly, subjects almost invariably selected the most attractive person available to be their date.

You may have noticed, however, that in real life we seldom have the opportunity to request a date without at least the possibility of being turned down. When experimental studies began to build in the possibility of rejection, an interesting effect emerged: Subjects stopped picking the most attractive candidate from a group and started selecting partners whose level of physical attractiveness was more similar to their own. This behavior has been called the **matching phenomenon,** and it is an effect that has been verified by naturalistic observation studies.

The effects of physical attractiveness carry over beyond romantic situations. Numerous studies (e.g., Dion, Berscheid, & Walster, 1972) suggest that attractive persons are assumed to have other desirable characteristics as well. Such persons are routinely judged to be more intelligent, to have happier marriages, to be more successful in their careers and social lives, and so on. This effect of overgeneralizing is referred to as the **physical attractiveness stereotype.**

Studies have indicated that there may be some potentially serious implications involved in the application of this stereotype. For instance, Anderson and Nida (1978) have shown that the same piece of work (in this case an essay) will be evaluated more favorably when a physically attractive person is thought to have produced it. Similarly, a study by Clifford and Hatfield (1973) found fifth-grade teachers to judge attractive children as more intelligent. Another study (Dion, 1972) found that women who were asked to recommend punishment for a child who had misbehaved were more lenient when the child was judged to be physically attractive.

Physical attractiveness is a powerful influence in interpersonal relationships. Numerous studies have found that physical attractiveness is, at least at first, the single most important factor in selecting friends and dates.

matching phenomenon
the tendency to select partners whose level of attractiveness matches our own

physical attractiveness stereotype
the tendency to associate desirable characteristics with a physically attractive person, solely on the basis of attractiveness

The more similar another person is to you, the more you will tend to like that person. Our friends tend to be people who share our attitudes and who like to do the things we like to do.

Similarity   There is a large body of research on the relationship between similarity and attraction, but the findings are consistent, and we can summarize them briefly. Much of this research has been done by Donn Byrne and his colleagues (e.g., Byrne, 1971). It indicates that there is an almost perfect relationship between liking and the proportion of attitudes held in common. To put it simply, the more similar another person is to you, the more you will tend to like that person (Buss, 1985).

Perhaps you know a happily married couple for whom this sweeping conclusion does not seem to fit. At least some of their behaviors seem to be quite dissimilar, almost opposite. Perhaps the wife appears to be the one who makes most of the decisions while the husband simply seems to follow orders. It may very well be the case, however, that this apparent dissimilarity in behavior exists only on the surface. There may be an important similarity that makes for a successful marriage here: both have the same idea of what a marriage should be like—wives decide and husbands obey. In such a case, the observed differences in behavior are reflecting a powerful similarity in the view of the roles of married couples.

That similarity enhances interpersonal attraction certainly makes sense in light of the simple theory of attraction we described earlier. Agreement with our attitudinal positions is reinforcing, and people who are similar to us tend to agree with us. Similarity is probably the glue that—over the long haul—holds together romances and friendships.

Before you go on

What are four determinants of interpersonal attraction, and how do they have the effect that they do?

Our discussion of interpersonal attraction in this topic has been quite general. The four principles we listed are thought to apply equally to both liking and loving relationships. Nevertheless, we all recognize a difference between the two in everyday life, and the distinction has also been of interest to the social psychologist.

Zick Rubin (1970, 1973) has proposed that while *liking* someone basically involves affection and respect, *loving* consists of three dimensions: attachment, caring, and intimacy. Rubin has developed separate scales to measure these two interpersonal experiences, and samples are reproduced in Figure 31.8. These scales have been used in a number of studies designed to explore the differences between liking and loving and have involved literally hundreds of dating couples.

Rubin's research offers solid evidence that the distinction between liking and loving is a valid one. Included in his findings are the following general conclusions: (1) The "love scale" scores of dating partners tended to be more similar than their "liking scale" scores. (2) Partners whose love scores indicated that they had a strong, serious relationship were observed to spend more time maintaining eye contact with one another than couples whose scores indicated a weak relationship. (3) Partners with strong relationships (high scores on the love scale) were more likely to anticipate marrying their partner. Such expectations were much less common among partners with high liking scale scores.

More recently, Keith Davis, a University of South Carolina social psychologist, has reported a new approach to differentiating between liking and loving (1985). Davis approached the concepts of "friendship" and "love" consistent

with the definition of concept proposed by Eleanor Rosch (see Topic 15). Davis and his colleagues searched for those dimensions or characteristics that defined the prototypic case for both friendship and love. Although friendship, for example, may be characterized as having many different components, which characteristics are absolutely necessary for us to characterize a relationship as being a friendship? Once these are determined, what additional characteristics are important in defining a loving relationship?

The model that evolved from their investigation indicated that there are eight required characteristics that define the prototype of friendship: (1) *Enjoyment*—friends enjoy each other's company. (2) *Acceptance*—friends are willing to take each other as they are, without trying to change them. (3) *Trust*—friends believe that each will act to benefit the other. (4) *Respect*—friends assume that each exercises good judgment. (5) *Mutual assistance*—friends help each other and can count on each other for help when needed. (6) *Confiding*—friends can and do share their private experiences and feelings. (7) *Understanding*—friends know what is important to one another, and why the other does whatever he or she may do. (8) *Spontaneity*—friends feel comfortable being themselves and not playing roles in each other's company. These characteristics, taken together, define a liking relationship, a friendship.

Loving relationships were believed to encompass each of these points, plus five others. First, love involves characteristics that Davis calls the passion cluster: *fascination*—being preoccupied and attentive to the other person, even when such attention is not necessary; *exclusiveness*—reserving this

Loving consists of attachment, caring, and intimacy. People who love each other enjoy each other's company and are willing to give the utmost for the other's benefit.

close, personal relationship for one person only; and *sexual desire*—wanting physical contact and sexual intimacy. The second major component of love Davis calls the caring cluster: *champion/advocate*—a willingness to support the partner's causes whatever they may be and regardless of personal price; and *giving the utmost*—a commitment to give to the other when the need arises, even to the extent of extreme self-sacrifice.

When this model of liking and loving was tested on 250 subjects (both single and married), it was largely confirmed as a sensible way to view these two interpersonal relationships. By and large, both friends and lovers shared most of the characteristics the model identified as friendship characteristics, and the so-called passion cluster provided a good means of differentiating between friends and lovers. There were a few surprises, however. Although lovers had higher scores than friends on the giving-the-utmost dimension, scores on the champion/advocate dimension showed no such difference. Even so, Davis and his associates feel that this dimension of a loving relationship should be kept as part of the model. A second surprise was that lovers endorsed statements of enjoying each other's company to a much greater degree than did friends. This was a dimension on which there was expected to be a small difference between friends and lovers. This research also indicated that relationships with best friends were viewed as being significantly more stable than spouse/lover relationships.

We might summarize Davis' research best in his own words: "If the findings of this research and of others cited are valid, then the typical love relationships will differ from even very good friendships in having higher levels of fascination, exclusiveness and sexual desire (the passion cluster), a greater depth of caring about the other person (which would be manifest in a willingness to give the utmost when needed) and a greater potential for enjoyment and other positive emotions. Love relationships will also have, however, a greater potential for distress, ambivalence, conflict and mutual criticism" (1985, p. 30).

Liking Scale

1 I think that _____ is unusually well adjusted.

2 I would highly recommend _____ for a responsible job.

3 In my opinion, _____ is an exceptionally mature person.

Love Scale

1 I feel that I can confide in _____ about virtually everything.

2 I would do almost anything for _____ .

3 If I could never be with _____ , I would feel miserable.

Figure 31.8
A list of sample items used to indicate the degree of liking and loving in a relationship. Each item is to be rated on a 9-point scale ranging from not at all true to moderately true to definitely true. (From Rubin, 1973.)

TOPIC SUMMARY

What are stereotypes and norms, and in what way are they cognitive?

Both stereotypes and norms are sets of ideas or beliefs (cognitions) that we form about our social world. Stereotypes are generalized mental representations that we have of other people and are often based on very little information. Norms are learned expectations or rules that guide and influence our behaviors in social situations. / 576

What is an attitude and what are its three components?

An attitude is an evaluative disposition directed toward some object. An attitude consists of feelings (affect), behaviors, and beliefs (cognition). Although the affective and cognitive components of attitudes are often consistent with each other, behavior may be inconsistent with the other two major components. / 577

What are some of the functions served by attitudes?

Attitudes may guide our behaviors, and they summarize the beliefs we hold. They also serve a social identification function; that is, they tell others about us and the attitudes of others give us useful information about them. When we carefully select the attitudinal information we make available to others, we say that an impression management function is being served. / 578

Briefly describe three ways in which attitudes might be acquired.

Attitudes may be acquired through classical conditioning; that is, after positive or negative experiences are associated with an attitudinal object, the object, by itself, comes to elicit a positive or negative feeling. Attitudes may also be directly reinforced (operant conditioning), or they may be reinforced vicariously (observational learning). / 579

What is cognitive dissonance, and how is it relevant to attitude change?

Cognitive dissonance is an unpleasant state of tension that generally occurs when we behave in a fashion inconsistent with the affective component of an attitude. Because we are motivated to eliminate dissonance, we may do so by changing our attitudes so that they become consistent with the way we behave. / 581

Other than cognitive dissonance, what are some factors associated with persuasion?

The quality of the arguments involved in a persuasive communication and one's ability to form supportive or counterarguments are likely to affect the degree of persuasion by influencing the cognitive responses that the communication produces. Communicators perceived as being expert or trustworthy are seen as credible sources of information, and, hence, are more persuasive. / 582

What are the two basic types of attribution, and how does the fundamental attribution error affect social judgment?

The two basic types of attribution are internal and external. An internal attribution finds the cause for a behavior within the person and is sometimes called a dispositional attribution. An external attribution finds the cause of behavior to be outside the person and is sometimes called a situational attribution. The fundamental attribution error leads us to overuse internal attributions in explaining the behavior of others, and to overuse external attributions in explaining our own behavior. / 584

What are four determinants of interpersonal attraction, and how do they have the effect that they do?

The principle of *reciprocity* states that we tend to like people who like us back. This is the most straightforward example of interpersonal attraction being based on a system of rewards. *Proximity* promotes attraction by means of the mere exposure phenomenon: being near another person on a frequent basis gives us the opportunity to see whether that other person has rewards to offer. We also tend to be attracted to people who are *physically attractive,* another characteristic that tends to be rewarding. Finally, the principle of *similarity* suggests that we tend to be attracted to others who are similar to ourselves; similarity is yet another characteristic that provides rewards. / 587

TOPIC

32 *Social Influence*

Doug's usual plan of action on Sundays includes staying in bed as late as possible. However, a good friend has asked Doug to join him at church this Sunday. Although Doug is not particularly interested in becoming a churchgoer, he decides that he has nothing to lose by going this once. If nothing else, he reasons, he might get an early start on the day and get some work done for a change.

Sunday morning arrives, and as Doug and his friend head off to church, Doug finds himself wondering about what the experience will be like. Doug can't remember having been to church since he was about 12 years old. When he went to church as a child, he had attended a Presbyterian church; he knows nothing about the Episcopal church he's attending today. Doug asks his friend about the service and is told to expect more ritual than is typically found in the Presbyterian church. All he needs to do, Doug is assured, is to follow what's happening in the prayer book, which contains a description of the service and will tell him exactly what to do.

As they enter the church, an usher stops Doug's friend and asks him to substitute for another usher who is ill today. Doug's friend agrees to usher, and Doug takes a seat just as the service is about to begin. Doug reaches for a prayer book, but finds only hymnals in the pew rack. For a second he considers moving to another seat, but just at that instant, the congregation stands as the service begins. Doug hesitates, then stands with everyone else.

The worship service that follows involves a lot of standing up, sitting down, and kneeling. By paying close attention to what everyone else is doing, Doug manages to get through it without embarrassing himself. There is one uncomfortable moment, however. It occurs when people start filing systematically out of their pews to go forward to take communion. Row by row, moving from the front to the rear of the sanctuary, the ceremony progresses. Nearly everyone, with the exception of a few individuals here and there, leaves his or her seat and goes forward. Fortunately, Doug is seated near the back of the church so he has a little time to ponder the situation. He wonders if the others who have remained in their seats are also visitors. Is communion restricted to members of this church? What should he do? To make matters worse, Doug is sitting at the very end of the pew, and he will have to be the first person in his row to make a move. The usher approaches Doug's pew. What will he do?

Why We Care

The scenario we have just described can serve to remind us that to function efficiently in the social world often depends on the accurate (and rapid) interpretation of social information. Our perception of the social world is sometimes ambiguous; when it is, we tend to rely on others to make matters clearer. Much of the time, other people are an excellent source of clues as to how we should behave. As was the case in the first part of the church service we described above, the actions of others can provide guidelines for our own behavior, and sometimes others actually tell us what we are to do. On other occasions, when social cues remain ambiguous, we may misinterpret the situation and behave inappropriately. At still other times, we may be so confused that we do nothing at all, and that can be inappropriate, too. Sitting at the end of the pew during a communion service meant that Doug either had to walk forward or step aside and allow others to pass; doing nothing would have interfered with the ceremony in progress.

A great deal of our behavior is influenced by others. In fact, we are probably so accustomed to this process of social influence that much of the time it escapes our awareness. You probably did not consider why you happened to walk on the right side of the sidewalk the last time you were downtown on a busy shopping day, or why you took a place at the end of the line the last time you bought tickets to a movie, or why you applauded and cheered at the last concert you attended. Nevertheless, all of these behaviors were the products of social influence.

In our last topic, we looked at social influences on our thinking, or cognitions. Here we examine how social forces affect our behaviors. Of course, it is somewhat artificial to separate thinking from acting since, as we have seen, the two processes are so intertwined. (In fact, thinking itself can be viewed as a type of behavior.) In this topic, however, we will focus on overt, directly observable forms of socially influenced behavior. We will consider the influences of conformity and obedience separately, although we'll note that they have much in common. We'll consider the phenomena of bystander apathy and intervention and list some of the factors that determine how, or if, someone will intervene on behalf of someone else. We'll briefly review a number of situations in which social influence is a force in our lives, and we will end our discussion with some comments about aggression. In each case, the theme will be the same: how the actions of others influence the behavior of the individual.

Other people provide us with clues as to how we should behave. By watching what others do, we learn appropriate behaviors in a wide variety of social settings. Even such a seemingly simple activity as boarding a bus has appropriate and inappropriate behaviors.

CONFORMITY

One of the most obvious and direct forms of social influence occurs whenever we modify our behavior so that it is consistent with the behavior of others, a social-psychological process usually referred to as **conformity.** Often this means that we follow some norm or standard that prescribes how we should act in a given situation. As we saw in our opening example involving the decision of how to act in an unfamiliar situation, to conform is natural and often desirable. Conformity helps to make social behaviors efficient.

conformity
changing one's behavior so that it is consistent with the behavior of others

Norm Formation and Conformity

Some of the first studies to demonstrate the power of conformity were performed by Muzafer Sherif (1936). Sherif used an interesting perceptual phenomenon called the **autokinetic effect** to show how social norms can develop

autokinetic effect
an illusion in which a stationary spot of light in a dark room appears to move

Figure 32.1

The type of stimuli used in Asch's conformity experiment. Subjects are to say which of the three lines on the right (A, B, or C) equals the line on the left. Associates of the experimenter will occasionally make incorrect choices.

A   B C

and induce conformity in ambiguous circumstances. If a person is seated in a completely darkened room and a small spot of light is projected on the wall, within a few moments the light will appear to move. This compelling, illusory movement is not at all regular—the light seems to dart from place to place.

When asked to estimate how far the light moves in this situation, people vary widely in their judgments, which may range from a few inches to several feet (remember that the light is actually stationary). Sherif first asked people to make judgments about the apparent movement of the light independently. Then, in each of several sessions that took place on different days, he had people experience the illusion and make their judgments with other subjects present in the room. The others were also to estimate how far the light moved.

As a result of the group experience, participants adjusted their judgments to match the estimates of others. That is, over the course of the study, the judgments of the different members of a typical group of subjects converged, and the end result was an agreement within the group as to how far the light had moved. A norm had emerged to guide behavior in this ambiguous situation, and the individuals in the study conformed to that norm.

The Asch Studies

The results of the demonstrations by Sherif may not be all that surprising. After all, the situation was completely ambiguous. The subjects had had no prior experience with the autokinetic effect, and there were no cues to guide their judgments—at least until the other subjects entered the picture. How might people respond to group pressure when the reality of the situation is much clearer?

Solomon Asch (1951, 1956) initially believed that people are not very susceptible to social pressure, particularly when the social situation is clear-cut and unambiguous. Asch hypothesized that subjects would behave inde-

After consistently disagreeing with the other subjects in Asch's study, the lone dissenter begins to doubt his judgment and looks again at the card, even though the correct answer is obvious.

pendently of group pressure whenever there was no question that their own judgments were accurate, and he developed an interesting technique for testing his hypothesis.

As discussed in Topic 2, a subject in Asch's procedure would join a face-to-face group seated around a table. In his original study, the group consisted of seven people. Unknown to the real subject, however, six individuals were actually confederates of the experimenter. The experimenter explained that the study dealt with the ability to make perceptual judgments. The participants would be doing nothing more than deciding which of three lines was the same length as a standard line (see Figure 32.1). The experimenter would show each set of lines to the group and then go around the table collecting responses from each member of the group. In fact, the only real subject was always the last one to respond.

It is important to note that each of the 18 judgments the subjects were asked to make involved unambiguous stimuli. The correct answer was always obvious. However, on 12 of the 18 trials, the confederates gave a unanimous, but *incorrect* answer. Now what should the subject do? How should he resolve this conflict? His own experience told him what the right answer was, but the group was saying something else. Should he trust the judgments of the others, or should he trust his own perceptual ability?

The results of his initial study surprised Asch, because they did not confirm his original hypothesis. Across all of the critical trials (when confederates gave "wrong" answers), conformity occurred 37 percent of the time. That is, subjects responded with an incorrect answer that agreed with the majority on more than one third of the critical trials. Even more striking is that 75 percent of Asch's subjects conformed to the group pressure at least once.

In subsequent studies, Asch tried several variations of his original procedure. In one experiment, he varied the size of the unanimous, incorrect majority. As you might now expect, the level of conformity increased as the size of the majority increased (leveling off at about three or four people). Subjects gave an erroneous judgment only 4 percent of the time when only one incorrect judgment preceded their own. In another study, Asch found that conformity decreased to 10 percent when there was one dissenter among the six confederates who voiced an accurate judgment before the subjects gave theirs. In short, when the subjects had at least some small social support for what their eyes had told them, they tended to trust their own judgment.

Before you go on
Briefly describe the methodology and the basic findings of the Sherif and Asch conformity studies.

OBEDIENCE TO AUTHORITY

Although the subjects in Asch's studies obviously took the procedure seriously, the consequences of either conforming or maintaining independence were rather trivial. At worst, Asch's subjects might have experienced some discomfort as a result of voicing their independent judgments. There certainly were no external rewards or punishments for their behavior. In some of the most famous (and most controversial) research in all of social psychology, Stanley Milgram went at least one large step beyond Asch's procedure. His experiments pressured subjects to comply with the demand of an author-

Extreme, unquestioning obedience to authority can have negative consequences. Consider concentration camp commander Franz Hoessler whose blind obedience to Hitler's decrees led to the brutal murder of millions of innocent people.

ity figure—a demand that was both troubling and unreasonable (Milgram, 1963, 1965, 1974).

The original impetus for Milgram's research was the extreme obedience to Nazi authority displayed by many German military personnel during World War II. Milgram initially wondered whether the mass executions and other forms of cruelty perpetrated by the Nazis might reflect something about the German character. The original goal of his research was to determine if people of different nationalities differ in the degree to which they will obey a request to inflict pain on another person. Milgram's research procedure was designed to serve as a basis for making such comparisons.

All of the studies carried out in this series involved the same basic procedure. Subjects arrived at the laboratory to find that they would be participating with a second person (once again, a confederate of the experimenter). The experimenter explained that the research was an investigation of the effects of punishment on learning, and that one person would serve as a teacher while the other would act as learner. These two roles were "randomly" assigned by a rigged drawing in which the actual subject was always assigned the role of teacher. The subject watched as the learner was taken into the next room and connected to electrodes that would be used for delivering punishments in the form of electric shocks.

The teacher then received his or her instructions. First, he or she was to read to the learner a list of four pairs of words. Then the teacher would read the first word of one of the pairs, and the learner was to supply the second word. The teacher sat in front of a rather imposing electric shock generator (see Figure 32.2) which had 30 switches, each with its voltage level labeled. From left to right, the switches increased by increments of 15 volts, ranging from 15 volts to 450 volts. Verbal labels were also printed under groups of switches on the face of the generator. These ranged from "Slight" to "Moderate" to "Extreme Intensity" to "Danger: Severe Shock." The label at the 450 volt end simply read "XXX."

As the task proceeded, the learner periodically made errors according to a prearranged schedule. The teacher had been instructed to deliver an electric shock for each incorrect answer. With each error, the teacher was to move up the scale of shocks on the generator, giving the learner a more potent shock with each new mistake. (The learner, remember, was part of the act, and no one was actually receiving any shocks.)

Whenever the teacher hesitated or questioned whether he or she should continue, the experimenter was ready with one of several verbal prods, such as "Please continue," or "The experiment requires that you continue." If the subject protested, the experimenter would become more assertive and offer one of his alternative prods: "You have no choice; you must go on," he or she might say. The degree of obedience—the behavior of interest to Milgram—was determined by the level of shock at which the teacher refused to go further.

Milgram was astonished by the results of his first study, and the results continue to amaze students of psychology more than 20 years later. Twenty-six of Milgram's 40 subjects, 65 percent, obeyed the experimenter's demands and went all the way to the highest shock value and closed all the switches. In fact, *no subject* stopped prior to the 300 volt level, the point at which the learner pounded on the wall of the adjoining room in protest. One later variation of this study added voice feedback from the learner, who delivered an increasingly stronger series of demands to be let out of the experiment. The level of obedience in this study was still unbelievably high: 25 of 40 subjects, or 62.5 percent, continued to administer shocks to the 450 volt level.

It is important to note that the behavior of Milgram's subjects did not at all indicate that they were unconcerned about the learner. They experienced genuine and extreme stress in this situation. Some fidgeted, some trembled, many perspired profusely. A number of subjects laughed nervously. In short, the people caught in this rather unusual situation showed obvious signs of conflict and anxiety. Nevertheless, they continued to obey the orders of the authoritative experimenter even though they had good reason to believe that they might well be harming the learner.

Milgram's first study was performed with male subjects ranging in age from 20 to 50. A later replication with adult women as subjects produced precisely the same results: 65 percent obeyed fully. Other variations of the basic procedure, however, uncovered that several factors could reduce the amount of obedience. Putting the learner and teacher in the same room, or having the experimenter deliver his orders over the telephone, for example, reduced obedience markedly. Another variation produced an interesting parallel to one of the Asch studies we discussed: When the shocks were delivered by a team consisting of the subject and two disobedient confederates, full obedience dropped to only 10 percent.

The Fundamental Attribution Error: A Word of Caution

When one first hears about these rather distressing results, there is a tendency for many people to think that Milgram's obedient subjects were cold, callous, unfeeling, unusual, or even downright cruel and sadistic people. Nothing could be further from the truth. As we have already seen, the participants in this research were truly troubled by what was happening. If you thought that Milgram's subjects must be strange or different, perhaps you were a victim of what we identified in our last topic as the *fundamental attribution error*. That is, you were attributing the subjects' behavior to personality characteristics instead of recognizing the powerful situational forces at work.

Figure 32.2
A shock generator apparatus of the sort the teacher would use to punish the learner in Stanley Milgram's research on obedience. In the photo on the bottom, the subject is given a sample shock.

Attributing such personality characteristics to the teachers is particularly understandable in light of the unexpected nature of the results. A number of psychologists in commenting on this research have suggested, in fact, that the most significant aspect of Milgram's findings is that they *are* so surprising to us. As part of his research, Milgram asked people (including a group of psychiatrists) to predict what they themselves would do under these circumstances, and he also asked them to predict how far others would go before refusing the authority. Needless to say, respondents in both cases predicted very little obedience, expecting practically no one to proceed all the way to the final switch on the shock generator.

Conformity and Obedience: An Interpretation

The unexpectedly high levels of conformity and obedience in the Asch and Milgram studies force us to conclude that these behaviors, under the circumstances involved, in no way reflect any sort of psychological or mental disorder. To use a frequently cited phrase from one prominent social psychologist, "People who do crazy things are not necessarily crazy" (Aronson, 1984, p. 8). If we accept as normal that which most people are likely to do, then the behavior of Asch's and Milgram's subjects was indeed normal. Both lines of research clearly point to the power of situational influences in determining social behaviors, and they remind us that we may not be nearly as capable of acting independently and controlling our own behavior as we might like to think we are.

We have already suggested that people tend to rely on others for help in determining social reality when ambiguity is present. The research procedures of Asch and Milgram created conflict for those subjects who tried to define the situations in which they found themselves. Asch created a discrepancy between what the subject perceived as true and what others said was true. In much the same way, Milgram created an inconsistency between what the subject felt was the right and proper thing to do and what an authority figure said must be done. The situation was probably made even more difficult for Milgram's subjects by the tendency that we have to accept perceived authority without questioning it. From very early in life, we are conditioned to obey our parents, teachers, police officers, and the like. We often tend to trust others when faced with tasks of resolving conflicts such as those presented in these two classic studies.

A Reminder on Ethics in Research

In reading about Milgram's research, it should have occurred to you that subjecting participants to such a stressful experience might be considered morally and ethically objectionable. Milgram himself was quite concerned with the welfare of his subjects, and he took great care to **debrief** them after each session had been completed. That is, he informed them that they had not really administered any shocks and explained why deception had been necessary. It is, of course, standard practice in psychological experiments to conclude the session by disclosing the true purpose of the study and alleviating any anxiety that might have arisen.

Milgram reported that the people in his studies were generally not upset over having been deceived, and that their principal reaction was one of relief when they learned that no electric shock had, in fact, been used. Milgram also indicated that a follow-up study performed a year later with some of the same subjects showed that no long-term adverse effects had been created by his procedure.

debriefing
explaining to a subject, after an experiment has been completed, the true nature of the experiment, making sure that there are no lasting negative consequences of participation

Despite these precautions, Milgram has been severely criticized for placing people in such an extremely stressful situation. Indeed, one of the effects of his research was to establish in the scientific community a higher level of awareness of the need to protect the well-being of human research participants. Today, as we have noted previously, virtually every college and university where research is conducted with humans has a review board or committee to screen all research proposals, making sure that no experimentation will be conducted if it runs any risk of harming the participants, either physically or psychologically. More specifically, psychologists doing research are expected to adhere to rather stringent ethical guidelines published by the American Psychological Association. It is probably safe to say that because of the extreme nature of Milgram's procedures, he would not be allowed to perform such experiments today.

Before you go on

What was responsible for the high level of obedience in Milgram's experiments?

Is it possible to predict what any individual would do in Milgram's experimental situation?

BYSTANDER INTERVENTION

In March of 1964, a New York City cocktail waitress named Kitty Genovese was brutally murdered in front of her apartment building as she returned from work at approximately 3:30 a.m. Although murders have become somewhat commonplace in our large urban centers, there were some unusual and particularly disturbing circumstances surrounding this incident:

> *For more than half an hour, thirty-eight respectable law-abiding citizens in Queens watched a killer stalk and stab a woman in three separate attacks in Kew Gardens.*
>
> *Twice the sound of their voices and the sudden glow of their bedroom lights interrupted him and frightened him off. Each time he returned, sought her out and stabbed her again. Not one person telephoned the police during the assault; one witness called after the woman was dead (New York Times, March 27, 1964).*

This tragic event stimulated public concern and sparked a good deal of commentary in the media. People wondered how the witnesses could have shown such a lack of concern for a fellow human being. Apathy and alienation were terms frequently used in describing what had happened. One outcome of this incident was that a program of research was begun that helped to establish a basic understanding of the social factors that can lead to such a situation.

Bibb Latané and John Darley, two social psychologists who at the time were at universities in New York City, were not satisfied that terms such as bystander apathy adequately explained what happened in the Genovese case. They were convinced that situational factors make such events possible.

Latané and Darley (1970) first pointed out that there are typically several logical reasons why people should *not* be expected to offer help in an emergency. Emergencies tend to happen quickly and without advance warning. Except for medical technicians, firefighters, and a few other select categories of individuals, people generally are not prepared to deal with emergencies when they do arise. By their very nature, emergencies are not commonplace

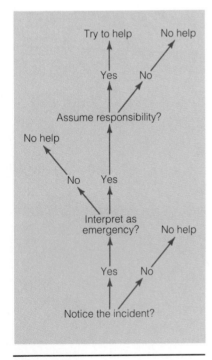

Figure 32.3
Some of the decisions and outcomes involved as a bystander considers intervening.
(After Darley & Latané, 1968.)

occurrences for most of us. It also goes without saying that the risk of physical injury, as was clearly present in the Genovese case, is an understandable deterrent to helping. Finally, people may fail to help because they genuinely want to avoid the legal consequences that might follow. They simply do not want to get involved.

A Cognitive Model of Bystander Intervention

Latané and Darley also suggested that a series of cognitive events must occur before a bystander can intervene in an emergency (Figure 32.3). First, the bystander must *notice* what is going on. A person who is window shopping and thus fails to see someone collapse on the opposite side of the street cannot be expected to rush over and offer assistance. If the bystander notices something happen, he or she still must *interpret* the event as an emergency; perhaps the person who has collapsed is simply drunk and not really having a stroke or a heart attack. The third step involves the bystander's deciding that it is his or her (and not someone else's) *responsibility* to do something.

Even if the bystander has noticed something occurring, has interpreted the situation as one calling for quick action, and has assumed responsibility for helping, he or she still faces the decision of what form of assistance to offer. Should he or she attempt to administer first aid; should he or she try to find the nearest telephone; or should he or she simply start shouting for help? As a final step in the process, the person must decide how to implement his or her decision to act. What is the appropriate first aid under the circumstances? Just where can a phone be found?

A negative outcome at any of these cognitive steps of decision-making will lead to a choice by the bystander not to offer assistance. When one considers the cognitive events necessary for actually helping, along with the many potential costs associated with intervention, it becomes apparent that the deck is stacked against the victim in an emergency. As Latané and Darley have suggested, perhaps we should be surprised that bystanders ever do offer help.

Psychological Effects of the Presence of Others

Although tragedies such as the Kitty Genovese murder may not happen every day, literally dozens of media reports involving the same sort of scenario have appeared repeatedly in the 20 years since that event. Rather ironically, it is the very presence of others that leads to this disturbing social-psychological phenomenon. There seem to be three psychological processes that account for the **social inhibition of helping,** or **bystander effect** (Latané & Darley, 1970; Latané & Nida, 1981).

Audience Inhibition   **Audience inhibition** refers to our tendency to be hesitant to do things in front of others, especially when the others are strangers. We tend to be concerned about how others evaluate us (a point we will return to later). In public, no one wants to do anything that might appear to be incompetent, improper, or silly. The bystander who intervenes risks embarrassment if he or she blunders. That risk is greater when the number of people present is larger.

Imagine that you are the one who steps out of a crowd to assist an unconscious man slumped against a wall. You might feel rather foolish if, as you turn him on his back to administer CPR, a couple of empty wine bottles were to roll out from beneath his coat. Audience inhibition, then, may frequently be sufficient to prevent intervention in an emergency.

Social Influence   A second process that Latané and Darley use to explain the social inhibition of helping is termed simply **social influence.** Emergencies tend to be ambiguous: Is the raggedly dressed man who has collapsed on the street ill or drunk? Is the commotion in a neighboring apartment an assault or a family quarrel that's a little out of hand? As we have already seen, when social reality is unclear, we turn to others for clues.

While a person is in the process of getting information from others, he or she will probably try to remain calm and collected, behaving as if there is no emergency. Everyone else, of course, is doing the very same thing, showing no outward sign of concern. The result is that everyone is led by the others present to think that the situation is really not an emergency after all, a psychological state called **pluralistic ignorance.** The group is paralyzed, in a sense, and the phenomenon can be interpreted as a type of conformity—conformity to the inaction of others.

This process was demonstrated clearly in a classic experiment by Latané and Darley (1968, 1970). Columbia University students reported to a campus building to participate in an interview. They were sent to a waiting room and were asked to complete some preliminary forms. While they did so, white smoke began to billow through a vent in the wall. After 6 minutes (the point at which the procedure was terminated if the "emergency" had not been reported), there was enough smoke in the room to interfere with breathing and prevent seeing across the room.

When subjects were alone in the waiting room, 75 percent of them emerged to report the smoke. However, when two passive confederates were in the room with the subject, only 10 percent responded; only 38 percent of groups consisting of three actual subjects reported the smoke. People who reported the smoke did so quickly. Those from the groups who failed to do so generated all sorts of explanations for the smoke: steam, vapors from the air conditioner, smog introduced to simulate an urban environment, and even "truth gas." In short, the unresponsive group members had been led by the inaction of their peers to conclude just about anything other than the obvious—that something was wrong.

social inhibition of helping (bystander effect)
the tendency for people to be less likely to offer help when they are in a group than when they are alone

audience inhibition
reluctance to intervene and offer assistance in front of others

social influence
(in the context of helping) relying on others to define whether or not a situation is a true emergency

pluralistic ignorance
a condition wherein the inaction of others leads each individual in a group to interpret a situation as a nonemergency, thus leading to general inactivity

Diffusion of Responsibility   In the Kitty Genovese murder that began this discussion, it was terribly clear that an emergency was in progress; there was very little ambiguity about what was happening. Furthermore, the 38 witnesses were not in a face-to-face group that would allow social influence processes to operate. Latané and Darley thus suggested that a third important process is necessary to complete the explanation of bystander behavior. A single bystander in an emergency situation must bear the full responsibility for offering assistance, but the witness who is part of a group shares that responsibility with other onlookers. The greater the number of other people present, the smaller is each individual's personal obligation to intervene. This process is referred to as **diffusion of responsibility** and has been demonstrated in another series of experiments by Latané and Darley (1968, 1970).

In this study, New York University students arrived at a laboratory to take part in a group discussion of some of the personal problems they experienced as college students in an urban environment. To reduce the embarrassment of talking about such matters in public, each group member (presumably) would be isolated in his or her own cubicle and would communicate with the others through an intercom system. Actually there were no other group members, only tape recorded voices. Thus, there was only one subject in each group, and the perceived size of the group could easily be manipulated to see whether diffusion of responsibility would occur.

The first person to speak mentioned that he was prone to seizures when under pressure, such as when studying for an exam. The others, including the actual subject, then took turns talking for about 10 minutes about their problems. A second round of discussion then began with the seizure-prone student who, shortly after he started talking, began to suffer one of his seizures.

Just as in the Genovese incident, it was obvious that something was wrong. As the "victim" began stammering, choking, and pleading for help, the typical subject became quite nervous; some trembled, some had sweaty palms. This experiment had another feature in common with the Genovese episode: Subjects could not be sure if any other bystanders (members of the group) had taken any action. (In fact, remember, there were no others.)

As expected, the likelihood of helping decreased as the perceived size of the group increased. Eighty-five percent of those in two-person groups (subject and victim) left the cubicle to report the emergency to the experimenter. When the subject thought that he or she was in a three-person group, 62 percent responded. Only 31 percent of the participants who believed that they were in a six-person group took any step to intervene. The responsibility for reporting the seizure was clearly divided among those thought to be present.

Incidentally, diffusion of responsibility does come in forms that are less serious in their implications. Those of you with a few siblings can probably recall times at home when the telephone has rung five or six times before anyone has made a move to answer it, even though the entire family was there at the time. And some of you have probably been at parties where the doorbell went unanswered. These examples involve the same sort of social-psychological process that we have been discussing.

The Bystander Effect: A Conclusion

The situational determinants of helping behavior continued to be a popular research topic for social psychologists throughout the 1970s. Many of these studies included a manipulation of the size of the group witnessing the event that created the need for help in the first place. Latané and Nida (1981) reviewed some 50 studies involving nearly 100 different comparisons between helping alone and in groups. Although these experiments involved a wide range of settings, procedures, and participants, the social inhibition of helping (the bystander effect) occurred in almost every instance. Latané and Nida combined the data from all of these studies in a single statistical analysis. Their conclusion: There is very little doubt that we are correct in concluding than an individual is more likely to help when he or she is alone rather than in a group. In other words, the bystander effect is a remarkably consistent phenomenon, perhaps as predictable as any phenomenon in social psychology.

Before you go on

What are audience inhibition, social influence, and diffusion of responsibility in the context of bystander and helping behavior?

How does the presence of others lead to nonintervention in an emergency?

OTHER EXAMPLES OF GROUP INFLUENCE

We have just reviewed in some detail how being a part of a group can alter one's behavior. Since a great deal of our behavior does occur in groups, group influence is an important topic in social psychology. In this section, we'll survey a few additional examples of behavioral phenomena that occur in groups.

Social Impact Theory and Social Loafing

Latané has gone on from his studies of bystander behavior to suggest that other social behaviors also show diffusion effects (Latané, 1981; Latané & Nida, 1980). In fact, this idea has become a major cornerstone of Latané's theory of social impact.

Latané has proposed a **psychosocial law** that parallels the psychophysical laws we reviewed in Topic 5. Fundamentally, this law specifies that each person that is added to a group has less impact on a target individual than the previous person to join the group. In terms of helping in an emergency, for example, this means that adding one other bystander besides yourself to the situation should decrease significantly your likelihood of responding. If, however, you are in a group of 49 bystanders, a fiftieth person would have little effect on the chances of your helping. The data from a typical diffusion of responsibility experiment follow a power function like that depicted in Figure 32.4.

For example, tipping in restaurants follows such a pattern. Freeman and his colleagues (1975) found that tipping declined systematically with increases in the size of the dining party. On the average, people eating alone left about a 19 percent tip, while those dining in groups averaged only about 13 percent of the total check.

Similarly, Latané, Williams, and Harkins (1979) have identified an effect they call **social loafing**, which refers to the tendency to work less as the size of the group in which one is working becomes larger. Their studies had participants shout or clap as loud as possible, either in groups or alone. Other studies (e.g., Petty et al., 1977) have used cognitive tasks, such as evaluating poetry. The results tend to be consistent: When people can hide in the crowd, their effort (and hence their productivity) declines.

Figure 32.4

The psychosocial law applied to helping. This theoretical curve predicts the likelihood that someone will help in an emergency. As the number of fellow bystanders increases, the likelihood of helping behavior drops rapidly. (After Latané, 1981.)

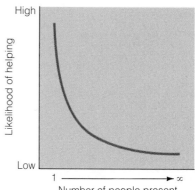

Social Facilitation

Many years ago, a psychologist by the name of Norman Triplett (1898) was struck by his observation that bicycle riders competing against other cyclists outperformed those racing against a clock. He then performed what is considered to be the first laboratory experiment in social psychology. Triplett had children wind a fishing reel as rapidly as possible. They performed this task either alone or with another child alongside doing the same. Just as he had noticed in his records of bicycle races, Triplett found that the children worked faster when another child was present. We now know that such an effect sometimes occurs not only with coactors (others performing the same task), but also if a person performs in front of an audience. These two types of effects are two forms of **social facilitation.**

Numerous studies of these phenomena were performed early in the twentieth century, but with a puzzling inconsistency in their results. Sometimes social facilitation would occur; but on other occasions, just the opposite would occur. Sometimes people actually performed more poorly in the presence of others than they did alone, an effect we call **social interference.** In fact, the inconsistency in these findings was so bewildering that psychologists for the most part eventually gave up investigating social facilitation.

In 1965, Robert Zajonc resurrected the topic of social facilitation by providing a plausible interpretation of this inconsistency in the appearance of social facilitation effects. In his examination of the research that had accumulated over the years, Zajonc noticed that social facilitation had occurred whenever the behavior under study was simple or very well learned. Social interference, on the other hand, tended to occur whenever the behavior involved was complex or not well practiced. On the basis of an old and established principle of experimental psychology, Zajonc suggested that the presence of others creates *arousal,* which in turn energizes the dominant (most likely) response under the circumstances. When the dominant response is correct, as with a simple, well-practiced task, social facilitation occurs. When the dominant response is incorrect, as with a complex task or one with which we have had little practice, the result is social interference.

Because of social facilitation, we perform better when we are in the presence of others. Bicycle racers ride faster when racing against other riders than when racing against the clock.

You may have experienced this effect yourself if you have ever tried to acquire a skill at a sport that is totally new to you. Whereas skilled athletes tend to perform better in front of audiences, the novice tends to do better when alone. You may have experienced (as a novice, that is) the frustration of finding it difficult to even hit a golf ball or tennis ball when there are others standing nearby watching you. One line of thought suggests that the arousal in Zajonc's model comes from being concerned over how others evaluate us (Cottrell, 1972). We call this state **evaluation apprehension.**

evaluation apprehension
one's concern about how others are evaluating one's performance

Decision-making in Groups

Many of the decisions that we face in our daily lives are the sort that must be made in groups. Committees, boards, family groups, and group projects for a class are only a few of the many possible examples. One might reason that problem solving ought to be more effective in a group because individuals can pool their resources. Having more people available should necessarily mean having more talent and knowledge available. It also seems logical that the cohesiveness of the group might contribute to a more productive effort (and for some groups and some problems, this is exactly the case). But how does the group itself affect the process of making a decision? Here we will look briefly at two curious phenomena that can occur in such circumstances.

Group Polarization   James Stoner (1961), an MIT graduate student in industrial management, gave subjects in his research a series of decision dilemmas to resolve. The result of each decision would be a statement of how much risk the fictitious character in the dilemma should take. To his surprise, Stoner found that the decisions rendered by groups were generally riskier than those that the individual group members had made prior to the group decision.

Several hundred studies later, we now know that this effect can occur in the opposite direction as well. In other words, the "risky shift" is simply a specific case of a more general **group polarization** phenomenon. The process of group discussion leads to an enhancement of the group member's average

group polarization
the tendency for members of a group to give more extreme judgments following a discussion than they gave initially

Many of the decisions we face daily are the sort that are best made in groups, whether committees, boards, or family groups.

tendency before the discussion. That is, the group process pushes members further in the direction in which they leaned initially. One explanation for group polarization suggests that the discussion gives group members an opportunity to hear persuasive arguments they have not previously considered, leading to a strengthening of their original attitudes. Another possibility is that after comparing attitudinal positions with one another, some group members feel pressure to catch up with other group members who have more extreme attitudes.

groupthink
a style of thinking of cohesive groups concerned with maintaining agreement to the extent that independent ideas are discouraged

Groupthink   Irving Janis (1972) has described a phenomenon of considerable social influence called **groupthink.** Janis maintains that this style of thinking emerges when group members are so interested in maintaining harmony that differences of opinion are suppressed. It is especially likely to occur in cohesive groups. Alternative courses of action are not considered realistically and the frequent result is a poor decision. Janis has analyzed several key historical events—including Pearl Harbor, the Bay of Pigs invasion, and the escalation of the Vietnam War—in terms of the operation of groupthink. Each of these situations involved a cohesive decision-making group that was relatively isolated from outside judgments, a directive leader who supplied pressure to conform to his position, an illusion of unanimity, and a number of other symptoms of groupthink listed by Janis.

Before you go on
Summarize some examples of group influence that may have positive or negative consequences.

SOCIAL INFLUENCE THROUGH AGGRESSION

aggression
behavior with the intent to do harm to another

Our final section in this topic deals with an especially unpleasant and even potentially dangerous form of social behavior. **Aggression** is generally defined as behavior with the intent of harming another.

In light of the power of social situations to affect behavior, all of us have the potential to be aggressive. In fact, there is one particular set of social circumstances that definitely tends to lead to aggressive and violent behaviors. We have already seen how groups can diffuse the responsibility for one's behavior. When the anonymity of being in a group is combined with a high level of arousal—such as is often present at a soccer match, a rock concert, or in an angry mob—an individual's attention may be drawn away from himself, and the person may feel lost in the crowd. This psychological state, called **deindividuation,** has been reliably demonstrated to lead to destructive, antisocial behavior in a wide range of research settings (Diener, 1980; Festinger, Pepitone & Newcomb, 1952; Zimbardo, 1970).

deindividuation
a process in which the person loses self-awareness and becomes anonymous within a group

Theoretical Explanations of Aggression

Although deindividuation may result in aggression, most aggression probably occurs in other social contexts. These other contexts are the focus of the major explanations of aggression.

Frustration-aggression Theory   Probably most of us at one time or another have kicked a soft drink machine that has taken our money, slammed down the telephone receiver after getting a busy signal for what seemed like the thirtieth time, or struck out at a disobedient pet. Such reac-

There are certain social situations that tend to lead to aggressive and violent behaviors. Simple partisanship at sporting events can turn to mob violence and destruction.

tions are predicted by the theoretical position established back in 1939 by John Dollard and his associates. They maintained that frustration (the blocking of goal-directed behavior) leads to aggression. Frustration is an unpleasant drive that can be reduced by behaving aggressively.

Although this notion certainly explains some aggression, it is evidently overstated since research has shown that frustration sometimes fails to produce aggression and, furthermore, aggression can occur without prior frustration. One later modification of the frustration-aggression theory (Berkowitz, 1978) suggests that frustration leads to anger, which in turn is released in the form of aggression if an appropriate aggressive cue is present. Nevertheless, there seems to be another, perhaps more important cause of aggression.

Frustration often leads to aggression. The frustration of being caught in a traffic jam can lead us to behave aggressively toward other motorists and even pedestrians.

Social Learning Theory   A famous program of research conducted primarily in the early 1960s (Bandura, 1973) provided solid evidence that aggression can be learned by observing others (see our discussion in Topic 12). Bandura's research demonstrated that greater amounts of aggressive behavior occur following the witnessing of aggression performed by either a live or filmed model. Imitation of aggression is even more pronounced if the observed aggression goes unpunished or if it is portrayed as justified. The observer is also likely to display an enhanced aggressive response if provoked or frustrated.

Television and Violent Behavior

Bandura's research obviously speaks directly to the issue of the harmfulness of violence in television programming. Although his typical findings seem, for the most part, to be restricted to laboratory experiments, the evidence for a social learning approach to aggression has convinced most people that we should be cautious about overexposure to televised violence, particularly with children. Many observers believe that violence is excessive in television programming, particularly in cartoons aimed at a young audience. Furthermore, there does seem to be a moderate but consistent relationship between the amount of violence in a child's television diet and a child's level of aggressiveness (e.g., Eron, 1982).

There are other theoretical positions that have been considered relevant to aggression and violence. Freud believed, for example, that aggression allows a person to release tension. Others have suggested that this same process of **catharsis** can occur vicariously; in other words, a person might be able to blow off steam by watching someone else behave violently on television. The evidence generally fails to support such an idea, however. Viewing violence tends to increase violent behavior, not reduce it.

Another important and relevant theoretical concept here is that of **perceptual adaptation.** In the context of sensation and perception, this process refers to our decreased sensitivity to stimuli that are presented constantly over a period of time. In the context of television violence, the concern is that the viewer who watches too much violence becomes adapted to it. Further violence becomes less objectionable because the viewer has become desensitized to it. This idea is well accepted even though there has been little social psychological research dealing with it, probably because the phenomenon occurs so reliably in the sensory context.

catharsis
the release of pent-up tension or negative emotions, such as in the release of aggression and violence by watching such behaviors in others

perceptual adaptation
(in the context of viewing violence) the idea that watching violence leads a person to become adapted or desensitized to it

Before you go on
Briefly describe four theoretical approaches to aggression and indicate the degree of support that exists for each.

In this topic, we have discussed a number of results of group influence, and many of them have been unfavorable: leading people not to help someone else in need, to exert less effort, to perform poorly, to think inefficiently, or to act aggressively. At the same time, groups are a major part of social life, and some goals simply cannot be reached alone, without group membership.

It is important to realize that effective group performance can be fostered by good morale, healthy communication, sound leadership, and teamwork that is accomplished through the appropriate division of responsibility. Hopefully, an awareness of the possible negative consequences of group activity and the conditions that produce them will enable us to counter obstacles to group productivity and satisfaction.

Basic principles of social psychology are currently being applied in a number of everyday situations, ranging from environmental design to energy conservation. One of the most thoroughly developed areas of applied social psychology is that of social psychology and the law. Questions about social influence processes are abundant and are relevant in the context of our legal system: What psychological factors affect arrests and plea bargaining? What characteristics of a defendant are most likely to have an effect on jurors and judges? How effective and accurate is eyewitness testimony? What are the effects of a judge's instructions to a jury? What are the group dynamics of a jury as it attempts to render a judgment? (See Topic 34.)

Research has been conducted on all of these questions, as well as many other issues involving social psychology in the courtroom. Let's briefly consider the group dynamics of a jury. A jury is, after all, a group charged with the task of making a decision; as such, it should be subject to many of the same social forces that operate in other decision-making groups.

Imagine that you are the only juror (out of 12) who favors acquittal. The other 11 jury members believe the defendant to be guilty as charged. Might you not feel pressure to conform to the majority's position? Although minorities occasionally succeed in swaying the majority to their side, some 90 percent of juries end up with the verdict initially favored by the majority (Kalven & Zeisel, 1966). This finding is consistent with the notion that strong pressures to conform do indeed operate within a jury.

The concern with pressure to conform also relates to another issue currently being debated: the question of whether smaller juries might be feasible. Assuming that

The impact of social influence is readily apparent in the behavior of juries. The members of juries are subject to enormous influences from witnesses, testifiers, lawyers, judges, and other members of the jury.

six-person juries would be less expensive and more efficient, several states have recently passed laws allowing six-person juries to sit in judgment in certain cases. However, social psychologists have been critical of this move. Why?

You will recall from our discussion of Asch's conformity research that his subjects tended not to conform if there was just one other dissenter in the group. That is, the person with the minority point of view who has an ally finds it easier to resist group pressure than if that person is a minority of one. Since a 12-person jury represents a larger sample than a six-person jury, it stands to reason that a juror with a minority opinion is less likely to stand alone in a 12-person group. The larger jury, then, should encourage fairer deliberations, or so the argument goes.

Social psychology has begun to have an impact on our legal system. Attorneys are becoming more aware of relevant social-psychological research, and some social psychologists now work as legal consultants who help in such tasks as jury selection and witness preparation. This rapidly developing area is one that you will certainly hear more about in the future.

TOPIC SUMMARY

Briefly describe the methodology and the basic findings of the Sherif and Asch conformity studies.

Sherif used the autokinetic phenomenon to explore the emergence of norms in groups. Over several days of judging how far a light moved, subjects adjusted their own estimates in the direction of estimates made by others. In the Asch studies, people made simple judgments about unambiguous perceptual stimuli. On some trials, confederates, answering before the actual subject, gave clearly incorrect judgments. Asch's subjects followed suit and yielded to the pressure of the group surprisingly often. / 595

What was responsible for the high level of obedience in Milgram's experiments?

Is it possible to predict what any individual would do in Milgram's experimental situation?

The individuals who obeyed in Milgram's experiments were neither cruel nor inhumane. Rather, the experimenter created a powerful social situation that made it very difficult to refuse the authority figure's orders. It is impossible to say, of course, what any one individual might do in this situation, but we have to remember that a large majority of the subjects in Milgram's project did yield to the authority of the experimenter. / 599

What are audience inhibition, social influence, and diffusion of responsibility in the context of bystander and helping behavior?

How does the presence of others lead to nonintervention in an emergency?

Audience inhibition refers to the hesitancy to intervene in front of others, perhaps for fear of embarrassing one's self. Social influence occurs when other bystanders lead one to think that nothing is really wrong in an ambiguous emergency situation. Diffusion of responsibility causes a bystander in a group to feel less obligated to intervene than if he or she were alone. Each of these processes tends to discourage bystander helping and each is more likely to operate as the number of persons present increases. / 603

Summarize some examples of group influence that may have positive or negative consequences.

The social inhibition of helping, social loafing, social interference, and groupthink all represent situations in which the group has a negative influence on behavior. However, having others present can produce favorable effects, too, as demonstrated by the social facilitation phenomenon and real-life groups that function effectively because of good organization, morale, and leadership. / 606

Briefly describe four theoretical approaches to aggression and indicate the degree of support that exists for each.

One of the first explanations of aggression was the frustration-aggression theory, which maintained that frustration leads to aggression. This position is now regarded as overstated because frustration does not always lead to aggression and aggression may occur without frustration. Social learning theory, for which laboratory research has produced a great deal of support, states that aggression is learned through observing a model behave aggressively. This is particularly true when the model's behavior is reinforced or goes unpunished. The catharsis hypothesis suggests that observing aggression (as on TV) allows a person to release tension, making aggression less likely. Unfortunately, there is little support for this theory. The process of perceptual adaptation, a well-established principle in psychology, suggests that watching televised violence (for example) eventually leads the viewer to become adapted or desensitized to it. / 608

CHAPTER FIFTEEN

APPLIED PSYCHOLOGY

TOPIC 33 Industrial/Organizational Psychology

Jack Phillips is vice-president of operations for Amalgamated Flange Fabrications, Inc., a small midwestern manufacturing company that is facing a number of problems. For one thing, the company needs to improve its level of productivity. Pressures from foreign imports and a reduced demand for the high-quality flanges that AFF produces have severely reduced profits for the last 2 years. For the first time in the company's history, the balance sheet for the last quarter showed a substantial loss. At the moment, Jack sees three ways in which he might make a significant improvement in productivity: instituting some organizational restructuring, providing a training program for present employees, and tightening present policies on personnel selection.

Jack sees the need for improved productivity as a once-in-a-lifetime opportunity to change the organizational structure of AFF. Jack feels that many of AFF's policies and procedures are antiquated and inefficient. Jack wants to make some changes on the production line, implementing some of the technological advances that have revolutionized flange manufacturing. But more than that, Jack realizes that to return AFF to its once highly-respected status in the industry, management will have to take a new look at leadership styles and means to motivate rank-and-file workers.

Installing new equipment and restructuring the organization will necessitate retraining at almost all levels within the company. In some cases, training will be directed at teaching new skills, but in others, it will be directed at bringing about changes in attitudes and styles of communication.

To complicate matters further, contract negotiations with the local labor union begin next week. Jack wants to be sure that the changes he is proposing can be implemented while maintaining—and perhaps even increasing—job satisfaction among AFF employees.

Finally, Jack needs to hire a new plant manager to help him put all these changes into practice. The last plant manager resisted change in any form. He proved to be an ineffective manager and had to be fired. Jack doesn't want to make a mistake in choosing a new plant manager.

Although by title Jack Phillips is a vice-president of operations of a manufacturing company, many of the tasks he has before him are psychological in nature. They reflect many of the concerns of industrial/organizational (I/O) psychology, which is the subject of this topic.

Why We Care

One of the themes we have maintained throughout this text is that psychology has many applications in everyday life. The scientific study of behavior and mental processes can be brought to bear on many of the problems we face from day to day. In this chapter, we will focus even more directly on the application of psychological principles to real world events and issues.

In this topic, our focus will be on **industrial/organizational psychology,** I/O for short. In large measure, the people in this field are concerned with applying psychological principles in order to improve the effectiveness and efficiency of business and industrial organizations. Approximately 1800 of the 28,500 members of the American Psychological Association claim industrial/organizational psychology as their specialty. Most I/O psychologists are employed by business and governmental agencies (approximately 67 percent), about 30 percent are employed in an academic setting, and the remainder are employed either in private consulting firms or in hospital and human services settings (Stapp & Fulcher, 1982).

I/O psychology
industrial/organizational psychology; concerned with applying principles of psychology to improve the efficiency and effectiveness of organizations

I/O psychologists may be involved in such diverse activities as personnel selection and training, improvement of employee satisfaction, improving the effectiveness of human/machine interactions, increasing effective communication, and providing individual counseling to employees. I/O psychologists can enter an organization at any level; some study the behaviors and effectiveness of executives and top management (McCall & Lombardo, 1983), while others are interested in the relationship between psychology and organized labor unions (Huszczo et al., 1984).

In this topic, we will examine three major thrusts of industrial/organizational psychology that mirror the problems facing our fictitious Jack Phillips of Amalgamated Flange Fabrications, Inc. First, we'll discuss personnel selection techniques, where the overriding question is how best to fit the right person to a given job. Then we'll consider what psychologists can contribute to discussions of how to increase productivity while increasing employee satisfaction and reducing stress in the workplace. Finally, we'll review some of the applications of psychology to the structuring of organizations in business and industry.

PERSONNEL SELECTION

One of the most important roles of industrial/organizational psychologists is assisting an employer in formulating procedures for making decisions about the hiring of employees. At least in theory, the task is a straightforward one: to find the best person for each and every job within the organization. In practice, the task is often quite difficult.

There are three major steps involved in personnel selection. The first is to generate an adequate *job analysis.* That is, before you can find the right person for a job, you will need to know, as specifically as possible, the exact nature of the position to be filled. Once a complete job analysis has been done, the second step is to agree on the procedures to be used to *evaluate the characteristics of the applicants* for that job. Here a number of assessment tools may be used: psychological testing, interviews, letters of recommendation, application forms, and the like. A third and integral part of this process is to build in procedures by which your *selection process can be evaluated* (Dunnette & Borman, 1979). That is, before a selection has been made, you must have in mind how the decision will be evaluated. You'll need to specify the criteria that will be used at a later date to determine whether the selection decision was a good one. In this section, we'll examine some of the considerations that need to be made at each of these three steps.

The Job Analysis

Before we can begin to find the right person for a given job, we need to know the exact nature of the position we are trying to fill. Mr. Phillips of Amalgamated Flange is looking for a plant manager. If I were an I/O psychologist, I could not tell Mr. Phillips what sort of person he was looking for. Rather, he would have to tell me. We might begin with a description of the responsibilities of an AFF plant manager. Then we would have to translate that job description into a set of measurable characteristics that a successful plant manager would possess. In other words, we would begin our selection efforts by doing a **job analysis.** A job analysis "seeks to identify personal qualities that contribute to or limit success" in that job (Cronbach, 1984, p. 360).

Typically, writing a complete job analysis is a two-step process. The first step involves compiling a complete description of what a person in that job is expected to do. There are many sources of information that a job analyst might use to generate this description. Most companies have developed official job descriptions for their employees, but these are usually stated in general terms, such as "supervise workers in the plant; maintain acceptable levels of production; oversee equipment operation and maintenance; schedule work loads," and the like.

To be useful, a job analysis must be more specific in describing the actual behaviors engaged in by someone in a given position. Does a plant manager have to know how to operate the machinery used in the plant? Does the plant manager deal with plant employees on a one-to-one basis or in groups? Are interactions with employees informal and hit-and-miss, or are there regularly scheduled, formal meetings that need to be organized? Is the plant manager in charge of meetings? To what extent is the plant manager responsible for employee training and development? Will the plant manager be involved in labor negotiations? Clearly this list of questions can be a long one. The basic underlying concern at this level of analysis is, "On a day-to-day basis, just what does a plant manager do?"

Much of this information can be accumulated through questionnaires and interviews with plant managers or with supervisors of plant managers. Valuable information can also be gained through careful observation. It is always advisable for the job analyst to spend some time watching a person actually performing the job being analyzed.

Once duties and responsibilities have been delineated, the next step requires that these be translated into terms of measurable personal characteristics. Again, what is involved here is usually a collaborative effort between a representative of the employer and a psychologist. The goal is to generate a list of characteristics that a person in a given position should have in order to do that job as well as possible. This list and the complete description are the job analysis. There are a number of different areas that might be explored at this point. How much previous experience is really necessary? What sorts of personal characteristics would be helpful? What sorts of specific skills and abilities are required to perform the tasks at hand? Plant managers, for example, may need to demonstrate some level of experience in plant operations, be well organized, and be able to deal with others. Workers in the plant—flange assemblers, for example—may need to demonstrate muscular coordination or physical strength and be able to tolerate continued exposure to loud noise.

job analysis
a complete and specific description of a job including personal qualities required to do it well

One of the most important roles of the industrial/organizational psychologist is helping employers make the best possible personnel selections—to choose the best person for each and every job. The first step is doing a job analysis to determine the personal qualities best suited to the job in question.

Once a job analysis has been completed—once we know what an applicant will be expected to do on the job *and* once we have translated those tasks into measurable personal characteristics—we are ready to begin designing an assessment process.

Before you go on

What is involved in doing a job analysis?

The Assessment Process

As you might imagine, a wide variety of techniques and sources of information are available to the employer (and to the psychologist who may assist) in screening and evaluating applicants for any given position. If the job analysis has been done properly, the psychologist has a complete list of those duties and characteristics in which the employer is interested and is charged with the task of finding the applicant who best reflects them.

Some useful information can be gleaned from a well-constructed job application form. An application form can serve three useful functions. (1) It can be used as a rough screening device. Some applicants will be unhirable because they do not meet requirements for the job, such as a minimal education level or specified job experience. (2) It can supplement and provide cues for interviewing. Bits and pieces of fragmented data from application forms can be pursued later during in-depth interviews. (3) It provides biographical data (called *biodata*) that may be useful in making direct predictions about a candidate's likelihood of success, such as length of previous employment and special training experiences (Landy, 1985, pp. 117–118).

An integral part of many selection procedures will be the employment interview. We have already commented (Topic 24) on the inherent dangers of relying too heavily on information gained through interviews. Unstructured interviews in particular are subject to many sources of error. Nonetheless, Tenopyr (1981) finds the interview to be the most widely used selection procedure in this country, despite the fact that the results of validity studies for interviews are "dismal" and that "despite various innovations over the years, [the interview] has never been consistently shown to improve selection" (p. 1123). For one thing, interviews, by their nature, involve the interaction of two people—the interviewer and the person being interviewed. As a result, the biases of the interviewer, conscious or unconscious, may flavor the results of an employment interview.

The most valid interviews are those that are highly structured and involve the combined evaluations from a number of interviewers. Training interviewers to be sensitive to personal biases can also improve the validity of the technique, but such training is expensive. According to Cronbach, "In employment practice, interviews have several functions and surely will continue to be used. The best general advice is to make sure that interviewer judgments are not given excessive weight in selection" (1984, p. 406).

Beyond the application form and the interview, personnel selection often involves the administration and interpretation of psychological tests. Many tests are narrow in their application and are designed to assess only one specific characteristic of the applicant (finger dexterity, for example, which might be very relevant for an assembly-line worker in an electronics plant). Other tests are more general and may assess a number of different skills and abilities. Tests of general intelligence and/or certain personality characteristics may be called for, particularly when evaluating candidates for manage-

The interview is an integral part of the employee selection process. A highly-structured, well-planned interview will bring out the best in the potential employee and will give the employer valuable evaluation information.

rial or supervisory positions. There are literally hundreds of published paper-and-pencil tests designed to measure a variety of characteristics, from mechanical aptitude, to leadership style, to motivation for sales work, to critical thinking skills. An I/O psychologist involved in personnel decisions will know about these tests and recommend specific instruments for specific selection tasks.

From time to time, it is necessary to construct one's own test to assess some unique or special ability not measured by available instruments. A common form of testing in employment settings is called *situational testing,* in which applicants are given the opportunity to role-play the task they may be hired to do. If you were going to hire someone to work at the counter of your dry cleaning business, for instance, you might ask an applicant how he or she would respond to an irate customer whose suit was damaged in cleaning. Actually role-playing the part of customer while the applicant plays the part of employee might provide useful information.

Validity and reliability are critical factors in any personnel selection procedure, and we'll discuss these separately in the next section. Another factor of no small consequence is cost of assessment. One of the difficult decisions that often has to be made in personnel selection is just how much time, effort, and money will be invested in the selection process for any job level. In the long run, it may not pay to invest thousands of dollars interviewing and testing persons for unskilled, low-paying positions. Choosing the right person for a top management or executive position, on the other hand, may justify such an investment.

In response to such cost/benefit concerns, some large corporations now use what is called an **assessment center** approach to select (or promote) management personnel. This approach provides evaluators with opportunities to observe applicants in a number of social situations and under stress. The assessment center was first introduced during World War II as a device for selecting candidates for the Office of Strategic Services, known today as the CIA. It wasn't until the 1960s that this approach was used for selecting executives in private business and industry, although the first application was by AT&T in the mid-1950s (Bray, Campbell & Grant, 1974).

The assessment center procedure involves an intensive period of evaluation, usually lasting 3 or 4 days. A number of applicants for a position are brought together along with executives of the company and a team of psychologists. In addition to batteries of standard paper-and-pencil tests and interviews, the applicants are given a number of situational tests in which their behaviors in situations similar to those they might encounter on the job can be observed. One assessment center method is called the **in-basket technique.** Here, applicants are provided with a number of tasks, memos, and assignments of the sort they might encounter in a typical day at the office (as previously determined through a job analysis). They can then be observed as they attempt to sort out and deal with the imaginary issues they find in the in-basket.

Assessment centers provide a sensible approach to selecting managers and other key persons in a business who often must function in social and stressful situations. Unfortunately, there is little data available regarding the effectiveness of the technique. "Although studies using combinations of techniques in assessment have generally resulted in moderate validity coefficients for the criterion of success at management, . . . the assessment center cannot be recommended unequivocally as a general alternative to tests" (Tenopyr, 1981, p. 1124). Other reviewers are equally skeptical about the quality of the research that supports the use of assessment centers. It seems

assessment center
a personnel selection mechanism whereby applicants are tested, interviewed, and observed in a number of situations by a team of evaluators

in-basket technique
an assessment device in which applicants are asked to respond to a number of situations that might be encountered in a typical workday

that in general, assessments of individuals are reasonably valid, but making specific predictions with regard to specific behaviors has proven neither reliable nor valid (Landy, 1985; Zedeck & Cascio, 1984).

Before you go on
What are some of the sources of information that can be used in making personnel decisions?

Evaluating the Selection Process

So far, what we have said about personnel selection has been reasonably straightforward: One analyzes the nature of the position to be filled, delineates those characteristics required to do the job well, assesses—through the use of a variety of sources—the characteristics of those persons who apply for the position, and hires the person who best fits the job analysis. This sounds simple enough, but as we suggested above, an integral part of personnel selection is building in mechanisms by which we can determine the success or failure of our selection procedures. In this regard, we should review two considerations: validity and fairness. In most cases, these define the bottom line of the success or failure of a selection procedure.

validity
the extent to which a test measures what it claims to be measuring

The Validity of Employee Assessment Techniques In the context of psychological testing, we have previously defined **validity** as the extent to which a test measures what it claims to be measuring. (Remember that concern over validity makes little sense without first determining that your tests are *reliable*. That is, before you concern yourself with validity, you should assure yourself that your tests are producing reliable, or consistent, results.) This same general concept can be applied to the process of personnel selection. In a sense, we go through a series of procedures that claim to be identifying the best person for a given job. To claim that our procedures are valid ones, we need to be able to demonstrate that the person we hire for a given position will in fact be better suited for that job than would be someone we simply chose at random to fill the position. In this sense, evaluating the validity of our assessment procedures has practical consequences. Jack Phillips is going to be justifiably upset if we recommend that he hire Candidate X as plant manager and Candidate X turns out to be a poor manager.

To establish the validity of our assessment device (or devices), we need to demonstrate a correlation between what we have measured (biodata, interview results, test performance, etc.) and an established criteria (usually, performance on the job). If applicants who perform well on a typing test turn out to be good typists and/or word processors, we may have a valid test for typists and word processors.

As you can imagine, there are a number of different sources of error in estimating the validity of any assessment technique. First, we may have made an error at the level of job analysis. We may have assumed that an office receptionist needs to have superior filing skills. We may then go out of our way to hire an applicant with such skills, only to discover later that filing is a job task that seldom arises.

Second, we may make an error in choosing a test to measure an important employee characteristic. We might know, for example, that Test S is a valid test for selecting retail salespersons and decide to use it as part of a testing program for salespersons who will be working at the wholesale level, dealing with purchasing agents rather than the general public.

Third, we may make an error in assessing the criteria against which our assessment program will be evaluated. That is, we may have found the very best person for our position, but because we did not have a good measure of on-the-job performance, we may not realize it. For example, we may hire a district sales manager, following advice based on the interpretation of a battery of tests. We then discover that the sales manager's supervisors (two regional sales managers) find the new employee totally unsatisfactory. Before we jump to conclusions concerning the lack of validity of our testing program, we ought to examine the validity of our criteria—the judgments of our regional sales managers. They may be in error. Here is where we go back to a point made earlier. A central aspect of doing a job analysis is to define those measurable characteristics of the job that will allow us to make judgments about the success or failure of a person in that job. If we have well-defined characteristics of a job well done in mind before we start, we will be better able to assess the validity of our selection procedures and won't have such problems.

Fairness and Legality   Title VII of the Civil Rights Act of 1964, as amended by the Equal Employment Opportunity Act of 1972, makes it illegal "to fail to hire or discharge any individual, or otherwise to discriminate against any individual with respect to his compensation, terms, conditions or privileges of employment because of such individual's race, color, religion, sex, or national origin." (Committee on Labor and Public Welfare, quoted in Howell & Dipboye, 1982, p. 247). Through many court cases, the issue involved in this federal law (and its many interpretations) is essentially an issue of fairness and validity.

A second means of determining the fairness of selection procedures is to consider if the procedures create an adverse impact on one of the affected, or protected, minority groups. Adverse impact is often interpreted in terms of what is called the *4/5 rule*. What this amounts to goes something like this. Assume that 50 white males apply for a job with a given company, and 5 are hired. If there are 50 black applicants, let's say, for jobs at the same company, hiring 4 of the 50 (4/5 or 80 percent of the number of white hires) would be acceptable. Hiring only 3 or fewer (fewer than 4/5 of the number of whites) would not be acceptable. Fair employment cases that make it to court (and most do not) first address the determination of adverse impact. "Although a number of fairness models exist, none enjoys unconditional acceptance either in the profession or in the courts. In short, disagreement over the appropriate means for implementing fairness and EEO has not been resolved in the almost 20 years since the passage of Title VII" (Zedeck & Cascio, 1984, p. 497).

In terms of validity, courts have held that psychological assessment devices must fairly measure the knowledge and skills required by a particular job, and it is the responsibility of the employer to *demonstrate* that its tests do just that (Bersoff, 1981). Abstract, even logical, arguments about the possible relationship between a selection device and a hire/no-hire decision will not suffice. An employer must demonstrate the validity of its personnel selection procedures.

What is fair is often determined in the eye of the beholder. Rulings based on adverse impact may seem fair to some, but may not seem fair to the individual applicant. It is safe to say that the final word on the legal status of psychological testing in the context of making decisions about employees has not been heard. As Bersoff puts it, "legal scrutiny of psychological testing is both a present and future reality" (1981, p. 1055).

Before you go on
How may we determine the validity of personnel selection procedures?

EMPLOYEE TRAINING, SATISFACTION, AND PRODUCTIVITY

Although personnel selection is an important aspect of the job of an industrial/organizational psychologist, it is just one of many. In this section, we'll examine three related concerns about employees already on the payroll: training and development, job satisfaction, and productivity. It is clear to all of us that these three aspects of life in the workplace should be interrelated, and they are, but not always in obvious ways. We'll consider each of these complex factors in turn.

Training and Employee Development

Retraining employees to learn new skills and procedures will help keep worker motivation high and will also help industries stay abreast of new technologies.

training
a systematic, intentional process of altering the behaviors of employees to increase organizational effectiveness

The training and development of employees is one of the major concerns of business and industry. The cost of training in business (and government) runs into billions of dollars every year (Landy, 1985, p. 263). After reviewing more than 200 experimental studies dealing with psychological approaches to productivity improvement, Katzell and Guzzo concluded that, "Training and instruction activities represent the most frequently reported approach to productivity improvement during 1971–1981" (1983, p. 469). Typically, training programs are found to be successful in a variety of organizational settings, with various types of personnel, and in terms of a number of productivity criteria, including quantity and quality of work, cost reduction, turnover, absenteeism, and accident reduction (Katzell & Guzzo, 1983).

For almost any job, the training of new employees will be a must. The training of existing employees is motivated by a number of factors, including newly introduced procedures or techniques for doing a given job, relocation or reassignment within the company, the introduction of a new line of products or services, or the desire to maintain workers' levels of motivation on the job or to improve their attitudes toward their job and the company. These are the very concerns that have led Jack Phillips to consider beginning a training program at AFF.

In the context of industrial/organizational psychology, **training** has a specific and somewhat narrow definition. Training is taken to mean "a systematic intentional process of altering behavior of organizational members in a direction which contributes to organizational effectiveness" (Hinrichs, 1976). This definition implies that training is an activity intended by an organization to increase the skills or abilities of employees to do the job to which they have been assigned. Training implies some systematic intervention, as opposed to a hit-or-miss approach to instruction.

In business and industry, we talk about *training programs.* Developing a successful training program is a multifaceted enterprise. We'll review here the steps involved in designing and implementing a training program. Our analysis is based on the system proposed by Goldstein (1974) and is summarized in Figure 33.1. You might want to follow along in this flow-chart of the major aspects of designing a training program.

Training programs are usually designed to address some need within the organization. As such, the first thing you will have to do is a complete assessment of instructional needs. In many ways, a needs assessment in this context is rather like a job analysis in personnel selection. There are a number of basic questions that must be raised and answered at this critical stage. Just what is the problem that training is supposed to solve? Is production down? Is there a new product that salespeople need to know about? Is the accident rate getting too high? The first stage of assessing instructional needs will be to state the general goals of your training program. The second step requires

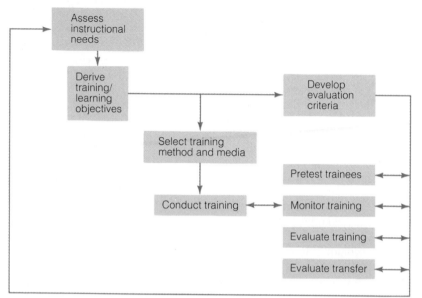

Figure 33.1
A flow-chart diagram of the steps involved in planning and conducting a training program.
(Adapted from Goldstein, 1984.)

translating these general goals into actual training objectives. At this stage, general statements of possible outcomes will no longer suffice. Here we need *specific* statements of what we expect the training program to accomplish. Just what do you want trainees to know or be able to do at the end of the training session that they do not know or do not do now? It is usually in terms of these specific learning or behavioral objectives that a training program will be evaluated.

With your objectives in mind, but before you begin actual training, you will want to specify criteria by which your training can be evaluated when it is over. Clearly, your criteria for evaluating your program will be closely related to the needs and objectives of the program. For your evaluation to be effective, it is important to list now, before training begins, how you will evaluate outcomes. There are many factors you might want to consider here. Did the trainees develop the skills and acquire the information you intended? How did the trainees feel about the program? And, importantly, did the training program have any impact on the organizational needs that prompted the training in the first place? To assist in this evaluation, you might want to consider designing a pretest procedure to assess your trainees in terms of their present skill or information level. Such pretesting may provide a means of determining the impact of your program.

With your listing of criteria for assessing outcomes determined, you now must turn your attention to how you will go about the actual training. Given what you know about your needs and objectives and what you know about your employees, what will be the most efficient type of training mechanism you can use to reach your specified goals? It goes without saying that the particular method for training that you choose to implement will depend at least in part on the training objectives and organizational needs you are facing at the moment.

There are many different methods that might be used in a training program. If there is any general conclusion we can draw concerning their effectiveness it might be than no one is universally better than any other. In some cases, bringing workers together for what amounts to classroom instruction works well. At the same time, there are certainly situations in which assembling large numbers of workers would be unrealistic. Automobile manufacturers, for example, can hardly be expected to have all car salespeople report to the home office for instruction on improvements in the new models of cars they will be selling. Occasionally, training has to go to the worker—in the form of printed material, audio cassettes, videotaped programs, and the like—rather than having the worker go to the training.

In either case, as designer of a training program, you will have many decisions to make about the methods you will use in your training program. Should you use "live" instructors, or should information be presented in the form of some media: print, audiotapes, videotapes, videodisks, and the like? Should training be formalized and time-limited, or can trainees be allowed to work individually, at their own pace? Will there need to be hands on experience? Will training be in groups or individually oriented? Will on-the-job training be efficient or disruptive? Can the job be simply simulated for the purposes of training? As you can see, your options are many, and all should be considered. Too many trainers fall into the habit of using only one or two training techniques for a range of different needs and objectives. For example, televised instruction may be very useful to point out new features of an automobile to a salesperson, but quite ineffective as a means of training a service person how to repair a new electronic ignition system.

Having decided on a training technique, you are ready to begin. If you have worked through the procedures outlined so far, actually conducting the training will be relatively easy. We should add, of course, that you will continually monitor the effectiveness of the training program as it runs its course. Even the best of plans sometimes need to be adjusted during actual training.

When you have finished your training program, you are ready to consider (again) what may be the most difficult part of training and development: evaluating the success of your training and the extent that your training transfers to the actual job in the workplace and thus meets the organizational needs that prompted the training originally. There are many difficulties involved in doing quality evaluations of training programs, and we need not review them here. We will only make two important points: (1) training programs that do not include ways and means of evaluating short and long term effectiveness will generally be of little value, and (2) the more effort put into the assessment of needs and the establishment of training objectives at the beginning of a training project, the easier it will be to evaluate the program when it is over.

Before you go on

List some of the factors that need to be considered in the design and implementation of a training program.

Job Satisfaction

Industrial/organizational psychologists have been studying the factors that lead to job satisfaction for many years. Indeed, studies of worker satisfaction were among the first major research efforts of I/O psychology (Hoppock, 1935; Mayo, 1933). If we know nothing else about job satisfaction, we know that it is a complex concept. For one thing, job satisfaction is a cognitive reaction and, hence, is not subject to direct observation. A worker's satisfaction with his or her job must be inferred, usually from questionnaire data.

I/O psychologists have found that regardless of the job, employee satisfaction is based on such things as physical conditions, job security, salary adequacy, fringe benefits, self-esteem, and relations with coworkers. Those who rank their jobs high in these areas are likely to be satisfied workers.

Although we may talk about job satisfaction in general terms, it is clear that an employee's level of satisfaction may vary considerably for different aspects of the job itself. As you know from your own work experience, an employee may be quite happy with physical working conditions, very unhappy with base salary, relatively pleased with the availability of fringe benefits, satisfied with the level of challenge provided by the job, very dissatisfied with relationships with coworkers, and so on. We may argue that there are as many sources of satisfaction and/or dissatisfaction as there are aspects to one's job.

It is often the task of the I/O psychologist to determine just which of all the factors that may influence one's satisfaction with the job are most important in any particular setting. There are many possible factors to be considered, including the physical characteristics of the workplace, the mental strain of the job, the challenge inherent in the job, the quality of reward for one's work, communication with supervisory personnel, the opportunity to influence company policy and procedure, opportunities for promotion or advancement, and so on.

Recently, I/O psychologists have become interested in a concept even broader than job satisfaction, which is called **quality of work life,** or **QWL,** and how to develop strategies to improve the quality of work life (Lawler, 1982; Tuttle, 1983). QWL is a difficult concept to define concisely, but may be taken to include such factors as:

quality of work life (QWL)
those aspects of the work situation that influence an employee's attitudes or evaluation of his or her position, including job satisfaction

1. Employment conditions (safety, health, physical environment).

2. Employee security (future of the job).

3. Income adequacy (now and in the future).

4. Equity of pay and other rewards.

5. Worker autonomy and independence.

6. Opportunities for social interaction.

7. Self-esteem.

8. Democracy (worker participation in decision making).

9. Worker satisfaction (Davis & Cherns, 1975).

Now that we have a sense of what we mean by job satisfaction and quality of work life, let's consider worker productivity and performance; then we can examine the relationship between the two.

Before you go on

What is meant by job satisfaction and quality of work life?

How are these concepts usually measured?

Productivity

You might think that defining *productivity* would be much simpler than defining satisfaction. Such is not the case. Even within the same company, productivity can be viewed from a number of varied perspectives, each valid in its own way (Tuttle, 1983). Accountants may view productivity in terms of bottom-line profits and losses; economists may take a somewhat broader view, examining input/output ratios; managers tend to find themselves defining productivity in terms of many variables, including absenteeism, employee turnover, and resources spent on training.

The psychologist studying productivity tends to focus on the effectiveness ("doing the right things") and efficiency ("doing things right") of employees within an organization (Tuttle, 1983, p. 483). Is everything being done *by* the organization, *in* the organization to make each and every employee as productive as possible? For example, if flange production is down for the month of February because a blizzard cut off supplies to the plant, Jack Phillips, as vice-president of operations, will be concerned about productivity and will try to locate other sources of supplies nearby. The I/O psychologist's view of productivity, however, will tend to be more concerned about the behaviors of employees (human resources) within the plant and less concerned about material resources.

In their review of factors that influence employee productivity, Katzell and Guzzo (1983) examined 11 intervention techniques that had been studied experimentally. Most worked to some extent, prompting the conclusion that "psychology has much to offer to the improvement of employee productivity" (p. 472). Of those factors that affect the productivity of workers, the most successful include two types of programs we've already reviewed: (1) a careful, well-designed program of employee *recruitment and selection,* and (2) programs for the *training and instruction* of present employees. Other factors found to have a significant influence on productivity were: (1) providing employees with individualized *feedback and counseling* concerning their jobs, (2) involving employees in *goal setting* (although these effects may not be long-lasting), and (3) *financial compensation,* where linking compensation to productivity (as in incentive programs) seems to be most effective (from Katzell & Guzzo, 1983).

Now we can return to an issue we alluded to earlier: the evidence concerning the relationship between quality of work life and employee productivity.

The Relationship Between Satisfaction and Productivity

There is a certain logic to the assertion that the happy worker is a productive worker—that increased job satisfaction will necessarily be reflected in increased worker productivity. For the last 50 years, many managers and executives have assumed without question a causal relationship between satisfaction and productivity. In many ways, satisfaction and productivity *may* be related, but the relationship is not a simple one.

Interest in how human relations issues relate to measures of employee performance date back at least to the Hawthorne studies of the 1920s and 1930s (see Topic Expansion). Yet even after all these years, the only conclusion we can safely draw about these two variables is that in some instances, they may be correlated. Cause-and-effect statements are out of the question.

In fact, research on job satisfaction refutes the contention that increased performance necessarily results from increased satisfaction. That is not to say that satisfaction is not important, but rather that improving a worker's job satisfaction will not *necessarily* increase his or her effectiveness or efficiency (Howell & Dipboye, 1982, p. 81). Over and over, we find contradictory evidence, which among other things reflects the difficulties involved in agreeing on operational definitions for both quality of work life and productivity. Tuttle (1983) argues that quality of working life and productivity are conceptually distinct but related concepts; he claims, too, that "most authors would agree that productivity improvements frequently accompany improvements in quality of working life" (p. 483). We simply need to remember that such relationships are not necessarily to be found, nor do they suggest a cause-and-effect relationship.

The lack of a consistent relationship between satisfaction and productivity may not be that difficult to explain. Some workers may hate their present jobs, but work very hard at them so that they may be promoted to some other position that they believe they will prefer. Some individuals may be very satisfied with their present positions simply because expectations for productivity are low—if demands for productivity increase, satisfaction may decrease, at least in this situation. Increasing productivity may have the effect of increasing satisfaction, rather than vice versa. A well-motivated employee, who wants to do her very best at her job, will be pleased to enter a training program to improve her on-the-job efficiency. Doing the job better leads to pride and an overall increase in satisfaction—for this worker; for another, the same training program may be viewed as a ploy on management's part to make life miserable for the worker.

As we have so often found in our study of psychology, even issues that appear simple on first inspection often become terribly complex. And, as is so often the case, at least some of the difficulties here revolve around matters of definition and measurement. It seems clear that for many years to come, research and programmatic interventions on the quality of work life and employee productivity will continue to be central issues in I/O psychology.

Before you go on
What is the relationship between job satisfaction and job productivity?

THE ORGANIZATION OF ORGANIZATIONS

One thing we all recognize about the world of work is that it almost always takes place within some structured organization. As our Mr. Phillips contemplates hiring a new plant manager and faces contract negotiations, one thing he will be thinking about is how the systems that together make up Amalgamated Flange Fabrications, Inc. can best be organized. In this context, *organization* usually means the policies and procedures by which things get done within a group. Policy and procedures generally are established by top management (or evolve slowly over the years) and are passed down, eventually to the rank and file worker. That is, within any organization, there are rules for how things are to be done: who one should see with a complaint, how much overtime is allowable, who may discuss what with whom, what is required for promotion, minimum standards of job performance, and so on.

There are many different philosophies, or theories, of how a business (for example) can best be organized. (Organizational psychology can certainly be applied to systems other than those in business and industry.) Some (classic) approaches see the worker as simply a cog in a physical structure or organization of production, where workers can be replaced and interchanged as easily as pieces of equipment. Other (human relations) approaches focus on organizing the workplace to accommodate human needs for safety, socialization, belongingness, recognition, and the like.

Some theories emphasize leadership styles and the characteristics of executives or managers as being central concerns. Some theories focus on the beliefs held by managers about the workers under their control (for example, the Theory X and Theory Y systems of McGregor, 1960).

Ouchi's (1981) popular *Theory Z* approach to organizational structure and function is an example of an organizational theory that has become widely accepted in the business community, without being very well tested. Essentially, Ouchi's position is that American businesses could profit from adapting some of their long-standing policies and procedures to more closely approximate those of Japanese companies. That is, there should be more concern with job stability, more involvement of the employee in the decision-making process, more slow and careful employee evaluation and promotion, and more concern for the worker beyond the confines of the workplace, for instance. Although many of these steps are sensible (and most of them are not new), they have not yet been put to the empirical test in a wide variety of situations. If we rely on past experience, what we may predict is that there are some businesses that will profit from attempts to follow Ouchi's advice, and there are some that will eventually fail.

Once again we find that the most consistent finding that we have about organizational structure and theory is that no one model or system is best. In fact, it is even difficult to suggest that any one organizational scheme is best for any one particular purpose.

Recently, psychologists have become increasingly interested in the implicit, or underlying, organization of groups. That is, there is for any organization an implicit set of rules and regulations (norms) that members know and react to that are not stated in official policy. "Everybody knows that you just don't contradict Charlie when he makes a suggestion." "If you've got a new idea, for goodness sake keep it to yourself!" "Complaining to Ruth will do no good at all; it's okay, though, to go over her head if you really feel that you should." Lists of this sort of insider's knowledge of organizations could go on and on. It is becoming an important job of I/O psychologists to determine the perception of these implicit policies and procedures, sometimes referred to as "corporate culture" (Kilman, 1985).

Management should know about such implicit policies, particularly the self-defeating and disruptive perceptions that employees have about an organization. Occasionally, what an I/O psychologist discovers about an organization is what a top executive wants to hear. It has been suggested that the culture and health of a company is most affected by its top executives, and some of them may have organizational styles that do not contribute to the well-being of the company. Manfred Kets de Vries, a professor of organizational behavior, and Danny Miller, a professor of management policy, suggest that such leadership styles deserve to be labeled as "neurotic" (1984). Neurotic managerial styles will ultimately be reflected in unhealthy companies (de Vries & Miller, 1984). When, for example, executives become suspicious and distrusting of employees—as well as competitors—the organization may take on "paranoid" characteristics, filled with searches for quality information and rumors about who's in trouble with whom. As a lack of trust generalizes throughout the organization, communication, problem solving, and decision making ultimately break down.

Before you go on

What are some of the concerns of psychologists who study organizations?

In this brief topic, we can hardly do more than begin to mention some of the areas of concern of those psychologists who work for and in business and industry. They are very much interested in theories and research, but most often the concerns they face day to day are of a practical and applied nature. In addition to the areas of personnel selection, training, quality of work life, productivity, and organization that we have discussed here, there are many other areas in which I/O psychologists are involved. These include such wide-ranging concerns as developing marketing strategies for a new product, developing assistance programs for employees with psychological problems, helping in the design of a piece of machinery so that it can be operated most efficiently and safely, and designing workshops to improve management/employee communication. To work most effectively in the setting of business and industry, the I/O psychologist falls back on a knowledge and understanding of many basic psychological principles, from sensation, perception, learning, memory, human development, motivation, personality theory and measurement, and social psychology.

One of the first experimental interventions in an industrial setting was begun in 1924 at the Hawthorne plant of the Chicago Western Electric Company in Cicero, Illinois. Among other things, the plant assembled electric relays used in the manufacture of telephones. The studies begun here lasted for more than a decade. In fact, a number of separate experiments were conducted through these years, but we will refer to them collectively as the Hawthorne studies. The results of these experiments were controversial when they were first described, and they continue to be controversial.

It all started innocently enough. The initial issue was whether or not the level of lighting in the factory had a measurable effect on production. What the researchers found was that as they varied illumination, production tended to increase. What was surprising was that production tended to increase whether illumination was increased or decreased, and in one study, production increased when the workers *thought* that illumination was being changed when in fact it was not changed at all. How curious! A noticeable effect was being produced on worker output, but there was no clear relationship between that output and the manipulations of the experimenters.

In another series of experiments, output also appeared to increase steadily regardless of specific manipulations of an independent variable. Five women were separated from other workers and put in a special room where a number of variables were studied. One factor that was changed was the style of the supervision these workers received. A number of physical changes were also introduced, including rest breaks, free lunch periods, and shorter working hours. When these benefits were intro-

duced, production increased, and when they were then eliminated, production also appeared to increase. As we shall see, the key word here is "appeared."

Two university psychologists, Elton Mayo (1933) and Fritz Roethlisberger (Roethlisberger & Dickson, 1939) analyzed the findings of the Hawthorne experiments and came to some rather sweeping generalizations about the nature of the workplace, relations between management and the worker, and the relationship between job satisfaction and productivity. One of their conclusions has become so entrenched in psychology it has been given a label: *the Hawthorne Effect*. The Hawthorne Effect is "the tendency of human beings to be influenced by special attention from others" (Stagner, 1982). The straightforward translation of this principle is that workers (or anyone else) will change (or improve) their behavior (or productivity) if they are led to believe that someone cares about what they are doing.

Mayo and Roethlisberger explained the improved performance of workers largely in terms of humane treatment and enlightened management practices that involved workers in decision making and tended to the personal and social needs of employees. For example, the output of the five assemblers increased because of changes in supervisory style and because they were clearly treated differently—given their own special room and work hours—regardless of what that difference was. At least that was the argument. It is commonly claimed that what we now call the *human relations movement* in industry began with this interpretation of the data from the Hawthorne plant experiments.

Three important points need to be made concerning the Hawthorne studies and their subsequent inter-

pretations. First, early analyses significantly overstated the actual effects of some of the experimental interventions. For example, weekly productivity *did* increase when workers were switched from a schedule that included breaks and a free lunch to a schedule of solid work time, *but* hourly production actually declined. Total output increased only because the workers spent more hours during each week actually working, even though they worked at a slower pace. Second, very little mention was made in early reports of significant flaws in experimental design and of the lack of naïvete of the subjects/workers who were often told what the experimenters were trying to do (Parsons, 1974). Finally, resistance on the part of workers to some of the changes instituted at the Hawthorne plant were downplayed in early analyses. In fact, two of the original five workers in the special room were dismissed from the experiment for "gross insubordination and low output" and were replaced with two other workers (Bramel & Friend, 1981, p. 871).

Even with these flaws, the Hawthorne studies are of significant and lasting historical importance. Though the Hawthorne Effect was overstated in early reports, it has been reliably observed in a wide range of situations. The fact that managers and psychologists today are showing renewed concern for the quality of work life is an idea that can be traced to the Hawthorne studies.

In brief, the experiments done at the Hawthorne plant were often basically flawed and misinterpreted (or overinterpreted), but they were landmark efforts of industrial psychology's early days. They led the way for the many other experimental manipulations that followed.

What is involved in doing a job analysis?

Doing a proper job analysis involves constructing a complete and specific description of the activities performed by someone in a given position, a listing of those characteristics required to do the job well, and a means of evaluating the performance of a person in that job. This information is accumulated through an inspection of official documents, interviews, questionnaires, and the direct observation of job activities. / 616

What are some of the sources of information that can be used in making personnel decisions.

Once a job analysis has been completed, personnel selection involves compiling a series of assessment tools to measure the relevant characteristics of applicants. Many such tools are available, including application forms, interviews, paper-and-pencil tests, projective tests, situational tests, and assessment center approaches. / 618

How may we determine the validity of personnel selection procedures?

In the context of personnel selection, validity deals with the extent to which selection devices actually determine the right person for a given job. Validity is commonly determined by correlations of selection devices with measurements of criteria behaviors, such as supervisor ratings, or some other on-the-job assessment of performance. / 619

List some of the factors that need to be considered in the design and implementation of a training program.

A number of factors need to be considered in the design and implementation of an employee training program. These include an assessment of the organization's instructional needs, the development of specific learning/training objectives, means by which training will be evaluated, and the selection of appropriate methods and media for the actual training. Once training has begun, it should be constantly monitored to see if objectives are being met, and after training has been completed, the program itself should be evaluated, as should the transfer of information and skills from training to actual on-the-job performance. / 622

What is meant by job satisfaction and quality of work life? How are these concepts usually measured?

Job satisfaction and quality of work life are complex concepts, usually inferred from interview and questionnaire data. In the broadest sense, job satisfaction is a measure of an employee's evaluation of his or her position in an organization. QWL involves many factors, such as appraisals of employment conditions, job security, compensation, autonomy and independence, opportunities for social interaction, self-esteem, and participation in the decision-making process. / 624

What is the relationship between job satisfaction and job productivity?

Although job satisfaction and productivity are related, there is very little evidence to suggest that one causes the other. Interventions designed to improve satisfaction often do increase production levels, but interventions designed to improve production often increase job satisfaction. We may say that quality of work life and productivity are conceptually distinct, but related concepts. / 625

What are some of the concerns of psychologists who study organizations?

Organizational theory is basically concerned with the policies and procedures of a group, usually a business or industry. Relevant policies often deal with leadership, communication, standards of performance, physical layout, policies for salary increments, and the like. The implicit, unwritten policies of a corporation or organization are often as powerful in determining individual behavior as are the formal official policies of an organization. / 627

TOPIC 34 Other Fields of Applied Psychology

PSYCHOLOGISTS BECOME INVOLVED IN RESEARCH ON AIDS

Acquired immune deficiency syndrome (AIDS) is a fatal disease that has become the number one priority of the U.S. Public Health Service. By mid-1985, more than 20,000 cases were detected. The disease largely affects gay and bisexual men (approximately 70 percent of reported cases). Recently, psychologists have joined with medical researchers and immunologists in the study of this silent killer. Psychologists are most involved in determining the characteristics and behavioral patterns of individuals most likely to contract the disease, in designing information and training programs to help prevent the spread of AIDS, and in addressing the psychological impact of the disease on the patient, friends, and family.

PSYCHOLOGICAL PREPARATION GIVES WORLD-CLASS ATHLETES AN ADVANTAGE

In addition to training their bodies to the peak of athletic perfection, Olympic athletes are also spending time training their minds to improve their performance. Sports psychologists have become an integral part of the training program of many athletes, both amateur and professional. "Physical preparation is no longer enough if you want to be a winner," said one track star.

THE STRESS OF OVERCROWDING MAKES CITY LIFE UNBEARABLE FOR SOME, CHALLENGING FOR OTHERS

Conditions of overcrowding have long been known to have adverse effects on rats, and it is usually assumed that people living in crowded urban settings suffer similar negative consequences. Recent research suggests that the crowded conditions of city life may also have benefits and may provide a sort of support for the individual that is not found elsewhere.

HELP FOR DIABETICS FOUND IN BEHAVIOR MODIFICATION AND BIOFEEDBACK TECHNIQUES

Diabetes is a disease that affects nearly 10 million Americans. At the moment, there is no cure for diabetes, but its symptoms can be treated and its progress arrested through the careful administration of insulin and by effecting changes in the patient's style of life. The psychological techniques of biofeedback and behavior modification have recently been demonstrated to be of significant value in helping patients monitor their own glucose levels (so the patient knows how much insulin to take and when to take it) and in actually reducing the need for medication.

PSYCHOLOGISTS URGE CAUTION IN ACCEPTANCE OF EYEWITNESS TESTIMONY

American courts have long relied heavily on the value of eyewitness testimony, particularly in criminal cases. Psychologists point out that many factors may lead to a distortion of the perception of reality and the memory of events, particularly in emotional and stress-laden situations. Basically irrelevant characteristics of the witness may also affect jury deliberations.

HOW AN INFANT CRIES MAY PROVIDE EARLY DIAGNOSIS OF DEVELOPMENTAL PROBLEMS

SEAT-BELT USE CAN BE INCREASED THROUGH PROGRAMS OF PSYCHOLOGICAL INTERVENTION

BEING THE HOME TEAM MAY NOT ALWAYS BE AN ADVANTAGE

CHRONIC PAIN CAN BE LESSENED BY BEHAVIORAL MEANS

THE SHAPE OF A ROOM DETERMINES ITS PERCEIVED SIZE

PSYCHOLOGISTS ARGUE FOR NEW STRATEGIES IN THE FIGHT AGAINST DRUNK DRIVING

PATIENTS WITH ORGAN TRANSPLANTS REQUIRE HELP WITH PSYCHOLOGICAL ADJUSTMENTS

These headlines are fictitious. The stories they represent, however, are real. Each provides an example of recent interventions by psychologists into the world of social problems. Together they provide just a glimpse of the sorts of applications of psychological principles to real-life problems that are becoming more and more common. In this topic, we'll examine some of these issues of applied psychology.

In our first topic, we said that one of the goals of psychology is to understand the laws of behavior and mental processes. It is also one of psychology's goals to apply what we have learned about our subject matter. Most commonly we think of applying psychology in the context of diagnosis and therapy for psychological disorders. Then we might think of the applications of the psychological principles of learning and memory to education and child rearing. In our last topic, we saw that there is a wide variety of psychological data and research that is relevant to business and industry.

In this topic, we'll briefly examine four additional areas in which behavioral and psychological principles have proven to be usefully applied: the environment, health, the law, and sports.

This topic is not meant to be a complete examination of the many areas of applied psychology. Rather, our goal here is to examine the sorts of issues in which psychologists are becoming involved and to point out some of the applications that psychologists have made in these areas.

PSYCHOLOGY AND THE ENVIRONMENT

environmental psychology
the field of applied psychology that studies the effect of the environment on persons in it

Some environmental psychologists are involved in designing physical spaces to maximize the purpose for which that space is intended, such as in shopping malls.

Environmental psychology is the field in which psychologists study how the environment affects the behavior and mental processes of persons living in it. Environmental psychologists are also concerned with how individuals, in turn, affect their environments. This field tends to be an interdisciplinary endeavor. Environmental psychologists often work with urban planners, sociologists, economists, clinical psychologists, interior decorators, architects, and builders.

The range of specific interests in environmental psychology is very large. Some psychologists are interested in such factors as how lighting and color, for example, might affect workers' productivity, or students' learning, or hospital patients' mental and physical health. Some are concerned with behavioral and psychological reactions to the poisons, or toxins, that are present in our environments. Some are interested in the design and construction of physical space that maximizes the purpose for which that space is constructed. Others focus on the impact of crowding, territoriality, and adjustment to the demands of city living. Of course, many of these issues are interrelated.

Environmental psychologists recognize that what will influence behavior most is one's *perception* of the environment. A room with 10 persons in it may appear to be terribly small and crowded if it is perceived as an office. The same room may appear quite large and uncrowded if the walls are painted white, the lighting is made brighter, and the furniture rearranged so that the room is perceived as a waiting area. In fact, two rooms of exactly the same area, one square and one rectangular, will not be perceived as being the same size; the rectangular room will appear larger than the square room (Sadalla & Oxley, 1984). Let's begin our introduction to environmental psychology by considering some of the issues involved in the perception of space and distance.

Before you go on

Define environmental psychology, and list some of the issues that environmental psychologists study.

Space and Territory

Imagine that you are seated in the library, studying at a large table. There is no one else at your table. Then another student enters the room and sits right next to you. Although there are seven other chairs at your table, this student chooses to sit in the one just to your left. Or imagine that you are in the process of buying a used car. While you are examining a late-model sports car, a salesperson approaches you, stands right in front of you (not more than 8 inches away) and begins to tell you about all the positive features of the car you are looking at. Or imagine that in your psychology class you always sit in the same seat. The semester is about over, and you have gotten to know some of the people who habitually sit near you. On Friday when you go to class, you find that there is someone else in "your seat." Or imagine that you are a suburban homeowner. You have spent a number of years getting your backyard to look just the way you want it to. Then, neighborhood children discover that going through your rose garden makes a good short-cut to school.

In each of these scenarios—and in hundreds of others we might easily imagine—you will probably feel a sense of discomfort. Your personal space or your territory has been invaded without invitation. The study of the effects of invading personal space and territory has been an active research area for environmental psychologists.

Personal space is mobile. It goes with you wherever you go. It is an imaginary bubble of space that surrounds you and into which others may enter comfortably by invitation only. The extent of your personal space depends on the situation, as well as a number of factors, including your age (Aiello & Aiello, 1974) and sex (Evans & Howard, 1973), and who the "intruder" happens to be. You will be much more likely to allow an invasion of your personal space by someone you know well or by an attractive member of the opposite sex.

personal space
the bubble of space around an individual which is reserved for intimate relationships and into which others may enter with welcome by invitation only

The anthropologist Edward Hall (1966) has demonstrated that the extent of one's personal space is also determined in part by one's culture. Westerners, for example, tend to require larger personal spaces than do either Arabs or Japanese. Hall also claims that within a cultural setting, personal space may be subdivided into a number of different distances, each relevant for a different type of social interaction. *Intimate distance,* for example, is defined as being between actual contact and approximately 18 inches. This space tends to be reserved for special, intimate communications: displays of affection by lovers, offerings of comfort, and the like. This space is usually reserved only for people whom you know very well and care about, and you will feel uncomfortable if someone else is in it.

Intimate distance extends from actual physical contact to about 18 inches from the body. It is usually reserved for displays of affection and offerings of comfort.

Personal distance, according to Hall, is reserved for day-to-day interactions with acquaintances and friends. It extends from about 18 inches to approximately 4 feet, just beyond arm's length. This space becomes relevant in social gatherings, such as parties, in which small clusters of persons gather around to share in conversation. Actual physical contact in this sort of situation is unusual and generally unwelcomed. We usually keep our bubble of personal space adjusted to this size.

Hall refers to the distance of 4 to 12 feet as our *social distance.* This distance is appropriate for social interactions with persons we do not know well. It may commonly include some sort of physical barrier, such as a desk or table, between us and others around us. Within this space, communication can still continue, but there is an implied message of lack of intimacy and aloofness. This is the distance one uses when conducting business or at formal meetings.

Personal distance is reserved for day-to-day interactions with acquaintances and friends—at a party, for example; while social distance is appropriate for social interactions with persons we do not know well—such as in business meetings.

Finally, there is *public distance,* in which personal contact is minimized, though communication remains possible. This distance is defined as being between 12 and 25 feet. Formal lectures in large classrooms, performances given from a stage, or after-dinner talks given from behind the head table may be examples. Because of the distances involved, communication in these settings tends to flow in one direction.

The point of this delineation of personal space is that we tend to feel pressured, stressed, or discomforted whenever these distances are violated. When that perfect stranger sits right next to you in the library, he or she is violating your personal space. The salesman with his or her nose almost touching yours is violating your intimate space. When a lecturer leaves the podium and begins to wander through the audience, we may feel strange because our defined social space is being invaded.

Territoriality is also related to an individual's use of space in the environment. It involves the setting off and marking of a piece of territory (a geographical location) as one's own. It is the tendency to want to declare that "this space is mine; it's my turf and someone else can enter here only at my request."

territoriality
the setting off and marking of a piece of territory (a location) as one's own

Territoriality was first studied extensively in nonhuman animals (e.g., Lorenz, 1969). Many species of animals have been observed to establish and defend geographical areas that they use either for finding and hunting food or for mating and rearing their young. These territories are often defended vigorously—most commonly with ritualistic posturing and threats of aggression, but occasionally with actual combat.

It seems clear that people, too, establish territories as their own, not to be entered without invitation. While reviewing the evidence for territoriality in humans, Altman (1975) noted that like personal space, our defined territories vary in their value to us. Some are *primary,* or personal, territories, defined by us as ours and no one else's. "This is my room, and you'd better stay out of it." We tend to invest heavily in our primary territories. We decorate our homes, yards, apartments, or dormitory rooms to put our mark on our space. Primary territories will be claimed for the long term, well marked, and defended. By controlling our primary territory, we can maintain a sense of privacy and a sense of identity. Evidence of such a territoriality among humans is all around us. The miles of chain-link fence that are sold each year

Animals often use postures and threats of aggression to establish and maintain their territories.

Humans generally have two types of territories: primary, which is space defined and marked as our own, and secondary, which is space for social interactions—such as on an elevated train.

provide testimony to the human need to establish a separate, primary territory.

Altman also suggests that we are sensitive to two other types of territory: *secondary* and *public*. As individuals, we are less concerned with secondary territories than we are with primary ones. Secondary territories are more flexible and less well defined. They tend to be areas we set aside for social gatherings, not so much for personal privacy. If you and your friends always sit at the same table in the cafeteria at lunchtime, you have established a secondary territory. Although you will feel upset if someone else claims "your table" for lunch, you will be less likely to start a major fuss to reclaim it than if someone had invaded a primary territory. Members of the faculty may stake out a room in a college building as a faculty lounge and will be quite upset to discover students using it, even if they are using it to study. Secondary territories are not owned by those who use them and tend not to be used for expressing personal identity. That is, there may be a sign on the door that says "Faculty Lounge," but the area can be used for other functions, and an occasional intrusion by nonfaculty will probably be tolerated.

Public territories are those we tend to occupy for only a short time. They are not ours in any literal sense, and we will not feel much distress if these territories are violated. While waiting for your plane, you sit in a seat in the airport terminal and place your luggage at your feet. You get up for just a minute to buy a newspaper, and when you return, you discover that someone has claimed your seat. In such a situation, you may be momentarily annoyed, but you will not have much difficulty simply finding another seat—rather than starting a confrontation.

Personal space and territories that we claim as our own serve many functions. They provide a sense of structure and continuity in what otherwise may seem to be a complex and ever-changing environment. They help us claim some sense of identity. They help us set ourselves apart from others. They regulate and reinforce needs for privacy. When space and territory are violated, we may predict negative outcomes: anxiety, distress, and sometimes even aggressive attempts of reclamation.

Before you go on
Define the concepts of personal space and territoriality.

Urban dwellers often face heavily crowded environments, which can lead to discomfort and stress.

Life in the City—An Example

In the early 1960s, Calhoun (e.g., 1962) first published the results of his experiments on overcrowding of rats. The data were impressive and intriguing. Calhoun raised colonies of rats in a number of different environments. In some, population density was allowed (encouraged) to increase to the point where the overcrowding began to affect the behavior of the rats within the colony. Male rats became aggressive; newborn rats were often cannibalized or ignored and left to die; female rats became less receptive to sexual advances from male rats; and when mating did occur, litter size tended to decrease, apparently in response to the pressures of colony overpopulation. As you might imagine, it didn't take long for a number of psychologists to apply the data from Calhoun's rat studies to life in modern cities. Indeed, early investigators found a number of correlations between population density and negative behavioral consequences, such as mental illness, crime, stress, and delinquency (Altman, 1975; Freedman, 1975).

As psychologists began to look more closely at the lives of people in urban environments, it became clear that the translation of the data from Calhoun's rats to residents of our metropolitan centers was not all that straightforward. The first thing we need to do is distinguish between two easily confused terms. The first is **population density;** it is the number of persons (or animals) per unit of area. It is an objective, descriptive concept. **Crowding,** on the other hand, is more of a psychological concept. It is a subjective feeling of discomfort or distress produced by a lack of space. Crowding may be quite independent of the number of persons involved. That is, you might feel very crowded and uncomfortable if you had to sit in the back seat of a small car with just two other people, and not at all crowded when you all get to the football stadium and are jammed together with 60,000 others to watch a football game.

Crowding is a negative condition, one that leads to discomfort and stress. As such, it tends to produce a number of negative consequences (see our discussion of stress in Topic 22 or the reviews by Altman and Freedman cited above). But it is incorrect to conclude, or assume, that living in a densely populated city *necessarily* produces negative consequences. Other potential stressors, such as noise, pollution, and the threat of crime, that we commonly associate with city life may be more than offset by better medical care, better sanitation, and systems for handling emergencies of all kinds (Creekmore, 1985). Many of the advantages of city living will be unavailable to residents of smaller communities. For example, few cities with populations of less than

population density
a quantitative measure of the number of persons (or animals) per unit of area

crowding
the subjective feeling of discomfort caused by a sense of lack of space

50,000 can support symphony orchestras, opera companies, museums, and art galleries. Nor can they afford stadiums and arenas for professional sports (Barker, 1966). The challenge for environmental psychologists is to help urban planners and architects design living spaces in areas of high population density that minimize the subjective experience of crowding while maintaining privacy and expressions of individual territoriality.

Before you go on

What is the difference between population density and crowding?

What are some of the positive and negative aspects of city living?

Noise, Temperature, and Environmental Toxins

In this section, we'll review some of the evidence that suggests that three classes of environmental variables can have a profound effect on behavior. We'll consider noise, temperature, and environmental toxins (poisons) and how they affect human performance.

Noise   Noise may be defined as any intrusive, unwanted, or excessive experience of sound. Almost any environment will be filled with some level of background noise, and noise per se need not be disruptive or stressful. As we have seen (Topic 7), the total absence of sound can induce stress. Noise becomes most stressful when it is loud, high-pitched, and unpredictable (Glass & Singer, 1972). Continued exposure to high intensity sound can produce lasting deafness (Scharf, 1978; Taylor et al., 1965), although prolonged exposure to high levels of noise seem to produce few other serious physical problems (Matlin, 1983). However, there is ample evidence that prolonged exposure to noise increases levels of stress and resultant increases in anxiety (and other psychological disorders), and also increases levels of aggressive behaviors (Bell, Fisher, & Loomis, 1978).

Noise levels also have predictable effects on the performance of cognitive tasks. Cohen and his associates (1980), for example, have demonstrated that children who attended schools near the busy Los Angeles airport tended to have higher blood pressure and were more easily distracted from their work than children who attended schools in quieter neighborhoods. Significantly, however, Glass and Singer (1972) suggest that absolute levels of background noise may not be the major determiner of disruption. What may matter more in the disruption of performance is the *predictability* of the noise. The results of one experiment (Glass, Singer, & Friedman, 1969) that demonstrated this phenomenon are presented in Figure 34.1.

Subjects were given the task of trying to solve problems that, in fact, had no solution. Subjects worked on these puzzles under three levels of background noise. In one condition, there was no noise; in a second, a soft (68 decibel) noise was presented; in the third, a loud (110 decibel) noise was introduced. In the conditions using background noise, the predictability of the noise was also manipulated. In one condition, the occurrence of the noise was regular and predictable; in the other, the noise was introduced on a random schedule. The introduction of predictable noise did not significantly alter the subjects' persistence in working on the problems. The unpredictable noise, however, significantly reduced the number of trials that the subjects were willing to invest in the problem task.

Temperature   It seems clear that extremes of temperature can have adverse effects on behavior. It is probably the case that any task can be

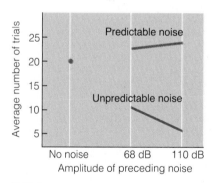

Figure 34.1
The effects of the predictability of noise as a distractor during a cognitive task. When stimulus noise occurred unpredictably, subjects spent fewer trials attempting to solve insolvable puzzles.
(Based on Glass, Singer & Friedman, 1969.)

Environmental neurotoxin pollution can pose a serious threat not only to people's health, but also to their entire way of life. Illegal chemical dumping has forced many families out of their homes.

neurotoxins
chemicals (poisons) that affect psychological processes through the nervous system

accomplished most effectively within a range of moderate environmental temperatures (Baron, 1977). It is no doubt important, for example, to try to keep the temperature of a workplace within reasonable limits. If temperatures become excessively hot or cold, performance will tend to decrease, although the effects of temperature on performance depend in large measure on the type of task being performed.

Environmental psychologists have also been concerned with the effects that extremely high temperatures have on social interactions and on aggression, in particular. There is a common perception that riots and other more common displays of aggressive, violent behaviors are more frequent during the long, hot days of summer. To a certain extent, this observation is supported by the evidence. Baron and Ransberger (1978) point out that riots are most likely to occur when the outside temperature is only moderately high, between about 75° and 90°. But when temperatures get much above 90°, energy (even for aggression) becomes rapidly depleted, and rioting is less likely to occur.

It seems that temperature's disruptive effect on behavior (in terms of stress, aggression, and impaired performance) may not be a simple one. For any person and any task, there may be an optimal temperature level. Deviations in temperature both above and below this optimal level could then lead to disruptions of behavior.

Environmental Toxins As societies become more heavily invested in technological advancement, one of the accompanying side-effects is often an increased level of environmental pollutants. Psychologists concerned with issues of the quality of life are becoming more involved in issues concerning the quality of the environment.

Of the nearly 100,000 chemicals in use in this country's industries, nearly 600 have been declared dangerous in large doses by the federal government (Anderson, 1982). Many of the chemicals that poison the environment are classified as **neurotoxins** because they have their poisonous effects on the human nervous system. Even in small doses, they may cause detectable behavioral and emotional changes in individuals.

Environmental psychologists are involved in research on neurotoxins at a number of different levels. On the one hand, there are efforts of education—workers and consumers need to know about the short- and long-term effects of contact with chemical toxins. Because many of the effects of pollutants are psychological, and particularly because these chemicals may affect the behaviors of young children (and the unborn), it is becoming more and more common to find psychologists involved in the actual diagnosis of the effects of toxins (Fein et al., 1983). That is, exposure to neurotoxins may be more readily diagnosed through behavioral, psychological means than through medical diagnosis.

Just to give you an idea of the extent of the effects that neurotoxins may have on behavior, refer to Figure 34.2, in which you'll find listed some of the more common neurotoxins and the effects they are likely to have through prolonged exposure. Although some toxins are more likely to be found in some industrial settings than in others, it is reasonable to assume that even those of us who are not employed in these settings may be at some risk.

Before you go on
What are some of the effects that noise, extreme temperature, and neurotoxins have on behavior?

Figure 34.2

Workers at risk from neurotoxins.

Below, the principal neurotoxins used in industry, the symptoms associated with them, and the number of workers chronically exposed according to government estimates. Dashes mean that figures are unavailable or that workers are exposed only by accident. Chemicals in capital letters pose the greatest risk. (Data from the National Institute for Occupational Safety and Health.)

Substance	Industry	Year of First Report of Neurotoxicity	Effect	Number of Workers Potentially at Risk
CARBON MONOXIDE (CO)	Industries using combustion processes	Before Christ	Reduced attention span	—
LEAD, INORGANIC	Smelters	Before Christ	Disorientation; blindness; nerve damage to hands and feet	649,000
Mercury, inorganic	Hat manufacturing	1557	Tremors in hands, face, and legs	33,600
CARBON DISULFIDE	Rubber vulcanization	1856	Nerve damage in hands and feet, psychosis	24,200
Thallium	Glass making	1862	Nerve damage in lower limbs; damage to optic nerves and eye	853,000
Mercury, organic	Chemical research	1865	Visual-field constriction; nerve damage in hands and feet	—
Triethyltin (organotins)	Pharmaceuticals	1880	General weakness; vertigo	—
METHYL BROMIDE	Fumigation	1899	Nerve damage in hands and feet	105,000
CARBON TETRACHLORIDE	Dry cleaning	1909	Visual-field constriction	2 million
METHYL CHLORIDE	Rubber and plastics	1914	Nerve damage in hands and feet; blurred vision; short-term memory loss	40,500
TRICHLOROETHYLENE	Degreasing, dry cleaning	1915	Loss of facial sensation; impaired memory and concentration; tremors	3.6 million
Cadmium	Metalworking	1930	Loss or impairment of sense of smell	1.4 million
Triorthocresylphosphate (TOCP)	Pesticides	1930s	Nerve damage in hands and feet	—
Manganese	Mining	1944	Psychosis; impaired speech; tremors; loss of coordination; muscular weakness	41,000
Acetone	Cellulose production	1955	Vertigo; weakness	—
Dieldrin (and aldrin)	Pesticide application	1957	Epileptic convulsions; loss of coordination; blurred vision; double vision; nystagmus (involuntary blinking)	10,400
PERCHLOROETHYLENE	Degreasing, dry cleaning	1957	Vertigo; lack of coordination; tremors; memory loss	—
N-HEXANE	Gluing, shoemaking	1960	Nerve damage in lower limbs	764,000
TOLUENE	Paints, explosives	1961	Tremors; vertigo; lack of coordination; bizarre behavior; emotional instability	4.8 million
Aluminum	Mining, refining	1962	Mental deterioration; aphasia; convulsions	—
Acetylene tetrachloride	Solvent—multiple uses	1963	Tremors; vertigo	—
STYRENE	Plastics, manufacturing	1963	Short-term memory loss; nerve damage in hands and feet	329,000
Methyl isobutyl ketone	Centrifuge operation	1964	Muscular weakness	—
Acrylamide	Chemical manufacturing	1966	Nerve damage in hands and feet	7,000
Paraquat	Pesticide	1966	Tremors; mental disturbance	1,130
METHYLENE CHLORIDE	Solvent—multiple uses	1967	Delusions; hallucinations	2.2 million
Pentachlorophenol	Pesticide	1971	Blind spot; corneal numbness and damage; autonomic nervous system impairment	—
Tetrachlorobiphenyl	Food (cooking-oil accident)	1971	Nerve damage in hands and feet	—
METHYL N-BUTYL KETONE (MBK)	Dyeing	1973	Nerve damage in lower limbs	—
POLYBROMINATED BIPHENYLS (PBBs)	Fire extinguishers	1973	Poor concentration; irritability; numbness in extremities; blurred vision; eye-movement impairment	—
CHLORDECONE (KEPONE)	Pesticide	1975	Tremors; nervousness	—
DIMETHYLAMINO-PROPIONITRILE (DMAPN)	Polyurethane foam	1977	Impotence; lack of urination control; tingling in hands and feet	—

PSYCHOLOGY AND HEALTH

Health psychology is a relatively new field of applied psychology. In general, it involves the study of psychological and behavioral factors affecting physical health and illness. It is a "problem-oriented field that has brought together researchers and practitioners from a wide variety of psychological subspecialties" (Krantz, Grunberg, & Baum, 1985, p. 350). The involvement of psychologists in the realm of physical health and well-being is based on at least four assumptions:

1. Behaviors increase the risk of certain chronic diseases.
2. Changes in behaviors can reduce the risk of certain diseases.
3. Behavior can be easily changed.
4. Behavioral interventions are cost effective (Kaplan, 1984). In this section, we'll look at the role of psychologists in the understanding, treatment, and prevention of disease.

The first thing we should recognize is the extent to which psychological and social factors are related to physical illness and disease. Today, the leading causes of death in this country are cardiovascular disorders and cancers. These diseases are caused and maintained by the interaction of a number of factors, including biological, social, environmental, and behavioral influences. Among the latter, such variables as cigarette smoking, nutrition, obesity, and stress have been identified as important risk factors (Krantz, Grunberg, & Baum, 1985).

One of the strongest links between psychology and health is stress. We discussed stress and sources of stress (called stressors) at length in Topic 22 and need not repeat that discussion here. But we should remember that one of the points we raised concerning stress was that its ultimate effect was often on the physical health of the individual under stress. The relationship between psychological stress and physical illness is not a simple one. In some people, stress has the direct effect of raising blood pressure levels and/or suppressing the body's natural abilities to ward off disease (called *immunosuppression*). These reactions may then lead to physical disorders such as hypertension, cardiac irregularities, or stroke (Baum et al., 1982). In other people, the effects of stress are less direct, leading first to behavioral reactions such as increases in alcohol and drug use, or an increase in cigarette smoking, which in turn lead to health problems.

The severity of health problems produced by stress (or even *if* such problems develop) often depends on situational variables, such as the amount of social support available, the individual's attitudes about himself or herself, and perceived level of control over stress-producing events (Cohen & McKay, 1984). Further, there is some evidence that single episodes of stress—even extreme stress—are less likely to lead to physical problems in the long run than are series of repeated stress events (DeLongis et al., 1982).

One area in which psychological intervention has proven successful is in helping patients comply with the orders of physicians. Even the best of medical advice will be useless if it is not followed. One estimate (Ley, 1977) suggests that as many as 50 percent of patients fail to follow doctor's orders with regard to taking prescribed medicines. There are many reasons why patients fail to comply with doctors' orders, including lack of good communication between patient and doctor, the financial burden imposed by expensive medications, and the extent of disruption of daily routine required to follow the regimen of daily medication.

Psychologists certainly can assist in improving patient/physician communications concerning medication. And psychologists can assist patients in

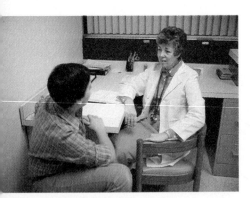

Health psychologists study the psychological and behavioral factors that affect physical health and illness. They may counsel people to change certain behaviors to improve their health.

monitoring their daily medications. As implied in one of our opening news stories, health psychologists have been making advances in the treatment of diabetes on a number of fronts. For example, biofeedback and behavior modification techniques have been used to assist patients in reducing their needs for insulin (Meer, 1985). Psychological techniques have also been used to help diabetics maintain their daily treatment regimens. A number of strategies have proven useful for this purpose including:

"1. *specific assignments* that unambiguously define what is to be done;

2. *skill training* to develop new behaviors relevant to treatment;

3. *cueing* specific behaviors with salient stimuli;

4. *tailoring* the regimen to meet the schedule and particular needs of the patient;

5. *contracts* between patient, therapist, and significant others for prescribed behavior change;

6. *shaping* successive approximations of the desired treatment regimen;

7. *self-monitoring* behaviors relevant to treatment; and

8. *reinforcement* of new desired behaviors" (Surwit, Feinglos, & Scovern, 1983, p. 260).

The last area of application in health psychology that we might mention here has to do with behavioral interventions with the aim of *prevention.* Indeed, "7 of the 10 leading causes of death in the United States are in large part behaviorally determined. We believe these unhealthy behaviors can be significantly reduced with help from psychologists" (Heffernan & Albee, 1985, p. 202). Interventions to prevent health problems from arising in the first place have been focused in a number of key areas, including smoking, misuse of alcohol, nutrition, physical fitness and exercise, control of stress, high blood pressure control, family planning, immunization, and sexually transmitted diseases (McGinnis, 1985).

Although efforts to effect attitudinal and behavioral change have been moving forward on all these fronts, none has received as much attention as efforts to discourage young people from smoking. Part of the reason for special efforts in this area is that the success rate of programs to persuade smokers to quit smoking have been less than encouraging: Nearly 80 percent of "quitters" relapse within a year. (In fact, most smokers who quit permanently do so without any special program of intervention.) Approaches that use role models and peers to teach specific skills to be used to resist pressures to begin smoking in the first place have been quite successful (e.g., Murray et al., 1984).

Psychologists involved in health psychology, then, are involved in a wide range of activities. Some are investigating the nature of the relationship between psychological variables and the incidence of disease; some look for ways to use psychological methods (such as biofeedback, behavior modification, and relaxation training) to help ease the symptoms of physical illness; some seek ways to help people change their attitudes and behaviors in order to become healthier and prevent health problems; some assist patients in complying with prescribed treatment plans; and still others fill a more traditional role, dealing directly with the psychological and emotional distress that often accompanies the knowledge that one has a serious or life-threatening disorder.

Health psychologists stress prevention of health problems through nonsmoking, good nutrition, and physical exercise.

Before you go on

What are some of the areas of activity in the field of health psychology?

PSYCHOLOGY AND THE LAW

There are a variety of ways in which the principles and practices of psychology can be applied to the criminal justice system. In Topic 32, we discussed how our understanding of social influence has affected decisions concerning the size of trial juries. Psychologists (and other social scientists) have had an impact on the legal system in many other ways. Certainly, issues of insanity pleas and the extent of a defendant's possible diminished capacity will involve the testimony of expert witnesses. Psychologists have also considered the psychological factors affecting a police officer's decision to make an arrest, a district attorney's decision to prosecute a case, a defense attorney's decision to take on a case, a jury's decision to convict a defendant, a judge's decision regarding a defendant's sentence, and the prison system's decision to parole a prisoner (Greenberg & Ruback, 1982). In this section, we'll focus our attention on two applications of psychological understanding to jury trials: the selection of jury members and the nature of eyewitness testimony.

Selecting Members of a Jury

If we were to draw our impressions of society from what we see on television and in the movies, we might reasonably conclude that most criminal lawyers and judges spend most of their time in the courtroom participating in jury trials. The right of an accused to a trial by an impartial jury of his or her peers is a right with which we are all familiar. But, in fact, very few criminal cases ever reach the stage of a courtroom trial. Fully 90 percent of those accused of a serious crime plead guilty in exchange for reduced charges and other favors from prosecutors. Of those persons brought to trial, most (60 percent charged with felonies, 95 percent charged with misdemeanors) are tried by judges, not juries (Greenberg & Ruback, 1982; Kalven & Zeisel, 1966).

Large numbers of legal cases do go to trial, however. One of the most critical aspects of a jury trial, of course, is the selection of those who will serve as jurors. Selection is generally a two-stage process, the first being a simple compilation of names of potential jurors, usually drawn up from voter registration lists. The second stage is when the defense attorney and the prosecutor (and the judge) interview prospective jurors from the general list. Either party (or the judge) may challenge a juror as biased and ask that that person be dismissed from jury duty. Clearly, it is in the best interests of both prosecution and defense to secure jurors they believe will be most sympathetic to the cases they are about to present. In fact, the argument goes, neither side is actually looking for a truly unbiased juror (Horowitz & Willging, 1984). To say the least, psychologists can be very useful in helping lawyers identify jurors who will help their case.

For example, one way in which psychologists can help is to assess prevailing attitudes concerning an upcoming trial. Then they attempt to see if attitudes in sympathy with the defense (let's say) are more common in any segment of the sampled population. If they are, the lawyer can then try to get jurors from that population. In the trial of a group of anti-Vietnam war protesters (the Harrisburg Seven) that was held in the early 1970s, for example, it was discovered that the juror most likely to be sympathetic with the arguments of the defense was in agreement with the antiwar movement, female, had no religious preference, held a skilled or white-collar position, and was a member of the Democratic party (Schulman et al., 1973).

Does this selection process really work? Can juries be rigged by applying scientific testing and psychological insights about factors affecting juror's decision making? It is true that the Harrisburg Seven were acquitted, and in other cases where scientific methods have been used to influence jury selection, the side using such methods has usually won. But, in truth, the effectiveness of such techniques "of juror selection has simply not been empirically demonstrated" (Horowitz & Willging, 1982, p. 175). That is, the effectiveness of scientific jury selection has not been adequately demonstrated in controlled experimental settings. And in experimental tests that have been conducted, the scientific method of jury selection has not been found to be superior to conventional methods. About the only characteristic of a potential juror that has been reliably related to the likelihood to attribute guilt is the sex of the juror in trials of rape cases (for example, Saks, 1976).

Before you go on

What is one way in which social scientists might affect the selection of jury members?

Is there any evidence that such scientifically constituted juries perform differently than conventionally constituted juries?

Eyewitness Testimony

In a large measure, we have already dealt with some of the issues related to eyewitness testimony when we discussed factors that affect perception (Topic 8) and when we discussed failures of memory retrieval (Topic 14). It seems reasonable to conclude that eyewitnesses should not be expected to recount with perfect accuracy and precision everything that they might have witnessed—particularly in the context of a stressful, emotion-laden situation of the sort that is often the focus of jury trials. We recognize that there are many sources of distortion, both of perception (seeing what one wants to see or expects to see instead of what actually happened) and memory (being led to recall events that never happened). Even most jurors may realize that there may be distortions of reality in eyewitness accounts, but the rate of convictions with eyewitness testimony is *four times* the rate of convictions without it (Loftus, 1974).

The basic problem for juries and judges is being able to tell the difference between reliable and unreliable witnesses, or, more correctly, in being able to determine the degree of reliability of eyewitness testimony. There is some evidence that jurors are willing to believe eyewitness testimony even if they are aware of potential problems associated with that testimony (Horowitz & Willging, 1984; Loftus, 1979).

Recently, psychologists have been debating the issue of whether or not psychologists themselves should serve the court as expert witnesses, testifying about the very nature of eyewitness testimony. One side of this argument (Loftus, 1983a, 1983b) claims that jurors tend to "overbelieve" eyewitnesses and should be cautioned against doing so in the light of psychological research on perception and memory. The other side of this issue (McCloskey & Egeth, 1983a, 1983b) claims that there is as yet incomplete and inconclusive evidence that jurors rely too heavily on eyewitness accounts, and that psychologists as experts might simply confuse the jury and, worse, foster "underbelief." Needless to say, this issue is a heated and important one, both in psychology and in law. We need to know more about factors that affect an eyewitness's accuracy of report, the extent to which juries are influenced by such reports, and the extent to which expert testimony might tip the delicate scales of justice.

Before you go on

What is the role of psychology in dealing with the credibility of eyewitness testimony in jury trials?

PSYCHOLOGY AND SPORT

Sport psychology is another exciting area of applied psychology. Although it has had a long history in Europe, sport psychology has become an organized focus of attention in this country only within the last 15–20 years. We may define sport psychology as have Browne and Mahoney in their recent review as "the application of psychological principles to sport and physical activity at all levels of skill development" (1984, p. 605). Although there are many potential applications of psychology to sports and athletes, we'll briefly review just two: psychological characteristics of athletes and maximizing athletic performance.

Psychology's history is filled with research dealing with the measurement of individual differences. Wouldn't it be useful to be able to predict who might become a world-class athlete on the basis of psychological testing? It is certainly the case that there are physiological differences between athletes and nonathletes—amount of muscle, muscle type, height, weight, lung capacity, and so on. Are there any differences between athletes and nonathletes on personality measures?

Generally, research in this area has been less than satisfactory, and results often simply tend to confirm the obvious. Although differences tend to be small, successful athletes tend to score higher than nonsuccessful athletes on tests of assertion, dominance, aggression, need for achievement, and a few other dimensions; they score lower on such traits as anxiety level, depression, and fatigue (Browne & Mahoney, 1984). Athletes in some sports, such as hockey and football, are more tolerant of pain than are athletes in other sports, such as golf and bowling (e.g., Ryan & Kovacic, 1966).

Of greatest practical importance to coaches and athletes (and to some sport psychologists) is the performance of the athlete in competition, and what can be done to maximize that performance. One area of interest has been the arousal level of the athlete. Clearly the athlete in competition needs to be fully aroused and motivated to perform—"psyched up" to his or her best. But psychologists also know that too much arousal can interfere with performance. They can help athletes be sensitive to maintaining high levels of arousal, while still maintaining appropriate levels of concentration on the task at hand. This often involves training athletes to monitor and control arousal levels (Harris, 1973; Landers, 1982).

In a similar vein, one psychologist has claimed recently that the so-called home-field advantage may often be overexaggerated, particularly in important games (Baumeister, 1985). The argument is that the frenzied, yelling, screaming hometown fans may raise arousal levels of the home team *beyond* the point of maximum efficiency.

One psychologist who researches sports and athletes, Michael Mahoney, commenting on Olympic athletes, has said, "At this level of competition, the difference between two athletes is 20 percent physical and 80 percent mental" (quoted in Kiester, 1984, pp. 20–21). To the extent that this observation is accurate, psychologists have been helpful in preparing athletes to do their best—to give what is called their *peak performance*. Mental practice, combined of course with physical practice, has proven to be quite beneficial. In addition to manipulating levels of arousal, mental practice is useful in:

1. mentally rehearsing a particular behavioral pattern (think about and mentally picture that golf swing and the flight of the ball before you step up to the tee);

2. reducing negative thoughts that may interfere with performance (forget about an earlier error and focus on positive experiences, perhaps past victories);

The home team advantage may, in fact, be a myth. The yelling, frenzied hometown fans may arouse the athletes to levels beyond peak performance. In effect, they get too psyched up and may make nervous errors.

3. rehearsing one's role in a team sport (know what you are supposed to do and when you are supposed to do it in different game situations);

4. setting realistic goals (don't get tense worrying about a competitor in this race, simply try to better your last performance) (e.g., Creekmore, 1984; Kiester, 1984a, 1984b; Ogilvie & Howe, 1984; Scott & Pelliccioni, 1982; Suinn, 1980).

Before you go on

What are some of the ways in which psychologists may become involved in sports and athletics?

In this topic, we have briefly reviewed four general areas in which psychological understanding can be brought to bear on a real-life situation or problem. We have seen that psychologists are concerned about how the environment affects our behavior, how psychological factors and physical disease may be interrelated, how psychology can be used to understand and/or influence the criminal justice system, and how even sports and athletics can benefit from our knowledge of human behavior.

Our sampling of examples in this topic was just that—a sampling and not a complete listing of psychological applications. There are a number of other applied fields of psychology that we might have included in this topic, including applied developmental psychology, consumer psychology, the psychology of marketing and advertising, engineering psychology, political psychology, and many others. Psychology is a science, and it is an academic discipline. It is also a field ready and willing to be a force of influence and change in the world.

For some time now, Scott Geller and some of his colleagues and students at Virginia Polytechnic Institute and State University in Blacksburg, Virginia, have been attempting to apply behavioral analyses to modify a socially important behavior—the wearing of seat belts (or perhaps better, safety belts). Programs designed to bring about changes in attitudes, and more importantly in behavior, have met with considerable success (Geller, 1985).

The common claim is that more than half of the nearly 500,000 injuries and 30,000 deaths that occur each year as the result of vehicle accidents could be prevented if safety belts were worn. Yet, Geller claims, fewer than 15 percent of American drivers (and passengers) actually "buckle up."

There are, of course, many reasons why people tend not to wear seat belts. Some hold false beliefs: "If I wreck my car and it catches on fire, I don't want to be trapped inside by my seat belt." Some simply deny: "I won't be in an accident, so it doesn't matter if I wear my seat belt or not." Some have often been reinforced for *not* wearing a safety belt: "I've never worn the darn thing before, and I haven't had any problems yet. I always get where I want to go without using it." There are few appropriate role models for seat belt use—fewer than 5 percent of television stars in action programs are shown wearing a seat belt. (Geller, 1985). And in many cases, neither drivers nor passengers receive any direct message to remind them that seat belts should be worn.

Geller's agenda for increasing safety-belt use centers around sound psychological research and theory, most notably the appropriate use of positive reinforcement. For example, in one program seat-belt usage more than doubled when police officers (and others) passed out coupons for fast-food restaurants and lottery tickets to motorists wearing seat belts. The cost of the program was minimal—the reinforcers had been donated by local merchants—and the potential benefits considerable. In another similar program, customers who arrived at a bank's drive-up window wearing a seat belt received a free number for a community bingo game.

Threats and warnings of dire consequences of *not* wearing a seat belt were eliminated in these programs. Appropriate behaviors were reinforced. Seat-belt usage increased and remained at or near increased levels even when the reinforcement programs were over, although intermittently reintroducing the reinforcers is suggested to help maintain safety-belt wearing for the long term. This is in keeping with the knowledge that intermittently reinforced responses are more resistant to extinction.

As it happens, programs such as the safety-belt one cannot be administered effectively by individuals. They require the cooperation and involvement of organizations, either community action groups, or corporations. Corporations can be easily persuaded to initiate seat-belt programs because of the demonstrated cost-effectiveness of such programs compared to lost time and turnover problems that arise from injuries sustained by employees in traffic accidents.

Public safety has undoubtedly become an important political issue for the 1980s. Many states are actively pursuing seat-belt laws of varying form that will, in some cases, impose fines on persons not wearing them. Legislating seat-belt usage has met with resistance from the general public and from groups concerned with governmental control of one's own life and property. Perhaps more positive strategies of the sort described by Geller, which use psychological theory and research applied to a very practical problem, will be more effective agents of change.

Define environmental psychology, and list some of the issues that environmental psychologists study.

Environmental psychology studies how the environment affects the behavior and mental processes of persons living within it. Environmental psychologists study a number of different issues, including personal space, crowding, territoriality, privacy, environmental pollutants and neurotoxins, and the effects of weather and noise. / 632

Define the concepts of personal space and territoriality.

Personal space is the imaginary bubble of area around an individual into which others enter only by invitation or in specified situations. It is mobile and goes with the person. There may be different types of personal space defined for different situations. Territoriality, on the other hand, is one's claim to certain areas (territories) in the environment. Territories may be defended against intrusion and are often used as statements of self-expression. Intrusion into one's personal space or territory leads to tension, stress, and even aggression. / 635

What is the difference between population density and crowding?

What are some of the positive and negative aspects of city living?

Population density is a quantitative measure of the number of people (for example) occupying a given geographic area. Crowding, on the other hand, is a psychological reaction of distress that occurs when individuals feel that their space or privacy has been invaded. City living increases the probability of living with crowding, noise, and other pollutants, but these stressors may be offset by the advantages of a wide range of opportunities not found outside large population centers, such as health care, police protection, and access to the arts. / 637

What are some of the effects that noise, extreme temperature, and neurotoxins have on behavior?

Noise, extreme temperatures, and neurotoxins may all be viewed as environmental pollutants and potentially stressful, if not directly harmful to physical and psychological well-being. Noise per se is less stressful than is unexpected, unpredictable, or uncontrollable noise. High temperatures may lead to aggressive reactions, but extremely high (and low) temperatures tend to decrease all levels of behavior. Many chemicals commonly found in the environment have negative consequences for behavior and mental activities; such chemicals are called neurotoxins. / 638

What are some of the areas of activity in the field of health psychology?

Health psychology, in general, is the study of psychological and behavioral factors that affect physical health and disease. Health psychologists are involved in a number of areas, including research on the effects of stress on physical health, the role of behaviors in the causes of disease, treatment of chronic diseases (such as helping patients comply with physicians' orders) and preventative programs (such as those directed at keeping young people from smoking). / 641

What is one way in which social scientists might affect the selection of jury members?

Is there any evidence that such scientifically constituted juries perform differently than conventionally constituted juries?

Social scientists may affect jury selection by discovering the personal characteristics of those who might be sympathetic to either the prosecution or the defense in a jury trial so as to advise the attorney what sorts of jurors to select. As it happens, there is little empirical evidence that the systematic application of scientific principles to jury selection is in any significant way more successful than conventional methods. / 643

What is the role of psychology in dealing with the credibility of eyewitness testimony in jury trials?

There is currently a debate in progress over the extent to which psychologists should intervene in the criminal justice system with regard to the credibility of eyewitness testimony. Some argue that psychologists have ample data to question the reliability of such testimony, while others argue that the data are not yet in on this question and that informing juries of the psychological factors that affect eyewitness testimony would be at best useless and at worst confusing or prejudicial. / 643

What are some of the ways in which psychologists may become involved in sports and athletics?

Psychologists have become involved in sports and athletics in a number of different ways, including trying to discover how athletes are different from nonathletes, attempting to improve an athlete's peak performance, studying the effects of audience reactions on athletic performance, and investigating the effects of participation on the athlete. / 645

APPENDIX

TOPIC

This brief topic is about measurement and statistics. Measurement and statistics involve numbers; when we measure something, we assign it a numerical value, and statistics help us to analyze and understand measurements once we have made them. So that we may have some numbers to work with in this topic, let's consider the following problem.

You and your best friend are enrolled in the same introductory psychology class this semester. You have just taken your first exam—a 50-item multiple-choice test. Somewhat concerned about the possibility of cheating, your instructor provided two forms of your first exam, Form A and Form B. They covered the same material, of course, but the questions were different on the two forms. By chance, you took Form A of the test, and your friend took Form B. You had studied together, and you thought that you both knew the material equally well. But, your score on the test was eight points lower than your friend's. You suspect that perhaps the two forms of your first test were not equally difficult. You believe that your test (Form A) was harder than your friend's (Form B). You ask your instructor for all the grades on the test, for both forms. Because of confidentiality, your instructor cannot provide you with names, but does supply you with all the grades from the exam.

There are 100 students in your class. Fifty took Form A and 50 took Form B. When you get the scores from your instructor, you find that they are arranged as follows:

Form A:

98	86	100	60	94
72	80	78	66	86
92	62	86	96	62
82	86	78	88	84
64	86	68	76	80
86	96	76	72	80
80	82	82	64	78
68	74	64	98	84
66	64	70	90	86
96	92	82	68	92

Form B:

82	100	90	80	60
72	86	82	88	80
82	76	84	74	84
86	74	78	78	78
78	74	84	80	80
90	84	68	78	86
80	80	80	84	80
76	76	80	82	82
86	74	70	78	76
82	82	80	76	80

What a mess. Just looking at all these numbers doesn't tell you much at all. Arranged as they are, it's difficult to see if either form yielded higher or lower scores. To answer your original question (was there a difference in performance on the two forms of the exam), you are going to have to manipulate these numbers somehow. Such manipulations involve statistics. As we'll repeat throughout this topic, statistics are tools we use to help us make sense out of data we have collected. Statistics will be very helpful in analyzing these data. Imagine how much more useful (or necessary) they would be if your data included two sets of 500 numbers each.

We begin this final topic by reminding ourselves of two points that we made back in our first topic. (1) The quality of a scientific endeavor is often a reflection of its ability to accurately and precisely *measure* its subject matter. (2) The subject matter of psychology—behavior and mental processes—is *variable*.

In this topic, we will do two things. First, we'll briefly consider the nature of measurement. What does it mean to measure something? We'll discover that measurement is a process that, at least in psychology, can occur at different levels. Secondly, we'll examine what we can do with the numbers that result from our measurement efforts.

It is one thing to be able to measure some psychological characteristic and something else again to make sense out of those measurements once they've been made. This is particularly true when we have a large number of measurements, either made repeatedly on the same individual or on many different subjects. After making a large series of measurements and generating a large number of numbers, we need to be able to summarize and describe our data. We may also want to make decisions on the basis of the numbers we have collected. That's where the use of statistics comes in. Statistics help us to summarize, describe, and make judgments about measurements. How they do so will be the principle subject of this topic.

Before we go on, I would like to insert a word of caution. In this topic we are going to be dealing with numbers and a few simple formulas. Please don't let the numbers make you anxious. Some students find dealing with numbers difficult and think that statistics are not relevant for psychology students. Keep in mind that statistics are tools, necessary tools, to help us understand our subject matter. I have long argued that (at this level at least) you don't need to be mathematically sophisticated to appreciate statistics. What is required is a positive attitude and a few arithmetic skills, such as addition, subtraction, multiplication, and division. If you haven't had much math background, just go slowly and think about the issues involved in our discussion. Don't let yourself get bogged down in the numbers.

LEVELS OF MEASUREMENT

Our ability to understand and make predictions about particular behaviors and/or mental processes often hinges on our ability to measure them. **Measurement** involves the assignment of numbers to some characteristic of interest according to rules or according to some agreed-upon system. The rules or system for most physical measurements are generally simple and well established. You are 5′10″ tall because from top to bottom your height equals 70 inches, where an inch is defined as a standard unit of length, and you have 70 of them.

The rules or systems for psychological measurement are seldom as clear-cut. Are you extroverted and outgoing, or are you shy and introverted? How extroverted are you? How much extroversion do you have? How do we know? What is the standard against which we can compare you and your behavior? As we have seen (Topic 24), much of the measuring that we do in psychology involves psychological tests. For now, let's deal with measurement in general, defining four types or levels of measurement; then we can consider what to do with measurements once they have been made.

measurement
the assignment of numbers to a characteristic of interest on the basis of rules

Before you go on
Provide a general definition of measurement.

Nominal Measurement

One of the simplest ways to measure things is to categorize them on the basis of some characteristic of interest. **Nominal measurement** is basically a sorting procedure. If subjects in an experiment, for example, are divided into two groups, female and male, the subjects have been measured, here on the basis of their sex. They have been placed into one of two categories. We could easily go another step and arbitrarily assign numbers to our categories: female = 1, male = 2 (or vice versa).

A social psychologist might be interested in the relationship between religious preference and voting patterns and do an initial survey using nominal measurement. To do so, one names (nominal means "name") people as being either Protestant, Catholic, Jewish, or other. The second categorization identifies subjects as Republican, Democrat, Independent, or other. Having made these measurements, one can then look for relationships among them.

If we know that something has been measured with a nominal scale, we really don't know much. We can make observations such as "If A and B are in the same group, and if B and C are in the same group, then obviously A and C are also in the same group." That's not saying a lot, but it is something; it does bring some organization to the events we are measuring. Note that there is no implication at this level of measurement that anything has more or less of the characteristic in which we are interested. All we can do is categorize, name categories, and then assign numbers to our categories if we so choose.

nominal measurement
sorting events into categories on the basis of some characteristic of interest

Ordinal Measurement

With **ordinal measurement,** we can go one step further. Now we can categorize events into groups *and* we can order (or rank order) events in terms of how much of some characteristic they have. That may not make much sense in the abstract, but you are quite familiar with ordinal measurement. Let's look at a couple of examples.

To produce an ordinal scale, one places things in some order on the basis of a rule. Don't college degrees fit the description of ordinal levels? We have 2-year associate degrees (AASs), 4-year bachelor degrees (BAs and BSs), graduate master's degrees (MAs and MSs), and PhDs (and others). At least in theory, each degree takes more effort, and certainly more time, than the preceding one. So we can sort people into categories on the basis of the highest degree they have earned, and then we can rank order categories. One thing that we *cannot* do with ordinal scales is talk about the *amount of difference* in the rankings. Is the difference between an AAS and a BA the same as the difference between a BA and an MA? With only a ranking of these degrees, we can't say.

High school class rank is another common example of an ordinal scale with which you are familiar. Is the difference between students who finish 2nd and 3rd in their high school class the same as the difference between those students who happen to finish 104th and 105th? Maybe, but maybe not. All class ranks do is order students without implying anything about the degree of difference between ranks. Many psychological tests yield numbers that allow us to rank people on the basis of some characteristic of interest— and little else.

ordinal measurement
placing categorized events in order, or ranked, in terms of extent or amount of some characteristic of interest

Interval Measurement

Interval measurement provides us with a much more sophisticated level of measurement. With interval measurement, we *can* make statements about the differences between events or people at different ranks. Here, not only

interval measurement
measurement in which we can specify equal differences between adjacent, ranked events

are things put in order, but the differences between each unit in the ordering are equal.

Standard thermometers provide the most common example of interval scale devices. The temperature of objects can be put in order, and each unit of measurement is equal to all others. That is, the difference between 28° (Fahrenheit, let's say) and 30° is the same as the difference between 104° and 106°. It takes the same amount of energy to raise a temperature by two degrees whether you start with 28° or 104°.

Ratio Measurement

Ratio measurement is rarely found in psychology. For a number of psychological characteristics, ratio scales do not even make much sense. They are, however, the most powerful type of measurement scales. Ratio measures have all of the characteristics of those scales listed above. They allow us to categorize events, rank them, and specify equal differences between adjacent ranks. In addition, they provide a true, meaningful zero point. With a meaningful zero point, we can form ratios, which is what gives this level of measurement its name.

Most common physical measurements (length, weight, time, etc.) are ratio measurements. Two feet is a distance twice as long as 1 foot, one half as long as 4 feet, and one third as long as 6 feet. We can make such statements— form such ratios—because we can comprehend the notion of zero length. Similarly, we are quite comfortable claiming that 60 minutes is twice as long a time period as 30 minutes, and that it comprises 1/24 of a day.

It makes less sense to claim, for example, that, "Bill is twice as smart as Tom," or that "John is one third as extroverted as George." Although we may occasionally say such things, we realize that we don't mean exactly "twice" or "one third." Our problem is that zero intelligence or zero extroversion have little significance. We certainly can rank order (use ordinal scales or even interval scales) and claim that Bill is smarter than Tom, but without a true zero point, we cannot form ratios.

Before you go on
Define four levels of measurement.

ORGANIZING DATA

We have seen that measurement can be a complex process and that events can be measured in a number of different ways: nominal, ordinal, interval, or ratio. Let us now assume that we have collected a large number of measurements. We want to make some decisions based on the measurements we have made. We first need to assemble our numbers, our data, in some sensible way so that we can quickly and easily get some idea of what our measurements indicate. At very least, we should put our data into the form of a frequency distribution. We might then consider some graphic representation of our data.

Frequency Distributions

Once we have collected a large number of numbers, we usually seek ways to organize and summarize them to make them useful and meaningful. One of the easiest things to do with our numbers is to arrange them in a **frequency distribution.** As its name suggests, a frequency distribution lists, in order, all

	Form A		Form B	
Score	Frequency		Frequency	
100	/	1	/	1
98	/ /	2		0
96	/ / /	3		0
94	/	1		0
92	/ / /	3		0
90	/	1	/ /	2
88	/	1	/	1
86	/ / / / / / / /	7	/ / / /	4
84	/ /	2	/ / / / /	5
82	/ / / /	4	/ / / / / / /	7
80	/ / / /	4	/ / / / / / / / / / /	11
78	/ / /	3	/ / / / / /	6
76	/ /	2	/ / / / /	5
74	/	1	/ / / /	4
72	/ /	2	/	1
70	/	1	/	1
68	/ / /	3	/	1
66	/ /	2		0
64	/ / / /	4		0
62	/ /	2		0
60	/	1	/	1
		N = 50		N = 50

Figure 35.1
Frequency distributions for our sample data of two forms (A and B) of a classroom exam. Scores, or measurements, are listed in order in the left column, and the frequency with which each occurs is indicated with either a hash mark (/) or a number.

of the numbers or scores that we have collected and indicates the frequency with which each occurs.

Figure 35.1 shows two types of frequency distribution for the scores earned on Form A and Form B of the example exam we introduced at the beginning of this topic. In this figure, we have placed the two frequency distributions side by side. You can easily see, just by inspection of these distributions, that there is a difference between the scores earned on Form A and Form B of our imaginary classroom exam.

Graphic Representations

It is often helpful to go one step beyond the simple frequency distribution and draw a graph of our data. There have been a number of different graphs used throughout this text. Graphs of frequencies of scores are among the most common types of graphs in psychology. For such a graph, our scores (in general referred to as *X-scores*) are plotted on the horizontal (X) axis of the graph, and frequencies (f) are plotted on the vertical (Y) axis of our graph.

Figures 35.2A and 35.2B show one way to graph frequencies of occurrence. This sort of bar graph is called a **histogram**. The frequency of each X-score is indicated by the height of the bar above the score. When we have few X-scores, and when frequencies are not too large, histograms provide clear depictions of our data. Figure 35.3 shows the same data in a simple line graph. The advantage of this sort of graph is obvious: We can easily show

histogram
a bar graph; a graphic representation of a frequency distribution

Figure 35.2 (A)

Histograms showing the frequency with which scores were earned on Form A and Form B of the classroom exam.

Figure 35.2 (B)

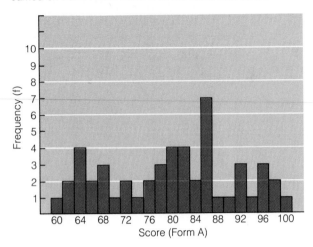

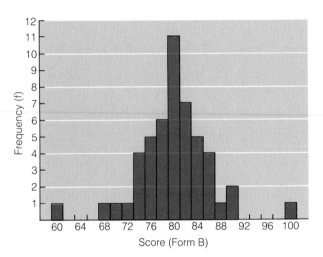

distributions of both test scores on the same axes. With such graphs, it is important to provide a key indicating which line represents each group of scores.

Before you go on

What is a frequency distribution and what is a histogram?

What are they used for?

DESCRIPTIVE STATISTICS

Let's continue working with our opening problem. We began with two sets of 50 numbers, scores earned on Form A and Form B of a classroom exam. Our basic question was whether or not these two forms of the same test were really equally difficult. To get started, we put the scores into frequency distributions and then constructed graphs that represented our data. That helped, but there is more we can do.

central tendency
a measure of the middle, or average, score in a set

When describing collections or distributions of data, our two major concerns are usually with (1) central tendency and (2) variability. Measures of **central tendency** are statistics that tell us where our scores tend to center. In general terms, measures of central tendency are called *averages*. If we want to know if performance on Form A was better or worse *on the average* than performance on Form B, we would have to compute some measure of central tendency for both distributions of scores. Measures of **variability** are statistics that tell us about the extent of dispersion, or spread of scores, within a distribution. Are the scores clustered closely around the average, or are they more variable, deviating considerably from the average? First, we'll deal with measures of central tendency, then with variability.

Measures of Central Tendency

There are three statistics we can use to represent the central tendency of a distribution of numbers. The most commonly used is the mean. The median and mode are also measures of central tendency, but they are used less frequently.

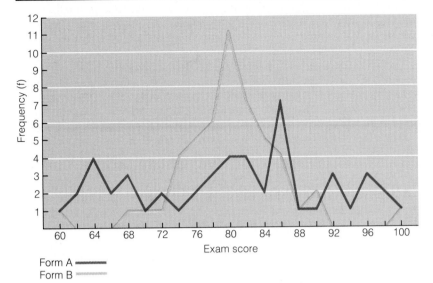

Form A ▬▬▬
Form B ▭▭▭

The Mean   When we think about computing the average of a distribution of scores, we are usually thinking about computing the mean. The **mean** of a set of scores is their total divided by the number of scores in the set. For example, if Max is 6 feet tall, and Ruth is 4 feet tall, their mean height is 5 feet. Four inches of snow yesterday and 2 inches today yields a mean snowfall of 3 inches for the 2 days ($4'' + 2'' = 6'' \div 2 = 3''$).

mean
(X), the sum of all X-scores (ΣX) divided by N, the number of X-scores

So, to compute the mean scores for Form A of our example, we add up all the scores and divide by 50, because there are 50 scores in the set. We'd do the same thing for the scores earned on Form B; add them up and divide by 50.

The mean of a set of numbers is symbolized by $\overline{X}$, read *X bar*. The upper case Greek letter sigma, Σ, stands for "take the sum of whatever follows." We use the symbol X to represent an individual score from a set of scores, and N for the number of scores in the set. So the formula for computing a mean looks like this:

$$\overline{X} = \frac{\Sigma X}{N}$$

This is just a fancy shorthand way of expressing what you already know: To find the mean of a set of scores ($\overline{X}$), add the scores (X) together and then divide by the number of scores (N). When we do this for Form A and Form B of our classroom exam example, we find that the mean for both sets of scores is 80. That is, $\Sigma X = 4000$ and $N = 50$ in each case, so $\Sigma X \div N = 80$ for both forms of the exam. In terms of average score (as indicated by the mean), there is clearly no difference between the two forms of the test.

The Median   Although the mean is generally the central tendency measure of choice, there are occasions when it may not be appropriate. These occasions occur when a distribution includes a few extreme scores. For a simple example, the mean of the numbers 2, 3, 3, 5, 7 is 4 ($\Sigma X = 20$; $N = 5$; so $\overline{X} = 4$). Even on inspection, 4 looks right; it is a value near the middle or center of the set. Now consider the numbers 2, 3, 3, 5, 37. What is their mean? Their sum is 50, so their mean equals 10. Here it seems by inspection that the extreme score of 37 is adding too much weight to our measure of central tendency. Imagine computing the average income of a small, working-class community that happened to include two millionaires. The *mean* income of this community would be unduly influenced by just two persons with unusually high incomes.

In such cases, we might prefer to use the **median** as our measure of central tendency. The median is the value of a set of numbers that divides it exactly in half. There are as many scores above the median as below it. Perhaps you recognize that the median is the same as the 50th percentile of a distribution—50 percent of the scores are higher, 50 percent are lower.

Don't fall for this trick: "What is the median of these test scores: 42, 58, 37, 62, 55?" There is a tendency to want to say "37" because it is in the middle of the list with two scores to the left and two scores to the right. But "37" certainly isn't at the center of these scores; it's the lowest of the five! Before you choose the median, the scores must first be placed in order: 37, 42, 55, 58, 62. *Now* the score in the middle, 55, is the median score, the one that divides the set in half. Whenever we have an even number of scores, or a large number of scores, the computation of the median becomes slightly more complicated. We can't always just put our scores in order and identify the median by inspection. For our example distributions, the median for Form A of the exam is 80.50; for Form B it is 79.04.

The Mode   No doubt the easiest measure of central tendency to calculate is the **mode**. The mode is the most frequently occurring value in a set or distribution of scores. If you have already constructed a frequency distribution, finding the mode is particularly easy. Just locate the X-value with the greatest frequency and you've found the mode. For many psychological characteristics measured for large numbers of subjects, the mode *does* tend to fall at or near the center of the distribution of scores. For our example problem, the mode of scores earned on Form A is 86, and on Form B the mode is 80.

As it happens, the mode is seldom used as a measure of average. For one thing, computing the mode disregards all of the other values in the distribution. For another, there is no guarantee that the most frequently occurring number will necessarily be at the middle, and there is always the possibility that no *one* number will be *the* most frequent.

median
the score of an ordered set above which and below which fall half the scores

mode
the most frequently occurring X-score in a set

Before you go on
Name and define three measures of central tendency.

Variability

If we know how two sets of scores, or distributions, differ "on the average," we know a lot. We would know, for instance, that there is no apparent difference in central tendency for the two sets of scores we have been using as an example problem. There is, however, a second descriptive characteristic of distributions of numbers that may be of interest: their spread, or dispersion, or **variability**.

It is quite possible to have two sets of scores that have identical means but that, at the same time, are clearly different from each other. This sort of difference can be seen in Figure 35.3 and is even more clearly obvious in Figure 35.4. In this figure, we can see that most of the scores of distribution A are clustered, or packed, around the mean of the distribution. The scores of distribution B are much more spread out, or variable, even though the mean of this set of scores equals the mean of distribution A.

variability
the extent of spread or dispersion in a set or distribution of scores

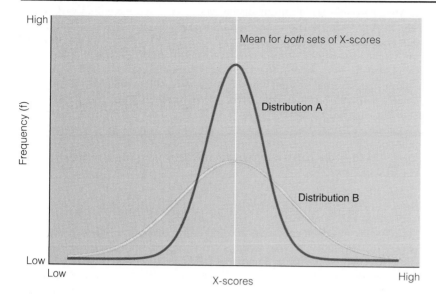

High

Mean for *both* sets of X-scores

Distribution A

Frequency (f)

Distribution B

Low

Low   High

X-scores

Figure 35.4
Two distributions of X-scores (A and B) that have identical means, but clearly different variability.

Imagine for a moment that the two graphs in Figure 35.4 represent grades earned by two large classes. Further imagine that the mean grade for each class is a C. If this is the case, then these graphs tell us that almost everyone in Class A received a C, a C+, or a C−. Some may have received a B− or a D+, but most grades were near the average C. In Class B, on the other hand, there were obviously many more As and Bs, and Ds and Fs than were earned by the other class, even though the mean grade for the two classes was a C. So knowing about a distribution's variability is to have some useful information. How shall we represent variability statistically?

One way to measure the spread of scores in a distribution is to use a statistic called the **range.** Range is one of the easiest statistics to calculate. It is found by subtracting the lowest score from the highest. Unfortunately, range (as a measure of variability) simply disregards all the other scores between the highest and lowest. Even when most scores are bunched tightly around the mean, if there are just a couple of extreme scores, the range will be large. The range would be an inappropriate measure of variability for our example problem. Scores on both Form A and Form B of the classroom exam range from a high score of 100 to a low score of 60. Thus, the range for both sets of scores is 40 points. An inspection of our Figure 35.3, however, indicates that scores on Form A are generally more variable than scores on Form B.

A measure of variability that does take into account all of the scores of a distribution is **standard deviation.** Standard deviation is usually symbolized by *s,* or *s. d.* What it amounts to is a kind of average of the extent to which all the scores in a distribution are different from (deviate from) their mean. Let's go through the procedures that reflect this definition of standard deviation.

The first thing we need to know is the mean of our distribution ($\overline{X}$). Then we find the difference between each score (X, remember) and the mean ($\overline{X}$). This is simple subtraction, so now we have a collection of (X − $\overline{X}$) scores. Because means are by definition in the middle of distributions, some X-scores will be above the mean (so X − $\overline{X}$ will be a positive number), and some X-scores will be below the mean (so X − $\overline{X}$ will be a negative number).

range
a measure of variability; the highest score in a distribution, minus the lowest

standard deviation
a type of average of the deviations of each X-score from the mean of the distribution;

$$\sqrt{\frac{\Sigma(X - \overline{X})^2}{N}}$$

If we simply add up all of our deviations, $\Sigma(X - \overline{X})$, we will always have a sum of zero. What we do to deal with this complication is simply square each deviation score, so that we have a set of $(X - \overline{X})^2$ scores. Any real number, even a negative one, that is squared, or multiplied by itself, will yield a positive number. *Now* we add together our squared deviations, $\Sigma(X - \overline{X})^2$. We then find an average by dividing this total by N, the number of scores we are dealing with. In formula form, what we have so far is: $\Sigma(X - \overline{X})^2/N$. This statistic is called *variance.*

Earlier we introduced a squaring operation just to get rid of negative numbers. We now reverse that operation by taking the square root of our result. What we end up with then is our formula for standard deviation, and it looks like this:

$$s.d. = \sqrt{\frac{\Sigma(X - \overline{X})^2}{N}}$$

You may never be called upon to actually compute a standard deviation using this formula. For one thing, even simple handheld calculators often come with a button that automatically yields a standard deviation value once you've punched in all the X-scores. For another, there are simpler, computational formulas that provide the same result in fewer, easier steps. But you should appreciate what standard deviations do. They tell us the extent to which scores in a distribution deviate, or are spread, from the distribution's mean. We use standard deviations often in psychology.

To reinforce our discussion, Figure 35.5 depicts the computation of a standard deviation for some simple data. When the procedure is applied to our example data, we find that the standard deviation for Form A of the exam is 11.29; for Form B, the s.d. is 6.18. This result conforms to our observation that the scores on Form A of the test are more variable than those earned on Form B.

Before you go on

What is the formula for standard deviation, and of what is it a measure?

INFERENTIAL STATISTICS

We have already seen that statistics can be used to summarize and describe some of the essential characteristics of large collections of data. Statistics can also be used to guide our decision making concerning the data we have collected. That is, statistics can allow us to make inferences about our data. **Inferential statistics** tell us about the *significance* of the results of our experimental or correlational studies. In general, they tell us the likelihood that the data we have collected might have occurred by chance. Let's use another example, again dealing with means.

Perhaps you'll recall the example we generated in Topic 1 having to do with studying under the influence of different sorts of background music. To keep matters simple, let's assume that you have two groups of volunteer subjects. Each group is to try to learn 50 words in a 5-minute study session. One group will practice in silence; the other group will have classical music playing in the background. We'll call the first group Group S and the second, Group C. For both groups, N = 40. After each group studies their word lists for 5 minutes, you test to see how many words have been learned. Then you construct a frequency distribution of your data and compute the means and

inferential statistics
statistical tests that tell us about the significance of the results of experimental or correlational studies

X-scores	$X - \bar{X}$	$(X - \bar{X})^2$
12	6.5	42.25
10	4.5	20.25
7	1.5	2.25
6	.5	.25
5	−.5	.25
5	−.5	.25
4	−1.5	2.25
4	−1.5	2.25
1	−4.5	20.25
1	−4.5	20.25
		$\Sigma(X - \bar{X})^2 = 110.50$

$$\Sigma X = 55$$
$$N = 10$$
$$\bar{X} = \Sigma X \div N = 5.5$$

$$\text{s.d.} = \sqrt{\frac{\Sigma(X - \bar{X})^2}{N}} = \sqrt{\frac{110.50}{10}} = \sqrt{11.05} = \underline{3.32}$$

Figure 35.5
The computation of the standard deviation for a small distribution of X-scores.

standard deviations for each set of data. What you discover is that Group S has a mean number of words learned equal to 26 and Group C's mean is 28.5. Now what? There's no doubt that 28.5 is larger than 26, but the difference is not very large. Is the difference large enough? We need to backtrack just a little.

Imagine that we had two groups of subjects in a similar experiment that received exactly the same treatment. That is, both groups performed the same task under the same conditions. Some dependent variable is measured for both groups (perhaps the number of words that were learned in a 5-minute study session). Even though both groups were treated exactly the same, would we expect the mean scores for the two groups to be *exactly* equal? Wouldn't we expect *some* chance variation in scores between the two groups? If we did this same experiment again tomorrow, or next week, would we expect (again) to get exactly the same mean scores, even though experimental conditions remain the same? No. We generally anticipate that simply because of chance factors alone there will be some difference between the scores earned by two different groups of subjects, even if they are doing the same thing under the same conditions. So if mean scores for our two groups turn out to be somewhat different, we aren't surprised; we can attribute the difference to chance. But what if the groups are treated differently? What if the differences in measured responses are large? Can these differences also be attributed to chance? Or do they reflect real, significant differences between the two groups? This is where inferential statistics come in.

Inferential statistics allow us to make probability statements. They help us determine if observed differences in our descriptive statistics (like means) are due to chance and random factors, or if they reflect some true difference between the groups we have measured. Differences that are not likely to have occurred by chance are called **statistically significant differences.** If the difference between two calculated means is found to be statistically significant, that difference may or may not be *important* or *meaningful,* but we can claim that the difference is not likely to be due to chance.

One way to think about statistical significance is in terms of replication. If, for example, two means are significantly different, it is likely that if the measurements were taken over and over again, the same difference in the

statistically significant differences
differences between some descriptive statistics not likely to have occurred by chance if the descriptive statistics were describing the same group

same direction would show up most of the time. Inferential statistics can be used to judge the statistical significance of any descriptive statistic. They can be used to tell us about the probability that means, medians, standard deviations, proportions, and correlation coefficients are truly different or, rather, different by chance alone.

Significance is usually stated as a proportion. We talk about means being different at the "0.05 level," for instance. What this means is that the likelihood of our finding a mean difference as large as we did by chance alone is less than 5 in 100. The "0.01 level of significance" is even more conservative. It implies that the difference that we have observed would have occurred by chance—if in fact no real differences exist—less than 1 time in a 100.

Let's return now to the example with which we are working in this section and add a small insight to this business of statistical significance. We have reported that the results of an experiment provide us with two mean scores: 26 and 28.5. Now we are interested in determining the extent to which these means are statistically different or due to chance factors. As we have implied, there is a statistical test of significance that can be applied to our data to answer this very question. The statistical test is called a *t-test*.

There are *three* factors that influence a test of significance such as the one that would be applied to our data for this example. One, of course, is the extent of the mean difference itself. *Everything else being equal,* the larger the measured difference, the more likely that the difference reflects a real difference and not chance factors. A second factor is the size of the sample, or the number of measurements being tested. *Everything else being equal,* differences based on large numbers of observations are more likely to be significant than differences based on fewer observations. The third factor that influences a measure of statistical significance is the variability of the data. To see why variability (usually standard deviation) matters in determining the significance of difference between means, refer to Figure 35.6. In the top part of Figure 35.6 we see two distributions of X-scores that have different means. The bottom part of the figure shows two other distributions that have the same mean difference. Because the variability (standard deviations) of distributions A and B are small, it is more likely that their means reflect

Figure 35.6

The possible outcomes of two experiments. In both cases, the mean differences ($\overline{B} - \overline{A}$) ($\overline{D} - \overline{C}$) are the same, and the Ns are also the same for each distribution. But because the variabilities in (A) are smaller, the difference between A and B is more likely to be significant than is the difference between C and D.

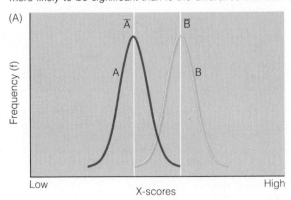
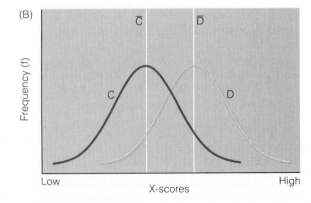

significant differences than is the case for distributions C and D—even though the actual mean difference is the same in either case. In fact, the formula for the t-test of the significance of the difference between means includes (1) the mean difference itself, (2) the size of the groups involved, or N, and (3) the standard deviations of the scores from each group. When applied to our original sample problem, we find that there is *no* statistically significant difference between the means of Forms A and B. This is hardly surprising because the means themselves were identical.

Before you go on

What is meant by "test of statistical significance"?

What does it mean to say that two means, for example, are statistically significant at the 0.01 level?

As we have suggested in our topics on personality assessment and on the measurement of intelligence, many of the measurements we make in psychology tend to fall into a similar pattern. Particularly when measurements are made on large numbers of subjects, we commonly find that they fall into a distribution we call the **normal curve** (see Figure 35.7). The normal curve is a frequency distribution that is symmetrical and bell-shaped. As you can see, scores that are normally distributed tend to bunch around the mean and become infrequent at the extreme values of X (whatever the X-scores may be). Because this

normal distribution of scores does occur so often, we tend to know a lot about the nature of this curve.

The normal curve is simply a graphic representation of a collection of numbers. As such, we can compute the mean and the standard deviation of the scores that make up the distribution. Because the normal distribution is symmetrical, the mean always falls precisely in the middle of the distribution and is coincident with the median. *That is, there are just as many scores above the mean as there are below it.* We also know how many scores (or what proportion or percentage) of scores fall within standard devia-

normal curve
a commonly found, symmetrical, bell-shaped frequency distribution

Figure 35.7
The percentage of cases in a normal distribution falling between ± 1 s.d. around the mean (68%), ± 2 s.d. (95%), and ± 3 s.d. (99%). Note that the curve is symmetrical and the mean divides it exactly in half, and that virtually all scores fall between 3 standard deviations below the mean and 3 standard deviations above the mean.

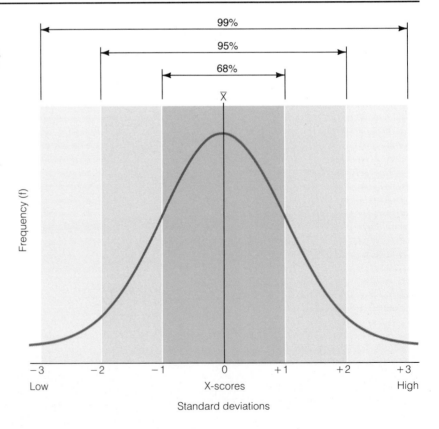

tion units around the mean. For example, we know that 68 percent of all scores fall between 1 standard deviation below the mean and 1 standard deviation above the mean (see Figure 35.7). It is also the case that 95 percent of the scores fall between ±2 standard deviations around the mean. Virtually all the cases in a normal distribution fall between −3 and +3 standard deviations around the mean. What good is this sort of information? Let's look at an example problem.

When many people are measured, IQ scores tend to fall in distributions that we may consider to be normal distributions. Figure 35.8 depicts a theoretical IQ distribution where, by definition, the mean equals 100 and the standard deviation is equal to 15 IQ points. We might want to know, for instance, what percentage of the population has an IQ score above 100. Well, that's an easy one. Because the mean equals 100, and because the mean divides the distribution exactly in half, 50 percent of the cases fall above 100 and 50 percent of the cases fall below an IQ of 100, so the answer is 50 percent.

What percentage of the population has an IQ score above 115? This takes a little more effort, and following along with Figure 35.8 might help. We might work backward. If we know the percentage of cases in the shaded portion of the curve (up to IQ = 115), then the difference between that percentage and 100 will be the percentage who have IQs above 115. We can't determine the shaded percentage by inspection, but we can do so in a few easy steps. One half, or 50 percent, of the cases fall below the mean (this we've already established). Now what about that segment between 100 and 115? What we do know (check on Figure 35.7

again) is that 68 percent of the cases fall between −1 standard deviation and +1 standard deviation. In a normal distribution, the mean divides this segment exactly in half, so that between the mean and 1 standard deviation above the mean are included 34 percent of the cases. (Note that IQ = 115 *is* 1 s.d. above the mean.) So now we have 50 percent to the mean of 100, and 34 percent from the mean to 115. We add the two together and determine that 84 percent of the cases fall below an IQ of 115, so 16 percent must fall above it. Using the same logic, we can convert any score to a percentage or proportion, if we are dealing with a normal curve. To do so for scores

that do not fall precisely on standard deviation units above or below the mean involves a slight complication, but the general method is the same as we have indicated here. What percentage of the population (in accord with our Figures 35.7 and 35.8) have earned IQ scores above 130? (The answer is 2.5 percent. Can you see where that comes from?)

Figure 35.8

A theoretical normal curve of IQ scores. Here we can see, with mean = 100 and s.d. = 15, that 84 percent of the population has an IQ of 115 or less (50% to the mean and 34% from the mean to 1 s.d. above the mean). Thus, only 16 percent have IQs above 115.

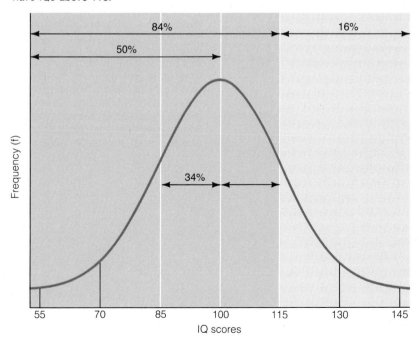

TOPIC SUMMARY

Provide a general definition of measurement.

In general, measurement involves assigning numbers to some characteristic of interest according to rules or some agreed-upon system. / 652

Define four levels of measurement.

Measurement may take place at four different levels, or with four different scales. Nominal scales name, sort, or categorize events on the basis of the presence of some characteristic of interest. Ordinal scales allow us to rank events on the basis of the amount or extent of some characteristic of interest. With interval scales, we can specify that there is an equal difference between adjacent ranked events. Ratio scales categorize, rank order with equal intervals, and include a real zero point. / 654

What is a frequency distribution and what is a histogram?

What are they used for?

As its name suggests, a frequency distribution is a way of organizing collected data by listing all scores (X-scores) in order and indicating the frequency with which each occurs. A histogram is a bar graph that represents the frequency with which X-scores occur by the height of a bar. Both histograms and frequency distributions help us summarize data so that we can make some determinations about its nature by visual inspection. / 656

Name and define three measures of central tendency.

There are three measures of central tendency, or average: (1) the *mean,* $\overline{X}$, the sum of X-scores divided by the number of scores (i.e., $\overline{X} = \Sigma X/N$); (2) the *median,* the score above which and below which fall 50 percent of the scores, and (3) the *mode,* the most frequently occurring score in the distribution. / 658

What is the formula for standard deviation, and of what is it a measure?

The standard deviation (s.d.) is a measure of the spread, or dispersion, of the scores in a distribution. It is, essentially, the average of the extent to which each score in the distribution deviates from its mean. The formula for standard deviation is:

$$\text{s.d.} = \sqrt{\frac{\Sigma(X - \overline{X})^2}{N}} \qquad / 660$$

What is meant by "test of statistical significance"?

What does it mean to say that two means, for example, are statistically significant at the 0.01 level?

A test of statistical significance tells us about the likelihood that an observed descriptive statistical difference might have occurred by chance. For example, to say that the difference between two means is "statistically significant at the 0.01 level" means that if there were no real difference between the groups from which the means came, the likelihood of discovering a mean difference as large as the one observed is less than 1 in 100. / 663

GLOSSARY

A

abnormal statistically uncommon, maladaptive cognitions, affect, and/or behaviors that are at odds with social expectations and that result in distress or discomfort (p. 501)

absolute threshold the intensity of a stimulus that one can detect 50 percent of the time (p. 84)

accommodation the process in which the shape of the lens is changed (by the ciliary muscles) in order to focus an image on the retina (pp. 100, 137)

acquisition the process in classical conditioning in which the strength of the CR increases with repeated pairings of the CS and UCS (p. 176)

adolescence the developmental period between childhood and adulthood, often begun at puberty, which ends when full physical growth is achieved (p. 340)

adrenal glands located on the kidneys, part of the ANS especially involved in emotional reactions (pp. 53, 387)

affect the feelings or mood that accompany emotional reactions (p. 7)

affective assessment the measurement of personality characteristics, one's typical behaviors (p. 440)

affective disorders disorders of mood or feeling; usually depression; less frequently mania and depression occurring in cycles (p. 525)

affirmative concepts concepts defined by the presence of one particular attribute (p. 267)

aggression behavior with the intent to do harm to another (p. 606)

agoraphobia a phobic fear of open places, of being alone, or of being in public places from which escape might be difficult (p. 508)

algorithm a problem-solving strategy in which all possible solutions are generated and tested and an acceptable solution is guaranteed (p. 288)

all-or-none-principle the notion that a neuron will either fire, and generate a full impulse, or will not fire at all (p. 46)

alpha activity an EEG pattern associated with quiet relaxation and characterized by slow waves in cycles of 8–12 per second (p. 150)

Alzheimer's disease a gradual, progressive loss of intellectual functioning (dementia) caused by abnormal changes in brain tissues (p. 533)

androgyny a social role that includes both feminine and masculine traits, attitudes, beliefs, values, and so on (p. 348)

antianxiety drugs chemicals, such as the meprobamates and benzodiazepines, that alleviate the symptoms of anxiety (p. 547)

antidepressant drugs chemicals, such as MAO inhibitors and tricyclics, that reduce and/or eliminate the symptoms of depression (p. 546)

antipsychotic drug chemicals, such as reserpine and chlorpromazine, that are effective in reducing psychotic symptoms (p. 546)

anxiety a general feeling of apprehension or dread, accompanied by predictable physiological changes (pp. 407, 507)

aphasia a disorder or loss of speech caused by damage to some portion of the brain (p. 76)

aqueous humor watery fluid found between the cornea and lens that nourishes the structures at the front of the eye (p. 100)

arousal one's level of activation or excitement; indicative of a motivational state (p. 360)

assessment center a personnel selection mechanism whereby applicants are tested, interviewed, and observed in a number of situations by a team of evaluators (p. 617)

association areas those areas in the frontal, parietal, and temporal lobes that are neither sensory nor motor in function where cognitive functioning is assumed to take place (p. 72)

attachment a strong, two-way emotional/social relationship, usually between a child and its mother or primary caregiver (p. 334)

attitude a general evaluative disposition directed toward some object, consisting of feelings, behaviors, and beliefs (p. 576)

attribution theory a theory that tries to describe how we explain the causes of behavior (p. 583)

audience inhibition reluctance to intervene and offer assistance in front of others (p. 601)

autokinetic effect an illusion in which a stationary source of light in an otherwise dark environment appears to move (pp. 140, 593)

autonomic nervous system (ANS) the system of nerves that serves the smooth muscles, glands, and internal, visceral organs (pp. 49, 387)

aversion therapy a technique of behavior therapy in which an aversive stimulus, such as a shock, is paired with an undesired behavior (p. 561)

avoidance conditioning a form of operant conditioning in which an organism learns to respond to a signal or cue in order to avoid a negative reinforcer (p. 193)

axon the long taillike extension of a neuron that carries an impulse away from the cell body toward the synapse (p. 42)

axon terminals a series of branching extensions at the end of an axon that form synapses with other neurons (p. 43)

B

basilar membrane a structure within the cochlea that vibrates and stimulates the hair cells of the inner ear (p. 116)

behavior any action or reaction of an organism that can be observed and measured (p. 5)

behavior modification a therapeutic technique of modifying behavior by reinforcing appropriate behaviors and extinguishing inappropriate behaviors (p. 196)

behavior therapy techniques of psychotherapy founded on principles of learning established in the psychological laboratory (p. 559)

behavioral observation the personality assessment technique in which one draws conclusions about an individual on the basis of observations of his or her behaviors (p. 446)

behaviorism the school of psychology, associated with Watson and Skinner, that focuses on the observable, measurable behavior of organisms (p. 12)

biofeedback the operant conditioning procedure of providing information to an individual about internal bodily processes so that those processes can be modified (p. 203)

blindspot the region of the retina, containing no photoreceptors, where the optic nerve leaves the eye (p. 102)

brain stem the portion of the brain just above the spinal cord, comprised of the medulla and the pons (p. 66)

brightness the psychological experience associated with a light's intensity or wave amplitude (p. 95)

brightness constancy the tendency to see objects as being of the same brightness regardless of the intensity of light reflected from them (p. 141)

British Empiricism the school of thought (associated with John Locke among others) that focused on the source of mental processes, claiming them to be learned through experience (p. 9)

C

case history an intensive, detailed study of certain aspects of one (or a few) individual(s) (p.36)

CAT scan (computerized axial tomography) a method of imaging brain structure through the computer enhancement of X-ray pictures (p. 65)

category clustering the tendency of subjects during recall to group words together into categories even if they are presented in random order (p. 236)

catharsis the release of pent-up tension or negative emotions, such as in the release of aggression and violence by watching such behaviors in others (p. 608)

cell body the largest mass of a nerve cell. The cell body contains the cell's nucleus and "receives" neural impulses (p. 42)

central nervous system (CNS) those neurons in the brain and the spinal cord (p. 49)

central tendency a measure of the middle, or average, score in a set (p. 656)

cerebellum spherical structure at lower rear of brain that is involved in the coordination and smoothing of muscular activity (p. 67)

cerebral cortex (cerebrum) the large, convoluted outer covering of the brain that is most fully developed in humans and is the seat of intellectual functions (p. 70)

chromosomes tiny threads of protein, found in pairs in the nucleus of a cell, that carry genes (p. 303)

chronological age (CA) a person's actual, biological age (p. 469)

ciliary muscles small muscles that control the shape (focusing capability) of the lens (p. 100)

classical conditioning learning in which an originally neutral stimulus comes to evoke a new response after having been paired with a stimulus that reflexively evokes that same response (p. 174)

client-centered therapy the humanistic psychotherapy associated with Rogers, which is aimed at helping the client grow and change from within (p. 558)

closure a Gestalt principle of organization concerning the tendency to perceive incomplete figures as whole and complete (p. 133)

cochlea the inner ear where sound waves become neural impulses (p. 116)

cognitions the mental process of "knowing," of thinking, attending, perceiving, remembering, and the like (pp. 7, 263)

cognitive having to do with cognitions—mental representations of information and knowledge (p. 208)

cognitive assessment the measurement of intelligence, ability, or aptitude, one's best performance (p. 440)

cognitive dissonance the state of tension or discomfort that exists when we hold inconsistent cognitions (p. 580)

cognitive map a mental representation of the learning situation or physical environment (p. 209)

cognitive processes the mental activities that involve forming and using cognitions (p. 263)

cognitive psychology the scientific psychology that studies the nature of cognitions: perceptions, thoughts, ideas, beliefs, concepts, problem solving, and memory (p. 14)

cognitive restructuring therapy a form of cognitive therapy in which patients are led to overcome negative self-images and pessimistic views of the future (p. 564)

compensation a mechanism through which extraordinary resources are invested in some trait or ability to offset deficits in other traits or abilities (p. 408)

compulsions constantly intruding, stereotyped, and essentially involuntary acts or behaviors (p. 509)

concept a mental event used to represent a category or class of events or objects (p. 265)

conception the uniting of a father's sperm cell and a mother's ovum (p. 302)

concurrent validity the extent to which a test is correlated with other tests claiming to measure the same characteristic (p. 444)

conditioned response (CR) in classical conditioning, the learned response (e.g., salivation) evoked by the CS after conditioning (p. 175)

conditioned stimulus (CS) in classical conditioning, an originally neutral stimulus (e.g., a tone) that, when paired with a UCS, comes to evoke a new response (p. 175)

conditioning demonstrated by a relatively permanent change in behavior that occurs as the result of practice or experience (p. 173)

cones the photoreceptor cells of the retina that are thought to operate best in bright light and to be responsible for perceiving colors (p. 102)

conflict a source of stress in which *some* goals can be reached only at the expense of others (p. 401)

conformity changing one's behavior so that it is consistent with the behavior of others (p. 593)

conjunctive concepts concepts that are defined by "and" rules; that is, having all attributes of the concept (p. 266)

consciousness our awareness, or perception, of the environment and of our own mental processes (p. 148)

conservation the understanding that changing something's form does not change its essential character (p. 327)

conservative focusing a concept formation strategy of choosing one attribute at a time to see if it forms part of a given concept (p. 270)

content validity the extent to which a test provides an adequate and fair sample of the behaviors being measured (p. 444)

continuity the Gestalt principle that a line or movement is perceived as continuing in the same smooth direction as first established (p. 133)

continuous reinforcement (CRF) a reinforcement schedule in which each and every response is followed by a reinforcer (p. 197)

contrast the extent to which a stimulus is in some physical way different from other surrounding stimuli (p. 129)

convergence the tendency of the eyes to move toward each other as we focus on objects up close (p. 136)

convergent thinking the reduction or focusing of many different ideas into one possible problem solution (p. 294)

conversion disorder the display of a (severe) physical disorder for which there is no medical explanation; often accompanied by an apparent lack of concern on the part of the patient (p. 511)

cornea the outermost structure of the eye that protects the eye and helps focus light waves (p. 99)

corpus callosum the network of nerve fibers that normally transmit impulses between the two hemispheres of the cerebral cortex (p. 73)

correlation a largely statistical method used to discover R-R relationships (p. 27)

correlation coefficient a statistic (a number, r) that indicates the nature (positive or negative) and strength of the relationship between measured responses (p. 28)

critical period the time interval during which an imprinted response is most easily and effortlessly acquired (p. 217)

cross-laterality the principle that, in general, sensory and motor impulses to and from the brain cross from the left side of the body to the right side of the brain, and vice versa (p. 71)

cross-sectional method a research method in which a number of subjects of different ages are compared on some measure at the same time (p. 489)

crowding the subjective feeling of discomfort caused by a sense of lack of space (p. 636)

D

death instincts (thanatos) those inborn impulses proposed by Freud that compel one toward destruction, including aggression (p. 421)

debriefing explaining to a subject, after an experiment has been completed, the true nature of the experiment, making sure that there are no lasting negative consequences of participation (p. 598)

decibel the unit of measurement for loudness in which O represents the absolute threshold and 140 is sensed as pain (p. 112)

deep structure in transformational grammar, the basic idea, cognition, or message that is to be communicated with language (p. 277)

defense mechanisms techniques, often beyond one's conscious control, employed to protect against the feelings of stress (p. 407)

degenerative dementia a marked loss of intellectual and cognitive abilities that worsens with age (p. 521)

deindividuation a process in which the person loses self-awareness and becomes anonymous within a group (p. 606)

delta wave an EEG wave pattern (.5 to 3 cycles per second) indicative of deepening levels (p. 151)

dendrite a branchlike extension of the neuron's cell body. Dendrites receive neural impulses (p. 42)

denial refusing to acknowledge the presence of stressors (p. 408)

dependent variables those responses or behaviors that are measured in an experiment and are expected to "depend" on manipulations of the independent variables (p. 29)

depressants those drugs (such as alcohol, opiates, sedatives, and heroin) that slow or reduce nervous system activity (p. 162)

difference threshold the minimal difference in some stimulus attribute, such as intensity, that one can detect 50 percent of the time (p. 84)

diffusion of responsibility the tendency to allow others to share in the obligation to intervene (p. 602)

discrimination the phenomenon in which an organism learns to make a CR in response to only one CS, but not to other stimuli (pp. 177, 199)

disjunctive concepts concepts defined by "either/or" rules; that is, either having some attributes or others (p. 266)

displacement directing one's motives at some substitute person or object rather than expressing them directly (p. 409)

dissociative disorders disorders in which one separates or dissociates from aspects of one's personality (p. 512)

distributed practice rehearsal in which practice is done in segments with rest intervals interspersed (p. 248)

divergent thinking the creation of many ideas or potential problem solutions from one idea (p. 294)

DNA (deoxyribonucleic acid) complex protein molecules that make up genes and that contain the blueprint for genetic transmission (p. 303)

dominant gene a gene whose characteristics will be expressed regardless of the gene with which it is paired (p. 305)

double-blind technique in an experiment, a protection against bias in which neither the subject(s) nor the experimenter(s) are told the hypothesis of the experiment (p. 33)

Down's syndrome a disorder leading to mental retardation that is caused by having three chromosomes, instead of the normal pair, in position 21 (p. 306)

drive the arousing and directing experience of a state of need, thus motivating behavior (p. 362)

duplicity theory of vision the theory that the rods are twilight receptors and color-blind, whereas the cones are daylight receptors and responsible for color vision (p. 104)

E

eardrum the outermost membrane of the ear which is set in motion by the vibrations of a sound and passes those vibrations to the ossicles (p. 116)

ego that aspect of personality that encompasses the sense of self; in contact with the real world; operates on the reality principle (p. 421)

egocentric seeing everything from one's own point of view, unable to appreciate someone else's perspective (p. 327)

elaborative rehearsal a mechanism for processing information into LTM that involves the meaningful manipulation of the information to be remembered (p. 234)

electroconvulsive therapy (ECT) a treatment (usually for the symptoms of severe depression) in which a high voltage current passed across a patient's head causes a seizure and loss of consciousness (p. 544)

electrode a fine wire used to either stimulate or record the electric activity of neural tissue (p. 62)

electroencephalogram (EEG) an instrument to measure and record the electrical activity of the brain using electrodes attached to the scalp (pp. 64, 149)

emotion a reaction involving subjective feelings, physiological response, cognitive interpretation, and behavioral expression (p. 383)

empathic able to understand and share the essence of another's feelings; to view from another's perspective (p. 558)

encoding the active process of putting information into memory (p. 225)

endocrine system a network of glands that secrete hormones directly into the bloodstream (p. 49)

environmental psychology the field of applied psychology that studies the effect of the environment on persons in it (p. 632)

epinephrine (adrenalin) a hormone produced by the adrenal glands that is involved in emotional activity, mostly affecting heart activity (p. 387)

episodic memory in LTM, where life events and experiences are stored (p. 235)

escape conditioning a form of operant conditioning in which an organism learns to escape from a negative reinforcer (p. 193)

estrogen a female sex hormone, produced by the ovaries, important in the sex drive and the development of secondary sex characteristics (p. 370)

etiology the cause of predisposing factors of a disturbance or disorder (p. 504)

evaluation apprehension one's concern about how others are evaluating one's performance (p. 605)

experiment the scientific method used to establish the relationship between manipulated events (independent variables) and measured events (dependent variables) while other events (extraneous variables) are controlled (p. 29)

experimental neurosis a condition of anxiety and agitation evidenced by subjects that are asked to make too fine a discrimination in a classical conditioning task (p. 178)

external attribution an explanation of behavior in terms of something outside the person; a situational attribution (p. 583)

extinction the process in classical conditioning in which the strength of the CR decreases with repeated presentations of the CS alone (p. 176)

extraneous variables those variables in an experiment that need to be controlled or eliminated so as not to affect the dependent variable (p. 29)

F

fantasy an escape from stress through imagination and daydreaming (p. 408)

Fechner's law the statement that the magnitude of psychological sensation is a logarithmic function of physical magnitude ($S = C \log I$) (p. 88)

fetal alcohol syndrome a collection of symptoms reflecting retardation of intellectual and physical development caused by a mother's ingestion of alcohol during pregnancy (p. 312)

figure-ground relationship the Gestalt psychology principle that stimuli are selected and perceived as figures against a ground or background (p. 129)

fixed interval (FI) schedule a system in which the first response that occurs after a fixed time interval is reinforced (p. 198)

fixed ratio (FR) schedule a system in which one reinforcer is administered only after a fixed number of responses (p. 198)

flooding a technique of behavior therapy in which a subject is confronted with the object of his or her phobic fear, while accompanied by the therapist (p. 560)

focus gambling a concept formation strategy of finding a positive instance of a concept and then guessing that other events that share some of the same attributes are also members of the concept (p. 271)

fovea the region of the retina of greatest acuity due to a high concentration of cones (p. 102)

free association the procedure in psychoanalysis in which the patient is to express whatever comes to mind without editing responses (p. 556)

frequency distribution an order listing of all X-scores indicating the frequency with which each occurs (p. 654)

frontal lobe the largest of the four lobes of the cerebrum; in front of the central fissure and above the lateral fissure (p. 70)

frustration the blocking or thwarting of goal-directed behavior (p. 400)

frustration-aggression hypothesis the point of view (now discredited) that all aggression stems from frustration (p. 406)

fugue state a condition of amnesia accompanied by unexplained travel or change of location (p. 512)

functional fixedness the phenomenon in which one is unable to see a new use or function for an object because of experience using the object in some other function (p. 293)

functionalism the school of psychology that studied the function of the mind and consciousness in helping the organism to adapt to its environment (p. 11)

fundamental attribution error the tendency to use internal attributions when explaining the behavior of other people (p. 583)

G

g-factor Spearman's name for general intelligence of the sort common to all intellectual tasks (p. 464)

ganzfeld an artificial environment in which physical cues to depth and distance have been removed (p. 141)

general adaptation syndrome (GAS) a pattern of physiological reactions to stressors including alarm, resistance, and exhaustion (p. 398)

generalization the process by which a response that was reinforced in the presence of one stimulus appears in response to other, similar stimuli (pp. 177, 199)

generalized anxiety disorder persistent, chronic, and distressingly high levels of unattributable anxiety (p. 508)

genes the basic structure of heredity; found on chromosomes (p. 303)

genotype an individual's characteristics as determined by his or her genes (p. 306)

gestalt whole, totality, configuration, or pattern; the whole (gestalt) being perceived as more than the sum of its parts (pp. 11, 129)

glaucoma a vision disorder caused by an increase in pressure of aqueous humor on the lens and cornea (p. 100)

group polarization the tendency for members of a group to give more extreme judgments following a discussion than they gave initially (p. 605)

groupthink a style of thinking of cohesive groups concerned with maintaining agreement to the extent that independent ideas are discouraged (p. 606)

H

hair cells the receptor cells for hearing, located in the cochlea, that are stimulated by the vibrating basilar membrane and transmit neural impulses to the brain (p. 116)

hallucinations perceptual experiences occurring without the benefit of sensory input; perceiving that which is not there to be perceived (p. 157)

hallucinogens drugs (such as LSD and PCP) whose major effects are the alteration of perceptual experience and mood (p. 164)

health psychology the field of applied psychology that studies the diagnosis, treatment, and prevention of physical disorders and disease from a behavioral and/or psychological perspective (p. 640)

hemispheres the two halves of the cerebral cortex, separated by a large, deep fissure running from front to back (p. 70)

hertz (Hz) the standard measure of sound wave frequency that is the number of wave cycles per second (p. 113)

heuristic a problem-solving strategy in which hypotheses about problem solutions are generated and tested in a time-saving and systematic way, but that does not guarantee an acceptable solution (p. 288)

hierarchy of needs Maslow's theoretical arrangement, in which needs are satisfied in order, from physiological needs to self-actualization (p. 376)

histogram a bar graph; a graphic representation of a frequency distribution (p. 655)

holophrastic speech using one word to communicate a range of intentions by changing gestures, intonation, and so on (p. 333)

homeostasis a state of balance or equilibrium among internal physiological conditions (p. 364)

homosexual an individual with sexual preference for and sexually aroused by members of his or her own sex (p. 371)

hormones chemical compounds, secreted by endocrine glands, carried through the bloodstream in order to have their effect on behavior (p. 49)

hue the psychological experience associated with a light's wavelength (p. 96)

humanism a point of view associated with Maslow and Rogers that focuses on the person or self as a central matter of concern (p. 13)

hypnosis an induced altered state of consciousness characterized by an increase in suggestibility, attention, and imagination (p. 156)

hypochondriasis a mental disorder involving the fear of developing some serious disease or illness (p. 510)

hypothalamus a small structure at the base of the brain involved in many drives, including thirst, hunger, sex, and temperature regulation (pp. 69, 365)

hypothesis a tentative proposition, or explanation, that can be tested, confirmed, or rejected (p. 5)

I

id that instinctive aspect of personality that seeks immediate gratification of impulses and operates on the pleasure principle (p. 421)

idealistic principle the impulse that governs the superego; opposed to the id, seeking adherence to standards of ethics and morality (p. 421)

identity crisis the struggle to define and integrate one's sense of self, and to decide what one's attitudes, beliefs, and values should be (p. 346)

identity status a level of commitment in the development of identity or a sense of self (p. 347)

implosive therapy a behavior therapy in which one imagines one's worst fears, experiencing extreme anxiety in the safe surroundings of the therapist's office (p. 561)

impression management function the selective presentation or misrepresentation of one's attitudes in an attempt to present one's self in a particular way (p. 578)

imprinting the simple acquisition of a response (e. g., following) based on exposure to the proper stimulus during a critical period (p. 217)

in-basket technique an assessment device in which applicants are asked to respond to a number of situations that might be encountered in a typical workday (p. 617)

incentive a goal that an organism may be motivated to approach or avoid (p. 362)

independent variables those events in an experiment, manipulated by the experimenter, that are expected to have an effect on behavior (p. 29)

inferential statistics statistical tests that tell us about the significance of the results of experimental or correlational studies (p. 660)

inferiority complex the Adlerian notion that, as children, we develop a sense of inferiority in dealing with our environment (p. 424)

insanity a legal term for diminished capacity and inability to tell right from wrong (p. 506)

insight the sudden reorganization of perceptions and cognitions that leads to the solution of a problem (p. 212)

insomnia the chronic inability to get an adequate amount of sleep (p. 166)

instinct an unlearned, complex pattern of behavior that occurs in the presence of particular stimuli (p. 360)

instinctive drift the tendency of behaviors that have been conditioned to eventually revert to more instinctive behaviors (p. 201)

intelligence the capacity to understand the world and the resourcefulness to cope with its challenges; that which an intelligence test measures (p. 462)

intelligence quotient (IQ) the quotient of mental age divided by chronological age (MA/CA) multiplied by 100, taken to represent one's level of tested intelligence (p. 469)

interactive dualism Descartes's notion that a separate body and mind interact and influence each other (p. 9)

internal attribution an explanation of behavior in terms of something within the person; a dispositional attribution (p. 583)

interneurons neurons within the brain or spinal cord (p. 44)

interval measurement measurement in which we can specify the difference between adjacent, ranked events (p. 653)

interview the personality assessment technique involving a conversational interchange between an interviewer and a subject to gain information about the subject (p. 447)

I/O psychology industrial/organizational psychology; concerned with applying principles of psychology to improve the efficiency and effectiveness of organizations (p. 614)

ion an electrically charged (either + or −) chemical particle (p. 44)

iris the structure of the eye that reflexively opens or contracts the pupil (p. 99)

J

job analysis a complete and specific description of a job including personal qualities required to do it well (p. 615)

just noticeable difference (j.n.d.) the minimum amount of change in a stimulus required for detection (p. 86)

K

kinesthetic sense the position sense that tells us where the different parts of our bodies are and what our muscles and joints are doing (p. 121)

L

language a collection of arbitrary symbols that have significance for a language-using community and that follow certain rules of combination (p. 272)

latent content the underlying meaning of a dream, thought to be symbolically representative (p. 155)

latent learning hidden learning that is not reflected in performance until performance is reinforced (p. 209)

learned helplessness a condition in which a subject does not attempt to escape from a painful or noxious situation after learning in a previous, similar situation that no escape was possible (p. 195)

learning demonstrated by a relatively permanent change in behavior that occurs as the result of practice or experience (p. 172)

learning set an acquired, expected way to go about learning or problem solving; learning to learn (p. 213)

lens the structure of the eye behind the iris that changes shape to focus visual images (p. 100)

lesion a cut or wound made on neural tissue to study the impact of the destruction of specific brain areas (p. 62)

libido the energy that activates the life (sexual) instincts (largely of the id) (p. 420)

life instincts (eros) those inborn impulses proposed by Freud that compel one toward survival, including hunger, thirst, and sex (p. 420)

light a radiant energy that can be represented as a wave form with wavelengths between 380 and 760 nanometers (p. 95)

limbic system a collection of small structures, including the amygdala, septal area, and hippocampus, involved in emotional and motivational responding and in the transfer of memories to long-term storage (pp. 68, 388)

lobotomy a psychosurgical procedure in which the connections of the frontal lobes are severed from the rest of the brain (p. 62)

locus of control a general belief that what happens is either under our control (internal locus) or a matter of chance and environmental factors (external locus) (p. 427)

long-term memory (LTM) a type of memory with virtually unlimited capacity and very long, if not permanent, duration (p. 232)

longitudinal method a research method in which measures are taken on the same subjects repeatedly over time (p. 489)

loudness the psychological experience correlated with the intensity, or amplitude, of a sound wave (p. 112)

M

magnitude estimation Stevens's method of psychophysical scaling in which subjects assign numbers directly to their psychological experience of the intensity of stimuli (p. 88)

maintenance rehearsal the technique of simple, rote repetition used to keep information in STM (p. 229)

malleus, incus, and stapes (collectively *ossicles*) three small bones that transmit sound wave vibrations from the eardrum to the oval window (p. 116)

manifest content the literal content of a dream as it is recalled by the dreamer (p. 155)

mantrum a soft word or sound chanted repeatedly to aid the meditation process (p. 158)

massed practice rehearsal in which there is no break in one's practice (p. 248)

masturbation self-stimulation of the genitals to the point of arousal, often to orgasm (p. 343)

matching phenomenon the tendency to select partners whose level of attractiveness matches our own (p. 586)

mean ($\overline{X}$), the sum of all X-scores (ΣX) divided by N, the number of X scores (p. 657)

meaningfulness the extent to which information to be retrieved evokes existing associations in one's memory (p. 251)

measurement the assignment of numbers to some characteristic of interest according to rules or some agreed upon system (pp. 440, 652)

median the score of an ordered set above which and below which fall half the scores (p. 658)

meditation the focusing of awareness in order to arrive at an altered state of consciousness and relaxation (p. 158)

medulla the lowest structure of the brain that controls reflex functions such as respiration and heartbeat and where many nerve fibers cross from the left side of the brain to the right side of body, and vice versa (p. 66)

memory the ability to encode, store, and retrieve information no longer physically present (p. 224)

menarche a female's first menstrual period; often taken as a sign of the beginning of adolescence (p. 342)

mental age (MA) on the Stanford-Binet test, the age level at which the subject is functioning intellectually (p. 469)

mental processes those activities of consciousness not normally observable by others, including cognitions and affect (p. 7)

mental retardation a condition, indicated by an IQ below 70, which begins during the developmental period and is associated with impairment in adaptive functioning (p. 491)

mental set a tendency to perceive or respond to something in a predetermined, set way; an expectation (pp. 131, 291)

mentally gifted demonstrating outstanding ability or aptitude in a number of possible areas; usually general intelligence, where an IQ of 130 is a standard criterion (p. 490)

mere exposure phenomenon the tendency to increase our liking of people and things the more we see of them (p. 585)

Minnesota Multiphasic Personality Inventory (MMPI) a paper-and-pencil inventory used to assess a number of personality dimensions (p. 448)

mnemonic devices strategies for improving retrieval that take advantage of existing memories in order to make new material more meaningful (p. 250)

mode the most frequently occurring X-score in a set (p. 658)

modeling the acquisition of a new appropriate response through the imitation of a model (p. 563)

monochromatic a pure light made up of light waves that all have the same wavelength (p. 98)

moro reflex the neonatal reflex, which is caused by a sudden noise or loss of support, in which a child thrusts its arms out to the sides with fingers open, only to quickly return the arms to the chest with fists clenched (p. 320)

morpheme the smallest unit of meaning in a language (pp. 274, 332)

motivation those forces that arouse and direct behavior in order to satisfy needs or reach goals (p. 360)

motor area that portion of the parietal lobe directly behind the central fissure in which are found the centers that control the voluntary movement of muscles (p. 71)

motor neurons neurons that carry impulses away from the brain or spinal cord toward the muscles and/or glands (p. 44)

multiple personality the existence within one individual of two or more distinct personalities, each of which is dominant at a particular time (p. 513)

myelin a white, fatty covering found on some axons that serves to protect the axon and increase the speed of neural impulses (p. 43)

N

nanometer the unit of measurement for the wavelength of light that is equal to one millionth of a millimeter (p. 96)

narcolepsy a disorder characterized by brief, uncontrollable sleep attacks and an immediate descent into REM sleep (p. 166)

naturalistic observation the psychological method in which behavior is observed as it occurs naturally (p. 34)

need lack or shortage of some biological essential that is required by an organism for survival (p. 361)

need for affiliation the need to be with others and to form friendships and associations (p. 374)

need for competence the need to meet the challenges (large and small) provided by one's environment (p. 374)

need for power the need to be in control of events or persons, usually at another's expense (p. 373)

need to achieve (nAch) the (learned) need to meet or exceed some standard of excellence in performance (p. 372)

negative reinforcer a stimulus that increases the rate of a response when that stimulus is removed after the response has been made (p. 193)

neo-Freudians those theorists of the psychoanalytic school who have taken issue with some parts of Freudian theory, including Adler, Jung, and Horney (p. 419)

neonate the newborn child, from birth through the first 2 weeks (p. 319)

neural impulse the discharge of electrically charged chemical ions through the neural membrane that travels down a neuron when it is active or fires (p. 44)

neural threshold the minimum amount of stimulation required to produce an impulse within a neuron (p. 46)

neuron a nerve cell that is the basic building block of the nervous system; transmits neural impulses (p. 42)

neurotoxins chemicals (poisons) that affect psychological processes through the nervous system (p. 638)

neurotransmitters chemical molecules released at the synapse that either excite a subsequent neuron or inhibit impulse transmission (p. 46)

NMR (nuclear magnetic resonance) a recently developed, high resolution method of imaging brain structures (p. 65)

nominal measurement sorting events into categories on the basis of some characteristic of interest (p. 653)

norepinephrine a hormone secreted by the adrenal glands; involved in emotional arousal (p. 387)

normal curve a commonly found, symmetrical, bell-shaped frequency distribution (p. 664)

norms results of a test taken by a large group of subjects whose scores can be used to make comparisons with or give meaning to new scores (p. 444)

norms rules or expectations that guide our behavior in certain social situations by prescribing how we ought to behave (p. 575)

nucleus the dense area of a cell (near its center) that contains genetic material and acts as master control for the cell's structure and function (p. 303)

O

object permanence the realization that objects that are not physically present are not gone forever and may still reappear (p. 327)

obsessions ideas or thoughts that involuntarily and persistently intrude into awareness (p. 509)

occipital lobe the lobe of the cerebrum at the back and lower back of the brain (p. 70)

operant conditioning changing the rate of a response on the basis of the consequences that result from that response (p. 187)

operational definition a definition given in terms of the operations used to measure or to create the concept being defined (pp. 6, 462)

optic nerve the layer of nerve cells that transmits neural impulses from the eye to the occipital lobe of the brain (p. 102)

ordinal measurement placing categorized events in order, or ranked, in terms of extent or amount of some characteristic of interest (p. 653)

overlearning the practice or rehearsal of material over and above what is needed to just barely learn it (p. 247)

overregularization overapplying a learned syntactic rule (for plural or tense, for example) in a situation where it is not appropriate (p. 333)

ovum the sex cell of the mother that contains 23 single chromosomes (p. 304)

P

panic disorders disorders in which anxiety attacks suddenly and unpredictably incapacitate; there may be periods free from anxiety (p. 509)

paranoid disorder a rare psychotic mental disorder characterized by delusions of persecution, influence, grandeur, or jealousy (p. 524)

parasympathetic division division of the ANS that maintains a calm, relaxed state of the organism (pp. 49, 387)

parietal lobe the lobe of the cerebrum behind the frontal lobe, in front of the occipital lobe, and above the lateral fissure (p. 70)

partial report method a recall procedure in which a subject is asked to recall only a specified portion of the material presented earlier (p. 227)

partial reinforcement schedules systems by which responses are not reinforced every time they occur (p. 197)

perception the complex internal process of selecting, identifying, organizing, and interpreting stimuli (p. 82)

perceptual adaptation (in the context of viewing violence) the idea that watching violence leads a person to become adapted or desensitized to it (p. 608)

peripheral nervous system (PNS) those neurons throughout the body that are not in the brain or spinal cord; that is, those located in the periphery (p. 49)

personal space the bubble of space around an individual which is reserved for intimate relationships and into which others may enter with welcome by invitation only (p. 633)

personality relatively enduring and unique traits (including cognitions, feelings, and behaviors) that can be used to characterize an individual in different situations (p. 419)

personality disorders enduring patterns of perceiving, relating to, and thinking about the environment and one's self that are inflexible and maladaptive (p. 513)

persuasion the process of intentionally attempting to change an attitude (p. 580)

PET scan (positron-emission tomography) a method of imaging the brain, and its activity, through the injection of radioactive substances into the brain (p. 65)

phenomenological an approach that emphasizes one's perception and awareness of events as being more important than the events themselves (p. 428)

phenotype an individual's characteristics as actually expressed (p. 306)

phenylketonuria (PKU) a genetically-caused disorder that produces mental retardation; it is now detectable and preventable (p. 493)

pheromones chemical molecules that produce an odor that is used as a method of communication between organisms (p. 119)

phi phenomenon the visual illusion that explains the apparent motion of stationary lights flashing on and off in sequence (p. 139)

phobic disorder an intense, irrational fear that leads a person to avoid the feared object, activity, or situation (p. 507)

phonemes the smallest unit of sound in the spoken form of a language (pp. 274, 331)

photoreceptors light-sensitive cells (rods and cones) of the retina (p. 102)

physical attractiveness stereotype the tendency to associate desirable characteristics with a physically attractive person, solely on the basis of attractiveness (p. 586)

pinna the outer ear which collects and funnels sound waves (p. 116)

pitch the psychological experience that corresponds to sound wave frequency and influences our perception of tones as being high or low (p. 113)

pituitary gland the master gland of the endocrine system that directly controls other glands and overall growth and development of the body (p. 53)

pleasure principle the impulse of the id to seek immediate gratification to reduce tensions (p. 421)

pluralistic ignorance a condition wherein the inaction of others leads each individual in a group to interpret a situation as a nonemergency, thus leading to general inactivity (p. 601)

pons part of the brain stem forming a bridge, or relay station, between the brain and spinal cord (p. 67)

population density a quantitative measure of the number of persons (or animals) per unit of area (p. 636)

positive reinforcer a stimulus that increases the rate of a response when that stimulus is presented to an organism after the response is made (p. 192)

preconscious that level of consciousness in which elements of memory and environment can quickly and easily be brought into awareness (p. 148)

predictive validity the extent to which a test can be used to predict future behaviors (p. 444)

prefrontal lobotomy a psychosurgical technique in which the prefrontal lobes of the cerebral cortex are severed from lower brain centers (p. 543)

Premack Principle the theory that more preferred activities can be used as reinforcers for less preferred activities (p. 192)

prenatal period the period of development from conception to birth (p. 308)

primary mental abilities according to Thurstone, the seven unique abilities that comprise intelligence (p. 465)

primary reinforcers stimuli (usually biologically or physiologically based) that increase the rate of a response with no previous experience required (p. 196)

proactive interference the inhibition of retrieval of recently learned material caused by material learned earlier (p. 256)

problem a situation in which there is a discrepancy between one's situation at the moment and one's desired situation with no clear way of getting from one to the other (p. 284)

process schizophrenia schizophrenia in which the onset of the symptoms is comparatively slow and gradual (p. 529)

progesterone a female sex hormone, produced by the ovaries, important in the sex drive and in preparing the female for pregnancy (p. 370)

projection seeing in others those very characteristics and motives that cause stress in one's self (p. 409)

projective technique a personality assessment technique requiring subjects to respond to ambiguous stimuli, thus projecting some of their selves into their responses (p. 453)

prototype the member of a concept or category that best typifies or represents that concept or category (p. 267)

proximity a Gestalt principle of organization in which stimuli are perceived as belonging together if they occur close together in space or time (p. 133)

psychoactive drug a natural or synthetic chemical that has an effect on psychological processes and consciousness (p. 160)

psychoanalysis the form of psychotherapy, begun by Freud, aimed at helping the patient gain insight into unconscious conflicts (p. 555)

psychoanalytic the approach to personality associated with Freud and his followers that relies on instincts and the unconscious as explanatory concepts (p. 419)

psychogenic amnesia a psychologically caused inability to recall important personal information (p. 512)

psycholinguistics the science that studies the cognitive processes involved in the acquisition and use of language (p. 272)

psychological test an objective, standardized measure of a sample of behavior (p. 440)

psychology the scientific study of behavior and mental processes (p. 4)

psychophysics the study of the relationship between the physical attributes of stimuli and the psychological experience that they produce (p. 82)

psychosexual disorders impairment or discomfort associated with sexual activity that is not organic in origin (p. 515)

psychosocial law the view that each person who joins a social situation adds less influence than the previous person to join the group (p. 604)

psychosurgery a surgical procedure designed to affect psychological or behavioral reactions (p. 543)

psychotherapy attempts to treat mental disorders through psychological means, effecting change in cognitions, affect, and/or behavior (p. 553)

psychotic disorders psychological disorders that involve gross impairment in functioning and a loss of contact with reality (p. 520)

puberty the stage of physical development at which one becomes capable of sexual reproduction (p. 342)

public verifiability the agreement (verifiability) of observers (public) that an event did or did not take place (p. 6)

punishment the administration of a punisher, which is a stimulus that decreases the rate or probability of a response that precedes it (p. 195)

pupil the opening in the iris that changes size in relation to the level of light available (p. 99)

Purkinje shift the phenomenon of perceived levels of brightness changing as a function of overall illumination levels (p. 105)

Q

quality of work life (QWL) those aspects of the work situation that influence an employee's attitudes or evaluation of his or her position, including job satisfaction (p. 623)

R

random assignment the assignment of subjects to groups (samples) so that each subject has an equal chance of being assigned to any one group (p. 33)

range a measure of variability; the highest score in a distribution, minus the lowest (p. 659)

ratio measurement measurement in which events can be categorized and ranked with equal differences between adjacent ranks, and in which there is a true zero point (p. 654)

rational-emotive therapy (RET) a form of cognitive therapy aimed at changing the subject's irrational beliefs or maladaptive cognitions (p. 564)

rationalization generating excuses to explain one's behaviors rather than dealing with the real reasons for one's behaviors (p. 408)

reactive schizophrenia schizophrenia in which the onset of the symptoms is comparatively sudden (p. 529)

reality principle the impulse that governs the ego, arbitrating between the demands of the id, the superego, and the real world (p. 421)

recall a method of retrieval in which the individual is provided with the fewest possible cues to aid retrieval (p. 245)

recessive gene a gene whose characteristics will be expressed only if it is paired with a similar recessive gene (p. 305)

recognition a method of retrieval in which the individual is asked to identify previously learned material as being familiar (p. 245)

regression when under stress, a return to earlier, childish levels of previously productive behaviors (p. 409)

reinforcer a stimulus that increases the rate or probability of the response that it follows (p. 191)

relational concepts concepts defined in terms of their comparative relation to other concepts (p. 267)

reliability consistency or dependability (p. 442)

REM sleep rapid eye movement sleep during which dreaming occurs; also called *paradoxical sleep* because of high levels of physiological activity (p. 151)

repression "motivated forgetting," in which stressful events are forced from awareness into the unconscious and cannot be remembered (pp. 258, 407)

resistance in psychoanalysis, the inability or unwillingness to freely discuss some aspect of one's life (p. 556)

response any observable or measurable reaction of an organism (p. 24)

reticular activating system (RAS) a network of nerve fibers extending from the brain stem to the cortex that is involved in the level of arousal or activation (p. 68)

retina layers of cells at the back of the eye that contain the photosensitive rods and cones (p. 101)

retinal disparity the phenomenon in which each retina receives a different (disparate) view of the same three-dimensional object (p. 136)

retrieval the process of locating, removing, and using information that is stored in memory (p. 225)

retroactive interference the inhibition of retrieval of previously learned material caused by material learned later (p. 255)

rods the photoreceptor cells of the retina that are thought to be most active at low levels of illumination and to be essentially color-blind (p. 102)

rooting reflex the neonatal reflex in which a child turns toward a light touch on its cheek and then makes sucking motions (p. 320)

Rorschach inkblot test a projective technique in which the subject is asked to say what he or she sees in a series of inkblots (p. 454)

R-R relationships statements of correlation that are used to tell us about the strength and nature of relationships between responses (p. 24)

S

s-factor Spearman's term for the intellectual skills that are appropriate for specific tasks (p. 464)

sample a chosen portion of the population of interest (p. 32)

saturation the psychological experience associated with the purity of a light wave; monochromatic lights are as highly saturated as possible (p. 98)

schizophrenia complex psychotic disorders characterized by impairment of cognitive functioning, delusions and hallucinations, social withdrawal, and inappropriate affect (p. 528)

science an organized body of knowledge gained through application of scientific methods (p. 4)

scientific methods systematic procedures involving observation, description, control, and replication used to gain knowledge (p. 5)

secondary reinforcers stimuli that increase the rate of a response because of their being associated with other (primary) reinforcers; also called conditioned *or* learned *reinforcers* (p. 196)

semantic memory in LTM, where vocabulary, facts, simple concepts, and rules are stored (p. 235)

sensation the process of receiving stimulus input from the environment and changing that input into nervous system activity (p. 82)

sensory adaptation a condition in which there is a reduction in the level of sensation as a function of exposure to a constant stimulus (p. 121)

sensory memory the type of memory that holds large amounts of information registered at the senses for very brief periods of time (p. 226)

sensory neurons neurons carrying impulses from receptor cells toward the brain or spinal cord (p. 44)

serial position effect the observation that items from the middle of a list are more difficult to recall than are items from either the beginning or end of a list (p. 238)

sex (or gender) roles social roles based on one's sex, or gender (p. 347)

shape constancy the tendency to see objects as being of constant shape regardless of the shape of the retinal image (p. 141)

shaping a procedure of reinforcing successive approximations of a desired response until the actual desired response is made (p. 189)

short-term memory (STM) a type of memory with limited capacity (7 ± 2 bits of information) and limited duration (15–20 seconds) (p. 229)

signal detection theory the view that stimulus detection is a matter of decision-making, of separating signal from noise (p. 89)

similarity in Gestalt psychology, the principle that stimuli are perceived together if they share common characteristic(s) (p. 133)

single-blind technique in an experiment, a protection against bias through which the subject(s) is not told the hypothesis of the experiment (p. 33)

size constancy the tendency to see objects as being of constant size regardless of the size of the retinal image (p. 141)

sleep apnea patterns of sleep during which breathing stops momentarily (p. 166)

sleep spindles very brief, high amplitude peaks in EEG pattern, found in stages 2 and 3 of sleep (p. 151)

social facilitation improved performance due to the presence of others (p. 604)

social identification function the observation that attitudes communicate information useful in social evaluation (p. 577)

social influence (in the context of helping) relying on others to define whether or not a situation is a true emergency (p. 601)

social inhibition of helping (bystander effect) the tendency for people to be less likely to offer help when they are in a group than when they are alone (p. 601)

social interference impaired performance due to the presence of others (p. 604)

social learning theory the theory that learning takes place through the observation and imitation of models (p. 214)

social loafing the tendency for a person to work less hard when part of a group in which everyone's efforts are pooled (p. 604)

social psychology the scientific study of how others influence the thoughts, feelings, and behaviors of the individual (p. 574)

social roles expectations that others form about us on the basis of our positions in society (p. 347)

somatic nervous system sensory and motor neurons outside the CNS that serve the sense receptors and skeletal muscles (p. 49)

somatization disorder a persistent distress over a chronic physical symptom for which there is no medical explanation (p. 511)

somatoform disorders psychological disorders that reflect imagined physical or bodily symptoms or complaints (p. 510)

sperm the sex cell of the father that contains 23 single chromosomes (p. 304)

spinal cord a collection of neurons within the spine that conveys impulses to and from the brain and is involved in some reflex behaviors (p. 50)

spinal reflex an automatic, involuntary response to a stimulus that involves sensory neurons, interneurons in the spinal cord, and motor neurons (p. 52)

split brain procedure the surgical procedure of separating the functioning of the two cerebral hemispheres by destroying the corpus callosum (p. 73)

split-half reliability a check on the internal consistency of a test, which is found by correlating one part of a test with another part of the same test (p. 443)

spontaneous recovery the phenomenon in classical conditioning in which a previously extinguished CR returns after a rest interval (p. 177)

S-R relationships cause and effect statements relating stimuli to the responses they produce (p. 25)

stage of the embryo in prenatal development, the period from 2 weeks to 8 weeks following conception (p. 309)

stage of the fetus in prenatal development, the period from 2 months after conception until birth (p. 310)

stage of the zygote in prenatal development, the period from conception through the first 2 weeks (p. 308)

standard deviation a type of average of the deviations of each X-score from the mean of the distribution:

$$\sqrt{\frac{\Sigma(X - \overline{X})^2}{N}}$$

(p. 659)

statistically significant differences differences between some descriptive statistics not likely to have occurred by chance if the descriptive statistics were describing the same group (p. 661)

stereotype a generalized mental (cognitive) representation of someone based on a small sample of experience (p. 575)

Stevens's law the statement that the magnitude of a psychological sensation is an exponential function of physical magnitude (S = CI^b) (p. 88)

stimulants those drugs (such as caffeine, cocaine, and amphetamines) that increase nervous system activity (p. 160)

stimulus any event or energy that produces a reaction or response in an organism (pp. 25, 83)

storage the process of holding encoded information until the time of retrieval (p. 225)

strategy a plan or procedure for identifying members of a particular category or concept (p. 270)

stress a complex pattern of reactions to real or perceived threats to one's sense of well-being that motivate adjustment (p. 397)

stressors real or perceived threats to one's sense of well-being; sources of stress (p. 397)

structuralism the school of psychology (associated with Wundt) interested in the structure or elements of the human mind or consciousness (p. 10)

subjective organization the tendency for subjects to impose some subjective, personal order on their recall of random events or items (p. 236)

superego that aspect of personality that refers to ethical or moral considerations and operates on the idealistic principle (p. 421)

surface structure in transformational grammar, the structure of an utterance as it is produced (p. 277)

survey a means of collecting data from large numbers of subjects, either by interview or questionnaire (p. 35)

sympathetic division division of the ANS that becomes active during emotional states (pp. 49, 387)

synapse the junction of two neurons where an impulse is relayed from the axon of one to the dendrite (or cell body) of another through the release of a neurotransmitter (p. 46)

synaptic cleft the space between the presynaptic membrane of one neuron and the postsynaptic membrane of the next neuron (p. 46)

syndrome a collection of symptoms used to describe a disorder (p. 521)

synesthesia a condition of cross-sensory experience—seeing sounds, hearing colors, tasting odors, and the like—associated with hallucinogen use (p. 164)

syntax the rules that govern how the morphemes of a language may be combined (p. 275)

systematic desensitization the application of classical conditioning procedures to alleviate extreme anxiety; anxiety-producing stimuli are presented while the subject is in a relaxed state (p. 560)

T

taste buds the receptors for taste which are located in the tongue (p. 119)

temporal lobe the lobe of the cerebrum located at the temples (p. 70)

territoriality the setting off and marking of a piece of territory (a location) as one's own (p. 634)

test-retest reliability a check of consistency made by correlating the results of a test taken by the same subjects at two different times (p. 443)

testosterone the male sex hormone, produced by the testes, important to the sex drive and the development of secondary sex characteristics (p. 370)

thalamus the final sensory relay station, just below the cerebral cortex that projects sensory fibers to the proper cortical location (p. 69)

thematic apperception test (TAT) a projective technique in which the subject is asked to tell a story about an ambiguous picture (pp. 372, 454)

theory a collection of related assumptions, used to explain some phenomenon, which lead through logical reasoning to testable hypotheses (p. 419)

thyroid gland an endocrine gland that regulates the rate, or pace, of the body's functioning (p. 53)

timbre the psychological experience relating to sound wave purity by which we perceive the sharpness, clearness, or quality of a tone (p. 115)

training a systematic, intentional process of altering the behaviors of employees to increase organizational effectiveness (p. 620)

traits distinguishable, relatively enduring ways in which individuals may differ (p. 430)

transference in psychoanalysis, the situation in which the patient comes to feel about the analyst in the same way he or she once felt about some other important person (p. 557)

tremors involuntary, trembling, jerky movements that are usually associated with damage in the cerebellum (p. 68)

U

unconditioned response (UCR) in classical conditioning, a response (e.g., salivation) reliably and reflexively evoked by a stimulus (the UCS) (p. 174)

unconditioned stimulus (UCS) in classical conditioning, a stimulus (e.g., food powder) that reflexively and reliably evokes a response (the UCR) (p. 174)

unconscious that level of consciousness from which memories or thoughts cannot be easily recalled into consciousness (p. 149)

V

validity the extent to which a test measures what it claims to be measuring (pp. 443, 618)

variability the extent of spread or dispersion in a set or distribution of scores (p. 658)

variable interval (VI) schedule a system in which a reinforcer is administered after the first response made following the end of a varying time interval (p. 198)

variable ratio (VR) schedule a system in which a reinforcer is administered only after a randomly varied number of responses has occurred (p. 198)

vesicles the small containers, or packets, of neurotransmitter substance found in axon terminals (p. 46)

vestibular sense the position sense that tells us about balance, where we are in relation to gravity, and movement or acceleration (p. 121)

viability the point at which a fetus can survive outside the uterus, usually in the seventh month (p. 310)

vicarious reinforcement (or) punishment the strengthening (reinforcement) or weakening (punishment) of responses due to observing the consequences of someone else's behaviors (p. 215)

vitreous humor the thick fluid behind the lens of the eye that functions to keep the eyeball spherical (p. 101)

W

wave amplitude a characteristic of wave forms (height of the wave) that indicates intensity (p. 95)

wavelength a characteristic of wave forms that indicates the distance between any point on a wave and the corresponding point of the next cycle of the wave (p. 95)

Weber's law the statement that the size of a j.n.d. divided by standard intensity is a constant ratio ($\Delta I/I = C$) (p. 86)

Wechsler Adult Intelligence Scale-Revised (WAIS-R); Wechsler Intelligence Scale for Children-Revised (WISC-R); Wechsler Preschool and Primary Scale of Intelligence (WPPSI). David Wechsler's IQ tests, each for a different age range of subjects and all composed of both verbal and performance subtests (p. 471)

white light a light of lowest possible saturation, containing a mixture of all visible wavelengths (p. 98)

white noise a sound composed of a random assortment of wave frequencies from the audible spectrum (p. 115)

whole report method a recall procedure in which a subject is asked to recall all of the material presented earlier (p. 227)

X

X and Y chromosomes the chromosomes that determine an individual's sex; paired as XX for females and XY for males (p. 304)

Z

zygote the single cell that results from conception; contains 23 chromosomes from the father's sperm and 23 chromosomes from the mother's ovum (p. 304)

REFERENCES

A

Abel, E. L. (1981). Behavioral teratology. *Psychological Bulletin, 90,* 564–581.

Abroms, K. I. & Bennett, J. W. (1981). Parental contributions to trisomy 21: Review of recent cytological and statistical findings. In P. Mittler (Ed.), *Frontiers of knowledge in mental retardation (Vol. 2).* Baltimore: University Park Press.

Adams, J. A. (1980). *Learning and memory: An introduction.* Homewood, IL: Dorsey.

Adams, J. L. (1974). *Conceptual blockbusting.* Stanford, CA: Stanford Alumni Association, Cited in A. L. Glass, K. J. Holyoak, & J. L. Santa, (1979). *Cognition.* Reading, MA: Addison-Wesley.

Agnew, H. W., Webb, W. B., & Williams, R. L. (1964). The effects of stage 4 sleep deprivation. *Electroencephalography and Clinical Neurophysiology, 17,* 68–70.

Aiello, J. R. & Aiello, T. D. (1974). The development of personal space: Proxemic behavior of children 6 through 16. *Human Ecology, 2,* 177–189.

Aiken, L. R. (1982). *Psychological testing and assessment (4th ed.),* Boston: Allyn & Bacon.

Aiken, L. R. (1984). *Psychological testing and assessment (5th ed.),* Boston: Allyn & Bacon.

Ainsworth, M. D. S. (1979). Infant-mother attachment. *American Psychologist, 34,* 932–937.

Albee, G. W. (1985). The answer is prevention. *Psychology Today, 19,* 60–64.

Allen, M. G. (1976). Twin studies of affective illness. *Archives of General Psychiatry, 33,* 1476–1478.

Allport, G. W. & Odbert, H. S. (1936). Trait-names: A psycholexical study. *Psychological Monographs, 47,* Whole No. 211.

Altman, I. (1975). *The environment and social behavior.* Monterey, CA: Brooks/Cole.

American Association on Mental Deficiency. (1974). *Adaptive behavior scale: Manual,* Washington, DC: Author.

American Psychiatric Association. (1980). *Diagnostic and statistical manual of mental disorders (3rd ed.).* Washington, DC: American Psychiatric Association.

American Psychological Association. (1973). *Ethical principles of psychologists.* Washington, DC: American Psychological Association.

American Psychological Association. (1981). Ethical principles of psychologists. *American Psychologist, 36,* 633–638.

Amoore, J. E. (1970). *Molecular basis of odor.* Springfield, IL: C. C. Thomas.

Anastasi, A. (1982). *Psychological testing (5th ed.).* New York: Macmillan.

Anderson, A. (1982). Neurotoxic follies. *Psychology Today, 16,* 30–42.

Anderson, R. & Nida, S. A. (1978). Effect of physical attractiveness on opposite- and same-sex evaluations. *Journal of Personality, 46* 401–413.

Anisfeld, M. (1984). *Language development from birth to three.* Hillsdale, NJ: Erlbaum.

Anisman, H. & Zacharko, R. M. (1982). Depression: The predisposing influence of stress. *The Behavioral and Brain Sciences, 5,* 89–137.

Apgar, V. & Beck, J. (1974). *Is my baby all right?* New York: Pocket Books.

Archer, S. L. (1982). The lower age boundaries of identity development. *Child Development, 53,* 1551–1556.

Aronson, E. (1984). *The social animal.* San Francisco: Freeman.

Aronson, E. & Linder, D. (1965). Gain and loss of esteem as determinants of interpersonal attractiveness. *Journal of Personality and Social Psychology, 1,* 156–171.

Aronson, E., Turner, J. A., & Carlsmith, J. M. (1963). Communicator credibility and communication discrepancy as a determinant of opinion change. *Journal of Abnormal and Social Psychology, 67,* 31–36.

Aronson, M. K. (1982). Alzheimer's disease: An overview. *Generations, 7,* 6–7.

Asch, S. (1952). *Social psychology.* Englewood Cliffs, NJ: Prentice-Hall.

Asch, S. E. (1951). The effects of group pressure upon the modification and distortion of judgment. In H. Guetzkow (Ed.), *Groups, leadership and men.* Pittsburgh: Carnegie.

Asch, S. E. (1956). Studies of independence and conformity: I. A minority of one against a unanimous majority. *Psychological Monographs: General and Applied, 70,* (Whole No. 416), 1–70.

Aserinsky, E., & Kleitman, N. (1953). Regularly occurring periods of eye mobility and concomitant phenomena during sleep. *Science, 118,* 273–274.

Atkinson, J. W. & Feather, N. T. (Eds.) (1966). *A theory of achievement motivation.* New York: Wiley.

Atkinson, J. W. & Litwin, G. H. (1960). Achievement motive and test anxiety conceived as motive to approach success and motive to avoid failure. *Journal of Abnormal and Social Psychology, 60,* 27–36.

Atkinson, R. C. (1975). Mnemotechnics in second-language learning. *American Psychologist, 30,* 821–828.

Atkinson, R. C. & Shiffrin, R. M. (1968). Human memory: A proposed system and its control processes. In K. W. Spence & J. T. Spence (Eds.), *The psychology of learning and motivation: Advances in research and theory.* New York: Academic Press.

Auletta, K. (1984). Children of children. *Parade, 17,* 4–7.

Avery, M. E. & Frantz, I. D. (1983). To breathe or not to breathe: What have we learned about apneic spells and Sudden Infant Death? *The New England Journal of Medicine, 309,* 107–108.

B

Babich, F. R., Jacobson, A. L., Bubash, S., & Jacobson, A. (1965). Transfer of a response to naive rats by injection of ribonucleic acid extracted from trained rats. *Science, 149,* 656–657.

Baddeley, A. D. (1966). Short-term memory for word sequences as a function of acoustic, semantic and formal similarity. *Quarterly Journal of Experimental Psychology, 18,* 362–365.

Bandura, A. (1965). Influence of models' reinforcement contingencies on the acquisition of imitative responses. *Journal of Personality and Social Psychology, 1,* 589–595.

Bandura, A. (1973). *Aggression: A social learning analysis:* Englewood Cliffs, NJ: Prentice-Hall.

Bandura, A. (1976). Modeling theory: Some traditions, trends and disputes. In W. S. Sahakian (Ed.), *Learning: Systems, models, and theories.* Chicago: Rand McNally.

Bandura, A. (1977). *Social learning theory.* Englewood Cliffs, NJ: Prentice-Hall.

Bandura, A. (1978). The self-system in reciprocal determinism. *American Psychologist, 33,* 344–358.

Bandura, A., Ross, D., & Ross, S. A. (1963). Imitation of film-mediated aggressive models. *Journal of Abnormal and Social Psychology, 66,* 3–11.

Barber, T. F. X. (1972). Suggested (hypnotic) behavior: The trance paradigm vs. an alternative paradigm. In E. Fromm & R. E. Shorr (Eds.), *Hypnosis: Research developments and perspectives.* Chicago: Aldine-Atherton.

Bard, P. (1934). The neurohormonal basis of emotion reactions. In C. A. Murchison (Ed.), *Handbook of general experimental psychology.* Worcester, MA: Clark University Press.

Barker, R. (1968). *Ecological psychology.* Stanford, CA: Stanford University Press.

Baron, R. A. (1977). *Human aggression.* New York: Plenum.

Baron, R. A. & Byrne, D. (1984). *Social psychology: Understanding human behavior (4th ed.).* Boston: Allyn and Bacon.

Baron, R. A. & Ransberger, V. M. (1978). Ambient temperature and the occurrence of collective violence: The "long hot summer" revisited. *Journal of Personality and Social Psychology, 36,* 351–360.

Bartlett, F. C. (1932). *Remembering: A Study in experimental and social psychology.* London: Cambridge University Press.

Bartlett, F. C. (1958). *Thinking.* London: Allen and Unwin.

Bartus, R. T., Dean, R. L., Beer, B., & Lippa, A. S. (1982). The cholinergic hypothesis of geriatric memory dysfunction. *Science, 217,* 408–417.

Baum, A., Grunberg, N. E., & Singer, J. E. (1982). The use of psychological and neuroendocrinological measurements in the study of stress. *Health Psychology, 1,* 217–236.

Baumeister, R. F. (1985). The championship choke. *Psychology Today, 19,* 48–52.

Bayley, N. & Schaefer, E. S. (1964). Correlations of maternal and child behaviors with the development of mental abilities: Data from the Berkeley Growth Study. *Monographs of the Society for Research in Child Development, 29,* 1–80.

Beck, A. T. (1967). *Depression: Clinical, experimental, and theoretical aspects.* New York: Harper & Row.

Beck, A. T. (1976). *Cognitive therapy and the emotional disorders.* New York: International Universities Press.

Bell, A. P., Weinberg, M. S., & Hammersmith, S. K. (1981). *Sexual preference: Its development in men and women.* Bloomington, IN: Indiana University Press.

Bell, P. A., Fisher, J. D., & Loomis, R. J. (1978). *Environmental Psychology.* Philadelphia: W. B. Saunders.

Bem, S. L. (1974). The measurement of psychological androgyny. *Journal of Consulting and Clinical Psychology, 42,* 155–162.

Bem, S. L. (1975). Sex role adaptability: One consequence of psychological androgyny. *Journal of Personality and Social Psychology, 31,* 634–643.

Ben-Yehuda, N. (1980). The European witch craze. *American Journal of Sociology, 86,* 1–31.

Bennett, T. L. (1982). *Introduction to physiological psychology.* Monterey, CA: Brooks/Cole.

Bennett, W. (1980). The cigarette century. *Science, 80,* 36–43.

Benson, H. (1975). *The relaxation response.* New York: Morrow.

Berkowitz, L. (1978). Whatever happened to the frustration-aggression hypothesis? *American Behavioral Scientist, 21,* 691–708.

Berkowitz, L. (1982). Aversive conditions as stimuli to aggression. *Advances in Experimental Social Psychology, 15,* 249–288.

Berne, E. (1960). *I'm okay, you're okay.* New York: Grove Press.

Berne, E. (1964). *Games people play.* New York: Grove Press.

Bernstein, I. (1978). Learned taste aversion in children receiving chemotherapy. *Science, 200,* 1302–1303.

Berscheid, E. & Walster (Hatfield), E. (1978). *Interpersonal attraction.* Reading, MA: Addison-Wesley.

Bersoff, D. N. (1981). Testing and the law. *American Psychologist, 36,* 1047–1056.

Birdwhistell, R. L. (1952). *Introduction to kinesics.* Louisville, KY: University of Louisville Press.

Birren, J. E. (1983). Aging in America: Roles for psychology. *American Psychologist, 38,* 298–299.

Block, J. (1965). *The challenge of response sets.* New York: Appleton-Century-Crofts.

Bloom, F. E., Lazerson, A., & Hotstadter, L. (1985). *Brain, mind, and behavior.* New York: W. H. Freeman.

Blum, J. E., Jarvik, L. F., & Clark, E. T. (1970). Rate of change on selective tests of intelligence: A twenty-year longitudinal study. *Journal of Gerontology, 25,* 171–176.

Bootzin, R. R. & Acocella, J. R. (1984). *Abnormal psychology: Current perspectives (4th ed.).* New York: Random House.

Boring, E. G. (1930). A new ambiguous figure. *American Journal of Psychology, 42,* 109–116.

Bouchard, T. J. & McGue, M. (1981). Familial studies of intelligence: A review. *Science, 212,* 1055–1059.

Bourne, L. E., Dominowski, R. L., & Loftus, E. F. (1979). *Cognitive processes.* Englewood Cliffs, NJ: Prentice-Hall.

Bousfield, W. A. (1953). The occurrence of clustering in the free recall of randomly arranged associates. *Journal of General Psychology, 49,* 229–240.

Bower, G. H. (1972). Mental imagery and associate learning. In L. W. Gregg (Ed.), *Cognition in learning and memory.* New York: Wiley.

Bower, G. H. & Clark, M. C. (1969). Narrative stories as mediators for serial learning. *Psychonomic Science, 14,* 181–182.

Bower, G. H. & Springston, F. (1970). Pauses as recoding points in letter series. *Journal of Experimental Psychology, 83,* 421–430.

Bower, T. G. R. (1976). Repetitive processes in child development. *Scientific American, 235,* 38–47.

Bowlby, J. (1969). *Attachment and loss (Vol. 1, Attachment).* New York: Basic Books.

Braine, M. D. S. (1976). Children's first word combinations. *Monographs for the Society for Research in Child Development, 41,* (Serial No. 164).

Bramel, D. & Friend, R. (1981). Hawthorne, the myth of the docile worker, and class bias in psychology. *American Psychologist, 36,* 867–878.

Bransford, J. D. (1979). *Human cognition: Learning, understanding and remembering.* Belmont, CA: Wadsworth.

Braun, P., Kochansky, G., Shapiro, R., Greenberg, S., Gudeman, J. E., Johnson, S., & Shore, M. (1981). Overview: Deinstitutionalization of psychiatric patients, a critical review of outcome studies. *American Journal of Psychiatry, 138,* 736–749.

Bray, D. W., Campbell, R. J., & Grant, D. L. (1974). *Formative years in business: A long-term AT&T study of managerial lives.* New York: Wiley.

Breland, K. & Breland, M. (1961). The misbehavior of organisms. *American Psychologist, 16,* 681–684.

Broadbent, D. E. (1958). *Perception and communication.* London: Pergamon Press.

Brown, J. (1958). Some tests of the decay theory of immediate memory. *Quarterly Journal of Experimental Psychology, 10,* 12–21.

Brown, J. I. (1973). *The Nelson-Denny Reading Test.* Boston: Houghton Mifflin.

Brown, J. S. (1948). Gradients of approach and avoidance responses and their relation to motivation. *Journal of Comparative and Physiological Psychology, 41,* 450–465.

Brown, R. W., Cazden, C. B., & Bellugi, U. (1969). The child's grammar from I to III. *Symposia on Child Psychology (Vol. 2).* Minneapolis: University of Minnesota Press.

Brown, R. W. & McNeill, D. (1966). The "tip of the tongue" phenomenon. *Journal of Verbal Learning and Verbal Behavior, 5,* 325–337.

Browne, M. A. & Mahoney, M. J. (1984). Sport psychology. *Annual Review of Psychology, 35,* 605–626.

Bruner, J. S., Goodnow, J. J., & Austin, G. A. (1956). *A study of thinking.* New York: Wiley.

Buckhout, R. (1975). Nearly 2000 witnesses can be wrong. *Social Action and the Law, 2,* 7.

Burisch, M. (1984). Approaches to personality inventory construction. *American Psychologist, 39,* 214–227.

Buss, D. (1985). Human mate selection. *American Scientist, 73,* 47–51.

Buss, D. M. (1984). Evolutionary biology and personality psychology. *American Psychologist, 39,* 1135–1147.

Butler, R. N. & Emr, M. (1982). SDAT research: Current trends. *Generations, 7,* 14–18.

Byrne, D. (1971). *The attraction paradigm.* New York: Academic Press.

Byrne, D. & Clore, G. L. (1970). A reinforcement model of evaluative responses. *Personality: An International Journal, 1,* 103–128.

C

Calhoun, J. B. (1962). Population density and social pathology. *Scientific American, 206,* 139–148.

Campos, J. J. (1976). Heart rates: A sensitive tool for the study of emotional development. In L. Lipsitt (Ed.), *Developmental psychobiology: The significance of infancy.* Hillsdale, NJ: Erlbaum.

Campos, J. J., Langer, A. & Krowitz, A. (1970). Cardiac responses on the visual cliff in prelocomotor human infants. *Science, 170,* 196–197.

Cannon, W. B. (1927). The James-Lange theory of emotions: A critical examination and an alternative theory. *American Journal of Psychology, 39,* 106–124.

Cannon, W. B. (1932). *The wisdom of the body.* New York: Norton.

Carson, R. C. (1983). The schizophrenias. In H. E. Adams & P. B. Sutker (Eds.), *Comprehensive handbook of psychopathology.* New York: Plenum.

Carson, T. P. & Carson, R. C. (1983). The affective disorders. In H. E. Adams & P. B. Sutker (Eds.), *Comprehensive handbook of psychopathology.* New York: Plenum.

Cattell, R. B. (1963). Theory of fluid and crystallized intelligence: A critical experiment. *Journal of Educational Psychology, 54,* 1–22.

Cattell, R. B. (1973). Personality pinned down. *Psychology Today, 7,* 40–46.

Cattell, R. B. (1979). *Personality and learning theory: The structure of personality in its environment (Vol. 1).* New York: Springer.

Cermak, L. S. & Craik, F. I. M. (Eds.), (1979). *Levels of processing in human memory.* Hillsdale, NJ: Erlbaum.

Cherry, C. (1953). Some experiments on the recognition of speech with one and two ears. *Journal of the Acoustical Society of America, 25,* 975–979.

Chi, M. T. H. (1978). Knowledge structures and memory development. In R. Siegler (Ed.), *Children's thinking: What develops?* Hillsdale, NJ: Erlbaum.

Chomsky, N. (1957). *Syntactic structures.* The Hague: Mouton.

Chomsky, N. (1965). *Aspects of the theory of syntax.* Cambridge, MS: M.I.T. Press.

Chomsky, N. (1967). *Aspects of the theory of syntax.* Cambridge: MIT Press.

Clark, H. H. & Clark, E. V. (1977). *Psychology and language.* New York: Harcourt, Brace, Jovanovich.

Clarke-Stewart, A., Friedman, S., & Koch, J. (1985). *Child development: A topical approach.* New York: Wiley.

Clifford, M. M. & Walster (Hatfield), E. (1973). The effect of physical attractiveness on teacher expectation. *Sociology of Education, 46,* 248–258.

Clore, G. L. & Byrne, D. (1974). A reinforcement-affect model of attraction. In T. L. Huston (Ed.), *Foundations of interpersonal attraction.* New York: Academic Press.

Cohen, G. D. (1980). *Fact sheet: Senile dementia (Alzheimer's disease). [No. (ADM) 80-929].* Washington, DC: (NIMH) Center for Studies of the Mental Health of the Aging.

Cohen, L. R., DeLoach, J., & Strauss, M. (1978). Infant visual perception. In J. Osofky (Ed.), *The handbook of infant development.* New York: Wiley.

Cohen, S., Evans, G. W., Krantz, D. S., & Stokols, D. (1980). Physiological, motivational, and cognitive effects of aircraft noise on children: Moving from the laboratory to the field. *American Psychologist, 35,* 231–243.

Cohen, S., Evans, G. W., Krantz, D. S., Stokols, D., & Kelly, S. (1981). Aircraft noise and children: Longitudinal and cross-sectional evidence on adaptation to noise and the effectiveness of noise abatement. *Journal of Personality and Social Psychology, 40,* 331–345.

Cohen, S. & McKay, G. (1984). Social support, stress, and the buffering hypothesis: A theoretical analysis. In A. Baum, J. E. Singer & S. E. Taylor (Eds.), *Handbook of psychology and health (Vol. 4—Social psychological aspects of health).* Hillsdale, NJ: Erlbaum.

Coleman, J. C., Butcher, J. N., & Carson, R. C. (1980). *Abnormal psychology and modern life (6th ed.).* Glenview, IL: Scott, Foresman.

Coleman, J. C., Butcher, J. N., & Carson, R. C. (1984). *Abnormal psychology and modern life (7th ed.),* Glenview, IL: Scott, Foresman.

College Entrance Examination Board (1982). *Profiles, college-bound seniors, 1981.* New York: Author.

Collins, A. M. & Quillian, M. R. (1969). Retrieval time from semantic memory. *Journal of Verbal Learning and Verbal Behavior, 8,* 240–247.

Conrad, R. (1963). Acoustic confusions and memory span for words. *Nature, 197,* 1029–1030.

Conrad, R. (1964). Acoustic confusions in immediate memory. *British Journal of Psychology, 55,* 75–84.

Conger, J. J. (1975). Sexual attitudes and behavior of contemporary adolescents. In J. J. Conger (Ed.), *Contemporary issues in adolescent development.* New York: Harper & Row.

Conger, J. J. & Peterson, A. C. (1984). *Adolescence and youth: Psychological development in a changing world.* New York: Harper & Row.

Cooper, L. A. & Shepard, R. N. (1973). Chronometric studies of the rotation of mental images. In W. G. Chase (Ed.), *Visual information processing.* New York: Academic Press.

Coryell, W. & Winokur, G. (1982). Course and outcome. In E. S. Paykel (Ed.), *Handbook of affective disorders.* New York: Guilford Press.

Costello, C. G. (1982). Fears and phobias in women: A community study. *Journal of Abnormal Psychology, 91,* 280–286.

Cottrell, N. B. (1972). Social facilitation. In C. G. McClintock (Ed.), *Experimental social psychology.* New York: Holt, Rinehart & Winston.

Coulter, W. A. & Morrow, H. W. (Eds.) (1978). *Adaptive behavior: Concepts and measurements.* New York: Grune & Stratton.

Craik, F. I. M. (1970). The fate of primary memory items in free recall. *Journal of Verbal Learning and Verbal Behavior, 9,* 143–148.

Craik, F. I. M. & Tulving, E. (1975). Depth of processing and the retention of words in episodic memory. *Journal of Experimental Psychology: General, 104,* 268–294.

Craik, F. I. M. & Watkins, M. J. (1973). The role of rehearsal in short-term memory. *Journal of Verbal Learning and Verbal Behavior, 12,* 598–607.

Cratty, B. J. (1970). *Perceptual and motor development in infants and children.* New York: Macmillan.

Creekmore, C. R. (1984). Games athletes play. *Psychology Today, 18,* 40–44.

Creekmore, C. R. (1985). Cities won't drive you crazy. *Psychology Today, 19,* 46–53.

Cronbach, L. J. (1984). *Essentials of psychological testing (4th ed.).* Cambridge, MA: Harper & Row.

D

Darley, J. M. & Latané, B. (1968). Bystander intervention in emergencies: Diffusion of responsibility. *Journal of Personality and Social Psychology, 8,* 377–383.

Darwin, C. (1872). *The expression of emotion in man and animals.* New York: Philosophical Library [reprinted in 1955 and 1965 by the University of Chicago Press, Chicago].

Darwin, C. T., Turvey, M. T., & Crowder, R. G. (1972). An auditory analogue of the Sperling partial report procedure: Evidence for brief auditory storage. *Cognitive Psychology, 3,* 255–267.

Davidson, J. M., Smith, E. R., Rodgers, C. H., & Bloch, G. J. (1968). Relative thresholds of behavioral and somatic responses to estrogen. *Physiology and Behavior, 3,* 227–229.

Davis, K. (1985). Near and dear: Friendship and love compared. *Psychology Today, 19,* 22–30.

Davis, L. E. & Cherns, A. B. (1975). *The quality of working life: Vol. I. Problems, prospects and the state of the art.* New York: The Free Press.

DeCasper, A. J. & Fifer, W. P. (1980). Of human bonding: Newborns prefer their mother's voice. *Science, 208,* 1174–1176.

DeLeon, P. H., Vandenbos, G. R., & Cummings, N. A. (1983). Psychotherapy—Is it safe, effective, and appropriate? The beginning of an evolutionary dialogue. *American Psychologist, 38,* 907–911.

DeLongis, A., Coyne, J. C., Dakof, G., Folkman, S., & Lazarus, R. S. (1982). Relationship of daily hassles, uplifts, and major life events to health status. *Health Psychology, 1,* 119–136.

Dember, W. N. (1960). *The psychology of perception.* New York: Holt, Rinehart and Winston.

Dember, W. N. & Warm, J. S. (1979). *Psychology and perception.* New York: Holt, Rinehart and Winston.

Dement, W. C. (1960). The effect of dream deprivation. *Science, 135,* 1705–1707.

Dement, W. C. (1974). *Some must watch while some must sleep.* San Francisco: Freeman.

Dement, W. C. & Kleitman, N. (1957). The relation of eye movements during sleep to dream activity: An objective method for the study of dreaming. *Journal of Experimental Psychology, 53,* 339–346.

DeVilliers, J. G. & deVilliers, P. A. (1978). *Language acquisition.* Cambridge: Harvard University Press.

De Vries, M. F. R. K. & Miller, D. (1984). Unstable at the top. *Psychology Today, 18,* 26–34.

Diener, E. (1980). Deindividuation: The absence of self-awareness and self-regulation in group members. In P. B. Paulus (Ed.), *Psychology of Group Influence.* Hillsdale, NJ: Erlbaum.

Dion, K. K. (1972). Physical attractiveness and evaluations of children's transgressions. *Journal of Personality and Social Psychology, 24,* 207–213.

Dion, K. K., Berscheid, E., & Walster (Hatfield), E. (1972). What is beautiful is good. *Journal of Personality and Social Psychology, 24,* 285–290.

Dirkes, M. A. (1978). The role of divergent production in the learning process. *American Psychologist, 33,* 815–820.

Dixon, F. (1971). *Subliminal perception: The nature of a controversy.* London: McGraw-Hill.

Doll, E. A. (1965). Vineland social maturity scale: Manual of directions (rev. ed.). Minneapolis: American Guidance Service.

Dollard, J., Doob, L., Miller, N., Mowrer, O. H., & Sears, R. R. (1939). *Frustration and aggression.* New Haven, CT: Yale University Press.

Dove, A. (1968). Taking the chitling test. *Newsweek,* July.

Drachman, D. A. (1977). Memory and cognitive function in man: Does the cholinergic system have a specific role? *Neurology, 27,* 783–790.

Duncker, K. (1945). On problem solving. *Psychological Monographs, 58,* Whole No. 270.

Dunnette, M. D. & Borman, W. C. (1979). Personnel selection and classification systems. *Annual Review of Psychology, 30,* 477–525.

E

Ebbinghaus, H. E. (1885/1964). *Memory: A contribution to experimental psychology.* New York: Dover.

Eisdorfer, C. (1983). Conceptual models of aging. *American Psychologist, 38,* 197–202.

Ekman, P. (1972). Universals and cultural differences in facial expression of emotion. In J. K. Cole (Ed.), *Nebraska Symposium on Motivation.* Lincoln, NB: University of Nebraska Press, 207–283.

Ekman, P. (1973). Cross-cultural studies in facial expression. In P. Ekman (Ed.), *Darwin and facial expressions: A century of research in review.* New York: Academic Press.

Ekman, P., Levenson, R. W., & Friesen, W. V. (1983). Autonomic nervous system activity distinguishes among emotions. *Science, 221,* 1208–1210.

Elliott, J. (1977). The power and pathology of prejudice. In P. G. Zimbardo & F. L. Ruch, *Psychology and life (9th ed., Diamond printing).* Glenview, IL: Scott, Foresman.

Ellis, A. (1970). *Reason and emotion in psychotherapy.* New York: Lyle Stuart.

Entwistle, D. (1966). *The word associations of young children.* Baltimore: Johns Hopkins University Press.

Epstein, S. M. (1967). Toward a unified theory of anxiety. In B. A. Maher (Ed.), *Progress in experimental personality research.* (Vol. 4). New York: Academic Press.

Ericsson, K. A. & Chase, W. G. (1982). Exceptional memory. *American Scientist, 70,* 607–615.

Erikson, C. W. (1956). Subception: Factor artifact. *Psychological Review, 63,* 74–80.

Erikson, E. H. (1963). *Childhood and society.* New York: Norton.

Erikson, E. H. (1968). *Identity, youth and crisis.* New York: Norton.

Erlenmeyer-Kimling, L. & Jarvik, L. F. (1963). Genetics and intelligence: A review. *Science, 142,* 1477–1479.

Eron, L. D. (1982). Parent-child interaction, television violence, and aggression in children. *American Psychologist, 37,* 197–211.

Erwin, E. (1980). Psychoanalytic therapy: The Eysenck argument. *American Psychologist, 35,* 435–443.

Etaugh, C. (1980). Effects on nonmaternal care on children. *American Psychologist, 35,* 309–316.

Evans: G. W. & Howard, R. B. (1973). Personal space. *Psychological Bulletin, 80,* 334–344.

Eysenck, H. J. (1952). The effects of psychotherapy: An evaluation. *Journal of Consulting Psychology, 16,* 319–324.

Eysenck, H. J. (1973). *The inequality of man.* London: Temple Smith.

Eysenck, H. J. & Eysenck, S. B. G. (1976). *Psychoticism as a dimension of personality.* London: Hodder & Stoughton.

F

Fantz, R. L. (1961). The origin of form perception. *Scientific American, 204,* 66–72.

Fantz, R. L. (1963). Pattern vision in newborn infants. *Science, 140,* 296–297.

Fast, J. (1970). *Body language.* New York: M. Evans.

Fein, G. G., Schwartz, P. M., Jacobson, S. W., & Jacobson, J. L. (1983). Environmental toxins and behavior development. *American Psychologist, 38,* 1188–1197.

Festinger, L. (1957). *A theory of cognitive dissonance.* Stanford, CA: Stanford University Press.

Festinger, L. & Carlsmith, J. M. (1959). Cognitive consequences of forced compliance. *Journal of Abnormal and Social Psychology, 58,* 203–210.

Festinger, L., Pepitone, A., & Newcomb, T. (1952). Some consequences of deindividuation in a group. *Journal of Abnormal and Social Psychology, 47,* 382–389.

Festinger, L., Schacter, S., & Back, K. (1950). *Social processes in informal groups: A study of human factors in housing.* New York: Harper.

Fishbein, M. & Ajzen, I. (1975). *Belief, attitude, intention, and behavior: An introduction to theory and research.* Reading, MA: Addison Wesley.

Fisher, S. & Greenberg, R. P. (1977). *The scientific credibility of Freud's theories and therapy.* New York: Basic Books.

Flavell, J. H. (1982). On cognitive development. *Child Development, 53,* 1–10.

Fleming, J. D. (1974). Field report: The state of the apes. *Psychology Today, 8,* January, 31–46.

Flynn, J. P., Vanegas, H., Foote, W., & Edwards, S. (1970). Neural mechanisms involved in a cat's attack on a rat. In R. E. Whalen, R. F. Thompson, M. Verzeano, & N. M. Weinberger (Eds.), *The neural control of behavior.* New York: Academic Press.

Forisha-Kovach, B. (1983). *The experience of adolescence.* Glenview, IL: Scott, Foresman.

Fox, H. E., Steinbrecher, M., Pressel, D., Inglis, J., Medvid, L., & Angel, E. (1978). Maternal ethanol ingestion and the occurrence of human fetal breathing movements. *American Journal of Obstetrics and Gynecology, 132,* 354–358.

Frankenberg, W. K. & Dodds, J. B. (1967). The Denver Developmental Screening Test. *Journal of Pediatrics, 71,* 181–191.

Frazier, T. M., Davis, G. H., Goldstein, H., & Goldberg, I. D. (1961). Cigarette smoking and prematurity: A prospective study. *American Journal of Obstetrics and Gynecology, 81,* 988–996.

Freedman, D. X. (1984). Psychiatric epidemiology counts. *Archives of General Psychiatry, 41,* 931–934.

Freedman, J. L. (1975). *Crowding and behavior.* New York: Viking.

Freeman, S., Walker, M. R., Borden, R., & Latané, B. (1975). Diffusion of responsibility and restaurant tipping: Cheaper by the bunch. *Personality and Social Psychology Bulletin, 1,* 584–587.

Freud, S. (1955). *The interpretation of dreams.* (orig. pub. 1900). New York: Basic Books.

Friedman, M. I. & Stricker, E. M. (1976). The physiological psychology of hunger: A physiological perspective. *Psychological Review, 83,* 409–431.

Friedman, S. (1972). Habituation and recovery of visual response in the alert human newborn. *Journal of Experimental Child Psychology, 13,* 339–349.

G

Gagné, R. M. (1984). Learning outcomes and their effects: Useful categories of human performance. *American Psychologist, 39,* 377–385.

Galanter, E. (1962). Contemporary psychophysics. In R. Brown *et al.* (Eds.), *New directions in psychology, Vol. 1.* New York: Holt, Rinehart and Winston.

Galton, F. (1879). Psychometric experiments. *Brain, 2,* 149–162.

Garcia, J., Ervin, F. R., & Koelling, R. A. (1966). Learning with prolonged delay of reinforcement. *Psychonomic Science, 5,* 121–122.

Gardner, E. (1963). *Fundamentals of neurology.* Philadelphia: W. B. Saunders.

Gardner, R. A. & Gardner, B. T. (1969). Teaching sign language to a chimpanzee. *Science, 165,* 664–672.

Gardner, B. T. & Gardner, R. A. (1975). Evidence for sentence constituents in the early utterances of child and chimpanzee. *Journal of Experimental Psychology: General, 104,* 244–267.

Garfield, S. L. (1981). Psychotherapy: A 40-year appraisal. *American Psychologist, 36,* 174–183.

Gazzaniga, M. S. & LeDoux, J. E. (1978). *The integrated mind.* New York: Plenum.

Geller, E. S. (1985). Seat belt psychology. *Psychology Today, 19,* 12–13.

Gelman, R. (1978). Cognitive development. *Annual Review of Psychology, 29,* 297–332.

George, S. & Jennings, L. (1975). Effect of subliminal stimuli on consumer behavior: Negative evidence. *Perceptual and Motor Skills, 41,* 847–854.

Gerow, J. R. & Murphy, D. P. (1980). The validity of the Nelson-Denny Reading Test as a predictor of performance in introductory psychology. *Educational and Psychological Measurement, 40,* 553–556.

Geschwind, N. (1979). Specializations of the human brain. *Scientific American, 241,* 180–199.

Gibson, E. & Walk, R. D. (1960). The visual cliff. *Scientific American, 202,* 64–71.

Gibson, G. E., Peterson, C., & Jenden, D. J. (1981). Brain acetylcholine synthesis declines with senescence. *Science, 213,* 674–676.

Ginott, H. G. (1969). *Between parent and teenager.* New York: Avon.

Glanzer, M. & Cunitz, A. R. (1966). Two storage mechanisms in free recall. *Journal of Verbal Learning and Verbal Behavior, 5,* 351–360.

Glaser, R. (1984). Education and thinking. *American Psychologist, 39,* 93–104.

Glass, A. L., Holyoak, K. J., & Santa, J. L. (1979). *Cognition.* Reading, MA: Addison-Wesley.

Glass, D. C. & Singer, J. E. (1972). *Urban stress.* Hillsdale, NJ: Erlbaum.

Glass, D. C., Singer, J. E., & Friedman, L. N. (1969). Psychic cost of adaptation to an environmental stressor. *Journal of Personality and Social Psychology, 12,* 200–210.

Glenn, N. D. & Weaver, C. N. (1981). The contribution of marital happiness to global happiness. *Journal of Marriage and the Family, 43,* 161–168.

Glucksberg, S. & Danks, J. H. (1968). Effects of discriminative labels and of nonsense labels upon availability of novel function. *Journal of Verbal Learning and Verbal Behavior, 7,* 72–76.

Golbus, M. S. (1980). Teratology for the obstetrician: Current status. *American Journal of Obstetrics and Gynecology, 55,* 269.

Goldiamond, I. (1966). Statement on subliminal advertising. In R. Ulrich, T. Stachnick, & J. Mabry (Eds.), *Control of human behavior.* Glenview, IL: Scott, Foresman.

Goldstein, I. L. (1974). *Training: Program development and evaluation.* Monterey, CA: Brooks/Cole.

Goleman, O. (1980). 1,528 little geniuses and how they grew. *Psychology Today, 14,* 28–53.

Gottlieb, B. H. (1981). *Social networks and social support.* Beverly Hills, CA: Sage.

Green, D. M. & Swets, J. A. (1966). *Signal detection theory and psychophysics.* New York: Wiley.

Greenberg, M. S. & Ruback, R. B. (1982). *Social psychology of the criminal justice system.* Monterey, CA: Brooks/Cole.

Greeno, J. G. (1974). Hobbits and orcs: Acquisition of a sequential concept. *Cognitive Psychology, 6,* 270–292.

Greeno, J. G. (1978). Natures of problem-solving abilities. In W. K. Estes (Ed.), *Handbook of learning and cognitive processes (Vol. 5).* Hillsdale, NJ: Erlbaum.

Greenwald, A. G. (1985). Lecture notes at Ohio State University.

Gregory, R. L. (1977). *Eye and brain: The psychology of seeing* (3rd ed.). New York: McGraw-Hill.

Grinspoon, L. (1977). *Marihuana reconsidered* (2nd ed.). Cambridge, MA: Harvard University Press.

Grossman, H. J. (Ed.) (1973). *Manual on terminology and classification in mental retardation.* Washington, DC: American Association on Mental Deficiency.

Guilford, J. P. (1959). *Personality.* New York: McGraw-Hill.

Guilford, J. P. (1967). *The nature of human intelligence.* New York: McGraw-Hill.

H

Haas, A. (1979). *Teenage sexuality: A survey of teenage sexual behavior.* New York: Macmillan.

Haas, R. G. (1981). Effects of source characteristics on cognitive responses and persuasion. In R. E. Petty, T. M. Ostrom & T. C. Brock (Eds.), *Cognitive responses in persuasion.* Hillsdale, NJ: Erlbaum.

Hall, C. (1966). *The meaning of dreams.* New York: McGraw-Hill.

Hall, E. T. (1966). *The hidden dimension.* Garden City, NY: Doubleday.

Hall, G. S. (1904). *Adolescence.* New York: Appleton-Century-Crofts.

Harlow, H. F. (1932). Social facilitation of feeding in the albino rat. *Journal of Genetic Psychology, 41,* 211–221.

Harlow, H. F. (1949). The formation of learning sets. *Psychological Review, 56,* 51–65.

Harlow, H. F. (1959). Love in infant monkeys. *Scientific American, 200,* 68–74.

Harlow, H. F., Harlow, M. K., & Suomi, S. J. (1971). From thought to therapy: Lessons from a private library. *American Scientist, 59,* 538–549.

Harris, B. (1979). What ever happened to little Albert? *American Psychologist, 34,* 151–160.

Harris, D. V. (1973). *Involvement in sport: A somatopsychic rationale for physical activity.* Philadelphia: Lea & Febiger.

Harris, L. & Associates (1975), (1981), (1983). *The myth and reality of aging in America.* Washington, DC: The National Council on Aging.

Harris, P. L. (1983). Infant cognition. In P. H. Mussen (Ed.), *Handbook of child psychology Vol. II.* New York: Wiley.

Harter, S. (1978). Effectance motivation reconsidered: Toward a developmental model. *Human Development, 21,* 34–64.

Hassett, J. (1980). Acupuncture is proving its points. *Psychology Today, 14,* December, 81–89.

Hauri, P. (1977). *The sleep disorders.* Kalamazoo, MI: Upjohn.

Hayes, C. (1952). *The ape in our house.* London: Gollancz.

Hayes, J. R. (1981). *The complete problem solver.* Philadelphia: Franklin Institute Press.

Haynes, S. G., McMichael, A. J., & Tyroler, H. A. (1978). Survival after early and normal retirement. *Journal of Gerontology, 33,* 872–883.

Heffernan, J. A. & Albee, G. W. (1985). Prevention perspectives. *American Psychologist, 40,* 202–204.

Heidbreder, E. (1946). The attainment of concepts. *Journal of Psychology, 23,* 93–138.

Held, R. & Hein, A. (1963). Movement-produced stimulation in the development of visually guided behavior. *Journal of Comparative and Physiological Psychology, 56,* 872–876.

Heron, W., Doane, B. K., & Scott, T. H. (1956). Visual disturbances after prolonged perceptual isolation. *Canadian Journal of Psychology, 10,* 13–18.

Hess, E. H. (1959). Imprinting. *Science, 130,* 133–144.

Hess, E. H. (1972). "Imprinting" in a natural laboratory. *Scientific American, 227,* 24–31.

Hilgard, E. R. (1975). Hypnosis. *Annual Review of Psychology, 26,* 19–44.

Hilgard, E. R. (1977). *Divided consciousness.* New York: Wiley.

Hilgard, E. R. (1978). Hypnosis and consciousness. *Human Nature.* January, 42–49.

Hilgard, E. R. & Hilgard, J. R. (1975). *Hypnosis in the relief of pain.* Los Altos, CA: W. Kaufman.

Hill, W. F. (1985). *Learning: A survey of psychological interpretations* (4th ed.). New York: Harper & Row.

Hinrichs, J. R. (1976). Personnel training. In M. Dunnette (Ed.) *Handbook of industrial and organizational psychology.* Chicago: Rand McNally.

Hockett, C. F. (1960). The origin of speech. *Scientific American, 203,* 88–96.

Holmes, D. S. (1984). Meditation and somatic arousal reduction: A review of the experimental evidence. *American Psychologist, 39,* 1–10.

Holmes, T. S. & Holmes, T. H. (1970). Short-term intrusions into the life-style routine. *Journal of Psychosomatic Research, 14,* 121–132.

Holmes, T. H. & Rahe, R. H. (1967). The social readjustment rating scale. *Journal of Psychosomatic Research, 11,* 213–218.

Hoppock, R. (1935). *Job satisfaction.* New York: Harper & Row.

Horn, J. L. (1976). Human abilities: A review of research and theory in the early 1970s. *Annual Review of Psychology, 27,* 437–485.

Horn, J. L. & Cattell, R. B. (1966). Refinement and test of the theory of fluid and crystallized intelligence. *Journal of Educational Psychology, 57,* 253–276.

Horn, J. L. & Donaldson, G. (1976). On the myth of intellectual decline in adulthood. *American Psychologist, 31,* 701–719.

Horner, M. S. (1969). Women's will to fail. *Psychology Today, 3,* March, 36.

Horowitz, I. A. & Willging, T. (1984). *The psychology of law.* Boston: Little, Brown.

Hothersall, D. (1984). *History of psychology.* New York: Random House.

Hovland, C. I. & Weiss, W. (1951). The influence of source credibility on communication effectiveness. *Public Opinion Quarterly, 15,* 635–650.

Howard, D. V. (1983). *Cognitive psychology.* New York: Macmillan.

Howell, W. C. & Dipboye, R. L. (1982). *Essentials of industrial and organizational psychology.* Homewood, IL: Dorsey Press.

Hubel, D. H. (1979). The brain. *Scientific American, 241,* 45–53.

Hubel, D. H. & Wiesel, T. N. (1979). Brain mechanisms of vision. *Scientific American, 241,* 150–162.

Hughes, F. P. & Noppe, L. D. (1985). *Human development: Across the life span.* St. Paul, MN: West.

Hughes, J., Smith, T. W., Kosterlitz, H. W., Fotergill, L. A., Morgan, G. A., & Morris, H. R. (1975). Identification of two related peptides from the brain with potent opiate antagonist activity. *Nature, 258,* 577–579.

Hull, C. L. (1943). *Principles of behavior.* New York: Appleton-Century-Crofts.

Huszczo, G. E., Wiggins, J. G., & Currie, J. S. (1984). The relationship between psychology and organized labor. *American Psychologist, 39,* 432–440.

I

Insko, C. A. (1965). Verbal reinforcement of attitude. *Journal of Personality and Social Psychology, 2,* 621–623.

Izard, C. E. (1971). *The face of emotion.* New York: Appleton-Century-Crofts.

Izard, C. E. (1972). *Patterns of emotions: A new analysis of anxiety and depression.* New York: Academic Press.

Izard, C. E. (1984). Emotion-cognition relationships and human development. In C. E. Izard, J. Kagan, & R. B. Zajonc (Eds.), *Emotions, cognition, and behavior* (pp. 17–37). New York: Cambridge University Press.

Izard, C. E., Huebner, R. R., Risser, D., McGinnes, G. C., & Dougherty, L. M. (1980). The young infant's ability to produce discrete emotional expressions. *Developmental Psychology, 16,* 132–141.

J

Jackaway, R. & Teevan, R. (1976). Fear of failure and fear of success: Two dimensions of the same motive. *Sex roles, 2,* 283–294.

James, W. (1890). *Principles of psychology.* New York: Holt.

James, W. (1892). *Psychology: Briefer course.* New York: Holt.

James, W. (1904). Does consciousness exist? *Journal of Philosophy, 1,* 477–491.

Janda, L. H. & Klenke-Hamel, K. E. (1980). *Human sexuality.* New York: Van Nostrand.

Janis, I. L. (1972). *Victims of groupthink.* Boston: Houghton-Mifflin.

Janis, I. L. (1983). The role of social support in adherence to stressful decisions. *American Psychologist, 38,* 143–160.

Jenkins, J. G. & Dallenbach, K. M. (1924). Oblivescence during sleep and waking. *American Journal of Psychology, 35,* 605–612.

Jensen, A. R. (1969). How much can we boost IQ and scholastic achievement? *Harvard Educational Review, 39,* 1–123.

Jensen, A. R. (1973). *Educability and group differences.* London: Methuen.

Jensen, A. R. (1980). *Bias in mental testing.* New York: Free Press.

Jensen, A. R. (1981). *Straight talk about mental tests.* London: Methuen.

Johnson, E. S. (1978). Validation of concept-learning strategies. *Journal of Experimental Psychology, 107,* 237–265.

Jones, K. L., Smith, D. W., Ulleland, C. N., & Streissgoth, A. P. (1973). Patterns of malformation in offspring of chronic alcoholic mothers. *Lancet, 3,* 1267–1271.

Jones, L. V. (1984). White-black achievement differences: The narrowing gap. *American Psychologist, 39,* 1207–1213.

Jones, M. C. (1957). The careers of boys who were early or late maturing. *Child Development, 28,* 113–128.

Jones, M. C. & Mussen, P. H. (1976). Self-conceptions, motivations, and interpersonal attitudes of early and late maturing girls. *Child Development, 29,* 491–501.

Julien, R. M. (1978). *A primer of drug action* (2nd ed.). San Francisco: Freeman.

K

Kalat, J. W. (1984). *Biological psychology* (2nd ed.). Belmont, CA: Wadsworth.

Kalish, R. A. (1976). Death and dying in a social context. In R. H. Binstock & E. Shanas (Eds.), *Handbook of aging and the social sciences.* New York: Van Nostrand.

Kalish, R. A. (1982). *Late adulthood: Perspectives on human development.* Monterey, CA: Brooks/Cole.

Kalish, R. A. & Reynolds, D. K. (1976). *Death and ethnicity: A psychocultural study.* Los Angeles: University of Southern California Press.

Kalven, Jr., H. & Zeisel, H. (1966). *The American jury.* Chicago: University of Chicago Press.

Kaplan, R. M. (1984). The connection between clinical health promotion and health status. *American Psychologist, 39,* 755–765.

Katchadourian, H. (1977). *The biology of adolescence.* San Francisco: Freeman.

Katzell, R. A. & Guzzo, R. A. (1983). Psychological approaches to productivity improvement. *American Psychologist, 38,* 468–472.

Kay, R. (1983). *Biofeedback.* Rockville, MD: U. S. Department of Health and Human Services.

Keesey, R. E. & Powley, T. L. (1975). Hypothalamic regulation of body weight. *American Scientist, 63,* 558–565.

Kelley, H. H. (1973). The process of causal attribution. *American Psychologist, 28,* 107–128.

Kellogg, W. N. (1968). Communication and language in the home-raised chimpanzee. *Science, 162,* 423–427.

Kennedy, G. C. (1953). The role of depot fat in the hypothalamic control of food intake in the rat. *Proceedings of the Royal Society,* Series B, *140,* 578–592.

Kermis, M. D. (1984). *The psychology of human aging.* Boston: Allyn & Bacon.

Kessler, S. (1980). The genetics of schizophrenia: A review. In S. J. Keith & L. R. Mosher (Eds.), *Special report: Schizophrenia.* Washington, DC: U. S. Government Printing Office.

Kientzle, M. J. (1946). Properties of learning curves under varied distributions of practice. *Journal of Experimental Psychology, 36,* 187–211.

Kiesler, C. A. (1982). Mental hospitals and alternative care. *American Psychologist, 37,* 349–360.

Kiesler, C. A. & Kiesler, S. B. (1969). *Conformity.* Reading, MA: Addison Wesley.

Kiester, E. (1984). The playing fields of the mind. *Psychology Today, 18,* 18–24. (a)

Kiester, E. (1984). The uses of anger. *Psychology Today, 18,* 26. (b)

Kilman, R. H. (1985). Corporate culture. *Psychology Today, 19,* 62–68.

Kimble, G. A. (1981). Biological and cognitive constraints on learning. In L. T. Benjamin (Ed.), *The G. Stanley Hall Lecture Series, Vol. 1.* Washington, DC: American Psychological Association.

Kimmel, H. D. (1967). Instrumental conditioning of autonomically mediated behavior. *Psychological Bulletin, 67,* 337–345.

Kimmel, H. D. (1974). Instrumental conditioning of autonomically mediated responses in human beings. *American Psychologist, 29,* 325–335.

Kinsbourne, M. (1982). Hemispheric specialization and the growth of human understanding. *American Psychologist, 37,* 411–420.

Kinsey, A. C., Pomeroy, W. B., & Martin, C. E. (1948). *Sexual behavior in the human male.* Philadelphia: Saunders.

Kinsey, A. C., Pomeroy, W. B., Martin, C. E., & Gebhard, P. H. (1953). *Sexual behavior in the human female.* Philadelphia: Saunders.

Kleitman, N. (1963). Patterns of dreaming. *Scientific American, 203,* 82–88.

Knittle, J. L. (1975). Early influences on development of adipose tissue. In G. A. Bray (Ed.), *Obesity in perspective.* Washington, DC: U. S. Government Printing Office.

Köhler, W. (1925). *The mentality of apes.* New York: Harcourt, Brace and World.

Köhler, W. (1969). *The task of Gestalt psychology.* Princeton, NJ: Princeton University Press.

Kohut, H. (1977). *The restoration of self.* New York: International Universities Press.

Korchin, S. J. & Schuldberg, D. (1981). The future of clinical assessment. *American Psychologist, 36,* 1147–1158.

Krantz, D. S., Grunberg, N. E., & Baum, A. (1985). Health psychology. *Annual Review of Psychology, 36,* 349–383.

Krueger, W. C. F. (1929). The effect of overlearning on retention. *Journal of Experimental Psychology, 12,* 71–78.

Kübler-Ross, E. (1969). *On death and dying.* New York: Macmillan.

L

Labov, W. (1973). The boundaries of words and their meanings. In C. J. N. Bailey & R. W. Shuy (Eds.), *New ways of analyzing variations in English.* Washington, DC: Georgetown University Press.

Lamb, M. (1979). Paternal influences and the father's role: A personal perspective. *American Psychologist, 34,* 938–943.

Landers, D. M. (1982). Arousal, attention, and skilled performance: Further considerations. *Quest, 33,* 271–283.

Landy, F. J. (1985). *Psychology of work behavior.* Homewood, IL: Dorsey Press.

Langer, S. K. (1951). *Philosophy in a new key.* New York: The New American Library.

Latané, B. (1981). The psychology of social impact. *American Psychologist, 36,* 343–356.

Latané, B. & Darley, J. M. (1968). Group inhibition of bystander intervention in emergencies. *Journal of Personality and Social Psychology, 10,* 215–221.

Latané, B. & Darley, J. M. (1970). *The unresponsive bystander: Why doesn't he help?* New York: Appleton-Century-Crofts.

Latané, B. & Nida, S. (1980). Social impact theory and group influence: A social engineering perspective. In P. B. Paulus (Ed.), *Psychology of group influence.* Hillsdale, NJ: Erlbaum.

Latané, B. & Nida, S. (1981). Ten years of research on group size and helping. *Psychological Bulletin, 89,* 308–324.

Latané, B., Williams, K., & Harkins, S. (1979). Many hands make light the work: The causes and consequences of social loafing. *Journal of Personality and Social Psychology, 37,* 822–832.

Lawler, E. E. (1982). Strategies for improving the quality of work life. *American Psychologist, 37,* 486–493.

Lazarus, R. S. (1981). Little hassles can be hazardous to health. *Psychology Today, 15,* 58–62.

Lazarus, R. S. (1982). Thoughts on the relations between emotion and cognition. *American Psychologist, 37,* 1019–1024.

Lazarus, R. S. (1984). On the primacy of cognition. *American Psychologist, 39,* 124–129.

Lazarus, R. S. & McCleary, R. A. (1951). Autonomic discriminations without awareness: A study of subception. *Psychological Review, 58,* 113–122.

Lempers, J. D., Flavell, E. R., & Flavell, J. H. (1977). The development in very young children of tactile knowledge concerning visual perception. *Genetic Psychology Monographs, 95,* 3–53.

Lenneberg, E. H. (1967). *Biological foundations of language.* New York: Wiley.

Leon, G. R. & Roth, L. (1977). Obesity: Psychological causes, correlations and speculations. *Psychological Bulletin, 84,* 117–139.

Leonard, J. (1970). Ghetto for blue eyes in the classroom. *Life,* May 8, p. 16.

Lerner, R. M. & Hultsch, D. F. (1983). *Human development: A lifespan approach.* New York: McGraw-Hill.

Levinson, D. J., Darrow, C. M., Klein, E. B., Levinson, M. H., & McKee, B. (1974). *The seasons of a man's life.* New York: Knopf.

Levinthal, C. F. (1983). *Introduction to physiological psychology* (2nd ed.). Englewood Cliffs, NJ: Prentice-Hall.

Levy, J., Trevarthen, C., & Sperry, R. W. (1972). Perception of bilateral chimeric figures following hemispheric disconnection. *Brain, 95,* 61–78.

Ley, P. (1977). Psychological studies of doctor-patient communication. In S. Rachman (Ed.), *Contributions to medical psychology (Vol. 1).* Oxford: Pergamon.

Lidz, T. (1973). *The origin and treatment of schizophrenic disorders.* New York: Basic Books.

Lidz, T., Fleck, S., & Cornelison, A. R. (1965). *Schizophrenia and the family.* New York: International University Press.

Lindsley, D. B., Bowden, J., & Magoun, H. W. (1949). Effect upon EEG of acute injury to the brain stem activating system. *Electroencephalography and Clinical Neurophysiology, 1,* 475–486.

Loftus, E. F. (1974). Reconstructing memory: The incredible witness. *Psychology Today, 8,* 116–119.

Loftus, E. F. (1979). *Eyewitness testimony.* Cambridge: Harvard University Press.

Loftus, E. F. (1983). Silence is not golden. *American Psychologist, 38,* 564–572. (a)

Loftus, E. F. (1983). Whose shadow is crooked? *American Psychologist, 38,* 576–577. (b)

Loftus, E. F. (1984). The eyewitness on trial. In B. D. Sales & A. Alwork (Eds.), *With liberty and justice for all.* Englewood Cliffs, NJ: Prentice-Hall.

Loftus, E. F. & Loftus, G. R. (1980). On the permanence of stored information in the human brain. *American Psychologist, 35,* 409–420.

Loftus, E. F., Miller, D. G., & Burns, H. J. (1978). Semantic integration of verbal information into a visual memory. *Journal of Experimental Psychology: Human Learning and Memory, 4,* 19–31.

Lorenz, K. (1969). *On aggression.* New York: Bantam Books.

Lorenz, K. (1981). *The foundation of ethology.* New York: Springer-Verlag.

Lott, A. J. & Lott, B. E. (1974). The role of reward in the formation of positive interpersonal attitudes. In T. L. Huston (Ed.), *Foundations of interpersonal attraction.* New York: Academic Press.

Lubin, B., Larsen, R. M., & Matarazzo, J. D. (1984). Patterns of psychological test usage in the United States: 1935–1982. *American Psychologist, 39,* 451–454.

Lucas, E. A., Foutz, A. S., Dement, W. C., & Mitler, M. M. (1979). Sleep cycle organization in narcoleptic and normal dogs. *Physiology and Behavior, 23,* 325–331.

Luchins, A. S. (1942). Mechanization in problem solving. *Psychological Monographs, 54,* No. 248.

Luh, C. W. (1922). The conditions of retention. *Psychological Monographs,* No. 142.

Lynn, D. (1974). *The father: His role in child development.* Monterey, CA: Brooks/Cole.

M

Maccoby, E. E. & Jacklin, C. N. (1974). *The psychology of sex differences.* Stanford: Stanford University Press.

Maccoby, E. E. & Jacklin, C. N. (1980). Sex differences in aggression: A rejoinder and reprise. *Child Development, 51,* 964–980.

Mace, N. L. & Rabins, P. V. (1981). *The 36-hour day.* Baltimore, MD: The Johns Hopkins University Press.

Mackenzie, B. (1984). Explaining race differences in IQ: The logic, the methodology, and the evidence. *American Psychologist, 39,* 1214–1233.

MacMillan, D. L. (1982). *Mental retardation in school and society* (2nd ed.). Boston: Little, Brown.

Magenis, R. E., Overton, K. M., Chamberlin, J., Brady, T., & Lovrien, E. (1977). Parental origin of the extra chromosome in Down's syndrome. *Human Genetics, 37,* 7–16.

Magnusson, D. & Edler, N. S. (Eds.) (1977). *Personality at the crossroads: An international perspective.* Hillsdale, NJ: Wiley-Erlbaum.

Maharishi, Mahesh Yogi. (1963). *The science of living and art of being.* London: Unwin.

Maier, N. R. F. (1931). Reasoning in humans II: The solution of a problem and its appearance in consciousness. *Journal of Comparative Psychology, 12,* 181–194.

Maier, S. F. & Seligman, M. E. P. (1976). Learned helplessness: Theory and evidence. *Journal of Experimental Psychology, 105,* 3–46.

Mandler, G. (1967). Verbal learning. In T. M. Newcomb (Ed.), *New directions in psychology III.* New York: Holt, Rinehart & Winston.

Mandler, G. (1980). Recognizing: The judgment of previous occurrence. *Psychological Review, 87,* 252–271.

Marcia, J. E. (1980). Identity in adolescence. In J. Adelson (Ed.), *Handbook of adolescent psychology.* New York: Wiley.

Marshall, G. D. & Zimbardo, P. G. (1979). Affective consequences of inadequately explained physiological arousal. *Journal of Personality and Social Psychology, 37,* 970–988.

Martindale, C. (1981). *Cognition and consciousness.* Homewood, IL: Dorsey Press.

Maslach, C. (1979). The emotional consequences of arousal without reason. In C. E. Izard (Ed.), *Emotions in personality and psychopathology.* New York: Plenum.

Maslow, A. H. (1943). A theory of human motivation. *Psychological Review, 50,* 370–396.

Maslow, A. H. (1954). *Motivation and personality.* New York: Harper.

Maslow, A. H. (1970). *Motivation and personality* (2nd ed.). New York: Harper and Row.

Massaro, D. W. (1975). *Experimental psychology and information processing.* Chicago: Rand McNally.

Masters, W. H. & Johnson, V. E. (1979). *Homosexuality in perspective.* Boston: Little, Brown.

Matlin, M. W. (1983). *Perception.* Boston: Allyn and Bacon.

Mayer, J. (1952). The glucostatic theory of regulation of food intake and the problem of obesity. *Bulletin of the New England Medical Center, 14,* 43.

Mayo, E. (1933). *The human problems of an industrial civilization.* Cambridge, MA: Harvard University Press.

McCall, J. & Lombardo, D. B. (1983). What makes a top executive? *Psychology Today, 17,* 48–56.

McCarley, R. W. & Hoffman, E. (1981). REM sleep, dreams, and the activation-synthesis hypothesis. *American Journal of Psychiatry, 138,* 904–912.

McClelland, D. C. (1958). Risk-taking in children with high and low need for achievement. In J. W. Atkinson (Ed.), *Motives in fantasy, action, and society.* Princeton, NJ: Van Nostrand.

McClelland, D. C. (1975). *Power: The inner experience.* New York: Irvingston-Halstead-Wiley.

McClelland, D. C. (1982). The need for power, sympathetic activation, and illness. *Motivation and Emotion, 6,* 31–41.

McClelland, D. C. (1985). *Human motivation.* Glenview, IL: Scott, Foresman.

McClelland, D. C., Atkinson, J. W., Clark, R. A., & Lowell, E. L. (1953). *The achievement motive.* New York: Appleton-Century-Crofts.

McClelland, D. C. & Winter, D. G. (1969). *Motivating economic development.* New York: Free Press.

McCloskey, M. & Egeth, H. E. (1983). Eyewitness identification. *American Psychologist, 38,* 550–563. (a)

McCloskey, M. & Egeth, H. E. (1983). A time to speak, or a time to keep silent? *American Psychologist, 38,* 573–575. (b)

McConnell, J. V. (1962). Memory transfer through cannibalism in planarians. *Journal of Neuropsychiatry, 3,* 42–48.

McConnell, J. V., Jacobson, A. L., & Kimble, D. P. (1959). The effects of regeneration upon retention of a conditioned response in the planarian. *Journal of Comparative and Physiological Psychology, 52,* 1–5.

McDougall, W. (1908). *An introduction to social psychology.* London: Methuen.

McGee, M. G. (1979). Human spatial abilities: Psychometric studies and environmental, genetic, hormonal, and neurological influences. *Psychological Bulletin, 86,* 889–918.

McGinnis, J. M. (1985). Recent history of federal initiatives in prevention policy. *American Psychologist, 40,* 205–212.

McGregor, D. (1960). *The human side of enterprise.* New York: McGraw-Hill.

McNeil, D. (1970). *The acquisition of language.* New York: Harper & Row.

Mednick, M. T. S. (1979). The new psychology of women: A feminist analysis. In J. E. Gullahorn (Ed.), *Psychology and women: In transition.* New York: Wiley.

Meer, J. (1985). Behavior mod and diabetes. *Psychology Today, 19,* 12.

Meichenbaum, D. (1977). *Cognitive-behavior modification: An integrative approach.* New York: Plenum.

Meltzoff, A. N. & Moore, M. K. (1977). Imitation of facial and manual gestures by human neonates. *Science, 198,* 75–78.

Melzack, R. (1973). *The puzzle of pain.* London: Penguin.

Melzack, R. & Wall, P. D. (1965). Pain mechanisms: A new theory. *Science, 150,* 971–979.

Milgram, S. (1963). Behavioral studies of obedience. *Journal of Abnormal and Social Psychology, 67,* 371–378.

Milgram, S. (1965). Some conditions of obedience and disobedience to authority. *Human Relations, 18,* 57–76.

Milgram, S. (1974). *Obedience to authority.* New York: Harper & Row.

Miller, G. A. (1956). The magical number seven, plus or minus two: Some limits on our capacity for processing information. *Psychological Review, 63,* 81–96.

Miller, G. A., Galanter, E., & Pribram, K. H. (1960). *Plans and the structure of behavior.* New York: Holt, Rinehart and Winston.

Miller, N. E. (1944). Experimental studies of conflict. In J. M. Hunt (Ed.), *Personality and the behavior disorders.* New York: Ronald Press, 431–465.

Miller, N. E. (1959). Liberalization of basic S-R concepts: Extensions to conflict behavior, motivation, and social learning. In S. Koch (Ed.), *Psychology: A study of a science (Vol. 2).* New York: McGraw-Hill.

Miller, N. E. (1969). Learning of visceral and glandular responses. *Science, 163,* 434–445.

Miller, N. E. (1978). Biofeedback and visceral learning. *Annual Review of Psychology, 29,* 373–404.

Miller, N. E. (1985). Rx: Biofeedback. *Psychology Today, 19,* February, 54–59.

Miller, R. C. & Berman, J. S. (1983). The efficacy of cognitive behavior therapies: A quantitative review of the research evidence. *Psychological Bulletin, 94,* 39–53.

Minami, H. & Dallenbach, K. M. (1946). The effect of activity upon learning and retention in the cockroach. *American Journal of Psychology, 59,* 682–697.

Mischel, W. (1968). *Personality and assessment.* New York: Wiley.

Mischel, W. (1973). Toward a cognitive social learning reconceptualization of personality. *Psychological Review, 80,* 252–283.

Mischel, W. (1979). On the interface of cognition and personality. *American Psychologist, 34,* 740–754.

Mischel, W. (1981). *Introduction to personality (3rd Ed.).* New York: Holt, Rinehart & Winston.

Mitler, M. M., Guilleminault, C., Orem, J., Zarcone, V. P. & Dement, W. C. (1975). Sleeplessness, sleep attacks and things that go wrong in the night. *Psychology Today,* December, 45–50.

Moore, K. L. (1982). *The developing human* (3rd ed.). Philadelphia: W. B. Saunders.

Morris, C. W. (1946). *Signs, language, and behavior.* New York: Prentice-Hall.

Moruzzi, G. & Magoun, H. W. (1949). Brain stem reticular formation and activation of the EEG. *Electroencephalography and Clinical Neurophysiology, 1,* 455–473.

Murch, G. M. (1973). *Visual and auditory perception.* Indianapolis, IN: Bobbs-Merrill.

Murdock, B. B. (1962). The serial position effect in free recall. *Journal of Experimental Psychology, 64,* 482–488.

Murray, D. M., Johnson, C. A., Luepker, R. V., & Mittelmark, M. B. (1984). The prevention of cigarette smoking in children: A comparison of four strategies. *Journal of Applied Social Psychology, 14,* 274–288.

Murray, D. J. (1983). *A history of western psychology.* Englewood Cliffs, NJ: Prentice-Hall.

Murray, H. A. (1938). *Explorations in personality.* New York: Oxford.

Myers, D. G. (1983). *Social psychology.* New York: McGraw-Hill.

N

National Council on Alcoholism (1979). *Facts on alcoholism.* New York.

National Institute of Mental Health. (1984). The NIMH epidemiologic catchment area program. *Archives of General Psychiatry, 41,* 931–1011.

Nelson, S. D. & Stapp, J. (1983). Research activities in psychology: An update. *American Psychologist, 38,* 1321–1329.

Newell, A., Shaw, J. C., & Simon, H. A. (1962). The process of creative thinking. In H. E. Gruber, G. Terrell, and M. Wetheimer (Eds.), *Contemporary approaches to creative thinking.* New York: Atherton Press.

Newell, A. & Simon, H. A. (1972). *Human problem solving.* Englewood Cliffs, NJ: Prentice-Hall.

Newman, B. M. & Newman, P. R. (1984). *Development through life: A psychosocial approach.* Homewood, IL: Dorsey.

Nisbett, R. & Wilson, T. (1977). Telling more than we can know: Verbal reports on mental processes. *Psychological Review, 84,* 231–259.

Nisbett, R. E. (1972). Hunger, obesity, and the ventromedial hypothalamus. *Psychological Review, 79,* 433–453.

O

Oden, M. H. (1968). The fulfillment of promise: 40-year follow-up of the Terman gifted group. *Genetic Psychology Monographs, 77,* No. 1, 3–93.

Ogilvie, B. C. & Howe, M. A. (1984). Beating slumps at their game. *Psychology Today, 18,* 28–32.

Olton, D. S. (1978). Characteristics of spatial memory. In S. H. Hule, H. F. Fowler, & W. K. Honig (Eds.), *Cognitive processes in animal behavior.* Hillsdale, NJ: Erlbaum.

Olton, D. S. (1979). Mazes, maps, and memory. *American Psychologist, 34,* 583–596.

Olton, D. S. & Samuelson, R. J. (1976). Remembrance of places passed. Spatial memory in rats. *Journal of Experimental Psychology: Animal Behavior Processes, 2,* 96–116.

Orne, M. (1969). Demand characteristics and the concept of quasicontrols. In R. Rosenthal & R. Rosnow (Eds.), *Artifact in behavioral research.* New York: Academic Press.

Ouchi, W. (1981). *Theory Z: How American business can meet the Japanese challenge.* Reading, MA: Addison-Wesley.

P

Parsons, H. M. (1974). What happened at Hawthorne? *Science, 183,* 922–932.

Patterson, F. & Linden, E. (1981). Ape language. *Science, 211,* 86–87.

Pavlov, I. (1927). *Conditioned reflexes.* Oxford: Oxford University Press.

Pavlov, I. (1928). *Lectures on conditioned reflexes: The higher nervous activity of animals.* (Vol. 1) translated by H. Gantt. London: Lawrence and Wishart.

Penfield, W. (1975). *The mystery of the mind.* Princeton, NJ: Princeton University Press.

Penfield, W. & Rasmussen, T. (1950). *The cerebral cortex of man.* New York: Macmillan.

Peters, W. A. (1971). *A class divided.* Garden City, NY: Doubleday.

Peterson, L. R. & Peterson, M. J. (1959). Short-term retention of individual verbal items. *Journal of Experimental Psychology, 58,* 193–198.

Petty, R. E. & Cacioppo, J. T. (1981). *Attitudes and persuasion: Classic and contemporary approaches.* Dubuque, IA: Wm. C. Brown.

Petty, R. E., Harkins, S. G., Williams, K. D., & Latané, B. The effects of group size on cognitive effort and evaluation. *Personality and Social Psychology Bulletin, 3,* 579–582.

Petty, R. E., Ostrom, T., & Brock, T. C. (Eds.) (1981). *Cognitive responses in persuasion.* Hillsdale, NJ: Erlbaum.

Petty, R. E., Wells, G. L., & Brock, T. C. (1976). Distraction can enhance or reduce yielding to propaganda: Thought disruption versus effort justification. *Journal of Personality and Social Psychology, 34,* 874–884.

Piaget, J. (1948). *The moral judgment of the child.* Glencoe, IL: Free Press.

Piaget, J. (1954). *The construction of reality in the child.* New York: Basic Books.

Piaget, J. (1967). *Six psychological studies.* New York: Random House.

Pines, M. (1982). Infant-stim: It's changing the lives of handicapped kids. *Psychology Today, 16,* 48–53.

Pines, M. (1983). Can a rock walk? *Psychology Today, 17,* November, 46–54.

Plutchik, R. (1980). *Emotion: A psychoevolutionary synthesis.* New York: Harper & Row. (a)

Plutchik, R. (1980). A language for the emotions. *Psychology Today, 14,* February, 68–78. (b)

Pola, J. & Matin, L. (1977). Eye movements following autokinesis. *Bulletin of the Psychonomic Society, 10,* 397–398.

Pollio, H. R. (1974). *The psychology of symbolic activity.* Reading, MS: Addison-Wesley.

Posner, M. I. (1973). *Cognition: An introduction.* Glenview, IL: Scott, Foresman.

Premack, D. (1965). Reinforcement theory. In D. Levine (Ed.), *Nebraska symposium on motivation.* Lincoln, NB: University of Nebraska Press.

Premack, A. J. & Premack, D. (1972). Teaching language to an ape. *Scientific American, 172,* 808–822.

President's Commission on Mental Health (1978). *Report to the President.* Washington, DC: U. S. Government Printing Office.

Pressley, M., Levin, J. R., & Delaney, H. D. (1982). The mnemonic keyword method. *Review of Educational Research, 52,* 61–91.

R

Rahe, R. H. & Arthur, R. J. (1978). Life changes and illness reports. In K. E. Gunderson & R. H. Rahe (Eds.) *Life stress and illness.* Springfield, IL: Thomas.

Rappaport, D. (1951). The autonomy of the ego. *Bulletin of the Menninger Clinic, 15,* 113–123.

Raven, J. C. (1962). *Advanced progressive matrices: Set II.* London: H. K. Lewis.

Raven, J. C., Court, J. H., & Raven, J. (1978). *Manual for Raven's Progressive Matrices and Vocabulary Scales.* London: H. K. Lewis.

Rechtschaffen, A. (1971). The control of sleep. In W. A. Hunt (Ed.), *Human behavior and its control.* (pp. 75–92). Cambridge, MA: Schenkman.

Rescorla, R. A. & Wagner, A. R. (1972). A theory of Pavlovian conditioning. In A. A. Black & W. F. Prokasky (Eds.), *Classical conditioning II.* New York: Appleton-Century-Crofts.

Restak, R. M. (1982). Islands of genius. *Science 82, 3,* 62–67.

Revusky, S. H. & Garcia, J. (1970). Learned associations over long delays. In G. H. Bower & J. T. Spence (Eds.), *The psychology of learning and motivation: IV.* New York: Academic Press.

Reynolds, A. G. & Flagg, P. W. (1983). *Cognitive psychology* (2nd ed.). Boston: Little, Brown.

Riesen, A. H. (1965). Effects of early deprivation of photic stimulation. In S. Osler & R. Cooke (Eds.), *The biosocial basis of mental retardation.* Baltimore: The Johns Hopkins University Press.

Roche, A. F. & Davila, G. H. (1972). Late adolescent growth in stature. *Pediatrics, 50,* 874–880.

Rodin, J. (1981). Current status of the internal-external hypothesis of obesity: What went wrong? *American Psychologist, 36,* 361–372.

Roffwarg, H. P., Munzio, J. N. & Dement, W. C. (1966). Ontogenic development of the sleep-dream cycle. *Science, 152,* 604–619.

Roethlisberger, F. J. & Dickson, W. J. (1939). *Management and the worker.* New York: Wiley.

Rosch, E. (1973). Natural categories. *Cognitive Psychology, 4,* 328–350.

Rosch, E. (1975). Cognitive representations of semantic categories. *Journal of Experimental Psychology: General, 104,* 192–253.

Rosch, E. (1978). Principles of categorization. In E. Rosch & B. B. Lloyd (Eds.), *Cognition and categorization.* Hillsdale, NJ: Erlbaum.

Rose, S. A. & Blank, M. (1974). The potency of context in children's cognition: An illustration through conservation. *Child Development, 45,* 499–502.

Rosenthal, D. (1970). *Genetic theory and abnormal behavior.* New York: McGraw-Hill.

Rosenthal, D. (1971). *Genetics of psychopathology.* New York: McGraw-Hill.

Ross, L. D. (1977). The intuitive psychologist and his shortcomings: Distortions in the attributional process. In L. Berkowitz (Ed.), *Advances in experimental social psychology (Vol. 10).* New York: Academic Press.

Rossi, A. S. (1980). Aging and parenthood in the middle years. In P. B. Baltes & O. G. Brim Jr. (Eds.), *Lifespan development and behavior (Vol III).* New York: Academic Press.

Rotter, J. B. (1982). *The development and application of social learning theory: Selected papers.* New York: Praeger.

Rubin, Z. (1970). Measurement of romantic love. *Journal of Personality and Social Psychology, 16,* 265–273.

Rubin, Z. (1973). *Liking and loving: An invitation to social psychology.* New York: Holt, Rinehart & Winston.

Rumbaugh, D. M. (Ed.) (1977). *Language learning by a chimpanzee: The Lana project.* New York: Academic Press.

Rundus, D. (1971). Analysis of rehearsal processes in free recall. *Journal of Experimental Psychology, 89,* 63–77.

Ryan, E. D. & Kovacic, C. R. (1966). Pain tolerance and athletic participation. *Journal of Personality and Social Psychology, 22,* 383–390.

S

Sadalla, E. K. & Oxley, D. (1984). The perception of room size: The rectangularity illusion. *Environment and Behavior, 16,* 394–405.

Saks, M. J. (1976). Social scientists can't rig juries. *Psychology Today, 10,* 48–57.

Samuelson, F. J. B. (1980). Watson's little Albert, Cyril Burt's twins, and the need for a critical science. *American Psychologist, 35,* 619–625.

Sarason, I. G., Johnson, J. H., & Siegel, J. M. (1978). Assessing the impact of life change: Development of the life experiences survey. *Journal of Consulting and Clinical Psychology, 46,* 932–946.

Scarr, S. & Weinberg, R. A. (1976). IQ test performance of black children adopted by white families. *American Psychologist, 31,* 726–739.

Scarr, S. & Weinberg, R. A. (1978). Attitudes, interests, and IQ. *Human Nature,* April, 29–36.

Schacter, S. (1971). Some extraordinary facts about obese humans and rats. *American Psychologist, 26,* 129–144.

Schacter, S. & Singer, J. (1962). Cognitive, social and physiological determinants of emotional states. *Psychological Review, 69,* 379–399.

Schacter, S. & Singer, J. (1979). Comments on the Maslach and Marshall-Zimbardo experiments. *Journal of Personality and Social Psychology, 37,* 989–995.

Schaie, K. W. (1974). Translations in gerontology—from lab to life: Intellectual functioning. *American Psychologist, 29,* 802–807.

Schaie, K. W. & Strother, C. R. (1968). A cross-sequential study of age changes in cognitive behavior. *Psychological Bulletin, 70,* 671–680.

Scharf, B. (1978). Loudness. In E. C. Carterette & M. P. Friedman (Eds.), *Handbook of Perception.* New York: Academic Press.

Schau, C. G., Kahn, L., Diepold, J. H., & Cherry, F. (1980). The relationships of parental expectations and preschool children's verbal sex typing to their sex-typed toy play behavior. *Child Development, 51,* 266–270.

Scheerer, M. (1963). Problem solving. *Scientific American, 208,* 118–128.

Schiffman, H. R. (1976). *Sensation and perception: An integrated approach.* New York: Wiley.

Schulman, J., Shaver, P., Coleman, R., Emricle, B., & Christie, R. (1973). Recipe for a jury. *Psychology Today, 7,* 37–44, 77, 79–84.

Schwartz, B. (1984). *Psychology of learning and behavior* (2nd ed.). New York: Norton.

Schwartz, P. (1983). Length of day-care attendance and attachment behavior in eighteen-month-old infants. *Child Development, 54,* 1073–1078.

Scott, M. D. & Pelliccioni, L., Jr. (1982). *Don't choke: How athletes become winners.* Englewood Cliffs, NJ: Prentice-Hall.

Sears, P. S. & Barbee, A. H. Career and life satisfaction among Terman's gifted women. In J. Stanley et al. (Eds.), *The gifted and the creative: Fifty-year perspective.* Baltimore: Johns Hopkins University Press.

Sears, R. R. (1977). Sources of life satisfactions of the Terman gifted men. *American Psychologist, 32,* 119–128.

Seligman, M. E. P. (1975). *Helplessness: On depression, development, and death.* San Francisco: Freeman.

Selye, H. (1956). *The stress of life.* New York: McGraw-Hill.

Selye, H. (1974). *Stress without distress.* Philadelphia: Lippincott.

Selye, H. (1976). *The stress of life* (rev. ed.). New York: McGraw-Hill.

Senden, M. V. (1960). *Space and sight.* New York: Free Press.

Shadish, W. R. (1984). Polict research: Lessons from the implementation of deinstitutionalization. *American Psychologist, 39,* 725–738.

Sheer, D. E. (Ed.) (1961). *Electrical stimulation of the brain.* Austin, TX: University of Texas Press.

Sheldon: W. H. (1940). *The varieties of human physique: An introduction to constitutional psychology.* New York: Harper.

Sheldon, W. H. (1942). *The varieties of temperament: A psychology of constitutional differences.* New York: Harper.

Sheldon, W. H. (1944). Constitutional factors in personality. In J. McV. Hunt (Ed.), *Personality and the behavior disorders.* New York: Ronald Press, 526–549.

Sheldon, W. H. (1954). *Atlas of men: A guide for somatotyping the adult male at all ages.* New York: Harper.

Sherif, M. (1936). *The psychology of social norms.* New York: Harper & Row.

Shevrin, H. & Dickman, S. (1980). The psychological unconscious: A necessary assumption for all psychological theory? *American Psychologist, 35,* 421–434.

Shipley, T. (Ed.) (1961). *Classics in psychology.* New York: Philosophical Library.

Siegler, R. S. (1983). Five generalizations about cognitive development. *American Psychologist, 38,* 263–277.

Silverman, L. H. (1976). Psychoanalytic theory: "The reports of my death are greatly exaggerated." *American Psychologist, 31,* 621–637.

Simkins, L. (1982). Biofeedback: Clinically valid or oversold? *The Psychological Record, 32,* 3–17.

Skinner, B. F. (1938). *The behavior of organisms: A behavioral analysis.* New York: Appleton-Century-Crofts.

Skinner, B. F. (1956). A case history in the scientific method. *American Psychologist, 11,* 221–233.

Skinner, B. F. (1983). *A matter of consequence.* New York: A. Knopf.

Skinner, B. F. (1983). Intellectual self-management in old age. *American Psychologist, 38,* 239–244.

Skinner, B. F. (1984). *A matter of consequence.* New York: A. Knopf.

Slobin, D. I. (1979). *Psycholinguistics.* Glenview, IL: Scott, Foresman.

Smith, G. E. & Berg, J. M. (1976). *Down's anomaly.* London: Churchill Press.

Smith, M. L., Glass, G. V., & Miller, T. I. (1980). *The benefits of psychotherapy.* Baltimore: Johns Hopkins University Press.

Snyder, S. H. (1977). Opiate receptors and internal opiates. *Scientific American, 236,* 44–56.

Snyder, S. H. (1980). *Biological aspects of mental disorder.* New York: Oxford University Press.

Snyder, S. H. (1980). Brain peptides as neurotransmitters. *Science, 209,* 976–983.

Snyder, S. H. (1984). Medicated minds. *Science 84,* November, 141–142.

Solomon, R. L. (1980). The opponent-process theory of acquired motivation: The costs of pleasure and the benefits of pain. *American Psychologist, 35,* 691–712.

Solomon, R. L. & Corbit, J. D. (1974). An opponent-process theory of motivation. I. Temporal dynamics of affect. *Psychological Review, 81,* 119–145.

Sorenson, R. C. (1973). *Adolescent sexuality in contemporary America.* New York: Abrams.

Spanos, N. P. & Barber, T. F. X. (1974). Toward convergence in hypnosis research. *American Psychologist, 29,* 500–511.

Spearman, C. (1904). "General intelligence" objectively determined and measured. *American Journal of Psychology, 15,* 201–293.

Sperling, G. (1960). The information available in brief visual presentations. *Psychological Monographs, 74,* Whole No. 498.

Sperling, G. (1963). A model for visual memory tasks. *Human Factors, 5,* 19–31.

Sperry, R. (1982). Some effects of disconnecting the cerebral hemispheres. *Science, 217,* 1223–1226.

Sperry, R. W. (1968). Hemispheric disconnection and unity in conscious awareness. *American Psychologist, 23,* 723–733.

Spitzer, R. L., Skodol, A. E., Gibbon, M., & Williams, J. B. W. (1981). *DSM-III case book.* Washington, DC: American Psychiatric Association.

Springer, J. P. & Deutsch, G. (1981). *Left brain, right brain.* San Francisco: W. H. Freeman.

Squire, L. R. & Slater, P. C. (1978). Bilateral and unilateral ECT: Effects on verbal and nonverbal memory. *American Journal of Psychiatry, 135,* 1316–1320.

Stager, S. F. & Burke, P. J. (1982). A reexamination of body build stereotypes. *Journal of Research in Personality, 16,* 435–446.

Stagner, R. (1982). The importance of historical context. *American Psychologist, 37,* 856.

Standing, L., (1973). Learning 10,000 pictures. *Quarterly Journal of Experimental Psychology, 25,* 207–222.

Standing, L., Conezio, J. & Haber, R. N. (1970). Perception and memory for pictures: Single-trial learning of 2500 visual stimuli. *Psychonomic Science, 19,* 73–74.

Stapp, J. & Fulcher, R. (1983). The employment of APA members: 1982. *American Psychologist, 38,* 1298–1320.

Stapp, J. & Vandenbos, G. R. (1983). Service providers in psychology: Results of the 1982 APA Human Resources Survey. *American Psychologist, 38,* 1330–1352.

Stechler, G. & Halton, A. (1982). Prenatal influences on human development. In B. B. Wolman (Ed.), *Handbook of developmental psychology.* Englewood Cliffs, NJ: Prentice-Hall.

Stene, J., Stene, E., Stengel-Rutkowski, S., & Murken, J. D. (1981). Parental age and Down's syndrome, data from prenatal diagnoses (DFG). *Human Genetics, 59,* 119–124.

Sternbach, R. A. (Ed.) (1978). *The psychology of pain.* New York: Raven.

Sternberg, R. J. (1979). The nature of mental abilities. *American Psychologist, 34,* 214–230.

Sternberg, R. J. (1981). Testing and cognitive psychology. *American Psychologist, 36,* 1181–1189.

Sternberg, R. J. (1982). Who's intelligent? *Psychology Today, 16,* 30–39.

Stevens, S. S. (1961). To honor Fechner and repeal his law. *Science, 133,* 80–86.

Stevens, S. S. (1970). Neural events and the psychophysical law. *Science, 170,* 1043–1050.

Stoner, J. A. F. (1961). *A comparison of individual and group decisions involving risk.* Unpublished master's thesis; Massachusetts Institute of Technology, Cambridge, MA.

Storandt, M. (1983). Psychology's response to the graying of America. *American Psychologist, 38,* 323–326.

Suinn, R. M. (1980). *Psychology in sports: Methods and applications.* Minneapolis: Burgess.

Surwit, R. S., Feinglos, M. N., & Scovern, A. W. (1983). Diabetes and behavior. *American Psychologist, 38,* 255–262.

Szasz, T. S. (1961). *The myth of mental illness.* New York: Harper & Row.

T

Tanner, J. M. (1973). Growing up. *Scientific American, 135,* 34–43.

Tanner, J. M., Whitehouse, R. H., & Takaishi, M. (1966). Standards from birth to maturity for height, weight, height velocity and weight velocity: British children, 1965. *Archives of Diseases in Childhood, 41,* 457–471, 613–635.

Taylor, W., Pearson, J., Mair, A., & Burns, W. (1965). Study of noise and hearing in jute weaving. *Journal of the Acoustical Society of America, 4,* 144–152.

Tenopyr, M. L. (1981). The realities of employment testing. *American Psychologist, 36,* 1120–1127.

Terman, L. M. & Merrill, M. A. (1972). *Stanford-Binet Intelligence Scale—manual for the third edition.* Boston: Houghton-Mifflin.

Terrace, H. S. (1979). Is problem-solving language? *Journal of the Experimental Analysis of Behavior, 31,* 161–175.

Terrace, H. S., Pettito, L. A., Sanders, R. J., & Bever, T. G. (1979). Can an ape create a sentence? *Science, 206,* 891–902.

Thompson, C. I. (1980). *Controls of eating.* Jamaica, NY: Spectrum.

Thompson, R. & McConnell, J. V. (1955). Classical conditioning in the planerian, *Dugesia dorotocephala. Journal of Comparative and Physiological Psychology, 48,* 65–68.

Thorndike, E. L. (1911). *Animal intelligence.* New York: Macmillan.

Thurstone, L. L. (1938). Primary mental abilities. *Psychometric Monographs,* (No. 1).

Tilley, A. J. & Empson, J. A. C. (1978). REM sleep and memory consolidation. *Biological Psychology, 6,* 293–300.

Tobin-Richards, M., Boxer, A., & Peterson, A. C. (1984). The psychological impact of pubertal change: Sex differences in perceptions of self during early adolescence. In J. Brooks-Gunn & A. C. Peterson (Eds.), *Girls at puberty: Biological, psychological and social perspectives.* New York: Plenum.

Tolman, C. W. (1969). Social feeding in domestic chicks: Effects of food deprivation of non-feeding companions. *Psychonomic Science, 15,* 234.

Tolman, E. C. (1932). *Purposive behavior in animals and men.* New York: Appleton-Century-Crofts.

Tolman, E. C. & Honzik, C. H. (1930). Introduction and removal of reward and maze performance in rats. *University of California Publications in Psychology, 4,* 257–275.

Torrey, T. W. & Feduccia, A. (1979). *Morphogenesis of the vertebrates.* New York: Wiley.

Triplett, N. (1898). The dynamogenic factors in pacemaking and competition. *American Journal of Psychology, 9*, 507–533.

Trotter, R. J. (1983). Baby face. *Psychology Today, 17*, August, 14–20.

Tucker, D. M. (1981). Lateral brain function, emotion, and conceptualization. *Psychological Bulletin, 89*, 19–46.

Tulving, E. (1962). Subjective organization in free recall of "unrelated" words. *Psychological Review, 69*, 344–354.

Tulving, E. (1972). Episodic and semantic memory. In E. Tulving & W. Donaldson (Eds.), *Organization of memory*. New York: Academic Press.

Tuttle, T. C. (1983). Organizational productivity: A challenge for psychologists. *American Psychologist, 38*, 479–486.

U

Underwood, B. J. (1957). Interference and forgetting. *Psychological Review, 64*, 49–60.

United States Office of Education. (1972). *Education of the gifted and talented, Vol. 2.* Washington, DC: U. S. Government Printing Office.

United States Surgeon General's Report. (1979). *Healthy people.* Washington, DC: U. S. Government Printing Office.

V

Valenstein, E. S. (1973). *Brain control.* New York: Wiley.

Valenstein, E. S. (1980). *The psychosurgery debate.* San Francisco: W. H. Freeman.

Verillo, R. T. (1975). Cutaneous sensation. In B. Scharf (Ed.), *Experimental sensory psychology.* Glenview, IL: Scott, Foresman.

Vernon, P. E. (1960). *The structure of human abilities (rev. ed.).* London: Methuen.

Vernon, P. E. (1979). *Intelligence: Heredity and environment.* San Francisco: W. H. Freeman.

Vinacke, W. E. (1974). *The psychology of thinking* (2nd ed.). New York: McGraw-Hill.

W

Wallace, P. (1977). Individual discrimination of humans by odor. *Physiology and Behavior, 19*, 577–579.

Wallace, R. K. & Benson, H. (1972). The physiology of meditation. *Scientific American, 226*, 85–90.

Wallas, G. (1926). *The art of thought.* New York: Harcourt, Brace.

Wallis, C. (1983). Slow, steady and heartbreaking. *Time*, July 11, 56–57.

Walster (Hatfield), E., Aronson, V., Abrahams, D., & Rottman, L. (1966). Importance of physical attractiveness in dating behavior. *Journal of Personality and Social Psychology, 4*, 508–516.

Walster, E. & Festinger, L. (1962). The effectiveness of "overheard" and persuasive communications. *Journal of Abnormal and Social Psychology, 65*, 395–402.

Watson, J. B. (1919). *Psychology from the standpoint of a behaviorist.* Philadelphia: Lippincott.

Watson, J. B. & Raynor, R. (1920). Conditioned emotional reactions. *Journal of Experimental Psychology, 3*, 1–14.

Watson, J. B. (1924). *Behaviorism.* New York: Norton.

Watson, J. B. (1925). *Behaviorism.* New York: Norton.

Webb, W. B. (1975). *Sleep, the gentle tyrant.* Englewood Cliffs, NJ: Prentice-Hall.

Webb, W. B. (1979). The nature of dreams. In D. Goleman & R. J. Davidson (Eds.), *Consciousness: Brain, states of awareness, and mysticism.* (pp. 76–78). New York: Harper & Row.

Webb, W. B. (1981). The return of consciousness. In L. T. Benjamin, Jr. (Ed.), *The G. Stanley Hall Lecture Series.* (Vol. I). Washington, DC: American Psychological Association.

Wechsler, D. (1958). *The measurement and appraisal of adult intelligence (4th ed.).* Baltimore: Williams & Wilkins.

Wechsler, D. (1975). Intelligence defined and undefined: A relativistic reappraisal. *American Psychologist, 30*, 135–139.

Weil, A. T., Zinberg, N., & Nelson, J. M. (1968). Clinical and psychological effects of marijuana in man. *Science, 162*, 1234–1242.

Weitzman, E. D. (1981). Sleep and its disorders. *Annual Review of Neurosciences, 4*, 381–417.

Welch, W. W., Anderson, R. E., & Harris, L. J. (1982). The effects of schooling on mathematics achievement. *American Educational Research Journal, 19*, 145–153.

White, R. W. (1959). Motivation reconsidered: The concept of competence. *Psychological Review, 66*, 297–333.

White, R. W. (1974). Strategies of adaptation: An attempt at a systematic description. In G. V. Coelheo, D. A. Hamburg, & J. E. Adams (Eds.), *Coping and adaptation.* New York: Basic Books.

Wickens, D. D. (1973). Some characteristics of word encoding. *Memory and cognition, 1*, 485–490.

Williams, R. L. (1972). *The BITCH Test (Black Intelligence Test of Cultural Homogeneity).* St. Louis: Williams and Associates.

Winter, D. G. & Stewart, A. J. (1978). The power motive. In H. London & J. E. Exner, Jr. (Eds.), *Dimensions of personality.* New York: Wiley.

Winters, K. C., Weintraub, S., & Neale, J. M. (1981). Validity of MMPI code types in identifying DSM-III schizophrenics, unipolars, and bipolars. *Journal of Consulting and Clinical Psychology, 49*, 486–487.

Wollen, K. A., Weber, A., & Lowry, D. H. (1972). Bizarreness versus interaction of mental images as determinants of learning. *Cognitive Psychology, 3*, 518–523.

Wolpe, J. (1958). *Psychotherapy by reciprocal inhibition.* Stanford, CA: Stanford University Press.

Wolpe, J. (1981). Behavior therapy versus psychoanalysis. *American Psychologist, 36*, 159–164.

Woodworth, R. S., & Schlosberg, H. (1954). *Experimental psychology* (rev. ed.). New York: Henry Holt.

Wurtman, R. J. (1985). Alzheimer's disease. *Scientific American, 247*, 62–74.

Y

Yates, A. J. (1980). *Biofeedback and the modification of behavior.* New York: Plenum.

Yates, F. A. (1966). *The art of memory.* Chicago: University of Chicago Press.

Z

Zadeh, L. (1965). Fuzzy sets. *Information and Control, 8*, 338–353.

Zajonc, R. B. (1965). Social facilitation. *Science, 149*, 269–274.

Zajonc, R. B. (1968). Attitudinal effects of mere exposure. *Journal of Personality and Social Psychology*, Monograph supplement, *9*, 1–27.

Zajonc, R. B. (1980). Feeling and thinking: Preferences need no inferences. *American Psychologist, 35*, 151–175.

Zajonc, R. B. (1984). On the primacy of affect. *American Psychologist, 39*, 117–123.

Zedeck, S. & Cascio, W. F. (1984). Psychological issues in personnel decisions. *Annual Review of Psychology, 35*, 461–518.

Zelnik, M. & Kantner, J. F. (1980). Sexual activity, contraceptive use, and pregnancy among metropolitan-area teenagers: 1971–1979. *Family Planning Perspectives, 12*, 230–237.

Zimbardo, P. G. (1970). The human choice: Individuation, reason, and order versus deindividuation, impulse, and chaos. In W. J. Arnold & D. Levine (Eds.), *Nebraska symposium on motivation, 1969, (Vol. 17).* Lincoln, NB: University of Nebraska Press.

ACKNOWLEDGMENTS

Credits for photographs, illustrations, and quoted material not given on the page where they appear are listed below.

PHOTO CREDITS

All photographs not credited are the property of Scott, Foresman. Cover and chapter opening photographs: Michael Goss/Scott, Foresman.

Chapter 1

6 Carl Mydans
8 Owen Franken/Stock, Boston
9 (left) Giraudon/Art Resource
9 (right) Library of Congress
10 (both) The Bettmann Archive
11 The Bettmann Archive
13 (left) UPI/The Bettmann Archive
13 (center left) Courtesy of Dr. B. F. Skinner
13 (center right, right) The Bettmann Archive
14 Courtesy of The National Portrait Gallery, London
17 Roe Di Bona
23 J. Berndt/The Picture Cube
31 Richard Wood/The Picture Cube
34 Marcia Weinstein

Chapter 2

43 Manfred Kage/Peter Arnold
59 Fig. 4.1. The Bettmann Archive
61 Fig. 4.2. Courtesy of the Warren Anatomical Museum, Harvard Medical School
63 Fig. 4.3. Courtesy of Dr. José M. Delgado
64 Fig. 4.4. From Louis P. Thorpe, Barney Katz, & Robert T. Lewis, *The Psychology of Abnormal Behavior: A Dynamic Approach* (2nd ed.). Copyright © 1961 by John Wiley & Sons, Inc.
65 Fig. 4.5. Dan McCoy/Rainbow
65 (right) Brookhaven National Laboratory and New York University Medical Center
75 Fig. 4.11. From "Perception of Bilateral Chimeric Figures Following Hemispheric Deconnexion" by Jerre Levy, Colwyn Trevarthen and R. W. Sperry. *Brain* vol. 95, page 68, 1972.

Chapter 3

82 Fig. 5.1. Courtesy of Cadillac Motor Car Division, General Motors Corporation
87 (both) The Granger Collection
94 Jim Hamilton/The Picture Cube
99 Fig. 6.5. (right) Courtesy of Munsell Color, Baltimore, Maryland
108 Fig. 6.13. MacMillan Science Co., Inc.

Chapter 4

130 (top) Steve Lissau
150 Christopher Springmann
154 (all) Patrick Ward © DISCOVER Magazine 2/83, Time Inc.

155 Courtesy of The Detroit Institute of Arts, Gift of Mr. and Mrs. Bert L. Smokler and Mr. and Mrs. Lawrence A. Fleischmann
157 Randa Bishop/DPI
159 Jean-Claude Lejeune
161 Charles Marden Fitch/Taurus
163 Dean Abramson/Stock, Boston
165 R. D. Ullmann/Taurus

Chapter 5

172 John Running/Stock, Boston
174 The Bettmann Archive
179 Jean-Claude Lejeune
180 Courtesy of Dr. Ben Harris, from Watson's 1919 film *Experimental Investigation of Babies*
181 Vloo/Stockphotos, Inc.
182 John Lei/Stock, Boston
188 The Granger Collection
195 Erika Stone/Photo Researchers
199 Elizabeth Crews
201 Animal Behavior Enterprises, Hot Springs, Arkansas
203 REPRINTED FROM PSYCHOLOGY TODAY MAGAZINE Copyright © 1985 American Psychological Association
207 Leonard Lee Rue III/Animals Animals
209 Courtesy of the Department of Psychology, University of California, Berkeley
211 Meri Houtchens-Kitchens/The Picture Cube
212 Fig. 12.3. From *The Mentality of Apes* by Wolfgang Köhler. Routledge & Kegan Paul Ltd., London, 1927. (Reprinted 1948, 1973).
214 Courtesy of Dr. Albert Bandura
215 Brent Jones
218 Fig. 12.4. Thomas McAvoy, LIFE Magazine © 1955 Time Inc.

Chapter 6

223 *Chicago's Consumer Yellow Pages 1985—The Red Book.* Published by Reuben H. Donnelley. Reprinted by permission.
228 Jean-Claude Lejeune
232 Nancy Bates/The Picture Cube
233 (both) Wide World
235 (left) Charles Gupton/Southern Light
235 (right) Bohdan Hrynewych/Southern Light
244 Cameramann International, Ltd.
251 J. D. Sloan/The Picture Cube
254 From *Congestorium Artificia Memoriae* by Johannes Romberch, Venice, 1553.

Chapter 7

265 Jean-Claude Lejeune
268 Adolahe/Southern Light
273 (left) Brent Jones
273 (right) Bob Daemmrich/TexaStock
274 Elizabeth Crews
279 Paul Fusco/Magnum
280 Yerkes Regional Primate Research Center of Emory University
285 (right) Charles Gupton/Southern Light

Chapter 8

301 Brent Jones
307 Wayne Sorce © DISCOVER Magazine 2/85, Time Inc.
315 Robert V. Eckert/Stock, Boston
318 Christopher Vail
320 Barbara Alper/Stock, Boston
321 Betsy Lee/Taurus
323 Fig. 18.3. William Vandivert
325 (top) Enrico Ferorelli/Dot
325 (bottom) Wide World
326 Fig. 18.5 (all) George Zimbel/Monkmeyer Press
330 Jon Erikson
334 Fig. 18.8. Martin Rogers/Stock, Boston
335 Charles Gupton/Southern Light
339 (top) Reggie Tucker/Taurus
339 (center) Jonathan L. Barkan/The Picture Cube
339 (bottom) Charles Gupton/Southern Light
344 (top) Summer Productions/Taurus
344 (bottom) Jeff Albertson/Stock, Boston
346 (left) Charles Gupton/Stock, Boston
346 (right) Pam Hasegawa/Taurus
349 Lenore Weber/Taurus
350 G. Cloyd/Taurus
351 Brent Jones
353 Elizabeth Crews

Chapter 9

361 (both) Robert P. Carr
363 Stewart M. Green/Tom Stack & Associates
364 (left) Chuck Beckley/Southern Light
364 (right) Brian Parker/Tom Stack & Associates
368 Charles Gupton/Stock, Boston
369 Lenore Weber/Taurus
371 Michael D. Sullivan/TexaStock
373 Fig. 20.2. Reprinted by permission of the publishers from Henry A. Murray, THEMATIC APPERCEPTION TEST, Cambridge, Mass.: Harvard University Press, Copyright © 1943 by the President and Fellows of Harvard College, © 1971 by Henry A. Murray.
374 (top) Charles Feil/Stock, Boston
374 (bottom) Marty Heitner/Taurus
380 Frank J. Staub/The Picture Cube
382 Elizabeth Crews
384 Fig. 21.3. (left) George Harrison, (right) John Chellman/Animals Animals
385 Fig. 21.4 From *Darwin and Facial Expression: A Century of Research in Review,* edited by Paul Ekman. Academic Press, 1973. By Permission of Dr. Paul Ekman, Ed Gallob, and Dr. Silvan Tomkins.
386 Fig. 21.5. From *Darwin and Facial Expression: A Century of Research in Review,* edited by Paul Ekman. Academic Press, 1973. By permission of Dr. Paul Ekman.
391 Ellis Herwig/Stock, Boston
392 Fig. 21.6. (both) Reprinted from C. E. Izard's contribution to the 1978 NEBRASKA SYMPOSIUM ON MOTIVATION, by permission of University of Nebraska Press. Copyright © 1979 by the University of Nebraska Press.
399 © Laszlo
400 Bohdan Hrynewych/Southern Light
412 David E. Kennedy/TexaStock

Chapter 10

420 Culver Pictures
422 (top) Tom Stack/Tom Stack & Associates
422 (bottom) Ken Robert Buck/Stock, Boston
423 (bottom) Wide World
424 (left) The Bettmann Archive
424 (right) Courtesy of the Association for the Advancement of Psychoanalysis of the Karen Horney Psychoanalytic Institute and Center
425 Brent Jones
426 Courtesy of Dr. Albert Bandura
429 Kevin Horan/Picture Group

430 Courtesy of Harvard University News Office
435 Cary Wolinsky/Stock, Boston
446 Judy S. Gelles/Stock, Boston
447 Bohdan Hrynewych/Southern Light

Chapter 11

461 Dave Schaefer/The Picture Cube
467 Jonathan L. Barkan/The Picture Cube
468 The Bettmann Archive
471 The Psychological Corporation
473 Courtesy Library of the National Academy of Sciences
475 Sidney Harris
482 (left) Jacques M. Chenet/NEWSWEEK
482 (right) © Michael Alexander 1983. All rights reserved.
483 Dave Schaefer/The Picture Cube

Chapter 12

499 Cameramann International, Ltd.
502 (left) Victor Englebert
502 (right) Philip Jon Bailey/The Picture Cube
503 (left) Evelyn Jones/Taurus
503 (top right) Bruno Barbey/Magnum
503 (bottom right) Historical Pictures Service, Chicago
504 Tom Damman/NYT Pictures
507 (left) Owen Franken/Stock, Boston
507 (right) Bill Binzen
512 Susan Greenwood/Gamma-Liaison
519 Eric Roth/The Picture Cube
522 (both) Dan McCoy/Rainbow
523 Courtesy National Council on Alcoholism Inc.
531 NIMH
533 (both) Ira Wyman/Sygma

Chapter 13

537 TWIXT game: Reproduced by permission of the Avalon Hill Game Company, Baltimore, Maryland.
539 Bulloz
540 The British Library
541 The Pierpont Morgan Library
542 (left) The Bettmann Archive
542 (right) The Trustees of Sir John Soane's Museum
543 (left, center) Historical Pictures Service, Chicago
543 (right) Brown Brothers
545 Andy Freeberg
549 David E. Kennedy/TexaStock
554 (left) Larry Smith/DPI
556 Historical Pictures Service, Chicago
560 Courtesy of Dr. Joseph Wolpe
561 Curt Gunther/Camera 5
562 Courtesy of Dr. Albert Bandura
564 UPI/The Bettmann Archive
565 Bohdan Hrynewych/Southern Light
566 Courtesy Grove Press

Chapter 14

575 (left) David E. Kennedy/TexaStock
575 (right) Bob Daemmrich/TexaStock
576 Owen Franken/Sygma
579 Fig. 31.3. Courtesy Evan-Picone Inc.
579 Fig. 31.4. Courtesy Diet Center Inc.
582 Dennis Brack/Black Star
586 David Woo/Stock, Boston
587 Philip Jon Bailey/The Picture Cube
588 Paul Conklin
592 Cameramann International, Ltd.
594 William Vandivert
596 Courtesy of World Federation of Bergen-Belsen Associations
597 Fig. 32.2. From the film *Obedience,* distributed by New York University Film Library; Copyright © 1965, by Stanley Milgram
600 James Ewing

604 Joseph A. DiChello, Jr.
605 Paul Conklin
607 (left) Gamma-Liaison
607 (right) Owen Franken/Stock, Boston
609 David Woo/Stock, Boston

Chapter 15

620 Yvonne Hemsey/Gamma-Liaison
623 (right) Charles Harbutt/Archive
632 Courtesy of The Rouse Company
633 Owen Franken/Stock, Boston
634 (top left) Bohdan Hrynewych/Southern Light
634 (bottom) Lynn M. Stone
636 Allan Price/Taurus
638 Fred Ward/Black Star

LITERARY, FIGURES, AND TABLES

Chapter 1

16 Fig. 1.2 "APA Division List" from *division and state association membership* (October, 1984). Copyright © 1984 by the American Psychological Association. Reprinted by Permission.

19, 20 Figs. 1.3 & 1.4 Adaptation of tables used in "The Employment of APA Members: 1982" by Joy Stapp and Robert Fulcher from *American Psychologist* (December, 1983). Copyright © 1983 by the American Psychological Association. Adapted by Permission.

Chapter 2

50 Fig. 3.6 From *Fundamentals of Neurology*, 4th Edition by Ernest Gardner. Copyright © 1963 by W. B. Saunders Company. Reprinted by permission.

74 Fig. 4.10 Adapted from *Seeing: Illusion, Brain and Mind* by John P. Frisby. Copyright © 1979 by John P. Frisby. Reprinted by permission of Oxford University Press.

Chapter 3

85 Fig. 5.3 From "Contemporary Psychophysics" by Eugene Galanter from *New Directions in Psychology*. Copyright © 1962 by Holt, Rinehart and Winston, Inc. Reprinted by permission of the author.

Chapter 4

144 Fig. 8.18 From "Movement-Produced Stimulation in the Development of Visually Guided Behavior" by Richard Held and Alan Hein, from *Journal of Comparative and Physiological Psychology* Volume 56, No. 5, 1963. Published by the American Psychological Association. Reprinted by permission of the authors.

150 Fig. 9.1 Figure 1, "EEG patterns of human sleep stages" from *The Sleep Disorders* by P. Hauri. Copyright © 1982 by The Upjohn Company, Kalamazoo, Michigan. Reprinted by permission.

152 Fig. 9.2 Figure 2, "Typical sleep pattern of a young adult" from *The Sleep Disorders* by P. Hauri. Copyright © 1982 by The Upjohn Company, Kalamazoo, Michigan. Reprinted by permission.

153 Fig. 9.3 "Ontogenetic Development of the Human Sleep-Dream Cycle" by H. P. Roffwarg, J. N. Muzio and W. C. Dement, from *Science* Volume 152: 604–619: 29 April, 1966. Copyright © 1966 by the American Association for the Advancement of Science. Reprinted by permission.

Chapter 5

210 Fig. 12.1 "Introduction and Removal of Reward, and Maze Performance in Rats" by E. C. Tolman and C. H. Honzik, from *University of California Publications in Psychology* Volume IV 1928–1931. Reprinted by permission.

210 Fig. 12.2 "Mazes, Maps, and Memory" by David S. Olton, from *American Psychologist* (July, 1979). Copyright © 1979 by the American Psychological Association, Inc. Reprinted by permission of the author.

Chapter 6

228 Fig. 13.2 "The Information Available in Brief Visual Presentations" by George Sperling from *Psychological Monographs.* Reprinted by permission of New York University.

229 Fig. 13.3 "Short-term Retention of Individual Verbal Items" by Lloyd R. Peterson and Margaret J. Peterson, from *Journal of Experimental Psychology* (September, 1959), the American Psychological Association. Reprinted by permission of the authors.

234 Fig. 13.4 From *Human Memory: The Processing of Information* by Geoffrey R. Loftus and Elizabeth F. Loftus, page 59. Copyright © 1976 by Lawrence Erlbaum Associates, Inc. Reprinted by permission of Lawrence Erlbaum Associates, Inc., and the author.

237 Fig. 13.5 From "Retrieval Time From Semantic Memory" by Allan M. Collins and M. Ross Quillian, from *Journal of Verbal Learning and Verbal Behavior* 8, 1969. Reprinted by permission of Academic Press, Inc. and the author.

238 Fig. 13.6 "The Serial Position Effect of Free Recall" by Bennet B. Murdock, Jr., from *Journal of Experimental Psychology*, Volume 64, No. 5, 1962. Copyright © 1962 by the American Psychological Association, Inc. Reprinted by permission of the author.

239, 240 Figs. 13.7 & 13.8 From "Two Storage Mechanisms in Free Recall" by Murray Glanzer and Anita R. Cunitz from *Journal of Verbal Learning and Verbal Behavior*, 1966. Reprinted by permission of Academic Press, Inc. and the author.

248 Fig. 14.2 From "The Conditions of Retention," by C. W. Luh, from *Psychological Monographs.* Psychological Review, Co., 1922.

249 Fig. 14.3 From "Properties of Learning Curves under Varied Distribution of Practice" by Mary J. Kientzle, from *Journal of Experimental Psychology* 36 (June, 1946). Published by the American Psychological Association, Inc. Reprinted by permission of the author.

252 Fig. 14.4 from "Narrative Stories as Mediators for Serial Learning" by Gordon H. Bower and Mical C. Clark, from *Psychonomic Science*, 1969, Volume 14(4). Copyright © 1969 by Psychonomic Journals, Inc. Reprinted by Permission.

252 Fig. 14.5 From "Mnemotechnics in Second-Language Learning" by Richard C. Atkinson, from *American Psychologist* Volume 30, August 1975, Number 8. Published by the American Psychological Association. Reprinted by permission of the author.

253 Fig. 14.6 From "Bizareness versus Interaction of Mental Images as Determinants of Learning" by Keith A. Wollen, Andrea Weber, and Douglas H. Lowry, from *Cognitive Psychology*, 1972. Copyright © 1972 by Academic Press, Inc. Reprinted by permission.

253 Fig. 14.7 From *Plans and the Structure of Behavior* by George A. Miller, Eugene Galanter, and Karl H. Pribram (Holt, Rinehart and Winston 1960). Reprinted by permission of the authors.

256 Fig. 14.8 Hiroshi Minami and Karl M. Dallenbach, "The Effect of Activity Upon Learning and Retention in the Cockroach." *The American Journal of Psychology*, January 1946.

256 Fig. 14.8 From "Obliviscence During Sleep and Waking" by John G. Jenkins and Karl M. Dallenbach, from *American Journal of Psychology.* Copyright © 1946, 1974 by the Board of Trustees of the University of Illinois. Reprinted by permission of the University of Illinois Press.

259 Fig. 14.10 From *Remembering: A Study in Experimental and Social Psychology* by Frederic C. Bartlett. Reprinted by permission of Cambridge University Press.

Chapter 7

268 Fig. 15.2 "Cognitive Representations of Semantic Categories" by Eleanor Rosch, from *Journal of Experimental Psychology: General* (September, 1975). Copyright © 1975 by the American Psychological Association, Inc. Reprinted by permission of the author.

269 Fig. 15.3 From "The Attainment of Concepts: I. Terminology and Methodology" by Edna Heidbreder, from *Journal of General Psychology* Vol. 35, 1946, p. 182, a publication of the Helen Dwight Reid Educational Foundation. Copyright 1946 by The Journal Press. Reprinted by permission.

283 From *Cognitive Psychology* by Allan G. Reynolds and Paul W. Flagg. Little, Brown and Company, 1983.

286 Fig. 16.1 From *The Task of Gestalt Psychology* by Wolfgang Köhler. Copyright © 1969 by Princeton University Press. Figure p. 146 reprinted with permission of Princeton University Press.

287 Fig. 16.2 From *Cognition*, by Arnold Glass, Keith Holyoak, and John Santa. Copyright © 1979 by Newbery Award Records, Inc. Reprinted by permission of Random House, Inc.

290 Fig. 16.3 From "An Analysis of Behavior in the Hobbits-Orcs Problem" by John C. Thomas, Jr. from *Cognitive Psychology* 6. Copyright © 1974 by Academic Press, Inc. Reprinted by permission of Academic Press, Inc. and the author.

292 Fig. 16.5 From "Problem-Solving" by Martin Scheerer, from *Scientific American*, Vol. 208, 1963.

293 Fig. 16.6 From "Reasoning in Humans. II. The Solution of a Problem and Its Appearance in Consciousness," by Norman R. F. Maier, from *The Journal of Comparative Psychology*. The Williams & Wilkins Company, 1931.

Chapter 8

309, 311 Figs. 17.4 & 17.5 Figures 1.2 and 8.14 from *The Developing Human, Third Edition: Clinically Oriented Embryology* by Keith L. Moore. Copyright © 1982 by W. B. Saunders Company. Reprinted by permission of W. B. Saunders and the author.

321 Fig. 18.1 From *The First Two Years* by Mary M. Shirley. Reprinted by permission of University of Minnesota Press.

322 Fig. 18.2 Bryant J. Cratty, *Perceptual and Motor Development in Infants and Children*, Copyright © 1979, p. 212. Reprinted by permission of Prentice-Hall, Inc., Englewood Cliffs, N.J.

341 Fig. 19.1 Figure 8 from "Standards from Birth to Maturity for Height, Weight, Height Velocity, and Weight Velocity: British Children, 1965" by J. M. Tanner, R. H. Whitehouse, and M. Takaishi from *Archives of Diseases in Childhood*, Vol. 41, October 1966. Copyright © 1966 by the British Medical Association. Reprinted by permission of the British Medical Journal and the authors.

345 Fig. 19.2 From "Sexual Activity, Contraceptive Use and Pregnancy Among Metropolitan-Area Teenagers: 1971–1979" by Melvin Zelnik and John K. Kantner. Adapted with permission from *Family Planning Perspectives*, Volume 12, Number 5, 1980.

350 Fig. 19.3 "Human Mate Selection" by David M. Buss, from *American Scientist* (January-February, 1985). Reprinted by permission of American Scientist.

355 Fig. 19.4 Two figures from "Growing Up" by J. M. Tanner from *Scientific American*, September 1973, Volume 229, Number 3. Copyright © 1973 by *Scientific American*, Inc. All rights reserved.

Chapter 9

383 Figs. 21.1 & 21.2 From "Language for the Emotions" by Robert Plutchik from *Psychology Today*, February 1980, p. 73 and graph on p. 74. Copyright © 1980 by American Psychological Association. Reprinted by Permission from *Psychology Today*.

385 Fig. 21.4 From "Cross-Cultural Studies of Facial Expressions" from *Darwin and Facial Expression: A Century of Research in Review* edited by Paul Ekman. Copyright © 1973 by Academic Press, Inc. Reprinted by permission of Academic Press, Inc. and the author.

392–393 "Baby Face" by Robert J. Trotter, from *Psychology Today* (August, 1983). Copyright © 1983 by The American Psychological Association. Reprinted with permission from Psychology Today Magazine.

398 Fig. 22.1 Figure 3 from "The Three Phases of General Adaptation Syndrome" (p. 39) in *Stress Without Distress* by Hans Selye, M.D. (J. B. Lippincott Co.). Copyright © 1974 by Hans Selye, M.D. Reprinted by permission of Harper & Row, Publishers, Inc.

405 Fig. 22.7 Reprinted with permission from *Journal of Psychosomatic Research*, Volume 11, 1967, by T. H. Holmes and R. H. Rahe, "The Social Readjustment Rating Scale," pp. 213–218.

Chapter 10

433 Fig. 23.4 From *The Inequality of Man* by H. J. Eysenck. Copyright © 1973 by Hans J. Eysenck. Reprinted by permission of Educational & Industrial Testing Services.

439 "Are You Naturally Sexy" by Barry Cooper, from *Womans World Advertising Supplement*, March 13, 1984. Reprinted by permission of *Womans World*.

450 Fig. 24.2 Table "Descriptions of MMPI scales and simulated items" from *Psychological Testing and Assessment* by Lewis R. Aiken. Copyright 1943, renewed © 1970 by the University of Minnesota. Reprinted by permission.

451 Fig. 24.3 Sample Minnesota Interpretive Report for the Minnesota Multiphasic Personality Inventory. Minnesota Multiphasic Personality Inventory Copyright the University of Minnesota 1943, renewed © 1970. This report © 1982. Reprinted by permission.

Chapter 11

463 Fig. 25.1 From "Who's Intelligent?" by Robert J. Sternberg, from *Psychology Today* 16 (April, 1982). Copyright © 1982 by the American Psychological Association. Reprinted with permission from Psychology Today Magazine.

466 Fig. 25.3 From *The Nature of Human Intelligence* by J. P. Guilford. Copyright © 1967 by McGraw-Hill, Inc. Reprinted by permission.

467 Fig. 25.4 From "The Structure of Human Abilities" by Philip E. Vernon. Copyright © 1961 by Methuen & Company, Ltd. Reprinted by permission of the publisher and author.

472 Fig. 25.6 From Wechsler Adult Intelligence Scale-Revised (WAIS-R) Manual by David Wechsler. Copyright © 1981 by The Psychological Corporation. Reprinted by permission of Harcourt Brace Jovanovich, Inc.

480 A. Dove, "Taking the Chitling Test" *Newsweek*, July, 1968.

480 From *The BITCH Test (Black Intelligence Test of Cultural Homogeneity)*, by R. L. Williams. Williams and Associates, 1972.

484 Fig. 26.1 From "Genetics and Intelligence: A Review" by L. Erlenmeyer-Kimling and L. F. Jarvik, from *Science* Vol. 142, pp. 1477–1479, Fig. 1, 13 December 1963. Copyright © 1963 by the American Association for the Advancement of Science. Reprinted by permission of the publisher and author.

488 Fig. 26.3 Adaptation of figure from *Correlations of Maternal and Child Behaviors with the Development of Mental Abilities: Data from the Berkeley Growth Study* by Bayley and Schaefer. Copyright © 1964 by the Society for Research in Child Development, Inc. Reprinted by Permission.

Chapter 12

514 Fig. 27.3 From *Diagnostic and Statistical Manual of Mental Disorders, Third Edition,* pp. 307–329. Washington, D.C., American Psychiatric Association. Copyright © 1980. Used with Permission.

524 From: *DSM-III Case Book* by Spitzer LR, Skodol AE, Gibbon M, Williams JBW, pp 67–68. Copyright © 1981, American Psychiatric Association. Reprinted with permission.

Chapter 13

539 From "Treatise on Insanity" by Phillippe Pinel from *Classics in Psychology.* Copyright © 1961 by Philosophical Library, Inc. Reprinted by permission.

564 Fig. 30.1 From *Reason and Emotion in Psychotherapy* by Albert Ellis (New York: Citadel, 1962) and *A New Guide to Rational Living* by Albert Ellis and Robert A. Harper (North Hollywood, CA: Wilshire Books, 1975). Copyright © by the Institute for Rational-Emotive Therapy.

567 Fig. 30.2 From table 5.1 from *The Benefits of Psychotherapy* by Mary Lee Smith, Gene V. Gloss, and Thomas I. Miller. Copyright © 1980 by The Johns Hopkins Press. Printed by Permission.

Chapter 14

578 Fig. 31.2 From Petty, Richard E. and John T. Cacioppo, *Attitudes and Persuasion: Classic and Contemporary Approaches.* Copyright © 1981 Wm. C. Brown Publishers, Dubuque, Iowa. All Rights Reserved. Adapted by permission.

581 Fig. 31.5 Adaptation of table 1 of "Cognitive Consequences of Forced Compliance" by Leon Festinger and James M. Carlsmith from *The Journal of Abnormal and Social Psychology,* March, 1959. Copyright © 1959 by the American Psychological Association. Adapted by permission of the author.

582 Fig. 31.6 From "Distraction Can Enhance or Reduce Yielding to Propaganda: Thought Disruption Versus Effort Justification" by Richard E. Petty, Gary L. Wells, and Timothy C. Brock from *Journal of Personality and Social Psychology* Vol. 34, No. 5, November, 1976. Copyright © 1976 by American Psychological Association. Reprinted by permission.

584 Fig. 31.7 From *Social Psychology: Understanding Human Interaction,* Fourth Edition, by Robert A. Baron and Donn Byrne, page 59. Copyright © 1984, 1981, 1977, 1974 by Allyn and Bacon, Inc. Reprinted by permission.

589 Fig. 31.8 From "Measurement of Romantic Love" by Zick Rubin, from *Journal of Personality and Social Psychology* (October, 1970). Copyright © 1970 by the American Psychological Association, Inc. Reprinted by permission of the author.

599 From "37 Who Saw Murder Didn't Call the Police" by Martin Gansberg from *The New York Times,* March 17, 1964. Copyright © 1964 by The New York Times Company. Reprinted by permission.

600 Fig. 32.3 From "When Will People Help In A Crisis?" by John M. Darley and Bibb Latané from *Psychology Today.* Copyright © 1968 by American Psychological Association. Reprinted by Permission from *Psychology Today.*

Chapter 15

621 Fig. 33.1 From *Training: Program Development and Evaluation,* by I. L. Goldstein. Copyright © 1974 by Wadsworth Publishing Company, Inc. Reprinted by permission of Brooks/Cole Publishing Company, Monterey, California.

639 Fig. 34.2 From "Workers At Risk From Neurotoxins" in "Neurotoxic Follies" by Alan Anderson, *Psychology Today,* July 1982. Copyright © 1982 by American Psychological Association. Reprinted by permission from *Psychology Today.*

NAME INDEX

SUBJECT INDEX

Conduction aphasia, 77
Cones, of eye, 102, 103–108, 109, 139, 200
Confidentiality, in research, 37
Conflict: during adolescence, 345–347, 356; in Freudian psychology, 421, 555–556, 557, 563, 569; and psychological disorders, 512; and stress, 401–403, 411, 413
Conflict-induced stress, 401–403, 413
Conformity, 18, 34, 37, 593–598, 601, 609
Conjunctive concepts, 266, 281
Connotative meaning, 181, 184
Conscience, 421, 437
Conscious and consciousness, 11, 15, 21, 91, 147–149, 157, 167–168; and drugs, 160–165, 522, 545–547; and hypnosis, 156–158; and meditation, 158–160; and memory, 257; and organic syndromes, 521, 535; and psychoanalytic theory, 420, 421, 437, 555–557; and sleep, 149–156, 166–167
Conservation, concept of, 326, 327–328, 329–330, 336
Conservative focusing, 270–271, 281, 288
Consistency: and attitudes, 580–581, 583, 590; in personality, 434, 435–436
Constancy, and perception, 141–142, 145
Constitutional theories of personality, 417–418
Contact comfort, 334
Contempt, 383, 392, 394
Content, and intelligence, 466
Content validity, 444, 458
Context, and perception, 12, 134–135
Contingency management, 562, 569
Continuity, and perception, 134, 145
Continuous reinforcement schedules (CRF), 197, 198
Contraception, 344–345, 350
Contracting, 562, 569, 570, 641
Contrast, and perception, 129–130, 132, 145
Control, of environment, 427, 437
Control groups, 32–33
Convergence, 136, 145
Convergent thinking, 294, 298
Conversion disorder, 505, 511, 512, 517, 556
Coordination, and the brain, 67–68, 78
Coping, 159, 411–412
Cornea, of eye, 99, 100, 102, 109
"Corporate culture," 626–627, 629
Corpus callosum, 69, 73, 74, 78, 365
Correlation, 27–29, 38; and body type, 417; of IQ and age, 488–489; of IQ in twin studies, 483–485; and tests, 444, 456–457
Correlation coefficient, 28, 443
Counseling, 552, 554, 565
Counseling psychologist, 554, 569
Counseling psychology, 17, 20
Counterbalance General Intelligence Test, 480
Countertransference, 557
Courtrooms, psychology in, 609, 642–643
Creative problem solving, 294–295, 298
Creativity, 74, 78, 490, 495
Credibility, and persuasion, 582, 590
Crisis, in development, 330–331, 337
Crisis intervention centers, 412
Criterion referenced test, 449
Critical periods, 217–218, 309

Cross-cultural studies, 36, 38, 330, 385–386, 393
Cross-dressing, 516
Cross-laterality, of brain, 71–72, 74–75
Cross-sectional method, 489
Crowding, 631, 632, 636, 647
Crystallized intelligence, 467, 478, 489, 495
Cues: and eating, 366–369, 378; and perception, 132, 136–139, 141, 145; and retrieval, 245, 246; and sexual behavior, 370–371; and thirst, 366, 378
Cultural bias, 476–477
Culture: and abnormality, 36, 38, 501, 502–503; corporate-, 626–627, 629; and emotions, 385–386, 393, 394; and intelligence tests, 476–477, 495; and personal space, 633
Culture Fair Intelligence Test, 477
Culture fair tests, 476–477, 480, 494
Culture-free tests, 476–477
Cutaneous sense, 87, 119–121, 124

D

Dark adaptation, 105, 109
Data organizing, 654–656
Daydreaming, 408–409, 414, 514
Death, 349, 352–353, 356, 413, 525
Death instincts, 420–421, 423, 428, 555
Debriefing, after research, 37, 598–599
Decibel, 112, 113, 114
Decision making: and drugs, 162, 164; and employment, 624, 629; by group, 605–606; and intervention, 600
Deep structure, 277, 281
Defense mechanisms, 407–410, 414, 421
Defensiveness scale (K), 450
Deficiency needs, 429
Degenerative dementia, 521–522, 533–534
Deindividualization, 606
Deinstitutionalization, 546, 548–549
Delirium, 521, 522, 523, 539
Delta wave, 151, 167
Delusions, 521, 523, 524, 528, 530, 535
Dementia, 523, 533–534
Dendrites, 42–43, 46, 47, 55, 57
Denial: of dying, 352–353; and stress, 408, 414
Dependence, on drugs, 160, 161, 163, 164, 168, 547, 550
Dependent personality disorder, 514
Dependent variables, 29–33, 38
Depressants, 162–163, 164, 166, 168
Depression, 166, 353, 421, 505, 525, 535, 544–545, 546–547, 550, 567
Deprivation: biological, 361–362; perceptual, 144; sensory, 111; sleep-, 152–154, 167–168
Depth perception, 135–139, 141, 144, 145, 322–323, 336
Desensitization, to violence, 608, 610
Development: in adolescence, 340–348; in adulthood, 348–353; cognitive, 324–333, 336; and heredity, 301–307, 310; motor, 320–322, 336; nature vs. nurture in, 301, 314–315; perceptual, 143–144; prenatal, 307–313, 492–493; psychosexual stages of, 422, 437; psychosocial, 330–331, 333, 336, 337, 340, 345–348; sensory, 322–324, 336
Developmental psychology, 17, 20
Diabetes, 631, 641
Diagnosis, assessment used for, 445–446, 458

Diagnostic and Statistical Manual of Mental Disorders (DSM-III), 503–505, 506, 507, 509, 511, 513, 515–516, 517, 520, 521–522, 525, 529, 530
Diet, and prenatal development, 311–312, 316
Difference thresholds, 85–86, 88, 92
Diffusion of responsibility, 602, 610
Diminishing returns phenomenon, 247–248
Discrimination: in classical conditioning, 177–178, 184; and employment, 619; in operant conditioning, 199–200, 205
Disease, 398, 404, 510, 517, 640–641, 647
Disgust, 383, 385, 392, 393, 394
Disjunctive concepts, 266
Disorganized schizophrenia, 530
Disorientation, 533
Displacement, 409, 414
Dispositional attributions, 583, 590
Dissociative disorders, 505, 512–513, 517, 528
Distance perception, 135–139, 141, 144, 145
Distractability, 526
Distraction, and persuasion, 581–582
Distress, 383, 392, 394
Distributed practice, 248–249, 260
Distribution curve, 486, 664–665
Divergent thinking, 294–295, 298
DNA (deoxyribonucleic acid), 303, 313, 314, 316
Dominant genes, 304–306, 316
Dopamine, 56, 527, 531, 535
Dorsal root, 51
Double-blind technique, 33, 38
Double messages, 532
Down's Syndrome, 306–307, 316, 492
Dream interpretation, 556, 569
Dreaming, 147, 151, 152, 155–156, 166, 168, 420, 523, 556, 559
Drives, 361–372, 376, 428
Drug therapy, 545–547, 549, 550; for anxiety, 547; for depression, 546–547; for psychosis, 546, 548, 549
Drugs, 160–165, 168, 640; and neurotransmitters, 55–56, 160, 161; and organic disorders, 521; and prenatal development, 310, 312, 316, 492, 495
Dual-center theories, 367
Dualism, interactive, 9, 21
Duplicity theory of vision, 104, 109

E

Ear, 113–114, 116–117
Eardrum, 116, 124
Early bloomers, 354–355
Eating behavior, 69, 78, 366–369, 378
Ectomorphs, 417
Educational psychology, 17, 20
Ego, 407, 421, 424, 437
Ego-dystonic homosexuality, 516
Ego-integrity vs. despair, 331, 352
Egocentrism, 326, 327, 329, 336, 514
Ejaculation, 516
Elaborative rehearsal, 234, 242, 250–254, 328
Elavil, 547
Elderly. *See* Old age
Electra complex, 422
Electrical activity, of brain, 63–64, 78
Electrical stimulation, of brain, 62–63, 68, 70, 78, 367, 388
Electroconvulsive therapy (ECT), 544–545, 550

Electroencephalogram (EEG), 64, 68; and meditation, 158; and sleep, 149–151, 153, 166, 167
Elephant model, of Alzheimer's disease, 534
Embryo, 309–310, 312, 313, 316
Emotions, 379–394; and attitudes, 576–577; blunting of, 519, 520, 528; defined, 382–384; and heredity, 315; in infants, 392–393; and the nervous system, 53–54, 57, 68, 69; and prenatal development, 312–313; physiological aspects of, 387–389, 394; theories of, 389–391, 394
Empathy, 558, 569
Empirical approach, and test, 456
Empiricists, 143
Employee assessment, 614, 616–619
Employee training, 620–622, 624, 625, 629
Employment, 339, 347, 613–629; and job satisfaction, 622–624; and productivity, 624–625, 628, 629. *See also* Industrial organizational psychology
Encapsulated nerve endings, 120
Encoding, 225, 242; long-term memory, 233–234; and mnemonic devices, 251–254; short-term memory, 229, 231
Endocrine system, 42, 48, 49, 53–54, 57, 69, 387–388
Endomorphs, 417
Endorphins, 56, 123
Environment: and attribution, 583–584; and IQ, 481–485, 494, 495; vs. heredity, 301, 314–315, 481–485; and perception, 143–144, and personality, 425–427, 428, 436; and prenatal development, 310–313
Environmental frustration, 400, 413
Environmental psychology, 632–639, 647; space and territory, 633–635; toxins, 632, 638–639; urban life, 636–637
Epilepsy, 74, 204
Epinephrine, 53–54, 390–391
Episodic memory, 235, 242
Equal Employment Opportunity Act (EEO), 619
Equanil, 547
Erection, 516
Erikson's theory of psychosocial development, 330–331, 333, 337, 340
Eros, 420
Escape: and psychological disorders, 510–511, 512, 517; and stress, 406, 411
Escape conditioning, 193, 194, 205
Esteem needs, 377
Estrogen, 342, 370
Ethics: and research, 30, 37, 180, 481–482, 598–599; and treatment, 561–562
Etiology, of disorders, 504, 521
Euphoria, drug-induced, 161, 163
Evaluation apprehension, 605
Evolution, and sleep, 154, 168
Exercise, and stress, 412
Exhaustion state, 399, 413
Exhibitionism, 516
Expectation: and abnormality, 501–502; and perception, 131–132, 134, 145
Experience, 9, 213, 440; vs. heredity, 143–144; and perception, 132, 134–135, 139, 143–144, 145; and personality, 425–427, 433, 434
Experimental bias, 33, 35, 38, 418

Experimental groups, 32–33
Experimental neurosis, 178
Experimental Psychology, 284
Experiments, 29–33, 38, 381, 382
Expressive aphasia, 76
External attribution, 583, 590
External cues: and drinking, 366; and eating, 367–368, 369; and sexual behavior, 370–371
External locus of control, 427
Extinction, in conditioning, 176–177, 184, 190, 191, 197–198, 199, 204
Extraneous variables, 29, 30, 31, 32, 38
Extroversion-introversion dimension, 432, 437, 442, 444–445
Eye, 83, 99–109, 136–137
Eyewitness testimony, 233, 631, 643, 647

F

Facial expression, and emotion, 385–386, 392–393, 394
Factor analysis, 431, 456–457
Failure, feelings of, 331, 337, 527
Fairness, and employment, 619
Fallopian tubes, 308
Family, 349, 356, 530, 531–532, 535, 565
Fantasy, 408–409, 414
Farsightedness, 100, 101
Fat cells, and obesity, 368, 378
Father: and development, 307, 316, 335, 371; role as, 350; and schizophrenia, 532
Fatigue, 162, 525
Fear of failure, 373
Fear of success, 373
Fears, 383, 384, 385, 391, 392, 394, 425, 509, 510, 517; of death, 352–353; in infants, 179–181, 184, 323, 392–393, 425; therapy for, 560–561, 563, 569. *See also* Phobia
Fechner's law, 87–88, 89, 92, 112
Feedback, and productivity, 624
Feelings: and attitudes, 576–577, 590; and emotion, 382, 383, 394
Females, 348, 352; during adolescence, 341, 343, 344, 347–348, 354–355, 356; and fear of success, 373; and IQ tests, 487–488; and motor development, 321, 322; and psychological disorders, 510, 511, 525, 535; and sexual activity, 343, 344, 356, 370, 371, 515
Fertilization, 308
Fetal alcohol syndrome, 312
Fetus, 309, 310, 311, 312, 313, 316, 492, 495
Figure-ground relationship, 129, 132, 143
Fixed interval (FI) schedule, 198, 205
Fixed ratio (FR) schedule, 198, 205
Flooding, in therapy, 560–561, 569
Fluid intelligence, 467, 478, 489, 495
Focus gambling, 271
Foreclosure, during adolescence, 347
Forgetting, 232, 247, 258, 259–260
Formal concepts, 265–267, 281
Formal operations stage, 326, 329, 337, 340
Four-fifths (4/5) rule, 619
Fovea, of eye, 100, 103, 104
Frame of reference, 12
Fraternal twins, and IQ, 483
Free association, 556, 569
Free nerve endings, 120, 123

Frequency distributions, 654–655, 656, 660–661, 666
Freud's personality theory, 156, 419–425, 437
Friendships, 374, 377, 584–589
Frontal lobes, of brain, 61, 62, 70, 71, 72, 73, 76
Frustration, 400–401, 403, 406, 409, 411, 413, 414, 606–607, 610
Frustration-aggression theory, 406–407, 414, 606–607, 610
Frustration-induced stress, 399–401, 406, 413
Fugue, 505, 512, 517
Functional dyspareunia, 516
Functional fixedness, 282, 293–294, 295, 296, 298
Functional vaginismus, 516
Functionalism, 11, 21
Fundamental attribution error, 583, 590, 597–598

G

g-factor, 464–465, 466
GABA (gamma-aminobutyric acid), 56
Galvanic skin response (GSR), 91
Games, in relationships, 565–566
Ganglion cells, of eye, 102, 108
Ganzfeld, 141
Gate-control theory, 123
Genain quadruplets, 531
Gender identity disorder, 505, 516
Gender roles, 347–348
General adaptation syndrome (GAS), 398–399, 413
Generalization, 32; in classical conditioning, 177–178, 180, 184; in operant conditioning, 199, 205
Generalized anxiety, 508–509, 517
Generativity, in adulthood, 350, 356
Generativity vs. stagnation, 331, 351
Genes, 303–307, 310, 313, 314–315, 316; and IQ, 483–485, 494, 495; and mental retardation, 492–493; and psychological disorders, 526–527, 534, 535
Genetic transmission, 304–306, 316
Genital stage of development, 340, 422, 437
Genotype, 306, 316
Gestalt psychology, 11–12, 21, 129, 133, 134, 143, 211
Ghost wars, and memory, 259–260
Giftedness, 490–491, 495
Glands, 53–54, 57
Glaucoma, 100
Global aphasia, 77
Glove anesthesia, 511
Goal state, of problem, 284–286, 288, 297
Goals: of adolescence, 347, 356; of adulthood, 349, 356; in childhood, 424; and employment, 620–621, 624; and motivation, 359, 362–363, 378, 429; and sports, 645; and stress, 399–401, 406, 411, 413, 414; of therapy, 553, 558, 563, 564, 566
Grammars, 273, 275–278, 280, 281
Graphs, 655–656, 666
Gray matter, 43, 51, 73
GRE (Graduate Record Exam), 474
Group intelligence tests, 473–474, 475, 478
Group polarization, 605–606

Wechsler Primary Scale of Intelligence (WPPSI), 471
Wernicke's aphasia, 77
Wernicke's area, 71, 76–77
White light, 98, 115
White matter, 43, 51, 52, 57
White noise, 115
Whole report method, 227
Witchcraft, mental illness as, 541, 550
Withdrawal: following deprivation, 334; from drugs, 160, 161, 162, 163, 521, 522, 523, 547; and psychological disorders, 528, 533
Word associations, 318, 453
Word Associations of Young Children, 318
"Word salads," 528, 530
Words, and meaning, 181, 184, 331, 332
Working backward strategy, 288, 289, 291
Working memory. *See* Short-term memory
Worthlessness, feelings of, 525
Wyatt vs. Stickney, 549

X

X chromosomes, 303, 304, 316

Y

Y chromosomes, 303, 304, 316
Young adulthood, 331, 346, 348–350, 356

Z

Zoophilia, 516
Zygote, 304, 308–309, 313, 316